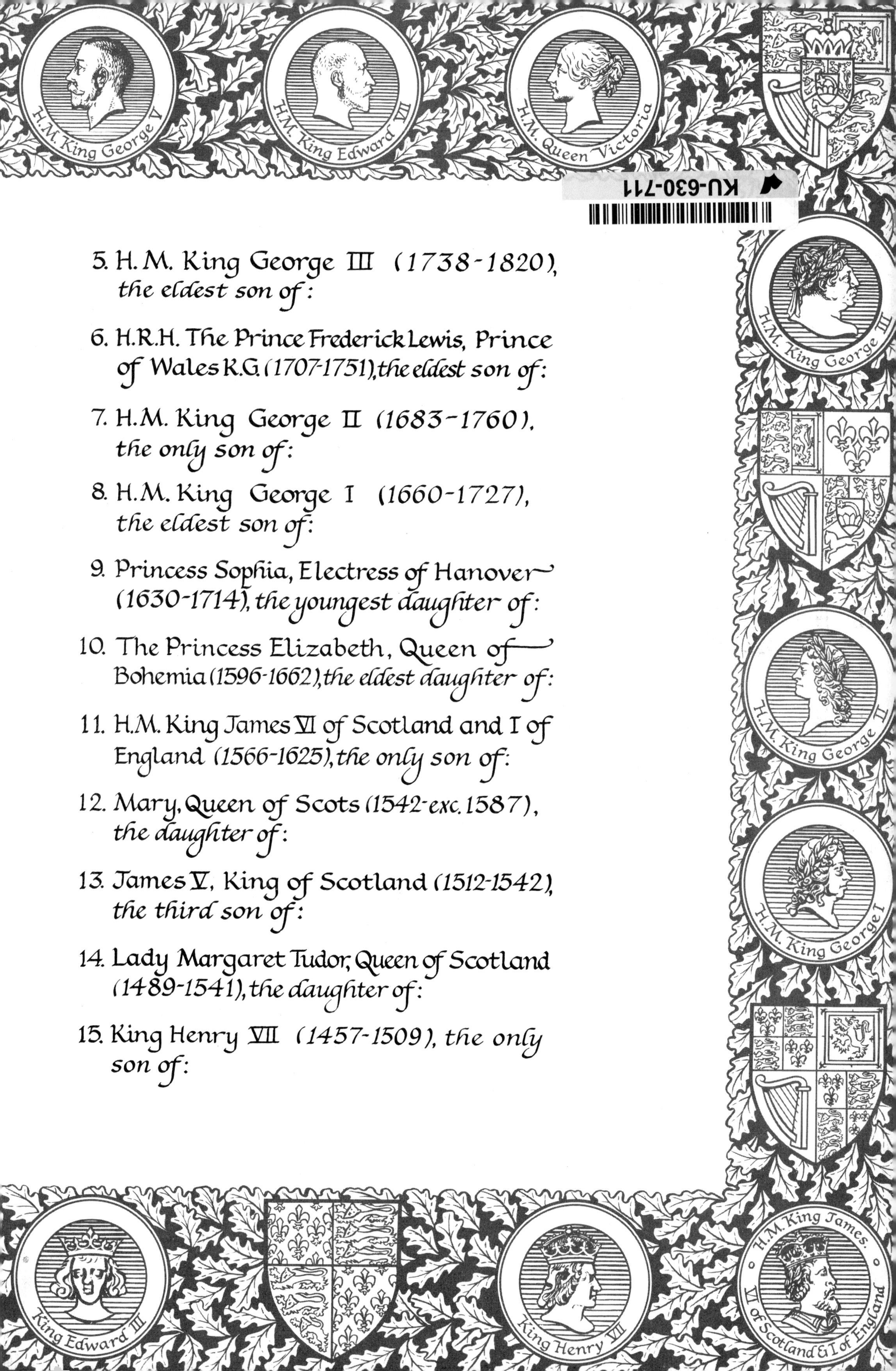

KU-630-711

5. H. M. King George III (1738-1820), *the eldest son of:*

6. H.R.H. The Prince Frederick Lewis, Prince of Wales K.G. (1707-1751), *the eldest son of:*

7. H.M. King George II (1683-1760), *the only son of:*

8. H.M. King George I (1660-1727), *the eldest son of:*

9. Princess Sophia, Electress of Hanover (1630-1714), *the youngest daughter of:*

10. The Princess Elizabeth, Queen of Bohemia (1596-1662), *the eldest daughter of:*

11. H.M. King James VI of Scotland and I of England (1566-1625), *the only son of:*

12. Mary, Queen of Scots (1542-exc. 1587), *the daughter of:*

13. James V, King of Scotland (1512-1542), *the third son of:*

14. Lady Margaret Tudor, Queen of Scotland (1489-1541), *the daughter of:*

15. King Henry VII (1457-1509), *the only son of:*

Standard Book Number SBN: 900424 04 4
Copyright 1971 by Guinness Superlatives Limited

Standard Book Number SBN: 900424 05 2
Southern African Edition
© 1971 by Guinness Superlatives Limited
World Copyright Reserved
Eighteenth Edition

Note.
In keeping with the standardization sought by The Booksellers' Association, The Library Association and The Publishers' Association, editions have been designated thus:—

Edition	*Published*	*Edition*	*Published*
First Edition	October 1955	Tenth Edition	November 1962
Second Edition	October 1955	Eleventh Edition	November 1964
Third Edition	November 1955	Twelfth Edition	November 1965
Fourth Edition	January 1956	Thirteenth Edition	October 1966
Fifth Edition	October 1956	Fourteenth Edition	October 1967
Sixth Edition	December 1956	Fifteenth Edition	October 1968
Seventh Edition	November 1958	Sixteenth Edition	October 1969
Eighth Edition	November 1960	Seventeenth Edition	October 1970
Ninth Edition	April 1961	Eighteenth Edition	October 1971

No part of this book may be reproduced or transmitted in any form or by any means electronic, chemical or mechanical, including photocopying, any information storage or retrieval system without a licence or other permission in writing from the copyright owners. Reviewers are welcome to quote brief passages should they wish.

Note.
No back numbers are now available. Orders for current editions published overseas will willingly be passed on to the publishers concerned. The date indicates the first year an edition was established in the country concerned.

Guinness Book of World Records 1956 Casebound U.S.A.
Guinness Book of World Records 1962 Paperback U.S.A.
Le Livre des Extrêmes 1962 Casebound French
Guinness Rekord bog Først og Størst Sidst og Mindst 1967 Casebound Danish
Guinness Das Buch Der Rekorde 1967 Paperback German
Guinness Rekord bok Først og Størst Sist og Minst 1967 Casebound Norwegian
Guinness Korega Sekai Ichi 1968 Paper (2 vols.) Japanese
Enciclopedia Guinness de Superlativos Mundiales 1968 Paperback Spanish
Il Guinness dei Primati 1968 Italian
Guinness Ennätysten Kirja 1968 Casebound Finnish
Guinness Rekord bok Först och Störst 1968 Casebound Swedish
Het Groot Guinness Rekord Boek 1971 Casebound Dutch
Guinnessova kniha rekordu 1972 Paperback Czech

Layout and illustrations by DENZIL REEVES

Filmset by Layton-Sun Limited
6-10 Kirby Street, London EC1N 8TU

Printed offset lithography by
Redwood Press Ltd. of Trowbridge,
Wiltshire, England
Made and Printed in Great Britain

GUINNESS SUPERLATIVES LIMITED, 2 CECIL COURT, LONDON ROAD, ENFIELD, MIDDX.

THE GUINNESS BOOK OF RECORDS

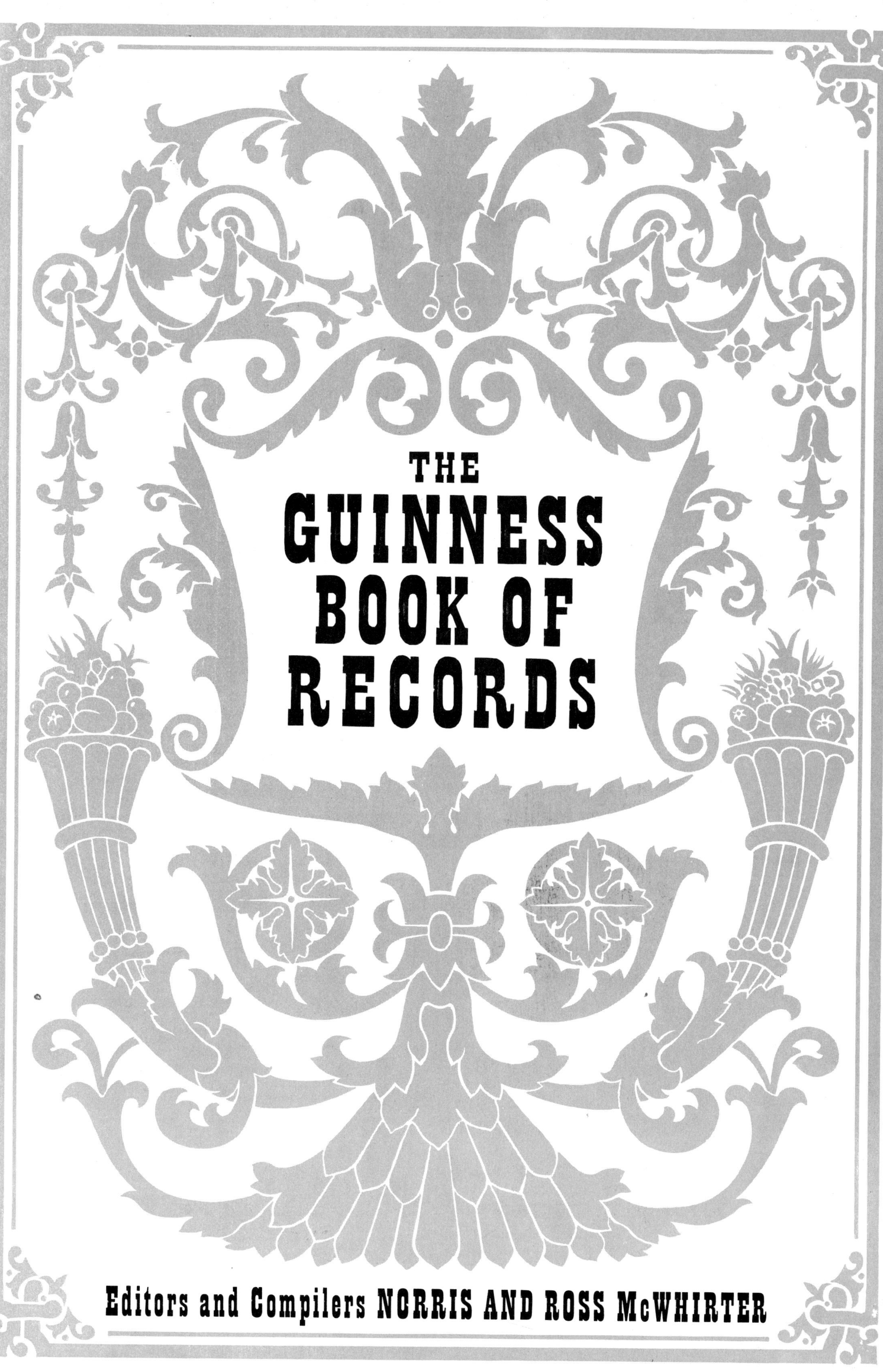

Editors and Compilers NORRIS AND ROSS McWHIRTER

ACKNOWLEDGEMENTS

Ian Allen & Co.
The Alpine Club
American Telephone & Telegraph Co.
J. W. Arblaster, Esq., A.I.M.
The Automobile Association
T. Banner, Esq.
James Bond
The Brewers' Society
The British Broadcasting Corporation
British European Airways
British Medical Association
British Museum (Natural History)
British Mycological Society
British Overseas Airways Corporation
British Rail
British Transport Commission
British Travel
British Waterworks Association
Burke's Peerage Ltd.
Central Electricity Generating Board
Central Office of Information
Dr. A. J. C. Charig
The Chemical Society
Church Commissioners
Conchological Society of Great Britain and Ireland
County Councils Association
Clerk of Dail Eireann
Department of Employment and Productivity
Eldon Pothole Club
Fédération Aéronautique Internationale
Fédération Internationale de l'Automobile
Fédération Internationale des Hôpitaux
George Fisher, Esq.
Frank L. Forster
Fortune
Dr. Francis C. Fraser
The Fur Trade Information Centre
General Motors Corporation
General Post Office
Geological Survey and Museum
The Gramophone Co. Ltd.
Greater London Council
W. T. Gunston, Esq., *Flight International*
John I. Haas Inc.
R. Hassell, Esq.
A. Herbert, Esq. (New Zealand)
Michael E. R. R. Herridge, Esq.
The Home Office
Imperial War Museum
The Inland Waterways Association
Institut International des Châteaux Historiques
Institute of Strategic Studies
International Association of Volcanology
International Civil Aviation Organization
The Kennel Club
D. G. King-Hele, Esq., F.R.S.
Kline Iron and Steel Company
Frank W. Lane, Esq.
Dr. L. S. B. Leakey
The Library of Congress, Washington, D.C.
Lloyd's Register of Shipping
London Transport Board
J. Lyons & Co. Ltd.
Marconi's Wireless Telegraph Co. Ltd.
The late T. L. Marks, Esq., O.B.E., T.D.
Prof. K. G. McWhirter, M.A., M.SC.
Meteorological Office
Metropolitan Police
Ministry of Agriculture, Fisheries and Food
Ministry of Defence
Ministry of Housing and Local Government
Ministry of Labour
Ministry of Public Buildings and Works
Ministry of Social Security
Ministry of Technology
Alan Mitchell, Esq.
The Museums Association
Music Research Bureau
National Aeronautics and Space Administration
National Coal Board
National Geographic Society
National Maritime Museum
National Physical Laboratory
The New York Times
The Patent Office Library
Photo Dealer Magazine
Port of New York Authority
Ransomes and Rapier Ltd.
Registrar General's Annual Report and Statistics Review
Registrar General's Office, Edinburgh
Jean Reville, Esq.
Rolls-Royce Ltd.
Royal Astronomical Society
Royal Botanic Gardens
Royal College of Surgeons of England
Royal Geographic Society
Royal National Life-boat Institution
Royal Norwegian Embassy
Sampson Low, Marston & Co. Ltd.
Dr. Albert Schwartz
B. A. Seaby Ltd.
Cdr. T. R. Shaw, R.N.
Siemens und Halske Aktiengesellschaft
Société Nationale des Chemins de Fer Français
Statutory Publications Office
John W. R. Taylor, Esq.
Time-Life International Inc.
The Treasury
Trinity House
U.N.E.S.C.O.
U.N. Statistical Office
United States Department of Agriculture
United States Department of the Interior
Water & Water Engineering
Gerry L. Wood, Esq., F.Z.S.
World Meteorological Organization
World Record Breakers Association
Zoological Society of London
Zoological Society of Philadelphia
Also to Mrs. Barbara Anderson, Mrs. Christine Bethlehem, Mrs. Rosemary Bevan, Signa. Wendy Cirillo, Mrs. Pamela Croome, Miss Trudy Doyle, Mlle. Béatrice Frei, Harold C. Harlow, Esq., Miss Tessa Hegley, E. C. Henniker, Esq., Mrs. Angela Hoaen, David Hoy, Esq., Mrs. Eileen Jackson, Mrs. Jane Mayo, G. M. Nutbrown, Esq., Mrs. Margaret Orr-Deas, Peter B. Page, Esq., Geoffrey Potter, Esq., John Rivers, Esq., Mrs. Judith Sleath, Mrs. Anne Symonds, Andrew Thomas, Esq. (Associate Editor 1964–68), Tony Thomas, Esq., Miss Hilary Tippett, Mrs. Winnie Ulrich, Miss Diana Wilford.

CONTENTS

FOREWORD

By the Rt. Hon. The Earl of Iveagh

When we first brought out this book, some sixteen years ago, we did so in the hope of providing a means for the peaceful settling of arguments about record performances in this record-breaking world in which we live. We realise, of course, that much joy lies in the argument, but how exasperating it can be if there is no final means of finding the answer.

In the event, we have found that the interest aroused by this book has exceeded our wildest expectations. We have now produced more than 6,000,000 copies, and ten editions in the United States. Translations into Czech, Danish, Dutch, French, Finnish, German, Italian, Japanese, Norwegian, Spanish and Swedish are showing the universality of its appeal. Whether the discussion concerns the smallest fish ever caught, the most expensive wine, the greatest weight lifted by a man, the furthest reached in space, the world's most successful racehorse, or—an old bone of contention—the longest river in the world, I can but quote the words used in introducing the first edition, "How much heat these innocent questions can raise: Guinness, in producing this book, hopes that it may assist in resolving many such disputes, and may, we hope, turn heat into light".

Iveagh

Chairman
Arthur Guinness, Son & Co., Ltd.
St. James's Gate Brewery, Dublin
Park Royal Brewery, London

October 1971

PREFACE

This eighteenth Edition has again been completely revised. We wish to thank correspondents from most of the countries of the world for raising or settling various editorial points. Strenuous efforts have been made to improve the value of the material presented and these will be continued in future editions.

We would like to stress that in the fast moving world of records that would-be record breakers should not rely on old editions nor indeed the current edition without consulting the stop press. Even then some categories of record are broken several times in a year.

Norris McWhirter

Editors and compilers

Ross McWhirter

October 1971

Guinness Superlatives Limited, 2 Cecil Court, London Road, Enfield, Middlesex.

1 THE HUMAN BEING

1. DIMENSIONS

TALLEST GIANTS

The height of human giants is a subject on which accurate information is frequently obscured by exaggeration and commercial dishonesty. The only admissible evidence on the true height of giants is that collected in recent years under impartial medical supervision.

The Biblical claim that Og, the Amorite king of Bashan and Gilead in *c.* 1450 B.C., stood 9 Hebrew cubits (13 feet 2½ inches) is based solely on the length of his basalt sarcophagus or "iron bedstead". The assertion that Goliath of Gath (*c.* 1060 B.C.) stood 6 cubits and a span (9 feet 6½ inches) suggests a confusion of units or some over-zealous exaggeration by the Hebrew chroniclers. The Jewish historian Flavius Josephus (born in A.D. 37 or 38, died after A.D. 93) and some of the manuscripts of the Septuagint (the earliest Greek translation of the Old Testament) attribute to Goliath the more credible height of 4 Greek cubits and a span (6 feet 10 inches).

Extreme medieval data, taken from bone measurements, invariably refer to specimens of extinct whale, giant cave bear, mastodon, woolly rhinoceros or other prehistoric non-human remains.

Paul Topinard (1830–1911), a French anthropometrist, stated that the tallest man who ever lived was Daniel Mynheer Cajanus (1714–49) of Finland, standing 283 centimetres (9 feet 3·4 inches). In 1872 his right femur, now in Leyden Museum, in the Netherlands, was measured by Prof. Carl Langer of Germany and indicated a height of 222 centimetres (7 feet 3·4 inches). Pierre Lemolt, a member of the French Academy, reported in 1847 that Ivan Stepanovich Lushkin (1811–44), a drum major in the Russian Imperial Regiment of Guards at Preobrazhenskiy, measured 3 arshin 9¼ vershok (8 feet 3¾ inches) and was "the tallest man that has ever lived in modern days". However, his left femur and tibia, which are now in the Museum of the Academy of Sciences in Leningrad, U.S.S.R., indicate a height of 7 feet 10¼ inches.

Circus giants and others who are exhibited are normally under contract not to be measured and are, almost traditionally, billed by their promoters at heights up to 18 inches in excess of their true heights. There are many notable examples of this, and 23 instances were listed in the *Guinness Book of Records* (14th edition). The acromegalic giant Eddie Carmel (b. Tel Aviv, Israel, 1938), formerly "The Tallest Man on Earth" of Ringling Bros. and Barnum & Bailey's Circus (1961–68) is allegedly 9 feet 0⅝ inches tall (peak weight 535 lb.), but photographic evidence suggests that his true height is about 7 feet 8 inches. He does not permit himself to be measured.

An extreme case of exaggeration concerned Siah Khān ibn Kashmir Khān (b. 1913) of Bushehr (Bushire), Iran. Prof. D. H. Fuchs showed photographs of him at a meeting of the Society of Physicians in Vienna, Austria, in January 1935, claiming that he was 320 centimetres (10 feet 6 inches) tall. Later, when Siah Khān entered the Imperial Hospital in Teheran for an operation, it was revealed that his actual height was 220 centimetres (7 feet 2·6 inches).

World Modern opinion is that the tallest recorded man of whom there is irrefutable evidence was Robert Pershing Wadlow, born at 6.30 a.m. on 22 Feb. 1918 in Alton, Illinois, U.S.A. Weighing 8½ lb. at birth, his abnormal growth began almost immediately. His height progressed as follows:

Age in Years	Height	Weight in lb.	Age in Years	Height	Weight in lb.
5	5′4″	105	15	7′8″	355
8	6′0″	169	16	7′10½″	374
9	6′2½″	180	17	8′0½″	315*
10	6′5″	210	18	8′3½″	—
11	6′7″	—	19	8′5½″	480
12	6′10½″	—	20	8′6¾″	—
13	7′1¾″	255	21	8′8¼″	491
14	7′5″	301	22·4†	8′11″	439

**Following severe influenza and infection of the foot.*
†Wadlow was still growing during his terminal illness.

Dr. C. M. Charles, Associate Professor of Anatomy at Washington University's School of Medicine in St. Louis, Missouri, measured Robert Wadlow at 272 centimetres (8 feet 11·1 inches) in St. Louis on 27 June 1940. Wadlow died 18 days later, at 1.30 a.m. on 15 July 1940, in Manistee, Michigan, as a result of cellulitis of the feet aggravated by a poorly fitted brace.

Robert Wadlow the tallest human of all time, with his father. Robert is the one wearing the glasses

He was buried in Oakwood Cemetery, Alton, Illinois in a coffin measuring 10 feet 9 inches in length, 32 inches wide and 30 inches deep. His greatest recorded weight was 491 lb. (35 stone 1 lb.), on his 21st birthday. He weighed 439 lb. (31 stone 5 lb.) at the time of his death. His shoes were size 37AA ($18\frac{1}{2}$ inches long) and his hands measured $12\frac{3}{4}$ inches from the wrist to the tip of the middle finger.

The only other men for whom heights of 8 feet or more have been reliably reported are the seven listed below. In each case gigantism was followed by acromegaly, a disorder which causes an enlargement of the nose, lips, tongue, lower jaw, hands and feet, due to renewed activity by the already swollen pituitary gland, which is located at the base of the brain.

John F. Carroll (1932–69) of Buffalo, New York State, U.S.A. (a) 8 feet $7\frac{3}{4}$ inches (263·5 centimetres).
John William Rogan (1871–1905), a Negro of Gallatin, Tennessee, U.S.A. (b) 8 feet 6 inches (259·1 centimetres).
Don Koehler (b. 1929–*fl.* 1969) of Denton, Montana, U.S.A. (c) 8 feet 2 inches (248·9 centimetres).
Väinö Myllyrinne (1909–63) of Helsinki, Finland (d) 8 feet 1·2 inches (247 centimetres).
Gabriel Estavão Monjane (b. 1944) of Monjacaze, Mozambique (e) 8 feet 1 inch (246·3 centimetres).
"Constantine" (1872–1902) of Reutlingen, West Germany (f) 8 feet 0·8 inch (246 centimetres).
Sulaimān 'Alī Nashnush (b. 1943) of Tripoli, Libya (g) 8 feet 0·4 inch (245 centimetres).

(a) *Severe kypho-scoliosis (two dimensional spinal curvature). The figure represents his height with assumed normal spinal curvature, calculated from a standing height of 8 feet 0 inches, measured on 14 Oct. 1959. His standing height was 7 feet $8\frac{1}{4}$ inches shortly before his death.*

(b) *Measured in a sitting position. Unable to stand owing to ankylosis (stiffening of the joints through the formation of adhesions) of the knees and hips.*

(c) *He has a twin sister who is 5 feet 9 inches tall.*

(d) *Stood 7 feet $3\frac{1}{2}$ inches at the age of 21 years. Experienced a second phase of growth in his late thirties and may have stood 8 feet 3 inches at one time.*

(e) *Abnormal growth started at the age of 10, following a head injury. Some kypho-scoliosis. Present height* c. *7 feet 10 inches. A height of 8 feet 6 inches is claimed.*

(f) *Height estimated, as both legs were amputated after they turned gangrenous. He claimed a height of 259 centimetres (8 feet 6 inches).*

(g) *Operation to correct abnormal growth in Rome in 1960 was successful.*

A table of the tallest giants of all-time in the 31 countries with men taller than 7 feet 4 inches (223·5 cms.) was listed in the 15th edition of the *Guinness Book of Records* (1968) at page 9.

The claim that Sa'īd Muhammad Ghazi (b. 1909) of Alexandria, Egypt (now the United Arab Republic) attained a height of 8 feet 10 inches in February 1941 is now considered unreliable. Photographic evidence suggests his height was more nearly 7 feet $10\frac{1}{2}$ inches, though he may have reached 8 feet at the time of his death.

England The tallest Englishman ever recorded was William Bradley (1788–1820), born in Market Weighton, in the East Riding of Yorkshire. He stood 7 feet 9 inches. John Middleton (1578–1623), the famous Childe of Hale, in Lancashire, was claimed to be 9 feet 3 inches. Hat pegs were accurately but inconclusively measured in October 1969 to be 12 feet 9 inches above the present floor of his cottage. James Toller (1795–1819) of St. Neots, near Huntingdon, was alleged to be 8 feet 6 inches but was actually 7 feet 6 inches. Albert Brough (1871–1919), a publican of Nottingham, reached a height of 7 feet $7\frac{1}{2}$ inches. Frederick Kempster (1889–1918) of Bayswater, London, was reported to have measured 8 feet $4\frac{1}{2}$ inches at the time of his death, but photographic evidence suggests that his height was 7 feet $8\frac{1}{2}$ inches. He measured 234 centimetres (7 feet 8·1 inches) in 1913. Henry Daglish, who stood 7 feet 7 inches, died in Upper Stratton, Wiltshire, on 16 March 1951, aged 25. The much-publicized Edward (Ted) Evans (1924–58) of Englefield Green, Surrey, was reputed to be 9 feet 3 inches but actually stood 7 feet $8\frac{1}{2}$ inches. The tallest fully mobile man now living in Great Britain is Christopher Paul Greener (b. 21 Nov. 1943 in New Brighton, Cheshire) of Hayes, Kent, who measures 7 feet $4\frac{3}{4}$ inches. Terence Keenan (b. 1942) of Rock Ferry, Birkenhead, Cheshire measures 7 feet 6 inches, but is unable to stand erect owing to a leg condition. His abnormal growth began at the age of 17 when he was only 5 feet 4 inches tall.

Scotland The tallest Scotsman, and the tallest recorded "true" (non-pathological) giant, was Angus Macaskill (1825–63), born on the island of Berneray, in the Sound of Harris, in the Outer Hebrides. He stood 7 feet 9 inches and died in St. Ann's, on Cape Breton Island, Nova Scotia, Canada. Lambert Quételet (1796–1874), a Belgian anthropometrist, considered that a Scotsman named MacQuail, known as "the Scotch Giant", stood 8 feet 3 inches. He served in the famous regiment of giants of Frederick William I (1688–1740), King of Prussia. His skeleton, now in the Staatliche Museum zu Berlin, East Germany, measures 220 centimetres (7 feet 2·6 inches). Sam McDonald (1762–1802) of Lairg in Sutherland, was reputed to be 8 feet tall but actually stood 6 feet 10 inches. The tallest Scotsman now living is George Gracie (b. 1938) of Forth, Lanarkshire. He stands 7 feet 3 inches and weighs 28 stone. His brother Hugh (b. 1941) is 7 feet $0\frac{1}{2}$ inch.

Wales The tallest Welshman ever recorded was George Auger (1886–1922), born in Cardiff, Glamorganshire. He stood 7 feet 7 inches and died in New York City, N.Y., U.S.A.

Ireland The tallest Irishman was Patrick Cotter O'Brian (1760–1806), born in Kinsale, County Cork. He died at Hotwells, Clifton, Bristol. He said that he was 8 feet

7¾ inches at the age of 26, but his actual living height was 7 feet 10·86 inches, calculated from measurements of his long bones made by Dr. Edward Fawcett, Professor of Anatomy at University College, Bristol, on 3 March 1906, after his coffin had been accidentally exposed during excavation work.

The tallest Irishman now living is believed to be Jim Cully (b. 1926) of Tipperary, a former boxer and wrestler. He stands 7 feet 2 inches.

Isle of Man The tallest Manxman ever recorded was Arthur Caley (b. 16 Nov. 1829) of Sulby. He was variously credited with heights of 8 feet 2 inches and 8 feet 4 inches, but actually stood 7 feet 6 inches. He died at Clyde, New Jersey, U.S.A., on 12 Feb. 1889 aged 59.

TALLEST GIANTESSES

World *All-time* Giantesses are rarer than giants and their heights less spectacular. The tallest on record is an unidentified acromegalic giantess who died in Northfield, Birmingham, England in 1921 aged *c.* 24 years. The skeleton has a mounted height of 7 feet 4 inches but she had a severe curvature indicating a height of *c.* 7 feet 9 inches when alive. The only other woman to exceed 7½ feet was Wassiliki Calliandji (1882–1904) of Corinth, Greece. She measured 230 centimetres (7 feet 6½ inches) and weighed 120 kilogrammes (18 stone 12½ lb.). The German giantess Pauline Marianne Wehde (1866–83), long hailed as the tallest woman of all time, was billed at 254 centimetres (8 feet 4 inches) but her true height was estimated to be 224 centimetres (7 feet 4·2 inches). She weighed 160 kilogrammes (25 stone 3 lb.). Anna Swan (1846–88) of Nova Scotia, Canada, was billed at 8 feet 1 inch but actually measured 7 feet 5½ inches. In 1871 she married Martin van Buren Bates (1845–1919) of Whitesburg, Letcher County, Kentucky, U.S.A., who stood 7 feet 2½ inches. The French giantess Emma-Aline Batallaid (1877–95), *alias* "Lady Aama", claimed to be 244 centimetres (8 feet 0 inches) tall but her height at the time of her death was 6 feet 7¾ inches. Ella Ewing (1875–1913) of Gorin, Missouri, U.S.A., was billed at 8 feet 2 inches and reputedly measured 6 feet 9 inches at the age of 10 (*cf.* 6 feet 5 inches for Robert Wadlow at this age). She measured 7 feet 4½ inches at the age of 23 and may have attained 7 feet 6 inches by the time of her death.

Living The tallest woman recently living was believed to be Delores Ann Johnson, *née* Pullard (b. August 1946), a negress from De Quincy, Louisiana, U.S.A. She measured 6 feet 10 inches in March 1961 and grew to 7 feet 5 inches by October 1964. She reportedly wore size 52 dresses and size 23 shoes and weighed 435 lb. (31 stone 1 lb.). She died in a hospital in Houston, Texas on 19 May 1971. In June 1969 a height of 7 feet 1½ inches was reported for Mildred Tshakayi (b. 1946), a Rhodesian bush dweller, who was reportedly still growing. Gwen Bachman (b. 1953) of Englewood, Colorado, measured 7 feet in October 1970. In December 1970 a height of 7 feet 5 inches was reported for a woman named Tiliya, living in the village of Saidpur in Bihar State, north-eastern India, but further information is lacking. Katja van Dyke, born in 1905 at Roosendaal, in the Netherlands, claims to be 8 feet 4 inches, but her height is estimated to be not more than 6 feet 11 inches. She measured 6 feet 4½ inches at the age of 16.

SHORTEST DWARFS

The strictures which apply to giants apply equally to dwarfs, except that exaggeration gives way to understatement. In the same way as 9 feet may be regarded as the limit towards which the tallest giants tend, so 23 inches must be regarded as the limit towards which the shortest mature dwarfs tend (*cf.* the average length of new-born babies is 18 to 20 inches). In the case of child dwarfs the age is often enhanced by their agents or managers.

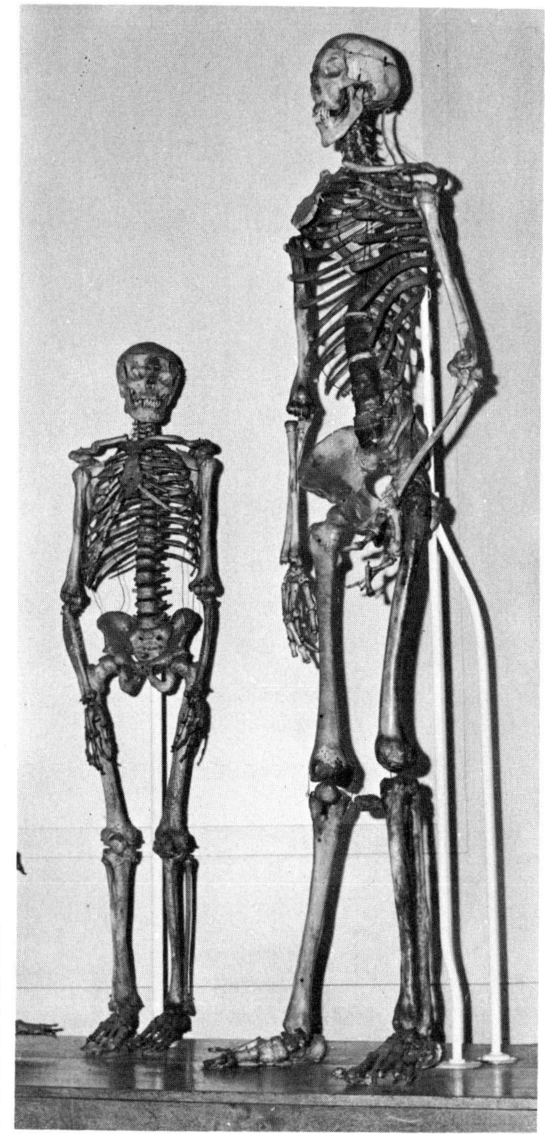

The skeleton of the tallest woman of all time at the Anatomical Museum in the Medical School, Birmingham University. Her identity remains a 50-year-old secret

The shortest type of dwarf is an ateliotic dwarf, known as a midget. In this form of dwarfism the skeleton tends to remain in its infantile state. Midgets seldom grow to more than 40 inches tall. The most famous midget in history was Charles Sherwood Stratton, *alias* "General Tom Thumb", born on 11 Jan. 1832 in Bridgeport, Connecticut, U.S.A. He measured 25 inches at the age of 5 months and grew to only 70 centimetres (27·6 inches) by the age of 13½. He was 30½ inches tall at the age of 18 and 35 inches at 30. He stood 40 inches tall at the time of his death from apoplexy on 15 July 1883.

Another celebrated midget was Józef ('Count') Boruwalaski (b. November 1739) of Poland. He measured only 8 inches long at birth, growing to 14 inches at the age of one year. He stood 17 inches at 6 years, 21 inches at 10, 25 inches at 15, 35 inches at 25 and 39 inches at 30. He died near Durham, England, on 5 Sept. 1837, aged 97.

World The shortest mature human of whom there is independent evidence was Pauline Musters ('Princess Pauline'), a Dutch midget. She was born at Ossendrecht, on 26 Feb. 1876 and measured 12 inches at birth. At the age of 9 she was 55 centimetres (21·65 inches) tall and weighed only 1½ kilogrammes (3 lb. 5 oz.). She died, at the age of 19, of pneumonia, with meningitis, her heart weakened from alcoholic excesses, on 1 March 1895 in New York City, N.Y., U.S.A. Although she was billed

at 19 inches, she was measured shortly before her death and was found to be 59 centimetres (23·2 inches) tall. A *post mortem* examination showed her to be exactly 24 inches (her body was slightly elongated after death). Her mature weight varied from 7½ lb. to 9 lb. and her "vital statistics" were 18½–19–17.

The Italian girl Caroline Crachami, born in Palermo, Sicily, in 1815, was only 20·2 inches tall when she died in London in 1824, aged 9. At birth she measured 7 inches long and weighed 1 lb. Her skeleton, measuring 19·8 inches, is now part of the Hunterian collection in the Museum of the Royal College of Surgeons, London.

Male The shortest recorded adult male dwarf was Calvin Phillips, born on 14 Jan. 1791 in Bridgewater, Massachusetts, U.S.A. He weighed 2 lb. at birth and stopped growing at the age of 5. When he was 19 he measured 26½ inches tall and weighed 12 lb. with his clothes on. He died two years later, in April 1812, from progeria, a rare disorder characterised by dwarfism and premature senility.

William E. Jackson, *alias* "Major Mite", born on 2 Oct. 1864 in Dunedin, New Zealand, measured 9 inches long and weighed 12 oz. at birth. In November 1880 he stood 21 inches and weighed 9 lb. He died in New York City, N.Y., U.S.A., on 9 Dec. 1900, when he measured 27 inches.

Another notable case was Max Taborsky, *alias* "Prince Kolibri", born in Vienna, Austria, in January 1863. He measured 35 centimetres (13·8 inches) at birth and stopped growing at the age of 9. When he died, aged 25, in 1888, he stood 69 centimetres (27·2 inches) tall and weighed 5 kilogrammes (11 lb.).

United Kingdom The shortest recorded British dwarfs were Hopkins Hopkins (1737–54) of Llantrisant, Glamorgan, and Miss Edith Barlow (1927–57) of Rotherham, Yorkshire, each 31 inches tall. Hopkins, who died from progeria (see above), weighed 19 lb. at the age of 7 and 13 lb. at the time of his death. Miss Barlow weighed 17 lb. William Butler of Plumstead, London, was reputedly 30 inches tall at the time of his death on 23 July 1737 aged 40, but this figure lacks confirmation. Harold Pyott (1887–1937) of Hemel Hempstead, Hertfordshire, may have been equally short. Although he claimed to be only 23 inches tall, his coffin measured 35 inches.

The famous 'Sir' Geoffrey Hudson (b. 1619) of Oakham, Rutlandshire, was reputedly 18 inches tall at the age of 30, but this extreme measurement is not borne out in portraits which show he was then about 3 feet 6 inches. At the time of his death in London in 1682 he measured 3 feet 9 inches.

Ireland The shortest recorded Irish adult dwarf was Mrs. Catherine Kelly (b. in August 1756), known as "the Irish fairy", who stood 34 inches tall and weighed 22 lb. She died in Norwich, Norfolk, on 15 Oct. 1785. David Jones (b. 28 April 1903) of Lisburn, County Antrim, Northern Ireland, reputedly measured 26 inches at the time of his death on 1 April 1970 aged 66. But as he weighed 4 stone (56 lb.), his height was probably nearer 36 inches.

Most variable stature Adam Rainer, born in Graz, Austria, in 1899, measured 1·18 metres (3 feet 10·45 inches) at the age of 21. But then he suddenly started growing upwards at a rapid rate, and by 1931 he had reached 2·18 metres (7 feet 1¾ inches). He became so weak as a result that he was bed-ridden for the rest of his life. He died on 4 March 1950 aged 51.

RACES

Tallest The tallest race in the world is the Tutsi (also called Batutsi, Watutsi, or Watussi), Nilotic herdsmen of Rwanda and Burundi, Central Africa whose males average 6 feet 1 inch, with a maximum of 7 feet 6 inches. The Tehuelches of Patagonia, long regarded as of gigantic stature (*i.e.* 7 to 8 feet), have in fact an average height (males) of 5 feet 10 inches with a maximum of just over 2 metres (6 feet 6¾ inches). A tribe with an average height of more than 6 feet was discovered in the inland region of Passis Manua of New Britain in December 1956. In May 1965 it was reported that the Crahiacoro Indians in the border district of the States of Mato Grosso and Pará, in Brazil, are exceptionally tall—certainly with an average of more than 6 feet. A report in May 1966 specifically attributed great stature to the Krem-Akarore Indians of the Xingu region of the Mato Grosso. In December 1967 the inhabitants of Barbuda, Leeward Islands were reported to have an average height in excess of 6 feet. The tallest people in Europe are the Montenegrins of Yugoslavia, with a male average of 5 feet 10 inches, compared with the men of Sutherland, at 5 feet 9½ inches. In 1912 the average height of the men living in Balmaclellan, Kirkcudbrightshire was reported to be 179 centimetres (5 feet 10·4 inches).

Tutsi (or Watutsi) tribesmen, the world's tallest ethnic group, indulging at what comes naturally—the sport of high jumping.

Shortest The world's shortest known race is the negrito Onge tribe, of whom only 22 (12 men, 10 women) survived on Little Andaman Island in the Indian Ocean by May 1956. Few were much more than 4 feet. The smallest pygmies are the Mbuti, with an average height of 4 feet 6 inches for men and 4 feet 5 inches for women, with some groups averaging only 4 feet 4 inches for men and 4 feet 1 inch for women. They live in the forests near the river Ituri in the Congo (Kinshasa), Africa. In June 1936 there was a report, not subsequently substantiated, that there was a village of dwarfs numbering about 800 in the Hu bei (Hupeh) province of Central China between Wu han and Lishan in which the men were all less than 4 feet tall and the women slightly taller. In October 1970 a tribe of pygmies, reportedly measuring only 1 metre (3 feet 3·4 inches) tall, was discovered in the border area of Bolivia, Brazil and Peru.

WEIGHT

Heaviest heavyweights *World Men* The heaviest recorded human of all time was the 6-foot 0½-inch tall Robert Earl Hughes (b. 4 June 1926) of Monticello, Illinois, U.S.A. An 11¼ lb. baby, he weighed 14½ stone at six years, 27 stone at ten, 39 stone at 13, 49½ stone at 18, 64 stone at 25 and 67½ stone at 27. His greatest recorded weight was 1,069 lb. (76 stone 5 lb.) in February 1958, and he weighed 1,041 lb. (74 stone 5 lb.) at the time of his death. His claimed waist of 122 inches, his chest of 104 inches and his upper arm of 40 inches were also the greatest on record. He died of uraemia (a condition caused by retention of urinary matter in the blood) in a trailer at Bremen, Indiana, on 10 July 1958, aged 32, and was buried in Binville Cemetery, near Mount Sterling, Illinois, U.S.A. His coffin, a converted piano case measuring 7 feet by 4 feet 4 inches and weighing nearly half a ton, had to be lowered by crane.

Johnny Alee (1853–87) of Carbon (now known as Carbonton) North Carolina, U.S.A. is reputed to have weighed 1,132 lb. (80 stone 12 lb.) at the time of his death, but the accuracy of this report has not yet been fully substantiated. He died from a heart attack after plunging through the flooring of his log cabin, which had been his "prison" for 19 years.

The only other men for whom weights of 800 lb. (57 stone 2 lb.) or more have been reliably reported are the 6 listed below:

	lb.	Stone	lb.
Mills Darden (1798–1857) U.S.A. (7 ft. 6 in.)	1,020	72	12
John Hanson Craig (1856–94) U.S.A. (6 ft. 5 in.)	907 (a)	64	11
Arthur Knorr (1914–60) U.S.A. (6 ft. 1 in.)	900 (b)	64	4
T. A. Valenzuela (1895–1937) Mexico (5 ft. 11 in.)	850	60	10
David Maquire (1904–*fl.* 1935) U.S.A. (5 ft. 10 in.)	810	57	12
William J. Cobb (b. 1926) U.S.A. (6 ft. 0 in.)	802 (c)	57	4

(a) *Won $1,000 in a "Bonny Baby" contest in New York City in 1858.*
(b) *Gained 300 lb. in the last 6 months of his life.*
(c) *Reduced to 232 lb. (16 stone 8 lb.) by July 1965.*

James Chasse (b. 1940) of Vineland, New Jersey, U.S.A., formerly the world's heaviest living man at 775 lb. (55 stone 5 lb.), was put on a low-calorie diet by doctors in November 1968. He hopes to get his weight down to 165 lb. (11 stone 11 lb.) by the end of 1972.

Women The heaviest woman ever recorded was a negress whose name was not recorded. She died in Baltimore, Maryland, U.S.A., on 4 Sept. 1888. Her weight was stated to be 850 lb. (60 stone 10 lb.).

A more reliable and better documented case was that of Mrs. Flora Mae (or May) Jackson (*née* King), a 5 ft. 9 in. negress born in 1930 at Sugar Lark, Mississippi, U.S.A. She weighed 10 lb. at birth, 267 lb. (19 stone 1 lb.) at the age of 11, 621 lb. (44 stone 5 lb.) at 25 and 840 lb. (60 stone) shortly before her death in Meridian, Florida, on 9 Dec. 1965. She was known in show business as "Baby Flo".

Great Britain Men The heaviest recorded man in Great Britain was William Campbell, who was born in Glasgow in 1856 and died on 16 June 1878, when a publican at High Bridge, Newcastle upon Tyne, Northumberland. He was 6 feet 3 inches tall and weighed 53 stone 8 lb., with an 85-inch waist and a 96-inch chest. His coffin weighed 1,500 lb. He was "a man of considerable intelligence and humour". The only other British man with a recorded weight of more than 50 stone (700 lb.) was the celebrated Daniel Lambert (1770–1809) of Leicester. He stood 5 feet 11 inches tall, weighed 52 stone 11 lb. shortly before his death and had a girth of more than 92 inches.

The resting place of England's "greatest" man—the celebrated colossus Daniel Lambert

The highest weight attained by any man living in Britain today was that of Arthur Armitage (born a 5 lb. baby on 28 June 1929) of Knottingley, Yorkshire, who scaled 40 stone 6 lb. (566 lb.) in his clothes on 15 Feb. 1970. He is 5 feet 9 inches tall and his vital statistics were 76–80–80. By June 1971 he had reduced by dieting (600 calories per day) to 21 stone 9 lb. (303 lb.).

George MacAree (b. 24 Dec. 1923) of Newham, London, who scaled 36 stone $9\frac{1}{2}$ lb. on 20 Feb. 1971 is now the heaviest man in Britain. He is 5 feet $10\frac{1}{2}$ inches tall and has vital statistics of $72\frac{1}{2}$–$69\frac{1}{2}$–80.

George MacAree at 36 stone, Britain's reigning heavyweight champion

Women The heaviest recorded woman in Great Britain was Miss Nellie Lambert (b. 3 April 1894) of Leicester, who weighed 40 stone 3 lb. at the age of 19 years. She stood 5 feet 3 inches tall, with a waist of 88 inches and 26-inch upper arm. She claimed to be a great-granddaughter of Daniel Lambert (see page 13), though he was never married.

Ireland The heaviest Irishman is reputed to have been Roger Byrne, who was buried in Rosenallis, County Laoighis (Leix), on 14 March 1804. He died in his 54th year and his coffin and its contents weighed 52 stone. Another Irish heavyweight was Lovelace Love (1731–66), born in Brook Hill, County Mayo. He weighed "upward of 40 stone" at the time of his death.

Heaviest twins The heaviest twins in the world are the McCreary twins (b. 1948), farmers of Hendersonville, North Carolina, U.S.A., who in March 1970 weighed 660 lb. (47 stone 2 lb.) and 640 lb. (45 stone 10 lb). Their names are Bill and Ben.

Lightest lightweights
World The lightest recorded adult was Lucia Zarate (b. San Carlos, Mexico 2 Jan. 1863, d. October 1889), an emaciated Mexican midget of $26\frac{1}{2}$ inches, who weighed $2\frac{1}{8}$ kilogrammes (4·7 lb.) at the age of 17. She "fattened up" to 13 lb. by her 20th birthday. At birth she weighed $2\frac{1}{2}$ lb. The lightest adult reported in the United Kingdom has been Hopkins Hopkins (Shortest dwarfs, see p. 12).

The thinnest recorded adults of normal height are those suffering from Simmonds' Disease (Hypophyseal cachexia). Losses up to 65 per cent. of the original body-weight have been recorded in females, with a "low" of 45 lb. In cases of anorexia nervosa (a morbid fear of growing up), weights of under 5 stone (70 lb.) have been reported. In cases of extreme muscular atrophy the bodyweight may be less than 40 lb., although the victims never attain normal stature. It was recorded that the American exhibitionist Rosa Lee Plemons (b. 1873) weighed 27 lb. at the age of 18. Edward C. Hagner (1892–1962), *alias* Eddie Masher, is alleged to have weighed only 48 lb. (3 stone 6 lb.) at a height of 5 feet 7 inches. He was also known as "the Skeleton Dude". In August 1825 the biceps measurement of Claude-Ambroise Seurat (b. 10 April 1797, d. 6 April 1826) of Troyes, France was 4 inches and the distance between his back and his chest was less than 3 inches.

Twins Bill and Ben McCreary —a two man traffic jam

The world's lightest recorded adult, Lucia Zarate

According to one report he stood 5 feet 7½ inches and weighed 78 lb. (5 stone 8 lb.) but in another account was described as 5 feet 4 inches and only 36 lb. (2 stone 8 lb.).

Slimming The greatest recorded slimming feat was that of William J. Cobb (b. 1926), *alias* 'Happy Humphrey', a professional wrestler of Macon, Georgia, U.S.A. It was reported in July 1965 that he had reduced from 802 lb. (57 stone 4 lb.) to 232 lb. (16 stone 8 lb.), a loss of 570 lb. (40 stone 10 lb.), in 3 years. His waist measurement declined from 101 inches to 44 inches.

The U.S. circus fat lady Mrs. Celesta Geyer (b. 1901), *alias* Dolly Dimples, reduced from 553 lb. to 152 lb. in 1950–51, a loss of 401 lb. in 14 months. Her vital statistics diminished *pari passu* from 79–84–84 to a *svelte* 34–28–36. Her book "How I lost 400 lbs." was not a best-seller because of the difficulty of would-be readers identifying themselves with the dressmaking problems of losing more than 28 stone when 4 feet 11 inches tall. In December 1967 she was reportedly down to 110 lb. (7 stone 12 lb.). The speed record for slimming was established by Paul M. Kimelman, 21, of Pittsburgh, Pennsylvania, U.S.A., who from 25 Dec. 1966 to August 1967 went on a crash diet of 300 to 600 calories per day to reduce from 427 lb. (30½ stone) to 130 lb. (9 stone 4 lb.). In his prime he wore size 56 trousers into one leg of which he can now step easily.

Arthur Armitage (see page 14) reportedly lost 12 stone in 6 weeks in November–December 1970 when reducing from 40 stone towards his target of 16 stone.

Weight gaining A probable record for gaining weight was set by Arthur Knorr (b. 17 May 1914), who died on 7 July 1960, aged 46, in Reseda, California, U.S.A. He gained 300 lb. (21 stone 6 lb.) in the last 6 months of his life and weighed 900 lb. (64 stone 4 lb.) when he died. Miss Doris James of San Francisco, California, U.S.A. is alleged to have gained 325 lb. (23 stone 3 lb.) in the 12 months before her death in August 1965, aged 38, at a weight of 675 lb. (48 stone 3 lb.). She was only 5 feet 2 inches tall.

Man *(Homo sapiens)* is a species in the sub-family Homininae of the family Hominidae of the super-family Hominoidea of the sub-order Simiae (or Anthropoidea) of the order Primates of the infra-class Eutheria of the sub-class Theria of the class Mammalia of the sub-phylum Vertebrata (Craniata) of the phylum Chordata of the sub-kingdom Metazoa of the animal kingdom.

2. ORIGINS

EARLIEST MAN

SCALE OF TIME

If the age of the Earth-Moon system (latest estimate at least 4,700 million years) is likened to a single year, Handy Man appeared on the scene at about 8.35 p.m. on 31 December, Britain's earliest known inhabitants arrived at about 11.32 p.m., the Christian era began about 13 seconds before midnight and the life span of a 113-year-old man (see page 16) would be about three-quarters of a second. Present calculations indicate that the Sun's increased heat, as it becomes a "red giant", will make life insupportable on Earth in about 10,000 million years. Meanwhile there may well be colder epicycles. The period of 1,000 million years is sometimes referred to as an aeon.

World The earliest known primates appeared in the Palaeocene period of about 70,000,000 years ago. The sub-order of higher primates, called Simiae (or Anthropoidea), evolved from the catarrhine or old-world sect nearly 30,000,000 years later in the Lower Oligocene period. During the Middle and Upper Oligocene the super-family Hominoidea emerged. This contains three accepted families, *viz* Hominidae (bipedal, ground-dwelling man or near man), Pongidae (brachiating forest apes) and Oreopithecidae, which includes *Apidium* of the Oligocene and *Oreopithecus* of the early Pliocene. Opinion is divided on whether to treat gibbons and their ancestors as a fourth full family (Hylobatidae) or as a sub-family (Hylobatinae) within the Pongidae. Some consider that Proconsulidae should also comprise a family, although others regard the genus *Proconsul*, who lived on the open savannah, as part of another sub-family of the Pongidae.

Earliest Hominid There is a conflict of evidence on the time during which true but primitive Hominidae were evolving. Fossil evidence indicates that it was some time during the Upper Miocene (about 10,000,000 to 12,000,000 years ago). The characteristics of the Hominidae, such as a large brain, very fully distinguish them from any of the other Hominoidea. Evidence published in August 1969 indicated that the line of descent of *Ramapithecus*, from the north-eastern Indian sub-continent, was not less than 8,000,000 years old and that of *Australopithecus*, from Eastern Africa possibly 6,000,000 years old.

Earliest Genus Homo The earliest known true member of the genus *Homo* was found between 6 Dec. 1960 and 1963 by Dr. Louis Seymour Bazett Leakey (b. 7 Aug. 1903 at Kabete, Kenya) Hon. Director of the Kenya National Museum's Centre for Pre-History and Palaeontology, in Nairobi, and his wife Mary in Bed I in the Olduvai Gorge, Tanganyika (now part of Tanzania). These remains have been determined by stratigraphic, radio-metric and fission-track dating to have existed between 1,750,000 and 2,300,000 years ago. They were first designated *"pre-Zinjanthropus"* but in March 1964 were renamed Handy Man *(Homo habilis)*, to differentiate them from the more primitive Nutcracker Man *(Zinjanthropus boisei)*, an East African australopithecine who was contemporary with Handy Man throughout Bed I and the greater part of Bed II times. Handy Man was about 4 feet tall.

In August 1965 a fragment of a *humerus* bone from a hominine upper arm was found near Kanapoi, Kenya, by Professor Bryan Patterson, a vertebrate palaeontolo-

The Olduvai Gorge, Tanzania where the earliest yet discovered artifacts of the genus *Homo* were found in 1960

gist of the Museum of Comparative Zoology at Harvard University, Cambridge, Massachusetts, U.S.A. It was announced in January 1967 that this bone dates from between 2,300,000 and 2,700,000 years ago.

Earliest Homo sapiens

The earliest recorded remains of the species *Homo sapiens*, variously dated from 300,000 to 450,000 years ago in the Middle Pleistocene, were discovered on 24 Aug. 1965 by Dr. Lászlo Vértes in a limestone quarry at Vértesszöllös, about 30 miles west of Budapest, Hungary. The remains, designated *Homo sapiens palaeo-hungaricus*, comprised an almost complete occipital bone, part of a skull with an estimated cranial capacity of nearly 1,400 cubic centimetres (85 cubic inches).

Earliest man in the Americas date from at least 50,000 B.C. and "more probably 100,000 B.C." according to Dr. Leakey after the examination of some hearth stones found in the Mojave Desert, California and announced in October 1970. The earliest human relic is a skull found in the area of Los Angeles, California dated in December 1970 to be from 22,000 B.C.

British Isles

The earliest known inhabitants of the British Isles who belonged to the genus *Homo* were Clactonian man (probably fewer than 200 of them), one of whose middens was discovered in Aug. 1969 by Dr. Waechter in the Lower Gravels of the Barnfield Pit at Swanscombe, Kent, together with some of their discarded choppers made of flint cores and blunted flake tools. They probably lived in the Thames valley area during the first third of the Great Interglacial 500,000–475,000 B.C. The oldest human remains ever found in Britain are pieces of a brain case from a specimen of *Homo sapiens fossilis*, believed to be a woman, recovered in June 1935 and March 1936 by Dr. Alvan T. Marston from the Boyn Hill terrace in the Barnfield Pit, near Swanscombe, northern Kent. This find is attributed to Acheulian man, type *III* or *IV*, dating from the warm Hoxnian interglacial period, about 250,000 years ago.

The mandible found in the Red Crag at Foxhall, near Ipswich, in 1863, but subsequently lost in the United States, has been claimed as a Clactonian relic and thus possibly anything up to 100,000 years older than Swanscombe man.

No remains from the Mesolithic period (*ante* 3500 B.C.) have yet been found but a site at Portland Bill is expected to yield some.

3. LONGEVITY

No single subject is more obscured by vanity, deceit, falsehood and deliberate fraud than the extremes of human longevity. Extreme claims are generally made on behalf of the very aged rather than by them.

Many hundreds of claims throughout history have been made for persons living well into their second century and some, insulting to the intelligence, for people living even into their third. The facts are that centenarians surviving beyond their 110th year are of the extremest rarity and the present absolute limit of proven human longevity does not admit of anyone living to celebrate a 114th birthday.

It is highly significant that in Sweden, where alone proper and thorough official investigations follow the death of every allegedly very aged citizen, none has been found to have surpassed 110 years. The most reliably pedigreed large group of people in the world, the British peerage, has, after ten centuries, produced only one peer who reached even his 100th birthday. However, this is possibly not unconnected with the extreme draughtiness of many of their residences.

Scientific research into extreme old age reveals that the correlation between the claimed density of centenarians

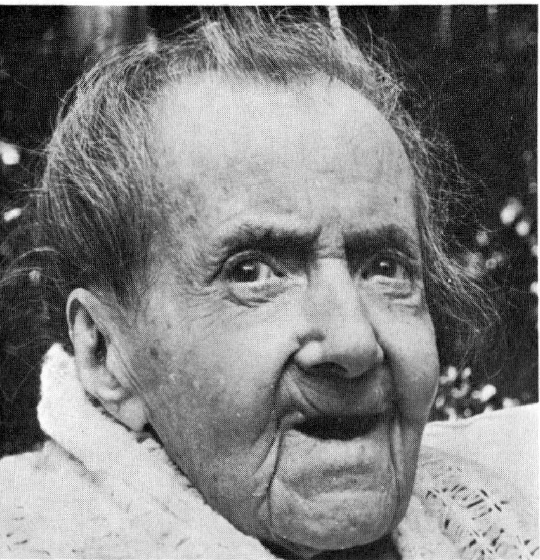

Miss Alice Stevenson, Britain's senior citizen in whose lifetime there have been 22 Prime Ministers from Lord Palmerston to Mr. Edward Heath

in a country and its regional illiteracy is 0·83 ±0·03. In late life, very old people often tend to advance their ages at the rate of about 17 years per decade. This was nicely corroborated by a cross analysis of the 1901 and 1911 censuses of England and Wales. Early claims must necessarily be without the elementary corroboration of birth dates. England was among the earliest of all countries to introduce local registers (1538) and official birth registration (1 July 1837), which was made fully compulsory only in 1874. Even in the United States, 45 per cent. of births occurring between 1890 and 1920 were unregistered.

Several celebrated super-centenarians are believed to have been double lives (father and son, brothers with the same names or successive bearers of a title). The most famous example is Christian Jakobsen Drackenberg allegedly born in Stavanger, Norway on 18 Nov. 1626 and died in Aarhus, Denmark aged seemingly 145 years 326 days on 9 Oct. 1772. A number of instances have been commercially sponsored, while a fourth category of recent claims are those made for political ends, such as the 100 citizens of the Russian Soviet Federative Socialist Republic (population about 132,000,000 at mid-1967) claimed in March 1960 to be between 120 and 156. From data on documented centenarians, actuaries have shown that only one 115-year life can be expected in 2,100 million lives (*cf.* world population was estimated to be 3,600 million at mid-1970).

The height of credulity was reached on 5 May 1933, when a news agency solemnly filed a story from China with a Peking date-line that Li Chung-yun, the "oldest man on Earth", born in 1680, had just died aged 256 years (*sic*). Currently the most extreme case of longevity claimed in the U.S.S.R. is 166 years for Shirali Muslimov of Barzavu, Azerbaijan, reputedly born on 19 May 1805.

Mythology often requires immense longevity; for example Larak the god-King lived according to Sumerian mythology 28,800 years and Dumuzi even longer. The most extreme biblical claim is that for Methuselah at 969 years (Genesis V, verse 27).

Oldest authentic centenarian *World*

The greatest authenticated age to which a human has ever lived is 113 years 124 days in the case of Pierre Joubert, a French-Canadian bootmaker. He was born in Charlesbourg, Québec Province, Canada, on 15 July 1701, son of Pierre Joubert (b. 1670) and Magdeleine Boesmier, and died in Québec on 16 Nov. 1814. His longevity was the subject of an investigation in 1870 by Dr. Tache, Official Statistician to the Canadian Government, and the proofs published are irrefutable. The following national records can be taken as authentic:

	Years	Days		Born	Died
Canada (a)	113	124	Pierre Joubert	15 July 1701	16 Nov. 1814
United States (b)	113	1	John B. Salling	15 Mar. 1846	16 Mar. 1959
United Kingdom (c)	111	339	Ada Rowe (*née* Giddings)	6 Feb. 1858	11 Jan. 1970
Ireland	111	327	The Hon. Katherine Plunket	22 Nov. 1820	14 Oct. 1932
South Africa (d)	111	151	Johanna Booyson	17 Jan. 1857	16 June 1968
Czechoslovakia	111	+	Marie Bernatkova	22 Oct. 1857	*fl.* Oct. 1968
Channel Islands	110	321	Margaret Ann Neve (*née* Harvey)	18 May 1792	4 April 1903
Yugoslavia	110	150+	Demitrius Philipovitch	9 Mar. 1818	*fl.* Aug. 1928
Japan (e)	110	114	Yoshigiku Ito	3 Aug. 1856	26 Nov. 1966
Netherlands	110	5	Baks Karnebeek (Mrs.)	2 Oct. 1849	7 Oct. 1959
France	109	309	Marie Philoméne Flassayer	13 June 1844	18 April 1954
Italy	109	179	Rosalia Spoto	25 Aug. 1847	20 Feb. 1957
Australia (f)	109	37	James Hull	3 Aug. 1852	9 Sept. 1961
Scotland	109	14	Rachel MacArthur (Mrs.)	26 Nov. 1827	10 Dec. 1936
Norway	109	+	Marie Olsen (Mrs.)	1 May 1850	*fl.* May 1959
Tasmania	109	+	Mary Ann Crow (Mrs.)	2 Feb. 1836	1945
Germany (g)	108	128	Luise Schwatz	27 Sept. 1849	2 Feb. 1958
Portugal	108	+	Maria Luisa Jorge	7 June 1859	*fl.* July 1967
Scotland	107	108	Jane Spier (Mrs.)	23 Nov. 1848	12 Mar. 1956
Finland	107	+	Marie Anderson	3 Jan. 1829	1936
Belgium	106	267	Marie-Joseph Purnode (Mrs.)	17 April 1843	9 Nov. 1949
Austria	106	231	Anna Migschitz	3 Feb. 1850	1 Nov. 1956
Sweden	106	98	Emma Gustaffsson (Mrs.)	18 June 1858	14 Sept. 1964
Isle of Man	105	221	John Kneen	12 Nov. 1852	9 June 1958
Spain (h)	105	217	Maria Cid Cabanes	25 Feb. 1845	30 Nov. 1950

(a) *Mrs. Ellen Carroll died in North River, Newfoundland, Canada on 8 December 1943, reputedly aged 115 years 49 days.*

(b) *Mrs. Betsy Baker (née Russell) was allegedly born 20 August 1842 in Brington, Northamptonshire, and died in Tecumseh, Nebraska, U.S.A. on 24 October 1955, reputedly aged 113 years 65 days. The 67-year-old son of Mrs. Tatzumbie Dupea, a Piute Indian at the Good Hope Convalescent Center, Los Angeles claimed that her birthday on 26 July 1969 was not her 112th but her 120th.*

(c) *London-born Miss Isabella Shepheard was allegedly 115 years old when she died at St. Asaph, Flintshire, North Wales, on 20 Nov. 1948, but her actual age was believed to have been 109 years 90 days. Charles Alfred Nunez Arnold died in Liverpool on 15 Sept. 1941 reputedly aged 112 years 66 days based on baptismal evidence.*

(d) *Mrs. Susan Johanna Deporter of Port Elizabeth, South Africa, was reputedly 114 years old when she died on 4 August 1954. Mrs. Sarah Lawrence, Cape Town, South Africa reputedly 112 on 3 March 1968.*

(e) *A man named Nakamura of Kamaishi, northern Japan, was reported to have died on 4 May 1969 aged 116 years 329 days.*

(f) *Reginald Beck of Sydney, New South Wales, Australia was allegedly 111 years old when he died on 13 April 1928.*

(g) *Friedrich Sadowski of Heidelberg reputedly celebrated his 111th birthday on 31 October 1936.*

(h) *Juana Ortega Villarin, Madrid, Spain, allegedly 112 in February 1962.*

In the face of the above data the claim published in the April 1961 issue of the Soviet Union's *Vestnik Statistiki* ('Statistical Herald') that there were 224 male and 368 female Soviet citizens aged in excess of 120 recorded at the census of 15 Jan. 1959 indicates a reliance on hearsay rather than evidence. Official Soviet insistence on the unrivalled longevity of the country's citizenry is curious in view of the fact that the 592 persons in their unique "over 120" category must have spent at least the first 78 years of their prolonged lives under Tsarism. It has recently been suggested that the extreme ages claimed by some men in Georgia, U.S.S.R., are the result of attempts to avoid military service when they were younger, by assuming the identities of older men.

Great Britain The oldest living Briton among an estimated 900 centenarians is Miss Alice Stevenson (b. 9 July 1861) now living at Brambleacres Old People's Home, Worcester Road, Sutton, Surrey.

Most reigns The greatest number of reigns during which any English subject could have lived is ten. A person born on the day (11 April) that Henry VI was deposed in 1471 had to live to only the comparatively modest age of 87 years 7 months and 6 days to see the accession of Elizabeth I on 17 Nov. 1558. Such a person could have been Thomas Carn of London, born 1471 and died 28 Jan. 1578 in his 107th year.

Thomas Carn, of London who lived through Ten Reigns.

Mrs Fyodor Vassilet with her 69 children

Mother Russia's most prolific mother was Madame Vassilet

4. REPRODUCTIVITY

MOTHERHOOD

Most children *World* The greatest number of children produced by a mother in an independently attested case is 69 by the first wife of Fyodor Vassilet, a peasant of the Moscow Jurisdiction, Russia, who, in 27 confinements, gave birth to 16 pairs of twins, 7 sets of triplets and 4 sets of quadruplets. Most of the children attained their majority. Mme. Vassilet (1816–72) became so renowned that she was presented at the court of Tsar Alexander II.

Currently the highest reliably reported figure is a 32nd child born on 11 Nov. 1970 to Maria Addolorata Casalini (b. 1929) of Brindisi, Italy. She was married at 17 and so far has had, in 23 confinements, two sets of quadruplets, one of triplets, one of twins and 19 single births. Only 15 children survive.

Great Britain The British record is probably held by Mrs. Elizabeth Greenhill (d. 1681) of Abbot's Langley, Hertfordshire. It is alleged that she gave birth to 39 children (32 daughters and 7 sons), all of whom attained their majority. She was married at 16, had a world record 38 confinements and died reputedly aged 64. Her last son Thomas (d. *c.* 1740) became surgeon to the 10th Duke of Norfolk and was the author of the "Art of Embalming" (1705). According to an inscription on a gravestone in Conway Church cemetery, Caernarvonshire, North Wales, Nicholas Hookes (d. 27 March 1637) was the 41st child of his mother Alice Hookes, but further details are lacking.

Great Britain's champion mothers of today are believed to be Mrs. Margaret McNaught, 48 of Balsall Heath, Birmingham (12 boys and 10 girls, all single births) and Mrs. Mable Constable, 51 of Long Itchington, Warwickshire who also has had 22 children including a set of triplets and two sets of twins.

Oldest mother *World* Medical literature contains extreme but unauthenticated cases of septuagenarian mothers. The oldest recorded mother of whom there is certain evidence is Mrs. Ruth Alice Kistler (*née* Taylor), formerly Mrs. Shepard, of Portland, Oregon, U.S.A. She was born at Wakefield, Massachusetts, on 11 June 1899 and gave birth to a daughter, Suzan, at Glendale, near Los Angeles, California, on 18 Oct. 1956, when her age was 57 years 129 days. The incidence of quinquagenarian births varies widely with the highest known rate in Albania (nearly 5,500 per million).

Great Britain The oldest British mother reliably recorded is Mrs. Winifred Wilson (*née* Stanley) of Eccles, Lancashire. She was born in Wolverhampton on 11 Nov. 1881 or 1882 and had her tenth child, a daughter Shirley, on 14 Nov. 1936, when aged 54 or 55 years and 3 days. At Southampton on 10 Feb. 1916, Mrs. Elizabeth Pearce gave birth to a son when aged 54 years 40 days. It is believed that live births to quinquagenarian mothers occur only twice in each million births in England and Wales.

Ireland The oldest Irish mother recorded was Mrs. Mary Higgins of Cork, County Cork (b. 7 Jan. 1876) who gave birth to a daughter, Patricia, on 17 March 1931 when aged 55 years 69 days.

Descendants In polygamous countries, the number of a person's descendants can become incalculable. The last Sharifian Emperor of Morocco, Moulay Ismail, known as "The Bloodthirsty", was reputed to have fathered a total of 548 sons and 340 daughters.

Capt. Wilson Kettle (b. 1860) of Grand Bay, Port aux Basques, Newfoundland, Canada, died on 25 Jan. 1963, aged 102, leaving 11 children by two wives, 65 grandchildren, 201 great-grandchildren and 305 great-great-grandchildren, a total of 582 living descendants. Mrs. Johanna Booyson (see page 17), of Belfast, Transvaal, was estimated to have 600 living descendants in South Africa in January 1968.

Mrs. Sarah Crawshaw (d. 25 Dec. 1844) left 397 descendants, according to her gravestone in Stones Methodist Church, Ripponden, Halifax, Yorkshire.

Multiple great grandparents Theoretically a great-great-great-great-grandparent is a possibility, though in practice countries in which young mothers are common generally have a low expectation of life. Mrs. Ella M. Prince of the U.S.A., who died, aged 91, on 29 May 1970, had three great-great-great-grandchildren among her 60 living descendants, while Hon. General Walter Washington Williams (1855–1959) of Houston, Texas, U.S.A., was reportedly several times a great-great-great-grandfather.

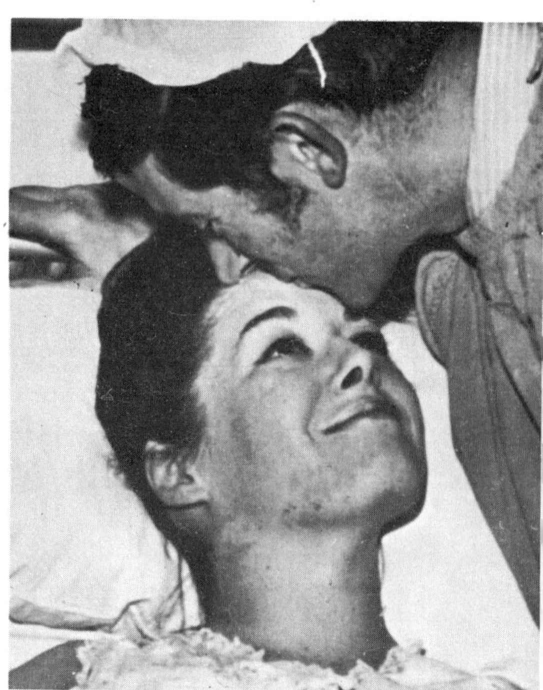

Mrs. Geraldine Mary Broderick who gave birth to nonuplets

MULTIPLE BIRTHS

World With multiple births, as with giants and centenarians, exaggeration is the rule. Since 1900 two cases of nonuplets, five cases of octuplets, 18 cases of septuplets and at least 23 cases of sextuplets have been reported. Mrs. Geraldine Broderick, 29, gave birth to 5 boys (two still-born) and 4 girls—the only certain nonuplets—at the Royal Hospital, Sydney, Australia on 13 June 1971. The last survivor, Richard (12 oz.) died on the sixth day. Jamaica has the highest incidence of multiple births (i.e. triplet and upward) at 4 per 1,000.

Octuplets The only confirmed case of live-born octuplets was the four boys and four girls born to Señora María Teresa Lopez de Sepulveda, aged 21, in a nursing home in Mexico City, Mexico, between 7 p.m. and 8 p.m. on 10 March 1967. They had an aggregate weight of 9 lb. 10 oz. and ranged between 1 lb. 3 oz. down to 14 oz. All the boys were named José and all the girls Josefina. They all died within 14 hours.

There have been four unconfirmed reports of octuplets since 1900: to Señora Enriquita Ruiba at Tampico, Mexico, in 1921; seven boys and one girl to Mme. Tam Sing at Kwoom Yam Sha, China, in June 1934; a case near Tientsin, China, on 29 Sept. 1947 (one baby died); and still-born babies to Señora Celia Gonzalez at Bahía Blanca, Argentina, on 2 May 1955.

Septuplets There have been five confirmed cases of septuplets since 1900: still-born babies to Britt Louise Ericsson, aged 34, in Uppsala, Sweden, in August 1964; five girls and two boys to Mme. Brigitte Verhaeghe-Denayer in Brussels, Belgium, on 25 March 1966 (all the babies died soon afterwards); four girls and three boys to Mrs. Sandra Cwikielnik in Boston, Massachusetts, U.S.A., on 1 Oct. 1966 (one was born dead and the others died within minutes); a case from Addis Ababa, Ethiopia in March 1969 of seven babies to Mrs. Verema Jusuf of whom two died immediately and a still-born set born in Sweden in 1966.

Sextuplets Among sextuplet births, the case of Mrs. Philip Speichinger provided the earliest irrefutable evidence in the person of a surviving daughter, Marjorie Louise of Mendon, Missouri, U.S.A., born on 9 Aug. 1936. The other five children were still-born. Mrs. Alinicia Parker (*née* Bushnell) was always cited as last survivor of the sextuplets reputedly born on 15 Sept. 1866 to Mrs. James B. Bushnell in Chicago, Illinois, U.S.A. She died, aged 85, in Warsaw, New York State, U.S.A., on 27 March 1952. The birth was registered by Dr. James Edwards but, for obscure reasons, was unrevealed until about 1912. The other children were identified as Lucy (died at 2 months), Laberto (died at 8 months), Norberto (died in 1934), Alberto (died in Albion, N.Y., in *c.* 1940) and Mrs. Alice Elizabeth Hughes (*née* Bushnell) who died in Flagstaff, Arizona, on 2 July 1941. From the sextuplets born to Maria Garcia wife of an Indian farmer in Michoacán State, Mexico, on 7 Sept. 1953, three (one boy and two girls) are reputedly still living. A woman living in a remote village in the Faridpur district of East Pakistan allegedly gave birth to six sons on 11 Nov. 1967.

Mrs. Sheila Ann Thorns (b. 2 Oct. 1938) of Northfield, Birmingham, England, gave birth to sextuplets at the New Birmingham Maternity Hospital on 2 Oct. 1968. In order of birth they were Lynne (2 lb. 6 oz., died 22nd), Ian (2 lb. 13 oz., died 13th), Julie (3 lb. 1 oz.), Susan (2 lb. 11 oz.), Roger (2 lb. 10 oz.) and a girl (died after one hour). A seventh child did not develop beyond the third month of this pregnancy which had been induced by a fertility drug. A second set of British sextuplets were delivered, after use of a fertility drug, of Mrs. Rosemary Letts (*née* Egerton) 23 of Rickmansworth, Hertfordshire by Caesarean section at University College Hospital, London on 15 Dec. 1969. One girl was still-born but the others Cara Dawn (2 lb. 13 oz.), Sharon Marie (2 lb. 9 oz.), Joanne (2 lb. 7 oz.), Gary John (1 lb. 11½ oz.) and Tanya (2 lb. 1 oz.) survived.

Quintuplets The earliest quintuplets in which all survived were: Émilie (died 6 Aug. 1954, aged 20), Yvonne (now in a convent), Cécile (now Mrs. Phillipe Langlois), Marie (later Mrs. Florian Houle died 1 March 1970) and Annette (now Mrs. Germain Allard), born in her seventh pregnancy to Mrs. Oliva Dionne, aged 25, near Callander, Ontario, Canada, on 28 May 1934 (aggregate weight 13 lb. 6 oz. with an average of 2 lb. 11 oz.).

Quintuplets were recorded in Wells, Somerset on 5 Oct. 1736 where four boys and a girl were all christened. Quins (three boys and two girls) were born to Mrs. Elspet Gordon of Rothes, Morayshire, Scotland in 1858 but all died within 12 hours and at Over Darwen, Lancashire on 24 April 1786 Mrs. Margaret Waddington produced five girls (three still-born) weighing a total of 2 lb. 12 oz.

Quins were born to Mrs. Irene Mary Hanson, 33 of Rayleigh, Essex at the Queen Charlotte's Maternity Hospital, Hammersmith, London on 13 Nov. 1969. They are Joanne Lesley (2 lb. 7 oz.), Nicole Jane (2 lb. 13 oz.), Julie Anne (2 lb. 15 oz.), Sarah Louise (3 lb. 7 oz.) and Jacqueline Mary (2 lb. 6½ oz.). A fertility drug was used.

Heaviest It was reported that quintuplets weighing 25 lb. were born on 7 June 1953 to Mrs. Lui Saulien of Chekiang province, China. A weight of 25 lb. was also reported for girl quins born to Mrs. Kamalammal in Pondicherry, India, on 30 Dec. 1956. All died shortly afterwards.

Quadruplets *Heaviest* The heaviest quadruplets ever recorded were Brucina Paula (5 lb. 7 oz.), Clifford (5 lb. 0 oz.), Stanford (4 lb. 15 oz.) and Stacey Lynn (4 lb. 7 oz.), totalling 19 lb. 13 oz., born by Caesarean section to Mrs. Ruth Becker, aged 28, between 5.15 a.m. and 5.18 a.m. on 3 Aug. 1962 at the Vancouver General Hospital in Vancouver, British Columbia, Canada.

United Kingdom The earliest recorded quadruplets to have all survived in the United Kingdom were the Miles quads, born at St. Neots, Huntingdon, on 28 Nov. 1935—Ann (now Mrs. Robert Browning), Ernest, Paul and Michael (total weight 13 lb. 15½ oz.). Sarah Coe, one of the quads born to Mrs. Henry Coe of Cambridge on 6–7 Oct. 1766 was reportedly still alive 42 years later in 1808. The other three died at 2, 15 and 20 months respectively. Quadruplets reputedly survived birth near Devil's Bridge, Cardiganshire, Wales in 1856 only to die of Cholera later in the same year. The heaviest set recorded were David John (5 lb. 7 oz.), Thelma Susan (4 lb. 1 oz.), Anthony James (5 lb. 1 oz.) and Beverley Margaret (3 lb. 14 oz.), totalling 18 lb. 7 oz., born on 14 Dec. 1957 to Mrs. Mary Bennett, aged 37, in the East End Maternity Hospital, Stepney, London. The lightest were Yana (3 lb. 8 oz.), Edward (3 lb. 3½ oz.), Lucille (3 lb. 8 oz.) and Christopher (2 lb. 7½ oz.), totalling 12 lb. 11 oz., born to Mrs. Phoebe Meacham (b. 1928) of Leigh-on-Sea in Rochford Hospital, Essex, on 3 Jan. 1962.

Ireland The first surviving quadruplets born in Ireland were those born on 23 Jan. 1965 to Mrs. Eileen O'Connell, aged 36, of Pallasgreen, County Limerick, in the Limerick Regional Hospital. On 31 Jan. 1965 they were weighed: Catherine Mary (2 lb. 2 oz.), Gerard Michael (3 lb. 6 oz.), John Paul (3 lb. 11 oz.) and Margaret Anne (3 lb. 0 oz.).

Triplets *Heaviest* There is an unconfirmed report of triplets weighing 23 lb., born in Australia in 1946 and one (two boys and a girl) of 26 lb. 6 oz. born to a 21-year-old Iranian woman reported on 18 March 1968. The heaviest recorded triplets born in the United Kingdom, were Robert (7 lb. 5 oz.), Geoffrey (6 lb. 2 oz.) and Paul (8 lb. 6 oz.), born between 8.10 p.m. and 8.25 p.m. on 8 Feb. 1965 to Mrs. Maureen Head, aged 25, of Colwyn Bay, Denbighshire, in the H.M. Stanley Hospital, St. Asaph,

Flintshire. They weighed an aggregate of 21 lb. 13 oz.

Most The greatest reported number of sets of triplets born to one woman is 15 (*cf.* 7 to Mme. Vassilet, page 18) to Maddalena Granata (1839–*fl.* 1886) of Nocera Superiore, Italy.

Oldest Giovanni, Leopoldo and Salvatore Zio of Palermo, Sicily, celebrated their 73rd birthday on 1 Sept. 1969.

Twins
Heaviest The heaviest recorded twins were two boys, the first weighing 17 lb. 8 oz. and the second 18 lb., born in Derbyshire. This was reported in a letter in *The Lancet* of 6 Dec. 1884. A more reliable recent case is that of Jerrald and Jerraldine, weighing 11 lb. each, born at 5.45 a.m. and 7.45 a.m. on 8 Jan. 1941 to Mrs. Beulah Paris (*née* Sehie), aged 34, at her home in Stanford, 4 miles from Louisville, Illinois, U.S.A.

Lightest The lightest recorded birthweight for surviving twins has been 3 lb. 2 oz. in the case of Wendy and Susan, born prematurely on 10 May 1961 to Mrs. Garner in St. Luke's Hospital, Huddersfield, Yorkshire.

Oldest The chances of identical twins both reaching 100 are said to be one in 1,000 million. The oldest recorded twins were Gulbrand and Bernt Morterud, born at Nord Odal, Norway, on 20 Dec. 1858. Bernt died on 1 Aug. 1960 in Chicago, Illinois, U.S.A. aged 101, and his brother died at Nord Odal on 12 Jan. 1964, aged 105. Twin sisters, Mrs. Vassilka Dermendjhieva and Mrs. Vassila Yapourdjieva of Sofia, Bulgaria allegedly celebrated their joint 104th birthday on 27 Sept. 1966.

"Siamese" Conjoined twins derived the name "Siamese" from the celebrated Chang and Eng Bunker, born at Maklong, Thailand (Siam), on 11 May 1811. They were joined by a cartilaginous band at the chest and married in April 1843 the Misses Sarah and Adelaide Yates and fathered ten and twelve children respectively. They died within three hours of each other on 17 Jan. 1874, aged 62. There is no genealogical evidence for the existence of the much-publicized Chalkhurst twins, Mary and Aliza, of Biddenden, Kent, allegedly born in *c.* 1550 (not 1100). Daisy and Violet Hilton, born in Brighton, Sussex on 5 Feb. 1908, were joined at the hip. They died in Charlotte, North Carolina, U.S.A., on 5 Jan. 1969 aged 60.

BABIES

Largest
World The heaviest normal new-born child recorded in modern times was a boy weighing 11 kilogrammes (24 lb. 4 oz.), born on 3 June 1961 to Mrs. Saadet Cor of Ceyhan, southern Turkey. There is an unconfirmed report of a woman giving birth to a 27 lb. baby in Essonnes, a suburb of Corbeil, central France, in June 1929. A deformed baby weighing 29¼ lb. was born in May 1939 in a hospital at Effingham, Illinois, U.S.A.

United Kingdom The greatest recorded live birth weight in the United Kingdom is 21 lb. for a child born on Christmas Day, 1852. It was reported in a letter to the *British Medical Journal* (1 Feb. 1879) from a doctor in Torpoint, Cornwall. The only other reported birth weight in excess of 20 lb. is 20 lb. 2 oz. for a boy born to a 33-year-old schoolmistress in Crewe, Cheshire, on 12 Nov. 1884. A baby of 33 lb. was reportedly born to a Mrs. Lambert of Wandsworth Road, London *c.* 1930 but its measurements indicate a weight of about 17 lb. The *British Medical Journal* reported in February 1935 the case of a boy aged 2 years 9 months who weighed 7 stone 2½ lb.

Ireland The heaviest baby recorded in Ireland was Anthony Michael Kinch, weighing 17 lb. 3 oz., who was born on 13 June 1950 to Mrs. Mary Kinch, aged 34, of Bray, County Wicklow.

Smallest The lowest birth weight for a surviving infant, of which there is definite evidence, is 10 oz. in the case of Marion Chapman, born on 5 June 1938 in South Shields, County Durham. She was 12¼ inches long. By her first birthday her weight had increased to 13 lb. 14 oz. She was born unattended and was nursed by Dr. D. A. Shearer, who fed her hourly through a fountain pen filler. Her weight on her 21st birthday was 7 stone 8 lb.

A weight of 8 oz. was reported on 20 March 1938 for a baby born prematurely to Mrs. John Womack, after she had been knocked down by a lorry in East Louis, Illinois, U.S.A. The baby was taken alive to St. Mary's Hospital, but further information is lacking. On 23 Feb. 1952 it was reported that a 6 oz. baby only 6½ inches long lived for 12 hours in a hospital in Indianapolis, Indiana, U.S.A. A twin was still-born. English law has accepted pregnancies with extremes of 174 days (*Clark v. Clark,* 1939) and 349 days (*Hadlum v. Hadlum,* 1949). The smallest viable baby reported from the United States has been Jacqueline Benson born at Palatine, Illinois on 20 Feb. 1936, weighing 12 oz.

Longest pregnancy The longest pregnancy reported is one of 389 days for a woman aged 25 in Woking Maternity Hospital, Surrey, England (*Lancet,* 3 Dec. 1954). The baby weighing 7 lb. 14 oz., was still-born. The average pregnancy is 273 days.

5. PHYSIOLOGY AND ANATOMY

BONES

Longest The thigh bone or *femur* is the longest of the 206 bones in the human body. It constitutes usually 27½ per cent. of a person's stature, and may be expected to be 19¾ inches long in a 6-foot-tall man. The longest recorded bone was the femur of the German giant Constantine who died in Mons, Belgium, on 30 March 1902, aged 30 (see page 10). It measured 76 centimetres (29·9 inches). The femur of Robert Wadlow, the tallest man ever recorded, measured approximately 29½ inches.

Smallest The *stapes* or stirrup bone, one of the three auditory ossicles in the middle ear, is the smallest human bone, measuring from 2·6 to 3·4 millimetres (0·10 to 0·17 of an inch) in length and weighing from 2·0 to 4·3 milligrammes (0·03 to 0·065 of a grain). Sesamoids are not included among human bones.

MUSCLES

Largest Muscles normally account for 40 per cent. of the body weight and the bulkiest of the 639 muscles in the human body is the *gluteus maximus* or buttock muscle, which extends the thigh.

Smallest The smallest muscle is the *stapedius,* which controls the *stapes* (see above), an auditory ossicle in the middle ear, and which is less than 1/20th of an inch long.

Smallest waists Queen Catherine de Medici (1519–89) decreed a waist measurement of 13 inches for ladies of the French court. This was at a time when females were more diminutive. The smallest recorded waist among women of normal stature in the 20th century is a reputed 13 inches in the case of the French actress Mlle. Polaire (1881–1939) and Mrs. Ethel Granger (b. 12 April 1905) of Peterborough, who reduced from a natural 22 inches over the period 1929–1939.

Largest chest measurements The largest chest measurements are among endomorphs (those with a tendency toward globularity). In the extreme case of Hughes (see page 13) this was reportedly 124 inches but in the light of his known height and weight a figure of 104 inches would be more supportable. George MacAree (see Britain's heaviest man) has a chest measurement of 72½ inches. Among muscular subjects (mesomorphs), chest measurements above 56 inches are extremely rare. The largest such chest measurement ever recorded was that of Angus Macaskill (1825–63) of Berneray, Scotland (see page 10), who may well have been the strongest man who ever lived. His chest must have measured 65 inches at his top weight of 37½ stone.

BRAIN

Largest The brain has 10^{10} cells each containing 10^{10} macromolecules. Each cell has 10^4 interconnections with other cells. After the age of 18 the brain loses some 10^3 cells per day but the macromolecular contingent of each cell is renewed 10^4 times in a normal life span. The brain of an average young adult male weighs 1,410 grammes (3 lb. 1·73 oz.) falling to 1,030 grammes (2 lb. 4·33 oz.). That of the average young adult female weighs 1,271 grammes (2 lb. 12·83 oz.). The heaviest brain ever recorded was that of Ivan Sergeyevich Turgenev (1818–83), the Russian author. His brain weighed 2,012 grammes (4 lb. 6·96 oz.). In January 1891 the *Edinburgh Medical Journal* reported the case of a 75-year-old man in the Royal Edinburgh Asylum whose brain weighed 1,829 grammes (4 lb. 0·5 oz.).

Smallest The brain of a microcephalous idiot may weigh as little as 300 grammes (10·6 oz.).

Longest necks The maximum measured extension of the neck by the successive fitting of copper coils, as practised by the Padaung or Mayan people of Burma, is 15¾ inches. From the male viewpoint the practice serves the dual purpose of enhancing the beauty of the female and ensuring fidelity. The neck muscles can become so atrophied that the removal of the support of the coils can produce asphyxiation.

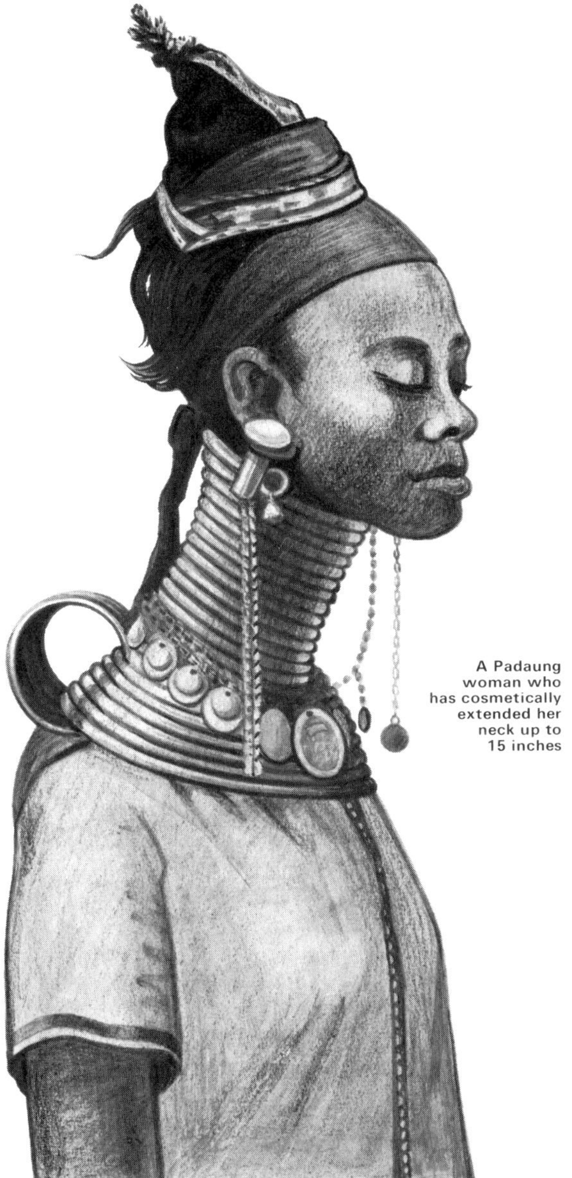

A Padaung woman who has cosmetically extended her neck up to 15 inches

Commonest illness The commonest illness in the world is coryza (acute nasopharyngitis) or the common cold. Only 4,600,000 working days were reportedly lost as a result of this illness in Great Britain between mid 1968 and mid 1969, since absences of less than three days are not reported. The greatest reported loss of working time in Britain is from bronchitis, which accounted for 37,490,000, or 11·39 per cent., of the total of 329,000,000 working days lost in the same period.

DISEASE

Commonest The commonest disease in the world is dental caries or tooth decay. In Great Britain 13 per cent. of people have lost all their teeth before they are 21 years old. During their lifetime few completely escape its effects. Infestation with pinworm *(Enterobius vermicularis)* approaches 100 per cent. in some areas of the world.

Rarest Medical literature periodically records hitherto undescribed diseases. Of once common diseases, rabies (hydrophobia) was last contracted in Britain in 1922 and last recorded in 1964. Kuru, or laughing sickness, afflicts only the Fore tribe of eastern New Guinea and is 100 per cent. fatal.

Most and least infectious The most infectious of all diseases is the pneumonic form of plague, with a mortality rate of about 99·99 per cent. Leprosy transmitted by *Mycobacterium leprae* is the least infectious of communicable diseases.

Highest morbidity Rabies in humans has been regarded as uniformly fatal when associated with the hydrophobia symptom. A 25-year-old woman Candida de Sousa Barbosa of Rio de Janeiro, Brazil, was believed to be the first ever survivor of the disease in November 1968. In 1969 all 515 cases reported were fatal.

Most notorious carrier The most notorious of all typhoid carriers has been Mary Mallon, known as Typhoid Mary, of New York City, N.Y., U.S.A. She was the source of the 1903 outbreak, with 1,300 cases. Because of her refusal to leave employment, often under assumed names, involving the handling of food, she was placed under permanent detention from 1915 until her death in 1938.

Touch sensitivity The extreme sensitivity of the fingers is such that a vibration with a movement of 0·02 of a micron can be detected. On 12 Jan. 1963 the Soviet newspaper *Izvestiya* reported the case of a totally blindfolded girl, Rosa Kulgeshova, who was able to identify colours by touch alone. Later reports suggested that the conditions of the experiment might not have excluded the possibility of collusion.

Most fingers Voight records a case of someone with 13 fingers on each hand and 12 toes on each foot.

Longest finger nails The longest recorded finger nails were reported from Shanghai in 1910, in the case of a Chinese priest who took 27 years to achieve nails up to 22¾ inches in length. Probably the longest nails now grown are those of Ramesh Sharma of Delhi whose thumb nail attained 9·4 inches after six years. He is a printer—presumably of the single-handed kind. Human nails normally grow from cuticle to cutting length in from 117 to 138 days.

Longest hair The longest recorded hair was that of Swami Pandarasannadhi, the head of the Thiruvadu Thurai monastery in India. His dead matted hair was reported in 1949 to be 26 feet in length.

Longest beard The longest beard recorded was that of Hans N. Langseth (b. 1846 in Norway) which measured 17½ feet at the time of his death in 1927 after 15 years residence in the United States. The beard was presented to the Smithsonian Institution, Washington, D.C. in 1967. R. Latter of Tunbridge Wells, Kent, who died in 1900 aged 77, reputedly had a beard 16 feet long. The beard of the bearded lady Janice Deveree (b. Bracken Co., Kentucky, U.S.A., 1842) was measured at 14 inches in 1884.

Longest moustache The longest moustache on record is that of Masuriya Din (b. 1908), a Brahmin of the Partabgarh district in Uttar Pradesh, India. It grew to an extended span of 8 feet 6 inches between 1949 and 1962, and costs £13 per annum in upkeep. The longest moustache in Great Britain is that of Mr. John Roy (b. 14 Jan. 1910), licensee of the "Cock Inn" at Beazely End, near Braintree, Essex. It attained a span of 41½ inches between 1939 and 1970.

Blood groups The preponderance of one blood group varies greatly from one locality to another. On a world basis Group O is the most common (46 per cent.), but in some areas, for example London and Norway, Group A predominates.

The full description of the commonest sub-group in Britain is O MsNs, P+, Rr, Lu(a−), K−, Le(a−b+), Fy(a+b+), Jk(a+b+), which occurs in one in every 270 people.

The rarest blood group on the ABO system, one of nine systems, is AB, which occurs in less than three per cent. of persons in the British Isles. The rarest type in the world is a type of Bombay blood (sub-type A-h) found so far only in a Czechoslovak nurse in 1961 and in a brother and sister in New Jersey, U.S.A. reported in February 1968. The American male has started a blood bank for himself.

Champion blood donor Joseph Elmaleh (b. 1915) of Marseilles, France, donated on 22 May 1968 his 597th pint of blood making a total of 74 gallons 5 pints since 1931. A 50-year-old haemophiliac Warren C. Jyrich required 2,400 pints of blood when undergoing open heart surgery at the Michael Reese Hospital, Chicago, U.S.A., in December 1970.

Largest vein The largest vein in the human body is the cardiac vein known as the vena cava.

Most alcoholic subject It is recorded that a hard drinker named Vanhorn (1750–1811), born in London, averaged more than four bottles of ruby port per day for the 23 years 1788 to his death aged 61 in 1811. The total of his "empties" was put at 35,688.

The United Kingdom's legal limit for motorists is 80 milligrammes of alcohol per 100 millilitres of blood. The hitherto recorded highest figure in medical literature of 490 mg. per 100 ml. was submerged when a 68-year-old male was carried from his kitchen in Tetbury, Gloucestershire, shortly after midnight on Boxing Day 1968. A figure of 600 mg. per 100 ml. was checked and rechecked by a disbelieving Dr. George Hickie. At the inquest the deceased was described by a close relative as "a fairly heavy drinker".

Longest coma The longest duration of human unconsciousness was 32 years 99 days endured by Karoline Karlsson (b. Mönsterås, Sweden in 1862) from 25 Dec. 1875 to 3 April 1908. She died on 6 April 1950 aged 88. The longest recorded coma of any person still living is that of Elaine Esposito (b. 3 Dec. 1934) of Tarpon Springs, Florida, U.S.A. She has never stirred since an appendicectomy on 5 Aug. 1941, when she was six, in Chicago, Illinois, U.S.A. She was still living in 1969.

Fastest reflexes The results of experiments carried out in 1943 have shown that the fastest messages transmitted by the nervous system travel at 265 m.p.h. With advancing age impulses are carried 15 per cent. more slowly.

BODY TEMPERATURE

Highest In Kalow's case (*Lancet*, 31 Oct. 1970) a woman following halothane anaesthesia ran a temperature of 112° F (44·4° C). She recovered after a procainamide infusion. Marathon runners in hot weather attain 105·8° F (41° C).

A temperature of 115° F was recorded in the case of Christopher Legge in the Hospital for Tropical Diseases, London, on 9 Feb. 1934. A subsequent examination of the thermometer disclosed a flaw in the bulb, but it is regarded as certain that the patient sustained a temperature of more than 110° F.

Lowest The lowest body temperature ever recorded for a living person was 60·8° F (16·0° C) in the case of Vickie Mary Davis (b. 25 Dec. 1953) of Milwaukee, Wisconsin, when she was admitted to the Evangelical Hospital, Marshalltown, Iowa, U.S.A., on 21 Jan. 1956. The house in which she had been found unconscious on the floor was unheated and the air temperature had dropped to −24° F (−31° C). Her temperature returned to normal (98·4° F or 36·9° C) after 12 hours and may have been as low as 59° F (15·0° C) when she was first found.

Heart stoppage The longest recorded heart stoppage is 3 hours in the case of a Norwegian boy, Roger Arntzen, in April 1962. He was rescued, apparently drowned, after 22 minutes under the waters of the River Nideelv, near Trondheim.

The longest recorded interval in a *post mortem* birth was one of at least 80 minutes in Magnolia, Mississippi, U.S.A. Dr. Robert E. Drake found Fanella Anderson, aged 25, dead in her home at 11.40 p.m. on 15 Oct. 1966 and he delivered her of a son weighing 6 lb. 4 oz. by Caesarean operation in the Beacham Memorial Hospital on 16 Oct. 1966.

Largest stone The largest stone or vesical calculus reported in medical literature was one of 13 lb. 14 oz. (6,294 grammes) removed from an 80-year-old woman by Dr. Humphrey Arthure at Charing Cross Hospital, London, on 29 Dec. 1952.

Earliest influenza An epidemic bearing symptoms akin to influenza was first recorded in 412 B.C. by Hippocrates (*c.* 460–*c.* 375 B.C.). The earliest description of an epidemic in Great Britain was in the *Chronicle of Melrose* in 1173, although the term influenza was not introduced until 1743 by John Huxham (1692–1768) of Plymouth, Devonshire.

Earliest duodenal ulcer The earliest description in medical literature of a duodenal ulcer was made in 1746 by Georg Erhard Hamberger (1696–1755).

Earliest slipped disc The earliest description of a prolapsed intervertebral cartilage was by George S. Middleton and John H. Teacher of Glasgow, Scotland, in 1911.

Pill-taking It is recorded that among hypochondriacs Samuel Jessup (b. 1752), a wealthy grazier of Heckington, Lincolnshire, has never had a modern rival. His consumption of pills from 1794 to 1816 was 226,934, with a peak annual total of 51,590 in 1814. He is also recorded as having drunk 40,000 bottles of medicine before death overtook him at the surprisingly advanced age of 65.

Most tattoos Vivian "Sailor Joe" Simmons, a Canadian tattoo artist, had 4,831 tattoos on his body. He died in Toronto on 22 Dec. 1965 aged 77. Britain's most tattooed man is Arthur (Eddy) Noble (b. 1924) of Newcastle, who filled in his last gaps with 114 more tattoos in 1970.

Hiccoughing The longest recorded attack of hiccoughs was that afflicting Jack O'Leary of Los Angeles, California, U.S.A. It was estimated that he "hicked" more than 160,000,000 times in an attack which lasted from 13 June 1948 to 1 June 1956, apart from a week's respite in 1951. His weight fell from 9 stone 12 lb. to 5 stone 4 lb. People sent 60,000 suggestions for cures of which only one apparently worked—a prayer to St. Jude, the patron saint of lost causes. The infirmary at Newcastle upon Tyne is recorded to have admitted a young man from Long Witton, Northumberland on 25 March 1769 suffering from hiccoughs which could be heard at a range of more than a mile.

Sneezing The most chronic sneezing fit ever recorded was that of June Clark, aged 17, of Miami, Florida, U.S.A. She started sneezing on 4 Jan. 1966, while recovering from a kidney ailment in the James M. Jackson Memorial Hospital, Miami. The sneezing was stopped by electric "aversion" treatment on 8 June 1966, after 155 days. The highest speed at which expelled particles have been measured to travel is 103·6 m.p.h.

Snoring *Loudest* Research at the Ear, Nose and Throat Department of St. Mary's Hospital, London, published in November 1968, shows that a rasping snore can attain a loudness of 69 decibels.

Yawning In Lee's case, reported in 1888, a 15-year-old female patient yawned continuously for a period of five weeks.

SWALLOWING

The worst known case of compulsive swallowing was reported in the *Journal of the American Medical Association* in December 1960. The patient, who complained only of swollen ankles, was found to have 258 items in his stomach, including a 3-lb. piece of metal, 26 keys, 3 sets of rosary beads, 16 religious medals, a bracelet, a necklace, 3 pairs of tweezers, 4 nail clippers, 39 nail files, 3 metal chains and 88 assorted coins.

Coins The most extreme recorded case of coin swallowing was revealed by Sedgefield General Hospital, County Durham, on 5 Jan. 1958, when it was reported that 366 halfpennies, 26 sixpences, 17 threepences, 11 pennies and four shillings (424 coins valued at £1 17s. 5d.), plus 27 pieces of wire totalling 5 lb. 1 oz., had been extracted from the stomach of a 54-year-old man.

Sword The longest length of sword able to be "swallowed" by a practised exponent, after a heavy meal, is 27 inches. Perhaps the greatest exponent is Alex Linton, born on 25 Oct. 1904 in Boyle, County Roscommon, Ireland. He stands 5 feet 3 inches tall and has "swallowed" four 27-inch blades at one time. He now lives in Sarasota, Florida, U.S.A.

An artist's representation of the assorted ironmongery swallowed in the Sedgefield case

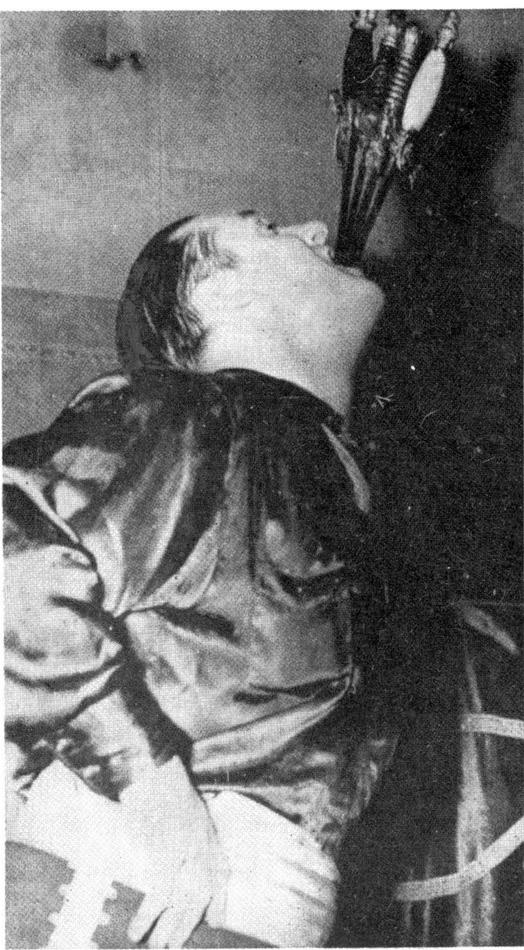

The world's most voracious sword swallower

DENTITION

Earliest The first deciduous or milk teeth normally appear in infants at five to eight months, these being the mandibular and maxillary first incisors. There are many records of children born with teeth, the most famous example being Prince Louis Dieudonné, later Louis XIV of France, who was born with two teeth on 5 Sept. 1638. Molars usually appear at 24 months, but in 1956 Bellevue Hospital in New York City, N.Y., U.S.A., reported a molar in a one-month-old baby, Robert R. Clinton.

Most Cases of the growth in late life of a third set of teeth have been recorded several times. A reference to an extreme case in France of a fourth dentition, known as Lison's case, was published in 1896. A triple row of teeth was noted in 1680 by Albertus Hellwigius.

OPTICS

Smallest visible object The resolving power of the human eye is 0·0003 of a radian or an arc of one minute (1/60th of a degree), which corresponds to 100 microns at 10 inches. A micron is a thousandth of a millimetre, hence 100 microns is 0·003937, or less than four thousandths, of an inch. The human eye can, however, detect a bright light source shining through an aperture only 3 to 4 microns across.

Colour sensitivity The unaided human eye, under the best possible viewing conditions, comparing large areas of colour, in good illumination, using both eyes, can distinguish 10,000,000 different colour surfaces. The most accurate photoelectric spectrophotometers possess a precision probably only one-half to one-third as good as this.

Colour blindness The most extreme form of colour blindness, monochromatic vision, is very rare. The highest recorded rate of red-green colour blindness is in Czechoslovakia and the lowest rate among Fijians and Brazilian Indians.

VOICE

Highest and lowest The highest and lowest recorded notes attained by the human voice before this century were a C in *alt-altissimo* (C^{iv}) by Lucrezia Agujari (1743–83), noted by the Austrian composer Wolfgang Amadeus Mozart (1756–91) in Parma, northern Italy, in 1770, and an A_1 (55 cycles per second) by Kaspar Foster (1617–73). Since 1950 singers have achieved high and low notes far beyond the hitherto accepted extremes. However, notes at the bass extremity of the register tend to lack harmonics and are of little musical value, while the topmost notes must be regarded as almost purely sinusoidal. Frl. Marita Günther, trained by Alfred Wolfsohn, has covered the range of the piano from the lowest note, A_{11}, to C^{v}. Of this range of $7\frac{1}{4}$ octaves, six octaves are considered to be of musical value. Mr. Roy Hart, also trained by Wolfsohn, has reached notes below the range of the piano. The highest note being sung by a tenor is G in *alt-altissimo* by Louis Lavelle, coached by Mr. S. Pleeth, in *Lovely Mary Donelly*. The lowest note put into song is a D_{11} by the singer Tom King, of King's Langley, Hertfordshire. The highest note called for in singing was an $f^{iv}\#$, which occurred twice in Zerbinetta's Recitative and Aria in the first (1912) version of the opera *Ariadne auf Naxos* by Richard Strauss (1864–1949). It was transposed down a tone in 1916.

Greatest range The normal intelligible outdoor range of the male human voice in still air is 200 yards. The *silbo*, the whistled language of the Spanish-speaking Canary Island of La Gomera, is intelligible across the valleys, under ideal conditions, at five miles. There is a recorded case, under freak acoustic conditions, of the human voice being detectable at a distance of $10\frac{1}{2}$ miles across still water at night. It was said that Mills Darden (see page 13) could be heard 6 miles away when he shouted at the top of his voice.

Lowest detectable sound The intensity of noise or sound is measured in terms of power. The power of the quietest sound that can be detected by a person of normal hearing at the most sensitive frequency of *c.* 2,750 Hz is $1{\cdot}0 \times 10^{-16}$ of a watt per square centimetre. One tenth of the logarithm (to the base of 10) of the ratio of the power of a noise to this standard provides a unit termed a decibel. Noises above 150 decibels will cause immediate permanent deafness, while a noise of 30 decibels is negligible.

Highest detectable pitch The upper limit of hearing by the human ear has long been regarded as 20,000 Hz (cycles per second), although children with asthma can often detect a sound of 30,000 cycles per second. It was announced in February 1964 that experiments in the U.S.S.R. had conclusively proved that oscillations as high as 200,000 cycles per second can be heard if the oscillator is pressed against the skull.

OPERATIONS

Longest The most protracted operations are those involving brain surgery. Such operations lasting up to 16 hours were reported from the United States as early as 1942.

Oldest subject The greatest recorded age at which a person has been subjected to an operation is 111 years 105 days in the case of James Henry Brett, Jr. (b. 25 July 1849, d. 10 Feb. 1961) of Houston, Texas, U.S.A. He underwent a hip operation on 7 Nov. 1960. The oldest age established in Britain was the case of Miss Mary Wright (b. 28 Feb. 1862) who died during an operation at Boston, Lincolnshire on 22 April 1971 aged 109 years 53 days.

Heart The first human heart transplant operation was performed on Louis Washkansky, aged 55, at the Groote Schuur Hospital, Cape Town, South Africa, between 1.00 a.m. and 6 a.m., on 3 Dec. 1967, by a team of 30 headed by Prof. Christiaan Neethling Barnard (b. 1924). The donor was Miss Denise Ann Darvall, aged 25. Washkansky died on 21 Dec. 1967. The transplant of the heart of Clive Haupt, a deceased 24-year-old Cape coloured, into Dr. Philip Blaiberg (b. 24 May 1909) of Wynberg, Cape Town, was performed at the same hospital between 10.35 a.m. and 4 p.m. on 2 Jan. 1968. Dr. Blaiberg died 564 days later on 17 Aug. 1969. Britain's longest-surviving heart transplant patient has been Mr. Charles Hendrick who died in Guy's Hospital of a lung infection on 31 Aug. 1969—107 days after his operation.

Earliest appendicectomy The earliest recorded successful appendix operation was performed in 1736 by Claudius Amyand (1680–1740). He was Serjeant Surgeon to King George II (reigned 1727–60).

Earliest anaesthesia The earliest recorded operation under general anaesthesia was for the removal of a cyst from the neck of James Venable by Dr. Crawford Williamson Long (1815–78), using diethyl ether ($(C_2H_5)_2O$), in Jefferson, Georgia, U.S.A., on 30 March 1842. The earliest use of ether in Great Britain was by Robert Liston (see also below) at the University College Hospital, London on 21 Dec. 1846 for an amputation.

Fastest amputation The shortest time recorded for the amputation of a limb in the pre-anaesthetic era was 33 seconds through a patient's thigh by Robert Liston (1794–1847) of Edinburgh, Scotland. This feat caused his assistant the loss of three fingers from his master's saw.

Surgical instruments The largest surgical instruments are robot retractors used in abdominal surgery introduced by Abbey Surgical Instruments of Chingford, Essex in 1968 and weighing 11 lb. Some bronchoscopic forceps measure 60 cms. ($23\frac{1}{2}$ inches) in length. The smallest is Elliot's eye trephine, which has a blade 0·078 of an inch in diameter.

Kim Ung-Yong of South Korea aged 4½, who established the highest ever recorded I.Q. of 210

Highest I.Q. On the Terman index for Intelligence Quotients, 150 represents "genius" level. The indices are sometimes held to be immeasurable above a level of 200 but a figure of 210 has been attributed to Kim Ung-Yong of Seoul, South Korea (b. 7 March 1963). He composed poetry and spoke four languages (Korean, English, German and Japanese), and performed integral calculus at the age of 4 years 8 months on television in Tokyo on "The World Surprise Show" on 2 Nov. 1967. Both his parents are University professors and were both born at 11 a.m. on 23 May 1934. Research into past geniuses at Stanford University, California, U.S.A., has produced a figure of "over 200" for John Stuart Mill (1806–73), who began to learn ancient Greek at the age of three. A similar rating has also been attributed to Johann Wolfgang von Goethe (1749–1832) of Frankfurt am Main, West Germany. More than 20 per cent. of the 15,000 members of the international Mensa society have an I.Q. of 161 or above on the Cattell index which is equivalent to 142 on the Terman index.

Human memory Mehmed Ali Halici of Ankara, Turkey on 14 Oct. 1967 recited 6,666 verses of the Koran from memory in six hours. The recitation was followed by six Koran scholars. Rare instances of eidetic memory—the ability to re-project and hence 'visually' recall material—are known to science.

Calculating ability Herbert de Grote of Baja, California, Mexico has been attested to have extracted the 13th root of a 100-digit number by exclusively mental process in 23 minutes in a test in Chicago, Illinois on 5 Oct. 1970. His answer was 46,231,597. No comparable feat has been recorded.

Sleeplessness Researches indicate that on the Circadian cycle for the majority peak efficiency is attained between 8 p.m. and 9 p.m. and the low point comes at 4 a.m. The longest recorded period for which a person has voluntarily gone without sleep, while under medical surveillance, is 282 hours 55 minutes (11 days 18 hours 55 minutes) by Mrs. Bertha Van Der Merwe, aged 52, a housewife of Cape Town, South Africa, ending on 13 Dec. 1968.

It was reported that Toimi Artturinpoika Silvo, a 54-year-old port worker of Hamina, Finland, stayed awake for 32 days 12 hours from 1 March to 2 April 1967. He walked 17 miles per day and lost 33 lb. in weight. Mr. Eustace Rushworth Burnett (b. 1880) of Hose, Leicestershire, claimed to have lost all desire to sleep in 1907 and that he never again went to bed. He died in January 1965, 58 years later, aged 85.

Motionlessness The longest that a man has voluntarily remained motionless is 4½ hours by Private (1st Class) William A. Fuqua of Fort Worth, Texas, U.S.A. He is a male mannequin or "fashioneer" in civil life earning up to $1,300 (£541) per hour for his ability to "freeze". The job is hazardous for it was reported in November 1967 that he was stabbed in the back by a man "proving" to his wife that he was only a dummy.

Fastest talker Few people are able to speak articulately at a sustained speed above 300 words per minute. The fastest broadcaster has been regarded as Jerry Wilmot, the Canadian ice hockey commentator in the post World War II period. Raymond Glendenning (b. Newport, Monmouth, 25 Sept. 1907) of the B.B.C. once spoke 176 words in 30 seconds while commentating on a greyhound race. In public life the highest speed recorded is a 327 words per minute burst in a speech made in December 1961 by John Fitzgerald Kennedy (1917–63), then President of the United States. In October 1965 it was reported that Peter Spiegel, 62, of Essen, West Germany, achieved 908 syllables in one minute at a rally of shorthand writers.

Dr. Charles Hunter of Rochdale, Lancashire, England on 14 Dec. 1968 demonstrated an ability to recite the 262 words of the soliloquy *To Be or Not To Be* from Shakespeare's *Hamlet* (Act III, Scene 1) in 41 secs. or at a rate of 383 words per minute. In March 1968 he covered the first 50 words in 7·2 secs. (a rate of 416·6 words per minute).

Fasting Most humans experience considerable discomfort after an abstinence from food for even 12 hours but this often passes off after 24–28 hours. Records claimed without unremitting medical surveillance are of little value.

The longest period for which anyone has gone without food is 382 days by Angus Barbieri (b. 1940) of Tayport, Fife, who lived on tea, coffee, water, soda water and vitamins in Maryfield Hospital, Dundee, Angus, from June 1965 to July 1966. His weight declined from 33 stone 10 lb. to 12 stone 10 lb. Dr. Stephen Taylor, 43, of Mount Roskill, New Zealand, fasted 40 days with only a glass of water per day in a political protest in 1970.

Hunger strike The longest recorded hunger strike was one of 94 days by John and Peter Crowley, Thomas Donovan, Michael Burke, Michael O'Reilly, Christopher Upton, John Power, Joseph Kenny and Seán Hennessy in Cork Prison, Ireland, from 11 Aug. to 12 Nov. 1920. These nine survivors (Joseph Murphy died on the 76th day) owed their lives to expert medical attention. The longest recorded hunger strike with forcible feeding in a British gaol is 375 days by Ronald Barker, 28, in Lincoln Jail and Armley Prison, Leeds from 23 Jan. 1970. He was protesting his innocence of a robbery in Louth, Lincolnshire in which he was found uninvolved in a re-trial at Northamptonshire Assizes on 2 Feb. 1971. The feeding was done with "Complan" by tube orally.

Most voracious fire-eater The hardest blowing fire-eater is Kjell Swing (Sweden), who can produce a flame 6½ feet long.

Underwater The world record for voluntarily staying under water is 13 minutes 42·5 seconds by Robert Foster, aged 32, an electronics technician of Richmond, California, who stayed under 10 feet of water in the swimming pool of the Bermuda Palms Motel at San Rafael, California, U.S.A., on 15 March 1959. He hyperventilated with oxygen for 30 minutes before his descent. His longest breath-hold without oxygen was 5 mins. 40 secs.

Human salamanders The highest dry-air temperature endured by naked men in U.S. Air Force experiments in 1960 was 400° F, and for heavily clothed men 500° F. Steaks require only 325° F. Temperatures of 140° C (284° F) have been found quite bearable in *Sauna* baths.

g forces The acceleration g, due to gravity, is 32 feet 1·05 inches per second per second at sea-level at the Equator. A *sustained* acceleration of 31 g was withstood for 5 seconds by R. Flanagan Gray, aged 39, at the U.S. Naval Air Development Center in Johnsville, Pennsylvania, in 1959. This makes the bodyweight of a 185 lb. (13 stone 3 lb.) man seem like 5,700 lb. (2·54 tons). The highest value endured in a dry capsule is 25 g. The highest g value endured on a water-braked rocket sled is 82·6 g for 0·04 of a second by Eli L. Beeding Jr. at Holloman Air Force Base, New Mexico, U.S.A., on 16 May 1958. He was put in hospital for 3 days. A man who fell off a 185-foot cliff has survived a *momentary* g of 209 in decelerating from 68 m.p.h. to stationary in 0·015 of a second.

Isolation The longest recorded period for which any volunteer has been able to withstand total deprivation of all sensory stimulation (sight, hearing and touch) is 92 hours, recorded in 1962 at Lancaster Moor Hospital, Lancashire.

Extra sensory perception The highest consistent performer in tests to detect powers of extra-sensory perception is Pavel Stepánek (Czechoslovakia) known in parapsychological circles as "P.S.". His performance on nominating hidden white or green cards from May 1967 to March 1968 departed from a chance probability yielding a Chi^2 value corresponding to $P < 10^{-50}$ or odds of more than 100 octillion to one against the achievement being one of chance. One of the two appointed referees recommended that the results should not be published. The highest published scores in any E.S.P. test were those of a 26-year-old female tested by Prof. Bernard F. Reiss of Hunter College, New York in 1936. In 74 runs of 25 guesses each she scored one with 25 all correct, two with 24 and an average of 18·24 instead of the random 5·00. Such a result would depart from chance probability by a factor $> 10^{700}$.

2 ANIMAL AND PLANT KINGDOMS

ANIMAL KINGDOM—GENERAL RECORDS

Note—Guinness Superlatives Ltd. will publish a specialist volume entitled *Animal Facts and Feats* during 1972, which will treat the dimensions and performances of all the Classes of the Animal Kingdom in greater detail giving also the sources and authorities for much of the material in this chapter.

Largest and heaviest

The largest and heaviest animal in the world (and probably also the biggest animal which has *ever* existed) is the blue or sulphur bottom whale (*Balænoptera musculus*), also called Sibbald's rorqual. Practical difficulties and commercial considerations combine to make data on weights very sparse, but it has now been established that the longest blue whale on record was a female taken near the South Shetlands in March 1926 which measured 33·27 metres (108 feet 11 inches) in length. Another female measuring 96$\frac{3}{4}$ feet, brought into the flensing station at Prince Olaf, South Georgia in *c.* 1931 was calculated to weigh 163·7 tons inclusive of blood. This figure was based on the number of cookers filled by the animal's blubber, meat and bones but the total weight was believed to have been 174 tons. Applying the cube rule, it seems probable that very long or very corpulent pregnant blue whales must at times have surpassed a weight of 200 tons, though none of this size has been weighed.

Tallest

The tallest living animal is the giraffe (*Giraffa camelopardalis*), now found only in the dry savannah and semi-desert of Africa south of the Sahara. The tallest ever recorded was a Masai bull (*G. camelopardalis tippelskirchi*), measuring 19 feet 3 inches in height from the tip of the forehoof to the tips of the "horns" with the neck erect, shot in Kenya before 1930 (weight *c.* 2 tons). It was thus 4$\frac{3}{4}$ feet taller than a London double-decker bus. Less credible heights of up to 23 feet have been claimed. A giraffe (10 feet 8 inches) was first seen in London in 1827.

Longest

The longest animal ever recorded is the jelly fish or coelenterate (*Cyanea arctica*), which inhabits the north-west Atlantic Ocean. One specimen washed up on the coast of Massachusetts, U.S.A. *c.* 1870 had a bell 7$\frac{1}{2}$ feet in diameter and tentacles measuring 120 feet, thus giving a theoretical tentacular span of some 245 feet. It weighed about 200 lb.

Smallest

The smallest of all free-living organisms are pleuro-pneumonia like organisms (P.P.L.O.) of the *Mycoplasma*. One of these, *Mycoplasma laidlawii*, first discovered in sewage in 1936, has a diameter during its early existence of only 100 millimicrons, or 0·000004 of an inch. Examples of the strain known as H.39 have a maximum diameter of 300 millimicrons and weigh an estimated $1{\cdot}0 \times 10^{-16}$ of a gramme. Thus a 174-ton blue whale would weigh $1{\cdot}77 \times 10^{23}$ or 177,000 trillion times as much.

Longest lived

Few animals live longer than humans. It would appear that chelonians are the longest lived animals. An age of 129 years has been attributed to a common box turtle (*Terrapene carolina*) from 1806 to 1935 and a span of 152 years, from 1766 to 1918, has been ascribed to a male Marion's tortoise (*Testudo sumerii*) at Port Louis, Mauritius. When the Royal Tongan tortoise, believed to be *Testudo radiata*, named "Tu'malilia" died on 19 May 1966, it was reputed to be over 200 years old, having been presented to the then King of Tonga by Captain James Cook (1728–79) on 22 Oct. 1773.

Fastest

The fastest reliably measured speed of any animal is 106·25 m.p.h. for the spine-tailed swift (*Chaetura caudacuta*) reported from the U.S.S.R. in 1951. In 1934 ground speeds ranging from 171·8 to 219·5 m.p.h. were reported for spine-tailed swifts over a 2-mile course in the Cachar Hills of north-eastern India. Details of these timings were published in March 1942, but the practical difficulties of the experiment indicated a large degree of probable error. This bird is probably the fastest moving living creature and has a blood temperature of 112·5° F. Speeds as high as 185 m.p.h. have been ascribed to peregrine falcons (*Falco peregrinus*) in a stoop, but in recent experiments in which miniature air speedometers were fitted the maximum recorded diving speed was 82 m.p.h. In June 1928 the unacceptable figure of 247 m.p.h. was attributed to frigate birds (genus *Fregata*) in level flight over a 25$\frac{1}{4}$-mile course off the Cardagos Garajos Islands, 250 miles north-east of Mauritius in the Indian Ocean.

Rarest

The best claimant to the title of the world's rarest land animal is the pygmy opposum (*Burramys parva*) which previously was known from 20,000-year-old fossil material from the Wombeyan Caves in New South Wales. On 19 Aug. 1966, however, a single male was found in the Melbourne University Ski Lodge on Mount Hotham, in the Victorian Alps, 130 miles north-east of Melbourne, Australia. This unique specimen was studied for 30 months at the Fisheries and Wildlife Department of Victoria in Melbourne.

ommonest It has been estimated that man shares the earth with about 3,000,000,000,000,000,000,000,000,000,000,000 (3,000 quintillion or 3×10^{33}) other living things. Of these, more than 75 per cent. are bacteria, namely 2,200 quintillion (or $2{\cdot}2 \times 10^{33}$).

eatest size difference between sexes The largest recorded female deep-sea angler fish of the species *Ceratias holboelli* weighed half a million times as much as the smallest known parasitic male. It has been suggested that this fish would make an appropriate emblem for the Women's Lib. Movement.

Fastest growth The fastest growth in the Animal Kingdom is that of the blue whale calf (see p. 26). A barely visible ovum weighing a fraction of a milligramme (0·000035 of an ounce) grows to a weight of *c.* 26 tons in 22¾ months, made up of 10¾ months gestation and the first 12 months of age. This is equivalent to an increase of 30,000 million-fold.

argest egg The largest egg of any living animal is that of the whale-shark (*Rhincodon typus*). One egg case measuring 12 inches in length, 5½ inches high and 3½ inches thick was picked up by the shrimp trawler "Doris" on 2 July 1953 at a depth of 31 fathoms (186 feet) in the Gulf of Mexico 130 miles south of Port Isabel, Texas, U.S.A. The egg contained a perfect embryo of a whale-shark 14½ inches long.

argest eye The giant squid *Architeuthis sp.* has the largest eye of any living animal. The diameter may exceed 45 centimetres (17·70 inches), compared to 10–12 centimetres (3·93 to 4·71 inches) for the largest blue whales (*Balænoptera musculus*).

1. MAMMALS *(Mammalia)*

argest and heaviest *World* For details of the blue whale (*Balænoptera musculus*) see page 26. Further information: a female blue whale taken by the *Slava* whaling fleet of the U.S.S.R. in the Antarctic on 17 March 1947 measured 27·6 metres (90 feet 8 inches) in length. Its tongue and heart weighed 4·22 tons and 1,540 lb. respectively.

Blue whales inhabit the colder seas and migrate to warmer waters in winter for breeding. Observations made in the Antarctic in 1946–7 showed that a blue whale can maintain speeds of 20 knots (23 m.p.h.) for 10 to 15 minutes. It has been calculated that a 90-foot blue whale travelling at 20 knots would develop 520 horsepower. The young measure up to 28·6 feet long at birth and weigh up to 3 tons.

It has been estimated that there were about 100,000 blue whales living throughout the oceans in 1935, but that less than 1,000 survived (most of them in the Southern Hemisphere) in 1969. The correct collective noun is a gam or a pod.

British waters A blue whale allegedly measuring 105 feet in length was stranded on the west coast of Lewis (Outer Hebrides), Scotland *c.* 1870, but the carcase was cut up by the local people before the length could be verified. There was also a report of a female blue whale measuring 101 feet being stranded in the River Humber in September 1750. These measurements, if correct, were probably taken along the curve of the body instead of from the tip of the upper jaw in a straight line to the notch in the flukes. Four blue whales have been stranded on British coasts since 1913. The last occurrence (*c.* 60 ft.) was at Wick, Caithness, Scotland, on 15 Oct. 1923.

Deepest dive The greatest recorded depth to which a whale has dived is 620 fathoms (3,720 feet) by a 47-foot bull sperm whale (*Physeter catodon*) found with his jaw entangled with a submarine cable running between Santa Elena, Ecuador and Chorillos, Peru on 14 Oct. 1955. At this depth the whale withstood a pressure of 1,680 lb. per square inch. Baird's beaked whale (*Berardius bairdii*) and the bottle-nosed whales (genus *Hyperoodon*) may dive even deeper. There is a record of a harpooned northern bottle-nose whale (*H. ampullatus*) staying underwater for 2 hours 3 minutes.

Largest on land The largest living land animal is the African bush elephant (*Loxodonta africana africana*). The average adult bull stands 10 feet 6 inches at the shoulder and weighs 5¾ tons. The largest specimen recorded was a bull shot in the Cuando River region of south-western Angola on 13 Nov. 1955. Lying on its side the animal measured 13 feet 2 inches in a straight line from the shoulder to the base of its forefoot, indicating that its living height was about 12 feet 6 inches. It had an overall length (from tip of trunk to tip of tail) of 33 feet 2 inches, a maximum girth of 19 feet 8 inches and its weight was estimated to be 24,000 lb. (10·7 tons). On 6 March 1959 the mounted specimen was put on display in the Museum of Natural History at the Smithsonian Institution, Washington, D.C., U.S.A. (See also Shooting, Chapter XII.) Another freak bull elephant known as Zhulamiti ('Taller than the Trees'), reputed to stand over 12 feet at the shoulder, was shot at Gona re Zhou, Mozambique in 1967 in unexplained circumstances.

The largest wild mammal in the British Isles, excluding the wild pony (*Equus caballus*), is the Scottish red deer (*Cervus elaphus scoticus*). A full-grown stag stands 3 feet 8 inches at the withers and weighs *c.* 208 lb. The heaviest ever recorded was a stag weighing 462 lb. killed in Glenmore Forest, Inverness-shire, in 1877. The record weight for a park red deer is 476 lb. and standing 4 feet 6 inches, killed at Woburn, Bedfordshire, in 1836. The wild population in 1968 was estimated at 180,000 to 185,000.

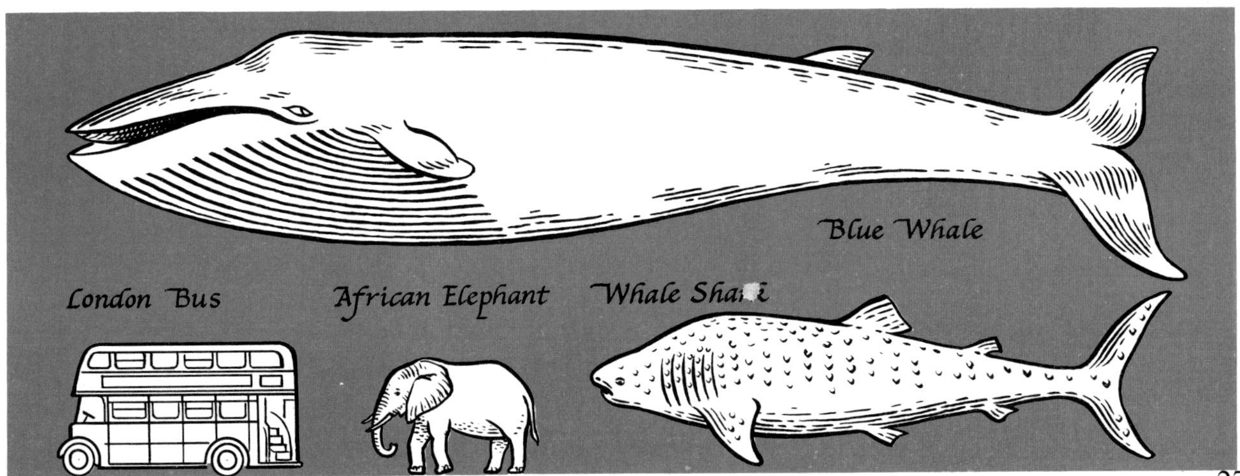

'omparative sizes of ·mpions in .e Animal Kingdom

Tallest The tallest mammal is the giraffe (*Giraffa camelopardalis*). For details see page 26.

Smallest *Land* The smallest recorded mammal is Savi's white-toothed pygmy shrew (*Suncus etruscus*) also known as the Etruscan shrew which is found along the coasts of the northern Mediterranean and southwards to Cape Province, South Africa. It has a total length of only 63·5 to 76·2 millimetres (2·5 to 3·0 inches) and weighs as little as 1½ grammes (0·06 of an ounce). The smallest mammal found in the British Isles is the European pygmy shrew (*Sorex minutus*), which has a total length of 76·2 to 108 millimetres (3·0 to 4·25 inches) and weighs between 2·4 and 6·1 grammes (0·084 to 0·213 of an ounce).

Marine The smallest marine mammal is the sea otter (*Enhydra lutris*), which is found in coastal waters off California, western Alaska and the Komandorskie and Kurile Islands in the Bering Sea. Males have a maximum length (including tail) of 156 centimetres (61·5 inches) and weigh up to 38·6 kilogrammes (85 lb.).

Rarest The rarest placental mammal in the world is now probably the Javan rhinoceros (*Rhinoceros sondaicus*). In 1970 there were an estimated 28 in the Udjung-Kulon (also called Oedjoeng Kuelon) Reserve of 117 square miles at the tip of western Java, Indonesia, but the number today may be as low as 10. There may also be a few in the Tenasserim area on the Thai-Burmese border. Among sub-species, there are believed to be only 7 or 8 specimens of the Javan tiger (*Panthera tigris sondaica*) left outside captivity, all of them in east Java. The rarest marine mammal is probably Hose's Sarawak dolphin (*Lagenodelphis hosei*), which is known only from a single specimen collected at the mouth of the Lutong River, Baram, Borneo in 1895 in an advanced state of decomposition. The skull is now in the British Museum (Natural History), London.

The rarest British land mammal is the pine marten (*Martes martes*), which is found in the highlands of Scotland, particularly in Coille na Glas, Leitire, Ross and Cromarty, and thinly distributed in North Wales and the Scottish border country. The largest specimens measure 34 inches from nose to tail and weigh up to 4 lb. 6 oz.

Fastest *World* The fastest of all land animals over a sustained distance (*i.e.* 1,000 metres or more) is probably the prong-horn antelope (*Antilocapra americana*) of the western United States. Specimens have been observed to travel at 35 m.p.h. for 4 miles, and 55 m.p.h. for ½ mile. On 14 Aug. 1936 at Spanish Lake, in Lake County, Oregon, a hard-pressed buck was timed by a car speedometer at 61 m.p.h. over 200 yards. Speeds of 81, 84 and even 90 m.p.h. have been quoted for the now rare cheetah or hunting leopard (*Acinonyx jubatus*), found on the plains of tropical Africa and India, but all appear to have been exaggerated. Tests in London in 1939 showed that on an oval greyhound track over 500 yards the cheetah's average speed over three runs was 43·4 m.p.h. (*cf.* 43·26 m.p.h. for the fastest racehorse). In 1957 a tame cheetah named "Okala" trained to run in a long enclosure recorded a speed of 56 m.p.h. on film at Ocala, Florida, U.S.A.

Britain The fastest British land mammal over a sustained distance is the roe deer (*Capreolus capreolus*) which can reach 40 m.p.h. On 19 Oct. 1970 a runaway red deer (*Cervus elaphus*) clocked 42 m.p.h. on a police radar trap as it charged through a street in Stalybridge, Cheshire.

Slowest The slowest moving land mammal is probably the three-toed sloth (*Bradypus tridactylus*) of Central and tropical South America. The usual ground speed is 6 to 8 feet a minute (0·068 to 0·098 m.p.h.), but one mother sloth, speeded up by the calls of her infant, was observed to cover 14 feet in one minute (0·155 m.p.h.). In the trees this speed may be increased to 2 feet a second (1·36 m.p.h.) (*cf.* these figures with the 0·03 m.p.h. of the common garden snail and the 0·17 m.p.h. of the giant tortoise).

Longest lived No mammal can match the extreme proven age of 113 years attained by Man (*Homo sapiens*) (see page 16). It is probable that the closest approach is over 90 years by the killer whale (*Orcinus orca*). A bull with distinctive markings, known as "Old Tom", was seen from 1839 to 17 Sept. 1930 when found floating dead in Twofold Bay, Eden, New South Wales, Australia.

The longest lived land mammal, excluding Man, is probably the Asiatic elephant (*Elephas maximus*). The greatest age that has been verified with reasonable certainty is an estimated 69 years in the case of a cow named "Jessie", who was taken in 1882 to the Taronga Zoological Park in Sydney, Australia, where she had to be destroyed, because of senile infirmity, on 26 Sept. 1939. Her age on arrival was probably 12 but may have been as high as 20 years. An elephant's age is determined by the persistence of its teeth, which generally wear out around the 50-55th year.

Highest living The highest living mammal in the world is probably the Tibetan pika (*Ochotona thibetana*), which has been found at an altitude of 18,000 feet in the Himalayas.

Largest herd The largest herds on record were those of the South African springbok (*Antidorcas marsupialis*) during migration in the 19th century. In 1849 Sir John Fraser of Bloemfontein reported seeing a herd of "Trek-Bokke" that took three days to pass through the settlement of Beaufort West, Cape Province. Another herd seen between Prieska and Bittersprut, Cape Province, in 1888, was estimated to contain 100,000,000 head.

Longest and shortest gestation periods The longest of all mammalian gestation periods is that of the Asiatic elephant (*Elephas maximus*), with a minimum of 17 months 17 days, an average of 19 to 21 months and a maximum of 25 months—more than 2½ times that of a human. A gestation period of 8 to 12 days has been reported for the water opossom or yapok (*Chironectes minimus*) of Central and northern South America.

Largest litter The greatest recorded number of young born to a mammal at a single birth is 32 (not all of which survived) in the case of the common tenrec (*Centetes ecaudatus*), found in Madagascar and the Comoro Islands. The average litter is about 14. In March 1961 a litter of 32 young was reported for a white mouse (*Mus musculus*) at Roswell Park Memorial Inst., Buffalo, N.Y., U.S.A.

An Animal Kingdom Speed Trial

Most prolific mammalian mother: the Tenrec

Fastest breeder The streaked tenrec (*Hemicentetes semispinosus*) of Madagascar is weaned after only 5 days, and females are capable of breeding 3–4 weeks after birth.

Heaviest brain The sperm whale (*Physeter catodon*) has the heaviest brain of any living animal. The brain of a 49-foot-long bull, processed aboard the Japanese factory ship *Nisshin Maru No. 2* in the Antarctic on 11 Dec. 1949, weighed 9,200 grammes (20·24 lb.), compared with 6,900 grammes (15·38 lb.) for a 90-foot blue whale. The heaviest brain recorded for an elephant is 6,654 grammes (14·6 lb.) in the case of *Loxodonta africana africana*.

Longest hibernation The common dormouse (*Glis glis*) spends more time in hibernation than any other mammal. The hibernation usually lasts between 5 and 6 months (October to April), but there is a record of an English specimen sleeping for 6 months 23 days without interruption. The common hedgehog (*Erinaceus europaeus*) also exceeds 6 months on occasion, but it is not a continuous sleep.

CARNIVORES

Largest *World Land* The largest living terrestrial member of the order Carnivora is the Kodiak bear (*Ursus arctos middendorffi*) of Alaska. The average adult male has a nose to tail length of 8 feet and weighs about 1,200 lb. In 1894 a weight of 1,656 lb. was recorded for a male shot at English Bay, Kodiak Island, whose *stretched* skin measured 13 feet 6 inches overall. This weight was exceeded by a male in the Cheyenne Mountain Zoological Park, Colorado Springs, Colorado, U.S.A., which scaled 1,670 lb. at the time of its death on 22 Sept. 1955.

The Peninsular brown bear (*Ursus arctos gyas*), also found in Alaska, is almost as large, adult males measuring $7\frac{3}{4}$ feet nose to tail length and weighing about 1,150 lb. A specimen 10 feet long, with an estimated weight of between 1,600 and 1,700 lb. was shot near Cold Bay, Alaska, on 28 May 1948. Another male shot in Clearwater Gap, Alberta, Canada, in November 1949 had a nose to tail measurement of over 9 feet and weighed an estimated 1,600 lb.

Weights in excess of 1,600 lb. have also been reported for the male polar bear (*Thalarctos maritimus*), which has an average nose to tail length of $7\frac{1}{2}$ feet and weighs about 900 lb. In 1960 a polar bear allegedly weighing 2,210 lb. was shot at the polar entrance to Kotzebue Sound, north-west Alaska. In April 1962 the mounted specimen, measuring 11 feet $1\frac{1}{4}$ inches, was put on display at the Seattle World Fair, Washington, U.S.A.

Sea The largest toothed mammal ever recorded is the sperm whale (*Physeter catodon*), also called the cachalot. The average adult bull is 47 feet long and weighs about 33 tons. The largest specimen ever to be measured accurately was a bull 20·7 metres (67 feet 11 inches) long, captured off the Kuril Islands in the north-west Pacific by a U.S.S.R. whaler during the summer of 1950. On 25 June 1903 a measurement of 68 feet was reported for a bull killed 60 miles west of Shetland and landed at the Norrona whaling station. The measurement, however, was made over the curve of the body and not in a straight line. In the summer of 1948 a bull with an alleged length of 90 feet was killed off the north-eastern coast of Vancouver Island, British Columbia, Canada, and brought into Nanaimo. Later, however, it was recorded that the longest of the 28 processed there in 1948 was 56 feet long. Nine cachalots have been stranded on British coasts since 1913.

Britain The largest British land carnivore is the badger (*Meles meles*). Average adult boars measure 3 feet in total length and weigh 27 lb., but specimens weighing up to 66 lb. have been reliably reported.

Smallest The smallest living carnivore is the least weasel (*Mustela rixosa*) of North America. Its total length (including tail) is up to $22\frac{1}{2}$ centimetres (8·9 inches) and mature specimens weigh between 35 and 70 grammes (from $1\frac{1}{4}$ to $2\frac{1}{2}$ oz.).

Rarest The rarest land carnivore is probably the Mexican grizzly bear (*Ursus nelsoni*), of which no more than 20–30 survive in a small patch of territory about 50 miles north of Chihuahua.

Largest feline The largest of the 36 members of the cat family (Felidae) is the long-haired Siberian tiger (*Panthera tigris longipilis*). The largest specimen ever recorded was one killed near Vladivostok *c.* 1895 which measured 13 feet 5 inches over the curves (10 feet 5 inches to the root of the tail) and probably weighed nearly 800 lb. This sub-species is now found only in the Khabarovsk and Primorskiy regions of the eastern U.S.S.R. In 1970 the total wild population, now strictly protected, was estimated at 50 to 90 animals.

The average adult male African lion (*Panthera leo*) measures 9 feet overall and weighs about 400 lb. The heaviest specimen found in the wild was one weighing 690 lb., shot near Hectorspruit, in the eastern Transvaal, South Africa in 1936. In September 1970 a weight of 826 lb. was reported for the 11-year-old lion "Simba" in Colchester Zoo, Essex, England. In 1953 an 18-year-old liger (a lion-tigress hybrid) at the Zoological Gardens of Bloemfontein, South Africa, was weighed at 750 lb.

The world's heaviest ever "big cat" Simba, the 59 stone lion

PINNIPEDS (Seals, Sea-lions and Walruses)

Largest The largest of the 32 known species of pinnipeds is the southern elephant seal (*Mirounga leonina*) which inhabits the sub-Antarctic islands. Adult bulls average $16\frac{1}{2}$ feet in length (snout to tip of tail), 12 feet in girth and weigh 6,000 lb. (2·67 tons). The largest specimen on record was a bull killed in Possession Bay, South Georgia, on 28 Feb. 1913 which measured *c.* $22\frac{1}{2}$ feet in length or 21 feet 4 inches after flensing and weighed nearly 5 tons. There are old records of bulls measuring 25, 27 and even 30 feet, but all lack confirmation. A length of 22 feet had been reported in 1870 for the northern elephant seal (*Mirounga angustirostris*), now restricted to islands off the coast of Mexico and southern California, but the measurement included the hind flippers. The largest seal elephant ever held in captivity is believed to have been "Goliath", a bull of the southern race, exhibited at the Philadelphia Zoological Gardens, Pennsylvania, U.S.A. In the winter of 1933–34, he measured 17 feet in length and weighed an estimated 6,000 lb. The largest among British fauna is the Atlantic or grey seal, the bulls of which have been recorded up to 9 feet in length and 658 lb. in weight.

Smallest The smallest pinniped is the ringed seal (*Pusa hispida*), found on the circumpolar Arctic coasts. Adult animals average $4\frac{1}{2}$ to $4\frac{3}{4}$ feet in length and weigh 170–200 lb.

Fastest and deepest The highest speed measured for a pinniped is 25 m.p.h. for a California sea-lion (*Zalophus californianus*). It was reported in March 1966 that a dive of 600 metres (1,970 feet) had been recorded by a depth gauge attached to a Weddell seal (*Leptonychotes weddelli*). The seal withstood a pressure of 875 lb. per square inch. An hour underwater has been exceeded. Some of this species have been measured to swim under ice for 19 miles, utilizing the layer of air sometimes trapped on the underside of the ice.

Longest lived A ringed seal (*Pusa hispida*) taken on the south-west coast of Baffin Island in 1954 was believed to be at least 43 years old based on a count of dental annuli.

Rarest The Caribbean or West Indies monk seal (*Monachus tropicalis*) was last seen on the beach of Isla Mujueres off the Yucatan Peninsula, Mexico in 1962 and is now believed to be on the verge of extinction. The Juan Fernandez fur seal (*Arctocephalus philippii philippii*), another sub-species thought to have become extinct in the 1890s, was "rediscovered" in November 1968 on the islands of Mas a Tierra and Mas Afvera in the Juan Fernandez Archipelago, 400 miles west of Chile in the South Pacific. In 1970 the total number of seals on the two islands was estimated at 60+, but there may also be other populations on Islas San Ambrosio and San Felix.

The fruit bat with its 5-foot 7-inch wing span

BATS

Largest The only flying mammals are bats (order Chiroptera), of which there are about 1,000 living species. That with the greatest wing span is *Pteropus niger*, also called the kalong, a fruit bat found in Indonesia. It has a wing span of up to 170 centimetres (5 feet 7 inches) and weighs up to 900 grammes (31·7 ounces). Some unmeasured specimens of *Pteropus neohibernicus*, another fruit bat found in New Guinea, may possibly reach 6 feet in wing span. The largest bat found in Britain is the noctule or great bat (*Nyctalus noctula*), which has a head and body length of 75 to 82 millimetres (2·9 to 3·2 inches), a wing span of up to 387 millimetres (15·23 inches) and weighs up to 40 grammes (1·4 oz.). The rare mouse-eared bat (*Myotis myotis*) has a wing span of up to 450 millimetres (17·71 inches), but it is not so heavy.

Smallest The smallest species of bat is *Pipistrellus nanulus*, found in West Africa. It has a wing span of about 6 inches and a length of $2\frac{1}{2}$ inches, of which one inch is tail. The average weight is about $2\frac{1}{2}$ grammes (0·09 of an ounce). The smallest British bat is the pipistrelle or common bat (*Pipistrellus pipistrellus*), which has a head and body length of 42 millimetres (1·6 inches) and a wing span of 200 to 230 millimetres (7·8 to 9·1 inches). Mature specimens weigh between 2·6 and 7·5 grammes (0·091 to 0·262 of an ounce).

Fastest The greatest speed attributed to a bat is 32 m.p.h. in the case of a free-tailed bat (*Tadarida mexicana*).

Rarest The rarest of the 13 species native to the British Isles is the mouse-eared bat (*Myotis myotis*). The first specimen to be positively identified (a male) was taken alive at Girton in Cambridgeshire in 1888 and is now preserved in the University Museum of Zoology at Cambridge. On 18 Feb. 1956 another specimen was found dead in an underground quarry on the Isle of Purbeck, near Swanage, Dorset, where several more have been found subsequently. In 1970 28 were recorded in Sussex.

Longest lived The greatest age reported for a bat is "at least 24 years" for a female little brown bat (*Myotis lucifugus*) found on 30 April 1960 in a cave on Mount Aeolus, East Dorset, Vermont, U.S.A. It had been banded at a summer colony in Mashpee, Massachusetts, on 22 June 1937.

Highest detectable pitch Because of their ultrasonic echolocation, bats have the most acute hearing in the animal world. The upper limit of hearing in some insect-eating varieties (families Vespertilionidae, Hipposideridae, Emballonuridae and Phyllostomatidae) is between 175,000 and 400,000 cycles per second.

PRIMATES

Largest The largest living primate is the eastern lowland gorilla (*Gorilla gorilla manyema*), which inhabits the lowlands in the eastern part of the Upper Congo (Kinshasa) and south-western Uganda. An average adult bull stands 5 feet 9 inches tall, weighs 360 lb. and has a chest measurement of 60 inches. The female averages 200 lb. The greatest height (crown to *heel*) reliably recorded is 196 centimetres (6 feet 5·1 inches) for a bull of the eastern highland race (*Gorilla gorilla beringei*) shot in the Angumu Forest, in the eastern Congo (Kinshasa) in March 1948. It had a chest measurement of 155 centimetres (61 inches) and weighed 230 kilogrammes (506 lb.). The heaviest gorilla ever kept in captivity was "Mbongo" (b. 1926), an obese 5-foot $7\frac{1}{2}$-inch bull of the eastern highland race, who died on 15 March 1942 in the San Diego Zoological Gardens, California, U.S.A. During an attempt to weigh him, shortly before his death, the scales fluctuated from 645 lb. to nearly 670 lb.

Smallest The smallest primate is probably the mouse lemur (*Microcebus murinus*) of Madagascar, with an overall length of up to 28 centimetres (11·0 inches), of which 15 cms. (5·9 inches) is tail. It weighs from 48 to 85 grammes (1·7 to 3·0 oz.).

Longest lived The greatest irrefutable age reported for a primate (excluding humans) is *c.* 50 years in the case of the male chimpanzee (*Pan troglodytes*) named "Heine" of Lincoln Park Zoological Gardens, Chicago, Illinois, U.S.A. He arrived there on 10 June 1924 when about 3 years of age.

Strength In 1923 "Boma", a 165 lb. male chimpanzee at New York Zoological Gardens, N.Y., U.S.A., recorded a right-handed pull (feet braced) of 847 lb. on a dynamometer (*cf.* 210 lb. for a man of the same weight). A 135 lb. female chimpanzee at the same zoo named "Suzette" recorded a two-handed pull of 1,260 lb.

MONKEYS

Largest The largest monkey is the mandrill (*Mandrillus sphinx*) of equatorial West Africa. Males weigh up to 54 kilogrammes (119 lb.), with a total length of up to 36 inches (tail 3 inches).

Smallest The smallest monkey is the pygmy marmoset (*Cebuella pygmaea*) of southern Colombia, eastern Ecuador, northern Peru and western Brazil. It was discovered in

1823 and has a body length of up to 16 centimetres (6·3 inches) and a tail of between 15 centimetres (5·9 inches) and 20 centimetres (7·9 inches). It weighs from 49 to 70 grammes (1·7 to 2·5 oz.) and rivals the mouse lemur for the title of smallest primate (see p. 30).

Rarest The rarest monkey is the Hairy-eared Dwarf Lemur (*Cheirogaleus trichotis*) of Madagascar, which has only been recorded four times. The last occasion was in 1966 when a live one was found on the east coast near Mananara.

est lived The greatest reliable age reported for a monkey is *c.* 47 years for a male mandrill (*Mandrillus sphinx*) named "George" of London Zoological Gardens, who died on 4 March 1916. He had been imported in 1869.

Iost and least telligent Of sub-human primates, chimpanzees appear to have the most superior intelligence. Lemurs have less learning ability than any monkey or ape and, in some tests, are inferior to dogs and even pigeons.

RODENTS

Largest The world's largest rodent is the capybara (*Hydrochoerus hydrocharis*), also called the carpincho or water hog, which is found in tropical South America. It grows up to 4½ feet in length (including short tail) and up to 150 lb. in weight. Britain's largest rodent is now the coypu (*Myocastor coypus*), introduced from Argentina in 1927 by East Anglian nutria fur breeders. Four escaped from Ipswich, Suffolk, in 1937. One was killed almost immediately, but the others founded a dynasty of wild specimens. Adult males measure up to 36 inches in total length (including tail) and weigh up to 26 lb. in the wild state (40 lb. in captivity).

Smallest The smallest rodent is the Old World harvest mouse (*Micromys minutus*), of which the British form weighs between 4·2 and 10·2 grammes (0·15 to 0·36 of an ounce) and measures up to 13·5 centimetres (5·3 inches) long, including the tail. It was announced in June 1965 than an even smaller rodent had been discovered in the Asian part of the U.S.S.R., but no details are yet available.

Rarest The rarest rodent in the world is believed to be the James Island rice rat (*Oryzomys swarthi*). Four were collected on this island in the Galapagos group in the eastern Pacific Ocean in 1906. The next trace was a skull of a recently dead specimen found in January 1966.

INSECTIVORES

Largest The largest insectivore (insect-eating mammal) is the moon rat (*Echinosorex gymnurus*) also known as the gymnura, found in Thailand, Malaysia, Sumatra and Borneo. It has an overall length of up to 65·5 centimetres (25·8 inches) and weighs up to 1,400 grammes (3·08 lb.).

Smallest The smallest insectivore is Savi's white-toothed shrew (see Smallest mammal, page 28).

ANTELOPES

Largest The largest antelope is the giant or Lord Derby eland (*Taurotragus derbianus*) of West and north-Central Africa which surpasses 2,000 lb. The common eland (*T. oryx pattersonianus*) of East and South Africa has the same shoulder height, of up to 72 inches, but is not quite so massive, although there is one record of a bull being shot in Malawi *c.* 1937 which weighed 2,078 lb.

Smallest The smallest known antelope, and the smallest ruminant, is the Royal antelope (*Neotragus pygmaeus*) of West Africa, measuring 10 to 12 inches at the shoulder and weighing only 7 to 8 lb. The slenderer Somali dik-dik (*Madoqua swaynei*), which stands 13 inches at the shoulder, weighs only 5 to 6 lb.

Rarest The rarest antelope is probably Jentink's duiker (*Cephalopus jentinki*) which is found only in a restricted area of tropical West Africa. Its total population may be only a few dozen.

DEER

Largest The largest deer is the Alaskan moose (*Alces gigas*). One standing 7 feet 8 inches at the withers, and weighing 1,800 lb., was shot in 1897 in the Yukon Territory, Canada. Unconfirmed measurements of up to 8½ feet at the withers and 2,600 lb. in weight have been claimed. The record antler span is 78½ inches.

Smallest The smallest deer is the mouse deer (*Tragulus javanicus*) or chevrotain of south-east Asia. It has a shoulder height of up to 33 centimetres (13 inches) and a maximum weight of 4·5 kg. (9·9 lb.).

Rarest The rarest deer in the world is Fea's muntjac (*Muntiacus feae*), which is known only from two specimens collected on the borders of Tenasserim, Burma and Thailand.

TUSKS

Longest The longest recorded elephant tusks are a pair from the eastern Congo (Kinshasa), presented in 1907 to the National Collection of Heads and Horns, kept by the New York Zoological Society in Bronx Park, New York City, N.Y., U.S.A. One measures 11 feet 5½ inches and the other measures 11 feet. Their combined weight is 293 lb. A single tusk of 11 feet 6 inches has been reported, but details are lacking.

Heaviest The heaviest recorded tusks are a pair in the British Museum (Natural History), London. They were first sold in Zanzibar (now part of Tanzania) in 1898, when the Museum acquired one of them. The other was bought by the Museum in 1933. They were measured in 1955, when the first was 10 feet 2¼ inches long, weighing 226½ lb., and the second 10 feet 5½ inches long, weighing 214 lb., giving a combined weight of 440½ lb. The tusks, when fresh, reportedly weighed 236 lb. and 226½ lb. so totalling 462½ lb. A tusk with an alleged weight of 117 kilogrammes (258 lb.), from Dahomey, West Africa, was exhibited at the Paris Exposition of 1900.

Longest horns The longest recorded animal horn was one measuring 81¼ inches on the outside curve, with a circumference of 18¾ inches, found on a specimen of domestic Ankole cattle (*Bos taurus*) near Lake Ngami, Botswana (formerly Bechuanaland).

Wild animal The longest horns grown by any wild animal are those of the Pamir argali (*Ovis poli*), also called Marco Polo's argali, a wild sheep found in Central Asia. One of these has been measured at 75 inches along the front curve, with a circumference of 16 inches.

Rhinoceros The longest recorded anterior horn of a rhinoceros is one of 62¼ inches, found on a female southern race white rhinoceros (*Ceratotherium simum simum*) shot in South Africa. The interior horn measured 22¼ inches. An unconfirmed length of 81 inches has also been once reported.

Blood temperatures The highest mammalian blood temperature is that of the domestic goat (*Capra hircus*), with an average of 103·8°F, and a normal range of from 101·7°F to 105·3°F. The blood temperature of the echidna or spiny anteater (*Tachyglossus aculeatus*), a monotreme found in Australia and New Guinea, is dependent on the temperature of its surroundings, and varies between 72°F and 97°F. The blood temperature of the golden hamster (*Mesocricetus auratus*) sometimes falls as low as 38·3°F during hibernation, and an extreme figure of 29·6°F has been reported for a Myotis bat (family Vespertilionidae) during deep sleep.

Most valuable furs The highest priced single skins are those of the mink-sable cross breed "mable" or "Kojah" of which 40 selected pelts from the Piampiano Fur Ranch, Zion, Illinois, U.S.A., realized $2,700 (£1,125) in New York City on 26 Feb. 1969. A "Kojah" coat costing $125,000 (£52,083) was sold by Neiman & Marcus of Dallas,

Texas to Richard Burton for his wife in May 1970. Individual pelts of sea otter (*Enhydra lutris*), known also as Kamchatka beaver, fetched up to $2,700 (then £675) before their 55-year-long protection began in 1912. The extremely rare solid white and solid black chinchilla mutations have not yet been marketed but would probably surpass all other furs in value.

Ambergris The heaviest piece of ambergris on record weighed 1,003 lb. and was recovered from a sperm whale (*Physeter catodon*) on 3 Dec. 1912 by a Norwegian whaling company in Australian waters. The lump was sold in London for £23,000.

MARSUPIALS

Largest The largest marsupial is the Red kangaroo (*Macropus rufus*) of Australia. Adult males stand 6–7 feet in height and measure up to 8 feet 11 inches from nose to tip of tail. The great grey kangaroo (*Macropus conguru*) or Forester as it is more commonly called, is slightly smaller, but one huge example measured 8 feet 8 inches from nose to tail (9 feet 7 inches along the body curve) and weighed 200 lb. The skin of this animal is preserved in the Australian Museum, Sydney, New South Wales.

Smallest The smallest known marsupials in the world are the very rare Kimberley planigale (*Planigale subtilissima*), which is found only in the Kimberley district, north Western Australia. It has a total length of 10 centimetres (3·93 inches) and weighs about 4 grammes (0·14 of an ounce).

Rarest The wolf-like thylacine or Tasmanian "tiger" (*Thylacinus cynocephalus*), the largest of the carnivorous marsupials, is now confined to the remotest parts of western Tasmania. The last thylacine kept in captivity was caught in a trapper's snare in the Florentine Valley, a few miles west of Mountain Field National Park, in 1933 and exhibited at Hobart Zoo. It died a few months later. Shortly before the Second World War there was evidence that "at least" half a dozen pairs survived in the coastal region of western Tasmania. On 2 Jan. 1957 it was reported that one had been kept in sight for two minutes and photographed by a helicopter pilot, Capt. J. Ferguson, on Birthday Bay beach, 35 miles south-west of Queenstown, Tasmania. Experts who examined the photograph, however, declared that the animal was a dog. In 1961 a young male was accidentally killed at Sandy Cape, western Tasmania, and in December 1966 traces of a lair (possibly a female with pups) was found in the boiler of a wrecked ship at Mawbanna on the north-west coast. On 3 Nov. 1969 the tracks of a thylacine were positively identified in the Cradle Mountain National Park, and other definite sightings have been made since in the Cardigan river area on the north-west coast and the Tooms Lake region.

Longest jump The greatest measured height cleared by a hunted kangaroo is 10 feet 6 inches, over a pile of timber. The longest recorded leap was reported in January 1951, when, in the course of a chase, a female Red kangaroo (*Macropus rufus*) made a series of bounds which included one of 42 feet. There is an unconfirmed report of a great grey kangaroo (*Macropus conguru*) jumping nearly 13·5 metres (44·7 feet) on the flat.

DOMESTICATED ANIMALS

HORSES

Oldest The greatest acceptable age for a horse (*Equus caballus*) is 52 years for a draught breed named "Monty", owned by Mrs. Marjorie Cooper of Albury, New South Wales, Australia, which died on 28 Jan. 1970. His jaw is now preserved in the School of Veterinary Science at Melbourne University. In 1919 an age of 54 years was reported for a pony living in France, but further details are lacking.

Largest The heaviest horse ever recorded was "Brooklyn Supreme", a pure-bred Belgian stallion weighing 3,200 lb. and standing 19½ hands (6 feet 6 inches). H died on 6 Sept. 1948, aged 20, in Callender, Iowa, U.S. The tallest horse ever recorded was "Dr. Le Gear", seal brown dapple Percheron gelding standing 21 han (7 feet 0 inches) and weighing 2,995 lb. (26·74 cwt Foaled in 1902, this horse, which measured 16 feet fro nose to tail, died in St. Louis, Missouri, U.S.A., in 191

The heaviest horse ever recorded in Britain is "Sal marsh Silver Crest" (b. 1955), a Percheron stallic weighing 2,772 lb. (24·75 cwt.), owned by George Sneath of Money Bridge, near Pinchbeck, Lincolnshir The horse stands 18·1 hands (6 feet 1 inch) tall. Th tallest horse in Britain is "Wandle Robert", a Shi stallion owned by Young & Co.'s Brewery of Wand worth, London. He stands 18·3 hands and weig 1 ton (2,240 lb.).

Heaviest draught The greatest load hauled by a pair of draught hors was 50 logs comprising 36,055 board-feet of timb (=53·8 tons) hauled on the Nester Estate at Ewe Ontonagon County, Michigan, U.S.A., in 1893.

DOGS

Largest The heaviest breed of domestic dog (*Canis familiaris*) the St. Bernard. The heaviest example has bee "Schwarzwald Hof Duke" owned by Dr. A. M. Brun of Oconomowoc, Wisconsin, U.S.A. He was whelpe on 8 Oct. 1964 and weighed 295 lb. (21 stone 1 lb.) c 2 May 1969, dying 3 months later aged 4 years 10 month The largest ever recorded in Britain was one name "Brandy", owned by Miss Gwendoline L. White Chinnor, Oxfordshire. He weighed 18 stone 7 l (259 lb.) on 11 Feb. 1966 and died on 6 March 196 aged 6½. "Westernisles Ross", known as "Lindwall a St. Bernard owned by Jean R. Rankin of Glasgo Scotland, whelped on 1 May 1962, weighed 18 stor 4 lb. (256 lb.) on 28 April 1966, and may have attain 19 stone (266 lb.) by the time of his death on 17 Au 1967 aged 5. The dog now living in Britain which h attained the heaviest weight has been "Montmoren of Hollesley", known as "Monty", owned by M Randolph Simon of Wilmington, Sussex and whelp on 1 May 1964. In April 1970 he was estimated weigh 19 stone (266 lb.).

Tallest The world's tallest breed of dog is the Irish wolfhoun The extreme recorded example was "Broadbrid Michael" (b. 1926), owned by Mrs. Mary Beynon, th of Sutton-at-Hone, Kent. He stood 39½ inches at t shoulder. The tallest dog now living in Britain is b lieved to be "Marron of Merrowlea" (b. Novemb 1968), a Great Dane owned by Mr. Gordon Jeffrey Banstead, Surrey, which stands 38 inches at t shoulder.

Smallest The world's smallest breed of dog is the Chihuahu from Mexico. Their *average* weight is 2 to 4 lb., b some specimens weigh only 16 oz. when fully grow The smallest British breed is the Yorkshire terrier, one which, named "Cody Queen of Dudley", was report in July 1968 to have weighed only 20 oz. at 16 month In January 1971 a fully grown 6-month-old white t poodle owned by Mrs. Sylvia Wyse of Buckna Staffordshire, called "Giles", was reported to wei only 13 oz. before being exported to Canada.

Fastest The fastest breed of untrained dog is the saluki, al called the Arabian gazelle hound or Persian greyhoun Speeds up to 43 m.p.h. have been claimed but tests the Netherlands have shown that it is not as fast as t present day greyhound which has attained a measur speed of 41¼ m.p.h. on a track.

Oldest Dogs of over 20 are very rare but even 34 years has be accepted by some authorities. The oldest reliab reported dog in the world was "Adjutant", a bla labrador gun-dog, who was whelped on 14 Aug. 193 and died on 20 Nov. 1963, aged 27 years and 3 mont in the care of his lifetime owner, James Hawkes,

Fat Olive's record

Fat Olive, a tomcat, has survived a 160-foot fall and broken the world distant record for feline survival.

He escaped with only two broken legs as he landed on a path of grass in Toronto after squeezing his way through a window 16 floors above ground. His feat easily beat the "greatest fall for cats" listed in the "Guinness Book of Records," which shows a record of 11 floors accredited to a British cat, called Pussycat, in 1965.

Despite his name, Fat Olive is male. His mother is named Bruce.—Reuter.

"L
hist
imm
Top
(see bel

/ Estate, near Boston, 37 the death of a collie, s owner, Mrs. Cole of 1951 an Irish terrier aged

Rarest the löwchen or lion dog (32 in Germany, four each in Belgium and Great Britain and one in Majorca) were reported in 1970. The breed was a famous lapdog of the nobility of southern Europe during the Renaissance period.

Largest litter The largest recorded litter of puppies is one of 23 thrown on 11 Feb. 1945 by "Lena", a foxhound bitch owned by Commander W. N. Ely of Ambler, Pennsylvania, U.S.A. A litter of 23 has also been reported for a St. Bernard.

ost prolific The dog who has sired the greatest recorded number of puppies is the greyhound "Low Pressure", nicknamed "Timmy", whelped in September 1957 and owned by Mrs. Bruna Amhurst of Regent's Park, London. From December 1961 to his death on 27 Nov. 1969 he had fathered 2,414 registered puppies with at least 600 others unregistered.

st popular The breed with the most Kennel Club registrations in 1970 was the Alsatian with 16,834. In 1971, Cruft's Dog Show (founded 1886 for terriers only) had an entry of 8,431, including 316 Alsatians, compared with the record entry of 10,650 dogs in 1936 before entrants were restricted to prize winners.

Most expensive In January 1956 Miss Mary de Pledge, of Bracknell, Berkshire, England, turned down an offer of £10,500 from an American dog-breeder for her 3½-year-old champion pekingese "Caversham Ku-Ku of Yam".

Top dog" The greatest altitude attained by any animal is 1,050 miles by the Samoyed husky (Russian, *laika*) bitch fired as a passenger in *Sputnik II*, on 3 Nov. 1957. The dog was variously named "Kudryavka" (feminine form of "Curly"), "Limonchik" (diminutive of lemon), "Malyshka", "Zhuchka" or by the breed name "Laika".

ghest and gest jump The canine "high jump" record is held by the British dog "Mikeve", who scaled a wall of 9 feet 6 inches off a springboard in a test in Kensington, London, in 1934. The longest recorded canine long jump was one of 30 feet by a greyhound named "Bang" made in jumping a gate in coursing a hare at Brecon Lodge, Gloucestershire in 1849.

Strongest The greatest load ever shifted by a dog was a sledge weighing 3,142 lb. (1·40 tons), pulled by "Charlie", a husky owned by Larry Clendenon, in a test at Anchor Point, Alaska, U.S.A., on 11 Feb. 1961.

Ratting Mr. James Searle's bull terrier bitch "Jenny Lind" killed 500 rats in 1 hour 30 minutes at "The Beehive" in Liverpool in 1853. Another bull terrier named "Jacko", owned by Mr. Jemmy Shaw, was credited with killing 1,000 rats in 1 hour 40 minutes, but the feat was performed over a period of ten weeks in batches of 100 at a time. The last 100 were accounted for in 5 min. 28 secs. in London on 1 May 1862.

Tracking The greatest tracking feat recorded was performed by the Doberman *Sauer*, trained by Detective-Sergeant Herbert Kruger. In 1925 he tracked a stock thief 100 miles across the Great Karroo, South Africa by scent alone. In Jan. 1969 a German Alsatian bitch was reported to have followed her master 745 miles from Brindisi to Milan, Italy in four months. The owner had left her when he went on a visit.

CATS

Heaviest The heaviest domestic cat (*Felis catus*) ever recorded has been the tabby "Gigi" owned by Miss Ann Clark of Carlisle, Cumberland. In 1970 he weighed 42 lb. and had a girth of 27 inches. The average weight is 11 lb.

Oldest According to the American Feline Society a cat living in Hazleton, Pennsylvania, celebrated its 37th birthday on 1 Nov. 1958, but further details are lacking. The oldest cat ever recorded in Britain was the tabby "Puss", owned by Mrs. T. Holway of Clayhidon, North Devon. He was 36 on 28 Nov. 1939. A more recent and better documented case was that of the female tabby "Ma" owned by Mrs. Alice St. George Moore of Drewsteignton, Devon. She was put to sleep on 5 Nov. 1957, aged 34. The oldest cat living in Britain today is a ginger tom named "Sandy" (b. 7 June 1943), owned by Mrs. Elsie Emmett of Isleworth, Middlesex, who is 28. "Flip", a black and white female Manx, and "Buncle", a female tabby, both owned by Mrs. Rosemary Morley of Brighton, celebrate their 27th birthdays this year. (November and December respectively.)

Largest litter The largest litter ever recorded was one of 12 kittens, born in March 1953 to "Brackledown Beauty", aged 2½, a blue-pointed Siamese cat owned by Mrs. E. F. Morrison of Hastings, Sussex. A litter of 13 has been reported for another Siamese cat, but details are lacking. The usual litter size is between 5 and 9.

Most prolific A cat named "Dusty", aged 17, living in Bonham, Texas, U.S.A., gave birth to her 420th kitten on 12 June 1952.

Greatest fall "Pussycat", owned by Miss Anne Walker of Maida Vale, London, fell 120 feet from the balcony of his owner's 11th-storey flat on 7 March 1965. He landed unhurt.

Most lives "Thumper", a 2½-year-old tabby owned by Mrs. Reg Buckett of Westminster, London was trapped in a lift shaft without food or water for 52 days from 29 March 1964.

Richest and most valuable Dr. William Grier of San Diego, California, U.S.A., died in June 1963, leaving his entire estate of $415,000 (£172,916) to his two 15-year-old cats, "Hellcat" and "Brownie". When the cats died in 1965 the money went to the George Washington University in Washington, D.C., U.S.A. In 1967 Miss Elspeth Sellar of Grafham, Surrey, turned down an offer of 2,000 guineas (£2,100) from an American breeder for her copper-eyed champion white Persian tom "Coylum Marcus" (b. 28 March 1965).

Rarest breed The rarest of the 52 recognized breeds in Britain is the red self Persian or long-haired red self.

Ratting A five-month-old tabby kitten named "Peter" living at Stonehouse railway station, Gloucestershire, killed 400 rats during a four week period in June-July 1938. Many of the kitten's victims seemed almost as large as itself. The greatest mouser on record was a tabby named "Mickey", owned by Shepherd & Sons Ltd. of Burscough, Lancashire, which killed more than 22,000 mice during 23 years with the firm. He died in November 1968.

Cat population The largest cat population is that of the U.S.A. with 28 million. Of Great Britain's cat population of 6 million an estimated 100,000 are "employed" by the Civil Service.

RABBITS

Largest and smallest The largest breed of rabbit (*Oryctolagus cuniculus*) is the Flemish giant, with an average weight of 14 lb. They measure up to 40 inches long from toe to toe, when fully extended. The heaviest specimen recorded was a male named "Floppy", who weighed 25 lb. and died in June 1963, aged 8. The smallest breed is the little Idaho or pygmy rabbit (*Sylvilagus idahoensis*) of the south-western United States, which has a total length of 8–11 inches and weighs up to 1 lb.

2. BIRDS *(Aves)*

Largest *Ratite* Of the 8,600 known living species, the largest is the North African ostrich (*Struthio camelus camelus*) which occurs south of the Atlas Mountains from Upper Senegal and Niger country across to the Sudan and Central Ethiopia. Male examples of this flightless or ratite bird reach 345 lb. in weight and stand 9 feet tall. Ostriches are able to run at a speed of 37 m.p.h.

Carinate The heaviest flying bird, or carinate, is the Kori bustard or paauw (*Otis kori*), which has a wing span of 8 feet or more. Cock birds weighing up to 40 lb. have been shot in South Africa, and one outsized specimen, killed in the Western Transvaal, was estimated to weigh 54 lb. The mute swan (*Cygnus olor*) has an average weight of 28 lb. A single instance has been recorded of one weighing 23 kilogrammes (50·7 lb.). Mute swans are resident in Britain where they have attained 44 lb. A weight of 46·2 lb. has also been reported for the great bustard (*Otis tarda*). The heaviest flying bird of prey is the Andean condor (*Vultur gryphus*), which weighs 20–25 lb. There is also a record of a female harpy eagle (*Harpia harpyja*) caught in Guyana which weighed 27 lb. (average weight 16–17 lb.).

Largest wing span The wandering albatross (*Diomedea exulans*) of the southern oceans has the largest wing span of any bird, adult males averaging 10 feet 3 inches with wings tightly stretched. The largest recorded specimen was one measuring 11 feet 10 inches caught by banders in Western Australia in *c.* 1957, but some unmeasured birds may exceed 12 feet. This size is closely matched by the Andean condor (*Vultur gryphus*), which has the greatest wing area of any bird. Adults commonly have a wing span of 9¾ to 10 feet, and some specimens may reach 11 feet. One example killed in the Ilo Valley, Southern Peru in *c.* 1714 reportedly measured 12 feet 3 inches, but this figure lacks confirmation. In extreme cases the wing span of the marabou stork (*Leptoptilus crumeniferus*) found in Africa, may also exceed 11 feet

The world's smallest bird, the male bee hummingbird compared with a house sparrow

(average span 9½ feet), and there is an unconfirmed record of 13 feet 4 inches for a specimen shot in Central Africa in the 1930s. In August 1939 a wing span of 12 feet was recorded for a mute swan (*Cygnus olor*) named "Guardsman" (d. 1945) at the famous swannery at Abbotsbury, near Weymouth, Dorset. The average span is 9 feet.

Smallest *World* The smallest bird in the world is the male bee hummingbird (*Mellisuga helenae*), also known as Helena's hummingbird or "the fairy hummer", found in Cuba. A fully-grown adult has a wing span of 1½ inches. The adult male weighs only 2 grammes or 1/18th of an ounce. This is less than a Sphinx moth. It has an overall length of 55 to 62 millimetres (2·2 to 2·4 inches), the bill and tail accounting for about 40 millimetres (1·6 inches). The adult females measure 57 to 66 millimetres (2·2 to 2·6 inches). The bee hummingbird (*Acestrura bombus*) of Ecuador is about the same size but is slightly heavier.

United Kingdom The smallest resident British bird is the goldcrest (*Regulus regulus*), measuring 3½ inches long and weighing 4½ grammes (0·16 of an ounce). It resembles a small olive warbler and has a bright orange and yellow crown with a black border. The firecrest (*Regulus ignicapillus*) is of almost equal diminutiveness.

Most abundant *World* The most abundant species of bird is the chicken, the domesticated form of the wild red jungle fowl (*Gallus gallus*) of India and south-east Asia. There are believed to be about 3,000 million in the world. The most abundant wild bird is believed to be the starling (*Sturnus vulgaris*). The most abundant and also the smallest of all sea birds is Wilson's petrel (*Oceanites oceanicus*), being only 7 inches in length. It is found as far south as Antarctica. The country with the most varied avifauna is Colombia with 1,700 species recorded to 1963 (*cf.* 755 for U.S.A.-Canada).

The most abundant species *ever* recorded was the passenger pigeon (*Ectopistes migratoria*) of North America. It has been estimated that there were between 5,000,000,000 and 9,000,000,000 of this species before *c.* 1880. Thereafter the birds were killed in vast numbers and the last recorded specimen died on 1 Sept. 1914 in the Zoological Gardens in Cincinnati, Ohio, U.S.A. This bird, a female, was mounted and is now on exhibition in the Smithsonian Institution, Washington, D.C., U.S.A.

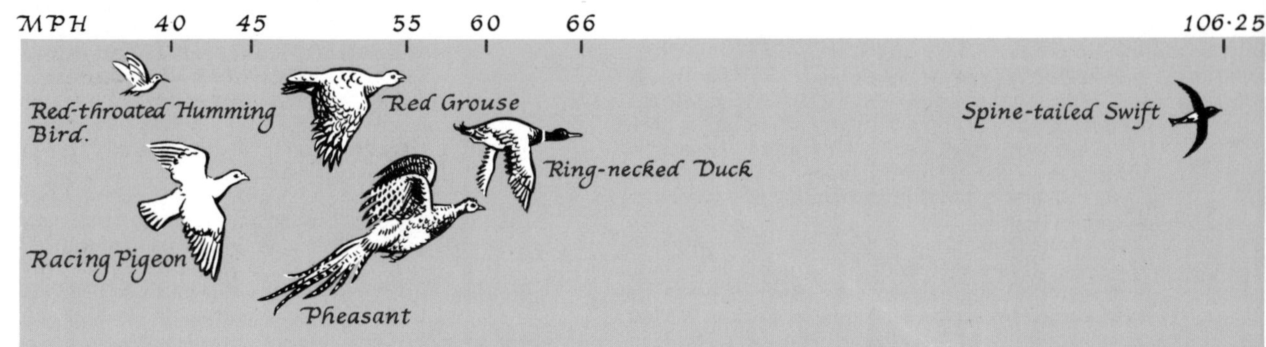

The avian champion and the fastest moving of all living things—the spine-tailed swift

United Kingdom The commonest wild breeding bird in Great Britain is the blackbird (*Turdus merula*) with just more than 10,000,000 or 8·3 per cent. of the total. The fowl stock was estimated at 90,000,000 in 1965, producing nearly 200,000,000 chicks each year. It was estimated in 1967 that 250,000 pigeon fanciers owned an average of 40 racing pigeons per loft, making a population of *c.* 10,000,000 in Great Britain.

Rarest *World* Perhaps the best claimants to this title would be the ten species last seen in the 19th century but still just possibly extant. They are the New Caledonian lorikeet (*Vini diadema*) (New Caledonia *ante* 1860); the Himalayan mountain quail (*Ophrysia superciliosa*) (eastern Punjab, 1868); Forest Spotted Owlet (*Athene blewitti*) (Central India, *c.* 1872); the Samoan wood rail (*Pareudiastes pacificus*) (Savaii, Samoa, 1873); the Fiji bar-winged rail (*Rallina poecilopterus*) (Ovalau and Viti Levu, 1890); the Kona "finches" (*Psittirostrata flaviceps* and *P. palmeri*) (Kona, Hawaii, 1891 and 1896); the Akepa (*Loxops coccinea*) (Oahu, Hawaii, 1893); the Kona "finch" (*Psittirostrata kona*) (Kona, Hawaii, 1894) and the Mamo (*Drepanis pacifica*) (Hawaii, 1898). The Ivory-billed woodpecker (*Campephilus principalis*) has been confirmed as surviving since 1963. The Maui nukupuu from Hawaii, considered extinct since 1896, was spotted in 1968 but is only a sub-species (*Hemignathus lucidus affinis*).

The osprey, which after 18 years' protection, has ceased to be Britain's rarest nesting bird

United Kingdom There are 36 species of birds (8 of them unconfirmed) which have been recorded only once in the British Isles. That which has not recurred for the longest period is the black capped petrel (*Pterodroma hasitata*), one of which was caught on a heath, at Southacre, Swaffham, Norfolk, in March or April 1850. The most tenuously established British bird is now probably the snowy owl (*Nyctea scandiaca*) now found only on Fetlar in the Shetland Islands.

Longest lived The greatest irrefutable age reported for any bird is 68 years in the case of a female European eagle-owl (*Bubo bubo*) living in 1899. Other records which are regarded as probably reliable include 80 years for a domestic goose (*Anser anser*), 73 years (1818–91) for a sulphur-crested cockatoo (*Cacatua galerita*), 72 years (1797–1869) for an African grey parrot (*Psittacus erithacus*), 70 years (1770–1840) for a mute swan (*Cygnus olor*), and 69 years for a raven (*Corvus corax*). An Egyptian vulture (*Neophron percnopterus*) which died in the menagerie at Schönbrunn, Vienna, Austria, in 1824 was stated to have been 118 years old, but the menagerie was not founded until 1752. Cases of three sulphur-crested cockatoos—all named "Cocky"—living according to hearsay evidence to 125, 115 and 114 have been recorded at Bridge Sollers, Hertfordshire, England; Nottingham Park Aviary, England and Tom Ugly's Point, New South Wales, Australia respectively.

Fastest flying The fastest flying bird is the spine-tailed swift (*Chaetura caudacuta*), for details see page 26.

The fastest running speed for any bird is 40 m.p.h. for the emu (*Dromiceius novae-hollandiae*).

Of standard game birds, the fastest is the spur-wing goose (*Plectropterus gambiensis*), with a recorded ground speed of 88 m.p.h. in level flight.

Fastest wing beats The fastest recorded wing beat of any bird is 90 beats per second by the hummingbirds of the species *Heliactin cornuta* of tropical South America. In 1951 wing beats of up to 200 per second were reported for the ruby-throated hummingbird (*Archilochus colubris*) and the rufous hummingbird (*Selasphorus rufus*) of the eastern United States during courtship flights. Large vultures (Vulturidae) can soar for hours without beating, their wings but sometimes exhibit a flapping rate as low as one beat per second.

Fastest swimmer Gentoo penguins (*Pygoscelis papua*) have been timed at 22½ m.p.h. under water, which is a respectable flying speed for some birds.

Longest flights The longest recorded banded recovery is one of 14,000 miles by an Arctic Tern (*Sterna paradisaea*), which was ringed in the Kandalaksha sanctuary, on the White Sea coast, U.S.S.R. on 5 July 1955, and caught by a fisherman off Freemantle, Western Australia, on 16 May 1956. The slender-billed shearwater (*Puffinus tenuirostris*) annually flies 20,000 miles around the Pacific Ocean.

Highest flying The celebrated example of a skein of 17 geese photographed by an astronomer crossing the Sun from Dehra Dun, India, on 17 Sept. 1919, at a height variously estimated at up to 29,500 feet, has been discredited by experts. The highest acceptable altitude is 8,200 metres (26,902 feet) by an alpine chough (*Pyrrhocorax graculus*) on Mount Everest in 1953 but its take-off point may have been as high as 20,000 feet. This height may be exceeded by the lammergeier (*Gypaetus barbatus*), a member of the vulture family, which has been seen at 25,000 feet on Mount Everest and probably reaches the summit (29,028 feet) on occasion. On three separate occasions in September 1959 a radar station in Norfolk picked up flocks of small passerine night migrants flying in from Scandinavia at 21,000 feet (3·97 miles). They were probably warblers, chats and fly catchers.

Most airborne The most "airborne" of all birds is the common swift (*Apus apus*), which flies non-stop for 9 months at a stretch and may remain aloft for as long as 21 months.

Most acute vision Tests have shown that owls are able to swoop on targets in an illumination of only 0·00000073 of a foot-candle (equivalent to the light from a candle lit 390 yards distant). This acuity is 50 times as great as that of human night vision. In good light and against a contrasting background, a falcon can spot a pigeon at a range of over 3,500 feet.

Eggs *Largest* Of living birds, that producing the largest egg is the North African ostrich (*Struthio camelus camelus*). The average egg weighs 3·63 to 3·88 lb., measures 6 to 7 inches in length, 4 to 6 inches in diameter and requires about 40 minutes for boiling. The shell is one-sixteenth of an inch thick and can support the weight of an 18 stone (252 lb.) man. The largest egg laid by any bird on the British list is that of the mute swan (*Cygnus olor*), whose eggs are from 4·3 to 4·9 inches long and between 2·8 and 3·1 inches in diameter.

Smallest The only recorded example of an egg of the bee hummingbird (*Mellisuga helenae*), the world's smallest bird (see page 34), is one measuring 11·4 millimetres (0·45 of an inch) long and 8 millimetres (0·32 of an inch) wide, now in the U.S. National Museum, Washington, D.C., U.S.A. This egg is closely matched in size by the eggs of the green and greyish white Vervain hummingbird (*Mellisuga minima*) of Jamaica, known as "the little doctor bird". Its egg looks like a large pearl and has an average length of 11·5 millimetres (0·45 of an inch) and a diameter of 8·25 millimetres (0·325 of an inch). The smallest eggs laid by any British bird are those of the goldcrest (*Regulus regulus*), which measure from 0·48 to 0·57 of an inch long and between 0·37 and 0·39 of an inch in diameter. The last confirmed nestings were in 1962 and 1965.

Incubation The shortest incubation period is that of the skylark (*Alauda arvensis*) and the brown-headed cowbird (*Molothrus ater*) at 11 days, and the longest that of the royal albatross (*Diomedea epomophora*) at up to 81 days. The idlest of cock birds are hummingbirds (family Trochilidae) among whom the hen bird does 100 per cent. of the incubation, whereas the female common or brown kiwi (*Apteryx australis*) leaves this entirely to the male.

Feathers *Longest* The longest feathers are those of the cock birds of the Japanese long-tailed fowls, or onagadori, from Kochi in Shikoku, with tail coverts up to 30 feet in length.

Most In a series of "feather counts" on various species of birds a whistling swan (*Cygnus columbianus*) was found to have 25,216 feathers. A ruby-throated hummingbird (*Archilochus colubris*) had only 940. The common house-sparrow (*Passer domesticus*) has about 3,500 in winter and 3,000 in summer.

Earliest and latest cuckoo It is unlikely that the cuckoo (*Cuculus canorus*) has ever been heard *and* seen in Great Britain earlier than 10 March, on which date one was observed in Devon in 1884 and in Wiltshire in 1938. The two latest dates recorded are 16 Dec. 1912 at Anstey's Cove, Torquay, Devon and 26 Dec. 1897 or 1898 in Cheshire.

Largest turkey The greatest recorded weight for a turkey (*Meleagris gallopavo*) is 70 lb., reported in December 1966 for a stag named "Tom" owned by a breeder in California, U.S.A. Turkeys were first brought to Britain *via* Germany from South America in 1549.

Domesticated birds The largest caged budgerigar (*Melopsittacus undulatus*) population is that of the United States with 19 million. Britain's population, 7 million in 1956, is now estimated as 4½ million. This small parakeet is wild in Australia.

Longest lived The average budgerigar life-span is 6-8 years. "Bluey," owned by Mrs. Dorothy Riddell, of Findern, near Derby, celebrated its 21st birthday on 10 Jan. 1955.

Most talkative The world's most talkative parrot is "Prudle" owned by Mrs. Lyn Logue of Golders Green, London which has won the "Best talking parrot-like bird" title at the National Cage and Aviary Bird Show in London for the six years 1965–70. "Prudle" is a male African Grey parrot taken from a nest in a tree about to be felled at Jinja, Uganda in 1958.

3. REPTILES *(Reptilia)*

(Crocodiles, snakes, turtles, tortoises and lizards.)

Largest and heaviest The largest reptile in the world is the salt-water or estuarine crocodile (*Crocodylus porosus*) of south-east Asia. Adult bulls average 12–14 feet in length and weigh about 1,200 lb. In *c.* 1823 a notorious man-eater measuring 27 feet in length and weighing an estimated 2 tons was shot at Jala Jala on Luzon Island in the Philippines after terrorising the neighbourhood for many years. Its skull, the largest on record, is now in the Museum of Comparative Zoology at Harvard University, Cambridge, Massachusetts, U.S.A. Another outsized example with a reputed length of 33 feet and a girth of 13 feet 8 inches was shot in the Bay of Bengal in 1840, but the size of its skull (now preserved in the Natural History Museum, London), suggests that its owner was more probably in the region of 23–24 feet. In April 1966 a salt-water crocodile measuring 20 feet 9 inches and weighing more than a ton was shot at Liaga, on the south-east coast of Papua.

Smallest The smallest species of reptile is believed to be *Sphaerodactylus parthenopiom*, a gecko found only on the island of Virgin Gorda, one of the British Virgin Islands, in the West Indies. It is known from 15 specimens, including some gravid females, found between 10 and 16 Aug. 1964. The three largest females measured 18 millimetres (0·71 of an inch) from snout to vent, with a tail of approximately the same length.

Two species of dwarf chameleon, *Evoluticauda tuberculata* and *Evoluticauda minima*, both found in Madagascar, are each known from only one specimen, each specimen having an overall length of 32 millimetres (1·3 inches). The tails measured 14 and 12 millimetres, respectively, so the specimen of *E. tuberculata* also had a snout-vent length of 18 millimetres. However, chameleons are more bulky than geckos and it is not known if the specimens discovered were fully grown.

It is possible that another gecko, *Sphaerodactylus elasmorhynchus*, may be even smaller. The only specimen ever discovered was an apparently mature female, with a snout-vent length of 17 millimetres (0·67 of an inch) and a tail of 17 millimetres, found on 15 March 1966 among the roots of a tree in the western part of the Massif de la Hotte in Haiti.

The smallest British reptile is the common or viviparous lizard (*Lacerta vivipara*), with a maximum length of 17·8 centimetres (7 inches).

Fastest The highest measured speed for any reptile on land is 18 m.p.h. by the race-runner lizard (*Cnemidophorus sexlineatus*) in Georgia, U.S.A. The highest speed claimed for any reptile in water is 22 m.p.h. by the leatherback turtle (see below).

Lizards *Largest* The largest of all lizards is the Komodo monitor or Ora (*Varanus komodoensis*), a dragonlike reptile first discovered on the Indonesian island of Komodo in 1912 and now found on Flores, Rintja and Padar. Lengths up to 23 feet (*sic*) have been quoted for this species, but the largest specimen to be accurately measured was a male presented to an American zoologist in 1928 by the Sultan of Bima which taped 3·05 metres (10 feet 0·8 inches). In 1937 this animal was put on display in St. Louis Zoological Park, Missouri, U.S.A. for a short period. It then measured 10 feet 2 inches in length and weighed 365 lb.

Oldest The greatest age recorded for a lizard is more than 54 years for a male slow worm (*Anguis fragilis*) kept in the Zoological Museum of Copenhagen from 1892 until 1946.

Chelonians *Largest* The largest of all chelonians is the Pacific leatherback turtle (*Dermochelys coriacea schlegelii*). The greatest weight reliably reported is 1,902½ lb. for a specimen captured near San Diego, California, U.S.A., on 20 June 1907 which had an overall length of 9 feet. The largest chelonian found in British waters is the Atlantic leatherback turtle (*Dermochelys coriacea coriacea*). One weighing 997 lb. and measuring more than 7 feet long was caught by a French fishing trawler in the English Channel on 8 May 1958. One described as weighing "nearly a ton" was netted off the Isles of Scilly on 18 June 1916, and one reportedly weighing 1,345 lb. in the North Sea on 6 Oct. 1951.

The heaviest recorded giant tortoise (*Testudo gigantea*) was one weighing 900 lb., collected in the Aldabra Islands, 270 miles north-east of Madagascar in 1847.

Longest lived The Royal Tongan tortoise named "Tu'imalila", believed to be a specimen of *Testudo radiata*, was reputedly presented to the King of Tonga by Captain James Cook (1728–79) in 1773 and died on 19 May 1966, thus indicating a possible age of about 200 years. The greatest proven age of a continuously observed tortoise is 116 years for a Mediterranean spur-thighed tortoise (*Testudo graeca*) which died in 1957 in Paignton Zoological Gardens, Devonshire. There is a reliable record of a common box turtle (*Terrapene carolina*) which lived for 129 years, from 1806 to 1935. It has been reported that a male Marion's tortoise (*Testudo sumeirii*) lived at Port Louis, Mauritius, for 152 years, from 1766 to 1918.

Slowest moving Tests on a giant tortoise (*Testudo gigantea*) in Mauritius show that even when hungry and enticed by a cabbage it cannot cover more than 5 yards in a minute (0·17 m.p.h.) on land. Over longer distances its speed is greatly reduced.

SNAKES

Longest *World* The longest (and the heaviest) of all snakes is the anaconda (*Eunectes murinus*) of South America. In 1944 a length of 37½ feet was reliably reported for a specimen killed on the upper Orinoco River in eastern Colombia. It must have weighed nearly 1,000 lb. compared with the normally acceptable limit of 500 lb. Another anaconda killed on the lower Rio Guaviare, in south-eastern Colombia, in November 1956 measured 10 metres 25 centimetres (33 feet 7½ inches) in length. The longest snake ever kept in a zoo was probably "Colossus", a female reticulated or regal python (*Python reticulatus*) who died of tuberculosis on 15 April 1963 in the Highland Park Zoological Gardens, Pittsburgh, Pennsylvania, U.S.A. She measured 28 feet 6 inches on 15 Nov. 1956, when she was growing at the rate of about 10 inches per year. Her girth, before a feed, was measured at 36 inches on 2 March 1955 and she weighed 320 lb. (22 stone 12 lb.) on 12 June 1957. A length of 10 metres (32·8 feet) was reported for a reticulated python killed in the jungles of Celebes, Indonesia, in 1912. An African rock python (*Python sebae*) measuring 9·81 metres (32 feet 2 inches) was killed at Bingerville, Ivory Coast, in 1932. A large standing reward of $5,000 (now £2,083) for any snake over 30 feet is offered by the New York Zoological Society, in Bronx Park, New York City, N.Y., U.S.A. It has not yet been collected.

Poisonous The longest poisonous snake in the world is the king cobra (*Ophiophagus hannah*), also called the hamadryad. A specimen measuring 18 feet 4 inches long was killed near Bangkok, in Thailand (Siam), in 1924.

British The longest British snake is the grass snake (*Natrix natrix*). A female measuring 5 feet 10 inches was seen at Hambledon, Surrey, in 1934–35. It is found throughout southern England, in Wales and in Dumfries-shire, Scotland, but is absent from Ireland.

Heaviest The heaviest snake is the anaconda (*Eunectes murinus*) (see above). The heaviest poisonous snake is the Eastern diamond-backed rattle-snake (*Crotalus adamanteus*), found in the south-eastern United States. A specimen 7 feet 9 inches in length weighed 34 lb. Less reliable lengths up to 8 feet 9 inches have been reported. A 15-foot 7-inch king cobra (*Ophiophagus hannah*), killed on Singapore Island in *c.* 1950 and presented to the Raffles Museum, weighed 26½ lb.

Shortest The shortest known snake is the worm snake (*Leptotyphlops bilineata*), found on the West Indian islands of Martinique, Barbados and St. Lucia. It has a maximum recorded length of 11·9 centimetres (4·7 inches).

Oldest The oldest snake ever recorded was a female anaconda (*Eunectes murinus*) who lived in Switzerland for more than 31 years. She was imported on 18 Aug. 1930 and died on 8 May 1962 in the Zoological Garden, Basel.

Fastest moving The highest measured speed for a snake is that of the black mamba (*Dendroaspis polylepis*). A speed of 7 m.p.h. was recorded on 23 April 1906 near Mbuyani on the Serengeti Plains of Kenya. Stories that mambas can overtake galloping horses (maximum speed 43·26 m.p.h.) are wild exaggerations, though a speed of 15 m.p.h. may be possible for short bursts. Some observers maintain that the African grass snake (*Psammophis furcatus*), also called the "lebitsi", can travel faster than the mamba. The British grass snake (*Natrix natrix*) has a maximum speed of 4·2 m.p.h.

Most poisonous *World* Authorities differ on which of the world's 300 poisonous snakes possess the venom which is most toxic. That of the Australian taipan (*Oxyuranus scutellatus*) is perhaps matched by that of the common krait (*Bungarus candidus*) of south-east Asia, and more likely by *Bothrops insularis*, a tree viper found only on the island of Queimada Grande, off south-eastern coast of Brazil. The tiger snake has a minimal lethal dose of only 2 milligrammes (1/14,000th of an ounce). It is believed that the venom of the beaked sea snakes (*Enhydrina schistosa*) found in the tropical and sub-tropical Indo-Pacific waters, may be even more toxic. The longest fangs of any snake are those of the Gaboon viper (*Bitis gabonica*), found in West, Central and South Africa, which measure up to 2 inches in length. A Gaboon viper bit itself to death on 12 Feb. 1963 in the Philadelphia Zoological Gardens, in Philadelphia, Pennsylvania, U.S.A. It was the only one of that species in the Zoo. They measure about 4 feet long and are brown and yellow. It is estimated that 40,000 people are killed by snakes every year of whom *c.* 25,000 are in India. Burma has the highest mortality rate with 15·4 deaths per 100,000 population per annum.

Britain The only poisonous snake in Great Britain is the adder (*Vipera berus*). Recently recorded deaths have been two in 1941 and one in 1957. The longest specimen recorded was one of 33½ inches, found in St. Leonard's Forest, near Horsham, Sussex, in July 1926.

4. AMPHIBIANS *(Amphibia)*

(Salamanders, toads, frogs, newts, caecilians, etc.)

Largest *World* The largest species of amphibian is the Japanese giant salamander (*Megalobatrachus japonicus*), which lives in deep mountain streams in southern Japan. The average length is 3–4 feet, but specimens measuring up to 6 feet have been reliably reported. In *c.* 1923 a length of 5 feet was recorded for a Chinese giant salamander (*M. davidianus*) killed in Kweichow (Guizhou) province, in southern China. A captive specimen weighed 40 kilogrammes (88 lb.) when alive and 45 kilogrammes (99 lb.) after death, thus indicating that its body had absorbed water from the aquarium.

Britain The largest British amphibian is the warty or great crested newt (*Triturus cristatus*). Males reach 14·6 centimetres (5·7 inches) in total length and females grow to 16·2 centimetres (6·37 inches). The maximum weight is 10½ grammes (0·37 of an ounce).

Newt The largest newt is the Waltl newt (*Pleurodeles waltl*), found in Morocco and the Iberian peninsula. It grows to a length of 40 centimetres (15¾ inches).

Frog The largest frog is the rare Goliath frog (*Rana* (or *Conraua*) *goliath*), first found in West Africa in 1906. It measures up to 14 inches snout to vent, or 30 inches long with its legs extended. One weighing 3,305 grammes (7 lb. 13 oz.) was caught in the rapids of the River Mbia, Rio Muni, Spanish Guinea on 23 Aug. 1960. This may be matched by a species in central New Guinea, known locally as "agak" or "carn-pnag", first reported in December 1960 which is said to measure 12 to 15 inches long and to weigh more than 6 lb. A giant frog was reported in 1969 in Sumatra.

Tree frog The largest species of tree frog is *Hyla vasta*, found on the island of Hispaniola (Haiti and the Dominican

Republic), in the West Indies. It has a maximum recorded length of 14·3 centimetres (5·6 inches) from snout to vent.

Toad The largest toad in the world is probably Blomberg's toad (*Bufo blombergi*), found in south-western Colombia, which measures up to 10 inches snout to vent. One specimen measuring 9 inches weighed 1 kilogramme (2·2 lb.). A snout to vent length of 10 inches has also been reported for the Rococo toad (*Bufo paracnemis*) of Brazil, Bolivia and northern Argentina, and the marine toad (*Bufo marinus*) of Central and South America, but no weights have yet been published.

Highest and lowest The common toad (*Bufo bufo*) is said to have been found at an altitude of 8,000 metres (26,200 feet) in Tibet, and at a depth of 340 metres (1,115 feet) in a mine.

Most poisonous The most active known venom is the batrachotoxin of the kokoi (*Phyllobates latinasus*), an arrow-poison frog of the Chocó in western Colombia, South America. Only about 1/100,000th of a gramme (0·0000004 of an ounce) is enough to kill a man.

Longest jump The record for three consecutive leaps is 32 feet 3 inches by a 2-inch-long South African sharp-nosed frog (*Rana oxyrhyncha*), recorded by Dr. Walter Rose of the South African Museum on Green Point Common, Cape Town on 16 Jan. 1954. It was named "Leaping Lena" (but later found to be a male). At the annual Calaveras County Jumping Frog Jubilee at Angels Camp, California, U.S.A. the swamp-bred *Corrosion*, owned by Leonard Hall, leaped 36 times his own length to reach 18 feet 0½ inch on 18 May 1970.

Smallest *World* The smallest species of amphibian is believed to be the arrow-poison frog *Sminthillus limbatus*, a frog found in Cuba. Fully-grown specimens have a maximum recorded length of 13 millimetres (0·51 of an inch).

Britain The smallest amphibian found in Britain is the palmate newt (*Triturus helveticus*), which measures 7·5 to 9·2 centimetres (2·95 to 3·62 inches) in length and weighs up to 2·39 grammes (0·83 of an ounce). The Natterjack or running toad (*Bufo calamita*), which has a maximum length of 8 centimetres (3·14 inches) from snout to vent, is shorter but is heavier.

Newt The smallest newt is the striped newt (*Notophthalmus perstriatus*), found in the south-eastern United States. Adults are just over 2 inches long.

Tree frog The smallest tree frog is the least tree frog (*Hyla ocularis*), found in the south-eastern United States. Adults are less than ¾ of an inch long.

Toad The smallest toad is probably Rose's toad (*Bufo rosei*), which lives on the mountain slopes above Cape Town, South Africa. It has an overall length of 1 inch.

Salamander The smallest species of salamander is *Desmognathus wrighti*, found in the Great Smoky Mountains (in Tennessee and North Carolina), in the U.S.A. Some mature specimens are only 1·4 inches long.

Longest lived A common toad (*Bufo bufo*) lived for 54 years in Copenhagen Zoological Garden, Denmark. A giant salamander (*Megalobatrachus japonicus*) lived for 50 or 52 years in Leyden Zoological Park, in the Netherlands, where it arrived from Japan in 1829 or 1831 and died on 3 June 1881. It was believed to be aged three when it arrived.

5. FISHES *(Pisces, Bradyodonti, Selachii, Marsipoli)*

LARGEST

Sea water *World* The largest species of fish is the whale-shark (*Rhincodon typus* or variously *Rhineodon typus*) first discovered in

The world's largest fish, the whale-shark, which may weigh more than 40 tons

Table Bay, Cape of Good Hope, South Africa, in April 1828 (length 15 feet). It is not, however, the largest marine animal, since it is smaller than the larger species of whales (mammals). A whale-shark measuring 59 feet long and weighing about 90,000 lb. (42·4 tons) was caught in a bamboo fish-trap at Koh Chik, in the Gulf of Siam, in 1919. Less reliable measurements up to 80 feet have been reported though the average length at maturity is 25 to 35 feet. The largest of the bony or "true" fishes (Pisces) is the Russian sturgeon or beluga (*Acipenser huso*), which is found in the Black Sea, Sea of Azov and the Caspian Sea, but enters rivers for spawning. Lengths up to 26 feet have been reliably reported, and a gravid female taken in the Volga-Caspian region in 1827 weighed 90 poods, equivalent to 1,474·2 kilogrammes (3,250½ lb.) or 1·44 tons.

Britain The largest fish recorded in the waters of the British Isles was a basking shark (*Cetorhinus maximus*) measuring 40 feet long and 25 feet in girth killed off Mutton Island, Galway Bay, Ireland on 3 May 1935 after becoming entangled in fishermen's nets. It weighed an estimated 14 tons. The largest bony fish found in British waters is the common sunfish (*Mola mola*) also known as the ocean sunfish, which grows up to 10 feet long between the tips of its dorsal and anal fins and weighs more than one ton.

Freshwater *World* The largest fish which spends its whole life in fresh water is the European catfish or wels (*Silurus glanis*). In September 1918 a specimen weighing 256·7 kilogrammes (564·74 lb.) was caught in the Desna river, six miles from Chernigov, U.S.S.R. Another specimen allegedly weighing 300 kilogrammes (660 lb.) was caught in the Dneiper river, near Kremenchug, U.S.S.R. The Arapaima (*Arapaima gigas*), also called the pirarucu, found in the Amazon and other South American rivers and often claimed to be the largest freshwater fish, averages 6½ feet and 150 lb. The largest "authentically recorded" measured 8 feet 1½ inches and weighed 324 lb.

Britain By far the largest of British freshwater fishes is the common sturgeon (*Acipenser sturio*). The heaviest recorded specimen was a female weighing 460 lb. taken in the River Esk, Yorkshire in 1810. Another specimen allegedly weighing "over 500 lb." was caught in the River Severn at Lydney, Glos. on 1 June 1937 but further details are lacking. Larger specimens have been taken at sea—notably one weighing 700 lb. and 10 feet 5 inches long netted by the trawler "Ben Urie" off the Orkneys and landed at Aberdeen on 18 Oct. 1956.

Shark The largest carnivorous fish (excluding plankton eaters) is the great white shark (*Carcharodon carcharias*), also called the man-eater or white pointer. In *c.* 1900 an

The sturgeon is the largest h ever found n freshwater (see page 38)

unconfirmed length of 43 feet was reported for a specimen which ran aground in False Bay, near the Cape of Good Hope, South Africa, but further information is lacking. Another great white shark measuring 37 feet was trapped in a herring weir at White Head Island, New Brunswick, Canada, in June 1930.

SMALLEST

Freshwater The shortest recorded freshwater fish and the smallest of all vertebrates is the dwarf pygmy goby (*Pandaka pygmaea*), an almost transparent goby fish found in streams and lakes of Luzon, Philippines. It measures only 7·5 to 11 millimetres long and weighs only 6 milligrammes (0·0002 of an ounce). It was first identified in 1927.

Sea water The shortest recorded marine fishes are the Marshall Islands goby (*Eviota zonura*), measuring 12 to 16 millimetres, and *Schindleria praematurus* from Samoa, measuring 12 to 19 millimetres, both in the Pacific Ocean. Mature specimens of the latter, largely transparent and first identified in 1940, have been known to weigh only 2 milligrammes, equivalent to 14,175 to the ounce—the lightest of all vertebrates and the smallest catch possible for any fisherman. The smallest British fish is the scorpion goby (*Gobios scorpoides*) found in the Thames with a maximum length of one inch.

Fastest The Atlantic sailfish (*Istiophorus americanus*) is generally considered to be the fastest species of fish, although the practical difficulties of measurement make data extremely difficult to secure. A figure of 68 m.p.h. (100 yards in 3 seconds) has been cited for one off Florida, U.S.A. The other species of spearfish (family Istiophoridae), including the Pacific sailfish (*Istiophorus greyi*) and the marlins (genus *Makaira*), are believed to be almost equally fast. A maximum of 50 knots (57·6 m.p.h.) has been calculated for a swordfish (*Xiphias gladius*) from a penetration of 22 inches by a bill into hard wood, but 30 to 35 knots (35 to 40 m.p.h.) is the most conceded by some experts. Speeds in excess of 35 knots (40 m.p.h.) have also been attributed to the mako shark (*Isurus oxyrinchus*) and the wahoo (*Acanthocybium solanderi*), and the bluefin tuna (*Thunnus thynnus*) has been scientifically clocked at 43·4 m.p.h. (in bursts of 10 to 20 seconds). The four-winged flying fish (*Cypselurus heterurus*) may also exceed 40 m.p.h. during its rapid rush to the surface before take-off (the average speed in the air is about 35 m.p.h.). Record flights of 42 seconds, 36 feet in altitude and 1,200 feet length have been recorded in the tropical Atlantic.

Longest lived Aquaria are of too recent origin to be able to establish with certainty which species of fish can fairly be regarded as the longest lived. Early indications are that it is the lake sturgeon (*Acipenser fulvescens*). One aged 82 years was reported from Wisconsin in 1954. Another lake sturgeon 81 inches long, and weighing 215 lb., caught on 15 July 1953 in the Lake of the Woods, Kenora, Ontario, Canada, was believed to be 150 years old, based on a growth ring (*annuli*) count in the spiny ray of its pectoral fin, but this figure has been questioned by some authorities. A figure of 150 years has also been attributed to the mirror carp (*Cyprinus carpio*), but the greatest authoritatively accepted age is "more than 50". Other long-lived fish include the European sterlet (*Acipenser ruthenus*) with 70 years, the European catfish or wels (*Silurus glanis*) with 60+ years, the European freshwater eel (*Anguilla anguilla*) with 55 years, the American eel (*Anguilla chrisypa*) with 50 years and the European pike (*Esox lucius*) with 40 years.

Oldest goldfish The exhibition life of a common goldfish (*Carassius auratus*) is normally about 17 years. On 22 Aug. 1970 Mrs. I. M. Payne, of Dawlish, Devon, announced that her pet goldfish had just celebrated its 34th birthday. In 1948 a figure of 40 years was reported for another goldfish that had been kept in a water butt, but further information is lacking.

Shortest lived The shortest lives of any vertebrate animals are those of the goby fishes (family Gobiidae), which are hatched, grow, reproduce and die in less than a year. The same may also be true of the ice fish (family Chaenichthyidae) of the Antarctic.

Deepest The greatest depth from which living organisms have been recovered is 35,137 feet by the U.S.S.R.'s research vessel *Vityaz* in the Tonga Deep area of the Pacific Ocean in September 1957. Dr. Jacques Piccard sighted a red shrimp one inch long and a flounder-type bottom feeder 12 inches long (tentatively identified as *Chascanopsetta lugubris*) from the bathyscaphe *Trieste* a few feet from its deepest ocean descent (calculated to be 35,802 feet) on 24 Jan. 1960. This sighting has been questioned by some authorities, who still regard 7,500 metres (24,600 feet) as the acceptable known limit for fish, in the case of brotulids of the genus *Bassogigas*.

Most eggs The common sunfish (*Mola mola*) produces up to 300,000,000 eggs 1/10th of an inch long and 1/20th of

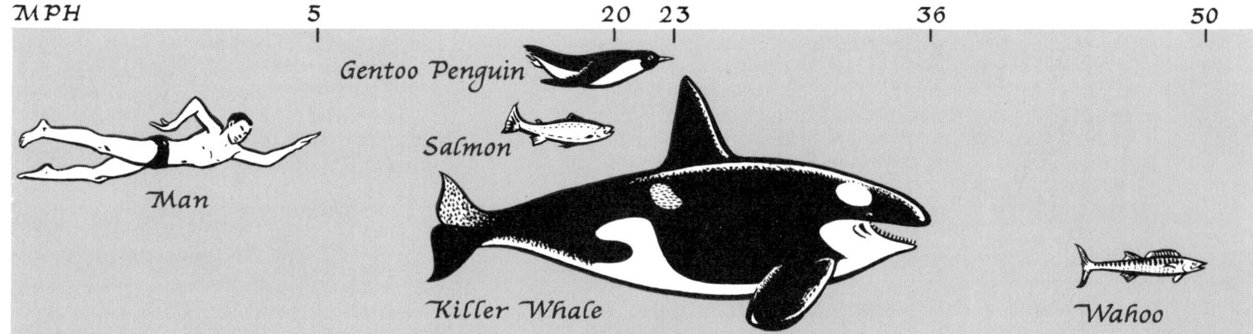

omparative eeds of fish behind the wahoo and ahead of a champion swimmer

an inch in diameter. The cichlids and certain catfish (order Ostariophysi) lay as few as 50.

Most venomous The most venomous fish in the world are the stonefish (*Synanceja verrucosa, S. horrida* and *S. trachynis*) of the tropical Indo-Pacific oceans. Contact with the spines of their fins usually proves fatal.

Most electric The electric eel (*Electrophorus electricus*) measuring up to 10 feet in length, 90 lb. in weight can discharge a shock of 650 volts at one ampere which is sufficient to stun a man 20 feet distant. It is found in the rivers of Brazil, Colombia and Peru.

6. STARFISHES *(Asteroida)*

Largest The largest recorded starfish is the 20-armed Sunflower Star (*Pycnopodia helianthoides*), found on the Pacific coast of North America. One specimen collected in Californian waters measured 3 feet 8 inches in diameter and weighed 11 lb. The largest species found in British waters is the spiny starfish (*Marthasterias glacialis*), which usually measures 9–12 inches in diameter, but has been recorded up to 28 inches.

Smallest The smallest recorded starfish is one of the genus Marginaster, which has a diameter of only half an inch when fully grown. The smallest starfish found in Britain is the cushion starfish (*Asterrina gibbosa*), which has a diameter of about one inch.

7. ARACHNIDS *(Arachnida)*

Most southerly In 1964 three previously unrecorded species of arachnids were found living in mosses at a height of 5,000 feet on a mountain near the snout of the Robert Scott Glacier, Antarctica, 309 miles from the South Pole. These included *Nano orchestes antarcticus*, a minute pink eight-legged mite 0·01 of an inch long. The temperature was −20° F.

SPIDERS (Order Araneae)

Largest *World* The world's largest known spider is the mygale or "bird-eating" spider (*Therόphosa leblondii*). A male specimen with a leg span of 10 inches, when fully extended and a body length of 3½ inches, was collected in April 1925 at Montagne la Gabrielle, French Guiana. It weighed nearly 2 oz. The heaviest spider ever recorded was a female tarantula of the genus *Lasiodora*, collected at Manaos, Brazil, in 1945. It measured 9½ inches across and weighed almost 3 ounces.

Britain Of the 603 known British species of spider, covering an estimated population of more than 500,000,000,000,000 the longest is the cardinal spider (*Tegenaria parietina*), a species of house spider, among which the males have a leg span sometimes exceeding 5 inches (length of body 19 mm. or 0·75 of an inch). An outsized specimen of the "Daddy Longlegs" spider (*Pholcus phalangioides*) in England has been measured 6 inches across. The spider *Segestria florentina* has a body measuring up to 23 millimetres (0·92 of an inch) long. The heaviest spider in Britain is *Araneus quadratus* (formerly called *Araneus reaumuri*), an orb-weaver. One specimen captured in October 1943 weighed 1·174 grammes (0·041 of an ounce) and measured 15 millimetres (0·58 of an inch) across the body.

Smallest *World* The smallest known spider in the world is *Microlinpheus bryophilus* (Family Argiopidae) discovered in Lorne, Victoria, Australia in 1932. The adult male has a body length of 0·6 of a millimetre or 1/35th of an inch. The smallest recorded spiders found in Britain are *Saloca diceros*, found among mosses in Dorset and Staffordshire, and *Glyphesis cottonae*, each of which has a body length of 1 millimetre (1/25th of an inch).

Largest web The largest webs are those spun by the female bird-eating golden orb-weaver (*Nephila pipipes*) found in Africa, Asia and Australasia with circumferences up to 12 feet.

Most poisonous The most poisonous spider recorded is the brown recluse spider (*Loxosceles reclusa*), also called the fiddler spider, which is found in the central and southern states of the U.S.A. The bite produces an ulcerating wound which often turns gangrenous. The bite or repeated bites of the female black widow spider (*Latrodectus mactans*) of South America, the Australian red-backed (*Latrodectus hasseltii*) spiders and funnel-web spiders (*Atrax robustus* and *A. formidabilis*) of Australia; and the button spider (*Lactrodectus indistinctus*) can be fatal.

Rarest The most elusive of all spiders are the primitive burrowing spiders (genus *Liphistius*) found in south-east Asia. The most elusive spider in Britain is the black and crimson *Eresus niger*, found in Hampshire, Dorset and Cornwall, which has been recorded less than a dozen times. In 1953 a specimen was reportedly seen at Sandown, Isle of Wight, but it escaped. Two male examples are preserved in the Natural History Museum, London.

Fastest The highest speed measured for a spider is 1·73 feet per second (1·17 m.p.h.) in the case of a specimen of *Tegenaria atrica*.

Longest lived Some of the large female "bird-eating" tarantulas (*Mygalomorphae*) have been kept in captivity for up to 25 years (the males only live 8–9 years). The longest lived of British spiders is probably the house spider (*Tegenaria derhamii*) which has been kept in captivity for as long as 7 years. Some wolf spiders (families Lycosidae and Pisauridae) may also live for 7 years.

8. CRUSTACEANS *(Crustacea)*

(Crabs, lobsters, shrimps, prawns, crayfish, barnacles, water fleas, fish lice, woodlice, sand hoppers, kril, etc.)

Largest *World* The largest of all crustaceans (although not the heaviest) is the scarlet giant spider crab (*Macrocheira kaempferi*), also called the stilt crab, which is found in deep waters off Japan. It usually has a foot-wide body and a claw span of 9–11 feet, but unconfirmed measurements up to 18 feet have been reported. A specimen with a claw span of 12 feet 1½ inches weighed 14 lb.

The largest species of lobster, and the heaviest of all crustaceans, is the American or North Atlantic lobster (*Homarus americanus*). One weighing 42 lb. 7 oz. and measuring 4 feet from tail to tip of claw was caught in a deep-sea trawl by the smack "Hustler" off the Virginia Capes, Virginia, U.S.A. in 1934 and is preserved in the Museum of Science, Boston, Mass. Another outsized specimen caught off Chatham, New England, U.S.A. in 1949 reportedly weighed 48 lb., but this claim has not yet been fully substantiated. The largest species of crayfish is the green crayfish (*Jasus verreauxi*), found in Australian waters. The average weight is 10–15 lb., but specimens have been recorded up to 25 lb.

Britain The largest crustacean found in British waters is the common or European lobster (*Homarus gammarus*), with an average length of 13 inches and an average weight of 8 lb. A specimen weighing 14½ lb., caught in September 1969 off St. Anne's Head, is now mounted in the bar of the Amroth Arms, Pembrokeshire, Wales. The largest crab found in British waters is the edible or great crab (*Cancer pagurus*). One weighing 14 lb. measuring 11 inches across was reported in 1895.

Smallest The smallest known crustaceans are water fleas of the genus *Alonella*, which may measure less than 1/100th of an inch long. They are found in British waters. The smallest British crab is the pea crab (*Pinnotheres pisum*), with a shell only 0·25 of an inch long.

Oldest The oldest of all known crustaceans is the *Hutchinsoniella*, similar to the trilobites of 500,000,000 years ago. First found in 1954, it is only 1/100th of an inch in length.

Deepest The marine crab *Ethusina abyssicola* has been taken at a depth of about 14,000 feet.

9. INSECTS *(Insecta)*

Largest *World* The bulkiest of all insects is the Goliath beetle (*Goliathus regius*), found in West Africa. It measures up to 5·85 inches in length, 4 inches across the back and weighs up to 3·52 oz. The beetle *Macrodontia cervicornis*, found in South America, is a little longer but less bulky. The longhorn beetle (*Batocera wallacei*) of New Guinea has a body length of 3½ inches but a total length of up to 11 inches, including antennae. Another longhorn beetle, *Titanus giganteus*, of French Guiana has a body length of 5·9 inches, excluding antennae. Some tropical stick-insects have a body length of up to 13 inches (*e.g. Phoboeticus fruhstorferi*) and, in the case of *Palophus titan* from Australia, a wing span of 10 inches.

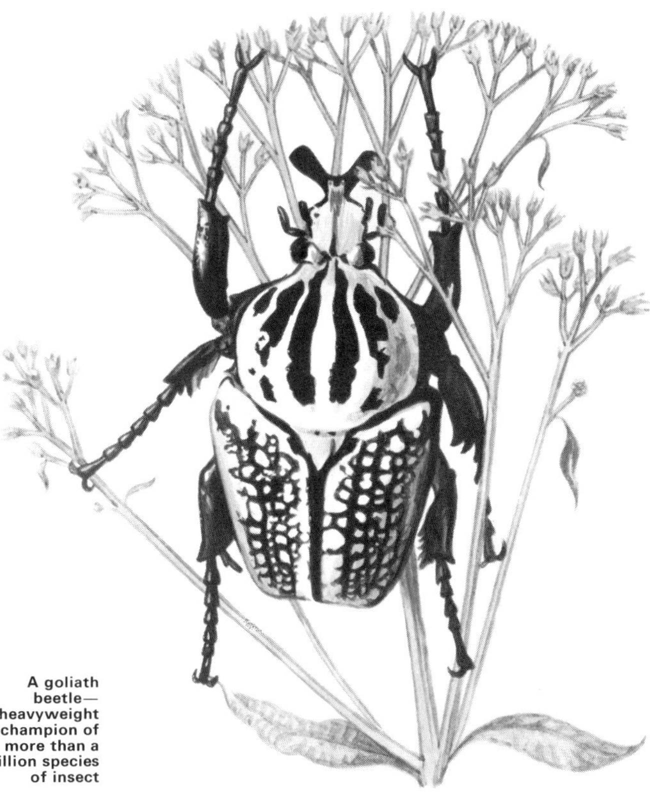

A goliath beetle—heavyweight champion of more than a million species of insect

Britain The largest British ground insect is the stag beetle (*Lucanus cervus*) found in Hampshire, which has a length of up to 2 inches, including antler-like mandibles. The heaviest ground insect found in Britain is the great silver beetle (*Hydrophilus piceus*), which has an overall length of 1¾ inches. Butterflies and moths (see page 42) have greater dimensions.

Smallest Several hundred new species of insect are discovered every year, but the smallest of those known are "hairy-winged" beetles of the family Trichopterygidae and the "battledore-wing fairy flies" of the family Mymaridae (parasitic wasps). They measure only 0·2 of a millimetre (0·008 of an inch) in length and the fairy flies have a wing span of only 1 millimetre (0·04 of an inch). The male bloodsucking banded louse (*Enderleinellus zonatas*), ungorged, and the parasitic wasp *Caraphractus cinctus* may each weigh as little as 0·005 of a milligramme, or 5,670,000 to an ounce. The eggs of the latter each weigh 0·0002 mg., or 141,750,000 to the ounce.

Fastest flying Experiments have proved that widely published statements that the female deer bot-fly could attain a speed of 820 m.p.h. are wildly exaggerated. Acceptable modern experiments have now established that the highest maintainable air-speed of any insect, including the deer bot-fly, is 24 m.p.h., rising to a maximum of 36 m.p.h. for short bursts. A relay of bees (maximum speed 14 m.p.h.) would use only a gallon of nectar in cruising 4,000,000 miles at an average speed of 7 m.p.h.

Longest lived The oldest recorded insect is *Buprestis splendens*, a wood-boring beetle which has been known to live for up to 37 years. Some queen termites (family Termitidae) are, however, believed to live for as long as 40 years.

Loudest The loudest of all insects is the male cicada (family (Cicadidae). At 7,400 pulses per minute its sounding membrane produces a noise (officially described by the United States Department of Agriculture as "Tsh-ee-EEEE-e-ou") detectable more than a quarter of a mile distant. The only British species is *Cicadetta montana*, confined to the New Forest area in Hampshire.

Southernmost The farthest south at which any insect has been found is 77° S. (900 miles from the South Pole) in the case of a springtail (order Collembola).

Largest swarm The greatest recorded swarm of locusts (family Acrididae) was one covering an estimated 2,000 square miles across the Red Sea in 1889. Such a swarm must have contained about 250,000 million insects weighing about 500,000 tons. A swarm of desert locusts (*Schistocerca gregaria*) can consume in 24 hours as much as 4 million elephants. Locusts fly at about 11 m.p.h.

Fastest wing beat The fastest wing beat of any insect is 57,000 per minute by the midge *Forcipomyia*. In experiments with truncated wings, at a temperature of 98·6° F., the rate increased to 133,080 beats per minute. The muscular contraction-expansion cycle in 0·00045 or 1/2,218th of a second, further represents the fastest muscle movement ever measured. Most butterflies beat their wings at a rate of 460 to 636 per minute.

Slowest wing beat The slowest wing beat of any insect is 300 per minute by the swallowtail butterfly (*Papilio machaon*).

Largest ants The largest of all ants is the great black ant (*Dinoponera gigantea*), found in the Amazon delta in South America. Females measure up to 33 millimetres (1·3 inches) overall and weigh up to 347 milligrammes. The largest of the 27 species found in Britain is the wood ant (*Formica rufa*), which grows up to 11 millimetres (0·43 of an inch) long. The smallest is the thief ant (*Solenopsis fugax*), with a maximum length of 3 millimetres (0·12 of an inch).

Largest grasshopper The largest of all grasshoppers is *Pseudophyllanax imperialis*, found on the island of New Caledonia, in the south-western Pacific Ocean. It has a wing span of nearly 10 inches and antennae extending 8 inches. The largest found in Britain is the great green grasshopper (*Phasgoneura viridissima*), which is up to 3 inches long.

Dragonflies The largest of the 43 species of dragonflies found in Britain is the golden-ringed dragonfly (*Cordulegaster boltonii*), which has been measured at up to 3·3 inches long and may have a wing span of more than 4 inches. The smallest dragonfly found in Britain is the scarce ischnura (*Ischnura pumilio*), with a body length of 1 inch and a wing span of 1·3 inches.

Oldest flea A Russian bird flea (Order Siphonaptera) is reported to have lived for 1,487 days or a little more than 4 years.

Longest flea jump The long jump record for a flea is 13 inches by a California rodent flea in 1910. The high jump record is 7¾ inches. In jumping 130 times its own height a flea subjects itself to a force of 200 g. Siphonapterologists recognize more than 1,300 varieties.

BUTTERFLIES AND MOTHS (Order Lepidoptera)

Largest *World* The largest known moth is the Hercules Emperor moth (*Coscinoscera hercules*) of Australia and New Guinea. It has a wing area of up to 40·8 square inches and a span of 10 inches. The Indian atlas moth (*Attacus atlas*) and the great owlet moth (*Thysania agrippina*) of Brazil each have a wing span of fully 12 inches but are less heavily built. The world's largest butterfly is the New Guinea birdwing (*Troides alexandrae*), the female of which has a span of 12 inches.

British The largest of the 21,000 species of insects found in the British Isles is the rare death's-head hawk moth (*Acherontia atropos*), which has a body length of about 6 centimetres (2·36 inches), an abdomen girth of 4 centimetres (1·57 inches) and a wing span of up to 13·3 centimetres (5·25 inches). It weighs up to 2 grammes (0·070 of an ounce). The largest butterfly found in the British Isles is the great monarch butterfly (*Danaus plexippus*), also called the milkweed or black-veined brown butterfly, which breeds in the southern United States and Central America. From 1876 to 1968, 215 were recorded in the United Kingdom. The wing span of a fully-grown specimen may exceed 4 inches, and weigh 0·75 of a gramme (0·026 of an ounce). The largest *native* butterfly is the swallowtail (*Papilo machaon*), with a wing span of 3–3½ inches and a weight of 0·5 of a gramme (0·017 of an ounce). This species is now confined to the fenlands of Cambridge and Norfolk.

Smallest *World and Britain* The smallest of the estimated 140,000 known species of Lepidoptera is the moth *Nepticula microtheiella*, with a wing span of 3 millimetres (0·12 of an inch) and a body length of 2 millimetres (0·08 of an inch). It is found in Britain. The smallest known butterfly is the dwarf blue (*Brephidium barberae*) from South Africa. It is 14 millimetres (0·55 of an inch) from wing-tip to wing-tip. The smallest known British butterfly is the small blue (*Cupido minimus*), with a wing span of 19 to 25 millimetres (0·75 to 1·0 inch).

Rarest The rarest of all butterflies is probably the birdwing *Ornithoptera allottei*, which is found only on Bougainville in the Solomon Islands. A specimen was sold for £750 in Paris on 24 Oct. 1966. A specimen of the Yellow Russian moth (*Rhyacia lucipeta*) taken in Sussex was exhibited in London in November 1968, and a Slender Burnished Brass moth (*Tlusia orichaleea*), whose home is India, was captured in southern England in October 1969. A grey Caradine of Mediterranean origin was first reported in August 1969 from Totteridge, London, N.20.

Highest The painted lady butterfly (*Vanessa cardui*) has been recorded at an altitude of 17,000 feet during migratory flights.

Most acute sense of smell The most acute sense of smell exhibited in nature is that of the male silkworm moth (*Bombyx mori*), or in Britain, the Emperor moth, which, according to German experiments in 1961, can detect sex attractant of the female at the almost unbelievable range of 11 kilometres (6·8 miles) upwind. This has been identified as one of the higher alcohols ($C_{16}H_{29}OH$) of which the female carries only $1·0 \times 10^{-13}$ of a gramme.

10. CENTIPEDE *(Chilopoda)*

Longest The longest of the 1,700 known species of centipede is the venomous giant scolopender (*Scolopendra gigantea*) of South and Central America. It has 23 segments (46 legs), and specimens have been measured up to 12 inches long and 1 inch across. In 1963 a length of 12½ inches was reported for a va waisted scolopender (*Scolopendra morsitans*) collected in West Africa. The centipede with most segments is a tropical species of the genus Geophilus, which has 173 pairs of legs. The longest centipede found in Britain is *Haplophilus subterraneus*, which has between 77 and 83 segments and measures up to 76 millimetres (3 inches) long and 1·4 millimetres (0·055 of an inch) across.

Shortest The shortest recorded centipede is one with only 8 segments and, therefore, 16 legs. The shortest centipede found in Britain is *Lithobius duboscqui*, which has 15 segments (30 legs) and measures up to 9·5 millimetres (0·38 of an inch) long and 1 millimetre (0·04 of an inch) across.

11. MILLIPEDES *(Diplopoda)*

Most legs The creatures with the greatest number of legs are millipedes of which there are about 6,500 species. These are distinguished from centipedes by having two instead of one pair of legs on most segments of the body. The largest number of legs reported for a millipede is 784 legs for a species found in Panama in July 1958. Millipedes range in length from 2 millimetres (0·078 of an inch) to 30 centimetres (11·8 inches).

A Gippsland earthworm—the world's longest species

12. SEGMENTED WORMS *(Annelida* or *Annulata)*

Longest earthworm The longest known species of earthworm is probably *Megascolides australis*, discovered in the Gippsland region of eastern Victoria, Australia in 1868. An average specimen measures 4 to 5 feet long and ¾ of an inch thick and weighs nearly a pound. The longest on record measured 11 feet when fully extended. The eggs of this worm measure 2 to 3 inches long and ¾ of an inch in diameter. In November 1967 a specimen of the African earthworm *Microschaetus rappi* measuring 11 feet long, and 21 feet when fully extended, was discovered at Debe Nek, near King William's Town, in the Eastern Cape. The *average* length of this species, however, is believed to be shorter than that of *Megascolides australis*. The longest segmented worm found in Britain is *Lumbricus terrestris*, which measures up to 35 centimetres (13¾ inches) in length.

13. MOLLUSCS *(Mollusca)*

(Squids, octopuses, shellfish, snails, etc.)

Largest squid The heaviest of all invertebrate animals is the Atlantic giant squid (*Architeuthis princeps*), which has been stranded on British shores on occasions. The largest specimen ever recorded was one measuring 55 feet overall (head and body 20 feet, tentacles 35 feet), captured on 2 Nov. 1878, after it had run aground in Tickle Bay, Newfoundland, Canada. Its eyes were 18 inches in diameter. The total weight was estimated to be two tons. Another giant squid washed up at Arnarnaesvick, Iceland, in November or December 1790 and cut up for cod-bait may have been even heavier. It had a head and body length of *c.* 6·60 metres (21 feet 8 inches) and measured 11·88 metres (39 feet) overall (the tentacles had been mutilated). Another specimen with an alleged total length of 88 feet (head and body 30 feet, longest tentacle 58 feet) was washed ashore on the coast of Newfoundland before 1892.

Largest octopus The largest octopus is *Octopus apollyon* of the North Pacific. A specimen caught off the coast of Alaska, U.S.A. had a span of 28 feet and weighed 360 lb. The Pacific octopus (*Octopus hongkongensis*) has been recorded up to 32 feet across, but its body is only about 18 inches long.

Most ancient The longest existing living creature is *Neopilina galatheae,* a deep-sea worm-snail which had been believed extinct for about 320,000,000 years, but which was found at a depth of 11,400 feet off Costa Rica by the Danish research vessel *Galathea* in 1952. Fossils found in New York State, U.S.A., in Newfoundland, Canada, and in Sweden show that this mollusc was also living about 500,000,000 years ago.

SHELLS

Largest The largest of all existing shells is the marine bivalve giant clam (*Tridacna gigas*), found on the Indo-Pacific coral reef. A specimen measuring 43 inches by 29 inches and weighing 579½ lb. (over a quarter of a ton) was collected from the Great Barrier Reef in 1917, and is now in the American Museum of Natural History, Central Park West, New York City, N.Y., U.S.A. The largest British shell is the fan mussel (*Pinna fragilis*), specimens of which, found at Tor Bay, Devon, measured 20 centimetres (7·87 inches) in height and 37 centimetres (14·56 inches) in length.

Smallest The smallest recorded shells are *Homalogyra atomus* and *H. rota,* marine gastropods found in the Atlantic Ocean. They are only 1/30th of an inch in diameter. The smallest British shell is the land gastropod *Punctum pygmaeum,* which has a height of 0·6 to 0·9 millimetres (0·023 to 0·035 of an inch) and a length of 1·2 to 1·5 millimetres (0·047 to 0·059 of an inch).

Rarest The most highly prized of all shells in the hands of conchologists is the white-tooth cowrie (*Cypraea leucodon*), measuring 3 inches long and found in deep water off the Cape of Good Hope, South Africa. Two examples are known, one in the British Museum (Natural History), London, and the other at Harvard University, Cambridge, Massachusetts, U.S.A. The highest price known to have been paid for a sea shell is £1,350 paid in a sale at Sotheby's, London on 4 March 1971 for one of the four known examples of *Conus bengalensis* Okutani, found off north-west Thailand in December 1970.

Longest lived Some experts regard the giant clam and the freshwater mussel (*Margaritan margaritifera*) as the longest lived shells, at up to 100 years.

SNAILS

Largest The largest recorded species of snail is the sea hare (*Aplysia californica*), which is found in coastal waters off California, U.S.A. The average weight is 7 to 8 lb. but specimens have been recorded up to 16 lb. The largest known land snail is the African giant land snail (*Achatina achatina*), measuring up to 10¾ inches long and weighing up to 1 lb. The largest found in Britain is the Roman or edible snail (*Helix pomatia*), which measures 4 inches long and weighs up to 3 oz.

Speed A snail's pace varies from as slow as 0·00036 m.p.h., or 23 inches per hour, up to 0·0313 m.p.h. or 55 yards per hour for the common garden snail (*Helix aspersa*). Tests were carried out at Maryland University, U.S.A.

14. RIBBON WORMS *(Nermertina or Rhynchopods)*

Longest worm The longest of the 550 recorded species of ribbon worms, also called nemertines (or nemerteans), is the "living fishing-line worm" found in the shallow waters of the North Sea. A specimen washed ashore at St. Andrews, Fifeshire, Scotland, in 1864 after a severe storm measured more than 180 feet in length, making it easily the longest recorded worm of any variety.

15. JELLY FISHES *(Scyphozoa or Scyphomedusia)*

Longest The longest jelly fish is the *Cyanea arctica*. For details see page 26.

The longest coelenterate found in British waters is the "lion's mane" jelly fish (*Cyanea capillata*) or the common sea blubber. It has been recorded up to 3 feet in diameter and 75 feet in length.

16. SPONGES *(Parazoa, Porifera or Spongida)*

Largest and smallest The largest sponges are the barrel-shaped loggerhead (*Spheciospongia vesparium*), measuring 3½ feet high and 3 feet in diameter, found in the West Indies and Florida, U.S.A., and the Neptune's cup or goblet (*Poterion patera*) of Indonesia, standing up to 4 feet in height. The smallest sponges, fully grown, are 3 millimetres (0·12 of an inch) high. The rarest coloration among the 20,000 known species is blue.

Deepest Sponges have been recovered from depths of up to 18,500 feet (3·5 miles).

17. EXTINCT ANIMALS

Largest *World* The first dinosaur to be scientifically described was *Megalosaurus bucklandi*, a 20-foot long bipedal theropod, in 1824. The bones of this animal had been discovered before 1818 in a slate quarry at Stonesfield, near Woodstock, Oxfordshire. It stalked across southern England about 130,000,000 years ago. The word "dinosaur" (great lizard) was not used for such reptiles until 1842. The longest recorded dinosaur was *Diplodocus carnegiei*, an attenuated sauropod which ranged over western North America about 150,000,000 years ago. A mounted skeleton in the Carnegie Museum, Pittsburgh, Pennsylvania, U.S.A. measures 87½ feet in length (neck 22 feet, body 15 feet, tail 50½ feet)—nearly the length of three London buses—and stands 11 feet 9 inches at the pelvis (the highest point on the body). This animal weighed an estimated 10·39 tons in life.

Heaviest The heaviest of all prehistoric animals was *Brachiosaurus,* which lived in East Africa (Rhodesia and Tanzania) and Colorado and Oklahoma, U.S.A., between 135,000,000 and 165,000,000 years ago. This sauropod measured up to 82 feet in length (height at shoulder 21 feet) and weighed up to 77 tons when alive, but isolated bones have been discovered which suggest that some individuals may have weighed as much as 100 tons. It could reach foliage 42 feet above the ground.

Britain Britain's largest prehistoric animal was the sauropod *Cetiosaurus leedsi,* which lived in England about 165,000,000 years ago. It measured up to 60 feet in length and weighed about 10 tons. The bones of this dinosaur were first located in the No. 1 Brickyard of the New Peterborough Brick Co., Peterborough in May 1898 and subsequently in Oxfordshire.

Largest predator The largest theropod was probably *Tyrannosaurus rex,* which lived about 75,000,000 years ago in what are now the states of Montana and Wyoming in the U.S.A., and Mongolia. It measured up to 47 feet in overall length, had a bipedal height of up to 18½ feet, a stride of 13 feet and weighed a calculated 6·78 tons. Its 4-foot long skull contained serrated teeth measuring up to 6 inches in length. Another theropod called Saurophagus maximus, which lived about 120,000,000 years ago in what is now the state of Oklahoma, U.S.A., may have been even heavier. It measured up to 42 feet overall, had a bipedal height of up to 16 feet, and was a much more massively built animal in proportion to its height.

Tusks *Longest* The longest tusks of any prehistoric animal were those of the straight-tusked elephant *Hesperoloxodon antiquus germanicus*, which lived in what is now northern Germany about 2,000,000 years ago. The average length in adult bulls was 5 metres (16 feet 4¾ inches). A single tusk of a woolly mammoth (*Mammonteus primigenius*) preserved in the Franzens Museum at Brno, Czechoslovakia, measures 5·02 metres (16 feet 5½ inches) along the curve. In 1933 a single tusk of an Imperial mammoth (*Archidiskodon imperator*) measuring 16 feet+ (anterior end missing) was unearthed near Post, Gorza County, Texas, U.S.A. In 1934 this tusk was presented to the American Museum of Natural History in New York City, N.Y., U.S.A.

Heaviest The heaviest single tusk on record is one weighing 330 lb., with a girth of 35 inches, now preserved in the Museo Archeologico, Milan, Italy. It measures 11 feet 9 inches in length. The tallest extinct elephant was the mammoth *Parelephas trogontherii*, which lived about 1,000,000 years ago in central Europe and North America. In February 1970 the skeleton of an unidentified extinct elephant reputedly measuring 16 feet at the shoulder was put on display at a museum in Azov, U.S.S.R. The specimen was believed to be 500,000 years old.

Longest horns The prehistoric Giant Deer (*Megaceros giganteus*), erroneously called the Irish elk, which lived in Northern Europe and Northern Asia as recently as 50,000 B.C. stood 7 feet at the shoulder and had greatly palmated antlers measuring up to 14 feet across.

Most brainless *Stegosaurus* ("plated reptile"), which measured up to 30 feet in length, 8 feet in height at the hips and weighed 1¾ tons, had a plum-sized brain weighing only 2½ ounces. It represented 0·004 of one per cent. of its bodyweight, compared with 0·074 of one per cent. for an elephant and 1·88 per cent. for a human. It roamed widely across the Northern Hemisphere about 150 million years ago, trying to remember where it had been.

Largest mammal The largest prehistoric mammal, and the largest land mammal ever recorded, was *Baluchitherium grangeri*, a long-necked, hornless rhinoceros found in central and western Asia between 20,000,000 and 40,000,000 years ago. It stood up to 17 feet 9 inches at the shoulder (27 feet to the crown of the head), measured 28 feet in length and weighed about 16 tons. The bones of this gigantic browser were first discovered near Chur-lando, Baluchistan, Pakistan in 1911.

Largest bird The largest prehistoric bird was the elephant bird (*Aepyornis maximus*), also known as the roc bird, which

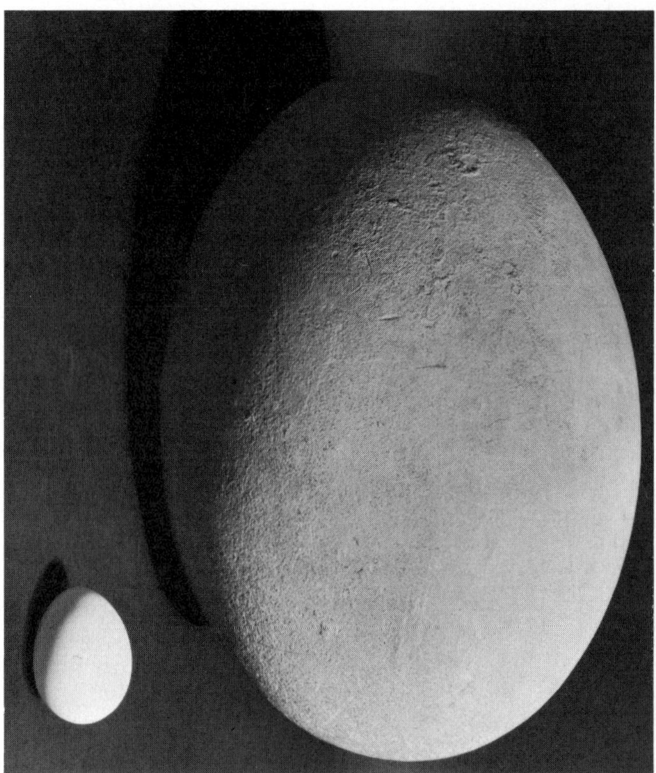

A roc egg compared with that of a hen

lived in southern Madagascar. It was a flightless bird standing 9 to 10 feet in height and weighing up to 965 lb. It also had the largest eggs of any living creature. One example measures 33¾ inches around the long axis with a circumference of 28½ inches, giving a capacity of 2·35 gallons—six times that of an ostrich egg. A more cylindrical egg preserved in the Academie des Sciences, Paris, France, measures 12⅝ inches by 15⅜ inches, and probably weighed about 27 lb. with its contents. This bird may have survived until *c.* 1660. The flightless moa *Dinornis giganteus* of South Island, New Zealand, was taller, attaining a height of over 13 feet, but probably weighed about 520 lb.

In May 1962 a single fossilized ankle joint of an enormous flightless bird was found at Gainsville, Florida, U.S.A. The largest actually to fly was probably the condor-like *Teratornis incredibilis*, which lived in North America about 125,000,000 years ago. The remains of one of this species, discovered in Smith Creek Cave, Nevada, in 1952 indicate a wing span of 5 metres (16 feet 4 inches), and the bird must have weighed at least 50 lb. Another gigantic flying bird named *Osteodontornis*, which lived in what is now the State of California, U.S.A. about 20,000,000 years ago, had a wing span of 16 feet and was probably even heavier. It was related to the pelicans and storks. The albatross-like *Gigantornis eaglesomei* has been credited with a wing span of 20 feet on the evidence of a single fossilized breastbone. It flew over what is now Nigeria between 34,000,000 and 58,000,000 years ago.

Largest flying creature The winged reptile *Pteranodon ingens,* which glided over what is now the State of Kansas, U.S.A. about 80,000,000 years ago, had a wing span of up to 27 feet and weighed an estimated 40 lb. Britain's largest extinct flying creature was *Ornithocheirus*, with a wing span of 10 feet, which flew over the Weald about 100,000,000 years ago.

Largest marine reptile The largest marine reptile ever recorded was the short-necked plesiosaur *Kronosaurus queenslandicus,* which swam in the seas around what is now Australia about 100,000,000 years ago. It measured about 50 feet in length, with a skull 9 feet long.

Largest crocodile The largest recorded crocodile was *Phobosuchus* ("horror crocodile"), which lived in the lakes and swamps of what are now the states of Montana and Texas, U.S.A., 75,000,000 years ago. It measured up to 54 feet in length and had a skull 6 feet long. The gavial *Rhamphosuchus*, which lived in northern India about 7,000,000 years ago, was nearly as large, attaining a length of 50 feet.

Largest chelonians The largest prehistoric marine turtle was *Archelon ischyros,* which lived in the shallow seas of North America about 80,000,000 years ago. An almost complete skeleton with a carapace (shell) 6½ feet long was discovered in August 1895 near the south fork of the Cheyenne River in Custer County, South Dakota. The skeleton, which has an overall length of 11 feet 4 inches (16 to 20 feet across the outstretched flippers), is now in the Peabody Museum of Natural History at Yale University, New Haven, Connecticut, U.S.A. This specimen is estimated to have weighed 6,000 lb. (2·7 tons) when it was alive.

The largest prehistoric tortoise was *Colossochelys atlas,* which lived in northern India between 7,000,000 and 12,000,000 years ago. An almost complete skeleton with a carapace 5 feet 5 inches long (7 feet 4 inches over the curve) and 2 feet 11 inches high was discovered in the Siwalik Hills in 1923. It is now in the American Museum of Natural History in New York City, U.S.A. This animal had a nose to tail length of 8 feet and is computed to have weighed 2,100 lb. when it was alive.

Longest snake The longest prehistoric snake was the python-like *Gigantophis garstini,* which inhabited the United Arab Republic (formerly Egypt) about 50,000,000 years ago. Parts of a spinal column discovered at El Faiyûm indicate a length of about 42 feet.

Largest reptile eggs The largest reptilian eggs so far discovered are those of a *Hypselosaurus priscus* in the valley of the Durance, near Aix-en-Provence, southern France, found in October 1960. The eggs of this 30-foot long sauropod, believed to be 80,000,000 years old, would have had, uncrushed, a length of 12 inches and a diameter of 10 inches.

Largest fish The largest fish ever recorded was the great shark *Carcharodon megalodon,* which lived between 1,000,000 and 25,000,000 years ago. The discovery of 6-inch long fossil teeth near Bakersfield, California, U.S.A. suggest a length of at least 80 feet.

Largest arachnid The largest arachnid ever recorded was *Pterygotus buffaloensis,* a sea scorpion (eurypterid), found off Wales, which lived about 400,000,000 years ago. It grew to a length of 9 feet.

Largest insect The largest prehistoric insect was the dragonfly *Meganeura monyi,* which lived between 280,000,000 and 325,000,000 years ago. Fossil remains from Commentry, central France indicate that it had a wing span reaching up to 70 centimetres (27½ inches).

Largest shelled mollusc The Cretaceous fossil ammonite (*Pachydiscus seppenradensis*) which lived about 75,000,000 years ago had a shell measuring up to 8 feet 5 inches in diameter.

Most southerly The most southerly creature yet found is a freshwater salamander-like amphibian *Labyrinthodont,* represented by a 2½-inch piece of jawbone found near Beardmore Glacier, Antarctica, 325 miles from the South Pole dating from the early Jurassic of 200,000,000 years ago. This discovery was made in December 1967.

18. PROTISTA AND MICROBES

PROTISTA

Protista were first discovered in 1676 by Anton van Leeuwenhoek of Delft (1632–1723), a Dutch microscopist. Among Protista characteristics common to both plants and animals are exhibited. The more plant-like are termed Protophyta (protophytes) and the more animal-like are placed in the phylum Protozoa (protozoans).

Largest The largest protozoans which are known to have existed were the now extinct Nummulites, which each had a diameter of 0·95 of an inch. The largest existing protozoan is *Pelomyxa palustris,* which may attain a length of up to 0·6 of an inch.

Smallest The smallest of all free-living organisms are pleuropneumonia-like organisms (P.P.L.O.) of the *Mycoplasma.* For fuller details see page 26. The smallest of all protophytes is *Micromonas pusilla,* with a diameter of less than 2 microns.

Fastest moving The protozoan *Monas stigmatica* has been measured to move a distance equivalent to 40 times its own length in a second. No human can cover even seven times his own length in a second.

Fastest reproduction The protozoan *Glaucoma,* which reproduces by binary fission, divides as frequently as every three hours. Thus in the course of a day it could become a "six greats grandparent" and the progenitor of 510 descendants.

Densest The most densely existing species in the animal kingdom is the sea water dinoflagellate *Gymnodinium breve,* which exists at a density of 240,000,000 per gallon of sea water in certain conditions of salinity and temperature off the coast of Florida, U.S.A.

Earliest of their type

Type	Scientific name and year of discovery	Location	Estimated years before present
Ape	*Aegyptopitherus zeuxis* (1966)	Fayum, U.A.R.	28,000,000
Primate	tarsier-like	Indonesia	70,000,000
	lemur	Madagascar	70,000,000
Social insect	*Sphecomyrma freyi* (1967)	New Jersey, U.S.A.	100,000,000
Bird	*Archaeopteryx lithographica* (1861)	Bavaria, W. Germany	140,000,000
Mammal	shrew-like (1966)	Thaba-ea-Litau, Lesotho	190,000,000
Reptiles	*Hylonomus, Archerpeton, Protoclepsybrops, Romericus*	all in Nova Scotia	290,000,000
Amphibian	*Ishthyostega* (first quadruped)	Greenland	350,000,000
Spider	*Palaeosteniza crassipes*	Aberdeenshire, Scotland	370,000,000
Insect	*Rhyniella proecursor*	Aberdeenshire, Scotland	370,000,000
Vertebrates	Agnathans (Jawless fish)	near Leningrad, U.S.S.R.	480,000,000
Mollusc	*Neophilina galatheae* (1952)	off Costa Rica	500,000,000
Crustacean	*Karagassiema* (12 legged)	Sayan Mts., U.S.S.R.	*c.* 650,000,000

BACTERIA

Largest The largest of the bacteria is the sulphur bacterium *Beggiatoa mirabilis,* which is from 16 to 45 microns in width and which may form filaments several millimetres long.

Highest In April 1967 the U.S. National Aeronautics and Space Administration reported that bacteria had been recently discovered at an altitude of 135,000 feet (25·56 miles).

Longest lived The oldest deposits from which living bacteria are claimed to have been extracted are salt layers near Irkutsk, U.S.S.R., dating from about 600,000,000 years ago. The discovery, not internationally accepted, of their survival was made on 26 Feb. 1962 by Dr. H. J. Dombrowski of Freiberg University, West Germany.

Toughest The bacterium *Micrococcus radiodurans* can withstand atomic radiation of 6·5 million röntgens or 10,000 times that fatal to the average man.

VIRUSES

Largest The largest true viruses are the brick-shaped pox viruses (*e.g.* smallpox, vaccina, orf etc.) measuring *c.* 250 × 300 millimicrons (mμ) or 0·0003 of a millimetre.

Smallest Of more than 1,000 identified viruses, the smallest are the pico-dna group including the adeno-viruses and the Kilhan rat virus measuring only 20 mμ in diameter.

Sub viral infective agents Evidence was announced from the Institute of Research on Animal Diseases at Compton, Berkshire, in January 1967 for the existence of a form of life more basic than both the virus and nucleic acid. It was named SF or Scrapie factor, from the sheep disease. If proven this will become the most fundamental replicating particle known. Its diameter is believed to be not more than 7 millionths of a millimetre. Having now been cultured, it has been allocated back to its former status of an ultra-virus.

19. PLANT KINGDOM *(Plantae)*

Earliest life *World* If one accepts the definition of life as the ability of an organism to make replicas of itself by taking as building materials the simpler molecules in the medium around it, life probably appeared on Earth about 3,200 million years ago. In April 1969 such a dating was reported for minute spherical bluish fluorescent organisms measuring up to 0·000008 of an inch in diameter found in Swaziland, Southern Africa.

United Kingdom The oldest micro-fossils found in Great Britain are those suggestive of blue-green algae mucilage identified in pre-Cambrian flint-like chert pebbles from north-west Scotland announced in April 1970. The age of the rock antedates the oldest Torridonian rocks of 935 million years and may derive from the fossiliferous Greenland sediments as old as 1,700 million years.

Earliest flower The oldest fossil of a flowering plant with palm-like imprints was found in Colorado, U.S.A., in 1953 and dated about 65,000,000 years old.

Largest forest *World* The largest afforested areas in the world are the vast coniferous forests of the northern U.S.S.R., lying mainly between latitude 55° N. and the Arctic Circle. The total wooded areas amount to 2,700,000,000 acres (25 per cent. of the world's forests), of which 38 per cent. is Siberian larch. The U.S.S.R. is 34 per cent. afforested.

Great Britain The largest forest in England is Kielder Forest (72,336 acres), in Northumberland. The largest forest in Wales is the Coed Morgannwg (Forest of Glamorgan) (42,555 acres). Scotland's most extensive forest is the Glen Trool Forest (51,376 acres) in Kirkcudbrightshire. The United Kingdom is 7 per cent. afforested.

PLANT

Rarest Plants thought to be extinct are rediscovered each year and there are thus many plants of which specimens are known in but a single locality. The flecked pink spurred coral-root (*Epipogium aphyllum*) is usually cited as Britain's rarest orchid, having been unrecorded between 1931 and 1953. The rose purple Alpine coltsfoot (*Homogyne alpina*), recorded by Don prior to 1814 in the mountains of Clova, Angus, Scotland, was not again confirmed until 1951. The only known location of the adder's-tongue spearwort (*Ranunculus ophioglossifolius*) in the British Isles is the Badgeworth Nature Reserve, Gloucestershire (see page 51).

Commonest The most widely distributed flowering plant in the world is *Cynodon dactylon,* a toothed grass found as far apart as Canada, Argentina, New Zealand, Japan and South Africa.

Northernmost The yellow poppy (*Papaver radicatum*) and the Arctic willow (*Salix arctica*) survive, the latter in an extremely stunted form, on the northernmost land (83° N.).

Southernmost The most southerly plant life recorded is seven species of lichen found in 1933-34 by the second expedition of Rear-Admiral Richard E. Byrd, U.S. Navy, in latitude 86° 03′ S. in the Queen Maud Mountains, Antarctica. The southernmost recorded flowering plant is the carnation (*Colobanthus crassifolius*), which was found in latitude 67° 15′ S. on Jenny Island, Margaret Bay, Graham Land (Palmer Peninsula), Antarctica.

Deepest roots The greatest recorded depth to which roots have penetrated is a calculated 150 feet in the case of a species of *Acacia,* probably *Acacia giraffae,* in a borehole on Okapanje Farm, about 60 miles east of Windhoek, in South West Africa, reported in 1948.

TREES

World's largest living thing The most massive living thing on Earth is the tallest know California big tree (*Sequoia gigantea*) named the "General Sherman", standing 272 feet 4 inches tall, in the Sequoia National Park, California, U.S.A. It has a true girth of 79·1 feet (at 5 feet above the ground). The "General Sherman" has been estimated to contain the equivalent of 600,120 board feet of timber, sufficient to make 40 five-roomed bungalows. The foliage is blue-green, and the red-brown tan bark may be up to 24 inches thick in parts. In 1968 the official published figure for its estimated weight was "2,145 tons" (1,915 long tons).

The seed of a "big tree" weighs only 1/6,000th of an ounce. Its growth at maturity may therefore represent an increase in weight of over 250,000 million fold.

Tallest *World* The world's tallest known species of tree is the coast redwood (*Sequoia sempervirens*), now found only growing indigenously in northern California and a small area of southern Oregon, U.S.A.

The tallest example is now believed to be the Howard Libbey Tree in Redwood Creek Grove, Humboldt County, California announced at 367·8 feet in 1964 but discovered to have an apparently dead top and re-estimated at 366·2 feet in 1970. The nearby tree announced to a Senate Committee by Dr. Rudolf W. Becking on 18 June 1966 to be 385 feet proved on re-measurement to be no more than 311·3 feet tall. It has a girth of 44 feet. The tallest non-sequoia is a Noble fir in Gifford Pinchot Park, Washington State, U.S.A., measured in 1964 to be 278 feet tall.

All-time The identity of the tallest tree of all-time has never been satisfactorily resolved. In 1872 a mountain ash (*Eucalyptus regnans*) found in Victoria, Australia, measured 435 feet from its roots to the point where the trunk had been broken off by its fall. At this point the trunk's diameter was 3 feet, so the overall height was probably at least 500 feet. Its diameter was 18 feet at 5 feet above the ground. Another specimen, known as the "Baron Tree", was reported to be 464 feet in 1868.

Nature's oldest living things—bristlecone pines from 3000 B.C.

Modern opinion tends to the view that the highest accurately measured Australian "big gum" tree is one 346 feet tall felled near Colac, Victoria, in 1890. Claims for a Douglas fir (*Pseudotsuga taxifolia*) of 417 feet with a 77-foot circumference felled in British Columbia in 1940 remain unverified. The tallest specimen now known in the U.S.A. is one of only 221 feet (California, 1966). The most probable claimant was thus a coast redwood of 367 feet 8 inches, felled in 1873 near Guernville, California, U.S.A., thus being the same height as the Howard Libbey Tree as originally measured.

Great Britain The tallest tree in Great Britain is a Douglas fir (*Pseudotsuga taxifolia*) at Powis Castle, Montgomeryshire, Wales, measured at 180 feet in 1970. The tallest in England is a Wellingtonia (*Sequoiadendron giganteum*) measured at 165 feet in February 1970 at Endsleigh, Devon. The tallest in Scotland is a Grand fir (*Abies grandis*) at Strone Cairndow, Argyllshire. Planted in 1876, this was 175 feet when measured in May 1969 and by October 1970 had added a good 2 feet.

Ireland The tallest tree in Ireland is a Sitka spruce (*Pitia sitchensis*) 162 feet tall at Shelton Abbey, County Wicklow. The Sitka spruce, planted in 1835, at Curraghmore, now 160 feet tall, will soon surpass the Shelton Abbey specimen.

Greatest girth *World* The Santa Maria del Tule Tree, in the state of Oaxaca, in Mexico, is a Montezuma cypress (*Taxodium mucronatum*) with a girth of 112–113 feet (1949) at a height of 5 feet above the ground. A figure of 204 feet in circumference was reported for the European chestnut (*Castanea sativa*) known as the "Tree of the 100 Horse" (Castagno di Cento Cavalli) on the edge of Mount Etna, Sicily, Italy in 1770.

Britain's greatest oaks The largest-girthed living British oak is a pollarded *Quercus pedunculata* at Bowthorp, Lincolnshire, with a girth of 39 feet 9 inches in 1965. The largest "maiden" oak is the Majesty Oak at Fredville, Kent, with a girth of 37 feet 5 inches. Another oak reported to be 43 feet in girth at Chirk, Denbighshire, is being checked.

OLDEST

World The oldest recorded living tree is a bristlecone pine (*Pinus aristata*) designated WPN–114, growing at 10,750 feet above sea-level on the north-east face of Wheeler Peak (13,063 feet) in eastern Nevada, U.S.A. During studies in 1963 and 1964 it was found to be about 4,900 years old. The oldest dated California big tree (*Sequoia gigantea*) is a 3,212-year-old stump felled in 1892, but larger standing specimens are estimated to be between 3,500 and 4,000 years as in the case of the "General Sherman" tree from a ring count from a core

TALLEST TREES IN GREAT BRITAIN AND IRELAND—BY SPECIES

		ft.
Alder (Italian)	Westonbirt, Gloucester	90
Alder (Common)	Sandling Park, Kent	85
Ash	Duncombe Park, Yorkshire	148
Beech	Yester House, East Lothian	142
Cedar	Petworth House, Sussex	132
Chestnut (Horse)	Petworth House, Sussex	125
Chestnut (Sweet)	Godinton Park, Kent	118
Cypress (Lawson)	Endsleigh, Devon	126
Cypress (Monterey)	Tregothnan, Cornwall	120
Douglas Fir	Powis Castle, Montgomery	180
Elm (Wych)	Rossie Priory, Nr. Dundee	128
Elm (Jersey)	Wilton, Wiltshire	121
Eucalyptus (Blue Gum)	Glengarriff, Co. Cork	140
Grand Fir	Strone, Argyllshire	177
Ginkgo	Linton Park (Maidstone), Kent	93
Hemlock (Western)	Benmore, Argyllshire	157
Holly	Staverton Thicks, Suffolk	74
Hornbeam	Durdans, Epsom, Surrey	105
Larch (European)	Parkhatch, Surrey	142
Larch (Japanese)	Blair Castle, Perthshire	121
Lime	Duncombe Park, Yorkshire	154
Metasequoia	Savill Gardens, Windsor, Berkshire	57
Monkey Puzzle	Endsleigh, Devon	86
Oak (Common)	Fountains Abbey, Yorkshire	120
Oak (Sessile)	Whitfield House, Hereford	135
Oak (Red)	West Dean, Sussex	115
Pine (Corsican)	Stanage Park, Radnor	147
Plane	Carshalton, Surrey	125
Poplar (Black Italian)	Fairlawne, Kent	140
Poplar (Lombardy)	Marble Hill, Twickenham	118
Silver Fir	Dupplin Castle, Perthshire	154
Spruce (Sitka)	Murthly, Perth	164
Sycamore	Drumlanrig Castle, Dumfries	112
Tulip-tree	Taplow Court, Buckingham	119
Walnut	Laverstoke Park, Hampshire	82
Wellingtonia	Endsleigh, Devon	165
Yew	Midhurst, Sussex	85

drilled in 1931. Dendrochronologists estimate the *potential* life-span of a bristlecone pine at nearly 5,500 years, but that of a "big tree" at perhaps 6,000 years. Ring count dating extends back to 5,150 B.C. by examination of fallen bristlecone pine wood.

Great Britain Of all British trees that with the longest life is the yew (*Taxus baccata*), for which a maximum age well in excess of 1,000 years is usually conceded. The oldest known is the Fortingall Yew near Aberfeldy, Perthshire, part of which still grows. In 1777 this tree was over 50 feet in girth and it cannot be much less than 1,500 years old today.

Earliest The earliest species of tree still surviving is the maidenhair tree (*Ginkgo biloba*) of China, which first appeared about 160,000,000 years ago, during the Jurassic era.

Fastest growing Discounting bamboo, which is not botanically classified as a tree, but as a woody grass, the fastest growing tree is *Eucalyptus deglupta*, which has been measured to grow 35 feet in 15 months in New Guinea. The youngest recorded age for a tree to reach 100 feet is 7 years for *E. regnans* in Rhodesia and for 200 feet is 40 years for a Monterey pine in New Zealand.

Slowest growing The speed of growth of trees depends largely upon conditions, although some species, such as box and yew, are always slow-growing. The extreme is represented by a specimen of Sitka spruce which required 98 years to grow to 11 inches tall, with a diameter of less than one inch, on the Arctic tree-line. The growing of miniature trees or *bonsai* is an oriental cult mentioned as early as *c.* 1320.

Most spreading The greatest area covered by a single clonal growth is that of the wild box huckleberry (*Gaylussacia brachyera*), a mat-forming evergreen shrub first reported in 1796. A colony covering 8 acres was discovered in 1845 near New Bloomfield, Pennsylvania. Another colony, covering about 100 acres, was "discovered" on 18 July 1920 near the Juniata River, Pennsylvania. It has been estimated that this colony began 13,000 years ago.

WOOD

Heaviest The heaviest of all woods is black ironwood (*Olea laurifolia*), also called South African ironwood, with a specific gravity of up to 1·49, and weighing up to 93 lb. per cubic foot. The heaviest British wood is boxwood.

Lightest The lightest wood is *Aeschynomene hispida,* found in Cuba, which has a specific gravity of 0·044 and a weight of only 2¾ lb. per cubic foot. The wood of the balsa tree (*Ochroma pyramidale*) is of very variable density—between 2½ and 24 lb. per cubic foot. The density of cork is 15 lb. per cubic foot.

BAMBOO

Tallest The tallest recorded species of bamboo is *Dendrocalamas giganteus,* native to southern Burma. It was reported in 1904 that there were specimens with a culm-length of 30 to 35 metres (100 to 115 feet) in the Botanic Gardens at Peradeniya, Ceylon. A growth rate up to 92 centimetres (36 inches) in 24 hours is possible.

Fastest growing Some species of the 45 genera of bamboo have attained growth rates of up to 36 inches per day (0·00002 m.p.h.), on their way to reaching a height of 100 feet in less than three months.

BLOOMS

Largest *World* The mottled orange-brown and white parasitic stinking corpse lily (*Rafflesia arnoldi*) has the largest of all blooms. These attach themselves to the cissus vines of the jungle in south-east Asia and measure up to 3 feet across and ¾ of an inch thick, and attain a weight of 15 lb.

The largest known inflorescence is that of *Puya raimondii*, a rare Bolivian plant with an erect panicle (diameter 8 feet) which emerges to a height of 35 feet. Each of these bears up to 8,000 white blooms (see also Slowest-flowering plant, below).

The world's largest blossoming plant is the giant Chinese wisteria at Sierra Madre, California, U.S.A. It was planted in 1892 and now has branches 500 feet long. It covers nearly an acre, weighs 225 tons and has an estimated 1,500,000 blossoms during its blossoming period of five weeks, when up to 30,000 people pay admission to visit it.

Great Britain The largest bloom of any indigenous British flowering plant is that of the wild white water lily (*Nymphaea alba*), which measures 6 inches across. Other species bear much larger inflorescences.

Smallest flowering plant The smallest of all flowering plants are duckweeds, seen on the surface of ponds. Of these the rootless *Wolffia punctata* has fronds only 1/50th to 1/35th of an inch long. Another species, *Wolffia arrhiza,* occurs in Great Britain but rarely, if ever, flowers there. The smallest plant regularly flowering in Britain is the chaffweed (*Cetunculus minimus*), a single seed of which weighs 0·00003 of a gramme.

Slowest flowering plant The slowest flowering of all plants is the rare *Puya raimondii,* the largest of all herbs, discovered in Bolivia in 1870. The panicle emerges after about 150 years of the plant's life. It then dies. (See also above under Largest blooms.)

LEAVES

Largest *World* The largest leaves of any plant belong to the raffia palm (*Raphia raffia*) of the Mascarene Islands, in the Indian Ocean, and the Amazonian bamboo palm (*R. toedigera*) of South America, whose leaf blades may measure up to 65 feet in length with petioles up to 13 feet.

The largest undivided leaf is that of *Alocasia macrorrhiza,* found in Sabah, East Malaysia. One found in 1966 measured 9 feet 11 inches long and 6 feet 3½ inches wide, and had an area of 34·2 square feet on one side.

Great Britain The largest leaves to be found in outdoor plants in Great Britain are that of *Gunnera manicata* from Brazil with leaves 6 to 10 feet across on prickly stems 5 to 8 feet long.

FRUIT

Most and least nutritive An analysis of the 38 commonly eaten fruits shows that the one with by far the highest calorific value is avocado (*Persea drymifolia*), with 1,200 calories per lb. That with the lowest value is rhubarb (*Rheum rhaponticum*), which is 94·9 per cent. water, with 80 calories per lb. The fruit with the highest percentage of invert sugar by weight is plantain or cooking banana (*Musa paradisiaca*), with 25·3 per cent., and that with the lowest is rhubarb, with 0·4 of one per cent. Apple (*Malus pumila*) and quince (*Cydonia oblonga*) are the least proteinous, at 0·3 of one per cent.

ORCHID

Largest The largest of all orchids is *Grammatophyllum speciosum,* native to Malaysia. A specimen recorded in Penang, West Malaysia, in the 19th century had 30 spikes up to 8 feet tall and a diameter of more than 40 feet. The largest orchid flower is that of *Selenipedium caudatum,* found in tropical areas of America. Its petals are up to 18 inches long, giving it a maximum outstretched diameter of 3 feet. The flower is, however, much less bulky than that of the stinking corpse lily (see Largest blooms, above).

Tallest The tallest of all orchids is the terrestrial tree-orchid (*Angraecum infundibulare*), which grows in the swamps of Uganda to a height of 12 feet.

Smallest The smallest orchid plant is believed to be *Notylia norae,* found in Venezuela. The smallest orchid flower

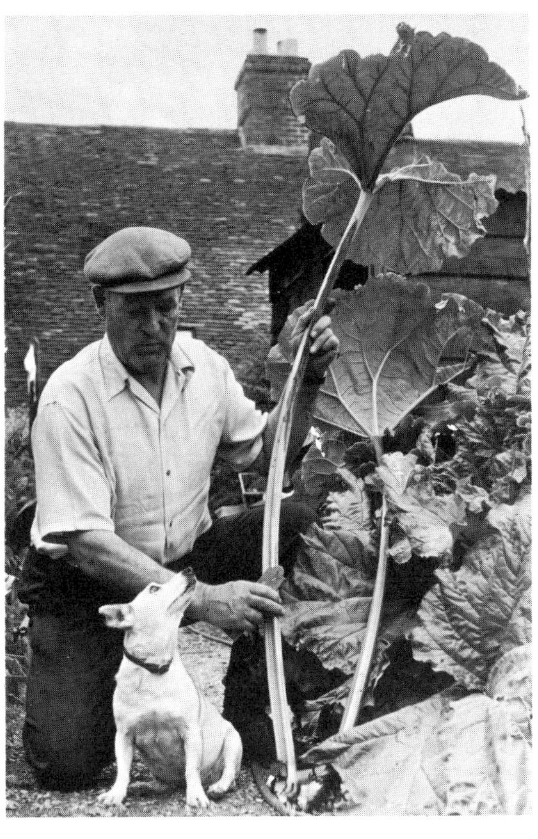

r. Setterfield the champion grower of rhubarb

is that of *Bulbophyllum minutissium*, found in Australia.

Highest priced The highest price ever paid for an orchid is 1,150 guineas (£1,207·50), paid by Baron Schröder to Sanders of St. Albans for an *Odontoglossum crispum* (variety *pittianum*) at an auction by Protheroe & Morris of Bow Lane, London, on 22 March 1906.

Longest seaweed Claims made that seaweed off Tierra del Fuego, South America, grows to 600 and even to 1,000 feet in length have gained currency. More recent and more reliable records indicate that the longest species of seaweed is the Pacific giant kelp (*Macrocyctis pyrifera*), which does not exceed 195 feet in length. It can grow 45 centimetres ($17\frac{3}{4}$ inches) in a day. The longest of the 700 species of seaweed recognized around the coasts of Britain is the brown seaweed *Corda filum* which grows up to a length of 20 feet.

Mosses The smallest of mosses is the pygmy moss (*Ephemerum*), and the longest is the brook moss (*Fontinalis*), which forms streamers up to 3 feet long in flowing water.

FUNGUS

Largest The largest recorded ground fungus was a specimen of the giant puff ball (*Calvatia gigantea*) which was 5 feet 3 inches long, 4 feet 5 inches wide and $9\frac{1}{2}$ inches high. It was discovered in New York State, U.S.A., in 1884.

The largest officially recorded tree fungus was a specimen of *Oxyporus (Fomes) nobilissimus*, measuring 56 inches by 37 inches and weighing at least 300 lb., found by J. Hisey in Washington State, U.S.A., in 1946. The largest recorded in the United Kingdom is an ash fungus

RECORD DIMENSIONS AND WEIGHTS FOR FRUIT, VEGETABLES AND FLOWERS GROWN IN THE UNITED KINGDOM

Most data subsequent to 1958 comes from the annual *Garden News* Giant Vegetable and Fruit Contest.

Apple	3 lb. 1 oz.	V. Loveridge	Ross-on-Wye, Hereford	1965
Artichoke	8 lb.	A. R. Lawson	Tollerton, Yorkshire	1964
Beetroot	23 lb. 2 oz.	A. Bratton	Ryton, Shropshire	1966
Broad Bean	$23\frac{3}{8}$ inches	T. Currie	Jedburgh, Roxburghshire	1963
Broccoli	28 lb. $14\frac{3}{4}$ oz.	J. T. Cooke	Funtington, Sussex	1964
Brussels Sprout	7 lb. 10 oz.	J. Marsh	Whitfield, Kent	1966
Cabbage[1]	69 lb. 8 oz.	P. Hayes	Uttoxeter, Staffordshire	1965
Carrot[2]	7 lb. 5 oz.	R. Clarkson	Freckleton, Lancashire	1970
Cauliflower	52 lb. $11\frac{1}{2}$ oz.	J. T. Cooke	Funtington, Sussex	1966
Celery	17 lb. 3 oz.	A. Bratton	Ryton, Shropshire	1965
Cucumber	10 lb. 2 oz. (indoor)	W. Hodgson	Birkenhead, Cheshire	1967
	4 lb. 14 oz. (outdoor)	M. Housden	Efford Hill, Hampshire	1966
Dwarf Bean	$14\frac{1}{2}$ inches	E. E. Jenkins	Shipston-on-Stour, Warwickshire	1970
Gourd	196 lb.	J. Leathes	Herringfleet Hall, Suffolk	1846
Kale	12 ft. tall	B. T. Newton	Mullion, Cornwall	1950
Leek	9 lb. 4 oz.	E. E. Jenkins	Shipston-on-Stour, Warwickshire	1968
Lemon	1 lb. 12 oz. (girth 15 inches)	T. P. Matthews	Iver Heath, Buckinghamshire	1969
Lettuce	16 lb. $2\frac{1}{4}$ oz.	J. T. Cooke	Funtington, Sussex	1966
Mangold	46 lb.	D. Bolland	Spalding, Lincolnshire	1964
Marrow[3]	60 lb.	A. V. Bishop	Snailwell, Cambridgeshire	1963
Mushroom[4]	54 inches circum.	—	Hasketon, Suffolk	1957
Onion	5 lb. 13 oz.	W. Taylor	Leicester	1965
Parsnip[5]	9 lb. 4 oz. (31 inches long)	P. C. Richardson	Heighington, Lincolnshire	1962
Pea Pod	$10\frac{1}{8}$ inches	T. Currie	Jedburgh, Roxburghshire	1964
Pear	1 lb. $12\frac{1}{4}$ oz.	A. Bratton	Shifnal, Shropshire	1966
Potato[6]	7 lb. 1 oz.	J. H. East	Spalding, Lincolnshire	1963
Pumpkin[7]	204 lb. 8 oz.	F. H. Smith	Coventry, Warwickshire	1970
Radish	16 lb. 8 oz.	E. E. Allen	Heston, Middlesex	1966
Red Cabbage	33 lb. 2 oz.	A. Bratton	Ryton, Shropshire	1963
Rhubarb	5 feet $1\frac{3}{8}$ inches	A. C. Setterfield	Englefield, Reading, Berkshire	1968
Runner Bean	$33\frac{3}{4}$ inches	A. Bratton	Ryton, Shropshire	1966
Savoy	38 lb. 8 oz.	W. H. Neil	Retford, Nottinghamshire	1966
Shallot	1 lb. 7 oz.	H. H. May	Inkpen, Berkshire	1962
Strawberry[8]	6 oz.	K. M. Muir	Clacton, Essex	1968
Sugar Beet	21 lb.	L. Hawcroft	Holme-on-Spalding Moor, Yorkshire	1971
Sunflower	15 feet 2 inches tall	Mrs. J. A. Hawkins	Capel, Surrey	1969
Swede[9]	32 lb. 8 oz.	R. T. Leeson	Irchester, Northamptonshire	1963
Tomato	3 lb.	B. Austin	Uttoxeter, Staffordshire	1964
Tomato Plant	20 ft. tall, 34 lb. fruit	—	Southport, Lancashire	1957
Turnip[10]	33 lb. 8 oz.	R. Speight	Cowplain, Hampshire	1963

1 *A 75 lb. cabbage has been reported (since 1930) from Bolton, Lancashire. The Swalwell, County Durham cabbage of 1865 grown by R. Collingwood reputedly weighed 123 lb.*

2 *One of 7 lb. 7 oz. (15 inches long) reported grown by Police Sgt. Alfred Garwood of Blidworth, Nottinghamshire in November 1970.*

3 *A 96 lb. marrow has been reported from Suffolk.*

4 *Same size reported by J. Coombes at Mark, Somerset on 28 July 1965.*

5 *50 inches long: G. Chesterton near Wyberton, Lincolnshire, April 1959.*

6 *One weighing 18 lb. 4 oz. reported dug up by Thomas Siddal in his garden in Chester on 17 Feb. 1795. A yield of 1,242 lb. 14 oz. from 6 plants reported on 28 Sept. 1969 by J. T. Cooke (see Broccoli above).*

7 *One weighing 245 lb. grown by M. Jean Giraud of France reported in 1968.*

8 *The top weight for an un-fasciated berry, also variety* Hummi-grundi, *was 3 oz.*

9 *One weighing 39 lb. 8 oz. claimed by E. R. Reay of Gaitsgill Hall, Dalston, Cumberland in 1940 (unratified).*

10 *A 73 lb. turnip was reported in December 1768, and one of 34 lb. grown by J. Orr of Preesall, Lancashire in November 1970.*

(Fomes fraxineus) measuring 50 inches by 15 inches wide, found by the forester A. D. C. LeSueur on a tree at Waddesdon, Buckinghamshire, in 1954.

Largest rose tree A "Lady Banksia" rose tree at Tombstone, Arizona, U.S.A., has a trunk 40 inches thick, stands 9 feet high and covers an area of 5,380 square feet, supported by 68 posts and several thousand feet of iron piping. This enables 150 people to be seated under the arbour. The original cutting came from Scotland in 1884.

Largest rhododendron The largest species of rhododendron is the scarlet *Rhododendron arboreum,* examples of which reach a height of 60 feet at Mangalbaré, Nepal.

Largest aspidistra The aspidistra (*Aspidistra elatior*) was introduced to Britain as a parlour palm from Japan and China in 1822. The height attained by these plants is up to 34 inches, although a plant growing in the shade may have its leaves elongated. A reported height of 42 inches is very much doubted by the Royal Botanic Gardens at Kew, Greater London. A specimen 34 inches tall grown by Leslie Holt of Stoke-on-Trent was reported in August 1968.

Largest vines The largest recorded grape vine was one planted in 1842 at Carpinteria, California, U.S.A. By 1900 it was yielding more than 9 tons of grapes in some years, and averaging 7 tons per year. It died in 1920. Britain's largest vine is at Kippen, Stirling with a girth, measured in 1956, of 5 feet. England's largest vine is the Great Vine, planted in 1768 at Hampton Court, Greater London. Its girth is 38 inches, with branches up to 110 feet long and an average yield of 1,200 lb.

Tallest hedge *World* The world's tallest hedge is the Meikleour beech hedge in Perthshire, Scotland. It was planted in 1746 and has now attained a trimmed height of 85 feet. It is 600 yards long.

Yew The tallest yew hedge in the world is in Earl Bathurst's Park, Cirencester, Gloucestershire. It was planted in 1720, runs for 130 yards, reaches 35 feet and takes 30 man-days to trim.

Largest cactus The largest of all cacti is the saguaro (*Cereus giganteus* or *Carnegieia gigantea*), found in Arizona, New Mexico and California, U.S.A., and Sonora, Mexico. The green fluted column is surmounted by candelabra-like branches rising to a height of 53 feet in the case of a specimen found in 1950 near Madrona, New Mexico. They have waxy white blooms which are followed by edible crimson fruit. A cardon cactus in Baja California, Mexico was reputed to reach 58 feet and a weight of 9 tons.

Most poisonous toadstool The yellowish-olive death cap (*Amanita phalloides*) is regarded as the world's most poisonous fungus. It is found in England. From six to fifteen hours after tasting, the effects are vomiting, delirium, collapse and death. Among its victims was Cardinal Giulio de' Medici, Pope Clement VII (1478–1534).

The Registrar General's Report states that between 1920 and 1950 there were 39 fatalities from fungus poisoning in the United Kingdom. As the poisonous types are mostly *Amanita* varieties, it is reasonable to assume that the deaths were predominantly due to *Amanita phalloides*. The most recent fatality was probably in 1960.

FERNS

Largest The largest of all the more than 6,000 species of fern is the tree fern (*Alsophila excelsa*) of Norfolk Island, in the South Pacific, which attains a height of up to 80 feet.

Smallest The world's smallest ferns are *Hecistopteris pumila,* found in Central America, and *Azolla caroliniana,* which is native to the United States.

The plant kingdom's champion-sized seed—Coco de Mer

SEED

Largest The largest seed in the world is that of the double coconut or Coco de Mer (*Lodoicea seychellarum*), the single-seeded fruit of which may weigh 40 lb. This grows only in the Seychelles Islands, in the Indian Ocean.

Smallest The smallest seeds are those of *Epiphytic* orchids, at 35,000,000 to the ounce (*cf.* grass pollens at up to 6,000,000,000 grains per ounce). A single plant of the American ragweed can generate 8,000,000,000 pollen grains in five hours.

Most viable The most viable of all known seeds are those of the Arctic Lupin (*Lupinus arcticus*) found in frozen silt at Miller Creek in the Yukon, Canada in July 1954. They were germinated in 1966 and dated by the radio carbon method to at least 8,000 B.C. and more probably to 13,000 B.C.

The largest of all cacti—a 53-foot saguaro

GRASS

Longest The tallest of the 160 grasses found in Great Britain is the common reed (*Phragmites communis*), which reaches a height of 9 feet 9 inches.

Shortest The shortest grass native to Great Britain is the very rare sand bent (*Mibora minima*) from Anglesey, which has a maximum growing height of under 6 inches.

Hay fever The highest recorded grass pollen count in Britain was one of 720 (mean number of grains per cubic metre of air noon to noon) near London on 15–16 June 1964. A figure of 1,460 for plane tree pollen was recorded on 9 May 1970. The lowest counts are nil.

'orst weeds The most intransigent weed is the mat-forming water weed *Salvinia auriculata,* found in Africa. It was detected on the filling of Kariba Lake in May 1959 and within 11 months had choked an area of 77 sq. miles rising by 1963 to 387 sq. miles. The world's worst land weeds are regarded as purple nut sedge, Bermuda grass, barnyard grass, junglerice, goose grass, Johnson grass, Guinea grass, cogon grass and lantana. The most damaging and widespread cereal weeds in Britain are the wild oats *Avena fatua* and *A. ludoviciana.* Their seeds can withstand temperatures of 240° F. for 15 minutes and remain viable.

20. PARKS, ZOOS, AQUARIA AND OCEANARIA

PARKS

Largest *World* The world's largest park is the Wood Buffalo National Park in Alberta, Canada (established 1922), which has an area of 11,172,000 acres (17,560 square miles).

Britain The largest National Park in Great Britain is the Lake District National Park which has an area of 866 square miles. The largest private park in the United Kingdom is Woburn Park (3,000 acres), near Woburn Abbey, the seat of the Dukes of Bedford. The largest common in the United Kingdom is Llansaintfread Cwmtoddyr (28,819 acres) in Radnorshire, Wales.

Smallest The world's smallest nature reserve is believed to be the Badgeworth Nature Reserve (346 square yards), near Cheltenham, Gloucestershire. Owned by the Society for the Promotion of Nature Reserves, it is leased to the Gloucestershire Trust for Nature Conservation to protect the sole site in the British Isles of the adder's-tongue spearwort (*Ranunculus ophioglossifolius*).

The smallest park in the world is Mill Ends Park on a safety island on S.W. Front Avenue, Portland, Oregon, U.S.A. It measures 45·8 square inches (*cf.* this page of 96·9 square inches) and was designated in 1948 at the behest of the city journalist Dick Fagan (d. 1969) for snail races and as a colony for leprechauns.

ZOOS

Largest game reserve It has been estimated that throughout the world there are some 500 zoos with an estimated annual attendance of 330,000,000. The largest zoological preserve in the world has been the Etosha Reserve, South West Africa established in 1907 with an area which grew to 38,427 square miles. In 1970 it was announced that the Kaokoveld section of 26,000 square miles had been de-proclaimed in the interests of the 10,000 Ovahimba and Ovatjimba living in the area.

Largest collection The largest collection in any zoo is that in the Zoological Gardens of West Berlin, Germany. At 1 Jan. 1971 the zoo had a total of 11,592 specimens from 2,414 species. This total included 1,045 mammals (230 species), 2,760 birds (746 species), 640 reptiles (286 species), 160 amphibians (59 species), 3,392 fishes (809 species) and 3,595 invertebrates (284 species).

Oldest The earliest known collection of animals was that set up by Wu-Wang, the first Emperor of the famous Chou Dynasty in China, about 1050 B.C. This 'Park of Intelligence' contained tigers, deer, rhinoceroses, birds, snakes, tortoises and fish. The oldest known zoo is that at Schönbrunn, Vienna, Austria, built in 1752 by the Holy Roman Emperor Franz Josef for his wife Maria Theresa. The oldest privately owned zoo in the world is that of the Zoological Society of London, founded in 1826. Its collection, housed partly in Regent's Park, London (36 acres) and partly at Whipsnade Park, Bedfordshire (541 acres, opened 1931), is the most comprehensive in the United Kingdom. At the stock-taking on 31 Dec. 1970 there were a total of 9,170 specimens including 1,787 mammals (225 species), 2,484 birds (569 species), 467 reptiles (192 species), 242 amphibians (62 species), 2,985 fishes (321 species) and 1,205 invertebrates (128 species). The record annual attendances are 3,013,571 in 1950 for Regent's Park and 756,758 in 1961 for Whipsnade. The most valuable animal is Chi-Chi, the great panda (*Ailuropoda melanoleuca*) once priced at £12,000. She was captured in China on 4 July 1957 when aged probably six months.

Largest aquarium The world's largest aquarium is the John G. Shedd Aquarium on 12th Street and Grant Park, Chicago, Illinois, U.S.A., completed in November 1929 at a cost of $3,250,000 (now £1,354,166). The total capacity of its display tanks is 375,000 gallons, with reservoir tanks holding 1,665,000 gallons. Exhibited are 10,000 specimens from 350 species. Salt water is brought in road and rail tankers from Key West, Florida, and a tanker barge from the Gulf of Mexico. The record attendances are 78,658 in a day on 21 May 1931, and 4,689,730 visitors in the single year of 1931.

OCEANARIA

Earliest and largest The world's first oceanarium is Marineland of Florida, opened in 1938 at a site 18 miles south of St. Augustine, Florida, U.S.A. Up to 5,800,000 gallons of sea-water are pumped daily through two major tanks, one rectangular (100 feet long by 40 feet wide by 18 feet deep) containing 375,000 gallons and one circular (233 feet in circumference and 12 feet deep) containing 330,000 gallons. The tanks are seascaped, including coral reefs and even a shipwreck. The salt water tank at the Marineland of the Pacific, Palos Verdes Peninsula, California, U.S.A. is $251\frac{1}{2}$ feet in circumference and 22 feet deep, with a capacity of 530,000 gallons. The total capacity of this whole oceanarium is 1,830,000 gallons.

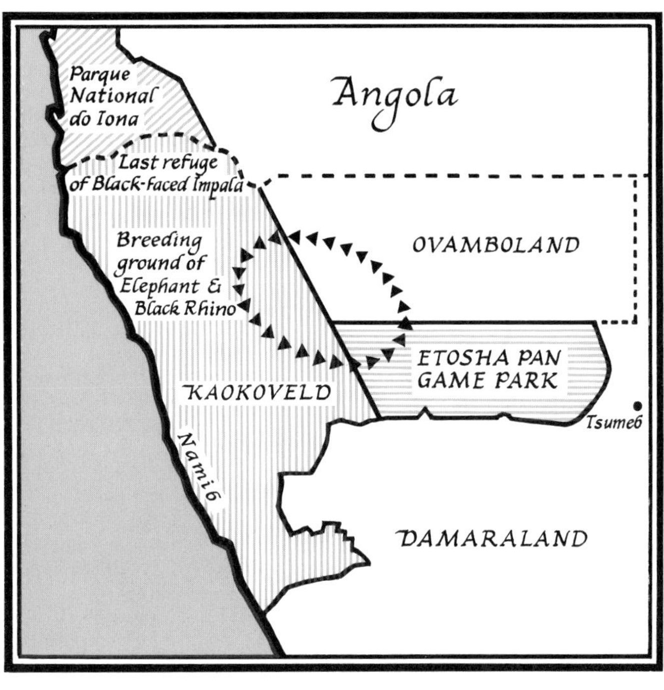

3 THE NATURAL WORLD

THE EARTH

The Earth is not a true sphere, but flattened at the poles and hence an ellipsoid. The polar diameter of the Earth (7,899·940 miles) is 26·466 miles less than the equatorial diameter (7,926·406 miles). The Earth also has a slight ellipticity of the equator since its long axis (about longitude 0°) is 174 yards greater than the short axis. The greatest departures from the ellipsoid form at sea-level are a protuberance of 62 feet in the neck of the English Channel and a depression of 79 feet to the south-west of Ceylon, in the Indian Ocean. The greatest circumference of the Earth, at the equator, is 24,901·55 miles, compared with 24,859·82 miles at the meridian. The area of the surface is estimated to be 196,938,800 square miles. The period of axial rotation, *i.e.* the true sidereal day, is 23 hours 56 minutes 4·0996 seconds, mean time.

The mass of the Earth is 5,882,000,000,000,000,000,000 tons and its density is 5·517 times that of water. The volume is an estimated 259,902,237,000 cubic miles. It is estimated that the Earth picks up about 2,000 tons of cosmic dust daily. Modern theory is that the Earth has an outer shell or lithosphere about 25 miles thick, then an outer and inner rock layer or mantle extending 1,800 miles deep, beneath which there is an iron-nickel core at an estimated temperature of 3,700° C. and at a pressure of 24,500 tons per square inch or 3,400 kilobars. If the iron-nickel core theory is correct, iron must be by far the most abundant element in the Earth.

1. NATURAL PHENOMENA

EARTHQUAKES

Greatest *World*

It is estimated that each year there are some 500,000 detectable seismic or micro-seismic disturbances of which 100,000 can be felt and 1,000 cause damage.

Using the comparative scale of Mantle Wave magnitudes (defined in 1968), the world's largest earthquake since 1930 has been the cataclysmic Alaska, U.S.A., or Prince William Sound earthquake (epicentre Latitude 61° 10′ N., Longitude 147° 48′ W.) of 28 March 1964 with a magnitude of 8·9. The Kamchatka, U.S.S.R., earthquake (epicentre Lat. 50° 45′ N., Long. 159° 30′ E.) of 4 Nov. 1952 and the shocks around Lebu, south of Concepción, Chile on 22 May 1960 are both now assessed at a magnitude of 8·8. Formerly the largest earthquake during this period had been regarded as the submarine shock (epicentre Lat. 39° 30′ N., Long. 144° 30′ E.) about 100 miles off the Sanriku coast of north-eastern Honshū, Japan on 2 March 1933 estimated at 8·9 on the Gutenberg-Richter scale (1956). It is possible that the earthquake in Lisbon, Portugal, on 1 Nov. 1755 would have been accorded a magnitude of between 8¾ and 9 if seismographs, invented in 1853, had been available to record traces. The first of the three shocks was at 9.40 a.m. and lasted for between 6 and 7 minutes. Lakes in Norway were disturbed. The energy of an earthquake of magnitude 8·9 is about 5·6 × 10^{24} ergs, which is equivalent to an explosion of 140 megatons (140,000,000 tons of trinitrotoluene [$C_7H_5O_6N_3$] called T.N.T.).

Worst death roll

The greatest loss of life occurred in the earthquake in Shensi Province, China, on 23 Jan. 1556, when an estimated 830,000 people were killed. The greatest material damage was in the earthquake (magnitude 8·2) on the Kwanto plain, Japan, at 11.58 a.m. (local time) on 1 Sept. 1923 (magnitude 8·2, epicentre in Lat. 35° 15′ N., Long. 139° 30′ E.). In Sagami Bay the sea-bottom in one area sank 1,310 feet. The official total of persons killed and missing in the *Shinsai* or great 'quake and the resultant fires was 142,807. In Tōkyō and Yokohama 575,000 dwellings were destroyed. The cost of the damage was estimated at £1,000 million (now more than £3,000 million).

Great Britain

The East Anglian or Colchester "twin" earthquake at 9.18 a.m. on 22 April 1884 (epicentres Lat. 51° 48′ N., Long. 0° 53′ E., and Lat. 51° 51′ N., Long. 0° 55′ E.) caused damage estimated at £10,000 to 1,200 buildings and the death of a child at Rowhedge. Langenhoe Church was wrecked. Windows and doors were rattled over an area of 53,000 square miles and the shock was felt in Exeter and Ostend, Belgium. The most marked since 1884 and the worst since instruments have been in use (*i.e.* since 1927) occurred in the Midlands at 3.43 p.m. on 11 Feb. 1957, showing a strength of between five and six. The strongest Scottish tremor occurred at Inverness at 10.45 p.m. on 13 Aug. 1816, and was felt over an area of 50,000 square miles. The strongest Welsh tremor occurred in Swansea at 9.45 a.m. on 27 June 190[illegible] (epicentre Lat. 51° 38′ N., Long. 4° W.). It was felt over an area of 37,800 square miles.

Ireland No earthquake with its epicentre in Ireland has ever been instrumentally measured, though the effects of remoter shocks have been felt. However, there was a shock in August 1734 which damaged 100 dwellings and five churches.

VOLCANOES

The total number of known active volcanoes in the world is 455 with an estimated 80 more submarine. The greatest concentration is in Indonesia, where 77 of its 167 volcanoes have erupted within historic times.

Greatest eruption The total volume of matter discharged in the eruption of Tambora, a volcano on the island of Sumbawa, in Indonesia, 5–7 April 1815, has been estimated at 36·4 cubic miles. The energy of this eruption was $8{\cdot}4 \times 10^{26}$ ergs. The volcano lost about 4,100 feet in height and a crater seven miles in diameter was formed. This compares with a probable 15 cubic miles ejected by Santoríni and 4·3 cubic miles ejected by Krakatoa (see below). The internal pressure causing the Tambora eruption has been estimated at 46,500,000 lb. per square inch or more than 20,000 tons per square inch.

Greatest explosion The greatest volcanic explosion in historic times was the eruption in *c.* 1470 B.C. of Thíra (Santoríni), a volcanic island in the Aegean Sea. It is highly probable that this explosion destroyed the centres of the Minoan civilization in Crete, about 80 miles away, with a *tsunami* 165 feet high. Evidence was published in December 1967 of an eruption that spewed lava over 100,000 square miles of Oregon, Idaho, Nevada and Northern California about 3,000,000 years ago.

The greatest explosion since then occurred at 9.56 a.m. (local time), or 2.56 a.m. G.M.T., on 27 Aug. 1883, with an eruption of Krakatoa, an island (then 18 square miles) in the Sunda Strait, between Sumatra and Java, in Indonesia. A total of 163 villages were wiped out, and 36,380 people killed by the wave it caused. Rocks were thrown 34 miles high and dust fell 3,313 miles away 10 days later. The explosion was recorded four hours later on the island of Rodrigues, 2,968 miles away, as "the roar of heavy guns" and was heard over 1/13th part of the surface of the globe. This explosion has been estimated to have had about 26 times the power of the greatest H-bomb test detonation but was still only a fifth part of the Santoríni cataclysm (see above).

Highest *Extinct* The highest extinct volcano in the world is Cerro Aconcagua (22,834 feet) on the Argentine side of the Andes. It was first climbed on 14 Jan. 1897 and was the highest climbed anywhere until 12 June 1907.

Dormant The highest dormant volcano is Volcán Llullaillaco (22,058 feet), on the frontier between Chile and Argentina.

Active The highest volcano regarded as active is Volcán Antofalla (20,013 feet), in Argentina, though a more definite claim is made for Volcán Guayatiri or Guallatiri (19,882 feet), in Chile, which erupted in 1959.

rthernmost and ıthernmost The northernmost volcano is Beeren Berg (7,470 feet) on the island of Jan Mayen (71° 05′ N.) in the Greenland Sea. It erupted on 20 Sept. 1970 and the island's 39 male inhabitants had to be evacuated. It was possibly discovered by Henry Hudson in 1607 or 1608, but definitely visited by Jan Jacobsz May (Netherlands) in 1614. It was annexed by Norway on 8 May 1929. The most southerly known active volcano is Mount Erebus (12,450 feet) on Ross Island (77° 35′ S.), in Antarctica. It was discovered on 28 Jan. 1841 by the expedition of Captain (later Rear-Admiral Sir) James Clark Ross, R.N. (1800–1862), and first climbed at 10 a.m. on 10 March 1908 by a British party of five, led by Professor (later Lieut.-Col. Sir) Tannatt William Edgeworth David (1858–1934).

The world's highest dormant volcano
Volcán Llullaillaco (22,058 feet)

Largest crater The world's largest *caldera* or volcano crater is that of Mount Aso (5,223 feet) in Kyūshū, Japan, which measures 17 miles north to south, 10 miles east to west and 71 miles in circumference. The longest lava flows known as *pahoehoe* (twisted cord-like solidifications) are 60 miles in length in Iceland.

GEYSERS

World's tallest The Waimangu geyser, in New Zealand, erupted to a height in excess of 1,000 feet in 1909, but has not been active since it erupted violently in 1917. Currently the world's tallest active geyser is the "Giant", discovered in 1870 in what is now the Yellowstone National Park, Wyoming, U.S.A., which erupts at intervals varying from 7 days to 3 months, throwing a spire 200 feet high at a rate of 580,000 gallons per hour. The *Geysir* ("gusher") near Mount Hekla in south-central Iceland, from which all others have been named, spurts, on occasions, to 180 feet.

OCEANS

Largest The area of the Earth covered by the sea is estimated to be 139,000,000 square miles, or 70·6 per cent. of the total surface. The mean depth of the hydrosphere was once estimated to be 12,450 feet, but recent surveys suggest a lower estimate, closer to 12,000 feet. The total weight of the water is estimated to be $1{\cdot}3 \times 10^{18}$ tons, or 0·022 per cent. of the Earth's total weight. The volume of the oceans is estimated to be 317,000,000 cubic miles compared with only 8,400,000 cubic miles of fresh water.

The largest ocean in the world is the Pacific. Excluding adjacent seas, it represents 45·8 per cent. of the world's oceans and is about 63,800,000 square miles in area. The shortest navigable trans-Pacific distance from Guayaquil, Ecuador to Bangkok, Thailand is 10,905 miles.

Most southerly The most southerly part of the oceans is 85° 34′ S., 154° W., at the snout of the Robert Scott Glacier, 305 miles from the South Pole, in the Pacific sector of Antarctica.

Deepest The deepest part of the ocean was first discovered in 1951 by H.M. Survey Ship *Challenger* in the Marianas Trench in the Pacific Ocean. The depth was measured by sounding and by echo-sounder and published as 5,960 fathoms (35,760 feet). Subsequent visits to the Challenger Deep have resulted in claims by echo-sounder only, culminating in one of 6,033 fathoms (36,198 feet) by the U.S.S.R.'s research ship *Vityaz* in March 1959. A metal object, say a pound ball of steel, dropped into water above this trench would take nearly 63 minutes to fall to the sea-bed 6·85 miles below. The average depth of the Pacific Ocean is 14,000 feet.

Sea temperature The temperature of the water at the surface of the sea varies from −2° C (28·5°F) in the White Sea to 35·6° C (96° F) in the shallow areas of the Persian Gulf in summer. A freak geo-thermal temperature of 56° C (132·8° F) was recorded in February 1965 by the survey ship *Atlantis II* near the bottom of Discovery Deep (7,200 feet) in the Red Sea. The normal sea temperature in the area is 22° C (71·6° F).

Remotest spot from land The world's most distant point from land is a spot in the South Pacific, approximately 48° 30′ S., 125° 30′ W., which is about 1,660 miles from the nearest points of land, namely Pitcairn Island, Ducie Island and Cape Dart, Antarctica. Centred on this spot, therefore, is a circle of water with an area of about 8,657,000 square miles—about 7,000 square miles larger than the U.S.S.R., the world's largest country (see Chapter X).

Largest sea The largest of the world's seas (as opposed to oceans) is the South China Sea, with an area of 1,148,500 square miles. The Malayan Sea comprising the waters between the Indian Ocean and the South Pacific, south of the Chinese mainland covering 3,144,000 square miles is not now an entity accepted by the International Hydrographic Bureau.

Largest gulf The largest gulf in the world is the Gulf of Mexico, with an area of 580,000 square miles and a shoreline of 3,100 miles from Cape Sable, Florida, U.S.A., to Cabo Catoche, Mexico.

Largest bay The largest bay in the world is the Bay of Bengal, with a shoreline of 2,250 miles from south-eastern Ceylon to Pagoda Point, Burma. Its mouth measures 1,075 miles across. Great Britain's largest bay is Cardigan Bay which has a 140 mile long shoreline and measures 72 miles across from the Lleyn Peninsula, Caernarvonshire to St. David's Head, Pembrokeshire in Wales.

Highest seamount The highest known submarine mountain, or seamount, is one discovered in 1953 near the Tonga Trench, between Samoa and New Zealand. It rises 28,500 feet from the sea bed, with its summit 1,200 feet below the surface.

STRAITS

Longest The longest straits in the world are the Malacca Straits between West Malaysia (formerly called Malaya) and Sumatra, in Indonesia, which extend for 485 miles.

Broadest The broadest straits in the world are the Mozambique Straits between Mozambique and Madagascar, which are at one point 245 miles across.

Narrowest The narrowest navigable straits are those between the Aegean island of Euboea and the mainland of Greece. The gap is only 45 yards wide at Chalkis. The Seil Sound, Argyllshire, Scotland, narrows to a point only 20 feet wide where a bridge joins the island of Seil to the mainland and is thus said to span the Atlantic.

HIGHEST WAVES

The highest officially recorded sea wave was measured by Lt. Frederic Margraff U.S.N. from the U.S.S. *Ramapo* proceeding from Manila, Philippines, to San Diego, California, U.S.A., on the night of 6–7 Feb. 1933, during a 68-knot (78·3 m.p.h.) gale. The wave was computed to be 112 feet from trough to crest. A stereo-photograph of a wave calculated to be 24·9 metres (81·7 feet) high was taken from the U.S.S.R.'s diesel-electric vessel *Ob'* in the South Pacific Ocean, about 600 kilometres (370 miles) south of Macquarie Island, on 2 April 1956. The highest instrumentally measured wave was one calculated to be at least 67 feet high, recorded by the British ship *Weather Reporter* in Lat. 52½° N., Long. 20° W., in the North Atlantic at 9.00 a.m. on 12 Sept. 1961. Its length was 1,150 feet and its period was 15 seconds. It has been calculated on the statistics of the Stationary Random Theory that one wave in more than 300,000 may exceed the average by a factor of 4.

On 9 July 1958 a landslip caused a wave to wash 1,740 feet high along the shore of Lituya Bay, Alaska, U.S.A.

Seismic wave The highest recorded *tsunami* (often wrongly called a tidal wave), was one of 220 feet which appeared off Valdez, south-west Alaska, after the great Prince William Sound earthquake of 28 March 1964. *Tsunami* (a Japanese word which is singular and plural) have been observed to travel at 490 m.p.h. Between 479 B.C. and 1967 there were 286 instances of devastating *tsunami*.

CURRENTS

Greatest The greatest current in the oceans of the world is the Antarctic Circumpolar Current, which was measured in 1969 in the Drake Passage between South America and Antarctica to be flowing at a rate of 9,500 million cubic feet per second—nearly treble that of the Gulf Stream. Its width ranges from 185 to 620 miles and has a surface flow rate of ¾ of a knot.

Strongest The world's strongest currents are the Saltstraumen in the Saltfjord, near Bodø, Norway, which reach 15·6 knots (18·0 m.p.h.). The flow rate through the 500 foot wide channel surpasses 500,000 cusecs. The fastest current in British territorial waters is 10·7 knots in the Pentland Firth between the Orkney Islands and Caithness.

GREATEST TIDES

World The greatest tides in the world occur in the Bay of Fundy, which separates Nova Scotia, Canada, from the United States' north-easternmost state of Maine and the Canadian province of New Brunswick. Burncoat Head in the Minas Basin, Nova Scotia, has the greatest mean spring range with 47·5 feet, and an extreme range of 53·5 feet.

United Kingdom The place with the greatest mean spring range in Great Britain is Beachley, on the Severn, with a range of 40·7 feet, compared with the British Isles' average of 15 feet. Prior to 1933 tides as high as 28·9 feet above and 22·3 feet below datum (total range 51·2 feet) were recorded at Avonmouth though an extreme range of 52·2 feet for Beachley was officially accepted. In 1883 a freak tide of greater range was reported from Chepstow, Monmouthshire.

Ireland The greatest mean spring tidal range in Ireland is 17·3 feet at Mellon, Limerick, on the banks of the River Shannon.

ICEBERGS

Largest The largest iceberg on record was an Antarctic tabular 'berg of over 12,000 square miles (208 miles long and 60 miles wide) sighted 150 miles west of Scott Island, in the South Pacific Ocean, by the U.S.S. *Glacier* on 12 Nov. 1956. The 200-foot-thick Arctic ice island T.1 (140 square miles) was discovered in 1946, and was still being plotted in 1963.

Most southerly Arctic The most southerly Arctic iceberg was sighted in the Atlantic in 30° 50′ N., 45° 06′ W., on 2 June 1934. The tallest on record was one calved off north-west Greenland with 550 feet above the surface. The southernmost iceberg reported in British home waters was one sighted 60 miles from Smith's Knoll, on the Dogger Bank, in the North Sea.

Most northerly Antarctic The most northerly Antarctic iceberg was a remnant sighted in the Atlantic by the ship *Dochra* in Latitude 26° 30′ S., Longitude 25° 40′ W., on 30 April 1894.

LAND

There is satisfactory evidence that at one time the Earth's land surface comprised a single primeval continent of 80 million square miles, now termed Pangaea, and that this split about 190,000,000 years ago, during the Jurassic period, into two super-continents, termed Laurasia (Eurasia, Greenland and Northern America) in the north and Gondwanaland (Africa, Arabia, India, South America, Oceania and Antarctica) and named after Gondwana, India. The South Pole was apparently in the area of the Sahara as recently as the Ordovician period of *c.* 450 million years ago.

2. STRUCTURE AND DIMENSIONS

ROCKS

The age of the Earth itself was revised in 1964 to at least 4,700 million years by the Isotope Geology Group at the Carnegie Institute in Washington, D.C., U.S.A. In June 1962 Dr. E. Gerling (U.S.S.R.) reported that there were some sub-crustal inclusions in younger rock with ages as high as 6,500 million years at Monchegorsk, south of Murmansk, in Russian Lapland. In view of the dating method used (potassium-argon) this figure has been treated with some suspicion. In March 1967 Dr. V. I. Baranov (U.S.S.R.) concluded that there was some evidence from the isotopic composition of lead which indicated an age of more than 6,000 million years.

Oldest *World* The greatest recorded age for any reliably dated rock is 3,400 ± 300 million years for G1 granite in Swaziland, southern Africa, according to the rubidium-strontium radio-dating method. A date of 3,300 million years is attributed by the same method to metamorphic rock in the Luiza Basement, Kasai, in the southern Congo (Kinshasa), indicating that this may be even older. Samples taken in 1964 from St. Peter and St. Paul Rocks (0° 56′ N., 29° 22′ W.) in the mid-Atlantic Ocean indicate that they may consist of primordial pieces of the Earth's mantle carried to the surface. These brown hornblende mylonites have been dated at about 4,500 million years old by the rubidium-strontium method. It was announced on 1 April 1966 that the U.S.S.R.'s survey ship *Vityaz* had retrieved a dark greenish iron-silicon-magnesium stone from a depth of $3\frac{1}{2}$ miles off eastern Madagascar. It was believed to be part of the Earth's upper mantle.

Britain The greatest age for any dated rock in the British Isles is 2,460 million years for a potassium felspar from Badcall, Sutherland, Scotland. This figure was calculated by the rubidium-strontium method.

Largest The largest exposed rocky outcrop is the 1,237 foot high Mount Augustus (3,627 feet above sea-level), discovered on 3 June 1858, 200 miles east of Carnarvon, Western Australia. It is an up-faulted monoclinal gritty conglomerate 5 miles long and 2 miles across and thus twice the size of the celebrated monolithic arkose Ayer's Rock (1,100 feet), 250 miles south-west of Alice Springs, in Northern Territory, Australia.

CONTINENTS

Largest Only 29·4 per cent., or an estimated 57,900,000 square miles, of the Earth's surface is land, with a mean height of 2,760 feet above sea-level. The Eurasian land mass is the largest, with an area (including islands) of 21,053,000 square miles.

Smallest The smallest is the Australian mainland, with an area of about 2,940,000 square miles, which, together with Tasmania, New Zealand, New Guinea and the Pacific Islands, is described as Oceania. The total area of Oceania is about 3,450,000 square miles, including West Irian (formerly West New Guinea), which is politically in Asia.

Land remotest from the sea *World* There is an as yet unpinpointed spot in the Dzoosotoyn Elisen (desert), northern Sinkiang, China, that is more than 1,500 miles from the open sea in any direction. The nearest large town to this point is Wulumuchi (Urumchi) to its south.

Great Britain The point furthest from the sea in Great Britain is a point near Meriden, Warwickshire, England, which is $72\frac{1}{2}$ miles equidistant from the Severn Bridge, the Dee and Mersey estuaries and the Welland estuary in the Wash. The equivalent point in Scotland is in the Forest of Atholl, Perthshire, $40\frac{1}{2}$ miles equidistant from the head of Loch Leven, Inverness Firth and the Firth of Tay.

Peninsula The world's largest peninsula is Arabia, with an area of about 1,250,000 square miles.

ISLANDS

Largest *World* Discounting Australia, which is usually regarded as a continental land mass, the largest island in the world is Greenland (part of the Kingdom of Denmark), with an area of about 840,000 square miles. There is some evidence that Greenland is in fact several islands overlayed by an ice-cap.

Great Britain The mainland of Great Britain (Scotland, England and Wales) is the eighth largest in the world, with an area of 84,186 square miles. It stretches $603\frac{1}{2}$ miles from Dunnet Head in the north to Lizard Point in the south and $287\frac{1}{2}$ miles across from Porthaflod, Pembrokeshire, Wales to Lowestoft, Suffolk. The island of Ireland (32,594 square miles) is the 20th largest island in the world.

LARGEST OFF-SHORE ISLANDS

	Sq. Miles	Name	County	Max. Dimension
Scotland	825·2	Lewis with Harris	Ross and Cromarty, Inverness-shire	$61\frac{1}{4}$ miles
Wales	278·08	Anglesey	Anglesey	23 miles
England	147·34	Isle of Wight	Hampshire	$22\frac{1}{4}$ miles
Republic of Ireland	56·83	Achill Island	County Mayo	$14\frac{1}{4}$ miles
N. Ireland	5·31	Rathlin Island	County Antrim	$4\frac{3}{4}$ miles

Freshwater The largest island surrounded by fresh water is the Ilha de Marajó (1,553 square miles), in the mouth of the River Amazon, Brazil. The world's largest inland island (*i.e.* land surrounded by rivers) is Ilha do Bananal, Brazil. The largest island in a lake is Manitoulin Island (1,068 square miles) in the Canadian (Ontario) section of Lake Huron. This island itself has on it a lake of 41·09 square miles called Manitou Lake, in which there are several islands. The largest lake island in Great

Rockall, 8 miles west of St. Kilda, annexed by itain in 1955 (see page 56)

Britain is Inchmurrin in Loch Lomond with an area of 284 acres.

Remotest
World
Uninhabited
The remotest island in the world is Bouvet Øya (formerly Liverpool Island), discovered in the South Atlantic by J. B. C. Bouvet de Lozier on 1 Jan. 1739, and first landed on by Capt. George Norris on 16 Dec. 1825. Its position is 54° 26′ S., 3° 24′ E. This uninhabited Norwegian dependency is about 1,050 miles from the nearest land—the uninhabited Queen Maud Land coast of eastern Antarctica.

Inhabited The remotest inhabited island in the world is Tristan da Cunha, discovered in the South Atlantic by Tristão da Cunha, a Portuguese admiral, in March 1506. It has an area of 38 square miles (habitable area 12 square miles) and was annexed by the United Kingdom on 14 Aug. 1816. The island's population was 235 in August 1966. The nearest inhabited land is the island of St. Helena, 1,320 miles to the north-east. The nearest continent, Africa, is 1,700 miles away.

British The remotest of the British islets is Rockall, 188 miles west of St. Kilda. This 70 foot high rock measuring 83 feet across was not formally annexed until 1955. The remotest British island which has ever been inhabited is North Rona which is 44 miles from the next nearest land at Cape Wrath and the Butt of Lewis. It was evacuated *c.* 1844. Muckle Flugga, off Unst, in the Shetlands, was the northernmost inhabited until the lighthouse was made automatic in 1970. Unst had a 1961 population of 1,148 and is in a latitude north of Southern Greenland.

Newest The world's newest island is a volcanic one about 100 feet high, which began forming in 1970 south of Gatukai Island in the British Solomon Islands, south-west Pacific.

Greatest archipelago The world's greatest archipelago is the 3,500-mile-long crescent of more than 3,000 islands which forms Indonesia.

Northernmost land The most northerly land is Kaffeklubben Øyen (the Coffee Club Island) off the north-east of Greenland, 440 miles from the North Pole, discovered by Dr. Lange Koch in 1921, but determined only in June 1969 to be in Latitude 83° 40′ 6″.

Largest atoll The largest atoll in the world is Kwajalein in the Marshall Islands, in the central Pacific Ocean. Its slender 176-mile-long coral reef encloses a lagoon of 1,100 square miles. The atoll with the largest land area is Christmas Island, in the Line Islands, in the central Pacific Ocean. It has an area of 184 square miles. Its two principal settlements, London and Paris, are 4 miles apart.

Longest reef The longest reef in the world is the Great Barrier Reef off Queensland, north-eastern Australia, which is 1,260 geographical miles in length. Between 1959 and 1969 a large section between Cooktown and Townsville was destroyed by the proliferation of the Crown of Thorns starfish *(Acanthaster planci)*.

MOUNTAINS

Highest
World
An eastern Himalayan peak of 29,028 feet above sea-level on the Tibet-Nepal border (in an area first designated Chu-mu-lang-ma on a map of 1717) was discovered to be the world's highest mountain in 1852 by the Survey Department of the Government of India, from theodolite readings taken in 1849 and 1850. In 1860 its height was computed to be 29,002 feet. The 5½-mile high peak was named Mount Everest after Sir George Everest, C.B. (1790–1866), formerly Surveyor-General of India. After a total loss of 11 lives since the first reconnaissance in 1921, Everest was finally conquered at 11.30 a.m. on 29 May 1953. (For details of ascents, see under Mountaineering in Chapter XII.) The mountain whose summit is farthest from the Earth's centre is the Andean peak of Chimborazo (20,561 feet), 98 miles south of the equator in Ecuador, South America. The highest mountain on the equator is Volcán Gayambe (19,285 feet), Ecuador in Long. 83°.

The highest insular island in the world is Mt. Sukarno (Carstensz Pyramide) (17,096 feet) in West Irian (formerly New Guinea), Indonesia.

In *The Guinness Book of Records* (seventh edition) a unique table of the highest points in 220 countries and other territories was published. Some additional data and amendments appeared in the 8th, 9th, 10th and 11th editions.

Highest
U.K. and Ireland
The highest mountain in the United Kingdom is Ben Nevis (4,406 feet, excluding the 12-foot cairn), 4¼ miles south-east of Fort William, Inverness-shire, Scotland. There is no record of its having been climbed before 1720 and it was not discovered to be higher than Ben Macdhui (4,300 feet) until 1870. In 1830 Bens Macdhui and Nevis (Gaelic, Beinn Nibheis) were respectively quoted as 4,418 feet and 4,358 feet.

There is some evidence that, before being ground down by the ice-cap, mountains in the Loch Bà area of the Island of Mull were 15,000 feet above sea-level.

There are 577 peaks and tops over 3,000 feet in the whole British Isles and 165 peaks and 136 tops in Scotland higher than Scafell Pike. The highest mountain off the mainland is Sgùrr Alasdair (3,309 feet) on Skye, named after Alexander (in Gaelic Alasdair) Nicolson, who made the first ascent in 1873.

Highest unclimbed Excluding subsidiary summits, the highest separate unclimbed mountain in the world is Gasherbrum III (26,090 feet) in the Karakoram, followed by Kangbachen (25,925 feet) in the Himalaya. These rank, respectively, 15th and 19th in height.

Largest The world's tallest mountain measured from its submarine base (3,280 fathoms) in the Hawaiian Trough to peak is Mauna Kea (Mountain White) on the Island of Hawaii, with a combined height of 33,476 feet, of which 13,796 feet are above sea-level. Another mountain whose dimensions, but not height, exceed those of Mount Everest is the Hawaiian peak of Mauna Loa (Mountain Long) at 13,680 feet. The axes of its elliptical base, 15,000 feet below sea-level, have been estimated at 74 miles and 53 miles. It should be noted that Cerro Aconcagua (22,834 feet) is more than 38,800 feet above the 16,000 foot deep abyssal plain or 42,834 feet above the Peru-Chile Trench which is 180 miles distant in the South Pacific.

Greatest ranges The world's greatest land mountain range is the Himalaya-Karakoram, which contains 96 of the world's 108 peaks of over 24,000 feet. The greatest of all mountain ranges is, however, the submarine mid-Atlantic Ridge, which is 10,000 miles long and 500 miles wide, with its highest peak being Mount Pico in the Azores, which rises 23,615 feet from the ocean floor (7,615 feet above sea-level).

Deepest halites Along the northern shores of the Gulf of Mexico for 725 miles there exist 330 subterranean "mountains" of salt, some of which rise more than 60,000 feet from bed rock and appear as the low salt domes first discovered in 1862.

Sand dunes The world's highest sand dunes are the Soussusvle Dunes near the village of Aus, South West Africa, which reach 830 feet. Claims for unstable dunes of 1,000 feet in the Sahara have not been pinpointed.

DEPRESSIONS

Deepest
World
The deepest depression so far discovered is beneath the Hollick-Kenyon Plateau in Marie Byrd Land, Antarctica, where, at a point 5,900 feet above sea-level, the ice depth is 14,000 feet, hence indicating a bed rock depression 8,100 feet below sea-level.

Highest points in the geographical counties of the United Kingdom and the Republic of Ireland

The data given below indicate the highest point of natural land in each geographical county, of which the Ordnance Survey has record. Readings frequently quoted as 4 feet or 2 feet higher than those listed, are accounted for by the addition of the 4-foot-high trigonometric point pillar or the point midway on such a pillar from which readings are actually taken. In a few other cases, heights are exaggerated by the addition of a cairn of stones on the summit, *e.g.* Ben Nevis is sometimes quoted at 4,418 ft.
Numbers in brackets indicate the order of the counties with the highest points.

ENGLAND

Geographical county	Height in feet	Location
Bedfordshire	801	Dunstable Downs
Berkshire	974	Walbury Hill
Buckinghamshire	857	N.E. corner of Alton Hill
Cambridgeshire and Isle of Ely	480	300 yards south of the Hall, Great Chishill
Cheshire	1,908	Black Hill
Cornwall	1,375	Brown Willy
Cumberland (1)	3,206[1]	SCAFELL PIKE
Derbyshire (9)	2,088	Kinder Scout
Devon (10)	2,038	High Willhays
Dorset	908	Pilsdon Pen
Durham, County (6)	2,449	Near Burnhope Seat
Essex	480	In High Wood, nr. Langley
Gloucestershire	1,083	Cleeve Cloud
Hampshire (Inc. Isle of Wight)	937	Pilot Hill, nr. Ashmansworth
Herefordshire (7)	2,306	Black Mountains
Hertfordshire	803	Hastoe
Huntingdon and Peterborough	267	South of Stamford
Kent	824	Westerham (old fort trig. point)
Lancashire (4)	2,631	Old Man of Coniston
Leicestershire	912	Bardon Hill, nr. Coalville
Lincolnshire	550	Normanby-le-Wold
London, Greater	809	33 yds. S.E. of "Westerham Height", (a house) on the Kent-G.L.C. boundary
Monmouthshire (8)	2,228	Chwarel-y-Fan
Norfolk	336	Roman Camp, Sheringham
Northamptonshire	734	Arbury Hill
Northumberland (3)	2,676	The Cheviot
Nottinghamshire	655	S. side of Herrods Hill
Oxfordshire	836	Portobello
Rutland	646	West of Oakham
Shropshire	1,790	Brown Clee Hill
Somerset	1,705	Dunkery Beacon
Staffordshire	1,684	Oliver Hill
Suffolk	420	Rede
Surrey	965	Leith Hill
Sussex	919	Blackdown Hill
Warwickshire	854	Ilmington Downs
Westmorland (2)	3,118	Helvellyn
Wiltshire	964	Milk Hill and Tan Hill
Worcestershire	1,394	Worcestershire Beacon
Yorkshire (5)	2,591	Mickle Fell

[1] *Formerly 3,210 feet.*

SCOTLAND

Geographical county	Height in feet	Location
Aberdeenshire (2)	4,300	Ben Macdhui (shared with Banffshire)
Angus (7)	3,504	Glas Maol
Argyll (6)	3,766	Bidean nam Bian
Ayrshire	2,565	Kirriereoch Hill
Banffshire (2)	4,300	Ben Macdhui (shared with Aberdeenshire)
Berwickshire	1,755	Meikle Says Law (shared with E. Lothian)
Bute	2,868	Goat Fell, Arran
Caithness	2,313	Morven
Clackmannanshire	2,363	Ben Cleugh (Clach) (Ochils)
Dumfries-shire	2,696	White Coomb
Dunbarton (10)	3,092	Ben Vorlich
East Lothian	1,755	Meikle Says Law (shared with Berwickshire)
Fife	1,713	West Lomond
Inverness-shire (1)	4,406	BEN NEVIS
Kincardineshire	2,555	Mount Battock (on Angus border)
Kinross-shire	1,630	Innerdouny Hill (Ochils)
Kirkcudbrightshire	2,770	Merrick
Lanarkshire	2,455	Culter Fell
Midlothian	2,137	Blackhope Scar
Moray	2,329	Càrn A'Ghille Chearr
Nairnshire	2,162	Càrn-Glas-Choire
Orkney	1,565	Ward Hill, Hoy
Peebles-shire	2,756	Broad Law (shared with Selkirkshire)
Perthshire (4)	3,984	Ben Lawers
Renfrewshire	1,713	Hill of Stake (on Ayrshire border)
Ross and Cromarty (5)	3,880	Carn Eige (on Inverness-shire border)
Roxburghshire	2,422	Nr. Auchope Cairn (on English border)
Selkirkshire	2,756	Broad Law (shared with Peebles-shire)
Shetland	1,486	Ronas Hill, Northmavine
Stirlingshire (9)	3,192	Ben Lomond
Sutherland (8)	3,273	Ben More Assynt
West Lothian	1,023	The Knock
Wigtownshire	1,051	Craigairie Fell

WALES

Geographical county	Height in feet	Location
Anglesey	720	Mynydd y Twr
Breconshire (3)	2,906	Pen-y-Fan (Cader Arthur)
Caernarvonshire (1)	3,560	SNOWDON (Y WYDDFA)
Cardiganshire	2,468	Plynlimon
Carmarthenshire (6)	2,500+	Carmarthen Fan Foel
Denbighshire (4)	2,713	Moel Sych (shared with Montgomeryshire)
Flintshire	1,820	Moel Fammau
Glamorgan	1,969	Craig-y-Llyn
Merionethshire (2)	2,972	Aran Fawddwy, nr. Bala
Montgomeryshire (4)	2,713	Moel Sych (shared with Denbighshire)
Pembrokeshire	1,760	Prescelly Top
Radnorshire	2,166	In Radnor Forest

NORTHERN IRELAND

Geographical county	Height in feet	Location
Antrim	1,817	Trostàn
Armagh	1,894	Slieve Gullion
Down (1)	2,796	SLIEVE DONARD
Fermanagh	2,188	Cuilcagh
Londonderry	2,240	Sawel Mountain
Tyrone	2,240	Sawel Mountain

REPUBLIC OF IRELAND

Geographical county	Height in feet	Location
Carlow (6)	2,610	Mount Leinster
Cavan	2,188	Cuilcagh
Clare	1,746	Glennagalliagh
Cork	2,321	Knockboy
Donegal	2,466	Errigal
Dublin	2,475	Kippure
Galway	2,395	Benbaun
Kerry (1)	3,414	CARRANTUOHILL
Kildare	1,248	Cupidstown Hill
Kilkenny	1,703	Brandon
Leitrim	2,113	Truskmore
Leix	1,734	Arderin
Limerick (3)	3,018	Galtymore
Longford	916	Cornhill
Louth	1,935	Slieve Foye
Mayo (5)	2,688	Mweelrea
Meath	911	Canbane East
Monaghan	1,255	Slieve Beagh
Offaly	1,734	Arderin
Roscommon	1,284	Corry Mountain
Sligo	2,113	Truskmore
Tipperary (3)	3,018	Galtymore
Waterford (8)	2,609	Knockmealdown
Westmeath	855	Mullaghmeen
Wexford (6)	2,610	Mount Leinster
Wicklow (2)	3,039	Lugnaquillia

The deepest exposed depression on land is the shore surrounding the Dead Sea, 1,291 feet below sea-level. The deepest point on the bed of the lake is 2,600 feet below the Mediterranean. The deepest part of the bed of Lake Baykal in Siberia, U.S.S.R., is 4,872 feet below sea-level.

Great Britain The lowest lying area in Great Britain is in the Holme Fen area of the Great Ouse, in northern Huntingdon and Peterborough, at nine feet below sea-level. The deepest depression in England is the bed of part of Windermere, 94 feet below sea-level, and in Scotland the bed of Loch Morar, 987 feet below sea-level.

Largest The largest exposed depression in the world is the Caspian Sea basin in the Azerbaydzhani, Russian, Kazakh and Turkmen Republics of the U.S.S.R. and northern Iran (Persia). It is more than 200,000 square miles, of which 143,550 square miles is lake area. The preponderant land area of the depression is the Prikaspiyskaya Nizmennost', lying around the northern third of the lake and stretching inland for a distance of up to 280 miles.

RIVERS

Longest *World* The river systems of the world are estimated to contain 55,000 cubic miles of fresh water.

In 1969 the National Geographic Society remeasured the length of the Amazon (*Amazonas*) from its source in Peru *via* its most navigable delta channel, the Pará River to the South Atlantic Ocean and found this, on a 200-foot-long mosaic of the best maps and charts, to be 4,195 miles. This figure finally ousts the historic claim of the Nile (*Bahr-el-Nil*) to have the world's largest watercourse.

The most authoritative survey of the Nile by M. Devroey of Belgium put its total length at 4,145 miles. In 1970 this 1·2% short fall of 50 miles was, however, widened by the loss of further miles of meanders with the filling of Lake Nasser, which backs up behind the new Aswan High Dam.

The true source of the Amazon was discovered in 1953 to be a stream named Huaraco, rising near the summit of Cerro Huagra (17,188 feet) in Peru.

The Huaraco progressively becomes the Toro then the Santiago then the Apurímac, which in its turn is known as the Ene and then the Tambo before its confluence with the Amazon prime tributary Ucayali.

The length of the Amazon from Cerro Huagra to the Atlantic Ocean *via* the more direct but less used Canal do Norte is 4,007 miles.

Ireland The longest river in Ireland is the Shannon, which is longer than any river in Great Britain. It rises 258 feet above sea-level, in County Cavan, and flows through a series of loughs to Limerick. It is 240 miles long, including the 56-mile long estuary to Loop Head. The basin area is 6,060 square miles.

Great Britain The longest river in Great Britain is the Severn, which empties into the Bristol Channel and is 220 miles long. Its basin extends over 4,409 square miles. It rises in south-western Montgomeryshire, in Wales and flows through Shropshire, Worcestershire and Gloucestershire. The longest river wholly in England is the Thames, which is 215 miles long to the Nore. Its remotest source is at Seven Springs, Gloucestershire, whence the River Churn joins the other head waters. The source of the Thames proper is Trewsbury Mead, Coate, Cirencester, Gloucestershire. The basin measures 3,841 square miles. The longest river wholly in Wales is the Towy, with a length of 64 miles. It rises in Cardiganshire and flows out into Carmarthen Bay. The longest river in Scotland is the Tay, with Dundee, Angus, on the shore of the estuary. It is 117 miles long from the source of its remotest head-stream, the Tummel, and has the greatest volume of any river in Great Britain, with a flow of up to 49,000 cubic feet per second. Its basin extends over 1,961 square miles.

Greatest flow The greatest flow of any river in the world is that of the Amazon, which discharges an average of 4,200,000 cubic feet of water per second into the Atlantic Ocean, rising to more than 7,000,000 "cusecs" in full flood. The lowest 900 miles of the Amazon averages 300 feet in depth.

Largest basin and longest tributary The largest river basin in the world is that drained by the Amazon (4,195 miles). It covers about 2,720,000 square miles. It has about 15,000 tributaries and sub-tributaries, of which four are more than 1,000 miles long. These include the Madeira, the longest of all tributaries, with a length of 2,100 miles, which is surpassed by only 14 rivers.

Longest sub-tributary The longest sub-tributary is the Pilcomayo (1,000 miles long) in South America. It is a tributary of the Paraguay (1,500 miles long), which is itself a tributary of the Paraná (2,500 miles).

Submarine river In 1952 a submarine river 250 miles wide, known as the Cromwell current, was discovered flowing eastward 300 feet below the surface of the Pacific for 3,500 miles along the equator. Its volume is 1,000 times that of the Mississippi.

Subterranean river In August 1958 a crypto-river was tracked by radio isotopes flowing under the Nile with a mean annual flow six times greater—560,000 million cubic metres (20 million million cubic feet).

Longest estuary The world's longest estuary is that of the Ob', in the northern U.S.S.R., at 450 miles.

Largest delta The world's largest delta is that created by the Ganga (Ganges) and Brahmaputra in East Pakistan and West Bengal, India. It covers an area of 30,000 square miles.

RIVER BORES

World The bore on the Ch'ient'ang'kian (Hang-chou-fe) in eastern China is the most remarkable in the world. At spring tides the wave attains a height of up to 25 feet and a speed of 13 knots. It is heard advancing at a range of 14 miles. The bore on the Hooghly branch of the Ganges travels for 70 miles at more than 15 knots. The annual downstream flood wave on the Mekong some-

The Severn River bore which can reach 9¼ feet high

times reaches a height of 46 feet. The greatest volume of any tidal bore is that of the Canal do Norte (10 miles wide) in the mouth of the Amazon.

reat Britain The most notable river bore in the United Kingdom is that on the River Severn, which attained a measured height of $9\frac{1}{4}$ feet on 15 Oct. 1966 downstream of Stonebench and a speed of 13 m.p.h. It travels 21 miles from Awre to Gloucester.

stest rapids The fastest rapids which have ever been navigated are the Lava Falls on the River Colorado in the United States. At times of flood these attain a speed of 30 m.p.h. (26 knots) with waves boiling up to 12 feet high.

WATERFALLS

Highest The highest waterfall in the world is the Angel Falls, in Venezuela, on a branch of the River Carrao, an upper tributary of the Caroní, with a total drop of 3,212 feet—the longest single drop is 2,648 feet. It was discovered in 1935 by a United States pilot named Jimmy Angel (died 8 Dec. 1956), who crashed nearby.

United Kingdom The tallest waterfall in the United Kingdom is Eas-Coul-Aulin, in the parish of Eddrachillis, Sutherland, Scotland, with a drop of 658 feet. England's highest fall is Caldron (or Cauldron) Snout, on the Tees, with a fall of 200 feet, in 450 feet of cataracts, but no sheer leap. It is at the junction of Durham, Westmorland and Yorkshire. The highest Welsh waterfall is the Pistyll Rhaiadr (240 feet), on the River Rhaiadr, in southern Denbighshire.

Ireland The highest falls in Ireland are the Powerscourt Falls (350 feet), on the River Dargle, County Wicklow.

Greatest On the basis of the average annual flow, the greatest waterfall in the world is the Guairá (374 feet high), known also as the Salto dos Sete Quedas, on the Alto Paraná River between Brazil and Paraguay. Although attaining an average height of only 110 feet, its estimated annual average flow over the lip (5,300 yards wide) is 470,000 cubic feet per second. The amount of water this represents can be imagined by supposing that it was pouring into the dome of St. Paul's Cathedral—it would fill it completely in three-fifths of a second. It has a peak flow of 1,750,000 cubic feet per second. The seven cataracts of the Stanley Falls in the Congo (Kinshasa) have an average annual flow of 600,000 cubic feet per second.

Widest The widest waterfalls in the world are the Khône Falls (50 to 70 feet high) in Laos, with a width of 6·7 miles and a flood flow of 1,500,000 cubic feet per second.

gest fjords d sea lochs *World* The world's longest fjord is the Nordvest fjord arm of the Scoresby Sund in eastern Greenland, which extends inland 195 miles from the sea. The longest of Norwegian fjords is the Sogne Fjord, which extends 183 kilometres (113·7 miles) inland from Sygnefest to the head of the Lusterfjord arm at Skjolden. It averages barely 3 miles in width and has a deepest point of 4,085 feet. If measured from Huglo along the Bømlafjord to the head of the Sørfjord arm at Odda, the Hardengerfjorden can also be said to extend 183 kilometres (113·7 miles). The longest Danish fjord is the Limfjorden (100 miles long).

eat Britain Scotland's longest sea loch is Loch Fyne, which extends 42 miles inland into Argyllshire.

LAKES AND INLAND SEAS

Largest *World* The largest inland sea or lake in the world is the Kaspiskoye More (Caspian Sea) in the southern U.S.S.R. and Iran (Persia). It is 760 miles long and its total area is 143,550 square miles. Of the total area some 55,280 square miles (38·6%) is in Iran, where it is named the Darya-ye-Khazar. Its maximum depth is 980 metres (3,215 feet) and its surface is 92 feet below sea-level. Its estimated volume is 21,500 cubic miles of saline water. Since 1930 it has diminished 15,000 square miles in area with a fall of 62 feet, while the shore line has retreated more than 10 miles in some places.

Freshwater lake *World* The freshwater lake with the greatest surface area is Lake Superior, one of the Great Lakes of North America. The total area is 31,800 square miles, of which 20,700 square miles are in the United States and 11,100 square miles in Ontario, Canada. It is 600 feet above sea-level. The freshwater lake with the greatest volume is Baykal (see Deepest lake, below) with an estimated volume of 5,750 cubic miles.

United Kingdom The largest lake in the United Kingdom is Lough Neagh (48 feet above sea-level) in Northern Ireland. It is 18 miles long and 11 miles wide and has an area of 147·39 square miles. Its extreme depth is 102 feet.

Great Britain The largest lake in Great Britain, and the largest inland loch in Scotland is Loch Lomond (23 feet above sea-level), which is 22·64 miles long and has a surface area of 32·81 square miles. It is situated in the counties of Stirling and Dunbarton and its greatest depth is 623 feet. The longest lake is Loch Ness which measures 22·75 miles. The largest lake in England is Windermere, in the county of Westmorland. It is $10\frac{1}{2}$ miles long and has a surface area of 5·69 square miles. Its greatest depth is 219 feet in the northern half. The largest *natural* lake in Wales is Llyn Tegid, with an area of 1·69 square miles, although it should be noted that the largest lake in Wales is that formed by the reservoir at Lake Vyrnwy, where the total surface area is 3·18 square miles.

Republic of Ireland The largest lough in the Republic of Ireland is Lough Corrib in the counties of Mayo and Galway. It measures 27 miles in length and is 7 miles across at its widest point with a total surface area of 41,616 acres (65·0 square miles).

Lake in a lake The largest lake in a lake is Manitou Lake (41·09 square miles) on Manitoulin Island (1,068 square miles) in the Canadian part of Lake Huron.

DEEPEST

World The deepest lake in the world is Ozero (Lake) Baykal in central Siberia, U.S.S.R. It is 620 kilometres (385 miles) long and between 20 and 46 miles wide. In 1957 the Olkhon Crevice was measured to be 1,940 metres (6,365 feet) deep and hence 4,872 feet below sea-level.

Great Britain The deepest lake in Great Britain is the 12-mile-long Loch Morar, in Inverness-shire. Its surface is 30 feet above sea-level and its extreme depth 1,017 feet. England's deepest lake is Wast Water (258 feet), in Cumberland.

HIGHEST

World The highest steam-navigated lake in the world is Lago Titicaca (maximum depth 1,214 feet), with an area of about 3,200 square miles (1,850 square miles in Peru, 1,350 square miles in Bolivia), in South America. It is 130 miles long and is situated at 12,506 feet above sea-level. There is a small unnamed lake north of Mount Everest by the Changtse Glacier, Tibet, at an altitude of 20,230 feet above sea-level.

United Kingdom The highest lake in the United Kingdom is the 1·9 acre Lochan Buidhe at 3,600 feet above sea-level in the Cairngorm Mountains, Scotland. England's highest is Broad Crag Tarn (2,746 feet above sea-level) on Scafell, Cumberland, and the highest in Wales is a pool above Llyn y Fign (*c.* 2,540 feet), 8 miles east of Dolgellau, Merionethshire.

Longest glaciers It is estimated that 6,020,000 square miles, or about 10·4 per cent. of the Earth's land surface, is permanently glaciated. The world's longest known glacier is the Lambert Glacier, discovered by an Australian aircraft crew in Australian Antarctic Territory in 1956–57. It is up to 40 miles wide and, with its upper section, known as the Mellor Glacier, it measures at least 250 miles in length. With the Fisher Glacier limb, the Lambert forms a continuous ice passage about 320 miles long. The longest Himalayan glacier is the Siachen (47 miles) in the Karakoram range, though the Hispar and Biafo combine to form an ice passage 76 miles long.

Greatest avalanches The greatest avalanches, though rarely observed, occur in the Himalaya but no estimates of their volume have been published. It was estimated that 3,500,000 cubic metres (120,000,000 cubic feet) of snow fell in an avalanche in the Italian Alps in 1885. (See also Disasters, end of Chapter XI.)

DESERT

Largest Nearly an eighth of the world's land surface is arid with a rainfall of less than 25 cms. (9·8 inches) per annum. The Sahara Desert in North Africa is the largest in the world. At its greatest length it is 3,200 miles from east to west. From north to south it is between 800 and 1,400 miles. The area covered by the desert is about 3,250,000 square miles. The land level varies from 436 feet below sea-level in the Qattâra Depression, United Arab Republic (formerly Egypt), to the mountain Emi Koussi (11,204 feet) in Chad. The diurnal temperature range in the western Sahara may be more than 80 degrees F. or 45 degrees C.

GORGE

Largest The largest gorge in the world is the Grand Canyon on the Colorado River in north-central Arizona, U.S.A. It extends from Marble Gorge to the Grand Wash Cliffs, over a distance of 217 miles. It varies in width from 4 to 13 miles and is up to 7,000 feet deep.

Deepest The deepest visible canyon in the world is Hell's Canyon, dividing Oregon and Idaho, U.S.A. It plunges 7,900 feet from the Devil Mountain down to the Snake River. The deepest submarine canyon yet discovered is one 25 miles south of Esperance, Western Australia, which is 6,000 feet deep and 20 miles wide.

CAVES

Largest *World* The largest known underground chamber in the world is the Big Room of the Carlsbad Caverns (1,320 feet deep) in New Mexico, U.S.A. It is 4,270 feet long and reaches 328 feet in height and 656 feet in width. The largest cavern in Britain is a cavern about 2,500 feet long, discovered on 13 April 1966 under Mynydd-dhu, a hill in Carmarthenshire, Wales. It contains stalagmites 12 feet tall and a waterfall with a drop of 100 feet.

The most extensive cave system in the world is said to be the Flint Ridge Cave system, discovered in 1799 in Kentucky, U.S.A. Its total length is reputed to be more than 150 miles, but it contains only 63·31 miles of actual mapped passageway. The world's longest surveyed cave is the Hölloch in Switzerland, with a measured length of 64·44 miles. The longest cave system in Great Britain is Ogof Ffynnon Dhu, Breconshire in South Wales, in which *c.* 20·40 miles of passages have so far been surveyed.

DEEPEST CAVES BY COUNTRIES

These depths are subject to continuous revisions.

Feet below Entrance		
4,300	Gouffre de la Pierre Saint-Martin, Pyrenees	France/Spain
3,750	Gouffre Berger, Sornin Plateau, Vercors	France
2,906	Spluga della Preta, Lessinische Alps	Italy
2,427	Hölloch, Moutatal, Schwyz	Switzerland
2,329	Gruberhorn Höhle, Hoher Göll, Salzburg	Austria
2,099	Sniezna, Tatra	Poland
2,040	Gouffre de Faour Dara	Lebanon
1,770	Abisso Vereo, Istria	Yugoslavia
1,690	Anou Boussouil, Djurdjura	Algeria
›1,300	Provetina, Mount Astraka	Greece
1,214	Cueva-Sima de Ormazaretta, Navarra	Spain
1,184	Neff's Cave, Utah	U.S.A.
1,115	Izvorul Tausoarelor, Rodna	Romania
1,070	Larshullet, Mo-i-Rana	Norway
800	Ogof Ffynnon Du, Breconshire	Wales
653	Oxlow Cavern, Giant's Hole, Derbyshire	England
527	Growling Swallet Cave, Tasmania	Australia
330	Pollnagollum-Poulelva, County Clare	Ireland

LONGEST CAVE SYSTEMS BY COUNTRIES

These surveyed lengths are subject to continuous revision.

Miles		
64·44	Hölloch, Schwyz	Switzerland
63·31	Flint Ridge Cave System, Kentucky	U.S.A.
32·74	Sistema Cavernavio de Cuyaguatega	Cuba
*26·10	Eisriesenwelt, Werfen, Salzburg	Austria
22·74	Peschtschera Optimistitshcheskaya, Pololien	U.S.S.R.
22·48	Complejo Palomera-Dolencias, Burgos	Spain
c. 20·4	Ogof Ffynnon Du, Breconshire	Wales
13·67	Goule de Foussoubie, Ardèche	France
13·67	Baradla Barlang-Jaskyna Domica, Magyarország	Hungary
10·50	Lancaster Hole—Easegill Caverns, Westmorland	England
7·39	Poulnagollum-Poulelva Caves, County Clare	Ireland
›6	Mullamullang Cave	Australia

* *Longest ice caves, discovered in 1879. Now rank as eighth longest known.*

Longest stalactite The longest known stalactite in the world is a wall-supported column extending 195 feet from roof to floor in the Cueva de Nerja, near Málaga, Spain. The rather low tensile strength of calcite (calcium carbonate) precludes very long free-hanging stalactites, but one of 38 feet exists in the Poll an Ionain cave in County Clare, Ireland.

Tallest stalagmite The tallest known stalagmite in the world is La Grande Stalagmite in the Aren Armand cave, Lozère, France, which has attained a height of 98 feet from the cave floor. It was found in September 1897.

SEA CLIFFS

Highest The location of the highest sea cliffs in the world has yet to be established. These may be in north-west Greenland. The highest cliffs in the British Isles are those on the north coast of Achill Island, in County Mayo, Ireland, which are 2,192 feet sheer above the sea at Croaghan. The highest cliffs in the United Kingdom are the 1,300 feet Conachair cliffs on St. Kilda, Scotland (1,397 feet). England's highest cliffs are at Countisbury, North Devon, where they drop 900 feet.

NATURAL BRIDGE

Longest The longest natural bridge in the world is the Landscape Arch in the Arches National Monument, Utah, U.S.A. This natural sandstone arch spans 291 feet and is set about 100 feet above the canyon floor. In one place erosion has narrowed its section to six feet.

3. WEATHER

The meteorological records given below necessarily relate largely to the last 125 to 145 years, since data before that time are both sparse and unreliable. Reliable registering thermometers were introduced as recently as *c.* 1820.

Palaeo-entomological evidence is that there was a southern European climate in England in *c.* 90,000 B.C., while in *c.* 6,000 B.C. the mean summer temperature reached 67° F, or 6 deg. F higher than the present. The earliest authentic British weather records relate to the period 26–30 Aug. 55 B.C. The earliest reliably known hot summer was in A.D. 664 during our driest ever century and the earliest known severe winter was that of A.D. 763–4. In 1683–84 there was frost in London from November to April. Frosts were recorded during August in the period 1668–89.

Progressive extremes The world's extremes of temperature have been noted progressively thus:

127·4° F	Ouargla, Algeria	27 Aug. 1884
130° F	Amos (formerly Mammoth Tank), California, U.S.A.	17 Aug. 1885
134° F	Death Valley, California, U.S.A.	10 July 1913
136·4° F	Al 'Aziziyah (el-Azizia), Libya*	13 Sept. 1922

* *Obtained by the U.S. National Geographic Society but not officially recognized by the Libyan Ministry of Communications.*

A reading of 140° F at Delta, Mexico, in August 1953 is not now accepted because of over-exposure to roof radiation. The official Mexican record of 136·4° F at San Luis, Sonora on 11 Aug. 1933 is not internationally accepted.

A freak heat flash reported from Coimbra, Portugal, in September 1933 to have caused the temperature to rise to 70° C (158° F) for 120 seconds is apocryphal.

−73° F	Floeberg Bay, Ellesmere Is., Canada		1852
−90·4° F	Verkhoyansk, Siberia, U.S.S.R.	3 Jan.	1885
−90·4° F	Verkhoyansk, Siberia, U.S.S.R.	5 & 7 Feb.	1892
−90·4° F	Oymyakon, Siberia, U.S.S.R.	6 Feb.	1933
−100·4° F	South Pole, Antarctica	11 May	1957
−102·1° F	South Pole, Antarctica	17 Sept.	1957
−109·1° F	Sovietskaya, Antarctica	2 May	1958
−113·3° F	Vostok, Antarctica	15 June	1958
−113·8° F	Sovietskaya, Antarctica	19 June	1958
−117·4° F	Sovietskaya, Antarctica	25 June	1958
−122·4° F	Vostok, Antarctica	7–8 Aug.	1958
−124·1° F	Sovietskaya, Antarctica	9 Aug.	1958
−125·3° F	Vostok, Antarctica	25 Aug.	1958
−126·9° F	Vostok, Antarctica	24 Aug.	1960

st equable mperature

The location with the most equable recorded temperature over a short period is Garapan, on Saipan, in the Mariana Islands, Pacific Ocean. During the nine years from 1927 to 1935, inclusive, the lowest temperature recorded was 19·6° C (67·3° F) on 30 Jan. 1934 and the highest was 31·4° C (88·5° F) on 9 Sept. 1931, giving an extreme range of 11·8 deg. C (21·2 deg. F). Between 1911 and 1966 the Brazilian off-shore island of Fernando de Noronha had a minimum temperature of 18·6° C (65·5° F) on 17 Nov. 1913 and a maximum of 32·0° C (89·6° F) on 2 March 1965, an extreme range of 13·4 deg. C (24·1 deg. F).

nidity and iscomfort

Human discomfort depends not merely on temperature but on the combination of temperature, humidity, radiation and wind-speed. The United States Weather Bureau uses a Temperature-Humidity Index, which equals two-fifths of the sum of the dry and wet bulb thermometer readings plus 15. When the THI reaches 75 in still air, at least half of the people will be uncomfortable while at 79 few, if any, will be comfortable. When the index reaches 86 inside a Federal building in Washington, D.C., everybody may be sent home. A reading of 92 (shade temperature 119° F, relative humidity 22%) was recorded at Yuma, Arizona, U.S.A., on 31 July 1957, but even this must have been surpassed in Death Valley, California, U.S.A.

Greatest mperature ranges

The greatest recorded temperature ranges in the world are around the Siberian "cold pole" in the eastern U.S.S.R. Olekminsk has ranged 189 deg. F from −76° F to 113° F and Verkhoyansk (67° 33′ N., 133° 23′ E.) has ranged 192 deg. F from −94° F (unofficial) to 98° F.

The greatest temperature variation recorded in a day is 100 deg. F (a fall from 44° F to −56° F) at Browning, Montana, U.S.A., on 23–24 Jan. 1916. The most freakish rise was 49 deg. F in 2 minutes at Spearfish, South Dakota, from −4° F at 7.30 a.m. to 45° F at 7.32 a.m. on 22 Jan. 1943. The British record is 50·9 deg. F (34·0° F to 84·9° F) in 9 hours at Rickmansworth, Hertfordshire, on 29 Aug. 1936.

gest freeze

The longest recorded unremitting freeze (maximum temperature 32° F and below) in the British Isles was one of 34 days at Moor House, Westmorland, from 23 Dec. 1962 to 25 Jan. 1963. This was almost certainly exceeded at the neighbouring Great Dun Fell, where the screen temperature never rose above freezing during the whole of January 1963.

Upper tmosphere

The lowest temperature ever recorded in the atmosphere is −143° C (−225·4° F) at an altitude of about 50 to 60 miles, during noctilucent cloud research above Kronogård, Sweden, from 27 July to 7 Aug. 1963. A jet stream moving at 408 m.p.h. at 154,200 feet was recorded by Skua rocket above South Uist, Outer Hebrides, Scotland on 13 Dec. 1967.

Deepest ermafrost

The greatest recorded depth of permafrost is 1·5 kilometres (4,921 feet) reported in April 1968 in the basin of the River Lena, Siberia, U.S.S.R.

Most intense rainfall

Difficulties attend rainfall readings for very short periods but the figure of 1·23 inches in one minute at Unionville, Maryland, U.S.A., at 3.23 p.m. on 4 July 1956, is regarded as the most intense recorded in modern times. There was reputedly a cloudburst of "near two foot . . . in less than a quarter of half an hour" at Oxford on the afternoon of 31 May (Old Style) 1682. Since 1860 the most intense rainfall recorded in Britain has been 1·25 inches in 5 minutes at Preston, Lancashire, on 10 Aug. 1893; and 2·21 inches at Bolton, Lancashire, on 18 July 1964.

Falsest St. Swithin's Days

The legend that the weather on St. Swithin's Day, celebrated on 15 July since A.D. 912, determines the rainfall for the next 40 days is one which has long persisted. There was a brilliant 13½ hours sunshine in London on 15 July 1924, but 30 of the next 40 days were wet. On 15 July 1913 there was a 15-hour downpour, yet it rained on only nine of the subsequent 40 days in London.

Lightning

The visible length of lightning strokes varies greatly. In mountainous regions, when clouds are very low, the flash may be less than 300 feet long. In flat country with very high clouds, a cloud-to-earth flash sometimes measures four miles, though in extreme cases such flashes have been measured at 20 miles. The intensely bright central core of the lightning channel is extremely narrow. Some authorities suggest that its diameter is as little as half an inch. This core is surrounded by a "corona envelope" (glow discharge) which may measure 10 to 20 feet in diameter.

The speed of a lightning discharge varies from 100 to 1,000 miles per second for the downward leader track, and reaches up to 87,000 miles per second (nearly half the speed of light) for the powerful return stroke. In Britain there is an average of six strikes per square mile per annum, and an average of 4,200 per annum over London alone. Every few million strokes there is a giant discharge, in which the cloud-to-earth and the return lightning strokes flash from the top of the thunder clouds. In these "positive giants" energy of up to 3,000 million joules (3×10^{16} ergs) is sometimes recorded. The temperature reaches about 30,000° C, which is more than five times greater than that of the surface of the Sun.

Highest waterspout

The highest waterspout of which there is a reliable record was one observed on 16 May 1898 off Eden, New South Wales, Australia. A theodolite reading from the shore gave its height as 5,014 feet. It was about 10 feet in diameter. A waterspout moved around Tor Bay, Devon on 17 Sept. 1969 which was according to press estimates 1,000 feet in height.

Cloud extremes

The highest standard cloud form is cirrus, averaging 27,000 feet and above, but the rare nacreous or mother-of-pearl formation sometimes reaches nearly 80,000 feet. The lowest is stratus, below 3,500 feet. The cloud form with the greatest vertical range is cumulo-nimbus, which has been observed to reach a height of nearly 68,000 feet in the tropics. Noctilucent "clouds", which were observed from Hampshire on 30 June 1950, are believed to pass at a height of over 60 miles.

Best and worst British summers

According to Prof. Gordon Manley's survey over the period 1728 to 1970 the best (*i.e.* driest and hottest) British summer was that of 1949 and the worst (*i.e.* wettest and coldest) that of 1879. The mean temperature for June, July and August 1911 at Shanklin, Isle of Wight was, however, 2·5 deg. F. higher than in 1949 at 64·9° F.

Most recent White Christmas and Frost Fair

London has experienced seven "White" Christmas Days since 1900. These have been in 1906, 1917 (slight), 1923 (slight), 1927, 1938, 1956 (slight) and 1970. These were more frequent in the 19th century and even more so before the change of calendar in 1752. The last of the nine recorded Frost Fairs held on the frozen river Thames was in December 1813 to 26 Jan. 1814.

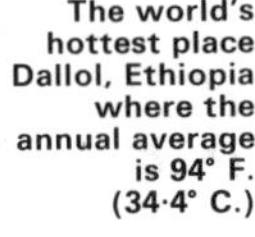
The world's hottest place Dallol, Ethiopia where the annual average is 94° F. (34·4° C.)

	World Records	United Kingdom & Ireland
Highest Shade Temperature:	136·4° F, Al' Aziziyah, Libya, 13.9.1922	100·5° F (38° C), Tonbridge, Kent, 22.7.1868
Lowest Screen Temperature:	−126·9° F, Vostok, Antarctica, 24.8.1960[2]	−17° F (−27·2° C), Braemar, Aberdeenshire Scotland, 11.2.1895[3]
Greatest Rainfall (24 hours):	73·62 in., Cilaos, La Réunion, Indian Ocean, 15–16.3.1952[4]	11·00 in., Martinstown, Dorset, 18–19.7.195
(Month):	366·14 in., Cherrapunji, Assam, India, July 1861	56·54 in., Llyn Llydau, Snowdon, Caernar vonshire, October 1909
(12 Months):	1,041·78 in., Cherrapunji, Assam, 1.8.1860–31.7.1861	257·0 in., Sprinkling Tarn, Cumberland, i 1954[5]
Greatest Snowfall[6] (12 Months):	1,000·3 in., Paradise Ranger Station (1,550 feet), Mt. Rainier, Washington State, U.S.A., 1955–56 (annual average 575·1 in.)	60 in., Upper Teesdale and Denbighshir Hills, 1947
Maximum Sunshine:[7]	97%+ (over 4,300 hours), eastern Sahara, annual average	78·3% (382 hours), Pendennis Castle, Fal mouth, Cornwall, June 1925
Minimum Sunshine:	Nil at North Pole—for winter stretches of 186 days	Nil in a month at Westminster, London, i December 1890[8]
Barometric Pressure (Highest):	1,083·8 mb. (32·00 in.), Agata, Siberia, U.S.S.R. (alt. 862 ft.), 31.12.1968	1,054·7 mb. (31·15 in.), Aberdeen, 31.1.190
(Lowest):	877 mb. (25·91 in.), about 600 miles north-west of Guam, Pacific Ocean, 24.9.1958	925·5 mb. (27·33 in.), Ochtertyre, near Crief Perthshire, 26.1.1884
Highest Surface Wind-speed:[9]	225 m.p.h., Mt. Washington (6,288 ft.), New Hampshire, U.S.A., 24.4.1934 (indicated speed 231 m.p.h.)	144 m.p.h. (125 knots), Coire Cas ski li (3,525 feet), Cairn Gorm, Inverness-shire 6.3.1967[10]
Thunder-Days (Year):[11]	322 days, Bogor (formerly Buitenzorg), Java, Indonesia (average, 1916–19)	38 days, Stonyhurst, Lancashire, 1912 an Huddersfield, Yorkshire, 1967
Hottest Place (Annual mean):[12]	Dallol, Ethiopia, 94° F (34·4° C) (1960–66).	Penzance, Cornwall, and Isles of Scilly, bot 52·7° F (11·5° C), average 1931–60
Coldest Place (Annual mean):	Pole of Cold (78° S., 96° E.), Antarctica, −72° F (16 deg. F lower than the Pole)	Braemar, Aberdeenshire, 43·7° F (6·5° C average 1931–60
Wettest Place (Annual mean):	Mt. Wai-'ale'ale (5,080 ft.), Kauai, Hawaii, U.S.A., 486·1 inches (average, 1920–58). About 335 rainy days per year	Styhead Tarn (1,600 ft.), Cumberland 172·9 in.
Driest Place (Annual mean):	Calama, in the Desierto de Atacama, Chile (rain never recorded)	Great Wakering, Essex 19·2 in. (1916–1950)
Longest Drought:	*c.* 400 years, Desierto de Atacama, Chile	73 days, Mile End, London, 4.3 to 15.5.189
Most Rainy Days (Year):	Bahía Felix, Chile, 348 days in 1916 (annual average 325 days)	Ballynahinch Castle, Galway, 309 days i 1923
Heaviest Hailstones:[14]	1·5 lb. (5·4 in. diameter, 17 in. circumference), Potter, Nebraska, U.S.A., 6.7.1928	5 oz., Horsham, Sussex, 5.9.1958
Longest Fogs (Visibility less than 1,000 yards):	Fogs persist for weeks on the Grand Banks, Newfoundland, Canada, and the average is more than 120 days per year	London, 26.11 to 1.12.1948 (4 days 18 hour London, 5.12 to 9.12.1952 (4 days 18 hour
Windiest Place:	The Commonwealth Bay, George V Coast, Antarctica, where gales reach 200 m.p.h.	Tiree, Argyllshire (89 ft.); annual averag 17·4 m.p.h.

1 *The shade temperature in London on 8 July 1808 may have reached this figure.*

2 *Vostok is 11,500 feet above sea-level. The coldest permanently inhabited place is the Siberian village of Oymyakon (63° 16′ N., 143° 15′ E.), in the U.S.S.R., where the temperature reached −96° F in 1964.*

3 *The −23° F at Blackadder, Berwickshire on 4 Dec. 1879, and the −20° F at Grantown-on-Spey on 24 Feb. 1955, were not standard exposures. The −11° F reported from Buxton, Derbyshire on 11 Feb. 1895 was not standard. The lowest official temperature in England is −6° F (−21·1° C) at Bodiam, Sussex on 20 Jan. 1940, at Ambleside, Westmorland on 21 Jan. 1940 and at Houghall, Durham on 5 Jan. 1941 and 4 March 1947.*

4 *This is equal to 7,435 tons of rain per acre. Elevation 1,200 metres (3,937 feet).*

5 *The record for Ireland is 154·4 in. near Derriana Lough, County Kerry, in 1948.*

6 *The record for a single snow storm is 175·4 in. at Thompson Pass, Alaska, on 26–31 Dec. 1955, and, for 24 hours, 76 in. at Silver Lake, Colorado, U.S.A., on 14–15 April 1921. London's earliest recorded snow was on 25 Sept. 1885, and the latest on 27 May 1821. Less reliable reports suggest snow on 12 Sept. 1658 and on 12 June 1791.*

7 *St. Petersburg, Florida, U.S.A. recorded 764 consecutive sunny days from 9 Feb. 1967 to 17 March 1969.*

8 *The south-eastern end of the village of Lochranza, Isle of Arran, Buteshire is in shadow of mountains from 18 Nov. to 8 Feb. each winter.*

9 *The highest speed yet measured in a tornado is 280 m.p.h. at Wichita Falls, Texa U.S.A., on 2 April 1958.*

10 *The figure of 177·2 m.p.h. at R.A.F. Saxa Vord, Unst, in the Shetlands, Scotlan on 16 Feb. 1962, was not recorded with standard equipment. There were gales great severity on 15 Jan. 1362 and 26 Nov. 1703.*

11 *Between Lat. 35° N. and 35° S. there are some 3,200 thunderstorms each 12 nigh time hours, some of which can be heard at a range of 18 miles.*

12 *In Death Valley, California, U.S.A., maximum temperatures of over 120° F we recorded on 43 consecutive days—6 July to 17 Aug. 1917. At Marble Bar, Weste Australia (maximum 121° F), 160 consecutive days with maximum temperatures over 100° F were recorded—31 Oct. 1923 to 7 April 1924. At Wyndham, Weste Australia, the temperature reached 90° F or more on 333 days in 1946.*

13 *The lowest rainfall recorded in a single year was 9·29 in. at one station in Marga Kent, in 1921.*

14 *Much heavier hailstones are sometimes reported. These are usually not single b coalesced stones. On 3 Sept. 1970 a 7½-inch diameter stone, 1·67 lb., was measur by a meteorologist at Coffeyville, Kansas, U.S.A. An 8½- oz. stone was recorded Bicester, Oxfordshire, on 11 May 1945.*

4 THE UNIVERSE AND SPACE

LIGHT-YEAR—that distance travelled by light (speed 186,282·42 ±0·06 miles per second or 670,616,722·8 m.p.h., *in vacuo*) in one tropical (or solar) year (365·24219878 mean solar days at January 0, 12 hours Ephemeris time in A.D. 1900) and is 5,878,500,600,000 miles. The unit was first used in March 1888.

MAGNITUDE—a measure of stellar brightness such that the light of a star of any magnitude bears a ratio of 2·511886 to that of a star of the next magnitude. Thus a fifth magnitude star is 2·511886 times as bright, while one of the first magnitude is exactly 100 (or $2{\cdot}511886^5$) times as bright, as a sixth magnitude star. In the case of such exceptionally bright bodies as Sirius, Venus, the Moon (magnitude −11·2) or the Sun (magnitude −26·7), the magnitude is expressed as a minus quantity.

PROPER MOTION—that component of a star's motion in space which, at right angles to the line of sight, constitutes an apparent change of position of the star in the celestial sphere.

The universe is the entirety of space, matter and anti-matter. An appreciation of its magnitude is best grasped by working outward from the Earth, through the Solar System and our own Milky Way galaxy, to the remotest extra-galactic nebulae.

METEOROIDS

Meteor shower

Meteoroids are mostly of cometary origin. A meteor is the light phenomenon caused by the entry of a meteoroid into the Earth's atmosphere. The greatest meteor "shower" on record occurred on the night of 16–17 Nov. 1966, when the Leonid meteors (which recur every 33¼ years) were visible between western North America and eastern U.S.S.R. It was calculated that meteors passed over Arizona, U.S.A., at a rate of 2,300 per minute for a period of 20 minutes from 5 a.m. on 17 Nov. 1966.

METEORITES

Largest *World*

When a meteoroid penetrates to the Earth's surface, the remnant is described as a meteorite. The largest known meteorite is one found in 1920 at Hoba West, near Grootfontein in South West Africa. This is a block about 9 feet long by 8 feet broad, weighing 132,000 lb. (59 tons). The largest meteorite exhibited by any museum is the "Tent" meteorite, weighing 68,085 lb. (30·4 tons), found in 1897 near Cape York, on the west coast of Greenland, by the expedition of Commander (later Rear-Admiral) Robert Edwin Peary (1856–1920). It was known to the Eskimos as the Abnighito and is now exhibited in the Hayden Planetarium in New York City, N.Y., U.S.A.

The largest piece of stony meteorite recovered is a piece of the Norton County meteorite which fell in Nebraska, U.S.A. on 18 Feb. 1948. The greatest amount of material recovered from any non-metallic meteorite is from the Allende fall of more than 1 ton in Chihuahua, Mexico on 8 Feb. 1969.

There was a mysterious explosion of about 35 megatons in Latitude 60° 55′ N., Longitude 101° 57′ E., in the basin of the Podkamennaya Tunguska river, 40 miles north of Vanavara, in Siberia, U.S.S.R., at 00 hours 17 minutes 11 seconds G.M.T. on 30 June 1908. The energy of this explosion was about 10^{24} ergs and the cause has been variously attributed to a meteorite (1927), a comet (1930), a nuclear explosion (1961) and to anti-matter (1965). This devastated an area of about 1,500 square miles and the shock was felt as far as 1,000 kilometres (more than 600 miles) away.

United Kingdom and Ireland

The heaviest of the 22 meteorites known to have fallen on the British Isles was one weighing at least 102 lb. (largest piece 17 lb. 6 oz.), which fell at 4.12 p.m. on 24 Dec. 1965 at Barwell, Leicestershire. Scotland's largest recorded meteorite fell in Strathmore, Perthshire, on 3 Dec. 1917. It weighed 22¼ lb. and was the largest of four stones totalling 29 lb. 6 oz. The largest recorded meteorite to fall in Ireland was the Limerick Stone of 65 lb., part of a shower of 106 lb. which fell near Adare, County Limerick, on 10 Sept. 1813. The larger of the two recorded meteorites to land in Wales was one weighing 28 oz., of which a piece weighing 25½ oz. went through the roof of a building in Beddgelert, Caernarvonshire, on 21 Sept. 1949.

Largest craters

Aerial surveys in Canada in 1956 and 1957 brought to light a gash, or astrobleme, 8½ miles across near Deep Bay, Saskatchewan, possibly attributable to a very old and very oblique meteorite. There is a possible crater-like formation 275 miles in diameter on the eastern shore of the Hudson Bay, where the Nastapoka Islands are just off the coast.

The largest proven crater is the Coon Butte or Baringer crater, discovered in 1891 near Canyon Diablo, Winslow, northern Arizona, U.S.A. It is 4,150 feet in diameter and now about 575 feet deep, with a parapet rising 130 to 155 feet above the surrounding plain. It has been estimated that an iron-nickel mass with a diameter of 200 to 260 feet, and weighing about 2,000,000 tons, gouged this crater in *c.* 25,000 B.C., with an impact force equivalent to an explosion of 30,000,000 tons of trinitrotoluene ($C_7H_5O_6N_3$), called T.N.T.

Evidence published in 1963 discounts a meteoric origin for the crypto-volcanic Vredefort Ring (diameter 26 miles), to the south-west of Johannesburg, South Africa, and also questions the meteoric origin of the New

Quebec (formerly the Chubb) "Crater", first sighted on 20 June 1943 in northern Ungava, Canada. This is now regarded as more likely to be a water-filled vulcanoid. It is 1,325 feet deep and measures 6·8 miles round its rim.

Tektites The largest tektite of which details have been published has been of 3·2 kilogrammes (7·04 lb.) found *c.* 1932 at Muong Nong, Saravane Province, Laos and now in the Paris Museum. Details of some larger finds are to be published in 1970.

AURORA

Most frequent Polar lights, known as Aurora Borealis or Northern Lights in the northern hemisphere and Aurora Australis in the southern hemisphere, are caused by electrical solar discharges in the upper atmosphere and occur most frequently in high latitudes. The maximum auroral frequencies, of up to 240 displays per year, have occurred in the Hudson Bay area of northern Canada. The extreme height of auroras has been measured at 1,000 kilometres (620 miles), while the lowest may descend to 45 miles.

Southernmost "Northern Lights" Displays occur 90 times a year (on average) in the Orkneys, 25 times a year in Edinburgh, seven times a year in London, and once a decade in southern Italy. On 25 Sept. 1909 a display was witnessed as far south as Singapore (1° 25′ N.). The greatest auroral displays over the United Kingdom in recent times occurred on 24–25 Oct. 1870 and 25 Jan. 1938.

THE MOON

The Earth's closest neighbour in space and only natural satellite is the Moon, at a mean distance of 238,856 statute miles centre to centre or 233,813 miles surface to surface. Its closest approach (perigee) and most extreme distance away (apogee) measured surface to surface are 216,420 and 247,667 miles respectively or 221,463 and 252,710 miles measured centre to centre. It has a diameter of 2,159·9 miles. The earliest radar echo from the Moon, which orbits at an average speed of 2,287 m.p.h., was achieved by the United States Army on 10 Jan. 1946.

The first direct hit on the Moon was achieved at 2 minutes 24 seconds after midnight (Moscow time) on 14 Sept. 1959, by the Soviet space probe *Lunik II* near the *Mare Serenitatis*. The first photographic images of the hidden side were collected by the U.S.S.R.'s *Lunik III* from 6.30 a.m. on 7 Oct. 1959, from a range of up to 43,750 miles, and transmitted to the Earth from a distance of 470,000 kilometres (292,000 miles). The first "soft" landing was made by the U.S.S.R.'s *Luna IX*, launched at about 11 a.m. G.M.T. on 31 Jan. 1966. It landed in the area of the Ocean of Storms (*Oceanus Procellarum*) at 18 hours 45 minutes 30 seconds G.M.T. on 3 Feb. 1966.

"Blue Moon" Owing to sulphur particles in the upper atmosphere from a forest fire covering 250,000 acres between Mile 103 and Mile 119 on the Alaska Highway in northern British Columbia, Canada, the Moon took on a bluish colour, as seen from Great Britain, on the night of 26 Sept. 1950. The Moon also appeared blue after the Krakatoa eruption of 27 Aug. 1883 (see page 53) and on other occasions.

Crater *Largest* Only 59 per cent. of the Moon's surface is directly visible from the Earth because it is in "captured rotation", *i.e.* the period of revolution is equal to the period of orbit. The largest visible crater is the walled plain Bailly, towards the Moon's South Pole, which is 183 miles across, with walls rising to 14,000 feet. On the averted side the Orientale Basin measures more than 600 miles in diameter.

Deepest The deepest crater is the Newton crater, with a floor estimated to be between 23,000 and 29,000 feet below its rim. The brightest directly visible spot on the Moon is *Aristarchus*.

Highest mountains As there is no water on the Moon, the heights of mountains can be measured only in relation to lower-lying terrain near their bases. The highest lunar mountains were, until 1967, thought to be in the Leibnitz and Doerfel ranges, near the lunar South Pole with a height of some 35,000 feet. On the discovery from Lunar Orbiter spacecraft of evidence that they were merely crater rims, the names have been withdrawn. Currently it is believed that such an elevation would be an exaggerated estimate for any feature of the Moon's surface.

Temperature extremes When the Sun is overhead, the temperature on the lunar equator reaches 243° F. (31 deg. F. above the boiling point of water). By sunset the temperature is 58° F., but after nightfall it sinks to −261° F.

Moon rocks The age attributed to the oldest of the first moon rocks brought back to Earth by the *Apollo XI* crew on 24 July 1969 was breccia aged 4,600 million years.

THE SUN

Distance extremes The Earth's 66,690 m.p.h. orbit of 584,000,000 miles around the Sun is elliptical, hence our distance from the Sun varies. The orbital speed varies between 65,600 m.p.h. (minimum) and 67,800 m.p.h. The average distance of the Sun is 92,956,000 miles (149,600,000 km.).

The closest approach (perihelion) is 91,342,000 miles and the farthest departure (aphelion) is 94,452,000 miles. The Solar System is revolving around the nucleus of the Milky Way at a speed of 481,000 m.p.h. and has a velocity of 42,500 m.p.h. relative to stars in our immediate region such as Vega.

Temperature and dimensions The Sun has an internal temperature of about 35,000,000° C., a core pressure of 500,000,000 tons per square inch and uses up 4,000,000 tons of hydrogen per second, thus providing a luminosity of 3×10^{27} candlepower, or 1,500,000 candlepower per square inch. The Sun has the stellar classification of a "yellow dwarf" and, although its density is only 1·41 times that of water, its mass is 333,430 times as much as that of the Earth. It has a mean diameter of 865,370 miles. The Sun with a mass of $1{\cdot}961 \times 10^{27}$ tons represents more than 99 per cent. of the total mass of the Solar System.

Sun-spots *Largest* To be visible to the *protected* naked eye, a Sun-spot must cover about one two-thousandth part of the Sun's hemisphere and thus have an area of about 500,000,000 square miles. The largest recorded Sun-spot occurred in the Sun's southern hemisphere on 8 April 1947. Its area was about 7,000 million square miles, with an extreme longitude of 187,000 miles and an extreme latitude of 90,000 miles. Sun-spots appear darker because they are more than 1,500 deg. C. cooler than the

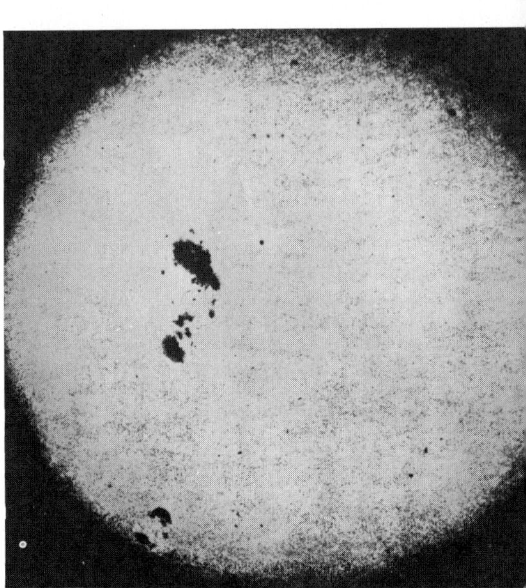

The largest recorded Sun-spot of 1947—90,000 by 187,000 miles

rest of the Sun's surface temperature of 5,660° C. The largest observed solar prominence was onc measuring 70,000 miles across its base and protruding 300,000 miles, observed on 4 June 1946.

…st frequent In October 1957 a smoothed Sun-spot count showed 263, the highest recorded index since records started in 1755 (*cf.* previous record of 239 in May 1778). In 1943 a Sun-spot lasted for 200 days from June to December.

ECLIPSES

Earliest recorded The earliest extrapolated eclipses that have been identified are 1361 B.C. (lunar) and 2136 B.C. (solar). For the Middle East only, lunar eclipses have been extrapolated to 3450 B.C. and solar ones to 4200 B.C. No line of totality for a solar eclipse crossed London for the 575 years from 20 March 1140 to 3 May 1715. The most recent occasion when a line of totality of a solar eclipse crossed Great Britain was on 29 June 1927, and the next instance may just clip the Cornish coast on 11 Aug. 1999. On 30 June 1954 a total eclipse was witnessed in Haroldswick, Unst, Shetland Islands but the line of totality was to the north of territorial waters.

Longest duration The maximum possible duration of an eclipse of the Sun is 7 minutes 31 seconds. The longest actually occurring since 13 June A.D. 717 was on 20 June 1955 (7 minutes 8 seconds), seen from the Philippines. The longest possible in the British Isles is 5½ minutes. Those of 15 June 885 and 3 May 1715 were both nearly 5 minutes, as will be the eclipse of 2381. An annular eclipse may last for 12 minutes 24 seconds. The longest totality of any lunar eclipse is 104 minutes. This has occurred many times.

…t and least frequent The highest number of eclipses possible in a year is seven, as in 1935, when there were five solar and two lunar eclipses; or four solar and three lunar eclipses, as will occur in 1982. The lowest possible number in a year is two, both of which must be solar, as in 1944 and 1969.

COMETS

Earliest recorded The earliest records of comets date from the 7th century B.C. The speeds of the estimated 2,000,000 comets vary from 700 m.p.h. in outer space to 1,250,000 m.p.h. when near the Sun. The successive appearances of Halley's Comet have been traced to 466 B.C. It was first depicted in the Nuremburg Chronicle of A.D. 684. The first prediction of its return by Edmund Halley (1656–1742) proved true on Christmas Day 1758, 16 years after his death. Its next appearance should be at 9·9 (viz. at 9.30 p.m.) February 1986, 75·81 years after the last, which was on 19 April 1910.

Closest approach On 1 July 1770, Lexell's Comet, travelling at a speed of 23·9 miles per second (relative to the Sun), came within 1,500,000 miles of the Earth. However, the Earth is believed to have passed through the tail of Halley's Comet, most recently on 19 May 1910.

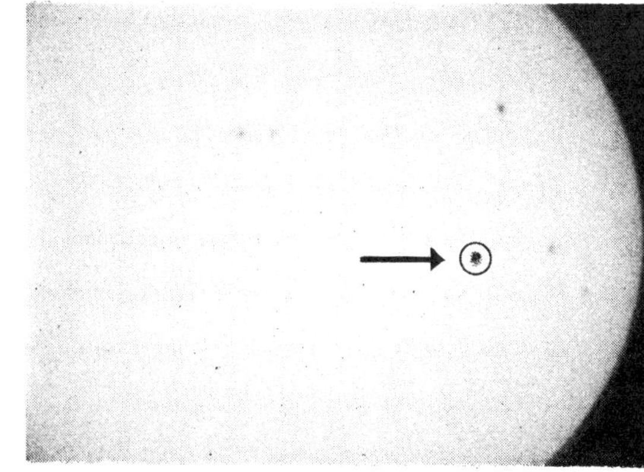

The solar system's …llest planet —Mercury …ght flitting …ss the face … the Sun at more than …,000 m.p.h.

Largest Comets are so tenuous that it has been estimated that even the head of one rarely contains solid matter much more than *c.* 1 kilometre in diameter. In the tail 10,000 cubic miles contain less than a cubic inch of solid matter. These tails, as in the case of the Great Comet of 1843, may trail for 200,000,000 miles.

Shortest period Of all the recorded periodic comets (these are members of the Solar System), the one which most frequently returns is Encke's Comet, first identified in 1786. Its period of 1,206 days (3·3 years) is the shortest established. Not one of its 48 returns (up to May 1967) has been missed by astronomers. Now increasingly faint, it is expected to "die" by 1993. The most frequently observed comets are Schwassmann-Wachmann I, Kopff and Oterma, which can be observed every year between Mars and Jupiter.

Longest period At the other extreme is the comet 1910a, whose path was not accurately determined. It is not expected to return for perhaps 4,000,000 years.

PLANETS

Largest Planets (including the Earth) are bodies which belong to the Solar System and which revolve round the Sun in definite orbits. Jupiter, with an equatorial diameter of 88,700 miles and a polar diameter of 82,790 miles, is the largest of the nine major planets, with a mass 318·354 times, and a volume 1,313 times that of the Earth. It also has the shortest period of rotation on its own equatorial axis, with a "day" of only 9 hours 50 minutes 30·003 seconds.

Smallest Of the nine major planets, Mercury, whose period of revolution round the Sun is only 87·9686 days, is the smallest, with a diameter of about 2,900 miles and a mass only 0·056 of that of the Earth, that is 330 trillion tons. Mercury has the highest average speed in orbit at 107,030 m.p.h. It rotates on its axis once every 58·65 days.

Hottest The U.S.S.R. probe *Venera 7* recorded a temperature of 480° C. (nearly 900° F.) on the surface of Venus on 17 Dec. 1970. The surface temperature of Mercury has been estimated at more than 800° F. on its hot side and may well exceed this at perihelion, when it is only 28,566,000 miles away from the Sun. The planet with a surface temperature closest to Earth's average figure of 59° F. is Mercury with a night-side figure of about 70° F.

Coldest The coldest planet is, not unnaturally, that which is the remotest from the Sun, namely Pluto, which has an estimated surface temperature of −420° F. (39 deg. F. above absolute zero). Its mean distance from the Sun is 3,664,000,000 miles and its period of revolution is 248·4302 years. Its diameter is about 3,700 miles. Pluto was first recorded by Clyde William Tombaugh (b. 4 Feb. 1906) at Lowell Observatory, Flagstaff, Arizona, U.S.A., on 18 Feb. 1930 from photographs taken on 23 and 29 January.

Nearest The fellow planet closest to the Earth is Venus, which is, at times, about 25,700,000 miles inside the Earth's orbit, compared with Mars's closest approach of 34,600,000 miles outside the Earth's orbit. Mars, known since 1965 to be cratered, has temperatures ranging from 85° F. to −130° F. but in which infusorians of the *genus* Colpoda *could* survive.

Brightest and faintest Viewed from the Earth, by far the brightest of the five planets visible to the naked eye (Uranus at magnitude 5·7 is only marginally visible) is Venus, with a maximum magnitude of −4·4. The faintest is Pluto, with a magnitude of 14.

Longest "day" The planet with the longest period of rotation is Venus, which spins on its own axis once every 243·16 days, so its "day" is longer than its "year" (224·7007 days). The shortest "day" is that of Jupiter (see above, Largest).

Conjunctions The most dramatic recorded conjunction (coming together) of the other seven principal members of the Solar System (Sun, Moon, Mercury, Venus, Mars, Jupiter and Saturn) occurred on 5 Feb. 1962, when 16° covered all seven during an eclipse in the Pacific area. It is possible that the seven-fold conjunction of September 1186 spanned only 12°. The next notable conjunction will take place on 5 May 2000.

SATELLITES

Most Of the nine major planets, all but Mercury, Venus and Pluto have natural satellites. The planet with the most is Jupiter, with four large and eight small moons. The Earth is the only planet with a single satellite. The distance of the Solar System's 32 known satellites from their parent planets varies from the 5,625 miles of *Phobos* from Mars to the 14,812,500 miles of *Hades* (or Satellite IX) from Jupiter.

Largest and smallest The largest satellite is Saturn's seventh, *Titan* (diameter 3,550 miles), and the smallest is Mars's outer "moon" *Deimos* (diameter 3·8 miles), discovered on 18 Aug. 1877 by Asaph Hill (U.S.).

The largest of the solar system's 32 "moons" Titan (see arrow), Saturn's 7th satellite which has a diameter of 3,550 miles.

Largest asteroids In the belt which lies between Mars and Jupiter, there are some 45,000 (only 3,100 charted) minor planets or asteroids which are, for the most part, too small to yield to diameter measurement. The largest and first discovered (by Piazzi at Palermo, Sicily on 1 Jan. 1801) of these is *Ceres*, with a diameter of 436 miles. The only one visible to the naked eye is *Vesta*, "discovered" on 29 March 1807 by Dr. Heinrich Wilhelm Olbers (1758–1840), a German amateur astronomer. The closest measured approach to the Earth by an asteroid was 485,000 miles, in the case of *Hermes* on 30 Oct. 1937.

STARS

Largest and most massive Of those measured, the star with the greatest diameter is the "red giant" *Epsilon Aurigae B* at 2,500 million miles. This star is so vast that our own Solar System of the Sun and the six planets out as far as Saturn could be accommodated inside it. The *Alpha Herculis* aggregation, consisting of a main star and a double star companion, is enveloped in a cold gas. This system, visible to the naked eye, has a diameter of 170,000 million miles. The fainter component of Plaskett's star discovered by J. S. Plaskett from the Dominion Astrophysical Observatory, Victoria, British Columbia, Canada *c.* 1920 is the most massive star known with a mass *c.* 55 times that of the Sun.

Smallest The smallest known star is LP 327-186, a "white dwarf" with a diameter only half that of the Moon, 100 light-years distant and detected in May 1962 from Minneapolis, Minnesota, U.S.A. The claim that LP 768-500 is even smaller is not widely accepted.

Oldest The Sun is estimated to be about 7,500 million years old and our galaxy between 10,000 million and 12,000 million years old.

Farthest The Solar System, with its Sun, nine major planets, 32 satellites, asteroids and comets, was discovered in 1921 to be about 27,000 light-years from the centre of the lens-shaped Milky Way galaxy (diameter 100,000 light-years) of about 100,000 million stars. The most distant star in our galaxy is therefore about 75,000 light-years distant.

Nearest Excepting the special case of our own Sun, the nearest star is the very faint *Proxima Centauri*, which is 4·3 light-years (25,000,000,000,000 miles) away. The nearest star visible to the naked eye is the southern hemisphere star *Alpha Centauri*, or *Rigil Kentaurus* (4·33 light-years), with a magnitude of 0·1.

Brightest Sirius A (*Alpha Canis Majoris*), also known as the Dog Star, is the brightest star in the heavens, with an apparent magnitude of −1·58. It is in the constellation *Canis Major* and is visible in the winter months of the northern hemisphere, being due south at midnight on the last day of the year. Sirius A is 8·7 light-years away and has a luminosity 26 times as much as that of the Sun. It has a diameter of 1,500,000 miles and a mass of 45,800,000,000,000,000,000,000,000 tons.

Most and least luminous If all stars could be viewed at the same distance, the most luminous would be the apparently faint variable *S. Doradûs*, in the Greater Magellanic Cloud (*Nebecula Major*), which can be 300,000 to 500,000 times brighter than the Sun, and has an absolute magnitude of −8·9. The faintest star detected visually is a very red star 30 light-years distant in *Pisces*, with one two-millionth of the Sun's brightness.

Coolest A 16th magnitude star with a surface temperature of only about 425° C. (800° F.) was detected in *Cygnus* in 1965.

Densest The densest stars are the "white dwarfs". A star with the mass of our Sun but the diameter of our Moon was discovered by W. J. Luyten of Harvard Observatory, U.S.A. in June 1966. The limit of stellar density is at the neutron state, when the atomic particles exist in a state in which there is no space between them. Each cubic inch would then weigh about 1,800 million tons (*sic*). Atoms measure a few Å units in diameter whereas the nuclei are five orders of magnitude smaller and hence have a diameter of 4 ten-trillionths (4×10^{-19}) of a centimetre.

Brightest super-nova Super-novae, or temporary "stars" which flare and then fade, occur perhaps five times in 1,000 years. The brightest "star" ever seen by historic man is believed to be the super-nova close to *Zeta Tauri*, visible by day for 23 days from 4 July 1054. The remains, known as the "Crab" Nebula, now have a diameter of about 30,000,000,000,000 miles and are still expanding at a rate of 800 miles per second. It is about 4,100 light-years away, indicating that the explosion actually occurred in about 3000 B.C.

Constellations The largest of the 88 constellations is *Hydra* (the Sea Serpent), which covers 1,302·84 square degrees and contains at least 68 stars visible to the naked eye (to 5·5 mag.). The constellation *Centaurus* (Centaur), ranking ninth in area embraces however at least 94 such stars. The smallest constellation is *Equuleus* (Little Horse) with an area of 71·64 square degrees and only 5 stars of 5½ magnitude.

Stellar planets Planetary companions, with a mass of less than 7 per cent. of their parent star, have been found to 61 *Cygni* (1942), Lalande 21185 (1960) and Barnard's Star (Munich 15040) in April 1963. Other near Sun-like stars, which could conceivably have a planetary system, are *Tau Ceti, Epsilon* and *Omicron-2 Eridani,* 70 *Ophiuchi* and *Epsilon Indi.* Listening operations ("Project Ozma") on the first two were maintained from 4 April 1960 to March 1961, using an 85-foot radio telescope at Deer Creek Valley, Green Bank, West Virginia, U.S.A. The apparatus was probably insufficiently sensitive for any signal from a distance of 11 light-years to be received.

THE UNIVERSE

According to Einstein's Special Theory time dilatation effect (published in 1905), time actually runs more slowly for an object as its speed increases. However time speeds up for an object as it moves away from a body exerting gravitational force. During their mission the crew of the Apollo VIII circum-lunar space flight aged a net 300 microseconds more than earthlings. No formal overtime claim was lodged.

Outside the Milky Way galaxy, which revolves once every 225,000,000 years, and moves around the centre of the local super-cluster of 2,500 neighbouring galaxies at a speed of 1,350,000 m.p.h., there exist 1,000,000 million other galaxies. These range in size up to 200,000 light-years in diameter. The nearest heavenly body outside our galaxy is the Large Magellanic Cloud near the Southern Cross, at a distance of 160,000 light-years. In 1967 it was determined by the astronomer G. Idlis (U.S.S.R.) that the Magellanic Clouds were detached from the Milky Way by another colliding galaxy, now in *Sagittarius*, about 3,800,000 years ago.

Farthest sible object The remotest heavenly body often visible to the naked eye is the Great Galaxy in *Andromeda* (Mag. 3·47). This is a rotating nebula in spiral form, and its distance from the Earth is about 2,200,000 light-years, or about 13,000,000,000,000,000,000 miles. It is just possible however that, under ideal seeing conditions, Messier 33, the Spiral in Triangulum (Mag. 5·79), is visible to the naked eye at a distance of 2,300,000 light-years.

Quasars In November 1962 the existence of quasi-stellar radio sources ("quasars" or QSO's) was established. No satisfactory model has yet been constructed to account for the immensely high luminosity of bodies apparently so distant and of such small diameter. The diameter of 3C 446 is only about 90 light-days, but there are measurable alterations in brightness in less than one day. It is believed to be undergoing the most violent explosion yet detected, since it has increased 3·2 magnitudes or 20-fold in less than one year.

"Pulsars" The discovery of the first pulsating radio source or "pulsar" CP 1919 was announced from the Mullard Radio Astronomy Observatory, Cambridge, England, on 29 Feb. 1968. The fastest so far discovered is NP 0532 in the Crab Nebula with a pulse of 33 milli-seconds. One theory is that it is a rotating neutron star of immense density.

Remotest object The greatest distance yet ascribed to a radio detected and visibly confirmed body is that claimed for the quasar designated 4C 05·34, identified from the Kitt Peak National Observatory, Arizona, U.S.A., and announced in May 1970. Though the Symposium on Relativistic Astrophysics in New York City, U.S.A., concluded in January 1967 that quasars "have no agreed distance from the Earth", a figure of at least 13,000 million light-years has been ascribed to quasars exhibiting a lesser red shift than the extreme figure of 2·87 measured for this body. PKS 0237—23 announced in March 1967 is the most luminous of observed heavenly bodies. Proponents of the oscillation theory of cosmology believe that the Universe is between 13 and 20,000 million years advanced on the expanding phase of an 80,000 million year expansion-contraction cycle. The number of previous cycles, if any, is not determinable.

ROCKETRY AND MISSILES

Earliest periments The origin of the rocket dates from war rockets propelled by a charcoal-saltpetre-sulphur gunpowder, made by the Chinese as early as *c.* 1100. These early rockets became known in Europe by 1258. The pioneer of military rocketry in Britain was Sir William Congreve, Bt., M.P. (1772–1828), Comptroller of the Royal Laboratory and Inspector of Military Machines, whose "six-pound rocket" was developed to a range of 2,000 yards by 1805 when used by the Royal Navy against Boulogne, France.

The earliest principles of reaction propulsion with the proposal of liquid fuel are usually ascribed to Konstantin Eduardovich Tsiolkovskiy (or Ziolkovsky) (1857–1935), a Russian-born Pole who did his work in 1898 (first published in 1903). However, plans of a three-stage solid fuel rocket and the modern cluster principle were published in *Artis Magnae Artilleriae* by Kazimierz Siemienowicz (Poland) as early as 1650. The first launching of a liquid-fuelled rocket (patented 14 July 1914) was by Dr. Robert Hutchings Goddard (1882–1945) of the United States, at Auburn, Massachusetts, U.S.A., on 16 March 1926, when his rocket reached an altitude of 341 feet and travelled a distance of 184 feet. The U.S.S.R.'s earliest rocket was the OR-1, built in 1929. The earliest British experiments were on Salisbury Plain in 1916 by Archibald Vivian Hill, C.H., O.B.E. (born 26 Sept. 1886), Director of the Anti-Aircraft Experimental Section (Munitions Inventions Dept.). Through the pioneer work of Prof. Hermann Julius Oberth (born 25 June 1894), a Hungarian-born German, and the Society for Space Travel (*Verein für Raumschiffahrt*), founded on 5 June 1927, Germany took the lead in 1931.

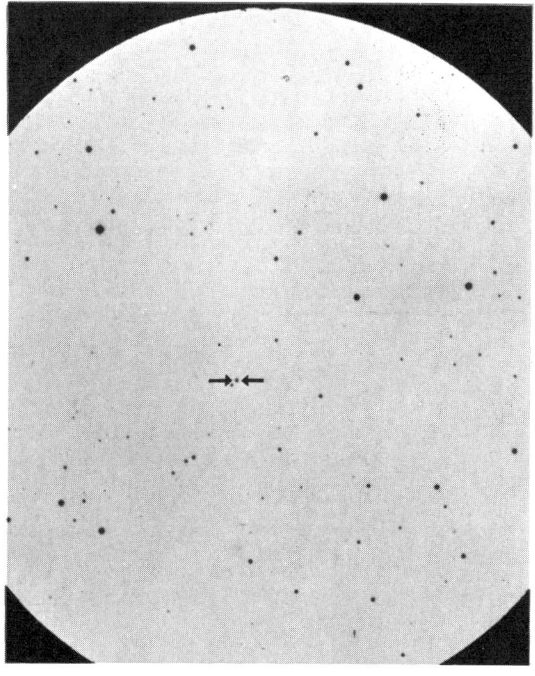

The quasar PKS 0237-23 which has the highest absolute luminosity of any heavenly body. It has been estimated to be about 80,000 trillion (80×10^{22}) miles distant

Longest ranges The longest range achieved in a ground-to-surface rocket test is 9,000 miles by a U.S. *Atlas,* measuring 85 feet long and weighing 120 tons, fired across the South Atlantic from Cape Canaveral (now Cape Kennedy), Florida, U.S.A., to a point 1,000 miles south-east of the Cape of Good Hope, South Africa, on 20 May 1960. The flight lasted about 53 minutes. The previous record was 7,760 miles by a Soviet rocket in the Pacific on 20 Jan. 1960. On 16 March 1962, Nikita Khrushchyov, then the Soviet Prime Minister, claimed in Moscow that the U.S.S.R. possessed a "global rocket" with a range of about 19,000 miles, *i.e.* more than the Earth's semi-diameter and therefore capable of hitting any target from either direction.

Most powerful *World* It has been suggested that the U.S.S.R. manned space-craft booster which blew up at Tyuratam in the summer (? July) of 1969 had a thrust of more than 10,000,000 lb. No further details have been released by the U.S.S.R. nor by the U.S. ELINT (Electronic Intelligence Section). It is known that the 25 megaton U.S.S.R. SS–9 I.C.B.M. has five times the weight of warhead of the U.S. Minuteman III.

The most powerful rocket that has been publicized is the *Saturn V,* used for the Project Apollo 3-man lunar exploration mission, on which development began in January 1962, at the John F. Kennedy Space Center, Merritt Island, Florida, U.S.A. The 6,218,558 lb. (2,776 ton) rocket is 363 feet 8 inches tall, with a payload of 45,000 lb., and gulps 13·4 tons of propellant per second for 2½ minutes (2,005 tons). Stage I (S-IC) is 138 feet tall and is powered by five Rocketdyne F-1 engines, using liquid oxygen (LOX) and kerosene, each delivering 1,514,000 lb. thrust. Stage II (S-II) is powered by five LOX and liquid hydrogen Rocketdyne J-2 engines with a total thrust of 1,141,453 lb., while Stage III (designated S-IVB) is powered by a single 228,290 lb. thrust J-2 engine. The whole assembly generates 175,600,000 horse-power and weighs up to 6,456,282 lb. (2,882 tons) fully loaded. It was first launched on 9 Nov. 1967.

The most powerful single rocket motor yet tested is the Aerojet-General Corporation SL-1 solid fuel motor with a diameter of 260 inches (21 feet 8 inches) and a length of 80 feet 8 inches. It was first tested on 25 Sept. 1965 at Homestead, Dade County, Florida, U.S.A. It was fired nose down and consumed 750 tons of solid fuel in 2 minutes 10 seconds, developing 3,600,000 lb. static thrust. The Aerojet-General SL-3, a solid fuel motor 70 feet long, with a diameter of 260 inches designed to produce 5,700,000 lb. static thrust was tested at Homestead on 17 June 1967.

United Kingdom The United Kingdom's largest rocket is the Hawker Siddeley *Blue Streak,* standing 69 feet 3 inches tall, weighing 94 tons and powered by twin Rolls-Royce kerosene-LOX RZ 2 engines with a thrust of 137,000 to 150,000 lb. each. The first test flight was at Lake Hart, Woomera, South Australia, on 5 June 1964.

Least powerful The least powerful rocket ever made is the Valveless Subliming Solid Control Rocket, manufactured for a U.S. Navy satellite programme by the Rocket Research Corporation of Seattle, Washington, U.S.A. It has a thrust of only one-millionth of 1 lb.

Ion rockets Speeds of up to 100,000 m.p.h. are envisaged for rockets powered by an ion discharge. It was announced on 13 Jan. 1960 that caesium vapour discharge had been maintained for 50 hours at the Lewis Research Center in Cleveland, Ohio, U.S.A. Ion rockets were first used in flight by the U.S.S.R.'s Mars probe *Zond II,* launched on 30 Nov. 1964.

A U.S. Saturn V Moon rocket being moved on the world's largest vehicle at Cape Kennedy, Florida. Note the scale with the ringed man

ARTIFICIAL SATELLITES

The dynamics of artificial satellites were first propounded by Sir Isaac Newton (1642–1727) in his *Philosophiae Naturalis Principia Mathematica* ("Mathematical Principles of Natural Philosophy"), begun in March 1686 and first published in the summer of 1687. The first artificial satellite was successfully put into orbit at an altitude of 142/588 miles and a velocity of more than 17,500 m.p.h. from a site north of the Caspian Sea on the night of 4 Oct. 1957. This spherical satellite, *Sputnik* ("Fellow Traveller") *I,* officially designated "Satellite 1957 Alpha 2", weighed 83·6 kilogrammes (184·3 lb.), with a diameter of 58 centimetres (22·8 inches), and its lifetime is believed to have been 92 days, ending on 4 Jan. 1958. It was designed under the direction of Dr. Sergey Pavlovich Korolyov (1906–1966).

Terrestrial escape velocity (25,022 m.p.h. at the surface but less at altitude) was first achieved by the U.S.S.R.'s

PROGRESSIVE ROCKET ALTITUDE RECORDS

Height in Miles	Rocket	Place	Launch Date
0·71 (3,762 ft.)	A 3-inch rocket	near London, England	April 1750
1·24 (6,560 ft.)	Rheinhold Tiling[1] (Germany) solid fuel rocket	Osnabrück, Germany	April 1931
nearly 3	OR-2 liquid fuel (U.S.S.R.)	U.S.S.R.	17 Aug. 1932
8·1	U.S.S.R. "Stratosphere" rocket	U.S.S.R.	1935
52·46	A.4 rocket (Germany)	Peenemünde, Germany	3 Oct. 1942
c. 85	A.4 rocket (Germany)	Heidelager, Poland	early 1944
118	A.4 rocket (Germany)	Heidelager, Poland	mid 1944
244	V-2/W.A.C. Corporal (2-stage) Bumper No. 5 (U.S.A.)	White Sands, N.M., U.S.A.	24 Feb. 1949
250	M.104 *Raketa* (U.S.S.R.)	? Tyuratam, U.S.S.R.	1954
682	Jupiter C (U.S.A.)	Cape Canaveral (now Cape Kennedy), Florida, U.S.A.	20 Sept. 1956
>2,700	Farside No. 5 (4-stage) (U.S.A.)	Eniwetok Atoll	20 Oct. 1957
70,700	Pioneer I-B Lunar Probe (U.S.A.)	Cape Canaveral (now Cape Kennedy), Florida, U.S.A.	11 Oct. 1958
215,300,000*	Luna I or Mechta (U.S.S.R.)	Tyuratam, U.S.S.R.	2 Jan. 1959
242,000,000*	Mars I (U.S.S.R.)	U.S.S.R.	1 Nov. 1962

* *Apogee in solar orbit.*

[1] *There is some evidence that Tiling may shortly after have reached 9,500 m. (5·90 miles) with a solid fuel rocket at Wangerooge, East Friesian Islands, West Germany.*

RECORDS

	Earth Orbits	**Moon Orbits**	**Solar Orbits**
Earliest Satellite	Sputnik I, 4 Oct. 1957	Luna X, 31 March 1966	Luna I, 2 Jan. 1959
Earliest Planetary Contact	Sputnik I rocket, 4 Oct. 1957—burnt out 1 Dec. 1957	Luna II hit Moon, 13 Sept. 1959	Venus III hit Venus, 1 Mar. 1966
Earliest Planetary Touchdown	Discoverer XIII capsule, landed 11 Aug. 1960	Luna IX soft landed on Moon 3 Feb. 1966	Venus VII soft landed on Venus 15 Dec. 1970
Earliest Rendezvous and Docking	Gemini 8 and Agena 8, 16 March 1966	Apollo X and LEM 4 docked 23 May 1969	None
Earliest Crew Exchange	Soyuz IV and V, 14–15 Jan. 1969	Apollo X and LEM 4, 18 May 1969	None
Heaviest Satellite	29·91 tons, Apollo IV, 9 Nov. 1967	28·41 tons, Apollo X, 18 May 1969	13·39 tons, Apollo X rocket, 18 May 1969
Lightest Satellite	1·47 lb. each, Tetrahedron Research Satellites (TRS), 2 and 3, 9 May 1963	150 lb., Interplanetary Monitoring Probe 6, 19 July 1967	13 lb., Pioneer IV, 3 March 1959
Longest First Orbit	42 days, Apollo XII rocket, 14 Nov. 1969	720 minutes, Lunar Orbiter 4, 4 May 1967	567 days, Mariner 4 (Mars Probe), 28 Nov. 1964
Shortest First Orbit	86 minutes 30·6 seconds, Cosmos 169, 17 July 1967	114 minutes, LEM 6 ascent stage (Apollo XII), 20 Nov. 1969	195 days, Mariner 5 (Venus Probe), 14 June 1967
Longest Expected Lifetime	>1 million years, Vela 12, 8 April 1970	Unlimited, IMP 6 (see above), 19 July 1967	All unlimited
Nearest First Perigee-Pericynthion-Perihelion	63 miles, Cosmos 169 rocket, 17 July 1967	10 miles, LEM 6 ascent stage (Apollo 12), 20 Nov. 1969	53,800,000 miles, Mariner 5 (Venus Probe), 14 June 1967
Furthest First Apogee-Apcynthion-Aphelion	535,522 miles, Apollo XII rocket, 14 Nov. 1969	4,900 miles, IMP 6 (see above), 19 July 1967	149,000,000 miles, Mars I, 1 Nov. 1962

The highest and lowest speeds in solar orbit are 89,300 m.p.h. and 47,000 m.p.h. by Mariner II *(27 Aug. 1962) and* Mars I *(see above), respectively.*
NOTE: *The largest artificial satellite measured by volume has been* Echo II *(diameter 135 feet), weighing 565 lb., launched into orbit (642/816 miles) from Vandenberg Air Force Base, California, U.S.A., on 25 Jan. 1964. It was an inflated sphere, comprising a 535 lb. balloon, whose skin was made of Mylar plastic 0·00035 of an inch thick, bonded on both sides by aluminium alloy foil 0·00018 of an inch thick, together with equipment.* Echo II *was the brightest of artificial satellites (its magnitude was about −1) and it has been claimed that it became the man-made object seen by more people than any other. Its lifetime was 1,960 days until it burned up on 7 June 1969.*

solar satellite Luna I (or Mechta), fired from Tyuratam on 2 Jan. 1959. This is sometimes termed the Second Cosmic velocity.

Solar escape velocity (36,800 m.p.h.) was first achieved in a limited way over the Hollomon Air Base, New Mexico, U.S.A., on 16 Oct. 1957, when aluminium pellets were fired at about 40,000 m.p.h. by a "shaped charge" from an Aerobee rocket at an altitude of 55 miles. The speed necessary for escape from the Milky Way galaxy is 815,000 m.p.h.

Earliest successful manned satellite

The first successful manned spaced flight began at 9.07 a.m. (Moscow time), or 6.07 a.m. G.M.T., on 12 April 1961. Flight Major (later Colonel) Yuriy Alekseyevich Gagarin (born 9 March 1934) completed a single orbit of the Earth in 89·34 minutes in the U.S.S.R.'s space vehicle *Vostok* ("East") *I* (10,417 lb.). The take-off was from Baikonur, in western Siberia, and the landing was 108 minutes later near the village of Smelovka, near Engels, in the Saratov region of the U.S.S.R. The maximum speed was 17,560 m.p.h. and the maximum altitude 327 kilometres (203·2 miles). Major Gagarin, invested a Hero of the Soviet Union and awarded the Order of Lenin and the Gold Star Medal, was killed in a jet plane crash near Moscow on 27 March 1968.

st woman in space

The first and only woman to orbit the Earth was Junior Lieutenant (now Lt.-Col.) Valentina Vladimirovna Tereshkova, now Mme. Nikolayev (b. 6 March 1937), who was launched in *Vostok VI* from Baikonur, U.S.S.R., at 9.30 a.m. G.M.T. on 16 June 1963, and landed at 8.16 a.m. on 19 June, after a flight of 2 days 22 hours 46 minutes, during which she completed over 48 orbits (1,225,000 miles) and came to within 3 miles of *Vostok V*.

admitted fatality

Col. Vladimir Mikhailovich Komarov (b. 16 March 1927) was launched in *Soyuz* ("Union") *I* at 00.35 a.m. G.M.T. on 23 April 1967. The spacecraft was in orbit for about 25½ hours but he died during the descent to the ground and was thus the first man indisputedly known to have died during space flight.

st "walk" in space

The first person to leave an artificial satellite during orbit was Lt.-Col. Aleksey Arkhipovich Leonov (b. 30 May 1934), who left the Soviet satellite *Voshkod II* at about 8.30 a.m. G.M.T. on 18 March 1965. Lt.-Col. Leonov was "in space" for about 20 minutes, and for 12 minutes 9 seconds he "floated" at the end of a line 5 metres (16 feet) long. His companion on this flight of over 17 orbits (about 447,000 miles) was Col. Pavel I. Belyayev (1925–1970).

Longest manned space flight

The longest space flight has been that of Col. Andrian G. Nikolayev and Flight Engineer Vitaliy I. Sevastiyanov in *Soyuz 9* lasting 17 days 16 hours 59 minutes, on 1–19 June 1970 landing near Vorkuta, U.S.S.R. Captain James A. Lovell, U.S.N., has the overall duration record away from Earth after his return from his fourth mission, the abortive *Apollo XIII* drama, with 715 hours 4 minutes 57 seconds.

Astronauts *Oldest and youngest*

The oldest of the 49 people in space has been Col. Georgiy T. Beregovoiy who was 47 years and 6 months when launched in *Soyuz 3* on 26 Oct. 1968. The youngest was Major Gherman Stepanovich Titov aged 25 years 11 months when launched in *Vostok II* on 6 Aug. 1961.

Longest lunar mission

The longest duration of any lunar mission was the fourth. *Apollo XII* was absent from Earth for 244 hours 38 minutes on 14–24 Nov. 1969 and was manned by the three U.S. Navy Commanders Charles Conrad, Richard F. Gordon and Alan L. Bean.

Duration record on the Moon

The longest stay on the Moon's surface has been 33 hours by Capt. Alan B. Shepard, 47, and Cdr. Edgar D. Mitchell, 40, in *Antares* on 5–6 Feb. 1971.

First Extra-terrestrial vehicle

The first wheeled vehicle landed on the Moon was *Lunokhod I* which began its travels on 17 Nov. 1970. Up to 6 April 1971 it had moved more than 7 kilometres (4·35 miles) and on gradients up to 30 degrees in the Mare Imbrium.

Most expensive project

The total cost of the U.S. space programme up to and including the lunar mission of *Apollo XIX* has been estimated at $25,241,400,000 (£10,517,250,000).

Accuracy record

The most accurate recovery from space was the splash-down of *Gemini IX* on 6 June 1966 only 769 yards from the *U.S.S. Wasp* in the Western Atlantic (27° 52′ N., 75° 0′ 24″ W.).

1. ELEMENTS

All known matter in the Solar System is made up of chemical elements. The total of naturally-occurring elements so far detected is 94, comprising, at ordinary temperature, two liquids, 11 gases and 81 solids. The so-called "fourth state" of matter is plasma, when negatively-charged electrons and positively-charged ions are in flux.

Lightest and heaviest sub-nuclear particles The number of fundamental sub-nuclear particles catered for by Unitary Symmetry Theory, or SU(3), published in 1964, was 34. The SU(6) system caters for 91 particles, while the later SU(12) system caters for an infinite number, some of which are expected to be produced by higher and higher energies, but with shorter and shorter lifetimes and weaker and weaker interactions. Of SU (3) particles the one with the highest mass is the omega minus, discovered on 24 Feb. 1964 at the Brookhaven National Laboratory, near Upton, Long Island, New York State, U.S.A. It has a mass of 1,672·5±0·5Mev and a lifetime of $1{\cdot}3 \times 10^{-10}$ of a second. Of all sub-atomic concepts only the neutrino calls for masslessness. There is experimental proof that the mass, if any, of an electron neutrino cannot be greater than one ten-thousandth of that of an electron, which itself has a rest mass of $9{\cdot}10956(\pm 0{\cdot}00005) \times 10^{-28}$ of a gramme, *i.e.* it has a weight of less than $1{\cdot}07 \times 10^{-31}$ of a gramme. The first neutrino observed in the world's deepest laboratory, 10,492 feet down in the East Rand Proprietary Mine at Boksburg, near Johannesburg, South Africa, was registered at 9.48 p.m. G.M.T. on 23 Feb. 1965.

Fastest particles A search for the existence of super-luminary particles, named tachyons (symbol T^+ and T^-), with a speed *in vacuo* greater than *c* the speed of light, was instituted in 1968 by Dr. T. Alvager and Dr. M. Kriesler of Princeton University, U.S.A. Such particles would create the conceptual difficulty of disappearing before they exist. Quarks and anti-quarks (q and $\bar{q}$) have similarly evaded detection.

Commonest The commonest element in the Universe is hydrogen, which has been calculated to comprise 90 per cent. of all matter and over 99 per cent. of matter in interstellar space.

Most and least isotopes The element with the most isotopes is the colourless gas xenon (Xe) with 30 and that with the least is hydrogen with 3. The metallic element with the most is platinum (Pt) with 29 and that with the least is lithium (Li) with 5. Of stable and naturally-occurring isotopes, tin (Sn) has the most with 10 whilst 20 elements exist in Nature only as single nuclides.

GASES

Lightest Hydrogen, a colourless gas discovered in 1766 by the Hon. Henry Cavendish (1731–1810), a British millionaire, is less than 1/14th the weight of air, weighing only 0·005611 of one lb. per cubic foot, or 89·88 milligrammes per litre.

Heaviest The heaviest elemental gas is radon, the colourless isotope Em 222 of the gas emanation, which was discovered in 1900 by Friedrich Ernst Dorn (1848–1916) of Germany, and is 111·5 times as heavy as hydrogen. It is also known as niton and emanates from radium salts.

Melting and boiling points *Lowest* Of all substances, helium has the lowest boiling point (−268·94° C.). This element, which is at normal temperatures a colourless gas, was discovered in 1868 by Sir Joseph Norman Lockyer, K.C.B. (1836–1920) working with Sir Edward Frankland, K.C.B. (1825–99) and the French astronomer Pierre Jules Cesar Janssen (1824–1907) working independently. Helium was first liquefied in 1908 by Heike Kamerlingh Onnes (1853–1926), a Dutch physicist. Liquid helium, which exists in two forms, can be solidified only under pressure of 26 atmospheres. This was first achieved on 26 July 1926 by W. H. Keesom (b. Netherlands 1876). At this pressure helium will melt at −272° C.

Highest Of the elements that are gases at normal temperatures, chlorine has the highest melting point (−101·0° C.) and the highest boiling point (−34·1°C.). This yellow-green gas was discovered in 1774 by the German-born Karl Wilhelm Scheele (1742–86) of Sweden.

Rarest The Earth's atmosphere weighs an estimated 5,187,000,000,000,000 tons, of which nitrogen constitutes 78·09 per cent. by volume in dry air. The heavy hydrogen isotope tritium exists in the atmosphere to an extent of only 5×10^{-23} of one per cent. by volume.

METALS

Lightest The lightest of all metals is lithium (Li), a metal, light golden brown (*in vacuo*), discovered in 1817 by Johan August Arfvedson (1792–1841) of Sweden. It has a density of 0·5333 of a gramme per cubic centimetre or 33·29 lb. per cubic foot. The isotope Li 6 (7·56 per cent. of naturally-occurring lithium) has a density of only 0·4616 g./cu. cm. compared with 0·5391 for Li 7.

Densest The densest of all metals and hence the most effective possible paperweight is osmium (Os), a grey-blue metal of the platinum group, discovered in 1804 by Smithson Tennant (1761–1815) of the United Kingdom. It has a density at 20° C. of 22·59 grammes per cubic centimetre or 1,410 lb. per cubic foot. A cubic foot of uranium would weigh 220 lb. less than a cubic foot of osmium. During the period 1955–70 iridium was thought by some inorganic chemists to be the densest metal but it has a density of 22·56.

elting and ling points *Lowest* Excluding mercury, which is liquid at normal temperatures, caesium (Cs), a silvery-white metal discovered in 1860 by Robert Wilhelm von Bunsen (1811–99) and Gustav Robert Kirchhoff (1824–87) of Germany, has the lowest metallic melting point at 28·5° C. (83·3° F.).

Excluding mercury which vaporizes at 356·66° C.), the metal which vaporizes at the lowest temperature and hence has the lowest boiling point is caesium with a figure of 669° C. (1236° F.).

Highest The highest melting point of any pure element is that of tungsten or wolfram (W), a grey metal discovered in 1783 by the Spanish brothers, Juan José d'Elhuyar and Fausto d'Elhuyar (1755–1833). It melts at 3417° C. ±10 deg. C.

The most refractory substances known are the tantalum carbide ($TaC_{0·88}$), a black solid, and the hafnium carbide ($HfC_{0·95}$), which melt at 4010° C. ±75 deg. C. and 3960° C. ±20 deg. C. respectively.

Expansion The highest normal linear thermal expansion of a metal is that of caesium which at 20° C., is $9·7 \times 10^{-5}$ of a cm. per cm. per one degree C. The trans-uranic metal plutonium will, however, expand and contract by as much as 8·9 per cent. of its volume when being heated to its melting point of 639·5° C. ±2 deg. C.

The lowest linear expansion is that of the alloy invar, containing 35 per cent. nickel, the remainder being iron, with one per cent. carbon and manganese. This has a linear thermal expansion of 9×10^{-7} of an inch per inch per one degree C. at ordinary temperatures. It was first prepared *c*. 1930 by Charles Edouard Guillaume (b. Switzerland 1861, d. 1938).

Highest ductility The most malleable, or ductile, of metals is gold. One ounce (avoirdupois) of gold can be drawn in the form of a continuous wire thread (diameter 2×10^{-4} of an inch) to a length of 43 miles. A cubic inch can be beaten into a leaf five-millionths of an inch thick, so as to cover nearly 1,400 square feet. It has been estimated that all the gold mined since A.D. 1500 could be stored in a vault with dimensions of $55 \times 55 \times 55$ feet.

Highest e strength The material with the highest known UTS (ultimate tensile strength) is sapphire whisker (Al_2O_3) at $6·2 \times 10^6$ lb. in.^{2}. This is equivalent to a whisker of the thickness of a human hair (an as yet unachieved 70 microns) which could support a weight of 621 lb.

Rarest The fourteen of the fifteen "rare earth" or "lanthanide" elements which have naturally-occurring isotopes (this includes lutetium) have now been separated into metallic purity exceeding 99·9%. The fifteenth member, the highly radioactive element promethium (Pm) has been produced artificially with a purity exceeding 99·8%. The radioactive elements 43 (technetium) and 61 (promethium) were chemically separated from pitchblende ore in 1961 and 1968 respectively. Because of their relatively short half-lives their existence in Nature is due entirely to the "spontaneous fission" radioactive decay of uranium.

The rarest naturally-occurring element is astatine (element 85) first produced artificially in 1940 and identified in Nature three years later. It has been calculated that only 0·3 of a gramme exists in the Earth's crust to a depth of 10 miles.

The isotope polonium 213 (Po 213) is, however, rarer by a factor of 5×10^5 which is equivalent to one atom in $3·5 \times 10^{37}$.

Several of the trans-uranium elements have been produced on an atom-to-atom basis so that at any one moment only single atoms of these elements may have existed.

Commonest Though ranking behind oxygen (46·60 per cent.) and silicon (27·72 per cent.) in abundance, aluminium is the commonest of all metals constituting 8·13 per cent. by weight of the Earth's crust.

Most magnetic and non-magnetic The most magnetic material, at ordinary temperatures, known is a cobalt-copper-samerium compound Co_3Cu_2Sm with a coercive force of 10,500 oersted. The most non-magnetic alloy yet discovered is 963 parts of copper to 37 parts of nickel.

Newest The newest trans-uranium element, number 105, was synthesised in the HILAC heavy-ion linear accelerator in the Lawrence Radiation Laboratory, University of California, Berkeley, California, U.S.A. by an American-Finnish team led by Dr. Albert Ghiorso. The element, for which the name "hahnium" has been proposed, was first produced on the 5th March 1970 with a mass of 260 and a half-life of 1·6 seconds. A previous claim to have produced the element in 1967–1968 in the Laboratory of Intra-Nuclear Reactions in the Joint Institute for Nuclear Research at Dubna, near Moscow, U.S.S.R. has now been withdrawn. A more definite, but still tentative, indentification of the element was achieved at Dubna during 1970.

Attempts initiated in November 1968 at Berkeley, California, U.S.A. to trace elements 110 (eka-platinum) to 114 (eka-lead) have so far proved to be unsuccessful. U.S.S.R. claims to have detected elements 108 and 114 in the Earth's crust have not been substantiated. Element 110 was apparently recorded by the Physics Department of Bristol University, England on emulsion plates sent aloft in a balloon 25 miles above Palestine, Texas, U.S.A. in September 1968, but the evidence must be regarded as being very tenuous. The heaviest isotope for which there is definite evidence is that of mass 261 of element 104 (rutherfordium or kurchatovium 261) synthesised in the Lawrence Radiation Laboratory in 1969.

Dr. Glenn Theodore Seaborg (b. 19 April 1912), Chairman of the United States Atomic Energy Commission, estimated in June 1966 that elements up to 126 would be produced by the year 2000.

Most expensive substance In October 1968 the U.S. Atomic Energy Commission announced that minuscule amounts of californium 252 (Element 98) were on sale at $100 for a tenth of a microgramme. A fanciful calculation would indicate that the price of an ingot weighing 1 lb. (if such were available) would at this rate have been £189,000 million or more than double the entire national wealth of the United Kingdom. It was announced in August 1970 that by using Am 243 and Cm 244, the price might be reduced to only $10 per microgramme.

Longest and shortest half-lives The half-life of a radio-active substance is the period taken for its activity to fall to half of its original value. The highest theoretical figure is $>2 \times 10^{18}$ years for bismuth 209, while the shortest is $2·4 \times 10^{-21}$ of a second for helium 5.

Purest The purest metal yet achieved is the grey-white metal germanium by the zone refining technique, first mooted in 1939 and published by William G. Pfann of Bell Laboratories, U.S.A. in 1952. By 1967 a purity of 99·99999999 per cent. had been achieved, which has been likened to one grain of salt in a freight car-load of sugar.

Hardest substances In February 1957 it was announced in the United States that, by dint of pressures of 65,000 atmospheres (426 tons per square inch) and temperatures of 1,700° C., a cubic form of boron nitride (BN) ("Borazon") had been produced which matched some diamonds for hardness, with a Mohs value of 10, or 7,000 on the Knoop K100 scale. Prof. Naoto Kawai of Osaka University, Japan announced in June 1967 the production by dint of a pressure of 150 tonnes/cm.^{2} (5,300,000 p.s.i.) of a single crystal of 1 part silica, 1 part magnesium and 4 parts oxygen which was "twice as hard as diamond".

Finest powder The finest powder produced is aluminium dust with an average diameter of 0·03 of a micron and a surface area of 75 square metres (807 square feet) per gramme. It was first marketed in the United States at $30 (then £10·70) per ounce in February 1959. Some particles measure only 0·005 of a micron.

SMELLIEST SUBSTANCE

The most pungent of the 17,000 smells so far classified is 4-hydroxy-3-methoxy benzaldehyde or vanillaldehyde. This can be detected in a concentration of 2×10^{-8} of a milligramme per litre of air. Thus $9{\cdot}7 \times 10^{-5}$ (about one ten-thousandth) of an ounce completely volatilized would still be detectable in an enclosed space with a floor the size of a full-sized football pitch (360 feet × 300 feet) and a roof 45 feet high. Only 2·94 ounces would be sufficient to permeate a cubic mile of the atmosphere. The most evil smelling substance must be a matter of opinion but ethyl mercaptan (C_2H_5SH) and butyl seleno-mercaptan (C_4H_9SeH), are powerful claimants, each with a smell reminiscent of a combination of rotting cabbage, garlic, onions and sewer gas.

Most expensive perfume The costliest perfume in the world is "Adoration", manufactured by Nina Omar of Puerto Real, Cadiz, Spain, and distributed in the United States at a retail price of $185 (£77) per half-ounce. Its most expensive ingredient is a very rare aromatic gum from Asia. The biggest and most expensive bottle of perfume sold is the one litre (1·76 pints) size of Chanel No. 5, from France. It retails in Great Britain at £120 per bottle.

Sweetest substance The sweetest naturally-occurring substance is exuded from the red serendipity berry (*Dioscoreophyllum cumminsii*) from Nigeria, which was announced in September 1967 to be 1,500 times as sweet as sucrose. The chemical 1-n-propoxy-2-amino-4-nitrobenzene was determined by Verkade in 1946 to be 5,600 times as sweet as 1 per cent. sucrose.

Bitterest substance The bitterest known substance is Bitrex, the proprietary name for benzyldiethyl (2:6-xylylcarbamoyl methyl) ammonium benzoate ($C_{28}H_{34}N_2O_3$), first reported from Macfarlan Smith Ltd. of Edinburgh, Scotland. This can be detected in solution at a concentration of one part in 20,000,000 and is thus about 200 times as bitter as quinine sulphate ($[C_{22}H_{24}N_2O_2]_2$, H_2SO_4, $2H_2O$).

Strongest acid The strength of acids and alkalis is measured on the pH scale. The pH of a solution is the logarithm to the base 10 of the reciprocal of the hydrogen-ion concentration in gramme ions per litre. The strongest simple acid is perchloric acid ($HClO_4$). Assessed on its power as a hydrogen-ion donor, the most powerful acid is a solution of antimony pentafluoride in fluosulphonic acid ($SbF_5 + FSO_3H$).

Strongest alkali The strength of alkalis is expressed by pH values rising above the neutral 7·0. The strongest bases are caustic soda or sodium hydroxide (NaOH), caustic potash or potassium hydroxide (KOH) and tetramethylammonium hydroxide ($N[CH_3]_4OH$), with pH values of 14 in normal solutions. True neutrality, pH 7, occurs in pure water at 22° C.

Most powerful fuel The greatest specific impulse of any rocket propulsion fuel combination is 435 lb. f. sec. per lb. produced by lithium fluoride and hydrogen. This compares with a figure of 300 for liquid oxygen and kerosene.

POISON

Quickest The barbiturate thiopentone, if given as a large intracardiac injection, will cause permanent cessation of respiration in one to two seconds.

Most potent Potentially the most poisonous substance yet discovered is the toxin of the bacterium *Pasteurella tularensis.* A *single* organism is believed to be able to institute tularemia variously called alkali disease, Francis disease or deerfly fever, though this is fatal in only 5 to 8 per cent. of cases.

The toxin of the bacterium *Clostridium botulinum* type A is in practice far more virulent. The normal lethal dose for a single adult male, by parenteral injection, would be about 0·12 of a microgramme. Hence 410 grammes (14·19 oz.) would suffice to eliminate the entire human population. *C. botulinum* is not easily disseminated and is not self-propagating. It prevents the release of acetylcholine, thus inducing a block to neuro-muscular transmission, which results in paralysis, asphyxia and death. The only major outbreak of botulism (first described in 1820) in Britain was that at Loch Maree, Ross and Cromarty, in August 1922, when eight persons died. Recent work suggests that a toxin from planktonic dinoflagellates producing "paralytic shellfish poisoning" is comparably lethal.

Historically, more deaths have resulted from the action of *Pasteurella pestis* than from any other organism. Some 140 strains have been identified but about 3,000 organisms are required to cause human fatality from bubonic plague (see Worst pandemic, Accidents and Disasters).

Most powerful nerve gas The nerve gas Sarin or GB (isopropylmethylphosphonofluoridate), a lethal colourless and odourless gas, has been developed since 1945 in the United States and is reputedly 30 times as toxic as phosgene ($COCl_2$) used in World War I. In the early 1950s substances known as V-agents, notably VX, 10 times more toxic than GB, were developed at the Chemical Defence Experimental Establishment, Porton Down, Wiltshire, which are lethal at 1 milligramme per man.

Most powerful drugs The most potent and, to an addict, the most expensive of all naturally-derived drugs is heroin, which is a chemically-processed form of opium from the juice of the unripe seed capsules of the white poppy (*Papaver somniferum*). An ounce, which suffices for up to 1,800 hypodermic shots or "fixes", may fetch up to $9,000 (£3,750) in the United States, or a 70,000 per cent. profit over the raw material price in Turkey. It has been estimated that an addict who has no income is impelled to steal $40,000's (£16,666) worth of goods per annum to keep him or herself in "fixes". The United States had 62,045 narcotics addicts recorded at 31 Dec. 1967, compared with the United Kingdom's 2,782 reported at the end of 1969. In 1969 the figure for New York City was believed to have surpassed the 1967 U.S. national total. The most potent analgesic drug is Etorphine or M-99, announced in June 1963 by Dr. Kenneth W. Bentley (b. 1925) and D. G. Hardy of Reckitt & Sons Ltd. of Hull, Yorkshire, with almost 10,000 times the potency of morphine.

2. DRINK

The strength of spirituous liquor is gauged by degrees proof. In the United Kingdom proof spirit is that mixture of ethyl alcohol (C_2H_5OH) and water which at 51° F. weighs 12/13ths of an equal measure of distilled water. Such spirit in fact contains 57·06 per cent. alcohol by volume, so that pure or absolute alcohol is 75·254° over proof (O.P.). A "hangover" is due to toxic congenerics such as amyl alcohol ($C_5H_{11}OH$).

alcoholic

The highest strength spirits which can be produced are raw rum and some Polish vodkas, up to 70° over proof or 97 per cent. alcohol. Royal Navy rum was 40° over proof (79·884 per cent. alcohol) before 1948, but was reduced to 4·5° under proof (U.P.) before its abolition after 278 years (introduced in 1692) on 31 July 1970. The strongest drink sold commercially is Polish White Spirit, produced by the State Spirits Monopoly of Poland. This is 40° O.P. The most powerful aquavit marketed is the Norwegian Vinmonopolet's "Brennevin 60 per cent.", having 60 per cent. alcohol by volume (5° O.P.).

BEER

Strongest

The world's strongest beer is draught Thomas Hardy ale brewed by Dorchester Brewery with 10·15 per cent. alcohol by weight and 12·58 per cent. by volume. The strongest regularly brewed nationally distributed beer in Britain is Gold Label Barley Wine brewed by Tennant Bros. of Sheffield, a subsidiary of Whitbread & Co. Ltd. It has an alcoholic content of 8·6 per cent. by weight and 10·6 per cent. by volume.

Weakest

The weakest liquid ever marketed as beer was a sweet ersatz beer which was brewed in Germany by Sunner, Colne-Kalk, in 1918. It had an original gravity of 1,000·96° and a strength 1/30th that of the weakest beer now obtainable in the United Kingdom.

Most xpensive

The most expensive beer marketed in the United Kingdom is the German lager Löwenbräu. It is brewed and bottled in Munich and is sold at a price which varies from 22½p to 40p per bottle (11·6 fluid oz.), according to the type of bar.

WINE

Most pensive

The most expensive purchaseable wine and the greatest oenological rarity is the Red Bordeaux *Château Lafite Rothschild* of 1806, which has appeared on wine lists at 750 francs (£61) per bottle. A bottle "sacrificed" in 1959 proved eminently drinkable but, not surprisingly, had lost its bouquet. On 16 Jan. 1965 a Jeroboam (equivalent to 8 wine bottles) of *Château Lafite Rothschild* 1925 was sold in Bordeaux, France for £850 (11,300 francs). A bottle of Tokay essence of the 'Comet' vintage of 1811, bottled *c.* 1840 for the now extinct princely family of Bretzenheim and imported into Britain in 1925 was auctioned for £220 at Christie's, London on 26 June 1969. It had been walled in during the Hungarian Revolution of 1849.

The highest priced wine on any general list is the German Wehlener Sonnenuhr *Trockenbeerauslese,* sold by O. W. Loeb at £25 from November 1970. Only 60 bottles were offered.

Most pensive iqueurs

The most expensive liqueur in France is the orange-flavoured *Le Grand Marnier Coronation.* Owing to excise duties, *Elixir Végétale de la Grande Chartreuse* which is 24 degrees O.P. is sold only by special order in miniature bottles of 2·8 fluid oz. at 90p per bottle in the United Kingdom. This liqueur has been produced since 1757 by Carthusian monks from a recipe of 1605, which reputedly contains 130 herbs including *Arnica montana.*

Ancient *Chartreuse* (before 1903) has been known to fetch more than £15 per litre bottle. An 1878 bottle was sold in 1954 for this price.

Most expensive spirits

The most expensive spirit is *Grande Fine Champagne Arbellot* 1749 brandy, retailed at Fauchon, Paris, at 667 francs (£55) per bottle. *Courvoisier Grande Fine Champagne Cognac* retails in Britain for £7·70 a bottle. Five bottles of 1811 *Cognac de Marnier* Napoleon brandy were offered for £1,000 each by A. E. Norman of Pinner, Greater London, on 19 Dec. 1962. In 1968 one was left, at a revised £1,000 5s. 4d. (owing to the increase in spirit duty), in the ownership of Mrs. Norman but withdrawn from offer.

Largest bottles

The largest bottle normally used in the wine and spirit trade is the Jeroboam or double magnum, with a capacity of up to 4 litres (7·04 pints), which is used only for liqueur brandy and champagne. A complete set of Monopole champagne bottles from the ¼ bottle, through the ½ bottle, bottle, magnum, Jeroboam, Rehoboam, Methuselah, Salmanezer and Balthazar, to the Nebuchadnezzar, which has a capacity of 16 litres (28·16 pints), is owned by Miss Denise Joan Wardle of Cleveleys, near Blackpool, Lancashire. In May 1958 a 5-foot-tall sherry bottle with a capacity of 20½ Imperial gallons was blown in Stoke-on-Trent, Staffordshire. This bottle, with the capacity of 131 normal bottles, was named an "Adelaide".

Smallest bottles

The smallest and meanest bottles of liquor sold are the Thistle bottles of Scotch whisky marketed by The Cumbrae Supply Co. of Glasgow. They contain 24 minims or $\frac{1}{20}$ of a fluid ounce and retail for 10p.

Champagne cork flight

The longest distance for a champagne cork to fly from an untreated and unheated bottle 4 feet from level ground is 49 feet 10½ inches popped by Leslie Ironside of Kirkintilloch, Scotland on 24 July 1970.

3. GEMS

Most precious

From 1955 the value of rubies rose, due to a drying up in supplies from Ceylon and Burma. A flawless natural stone of good colour was carat for carat more valuable than emerald, diamond or sapphire and, in some cases have attained a price of £4,000 per carat. The ability to produce very large corundum crystals in the laboratory must now have a bearing on the gem market.

Largest

The largest recorded stone of gem quality was a 520,000 carat (2 cwt. 5 lb.) aquamarine ($Al_2Be_3[Si_6O_{18}]$) found near Marambaia, Brazil, in 1910. It yielded over 200,000 carats of gem quality stones.

Rarest

Only two stones are known of the pale mauve gem Taaffeite ($Be_4Mg_4Al_{16}O_{32}$), first discovered in a cut state in Dublin, Ireland, in November 1945. The larger of the two examples is 0·84 of a carat. There are minerals of which only single examples are known.

Hardest

The hardest of all gems, and the hardest known naturally-occurring substance, is diamond, which is,

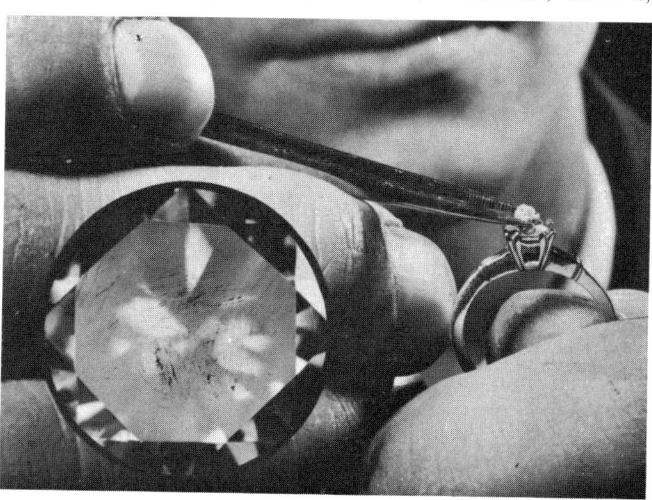

Evidence that boron is harder than diamond—a U.S. scientist here seen scratching a girl's best friend

chemically, pure carbon. Diamond is 90 times as hard as the next hardest mineral, corundum (Al_2O_3), and those from Borneo, in Indonesia, and New South Wales, Australia, have a particular reputation for hardness. Hardnesses are compared on Mohs' scale, on which talc is 1, a finger-nail is $2\frac{1}{2}$, window glass 5, topaz 8, corundum 9 and diamond 10. Diamonds average 7,000 on the Knoop scale, with a peak value of 8,400. This index represents a micro-indentation index based on Kilogrammes per one hundredth of a square millimetre $(kg/(mm^2)^{-2})$.

Densest The densest of all gem minerals is cassiterite or tinstone (SnO_2), a colourless to yellow stone found in Australia, Bolivia, West Malaysia (formerly called Malaya), Mexico and in Cornwall, England. It has a specific gravity of 6·90, rising to 7·1 in opaque form.

Diamonds The largest diamond ever discovered was a stone of 3,106 metric carats (over $1\frac{1}{4}$ lb.) found by Captain M. F. Wells in the Premier Mine, Pretoria, South Africa, on 26 Jan. 1905. It was named after Mr. (later Sir) Thomas Major Cullinan, D.S.O. (1862–1936), discoverer of the mine in 1902 and chairman of the mining company. It was purchased by the Transvaal government in 1907 and presented to King Edward VII. The Star of Africa No. 1 in the Royal Sceptre, cut from it by Jak Asscher in Amsterdam in 1908, is the largest cut diamond in the world with 74 facets and a weight of 530·2 metric carats.

The world's largest cut diamond—the 530·2 carat Star of Africa No. 1 in the British Royal Sceptre

The rarest coloured diamonds are blue and pink. The largest known are the 44·4 carat vivid blue Hope diamond, probably part of a $112\frac{1}{2}$ carat stone found in the Killur mines, Golconda, India, and purchased in 1642 by Jean Baptiste Tavernier (1605–89); and a 24 carat pink diamond, worth an estimated £450,000, presented to the Queen in 1947 by Dr. John Thoburn Williamson (1907–58), a Canadian geologist. In November 1958 the Hope diamond was presented to the Smithsonian Institution, Washington, D.C., U.S.A., by Mr. Harry Winston, a jeweller, who had paid a sum variously reported between $700,000 (£289,583) and $1,500,000 (£625,000).

The highest priced diamond—the 69·42-carat Cartier stone bought for Elizabeth Taylor by her husband Richard Burton for a reported £500,000

Highest auction price The auction record for any diamond piece is $1,050,00 (£437,500) paid by Cartier, Inc. of Fifth Avenue, New York City at Parke-Bernet Galleries on 23 Oct. 196 for a single flawless 69·42 carat stone set in a platinum ring from the estate of Mrs. Florence Gould Sturgeon. It was acquired one day later by Richard Burton by private treaty for a reported $1,200,000 (£500,000) for his wife Elizabeth Taylor.

Emeralds Emerald is green beryl. Hexagonal prisms measurin up to $15\frac{3}{4}$ inches long and $9\frac{3}{4}$ inches in diameter, an weighing up to 125 lb., have been recorded from th Ural mines in the U.S.S.R. An 11,000 carat emeral was reported to have been found by Charles Kempt an J. Botes at Letaba, northern Transvaal, South Africa on 16 Oct. 1956. The largest cut green beryl crystal is th Austrian Government's 2,680 carat unguent jar carve by Dionysio Miseroni in the 17th century. Of ger quality emeralds, the largest known is the Devonshir stone of 1,350 carats from Muso, Colombia.

Sapphires Sapphire is blue corundum (Al_2O_3). The largest cut ge sapphire in existence is the "Black Star Sapphire o Queensland", weighing 1,444 carats, carved in 1953–5 from a rough stone of 2,097 carats. It is in the form of bust of General Dwight David Eisenhower (1890–1969 formerly President of the United States. A carved da blue sapphire of the head of President Abraham Linco (1809–65), weighing 1,318 carats, is also in the custod of the Kazanjian Foundation of Los Angeles, Californi U.S.A. It was cut in 1949–51 from a 2,302-carat sto also found at Anakie, Queensland, Australia, in *c.* 193

Rubies Ruby is red corundum (Al_2O_3) with chromic oxi impurities. The largest natural gem stone known was 1,184 carat stone of Burmese origin. In July 1961 broken red corundum of an original 3,421 carats w reported to have been found in the United States. T largest piece weighed about 750 carats. Laborator made ruby prisms for laser technology reach ov 12 inches in length.

Pearl Pearls are protective secretionary bodies produced bivalved molluscs. Gem pearls come chiefly from t western Pacific genus *Pinctada* and the fresh wat mussel genus *Quadrula*. The largest known natural pe is the "Pearl of Lao-tze", also called the Pearl of Alla measuring $9\frac{1}{2}$ inches long and $5\frac{1}{2}$ inches in diameter, a weighing 14 lb. 1 oz. It was discovered in the shell o giant clam (*Tridacna gigas*), the largest of all bivalves Palawan, Philippines on 7 May 1934. Since 1936 t pearl has been owned by Wilburn Dowell Cobb San Francisco, U.S.A. It was valued at $3,500,0 (now £1,458,333) in 1939.

Opal The largest known opal is a yellow-orange one of 2 troy oz. unearthed by a bulldozer at Anda Moo South Australia, in January 1970, and valued $A168,000 (£78,113). The largest gem opal is the 17,7 carat "Olympic Australis" found at Coober Pe South Australia in August 1956.

Crystal The largest crystal ball is the Warner sphere of $106\frac{3}{4}$ and $12\frac{7}{8}$ inches diameter ground from a 1,000 lb. pi

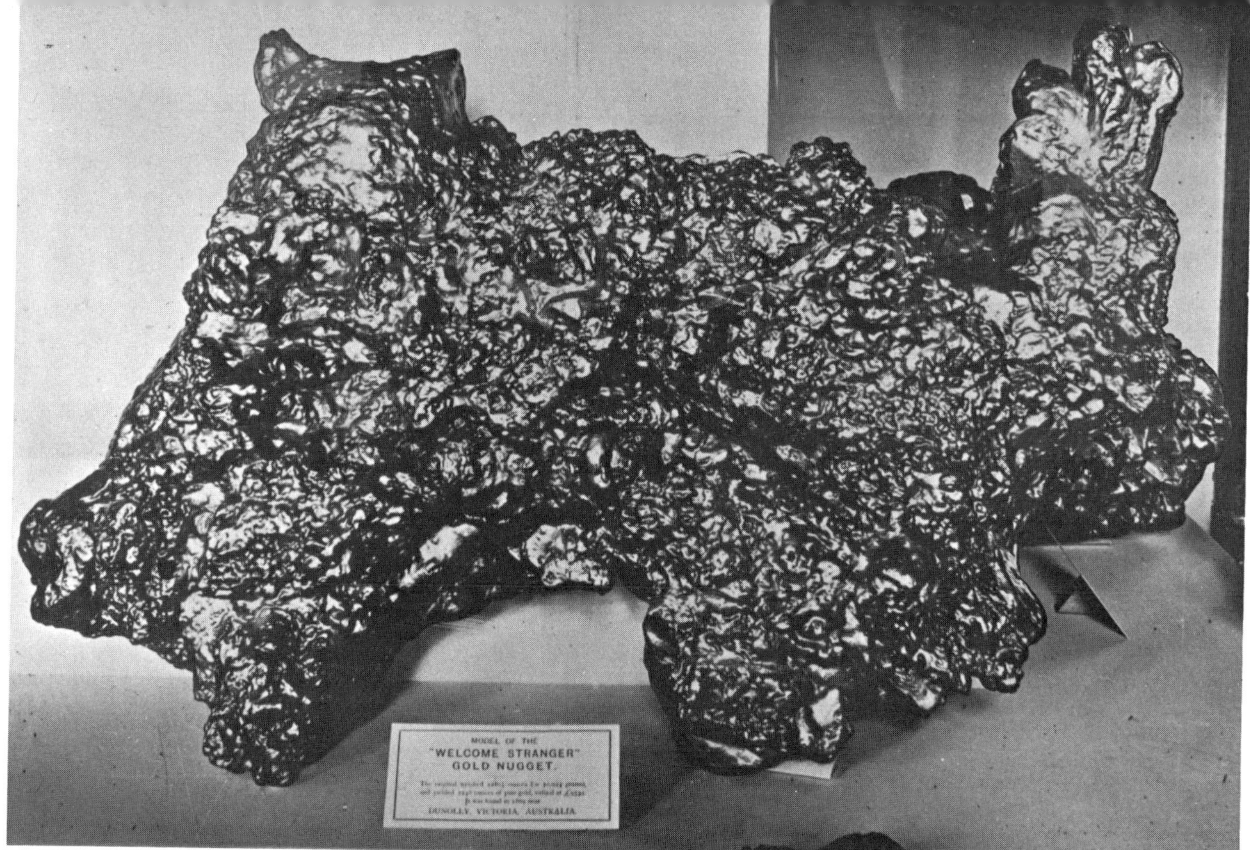

odel of the gest nugget of gold ever picked up e Welcome Stranger"

of Burmese quartz and now in the U.S. National Museum in Washington, D.C. A single rock crystal weighing 1,728 lb. was placed in the Ural Geological Museum in Sverdlovsk, U.S.S.R. in November 1968. A piezo-quartz crystal weighing 70 tons was reported to have been found in Kazakhstan, U.S.S.R., in September 1958.

Topaz The largest known topaz is a low quality transparent crystal weighing 596 lb., from a pegmatite in the province of Minas Gerais, Brazil. Since 1951 it has been on exhibition in the American Museum of Natural History, New York City, N.Y., U.S.A. The Museum also has a gem topaz of 7,725 carats.

NUGGETS

Gold The largest lump of reef gold ever found *in situ* was the Holtermann Nugget, weighing 7,560 oz. (472½ lb.), taken from the Beyers & Holtermann Star of Hope Gold Mining Co., Hill End, New South Wales, Australia, on 19 Oct. 1872. It was interlaced with quartz and had a total weight of 10,080 oz. (630 lb.). A nugget weighing 2,280¼ troy oz., named the "Welcome Stranger", was picked up in 1869 at Tarnagulla, near Moliagul, in Victoria, Australia. It yielded 2,248 oz. of pure gold.

Silver The largest silver nugget ever recorded was one of 2,750 lb. troy (2,263 lb. avoirdupois), found in Sonora, Mexico, and appropriated by the Spanish Government before 1821.

gest slab marble The largest piece of used marble in the world is the coping stone of the Tomb of the Unknown Soldier in Arlington National Cemetery, Arlington, Virginia, U.S.A. It weighs more than 45 tons and was cut from a 90-ton slab taken from a quarry at Yule, Colorado, U.S.A.

Amber The largest piece of amber ever reported was a piece weighing 33 lb. 10 oz. reputedly from Burma, bought by John Charles Bowring (1801–1893) in 1860 from a dealer in Canton, China for £300. It was placed in the Natural History Museum, London in 1940.

Jade The largest piece of gem quality jade recorded is a four-ton boulder of dark green chrome jade found in Noel Creek, British Columbia, Canada by Harry Street in September 1969 and worth $50,000. Local prospectors have taken to tiling their bathrooms with jade. Jade exists from dead white to jet black and from bright blue to blood red.

4. TELESCOPES

Earliest Although there is evidence that early Arabian scientists understood something of the magnifying power of lenses, their first use to form a telescope has been attributed to Roger Bacon (*c.* 1214–92) in England. The prototype of modern refracting telescopes was that completed by Johannes Lippershey for the Dutch government on 2 Oct. 1608.

Largest *Refractor* The largest refracting (*i.e.* magnification by lenses) telescope in the world is the 62-foot-long 40-inch telescope completed in 1897 at the Yerkes Observatory, Williams Bay, Wisconsin, and belonging to the University of Chicago, Illinois, U.S.A. The largest in the British Isles is the 28-inch at the Royal Greenwich Observatory completed in 1894.

Reflector World The largest operational telescope in the world is the 6 metre (236·2 inch) telescope sited near Zelenchukskaya in the Caucasus Mountains, U.S.S.R., at an altitude of 6,830 feet. The mirror, weighing 70 tons, was completed in November 1967 and assembled by October 1970. The overall weight of the 80-foot long assembly is 850 tons. Being the most powerful of all telescopes its range, which includes the location of objects down to the 25th magnitude, represents the limits of the observable Universe. Its light-gathering power would enable it to detect the light from a candle at a distance of 15,000 miles.

United Kingdom The largest reflector in the British Isles is the Isaac Newton 98·2-inch reflector at the Royal Greenwich Observatory, Herstmonceux Castle, Sussex. It was built in Newcastle upon Tyne, Northumberland, weighs 92 tons, cost £641,000 and was inaugurated on 1 Dec. 1967.

Radio *Earliest* The world's first fully steerable radio telescope is the Mark I telescope at the University of Manchester Department of Radio Astronomy, Nuffield Radio Astronomy Laboratories, Jodrell Bank, Macclesfield, Cheshire, on which work began in September 1952. The 750-ton 250-foot diameter bowl of steel plates and 180-foot-high supports weigh 2,000 tons. Its cost is believed to have been about £750,000 when it was completed in 1957. The Manchester University Mark V radio telescope at Meifod, Montgomeryshire will have a diameter of 400 feet and is due for completion at a cost of some £5 million in 1975.

Largest steerable dish The world's largest trainable dish-type radio telescope is the $850,000 (£354,165) installation completed for the United States National Radio Astronomy Observatory at Green Bank, West Virginia, U.S.A., in 1962. It has a diameter of 300 feet. Work started in November 1967 on the £2·35 million, 3,000-ton 328-foot diameter double-swivelling steerable dish for the Max Planck Institute for Radio Astronomy of Bonn in the Effelsberger Valley, West Germany.

Largest dish The world's largest dish radio telescope is the non-steerable ionospheric assembly built over a natural bowl at Arecibo, Puerto Rico, completed in November 1963 at a cost of about $9,000,000 (£3·75 million). It has a diameter of 1,000 feet and the dish covers 18½ acres. Its sensitivity could be raised by a factor of 2,000 by the fitting of new aluminium plates at a cost of $4·5 million (£1,875,000).

Largest World The most extensive radio telescope in the world is the C.S.I.R.O. (Commonwealth Scientific and Industrial Research Organization) radio-heliograph installation, completed in September 1967, at Culgoora, N.S.W., Australia where 96 receivers are on the 6-mile long circumference of a circle covering 1,833 acres. Plans for an assembly of 8 130-foot diameter movable dishes on a T-track measuring 3,000 yards across and 5,333 yards down were announced by the California Institute of Technology in August 1967. The $16,700,000 (£6,958,333) assembly will be erected in Owens Valley, California, U.S.A.

The British Science Research Council 5 kilometre radio telescope at Lord's Bridge, Cambridgeshire and Isle of Ely to be operated by the Mullard Radio Astronomy Observatory of Cambridge University will utilize 8 mobile 42-foot rail-borne computer-controlled dish aerials, which will be equivalent to a single steerable dish 5 kilometres in diameter. The project, to be operational before the end of 1973, will cost more than £2,100,000.

Solar The world's largest solar telescope is the 480-foot-long McMath telescope at Kitt Peak National Observatory near Tucson, Arizona, U.S.A. It has a focal length of 300 feet and an 80-inch heliostat mirror. It was completed in 1962 and produces an image measuring 33 inches in diameter.

Observatory *Highest* The highest altitude observatory in the world is the Mauna Kea Observatory, Hawaii at an altitude of 13,824 feet, opened in 1969. The principal instrument is an 88-inch (224 cm.) telescope.

Oldest The earliest astronomical observatory in the world is the Chomsong-dae built in A.D. 632 in Kyongju, South Korea and still extant.

Planetaria *World* The ancestor of the planetarium is the rotatable Gottorp Globe, built by Andreas Busch in Denmark between 1654 and 1664 to the orders of Duke Frederick III of Holstein's court mathematician Olearius. It is 34·6 feet in circumference, weighs nearly 3½ tons and is now preserved in Leningrad, U.S.S.R. The stars were painted on the inside. The earliest optical installation was not until 1923 in the Deutsches Museum, Munich, by Zeiss of Jena, Germany. The world's largest planetarium, with a diameter of 85 feet, is now being completed, at a cost of $1,500,000 (£625,000), on Dangerfield Island, on the Potomac, Washington, D.C., U.S.A.

United Kingdom The United Kingdom's first planetarium was opened at Madame Tussaud's, Marylebone Road, London, on 19 March 1958. Accurate images of 8,900 stars are able to be projected on the 70-foot high copper dome.

5. PHOTOGRAPHY

It is estimated that the total expenditure on photography in the United States in 1969 was $3,976,718,000 (£1,657 million) and that 69,120,000 still cameras and 7,800,000 cine cameras were in use. In the United Kingdom the expenditure on amateur photography in 1969 was £95,000,000.

CAMERAS

Earliest The earliest photograph was taken in the summer of 1826 by Joseph Nicéphore Niépce (1765–1833), a French physician and scientist. It showed the courtyard of his country house at Gras, near St. Loup-de-Varennes. It probably took eight hours to expose and was taken on a bitumen-coated polished pewter plate measuring 8 inches by 6½ inches. The earliest photograph taken in England was one of a diamond-paned window in Laycock (or Lacock) Abbey, Wiltshire, taken in 1835 by William Henry Fox Talbot (1800–1877), the inventor of the negative-positive process. This was bought by the Johannesburg City Council for £480 in November 1970. The world's earliest aerial photograph was taken in 1858 by Gaspard Félix Tournachon (1820–1910), *alias* Nadar, from a balloon near Villacoublay, on the outskirts of Paris, France.

The earliest photograph ever taken in England—the latticed window at Laycock Abbey, Wilts. taken in August 1835

Largest The largest camera ever built was the Anderson Mammoth camera, built in Chicago, Illinois, U.S.A. in 1900. When extended, it measured 9 feet high, 6 feet wide and 20 feet long. Its two lenses were a wide-angle Zeiss with a focal length of 68 inches and a telescope Rapid Rectilinear of 120 inches focal length. Exposures averaged 150 seconds and 15 men were required to work it.

Smallest Apart from cameras built for intra-cardiac surgery and espionage, the smallest camera generally marketed is the Japanese Kiku 16 Model II, which measures 2⅜ inches × 1 inch × ⅝ of an inch.

Fastest A paper on a camera of highly limited application with a time resolution of $1{\cdot}0 \times 10^{-11}$ of a second has been published by Butslov *et al.* of the U.S.S.R. Academy of Sciences. In June 1969 a camera from the U.S.S.R. was demonstrated at the N.P.L., Teddington, London with "events" moving across image tubes at 167 million m.p.h. or one quarter of the speed of light. Britain's fastest camera is the E.12 image tube camera announced by the Optical Group of the Atomic Weapons Research Establishment at Aldermaston, Berkshire in January 1966, with a rate of 60,000,000 exposures per second. The camera is marketed under the title of TE.12 by Telford Products Ltd., of Greenford, Middlesex, and Imacon by John Hadland (P.I.) Ltd., of Bovingdon, Hertfordshire.

Most expensive The most expensive amateur roll-film camera is the Rolleiflex SL.66 made by Franke und Heidecke

The world's largest camera built in 1900 in Chicago which required a crew of 15 to work it

Brunswick, West Germany, with an 80 mm. F/2·8 Planar lens, which retailed for £661 in 1969.

The most expensive miniature camera is the Zeiss Contarex, Pentaprism, Reflex with a built-in photoelectric meter and Zeiss Planar f/1·4 55 mm. lens. With a range of accessories, including two wide-angle and three telephoto lenses, this would cost £1,623·14.

Largest print The largest photographic print ever produced was an enlargement of a hand-drawn map of Europe, measuring over 4,000 square feet, made for the British Broadcasting Corporation by the Newbold Wells Organisation Limited of London. In 1964 this company produced the largest colour transparency, a hand-coloured transparency of the London sky-line, measuring 212 feet long by 12½ feet high, for the Vickers stand at the Sydney Exhibition in Australia.

Highest photograph The greatest height from which a man has taken a photograph is 248,400 miles by the crew of Apollo X on 22 May 1969 on the far side of the moon. (See Progressive Human Altitude table.)

X-ray *Largest* The largest X-ray ever made was of a 17-foot long Mercedes 280 SL car using Agfa-Gevaert Structurix D4 film and a 50-hour exposure in September 1959.

6. NUMEROLOGY

In dealing with large numbers, scientists use the notation of 10 raised to various powers to eliminate a profusion of noughts. For example, 19,160,000,000,000 miles would be written $1{\cdot}916 \times 10^{13}$ miles. Similarly, a very small number, for example 0·0000154324 of a grain, would be written $1{\cdot}5432 \times 10^{-5}$ of a grain. Of the prefixes used before numbers the smallest is "atto-" from the Danish *atten* for 18, indicating a trillionth part (10^{-18}) of the unit, and the highest is "tera-" (Greek, *teras*=monster), indicating a billion (10^{12}) fold.

NUMBERS

Highest The highest generally accepted named number is the centillion, which is 10 raised to the power 600, or one followed by 600 noughts. Higher numbers are named in linguistic literature the most extreme of which is the milli-millimillillion (10 raised to the power 6,000,000,000) devised by Rudolf Ondrejka. The number Megiston written with symbol ⑩ is a number too great to have any physical meaning. The highest named number outside the decimal notation is the Buddhist *asankhyeya*, which is equal to 10^{140} or 100 tertio-vigintillions (British system) or 100 quinto-quadragintillions (U.S. system).

The number 10^{100} (10,000 sexdecillion) is designated a Googol. This was invented by Dr. Edward Kasner (U.S.) (d. 1955). Ten raised to the power of a Googol is described as a Googolplex. Some conception of the magnitude of such numbers can be gained when it is said that the number of atoms in the observable Universe probably does not exceed 10^{85}. However, it has been said that the theoretical number of patterns of nucleotides (adenine, thymine, guanine and cytosine) in the massive deoxyribonucleic acid (D.N.A.) molecule is 10^{12000}.

The largest number to have become sufficiently well-known in mathematics to have been named after its begetter is the larger of the two Skewes numbers which is 10 to the power 10 to the power 10 to the power 10 to the power 3, obtained by Prof. Stanley Skewes, M.A., Ph.D., now of Cape Town University, South Africa, and published in two papers of 1933 and 1955 concerning the occurrence of prime numbers.

Prime numbers A prime number is any positive integer (excluding 1) having no integral factors other than itself and unity, *e.g.* 2, 3, 5, 7 or 11. The lowest prime number is thus 2. The highest known prime number is $2^{11213}-1$, discovered on 2 June 1963 by Prof. Donald B. Gillies, using the ILLIAC II computer at the University of Illinois, Urbana, Illinois, U.S.A. This number contains 3,376 digits.

Perfect numbers A number is said to be perfect if it is equal to the sum of its divisors other than itself, *e.g.* 1+2+4+7+14=28. The lowest perfect number is 6 (1+2+3). The highest known, and the 23rd so far discovered, is $2^{11212} \times (2^{11213}-1)$, with 6,751 digits.

Most primitive The lowest limit in enumeration among primitive peoples is among the Yancos, an Amazon tribe who cannot count beyond *poettarrarorincoaroac,* which is their word for "three". The Temiar people of West Malaysia (formerly called Malaya) also stop at three. Investigators have reported that the number "four" is expressed by a look of total stupefaction indistinguishable from that for any other number higher than three. It is said that among survivors of the Aimores, naked nomads of Eastern Brazil, there is no apparent word for "two".

Most accurate version of "pi" The greatest number of decimal places to which *pi* (π) has been calculated is 100,265 by Daniel Shanks and John W. Wrench, Jr., on an IBM 7090 machine in the IBM Data Processing Center, New York City, N.Y., U.S.A., on 29 July 1961. The calculation took 8 hours 43 minutes and the check 4 hours 22 minutes. It was estimated that the same calculation would take 30,000 years for a mathematician with a 10-place electric desk computer. The published value to 100,000 places was 3·141592653589793 . . . (omitting the next 99,975 places) . . . 5493624646.

Earliest measures The earliest known measure of weight is the *beqa* of the Amratian period of Egyptian civilization *c.* 3,800 B.C. found at Naqada, United Arab Republic. The weights are cylindrical with rounded ends from 188·7 to 211·2 grammes and are the basis of the English troy ounce. The unit of length used by the megalithic tomb-builders in Britain *c.* 2300 B.C. appears to have been 2·72±0·003 feet.

TIME MEASURE

Longest The longest measure of time is the *kalpa* in Hindu chronology. It is equivalent to 4,320 million years. In astronomy a cosmic year is the period of rotation of the Milky Way galaxy at the Sun's distance from the centre, *i.e.* about 225,000,000 years. In the Late Cretaceous Period of *c.* 85 million years ago the Earth rotated faster so resulting in 370·3 days per year.

Shortest Owing to variations in the length of a day, which is estimated to be increasing irregularly at the average rate of about two milliseconds per century due to the Moon's tidal drag, the second has been redefined. Instead of being 1/86,400th part of a mean solar day, it has, since 1960, been reckoned as 1/31,556,925·9747th part of the solar (or tropical) year at A.D. 1900, January 0 at 12 hours, Ephemeris time. In 1958 the second of Ephemeris time was computed to be equivalent to 9,192,631,770±20 cycles of the radiation corresponding to the transition of a caesium 133 atom when unperturbed by exterior fields. In a nano-second ($1{\cdot}0 \times 10^{-9}$ of a second) light travels 11·7 inches.

SMALLEST UNITS

The shortest unit of length is the atto-metre which is $1{\cdot}0 \times 10^{-16}$ of a centimetre. The smallest unit of area is a "shed", used in sub-atomic physics and first mentioned in 1956. It is $1{\cdot}0 \times 10^{-48}$ of a square centimetre. A "barn" is equal to 10^{24} "sheds". The reaction of a neutrino occurs over the area of 1×10^{-41} of a square millimetre.

7. PHYSICAL EXTREMES

TEMPERATURES

Highest The highest man-made temperatures yet attained are those produced in the centre of a thermonuclear fusion bomb, which are of the order of 300,000,000 to 400,000,000° C. Of controllable temperatures, the highest effective laboratory figure reported is 50,000,000° C. for 2/100ths of a second by Prof. Lev A. Artsimovich at Tokamuk in the U.S.S.R. in 1969. At very low particle densities even higher figures are obtainable. In 1963 a figure of 3,000 million °C. was reportedly achieved in the U.S.S.R. with Ogra injection-mirror equipment.

Lowest The lowest temperature reached is 1×10^{-6} K, achieved by Dr. Nicholas Kurti (b. 1908) at the Clarendon Laboratory, Oxford, in 1959. This temperature was also achieved in the Mullard Cryomagnetic Laboratory, Oxford, in June 1965. Absolute temperatures are defined in terms of ratios and not of differences, so that the temperature of melting ice (273·16° K, 0° C. or 32° F.) is said to be $3{\cdot}7 \times 10^{9}$ times as high as the lowest temperature ever attained. Absolute zero approximates to −273·16° C. or −459·69° F.

Highest pressures The highest sustained laboratory pressures yet reported are of 5,000,000 atmospheres (32,800 tons per square inch), achieved in the U.S.S.R. and announced in October 1958. Using dynamic methods and impact speeds of up to 18,000 m.p.h., momentary pressures of 75,000,000 atmospheres (490,000 tons per square inch) were reported from the United States in 1958.

Greatest tensile strength The highest tensile strength value reported is one of 3,500,000 lb. per sq. inch (lbf/in^2 or p.s.i.) by Anderegg for a very small glass fibre tested *in vacuo* at −200° C. In February 1967 a load of 3,270,000 p.s.i. was achieved on a thread of tungsten at Kharkov, U.S.S.R. Theoretical considerations indicate that amorphous boron has a maximum cohesive strength of 3,900,000 p.s.i. A boron wire 189·4 miles long could theoretically be suspended without parting.

Highest vacuum The highest (or 'hardest') vacuums obtained in scientific research are of the order of $1{\cdot}0 \times 10^{-16}$ of an atmosphere. This compares with an estimated pressure in inter-stellar space of $1{\cdot}0 \times 10^{-19}$ of an atmosphere. At sea-level there are 3×10^{19} molecules per cubic centimetre in the atmosphere, but in inter-stellar space there are probably less than 10 per cubic centimetre.

Fastest centrifuge The highest man-made rotary speed ever achieved is 1,500,000 revolutions per second, or 90,000,000 revolutions per minute, on a steel rotor with a diameter of about 1/100th of an inch suspended in a vacuum in an ultra-centrifuge installed in March 1961 in the Rouss Physical Laboratory at the University of Virginia in Charlottesville, Virginia, U.S.A. This work is led by Prof. Jesse W. Beams. The edge of the rotor is travelling at 2,500 m.p.h. and is subject to a stress of 1,000,000,000 g.

Most powerful microscopes Electron microscopes have now reached the point at which individual atoms are distinguishable. In March 1958 the U.S.S.R. announced an electronic point projector with a magnification approaching ×2,000,000, in which individual atoms of barium and molecules of oxygen can be observed. In 1970 a resolution of 0·88 of an Ångström unit diameter was achieved by Dr. K. Yada (Japan) using a Hitachi instrument. In February 1969 it was announced from Pennsylvania State University, U.S.A., that the combination of the field ion microscope invented by their Prof. Erwin W. Müller in 1956 and a spectrometer enabled single atoms to be identified.

Electron microscope The most powerful electron microscope in the world is the 3,500 kV installation at the National Scientific Research Centre, Toulouse, France which reached testing stage in October 1969. The high voltage generator and accelerator fill a cylinder 15 feet in diameter and 30 feet high. Its six lenses form a column 3 feet by 11 feet and weigh 20 tons.

Highest note The highest note yet attained is one of 60,000 megahertz (MHz) (60,000 million vibrations per second), generated by a "laser" beam striking a sapphire crystal at the Massachusetts Institute of Technology in Cambridge, Massachusetts, U.S.A., in September 1964. This is 1,000,000 times as high in pitch as the upper limit of human audibility.

oudest noise The loudest noise created in a laboratory is 210 decibels or 400,000 acoustic watts reported by N.A.S.A. from Huntsville, Alabama, U.S.A. in October 1965. Holes can be bored in solid material by this means.

uietest place The "dead room", measuring 35 feet by 28 feet, in the Bell Telephone System laboratory at Murray Hill, New Jersey, U.S.A., is the most anechoic room in the world, eliminating 99·98 per cent. of reflected sound.

nest balance The most accurate balance in the world is the Q01 quartz fibre decimicro balance made by L. Oertling Ltd. of Orpington, Kent, England which has a read-out scale on which one division corresponds to 0·0001 of a milligramme. It can weigh to an accuracy of 0·0002 of a milligramme which is equivalent to little more than one third of the weight of ink on this full stop.

Lowest viscosity The California Institute of Technology, U.S.A. announced on 1 Dec. 1957 that there was no measurable viscosity, *i.e.* perfect flow, in liquid helium II, which exists only at temperatures close to absolute zero (−273·15° C. or −459·67° F.).

west friction The lowest coefficient of static and dynamic friction of any solid is 0·02, in the case of polytetrafluoroethylene ($[C_2F_4]_n$), called P.T.F.E.—equivalent to wet ice on wet ice. It was first manufactured in quantity by E. I. du Pont de Nemours & Co. Inc. in 1943, and is marketed from the U.S.A. as Teflon. In the United Kingdom it is marketed by I.C.I. as Fluon.

At the University of Virginia (see above, Fastest centrifuge) a 30 lb. rotor magnetically supported has been spun at 1,000 revolutions per second in a vacuum of 10^{-6} mm. of mercury pressure. It loses only one revolution per second per day, thus spinning for years.

st powerful adhesive The most powerful adhesive known is epoxy resin, which, after being supercooled to −450° F., can withstand a shearing pull of 8,000 lb. per square inch.

Most powerful electric current The most powerful electric current generated is that from the Zeus capacitor at the Los Alamos Scientific Laboratory, New Mexico, U.S.A. If fired simultaneously the 4,032 capacitors would produce for a few microseconds twice as much current as that generated elsewhere on Earth.

Most powerful particle accelerator The world's most powerful particle accelerator is the U.S.S.R. Institute for High Energy Physics' proton synchrotron at Serpukhov, south of Moscow. On 13 Oct. 1967 it was reported to have attained an output of 76 GeV ($7{\cdot}6 \times 10^{10}$ electron volts). Construction had begun in 1960 and was completed at a cost of nearly £30,000,000.

A minimal output of 200 GeV is expected by 1973 from the 1·24 mile diameter ring at the National Accelerator Laboratory at Weston, Illinois, U.S.A. The plant will cost $250,000,000 or, if 400 GeV is required, $280,000,000 (£116·6 million). A capacity "stretched" to 500 GeV is regarded as feasible. The construction of the CERN II 300 GeV accelerator on the French-Swiss border at Megrin near Geneva was authorized on 19 Feb. 1971.

The building of SLAC, the underground linear accelerator, two miles long, for Stamford University, California, U.S.A. was completed, at a cost of $114,000,000 (£47,500,000), in November 1966. It is believed that it will enable the two intersecting storage rings to yield 20 GeV each in "centre of mass" experiments, producing the equivalent energy of a 1,000 GeV electron hitting a stationary target. The £30 million CERN intersecting storage rings (ISR) project, started in September 1966, using two 28 GeV proton beams, should yield the equivalent of 1,700 GeV in its centre of mass experiments due to run in mid-1971. Within a few weeks of the start-up on 27 Jan. 1971 interactions of more than 1,000 GeV were detected.

World's largest bubble chamber The largest bubble chamber in the world is at the Argonne National Laboratory, Illinois, U.S.A. It is 12 feet in diameter and contains 5,330 gallons of liquid hydrogen at a temperature of −247° C. The magnet is

The world's ost powerful particle ccelerator at Dubna near Moscow, U.S.S.R.

The world's most powerful magnet which can sustain a field of 255 kilogauss

18 Kilogauss and the plant went into operation in October 1969 after an expenditure of $18,000,000 (£7½ million).

Strongest magnet The heaviest magnet in the world is one measuring 200 feet in diameter, with a weight of 36,000 tons, for the 10 GeV synchrophasotron in the Joint Institute for Nuclear Research at Dubna, near Moscow, U.S.S.R. The largest super-conducting magnet is a niobium-zirconium magnet, weighing 15,675 lb., completed in June 1966 by Avco Everett Research Laboratory, Massachusetts, U.S.A. It produces a magnetic field of 40,000 gauss and the windings are super-cooled with 6,000 litres of liquid helium.

Strongest magnetic field The strongest recorded magnetic fields are ones of more than 1,000,000 gauss, fleetingly produced by declassified atomic bomb technology at the Illinois Institute of Technology, U.S.A. The first megagauss field was announced in March 1967.

The strongest steady magnetic field yet achieved is one of 220,000 gauss in a cylindrical bore of 1·25 inches, using 10 megawatts of power, called the "1J" magnet designed by D. Bruce Montgomery, which was put into operation at the Francis Bitter National Magnet Laboratory at Massachusetts Institute of Technology in 1964.

WIND TUNNELS

World The world's largest wind tunnel is a low-speed tunnel with a closed test section measuring 40 feet by 80 feet, built in 1944 at the Ames Research Center, Moffett Field, California, U.S.A. The tunnel encloses 800 tons of air and cost approximately $7,000,000 (now £2,916,666). The maximum volume of air that can be moved is 60,000,000 cubic feet per minute. The most powerful is the 216,000 h.p. installation at the Arnold Engineering Test Center at Tullahoma, Tennessee, U.S.A. opened in September 1956. The highest Mach number attained with air is Mach 27 at the works of the Boeing Company in Seattle, Washington State, U.S.A. For periods of micro-seconds, shock Mach numbers of the order of 30 have been attained in impulse tubes at Cornell University, Ithaca, New York State, U.S.A.

United Kingdom The largest wind tunnel in the United Kingdom is the transonic installation at the Aircraft Research Association at Bedford, with a working area 9 feet × 8 feet, and a tunnel power of 25,000 h.p. (18·5 Mw). This machine is capable of producing Mach 1·4, which is equivalent to 1,065 m.p.h. at sea level.

Finest cut Biological specimens embedded in epoxy resin can be sectioned by a glass knife microtome under ideal conditions to a thickness of 1/875,000th of an inch or 290 Ångström units.

Brightest light The brightest steady artificial light sources are "laser" beams (see below), with a luminosity exceeding the Sun's 800,000 candles per square inch by a factor well in excess of 1,000. In May 1969 the U.S.S.R. Academy of Sciences announced blast waves travelling through a luminous plasma of inert gases heated to 90,000° K. The flare-up for up to 3 micro-seconds shone at 50,000 times the brightness of the Sun *viz.* 40,000 million candles per square inch. Of continuously burning sources, the most powerful is a 200 kW high-pressure xenon arc lamp of 600,000 candle-power, reported from the U.S.S.R. in 1965. The most powerful searchlight ever developed was one produced during the 1939–45 war by the General Electric Company Ltd. at the Hirst Research Centre in Wembley, Greater London. It had a consumption of 600 kW and gave an arc luminance of 300,000 candles per square inch and a maximum beam intensity of 2,700,000,000 candles from its parabolic mirror (diameter 10 feet).

Most durable light The electric light bulb was invented in New York City, U.S.A. in 1860 by Heinrich (later Henry) Goebel (1818–93) of Springe, Germany. The average bulb lasts for 750 to 1,000 hours. On 21 Sept. 1908 a stagehand named Barry Burke at the Byers Opera House (now the Palace Theater), Fort Worth, Texas screwed in a new light bulb. The bulb is still burning six years after Burke's death and has been logged by an increasingly mystified Texas Electric Service since 1929. Most Texans believe that the filament escaped from a research laboratory.

Most powerful "laser" beams The first illumination of another celestial body was achieved on 9 May 1962, when a beam of light was successfully reflected from the Moon by the use of an optical "maser" (microwave amplification by stimulated emission of radiation) or "laser" (light amplification by stimulated emission of radiation) attached to a 48-in. telescope at Massachusetts Institute of Technology, Cambridge, Massachusetts, U.S.A. The spot was estimated to be 4 miles in diameter on the Moon. A "maser" light flash is focused into a liquid nitrogen-cooled ruby crystal. Its chromium atoms are excited into a high energy state in which they emit a red light which is allowed to escape only in the direction desired. The device was invented in 1958 by Dr. Charles Hard Townes (born 1915) of the U.S.A. Such a flash for 1/2,000th of a second can bore a hole through a diamond by vaporization at 10,000° C., produced by 2×10^{23} photons.

COMPUTERS

World The world's most powerful computer is the Control Data Corporation CDC 7600 first delivered in January 1969. It can perform 36 million operations in one second and has an access time of 27 nano-seconds. It has two internal memory cores of 655,360 and 5,242,880 characters (6 bits per character) supplemented by a Model 817 disc file of 800 million characters. Commercial deliveries have been scheduled from 1972 at a cost of $9 to $15 million (£3¾ to £6¼ million) depending on peripherals. Precision Instrument Co., Palo Alto, announced in June 1970 a contract to supply a "trillion bit" ($1{\cdot}0 \times 10^{12}$) Unicorn memory storage unit system for *Illiac IV* at the University of Illinois, U.S.A. Unicorn is the acronym for the uni-density coherent light recording computer laser mass memory system.

United Kingdom The largest computer built in the United Kingdom is the £2,500,000 Ferranti "Atlas I". The largest of these was installed in 1964 in the Atlas Computer Laboratory of the Science Research Council, Chilton, Didcot, Berkshire. This machine can perform 500,000 arithmetic operations in a second and 25,000,000 48-bit multiplications in two minutes. It has a capacity of 1·2 million characters supplemented by a disc store of 134 million characters. The ICL 1907 computer, manufactured by International Computers Ltd. of London, S.W.6, is capable of 600,000 arithmetic operations per second. The ICL 1906A announced in October 1967 is expected to attain double the capacity of an Atlas by 1970.

6 THE ARTS AND ENTERTAINMENTS

1. PAINTING

Earliest Evidence of Palaeolithic art was first found in 1834 at Chaffaud, Vienne, France by Brouillet when he recognised an engraving of two deer on a piece of flat bone from the cave, dating to about 20,000 B.C. The number of stratigraphically-dated examples of cave art is very limited. The oldest known dated examples came from La Ferrassie, near Les Eyzies in the Périgord, where large blocks of stone engraved with animal figures and symbols were found in the Aurignacian II layer (*c.* 25,000 B.C.); similarly engraved blocks and with traces of paint possibly representing a cervid (a deer-like form) came from the Aurignacian III layer (*c.* 24,000 B.C.).

LARGEST

World *All time* *Panorama of the Mississippi,* completed by John Banvard (1815–91) in 1846, showing the river scene for 1,200 miles in a strip probably 5,000 feet long and 12 feet wide, was the largest painting in the world, with an area of more than 1·3 acres. The painting is believed to have been destroyed when the rolls of canvas, stored in a barn at Cold Spring Harbor, Long Island, New York State, U.S.A., caught fire shortly before Banvard's death on 16 May 1891.

Existing The largest painting now in existence is probably *The Battle of Gettysburg*, completed in 1883, after 2½ years of work, by Paul Philippoteaux (France) and 16 assistants. The painting is 410 feet long, 70 feet high and weighs 5·36 tons. It depicts the climax of the Battle of Gettysburg, in southern Pennsylvania, U.S.A., on 3 July 1863. In 1964 the painting was bought by Joe King of Winston-Salem, North Carolina, U.S.A. after being stored by E. W. McConnell in a Chicago warehouse since 1933.

"Old Master" The largest "Old Master" is *Il Paradiso*, painted between 1587 and 1590 by Jacopo Robusti, *alias* Tintoretto (1518–94), and his son Domenico on Wall "E" of the Sala del Maggior Consiglio in the Palazzo Ducale (Doge's Palace) in Venice, Italy. The work is 22 metres (72 feet 2 inches) long and 7 metres (22 feet 11½ inches) high and contains more than 100 human figures.

United Kingdom The largest painting in the United Kingdom is the giant oval *Triumph of Peace and Liberty* by Sir James Thornhill (1676–1734), on the ceiling of the Painted Hall in the Royal Naval College, Greenwich, London. It measures 106 feet by 51 feet and took 20 years (1707–1727) to complete.

MOST VALUABLE

World It is not possible to state which is the most valuable painting in the world since many very valuable works are permanent museum and gallery acquisitions unlikely ever to come on to the market. Neither can they have an insurance replacement value. Valuations thus tend to be hypothetical. The "Mona Lisa" (*La Gioconda*) by Leonardo da Vinci (1452–1519) in the Louvre, Paris, was assessed for insurance purposes at $100,000,000 (then £35·7 million) for its move for exhibition in Wäshington, D.C., and New York City, N.Y., U.S.A., from 14 Dec. 1962 to 12 March 1963. However, insurance was not concluded because the cost of the closest security precautions was less than that of the premiums. It was painted in *c.* 1503–07 and measures 77 × 53 centimetres or 30·5 × 20·9 inches. It is believed to portray Mona (short for Madonna) Lisa Gherardini, the wife of Francesco del Giocondo of Florence, who disliked it and refused to pay for it. Francis I, King of France, bought the painting for his bathroom for 4,000 gold florins (now equivalent to £225,000) in 1517. The painting was stolen from the Louvre by the Italian Vicenzo Perruggia (b. 1881) on 21 Aug. 1911 but was recovered in Italy in 1913.

HIGHEST PRICE

Old Master On 6 Feb. 1967 the National Gallery of Art in Washington, D.C., U.S.A., acquired for an undisclosed amount, the oil painting *Ginevra de' Benci*, a portrait of a young Florentine woman, painted in *c.* 1480 by Leonardo da Vinci (1452–1519) of Italy. It was reported on 19 Feb. 1967 that the price was between $5,000,000 and $6,000,000 (then between £1·78 and £2·14 million) paid to Prince Franz Josef II of Liechtenstein. The painting, on poplar wood, measured 15⅛ inches by 14½ inches and thus possibly realized £9,772 per square inch. Said to portray "sombreness without dejection", it is one of the only nine undisputed Leonardos in existence.

Auction price *World* The highest price ever bid in a public auction for any painting is £2,310,000 for *Portrait of Juan de Pareja*, also known as *The Slave of Velázquez*, painted in Rome in 1649 by Diego Rodríguez de Silva Velázquez (1599–1660) and sold on 27 Nov. 1970 at the salerooms

The painting which attracted the highest ever auction price—the £2,310,000 Velazquez, the portrait of Juan de Pareja painted in 1649

of Christie, Manson & Woods, London to the Wildenstein Gallery, New York. The painting had been sold at Christie's at auction in 1801 for 39 guineas (£40·95). It was in the possession of the Earls of Radnor from May 1811 until 1970.

By British artist The highest auction price for any painting by a British artist is £220,000 for *A Cheetah with two Indians* by George Stubbs, R.A. (1724–1806) at Sotheby's on 18 March 1970. It was sold by the Trustees of Sir George Pigot's Will Trust to Thomas Agnew & Sons Ltd. on behalf of City Art Gallery, Manchester. The painting measures 71 × 107 inches and was painted *c.* 1765.

Modern painting The highest price paid for a modern painting is $1,550,000 (£645,833) paid by the Norton Simon Foundation of Los Angeles, California, U.S.A. at the Parke-Bernet Galleries, New York City on 9 Oct. 1968 for *Le Pont des Arts* painted by Pierre Auguste Renoir (1841–1919) of France in 1868. Renoir sold the picture to the Paris dealer Durand-Ruel for about £16.

Living artist *World* The highest price paid for paintings in the lifetime of the artist is $1,950,000 (£812,500) paid for the two canvases *Two Brothers* (1905) and *Seated Harlequin* (1922) by Pablo Diego José Francisco de Paula Juan Nepomuceno Crispín Crispiano de la Santisima Trinidad Ruiz y Picasso (b. 25 Oct. 1881) of Spain. This was paid by the Basle City Government to the Staechelin Foundation to enable the Basle Museum of Arts to retain the painting after an offer of $2,560,000 (£1,066,666) had been received from the United States in December 1967. The highest price for a single work at auction for a living artist is the £190,000 paid by the New York dealer David Mann for the blue period Picasso *Mère et enfant de profil* at Sotheby's, London, on 26 April 1967. It had been painted in Barcelona, Spain in 1902 and had been first sold to settle a doctor's bill. Over a period of two years (1968–70) a total sum of £4,460,663 was made at auctions of Picasso's work. Numerically this represented only 1/70th of his total output. Therefore it can be estimated that his life-time's *oeuvre* is worth more than £300,000,000.

British The highest price for any painting by a living British artist is £26,000 for a painting of a Pope in "convulsive hysteria" by Francis Bacon, completed in 1953, sent in anonymously and bought by Lefevre Gallery at auction at Sotheby's in 1970.

Pop Art The highest price for an item of Pop Art was for "Soup Can", the 72 × 54 inch "masterpiece" by Andy Warhol (U.S.A.) sold at Parke-Bernet Galleries, New York City in May 1970 for $60,000 (£25,000).

Drawing The highest price ever attached to any drawing is £800,000 for the cartoon *The Virgin and Child with St. John the Baptist and St. Anne*, measuring 54¼ inches by 39¾ inches, drawn in Milan, probably in 1499–1500, by Leonardo da Vinci (1452–1519) of Italy. On 31 July 1962 the United Kingdom Government announced that it would add £350,000 to the money collected by public subscription (£404,361 by October 1962) and the £50,000 grant from the National Art-Collections Fund to ensure that the work would remain as a national treasure under the trusteeship of the National Gallery, London. Three United States bids of over $4,000,000 (then £1,428,570) were reputed to have been made for the cartoon.

Most prolific painter Antoine Joseph Wiertz (1806–1865) of Belgium painted 131 canvases 50 feet wide and 30 feet high, totalling over 4·5 acres. This is believed to be the greatest area covered by any painter of note.

Largest gallery The world's largest art gallery is the Winter Palace and the neighbouring Hermitage in Leningrad, U.S.S.R. One has to walk 15 miles to visit each of the 322 galleries, which house nearly 3,000,000 works of art and archaeological remains.

Oldest and youngest R.A. The oldest ever Royal Academician has been (Thomas) Sidney Cooper C.V.O., who died on 8 Feb. 1902 aged 98 years 136 days, having exhibited 266 paintings over the record span of 67 consecutive years (1833–1902). The youngest ever R.A. has been Mary Moser (later Mrs. Hugh Lloyd), who was elected on the foundation of the Royal Academy in 1768 when aged 24.

Youngest exhibitor at R.A. The youngest ever exhibitor at the Royal Academy of Arts Annual Summer Exhibitions is Lewis Melville ("Gino") Lyons (b. 30 April 1962) at their 199th exhibition in 1967 when aged just over 5 years. His picture "Trees and Monkeys" was hung in Gallery IX having been accepted on 7 May 1967. The previous record had been set by Sir Edwin H. Landseer (1802–73) at the age of 13 in 1815.

Upside down duration record The longest period of time for which a modern painting has hung upside down in a public gallery unnoticed is 47 days. This occurred to *Le Bateau*, by Henri Émile Benoît Matisse (1869–1954) of France, in the Museum of Modern Art, New York, between 18 Oct. and 4 Dec. 1961. In this time 116,000 people had passed through the gallery.

MURALS

Earliest The earliest known murals on man-made walls are those at Çatal Hüyük in southern Anatolia, Turkey, dating from *c.* 5850 B.C.

Largest The world's largest mural is *The March of Humanity*, a mural of 54 panels, covering 48,000 square feet, by David Alfaro Siqueiros, which was unveiled in 1968 in the Olimpico Hotel, Mexico City, Mexico. A rainbow mural stretching nearly 300 feet up the sides of the Hilton Rainbow Hotel, Waikiki, Honolulu was completed in 1968.

Largest mobile The largest mobile in the world is one measuring 45 feet by 17 feet and weighing 600 lb., suspended in December 1957 in the main terminal building of the John F. Kennedy International Airport (formerly Idlewild), Long Island, New York State, U.S.A. It was created by

HIGHEST-PRICED PAINTINGS—PROGRESSIVE RECORDS

Price	Painter, title, sold by and sold to	Date
£6,500	Correggio's *The Magdalen Reading* (in fact spurious) to Elector Friedrich Augustus II of Saxony.	1746
£8,500	Raphael's *The Sistine Madonna* to Elector Friedrich Augustus II of Saxony.	1759
£16,000	Van Eyck's *Adoration of the Lamb*, 6 outer panels of Ghent altarpiece by Edward Solby to the Government of Prussia.	1821
£24,600*	Murillo's *The Immaculate Conception* by estate of Marshall Soult to the Louvre (against Czar Nicholas I) in Paris.	1852
£70,000	Raphael's *Ansidei Madonna* by the 8th Duke of Marlborough to the National Gallery.	1885
£100,000	Raphael's *The Colonna Altarpiece* by Sedelmeyer to J. Pierpoint Morgan.	1901
£102,880	Van Dyck's *Elena Grimaldi-Cattaneo* (portrait) by Knoedler to Peter Widener (1834–1915).	1906
£102,880	Rembrandt's *The Mill* by 6th Marquess of Lansdowne to Peter Widener.	1911
£116,500	Raphael's smaller *Panshanger Madonna* by Joseph (later Baron) Duveen (1869–1939) to Peter Widener.	1913
£310,400	Leonardo da Vinci's *Benois Madonna* to Czar Nicholas II in Paris.	1914
c. £400,000	Vermeer's *Girl's Head* by Prince d'Arenburg to Charles B. Wrightsman (U.S.).	1959
£821,429*	Rembrandt's *Aristotle Contemplating the Bust of Homer* by estate of Mr. and Mrs. Alfred Erickson to New York Metropolitan Museum of Art.	1961
£1,785,714	Leonardo da Vinci's *Ginevra de' Benci* (portrait) by Prince Franz Josef II of Liechtenstein to National Gallery of Art, Washington, D.C., U.S.A.	1967
£2,310,000	Velázquez's *Portrait of Juan de Pareja* by the Earl of Radnor to the Wildenstein Gallery, New York.	1970

** Indicates price at auction, otherwise prices were by private treaty.*

Alexander Calder (b. 1898), who invented this art form in 1930 as a reaction to sculptures or "stabiles". The heaviest of all mobiles is *Spirale*, weighing 4,000 lb., outside the U.N.E.S.C.O. headquarters in Paris, France. The word "mobile" was coined by Marcel Duchamp on 1932.

Largest mosaic The world's largest mosaic is on the walls of the central library of the Universidad Nacional Autónomao de México, Mexico City. There are four walls, the two largest measuring 12,949 square feet each represent the pre-Hispanic past.

2. SCULPTURE

Earliest *World* The earliest known examples of sculpture are the so-called Venus figurines from Aurignacian sites, dating to *c.* 25,000–22,000 B.C., *e.g.* the famous Venus of Willendorf from Austria and the Venus of Brassempouy (Landes, France).

Britain The earliest British art object is an engraving of a horse's head on a piece of rib-bone from Robin Hood Cave, Creswell Crag, Derbyshire. It dates from the Upper Palaeolithic period (*c.* 15,000 to 10,000 B.C.).

Most expensive The highest price paid for any sculpture is $160,000 (£66,666) for *Reclining Figure* ("Festival Figure") in bronze with a golden patina by Henry Moore, O.M., C.H. (b. Castleford, Yorkshire, 30 July 1898) at the Parke-Bernet Galleries, New York City, U.S.A. on 4 April 1968. Three such sculptures were cast in 1951.

Largest The world's largest sculptures are the mounted figures of Jefferson Davis (1808–89), Gen. Robert Edward Lee (1807–70) and Gen. Thomas Jonathan ("Stonewall") Jackson (1824–63), covering 1·33 acres on the face of Stone Mountain, near Atlanta, Georgia. They are 20 feet higher than the more famous Rushmore sculptures. When completed the world's largest sculpture will be that of the Indian chief Tashunca-Uitco, known as Crazy Horse, of the Oglala tribe of the Dakota or

The world's ...st expensive sculpture "Reclining Figure" by ...enry Moore, in bronze, ...d for £66,666

Nadowessioux (Sioux) group. He is believed to have been born in about 1849, and he died at Fort Robinson, Nebraska, on 5 Sept. 1877. The sculpture was begun on 3 June 1948 near Mount Rushmore, South Dakota, U.S.A. A projected 561 feet high and 641 feet long, it will require the removal of 5,000,000 tons of stone and is the life work of one man, Korczak Ziolkowski. The work will take until 1990.

Ground figures In the Nazia Desert, south of Lima, Peru there are straight lines (one 5 miles long), geometric shapes and plants and animals drawn on the ground by still unknown persons for an unknown purpose.

Hill figures The largest human hill carving in Britain is the "Long Man" of Wilmington, Sussex, 226 feet in length.

The oldest of all White Horses in Britain is the Uffington White Horse in Berkshire, dating from the late Iron Age (*c.* 150 B.C.) and measuring 374 feet from nose to tail and 120 feet from ear to heel.

3. LANGUAGE

Earliest Anthropologists believe that Handy Man (*Homo habilis*), the earliest known man whose skull survives (see Chapter 1), possessed the physiological capability for speech. The oldest known formally written language has been held to be Sumerian, dating from *c.* 3300 B.C. on the evidence of pictographs on clay tablets unearthed in 1952 from the Uruk IV level of the Temple of Inanna at Erech (called Uruk in Sumerian), now Warka, Iraq. In July 1967, however, clay tablets of the neolithic Danubian culture discovered 8 months earlier at Tataria, Moros River, Romania were dated to the fifth or fourth millennium B.C. The tablets bear symbols of bows and arrows, gates and combs. In 1970 it was announced that writing tablets bearing an early form of the Elamite language dating from 3,500 B.C. had been found in south-eastern Iran.

Oldest words in English Recent research indicates that several river names in Britain date from pre-Celtic times (*ante* 550 B.C.). These include Ayr, Hayle and Nairn. This ascendant, Indo-Germanic tongue, which was spoken from *c.* 3000 B.C. on the Great Lowland Plain of Europe, now has only fragments left in Old Lithuanian, from which the modern English word *eland* derives. Part of the language brought by the Celts of *c.* 550 B.C. six centuries before the Roman occupation survives in probably not more than 20 words in modern English. Examples include bin, brock, coomb, crag, down/dune, dun, and tor. Of even more extreme antiquity is the word *land* which is traceable to the Old Celtic *landa*, a heath and therefore must have been in use on the continent before the Roman Empire grew powerful in the 6th century B.C.

English became the language of court proceedings in October 1362 and the language for teaching in universities in *c.* 1380. Henry IV (1399–1413) was the first post-Conquest monarch whose mother-tongue was English. The earliest surviving document in English is the proclamation by Henry III, known as the Oxford Provision dated 1258.

Commonest language The language spoken by more people than any other is Northern Chinese, or Mandarin, by an estimated 590,000,000 people at mid-1970. The so-called national language (*guoyu*) is a standardized form of Northern Chinese as spoken in the Peking area. This was alphabetized into *zhuyin zimu* of 39 letters in 1918. In 1958 the *pinyin* system, using a Latin alphabet, was introduced. The next most commonly spoken language and the most widespread is English, by an estimated 320,000,000 in mid-1969. English is spoken by 10 per cent. or more of the population in 29 sovereign countries. Today's world total of languages and dialects still spoken is about 5,000 of which some 845 come from India.

Mr. Ned Maddrell, the last surviving speaker of the Manx language

In Great Britain and Ireland there are six indigenous tongues: English, Scots Gaelic, Welsh, Irish Gaelic (Erse), Manx and Romany (Gipsy). Of these English is, of course, predominant, while Manx has almost followed Cornish (last spoken in 1777) into extinction. By 1971 there remained only Mr. Edward (Ned) Maddrell (b. 20 Aug. 1877) of Glen Chass, Port St. Mary, Isle of Man, whose first language, in which he would converse if he had the choice, is Manx. In the Channel Islands, apart from Jersey and Guernsey *patois*, there survive words of Sarkese, in which a prayer book was published in 1812. A movement exists to revive the use of Cornish.

Most complex The following extremes of complexity have been noted: Chippewa, the North American Indian language of Minnesota, U.S.A., has the most verb forms with up to 6,000; Tillamook, the North American Indian language of Oregon, U.S.A., has the most prefixes with 30; Tabassaran, a language in Daghestan, U.S.S.R., uses the most noun cases with 35, while Eskimaux uses 63 forms of the present tense and simple nouns have as many as 252 inflections. In Chinese the *Chung-wên Ta Tz'û-tien* dictionary lists 49,905 characters. The fourth tone of "i" has 84 meanings, varying as widely as "dress", "hiccough" and "licentious". The written language provides 92 different characters for "i⁴". The most complex written character in Chinese is that representing the sound of thunder which has 52 strokes and is somewhat surprisingly pronounced *ping*. The most complex in current use consists of 36 strokes representing a blocked nose and less surprisingly pronounced *nang*.

Rarest and commonest sounds The rarest speech sound is probably the sound written *ř* in Czech which occurs in no other language and is the last sound mastered by Czech children. The commonest sound is the vowel *a* (as in the English father); no language (even Wishram) is known to be without it.

Most and least regular verbs Esperanto was devised in 1887 without irregular verbs and now has a million speakers. Swahili has a strict 6-class pattern of verbs and no verbs which are irregular to this pattern. According to the more daunting grammars published in West Germany, English has 194 irregular verbs though there are arguably 214.

Vocabulary The English language contains about 490,000 words plus another 300,000 technical terms, the most in any language, but it is doubtful if any individual uses more than 60,000. "Basic English", devised in 1930 by Charles K. Ogden, consists of 850 words. Written English contains about 10,000 words, while spoken English among the better educated has about 5,000 words.

ALPHABET

Oldest The development of the use of an alphabet in place of pictograms occurred in the Sinaitic world between 2000 and 1700 B.C. This northern Semitic language developed the consonantal system based on phonetic and syllabic principles. Its "O" has remained unchanged and is thereby the oldest of all letters in the 65 alphabets now in use.

Longest and shortest The language with most letters is Cambodian with 74, and Hawaiian has least with 12 (just A, E, H, I, K, L, M, N, O, P, U, W). Amharic has 231 formations from 33 basic syllabic forms, each of which has seven modifications, so this Ethiopian language cannot be described as alphabetic.

Most and least consonants and vowels The language with most consonants is the Caucasian mountain language Ubyx, with 80 and that with least is Mohawk, an Amerindian language of the Iroquoian family, with only 7 distinct consonantal speech sounds. The language with the most vowels is Sedang, a central Vietnamese language with 55 distinguishable vowel sounds and that with the least is Wishram, the north-western American Indian tongue of the Chinookian family with the single pure vowel *a*. The Hawaiian word for "certified" has 8 consecutive vowels—hooiaioia.

Largest letter The largest permanent letter in the world is the giant "W" on the north side of Mount Tenderfoot, behind Western State College in Gunnison, Colorado, U.S.A. The "W" was made with flat stones on 2 May 1923, when it measured 400 feet high and 300 feet wide, with "legs" 16 feet wide. In *c.* 1932 the size of the "W" was increased to 420 feet high and 320 feet wide, making a total area of 25,560 square feet of rock. In sky-writing (normally at *c.* 8,000 feet) a seven letter word may stretch for six miles in length and can be read from 50 miles. The world's earliest example was over Epsom racecourse, Surrey on 30 May 1922 when Cyril Turner "spelt out" "London Daily Mail" from an S.E.5A biplane.

Greatest linguist The most accomplished linguist ever known was Cardinal Giuseppe Caspar Mezzofanti (b. 17 Sept. 1774 at Bologna, d. 1849), the former chief keeper of the Vatican library in Rome, Italy. He could translate 114 languages and 72 dialects, and spoke 39 languages fluently, 11 others passably and understood 20 others along with 37 dialects. The claims made on behalf of Prof. Rasmus Christian Rask (1787–1832) of Copenhagen in 1837 have proved highly exaggerated. The greatest living linguist is probably Georges Schmidt (b. Strasbourg, France in 1915) of the United Nations Translation Department in New York City, U.S.A. who can speak fluently in 30 languages and can translate 66.

Longest chemical name The longest chemical term is that describing tryptophan synthetase A protein, which has the formula $C_{1289}H_{2051}N_{343}O_{375}S_8$ and the 1,913 letter name: Methionylglutaminylarginyltyrosylglutamylserylleucylphenylalanylalanylglutaminylleucyllysylglutamylarginyllysyglutamylglycylalanylphenylalanylvalylprolylphenylalanylvalylthreonylleucylglycylaspartylprolylglycylisoleucylglutamylglutaminylserylleucyllysylisoleucylaspartylthreonylleucylisoleucylglutamylalanylglycylalanylaspartylalanylleucylglutamylleucylglycylisoleucylprolylphenylalanylserylaspartylprolylleucylalanylaspartylglycylprolylthreonylisoleucylglutaminylasparaginylalanylthreonylleucylarginylalanylphenylalanylalanylalanylglycylvalylthreonylprolylalanylglutaminylcysteinylphenylalanylglutamylmethionylleucylalanylleucylisoleucylarginylglutaminyllysylhistidylprolylthreonylisoleucylprolylisoleucylglycylleucylleucylmethionyltyrosylalanylasparaginylleucylvalylphenylalanylasparaginyllysylglycylisoleucylaspartylglutamylphenylalanyltyrosylalanylglutaminylcysteinylglutamyllysylvalylglycylvalylaspartylserylvalylleucylvalylalanylaspartylvalylprolylvalylglutaminylglutamylserylalanylprolylphenylalanylarginylglutaminylalanylalanylleucylarginylhistidylasparaginylvalylalanylprolylisoleucylphenylalanylisoleucylcysteinylprolylprolylaspartylalanylaspartylaspartylaspartylleucylleucylarginylglutaminylisoleucylalanylseryltyrosylglycylarginylglycyltyrosylthreonyltyrosylleucylleucylserylarginylalanylglycylvalylthreonylglycylalanylglutamylasparaginylarginylalanylalanylleucylprolylleucylasparaginylhistidylleucylvalylalanyllysylleucyllysylglutamyltyrosylasparaginylalanylalanylprolylprolylleucylglutaminylglycylphenylalanylglycylisoleucylserylalanylprolylaspartylglutaminylvalyllysylalanylalanylisoleucylaspartylalanylglycylalanylalanylglycylalanylisoleucylserylglycylserylalanylisoleucylvalyllysylisoleucylisoleucylglutamylglutaminylhistidylasparaginylisoleucylglutamylprolylglutamyllysylmethionylleucylalanylalanylleucyllysylvalylphenylalanylvalylglutaminylprolylmethionyllysylalanylalanylthreonylarginylserine.

Longest words *World* The longest word ever to appear in literature occurs in *The Ecclesiazusae,* a comedy by Aristophanes (448–380 B.C.). In the Greek it is 170 letters long but transliterates into 182 letters in English, thus: lopadotemachoselachogaleokranioleipsanodrimhypotrimmatosilphioparaomelitokatakechymenokichlepikossyphophattoperisteralektryonoptekephalliokigklopeleiolagoiosiraiobaphetraganopterygon. The term describes a fricassee of 17 sweet and sour ingredients including mullet, brains, honey, vinegar, pickles, marrow and ouzo (a Greek drink laced with anisette).

The longest word in modern use is probably spårvagn-

LONGEST WORDS IN VARIOUS LANGUAGES

Serbo-Croatian	Prestolonaslednikovica (22 letters) —wife of an heir apparent.
French	Anticonstitutionnellement (25 letters) —anticonstitutionally.
Italian	Precipitevolissimevolmente (26 letters) —as fast as possible.
Russian	Dyeryevopyeryerabatyvayushchego (31 letters representing 23 Cyrillic letters) —of the timber processing (Genitive singular).
Japanese	Ryāgū-no-otohime-no-motoyui-no-kirihanshi (35 letters) —a seaweed, literally of small pieces of the paper hair streamers of the underwater princess.
Dutch	Ryksluchtvaartdienstweerschepenpersoneel (40 letters) —Government aviation department weather ship personnel.
Hungarian	Legmegengedelmeskedhetetlenségeskeidetekért (43 letters) —because of your continued greatest disobedience.

saktiebolagsskensmutsskjutarefackföreningspersonalbeklädnadsmagasinsförrådsförvaltaren, a Swedish word of 94 letters meaning "the manager of the depot for the supply of uniforms to the personnel of the track cleaners' union of the street railway company".

English The longest word in the Oxford English Dictionary is floccipaucinihilipilification (alternatively spelt in hyphenated form with "n" in seventh place), with 29 letters, meaning "the action of estimating as worthless", first used in 1741, and later by Sir Walter Scott (1771–1832). Webster's Third International Dictionary lists among its 450,000 entries pneumonoultramicroscopicsilicovolcanoconiosis (45 letters), the name of a miners' lung disease. It is understood that the inclusion of this entry is largely prompted by the convenience of being able to quote it in reply to unending inquiries as to the longest word in the American version of the English language.

The longest word in an English classic is the nonce word honorificabilitudinitatibus (27 letters), occurring in Act V, scene I of *Love's Labour's Lost* by William Shakespeare (1564–1616), but used with the ending "-tatatibus", making 29 letters, in *The Water Poet* by John Taylor (1580–1653).

In this category may also be placed the 52-letter word used by Dr. Edward Strother (1675–1737) to describe the spa waters at Bristol—aequeosalinocalcalinoceraceoaluminosocupreovitriolic. In his novel *Headlong Hall,* Thomas Love Peacock (1785–1866) described the human physique as "osseocarnisanguineoviscericartilaginonervomedullary"—51 letters.

The longest regularly formed English words are antidisestablishmentarianismically (34 letters), used by Mark McShane in his novel *Untimely Ripped,* published in 1963; and praetertranssubstantiationalistically (37 letters). The medical term hepaticocholangiocholecystenterostomies (39 letters) refers to the surgical creations of new communications between gallbladders and hepatic ducts and between intestines and gallbladders. The longest in common use is disproportionableness (21 letters).

Longest palindromic words The longest known palindromic word is *saippuakauppias* (15 letters), the Finnish word for soap-seller. The longest in the English language are *evitative* and *redivider* (each nine letters), while another nine-letter word, *Malayalam,* is a proper noun given to the language of the Malayali people in Kerala, southern India. The nine-letter word Rotavator is becoming accepted more widely than a brand name for a horticultural cultivating machine. The contrived chemical term *detartrated* has 11 letters, as does *kinnikinnik* (sometimes written *kinnik-kinnik*, a 12-letter palindrome), the word for the dried leaf and bark mixture which was smoked by the Cree Indians of North America. Some baptismal fonts in Greece and Turkey bear the circular 25 letter inscription ΝΙΨΟΝ ΑΝΟΜΗΜΑΤΑ ΜΗΜΟΝΑΝΟΨΙΝ meaning "wash (my) sins not only (my) face". This appears at St. Mary's Church, Nottingham, St. Paul's, Woldingham, Surrey and other churches. The longest palindromic sentence devised is one of 242 words by Howard Bergeson of Oregon, U.S.A. It begins "Deliver no evil, avid diva . . . and hence predictably ends . . . avid diva, live on reviled.

Most frequently used letters In English the most frequently used letters are in order: e, t, a, i, s, o, n, h, r, d and u. The most frequent initial letters are found by indexers to be s, e, p, a, t, b, m, d, r, f and h.

Commonest words In written English the most frequently used words are in order: the, of, and, to, a, in, that, is, I, it, for *and* as. The most used in conversation is I.

Most meanings The most over-worked word in English is the word *jack* which has 10 main substantive uses with 40 subuses and two verbal uses.

Most accents The French word with most accents is *hétérogénéité,* meaning heterogeneity. An atoll in the Pacific Ocean 320 miles E.S.E. of Tahiti is named Héréhérétué.

Worst tongue twisters The most difficult tongue twister in the only anthology of its type *Anthology of British Tongue-Twisters* by Ken Parkin of Teesside, is deemed by the author to be "The sixth sick sheik's sixth sheep's sick"—especially when spoken quickly.

Perhaps the most difficult in the world is the Xhosa (from Natal, South Africa) for "The skunk rolled down and ruptured its larynx" Iqaqa laziqikaqika kwaze kwaqhawaka uqhoqhoqha. The last word contains three "clicks". A European rival is the vowelless *Strch prst skrz krk,* the Czech for "stick a finger in the throat".

Longest abbreviation The longest known abbreviation is S.O.M.K.H.P.B.K. J.C.S.S.D.P.M.W.D.T.B., the initials of the Sharikat Orang-Orang Melayu Kerajaani Hilir Perak Berkerjasama-Serkerjasama Kerama Jimat Chermat Serta Simpanan Dan Pinjam Meminjam Wang Dengan Tanggonan Berhad. This is the Malay name for the Lower Perak Malay Government Servants' Co-operative Thrift and Loan Society Limited, in Telok Anson, Perak State, West Malaysia (formerly Malaya). The abbreviation for this abbreviation is not recorded.

Longest anagrams The longest regular English words which can form anagrams are the 16-letter pair "interlaminations" and "internationalism".

Shortest holo-alphabetic sentence The contrived headline describing the annoyance of an eccentric in finding inscriptions on the side of a fjord in a rounded valley as "Cwm fjord-bank glyphs vext quiz" represents the ultimate in containing all 26 letters in 26 letters.

Longest sentence The longest sentence in classical western literature is one in *Les Misérables* by Victor Marie Hugo (1802–85) which runs to 823 words punctuated by 93 commas, 51 semi-colons and 4 dashes. A sentence of 958 words appears in "Cities of the Plain" by the French author, Marcel Proust (1871–1922), while some authors such as James Joyce (1882–1941) appear to eschew punctuation altogether. The first 40,000 words of *The Gates of Paradise* by George Andrzeyevski (Panther) appear to lack any punctuation.

PLACE-NAMES

Longest *World* The official name for Bangkok, the capital city of Thailand, consists of the Thai words Krungt'ep ("city of the divine messenger"), plus a long list of Pali titles, as proclaimed at the city's foundation in 1782. A *shortened version* of this name is Krungtepmahanakornbowornratanakosinmahintarayudhayamahadilokpopnoparatanarajthaniburiromudomrajniwesmahasatarnamornpimarnavatarsatitsakatattiyavisanukamprasit (158 letters). The longest place-name now in use in the world is Taumatawhakatangihangakoauauotamatea (turipukakapikimaungahoronuku)pokaiwhenuakitanatahu, the unofficial 85-letter version of the name of a hill (1,002 feet above sea-level) in the Southern Hawke's Bay district of North Island, New Zealand. This Maori name means "the place where Tamatea, the man with the big knee who slid, climbed and swallowed mountains, known as Land-eater, played on his flute to his loved one". The official version has 57 letters (1 to 36 and 65 to 85).

United Kingdom The longest place-name in the United Kingdom is the concocted 58-letter name Llanfairpwllgwyngyllgogerychwyrndrobwllllantysiliogogogoch, which is translated: "St. Mary's Church in a hollow by the white hazel, close to the rapid whirlpool, by the red cave of St. Tysilio". This is the name given to a village in Anglesey, Wales, but the official name consists of only the first 20 letters. The longest genuine Welsh place-name listed in the Ordnance Survey Gazetteer is Lower Llanfihangel-y-Creuddyn (26 letters), a village near

Aberystwyth, Cardiganshire.

England The longest single word (unhyphenated) place-name in England is Blakehopeburnhaugh, a hamlet between Burness and Rochester in Northumberland, of 18 letters. The hyphenated Sutton-under-Whitestonecliffe, Yorkshire has 27 letters. The longest multiple name is North Leverton with Habbelsthorpe (30 letters), Nottinghamshire, while the longest parish name is Saint Andrew, Holborn above the Bars, with Saint George the Martyr (54 letters), in London.

Scotland The longest single word place-names in Scotland are Claddochknockline, with a population of 18 in 1961, on the island of North Uist, in the Outer Hebrides and the nearby Claddochbaleshare both with 17 letters. The statutory name for Kirkcudbrightshire (18 letters) is however County of Kirkcudbright. A 12-acre loch nine miles west of Stornoway on Lewes is named Loch Airidh Mhic Fhionnlaidh Dhuibh (31 letters).

Ireland The longest place-name in Ireland is Muckanaghederdauhaulia (22 letters), 4 miles from Costello in Carris Bay, County Galway. The name means "soft place between two seas".

Shortest The shortest place-names in the world are the French village of Y (population 143), so named since 1241, in the Somme, and the Norwegian village of Å (pronounced "Aw"). The shortest place-names in Great Britain are the two-lettered villages of Ae (population 199 in 1961) in Dumfriesshire, Oa on the island of Islay off western Scotland. In the Shetland Islands there are skerries called Ve and two stacks called Aa. The island of Iona was originally I. The River E flows into the southern end of Loch Mhór, Inverness-shire, Scotland. The shortest place-name in Ireland is Ta (or Lady's Island) Lough, a sea-inlet off the coast of County Wexford. Tievelough, in County Donegal, is also called Ea. In the United States there are seven two-lettered place-names, including both Ed and Uz in the State of Kentucky.

Earliest The earliest recorded British place-name is Belerion, the Penwith peninsula of Cornwall, referred to as such by Pytheas of Massalia in *c.* 308 B.C. The earliest reference to Britain was as *Pretanic* (implying an earlier *Qrtanic*). The oldest name among England's 41 counties is Kent, first mentioned in its Roman form of Cantium (from the Celtic *canto*, meaning a rim, *i.e.* a coastal district) from the same circumnavigation by Pytheas. The youngest is Lancashire, first recorded in the 12th century. The earliest mention of England is the form *Angelcynn*, which appeared in the Anglo-Saxon Chronicle in A.D. 880.

Commonest The commonest place-name in England and Wales is Newtown or New Town, with 129 entries in the 1961 Census Gazetteer, and Newton with 47. The British place-name most widely used overseas is Richmond, Yorkshire, which has given its name, according to a list compiled by Mr. David Ball, to 43 other villages, towns and cities, including examples in 20 of the 50 states of the U.S.A.

PERSONAL NAMES

Earliest The earliest personal name which has survived is uncertain. Some experts believe that it is En-lil-ti, a word which appears on a Sumerian tablet dating from *c.* 3300 B.C., recovered before 1936 from Jamdat Nasr, 40 miles south-east of Baghdad, Iraq. Other antiquarians regard it purely as the name of a deity, Lord of the air, and claim that the names Lahma and Lahamu, Sumer gods of silt, are older still. N'armer, the father of Men (Menes), the first Egyptian pharaoh, dates from about 2900 B.C. The earliest known name of any resident of Britain is Divitiacus, the Gaulish ruler of the Kent area *c.* 75 B.C.

Longest The longest name used by anyone is Adolph Blaine

World Charles David Earl Frederick Gerald Hubert Irvin John Kenneth Lloyd Martin Nero Oliver Paul Quincy Randolph Sherman Thomas Uncas Victor William Xerxes Yancy Zeus Wolfeschlegelsteinhausenbergerdorff, Senior, who was born at Bergedorf, near Hamburg, Germany, on 29 Feb. 1904. On printed forms, he uses only his eighth and second Christian names and the first 35 letters of his surname. The full version of the name of 590 letters appeared in the 12th edition of *The Guinness Book of Records*. He now lives in Philadelphia, Pennsylvania, U.S.A., and has recently shortened his surname to Mr. Wolfe+590, Senior.

The longest Christian or given name on record is Napuamahalaonaonekawehiwehionakuahiweanenawawakehoonkakehoaalekeeaonanainananiakeao'Hawaiikawao (94 letters) in the case of Miss Dawn N. Lee so named in Honolulu, Hawaii, U.S.A. in February 1967. The name means "The abundant, beautiful blossoms of the mountains and valleys begin to fill the air with their fragrance throughout the length and breadth of Hawaii".

United Kingdom The longest surname in the United Kingdom was the six-barrelled one borne by the late Major L. S. D. O. F. (Leone Sextus Denys Oswolf Fraudati filius) Tollemache-Tollemache de Orellana Plantagenet Tollemache Tollemache, who was born in 1884 and died of pneumonia in France on 20 Feb. 1917. Of non-repetitious surnames, the last example of a five-barrelled one was that of the Lady Caroline Jemima Temple-Nugent-Chandos-Brydges-Grenville (1858–1946). The longest single English surname is Featherstonehaugh, usually pronounced "Fanshaw". Fetherstonhaugh (pronounced "Freestonhugh") is used recurringly as a Christian name in one English family.

Scotland In Scotland the surname Macghillesheathanaich (21 letters) was first recorded in 1506 on the island of Islay, Argyllshire.

Shortest in Britain There exist among the 42,500,000 names on the Ministry of Social Security index four examples of a one-lettered surname. Their identity has not been disclosed, but they are "E", "J", "M" and "X". Two-letter British surnames include By and On.

Commonest *World* The commonest surname in the world is the Chinese name Chang which is borne, according to estimates, by between 12·1% and 9·7% of the Chinese population, so indicating even on the lower estimate that there are at least some 75,000,000 Changs—more than the entire population of all but 7 of the 145 other sovereign countries of the world.

English The commonest surname in the English-speaking world is Smith. There are 671,550 nationally insured Smiths in Great Britain, of whom 7,081 are plain John Smith and another 22,550 are John (plus one or more given names) Smith. Including uninsured persons, there are over 800,000 Smiths in England and Wales alone, of whom 90,000 are called A. Smith. There were an estimated 1,678,815 Smiths in the United States in 1964.

"Macs" There are, however, estimated to be 1,600,000 persons in Britain with M', Mc or Mac (Gaelic "son of") as part of their surnames. The commonest of these is Macdonald which accounts for about 55,000 of the Scottish population.

The most common forenames in Britain would appear from C. V. Appleton's study of a large sample of Smiths (11,568 born in 1968) to be Mark, Paul, Andrew, David and Michael for boys and Julie, Deborah, Karen, Amanda and Joanne for girls. In the period 1196–1307 William was the commonest boy's name but since 1340 to recent times this had been John.

Most contrived name The palm for the most determined attempt to be last in the local telephone directory must be awarded to Mr.

Zeke Zzzypt of Chicago, Illinois, U.S.A. He outdid the previous occupant who was a mere Mr. Zyzzy Zzyryzxxy. In September 1970 Mr. Zero Zzyzz (rhymes with "fizz") was ousted by Mr. Vladimir Zzzyd (rhymes with outdid) in the Miami directory.

THE WRITTEN WORD

Smallest handwriting The smallest writing achieved is a density of 85 letters per square millimetre with an engraving tool on metal by Dr. Anto Leikola of Helsinki, Finland.

In 1968 Mr. C. N. Swift of Edgbaston, Birmingham, England, wrote the Lord's Prayer 25 times on a piece of paper half the size of a standard United Kingdom postage stamp, *i.e.* 22 millimetres (0·87 of an inch) by 18 millimetres (0·71 of an inch) with a density of nearly 37 letters per square millimetre.

TEXTS

Oldest The oldest known written text is the pictograph expression of Sumerian speech (see Earliest Language, p. 84). The earliest known vellum document dates from the 2nd century A.D.; it contains paragraphs 10 to 32 of Demosthenes' *De Falsa Legatione*. Demosthenes died in the 4th century B.C.

Oldest printed The oldest surviving printed work is a Korean scroll or *sutra* from wooden printed blocks found in the foundations of the Pulguk Sa pagoda, Kyongju, Korea, on 14 Oct. 1966. It has been dated no later than A.D. 704.

Mechanically printed It is generally accepted that the earliest mechanically printed book was the 42-line Gutenberg Bible, printed at Mainz, Germany, in *c.* 1455 by Johann zum Gensfleisch zur Laden, called "zu Gutenberg" (*c.* 1398–*c.* 1468). Recent work on water marks published in 1967 indicates a copy of a surviving printed Latin grammar was made from paper made in *c.* 1450. The earliest exactly dated printed work is the Psalter completed on 14 Aug. 1457 by Johann Fust (*c.* 1400–1466) and Peter Schöffer (1425–1502), who had been Gutenberg's chief assistant. The earliest printing in Britain was an Indulgence dated 13 Dec. 1476, issued by Abbot Sant of Abingdon, Berkshire, and printed by William Caxton (*c.* 1422–1491).

Largest The largest book in the world is *The Little Red Elf*, a story in 64 verses by William P. Wood, who designed, constructed and printed the book. It measures 7 feet 2 inches high and 10 feet across when open. The book is at present on show in a case at the Red Elf Cave, Ardentinny near Dunoon. The largest art book ever produced was one 210 centimetres (82·7 inches) high and 80 centimetres (31·5 inches) wide, first shown in Amsterdam, in the Netherlands, in May 1963. It contained five "pages", three the work of Karel Appel (b. 1921), an abstract painter, and two with poems by Hugo Claus. The price was $5,255 (now £2,177).

Largest publication The largest publication in the world is the 263 volume British Museum Catalogue of Printed Books, 1455–1955, at £1,709·50 per set. *The National Union Catalog, Pre-1956 Imprints* is in process of publication for the American Library Association, by Mansell Information/Publishing Ltd. of London, in 610 volumes of 704 pages (429,440 pages) for $14,640 (£6,161) per set. The contract was won as a result of the harnessing of the Williamson Abstractor camera which is handling the 12,000,000 cards. By 30 May 1974 the 263 volume mark should be surpassed.

Smallest The smallest book in the world is a handwritten one—*Poems by Edgar Guest*. It was written in 1942 by Burt Randle. It is less than $\frac{1}{8}$ of an inch square and is held by a metal clasp. Edgar Albert Guest (1881–1959) was born in Birmingham, England.

An edition of 150 copies of *The Rubá'iyát of Omar Khayyám* by Edward FitzGerald (1809–83) was published in 1956 in Massachusetts, U.S.A., and weighed a total of 0·34 of an ounce. This book is a collection of *ruba'is,* or quatrains, attributed to Ghiyās-ud-din Abū'l-Fath 'Omar ibn Ibrāhīm al-Khayyāmi (d. 1123 or 1132), a Persian mathematician, astronomer and poet.

The smallest book printed in metal type as opposed to any photographic process is one printed for the Gutenberg Museum, Mainz, West Germany. It measures 3·5 millimetres by 3·5 millimetres (0·13 of an inch square) and consists of the Lord's Prayer in seven languages.

Most valuable The most valuable printed books are the three surviving perfect vellum copies of the Gutenberg Bible, printed in Mainz, Germany, in *c.* 1455 by Gutenberg (see above). The United States Library of Congress copy, bound in three volumes, was obtained in 1930 from Dr. Otto Vollbehr, who paid about $330,000 (now £137,500) for it. During 1970, according to an informed source, a paper edition in the hands of the New York book dealer, Hans Peter Krauss, was privately bought for $2,500,000 (£1,041,666). The highest priced newly published book was a single jewel-encrusted parchment edition of lithographs entitled *The Apocalypse*, weighing 226 lb., by Salvador Dalí (b. 11 May 1904) of Spain, published in Paris by Joseph Foret in March 1961 and priced at 1,000,000 francs (then £72,339).

Broadsheet The highest price ever paid for a broadsheet has been $404,000 (£168,333) for one of the 16 known copies of *The Declaration of Independence*, printed in Philadelphia in 1776 by Samuel T. Freeman & Co., to a Texan in May 1969.

Highest priced 20th century book The highest price paid for any book printed in this century in a standard binding and not illustrated with original lithographs is $4,000 (£1,667) paid at the Parke-Bernet Galleries in New York City for one of the first 100 copies of the first edition of *Ulysses* by James Joyce, published in Paris in 1922.

Longest novel The longest important novel ever published is *Les hommes de bonne volonté* by Louis Henri Jean Farigoule (b. 26 Aug. 1885), *alias* Jules Romains, of France, in 27 volumes in 1932–46. The English version *Men of Good Will* was published in 14 volumes in 1933–46 as a "novel-cycle". The novel *Tokuga-Wa Ieyasu* by Sohachi Yamaoka has been serialized in Japanese daily newspapers since 1951. When completed it will run to 40 volumes.

Encyclopaedias *Most comprehensive* The most comprehensive present day encyclopaedia is the *Encyclopaedia Britannica,* first published in Edinburgh, Scotland, in December 1768. A group of booksellers in the United States acquired reprint rights in 1898 and complete ownership in 1899. In 1943 the *Britannica* was given to the University of Chicago, Illinois, U.S.A. The current 24-volume edition contains 28,380 pages, 34,696 articles and 2,247 other entries, 36,674,000 words and 22,670 illustrations. It is now edited in Chicago and in London. There are 10,326 contributors.

Largest The largest encyclopaedia ever compiled was the *Great Standard Encyclopaedia* of Yung-lo ta tien of 22,937 manuscript chapters (370 still survive), written by 2,000 Chinese scholars in 1403–08.

Top-selling The world's top-selling encyclopaedia is *The World Book Encyclopaedia* published by Field Enterprises Educational Corporation of Chicago, Illinois, U.S.A. Since 1961 the annual average sales have exceeded 450,000 sets per annum.

Largest dictionary The largest dictionary ever published is the 12-volume Royal quarto *The Oxford English Dictionary* of 15,487 pages published between 1884 and 1928 with a first supplement of 963 pages in 1933 with a further 2-volume supplement, edited by R. W. Burchfield, due in 1974. The work contains 414,825 words, 1,827,306 illustrative

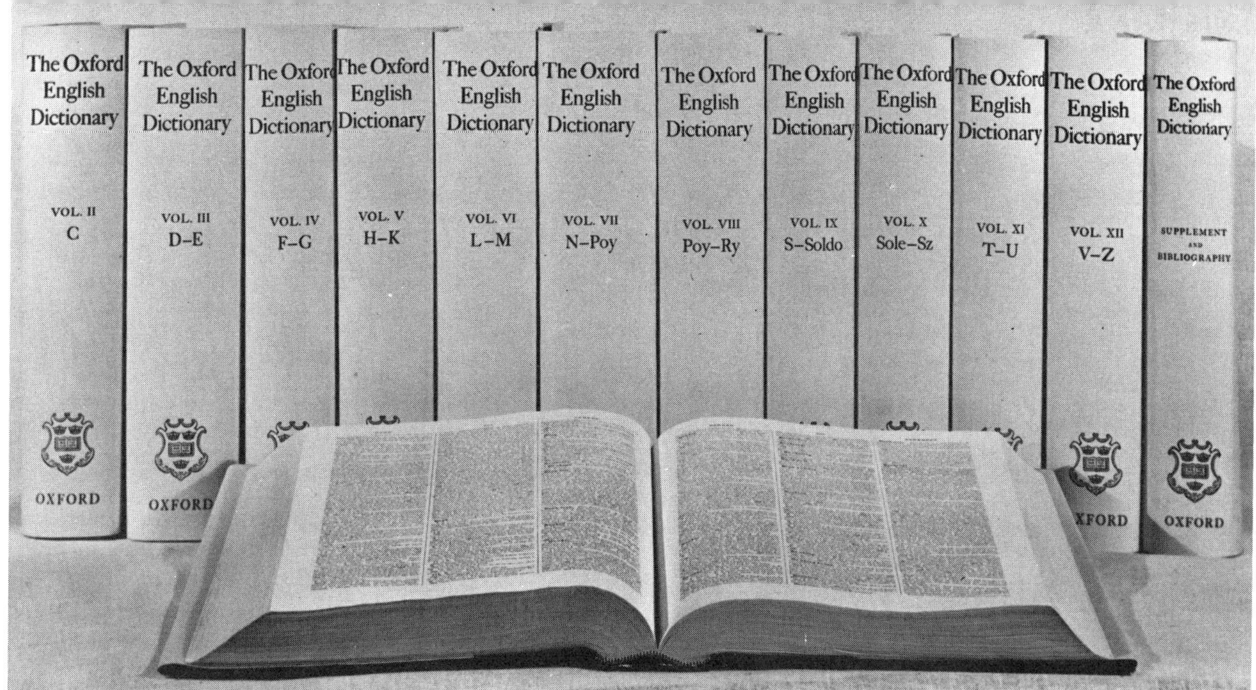

The world's largest dictionary—the 13-volume Oxford English Dictionary published by the Oxford University Press

quotations and 227,779,589 letters and figures.

Manuscripts
Highest price

The highest price ever paid for any manuscript is £100,000, paid in December 1933 by the British Museum, London, to the U.S.S.R. Government for the manuscript Bible *Codex Sinaiticus* originally from the Monastery of St. Catherine on Mt. Sinai, Egypt (now the United Arab Republic). It consists of 390 of the original 730 leaves, measuring 16 inches by 28 inches, of the book, dictated in Greek and written by three scribes in about A.D. 350 and rescued from a waste paper basket in May 1844 by Lobegott Friedrich Konstantin von Tischendorf (1815–74), a German traveller and Biblical critic. The highest price at auction is 1,100,000 New Francs (£94,933 incl. tax) paid by H. P. Krauss, the New York dealer, at the salerooms of Rheims et Laurin, Paris on 24 June 1968 for the late 13th-century North Italian illuminated vellum Manuscript of the Apocrypha.

The highest auction price ever paid for any literary manuscript is £90,000 for the long-lost illustrated manuscript of Books 1 to 9 of the translation in 15 parts by William Caxton (*c.* 1422–1491) of the *Metamorphoses* ("Transfigurations") by Publius Ovidius Naso (43 B.C.–A.D. 18), the Roman poet known as Ovid. This manuscript belonged to the collection of Sir Thomas Phillipps and was sold to Mr. L. D. Feldman of the House of El Dieff, in New York City, at the salerooms of Sotheby & Co., London, on 27 June 1966. An export licence was refused and it was announced on 5 Jan. 1967 that the manuscript would stay in Britain, as the result of a loan of $200,000 (then £71,000) from Mr. Eugene Power of Ann Arbor, Michigan, and George Braziller (U.S.A.), a publisher. The manuscript was donated to the library of Magdalene College, Cambridge (which possessed the manuscript of Books 10 to 15), in return for facsimile rights on all 15 Books.

The highest price ever paid for the manuscript of a living author is $18,200 (then £6,500), paid in May 1960 by a New York dealer for the handwritten copy of *A Passage to India* (published in 1924) by E. M. (Edward Morgan) Forster (1879–1969) of Britain.

20th century manuscript

The highest price paid for a 20th century manuscript is believed to be £30,000 by M. Alan Delon for the two-page appeal written in August 1940 by the then Col. Charles de Gaulle in London beginning "France has lost a battle, it has not lost a war". It had been secured by M. Andre Bernheim. The highest price for a 20th century British manuscript is the £8,500 given on 8 July 1969 at Sotheby's for the handwritten manuscript of Evelyn Waugh's novel *"Scoop. A Novel about Journalists"*.

Personal papers

The highest price paid for personal papers has been $Can.600,000 (£231,213), announced in April 1968, for those of Earl Russell (1872–1970) by McMaster University, Hamilton, Ontario.

BIBLE

Oldest

The oldest known Bible is the Yonan manuscript of the complete New Testament, written in Syriac-Aramaic in about A.D. 350 and presented to the United States Library of Congress in Washington, D.C., on 27 March 1955. The longest of the Dead Sea scrolls is the Temple Scroll measuring 28 feet which first became available for study in June 1967. The earliest Bible printed in English was one edited by Miles Coverdale (*c.* 1488–1569), printed in 1535 at Marberg in Hesse, Germany.

Longest and shortest books

The longest book in the Bible is the Book of Psalms, while the longest prose book is the Book of the Prophet Isaiah, with 66 chapters. The shortest is the Third Epistle of John, with 294 words in 14 verses. The Second Epistle of John has only 13 verses but 298 words.

Longest Psalm, verse, sentence and name

Of the 150 Psalms, the longest is the 119th, with 176 verses, and the shortest is the 117th, with two verses. The shortest verse in the English language version of the Bible is verse 35 of Chapter XI of the Gospel according to St. John, consisting of the two words "Jesus wept". The longest is verse 9 of Chapter VIII of the Book of Esther, which extends to a 90-word description of the Persian empire. The total number of letters in the Bible is 3,566,480. The total number of words depends on the method of counting hyphenated words, but is usually given as between 773,692 and 773,746. The word "and" appears 46,399 times. The longest name in the Bible is Maher-shalal-hash-baz, the symbolic name of the second son of Isaiah (Isaiah, Chapter VIII, verses 1 and 3).

MOST PROLIFIC WRITERS

The most prolific writer for whom a word count has been published was Charles Hamilton, *alias* Frank Richards (1875–1961), the Englishman who created Billy Bunter. At his height in 1908 he wrote the whole of the boys' comics *Gem* (founded 1907) and *Magnet* (founded 1908) and most of two others, totalling 80,000 words a week. His lifetime output was at least 72,000,000 words. He enjoyed the advantages of the use of electric light rather than candlelight and of being unmarried.

Novels

The Belgian writer Georges Simenon (b. Georges Sim in Liège on 13 Feb. 1903), creator of Inspector Maigret, writes a novel of 200 pages in 11 days and in February 1969 completed his 200th under his own name of which 74 were about Inspector Maigret. He has also written

John Creasey, whose total of fiction titles reached 555 in 1971

300 other novels under 19 other pen-names. These are published in 31 countries in 43 languages and have sold more than 300,000,000 copies. He hates adverbs and has had his children's playroom soundproofed. Since 1931 the British novelist John Creasey (b. 1908) has, under his own name and 13 *aliases*, written 529 books totalling more than 40,000,000 words. The authoress with the greatest total of published books is Miss Ursula Bloom (Mrs. A. C. G. Robinson), with 420 full-length works, starting in 1922 with *The Great Beginning* and including the best sellers *The Ring Tree* (novel) and *The Rose of Norfolk* (non-fiction).

Short stories The highest established count for published short stories is 3,500 in the case of Michael Hervey (born London, 1914) of Henley, New South Wales, Australia. Aided by his wife Lilyan Brilliant, he has also written 60 detective novels and 80 stage and television plays. The most prolific short story writer in Britain is Herbert Harris (born 1911) of Leatherhead, Surrey, with nearly 3,000 published in Britain and in 28 other countries.

Fastest novelist The world's fastest novelist has been Erle Stanley Gardner (1889–1970) of U.S.A., the mystery writer who created Perry Mason. He dictated up to 10,000 words per day and worked with his staff on as many as seven novels simultaneously. His sales on 140 titles reached 170 million by his death. The British novelist John Creasey (see above) has an output of 15 to 20 novels per annum, with a record of 22. He once wrote two books in a week with a half-day off.

Highest paid writer The highest rate ever offered to a writer was $30,000 (now £12,500) to Ernest Miller Hemingway (1899–1961) for a 2,000-word article on bullfighting by *Sports Illustrated* in January 1960. This was a rate of $15 (£6·25) per word. In 1958 a Mrs. Deborah Schneider of Minneapolis, Minnesota, U.S.A., wrote 25 words to complete a sentence in a competition for the best blurb for Plymouth cars. She won from about 1,400,000 entrants the prize of $500 (£208) every month for life. On normal life expectations she will collect $12,000 (£5,000) per word. No known anthology includes Mrs. Schneider's deathless prose.

Top selling author It was announced on 13 March 1953 that 672,058,000 copies of the works of Marshal Iosif Vissarionovich Dzhugashvili, *alias* Stalin (1879–1953), had been sold or distributed in 101 languages.

Among writers of fiction, sales alone of over 300,000,000 have been claimed for Georges Simenon (see above) and for the British authoress Agatha Christie (born Agatha Mary Clarissa Miller), now Lady Mallowan (formerly Mrs. Archibald Christie). Her paperback sales in the United Kingdom alone are 1½ million per annum.

Youngest The youngest recorded commercially-published author is Janet Aitchison of Reigate, Surrey, who wrote *The Pirates' Tale* when aged 5½ years. It was published as a Puffin Book by Penguin in April 1969 when she was 6½.

Janet Aitchison the world's youngest published authoress aged 7

POETS LAUREATE

Earliest The earliest official Poet Laureate was John Dryden (1631–1700), appointed in April 1668. It is recorded that Henry I (1100–1135) had a King's versifier named Wale.

Youngest and oldest The youngest Poet Laureate was Laurence Eusden (1688–1730), who received the bays on 24 Dec. 1718, at the age of 30 years and 3 months. The greatest age at which a poet has succeeded is 73 in the case of William Wordsworth (1770–1850) on 6 April 1843. The longest lived Laureate was John Masefield, O.M., who died on 12 May 1967, aged 88 years 11 months. The longest which any poet has worn the laurel is 41 years 322 days, in the case of Alfred (later the 1st Lord) Tennyson (1809–92), who was appointed on 19 Nov. 1850 and died in office on 6 Oct. 1892.

Longest poem The longest poem ever written was the *Mahabharata* which appeared in India in the period *c.* 400 to 150 B.C. It runs to 220,000 lines and nearly 3,000,000 words.

The longest poem ever written in the English language is *Poly-Olbion* or *A Chorographicall Description of Tracts, Rivers, Mountains, Forests, etc.*, written in Alexandrines in 30 books, comprising nearly 100,000 lines, by Michael Drayton (1563–1631) between 1613 and 1622.

BEST SELLERS

World The world's best seller is the Bible, portions of which have been translated into 1,280 languages. It has been estimated that between 1800 and 1950 some 1,500,000,000 were printed of which 1,100,000,000 were handled by Bible Societies. The total production of Bibles or parts of the Bible in the United States in the year 1963 alone was reputed to be 50,000,000.

It has been reported that 800,000,000 copies of the red-covered booklet *Quotations from the Works of Mao Ze dong* were sold or distributed between June 1966, when possession became virtually mandatory in China, and November 1970. The name of Mao Tse-tung (b. 26 Dec. 1893) means literally "Hair Enrich-East".

Non-fiction The next best selling non-fiction book is *The Common Sense Book of Baby and Child Care* by Dr. Benjamin McLane Spock (b. 2 May 1903) of New Haven, Connecticut, U.S.A. It was first published in New York in May 1946 and the total sales were 19,076,822 by December 1965 and probably over 22,000,000 by January 1969. Dr. Spock's book was written with a ball-point pen and typed by his wife, a silk heiress. Of perennials, the one with the highest aggregate sale is probably *Le Nouveau Petit Larousse Illustré*, which has sold nearly 20,000,000 copies since 1906. This total has also been attributed to *Baking is Fun*, by Dr. August Otker of Germany, first published in 1890. The top-selling H.M. Stationery Office publication has been The Highway Code with 70,000,000 copies.

The best seller among Government reports has been "The Beveridge Report" (1942) which has sold 280,000 copies.

Fiction The novel with the highest sales has been *Peyton Place* (first published in 1956) by Mrs. Grace de Repentigny Metalious (1924–64) of the United States, with a total of 11,919,660 copies by November 1970. Six million were sold in the first six months. In the United Kingdom the highest print order has been 3,000,000 by Penguin Books Ltd. for their paperback edition of *Lady Chatterley's Lover*, by D. H. (David Herbert) Lawrence (1885–1930). The total sales to January 1968 were 3,600,000 copies.

Post-card The top-selling post-card of all time is reputed to be a drawing by Donald Fraser McGill (1875–1962) with the caption: He: "How do you like Kipling?" She: "I don't know, you naughty boy, I've never Kippled". It sold about 6,000,000. Between 1904 and his death McGill sold more than 350,000,000 cards to users and deltiologists (picture post-card collectors).

LARGEST PUBLISHERS

A U.N.E.S.C.O. survey has shown that 22 per cent. of the world's books are in the English language, followed by 17 per cent. in Russian. The most active publishing country in the world is the U.S.S.R., where 1,252,000,000 copies of books *and pamphlets*, comprising 78,204 titles, including more than 30,000 for free distribution, were produced in 1964. The 1967 total of titles was 74,081. Total production of more than 1,500 million copies had been planned for 1970.

The U.K. published a record 31,420 book titles in 1968, of which 22,642 were new titles.

The largest publisher in the world is the United States Government Printing Office in Washington, D.C., U.S.A. The Superintendents of Documents Division dispatches more than 150,000,000 items every year. The annual list of new titles and annuals is about 6,000.

Fastest publishing The shortest interval between the receipt of a manuscript and the publication of a book is 66½ hours, in the case of *The Pope's Journey to the United States—the Historic Record*, a paperback of 160 pages, costing 75 cents (31p), written by 51 editors of the strike-bound *New York Times* and published by Bantam Books Inc. of Madison Avenue, New York City, N.Y., U.S.A. It was printed by the W. F. Hall Printing Co. of Chicago, Illinois, U.S.A. The first article reached the publishers at 1.30 p.m. on 4 Oct. 1965 and completed copies came off the printers' presses at 8.00 a.m. on 7 Oct. 1965.

Example of work of Donald McGill

PLEASE, LORD, EXCUSE ME A MINUTE WHILE I KICK FIDO!

LARGEST PRINTERS

World The largest printers in the world are R. R. Donnelly & Co. of Chicago, Illinois, U.S.A. The company, founded in 1864, has plants in seven main centres, turning out $200,000,000 (£83,300,000) worth of work per year from 180 presses, 125 composing machines and more than 50 binding lines. Nearly 18,000 tons of inks and 450,000 tons of paper and board are consumed every year.

Print order The largest printing job in the United Kingdom is the annual production by H.M. Stationery Office Press at Harrow, Greater London, of about 13,000,000 telephone directories. The task involves 200 employees, 9,000 tons of paper, and the setting, revising, printing and binding of 20,000 pages at a cost of about £1,000,000.

The print order for the 46th Automobile Association Handbook (1970–71) was 5,130,000 copies. The total print since 1908 has been 53,510,000. It is currently printed by web offset by Petty & Sons of Leeds.

Largest cartoon The largest cartoon ever published was one covering two floors (35 feet by 30 feet) on a building opposite the United Nations Headquarters in New York City, N.Y., U.S.A., depicting the enslavement by the U.S.S.R. of eight Eastern European nations.

Longest lived strip The most durable newspaper comic strip has been the Katzenjammer Kids (Hans and Fritz) first published in the United States in 1897 and currently drawn by Joe Musial. The most read is believed to be "Peanuts" by Charles M. Schulz (b. 1922) which since 1950 has grown to be syndicated to 1,000 U.S. newspapers with a total readership of 90,000,000.

LETTERS

Longest Physically the longest letter ever written was one of

3,696 feet 10 inches in length. It was written on an adding machine roll by Miss Terry Finch of Southsea, Hampshire to her boyfriend Sergeant Jerry Sullivan of Texas, U.S.A. and posted on 11 June 1969.

To an editor *Longest* The longest recorded letter to an editor was one of 13,000 words (a third of a modern novel) written to the editor of the *Fishing Gazette* by A.R.I.E.L. and published in 7-point type spread over two issues in 1884.

Most Britain's, and seemingly the world's, most indefatigable writer of letters to the editors of newspapers is Raymond L. Cantwell, 51 of Oxford, who since 1948 has had more than 12,000 letters published in print or on the air.

Shortest The shortest correspondence on record was that between Victor Marie Hugo (1802–85) and his publisher Hurst and Blackett in 1862. The author was on holiday and anxious to know how his new novel *Les Misérables* was selling. He wrote "?". The reply was "!".

SIGNATURES

Earliest Not counting attested crosses in a few charters of the early Norman kings ostensibly affixed by their own hands, the earliest English sovereign whose handwriting is known to have survived is Henry III (1207–72). The earliest signature to have survived is that of Richard II (dated 26 July 1386). The Magna Carta does not bear even the mark of King John (reigned 1199–1216), but carries his seal. In 1932 an attested cross of William I (reigned 1066–87) was sold in London.

Most expensive The highest price ever paid on the open market for a single letter is $51,000 (now £18,214), paid in 1927 for a letter written by the Gloucestershire-born Button Gwinnett (1732–77), one of the three men from Georgia to sign the United States' Declaration of Independence in Philadelphia on 4 July 1776. Such an item would probably attract bids of up to $250,000 (£104,163) today. If one of the six known signatures of William Shakespeare (1564–1616) were to come on the market or a new one was discovered the price would doubtless set a record. There is no known surviving signature of Christopher Marlowe (1564–1593).

The highest price ever paid for an autographed letter signed by a living person is $3,000 (£1,071) for a four-page letter signed by Mrs. Jacqueline Lee Kennedy Onassis (*née* Bouvier) (b. Southampton, N.Y., 22 July 1929), paid in New York City, N.Y., U.S.A., in May 1964.

CROSSWORDS

First The earliest crossword was one with 32 clues invented by Arthur Wynne (b. Liverpool, England, d. 1945) and published in the *New York World* on 21 Dec. 1913. The first crossword published in a British newspaper was one furnished by C. W. Shepherd in the *Sunday Express* of 2 Nov. 1924.

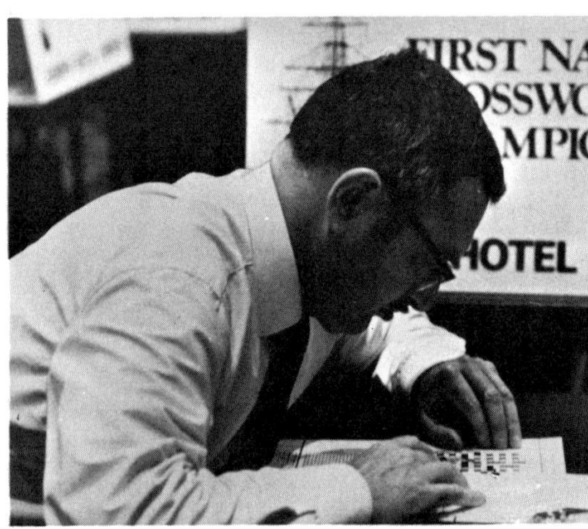

Roy Dean, the fastest solver of *The Times* crossword

Largest The largest crossword ever published is one with 3,185 clues across and 3,149 clues down, compiled by Robert M. Stilgenbauer of Los Angeles in 7½ years of spare time between 15 May 1938 and publication in 1949. Despite the 125,000 copies distributed not one copy has been returned worked out or even partially worked out.

Fastest The fastest recorded time for completing *The Times* crossword under test conditions is 3 minutes 45·0 seconds by Roy Dean, 43, of Bromley, Kent in the B.B.C. "Today" studio on 19 Dec. 1970.

Slowest In May 1966 *The Times* of London received an announcement from a Fijian woman that she had just succeeded in completing their crossword No. 673 in the issue of 4 April 1932.

Oldest map The oldest known map is the Turin Papyrus, showing the layout of an Egyptian gold mine, dated about 1320 B.C.

Christmas cards The greatest number of personal Christmas cards sent out is believed to be 40,000 in 1969 by President and Mrs. Nixon to friends and others, some of whom must have been unilateral acquaintances.

LIBRARIES

Largest *World* The largest library in the world is the United States Library of Congress (founded on 24 April 1800), on Capitol Hill, Washington, D.C. On 30 June 1969 it contained more than 59,000,000 items, including 14,846,000 books and pamphlets. The two buildings cover six acres and contain 327 miles of book shelves.

The Lenin State Library in Moscow, U.S.S.R., claims to house more than 20,000,000 books, but this total is understood to include periodicals.

The largest non-statutory library in the world is the New York Public Library (founded 1895) on Fifth Avenue with a floor area of 525,276 square feet. The main part of its collection is in a private research library which has 4,662,326 volumes on 80 miles of shelves, 9,000,000 manuscripts, 120,000 prints, 150,000 gramophone records, and 275,000 maps. There are also 81 tax-supported branch libraries with 3,231,696 books. The central research library is open until the civilized hour of 10 p.m. on every day of the year.

United Kingdom The largest library in the United Kingdom is that in the British Museum, London. It contains more than 9,000,000 books, about 115,000 manuscripts and 101,000 charters on 158 miles of shelf. There are spaces for 370 readers in the domed Reading Room, built in 1854. The largest public library in the United Kingdom will be the new Birmingham Public Library with a floor area of 230,000 square feet or more than 5¼ acres; seating for 1,200 people and an ultimate reference capacity for 1,500,000 volumes on 31 miles of shelving. The oldest public library in Scotland is in Kirkwall, Orkney, founded in 1683.

Overdue books It was reported on 7 Dec. 1968 that a book checked out in 1823 from the University of Cincinnati Medical Library on Febrile Diseases (London, 1805 by Dr. J. Currie) was returned by the borrower's great-grandson Richard Dodd. The fine was calculated as $22,646 (£9,435).

NEWSPAPERS

Most It has been estimated that the total circulation of newspapers throughout the world averaged 320,000,000 copies per day in 1966. The country with the greatest number is the U.S.S.R., with 7,967 in 1966. Their average circulation in 1966 was 110,400,000.

The United States had 1,749 English language daily newspapers at 1 Jan. 1968. They had a combined net paid circulation of 61,397,000 copies per day at 30 Sept. 1966. The peak year for U.S. newspapers was 1910, when there were 2,202. The leading newspaper readers in the world are the people of Sweden, where 515 newspapers were sold for each 1,000 of the population in 1967–68. The U.K. figure was 488.

Oldest *World* The oldest existing newspaper in the world is the Swedish official journal *Post och Inrikes Tidningar*, founded in 1644. It is published by the Royal Swedish Academy of Letters. The oldest existing commercial newspaper is the *Haarlems Dagblad/Oprechte Haarlemsche Courant*, published in Haarlem, in the Netherlands. The *Courant* was first issued as the *Weeckelycke Courante van Europa* on 8 Jan. 1656 and a copy of issue No. 1 survives.

United Kingdom The oldest continuously produced newspaper in the United Kingdom is *Berrow's Worcester Journal* (originally the *Worcester Post Man*), published in Worcester. It was traditionally founded in 1690 and has appeared weekly since June 1709. The oldest newspaper title is that of the *Stamford Mercury* dating back to at least 1714 and traditionally to 1695. The oldest daily newspaper in the United Kingdom is *Lloyd's List*, the shipping intelligence bulletin of Lloyd's, London, established as a weekly in 1726 and as a daily in 1734. The *London Gazette* (originally the *Oxford Gazette*) was first published on 16 Nov. 1665. In November 1845 it became the most expensive daily newspaper ever sold in the United Kingdom, priced at 2s. 8d. per copy. The oldest Sunday newspaper in the United Kingdom is *The Observer*, first issued on 4 Dec. 1791. The 9,378th issue was on 18 April 1971.

Largest The most massive single issue of a newspaper was the *New York Times* of Sunday 17 Oct. 1965. It comprised 15 sections with a total of 946 pages, including about 1,200,000 lines of advertising. Each copy weighed 7 lb. 14 oz. and sold for 30 cents (11p).

The largest page size ever used has been 51 inches by 35 inches for *The Constellation*, printed in 1895 by George Roberts as part of the Fourth of July celebrations in New York City, N.Y., U.S.A. The *Worcestershire Chronicle* was the largest British newspaper. A surviving issue of 16 Feb. 1859 measures 32¼ inches by 22½ inches. The largest page size of any present newspaper is 30 inches by 22 inches in *The Nantucket Inquirer and Mirror*, published every Friday in Nantucket, on Nantucket Island, Massachusetts, U.S.A.

The smallest recorded page size has been 3½ inches by 4½ inches, as used in *El Telegrama* of Guadalajara, Spain.

HIGHEST CIRCULATION

The first newspaper to achieve a circulation of 1,000,000 was *Le Petit Journal*, published in Paris, France, which reached this figure in 1886, when selling at 5 centimes (now about ½p) per copy.

World The claim exercised for the world's highest circulation is that by the *Ashashi Shimbun* (founded 1879) of Japan with a figure which attained more than 10,000,000 copies in October 1970. This, however, has been achieved by totalling the figures for editions published in various centres with a morning figure of 6,100,000 and an evening figure of 3,900,000. The highest circulation of any single newspaper in the world is that of the Sunday newspaper *The News of the World*, printed in Bouverie Street, London. Single issues have attained a sale of 9,000,000 copies, with an estimated readership of more than 19,000,000. The paper first appeared on 1 Oct. 1843, averaged 12,971 copies per week in its first year and surpassed the million mark in 1905. To provide sufficient pulp for the 1,500 reels used per week, each measuring 5 miles long, more than 780,000 trees have to be felled each year. The latest sales figure is 6,242,270 copies per issue (average for 1 July to 31 Dec. 1970), with a last published estimated readership of 16,208,000.

Daily *World* The highest circulation of any daily newspaper is that of the U.S.S.R. government organ *Izvestia* (founded in Leningrad on 12 March 1917 as a Menshevik newssheet and meaning "Information") with a figure of 8,670,000 in March 1967. The daily tabloid *Pionerskaya Pravda* had an average circulation of 9,181,000 copies per issue in 1966. This is the news organ of the Pioneers, a Communist youth organization founded in 1922.

United Kingdom The highest daily net sale of any newspaper in the United Kingdom is that of *The Daily Mirror*, founded in London in 1903. A print of 7,161,704 was sold out on 3 June 1953. The latest sales figure is 4,443,584 (for July–December 1970), with an estimated readership of 14,433,000.

Evening The highest circulation of any evening newspaper is that of *The Evening News*, established in London in 1881. The average daily net sale reached 1,752,166 in the first six months of 1950. The latest figure is 1,016,000 copies per issue (average for 1 July to 31 Dec. 1970), with an average readership of 2,973,000.

"Earliest" newspaper The first newspaper to be published in the world each day is sometimes said to be the *Fiji Times* because it is closest to the international date-line.

Most read The newspaper which achieves the closest to a saturation circulation is *The Sunday Post*, established in Glasgow in 1914. In 1969 its total estimated readership of 2,931,000 represented more than 80 per cent. of the entire population of Scotland aged 16 and over.

Most smoked newspaper New Guinea's *South Pacific Post*, which circulated only 5,200 copies over about 178,000 square miles, was the most sought after newspaper for smoking and sold for 6d. per lb. for this purpose. Since 1962 the arrival of the *Nu Gini Toktok* has eased the paper shortage.

PERIODICALS

Largest circulation *World* The largest circulation of any weekly periodical is that of *This Week Magazine*, produced in the United States to circulate with 43 newspapers which find it uneconomical to run their own coloured Sunday magazine section. The circulation was 11,889,211 copies at 31 March 1967. In its 30 basic international editions *The Reader's Digest* (established February 1922) circulates more than 29,000,000 copies monthly, in 14 languages, including a United States edition of 17,586,127 copies (average for July to December 1969) and a United Kingdom edition (established 1939) of 1,500,000 copies.

United Kingdom The highest circulation of any periodical in the United Kingdom is that of *The Radio Times* (instituted in September 1923). The average weekly sale for 1969 was 3,806,847 copies. The highest sale of any issue was 9,778,062 copies for the Christmas issue of 1955. The materials used include 885 tons of paper, 9½ tons of ink and 355 miles of stapling wire per issue.

Annual *Old Moore's Almanack* has been published annually since 1697, when it first appeared as a broadsheet, by Dr. Francis Moore (1657–1715) of Southwark, London to advertise his "physiks". The annual sale certified by its publishers W. Foulsham & Co. Ltd. of Slough, England is 1,150,000 copies and its aggregate sale must well exceed 100,000,000 copies.

ADVERTISING RATES

The highest price asked for advertising space *pro rata* is $98,200 (£35,071) for a four-colour centre-spread in *This Week*. The highest price for a single page is $76,420 (£31,841) for a four-colour back cover in *Life* magazine (circulation 8 million per week).

The colour page rate for the *Radio Times* is £5,800.

The highest expenditure ever incurred on a single advertisement in a periodical is $950,000 (£395,833) by

Uniroyal Inc. for a 40-page insert in the May 1968 issue of the U.S. edition of *The Reader's Digest*.

The British record is £30,000 for a 28-page booklet by Morphy-Richards Ltd. in *The Reader's Digest* of October 1964.

Longest editorship On 6 Jan. 1963 Sir Bruce Stirling Ingram, O.B.E., M.C. (1877–1963) celebrated his 63rd completed year as editor of *The Illustrated London News* in 3,272 weekly issues, and died two days later. This span was interrupted only by service in World War I.

4. MUSIC

INSTRUMENTS

Oldest The world's oldest surviving musical notation is a heptonic scale deciphered from a clay tablet by Dr. Duchesne-Guillemin in 1966–67. The tablet has been dated to *c.* 1800 B.C. and was found at a site in Nippur, Sumeria, now Iraq. Musical history is, however, able to be traced back to the 3rd millennium B.C., when the yellow bell (*huang chung*) had a recognized standard musical tone in Chinese temple music. It is possible that either a flute or a mouth bow is the object depicted in a painting from the Magdalenian period (*c.* 18,000 B.C.) in the Trois Frères Caves in the Pyrenees. Rock-gongs probably existed even earlier.

Earliest piano The earliest piano in existence is one built in Florence, Italy, in 1720 by Bartolommeo Cristofori (1655–1731) of Padua, and now preserved in the Kraus Museum of Florence.

Organ Largest *World* The largest and loudest musical instrument ever constructed is the Auditorium Organ in Atlantic City, New Jersey, U.S.A. Completed in 1930, this heroic instrument has two consoles (one with seven manuals and another movable one with five), 1,477 stop controls and 33,112 pipes ranging from $\frac{3}{16}$ of an inch to 64 feet in length. It is powered with blower motors of 365 horsepower, cost $500,000 (now £208,333) and has the volume of 25 brass bands, with a range of seven octaves. The world's largest church organ is that in Passau Cathedral, Germany. It was completed in 1928 by D. F. Steinmeyer & Co. It has 16,000 pipes and five manuals.

United Kingdom The largest organ in the United Kingdom is that installed in Liverpool Cathedral in 1926, with one five-manual and one four-manual console, and 10,936 pipes.

Loudest stop The loudest organ stop in the world is the Ophicleide stop of the Grand Great in the Solo Organ in the Atlantic City Auditorium (see above). It is operated by a pressure of 100 inches of water ($3\frac{1}{2}$ lb. per square inch) and has a pure trumpet note of ear-splitting volume, more than six times the volume of the loudest locomotive whistles.

Organ marathon The longest organ recital ever sustained was one of $43\frac{1}{4}$ hours at Handsworth College Chapel, Birmingham, England, by the Rev. Ian Yates on 9–11 May 1970. The duration for playing an electric organ is $49\frac{1}{2}$ hours by James A. Barron at the Sundale Shopping Centre, Southport, Queensland, Australia on 11–13 Nov. 1970. A British record of 40 hours was set by Graham Whitelaw, 20, at Glasgow University Men's Union on 14–16 Jan. 1970.

Harmonium marathon The longest recorded non-stop harmonium marathon is 72 hours by Iain Stinson and John Whiteley, both of the Royal Holloway College at Englefield Green, Surrey on 6–9 Feb. 1970.

Brass instrument *Largest* The largest recorded brass instrument is a tuba standing $7\frac{1}{2}$ feet tall, with 39 feet of tubing and a bell 3 feet 4 inches across. This contrabass tuba was constructed for a world tour by the band of John Philip Sousa (1854–1932), the Unites States composer, in *c.* 1896–98, and is still in use. This instrument is now owned by Mr. Ron Snyder (G.B.).

The world's largest brass instrument—the contrabass tuba

Longest alphorn The longest Swiss alphorn, which is of wooden construction, is 23 feet $7\frac{3}{8}$ inches long and was completed in 1968.

Stringed instrument *Largest* The largest stringed instrument ever constructed was a pantaleon with 270 strings stretched over 50 square feet, used by George Noel in 1767.

Most players The greatest number of musicians required to operate a single instrument was the six required to play the gigantic orchestrion, known as the Apollonican, built in 1816 and played until 1840.

Largest guitar The largest and presumably also the loudest playable guitar in the world is one 8 feet 10 inches tall, weighing 80 lb. and with a volume of 16,000 cubic inches (*c.f.* the standard 1,024 cubic inches) built by The Harmony Company of Chicago and completed in April 1970.

Largest double bass The largest bass viol ever constructed was an octo-bass 10 feet tall, built in *c.* 1845 by J. B. Vuillaume (1798–1875) of France. Because the stretch was too great for any musician's finger-span, the stopping was effected by foot levers. It was played in London in 1851.

Violin *Most valuable* The highest recorded auction price for a violin is the £29,000 paid in 1970 in Washington D.C. for the Delgesa Guarnerius violin of 1743 sold by the Phipps

Foundation. The "Messie" Stradivarius in the Ashmolean Museum at Oxford, England, has been hypothetically valued at £30,000 for many years.

Smallest The smallest fully-functional violin made is one $5\frac{1}{2}$ inches overall, constructed by Mr. T. B. Pollard of Rock Ferry, Birkenhead, Cheshire, England.

rgest drum The largest drum in the world is the Disneyland Big Bass Drum with a diameter of 10 feet 6 inches and a weight of 450 lb. It was built in 1961 by Remo Inc. of North Hollywood, California, U.S.A. and is mounted on wheels and towed by a tractor.

ORCHESTRAS

Most The greatest number of professional orchestras maintained in one country is 94 in West Germany. The total number of symphony orchestras in the United States, including "community" orchestras, was estimated to be 1,436 including 30 major and 66 metropolitan ones (as of August 1970).

Largest The vastest "orchestra" ever recorded was that assembled for the Norwegian National Meeting of School Brass Bands at Trondheim in August 1958. The total number of instrumentalists was 12,600. On 17 June 1872, Johann Strauss the younger (1825–99) conducted an orchestra of 2,000, supported by a choir of 20,000, at the World Peace Jubilee in Boston, Massachusetts, U.S.A. The number of violinists was more than 350.

Greatest attendance The greatest attendance at any classical concert was 90,000 for a presentation by the New York Philharmonic Orchestra, conducted by Leonard Bernstein, at Sheep Meadow in Central Park, New York City, N.Y., U.S.A., on 1 Aug. 1966.

op Festival The greatest estimated attendance at a Pop Festival has been 400,000 for the Woodstock Music and Art Fair at Bethel, New York State, U.S.A. on 15–17 Aug. 1969. According to one press estimate "at least 90 per cent." were smoking marijuana. The attendance at the Pop Festival at Freshwater, Isle of Wight, England on 31 Aug. 1970 was claimed by its promoters, Fiery Creations, also to be 400,000.

ighest and west notes The extremes of orchestral instruments (excluding the organ) range between the piccolo or octave flute, which can reach e^{v} or 5,274 cycles per second, and the sub-contrabass clarinet, which can reach C_{11} or 16·4 cycles per second. The highest note on a standard pianoforte is c^{v} (4,186 cycles per second), which is also the violinist's limit. In 1873 a sub double bassoon able to reach $B_{111}\#$ or 14·6 cycles per second was constructed but no surviving specimen is known. The extremes for the organ are g^{vi} (the sixth G above middle C) (12,544 cycles per sec.) and C_{111} (8·12 cycles per sec.) obtainable from $\frac{3}{4}$-inch and 64-foot pipes respectively.

COMPOSERS

Most prolific The most prolific composer of all time was probably Georg Philipp Telemann (1681–1767) of Germany. He composed 12 complete sets of services (one cantata every Sunday) for a year, 78 services for special occasions, 40 operas, 600 to 700 orchestral suites, 44 Passions, plus concertos and chamber music. The most prolific symphonist was Johann Melchior Molter (*c.* 1695–1765) of Germany who wrote 169. Joseph Haydn (1732–1809) of Austria wrote 104 numbered symphonies some of which are regularly played today.

Most rapid Among composers of the classical period the most prolific was Wolfgang Amadeus Mozart (1756–91) of Austria, who wrote 600 operas, operettas, symphonies, violin sonatas, divertimenti, serenades, motets, concertos for piano and many other instruments, string quartets, other chamber music, masses and litanies, of which only 70 were published before he died, aged 35. His opera *The Clemency of Titus* (1791) was written in 18 days and three symphonic masterpieces, *Symphony No. 39 in E flat major, Symphony in G minor* and the *Jupiter Symphony in C,* were reputedly written in the space of 42 days in 1788. His overture *Don Giovanni* was written in full score at one sitting in Prague in 1787 and finished on the day of its opening performance.

National anthems The oldest national anthem is the *Kimigayo* of Japan, in which the words date from the 9th century. The anthem of Greece constitutes the first four verses of the Solomos poem, which has 158 verses. The shortest anthems are those of Japan, Jordan and San Marino, each with only four lines. The anthems of Bahrain and Qatar have no words at all.

Longest rendering "God Save the King" was played non-stop 16 or 17 times by a German military band on the platform of Rathenau Railway Station, Brandenburg, on the morning of 9 Feb. 1909. The reason was that King Edward VII was struggling inside the train with the uniform of a German Field-Marshal before he could emerge.

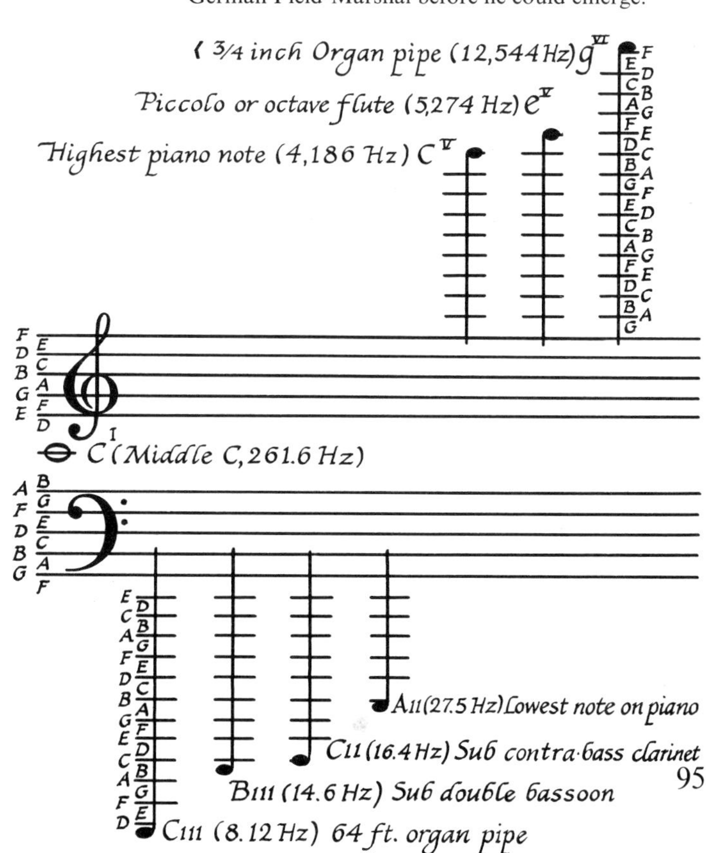

Longest symphony The longest of all symphonies is the orchestral symphony No. 3 in D minor by Gustav Mahler (1860–1911) of Austria. This work, composed in 1895, requires a contralto, a women's and a boys' choir and an organ, in addition to a full orchestra. A full performance requires 1 hour 34 minutes, of which the first movement alone takes 45 minutes. The Symphony No. 2 (the Gothic, now renumbered as No. 1), composed in 1919–22 by Havergal Brian, has been performed only twice, on 24 June 1961 and 30 Oct. 1966. The total *ensemble* included 55 brass instruments, 31 wood wind, six kettle-drummers playing 22 drums, four vocal soloists, four large mixed choruses, a children's chorus and an organ. The symphony is continuous and required, when played as a recording on 27 Nov. 1967, 100 minutes. Brian has written an even vaster work based on Shelley's "Prometheus Unbound" but the sheer expense of putting it on makes its performance unlikely. He wrote 18 symphonies between 1956, when he was 80 and 1967.

Longest piano composition The longest continuous non-repetitious piece for piano ever composed has been the Opus Clavicembalisticum by Kaikhosru Shapurji Sorabji (b. 1892). The composer himself gave it its only public performance on 1 Dec. 1930 in Glasgow, Scotland. The work is in 12 movements with a theme and 49 variations and a Passacaglia with 81 and a playing time of 2¾ hours.

The longest piano piece of any kind is *Vexations* by Erik Satie which consists of a 180-note composition which on the composer's orders must be repeated 840 times such that the whole lasts 18 hours 40 minutes. Its first reported public performance in September 1963 in the Pocket Theater, New York City required a relay of ten pianists. The *New York Times* critic fell asleep at 4 a.m. and the audience dwindled to six masochists. At the conclusion a sado-masochist shouted "Encore".

Longest silence The most protracted silence in a modern composition is one entitled *4 minutes 33 seconds* in a totally silent *opus* by John Cage (U.S.A.). Commenting on this trend among young composers, Igor Fyodorovich Stravinsky (1882–1971) said that he looked forward to their subsequent compositions being "works of major length".

HIGHEST PAID MUSICIANS

Pianist The highest-paid concert pianist was Ignace Jan Paderewski (1860–1941), Prime Minister of Poland from 1919 to 1921, who accumulated a fortune estimated at $5,000,000 (now about £1,800,000), of which $500,000 (£180,000) was earned in a single season in 1922–23. He once received $33,000 (£11,800) for a concert in Madison Square Garden, New York City, the highest fee ever paid for a single performance.

Singers Of great fortunes earned by singers, the highest on record are those of Enrico Caruso (1873–1921), the Italian tenor, whose estate was about $9,000,000 (£3,750,000), and the Italian-Spanish coloratura soprano Amelita Galli-Curci (1889–1963), who received about $3,000,000 (£1,250,000). In 1850, up to $653 (now £272) was paid for a single seat at the concerts given in the United States by Johanna ("Jenny") Maria Lind, later Mrs. Otto Goldschmidt (1820–87), the "Swedish Nightingale". She had a range from go to e'''', of which the middle register is still regarded as unrivalled.

Violinist The Austrian-born Fritz Kreisler (1875–1962) is reputed to have received more than £1,000,000 in his career.

Drummer The most highly paid drummer, or indeed "side man" of any kind, is Bernard ("Buddy") Rich (b. 1917) in the band of Harry James, at more than $75,000 (£31,250) per annum.

OPERA

Longest The longest of commonly performed operas is *Die Meistersinger von Nurnberg* by Wilhelm Richard Wagner (1813–83) of Germany. A normal uncut performance of this opera as performed by the Sadler's Wells company between 24 Aug. and 19 Sept. 1968 entailed 5 hours 15 minutes of music. *William Tell* by Rossini, never now performed uncut, would according to the *tempi* require some 7 or more hours if performed in full.

Aria The longest single aria, in the sense of an operatic solo, is Brünnhilde's immolation scene in Wagner's *Götterdämmerung*. A well-known recording of this has been precisely timed at 14 minutes 46 seconds.

Cadenza The longest recorded cadenza in operatic history occurred in *c.* 1815, when Crevilli, a tenor, sang the two words *felice ognora* ("always happy") as a cadenza for 25 minutes in the Milan Opera House, Italy.

Opera houses *Largest* The largest opera house in the world is the Metropolitan Opera House, Lincoln Center, New York City, N.Y., U.S.A., completed in September 1966 at a cost of $45,700,000 (£16,320,000). It has a capacity of 3,800 seats in an auditorium 451 feet deep. The stage is 234 feet in width and 146 feet deep. The tallest opera house is one housed in a 42-storey building on Wacker Drive in Chicago, Illinois, U.S.A.

Most tiers The Teatro della Scala (La Scala) in Milan, Italy, shares with the Bolshoi Theatre in Moscow, U.S.S.R., the distinction of having the greatest number of tiers. Each has six, with the topmost in Moscow being termed the Galurka.

BELLS

Heaviest *World* The heaviest bell in the world is the Tsar Kolokol, cast in 1733 in Moscow, U.S.S.R. It weighs 193 tons, measures 22 feet 8 inches in diameter and over 19 feet high, and its greatest thickness is 24 inches. The bell is cracked, and a fragment, weighing about 11 tons, broken from it. The bell has stood on a platform in the Kremlin, in Moscow, since 1836.

The world's largest bell, the 193-ton Tsar Kolokol in Moscow

The heaviest bell in use is the Mingoon bell, weighing 87 tons, in Mandalay, Burma, which is struck by a teak boom from the outside. The heaviest swinging bell in the world is the Kaiserglock in Cologne Cathedral, Germany, which was recast in 1925 at 25 tons. The heaviest change ringing peal in the world is the 13 bells weighing 16½ tons, in Liverpool Cathedral of which the tenor alone weighs 82 cwt.

United Kingdom The heaviest bell hung in the United Kingdom is "Great Paul" in St. Paul's Cathedral, London. It was cast in 1881, weighs 16 tons 14 cwt. 2 quarters 19 lb. and has a diameter of 9 feet 6½ inches. "Big Ben", the hour bell in the clock tower of the House of Commons, was cast in 1858 and weighs 13 tons 10 cwt. 3 quarters 15 lb. The heaviest peal is the 13 with a tenor bell weighing 72 cwt. donated by Bishop Grandison (1327–1369).

The heaviest bell ever cast in England and the heaviest tuned bell in the world is the bourdon bell of the Laura Spelman Rockefeller Memorial carillon in Riverside Church, New York City, N.Y., U.S.A. It weighs 18 tons 5 cwt. 1 quarter 18 lb. and is 10 feet 2 inches in diameter.

Oldest *World* The oldest bell in the world is reputed to be that found in the Babylonian Palace of Nimrod in 1849 by Mr. (later Sir) Austen Henry Layard (1817–94). It dates from *c.* 1000 B.C.

United Kingdom The oldest *dated* bell in England is that hung in St. Chad's, Claughton, in the parish of Hornby with Claughton, Lancashire. It weighs about 2½ cwt., is 21¼ inches in diameter and 16½ inches high. Still in perfect condition and in regular use, it is dated 1296. A claim that the church bell at Enborne, Berkshire dates from *c.* A.D. 1260 is accepted by some experts.

CARILLON

Largest The largest carillon in the world is the Laura Spelman Rockefeller Memorial carillon in Riverside Church, New York City, N.Y., U.S.A. It consists of 72 bells with a total weight of 102 tons.

Heaviest The heaviest carillon in the United Kingdom is in St. Nicholas Church, Aberdeen, Scotland. It consists of 48 bells, the total weight of which is 25 tons 8 cwt. 2 quarters 13 lb. The bourdon bell weighs 4 tons 9 cwt. 3 quarters 26 lb. and the carillon comprises four octaves, less the bottom semi-tone.

BELL RINGING

Eight bells have been rung to their full "extent" (a complete "Bob Major" of 40,320 changes) only once without relays. This took place in a bell foundry at Loughborough, Leicestershire, beginning at 6.52 a.m. on 27 July 1963 and ending at 12.50 a.m. on 28 July, after 17 hours 58 minutes. The peal was composed by Kenneth Lewis of Altrincham, Cheshire, and the eight ringers were conducted by Robert B. Smith, aged 25, of Marple, Cheshire. Theoretically it would take 37 years 355 days to ring 12 bells (maximus) to their full extent of 479,001,600 changes.

SONG

Oldest The oldest known song is the *chadouf* chant, which has been sung since time immemorial by irrigation workers on the man-powered treadwheel Nile water mills (or *saqiyas*) in Egypt (now the United Arab Republic). The English song *Sumer is icumen in* dates from *c.* 1240.

Top songs of all time The most frequently sung songs in English are *Happy Birthday to You* (based on the original *Good morning to all*), by Mildred and Patty S. Hill of New York (published in 1936 and in copyright until 1996); *For He's a Jolly Good Fellow* (originally the French *Malbrouk*), known at least as early as 1781, and *Auld Lang Syne* (originally the Strathspey *I fee'd a Lad at Michaelmass*), some words of which were written by Robert Burns (1759–96). *Happy Birthday* was sung in space by the Apollo IX astronauts on 8 March 1969.

Top selling sheet music Sales of three non-copyright pieces are known to have exceeded 20,000,000 namely *The Old Folks at Home*, *Listen to the Mocking Bird* (1855) and *The Blue Danube* (1867). Of copyright material the two top-sellers are *Let Me Call You Sweetheart* (1910, by Whitson Friedman) and *Till We Meet Again* (1918, by Egan Whiting) each with some 6,000,000 by 1967.

Most monotonous The longest song sung on one note is *Ein Ton*, written in 1859 by Peter Cornelius (1824–74) of Germany. The single note (the B above middle C) is repeated 80 times for 30 bars.

Most successful song writers In terms of sales of single records, the most successful of all song writers have been John Lennon and Paul McCartney (see also Gramophone, Fastest sales, p. 101) of the Beatles. Between 1962 and 1 Jan. 1970 they together wrote 30 songs which sold more than 1,000,000 records each.

HYMNS

Earliest There are believed to be more than 500,000 Christian hymns in existence. "Te Deum Laudamus" dates from about the 5th century, but the earliest exactly datable hymn is the French one "Jesus soit en ma teste et mon entendement" from 1490, translated into the well-known "God be in my head" in 1512.

Longest and shortest The longest hymn is "Hora novissima tempora pessima sunt; vigilemus" by Bernard of Cluny (12th century), which runs to 2,966 lines. In English the longest is "The Sands of Time are sinking" by Mrs. Anne Ross Cousin, *née* Cundell (1824–1906), which is in full 152 lines, though only 32 lines in the Methodist Hymn Book. The shortest hymn is the single verse in Long Metre "Be Present at our Table, Lord", anonymous but attributed to "J. Leland".

Most prolific hymnists Mrs. Frances (Fanny) Jan Van Alstyne, *née* Crosby (1820–1915), of the U.S.A., wrote more than 8,000 hymns although she had been blinded at the age of 6 weeks. She is reputed to have knocked off one hymn in 15 minutes. Charles Wesley (1707–88) wrote about 6,000 hymns. In the seventh (1950) edition of *Hymns Ancient and Modern* the works of John Mason Neale (1818–66) appear 56 times.

Longest hymn-in The Cambridge University Student Methodist Society sang through the 984 hymns in the Methodist Hymn Book in 45 hours 42 minutes, and completed 1,000 hymns with 16 more requests in 88 minutes on 7–9 Feb. 1969 in the Wesley Church, Cambridge.

5. THEATRE

Origins Theatre in Europe has its origins in Greek drama performed in honour of a god, usually Dionysus. The earliest amphitheatres date from the 5th century B.C. The largest of all known *orchestras* is one at Megalopolis in central Greece, where the auditorium reached a height of 75 feet and had a capacity of 17,000.

Oldest *World* The oldest indoor theatre in the world is the Teatro Olimpico in Vicenza, Italy. Designed in the Roman style by Andrea di Pietro, *alias* Palladio (1508–80), it was begun three months before his death and finished in 1582 by his pupil Vicenzo Scamozzi (1552–1616). It is preserved today in its original form.

United Kingdom The earliest London theatre was James Burbage's "The Theatre", built in 1576 near Finsbury Fields, London. The oldest theatre still in use in the United Kingdom is the Theatre Royal, Bristol. The foundation stone was laid on 30 Nov. 1764, and the theatre was opened on 30 May 1766 with a "Concert of Music and a Specimen of Rhetorick". Since then it has been more or less continuously in use as a theatre. It is the home of the Bristol Old Vic Company. Actors were legally rogues and vagabonds until the passing of an act (5 Geo. IV C.38) in 1824. The first honour for work on the stage was to Henry Irving (1838–1905), b. John Henry Brodribb, who was knighted in 1895. The earliest Dame was Geneviève Ward made D.B.E. in 1921. The first stage peer has been Sir Laurence Kerr Olivier (b. 22 May 1907), created a life Baron on 13 June 1970.

Largest *World* The world's largest building used for theatre is the National People's Congress Building (*Ren min da hui* *tang*) on the west side of Tian an men Square, Peking, China. It was completed in 1959 and covers an area of 12·9 acres. The theatre seats 10,000 and is occasionally used as such as in 1964 for the play "The East is Red". The largest regular theatre in the world is Radio City Music Hall in Rockefeller Center, New York City, N.Y., U.S.A. It seats more than 6,200 people and the average annual attendance is more than 8,000,000. The stage is 144 feet wide and 66 feet 6 inches deep, equipped with a revolving turntable 43 feet in diameter and three elevator sections, each 70 feet long.

The greatest seating capacity of any regular theatre in the world is that of the "Chaplin" (formerly the "Blanquita") in Havana, Cuba. It was opened on 30 Dec. 1949 and has 6,500 seats.

United Kingdom The highest capacity theatre is the Odeon, Hammersmith, West London, with 3,485 seats in 1971. The largest theatre stage in the United Kingdom is the Opera House in Blackpool, Lancashire. It was re-built in July 1939 and has seats for 2,975 people. Behind the 45-foot-wide proscenium arch the stage is 110 feet high, 60 feet deep and 100 feet wide, and there is dressing room accommodation for 200 artists.

Smallest The smallest regularly operated professional theatre in the United Kingdom is the Little Theatre, Tobermory, Isle of Mull, Scotland with a capacity of 36 seats.

Largest amphitheatre The largest amphitheatre ever built is the Flavian amphitheatre or Colosseum of Rome, Italy, completed in A.D. 80. Covering 5 acres and with a capacity of 87,000, it has a maximum length of 612 feet and maximum width of 515 feet.

Longest runs *World* The longest run of any show at one theatre anywhere in the world was by the play *The Drunkard*, written by W. H. Smith and "a gentleman". First produced, as a moral lesson, in 1844 by Phineas Taylor Barnum (1810–91), a United States showman, it was not performed commercially again until it was revived on 6 July 1933 at the Theatre Mart in Los Angeles, California, U.S.A. From that date it ran continuously, one show a night, for 7,510 performances, until 3 Sept. 1953. Starting on 7 Sept. 1953, a new musical adaptation of *The Drunkard*, called *The Wayward Way*, started to play alternate nights with the original version. On 17 Oct. 1959 it played its 9,477th and final time. It was seen by more than 3,000,000 people. The producer, Miss Mildred Ilse, was with the play throughout. In Britain, the Brighton Corporation's variety show *Tuesday Night at the Dome* reached its 1,200th performance in 24 years on 1 Dec. 1970.

Broadway The Broadway record is 3,213 performances of *Life with Father* at the Empire, which opened on 8 Nov. 1937 and closed at the end of 1947. The Broadway record for musicals was set by *Hello Dolly*, which opened on 16 Jan. 1964 and closed after 2,844 performances on 27 Dec. 1970. It grossed at least $60 million (£25 million) in New York and "on the road" playing to 8,000,000 people in the U.S. alone. In the Broadway version seven stars have played the role of Dolly: Carol Channing (1,272 performances), Ginger Rogers, Martha Raye, Betty Grable, Pearl Bailey, Phyllis Diller and Ethel Merman. The percussionist Mr. Louis M. Gatti played throughout. In Japan it enjoyed success as "*Haro, Dori*".

London The longest continuous run of any show at one theatre

Britain's longest ever running musical show, The Black and White Minstrels in action

in the United Kingdom is by *The Mousetrap* by Dame Agatha Mary Clarissa Christie, D.B.E. (*née* Miller, now Lady Mallowan) (b. Torquay, Devon, 15 Sept. 1890) at the Ambassadors Theatre (capacity 453). This thriller opened on 25 Nov. 1952, and had its 7,511th performance on 23 Dec. 1970. On 19 Aug. 1969 a power failure caused one performance to be missed. So far 111 actors have played its 8 roles. More than 2,750,000 people have seen the play and it has been calculated that, with the United Kingdom's present rate of natural increase, it can be expected to go on indefinitely.

The longest-running musical show ever performed in Britain was *The Black and White Minstrel Show*, a musical variety presentation which opened at the Victoria Palace, London, on 25 May 1962, was performed *twice* nightly and continued until 24 May 1969 reaching 4,354 performances. The total attendance had been recorded at 5,614,077. One chorus girl claims a pedometer strapped to a leg registered 6½ miles in one night. It reopened as *Magic of the Minstrels* on 24 Nov. 1969.

One-man show The longest run of any one-man show has been 213 performances of *Brief Lives* by Roy Dotrice (b. Guernsey, 5 May 1923) at the Criterion, London from 25 Feb. to 6 Sept. 1969. It also ran 16 nights on Broadway, New York City.

ortest runs *World* The shortest run on record was that of *The Intimate Revue* at the Duchess Theatre, London, on 11 March 1930. Anything which could go wrong did. With scene changes taking up to 20 minutes apiece, the management scrapped seven scenes to get the finale on before midnight. The run was described as "half a performance". Even this fractional first night was surpassed by *As You Like It* by William Shakespeare (1564–1616) at the Shaftesbury Theatre, London, in 1888. On the opening night the fire curtain was let down, jammed, and did not rise again that night or ever again on this production.

Broadway Of the many Broadway shows for which the opening and closing nights coincided, the most costly was *Kelly*, a musical costing $700,000 (then £250,000) which suffered its double ceremony on 6 Feb. 1965.

ngest play The Oberammergau *Passionsspiel* ("Passion Play"), performed every ten years since 1633, was performed with 125 speaking parts, 102 times in 1970, each performance occupying 5½ hours or 8½ hours including intervals. The audience for this 37th presentation ending on 30 September was 530,000.

akespeare The first all amateur company to have staged all 37 of Shakespeare's plays was The Southsea Shakespeare Actors, Hampshire, England, when in October 1966 they presented *Cymbaline*. The director throughout was Mr. K. Edmonds Gateley. Fifteen members of Manchester University completed a dramatic reading of all the plays, 154 sonnets and five narrative poems in 56 hours 25 minutes outdoors on the steps of the Catholic Chaplaincy on 19–21 Feb. 1971. The longest is *Richard III*.

ngest title The longest title of any play was that of 122 words on *The Fire of London*, which in full went on for another 118 words and was presented at The Mermaid Theatre, London on 4 Sept. 1966. This 17th century documentary was written by Peter Black, TV critic of the *Daily Mail*.

Longest chorus line The world's longest permanent chorus line is that formed by the Rockettes in the Radio City Music Hall, which opened in December 1932 in New York City, U.S.A. The 36 girls dance precision routines across the 144-foot-wide stage. The whole troupe, which won the *Grand Prix* in Paris in July 1937, is 46 strong, but 10 girls are always on alternating vacation or are undergoing repairs. The troupe is sometimes augmented to 64.

A scene from the longest play—The Oberammergau Passionsspiel

6. GRAMOPHONE

Origins The gramophone (phonograph) was first described on 30 April 1877 by Charles Cros (1842–88), a French poet and scientist. The first successful machine was constructed by Thomas Alva Edison (1847–1931) of the U.S.A., who gained his first patent on 19 Feb. 1878. It was on 15 Aug. 1877 that he shouted "Mary had a little Lamb". The first practical hand-cranked foil cylinder phonograph was manufactered in the United States by Chichester Bell and Charles Sumner Tainter in 1886.

The country with the greatest number of record players is the United States, with a total of 53,800,000 at mid-1968. A total of more than half a billion dollars (now £209 million) is spent annually on 500,000 juke boxes in the United States.

World sales of records for 1968 have been estimated at 1,141 million. The first year in the United States that retail sales of discs and tapes surpassed $1·5 billion (£625 million) was 1969. This compares with $48,000,000 in 1940.

The peak year for value in U.K. sales of records was 1970 with £39,214,000 for 112,941,000 records.

OLDEST RECORD

The oldest record in the British Broadcasting Corporation's gramophone library is a record made by Emile Berliner (b. Berlin, 1851) of himself reciting the Lord's Prayer. It was made in 1884. Berliner invented the flat disc to replace the cylinder in 1888.

The B.B.C. library, the world's largest, contains over 750,000 records, including 5,250 with no known matrix.

Bing Crosby's platinum disc to commemorate his surpassing the 300 million mark in lifetime sales

Earliest jazz records The earliest jazz record made was *Indiana* and *The Dark Town Strutters Ball*, recorded for the Columbia label in New York City, N.Y., U.S.A., on or about 30 Jan. 1917, by the Original Dixieland Jazz Band, led by Dominick (Nick) James La Rocca (1889–1961). This was released on 31 May 1917. The first jazz record to be released was the O.D.J.B.'s *Livery Stable Blues* (recorded 24 Feb.), backed by *The Dixie Jass Band One-Step* (recorded 26 Feb.), released by Victor on 7 March 1917.

Most successful solo recording artist On 9 June 1960 the Hollywood Chamber of Commerce presented Harry Lillis (*alias* Bing) Crosby, Jr. (b. 2 May 1904 at Tacoma, Washington) with a platinum disc to commemorate a sale of 200,000,000 records from the 2,600 singles and 125 albums he had recorded. On 15 Sept. 1970 he received a second platinum disc for selling 300,650,000 discs with Decca. It was then estimated that his global life-time sales on 88 labels in 28 countries totalled, according to his royalty reports, 362,000,000. His first commercial recording was "*I've Got the Girl*" recorded on 18 Oct. 1926 (master number W142785 (Take 3) issued on the Columbia label).

Most successful group The singers with the greatest sales of any group are the Beatles. This group from Liverpool, Lancashire, comprised George Harrison, M.B.E. (b. 25 Feb. 1943), John Ono (formerly John Winston) Lennon, M.B.E. (b. 9 Oct. 1940), James Paul McCartney, M.B.E. (b. 18 June 1942) and Richard Starkey, M.B.E., *alias* Ringo Starr (b. 7 July 1940). Between February 1963 and September 1970 their sales have been estimated at 133 million (74 million singles, 3 million E.P.s and 56 million albums) which represents 416 million in singles' equivalents.

GOLDEN DISCS

Earliest The earliest recorded piece eventually to aggregate a total sale of a million copies were performances by Enrico Caruso (b. Naples, Italy, 1873, and d. 1921) of the aria *Vesti la giubba (On with the Motley)* from the opera *I Pagliacci* by Ruggiero Leoncavallo (1858–1919), the earliest version of which was recorded with piano on 12 Nov. 1902. The first single recording to surpass the million mark was Alma Gluck's *Carry me back to old Virginny* on the Red Seal Victor label on the 12-inch single faced (later backed) record 74420. The first actual golden disc was one sprayed by R.C.A. Victor for presentation to the U.S. trombonist and band-leader Alton 'Glenn' Miller (1904–44) for his *Chattanooga Choo Choo* on 10 Feb. 1942.

Most The singer with the most golden discs claimed is Elvis Aaron Presley (b. Tupelo, Mississippi, U.S.A., 8 Jan. 1935). By 1 Sept. 1970 he had 86 golden discs (78 for singles, 1 E.P. and 7 for L.P.s), which are said to mark each sale of each 1,000,000 copies among his best-selling records. His total global sales were estimated at 130,000,000 discs by that date representing 275 million singles equivalents. The only *audited* measure of million-selling records within the U.S., however, is certification by the Recording Industry Association of America (R.I.A.A.) introduced in 1958. By their yardstick on U.S. sales, Presley has 10 Golden Discs with an additional 9 for million *dollar* sales (based on one third of list price plus sales of tapes). The champions for R.I.A.A. awards are The Beatles with 21 for singles which sold more than 1 million *copies* and 17 for L.P.s each of which sold more than $1 million worth by 1 Sept. 1970. The Beatles' global total of million-selling titles was believed to stand at 57 by 1 Sept. 1970.

Youngest The youngest age at which an artist has achieved sales of 1,000,000 copies of a record is 6 years by Osamu Minagawa of Tōkyō, Japan for his single *Kuro Neko No Tango (Black Cat Tango)* released on 5 Oct. 1969.

Most recorded song Two songs have each been recorded between 900 and 1,000 times in the United States alone—*St. Louis Blues*, written in 1914 by W. C. (William Christopher) Handy (b. Florence, Alabama 1873 and d. 1958), and *Stardust*,

Enrico Caruso, the first million-seller in the pioneer days of the phonograph

Elvis Presley for whom 86 golden discs have been claimed

written in 1927 by Hoagland ("Hoagy") Carmichael (b. Bloomington, Indiana, 22 Nov. 1899).

Most recordings Ben Selvin (b. 1898) of the U.S.A. has made 9,000 recordings as a violinist, band-leader or recording manager from 1919 to 1966.

Biggest sellers The greatest seller of any gramophone record to date is *White Christmas* by Irving Berlin (b. Israel Baline, at Tyumen, Russia, 11 May 1888). First recorded in 1941, it sold an estimated 100,000,000 to 1 Jan. 1971. This figure includes Bing Crosby's recording of this song (made for the film *Holiday Inn* in 1942) which, alone, accounted for over 30,000,000 by December 1967. The top-selling "pop" record has been *Rock Around the Clock* by William John Clifton Haley, Jr. (b. Detroit, Michigan, March 1927) and the Comets, recorded on 12 April 1954, with collective sales of 22,000,000 by January 1970. The top-selling British record of all-time is *I Want to Hold Your Hand* by the Beatles (see right), with world sales of 11,000,000 to mid-1967, including 5,000,000 in the United States.

est-sellers' charts Radio Luxembourg's "Top Twenty" Sunday night programme, launched in the autumn of 1948, was the first programme based on current selling strength though best-selling lists had been appearing in the U.S. periodical *Billboard* seven years before this. Based on *New Musical Express* data the longest continuous period for which any record has been in the "Top 30" is 39 weeks by *Stranger on the Shore* by Bernard Stanley ("Mr. Acker") Bilk (b. Clutton, Somerset, England, 28 Jan. 1929) from 25 Nov. 1961 to 18 Aug. 1962. The longest in the "Top 20" was 36 weeks by Frankie Laine (b. Frank Paul LoVecchio in Chicago, Illinois, U.S.A., on 30 March 1913) with his *I Believe* (Philips) from 28 March to 28 Nov. 1953. This recording also set records with 35 weeks in the top 10 (4 April to 28 Nov.) and 18 weeks at No. 1 (18 April to 13 June, 27 June to 1 Aug. and 15 Aug. to 29 Aug. 1953). The record for consecutive weeks at No. 1 is 11 by Otis Dewey 'Slim' Whitman, Jr. (b. 20 Jan. 1924 at Tampa, Florida, U.S.A.) with his *Rose Marie* from 23 July to 1 Oct. 1955. Only four records have reached the number one position (based on sales, as opposed to sales plus orders) in their week of release—Elvis Presley's *Jailhouse Rock* (released 17 Jan. 1958), *It's Now or Never* (28 Oct. 1960) and *Surrender* (19 May 1961); and *My Old Man's a Dustman* by Anthony (Lonnie) Donegan (b. Glasgow, Scotland, 29 April 1931) on 18 March 1960.

Greatest monopoly The greatest monopolizing of the sales charts was attained by the Beatles on 31 March 1964. On that date they were No. 1, 2, 3, 4 and 5 in the U.S. charts for the week ending 21 March 1964 with *Twist and Shout, Can't Buy Me Love, She Loves You, I Want to Hold Your Hand* and *Please Please Me*. They were also No. 1 and 2 on the L.P. charts with *Meet the Beatles* and *Introducing the Beatles*.

Long players The longest stay in the L.P. charts in the U.S.A. has been 490 weeks from late in 1958 to July 1968 by the Columbia album *Johnny's Greatest Hits* (Johnny Mathis). The longest in the U.K. has been *South Pacific* (sound track) with 306 weeks to 18 July 1964.

Top-selling L.P. The best-selling L.P. is the 20th Century Fox album *Sing We now of Christmas*, issued in 1958 and re-entitled *The Little Drummer Boy* in 1963. Its sales were reported to be 13,000,000 by 1 Jan. 1970. The first British L.P. to sell 1,000,000 copies was *With the Beatles* (Parlophone), from November 1963 to January 1964 in the United States and to September 1965 in Britain. The top-selling British L.P. is *Sergeant Pepper's Lonely Hearts Club Band* by the Beatles with more than 7,000,000 to 1 Jan. 1970.

Top-selling L.P. sound track The all-time best-seller among long-playing records of musical film shows is *The Sound of Music* sound track album, released by R.C.A. Victor in U.S.A. on 2 March and in Britain on 9 April 1965, with 13,000,000 to 1 Jan. 1970.

Top-selling classical L.P. The first classical long-player to sell a million was a performance featuring the pianist Harvey Lavan (Van) Cliburn, Jr. (b. Kilgore, Texas, 12 July 1934) of the *Piano Concerto No. 1* by Pyotr Ilyich Tchaikovsky (1840–93) (more properly rendered Chaykovskiy) of Russia. This recording was made in 1958 and sales reached 1,000,000 by 1961, 2,000,000 by 1965 and about 2,500,000 by January 1968.

Longest L.P. set The longest long-playing record is the 137-disc set of the complete works of William Shakespeare (1564–1616). The recordings, which were made in 1957–1964, cost £260·62½ per set, and are by the Argo Record Co. Ltd., London, S.W.3. The Vienna Philharmonic's playing of Wagner's "The Ring" covers 19 L.P.s, was eight years in the making, and requires 14½ hours playing time.

Fastest selling L.P.s The fastest selling record of all time is *John Fitzgerald Kennedy—A Memorial Album* (Premium Albums), an L.P. recorded on 22 Nov. 1963, the day of Mr. Kennedy's assassination, which sold 4,000,000 copies at 99 cents (then 35p) in six days (7–12 Dec. 1963), t[illegible] ironically beating the previous speed record set [illegible] satirical L.P. *The First Family* in 1962–63. The [illegible] selling British record has been the Beatles' d[illegible] album *The Beatles* (Parlophone) with "nearly 2 million" in its first week in November 1968.

Advance sales The greatest advance sale was 2,100,000 for *Can't Buy Me Love* by the Beatles, released in the United States on 16 March 1964. The Beatles also equalled their British record of 1,000,000 advance sales, set by *I Want to Hold Your Hand* (Parlophone) on 29 Nov. 1963, with this same record on 20 March 1964. The U.K. record for advance sales of an L.P. is 750,000 for the Parlophone album *Beatles for Sale* on the 4th Dec. 1964.

Highest fee The highest fee ever paid to recording artists for a single performance is $189,000 (then £67,500), paid to The Beatles for a performance in the William A. Shea Stadium baseball park, New York City, N.Y., U.S.A., on 23 Aug. 1966.

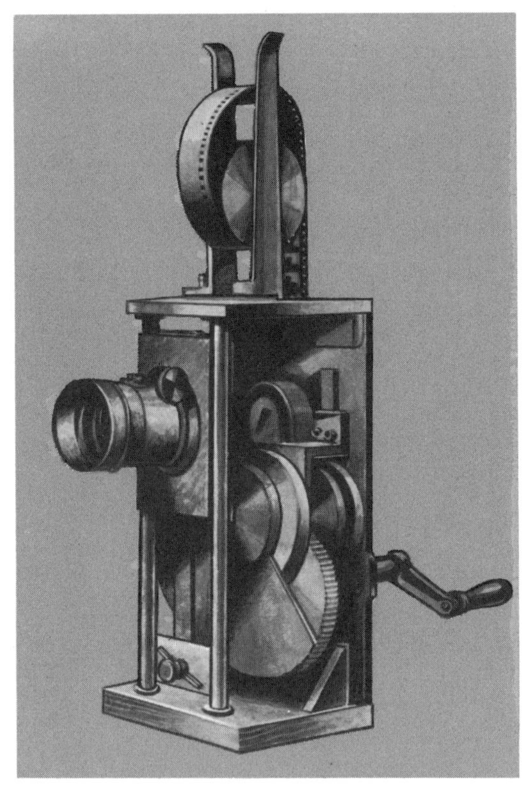

An early hand-cranked Lumière projector

7. CINEMA

EARLIEST

Origins The greatest impetus in the development of cinematography came from the inventiveness of Etienne Jules Marey (1830–1903) of France.

Earliest silent showings The earliest demonstration of a celluloid cinematograph film was given at Lyon (Lyons), France on 22 March 1895 by Auguste Marie Louis Nicolas Lumière (1862–1954) and Louis Jean Lumière (1864–1948), the French brothers. The first public showing was at the Indian Salon of the Hotel Scribe, on the Boulevard des Capucines, in Paris, on 28 Dec. 1895. The 33 patrons were charged 1 franc each and saw ten short films, including *Baby's Breakfast, Lunch Hour at the Lumière Factory* and *The Arrival of a Train*. The same programme was shown on 20 Feb. 1896 at the Polytechnic Institute in Regent Street, London.

Earliest 'Talkie' The earliest sound-on-film motion picture was demonstrated by Joseph Tykociner of the University of Illinois, U.S.A. in 1922. The event is more usually attributed to Dr. Lee de Forest (1873–1961) in New York City, N.Y., U.S.A., on 13 March 1923. The first all-talking picture was *Lights of New York*, shown at The Strand, New York City, on 6 July 1928.

Highest production Japan annually produces most full length films, with 607 films of 1,500 metres (4,921 feet) or more completed in 1967, compared with 304 films of 3,400 metres (11,155 feet) or more approved by the censor in India in 1964. This compares, however, with Japan's production of 1,000 films in 1928. The average seat price in Japan is 70 yen (7p). In the United Kingdom 66 feature films of 72 or more minutes duration were registered in the year ending 30 Sept. 1970.

Highest cinema-going The people of Taiwan go to the cinema more often than those of any other country in the world with an average of 66 attendances per person in 1967. The Soviet Union has the most cinemas in the world, with 154,950 in 1968 including those projecting only 16 mm. film. The number of cinemas in the U.K. declined from 4,542 in 1953 to 1,611 at 31 March 1970. The average weekly admissions declined from 24,700,000 in 1953 to 4,210,000 in 1969.

Most cinema seats The Falkland Islands have more cinema seats per total population than any other country in the world, with 230 seats for each 1,000 inhabitants. Burundi with 7 cinemas has one seat per 3,000. Excluding "captive" projectionists, the most persistent voluntary devotee of a film has been Mrs. Myra Franklin (b. 1919) of Cardiff, Wales, who saw *The Sound of Music* more than 900 times.

CINEMAS

Largest *World* The largest open-air cinema in the world is in the British Sector of West Berlin, Germany. One end of the Olympic Stadium, converted into an amphitheatre, seats 22,000 people.

United Kingdom The United Kingdom's largest cinema is the Odeon Theatre, Hammersmith, London, with 3,485 seats.

Oldest The earliest cinema was the "Electric Theatre", part of a tented circus in Los Angeles, California, U.S.A. It opened on 2 April 1902. The oldest building designed as a cinema is the Biograph Cinema in Wilton Road, Victoria, London. It was opened in 1905 and originally had seating accommodation for 500 patrons. Its present capacity is 700.

Biggest screen The largest cinema screen in the world is one measuring 130 feet by 39 feet (5,070 square feet) built by Andrew Smith Harkness Ltd. of Boreham Wood, Hertfordshire and shipped to South Africa in December 1967.

Most expensive film The most expensive film ever made is the 6 hour 12 min. long *War and Peace*, the U.S.S.R. government adaptation of the masterpiece of Tolstoy produced by Sergei Bondarchuk (b. 1921) over the period 1962–67. The total cost has been officially stated to be more than £40,000,000. More than 165,000 uniforms had to be made. The re-creation of a Napoleonic battle involved 12,000 men and 800 horses on a location near Smolensk in 1964. The greatest number of "extras" used in a film is more than 20,000 Red Army soldiers, at 3 roubles (£1·38) per month, in the joint Hollywood-Columbia, Paramount-Mosfilms production *Waterloo*, filmed in the Ukraine on a \$33 million (£13¾ million) budget and released in 1970.

Most expensive musical The most expensive musical made has been *Dr. Dolittle* which cost \$19,500,000 (£8,125,000) and which had its *première* at the Odeon, Marble Arch, London, W.1, on 12 Dec. 1967.

Most expensive film rights The highest price ever paid for film rights is \$5,500,000 (£1,964,284), paid on 6 Feb. 1962 by Warner Brothers for *My Fair Lady*, which cost \$17,000,000 (£6,070,000),

Helene Costello in "Lights of New York"—the earliest all-talking film

thus making it the most expensive musical film then made.

Longest film The longest film ever shown is *The Human Condition*, directed in three parts by Masaki Kobayashi of Japan. It lasts 8 hours 50 minutes, excluding two breaks of 20 minutes each. It was shown in Tōkyō in October 1961 at an admission price of 250 yen (24½p). The longest film ever released was **** by Andy Warhol which lasted 24 hours. It proved, not surprisingly except reportedly to its creator, a commercial failure and was withdrawn and re-released in 90-minute form as *The Loves of Ondine*.

Longest run It was reported in September 1969 that *Me Tarzan You Jane* was still running in one Egyptian cinema after 20 years since September 1949.

Longest title The longest film title is: *Persecution and Assassination of Jean-Paul Marat as performed by the Inmates of the Asylum of Charenton under the direction of the Marquis de Sade,* first distributed by United Artists in March 1967.

Highest box office gross The film which has had the highest gross earnings (amount paid by cinema owners) is *The Sound of Music* (released in February 1965) which reached $112,481,000 (£46,867,000) by September 1969 having cost 20th Century Fox $8,100,000 to produce. The Producer/Director Robert Wise reportedly received $11¼ million or 10 per cent. of the gross. The most successful black-and-white film has been *The Longest Day*, which cost $10,000,000 (then £3,570,000) to make and grossed $35,000,000 (now £14·58 million) from November 1962 to January 1968.

The fastest-earning film has been *Goldfinger*, the third in the series of films based on stories of James Bond (Agent 007 in the Secret Service) by Ian Lancaster Fleming (1908–64). The film grossed $10,300,000 (£3,678,000) in its first 14 weeks in the United States in 1965.

Highest earnings by an actor The greatest earnings by any film star for one film is expected to be that of Elizabeth Taylor in *Cleopatra*. Her undisputed share of the earnings is $3,000,000 (£1,070,000) and could eventually reach $7,000,000 (£2,500,000).

OSCARS

Most Walter (Walt) Elias Disney (1901–1966) won more "Oscars"—the awards of the United States Academy of Motion Picture Arts and Sciences, instituted on 16 May 1929 for 1927–28—than any other person. His total was 35 from 1931 to 1969. The only actress to win three Oscars in a starring rôle has been Miss Katharine Hepburn, formerly Mrs. Ludlow Ogden Smith (b. Hartford, Conn., 9 Nov. 1909) in *Morning Glory* (1932–3), *Guess Who's Coming to Dinner* (1967) and *The Lion in Winter* (1968). Oscars are named after Mr. Oscar Pierce of Texas, U.S.A. The films with most awards have been *Ben Hur* (1959) with 11, followed by *West Side Story* (1961) with 10. The film with the highest number of nominations was *All About Eve* (1950) with 14.

Newsreels The world's most durable newsreel commentator has been Bob Danvers Walker (b. Cheam, Surrey, 11 Oct. 1906), who commentated for Pathé "Gazette" from June 1940 until its demise in February 1970. He is the owner of the car registration numbers TV 1 and RAD 10.

8. RADIO BROADCASTING

Origins The earliest description of a radio transmission system was written by Dr. Mahlon Loomis (U.S.A.) (b. Fulton County, N.Y., 21 July 1826) on 21 July 1864 and demonstrated between two kites more than 14 miles apart at Bear's Den, Loudoun County, Virginia in October 1866. He received U.S. patent No. 129,971 entitled Improvement in Telegraphing on 20 or 30 July 1872. He died in 1886.

Earliest patent The first patent for a system of communication by means of electro-magnetic waves, numbered No. 12039, was granted on 22 June 1896 to the Italian-Irish Marchese Guglielmo Marconi (1874–1937). A public demonstration of wireless transmission of speech was, however, given in the town square of Murray, Kentucky, U.S.A. in 1892 by Nathan B. Stubblefield. He died destitute on 28 March 1928. The first permanent wireless installation was at The Needles on the Isle of Wight, Hampshire, by Marconi's Wireless Telegraph Co., Ltd., in November 1896.

Earliest broadcast *World* The world's first advertised broadcast was made on 24 Dec. 1906 by Prof. Reginald Aubrey Fessenden (1868–1932) from the 420-foot mast of the National Electric Signalling Company at Brant Rock, Massachusetts, U.S.A. The transmission included the *Largo* by Georg Friedrich Händel (1685–1759) of Germany. Fessenden had achieved the broadcast of highly distorted speech as early as November 1900.

United Kingdom The first experimental broadcasting transmitter in the United Kingdom was set up at the Marconi Works in Chelmsford, Essex, in December 1919, and broadcast a news service in February 1920. The earliest regular broadcast of entertainment was made from the Marconi transmitter "2 MT" at Writtle, Essex, on 14 Feb. 1922.

Transatlantic transmissions The earliest transatlantic wireless signals (the letter S in Morse Code) were sent by Marconi from a 10-kilowatt station at Poldhu, Cornwall, and received by Percy Wright Paget and G. S. Kempon at St. John's, Newfoundland, Canada, on 11 Dec. 1901. Human speech was first heard across the Atlantic in November 1915 when a transmission from the U.S. Navy station at Arlington, Virginia was received by U.S. radio-telephone engineers on the Eiffel Tower, Paris.

Most stations The country with the greatest number of radio transmitters is the United States, where there were 7,249 authorized transmitting stations in 1969 of which 4,263 were AM (Amplitude modulation) and 2,324 FM (Frequency modulation).

Radio sets There were an estimated 586,000,000 radio sets in use throughout the world at 30 June 1968, equivalent to 169 for each 1,000 people. Of these about 290,000,000 were in the United States (including Puerto Rico and the U.S. Virgin Islands) at 31 Dec. 1968. Of the U.S. total of 310 million for the end of 1969, 80,000,000 were in cars. The equivalent United Kingdom figure is 328 per 1,000 on the basis of 18,589,666 broadcast and broadcast/television licences current on 1 Jan. 1971. Of these only 2,074,034 were for sound only.

Longest The longest B.B.C. broadcast was the reporting of the Coronation of Queen Elizabeth II on 2 June 1953. It began at 10.15 a.m. and finished at 5.30 p.m., after 7 hours 15 minutes. This was well surpassed by Radio Station ELBC, Monrovia, on 23 Nov. 1961 when a transmission of 14 hours 20 minutes was devoted to the coverage of the Queen's visit to Liberia.

Most durable B.B.C. programmes The most durable B.B.C. radio series is *The Week's Good Cause* beginning on 24 Jan. 1926. *Any Questions* was first broadcast on 1 Jan. 1941 and the longest running record programme is *Desert Island Discs* which began on 29 Jan. 1942 and on which programme the only guest to be thrice stranded has been Arthur Bowden Askey, O.B.E. (b. 6 June 1900), most recently in 1955 and 1968. The *Desert Island* programme has been presented since its inception by Roy Plomley, who also devised the idea. The longest running solo radio feature is *Letter from America* by (Alfred) Alistair Cooke (b. 20 Nov. 1908), first commissioned as a series of 13 talks on 6 March 1946. The longest running comedy show has been *The Clitheroe Kid* started in 1958, which entered its 14th successive year in 1971.

John Logie Baird (1888–1946), the Scots-born pioneer of monochrome, colour and 3D television

9. TELEVISION

Invention The invention of television, the instantaneous viewing of distant objects, was not an act but a process of successive and inter-dependent discoveries. The first commercial cathode ray tube was introduced in 1897 by Karl Ferdinand Braun (1850–1918), but was not linked to "electric vision" until 1907 by Boris Rosing of Russia in St. Petersburg (now Leningrad). The earliest public demonstration of television was given on 26 Jan. 1926 by John Logie Baird (1888–1946) of Scotland, using a development of the mechanical scanning system suggested by Paul Nipkov in 1884. A patent application for the Iconoscope (No. 2,141,059) had been filed on 29 Dec. 1923 by Vladimir Kosma Zworykin (born in Russia on 30 July 1889, became a U.S. citizen in 1924), and a short range transmission of a model windmill had been made on 13 June 1925 by C. Francis Jenkins in Washington, D.C., U.S.A.

Earliest service The world's first public television broadcasting service was opened from Alexandra Palace, London, N.22, on 2 Nov. 1936, when there were about 100 sets in the United Kingdom. A television station at Berlin-Witzleben, Germany, made its first transmission on 4 April 1936.

Transatlantic transmission The earliest transatlantic transmission by satellite was achieved at 1 a.m. on 11 July 1962, *via* the active satellite *Telstar I* from Andover, Maine, U.S.A., to Pleumeur Bodou, France. The picture was of Mr. Frederick R. Kappel, chairman of the American Telephone and Telegraph Company, which owned the satellite. The first "live" broadcast was made on 23 July 1962. The earliest satellite transmission was one of 2,700 miles from California to Massachusetts, U.S.A., *via* the satellite *Echo I*, on 3 May 1962—the letters M.I.T.

Most sets In late 1968 the total estimated number of television transmitters in use or under construction was 5,450 serving 217,000,000 sets (63 for each 1,000 of the world population). Of these, about 94,200,000 were estimated to be in use in the United States where 96 per cent. of the population is reached. The number of colour sets in the U.S.A. has grown from 200,000 in 1960 to 25,400,000 by January 1970. The number of licences current in the United Kingdom was 16,515,626 on 1 Jan. 1971 of which 727,707 were for colour sets.

Greatest audience The greatest number of viewers for a televised event is an estimated 600,000,000 for the live and recorded transmissions of man's first lunar landing with the *Apollo XI* mission on 20–21 July 1969. This total was reportedly matched by the viewership of the landing of the nearly disastrous *Apollo XIII* space mission on 17 April 1970.

Largest T.V. prizes *World* The greatest amount won by an individual in T.V. prizes was $264,000 (then £94,286) by Teddy Nadler on quiz programmes in the United States up to September 1958. In March 1960 he failed a test to become a census enumerator because of his inability to distinguish between east and west. His comment was, reportedly, "Those maps threw me". In Australia, where T.V. prizes were not subject to income tax, the most successful contestant has been Barry O. Jones, a schoolteacher of Windsor, Victoria, who won $A52,620 (then £21,012 sterling) between June 1960 and June 1966.

United Kingdom The largest T.V. prize won in the U.K. is £5,580 by Bernard Davis, aged 33, on Granada T.V.'s "Twenty-one" quiz programme, reached on 24 Sept. 1958.

Most successful appeal The greatest amount raised by any B.B.C. T.V. or Radio Appeal was £1,500,000, raised as a result of an appeal by Richard Samuel Attenborough, C.B.E. (b. Cambridge, 29 Aug. 1923) on behalf of the East Pakistan Cyclone Disaster Fund.

LARGEST CONTRACTS

World The largest T.V. contract ever signed was one for $34,000,000 (£14,166,666) in a three-year no-option contract between Dino Paul Crocetti (b. 7 June 1917) otherwise Dean Martin, and N.B.C. Dean Martin was acclaimed in September 1968 as the top-earning show-business personality of all-time with $5,000,000 (over £2 million) in a year. Television's highest-paid interviewer has been Garry Moore (b. Thomas Garrison Morfit on 31 Jan. 1915), who was earning $43,000 (£15,357) a week in 1963, equivalent to $2,236,000 (nearly £800,000) per year.

United Kingdom The largest contract in British television was one of a reported £9,000,000, inclusive of production expenses, signed by Tom Jones (b. Thomas Jones Woodward, 7 June 1940) of Treforest, Glamorgan, Wales in June 1968 with ABC-TV of the United States and ATV in London for 17 one-hour shows per annum from January 1969 to January 1974.

Hourly The world's highest paid television performer based on an hourly rate is Perry Como (b. Pierino Como, Canonsburg, Pennsylvania, U.S.A., on 18 May 1912) who began as a barber. In May 1969 he signed a contract with N.B.C. to star in four one-hour video specials at $5,000,000 (£2,083,333) or at the rate of £8,680·55 per minute. The contract requires him to provide supporting artistes.

Longest telecast The longest pre-scheduled telecast on record was *The Jerry Lewis Telethon,* soliciting donations for muscular distrophy treatment lasting 18¼ hours on 6–7 Sept. 1970 and raising more than $5,000,000 (£2,083,333).

Most durable B.B.C. programme The longest running T.V. programme on B.B.C. is *Panorama* which was first transmitted, introduced by Max Robertson (b. Dacca, East Pakistan, 28 Aug. 1915) on 11 Nov. 1953. The News has been featured since 23 March 1938.

Earliest T.V. critic The first man in the world appointed to be a T.V. critic and correspondent was Leonard Marsland Gander (b. 27 June 1902) by the London *Daily Telegraph* in 1935—the year before the B.B.C.'s 405 line transmissions. He retired in July 1970 after 35 years with T.V. and 44 years with radio. The first "clearly recognizable" face he was able to see on the 30 line transmission was that of Leslie Mitchell (b. Edinburgh, 1905).

7 THE WORLD'S STRUCTURES

EARLIEST STRUCTURES

World The earliest known human structure is a rough circle of loosely piled lava blocks found in 1960 on the lowest cultural level at the Lower Palaeolithic site at Olduvai Gorge in Tanganyika (now part of Tanzania). The structure was associated with artifacts and bones and may represent a work-floor, dating to *c.* 1,750,000 B.C. (see Chapter 1, Early Man). The earliest evidence of buildings yet discovered is that of 21 huts with hearths or pebble-lined pits and delimited by stake holes found in October 1965 at the Terra Amata site in Nice, France originally dated to 300,000 B.C. but now thought to be more likely belonging to the Acheulian culture of 120,000 years ago. Excavation carried out between 28 June and 5 July 1966 revealed one hut with palisaded walls with axes of 49 feet and 20 feet. There is however, evidence of man's ability to make fire in the Abbevillian period *c.* 500,000 B.C. but no evidence as yet of the earliest hearths being surrounded by structures.

United Kingdom A rudimentary platform of birch branches, stones and wads of clay thrown down on the edge of a swamp at Star Carr, south of Scarborough, Yorkshire, may possibly represent the earliest man-made "dwelling" yet found in Britain (Mesolithic, *c.* 7650 B.C.). Remains of the earliest dated stone shelter and cooking pit were discovered in 1967 on the Isle of Portland, Dorset (Mesolithic, *c.* 5200 B.C.). The rock shelter on Oldbury Hill, ¾ of a mile south-west of Ightham, Kent, is believed to have been occupied by the Mousterian people before the onset of the Last Glaciation of the Ice Age, *c.* 80,000 B.C.

1. BUILDINGS FOR WORKING

LARGEST BUILDINGS

Manufacturing The largest ground area covered by any building in the world is the main assembly building at the Boeing Company's works at Everett, Washington State, U.S.A. It encloses a floor area of 1,565,000 square feet (36·0 acres). Construction was begun in August 1966 and parts were in use by late 1967. The building, constructed for the manufacture of Boeing 747 jet airliners, has a maximum height of 115 feet and has a capacity of 200 million cubic feet.

Scientific The most capacious scientific building in the world is the Vehicle Assembly Building (VAB) at Complex 39, the selected site for the final assembly and launching of the Apollo moon spacecraft on the Saturn V rocket, at the John F. Kennedy Space Center (KSC) on Merritt Island, near Cape Kennedy (formerly Cape Canaveral), Florida, U.S.A. It is a steel-framed building measuring 716 feet in length, 518 feet in width and 525 feet high. The building contains four bays, each with its own door 460 feet high. Construction began in April 1963 by the Ursum Consortium. Its floor area is 343,500 square feet (7·87 acres) and its capacity is 129,482,000 cubic feet. The building was "topped out" on 14 April 1965 at a cost of $108,700,000 (£45·3 million).

Administrative The largest ground area covered by any office building is that of the Pentagon, in Arlington County, Virginia, U.S.A. Built to house the U.S. Defense Department's offices, it was completed on 15 Jan. 1943 and cost about $83,000,000 (now £34,583,000). Each of the outermost sides of the Pentagon is 921 feet long and the perimeter of the building is about 1,500 yards. The five storeys of the building enclose a floor area of 6,500,000 square feet. During the day 29,000 people work in the building. The telephone system of the building has over 44,000 telephones connected by 160,000 miles of cable and its 220 staff handle 280,000 calls a day. Two restaurants, six cafeterias and ten snackbars and a staff of 675 form the catering department of the building. The corridors measure 17 miles in length and there are 7,748 windows to be cleaned.

Commercial The largest commercial or office buildings in the world are The World Trade Center in New York City, U.S.A. with a total of 9,000,000 square feet (206·6 acres) of rentable space.

Single office *Largest in U.K.* The largest single office in the United Kingdom is that of the West Midlands Gas Board at Solihull, Warwickshire, set up in 1962. It measures 565 feet by 160 feet (2·07 acres) in one open plan room accommodating 1,570 clerical and managerial workers.

TALLEST BUILDINGS

World The tallest inhabited building in the world is the Port of New York Authority's World Trade Center with twin towers of 110 storeys, standing 1,353 feet tall. Work started in August 1966 on Barclay and Liberty Streets, Lower West Side, Manhattan Island, New York City, N.Y., U.S.A. and the North Tower was topped out on 14 Dec. 1970, having surpassed the

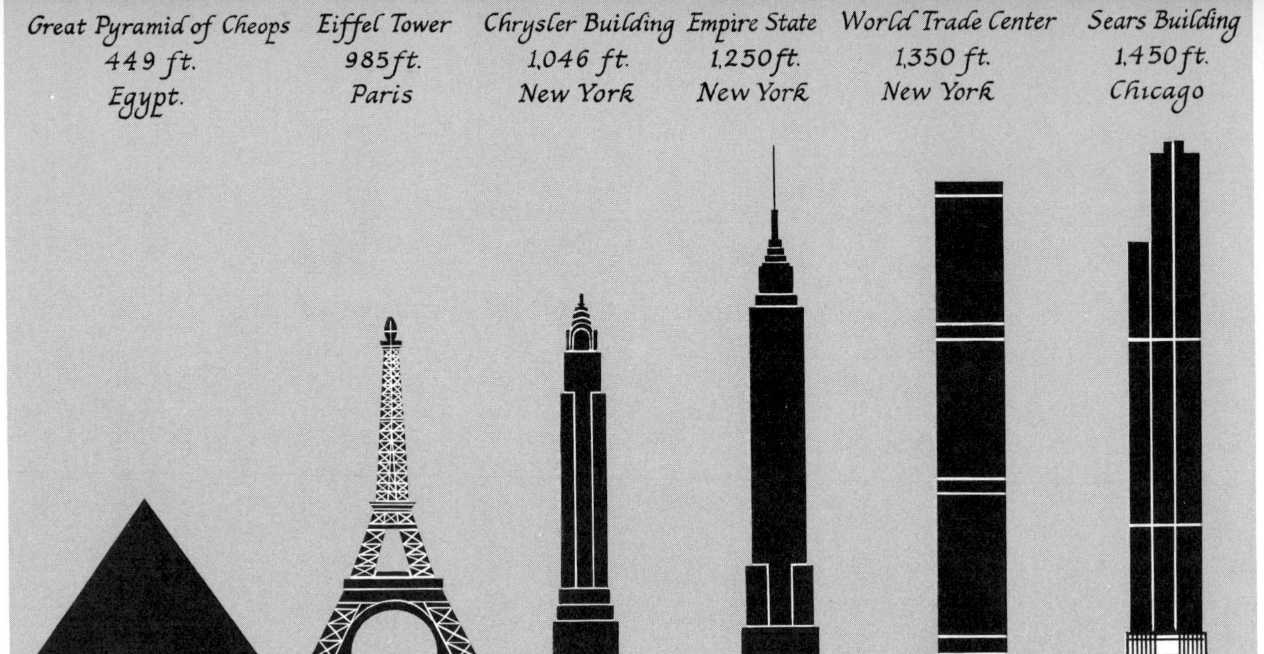

Champion Tall Buildings from the Eiffel Tower of 1889 to the Sears Tower due for completion in 1974

Empire State Building on 21 Oct. 1970. The total cost is estimated at $650,000,000 (£270·8 million). A 365-foot antenna tower will bring the total height of the North Tower to 1,718 feet. Completion will be in 1973. Each tower will have 21,800 windows and 104 elevators. The World Trade Center will be overtopped by the Sears Tower, the national headquarters of Sears Roebuck in Wacker Drive, Chicago, Illinois. It will have 109 storeys, rising to 1,451 feet and be due for completion in 1974. Its gross area will be 4,400,000 square feet (101·0 acres).

The maximum sway allowed for in a 150 m.p.h. hurricane would be 11 inches.

Most storeys The World Trade Center (see above) has 110 storeys—eight more than the Empire State Building. The projects for the 1,300-foot Schaumburg Planet Corporation Building with a 250-foot antenna and the 1,610-foot Barrington Space Needle, Barrington, Illinois, call for 113 and 120 storeys respectively.

United Kingdom The tallest office block in Britain is The National Westminster tower block in Bishopsgate, City of London due to be topped out in 1972, it will be 600 feet above street level.

HABITATIONS

Greatest altitude The highest inhabited buildings in the world are those in the Chilean mining village of Aucanquilca, at 17,500 feet above sea-level (see also Chapter XI). During the 1960–61 Himalayan High Altitude Expedition, the "silver hut", a prefabricated laboratory, was inhabited for four months in the Ming Bo Valley at 18,765 feet. In April 1961, however, a 3-room dwelling was discovered at 21,650 feet on Cerro Llullaillaco (22,058 feet), on the Argentine-Chile border, believed to date from the late pre-Columbian period *c.* 1480.

The Silver Hut in the Ming Bo Valley at 18,765 feet

Northernmost The most northerly habitation in the world is the Danish scientific station set up in 1952 in Pearyland, northern Greenland, over 900 miles north of the Arctic Circle. Eskimo hearths dated to before 1,000 B.C. were discovered in Pearyland in 1969. The U.S.S.R. and the United States have maintained research stations on ice floes in the Arctic. The U.S.S.R.'s "North Pole 15" which drifted 1,250 miles passed within 1¼ miles of the North Pole in December 1967.

Southernmost The most southerly permanent human habitation is the United States' Scott-Amundsen I.G.Y. (International Geophysical Year) base 800 yards from the South Pole.

EMBASSIES

Largest The largest embassy in the world is the U.S.S.R. embassy on Bei Xiao Jie, Peking, China, in the north-eastern corner of the Northern walled city. The whole 45-acre area of the old Orthodox Church mission (established 1728), now known as the *Bei guan*, was handed over to the U.S.S.R. in 1949. The largest in Great Britain is the United States of America Embassy in Grosvenor Square, London. The Chancery Building, completed in 1960, alone has 600 rooms for a staff of 700, on seven floors with a usable floor area of 255,000 square feet (5·85 acres).

PLANTS

Atomic The largest atomic plant in the world is the Savannah River Project, near Aiken, South Carolina, U.S.A., extending 27 miles along the river and over a total area of 315 square miles. The plant, comprising 280 permanent buildings, cost $1,400 million (£583 million). Construction was started in February 1951 and by September 1952 the labour force had reached 38,500. The present operating strength is 8,500.

Underground The world's largest underground factory was the Mittelwerk Factory, near Nordhausen in the Kohnstein Hills, south of the Harz Mountains, Germany. It was built with concentration camp labour during World War II and had a floor area of 1,270,000 square feet and an output of 900 V-2 rockets per month.

Tallest chimneys The world's tallest chimney is the $5·5 million International Nickel Company's stack 1,250 feet 9 inches tall at Copper Cliff, Sudbury, Ontario, Canada, completed in 1970. It was built by The M. W. Kellogg Company and the diameter tapers from 116·4 feet at the base to 51·8 feet at the top. It weighs 38,390 tons and became operational in 1971. The tallest chimney in Great Britain is one of 850 feet at Drax Power Station, Yorkshire, begun in 1966 and topped out on 16 May 1969. It was built by Holst & Co. Ltd. of Watford, Hertfordshire.

Cooling towers The largest cooling towers in the United Kingdom are the Ferrybridge "C" power station, Yorkshire, type measuring 375 feet tall and 300 feet across the base.

Each of the first 24 of the eventual 38 of this type throughout the country cost £340,000.

LARGEST HANGARS

World The world's largest hangar is the Goodyear Airship hangar at Akron, Ohio, U.S.A. which measures 1,175 feet long, 325 feet wide and 200 feet high. It covers 364,000 square feet (8·35 acres) and has a capacity of 55,000,000 cubic feet. The world's largest single fixed-wing aircraft hangar is the Lockheed-Georgia engineering test center at Marietta, Georgia measuring 630 feet by 480 feet (6·94 acres) completed in 1967.

The world's largest hangar at Akron, Ohio

The largest group of hangars in the world is at the U.S. Air Force Base near San Antonio, Texas, U.S.A. These, including covered maintenance bays, cover 23 acres.

United Kingdom The largest hangar building in the United Kingdom is the Britannia Assembly Hall at the Bristol Aeroplane Company's works at Filton, Bristol. The overall width of the Hall is 1,054 feet and the overall depth of the centre bay is 420 feet. It encloses a floor area of $7\frac{1}{2}$ acres. The cubic capacity of the Hall is 33,000,000 cubic feet. The building was begun in April 1946 and completed by September 1949.

GRAIN ELEVATOR

The world's largest single-unit grain elevator is that operated by the C-G-F- Grain Company at Wichita, Kansas, U.S.A. Consisting of a triple row of storage tanks, 123 on each side of the central loading tower or "head house", the unit is 2,717 feet long and 100 feet wide. Each tank is 120 feet high, with an inside diameter of 30 feet, giving a total storage capacity of 20,000,000 bushels of wheat. The largest collection of elevators in the world is at Port Arthur, Ontario, Canada, on Lake Superior.

GARAGES

Largest The largest garage in the world is that completed in September 1961 for the Austin Motor Works at Longbridge, near Birmingham. It has nine storeys and cost £500,000. It has a capacity of 3,300 cars. The United Kingdom's largest underground garage is Normand Ltd.'s Park Lane Garage, London, W.1, extending over nearly seven acres, 350 yards long by 96 yards wide with a capacity of 1,100 cars. It was opened on 15 Oct. 1962 at a cost of £1,051,915. The air can be changed six times per hour. The East corridor to Marble Arch tube station is 534 yards, or more than three-tenths of a mile, long.

Private The largest private garage ever built was one for 100 cars at the Long Island, New York mansion of William Kissam Vanderbilt (1849–1920).

Filling station The largest filling station of 36,000 in the United Kingdom is the Blue Star service station on the M6 at Charnock Richard, Lancashire. It has 50 petrol pumps supplying five brands and 10 derv pumps (for *d*iesel-*e*ngined *r*oad *v*ehicles) supplying five brands of diesel fuel and extends over 14 acres.

SEWAGE WORKS

Largest *World* The largest single sewage works in the world is the West-Southwest Treatment Plant, opened in 1940 on a site of 501 acres in Chicago, Illinois, U.S.A. It serves an area containing 2,900,000 people. It treated an average of 735,000,000 gallons of wastes per day in 1965.

United Kingdom The highest average flow in the United Kingdom is that of the G.L.C. (Greater London Council) Beckton Sewage Treatment Works, London, E.6, completed in October 1959 with major extensions due for completion in September 1973. The amount of sewage treated daily varies between 200 million gallons (dry weather) and 650 million gallons (wet weather). It serves an area of 112 square miles and more than 3,000,000 residents. The total B.O.D. (biological oxygen demand) load removed in a year is more than 135,340 tons.

WAREHOUSES

Largest *World* The world's largest warehouse is the Eurostore, built by the Garonor warehousing firm on a 240-acre site near Le Bourget, in north-east Paris, France. The building provides 5,400,000 square feet (124 acres) of floor-space.

United Kingdom The largest in the United Kingdom is the tobacco warehouse at Stanley Dock, Liverpool, with 11 storeys giving a total floor space of 36 acres, and a frontage of 625 feet.

Glasshouse The largest glasshouse in the United Kingdom is one 826 feet long and 348 feet wide, covering 6·5 acres at Brough, East Yorkshire, completed in 1971. A total of 420 tons of glass was used in glazing it.

2. BUILDINGS FOR LIVING

WOODEN BUILDINGS

Oldest The oldest wooden building in the world is the Temple of Horyu (Horyu-ji), built at Nara, Japan, in A.D. 708–715. The largest wooden building in the world, the nearby Daibutsuden, built in 1704–11, measures 285·4 feet long, 167·3 feet wide and 153·5 feet tall.

Largest The municipal building occupied by the Department of Education in Wellington, New Zealand built in 1876 has the largest floor area of any wooden building with 101,300 square feet.

CASTLES

Earliest *World* Castles in the sense of unfortified manor houses existed in all the great early civilizations, including that of ancient Egypt from 3,000 B.C. Fortified castles in the more accepted sense only existed much later. The oldest in the world is that at Gomdan, in the Yemen, which originally had 20 storeys and dates from before A.D. 100.

British Isles The oldest stone castle extant in Great Britain is Richmond Castle, Yorkshire, built in *c.* 1075. Iron Age relics from the first century B.C. or A.D. have been found in the lower levels of Dover Castle.

Ireland The oldest Irish castle is Ferrycarrig near Wexford dating from *c.* 1180. The oldest castle in Northern Ireland is Carrickfergus Castle, County Antrim, which dates from before 1210.

Largest *World* The largest castle in the world is the Qila (Citadel) at Halab (Aleppo) in Syria. It is oval in shape and has a surrounding wall 1,230 feet long and 777 feet wide. It dates, in its present form, from the Humanid dynasty of the 10th century A.D.

Thickest walls The most massive keep in the world was that in the 13th-century château at Coucy-le-Chateau-Auffrique, in the Department of L'Aisne, France. It was 177 feet high, 318 feet in circumference and had walls over $22\frac{1}{2}$ feet in thickness. It was levelled to its foundations by the Germans in 1917. The walls of Babylon north of

Doune Castle, Perthshire, built in the 15th century

Al Hillah, Iraq, built in 600 B.C., were up to 85 feet in thickness. The walls of part of Dover Castle, Kent, measure 20 feet in thickness. The largest Norman keep in Britain is that of Colchester Castle measuring 152½ feet by 111½ feet.

United Kingdom and Ireland The largest castle in the British Isles and the largest inhabited castle in the world is the Royal residence of Windsor Castle at New Windsor, Berkshire. It is primarily of 12th century construction and is in the form of a parallelogram, 1,890 feet by 540 feet. The overall dimensions of Carisbrooke Castle (450 feet by 360 feet), Isle of Wight, if its earthworks are included, are 1,350 feet by 825 feet. The largest castle in Scotland was the now ruined Doune Castle, Perthshire, built *c.* 1425. The most capacious of all Irish castles is Carrickfergus (see p. 107) in Antrim but that with the most extensive fortifications is Trim Castle, County Meath, built in *c.* 1205 with a curtain wall 485 yards long.

PALACES

Largest *World* The largest palace in the world is the Imperial Palace (*Gu gong*) in the centre of Peking (*Bei jing*, the northern capital), China, which covers a rectangle 1,050 yards by 820 yards, an area of 177·9 acres. The outline survives from the construction of the third Ming emperor Yong le of 1307–20, but due to constant re-arrangements most of the intra-mural buildings are 18th century. These consist of 5 halls and 17 palaces of which the last occupied by the last Empress was the Palace of Accumulated Elegance (*Chu xia gong*) until 1924.

Residential The largest residential palace in the world is the Vatican Palace, in the Vatican City, an enclave in Rome, Italy. Covering an area of 13½ acres, it has 1,400 rooms, chapels and halls, of which the oldest date from the 15th century.

United Kingdom The largest palace in the United Kingdom in Royal use is Buckingham Palace, London, so named after its site, bought in 1703 by John Sheffield, the 1st Duke of Buckingham and Normanby (1648–1721). Buckingham House was reconstructed in the Palladian style between 1835 and 1836, following the design of John Nash (1752–1835). The 610-foot-long East Front was built in 1846 and refaced in 1912. The Palace, which stands in 39 acres of garden, has 600 rooms including a ballroom 111 feet long.

The largest ever Royal palace has been Hampton Court Palace, Greater London, acquired by Henry VIII from Cardinal Wolsey in 1525 and greatly enlarged by the King and later by William III, Anne and George I, whose son George II was its last resident monarch.

Largest moat The world's largest moats are those which surround the Imperial Palace in Peking (see left). From plans drawn by French sources it appears to measure 54 yards wide and have a total length of 3,600 yards.

FLATS

Largest The largest block of flats in Britain is Dolphin Square, London, covering a site of 7½ acres. The building occupies the four sides of a square enclosing gardens of about three acres. Dolphin Square contains 1,220 separate and self-contained flats, an underground garage for 300 cars with filling and service station, a swimming pool, eight squash courts, a tennis court and an indoor shopping centre. It cost £1,750,000 to build in 1936 but was sold to Westminster City Council for £4,500,000 in January 1963. Its nine storeys house 3,000 people.

The largest municipal block of flats in Britain is the Quarry Hill development, Leeds, Yorkshire, completed in 1940. The £497,140 building covers 3·65 acres and contains 938 dwellings, comprising 3,188 rooms housing 3,280 people. The Hyde Park development in Sheffield, Yorkshire, comprises 1,322 dwellings and an estimated population of 4,675 persons. It was built between 1959 and 1966.

Tallest *World* The tallest block of flats in the world are Lake Point Towers of 70 storeys, and 645 feet in Chicago, Illinois, U.S.A.

Britain The highest in the United Kingdom are at Red Road, Balornock, Glasgow, which have 31 storeys, a height of 265 feet and were completed in 1967. The tallest residential blocks in the United Kingdom are the three tower blocks in the Barbican in the City of London, E.C.2, which have between 39 and 41 levels of flats and rise to a height of 417 feet above the street. The first tower was topped out in May 1971.

HOTELS

Largest *World* The world's largest hotel is the Hotel Rossiya in Moscow, U.S.S.R., with 3,200 rooms providing accommodation for 6,000 guests, in three buildings, each of 14 storeys completed in December 1967. The largest hotel in a single building is the Conrad Hilton (formerly the Stevens) on Michigan Avenue, Chicago, Illinois, U.S.A. Its 25 floors contain 2,600 (originally 3,000) guest rooms. It would thus take more than seven years to spend one night in each room of the hotel. The hotel employs about 2,000 people, of whom more than 70 are telephone operators and supervisors, and 72 are lift operators. The laundry of the hotel, with 195 employees, handles 535 tons of flat work each month.

The world's largest private house—Biltmore House, North Carolina, U.S.A.

The largest hotel building in the world, on the basis of volume, is the Waldorf Astoria, on Park Avenue, New York City, N.Y., U.S.A. It occupies a complete block of 81,337 square feet (1·87 acres) and reaches a maximum height of 625 feet 7 inches. The Waldorf Astoria has 47 storeys and 1,900 guest rooms and maintains the largest hotel radio receiving system in the world. The Waldorf can accommodate 10,000 people at one time and has a staff of 1,700. The restaurants have catered for parties up to 6,000 at a time. The coffee-makers' daily output reaches 1,000 gallons. The electricity bill is about $360,000 (£150,000) each year.

United Kingdom The greatest capacity of any hotel in the United Kingdom is that of the Regent Palace Hotel, Piccadilly Circus, London (opened on 20 May 1915). It has 1,140 rooms accommodating 1,670 guests. The total staff numbers 1,200. The largest hotel is the Grosvenor House Hotel, Park Lane, London, which was opened in 1929. It is of 8 storeys covering 2½ acres and caters for more than 100,000 visitors per year in 470 rooms. The Great Room is the largest hotel room in Great Britain measuring 181 feet by 131 feet with a height of 23 feet. Banquets for 1,500 are frequently handled.

Tallest The world's tallest hotel is the 34-storey Ukrania in Moscow, U.S.S.R., which, including its tower, is 650 feet tall. The highest hotel rooms in the world are those on the topmost 50th storey of the 509-foot-tall Americana Hotel, opened on 24 Sept. 1962 on 7th Avenue at 52nd Street, New York City, N.Y., U.S.A. Britain's tallest hotel is the 33-storey London Hilton (328 feet tall), completed in Park Lane, London, W.1, in 1962. It was opened on 17 April, 1963.

Most expensive The world's costliest hotel is the Mauna Kea Beach Hotel on Hawaii Island, U.S.A., which was built at a cost of $15,000,000 (£6,250,000) and has only 154 rooms. This implies a construction and amenity cost of more than £40,600 per room.

The Presidential Suite (8 rooms) in the New York Hilton cost $500 (then £178·50) in 1963. The most expensive hotel suites in Britain are the luxury suites in the London Hilton, Park Lane, London, W.1. Some suites are 80 guineas (£84) per night.

SPAS

The largest spa in the world measured by number of available hotel rooms is Vichy, Allier, France, with 14,000 rooms. Spas are named after the watering place in the Liège province of Belgium where hydropathy was developed from 1626. The highest French spa is Barèges, Hautes-Pyrénées, at 4,068 feet above sea level.

HOUSING

Largest estate The largest housing estate in the United Kingdom is the 1,670-acre Becontree Estate, on a site of 3,000 acres in Barking and Redbridge, Greater London, built between 1921 and 1929. The total number of homes is 26,822, with an estimated population of nearly 90,000.

New towns Of the 23 new towns being built in Great Britain that with the largest eventual planned population will be Milton Keynes, Buckinghamshire, with 250,000 by 1992.

Largest house *World* The largest private house in the world is the 250-room Biltmore House in Asheville, North Carolina, U.S.A. It is owned by George and William Cecil, grandsons of George Washington Vanderbilt II (1862–1914). The house was built between 1890 and 1895 in an estate of 119,000 acres, at a cost of $4,100,000 (now £1,708,333) and now valued at $55,000,000 with 12,000 acres. The most expensive private house ever built is La Cuesta Encunada at San Simeon, California, U.S.A. It was built in 1922–39 for William Randolph Hearst (1863–1951), at a total cost of more than $30,000,000 (now £12,500,000). It has more than 100 rooms, a 104-foot-long heated swimming pool, an 83-foot-long assembly hall and a garage for 25 limousines. The house required 60 servants to maintain it.

United Kingdom The largest house in the United Kingdom is Wentworth Woodhouse, near Rotherham, Yorkshire, formerly the seat of the Earls Fitzwilliam. The main part of the house, built over 300 years ago, has more than 240 rooms with over 1,000 windows, and its principal facade is 600 feet long. The Royal residence, Sandringham House, Norfolk, has been reported to have 365 rooms. The largest house in Ireland is Castletown in County Kildare, formerly owned by Lord Carew. Scotland's largest house is Hopetoun House, West Lothian, built between 1696 and 1756 with a west facade 675 feet long.

Stately home most visited The most visited stately home in the United Kingdom is Beaulieu, Hampshire, owned by Lord Montagu of Beaulieu with 502,109 visitors in 1970. The figures for Woburn Abbey, Bedfordshire, owned by the Duke of Bedford, have not been published since 1963 but reached 470,000 as early as 1961.

Smallest The smallest house in Britain is the 19th-century fisherman's cottage on Conway Quay, Caernarvonshire, North Wales. It has a 72-inch frontage, is 122 inches high and has two tiny rooms and a staircase.

Most expensive The most expensive private house in Britain is Ramsbury Manor, Wiltshire, which was bought by an American property dealer as a residence for a price, including the 460-acre grounds, of reportedly £650,000 in May 1965. The house itself, which dates from *c.* 1660, cost £275,000.

3. BUILDINGS FOR ENTERTAINMENT

STADIUMS

Largest *World* The world's largest stadium is the Strahov Stadium in Praha (Prague), Czechoslovakia. It was completed in 1934 and can accommodate 240,000 spectators for mass displays of up to 40,000 Sokol gymnasts.

Football The largest football stadium in the world is the Maracaña Municipal Stadium in Rio de Janeiro, Brazil, where the football ground has a normal capacity of 205,000, of whom 155,000 may be seated. A crowd of 199,854 was accommodated for the World Cup final between Brazil and Uruguay on 16 July 1950. A dry moat, 7 feet wide and over 5 feet deep, protects players from spectators and *vice versa*. The stadium also has facilities for indoor sports, such as boxing, and these provide accommodation for an additional 32,000 spectators.

Covered The largest covered stadium in the world is the Empire Stadium, Wembley, London, opened in April 1923. It was the scene of the 1948 Olympic Games and the final of the 1966 World Cup. In 1962–63 the capacity under cover was increased to 100,000, of whom 45,000 may be seated. The original cost was £1,250,000. The Azteca Stadium, Mexico City, Mexico, opened in 1968, has a capacity of 107,000 of whom nearly all are under cover.

Roofed Tenders for the construction of a transparent "tent" roof over the Munich Olympic Stadium, West Germany were issued in August 1969 which called for a size of 914,940 square feet (21·0 acres) in area. It will rest on a steel net supported by masts.

Indoor The world's largest indoor stadium is the Harris County Sports Stadium, or Astrodome, in Houston, Texas, U.S.A. opened in April 1965. It has a capacity of 45,000 for baseball and 66,000 (maximum) for boxing. The domed stadium covers 9½ acres and is so large that an 18-storey building could be built under the roof (208 feet high). The total cost was $38,000,000 (£15,830,000). In some conditions of humidity it would rain if the air conditioning equipment, which has a cooling capacity of 79,200,000 British Thermal Units per hour, were turned off (see also Largest dome, p. 119).

United Kingdom The highest capacity stadium in the United Kingdom is that at Hampden Park, Glasgow, which accommodated a football crowd of 149,547 on 17 April 1937.

Largest ballroom The largest ballroom in the United Kingdom is the Orchid Ballroom, Purley, Surrey. The room is over 200 feet long and 117 feet wide, and has a total floor area of 23,320 square feet. When laid out for dance championships, the floor of the Earl's Court Exhibition Hall is 256 feet in length. The Empress Ballroom, Blackpool, Lancashire, when used for dances, can accommodate 4,500 couples.

Amusement resort The world's largest amusement resort is Disneyland, in Anaheim, California, U.S.A. It was opened on 18 July 1955 and has an area of 230 acres. The investment had increased from an initial $17,000,000 (£7,083,000) to $95,000,000 (£39,583,000) by 1968. The total attendance surpassed 70,000,000 in 1968. In October 1965 27,443 acres were purchased in Orange and Osceola counties, near Orlando in central Florida, for "Disney World", due to be opened in 1971.

RESTAURANTS

Highest The highest restaurant in Great Britain is the Ptarmigan Observation Restaurant at 3,650 feet above sea-level on Cairngorm (4,084 feet) near Aviemore, Inverness-shire, Scotland.

NIGHT CLUBS

Oldest The oldest night club (*boîte de nuit*) is "Le Bal des Anglais" at 6 Rue des Anglais, Paris 5*me*, France. It was founded in 1843.

Largest The largest night club in the world is that in the Imperial Room of the Concord Hotel in the Catskill Mountains, New York State, U.S.A., with a capacity of 3,000 patrons. In the more classical sense the largest night club in the world is "The Mikado" in the Akasaka district of Tōkyō, Japan, with a seating capacity of 2,000. It is "manned" by 1,250 hostesses, some of whom earn an estimated £4,800 per annum. Long sight is essential to an appreciation of the floor show.

Loftiest The highest night club will be that on the 52nd storey of the Antigone Building, now under construction, in Montparnasse, Paris, at 187 metres (613·5 feet) above street level.

Lowest The lowest night club is the "Minus 206" in Tiberias, Israel, on the shores of the Sea of Galilee. It is 206 metres (676 feet) below sea-level.

PLEASURE BEACH

Largest The largest pleasure beach in the world is Virginia Beach, Virginia, U.S.A. It has 28 miles of beach front on the Atlantic and 10 miles of estuary frontage. The area embraces 255 square miles and 134 hotels and motels.

Longest pleasure pier The longest pleasure pier in the world is Southend Pier at Southend-on-Sea in Essex. It is 1·33 miles in length. It was built in 1889, with final extensions made in 1929. It is decorated with more than 75,000 lamps.

FAIRS

Largest The largest fair ever held was the New York World's Fair, covering 1,216½ acres of Flushing Meadow Park, Queens Borough, Long Island, New York, U.S.A. The fair was open at times between 20 April 1939 and 21 Oct. 1940 and there were 25,817,265 admissions and an attendance of 51,607,037 for the 1964–65 Fair there.

Record attendance The record attendance for any fair was 65,000,000 for Expo 70 held on an 815-acre site at Osaka, Japan from March to 13 Sept. 1970. It made a profit of more than £11,000,000.

Big wheel The original Ferris Wheel, named after its constructor, George W. Ferris (1859–96), was erected in 1893 at the Midway, Chicago, Illinois, U.S.A., at a cost of $300,000 (now £125,000). The wheel was 250 feet in diameter, 790 feet in circumference, weighed 1,070 tons, and carried 36 cars each seating 40 people, making a total of 1,440 passengers. The structure was removed in 1904 to St. Louis, Missouri, and was eventually sold as scrap for $1,800 (now £750). In 1897 a Ferris Wheel with a diameter of 300 feet was erected for the Earls Court Exhibition, London. It had ten 1st-class and 30 2nd-class cars. The largest wheel now operating is the Riesenrad in the Prater Park, Vienna, Austria with a diameter of 218 feet. It was built by the British engineer Walter Basset in 1896 and carried 15 million people in its first 75 years.

Fastest switchback The world's fastest gravity switchback has been the "Bobs" in the Belle Vue Amusement Park, Manchester, Lancashire. The cars attained a peak speed of 61 m.p.h. The track was 862 yards 2 inches long with a maximum height of 76 feet. It had been imported from the U.S.A. in 1929.

PUBLIC HOUSES

Largest *World* The largest beer-selling establishment in the world is the Mathäser, Bayerstrasse 5, München (Munich), West Germany, where the daily sale reaches 84,470 pints. It was established in 1829, was demolished in World War II and re-built by 1955 and now seats 5,500 people. The through-put at the Dube beer halls in the Bantu township of Soweto, Johannesburg, South Africa may, however, be higher on some Saturdays when the average consumption of 6,000 gallons (48,000 pints) is far exceeded.

United Kingdom The largest public house in the United Kingdom is The Swan at Yardley, Birmingham. It has eight bars with a total drinking area of 13,852 square feet. The sale of beer is equivalent to 31,000 bottles per week. The pub can hold well over 1,000 customers and 320 for banqueting. The permanent staff totals 60 with seven resident. The Swan is owned by Allied Breweries and administered by Ansells Limited.

The Swan at Yardley, Birmingham

Smallest The smallest pub in the United Kingdom is "The Smith's Arms" in Godmanstone, Dorset, which is only 10 feet wide and 4 feet high at the eaves. It has a licence granted personally by Charles II (reigned 1660–85).

Highest The highest public house in the United Kingdom is the Tan Hill Inn in Yorkshire. It is 1,732 feet above sea-level, on the moorland road between Reeth in Yorkshire and Brough in Westmorland. The White Lady Restaurant, 2,550 feet up on Cairngorm (4,084 feet) near Aviemore, Inverness-shire, Scotland, is the highest licensed restaurant.

Oldest There are various claimants to the title of the United Kingdom's oldest inn. The foremost claimants include "The Angel and Royal" (*c.* 1450) at Grantham, Lincolnshire, which has cellar masonry dated 1213; the "George" (early 15th century) at Norton St. Philip, Somerset; "The George and Vulture" off Lombard Street, in the City of London, first mentioned in 1175; the oldest inn in Wales the Skirrid Mountain Inn, Llanvihangel Crucorney, Monmouthshire recorded in 1110; and "The Trip to Jerusalem" in Nottingham, with foundations believed to date back to 1070. An origin as early as A.D. 560 has been claimed for Ye Olde Ferry Boat Inn at Holywell, Huntingdonshire. There is some evidence that it ante-dates the local church, built in 980, but the earliest documents are not dated earlier than 1100. There is evidence that the Bingley Arms, Bardsey, near Leeds, Yorkshire, re-built in 1738, existed as the Priest's Inn according to Bardsey Church records dated 953.

Longest name The English pub with the longest name was the 39 letter "The Thirteenth Mounted Cheshire Rifleman Inn" at Stalybridge, Cheshire. The word "Mounted" is now omitted making "The Shoulder of Mutton and Cucumbers Inn" at Yapton, Sussex, a 34 letter candidate.

Shortest name There is one public house in the United Kingdom with a name of only two letters: the "C.B." Hotel, Arkengarthdale, near Richmond, Yorkshire.

Longest bars *World* The longest permanent bar with beer pumps is that built in 1938 at the Working Men's Club, Mildura, Victoria, Australia. It has a counter 287 feet in length, served by 32 pumps. Temporary bars have been erected of greater length. The Falstaff Brewing Corp. put up a temporary bar 336 feet 5 inches in length on Wharf St., St. Louis, Missouri, U.S.A., on 22 June 1970.

United Kingdom The longest bar in the United Kingdom with beer pumps is the French Bar (198 feet 5½ inches) at Butlin's Holiday Camp, Filey, Yorkshire. It has 20 beer pumps, 12 tills and stillage for 30 barrels, and is operated by 30 barmaids, 20 floor waiters and 20 other hands. The Grand Stand Bar at Galway Racecourse, Ireland completed in 1955, measures 210 feet.

Wine cellar The largest wine cellars in the world are at Paarl, those of the Ko-operative Wijnbouwers Vereeniging (K.W.V.) near Cape Town, in the centre of the wine-growing district of South Africa. They cover an area of 25 acres and have a capacity of 30,000,000 gallons. The largest blending vats have a capacity of 45,700 gallons and are 17 feet high, with a diameter of 26 feet.

4. MAJOR CIVIL ENGINEERING STRUCTURES

TALLEST STRUCTURES

World *Completed* The tallest structure in the world is a stayed television transmitting tower 2,063 feet tall, between Fargo and Blanchard, North Dakota, U.S.A. It was built at a cost of about $500,000 (£208,000) for Channel 11 of KTHI-TV, owned by the Pembina Broadcasting Company of North Dakota, a subsidiary of the Polaris Corporation from Milwaukee, Wisconsin, U.S.A. The tower was erected in 30 days (2 Oct. to 1 Nov. 1963) by 11 men of the Kline Iron and Steel Company of Columbia, South Carolina, U.S.A., who designed and fabricated the tower. The cage elevator in the centre rises to 1,948 feet. The tower is built to allow for a sway of up to 13·9 feet in a wind gusting to 120 m.p.h. and is so tall that anyone falling off the top would no longer be accelerating just before hitting the ground.

Uncompleted Work was begun in July 1970 on a tubular steel guyed T.V. tower near Plock, north-west Poland, which will rise to 2,100 feet. The structure, designed by Jan Polak, will weigh 550 tons and is due for completion in 1974.

United Kingdom The tallest structure in the United Kingdom is the Independent Television Authority's mast at Belmont, north of Horncastle, Lincolnshire, completed in 1965 to a height of 1,265 feet with 7 feet added by meteorological equipment installed in September 1967. It serves Anglia T.V. and was severely threatened by the icing on 21 March 1969 which two days earlier felled the 1,265-foot Emley Moor mast in Yorkshire.

TALLEST TOWERS

World The tallest self-supporting tower (as opposed to a guyed mast) in the world is the 1,749-foot-tall tower at Ostankino, Greater Moscow, U.S.S.R., topped out in May 1967. It is of reinforced concrete construction and weighs over 22,000 tons. A three-storey restaurant revolves at the 882-foot level and there is a balcony at 1,050 feet. In a high wind the T.V. antennae may sway up to 26 feet but the restaurant only 3·14 inches. The tower was designed by N. V. Nikitin.

The tallest tower built before the era of television masts

TALLEST STRUCTURES IN THE WORLD—PROGRESSIVE RECORDS

Height in feet	Structure	Location	Material	Building or Completion Dates
204	Djoser step pyramid (earliest Pyramid)	Saqqâra, Egypt	Tura limestone	*c.* 2650 B.C.
294	Pyramid of Meidun	Meidun, Egypt	Tura limestone	*c.* 2600 B.C.
c. 336	Snefru Bent pyramid	Dahshûr, Egypt	Tura limestone	*c.* 2600 B.C.
342	Snefru North Stone pyramid	Dahshûr, Egypt	Tura limestone	*c.* 2600 B.C.
480·9[1]	Great Pyramid of Cheops (Khufu)	El Gizeh, Egypt	Tura limestone	*c.* 2580 B.C.
525[2]	Lincoln Cathedral, Central Tower	Lincoln, England	lead sheathed wood	*c.* 1307–1548
489[3]	St. Paul's Cathedral	London, England	lead sheathed wood	1315–1561
465	Minster of Notre Dame	Strasbourg, France	Vosges sandstone	1420–1439
502[4]	St. Pierre de Beauvais	Beauvais, France	lead sheathed wood	–1568
475	St. Nicholas Church	Hamburg, Germany		1846–1874
485	Rouen Cathedral	Rouen, France	cast iron	1823–1876
513	Köln Cathedral	Cologne, West Germany	stone	–1880
555	Washington Memorial	Washington, D.C., U.S.A.	stone	1848–1884
985·9[5]	La Tour Eiffel	Paris, France	steel	1887–1889
1,046	Chrysler Building	New York City, U.S.A.	steel and concrete	1929–1930
1,250[6]	Empire State Building	New York City, U.S.A.	steel and concrete	1929–1930
1,572	KWTV Television Mast	Oklahoma City, U.S.A.	steel	Nov. 1954
1,610[7]	KSWS Television Mast	Roswell, New Mexico, U.S.A.	steel	Dec. 1956
1,619	WGAN Television Mast	Portland, Maine, U.S.A.	steel	Sept. 1959
1,676	KFVS Television Mast	Cape Girardeau, Missouri, U.S.A.	steel	June 1960
1,749	WTVM & WRBL TV Mast	Columbus, Georgia, U.S.A.	steel	May 1962
1,749	WBIR-TV Mast	Knoxville, Tennessee, U.S.A.	steel	Sept. 1963
2,063	KTHI-TV Mast	Fargo, North Dakota, U.S.A.	steel	Nov. 1963
c. 2,100	Polish T.V. Service Tower	Plock, Poland	galvanised steel	1970–1974

[1] *Original height. With loss of pyramidion (topmost stone) height now 449 ft. 6 in.*
[2] *Fell in a storm.*
[3] *Struck by lightning and destroyed 4 June 1561.*
[4] *Fell April 1573, shortly after completion.*
[5] *Original height. With addition of T.V. antenna in 1957, now 1,052 ft. 4 in.*
[6] *Original height. With addition of T.V. tower on 1 May 1951 now 1,472 ft.*
[7] *Fell in gale in 1960.*

TALLEST TELEVISION AND RADIO MASTS BY COUNTRIES

Country		Structure	Height in feet
United States		KTHI-TV Mast, Fargo, North Dakota	2,063
U.S.S.R.		Ostankino T.V. Tower, Greater Moscow	1,749
Hawaiian Is., U.S.A.	(2)	U.S. Navy twin antennae, Lualualei, Oaha	1,500
Iceland		Loran Mast, Snaefellsnes	1,378
Greenland		Danish Government Navigational Mast, Thule	1,345
West Germany		West Berlin T.V. Tower	1,312
China (mainland)		Peking Radio Mast	1,312
United Kingdom		I.T.A. Mast, Belmont, Lincolnshire	1,272
Australia		Tower Zero, North West Cape, Western Australia	1,271
Netherlands		Zender Lopik (T.V. Mast), near Lopik	1,253
East Germany		East Berlin T.V. Tower	1,185
Pacific Islands		Loran Tower, Tomil, Yap	1,100
Puerto Rico		WAPA-TV Mast, Cayey	1,100
Canada		CHTV Channel 11 Mast, Hamilton, Ontario	1,093
Japan		Tōkyō Television Tower (self-supporting)	1,092
France		Tour Eiffel, Paris	1,052
Finland	(10)	Masts at Jyväskylä, Lapua, Kerimäki, Tervola, Eurajoki, Pyhätunturi, Kiiminki, Kuusisto, Sippola and Tiirismaa	1,050
Czechoslovakia		"Jizní Morava" T.V. Mast, Kojál	1,033
Hungary		Lakihegg Mast	1,006
Northern Ireland		I.T.A. Mast, Strabane, County Tyrone	1,000
Scotland	(2)	I.T.A. Mast, Black Hill, Lanarkshire, and Durris, Kincardineshire	1,000
Wales		I.T.A. Mast, Brynchain, Caernarvonshire	1,000

is the Eiffel Tower, in Paris, France, designed by Alexandre Gustav Eiffel (1832–1923) for the Paris exhibition and completed on 31 March 1889. It was 300·51 metres (985 feet 11 inches) tall, now extended by a T.V. antenna to 1,052 feet 4 inches, and weighs 6,900 tons. The maximum sway in high winds is 5 inches. The whole steel edifice which has 1,792 steps, took 2 years, 2 months and 2 days to build and cost 7,799,401 francs 31 centimes. The 352nd suicide committed from the tower had occurred by 1 Jan. 1970.

The architects André and Jean Polak put forward a design in February 1969 for a tower 2,378·6 feet (725 metres) in height to be erected at La Défense in Paris.

United Kingdom The tallest tower in the United Kingdom is the Post Office Tower, opened on 8 Oct. 1965 in Maple Street, off Tottenham Court Road, London, W.1. It is 580 feet tall to the top of the concrete structure and 620 feet to the top of the lattice mast.* The weight of the tower and its foundations has been estimated at 13,000 tons.

* *The fastest times recorded for racing up the 814 steps to the top observation floor are:—Male: Norman Harrison (Imperial College, London) 4 mins. 21·4 secs. on 6 Feb. 1970. Female: Hillary Tanner (Hull University) 6 mins. 39 secs. on 12 Feb. 1971. Competition is limited to students.*

5. BRIDGES

OLDEST

World Arch construction was understood by the Sumerians as early as 3200 B.C. but the oldest surviving bridge in the world is the slab stone single arch bridge over the River Meles in Smyrna (now Izmir), Turkey, which dates from *c.* 850 B.C.

Britain The clapper bridges of Dartmoor and Exmoor (*e.g.* the Tarr Steps over the River Barle, Exmoor, Somerset) are thought to be of prehistoric types although none of

Britain's [l]ongest railway bridge—the 84-year-old Tay Bridge

the existing examples can be certainly dated. They are made of large slabs of stone placed over boulders. The Romans built stone bridges in England and remains of these have been found at Corbridge (the 2nd century A.D. Roman Corstopitum), Northumberland; Chester, Northumberland and Willowford, Cumberland. Remains of a wooden bridge have been found at Ardwinkle, Northamptonshire.

LONGEST

Cable suspension *World* The world's longest single span bridge is the Verrazano-Narrows Bridge stretching across the entrance to New York City harbour from Richmond, Staten Island to Brooklyn. Work on the $305,000,000 (then £109 million) project began on 13 Aug. 1959 and the bridge was opened to traffic on 21 Nov. 1964. It measures 6,690 feet between anchorages and carries two decks, each of six lanes of traffic. The centre span is 4,260 feet and the tops of the main towers (each 690 feet tall) are $1\frac{5}{8}$ inches out of parallel, to allow for the curvature of the Earth. The traffic in the first 12 months was 17,000,000 vehicles, and is rising towards 48,000,000 with the completion of the second deck. The bridge was designed by Othmar H. Ammann (1879–1965), a Swiss-born engineer.

The Mackinac Straits Bridge between Mackinaw City and St. Ignace, Michigan, U.S.A., is the longest suspension bridge in the world measured between anchorages (8,344 feet) and has an overall length, including viaducts of the bridge proper measured between abutment bearings, of 19,203 feet 4 inches. It was opened in November 1957 (dedicated 28 June 1958) at a cost of $100 million (then £35,700,000) and has a main span of 3,800 feet.

Detailed plans have been published for the building of a $333 million (£138·7 million) suspension bridge with a central span of 1,300 metres (4,265 feet), across the Akashi Straits, west of Kobe, Japan. It will have an overall length of 4,900 metres (16,076 feet or 3·04 miles), including all main and side spans. The distance between the main anchors will be 8,530 feet and the cables will be 126 centimetres (50 inches) in diameter. Even longer main spans are planned for completion in 1976 across the Humber Estuary (4,580 feet), a bridge of 4,600 feet across Tōkyō Bay, Japan, and one of 5,000 feet, with piers 400 feet deep, across the Messina Straits, Italy.

United Kingdom The longest span bridge in the United Kingdom is the Firth of Forth Road Bridge with a main channel span of 3,300 feet and side spans of 1,340 feet each, opened on 4 Sept. 1964. The main towers each stand 512 feet high. It is the sixth longest span in the world and cost £11,000,000 excluding the approaches.

Cantilever *World* The Quebec Bridge (Pont de Québec) over the St. Lawrence River in Canada has the longest cantilever truss span of any in the world—1,800 feet between the piers and 3,239 feet overall. It carries two railway tracks. Begun in 1899, it was finally opened to traffic on 3 Dec. 1917 at a cost of 87 lives, and $Can.25,000,000 (now £9,633,000).

United Kingdom The longest cantilever bridge in the United Kingdom is the Forth Bridge. Its two main spans are 1,710 feet long. It carries a double railway track over the Firth of Forth 150 feet above the water level. Work commenced in November 1882 and the first test trains crossed on 22 Jan. 1890 after an expenditure of £3 million. It was officially opened on 4 March 1890. Of the 4,500 workers who built it, 57 were killed in various accidents.

Longest steel arch *World* The longest steel arch bridge in the world is the Bayonne Bridge over the Kill Van Kull, which has connected Bayonne, New Jersey, to Staten Island, New York, since its completion in November 1931. Its span is 1,652 feet 1 inch—25 inches longer than the Sydney Harbour Bridge, Australia (see below).

United Kingdom The longest steel arch bridge in the United Kingdom is the Runcorn-Widnes bridge from Widnes, Lancashire, to Runcorn, Cheshire, opened on 21 July 1961. It has a span of 1,082 feet and a total length including approaches of 3,489 feet.

Largest steel arch The largest steel arch bridge in the world is the Sydney Harbour Bridge in Sydney, New South Wales, Australia. Its main arch span is 1,650 feet long and it carries two electric overhead railway tracks, eight lanes of roadway, a cycleway and a footway, 172 feet above the waters of Sydney Harbour. It took seven years to build and was officially opened on 19 March 1932 at a cost of $A9,500,000 (then £7,600,000). Its total length is 3,770 feet excluding complex viaducts.

Floating bridge *Longest* The longest floating bridge in the world is the Second Lake Washington Bridge, Seattle, Washington State, U.S.A. completed in 1963. Its total length is 12,596 feet and its floating section measures 7,518 feet (1·42 miles). It was built at a cost of $15,000,000 (£6,250,000) and completed in August 1963.

Railway bridge *Longest* The longest railway bridge in the world is the Huey P. Long Bridge, Metaire, Louisiana, U.S.A. with a railway section 22,996 feet (4·35 miles) long. It was completed on 16 Dec. 1935 with a longest span of 790 feet. The longest railway bridge in Britain is the second Tay Bridge (11,653 feet), joining Fife and Angus, opened on 20 June 1887. Of the 85 spans, 74 (length 10,289 feet) are over the waterway.

HIGHEST

World The highest bridge in the world is the bridge over the Royal Gorge of the Arkansas River in Colorado, U.S.A. It is 1,053 feet above the water level. It is a suspension bridge with a main span of 880 feet and was constructed in 6 months, ending on 6 Dec. 1929. The highest railway bridge in the world is the single track span at Fades, outside Clermont-Ferrand, France. It

PROGRESSIVE RECORD OF WORLD'S LONGEST BRIDGE SPANS

Feet	Location	Type	Completion
121	Martorell, Spain	Stone Arch	219 B.C.
142	Nera River, Lucca, Italy	Stone Arch	14 A.D.
170	Trajan's Bridge, Danube River	Timber Arch	104
251	Trezzo, Italy	Stone Arch	1377
390	Wettingen, Switzerland	Timber Arch	1758
408	Schuylkill Falls, Philadelphia, Pa.	Suspension	1816
449	Union Bridge, Berwick, England	Chain	1820
580	Menai Straits, Wales	Chain	1826
870	Fribourg, Switzerland	Suspension	1834
1,008½	Wheeling-Ohio Bridge (re-built 1856)	Suspension	1849
1,043	Lewiston Bridge, Niagara River	Suspension	1851
1,057	Covington-Cincinnati Bridge (re-built 1898)	Suspension	1867
1,268	Clifton Bridge, Niagara Falls	Suspension	1869
1,595½	Brooklyn Bridge, New York City	Suspension	1883
1,710	Forth Bridge, Scotland	Cantilever	1890
1,800	Quebec Bridge, Canada	Cantilever	1917
1,850	Ambassador Bridge, Detroit	Suspension	1929
3,500	George Washington Bridge, New York City	Suspension	1931
4,200	Golden Gate, San Francisco	Suspension	1937
4,260	Verrazano-Narrows Bridge, New York City	Suspension	1964

LONGEST BRIDGE SPANS IN THE WORLD—BY TYPE

Type	feet	metres	Location	Built
Cable Suspension	4,260	1,298·4	Verrazano-Narrows, New York, N.Y., U.S.A.	1964
Cantilever Truss	1,800	548·6	Quebec Railway Bridge, Quebec, Canada	1917
Steel Arch	1,652	503·6	Bayonne (Kill Van Kull), New York, N.Y., U.S.A.	1931
Continuous Truss	1,232	375·5	Astoria, Columbia River, Oregon, U.S.A.	1966
Cable-Stayed	1,148	350·7	Duisberg-Nuenkamp, West Germany	1970
Chain Suspension	1,114	339·5	Florianopolis, Santa Catarina, Brazil	1926
Concrete Arch	1,000	304·8	Gladesville, Sydney, Australia	1964
Plate and Box Girder	984	300·0	Río Niterói, Rio de Janeiro, Brazil	1971

was built in 1901–09 with a span of 472 feet and is 430 feet above the River Sioule.

United Kingdom The highest railway bridge in the United Kingdom was the Crumlin Viaduct, Monmouthshire, completed in June 1857 to a height of 200 feet.

WIDEST

The world's widest long-span bridge is the Sydney Harbour Bridge (160 feet wide). The Crawford Street Bridge in Providence, Rhode Island, U.S.A., has a width of 1,147 feet. The River Roch is bridged for a distance of 1,460 feet where the culvert passes through the centre of Rochdale, Lancashire.

Deepest foundations The deepest foundations of any structure are those of the 3,323-foot-span Ponte de Salazar, which was opened on 6 Aug. 1966, at a cost of £30,000,000, across the Rio Tejo (the River Tagus), in Portugal. One of the 625-foot-tall towers extends 260 feet down.

Longest viaduct The world's longest viaduct is the second Lake Ponchartrain Causeway, completed on 23 March 1969, joining Mandeville and Jefferson, Louisiana, U.S.A. It has a length of 126,055 feet (23·87 miles). It cost $29,900,000 (£12·45 million) and is 228 feet longer than the adjoining First Causeway completed in 1956. The longest railway viaduct in the world is the rock-filled Great Salt Lake Railroad Trestle, carrying the Southern Pacific Railroad 11·85 miles across the Great Salt Lake, Utah, U.S.A. It was opened as a pile and trestle bridge on 8 March 1904, but converted to rock fill in 1955–60.

AQUEDUCTS

World Longest *Ancient* The greatest of ancient aqueducts was the Aqueduct of Carthage in Tunisia, which ran 141 kilometres (87·6 miles) from the springs of Zaghouan to Djebel Djougar. It was built by the Romans during the reign of Publius Aelius Hadrianus (A.D. 117–138). By 1895, 344 arches still survived. Its original capacity has been calculated at 7,000,000 gallons per day. The triple-tiered aqueduct Pont du Gard, built in A.D. 19 near Nîmes, France, is 160 feet high. The tallest of the 14 arches of the Aguas Livres Aqueduct, built in Lisbon, Portugal, in 1748 is 213 feet 3 inches.

Modern The world's longest aqueduct, in the modern sense of a water conduit, is the Colorado River Aqueduct in south-eastern California, U.S.A. The system, complete with aqueduct conduit, tunnels and syphons, is 242 miles long and was completed in 1939. The California Aqueduct (completion due 1972) will be 444 miles long.

United Kingdom The longest aqueduct in the United Kingdom is the Pontcysyllte in Denbighshire, Wales, on the Frankton to Llantisilio branch of the Shropshire Union Canal. It is 1,007 feet long, has 19 arches up to 121 feet high and crosses the valley of the Dee. It was designed by Thomas Telford (1757–1834) of Scotland, and was opened for use in 1803.

6. CANALS

EARLIEST

World Relics of the oldest canals in the world, dated by archaeologists to 5000 B.C., were discovered near Mandali, Iraq early in 1968.

Britain The first canals in Britain were undoubtedly cut by the Romans. In the Midlands the 11-mile-long Fossdyke Canal between Lincoln and the River Trent at Torksey was built in about A.D. 65 and was scoured in 1122. Part of it is still in use today. Though Exeter Canal was cut as early as 1564–68, the first wholly artificial major navigation canal in the United Kingdom was the Bridgewater canal, dug in 1759–61. It ran from Worsley to Manchester, Lancashire. Parts of the Sankey Canal from St. Helens to Widnes, Lancashire, were however, dug before the Bridgewater Canal.

LONGEST

World The largest canalized system in the world is the Volga-Baltic Canal opened in April 1965. It runs 1,850 miles from Astrakhan up the Volga, *via* Kuybyshev, Gor'kiy and Lake Ladoga, to Leningrad, U.S.S.R. The longest canal of the ancient world has been the Grand Canal of China from Peking to Hangchou. It was begun in 540 B.C. and not completed until the 13th century by which time it extended for 1,107 miles. Having been allowed by 1950 to silt up to the point that it was in no place more than 6 feet deep, it is reported to have been reconstructed.

The Beloye More (White Sea) Baltic Canal from Belomorsk to Povenets, in the U.S.S.R., is 141 miles long with 19 locks. It was completed with the use of forced labour in 1933 and cannot accommodate ships of more than 16 feet in draught.

The world's longest big ship canal is the still inoperative (since June 1967) Suez Canal in the United Arab Republic, opened on 16 Nov. 1869 by the Khedive, Isma'il Pasha, and officially inaugurated on the following day by a procession of 68 vessels, headed by the French imperial yacht *L'Aigle*, with the Empress Marie Eugénie Ignace Augustine (1826–1920) on board. The canal was planned by the French diplomatist Count Ferdinand de Lesseps (1805–94) and work began on 25 April 1859. It is 100·6 miles in length from Port Said lighthouse to Suez Roads, 60 metres (197 feet) wide and dredged to 34 feet. The original excavation was 97,000,000 cubic yards, which had, by continual dredging, been trebled. It had been intended to dredge to the point that ships drawing 40 feet could transit by 1970.

United Kingdom The longest inland waterway in the United Kingdom is the Grand Union Canal Main Line from Brentford Lock Junction, Middlesex, to Langley Mill, a total distance of 167⅜ miles. The Grand Union System was originally 255 miles long when nine canals, including the Grand Junction, were amalgamated in 1929. The voyage along the whole length of the Grand Union Canal, Main Line, would involve the negotiation of 169 locks.

Largest seaway The world's longest artificial seaway is the St. Lawrence Seaway (189 miles long) along the New York State-Ontario border from Montreal to Lake Ontario, which enables 80 per cent. of all ocean-going ships, and bulk carriers with a capacity of 26,000 tons, to sail 2,342 miles from the North Atlantic, up the St. Lawrence estuary and across the Great Lakes to Duluth, Minnesota, U.S.A., on Lake Superior (602 feet above sea-level). The project cost $470,000,000 (then £168 million) and was opened on 25 April 1959.

Irrigation canal The longest irrigation canal in the world is the Kara-kumskiy Kanal, stretching 546 miles from Haun-Khan to Ashkhabad, Turkmenistan, U.S.S.R. In February 1967 the operative length was reported to have reached 520 miles.

LOCKS

Largest *World* The world's largest locking system is the Miraflores lock system in the Panama Canal, opened on 15 Aug. 1914. The two lower locks are 1,050 feet long, 110 feet wide and have gates 82 feet high, 65 feet long and 7 feet thick, with doors weighing 652 to 696 tons each. The largest liner ever to transit was S.S. *Bremen* (51,730 gross tons), with a length of 899 feet, a beam of 101·9 feet and a draught of 48·2 feet, on 15 Feb. 1939.

The world's largest single lock is that connecting the Schelde with the Kanaaldok system at Zandvliet, west of Antwerp, Belgium. It is 500 metres (1,640 feet) long and 187 feet wide and is an entrance to an impounded sheet of water 18 kilometres (11·2 miles) long.

United Kingdom The largest lock on any canal system in the United Kingdom is the Eastham Large Lock, Eastham, Cheshire, on the Manchester Ship Canal. It can handle craft up to 600 feet long and 80 feet beam.

Deepest The world's deepest lock is the Donzère-Mondragon lock on the River Rhône at Drôme, France. It is 86 feet deep and takes 8 minutes to fill.

Longest flight The world's highest lock elevator is at Arzwiller-Saint Louis in France. The lift was completed in 1969 to replace 17 locks on the Marne-Rhine canal system. It drops 146 feet over a ramp 383·8 feet long on a 41 degree gradient.

The longest flight of locks in the United Kingdom is on the Worcester and Birmingham Canal at Tardebigge, Worcestershire, where a 2½-mile-long flight of 30 consecutive locks raises the canal level 217 feet.

Largest cut The Gaillard Cut (known as "the Ditch") on the Panama Canal is 270 feet deep between Gold Hill and Contractor's Hill with a bottom width of 300 feet. In one day in 1911 as many as 333 dirt trains each carrying 357 tons left this site. The total amount of earth excavated for the whole Panama Canal was 8,910,000 tons, which total will be raised by the widening of the Gaillard Cut to 500 feet. In 1968 there were a record 14,807 transits.

7. DAMS

Earliest The earliest dam ever built was the Sadd al-Kafara, seven miles south-east of Helwan, United Arab Republic. It was built in the period 2950 to 2750 B.C. and had a length of 348 feet and a height of 37 feet.

Most massive Measured by volume, the largest dam in the world is the Fort Peck Dam, completed in 1940 across the Missouri River in Montana, U.S.A. It contains 125,628,000 cubic yards of earth and rock fill, and is 21,026 feet (3·98 miles) long and up to 251 feet high. It maintains a reservoir with a capacity of 19·1 million acre-feet. Work started in December 1967 on the Tarbela Dam across the River Indus, in the Sind, West Pakistan. The total cost of the 485-foot-tall, 9,000-foot-long construction is expected to reach $815 million (£339·6 million) by completion in 1975 including the $623 million contract awarded to the Impregilo Consortium. The total volume of the dam will be 186,000,000 cubic yards.

Largest concrete The world's largest concrete dam, and the largest concrete structure in the world, is the Grand Coulee Dam on the Columbia River, Washington State, U.S.A. Work on the dam was begun in 1933, it began working on 22 March 1941 and was completed in 1942 at a cost of $56 million. It has a crest length of 4,173 feet and is 550 feet high. It contains 10,585,000 cubic yards of concrete, and weighs about 19,285,000 tons. The hydro-electric power plant (completed in 1951) has a capacity of 1,974,000 kilowatts.

Highest The highest dam in the world is the Grande Dixence in Switzerland, completed in September 1961 at a cost of 1,600 million Swiss francs (£151,000,000). It is 932 feet from base to rim, 2,296 feet long and the total volume of concrete in the dam is 7,792,000 cubic yards. The earth fill Nurek dam on the Vakhsh-Amu Darya river, U.S.S.R. will be 1,017 feet high, have a crest length of 2,280 feet and a volume of 75,900,000 cubic yards. The concrete Ingurskaya dam in western Georgia, U.S.S.R., is planned to have a final height of 988 feet, a crest length of 2,240 feet and a volume of 3,920,000 cubic yards.

Longest The longest river dam in the world is the Hirakud Dam on the Mahanadi River, near Sambalpur, Orissa, India completed in 1956. It consists of a main concrete and masonry dam (3,768 feet), an Earth Dam (11,980 feet), the Left Dyke (five sections of 32,275 feet) and the Right Dyke (35,500 feet), totalling 15·8 miles altogether.

The longest sea dam in the world is the Afsluitdijk stretching 20·195 miles across the mouth of the Zuider

PROGRESSIVE WORLD RECORDS

Highest Dams since 1866

Name	River	Location	Year Completed	Feet
Gouffre d'Enfer (Furan)	Le Furan	France	1866	197
Ponthook*	Androscoggen	New Hampshire, U.S.A.	1887	276
Cheeseman	South Platte	Colorado, U.S.A.	1904	236
New Croton	Croton	New York, U.S.A.	1905	297
Buffalo Bill	Shoshone	Wyoming, U.S.A.	1910	326
Arrowrock	Boise	Idaho, U.S.A.	1915	350
Schrah	Aa	Switzerland	1924	364
Diablo	Skagit	Washington, U.S.A.	1929	389
Owyhee	Owyhee	Oregon, U.S.A.	1932	417
Chambon	Romanche	France	1934	446
Hoover	Colorado	Nevada–Arizona, U.S.A.	1936	726
Mauvoisin	Drance de Bagnes	Switzerland	1958	777
Vaiont	Vaiont	Italy	1961	858
Grande Dixence	Dixence	Switzerland	1961	932
Inguri	Inguri	Georgia, U.S.S.R.	—	988
Nurek	Vakhsh	U.S.S.R.	—	1,017

** Double-walled masonry earth-filled embankment, 13-foot crest length.*

Zee in two sections of 1·553 miles (mainland of North Holland to the Isle of Wieringen) and 18·641 miles from Wieringen to Friesland. It has a sea-level width of 293 feet and a height of 24 feet 7 inches.

United Kingdom The most massive (5,630,000 cubic yards), the highest (240 feet) and longest high dam (2,050 feet crest length) in the United Kingdom is the Scammonden Dam, West Riding of Yorkshire, begun in November 1966 and completed in the summer of 1970. This rock fill dam carries the M62 on its crest and was built by Sir Alfred McAlpine's. The cost of the project together with the 6½-mile motorway was £8,400,000. There are longer low dams or barrages of the valley cut-off type notably the Hanningfield Dam, Essex, built from July 1952 to August 1956 to a length of 6,850 feet and a height of 64·5 feet. The Llyn Brianne Dam in Carmarthenshire, also rock fill, will reach 300 feet in 1972 thus surpassing the concrete Clywedog Dam (built April 1964–April 1968), Montgomeryshire, of 237 feet as the highest in the United Kingdom.

LARGEST RESERVOIR

World The largest man-made is Bratsk Lake on the Angara river, U.S.S.R., with a volume of 137,214,000 acre-feet. The dam was completed in 1964. A volume of 149,000,000 acre-feet was quoted for Kariba Lake, Zambia-Rhodesia in 1959 but is now more reliably estimated at 130,000,000 acre-feet. The Volta Lake, Ghana, which filled behind the Akosombo dam from May 1964 to late 1968, also often referred to as the world's largest man-made lake, has a capacity of 120,000,000 acre-feet.

The completion in 1954 of the Owen Falls Dam near Jinja, Uganda, across the northern exit of the White Nile from the Victoria Nyanza marginally raised the level of that lake by adding 166,000,000 acre-feet, and technically turned it into a reservoir with a surface area of 17,169,920 acres (26,828 square miles).

The most grandiose reservoir project mooted is the Xingu-Araguaia river plan in central Brazil for a reservoir behind a dam at Ilha da Paz with a volume of 780,000 million cubic yards extending over 22,800 square miles. A dam at Obidos on the Amazon would produce a 744-mile-long back-up and a 68,400-square-mile reservoir at an estimated cost of $3,000 million (£1,250 million).

United Kingdom The largest wholly artificial reservoir in the United Kingdom is the Queen Mary Reservoir, built from August 1914 to June 1925, at Littleton, near Staines, with an available storage capacity of 8,130 million gallons and a water area of 707 acres. The length of the perimeter embankment is 20,766 feet (3·93 miles). Of valley cut-off type reservoirs the most capacious is Llyn Celyn, North Wales with a capacity of 17,800,000,000 gallons. The capacity of Haweswater, Westmorland, was increased by 18,660 million gallons by the building in 1929–41 of a 1,540-foot-long concrete buttress dam 120 feet high. The natural surface area was trebled to 1,050 acres. The deepest reservoir in Europe is Loch Morar, in Inverness-shire, Scotland, with a maximum depth of 1,017 feet (see also Chapter 3).

Largest polder The largest of the five great polders in the old Zuider Zee, Netherlands, will be the 149,000 acre (232·8 square miles) Markerwaard. Work on the 66-mile-long surrounding dyke was begun in 1957. The water area remaining after the erection of the 1927–32 dam is called IJssel Meer, which will have a final area of 487·5 square miles.

Largest levees The most massive earthworks ever carried out are the Mississippi levees begun in 1717 but vastly augmented by the U.S. Federal Government after the disastrous floods of 1927. These extend for 1,732 miles along the main river from Cape Girardeau, Missouri, to the Gulf of Mexico and comprise more than 1,000 million cubic yards of earthworks. Levees on the tributaries comprise an additional 2,000 miles.

8. TUNNELS

LONGEST

Water supply *World* The world's longest tunnel of any kind is the New York City-West Delaware water supply tunnel begun in 1937 and completed in 1945. It has a diameter of 13 feet 6 inches and runs for 85·0 miles from the Rondout Reservoir into the Hillview Reservoir, in the northern part of Manhattan Island, New York City, N.Y., U.S.A.

United Kingdom The longest water supply tunnel in the United Kingdom is the Thames water tunnel from Hampton-on-Thames to Walthamstow, Greater London, completed in 1960 with a circumference of 26 feet 8 inches and a length of 18·8 miles.

RAILWAY

World The world's longest main-line tunnel is the Simplon II Tunnel, completed after 4 years' work on 16 Oct. 1922. Linking Switzerland and Italy under the Alps, it is 12 miles 559 yards long. Over 60 were killed boring this and the Simplon I (1898–1906), which is 22 yards shorter. Its greatest depth below the surface is 7,005 feet.

Subway tunnel The world's longest continuous vehicular tunnel is the London Transport Board underground railway line from Morden to East Finchley, *via* Bank. In use since 1939, it is 17 miles 528 yards long and the diameter of the tunnel is 12 feet and the station tunnels 22·2 feet.

United Kingdom The United Kingdom's longest main-line railway tunnel is the Severn Tunnel (4 miles 628 yards), linking Gloucestershire and Monmouthshire, completed with 76,400,000 bricks between 1873 and 1886.

ROAD

World The world's longest road tunnel is the tunnel 7·2 miles long under Mont Blanc (15,771 feet) from Pèlerins, near Chamonix, France, to Entrèves, near Courmayeur in Valle d'Aosta, Italy, on which work began on 6 Jan. 1959. The holing through was achieved on 14 Aug. 1962 and it was opened on 16 July 1965, after an expenditure of £22,800,000. The 29½-foot-high tunnel with its carriage-way of two 12-foot lanes is expected to carry 600,000 vehicles a year. There were 23 deaths during tunnelling.

Sub-aqueous The world's longest sub-aqueous road tunnel is the Kanmon Tunnel, completed in 1958, which runs 6·15 miles from Shimonseki, Honshū, to Kyūshū, Japan. The Seikan Tunnel (38·6 miles), 100 metres (328 feet) beneath the sea-bed of the Tsugaru Strait between Tappi Saki, Honshū, and Fukushima, Hokkaidō, Japan, was due to be completed in 1973. Tests started on the sub-aqueous section (14·5 miles) in 1963.

Channel tunnel On 8 July 1966 the United Kingdom and French governments reached agreement on a Channel Tunnel for electric trains. It would run in two passages, each of 35·6 miles, 21 miles being sub-aqueous, between Westenhanger, near Dover, Kent, and Sangatte, near Calais. The project, now known as the "Chunnel", was first mooted in 1802. It will cost more than £350,000,000, if proceeded with.

United Kingdom The longest road tunnel in the United Kingdom is the Mersey Tunnel, joining Liverpool, Lancashire, and Birkenhead, Cheshire. It is 2·13 miles long, or 2·87 miles including branch tunnels. Work was begun in December 1925 and it was opened by H.M. King George V on 18 July 1934. The total cost was £7¾ million. The 36-foot-wide 4-lane roadway carries nearly 7½ million vehicles a year. A second Mersey Tunnel was begun in 1966.

Largest The largest diameter road tunnel in the world is that blasted through Yerba Buena Island, San Francisco, California, U.S.A. It is 76 feet wide, 58 feet high and 540 feet long. Up to 35,000,000 vehicles pass through on its two decks every year.

HYDRO-ELECTRIC

World The longest hydro-electric tunnel in the world will be the 51·5-mile-long Orange-Fish Rivers Tunnel, South Africa, begun in 1967 at an estimated cost of £250 million. A 30-mile-long tunnel joining the River Arpa with Lake Sevan at an altitude of 6,500 feet in the Armenian Mountains, U.S.S.R. was also reported under construction in 1967.

United Kingdom The longest in the United Kingdom is that at Ben Nevis, Inverness-shire, which has a mean diameter of 15 feet 2 inches and a length of 15 miles. It was begun in June 1926 and was holed through into Loch Treig on 3 Jan. 1930.

BRIDGE-TUNNEL

The world's longest bridge-tunnel system is the Chesapeake Bay Bridge-Tunnel, extending 17·65 miles from the Delmarva Peninsula to Norfolk, Virginia, U.S.A. It cost $200,000,000 (then £71·4 million) and was completed after 42 months and opened to traffic on 15 April 1964. The longest bridged section is Trestle C (4·56 miles long) and the longer tunnel is the Thimble Shoal Channel Tunnel (1·09 miles).

CANAL TUNNELS

Longest *World* The world's longest canal tunnel is that on the Rove canal between the port of Marseilles, France and the river Rhône, built in 1912–27. It is 4·53 miles long, 72 feet wide and 50 feet high, involving 2¼ million cubic yards of excavation.

United Kingdom The longest of the 49 canal tunnels in the United Kingdom is the Standedge Tunnel in the West Riding of Yorkshire on the Huddersfield Narrow Canal built from 1794 to 4 April 1811. It measures 3 miles 135 yards

Longest Tunnels

Miles	Yards	Name	Location	Built
	1,015	Euphrates river	Babylon (near Al Hillah), Iraq	2180–2160 B.C.
	1,093	Sámos water supply	Sámos, Aegean Is.	687 B.C.
1	650	Baebelo silver mine	Cazlona, Spain	c. 240 B.C.
3	886	Fucinus Emissarium	Monte Salvino, Celano, Italy	41–51 A.D.
7	800	Noirieu Canal tunnel	St. Quentin, France	–1822
31	880	Rothschönberg	Felberg, Saxony	–1877
33	220	New Croton water tunnel	Croton Dam–Manhattan, New York	–1888
85		West Delaware water supply	Rondout–Hillview, New York	1937–1945

Longest Rail Tunnels

Miles	Yards	Name	Location	Built
3	13	Woodhead No. 1	Cheshire, England	1 Oct. 1838–20 Dec. 1845
3	62	Standedge No. 2	Yorkshire, England	1846–1 Aug. 1849
3	62	Standedge No. 3	Yorkshire, England	April 1868–Oct. 1870
4	1,146	Hoosac	Massachusetts, U.S.A.	1855–1 July 1876
7	1,045	Fréjus (Mont Cenis)	Modane, France-Bardonecchia, Italy	18 Aug. 1857–17 Sept. 1871
9	452	St. Gotthard	Göschenen-Airolo, Switz.	13 Sept. 1872–23 May 1882
12	537	Simplon I	Brigue, Switz.–Iselle, Italy	1 Aug. 1898–25 Jan. 1906
12	559	Simplon II	Brigue, Switz.–Iselle, Italy	1918–16 Oct. 1922

Longest Road Tunnels

Miles	Yards	Name	Location	Built
	1,015	*Euphrates river	Babylon (near Al Ḥillah), Iraq	2180–2160 B.C.
	1,610	Pausilippo	Naples–Pozzuoli, Italy	36 B.C.
1	189	Vicoforte	Piedmont, Italy	c. 1650
1	382	Castel Hill	Budapest, Hungary	1847
1	628	Col de Rousset	Drôme, France	1867
1	1,724	Dell Colle di Tenda	Limone Piemonte, Italy–Tende, France	1882–89
2	231	*First Mersey Tunnel	Liverpool–Birkenhead, England	1925–34
6	265	*Kanmon	Honshū-Kyūshū, Japan	1939–58
7	476	Le Tunnel Routier de Mont Blanc	Pèlerins, France–Entrèves, Italy	1959–65
35	1,056	*Seikan Tunnel	Tsugaru Strait, Japan	1963–73

* *Sub-aqueous.*

in length and was closed on 21 Dec. 1944. The Huddersfield Narrow Canal is also the highest in the United Kingdom, reaching a height at one point of 638 feet above sea-level.

Tunnelling record The world's record for rapid tunnelling was set on 18 March 1967 in the 8·6-mile-long Blanco Tunnel, in Southern Colorado when the "mole" (giant boring machine) crew advanced the 10-foot diameter heading 375 feet in one day.

9. SPECIALISED STRUCTURES

SEVEN WONDERS OF THE WORLD

The Seven Wonders of the World were first designated by Antipater of Sidon in the 2nd century B.C. They included the Pyramids of Gîza, built by three Fourth Dynasty Egyptian Pharaohs, Hwfw (Khufu or Cheops), Kha-f-Ra (Khafre, Khefren or Chephren) and Menkaure (Mycerinus) near El Gîza (El Gizeh), south-west of El Qâhira (Cairo) in Egypt (now the United Arab Republic). The Great Pyramid ("Horizon of Khufu") was built in *c.* 2580 B.C. Its original height was 480 feet 11 inches (now, since the loss of its topmost stone or pyramidion, reduced to 449 feet 6 inches) with a base line of 756 feet and thus originally covering slightly more than 13 acres. It has been estimated that a work force of 4,000 required 30 years to manoeuvre into position the 2,300,000 limestone blocks averaging 2½ tons each, totalling about 5,750,000 tons and a volume of 90,700,000 cubic feet.

Of the other six wonders only fragments remain of the Temple of Artemis (Diana) of the Ephesians, built in *c.* 350 B.C. at Ephesus, Turkey (destroyed by the Goths in A.D. 262), and of the Tomb of King Mausolus of Caria, built at Halicarnassus, now Bodrum, Turkey, in *c.* 325 B.C. No trace remains of the Hanging Gardens of Semiramis, at Babylon, Iraq (*c.* 600 B.C.); the 40-foot-tall marble, gold and ivory statue of Zeus (Jupiter), by Phidias (5th century B.C.) at Olympia, Greece (lost in a fire at Istanbul); the 117-foot-tall statue by Charles of Lindus of the figure of the god Helios (Apollo), called the Colossus of Rhodes (sculptured 292–280 B.C., destroyed by an earthquake in 224 B.C.); or the 400-foot-tall lighthouse built by Soscratus of Cnidus during the 3rd century B.C. (destroyed by earthquake in A.D. 1375) on the island of Pharos (Greek, *pharos*=lighthouse), off the coast of El Iskandarîya (Alexandria), Egypt (now the United Arab Republic).

PYRAMIDS

Largest The largest pyramid, and the largest monument ever constructed, is the Quetzalcóatl at Cholula de Rivadahia, 63 miles south-east of Mexico City, Mexico. It is 177 feet tall and its base covers an area of nearly 45 acres. Its total volume has been estimated at 4,300,000 cubic yards, compared with 3,360,000 cubic yards for the Pyramid of Cheops (see above). The pyramid-building era here was between the 6th and 12th centuries A.D.

Oldest The oldest known pyramid is the Djoser step pyramid at Saqqâra, Egypt constructed to a height of 204 feet of Tura limestone in *c.* 2650 B.C. The oldest New World pyramid is that on the island of La Venta in south-eastern Mexico built by the Olmec people *c.* 800 B.C. It stands 100 feet tall with a base diameter of 420 feet.

TALLEST FLAGSTAFF

World The tallest flagstaff ever erected was that outside the Oregon Building at the 1915 Panama-Pacific International Exposition in San Francisco, California, U.S.A. Trimmed from a Douglas fir, it stood 299 feet 7 inches in height and weighed 45 tons. The tallest unsupported flag pole in the world is a 220-foot-tall metal pole weighing 28,000 lb. erected in 1955 at the U.S. Merchant Marine Academy in King's Point, New York, U.S.A. The pole, built by Kearney-National Inc., tapers from 24 inches to 5½ inches at the jack.

United Kingdom The tallest flagstaff in the United Kingdom is a 225-foot-tall Douglas fir staff at Kew, London. Cut in Canada, it was shipped across the Atlantic and towed up the River Thames on 7 May 1958, to replace the old 214-foot-tall staff of 1919.

Tallest totem pole The tallest totem pole in the world is one 160 feet tall in McKinleyville, California, U.S.A. It weighs 57,000 lb. (25·4 tons), was carved from a 500-year-old tree and was erected in May 1962.

MONUMENTS

Tallest The world's tallest monument is the stainless steel Gateway to the West Arch in St. Louis, Missouri, U.S.A., completed on 28 Oct. 1965 to commemorate the westward expansion after the Louisiana Purchase of 1803. It is a sweeping arch spanning 630 feet and rising to a height of 630 feet, and costing $29,000,000 (£12,083,000). It was designed in 1947 by Eero Saarinen (died 1961).

The tallest monumental column in the world is that commemorating the battle of San Jacinto (21 April 1836), on the bank of the San Jacinto river near Houston, Texas, U.S.A. General Sam Houston (1793–1863) and his force of 743 Texan troops killed 630 Mexicans (out of a total force of 1,600) and captured 700 others, for the loss of nine men killed and 30 wounded. Constructed in 1936–39, at a cost of $1,500,000 (now £625,000), the tapering column is 570 feet tall, 47 feet square at the base, and 30 feet square at the observation tower, which is surmounted by a star weighing 196·4 tons. It is built of concrete, faced with buff limestone, and weighs 31,384 tons.

Prehistoric *Largest* Britain's largest monolithic prehistoric monuments are the 28½-acre earthworks and stone circles of Avebury, Wiltshire, rediscovered in 1646. This is believed to be the work of the Beaker people of the later Neolithic period of *c.* 1700 to 1500 B.C. The whole work is 1,200 feet in diameter with a 40-foot ditch around the perimeter. The largest trilithons exist at Stonehenge, to the south of Salisbury Plain, Wiltshire, with single sarsen blocks weighing over 45 tons and requiring over 550 men to drag them up a 9° gradient. The dating of the site was in 1969 revised to the period *c.* 2400–2200 B.C.

Largest earthwork The greatest prehistoric earthwork in Britain is Wansdyke, originally Woden's Dyke, which ran 86 miles from Portishead, Somerset to Inkpen Beacon and Ludgershall, south of Hungerford, Berkshire. It is believed to have been built by the pre-Roman Wessex culture. The most extensive single site earthwork is the Dorset Cursus near Gussage St. Michael, dating from *c.* 1900 B.C. The workings are 6 miles in length, involving an estimated 250,000 cubic yards of excavations. The largest of the Celtic hill-forts is that known as Mew Dun, or Maiden Castle, two miles south-west of Dorchester, Dorset. It covers 115 acres and was abandoned shortly after A.D. 43.

Largest mound The largest artificial mound in Europe is Silbury Hill, 6 miles west of Marlborough, Wiltshire, which involved the moving of an estimated 670,000 tons of chalk to make a cone 130 feet high with a base of 5½ acres. Prof. Richard Atkinson in charge of the 1968 excavations showed that it is based on an innermost central mound, similar to contemporary round barrows, and may be dated to *c.* 2200 B.C. The largest long barrow in England is that inside the Neolithic camp and Iron Age Hill-fort at Maiden Castle (see above). It originally had a length of 1,800 feet and had several enigmatic features such as a ritual pit with pottery, limpet shells and animal bones. In 1934–37 the remains of a man of 25–35 was discovered, who had been hacked to pieces after death. The longest long barrow containing a megalithic chamber is that at West Kennet (*c.* 2200 B.C.), near Silbury, measuring 385 feet in length.

The 4,000-year-old Silbury Hill earthwork near Marlborough, Wiltshire

Youngest Ancient Monument Of all the ancient monuments scheduled in Great Britain, the youngest is Fort Wallington, near Portsmouth, Hampshire. It was begun in 1860, when a French invasion was thought possible, and was not completed until 1870.

OBELISKS (Monolithic)

Oldest The longest an obelisk has remained *in situ* is that at Heliopolis (now Masr-el-Gedîda) United Arab Republic (Egypt), erected by Senusret I *c.* 1750 B.C.

Largest The largest standing obelisk in the world is that in the Piazza of St. John in Lateran, Rome, erected in 1588. It came originally from the Circus Maximus (erected A.D. 357) and before that from Heliopolis, Egypt (erected *c.* 1450 B.C.). It is 110 feet in length and weighs 450 tons. The largest obelisk in the United Kingdom is Cleopatra's Needle on the Embankment, London, which is 68 feet 5½ inches tall and weighs 186·36 tons. It was towed down the Thames from Egypt on 20 Jan. 1878.

Largest tomb The largest tomb in the world is that of Emperor Nintoku (died *c.* A.D. 428) south of Ōsaka, Japan. It measures 1,594 feet long by 1,000 feet wide by 150 feet high.

Largest ziqqurat The largest surviving ziqqurat (from the verb *zaqaru*, to build high) or stage-tower is the Ziqqurat of Ur (now Muqqayr, Iraq) with a base 200 feet by 150 feet built to at least three storeys of which only the first and part of the second now survive to a height of 60 feet. It was built by the Akkadian King Ur-Nammu (*c.* 2113–2006 B.C.).

STATUES

Tallest The tallest free-standing statue in the world is that of "Motherland", an enormous female figure on Mamayev Hill, outside Volgograd, U.S.S.R., designed in 1967 by Yevgenyi Vuchetich, to commemorate victory in the Battle of Stalingrad (1942–43). The statue from its base to the tip of the sword clenched in her right hand measures 270 feet.

Longest Near Bamiyan, Afghanistan there are the remains of the recumbent Sakya Buddha, built of plastered rubble, which was "about 1,000 feet" long and is believed to date from the 3rd or 4th century A.D.

LARGEST DOME

World The world's largest dome is the "Astrodome" of the Harris County Sports Stadium, in Houston, Texas, U.S.A. It has an outside diameter of 710 feet and an inside diameter of 642 feet. (See page 110 for further details.) The largest dome of ancient architecture is that of the Pantheon, built in Rome in A.D. 112, with a diameter of 142½ feet.

Britain The largest dome in Britain is that of the Bell Sports Centre, Perth, Scotland with a diameter of 222 feet, designed by D. B. Cockburn and constructed in Baltic whitewood by Muirhead & Sons Ltd. of Grangemouth, Stirlingshire.

Tallest columns The tallest columns (as opposed to obelisks) in the world are the sixteen 82-foot-tall pillars in the Palace of Labour in Torino (Turin), Italy, for which the architect was Pier Luigi Nervi (born 21 June 1891). They were built of concrete and steel in only 8 days. The tallest load-bearing stone columns in the world are those measuring 69 feet in the Hall of Columns of the Temple of Amun at Al Karnak, the northern part of the ruins of Thebes, the Greek name for the ancient capital of Upper Egypt (now the United Arab Republic). They were built in the 19th dynasty in the reign of Rameses II in *c.* 1270 B.C.

HARBOUR WORKS

Longest jetty The longest deep water jetty in the world is the Quai Hermann du Pasquier at Le Havre, France, with a length of 5,000 feet. Part of an enclosed basin, it has a constant depth of water of 32 feet on both sides.

Longest pier *World* The world's longest pier is the Dammam Pier at El Hasa, Saudi Arabia, on the Persian Gulf. A rock-filled causeway 4·84 miles long joins the steel trestle pier 1·80 miles long, which joins the Main Pier (744 feet long), giving an overall length of 6·79 miles. The work was begun in July 1948 and completed on 15 March 1950.

United Kingdom The longest pier in Great Britain is the Bee Ness Jetty, completed in 1930, which stretches 8,200 feet along the west bank of the River Medway, 5 to 6 miles below Rochester, at Kingsnorth, Kent.

Longest breakwater *World* The world's longest breakwater system is that which protects the Ports of Long Beach and Los Angeles, California, U.S.A. The combined length of the four breakwaters is 43,602 feet (8·26 miles) of which the Long Beach section, built between 1941 and February 1949, is the longest at 13,350 feet (2·53 miles). The North breakwater at Tuticorin, Madras Province, Southern India on which construction began in 1968 will extend when complete to 13,589 feet.

United Kingdom The longest breakwater in the United Kingdom is the North Breakwater at Holyhead, Anglesey, which is 9,860 feet (1·86 miles) in length and was completed in 1873.

LARGEST DRY DOCK

World The largest dry dock in the world is the Belfast Harbour Commission and Harland and Wolff building dock at Belfast, Northern Ireland. It has been excavated by Wimpey's to a length of 1,825 feet and a width of 305 feet and can accommodate tankers of 1,000,000 d.w.t. Work was begun on 26 Jan. 1968 and completed on 30 Nov. 1969 and involved the excavation of 400,000 cubic yards. See also Largest crane.

Work started at Nagasaki, Japan on 16 Sept. 1970 on a building dock capable of taking a tanker of 1,200,000 d.w.t. for Mitsubishi Heavy Industries Co. at a cost of £32,000,000.

LARGEST FLOATING DOCKS

Sectional The largest floating docks ever constructed are the United States Navy's advanced base sectional docks (A.B.S.D.). These consist of 10 sectional units giving together an effective keel block length of 827 feet and clear width of 140 feet, with a lifting capacity of 71,000 tons. One designated AFDB 3 at Green Cove Springs, Florida, U.S.A. has a nominal lifting capacity of 80,000 tons.

Single unit The largest single unit floating dock is Admiralty Floating Dock (AFD) 35, which was towed from the Royal Navy's dockyard in Malta to the Cantieri Navali Santa Maria of Genoa, Italy, in May 1965. It has a lifting capacity of 65,000 tons and an overall length of

857 feet 8 inches. It had been towed to Malta from Bombay, India, where it was built in 1947.

LIGHTHOUSES

Brightest *World* The lighthouse with the most powerful light in the world is Créac'h d'Ouessant lighthouse, established in 1638 and last altered in 1939 on l'Île d'Ouessant, Finistère, Brittany, France. It is 163 feet tall and, in times of fog, has a luminous intensity of up to 500,000,000 candelas.

The lights with the greatest visible range are those 1,092 feet above the ground on the Empire State Building, New York City, N.Y., U.S.A. Each of the four-arc mercury bulbs has a rated candlepower of 450,000,000, visible 80 miles away on the ground and 300 miles away from aircraft. They were switched on on 31 March 1956.

United Kingdom The lighthouse in the United Kingdom with the most powerful light is the shorelight Orfordness, Suffolk. It has an intensity of 7,500,000 candelas. The Irish light with the greatest intensity is Aranmore on Rinrawros Point, County Donegal.

Tallest The world's tallest lighthouse is the steel tower 348 feet tall near Yamashita Park in Yokohama, Japan. It has a power of 600,000 candles and a visibility range of 20 miles.

Remotest The most remote Trinity House lighthouse is The Smalls, about 16 sea miles (18·4 statute miles) off the Pembrokeshire coast. The most remote Scottish lighthouse is Sule Skerry, 35 miles off shore and 45 miles north-west of Dunnet Head, Caithness. The most remote Irish light is Blackrock, about 9 miles off the Mayo coast.

WINDMILLS

Earliest The earliest recorded windmills are those used for grinding corn in Iran (Persia) in the 7th century A.D. The earliest known in England was the post-mill at Bury St. Edmunds, Suffolk, recorded in 1191. The oldest working mill in England is the post-mill at Outwood, Surrey, built in 1665, though the Ivinghoe Mill in Pitstone Green Farm, Buckinghamshire, dating from 1627, has been restored. The largest conventional windmill in England is a disused one at Sutton, Norfolk.

England's oldest windmill at Pitstone, Buckinghamshire

The world's largest working waterwheel at Laxey, Isle of Man

WATERWHEEL

Largest *World* The largest waterwheel in the world is the Lady Isabella wheel at Laxey, Isle of Man. It was built in Liverpool for draining a lead mine and completed on 27 Sept. 1854, has a circumference of 228 feet, a diameter of 72½ feet and an axle weighing 9 tons.

Barns The largest barn in Britain is one at Manor Farm, Cholsey, near Wallingford, Berkshire. It is 303 feet in length and 54 feet in breadth (16,362 square feet). The Ipsden Barn, Oxfordshire, is 385½ feet long but 30 feet wide (11,565 square feet).

The longest tithe barn in Britain is one measuring 268 feet long at Wyke Farm, near Sherborne, Dorset.

NUDIST CAMP

Largest The first nudist camps were established in Germany in 1912. The largest such camp in the world was that at l'Île du Levant, southern France, which had up to 15,000 *adeptes* before it was taken over for defence purposes by the French Navy in 1965. Currently the largest nude sea and sunbathing centre is Montalivet on the west coast of France with up to 10,000 "naturists". The term "nudist camp" went out of favour in the early 'sixties.

LONGEST WALL

World The Great Wall of China, completed during the reign of Shih Huang-ti (246–210 B.C.), is 1,684 miles in length, with a height of from 15 to 39 feet and up to 32 feet thick. Its erection is the most massive construction job ever undertaken by the human race. It runs from Shanhaikuan, on the Gulf of Pohai, to Chiayukuan in Kansu and was kept in repair up to the 16th century.

Britain The longest of the Roman Walls built in Britain was the 15–20-foot-tall Hadrian's Wall, built in the period A.D. 122–126. It ran across the Tyne-Solway isthmus of 74½ miles from Bowness-on-Solway, Cumberland, to Wallsend-on-Tyne, Northumberland, and was abandoned in A.D. 383.

LONGEST FENCE

The longest fence in the world is the dingo-proof fence enclosing the main sheep areas of Queensland, Australia. The wire fence is 6 feet high, one foot underground and stretches for 3,437 miles.

DOORS

Largest *World* The largest doors in the world are the four in the Vertical Assembly Building near Cape Kennedy,

Florida, with a height of 460 feet (see page 105).

The largest doors in the United Kingdom are those to the Britannia Assembly Hall, at Filton, Bristol. The doors are 1,035 feet in length and 67 feet high, divided into three bays each 345 feet across. The largest simple hinged door in Britain is that of Ye Old Bull's Head, Beaumaris, Anglesey, Wales, which is 12 feet wide and 30 feet high.

Oldest The oldest doors in Britain are those of Hadstock Church, Essex, which date from *c.* 1040 and exhibit evidence of Danish workmanship.

LARGEST WINDOWS

The largest sheet of glass ever manufactured was one of 50 square metres (538·2 square feet), or 20 metres (65 feet 7 inches) by 2·5 metres (8 feet 2½ inches), exhibited by the Saint Gobain Company in France at the *Journées Internationales de Miroiterie* in March 1958. The largest windows in the world are the three in the Palace of Industry and Technology at Rond-point de la Défense, Paris, with an extreme width of 218 metres (715·2 feet) and a maximum height of 50 metres (164 feet).

LONGEST STAIRS

The world's longest stairs are reputedly at the Mår power station, Øverland, western Norway. Built of wood, these are 4,101 feet in length, rising in 3,875 steps at an angle of 41 degrees inside the pressure shaft. The length of a very long, now discontinuous, stone stairway in the Rohtang Pass, Manali, Kulu, Northern India, is still under investigation.

TALLEST FIRE ESCAPE

The world's tallest mobile fire escape is a 250-foot-tall turntable ladder built in 1962 by Magirus, a West German firm.

LARGEST MARQUEE

World The largest tent ever erected was one covering an area of 188,368 square feet (4·32 acres) put up by the firm of Deuter from Augsburg, West Germany, for the 1958 "Welcome Expo" in Brussels, Belgium.

Britain The largest marquee in Britain is one made by Piggot Brothers in 1951 and used by the Royal Horticultural Society at their annual show (first held in 1913) in the grounds of the Royal Hospital, Chelsea, London. The marquee is 310 feet long × 480 feet wide, and consists of 18¾ miles of 36-inch-wide canvas covering a ground area of 148,800 square feet. A tent 390 feet long was erected in one lift by the Army at the 1970 Colchester Tattoo in Kings Head Meadow with 135 men.

LARGEST VATS

The largest vats in the United Kingdom are those used in cider brewing by H. P. Bulmer & Company. Their standard oak vats hold 60,000 gallons and reinforced concrete vats hold up to 100,000 gallons. Largest of all is a lined steel vat with a capacity of 550,000 gallons at Hereford.

The world's largest fermentation vessel is the giant stainless steel container, No. 26M, built by the A.P.V. Co. Ltd. of Crawley, Sussex, for the Guinness Brewery, St. James's Gate, Dublin, Ireland. This has a nominal capacity of 8,000 standard barrels, or 2,304,000 Imperial pints, and dimensions of 63 feet long by 28 feet 9 inches wide by 29 feet 7 inches high.

ADVERTISING SIGNS

Largest The greatest advertising sign ever erected was the electric Citroën sign on the Eiffel Tower, Paris. It was switched on on 4 July 1925, and could be seen 24 miles away. It was in six colours with 250,000 lamps and 56 miles of electric cables. The letter "N" which terminated the name "Citroën" between the second and third levels measured 68 feet 5 inches in height. The whole apparatus was taken down after 11 years in 1936.

The world's largest neon sign was that owned by the Atlantic Coast Line Railroad Company at Port Tampa, Florida, U.S.A. It measured 387 feet 6 inches long and 76 feet high, weighed 175 tons and contained about 4,200 feet of red neon tubing. It was demolished on 19 Feb. 1970. Broadway's largest billboard in New York City is 11,426 square feet in area—equivalent to 107 feet by 107 feet. Britain's largest illuminated sign is the word PLAYHOUSE extending 90 feet across the frontage of the new theatre in Leeds, Yorkshire opened in 1970.

The world's largest working sign was that in Times Square at 44 & 45th Streets, New York City, U.S.A., in 1966. It showed two 42½-foot-tall "bottles" of Haig Scotch Whisky and an 80-foot-long "bottle" of Gordon's Gin being "poured" into a frosted glass. The world's tallest free-standing advertising sign is the 188-foot-tall, 93-foot-wide Stardust Hotel sign at Las Vegas, Nevada, U.S.A. completed in February 1968. It uses 25,000 light bulbs and 2,500 feet of neon tubing and has letters up to 22 feet tall.

Highest *World* The highest advertising sign in the world is the "R.C.A." on the Radio Corporation of America Building in Rockefeller Plaza, New York City, U.S.A. The top of the 25-foot-tall illuminated letters is 825 feet above street level.

United Kingdom The highest advertising sign in the United Kingdom was the revolving name board of the contractors "Peter Lind" on the Post Office Tower, London (see Towers). The illuminated letters were 12 feet tall and 563 to 575 feet above the street.

LARGEST GASHOLDER

World The world's largest gasholder is that at Fontaine l'Evêque, Belgium, where disused mines have been adapted to store up to 500 million cubic metres (17,650 million cubic feet) of gas at ordinary pressure. Probably the largest conventional gasholder is that at Wien-Simmering, Vienna, Austria, completed in 1968, with a height of 274 feet 8 inches and a capacity of 10·59 million cubic feet.

United Kingdom The largest gasholder ever constructed in the United Kingdom is the East Greenwich Gas Works No. 2 Holder built in 1891 with an original capacity for 12,200,000 cubic feet. As reconstructed its capacity is 8·9 million cubic feet with a water tank 303 feet in diameter and a full inflated height of 148 feet. The No. 1 holder (capacity 8·6 million cubic feet) has a height of 200 feet. The River Tees Northern Gas Board's 1,186-foot-deep underground storage in use since January 1959 has a capacity of 330,000 cubic feet.

TALLEST FOUNTAIN

World The world's tallest fountain is the "Delacorte Geyser"

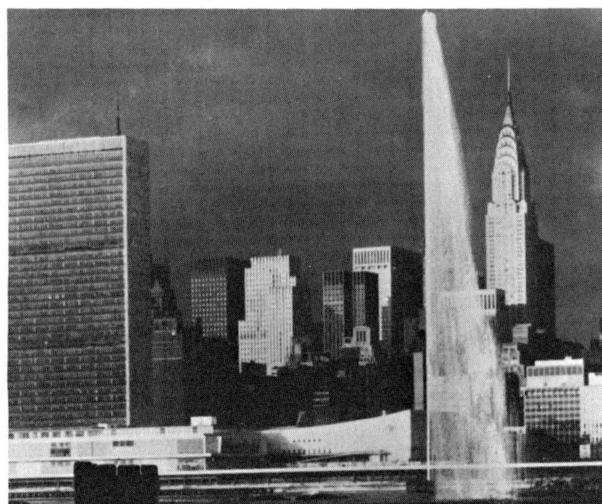

The world's tallest fountain in New York City

in Welfare Park, Manhattan, New York City which can attain a height of 600 feet. It was installed in June 1969 at a cost of $350,000 (£145,833) and given to the City by George T. Delacorte, founder of the Dell Publishing Company.

United Kingdom The tallest fountain in the United Kingdom is the Emperor Fountain at Chatsworth, Bakewell, Derbyshire. When first tested on 1 June 1844, it attained the then unprecedented height of 260 feet. Since the war it has not been played to more than 250 feet and rarely beyond 180 feet.

Bonfire *Largest* The largest Guy Fawkes bonfire constructed was one using 150 tons of timber and 1,330 tyres built to a height of 53 feet surmounted by a 10-foot flag pole by The First Company of Torrington Cavaliers in Torrington, Devon for 5 Nov. 1970.

CEMETERIES

The world's largest cemetery is that in Leningrad, U.S.S.R., which contains over 500,000 of the 1,300,000 victims of the German army's siege of 1941–42. The largest cemetery in the United Kingdom is Brookwood Cemetery, Brookwood, Surrey. It is owned by the London Necropolis Co. and is 500 acres in extent with 225,560 interments to May 1971.

CREMATORIA

Earliest The oldest crematorium in Britain is one built in 1879 at Woking, Surrey. The first legal cremation took place there on 20 March 1885.

Largest The largest crematorium in Europe is the Golders Green Crematorium, in north London. It extends over 14 acres and currently carries out about 5,500 cremations a year.

10. BORINGS

DEEPEST

World Man's deepest penetration into the Earth's crust was the test bore-hole made by the Phillips Petroleum Co. with the No. 1 well on their EE University Lease in Pecos County, Texas, U.S.A. After 730 days, the drilling crew reached 25,340 feet (4·80 miles) on 12 Oct. 1958. The well was spudded on 12 Oct. 1956, and plugged and abandoned as a "duster", without producing a drop of oil, on 9 Feb. 1959, having cost more than $3,000,000 (£1,250,000). The highest hole temperature was 351° F. A conception of the depth of this hole can be gained by the realization that it was sufficient in depth to lower the Empire State Building down it 20 times. The bore is however only 3 inches in diameter. The immense weight of drill pipe caused a stretch of up to 20 feet over the unstressed length.

The U.S.S.R. Ministry of Geology announced in March 1966 the start of operations to drill to a depth of 15 kilometres (9·32 miles or 49,213 feet) into the magmatic layer near the Finnish border in Karelia. Completion is scheduled for 1971–72. Early in 1967 it was announced that five other boreholes were to be sunk to a depth of up to 11 miles in "Project Anti-Cosmos". The other sites will be north of the Caspian Sea, in the north of the Russian S.F.S.R., in the outlying Urals, in the Caucasus, and in the Kurile Islands.

It was reported in February 1969 that two of the five super-deep borehole projects in the U.S.S.R. some in the Kola Peninsular and in the Caspian depression at Aral Sor (see Chapter 3) have completed their main first-stage to "some 7 to 8 kilometres" (22,966 to 26,247 feet). No formal announcement of having surpassed the 1958 world record of 7·72 km. (25,340 feet) was however made. The other sites will be at Saatly, Azerbaijan (first stage 1970; second stage 1972); and in the Urals and the Kurile Islands.

United Kingdom The deepest oil well in the United Kingdom is the British Petroleum well drilled to a depth of 9,355 feet at Tetney Lock, near Cleethorpes, Lincolnshire, in 1963. A depth of 19,171 feet was attained at an undisclosed site in the U.K. North Sea fields in 1970.

OIL FIELDS

Largest The largest oil field in the world is that at Oktyabr'skiy, U.S.S.R., which extends over 1,800 square miles (60 miles by 30 miles). It has been asserted that the Groningen gas field in the Netherlands is the largest discovered. It was estimated in 1968 that the United Kingdom's segment of the North Sea gas field contains $2{\cdot}5 \times 10^{13}$ cubic feet of almost pure methane of which the Leman Field (discovered April 1966), operated by the Shell-Esso-Gas Council-Amoco group, accounts for about half.

Greatest gusher The most prolific wildcat recorded is the 1,160-foot-deep Lucas No. 1, at Spindletop, about 3 miles north of Beaumont, Texas, U.S.A., on 10 Jan. 1901. The gusher was heard more than a mile away and yielded 800,000 barrels during the 9 days it was uncapped. The surrounding ground subsequently yielded 142,000,000 barrels.

Greatest flare The greatest gas fire was that which burnt at Gassi Touil in the Algerian Sahara from noon on 13 Nov. 1961 to 9.30 a.m. on 28 April 1962. The pillar of flame rose 450 feet and the smoke 600 feet. It was eventually extinguished by Paul Neal ("Red") Adair, aged 47, of Austin, Texas, U.S.A., using 550 lb. of dynamite. His fee was understood to be about $1,000,000 (then £357,000).

WATER WELLS

Deepest *World* The world's deepest water bore is the Stensvad Water Well 11-W1 of 7,320 feet drilled by the Great Northern Drilling Co. Inc. in Rosebud County, Montana, U.S.A. in October-November 1961.

United Kingdom The deepest well in the United Kingdom is a water table well 2,842 feet deep in the Staffordshire coal measures at Smestow. The deepest artesian well in Britain is that at the White Heather Laundry, Stonebridge Park, Willesden, London, N.W.10, bored in 1911 to a depth of 2,225 feet.

Largest *Hand-dug* The largest hand-dug well was one 100 feet in circumference and 109 feet deep dug in 1877–8 at Greensburg, Kansas, U.S.A.

MINES

Earliest The earliest known mining operations were in the Ngwenya Hills of the Hhohho District of north-western Swaziland where haematite (iron ore) was mined for body paint *c.* 41,000 B.C.

Deepest *World* The world's deepest mine is the East Rand Proprietary Mine at Boksburg, Transvaal, South Africa. In November 1959 a depth of 11,246 feet (2·13 miles) below the ground and 5,875 feet below sea-level was first attained. Mining does not now proceed below 10,788 feet where the rock temperature is two degrees cooler at 124° F. The deepest terminal below any vertical mine shaft in the world is No. 3 sub-vertical main shaft on the Western Deep Levels Mine reaching 9,783 feet below the surface. The longest vertical shaft is No. 3 Ventilation Shaft at the mine which measures 9,673 feet in one continuous hole. The longest sub-incline shaft is the Angelo Tertiary at E.R.P.M. (see above) with a length of 6,656 feet (1·26 miles).

United Kingdom The all-time record depth is 4,132 feet in the Arley Seam of the Parsonage Colliery, Leigh, Lancashire in Feb. 1949. The record in Scottish coalmines was 3,093 feet in the Michael Colliery, Barncraig, Fife, reached in August 1939. The deepest present mine workings are the Hem Heath Colliery (Moss Seam), Trentham, Staffordshire, England at 3,300 feet. The deepest in Scotland is the Great Seam at Monkton Hall Colliery,

Britain's deepest ever colliery, the arsonage pit, Leigh, Lancashire

Millerhill, Midlothian, at 2,930 feet. The deepest shaft in England was No. 2 shaft at Wolstanton Colliery, Stoke-on-Trent, Staffordshire, at 3,434 feet and the deepest in Scotland was Monkton Hall No. 1, Midlothian at 3,054 feet. The deepest Cornish tin mine was Dolcoath mine, near Camborne. The Williams shaft was completed in 1910 to 550 fathoms (3,300 feet) from adit or approximately 3,600 feet from the surface.

PROGRESSIVE DEEP MINING RECORDS

Depth		
2,764	Kitzbuhel copper mine, Austria	*1835
3,280	St. Vojtech mine, Príbram, Czechoslovakia (later reached 4,355 feet). Started 1779	May 1875
5,419	Ooregum goldmine, Kolar, Mysore, India	1919
7,640	Robinson Deep goldmine, Witwatersrand, South Africa	1931
8,051	Morro Vehlo goldmine, Nova Lima, Brazil	1933
8,198	Robinson Deep goldmine, Turf Section, South Africa	31 Dec. 1933
8,400	Robinson Deep goldmine (Old Village Deep) Turf Section, South Africa	1934
8,527	Crown Mines, Johannesburg, South Africa	1938
8,604	Champion Reef Mines, Kolar, Mysore, India	31 Dec. 1939
9,071	Crown Mines, Johannesburg, South Africa	31 Dec. 1949
9,288	East Rand Proprietary Mine, Boksburg, South Africa	Aug. 1953
11,000	East Rand Proprietary Mine, Boksburg, South Africa	8 Aug. 1958
11,246	East Rand Proprietary Mine, Boksburg, South Africa	Nov. 1959

**The deepest reached below sea level by this date was 1,513 feet in the Monkwearmouth Colliery, Durham, England.*

GOLDMINES

argest area The largest goldmining area in the world is the Witwatersrand gold field extending 30 miles east and west of Johannesburg, South Africa. Gold was discovered there in 1886 and by 1944 more than 45 per cent. of the world's gold was mined there by 320,000 Bantu and 44,000 Europeans. Currently 74 per cent. of the free world's supply comes from this area which now has a total labour force of 650,000.

Largest *World* The largest goldmine in area is the East Rand Proprietary Mines Ltd., whose 8,785 claims cover 12,100 acres. The largest, measured by volume extracted, is Randfontein Estates Gold Mine Co. Ltd. with 170 million cubic yards—enough to cover Manhattan Island to a depth of 8 feet. The main tunnels if placed end to end would stretch a distance of 2,600 miles.

United Kingdom The largest goldmine in Britain was Gwynfyngdd, Merionethshire, Wales, where gold was discovered in 1834 and which was worked from 1864 till 1961. Alluvial gold deposits are believed to have been worked in the Wicklow Mountains, Ireland, as early as 1800 B.C.

Richest The richest goldmine has been Crown Mines with nearly 45 million ounces and still productive. The richest in yield per year was West Driefontein which averaged more than 2½ million ounces per year until disrupted in November 1968 by flooding. The only large mine in South Africa yielding more than one ounce per ton milled is Free State Geduld.

Iron The world's largest iron-mine is at Lebedinsky, U.S.S.R., in the Kursk Magnetic Anomaly which has altogether an estimated 20,000 million tons of rich (45–65 per cent.) ore and 10,000,000 million tons of poorer ore in seams up to 2,000 feet thick. The world's greatest reserves are, however, those of Brazil, estimated to total 58,000 million tons, or 35 per cent. of the world's total surface stock.

Copper Historically the world's most productive copper mine has been the Bingham Canyon Mine (see below) belonging to the Kennecott Copper Corporation with over 9,000,000 short tons in the 65 years 1904–68. Currently the most productive is the Chuquicamata mine of the Anaconda Company 150 miles north of Antofagasta, Chile with 334,578 short tons in 1966.

The world's largest underground copper mine is at El Teniente, 50 miles south-east of Santiago, Chile, with more than 200 miles of underground workings and an annual output of nearly 11,000,000 tons of ore.

Silver, lead and zinc The world's largest lead, zinc and silver mine is the Sullivan Mine at Kimberley, British Columbia, Canada, with 248 miles of tunnels. The mines at Broken Hill, New South Wales, Australia, found in September 1883, produce annually 2,300,000 tons of ore, from which is extracted some 10 per cent. of the world's output of lead. The world's largest zinc smelter is the Cominco Ltd. plant at Trail, British Columbia, Canada which has an annual capacity of 263,000 tons of zinc and 800 tons of cadmium.

Spoil heap The world's largest artificial heap is the sand dump on the Randfontein Estates Gold Mine, South Africa, which comprises 42 million tons of crushed ore and rock waste and has a volume six times that of the Great Pyramid. The largest colliery tip in Great Britain covers 114 acres (maximum height 130 feet) with 18 million tons of slag at Cutacre Clough, Lancashire.

QUARRIES

Largest *World* The world's largest excavation is the Bingham Canyon Copper Mine, 30 miles south of Salt Lake City, Utah, U.S.A. From 1906 to mid-1969 the total excavation has been 2,445 million long tons over an area of 2·08 square miles to a depth of 2,280 feet. This is five times the amount of material moved to build the Panama Canal. Three shifts of 900 men work round the clock with 38 electric shovels, 62 locomotives hauling 1,268 wagons and 18 drilling machines for the 28 tons of explosive used daily. The average daily extraction is 96,000 tons of one per cent. ore and 225,000 tons of overburden.

The world's deepest open pit is the Kimberley Open Mine in South Africa, dug over a period of 43 years (1871 to 1914) to a depth of nearly 1,200 feet and with a diameter of about 1,500 feet and a circumference of nearly a mile, covering an area of 36 acres. Three tons (14,504,566 carats) of diamonds were extracted from the 21,000,000 tons of earth dug out. The inflow of water has now made the depth 845 feet to the water surface. The "Big Hole" was dug by pick and shovel.

United Kingdom The largest quarry in Britain is Imperial Chemical Industries Ltd.'s Tunstead Quarry, near Buxton, Derbyshire. The working face is 1½ miles long and 120 feet high.

Largest stone The largest mined slab of quarried stone is one measuring 68 feet by 14 feet by 14 feet, weighing about 1,590 tons, at Ba'labakk (Baalbeck), in the Lebanon. The largest able to be moved from this mine were slabs of 805 tons for the trilithon of the nearby Temple of Jupiter.

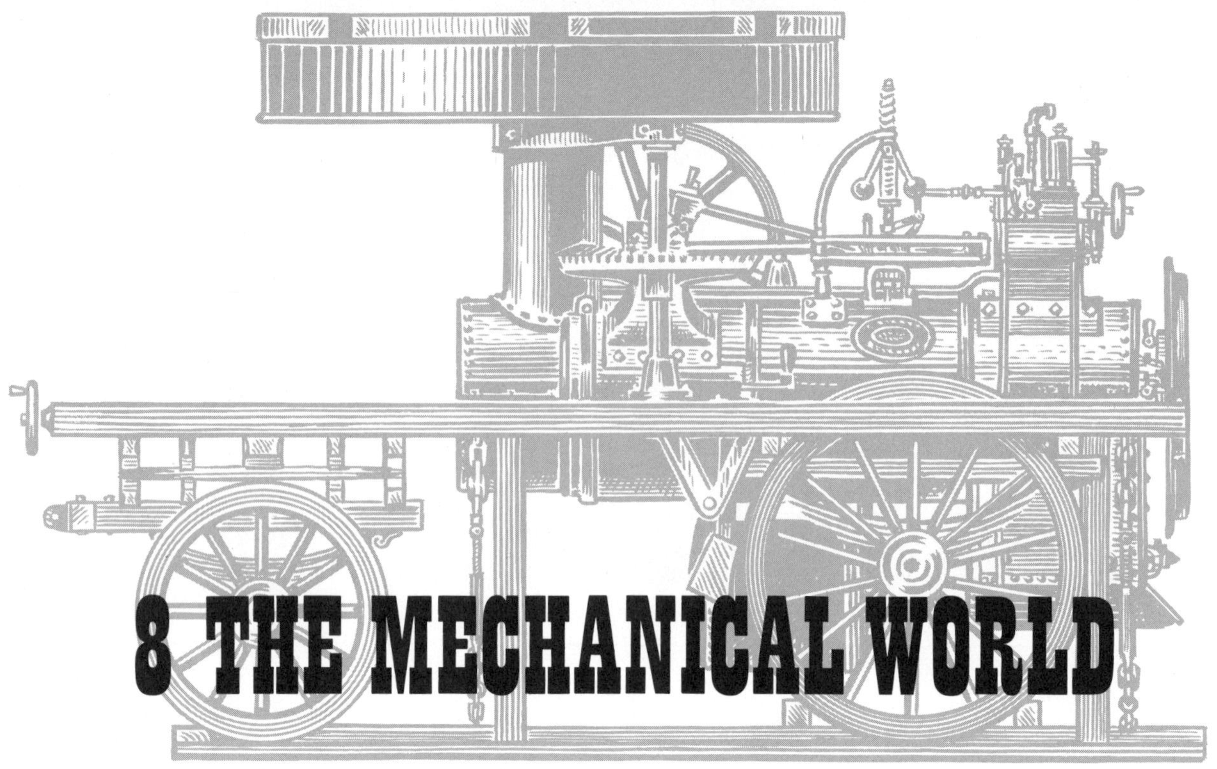

8 THE MECHANICAL WORLD

1. SHIPS

EARLIEST BOATS

The earliest known vessel which is still sea-worthy is a 102-foot-long sailing vessel dated to the Egyptian sixth dynasty from *c.* 2420 B.C. Oars found in bogs at Magle Mose, Sjaelland, Denmark and Star Carr, Yorkshire, England, have been dated to *c.* 8000 B.C.

Earliest power The earliest experiments with marine steam engines date from those on the river Seine, France, in 1775. Propulsion was first achieved when in 1783 the Marquis Jouffroy d'Abbans ascended a reach of the river Saône near Lyons, France, in the 180-ton paddle steamer *Pyroscaphe*.

The tug *Charlotte Dundas* was the first successful power-driven vessel. She was a paddle-wheel steamer built in Scotland in 1801–02 by William Symington (1763–1831), using a double-acting condensing engine constructed by James Watt (1736–1819). The earliest regular steam run was by the *Clermont*, built by Robert Fulton (1765–1815), a U.S. engineer, which maintained a service from New York to Albany from 17 Aug. 1807.

The 'Skibladner' of Norway now in her 115th year

Oldest steam vessel The oldest steamer is believed to be the *Skibladner* (206 gross tons), which was built in Motala, Sweden, in 1856 and sank on Lake Mjøsa, Norway, in February 1967 but was raised and refitted for re-commission. Mr. G. H. Pattinson's 40-foot steam launch, raised from Ullswater in 1962 and now on Lake Windermere, may date from a year or two earlier.

Earliest turbine The first turbine ship was the *Turbinia*, built in 1894 at Wallsend-on-Tyne, Northumberland, to the design of the Hon. Sir Charles Algernon Parsons, O.M., K.C.B. (1854–1931). The *Turbinia* was 100 feet long and of 44½ tons displacement with machinery consisting of three steam turbines totalling about 2,000 shaft horse-power. At her first public demonstration in 1897 she reached a speed of 34·5 knots (39·7 m.p.h.).

Atlantic crossings *Earliest* The earliest crossing of the Atlantic by a power vessel, as opposed to an auxiliary engined sailing ship, was a 22-day voyage begun in April 1827, from Rotterdam, Netherlands, to the West Indies by the *Curaçao*. She was a wooden paddle boat of 438 registered tons, built in Dundee, Angus, in 1826 and purchased by the Dutch Government for the West Indian mail service. The earliest Atlantic crossing entirely under steam (with intervals for desalting the boilers) was by H.M.S. *Rhadamanthus* from Plymouth to Barbados in 1832. The earliest crossing of the Atlantic under continuous steam power was by the condenser-fitted packet ship *Sirius* (703 tons) from Queenstown (now Cóbh), Ireland, to Sandy Hook, N.Y., U.S.A., in 18 days 10 hours on 4–22 April 1838.

Fastest *World* The fastest Atlantic crossing was made by the *United States* (then 51,988, now 38,216 gross tons), flagship of the United States Lines Company. On her maiden voyage between 3 and 7 July 1952 from New York City, N.Y., U.S.A., to Le Havre, France, and Southampton, England, she averaged 35·59 knots, or 40·98 m.p.h., for 3 days 10 hours 40 minutes (6.36 p.m. G.M.T. 3 July to 5.16 a.m. 7 July) on a route of 2,949 nautical miles from the Ambrose Light Vessel to the Bishop Rock Light, Isles of Scilly, Cornwall. During this run, on 6–7 July 1952, she steamed the greatest distance ever covered by any ship in a day's run (24 hours)—868 nautical miles, hence averaging 36·17 knots (41·65 m.p.h.). Her maximum speed is 41·75 knots (48 m.p.h.) on a full power of 240,000 shaft horse-power. The s.h.p. figure was only revealed by the U.S. Defense Department in 1968.

British The fastest crossing of the Atlantic by a British ship is 3 days 15 hours 48 minutes by the Cunard liner *Queen Mary* in September 1946 on a 2,710-mile voyage from Halifax, Nova Scotia, Canada, to Southampton at an average of 30·86 knots (35·54 m.p.h.). On her 2,938-mile crossing from the Ambrose Light to Bishop Rock on 10–14 Aug. 1938, she averaged 31·69 knots (36·49 m.p.h.) for 3 days 20 hours 42 minutes.

Submerged The fastest disclosed submerged Atlantic crossing is

The world's longest ever and largest surviving passenger liner

PROGRESSIVE LIST OF WORLD'S LARGEST AND LONGEST LINERS

Gross Tonnage	Name	Propulsion	Overall Length in Feet	Dates
1,340	Great Western (U.K.)	Paddle wheels	236	1838–1856
1,862	British Queen (U.K.)	Paddle wheels	275	1839–1844
2,360	President (U.K.)	Paddle wheels	268	1840–1841
3,270	Great Britain (U.K.)	Single screw	322	1845–1937
4,690	Himalaya (U.K.)	Single screw	340	1853–1927
18,914[1]	Great Eastern (U.K.)	Paddles and screw	692	1858–1888
10,650	City of New York (later Harvard, Pittsburgh) (U.S.)	Twin screw	528	1888–1923
17,274	Oceanic (U.K.)	Twin screw	705	1899–1914
20,904	Celtic (U.K.)	Twin screw	700	1901–1928
21,227	Cedric (U.K.)	Twin screw	700	1903–1932
23,884	Baltic (U.K.)	Twin screw	726	1904–1933
31,550	Lusitania (U.K.)	4 screws	790	1907–1915
31,938	Mauretania (U.K.)	4 screws	787	1907–1935
45,300	Olympic (U.K.)	Triple screw	892	1911–1935
46,300	Titanic (U.K.)	Triple screw	882	1912–1912
52,022	Imperator (Germany) (later Berengaria [U.K.])	4 screws	919	1913–1938
54,282[2]	Vaterland (Germany) (later Leviathan [U.S.])	4 screws	950	1914–1938
56,621	Bismarck (Germany) (later Majestic [U.K.] and H.M. Troopship Caledonia)	4 screws	954	1922–1939
79,280[3]	Normandie (France) (later U.S.S. Lafayette)	4 screws	1,029	1935–1946
80,774[4]	Queen Mary (U.K.) (later sold to U.S. interests)	4 screws	1,019	1936–
83,673[5]	Queen Elizabeth (U.K.) (later sold to U.S., then Hong Kong interests)	4 screws	1,031	1940–
66,348	France (France)	4 screws	1,035	1961–

1 *Originally 22,500 tons.*
2 *Listed as 59,957 gross tons under U.S. registration, 1922–31, but not internationally accepted as such.*
3 *Gross tonnage later raised by enclosure of open deck space to 83,423 gross tons.*
4 *Later 81,237 gross tons.*
5 *Later 82,998 gross tons.*

6 days 11 hours 55 minutes by the U.S. nuclear-powered submarine *Nautilus*, which travelled 3,150 miles from Portland, Dorset, to New York City, N.Y., U.S.A., arriving on 25 Aug. 1958.

Most crossings Between 1856 and June 1894 Captain Samuel Brooks (1832–1904) crossed the North Atlantic 690 times—equal to 2,437,712 statute miles. In 1850–51 he had sailed in the brig *Bessie* as an A.B. round The Horn to Panama coming home to Liverpool as her master. His life-time sailing distance was at least 2,513,000 miles.

Pacific crossing The fastest crossing of the Pacific Ocean (Yokohama, Japan to San Francisco, U.S.A.) is 8 days 35 minutes achieved by the 14,114-ton diesel cargo liner *Italy Maru* in August 1967.

EXTREMITIES REACHED

rthernmost The farthest north ever attained by a surface vessel is 86° 39′ N. in 47° 55′ E. by the drifting U.S.S.R. ice-breaker *Sedov* on 29 Aug. 1939. She was locked in the Arctic ice floes from 23 Oct. 1937 until freed on 13 Jan. 1940.

thernmost The farthest south ever reached by a ship was achieved on 3 Jan. 1955, by the Argentine icebreaker *General San Martin* in establishing the General Belgrano Base, Antarctica, on the shores of the Weddell Sea at 78° S., 39° W., 830 miles from the South Pole.

PASSENGER LINERS

Longest The world's longest and largest active liner (66,348 gross tons) is the *France*, built at St. Nazaire, owned by the Compagnie Générale Transatlantique. She measures 1,035 feet 2 inches overall and made her official maiden voyage from Le Havre, France, to New York City, N.Y., U.S.A., on 3 Feb. 1962, and cost £29,000,000.

Largest ever The R.M.S. *Queen Elizabeth* (finally 82,998 but formerly 83,673 gross tons), of the Cunard fleet, was the largest passenger vessel ever built and had the largest displacement of any liner in the world. She has an overall length of 1,031 feet and is 118 feet 7 inches in breadth. She was powered by steam turbines which develop 168,000 h.p. Her last passenger voyage ended on 15 Nov. 1968. The *Queen Elizabeth's* normal sea speed was 28½ knots (32·8 m.p.h.). She was sold at Port Everglades, Fort Lauderdale, Florida, U.S.A. as a tourist centre to a United States consortium for $8,600,000 (£3,583,333) on 19 July 1969 but was, in 1970, removed to Hong Kong to serve as a floating marine university by the Associated Maritime Industries Inc. of New York after purchase for $3,250,000 (£1,354,167).

WARSHIPS

Battleships *Largest World* The largest battleships in the world are now the U.S.S. *Iowa* (completed 22 Feb. 1943) and U.S.S. *Missouri* (completed 11 June 1944), each of which has a full load displacement of 57,950 tons and mounts nine 16-inch and 20 5-inch guns. The U.S.S. *New Jersey* (57,216 tons full load displacement) is, however, longer than either by nine inches, with an overall length of 888 feet. She was, in 1968, the last battleship on active service in the world.

Largest all-time The Japanese battleships *Yamato* (completed on 16 Dec. 1941 and sunk in the Bungo Strait off Kyūshū, Japan, by U.S. planes on 7 April 1945) and *Musashi* (sunk in the Philippine Sea by 11 bombs and 16 torpedoes on 24 Oct. 1944) were the largest battleships ever constructed, each with a full load displacement of 72,809 tons. With an overall length of 863 feet, a beam of 127 feet and a full load draught of 35½ feet, they mounted nine 460 mm. (18·1 inch) guns in three triple turrets. Each gun weighed 162 tons and was 75 feet in length, firing a 3,200 lb. projectile.

Britain Britain's largest ever and last battleship was H.M.S. *Vanguard* with a full load displacement of 51,420 tons, overall length 814 feet, beam 108½ feet, with a maximum draught of 36 feet. She mounted eight 15-inch and 15 5·25-inch guns. A shaft horse-power of 130,000 gave her a sea speed of 29½ knots (34 m.p.h.). The *Vanguard* was laid down in John Brown & Co. Ltd.'s yard at Clydebank, Dunbartonshire, on 20 Oct. 1941, launched on 30 Nov. 1944 and completed on 25 April 1946. She was sold for scrap in August 1960 for £500,000 having cost a total of £14,000,000.

Largest guns The largest guns ever mounted in any of H.M. ships were the 18-inch pieces in the light battle cruiser (later aircraft carrier) H.M.S. *Furious* in 1917. In 1918 they were transferred to the monitors H.M.S. *Lord Clive* and *General Wolfe*. The thickest armour ever carried wa… H.M.S. *Inflexible* (completed 1881), measurin… inches.

H.M.S. Furious, the only warship to mount an 18-inch gun

AIRCRAFT CARRIERS

Largest *World* The warship with the largest full load displacement in the world is the aircraft carrier U.S.S. *Nimitz* at 95,100 tons. She was launched in January 1971 and will be commissioned in 1972. U.S.S. *Enterprise* is, however, 1,101½ feet long and thus 65½ feet longer. U.S.S. *Nimitz*, which will have a speed well in excess of 30 knots, will cost $536,000,000 (£223·3 million). She will be followed by a sister ship U.S.S. *Eisenhower*, which will be only 9½ feet shorter than the *Enterprise*.

Britain Britain's largest ever aircraft carrier is H.M.S. *Ark Royal*, completed on 25 Feb. 1955, with a full load displacement of 50,786 tons (previously 53,340 tons),

H.M.S. Ark Royal, the Royal Navy's largest warship

Naval pilot Capt. Eric Brown, R.N., world record holder for deck landings

845 feet overall, 166 feet wide, maximum draught 36 feet, with a full complement of 2,640 and a capacity of 30 naval jet aircraft and 6 helicopters. Her 152,000 shaft horse-power give her a maximum speed of 31·5 knots (36·27 m.p.h.).

Most deck landings The pilot who has made the greatest number of deck landings is Capt. Eric M. Brown, C.B.E., D.S.C., A.F.C., R.N. with 2,407. Capt. Brown, who retired in 1970, flew a record 325 types of aircraft during his career and also set a world record with 2,721 catapult launchings.

Most powerful cruiser The Fleet Escort Ships (formerly cruisers) with the greatest fire power are the three Albany class ships U.S.S.'s *Albany, Chicago* and *Columbia* of 13,700 tons and 673 feet overall. They carry 2 twin Talos and 2 twin Tartar surface to air missiles and an 8-tube Asroc launcher.

Fastest destroyer The highest speed attained by a destroyer was 45·02 knots (51·84 m.p.h.) by the 3,750-ton French destroyer *Le Terrible* in 1935. She was powered by four Yarrow small tube boilers and two geared turbines giving 100,000 shaft horse-power. She was removed from the active list at the end of 1957.

Fastest warship The world's fastest warship is H.M.C.S. *Bras d'Or*, the 180-ton 150·8-foot-long Canadian Navy Hydrofoil commissioned in 1967. On 17 July 1969 outside Halifax harbour, Nova Scotia she attained 61 knots (70·2 m.p.h.).

SUBMARINES

Largest The world's largest submarine is the nuclear-powered ship *Le Redoubtable*, launched for the French navy at Cherbourg, France, on 29 March 1967. She has a submerged displacement of 9,000 tons, a surface displacement of 7,780 tons, a length of 419·9 feet and will be armed with 16 nuclear MSBM (*mer-sol balistique stratégique*) missiles. The largest submarines built for the Royal Navy are the four atomic-powered nuclear missile R class boats with a surface displacement of 7,500 tons and 8,400 tons submerged, a length of 425 feet, a beam of 33 feet and a draught of 30 feet.

Fastest The world's fastest submarines are the 35-knot U.S. Navy's tear-drop hulled nuclear vessels of the *Skipjack* class. They have been listed semi-officially as capable of a speed of 45 knots (51·8 m.p.h.) submerged. In November 1968 the building of attack submarines with submerged speeds in the region of 50 knots was approved for the U.S. Navy.

Deepest The greatest depth recorded by a true submarine was 8,310 feet by the Lockheed *Sea Quest* off California, U.S.A., on 29 Feb. 1968. The 51-foot-long *Aluminaut* launched by the Reynolds Metals Co. on 2 Sept. 1964 is designed for depths of up to 15,000 feet but is prevented from descending below 6,250 feet by prohibitive insurance costs. The U.S. Navy's nuclear-powered NR-1 being built by General Dynamics Inc. will be able to operate at a "very great" but classified depth which is assumed to be lower than the published figure of 20,000 feet for the first 7-man Deep Submergence Search Vehicle DSSV due in service in 1972.

Largest fleet The largest submarine fleet in the world is that of the U.S.S.R. Navy or *Krasni Flot*, which numbers about 375 boats, of which 45 (15 ballistic) are nuclear-powered and missile armed. The U.S. Navy has 41 such submarines in service.

TANKERS

Largest The world's largest tanker is the *Nisseki Maru* of 366,518 tons deadweight and 1,137 feet 7½ inches length overall built by Ishikawajima-Harima Heavy Industries Co. Ltd. at Kure, Japan, launched in April 1971 and completed in September 1971. She is 178 feet 9½ inches in the beam and draws 88 feet 7 inches. She is powered by a set of I.H.I. steam turbines delivering 39,450 s.h.p. at 90 revs. per minute giving 15 knots. The even larger *Globtik Tokyo* of 477,000 tons deadweight and 1,243 feet 5 inches length overall is scheduled for delivery by the same yard at a cost of £11·5 million in February 1973. She will be 203 feet 5 inches in the beam, will draw 91 feet 10 inches and will be powered by an I.H.I. turbine set rated at 44,385 s.h.p. Plans for these mammoth tankers were approved by the Japanese Transport Ministry on 23 June 1970.

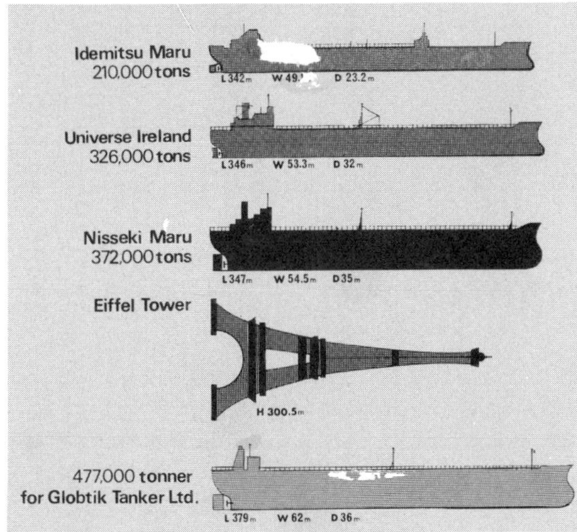

The world's largest tankers to scale against the Eiffel Tower

Longest The longest ships in the world of any kind are the Esso class tankers, which have a length of 1,141 feet 1 inch—106 feet longer than the world's longest ever liner, *France*. They have a deadweight tonnage of 252,000 tons, a gross registered tonnage of 127,150 and a beam of 170 feet 2 inches. Some idea of this length can be conveyed by the thought that it would take a golfer, standing on the stem, a full-blooded drive and a chip shot to reach the stern. The largest vessels launched in a United Kingdom shipyard are those of this class, the first of which was, on 2 May 1969, the *Esso Northumbria* launched for Esso Petroleum at the yard of Swan Hunter and Tyne Shipbuilders. She is 110 feet longer than the *Queen Elizabeth*.

CARGO VESSELS

Largest The largest dry cargo vessel in the world is the *Polysaga* (95,405 tons gross) which sails under the Norwegian flag. She is 1,009 feet 11 inches in length and has a beam of 144 feet 5 inches.

Fastest built During the Second World War "Liberty ships" of prefabricated welded steel construction were built at seven shipyards on the Pacific coast of the United States, under the management of Henry J. Kaiser (1882–1967). The record time for assembly of one ship of 7,200 gross tons (10,500 tons deadweight) was 4 days 15½ hours. In January 1968, 900 Liberty ships were still in service.

Largest cable ship The world's largest cable-laying ship is the American Telephone & Telegraph Co.'s German-built *Long Lines* (11,200 gross tons), completed by Deutsche Werft of Hamburg in April 1963, at a cost of £6,800,000. She has a fully-laden displacement of 17,000 tons, measures 511 feet 6 inches overall and is powered by twin turbine electric engines.

Largest whale factory The largest whale factory ship is the U.S.S.R.'s *Sovietskaya Ukraina* (32,034 gross tons), with a summer deadweight of 46,000 tons, completed in October 1959. She is 714·6 feet in length and 94 feet 3 inches in the beam.

The world's most powerful tug—*Oceanic*

Most powerful tug *World* The world's largest and most powerful tug is the 17,500 i.h.p. M.T. *Oceanic* (2,046 gross tons). She was built by Bugsier—und Bergungs—Aktiengesellschaft of Hamburg, West Germany and was commissioned in 1969. She is 284 feet 5 inches long, 46 feet 11 inches in the beam, has a speed of 22 knots (25 m.p.h.) and a range of 20,000 miles. She is being followed by an identical twin tug to be named *Arctic*.

British The most powerful tug ever built for a British owner is M.T. *Lloydsman* completed in June 1971 for United Towing Limited of Hull at the Victoria shipyard of Robb Caledon Shipbuilders Ltd., Leith. She is rated at 16,000 h.p. with a bollard full of 115 tons.

Fastest tow H.M.S. *Scylla* towed her sister ship, H.M.S. *Penelope* (Cdr. S. Idiens, R.N.), in the Western Mediterranean on 25 Sept. 1970 with an 11-inch mile-long nylon rope (breaking strain 165 tons) at a speed of 24 knots. The £10,000 Viking Nylon Braidline hawser, made by British Ropes, stretched 38% to 7,325 feet.

Largest car ferry The world's largest car and passenger ferry is the 502-foot-long *Finlandia* (8,100 gross tons), delivered by Wärtsilä Ab. of Helsinki in May 1967, for service between Helsinki and Copenhagen with Finska Angfartygs Ab. She can carry 321 cars and up to 1,200 passengers and achieved a speed of 22 knots (25 m.p.h.) during trials.

Largest hydrofoil The world's largest naval hydrofoil is the 212-foot-long *Plainview* (310 tons full load), launched by the Lockheed Shipbuilding and Construction Co. at Seattle, Washington, U.S.A., on 28 June 1965. She has a service speed of 50 knots (57 m.p.h.). A larger hydrofoil, carrying 150 passengers and 8 cars at 40 knots to ply the Göteborg-Ålborg crossing, came into service in June 1968. It was built by Westermoen Hydrofoil Ltd. of Mandal, Norway.

Most powerful icebreaker The world's most powerful icebreaker and first atomic-powered ship is the U.S.S.R.'s 44,000 s.h.p. *Lenin* (16,000 gross tons), which was launched at Leningrad on 2 Dec. 1957 and began her maiden voyage on 18 Sept.

1959. She is 439¾ feet long, 90½ feet in the beam and has a maximum speed of 18 knots (20·7 m.p.h.). In March 1970 the U.S.S.R. announced the building of a more powerful atomic-powered icebreaker to be named *Arctika*, able to go through ice 7 feet thick at 4 knots.

The largest converted icebreaker is the 1,007-foot-long S.S. *Manhattan* (43,000 s.h.p.), which was converted by the Humble Oil Co. into a 150,000-ton icebreaker with an armoured prow 69 feet 2 inches long. She made a double voyage through the North-West Passage in arctic Canada from 24 Aug. to 12 Nov. 1969.

Largest dredger The world's largest dredger is one reported to be operating in the lower Lena basin in May 1967, with a rig more than 100 feet tall and a cutting depth of 165 feet. The pontoon is 750 feet long. The largest dredging grabs in the world are those of 635 cubic feet capacity built in 1965 by Priestman Bros. Ltd. of Hull, Yorkshire for the dredging pontoon *Biarritz*.

Most successful trawler The greatest tonnage of fish ever landed from any British trawler in a year is 4,169 tons in 1969 from the freezer stern trawler *Lady Parkes* owned by Boston Deep Sea Fisheries Ltd. (est. 1894).

Britain's most successful-ever trawler—*Lady Parkes*

Wooden ship The heaviest wooden ship ever built was H.M. Battleship *Lord Clive* at 7,750 tons. She was completed at Pembroke Dock, Wales, on 2 June 1866. She measured 280 feet in length and was sold in 1875.

SAILING SHIPS

Largest The largest sailing vessel ever built was the *France II* (5,806 gross tons), launched at Bordeaux in 1911. The *France II* was a steel-hulled, five-masted barque (square-rigged on four masts and fore and aft rigged on the aftermost mast). Her hull measured 418 feet overall. Although principally designed as a sailing vessel with a stump topgallant rig, she was also fitted with two steam engines. She was wrecked in 1922.

Largest junks The largest junk on record was the sea-going *Cheng Ho* of *c.* 1420, with a displacement of 3,100 tons and a length variously estimated at from 300 feet to 440 feet.

A river junk 361 feet long, with treadmill-operated paddle-wheels, was recorded in A.D. 1161. In *c.* A.D. 280 a floating fortress 600 feet square, built by Wang Chün on the Yangtze, took part in the Chin-Wu river war. Modern junks do not, even in the case of the Chiangsu traders, exceed 170 feet in length.

Longest day's run under sail The longest day's run by any sailing ship was one of 465 nautical miles (535·45 statute miles) by the clipper *Champion of the Seas* (2,722 registered tons) of the Liverpool Black Ball Line running before a north-westerly gale in the south Indian Ocean under the command of Capt. Alex. Newlands. The elapsed time between the fixes was 23 hours 17 minutes giving an average of 19·97 knots.

Greatest speed The highest recorded speed by a sailing ship is 22 knots (25·3 m.p.h.) by *Sovereign of the Seas* on a run to Sydney on 18 March 1853. She was built in 1852 by Donald McKay of East Boston, Massachusetts, U.S.A.

Slowest voyage Perhaps the slowest passage on record was that of the *Red Rock* (1,600 tons), which was posted missing at Lloyd's of London after taking 112 days for 950 miles across the Coral Sea from 20 Feb. to 12 June 1899, at an average speed of less than 0·4 of a knot.

H.M. Battleship *Lord Clive*—the heaviest wooden ship ever built

Largest sails The largest spars ever carried were those in H.M. Battleship *Temeraire*, completed at Chatham, Kent, on 31 Aug. 1877. The fore and main yards measured 115 feet in length. The mainsail contained 5,100 feet of canvas, weighing 2 tons, and the total sail area was 25,000 square feet. At 8,540 tons the *Temeraire* was the largest brig ever built. The main masts of H.M.S. *Achilles, Black Prince* and *Warrior* all measured 175 feet from truck to deck.

Largest propeller The largest ship's propeller will be one of 30 feet 2 inches diameter from blade tip to blade tip built for the 477,000-ton tanker *Globtik Tokyo* due to be delivered in February 1973.

Largest Dracones The largest Dracones (flexible plastic containers used for bulk transport of liquids) ever built were completed by Frankenstein and Sons (Manchester) Ltd., in July 1962. They are 300 feet in length and can transport 1,200 tons (250,000 gallons) of water.

Deepest anchorage The deepest anchorage ever achieved is one of 24,600 feet in the mid-Atlantic Romanche Trench by Capt. Jacques-Yves Cousteau's research vessel *Calypso*, with a 5½-mile-long nylon cable, on 29 July 1956.

Largest wreck The largest ship ever wrecked has been the Japanese-built, Royal Dutch/Shell owned, 206,600-ton (deadweight) tanker *Marpessa* after a tank explosion when sailing in ballast from Rotterdam, 50 miles northwest of Dakar, Senegal on 15 Dec. 1969. She was 1,067 feet 5 inches long. The largest vessel ever to be wrecked in British waters has been the 965-foot-long tanker, *Torrey Canyon*, of 61,275 tons gross and 118,285 tons deadweight, which struck the Pollard Rock of the Seven Stones Reef between the Isles of Scilly and Land's End, Cornwall, England, at 08.50 on 18 March 1967. The resultant oil pollution from some 30,000 tons of Kuwait crude was "on a scale which had no precedent anywhere in the world". In an attempt to fire the remaining oil, the ship was bombed to virtual destruction on 28–30 March 1967.

Oldest wreck The oldest vessel regarded as salvageable in British waters is the carrack *Mary Rose*, which sank off Ryde, Isle of Wight in 1545. On 18 Sept. 1970 a 4 cwt. 8-foot-long breech-loader was recovered from her hull, which appears to have been preserved in a blue clay layer of the sea bed.

Guinness Superlatives has now published automotive records in much greater detail in the more specialist publication "Car Facts and Feats" *(price £2·20) and obtainable from the address in the front of this volume.*

2. ROAD VEHICLES

COACHING

Before the advent of the McAdam road surfaces in *c.* 1815 coaching was slow and hazardous. The zenith was reached on 13 July 1888 when J. Selby, Esq., drove the "Old Times" coach 108 miles from London to Brighton and back with 8 teams and 14 changes in 7 hours 50 minutes to average 13·79 m.p.h. Four-horse carriages could maintain a speed of $21\frac{1}{4}$ m.p.h. for nearly an hour.

MOTOR CARS

Earliest ıtomobiles *Model* The earliest automobile of which there is record is a two-foot-long model constructed by Ferdinand Verbiest (d. 1687) a Jesuit priest, and described in his *Astronomia Europaea.* His model was possibly inspired either by Giovanni Branca's description of a steam turbine, published in 1629, or by writings on "fire carts" during the Chu dynasty (*c.* 800 B.C.) in the library of the Emperor Khang-hi of China, to whom he was an astronomer during the period *c.* 1665–80.

Passenger-carrying The earliest mechanically-propelled passenger vehicle was the first of two military steam tractors, completed in Paris in 1769 by Nicolas-Joseph Cugnot (1725–1804). This reached $2\frac{1}{4}$ m.p.h. Cugnot's second, larger tractor, completed in May 1771, today survives in the *Conservatoire Nationale des Arts et Metiers* in Paris. Britain's first successful steam carriage carried eight passengers on 24 Dec. 1801 and was built by Richard Trevithick (1771–1833) at Redruth, Cornwall though a 3-wheeled model steam locomotive was built by William Murdoch in 1785–6.

Internal ombustion The first internal-combustion automobile was that built by Jean Joseph Étienne Lenoir (1822–1900), based on his electrically-ignited two-stroke gas engine (patented in 1860) fitted to a horse brake. In May 1862 it was driven from Rue la Roquette, Paris to Vincennes.

Earliest rol-driven cars The first successful petrol-driven car, the Motorwagen, built by Karl-Friedrich Benz (1844–1929) of Karlsruhe, ran at Mannheim, Germany, in late 1885. It was a 5 cwt. 3-wheeler reaching 8–10 m.p.h. Its single cylinder chain-drive engine (bore 91·4 mm., stroke 160 mm.) delivered 0·85 h.p. at 200 r.p.m. It was patented on 29 Jan. 1886. Its first 1 kilometre road test was reported in the local newspaper, the *Neue Badische Landeszeitung*, of 4 June 1886, under the heading "Miscellaneous". Two were built in 1885 of which one has been preserved in "running order" at the Deutsche Museum, Munich since 1959.

Earliest ritish cars In Britain F. H. Butler built a petrol-engined 3-wheeled automobile in 1887 but the earliest successful British cars were the 3-wheeled air-cooled 2 h.p. Wolseley built in 1895 by Herbert (the first and last Lord) Austin (1866–1941) and John H. Knight's Surrey-built 3-wheeler of July of the same year. The first car to run on an English road was an 1894 4 h.p. twin-cylinder Panhard-Levassor built in France, driven in June 1895 by the Hon. Evelyn Henry Ellis (1843–1913).

Oldest The oldest internal-combustion engine car seen on British roads has been the Danish "Hammel". Designed by Albert Hammel, who took out the original patents in 1886, it was completed in 1887. In 1954 it completed the London-to-Brighton run in $12\frac{1}{2}$ hours, averaging $4\frac{1}{2}$ m.p.h. The engine is a twin-cylinder, horizontal water-cooled four-stroke with a capacity of 2,720 c.c., bore and stroke 104·5 mm. × 160 mm., and a compression ratio of 3·5:1.

Earliest gistrations The world's first plates were introduced in Mallorca, Spain. The number PM 1 was issued to Don Jose Sureda y Fuentas for his 2 h.p. Clement on 11 Oct. 1900 at Palma. Registration plates were introduced in Britain in 1903. The original A1 plate was secured by the 2nd Earl Russell (1865–1931) for his 12 h.p. Napier. This plate, willed in September 1950 to Mr. Trevor T. Laker of Leicester, was sold in August 1959 for £2,500 in aid of charity. The Rolls-Royce bearing the registration plate RR1 was sold by tender to R. H. Owen Ltd. by the executors of Mr. Sydney Black on 22 July 1968 for £10,800—£3,300 more than the price of the Silver Shadow to which the number plate was affixed.

FASTEST CARS

Rocket engined The highest speed attained by any wheeled land vehicle is 627·027 m.p.h. in the second run of *Blue Flame*, a liquid natural gas-powered 4-wheeled vehicle driven by Gary Gabelich on the Bonneville Salt Flats, Utah, on 23 Oct. 1970. The earlier run was timed at 617·602 m.p.h. giving an average speed of 622·407 m.p.h. The tyres were made by Goodyear. The car is powered by a liquid natural gas/hydrogen peroxide rocket engine delivering 27,000 lb.s.t. maximum and thus theoretically capable of 900 m.p.h.

(Top) *Blue Flame*, the world's fastest ever land vehicle
(Bottom) Gary Gabelich, the driver, now aiming to break the sound barrier

Jet The highest speed attained by any jet-engined car is 613·995 m.p.h. over a flying 666·386 yards by the 34-foot 7-inch long 9,000 lb. *Spirit of America—Sonic I*, driven by Norman Craig Breedlove (b. 23 March 1938, Los Angeles) on Bonneville Salt Flats, Tooele County, Utah, U.S.A., on 15 Nov. 1965. The car was powered by a General Electric J79 GE-3 jet engine, developing 15,000 lb. static thrust at sea-level.

Wheel-driven The highest speed attained by a wheel-driven car is 429·311 m.p.h. over a flying 666·386 yards by Donald Malcolm Campbell, C.B.E. (1921–67), a British engineer, in the 30-foot-long *Bluebird*, weighing 9,600 lb., on the salt flats at Lake Eyre, South Australia, on 17 July 1964. The car was powered by a Bristol-Siddeley 705 gas-turbine engine developing 4,500 s.h.p. Its peak speed was *c.* 440 m.p.h. It was rebuilt in 1962, after a crash at about 360 m.p.h. on 16 Sept. 1960.

Piston engine The highest speed attained by a piston-engined car is 418·504 m.p.h. over a flying 666·386 yards by Robert Sherman Summers (born 4 April 1937, Omaha, Nebraska) in *Goldenrod* at Bonneville Salt Flats on 12 Nov. 1965. The car, measuring 32 feet long and weighing 5,500 lb., was powered by four fuel-injected Chrysler Hemi engines (total capacity 27,924 c.c.) developing 2,400 b.h.p.

Production The world's fastest and most powerful production car (more than 25 examples produced within 12 months) ever produced is the German Porsche 4·9 litre Type 917 launched in March 1969. It has a 12-cylinder air-cooled engine developing more than 550 b.h.p. at 8,000 plus r.p.m. A 4·9 litre Type 917L with an aerodynamic tail was timed at 234 m.p.h. in a test on the Le Mans Mulsanne straight in April 1971.

The world's fastest ever production car—the Porsche 917L at 234 m.p.h.

LARGEST

World Of cars produced for private road use, the largest has been the Bugatti "Royale", type 41, known in Britain as the "Golden Bugatti", of which only six (not seven) were made at Molsheim, France by the Italian Signor Ettore Bugatti, and some survive. First built in 1927, this machine has an 8-cylinder engine of 12·7 litres capacity, and measures over 22 feet in length. The bonnet is over 7 feet long. The longest present-day car is the Aerocar limousine built by Checker Motors Corporation of Kalamazoo, Michigan, U.S.A. This 8-door 12-seat model, announced in July 1965, is 22 feet $5\frac{3}{4}$ inches long. (For cars not intended for private use, see Largest engines.)

The largest ever private car, the Bugatti Royale built in 1927–31

Widest The widest standard production car is the U.S.S.R.'s Zil 114, measuring 6 feet 8·3 inches across. The Rolls-Royce Phantom VI is 6 feet 7 inches wide.

MOST EXPENSIVE

The most expensive car ever built is the U.S. Presidential 1969 Lincoln Continental Executive delivered to the U.S. Secret Service on 14 Oct. 1968. It has an overall length of 21 feet 6·3 inches with a 13-foot 4-inch wheelbase and with the addition of two tons of armour plate weighs 5·35 tons (12,000 lb.). The cost was estimated at $500,000 (£208,000) but it is rented at a nominal $1,200 (£500) per annum. Even if all four tyres were shot out it can travel at 50 m.p.h. on inner rubber-edged steel discs.

The most expensive standard car now available is the 19-foot 10-inch-long 7-seat Rolls-Royce Phantom VI (V8, 6,230 c.c. engine) with coachwork by Park Ward at £14,559 ($34,941) including purchase tax, when introduced in November 1968. The cost of a 4·9 litre Porsche Type 917 (see left) *ex* works with import duty and purchase tax would be more than £20,000 but none has been imported. The all-time dollar record was a Bugatti Royale in 1931 for $55,000 (then £14,850).

Vintage The greatest price paid for any vintage car has been $65,000 (£27,000) for a 1905 Rolls-Royce paid in U.S.A. in January 1969. The greatest collection of vintage cars is the William F. Harrah Collection of 1,440, estimated to be worth more than $3 million (£$1\frac{1}{4}$ million), at Reno, Nevada, U.S.A. Mr. Harrah is still looking for a Chalmer's Detroit 1909 Tourabout, an Owen car of 1910–12 and a Nevada Truck of 1915.

Most inexpensive The cheapest car of all-time was the U.S. 1908 Brownicker for children, but designed for road use, which sold for $150 (then £30 17s. 3d.). The Kavan of 1905, also of U.S. manufacture, was listed at $200 (then £41 3s.). The early models of the King Midget cars were sold in kit form for self-assembly for as little as $100 (then £24 16s.) as late as 1948.

Longest production The longest any car has been in production is 42 years (1910–52), including wartime interruptions, in the case of the "Flat Twin" engined Jowett produced in Britain. The Ford Model T, produced "in any color provided it is black" from 1 Oct. 1908 to 1927, totalled 15,007,033 models and will be overtaken by the Volkswagen "Beetle" from 1946 to mid-1972.

LARGEST ENGINES

Cars are compared on the basis of engine capacity. Distinction is made between those designed for normal road use and machines specially built for track racing and outright speed records.

All-time record The largest car ever built is the "Quad Al", constructed in 1965 in California, U.S.A. Intended for drag racing, the car has four-wheel drive and is powered by four V12 Allison V-1710 aircraft engines with a total capacity of 112,088 c.c., developing 12,000 b.h.p. It was first exhibited in January 1966 at the San Mateo Auto Show in California but is unable to move under its own power.

The largest car ever used was the "White Triplex", sponsored by J. H. White of Philadelphia, Pennsylvania, U.S.A. Completed early in 1928, after two years' work, the car weighed about 4 tons and was powered by three Liberty V12 aircraft engines with a total capacity of 81,188 c.c., developing 1,500 b.h.p. at 2,000 r.p.m. It was used to break the world speed record.

The largest racing car was the "Higham Special", which first raced in 1923 at Brooklands driven by its owner Count Louis Vorow Zborowski, the younger (k. 1924). It was powered by a V12 Liberty aircraft engine with a capacity of 27,059 c.c., developing 400 to 500 b.h.p. at 2,000 r.p.m. John Godfrey Parry Thomas renamed the car "Babs" and used it to break the land speed record. The car was wrecked, and Thomas killed, during an attempt on this record at Pendine Sands, Carmarthenshire, Wales, on 3 March 1927.

Production car The highest engine capacity of a production car was $13\frac{1}{2}$ litres (824 cubic inches), in the case of the Pierce-Arrow 6–66 Raceabout of 1912–18, the Peerless 6–60 of 1912–14 and the Fageol of 1918. The largest currently available is the V8 engine of 500·1 cubic inches (8,195 c.c.), developing 400 b.h.p., used in the 1971 Cadillac Fleetwood Eldorado.

Petrol nsumption The world record for fuel economy on a closed circuit course (one of 14·08 miles) was set by R. J. 'Bob' Greenshields, C. A. 'Skeeter' Hargrave, Jan Evans and Earl Elmqvist in a highly modified 1956 Austin Healey in the annual Shell Research Laboratory contest at Wood River, Illinois on 19 Sept. 1970 with 302·7 ton miles per U.S. gallon and 145·5 miles on one U.S. gallon. These figures are equivalent to 324·57 ton miles and 174·7 miles on an Imperial gallon.

In August 1969 a 4-seat Reliant 3-wheeler driven by Brian Lodwick plus an R.A.C. observer, described as 'large', achieved 103·5 miles on one gallon at Mallory Park, Leicestershire.

The best recorded figure in an unmodified 4-wheeled car using pump petrol is 96·59 m.p.g. by a Fiat 500 driven on an out and home course from Cheltenham to Evesham, Gloucestershire, England, by W. (Featherfoot Joe) Dembowski on 1 July 1965.

powerful rocket). It measures 131 feet 4 inches by 114 feet and cost $12,300,000 (£5,125,000). The loaded train weight is 8,036 tons. Its windscreen wipers with 42-inch blades are the world's largest. Two were built.

Largest lorry The world's largest lorry is the M-200 Lectra Haul built by Unit Rig and Equipment Co. of Fort Worth, Texas with a capacity of 200 tons. It is powered by a 1,650 h.p. diesel and twin 750 h.p. electric motors. It is 43 feet long and 20 feet high.

The most powerful British-engined prime mover is the Rotinoff Tractor Super Atlantic with a 400 b.h.p. Rolls-Royce engine. In May 1958, one of these hauled the first of 12 atomic power station heat-exchangers at Bradwell, Essex. The gross train weight was 370 tons. The Aveling Barford Sn 35 Dump Truck is fitted with a 450 b.h.p. engine.

Longest vehicle The longest vehicle in the world is the 572-foot-long, 54-wheeled U.S. Army Overland Train Mk. II, built by R. G. Le Tourneau Inc. of Longview, Texas, U.S.A. Its gross weight is 400 tons and it has a top speed of 20 m.p.h. It is driven by a 6-man crew, who control 4 engines with a combined s.h.p. of 4,680, which require a capacity of 6,522 Imperial gallons of fuel. It can carry a 150-ton pay-load at 15 m.p.h. for 400 miles.

The world's first bus fleet at Eastbourne, Sussex, England in 1903

The 190-yard-long U.S. Army Overland Train under test in Texas, U.S.A. —the longest ever vehicle

BUSES

Earliest The first municipal motor omnibus service in the world was inaugurated on 12 April 1903 between Eastbourne railway station and Meads, Sussex, England.

Largest The longest buses in the world are the 60-foot-long articulated 63-seater $64,400 Super Golden Eagles of the Continental Trailways of Dallas, Texas, U.S.A., built by Karl Kassbohrer Fahrzeugwerke of Ulm, West Germany. They have a speed of 70 m.p.h. despite a loaded weight of 20 tons.

gest route The longest regularly scheduled bus route is the Greyhound "Supercruiser" Miami, Florida to San Francisco, California route over 3,240 miles in 81 hours 50 minutes (average speed of travel 39·59 m.p.h.). The total Greyhound fleet numbers 5,500 buses.

Largest olleybuses The largest trolleybuses in the world are the articulated vehicles put into service in Moscow, U.S.S.R., in May 1959, with a length of 57 feet and a capacity of 200.

st massive vehicle The most massive vehicle ever constructed is the Marion eight-caterpillar crawler used for conveying *Saturn V* rockets to their launching pads at the John F. Kennedy Space Center, Florida (see Chapter 4, Most

Largest bulldozers The world's largest bulldozer is the Le Tourneau Crash Pusher CP-1, measuring 67 feet long and weighing 67 tons. It is driven on 6 tyres 31 feet 5 inches in circumference and 4 feet wide. The most powerful ground clearer is the $196,000 (then £70,000) 125-ton Le Tourneau Electric Tree Crusher built in 1962. It is 74 feet 4 inches long and can clear 4 acres an hour. The largest road grader in the world is the 18·3 ton 28 feet 2 inch long Galion T.700 Grad-o-matic with a 190 h.p. 6-cylinder Cummins diesel engine built in 1960. Mr. Le Tourneau's (1888–1969) autobiography was entitled "Mover of Men and Mountains".

Largest tractor The most powerful tractor in the world is the 142·8 ton K-205 Pacemaker with a 1,260 horse-power rating. It is built by R. G. Le Tourneau, Inc., of Longview, Texas, U.S.A.

Largest taxi fleet The largest taxi fleet was that of New York City, which amounted to 29,000 cabs in October 1929, compared with the 1969 figure of 11,500.

Fastest caravan The world record for towing a caravan in 24 hours is 1,689 miles (average speed 70·395 m.p.h.) by a Ford Zodiac Mk. IV towing a Sprite Major 5-berth caravan, 16 feet long and weighing $14\frac{1}{2}$ cwt., at Monza Autodrome near Milan, Italy, on 15–16 Oct. 1966. The drivers were Ian Mantle, John Risborough and Michael Bowler, all of Great Britain.

Longest motor caravan journey The longest motor caravan journey on record is one of 44,000 miles carried out in a 1966 Commer Highwayman through 46 sovereign countries between 27 Dec. 1966 and 24 July 1968 by Sy Feldman, his wife Christine, and two sons, Greg and Tim. The journey included nearly 4,000 miles through the U.S.S.R. and 12 trans-shipments beginning in Scotland and ending in Canada.

LOADS

Heaviest and largest The heaviest road loads moved in the United Kingdom were transformers involving a train weight of 422 tons, carried from Newcastle upon Tyne to Fawley, Southampton, by Robert Wynn & Sons Ltd. of Newport, Monmouthshire, on four occasions starting in February 1967. The longest load moved on British roads was a 170-foot-long distillation column moved 2 miles by Messrs. Pickford from Barry Dock to Sully, Glamorganshire, South Wales, on 29 Nov. 1965. The bulkiest load moved was an air separation unit 93 feet long, 15 feet 3 inches wide and 15 feet 7 inches high for a distance of 14 miles by Robert Wynn & Sons Ltd., from Edmonton, London N.9, to the Royal Victoria Docks for export to Texas, U.S.A. in 1969. Plans were begun in April 1971 for the moving by Wynn's of the first load exceeding 450 tons in early 1972.

Tallest The tallest load ever conveyed by road comprised two 98-foot-tall cableway towers, each weighing 70 tons, which were taken 25 miles from Ohakuri to Aratiatia, New Zealand, in June 1961. The loads were carried on a 68-wheel trailer, towed by a 230 h.p. Leyland Buffalo tractor, for George Dale and Son Ltd.

Amphibious vehicle The first Channel crossing by an amphibious vehicle was achieved in 7 hours 33 minutes by Mr. and Mrs. Ben Carlin in an amphibious jeep called "Half-Safe" from Calais, France, to Walmer, England, on 24 Aug. 1951.

Longest skid marks The longest recorded skid marks on a public road have been those 950 feet long left by a Jaguar car involved in an accident on the M1 near Luton, Bedfordshire, on 30 June 1960. Evidence given in the High Court case *Hurlock v. Inglis and others* indicated a speed "in excess of 100 m.p.h." before the application of the brakes. The skid marks made by the jet-powered *Spirit of America*, driven by Craig Breedlove, after the car went out of control at Bonneville Salt Flats, Utah, U.S.A., on 15 Oct. 1964, were nearly 6 miles long.

Largest tyres The world's largest tyres are mounted on the Le Tourneau twin bucket scraper LT-300. They measure 10 feet 2 inches in diameter, are 5 feet wide and weigh 5,800 lb. (2·59 tons). They are made by the B. F. Goodrich Co. of Miami, Oklahoma, U.S.A.

"L" test *Most failures* The record for persistence in taking the Ministry of Transport's Learners' Test is held by Mrs. Miriam Hargrave, 62, of Wakefield, Yorkshire, who failed her 39th driving test in eight years on 29 April 1970. She triumphed at her 40th attempt on 3 Aug. 1970 but stated that the cost of so many lessons had precluded the purchase of a car. The examiner was alleged not to have known about her previous 39 tests.

MOTORCYCLES

Earliest The earliest internal combustion-engined motorized bicycle was a wooden-framed machine built in 1885 by Gottlieb Daimler (1834–1900) of Germany. It had a top speed of 12 m.p.h. and developed one-half of one horse-power from its single cylinder 264 c.c. engine at 700 r.p.m. The earliest factory which made motorcycles in quantity was opened in 1894 by J. Hildebrand and A. Wolfmüller at München (Munich), Bavaria, Germany. In its first two years this factory produced over 1,000 machines, each having a water-cooled 1,488 c.c. twin-cylinder engine developing about 2·5 b.h.p. at 600 r.p.m.

Fastest road machine The fastest standard motorcycle ever produced is the Dunstall Norton Commando powered by a twin-cylinder 810 c.c. engine developing 70 b.h.p. at 7,000 r.p.m. and capable of 133 m.p.h.

Fastest racing machine The fastest racing motorcycle ever has been the 1957 498·6 c.c. 82 b.h.p. Moto Guzzi V8 capable of 178 m.p.h. (see also Motorcycle racing, Chapter 12). Of British machines the fastest ever are the 741 c.c. 3-cylinder B.S.A. Rocket 3 and Triumph Trident racers used in the "Daytona 200" on 14 March 1971. They develop 84 b.h.p. and are capable of 170 m.p.h

Largest The largest motorcycle ever put into production was the 1,301 c.c. in-line 4-cylinder Henderson, manufactured in the United States in the period 1926–29.

Most expensive The most expensive motorcycles in current production are the Harley-Davidson FLHB and FLHFB Super Sports Electra Glide machines, made in the U.S.A., with an engine capacity of 1,213 c.c. Extensively used for highway patrol work by State Police Departments, they weigh 661 lb. and sell for £1,400 in the United Kingdom (May 1971).

The most expensive British-made motorcycle in current production is the 810 c.c. Dunstall Norton Commando with a front disc brake. It retailed at £888 in April 1971.

BICYCLES

Earliest Though there were many velocipedes before that time, the term bicycle was first used in 1868. The earliest portrayal of such a vehicle is in a stained glass window, dated 1642, in Stoke Poges Church, Buckinghamshire, depicting a man riding a hobby horse or celeripede.

The first machine propelled by cranks and pedals, with connecting rods, was that invented in 1839 by Kirkpatrick Macmillan (1810–78) of Dumfries. It is now in the Science Museum, South Kensington, London.

Penny-Farthing record The record for riding from London to John o' Groats on Ordinary Bicycles, more commonly known as Penny-Farthings, is 10½ days by Cyril Mundy, 54, and Brian Thompson, 33, on 31 Aug. to 10 Sept. 1969. This performance broke a 96-year-old record set in June 1873.

Longest The longest tandem bicycle ever built is the 21-man vigintipede, measuring 35 feet 4 inches long, completed by Rickman Bros. and Hugh Stevenson Engineering Ltd. of New Milton, Hampshire, England, on 29 July 1968. It weighs 880 lb. and 2 tons laden. The most capacious cycle built is the double banked 28-seat 30-wheeler built in 1968 by the Zug Teachers' College, Switzerland.

Largest tricycle The largest tricycle ever made was one manufactured in 1897 for the Woven-Hose and Rubber Company of Boston, Massachusetts, U.S.A. Its side wheels were 11 feet in diameter and it weighed nearly a ton. It could carry eight riders.

Tallest unicycle The tallest unicycle ever mastered is one 32 feet tall ridden by Steve McPeak of Seattle Pacific College, U.S.A., in 1969. McPeak set a duration record when on 26 Nov. 1968 he completed a 2,000 mile journey from Chicago, Illinois to Las Vegas, Nevada, U.S.A. in 6 weeks on a 13-foot unicycle. He covered 80 miles on some days.

LAWN MOWER

Largest The widest gang mower on record is one of 15 overlapping sections manufactured by Lloyds & Co. of Letchworth Ltd., Hertfordshire, England used by The Jockey Club to mow 2,500 acres on Newmarket Heath. Its cutting width is 41 feet 6 inches and has a capacity,

The world's widest mower at Newmarket racecourse, England

with a 15 m.p.h. tractor, of up to 70 acres per hour.

Fastest The inaugural Motor Powered Lawn mower Grand Prix on Mersey Cricket Club ground, Sale, Cheshire, on 6 Oct. 1968 was won by Colin Dunne with 2 minutes 45·28 seconds over the ½-mile course for an average of 10·88 m.p.h.

PEDAL CARS
The record for propelling a pedal car from John o' Groats to Land's End (936 miles) is 166 hours 55 minutes set by Kenneth Budby, Ronald Oldroy, Tony Bradbury, Richard May and Martin Cave on 1–5 Aug. 1968. The record from Marble Arch, London to the Arc de Triomphe, Paris including a channel crossing by boat is 27 hours 57 minutes by a team of six from High Wycombe, Buckinghamshire on 19–20 May 1970.

3. RAILWAYS

EARLIEST
Railed trucks were used for mining as early as 1550 at Leberthal, Alsace and by Ralph Allen from Combe Down to the River Avon in 1731, but the first self-propelled locomotive ever to run on rails was that built by Richard Trevithick (1771–1833) and demonstrated over 9 miles with a 10-ton load and 70 passengers in Penydarren, Glamorganshire, on 21 Feb. 1804. The earliest established railway to have a steam-powered locomotive was the Middleton Colliery Railway, set up by an Act of 1758 running between Middleton Colliery and Leeds Bridge, Yorkshire. This line went over to the use of steam locomotives, built by Matthew Murray, in 1812. The Stockton and Darlington colliery line, County Durham, which ran from Shildon through Darlington to Stockton, opened on 27 Sept. 1825. The 7-ton *Locomotion I* (formerly *Active*) could pull 48 tons at a speed of 15 m.p.h. It was built and driven by George Stephenson (1781–1848). The first regular steam passenger run was inaugurated over a one mile section (between Bogshole Farm and South Street) on the 6¼-mile track between Canterbury and Whitstable, Kent, on 3 May 1830 hauled by the engine *Invicta*. The first electric railway was Werner von Siemen's 300-yard-long Berlin electric tramway opened for the Berlin Trades' Exhibition on 31 May 1879.

The birthplace, in 1781, of the railway pioneer George Stephenson

FASTEST
Electric The world rail speed record is held jointly by two French Railway electric locomotives, the CC7107 and the BB9004. On 28 and 29 March 1955, hauling three carriages of a total weight of 100 tons, they each achieved a speed of 205·6 m.p.h. The runs took place on the 1,500-volt D.C. Bordeaux-Dax line, from Facture to Morcenx, and the top speed was maintained by the drivers, H. Braghet and J. Brocca, for 2 kilometres (1·24 miles). The CC7107 weighs 106 tons and has a continuous rating of 4,300 h.p. at 1,500 volts, but developed 12,000 h.p. over the timing stretch. The BB9004 weighs 81 tons and has a continuous rating of 4,000 h.p.

Steam The highest speed ever recorded by a steam locomotive was 126 m.p.h. over 440 yards by the L.N.E.R. 4-6-2 No. 4468 *Mallard* (later numbered 60022), which hauled seven coaches weighing 240 tons gross, near Essendine, down Stoke Bank, between Grantham, Lincolnshire, and Peterborough on 3 July 1938. Driver Duddington was at the controls.

Fastest regular run The fastest point-to-point schedule in the world is that of the "New Tokaido" service of the Japanese National Railways from Tōkyō to Osaka, inaugurated on 1 Nov. 1965. The train covers 320·2 miles in 3 hours 10 minutes, at an average speed of 101·16 m.p.h. and the 212·4 miles between Tōkyō and Nagoya in 120 minutes, to average 106·2 m.p.h. The maximum speed is being raised from 130·5 to 155 m.p.h. The 72-ton 12-car unit has motors generating 8,160 kW on a single-phase 25,000 volt A.C.

he L.N.E.R. 6-2 engine *Mallard*, h attained 126 m.p.h. in 1938

system. A peak speed of 159 m.p.h. is eventually expected from the Hikari engine. The fastest regular run on British Rail is over the 140-mile 47-chain stretch from Crewe to Watford Junction in 101½ minutes giving an average of 83·1 m.p.h.

LONGEST NON-STOP

The world's longest daily non-stop run is that of the "Sud Express", which runs for 359·8 miles between Paris and Bordeaux, France. The longest run on British Rail without any advertised stop is the "Motorail Service", which runs from King's Cross, London to Aberdeen, Scotland, a distance of 523½ miles.

MOST POWERFUL

World The world's most powerful compound type steam locomotive was No. 700, a triple articulated or triplex 2-8-8-8-4, the Baldwin Locomotive Co. 6-cylinder engine built in 1916 for the Virginian Railway. It had a tractive force of 166,300 lb. working compound and 199,560 lb. working simple. In 1918 this railway operated a 4-cylinder compound 2-10-10-2 engine, built by the American Locomotive Co., with a starting (*i.e.* working simple) tractive effort of 176,000 lb. Probably the heaviest train ever hauled by a single engine was one of 15,300 tons made up of 250 freight cars stretching 1·6 miles by the Matt H. Shay (No. 5014), a 2-8-8-8-2 engine which ran on the Erie Railroad from May 1914 until 1929.

PERMANENT WAY

The greatest length of unbroken four-lane track in the world is between Castleton and Dunkirk, New York in the United States, and is 342½ miles in length. The longest stretch of continuous four-lane track in the United Kingdom is between St. Pancras, London, and Glendon North Junction, Northamptonshire, and is 75 miles in length.

Longest straight The longest straight in the world is on the Commonwealth Railways Trans Australian line over the Nullarbor Plain from Mile 496 between Nuringa and Loongana, Western Australia, to Mile 793 between Ooldea and Watson, South Australia, 297 miles dead straight although not level. The longest straight on British Rail is the 18 miles between Selby and Kingston-upon-Hull, Yorkshire.

Longest electric line The world's longest stretch of electrified line is the 3,240 miles between Moscow and Irkutsk in Siberia, U.S.S.R., completed in late 1960.

Widest The widest gauge in standard use is 5 feet 6 inches. This width is used in India, Pakistan, Ceylon, Spain, Portugal, Argentina and Chile. In 1885 there was a lumber railway in Oregon, U.S.A., with a gauge of 8 feet.

HIGHEST

World The highest standard gauge (4 feet 8½ inches) track in the world is on the Central Railway of Peru (owned by the Peruvian Corporation Ltd.) at La Cima, where a branch siding rises to 15,844 feet above sea-level. The highest point on the main line is 15,688 feet in the Galera tunnel.

PROGRESSIVE RAILWAY SPEED RECORDS

Speed m.p.h.	Engine	Place	Date
29·1	The *Rocket* (Stephenson and Booth's 0-2-2)	Liverpool–Manchester	8 Oct. 182
59	Grand Junction Rly., 2-2-2 *Lucifer*	Madeley Bank, Staffordshire	13 Nov. 183
c. 85[1]	Atmospheric railway (Frank Elrington)	Dun Laoghaire–Dalkey, Co. Dublin	19 Aug. 184
74½	Great Western Rly., 8 ft. single 4-2-2 *Great Britain*	Wootton Bassett, Wiltshire	11 May 184
74½	Great Western Rly., 8 ft. single 4-2-2 *Great Western*	Wootton Bassett, Wiltshire	1 June 184
78	Great Western Rly., 8 ft. single 4-2-2 *Great Britain*	Wootton Bassett, Wiltshire	11 May 184
81·8	Bristol & Exeter Rly., 9 ft. single 4-2-4 tank No. 41	Wellington Bank, Somerset	June 185
89·48	Crompton No. 604 engine	Champigny Pont sur Yvonne, France	20 June 189
98·4[2]	*Philadelphia & Reading Rly., Engine 206*	*Skillmans to Belle Mead, New Jersey*	*July 189*
102·8[2]	*N.Y. Central & Hudson River Rly. Empire State Express No. 999*	*Grimesville, N.Y., U.S.A.*	*9 May 189*
112·5[2,3]	*N.Y. Central & Hudson River Rly. Empire State Express No. 999*	*Crittenden West, N.Y., U.S.A.*	*11 May 189*
90·0	Midland Rly., 7 ft. 9 in. single 4-2-2	Melton Mowbray–Nottingham	Mar. 189
130[2]	*Burlington Route*	*Siding to Arion, Iowa, U.S.A.*	*Jan. 189*
101·0	Siemens und Halske Electric	near Berlin	190
120·0[2,4]	*Savannah, Florida and Western Rly. mail train*	*Screven, Florida, U.S.A.*	*1 Mar. 190*
124·89	Siemens und Halske Electric	Marienfeld-Zossen, nr. Berlin	6 Oct. 190
128·43	Siemens und Halske Electric	Marienfeld-Zossen, nr. Berlin	23 Oct. 190
130·61	Siemens und Halske Electric	Marienfeld-Zossen, nr. Berlin	27 Oct. 190
99-100[5]	Great Western Rly., 4-4-0 *City of Truro*	Wellington Bank, Somerset	9 May 190
143·0	Kruckenberg (propeller-driven)	Karstädt-Dergenthin, Germany	21 June 193
150·9	Co-Co S.N.C.F. No. 7121	Dijon-Beaune, France	21 Feb. 195
205·6	Co-Co S.N.C.F. No. 7107	Facture-Morcenx, France	28 Mar. 195
205·6	Bo-Bo S.N.C.F. No. 9004	Facture-Morcenx, France	29 Mar. 195
235	*L'Aerotrain* (jet aero engines)	Gometz le Chatel-Limours, France	4 Dec. 196

1 *Speed attributed to runaway compressed air train. No independent timings.*
2 *Not internationally regarded as authentic.*
3 *Later alleged to be unable to attain 82 m.p.h. on this track when hauling 4 coaches.*
4 *5 miles in 2½ minutes to a stop, hence fictitious.*
5 *Previously unauthenticated at 102·3 m.p.h.*

Great Britain The highest point on the British Rail system is at the pass of Drumochter (or Drumouchter) on the Perth-Inverness border, where the track reaches an altitude of 1,484 feet above sea-level. The highest railway in Britain is the Snowdon Mountain Railway, which rises from Llanberis to 3,493 feet above sea-level, just below the summit of Snowdon (Yr Wyddfa). It has a gauge of 2 feet 7½ inches.

Lowest The lowest point on British Rail is in the Severn Tunnel—144 feet below sea-level.

STEEPEST GRADIENTS

World The world's steepest standard gauge gradient by adhesion is 1:11. This figure is achieved by the Guatemalan State Electric Railway between the River Samala Bridge and Zunil.

[Gre]at Britain The steepest sustained adhesion-worked gradient on a main line in the United Kingdom is the two-mile Lickey incline of 1:37·7 in Worcestershire. From the tunnel bottom to James Street, Liverpool, on the former Mersey Railway, there is a stretch of 1:27; just south of Ilfracombe, Devon, two miles of 1:36; and between Folkestone Junction and Harbour a mile of 1:30.

[S]hallowest The shallowest gradient posted on the British Rail system is one indicated as 1 in 13,707 between Sturt Lane Junction and Farnborough, Hampshire. This could, perhaps, also be described as England's most obtuse summit.

BUSIEST

[Ra]il system The world's most crowded rail system is the Tōkyō service of the Japanese National Railways, which carries about 4,200,000 passengers daily. Professional pushers are employed to squeeze in passengers before the doors can be closed. Among articles reported lost in the crush in 1964 were 380,353 umbrellas, 256,031 spectacles and hats, 170,189 shoes, and also an assortment of false teeth and artificial eyeballs.

Station The world's busiest stations are Tōkyō Central, which, in 1969, handled 2,600 trains, and Shinjuku, 2,200,000 passengers daily. The busiest railway junction in Great Britain is Clapham Junction on the Southern Region of British Rail, with over 2,070 trains passing through each 24 hours.

STATIONS

Largest *World* The world's largest railway station is Grand Central Terminal, Park Avenue and 43rd Street, New York City, N.Y., U.S.A., built 1903–13. It covers 48 acres on two levels with 41 tracks on the upper level and 26 on the lower. On average more than 550 trains and 180,000 people per day use it, with a peak of 252,288 on 3 July 1947.

United [K]ingdom The largest railway station in extent on the British Rail system is the 17-platform Clapham Junction, London, covering 27¾ acres and with a total face of 11,165 feet. The station with the largest number of platforms is Waterloo, London (24½ acres), with 21 main line and two Waterloo and City Line platforms, with a total face of 15,352 feet. Victoria Station (21¾ acres) with 17 platforms has, however, a total face length of 18,412 feet. The oldest station in Britain is Liverpool Road Station, Manchester, first used on 15 Sept. 1830.

Highest The highest station in the world on standard gauge railways is Ticlio, at 15,685 feet above sea-level, on the Central Railway of Peru, in South America. The highest passenger station on British Rail is Corrour, Inverness-shire, at an altitude of 1,347 feet above sea-level.

Waiting rooms The world's largest waiting rooms are those in Peking Station, Changan Boulevard, Peking, China, opened in September 1959, with a capacity of 14,000.

Longest platform The longest railway platform in the world is the Kharagpur platform, Bihar, India, which measures 2,733 feet in length. The State Street Center subway platform staging on "The Loop" in Chicago, Illinois, U.S.A., measures 3,500 feet in length.

The longest platform in the British Rail system is the 1,975-foot-long platform at Colchester, Essex.

Longest freight train The longest and heaviest freight train on record was one about 4 miles in length consisting of 500 coal cars with three 3,600 h.p. diesels pulling and three more pushing on the Iaeger, West Virginia to Portsmouth, Ohio stretch of 157 miles on the Norfolk and Western Railway on 15 Nov. 1967. The total weight was nearly 42,000 tons.

Greatest load The heaviest single piece of freight ever conveyed by rail was a 1,230,000-lb. (549·2-ton) 106-foot-tall hydro-cracker reactor which was carried from Birmingham, Alabama, to Toledo, Ohio, U.S.A., on 12 Nov. 1965.

The heaviest load carried by British Rail was a 122-foot-long boiler drum, weighing 275 tons, which was carried from Immingham Docks to Killinghome, Lincolnshire in September 1968.

Greatest mileage The greatest mileage covered with a weekly roving ticket on British Rail is 8,098 miles between 27 July and 3 Aug. 1969 by Mike Howell and Graham Roberts, who are both blind.

UNDERGROUND RAILWAYS

Most extensive The most extensive and oldest (opened 10 Jan. 1863) underground railway system in the world is that of the London Transport Board, with 254 miles of route, of which 67 miles is bored tunnel and 23 miles is "cut and cover". This whole Tube system is operated by a staff of 20,000 serving 277 stations. The 473 trains comprising 3,373 cars carried 655,000,000 passengers in 1968. The record for a day is 2,073,134 on V.E. Day, 8 May 1945. The greatest depth is 192 feet at Hampstead. The record for touring all 277 stations is 15 hours precisely by Leslie R. V. Burwood on 3 Sept. 1968. The record for the Paris Metro's 270 stations (7 closed) is 11 hours 13 minutes by Alan Paul Jenkins of Bushey, Hertfordshire on 30 Aug. 1967.

Busiest The busiest subway in the world is the New York City Transit Authority (opened on 27 Oct. 1904) with a total of 239·87 miles of track and 1,305,854,341 passengers in 1968. The stations are closer set and total 475, while the peak of passengers carried was 2,051,400,973 in 1947. The record for travelling the whole system is 23 hours 16 minutes by Michael Feldman and James Brown on 1 June 1966.

Model railway The record run for a model train was set at Berkeley Square, London, on 2–6 Sept. 1966, when the Hornby engine *Cardiff Castle* ran 153 miles. The run was equivalent, at scale, to 11,600 miles averaging 123·9 m.p.h.

MONORAIL

Highest speed The highest speed ever attained on rails is 3,090 m.p.h. (Mach 4·1) by an unmanned rocket-powered sled on the 6·62-mile-long captive track at the U.S. Air Force Missile Development Center at Holloman, New Mexico, U.S.A., on 19 Feb. 1959. The highest speed reached carrying a chimpanzee is 1,295 m.p.h.

The highest speed attained by a tracked hovercraft is 235 m.p.h. by the jet-powered *L'Aerotrain*, invented by Jean Bertin (see Progressive speed table page 134).

Speeds as high as Mach 0·8 (608 m.p.h.) are planned in 1973 from The Onsoku Kasotai (sonic speed sliding vehicle), a wheelless rocket-powered train running on rollers designed by Prof. H. Ozawa (Japan) and announced in March 1968.

Note—The use of the Mach scale for aircraft speeds was introduced by Prof. Acherer of Zürich, Switzerland. The Mach number is the ratio of the velocity of a moving body to the local velocity of sound. This ratio was first employed by Dr. Ernst Mach (1838–1916) of Vienna, Austria in 1887. Thus Mach 1·0 equals 760·98 m.p.h. at sea-level at 15° C. and is assumed, for convenience, to fall to a constant 659·78 m.p.h. in the stratosphere, *i.e.* above 11,000 metres (36,089 feet).

4. AIRCRAFT

EARLIEST FLIGHTS

World The first controlled and sustained power-driven flight occurred near Kill Devil Hills, Kitty Hawk, North Carolina, U.S.A., at 10.35 a.m. on 17 Dec. 1903, when Orville Wright (1871–1948) flew the 16 h.p. chain-driven *Flyer 1* at an airspeed of 30–35 m.p.h., a ground speed of less than 8 m.p.h. and an altitude of 8–12 feet for 12 seconds, watched by his brother Wilbur (1867–1912) and five coastguards. Both brothers, from Dayton, Ohio, were bachelors because, as Orville put it, they had not the means to "support a wife as well as an aeroplane". The plane is now in the Smithsonian Institution, Washington, D.C.

The first man-carrying powered aeroplane to fly, but not entirely under its own power, was a monoplane with a hot-air engine built by Félix Du Temple de la Croix (1823–90), a French naval officer, and piloted by a young sailor who made a short hop after taking off, probably down an incline, at Brest, France, in *c.* 1874. The first hop by a man-carrying aeroplane entirely under its own power was made when Clément Ader (1841–1925) of France flew in his *Eole* for about 50 metres (164 feet) at Armainvilliers, France, on 9 Oct. 1890.

British Isles The first officially recognised flight in the British Isles was by "Colonel" Samuel Franklin Cody (1861–1913) of the U.S.A., who flew 1,390 feet in his own biplane at Farnborough, Hampshire, on 16 Oct. 1908. Horatio Frederick Phillips (1845–1926) almost certainly covered 500 feet in his "Venetian blind" aeroplane at Streatham, in 1907. The first British citizen to fly was Griffith Brewer (1867–1948), as a passenger of Wilbur Wright, on 8 Oct. 1908 at Auvours, France.

Cross-Channel The earliest cross-Channel flight by an aeroplane was made on 25 July 1909, when Louis Blériot (1872–1936) of France flew his *Blériot XI* monoplane, powered by a 23 h.p. Anzani engine, from Les Baraques, France, to a meadow near Dover Castle, England, in 37 minutes, after taking off at 4.41 a.m.

TRANS-ATLANTIC

The first crossing of the North Atlantic by air was made by Lt.-Cdr. (later Rear Admiral) Albert C. Read (1887–1967) and his crew (Stone, Hinton, Rodd, Rhoads and Breese) in the Curtiss flying-boat NC-4 of the U.S. Navy from Trepassey Harbour, Newfoundland, *via* the Azores, to Lisbon, Portugal, on 16 to 27 May 1919. The whole flight of 3,936 miles originating from Rockaway Air Station, Long Island, N.Y. on 8 May required 53 hours 58 minutes.

First non-stop The first non-stop trans-Atlantic flight was achieved from 4.13 p.m. G.M.T. on 14 June 1919, from Lester's Field, St. John's Newfoundland, 1,960 miles to Derrygimla bog near Clifden, County Galway, Ireland, at 8.40 a.m. G.M.T., 15 June, when Capt. John William Alcock, D.S.C. (1892–1919), and Lt. Arthur Whitten-Brown (1886–1948) flew across in a Vickers *Vimy*, powered by two 360 h.p. Rolls-Royce *Eagle VIII* engines. Both men were created K.B.E. on 21 June 1919 when Alcock was aged 26 years 286 days and won the *Daily Mail* prize of £10,000.

First solo The first solo trans-Atlantic flight was achieved by Capt. Charles Augustus Lindbergh (b. 4 Feb. 1902, Detroit) who took off in his 220 h.p. Ryan monoplane "Spirit of St. Louis" at 12.52 p.m. G.M.T. on 20 May 1927 from Roosevelt Field, Long Island, New Yor State, U.S.A. He landed at 10.21 p.m. G.M.T. o 21 May 1927 at Le Bourget airfield, Paris, France. Hi flight of 3,610 miles lasted 33 hours 29½ minutes and h won a prize of $25,000 (then £5,300).

Fastest The present New York–Paris trans-Atlantic record i 3 hours 19 minutes 44·5 seconds by a Genera Dynamics/Convair B-58A *Hustler* "Firefly", piloted b Major William R. Payne, U.S.A.F., on 26 May 196 The 3,626 miles were covered at an average of 1,08 m.p.h. The B-58 was withdrawn from operationa service in January 1970.

The fastest time between New York and London i 4 hours 36 minutes 30·4 seconds by Lt.-Cdr. Bria Davies, 35, and Lt.-Cdr. Peter M. Goddard, R.N., 3 of No. 892 Squadron, Royal Navy, on 11 May 196 flying a McDonnell Douglas F-4K. *Phantom II* wi Rolls-Royce *Spey* engines. Lt.-Cdr. Goddard wa participating in the *Daily Mail* trans-Atlantic air rac which he won (prize of £5,000) with an overall time o 5 hours 11 minutes 22 seconds from the top of th Empire State Building, New York, to the top of th Post Office Tower, London.

CIRCUMNAVIGATION

Earliest The earliest flight round the world was completed b two U.S. Army Air Service Douglas aircraft "Chicago (Lt. Lowell H. Smith and Sgt. L. L. Arnold) and "Ne Orleans" (Lt. Erik H. Nelson and Sgt. J. Harding) o 28 Sept. 1924 at Seattle, Washington, U.S.A. The 17 day flight of 26,100 miles began on 24 April 1924 an involved 57 "hops" and a flying time of 351 hou 11 minutes. These aircraft had interchangeable whee and floats. The earliest solo flight round the world wa made from 15 to 22 July 1933 by Wiley Hardeman Po (1899–1935) (U.S.A.) in the Lockheed *Vega* "Winn Mae" starting and finishing at Floyd Bennett Fiel New York City, U.S.A. He flew the 15,596 miles eas about in 7 days 18 hours 49 minutes—in 10 hops wi a flying time of 115 hours 36 minutes.

Fastest The fastest circumnavigation of the globe was achiev by three U.S.A.F. B-52 *Stratofortresses*, led by Ma Gen. Archie J. Old, Jr., chief of the U.S. 15th Air Forc They took off from Castle Air Force Base, Merce California, at 1 p.m. on 16 Jan. and flew eastward arriving 45 hours 19 minutes later at March Air For Base, Riverside, California, on 18 Jan. 1957, after flight of 24,325 miles. The planes averaged 525 m.p. and were refuelled four times in flight by KC-97 aer tankers.

Jet-engined Proposals for jet propulsion date back to Capta Marconnet (1909) of France, and to the turbojet pr posals of Maxime Guillaume in 1921. The earliest te bed run was that of the British Power Jets Ltd.'s expe mental W.U. (Whittle Unit) on 12 April 1937, invent by Flying Officer (now Air Commodore Sir) Fra Whittle (b. Coventry, 1 June 1907), who had applied f a patent on jet propulsion in 1930. The first flight by aeroplane powered by a turbojet engine was made the Heinkel He 178, piloted by Flug Kapitan Eri Warsitz, at Marienehe, Germany, on 27 Aug. 1939. was powered by a Heinkel S-3b engine (838 lb.s.t. installed with long tail-pipe) designed by Dr. Pabst v Ohain and first tested in August 1937.

The first British jet flight occurred when Fl. Lt. P. E. "Jerry" Sayer, O.B.E., flew the Gloster-Whittle E.28/ (wing span 29 feet, length 25 feet 3 inches) fitted with 860 lb.s.t. Whittle W-1 engine for 17 minutes Cranwell, Lincolnshire, on 15 May 1941. The seco prototype attained 466 m.p.h.

Supersonic flight The first supersonic flight was achieved on 14 Oct. 19 by Capt. (now Lt.-Gen.) Charles ("Chuck") E. Yeag U.S.A.F. (b. 13 Feb. 1923), over Edwards Air For Base, Muroc, California, U.S.A., in a U.S. Bell XS

The BAC/ érospatiale *Concorde* h exceeded Mach 2 on 4 Nov. 1970

rocket plane ("Glamorous Glennis"), with Mach 1·015 (670 m.p.h.) at an altitude of 42,000 feet.

LARGEST AIRCRAFT

Heaviest The greatest weight at which an aeroplane has taken off is 820,700 lb. (366·38 tons), achieved by the prototype Boeing Model 747B commercial transport at Edwards Air Force Base, California, in November 1970. The basic aeroplane weighed 320,000 lb. (142·9 tons), the remaining weight representing fuel, flight test equipment and an artificial payload of sand and water. The 747B has a wing span of 195 feet 8 inches, is 231 feet 4 inches long and has a normal maximum take-off weight of 775,000 lb. (346 tons), with a payload of 165,284 lb. (73·8 tons).

Largest wing span The aircraft with the largest wing span ever constructed was the Hughes H.2 *Hercules* flying-boat, which was raised 70 feet into the air in a test run of 1,000 yards, piloted by Howard Hughes, off Long Beach Harbor, California, U.S.A., on 2 Nov. 1947. The eight-engined 190-ton aircraft had a wing span of 320 feet and a length of 219 feet. It never flew again.

Most powerful The most powerful aircraft ever built was the U.S.A.'s delta-winged North American XB-70A *Valkyrie*. It had a maximum take-off weight of 550,000 lb. (245·53 tons) and was 196 feet long overall, with a wing span of 105 feet. Designed as a bomber but used only for research, it was powered by six General Electric YJ93-3 turbojet engines, which delivered a combined thrust of 186,000 lb. It had its maiden test flight from Palmdale on 21 Sept. 1964 and attained a speed of Mach 3·0 (about 2,000 m.p.h.) on 14 Oct. 1965. It climbed to 74,000 feet. Its last and longest flight was made on 4 Feb. 1969, from Edwards AFB, California, to Wright-Patterson AFB, Ohio, where it is now exhibited in the Air Force Museum, Dayton, Ohio.

Lightest The lightest aeroplane ever flown was the Beecraft *Wee Bee*, built in 1948 by four Convair employees, at a cost of $200 (then £50), in San Diego, California, U.S.A. It had a wing span of 15 feet, an empty weight of 170 lb. and a loaded weight of 360 lb. It was powered by an $18\frac{1}{2}$ h.p. Navy drone-type engine. The *Gnome*, built by Michael Ward of North Scarle, Lincolnshire and flown in August 1967 weighs 210 lb. or 380 lb. loaded. It has a span of 15 feet 9 inches and is powered by a 1925 Douglas engine with a capacity of some 14 h.p.

Smallest The smallest aeroplane ever flown is the Stits *Skybaby* biplane, designed, built and flown by Ray Stits at Riverside, California, U.S.A., in 1952. It was 9 feet 10 inches long, with a wing span of 7 feet 2 inches, and weighed 452 lb. empty. It was powered by an 85 h.p. Continental C85 engine giving a top speed of 185 m.p.h.

BOMBERS

Heaviest The world's heaviest bomber is the eight-jet sweptwing Boeing B-52H *Stratofortress*, which has a maximum take-off weight of 488,000 lb. (217·86 tons). It has a wing span of 185 feet and is 157 feet $6\frac{3}{4}$ inches in length, with a speed of over 650 m.p.h. The B-52 can carry 12 750-lb. bombs under each wing and 84 500-lb. bombs in the fuselage giving a total bomb load of 60,000 lb. or 26·78 tons. The ten-engined Convair B-36J, weighing 183 tons, had a greater wing span, at 230 feet, but is no longer in service. It had a top speed of 435 m.p.h.

Fastest The world's fastest operational bombers are the French Dassault *Mirage IV*, which can fly at Mach 2·2 (1,450 m.p.h.) at 36,000 feet, and the American General Dynamics FB-111A, which also flies above Mach 2. The North American XB-70A *Valkyrie* was designed to cruise at a speed of Mach 3 (about 2,000 m.p.h.) but was used only for research (see Most powerful aircraft, left). The fastest Soviet bomber is the Tupolev Tu-22 "Blinder", with an estimated speed of Mach 1·4 (925 m.p.h.) at 36,000 feet.

AIRLINERS

Largest *World* The highest capacity jet airliner is the Boeing 747, "Jumbo Jet", first flown on 9 Feb. 1969, which by November 1970 had set a record for gross take-off weight with 820,700 lb. (366·38 tons) (see left, Heaviest aircraft) and has a capacity of from 362 to 490 passengers with a cruising speed of 595 m.p.h. Its wing span is 195·7 feet and its length 231·3 feet. It entered service on 21 Jan. 1970.

United Kingdom The heaviest airliner built in the United Kingdom is the B.A.C. Super VC10, which first flew on 7 May 1964. It weighs 335,000 lb. (149·5 tons) and is 171·7 feet long, with a wing span of 146·2 feet. The largest ever British aircraft was the prototype Bristol Type 167 *Brabazon*, which had a maximum take-off weight of 129·4 tons but a wing span of 230 feet and a length of 177 feet. This eight-engined aircraft first flew on 4 Sept. 1949.

Fastest *World* The world's fastest airliner in service is the Convair CV-990 *Coronado*, one of which flew at 675 m.p.h. at 22,500 feet (Mach 0·97) on 8 May 1961. Its maximum cruising speed is 625 m.p.h. A Douglas DC-8 Series 40, with Rolls-Royce Conway engines, exceeded the speed of sound in a shallow dive on 21 Aug. 1961. Its true air speed was 667 m.p.h. or Mach 1·012 at a height of 40,350 feet. The U.S.S.R.'s Tu-144 supersonic airliner, with a capacity of 121 passengers, first flew on 31 Dec. 1968. Its design speed is Mach 2·35 (1,553 m.p.h.) with a ceiling of 65,000 feet and it "went" supersonic on 5 June 1969. It first exceeded Mach 2 on 26 May 1970, flying at 1,335 m.p.h. at a height of 53,475 feet for several minutes.

Britain The fastest British airliner in service is the three-engined Hawker Siddeley *Trident 1C* which has reached 627 m.p.h. (Mach 0·9) in level flight and 667 m.p.h. (Mach 0·96) in a shallow dive at 24,000 feet. The supersonic BAC/Aérospatiale *Concorde*, first flown on 2 March 1969, with a capacity of 128 passengers, is

The world's shortest scheduled flight in Scotland's Orkney Islands

expected to cruise at 1,320—1,450 m.p.h. It flew at Mach 1·05 on 10 Oct. 1969 and exceeded Mach 2 for the first time on 4 Nov. 1970.

Scheduled flights *Longest* The longest scheduled non-stop flight is the Buenos Aires, Argentina to Madrid, Spain stage of 6,462 statute miles, by Aerolineas Argentinas and Iberia inaugurated on 7 Aug. 1967. The Boeing 707-320B requires 11½ hours.

Shortest The shortest scheduled flight in the world is that by Loganair between the Orkney Islands of Westray and Papa Westray which has been flown since September 1967. Though scheduled for 2 minutes, in favourable wind conditions it is accomplished in 70 seconds.

HIGHEST SPEED

Official record The official air speed record is 2,070·102 m.p.h. by Col. Robert L. Stephens and Lt.-Col. Daniel André (U.S.A.) in a Lockheed YF-12A near Edwards Air Force Base, California, U.S.A., on 1 May 1965.

Air-launched record The fastest fixed-wing aircraft in the world is the U.S. North American Aviation X-15A-2, which flew for the first time (after conversion) on 28 June 1964 powered by a liquid oxygen and ammonia rocket propulsion system. Ablative materials on the airframe have once enabled a temperature of 3,000° F. to be withstood. The landing speed was 210 knots (241·8 m.p.h.) momentarily. The highest speed attained was 4,534 m.p.h. (Mach 6·72) when piloted by Major William J. Knight, U.S.A.F. (b. 1930), on 3 Oct. 1967. An earlier version piloted by Joseph A. Walker (1920–66), reached 354,200 feet (67·08 miles) also over Edwards Air Force Base, California, U.S.A., on 22 Aug. 1963. The programme was suspended after the final flight of 24 Oct. 1968.

Fastest jet The world's fastest jet aircraft is the U.S.A.F. Lockheed SR-71 reconnaissance aircraft (a variant of the YF-12A, left) which first flew on 22 Dec. 1964 and is reportedly capable of attaining a speed of 2,200 m.p.h. and an altitude ceiling of close to 100,000 feet. The SR-71 has a span of 55·6 feet and a length of 107·4 feet and weighs 170,000 lb. (75·9 tons) at take-off. Its reported range is 2,982 miles at Mach 3 at 78,750 feet. Only 23 are believed to have been built and 9 had been lost by April 1969. The fastest Soviet jet aircraft in service is the Mikoyan MiG-23 fighter (code name "Foxbat") with a speed of about Mach 3 (1,980 m.p.h.) at height.

Fastest biplane The fastest recorded biplane was the Italian Fiat C.R.42B, with a 1,010 h.p. Daimler-Benz DB601A engine, which attained 323 m.p.h. in 1941. Only one was built.

Fastest piston-engined aircraft The fastest speed at which a piston-engined aeroplane has ever been measured was for a cut-down privately owned Hawker *Sea Fury* which attained 520 m.p.h. in level flight over Texas, U.S.A., in August 1966 piloted by the late Mike Carroll of Los Angeles. The official record for a piston-engined aircraft is 482·462 m.p.h. over Edwards AFB, California by Darryl C. Greenmyer, 33 (U.S.) in a Grumman F8F-2 *Bearcat* on 16 Aug. 1969.

Fastest propeller-driven aircraft The Soviet Tu-114 turboprop transport is the world's fastest propeller-driven aeroplane. It has achieved average speeds of more than 545 m.p.h. carrying heavy

The holder of the unofficial all-time piston-engined speed record —a 520-m.p.h. Hawker *Sea Fury*

payloads over measured circuits. It is developed from the Tupolev Tu-95 bomber, known in the West as the "Bear", and has 14,795-horse-power engines.

Largest propeller The largest aircraft propeller ever used was the 22 feet 7½ inches diameter Garuda propeller, fitted to the Linke-Hofmann R II built in Breslau, Germany, which flew in 1919. It was driven by four 260 h.p. Mercédès engines and turned at only 545 r.p.m.

ALTITUDE

Official record The official world altitude record by an aircraft which took off from the ground under its own power is 113,892 feet (21·57 miles) by Lt.-Col. Georgiy Mosolov (U.S.S.R.) in a Mikoyan E-66A aircraft, powered by one turbojet and one rocket engine, on 28 April 1961. Major R. W. Smith of the U.S. Air Force reached an unofficial record height of 118,860 feet (22·15 miles) in a Lockheed NF-104A over Edwards Air Force Base, California, U.S.A., early in November 1963.

DURATION

The flight duration record is 64 days, 22 hours, 19 minutes and 5 seconds, set up by Robert Timm and John Cook in a Cessna 172 light aircraft. They took off from McCarran Airfield, Las Vegas, Nevada, U.S.A., just before 3.53 p.m. local time on 4 Dec. 1958, and landed at the same airfield just before 2.12 p.m. on 7 Feb. 1959. They covered a distance equivalent to six times around the world.

AIRPORTS

Largest *World* The world's largest airport is the Dulles International Airport, Washington, D.C., U.S.A., which extends over an area of 9,880 acres (15·59 square miles). The largest international airport terminal is that at John F. Kennedy International Airport (opened as Idlewild in July 1948) on Long Island, New York, U.S.A. Terminal City covers an area of 655 acres. Work was started in December 1968 on an 18,000 acre complex at Grapevine between Dallas and Fort Worth, Texas, U.S.A., for completion at a cost of $360 million (£150 million) by 1972. The five terminals will be able to handle 90 jumbo jets simultaneously. The airport under construction between Miami and Naples, Florida, will cover approximately 25,000 acres (39 square miles).

United Kingdom Fifty-nine airline companies from 49 countries operate scheduled services into London (Heathrow) Airport (2,765 acres), and during 1970 there were a total number of 270,302 air transport movements handled by a staff of over 48,059, employed by the various companies and the British Airports Authority. The total number of passengers, both incoming and outgoing, was 15,606,719 in 1970. The most flights in a day was 928 on 31 July 1969 and the largest number of passengers yet handled in a day was 65,798 on the same day. Aircraft fly to 93 countries.

Busiest The world's busiest airport is the Chicago International Airport, O'Hare Field, Illinois, U.S.A., with a total of 675,451 movements (632,030 air carrier movements) in 1969. This represents a take-off or landing every 47 seconds.

The busiest landing area is, however, Bien Hoa Air Base, South Vietnam, which handled 857,679 take-offs and landings in 1968. The world's largest "helipad" is An Khe, South Vietnam, which services U.S. Army and Air Force helicopters.

Highest and lowest The highest airport in the world is El Alto, near La Paz, Bolivia, at 13,599 feet above sea-level. Ladakh airstrip in Kashmir has, however, an altitude of 14,270 feet. The highest landing ever made is 6,080 metres (19,947 feet) on Dhaulagri in the Nepal Himalaya by a high-wing monoplane, named *Yeti*, supplying the 1960 Swiss Expedition. The lowest landing field is El Lisan on the east shore of the Dead Sea, 1,180 feet below sea-level, but the lowest international airport is Schiphol, Amsterdam, at 13 feet below sea-level.

LONGEST RUNWAY

World The longest runway in the world is one of 7 miles in length (of which 15,000 feet is concreted) at Edwards Air Force Base on the bed of Rogers Dry Lake at Muroc, California, U.S.A. The whole test centre airfield extends over 65 square miles. In an emergency an auxiliary 12-mile strip is available along the bed of the Dry Lake. The world's longest civil airport runway is

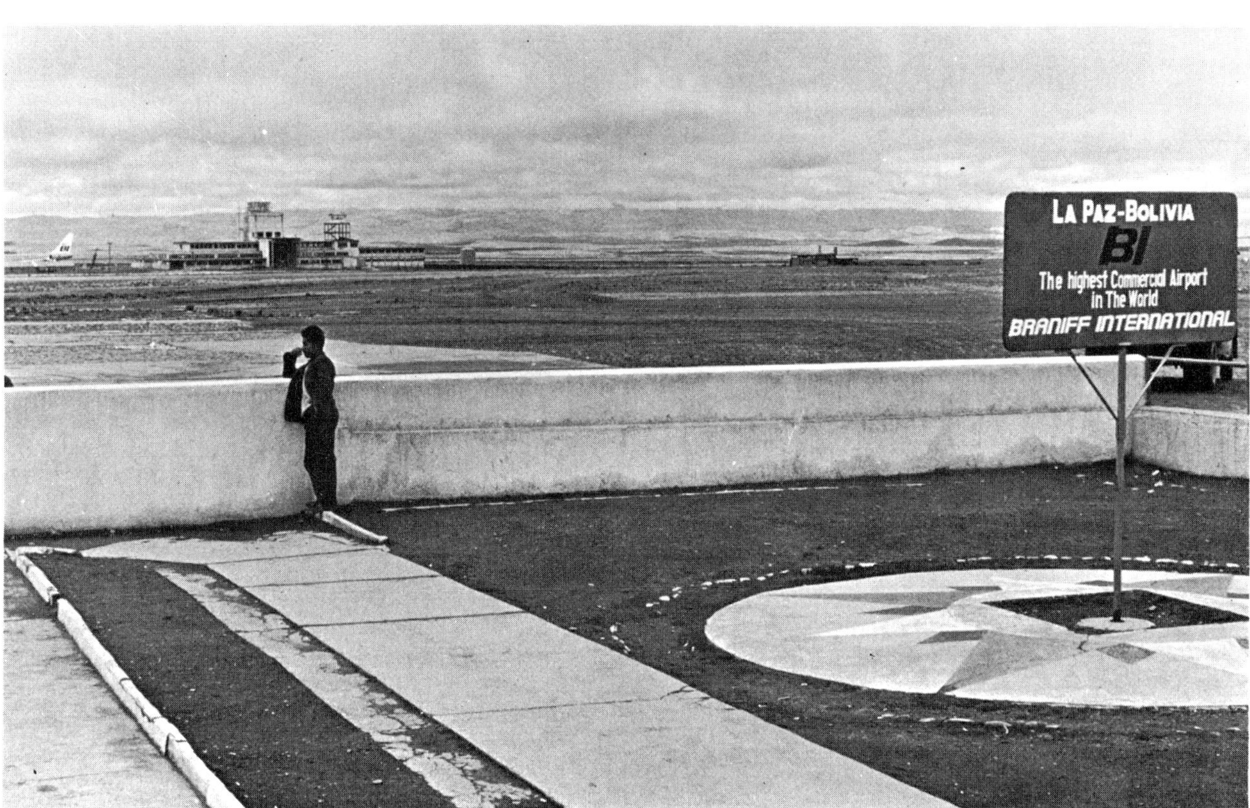

The world's highest international airport, El Alto, La Paz, Bolivia (13,599 feet)

The world's longest civil runway at Salisbury, Rhodesia

one of 15,500 feet (2·95 miles) at Salisbury, Rhodesia, completed in 1969.

United Kingdom The longest runway available normally to civil aircraft in the United Kingdom is Number 1 at London (Heathrow) Airport, measuring 12,799 feet (2·42 miles).

HELICOPTERS

Fastest rotating wing A Bell YUH-1B Model 533 compound research helicopter, boosted by two auxiliary turbojet engines, attained an unofficial speed record of 316·1 m.p.h. over Arlington, Texas, U.S.A., in April 1969.

Largest The world's largest helicopter is the Soviet Mi-12 ("Homer"), also known as the V-12, which set up an international record by lifting a payload of 88,636 lb. (39·5 tons) to a height of 7,398 feet on 6 Aug. 1969. It is powered by four 6,500 h.p. turboshaft engines and has an estimated span of 240 feet over its rotor tips with a fuselage length of 200·5 feet.

Fastest The world's speed record for a helicopter, subject to official confirmation, is 220·6 m.p.h. by a Sikorsky S-67 Blackhawk, flown by test pilot Kurt Cannon, between Milford and Branford, Connecticut, U.S.A., on 19 Dec. 1970.

Highest The altitude record for helicopters is 36,027 feet by Jean Boulet in a Sud-Aviation S.E.3150 *Alouette II* at Brétigny-sur-Orge, France, on 13 June 1958.

FLYING-BOAT

The fastest flying-boat is the Soviet twin-jet Beriev Be-10 (code name "Mallow"), which set up an official speed record of 566·69 m.p.h. over a measured course on 7 Aug. 1961, piloted by Nikolay Andrievskiy. This aircraft also holds the altitude record for flying-boats, with 49,088 feet, and lifted a record payload of 33,523 lb. (14·96 tons) to 2,000 metres (6,562 feet) on 12 Sept. 1961.

AIRSHIPS

Largest *Rigid World* The largest rigid airship ever built was the German *Graf Zeppelin II* (LZ130), with a length of 803 feet and a capacity of 7,063,000 cubic feet. She made her maiden flight on 14 Sept. 1938 and in May and August 1939 made radar spying missions in British air space. She was dismantled in April 1940.

British The largest British airship was the R101 built by the Royal Airship Works, Cardington, Bedfordshire and completed in 1929. She was 777 feet in length and had a capacity of 5,500,000 cubic feet. She crashed near Beauvais, France, killing 48 aboard on 5 Oct. 1930.

Non-rigid The largest non-rigid airship ever constructed was the U.S. Navy ZPG 3-W. It had a capacity of 1,516,300 cubic feet, was 403·4 feet long and 85·1 feet in diameter with a crew of 21. It first flew on 21 July 1958, but crashed into the sea in June 1960.

Earliest licence The Royal Aero Club's airship pilot's certificate No. 1 was issued to Ernest T. Willows (d. 1926) who on 4 Nov. 1910 in his flight from Wormwood Scrubs, London to Douai, France, in *Willows III* became the first to make the crossing from England to France.

BALLOONS

Distance record The record distance travelled is 3,052·7 kilometres (1,896·9 miles) by H. Berliner (Germany) from Bitterfeld, Germany, to Kirgishan in the Ural Mountains, Russia, on 8–10 Feb. 1914. The longest recorded stay aloft is 94½ hours by the *Small World* (Messrs. Timothy and Arnold B. Eiloart and Mr. and Mrs. Colin Mudie), which left Teneriffe on 12 Dec. 1958, and later ditched in the Atlantic after a flight of 1,200 miles. The official duration record is 87 hours by H. Kaulen (Germany) set on 13–17 Dec. 1913.

Largest The largest balloon ever to fly is the 800-foot-tall balloon built by G. T. Schjeldahl for the U.S.A.F. first tested on 18 July 1966. It was used for a Martian re-entry experiment by N.A.S.A. 130,000 feet above Walker AFB, New Mexico, U.S.A., on 30 Aug. 1966. Its capacity is 260 million cubic feet.

Human-powered flight The earliest successful attempt to fly over half a mile with a human-powered aircraft was made by John C. Wimpenny, who flew 993 yards at an average altitude of 5 feet (maximum 8 feet) and an average speed of 19·5 m.p.h. in a pedal-cranked propeller-driven aircraft called "Puffin I" at Hatfield, Herts., on 2 May 1962.

HOVERCRAFT

Earliest The inventor of the ACV (air-cushion vehicle) is Sir Christopher Cockerell, C.B.E., F.R.S. (b. 4 June 1910), a British engineer who had the idea in 1954, published his Ripplecraft Report 1/55 on 25 Oct. 1955 and patented it on 12 Dec. 1955. The earliest patent relating to an air-cushion craft was taken out in 1877 by John I. Thornycroft (1843–1928) of Chiswick, London. The first flight by a hovercraft was made by the 4-ton Saunders Roe SR-N1 at Cowes on 30 May 1959. With a 1,500-lb. thrust Viper turbojet engine, this craft reached 68 knots in June 1961. The first hovercraft public service was run across the Dee Estuary by the 60-knot 24-passenger Vickers-Armstrong VA-3 between July and September 1962.

Largest The largest is the £1,500,000 Westland SR-N4, "Mountbatten", weighing 168 tons, first run on 4 Feb. 1968. It has a top speed of 77 knots powered by 4 Bristol Siddeley Marine Proteus engines with 19-foot propellers. It carries 34 cars and 174 passengers and is 130 feet 2 inches long with a 76-foot 10-inch beam.

Longest flight The longest hovercraft journey was one of 5,000 miles through 8 West African countries between 15 Oct. 1969 and 3 Jan. 1970 by the British Trans-African Hovercraft Expedition. The longest non-stop journey on record is one of 550 miles lasting 33 hours by a Denny Mark II piloted by Sir John Onslow from Poole, Dorset to Fleetwood, Lancashire on 4–5 July 1968.

MODEL AIRCRAFT

The world record for altitude is 22,939 feet by Maynard L. Hill (U.S.A.) on 1 Sept. 1969 using a radio-controlled model. The speed record is 203·19 m.p.h. by E. Zanin (Italy) with a Zanin control-line jet in Rome on 26 April 1964. The best British performance is 101·5 m.p.h. by an unsponsored home-built 7·9 c.c. engined model of 32-inch wing span by John Crampton at Dunsfold, Surrey on 20 Oct. 1968.

Hypnosis from the air The first recorded example of hypnosis being performed from the air was when Mr. Henry Blythe hypnotized several people by radio telephone from an aircraft circling 1,500 feet above a marquee at Gloucester, England on 3 Aug. 1963.

5. POWER PRODUCERS

LARGEST POWER PLANT

World The world's largest power station is the U.S.S.R.'s hydro-electric station at Krasnoyarsk on the river Yenisey, Siberia, U.S.S.R. with a power of 6,096,000 kW. Its third generator turned in March 1968 and the twelfth became operative in December 1970. The turbine hall, completed in June 1968, is 1,378 feet long. The turbine hall at the Volga-V.I. Lenin Power Plant, Kuybyshev is more than 2,100 feet long. The underground turbine hall at the Canadian Churchill Falls (5,225,000 kW) installation is 972 feet long.

The largest non-hydro-electric generating plant in the world is the 2,500,000 kW Tennessee Valley Authority installation under construction at Paradise, Kentucky, U.S.A. with an annual consumption of 8,150,000 tons of coal. It cost $189,000,000 (£78,750,000).

The world's largest pumped storage plant is the 900,000 kW plant at Vianden, Luxembourg, completed in 1964.

United Kingdom The power stations with the greatest installed capacity in the United Kingdom are Ferrybridge "C" near Pontefract, Yorkshire, which reached full power of 2,000 MW in December 1967. With Ferrybridge "A" and "B" this complex contributes 2,430 MW. A single station in Longannet, Fife, Scotland began building up towards a delivery of 2,400 MW in 1971. A 3,960 MW station is under construction at Drax, Yorkshire, the first half of which (3 × 660 MW sets) will be completed in 1973.

The largest hydro-electric plant in the United Kingdom is the North of Scotland Hydro-electricity Board's Power Station at Loch Sloy, Dunbartonshire. The installed capacity of this station is 130,450 kW or 175,000 h.p. The Ben Cruachan Pumped Storage Scheme was opened on 15 Oct. 1965 at Loch Awe, Argyll, Scotland. It has a capacity of 400,000 kW and cost £24,000,000.

Biggest black-out The greatest power failure in history struck seven north-eastern U.S. States and Ontario, Canada, on 9–10 Nov. 1965. About 30,000,000 people in 80,000 square miles were plunged into darkness. Only two were killed. In New York City the power failed at 5.27 p.m. Supplies were eventually restored by 2 a.m. in Brooklyn, 4.20 a.m. in Queens, 6.58 a.m. in Manhattan and 7 a.m. in the Bronx.

ATOMIC POWER

Earliest The world's first atomic pile was built in a disused squash court at the University of Chicago, Illinois, U.S.A. It "went critical" on 2 Dec. 1942.

Largest The world's largest atomic power station is the 1,180 MW plant at Wylfa, Anglesey, North Wales, which began to contribute to the grid in February 1971. The Dungeness "B" station in Kent, due to be completed in July 1971, has a capacity of 1,200 MW followed by Hinkley "B" (1,250 MW) and Heysham, Lancashire (2,500 MW). The largest atomic plant scheduled in the United States is the Sequoyah Nuclear Power Plants Units 1 and 2 each of 1,124 MW due to be completed at Daisy, Tennessee in 1973 and 1974.

LARGEST REACTOR

The largest single atomic reactor in the world is the 873 MW Westinghouse Electric Corporation pressurized water type reactor installed at Indian Point No. 2 Station, New York, U.S.A. which became operative in 1969.

TIDAL POWER STATION

The world's first major tidal power station is the *Usine marémotrice de la Rance*, officially opened on 26 Nov. 1966 at the Rance estuary in the Golfe de St. Malo, Britanny, France. It was built in five years, at a cost of 420,000,000 francs (£34,685,000), and has a net annual output of 544,000,000 kWh. The 880-yard barrage contains 24 turbo alternators. This harnessing of the tides has imperceptibly slowed the Earth's rate of revolution. The $1,000 million (£416 million) Passama-

THE WORLD'S LARGEST HYDRO-ELECTRIC GENERATING PLANTS (Progressive List)

Ultimate Kilowattage	First Operational	Location	River
38,400	1898	De Cew Falls No. 1 (old plant)	Welland Canal
132,500	1905	Ontario Power Station	Niagara
403,900	1922	Sir Adam Beck No. 1 (formerly Queenston-Chippawa)	Niagara
1,641,000	1942	Beauharnois, Quebec, Canada	St. Lawrence
1,974,000*	1941	Grand Coulee, Washington State, U.S.A.	Columbia
2,100,000	1955	Volga-V.I. Lenin Station, Kuybyshev, U.S.S.R.	Volga
2,543,000	1958	Volga-22nd Congress Station, Volgograd, U.S.S.R.	Volga
4,500,000	1961	Bratsk, U.S.S.R.	Angara
6,096,000	1967	Krasnoyarsk, U.S.S.R.	Yenisey
6,300,000	—	Sayano-Shushensk, U.S.S.R.	Yenisey
c. 20,000,000	—	Lower Lena, near Verkoyansk, U.S.S.R.	Lena

* *Ultimate long-term planned kilowattage will be 9,771,000 kW with the completion of the "Third Powerplant" (capacity 7,200,000 kW).*

quoddy project for the Bay of Fundy in Maine, U.S.A., and New Brunswick, Canada, is not expected to be operative before 1978. The first ever tidal power station was the Dee Hydro Station, Cheshire with a capacity of 635 kW which began producing in October 1913.

LARGEST BOILER
The largest boilers ever designed are those ordered in the United States from The Babcock & Wilcox Company (U.S.A.) with a capacity of 1,330 MW so involving the evaporation of 9,330,000 lb. of steam per hour. The largest boilers now being installed in the United Kingdom are the three 660 MW units for the Drax Power Station (see page 141) designed and constructed by Babcock & Wilcox Ltd.

LARGEST GENERATOR
The largest generator in the world is now a double shaft steam generator with a designed capacity of 800,000 kW, being built since August 1963 at the Elektrosila works, Leningrad, in the U.S.S.R. This is destined for the Lower Lena Hydro-electric works (see p. 141). An 800,000 kW single-shaft steam turbine was reported from the U.S.S.R. in February 1971 and design work was in process on a 1,200,000 kW generator. The first 500,000 kW generator in Britain went into service at Ferrybridge, Yorkshire, in 1967. At Drax Power Station, Yorkshire, 660,000 kW generators will be installed by 1972.

LARGEST TURBINES
The largest turbines under construction are those rated at 820,000 h.p. with an overload capacity of 1,000,000 h.p., 32 feet in diameter with a 401-ton runner and a 312½-ton shaft for the Grand Coulee "Third Powerplant" (see page 141).

GAS TURBINE
The largest gas turbine in the world is that installed at the Krasnodar thermal power station in August 1969 with a capacity of 100,000 kW. It was built in Leningrad, U.S.S.R.

LARGEST PUMP TURBINE
The world's largest integral reversible pump-turbine is that made by Allis-Chalmers for the $50,000,000 Taum Sauk installation of the Union Electric Co. in St. Louis, Missouri, U.S.A. It has a rating of 240,000 h.p. as a turbine and a capacity of 1,100,000 gallons per minute as a pump. The Tehachapi Pumping Plant, California will in 1972 pump 18,300,000 gallons per minute over 1,700 feet up.

SOLAR POWER PLANT
The largest solar furnace in the world is the Laboratoire de l'Energie Solaire, at Mont Louis in the eastern Pyrenees, France. Its parabolic reflector, 150 feet in diameter, is the largest mirror in the world and concentrates the Sun's rays to provide a temperature of 5,432° F. In April 1958 it was announced that Soviet scientists had designed a solar power station for the Ararat Valley, Armenia, U.S.S.R., using 1,300 moving mirrors, totalling 5 acres in area, to provide 2,500,000 kW hours in a year. The U.S. Air Force solar furnace at Cloudcroft, New Mexico, U.S.A., has a parabolic mirror 108 feet in diameter and a flat mirror 154 feet square, yielding temperatures of *c.* 8,500° F.

LARGEST GAS WORKS
The flow of natural gas from the North Sea is diminishing the manufacture of gas by the carbonisation of coal and the reforming process using petroleum derivatives. Britain's largest ever gasworks covering 300 acres at Beckton, Essex, still had in December 1967, a production capacity of 700 million cubic feet per day of which 28 per cent. was by carbonisation requiring over 6,000 tons of coal per day.

MOST POWERFUL JET ENGINE
The world's most powerful jet engine was the General Electric GE4/J5 which attained a thrust of 63,200 lb., with after-burning, on 19 Sept. 1968. The thrust of the Thiokol XLR99-RM-2 rocket motor in each of the three experimental U.S.X-15 aircraft was 56,880 lb. at sea-level, reaching 70,000 lb. at peak altitudes. The Rolls-Royce RB 211-22, first ran on 31 Aug. 1968, reached 40,600 lb. in April 1969. It powers the Lockheed L-1011-1 'Tristar', which first flew on 16 Nov. 1970. The -22B version (45,000 lb.) will be used when the 'Tristar' goes into production.

6. ENGINEERING

OLDEST MACHINERY

World The earliest machinery still in use is the *dâlu*—a water raising instrument known to have been in use in the Sumerian civilization which originated *c.* 3,500 B.C. in Lower Iraq.

Britain The oldest piece of machinery operating in the United Kingdom is the snuff mill driven by a water wheel at Messrs. Wilson & Co.'s Sharrow Mill in Sheffield, Yorkshire. It is known to have been operating in 1797 and more probably since 1730.

LARGEST PRESS
The world's two most powerful production machines are forging presses in the U.S.A. The Loewy closed-die forging press, in a plant leased from the U.S. Air Force by the Wyman-Gordon Company at North Grafton, Massachusetts, U.S.A. weighs 9,469 tons and stands 114 feet 2 inches high, of which 66 feet is sunk below the operating floor. It has a rated capacity of 44,600 tons, and went into operation in October 1955. The other similar press is at the plant of the Aluminium Company of America at Cleveland, Ohio. There has been a report of a press in the U.S.S.R. with a capacity of 75,000 tonnes (73,800 tons), at Novo Kramatorsk. The most powerful press in Great Britain is the closed-die forging and extruding press installed in 1967 at the Cameron Iron Works, near Edinburgh, Scotland. The press is 92 feet tall (27 feet below ground) and exerts a force of 30,000 tons.

LATHE
The world's largest lathe is the 72-foot-long 385-ton giant lathe built by the Dortmunder Rheinstahl firm of Wagner in 1962. The face plate is 15 feet in diameter and can exert a torque of 289,000 ft. lb. when handling objects weighing up to 200 tons.

EXCAVATOR
The world's largest excavator is the 33,400 h.p. Marion 6360 excavator, weighing 12,500 tons. This vast machine can grab 241 tons in a single bite in a bucket of 85 cubic yards capacity.

DRAGLINE

World The Ural Engineering Works at Ordzhonikdze, U.S.S.R., completed in March 1962, has a dragline known as the ES-25(100) with a boom of 100 metres (328 feet) and a bucket with a capacity of 31·5 cubic yards. The world's largest walking dragline is the Bucyrus-Erie 4250W with an all-up weight of 12,000 tons and a bucket capacity of 220 cubic yards on a 310-foot boom. This machine, the world's largest mobile land machine is now operating on the Central Ohio Coal Company's Muskingum site in Ohio, U.S.A.

United Kingdom The largest dragline excavator in Britain is "Big Geordie", the Bucyrus-Erie 1550W 6250 gross h.p., weighing 3,000 tons and a forward mast 160 feet high. On open cast coal workings at Widdrington, Northumberland in February 1970, it proved able to strip 100 tons of overburden in 65 seconds with its 65 cubic yard bucket on a 265-foot boom. It is operated by Derek Crouch (Contractors) Ltd.

BLAST FURNACE
The world's largest blast furnace is the No. 3 Blast

Furnace at the Nippon Steel Corporation's Kimitsu Steel Works completed in April 1971. It has a daily pig iron production capacity of 10,000 tons.

Largest forging The largest forging on record is one 53 feet long weighing 396,000 lb. (176·79 tons) forged by Bethlehem Steel for the Tennessee Valley Authority nuclear power plant at Brown Ferry, Alabama, U.S.A. in Nov. 1969.

LONGEST PIPELINES

Oil The longest crude oil pipeline in the world is the Interprovincial Pipe Line Company's installation from Edmonton, Alberta, to Buffalo, New York State, U.S.A., a distance of 1,775 miles. Along the length of the pipe 13 pumping stations maintain a flow of 6,900,000 gallons of oil per day. In Britain the longest pipeline for crude oil is the 245-mile-long British Petroleum–Royal Dutch/Shell line from Merseyside to Greater London opened on 19 March 1969 at a cost of £8½ million.

The eventual length of the Trans-Siberian Pipeline will be 2,319 miles, running from Tuimazy through Ormsk and Novosibirsk to Irkutsk. The first 30-mile section was opened in July 1957.

Natural gas The longest natural gas pipeline in the world is the TransCanada Pipeline which by mid-1971 had 3,769 miles of pipe up to 36 inches in diameter. The mileage will be increased to 4,464 miles, some of it in 42-inch pipe, by mid-1973. A system 5,625 miles in length, with a 3,500-mile trunk from northern Russia to Leningrad, is under construction in the U.S.S.R., for completion by 1976.

Largest Cat Cracker The world's largest catalyst cracker is the American Oil Company's installation at the Texas City Refinery, Texas, U.S.A., with a capacity of 3,322,000 gallons per day.

Largest nut The largest nuts ever made weigh 26 cwt. (1·3 tons) each and have an inside diameter of 23 inches and an outside diameter of 26 inches. Known as the Pilgrim Nuts, they are manufactured by Moorside Components Ltd. of Oldham, Lancashire, for securing propellers.

TRANSFORMER

The world's largest transformer is one rated at 700,000 kVa at Longannet, Fife, Scotland, completed in January 1970.

HIGHEST ROPEWAY OR TELEPHERIQUE

World The highest and longest aerial ropeway in the world is the Teleferico Mérida (Mérida téléphérique) in Venezuela, from Mérida City (5,379 feet) to the summit of Pico Espejo (15,629 feet), a rise of 10,250 feet. The ropeway is in four sections, involving 3 car changes in the 8 mile ascent in one hour. The fourth span is 10,070 feet in length. The two cars work on the pendulum system—the carrier rope is locked and the cars are hauled by means of three pull ropes powered by a 230 h.p. motor. They have a maximum capacity of 45 persons and travel at 32 feet per second (21·8 m.p.h.). The longest single span ropeway is the 13,500-foot-long span from the Coachella Valley to Mt. San Jacinto (10,821 feet), California, U.S.A., inaugurated on 12 Sept. 1963. The largest cable cars in the world are those at Squaw Valley, California, U.S.A., with a capacity of 121 persons built by Carrosseriewerke A.G. of Aarburg, Switzerland, and first run on 19 Dec. 1968. The breaking strain on the 7,000-foot cable is 279 tons.

Great Britain Britain's longest cabin lift is that at Llandudno, Caernarvonshire, Wales opened in June 1969. It has 42 cabins each with a capacity of 1,000 people per hour and is 5,320 feet in length.

PASSENGER LIFTS

Fastest *World* The fastest domestic passenger lifts in the world are those fitted in the 100-storey, 1,107-foot-tall John

Britain's longest cable car lift at Llandudno, Wales

Hancock Building in Chicago, Illinois, U.S.A. They operate at a speed of 1,600 feet per minute. Much higher speeds are achieved in the winding cages of mine shafts. A hoisting shaft 6,800 feet deep, owned by Western Deep Levels Ltd. in South Africa, winds at speeds of up to 40·9 m.p.h.

United Kingdom The longest lift in the United Kingdom is one 930 feet long inside the B.B.C. T.V. tower at Bilsdale, West Moor, North Riding, Yorkshire built by J. L. Eve Construction Co. Ltd. It runs at 130 feet/min. The longest fast lifts are the two 15-passenger cars in the Post Office Tower, Maple Street, London W1 which travel 540 feet up at up to 1,000 feet/min.

Shortest shaft The shortest shaft on record is one of 2 feet 9 inches at St. Woolo's Hospital, Newport, Monmouthshire.

FASTEST ESCALATORS

The fastest escalators in the United Kingdom are those at the Leicester Square underground station on the London Transport Board railway. They have a step speed of 180 feet per minute. Escalators were introduced at Earl's Court station on 3 Oct. 1911.

The world's longest "moving sidewalk" is the Speedwalk Passenger Conveyor System at San Francisco Airport, California, U.S.A., comprising two conveyors measuring 450 feet each, and each with a capacity of 7,200 passengers per hour. It was opened on 20 May 1964.

The longest "travolators" in Great Britain are the pair of 360 feet and 375 feet in tandem at Terminal No. 3, London Airport, installed by Fletcher, Sutcliffe and Wild of Horbury, Leeds, Yorkshire in March-May 1970.

FASTEST PRINTER

The world's fastest printer is the Radiation Inc. electro-sensitive system at the Lawrence Radiation Laboratory, Livermore, California. High speed recording of up to 30,000 lines each containing 120 alphanumeric characters is attained by controlling electronic pulses through chemically impregnated recording paper which is rapidly moving under closely spaced fixed styli. It can thus print the wordage of the whole Bible (773,692 words) in 65 seconds—3,333 times as fast as the world's fastest typist.

TRANSMISSION LINES

Longest The longest span between pylons of any power line in the world is that across the Sogne Fjord, Norway, between Rabnaberg and Flatlaberg. Erected in 1955, by the Whitecross Co. Ltd. of Warrington, England, as part of the high-tension power cable from Refsdal power station at Vik, it has a span of 16,040 feet and a weight of 12 tons. In 1967 two further high tensile steel/aluminium lines 16,006 feet long, and weighing 33 tons, manufactured by Whitecross and B.I.C.C. (see below), were erected here. The longest in Britain are the 5,310-foot lines built by J. L. Eve Co. across the Severn with main towers each 488 feet high.

Highest The world's highest are those across the Straits of Messina, with towers of 675 feet (Sicily side) and 735 feet (Calabria) and 11,900 feet apart. The highest lines in Britain are those made by British Insulated Callender's Cables Ltd. at West Thurrock, Essex, which cross the Thames estuary suspended from 630-foot-tall towers at a minimum height of 250 feet, with a 130-ton breaking load. They are 4,500 feet in length.

Highest voltages The highest voltages now carried are 765,000 volts A.C. in the United States since 1969. The Swedish A.S.E.A. Company is experimenting with a possible 1,000,000 volt D.C. transmission line.

LONGEST CONVEYOR BELT

The world's longest single flight conveyor belt is one of 5½ miles installed at the N.C.B. power station at Longannet, Fife, Scotland by Cable Belt Ltd. of Camberley, Surrey. Cable Belt Ltd. are also installing a 9-mile-long single-flight conveyor at Cumberland, Tennessee, U.S.A., with a weekly capacity of 140,000 short tons of coal on a 42-inch-wide 800 ft./min. belt.

LONGEST WIRE ROPE

The longest wire rope ever spun in one piece was one measuring 46,653 feet (8·83 miles) long and 3⅛ inches in circumference, with a weight of 28½ tons, manufactured by British Ropes Ltd. of Doncaster, Yorkshire.

CLOCKS

Oldest The earliest mechanical clock, that is one with an escapement, was completed in China in A.D. 725 by I'Hsing and Liang Ling-tsan.

The oldest surviving working clock in the world is one dating from 1386, or possibly earlier, at Salisbury Cathedral, Wiltshire, which was restored in 1956. Earlier dates, ranging back to *c.* 1335, have been attributed to the weight-driven clock in Wells Cathedral, Somerset, but only the iron frame is original. A model of Giovanni de Dondi's heptagonal astronomical clock of 1348–64 was completed in 1962.

Largest *World* The world's most massive clock is the Astronomical Clock in Beauvais Cathedral, France, constructed between 1865 and 1868. It contains 90,000 parts and measures 40 feet high, 20 feet wide and 9 feet deep. The Su Sung clock, built in China at Khaifeng in 1088–92, had a 20-ton bronze armillary sphere for 1½ tons of water. It was removed to Peking in 1126 and was last known to be working in its 40-foot-high tower in 1136.

United Kingdom The largest clock in the United Kingdom was on the Singer Sewing Machine factory at Clydebank, Dunbartonshire, Scotland. It had four faces, each 26 feet in diameter, the minute hand was 12 feet 9 inches long and the hour hand 8 feet 9 inches. It was built in 1882, re-modelled in 1926 and operated until 5 p.m. on 5 March 1963. The largest clock face constructed in Britain is the Synchronome turret clock (diameter 60 feet) exhibited at Earl's Court, London, in March 1959. The largest clock wheel in the world is the World Time Clock installed at 120 Cheapside, London, E.C.2. It has a diameter of 10 feet and enables the zone times in the major cities of the world to be read off. This was commissioned by J. Henry Schroder Wagg & Co. Ltd., from Martin Burgess.

Public clocks The largest four-faced clock in the world is that on the building of the Allen-Bradley Company of Milwaukee, Wisconsin, U.S.A. Each face has a diameter of 40 feet 3½ inches with a minute hand 20 feet in overall length. The tallest four-faced clock in the world is that of the Williamsburgh Savings Bank in Brooklyn, New York City, N.Y., U.S.A. It is 430 feet above street level.

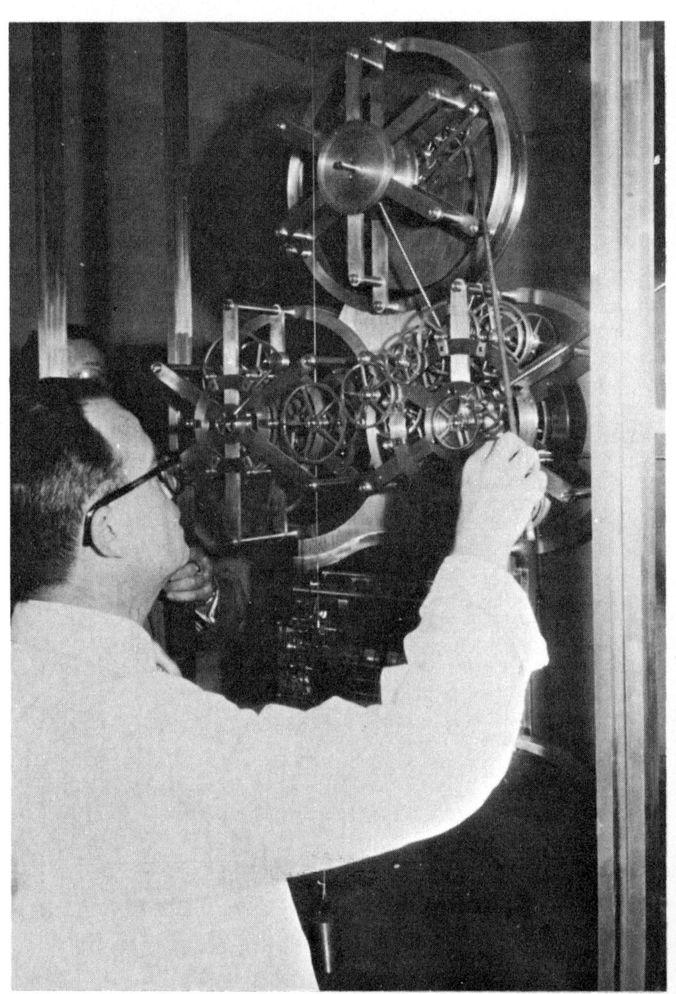

The world's most accurate clockwork clock—in Copenhagen, Denmark

Most accurate The most accurate and complicated clock in the world is the Olsen clock, installed in the Copenhagen Town Hall, Denmark. The clock, which has more than 14,000 units, took 10 years to make and the mechanism of the clock functions in 570,000 different ways. The celestial pole motion of the clock will take 25,753 years to complete a full circle and is the slowest moving designed mechanism in the world. The clock is accurate to 0·5 of a second in 300 years.

Most expensive The highest auction price for any English clock is £15,500 for an ebony bracket clock made by Thomas Tompian (*c.* 1639–1713) sold at the salerooms of Sotheby & Co., London on 29 April 1968.

WATCHES

Oldest The oldest watch (portable clock-work time-keeper) is one made of iron by Peter Henlein (or Hele) in Nürnberg

(Nuremberg), Bavaria, Germany, in *c.* 1504 and now in the Memorial Hall, Philadelphia, Pennsylvania, U.S.A. The earliest wrist watches were those of Jacquet-Droz and Leschot of Geneva, Switzerland, dating from 1790.

Most expensive Excluding watches with jewelled cases, the most expensive standard men's wrist watch is the Swiss Patek-Philippe which in May 1970 was retailed for £1,600. On 1 June 1964, a record £27,500 was paid for the Duke of Wellington's watch made in Paris in 1807 by Abraham Louis Bréguet, at the salerooms of Sotheby & Co., London, by the dealers Messrs. Ronald Lee for a Portuguese client.

Smallest The smallest watches in the world are produced by Jaeger Le Coultre of Switzerland. Equipped with a 15-jewelled movement they measure just over half-an-inch long and three-sixteenths of an inch in width. The movement, with its case, weighs under a quarter of an ounce.

TIME MEASURER

Most accurate *World* The most accurate time-keeping devices are the twin atomic hydrogen masers installed in 1964 in the U.S. Naval Research Laboratory, Washington, D.C. They are based on the frequency of the hydrogen atom's transition period of 1,420,450,751,694 cycles per second. This enables an accuracy to within one second per 1,700,000 years.

United Kingdom The most accurate time measurer in the United Kingdom is the 14-foot-long rubidium resonance Standard Atomic Clock at the National Physical Laboratory, Teddington, Greater London, devised by Dr. Louis Essen, O.B.E. and Mr. J. V. L. Parry and completed in 1962. It is accurate to within one second in 1,000 years.

RADAR INSTALLATIONS

Largest The largest of the three installations in the U.S. Ballistic Missile Early Warning System (B.M.E.W.S.) is that near Thule, in Greenland, 931 miles from the North Pole, completed in 1960 at a cost of $500,000,000 (now £208·3 million). Its sister stations are one at Clear, Alaska, U.S.A., completed in July 1961, and a $115,000,000 (now £47·9 million) installation at Fylingdales Moor, Yorkshire, completed in June 1963. A 187-mast installation costing £55 million has been erected at Orfordness, Suffolk for the U.S.A.F. and R.A.F.

Smallest tubing The smallest tubing in the world is made by Accles and Pollock, Ltd. of Oldbury, Worcestershire. It is of pure nickel with an outside diameter of 0·0005 of an inch and was announced on 9 Sept. 1963. The average human hair measures from 0·002 to 0·003 of an inch in diameter. The tubing, which is stainless, can be used for the artificial insemination of bees and for the medical process of "feeding" nerves, and weighs only 5 oz. per 100 miles.

LARGEST CRANE

World The crane with the world's greatest lifting capacity is the Goliath crane installed at Harland and Wolff's shipbuilding dock, Belfast, Northern Ireland, in 1969. The crane spans 460 feet and has a working safe load of 840 tons, but on a test lifted 1,050 tons. It was built to the design of Krupper-Ardelt of Wilhelmshaven, West Germany. A 32-wheeled gantry hydraulic crane with a span of 95 feet with a capacity of 2,000 short tons (1,785·7 tons) is under construction at the Grand Coulee Third Powerplant, Washington, U.S.A. The highest crane reported is a mobile crane, owned by Van Twist N.V. of Dordrecht, Netherlands, of 400 tons capacity which overtopped a 540-foot-high high-tension power pylon during its erection on the bank of the River Scheldt, near Antwerp, Belgium in 1970.

Hoisting tackle The greatest weight lifted by hoisting tackle is 700 tons by the Fluor Corporation of Los Angeles, California, U.S.A., in the case of an Isomax reactor 90 feet in length at Shuaiba, Kuwait, on 26 Aug. 1968.

Floating crane The world's largest floating cranes are the Foster Parker, *Atlas Number 1* and the *Hercules* derrick barges operated by Brown & Root Inc. of Houston, Texas. These are 350 feet long and 100 feet in the beam and carry a crew of 80 men. The main crane in fixed position at 65 feet radius is capable of hoisting 714 tons.

The world's most powerful floating crane, the *Atlas Number 1* (see above)

9 THE BUSINESS WORLD

1. COMMERCE

OLDEST INDUSTRY

Agriculture is often described as "the oldest industry in the world", whereas in fact there is no evidence that it was practised before *c.* 9000 B.C. The oldest industry is believed to be flint knapping, which is allied to the construction of hand axes, which are the earliest human artifacts, dating from between 1,750,000 and 2,300,000 years ago.

OLDEST COMPANY

World The oldest company in the world is believed to be Stora Kopparbergs Bergslags Aktiebolag ("The Great Copper Mountain Mining Corporation") of Falun, Sweden, in which there have been recorded share dealings since 16 June 1288. The earliest trading in share certificates was in those of the Dutch East India Company (*Verenigde Oost Indische Compagnie*) soon after its foundation on 20 March 1602. A share certificate dated 8 Dec. 1606 is in the possession of the Vereniging voor den Effectenhandel, Amsterdam.

Britain The oldest company in Britain is the Faversham Oyster Fishery Co., referred to the Faversham Oyster Fishing Act 1930, has existed "from time immemorial", *i.e.* from before 1189. The Royal Mint has origins going back to A.D. 287. The Whitechapel Bell Foundry of Whitechapel Road, London, E.1, has been in business since 1570. The oldest retail business in Britain is B. Smith, Ltd., in the market place of Thirsk, Yorkshire. Founded in 1580, the company is a firm of drapers, furnishers and caterers. R. Durtnell & Sons, builders, of Brasted, Kent, has been run by the same family since 1591.

GREATEST ASSETS

World The business with the greatest amount in physical assets is the Bell System, which comprises the American Telephone and Telegraph Company, with headquarters at 195 Broadway, New York City, N.Y., U.S.A., and its subsidiaries. The group's total assets on the consolidated balance sheet at 31 Dec. 1970 were valued at $49,641,509,000 (£20,684 million). The plant involved included 96,561,000 telephones. The number of employees was 1,005,380. The shareholders at 1 Jan. 1970 numbered more than those of any other company, namely 3,062,973. A total of 20,109 attended the Annual Meeting in April 1961, thereby setting a world record. The total of operating revenues and other income in 1970 was $16,954,881,000 (£7,064 million), from which the net income, after taxes, was $2,189,400,000 (£912 million). The first company to have assets in excess of $1 billion was the United States Steel Corporation with $1,400 million (then £287·73 million) at the time of its creation by merger in 1900.

United Kingdom The enterprise in the United Kingdom, excluding banks, with the greatest capital employed is the Electricity Council and the Electricity Boards in England and Wales with £4,754,400,000 in 1970. This ranks third in the western world to Standard Oil and General Motors.

The manufacturing company with the greatest net assets is Imperial Chemical Industries, Ltd., with £1,716,000,000, subsequent to its take-over of Atlas Chemical Industries Inc., in April 1971. Its staff and payroll then totalled 202,000. The company, which has 350 U.K. and overseas subsidiaries, was formed on 7 Dec. 1926 by the merger of four concerns—British Dyestuffs Corporation Ltd.; Brunner, Mond & Co. Ltd.; Nobel Industries Ltd. and United Alkali Co. Ltd. The first chairman was Sir Alfred Moritz Mond (1868–1930), later the 1st Lord Melchett.

The net assets of The "Shell" Transport and Trading Co. Ltd., at 31 Dec. 1970, were valued at £1,486,467,941. Of this, £1,480,377,600 represented a 40 per cent. holding of the net assets of the Royal Dutch/Shell Group, which stands at £3,700,944,000. Group companies have 184,000 employees. "Shell" Transport was formed in 1897 by Marcus Samuel (1853–1927), later the 1st Viscount Bearsted.

Greatest sales The first company to surpass the $1 billion (U.S.) mark in annual sales was the United States Steel Corporation in 1917. Now there are more than 120 billion dollar corporations in the world. The list is headed by General Motors (see Motor car manufacturer) with sales in 1970 of $18,752,353,515 (£7,813 million). Measured in terms of sales, there were in 1970, 42 U.S., 7 U.K. and 10 other European industrial companies totalling 59 with figures of more than £1,000 million.

Greatest profit and loss The greatest net profit ever made by one company in a year is $2,125,606,440 (now £885·7 million) by General

Motors Corporation of Detroit in 1965. The greatest loss ever sustained by a commercial concern in a year is $431·2 million (£179·6 million) by Penn Central Transportation Co. in 1970—a rate of $13·67 (£5·69) per second. The year 1971 however, had a better start when the 1970 January and February loss figure of $73·1 million (£30·45 million) was "surpassed" with a loss of $66·3 million (£27·62 million) for the two opening months. The top profit earner in the United Kingdom in 1970 was British Petroleum with £384·3 million and the biggest loss maker among non-bankrupt companies was £3,615,000 by the Sheffield plant manufacturers Davy-Ashmore.

ost efficient The major United Kingdom company with highest return on capital employed in 1970 was Holco Trading Company. The chairman, Mr. H. S. Schenk, of these London-based produce merchants (cocoa, rubber, etc.) reported a pre-tax profit of £447,000 on a capital employed of £498,000 thus showing a return of 89·2 per cent.

Biggest work force The greatest payroll in any civilian organization in the world is that of the United States Post Office with 726,472 on 1 July 1970. The biggest employer in the United Kingdom is the Post Office with 417,038 employees in 1970.

ADVERTISING AGENTS

The largest advertising agency in the world is J. Walter Thompson Co. Ltd., which in 1970 had total billings of $772,000,000 (£321·6 million).

Biggest advertiser The world's biggest advertiser is Unilever, the Anglo-Dutch group formed on 2 Sept. 1929 whose origins go back to 21 June 1884. The group has more than 500 companies in more than 60 countries and employs 326,600 people, mainly in the production of foods, detergents and toiletries. The advertising bill for over 1,000 branded products was £111,000,000 in 1970.

Aircraft anufacturer The world's largest aircraft manufacturer is the Boeing Company of Seattle, Washington, U.S.A. The corporation's sales totalled $3,677,073,000 (£1,532 million) in 1970, and it had about 79,100 employees and assets valued at $2,621,819,000 (£1,092 million) at 31 Dec. 1970. Cessna Aircraft Company of Wichita, Kansas, U.S.A., produced 4,229 civil (37 models) and 400 military aircraft in the year ending 31 Dec. 1970, with total sales of $227 million (£94·58 million). The company has produced more than 96,000 aircraft since Clyde Cessna's first was built in 1911. Their record year was 1965–66 with 7,922 aircraft completed.

AIRLINES

Largest The largest airline in the world is the U.S.S.R. State airline "Aeroflot", so named since 1932. This was instituted on 9 Feb. 1923, with the title of Civil Air Fleet of the Council of Ministers of the U.S.S.R., abbreviated to "Dobrolet". It operates nearly 1,300 aircraft over about 373,000 miles of routes, employs 400,000 people and carried 74,000,000 passengers in 1970 to 57 countries. The commercial airline carrying the greatest number of passengers in 1970 was United Air Lines of Chicago, Illinois, U.S.A. (formed 1931) with 28,537,000 passengers. The company had 51,679 employees and a fleet of 376 jet planes. The commercial airline serving the greatest mileage of routes is Air France, with 259,000 miles of unduplicated routes in 1971. In 1970 the company carried 6,135,000 passengers. In May 1971 the British European Airways (formed in August 1946) were operating a fleet of 103 aircraft, with 26 on order. BEA employed 27,305 staff and carried 8,400,000 passengers in 1970.

Oldest The oldest commercial airline is Koninklijke-Luchtvaart-Maatschappij N.V. (KLM) of the Netherlands, which opened its first scheduled service (Amsterdam-London) on 17 May 1920, having been established in 1919. One of the original constituents of B.O.A.C., Aircraft Transport and Travel Ltd., was founded in 1918 and merged into Imperial Airways in 1924, and one of the holding companies of S.A.S., Det Danske Luftfartselskab, was established on 29 Oct. 1918 but operated a scheduled service only between August 1920 and 1946.

Aluminium producer The world's largest producer of aluminium is Alcan Aluminium Limited, of Montréal, Québec, Canada. With its affiliated companies, the company had an output of 1,730,000 short tons (1,549,000 U.K. tons) and record sales of U.S.$1,389,000 (£579 million) in 1970. The company's principal subsidiary, the Aluminium Company of Canada, Ltd., owns the world's largest aluminium smelter, at Arvida, Québec, with a capacity of 450,000 short tons (402,000 U.K. tons) per annum.

Art auctioneering The largest and oldest firm of art auctioneers in the world is Messrs. Sotheby and Co., of New Bond Street, London founded in 1744. The turnover in 1970 was £45,211,484 including £15,981,007 turnover in their Parke-Bernet Galleries in New York City. The highest total of any single art sale has been $5,852,250 (£2,438,437) paid at Parke-Bernet on 25 Feb. 1970 for 73 impressionist and modern paintings.

Bicycle factory The 54-acre plant of Raleigh Industries Ltd. at Nottingham is the largest factory in the world producing complete bicycles. The company employs 9,865 and in 1970 made 1,504,860 bicycles and 604,000 wheeled toys.

Book shop The world's largest book shop is that of W. & G. Foyle Ltd., of London, W.C.2. First established in 1904 in a small shop in Islington, the company is now at 119–125 Charing Cross Road. The area on one site is 75,825 sq. ft. The largest single display of books in one room in the world is in the Norrington Room at Blackwell's Bookshop, Broad Street, Oxford. This subterranean adjunct was opened on 16 June 1966 and contains 160,000 volumes on 2½ miles of shelving in 10,000 square feet of selling space.

BREWERY

Largest *World* The largest single brewing plant in the world is that of Anheuser-Busch, Inc. in St. Louis, Missouri, U.S.A. This plant covers 95 acres and has a capacity of 8,900,000 U.S. barrels. In 1970 the whole company produced 22,201,811 U.S. barrels, equivalent to 15,916,531 Imperial barrels (4,584 million Imperial pints), the greatest annual volume ever produced by a brewing company.

Europe The largest brewery in Europe is the Guinness Brewery at St. James's Gate, Dublin, Ireland, which extends over 58·03 acres. The business was founded in 1759.

An aerial view of the Guinness Brewery, Park Royal, London, where the *Guinness Book of Records* was hatched in September 1954.

United Kingdom The largest brewing company in the United Kingdom is Bass-Charrington Ltd. with 9,450 public houses and hotels with full on-licences, and 1,416 off-licence premises and 124 hotels. The company has net assets of £329,680,000, a staff of 18,318 plus 38,555 on licensed premises and controls 20 breweries. Their sales figure of £343,071,000 for the year ending 30 Sept. 1970 was, however, surpassed by Allied Breweries Ltd. with £384,391,000 for the same period.

Greatest exports The largest exporter of beer, ale and stout in the world is Arthur Guinness, Son & Co. Ltd., of Dublin, Ireland. Exports of Guinness from the Republic of Ireland in 1970 were 1,135,000 Imperial barrels, which is equivalent to 1,795,886 half-pint glasses per day.

The world's largest brickworks in Bedfordshire, England

Brickworks The largest brickworks in the world is the London Brick Company plant at Stewartby, Bedford. The works, established in 1898, now cover 221 acres and produce 17,000,000 bricks and brick equivalent every week.

Building contractors The largest construction company in the United Kingdom is George Wimpey & Co., Ltd. (founded 1880), of London, who undertake building, civil, mechanical, electrical and chemical engineering work. With assets of £110,500,000 and over 32,000 employees, the turnover of work was £225,000,000 in 29 countries in 1970.

The world's largest shipbuilding dock, built by George Wimpey & Co.

Building societies The largest building society in the world is the Halifax Building Society of Halifax, Yorkshire. It was established in 1853 and had total assets of £1,995,660,839 at 31 Jan. 1971. It had 4,312 employees and 217 branches and 820 agencies. The oldest building society in the world is the Chelmsford and Essex Society, established in July 1845.

(Top) Jesse Boot, later Lord Trent, the founder of Boots Pure Drug Co. (Bottom) One of the newest of Boots' branches

Chemist shop chain The largest chain of chemist shops in the world is Boots Pure Drug Co. which has 1,636 retail branches. The firm was founded by Jesse Boot (b. Nottingham, 1850), later the 1st Baron Trent, who died in 1931.

Chemical company The world's largest chemical company is Imperial Chemical Industries Ltd. with sales, including those of Atlas Chemicals, of £1,526 million in 1970. The company, after the merger, had 202,000 employees and assets totalling £1,716 million as at 1 Jan. 1971.

Chocolate factory The world's largest chocolate factory is that built by Hershey Foods Inc. of Hershey, Pennsylvania, U.S.A., in 1905. In 1970 sales were $349,636,499 (£145,681,874) and the payroll was over 8,000 employees.

DEPARTMENT STORES

World The largest department store chain, in terms of number of stores, is J. C. Penney Company, Inc., founded in Wyoming, U.S.A., in 1902. The company operates 1,656 stores covering a gross area of 68,000,000 square feet. Its turnover was $3,756,091,636 (£1,565 million) in the 53 weeks ending 31 Jan. 1970, the fifteenth consecutive year of record sales.

United Kingdom The largest department store in the United Kingdom is Harrods Ltd. of Knightsbridge, London, S.W.1 named after Henry Charles Harrod, who opened a grocery in Knightsbridge Village in 1849. It has a total selling floor space of 19 acres, employs 5,300 people and has a total of approximately 10,000,000 transactions a year.

Most profitable The department store with the fastest-moving stock in the world is the largest of the 246 branches of Marks & Spencer Ltd. known as the Marble Arch branch at 458 Oxford Street, London, W.1. The figure of £200-worth of goods per square foot of selling space per year is believed to have become an understatement when the selling area was raised to 72,000 sq. ft. in October 1970.

Sorting "Monopoly" dollars which exceed the output of real dollars by the U.S. Treasury (see below)

Games manufacturer The largest company manufacturing games is Parker Bros. Inc. of Salem, Massachusetts, U.S.A. The company's top-selling line is the real estate game "Monopoly", acquired in 1935. More than 60,000,000 sets were sold by April 1971. The daily print of "money" is equivalent to 215,000,000 "dollars", thus exceeding the dollar output of the U.S. Treasury. The most protracted "Monopoly" session was one of 85 hours by 7 players at Didsbury College, Manchester in March 1971. The two-man record is 75½ hours by Kevin Daniel and Steve Skaggs on 25–28 March 1971 at Topeka, Kansas, U.S.A. They served 104 jail terms.

Distillery The world's largest distilling company is Distillers Corporation-Seagrams Limited of Canada. Its sales in the year ending 31 July 1970 totalled U.S.$1,437,234,000 (£598 million), of which $1,158,777,000 (£482 million) were from sales by Joseph E. Seagram & Sons, Inc. in the United States. The group employs about 15,000 people, including about 9,000 in the United States.

The largest of all Scotch whisky distilleries is Carsebridge at Alloa, Clackmannanshire, Scotland, owned by Scottish Grain Distillers Limited. This distillery is capable of producing more than 12,000,000 proof gallons per annum. The largest establishment for blending and bottling Scotch whisky is owned by John Walker & Sons Limited at Kilmarnock, Ayrshire, with a potential annual output of 120,000,000 bottles. "Johnnie Walker" is the world's largest-selling brand of Scotch whisky. The largest malt Scotch whisky distillery is the Tomatin Distillery, Inverness-shire, established at 1,028 feet above sea-level in 1897, with an annual capacity well in excess of 2 million proof gallons. The world's largest-selling brand of gin is Gordon's.

General merchandise The largest general merchandising firm in the world is Sears, Roebuck and Co. (founded by Richard W. Sears in Redwood North railway station, Minnesota in 1886) of Chicago, Illinois, U.S.A. The net sales were $9,262,161,819 (£3,859 million) in the year ending 31 Jan. 1971, when the corporation had 827 retail stores and 2,310 catalogue, retail and telephone sales offices and independent catalogue merchants, and total assets valued at $7,623,096,110 (£3,176 million).

Grocery stores The largest grocery chain in the world is The Great Atlantic and Pacific Tea Company, Inc., of New York City, N.Y., U.S.A. At 27 Feb. 1971 the company owned 4,427 stores, including more than 3,000 supermarkets. It operates 24 bakeries, two laundries for the uniforms of its 115,000 employees. The total sales, including subsidiary companies, for the 52 weeks ending 27 Feb. 1971 were $5,664 million (£2,360 million).

Hotelier Hilton form the largest luxury hotel group in the world. Hilton Hotels Corporation operates 39 hotels, with 30,809 rooms, in the continental U.S.A.; Hilton International Co. operates 51 hotels in 33 countries (48 cities), with 16,589 rooms. In 1969, Hilton Hotels Corporation had an operating revenue of more than $210,000,000 (£87·5 million) and 20,000 employees. Hilton International Co. had an operating revenue of $190,785,400 and 20,000 employees. The original corporation was founded by Conrad Nicholson Hilton (b. 25 Dec. 1887) who started in 1919 with the Mobley Hotel in Cisco, Texas. Hilton International Co. began operations in 1949 as a subsidiary of Hilton Hotels Corporation and was spun off from the corporation as a separate company to operate independently in December 1964. In May 1967, Hilton International Co. became a wholly-owned subsidiary of Trans World Airlines Inc.

The top revenue-earning hotel business is Holiday Inns Inc. with a 1969 revenue of $541,301,234 (£225·5 million).

INSURANCE COMPANIES

World The company with the highest volume of insurance in force in the world is the Metropolitan Life Insurance Company of 1 Madison Avenue, New York City, N.Y., U.S.A. The company had total assets of $27,865,762,284 at 1 Jan. 1971. The life assurance in force amounted to $167,283,940,423 (£69,701 million), which amount is far greater than the United Kingdom's National Debt. It insured 47,650,000 people.

The New York City headquarters of the world's largest insurance company

United Kingdom The largest insurance company in the United Kingdom is the Prudential Assurance Co. Ltd. At 1 Jan. 1971 the total funds were £2,306,025,000 and the total amount assured was £8,863,711,874.

Largest life policy The largest life assurance policy ever written was one of $10,800,000 (£4,500,000) reported on 18 March 1969 taken out by Mr. Michael Davis, 34 from Hollywood, California, U.S.A., chairman of NEBA International Inc., a chain of sandwich stands. His annual premium is $92,200 (£38,000).

Marine insurance The greatest insured value of any ship lost has been the $16·5 million (then £5·89 million) on the *Torrey Canyon.* The greatest loss withstood on the London market was $10·8 million (£4·5 million) on the *Marpessa* though the loss on the *Andrea Doria* in 1956 was £3·93 million (then $11·0 million). The cost of the repairs to the U.S.S. *Guittaro*, the nuclear submarine flooded on 15 May 1969 while fitting out at Mare Island, San Francisco, cost $25 million (£10·42 million). The Cunard liner QE2 was insured (builder's value only) on its sea trials in 1969 for £25·5 million ($61·2 million).

Highest pay-out The highest pay-out on a single life has been some $14 million (nearly £6 million) to Mrs. Linda Mullendore, wife of an Oklahoma rancher, reported on 14 Nov. 1970. Her murdered husband had paid $300,000 in premiums in 1969.

Mineral water The world's largest mineral water firm is Source Perrier, near Nîmes, France with an annual production of more than 1,400,000,000 bottles, of which more than 330,000,000 come from the single spring near Nîmes. The net profits for 1970 were 20,323,019·31 francs (£1,524,607). The French drink 36 litres (63·3 pints) of mineral water per person per year.

MOTOR CAR MANUFACTURER

The largest manufacturing company in the world is General Motors Corporation of Detroit, Michigan, U.S.A. During its peak year of 1969 world-wide sales totalled $24,295,141,357 (now £10,122 million), including 7,159,526 cars and trucks. Its assets at 31 Dec. 1970 were valued at $14,174,359,767 (£5,905 million). Its total 1970 payroll was $6,259,840,549 (£2,608 million) to an average of 695,796 employees. The greatest total of dividends ever paid for one year was $1,509,740,939 (£629 million) by General Motors for 1965.

Production in the United Kingdom in 1969 totalled 1,717,073 cars and 465,720 commercial vehicles. The largest manufacturer was the British Leyland Motor Corporation, with 830,874 cars and 186,732 commercial vehicles. The company is the United Kingdom's largest exporter with direct exports valued at £322 million in 1969. The Austin-Morris 1100/1300 was the best-selling car in 1969/70 with U.K. sales of 133,036 units representing 12·8 per cent. of that market.

An aerial view of the world's largest single automotive plant—the Volkswagen works, Wolfsburg, West Germany

Largest plant The largest single automobile plant in the world is the Volkswagenwerk, Wolfsburg, West Germany, with more than 61,000 employees turning out up to 5,000 cars daily. The surface area of the factory buildings is 291½ acres and that of the whole plant 1,730 acres with 43½ miles of rail sidings.

Oil company refineries The world's largest oil company is the Standard Oil Company (New Jersey), with 143,000 employees and assets valued at $19,241,784,000 (£8,017 million) on 1 Jan. 1971. The world's largest refinery is the Pernis refinery in the Netherlands, operated by the Royal Dutch/Shell Group of companies with a capacity of 25,000,000 long tons. The largest oil refinery in the United Kingdom is the Esso Refinery at Fawley, Hampshire. Opened in 1921 and much expanded in 1951, it has a capacity of 16,500,000 tons per year. The total investment on the 1,300-acre site is more than £120,000,000.

Paper mills The world's largest paper mill is that established in 1936 by the Union Camp Corporation at Savannah, Georgia, U.S.A., with an output of 903,124 short tons (806,361 long tons). The largest paper mill in the United Kingdom is the Bowater Paper Corporation Ltd.'s Kemsley Mill with an output of 4,600 tons of newsprint and 1,700 tons of fluting medium per week.

Public relations The world's largest public relations firm is Hill and Knowlton, Inc. of 150 East 42nd Street, New York City, N.Y., U.S.A. The firm employs a full-time staff of more than 325 and also maintains offices of wholly-owned subsidiary companies in Brussels, Frankfurt, Geneva, London, Paris, Madrid, Milan, Rome and Tōkyō.

Publishing The world's largest mass media publishing enterprise is the International Publishing Corporation Ltd. of London with 15 newspapers and 229 periodicals, 30,600 employees and a turnover of £156,022,000 in 1970. On 23 Jan. 1970 I.P.C. merged with Reed Paper Group.

Restaurateurs The largest restaurant chain in the world is that operated by F. W. Woolworth and Co. with 2,070 throughout six countries. The largest restaurateurs in the United Kingdom are J. Lyons & Co. Ltd. (incorporated in 1894). The company has a total of 160 teashops, four Corner Houses, and special restaurants and staff canteens, in which about 280,000,000 meals are served every year. Some of the 35,000 staff produce 40 miles of Swiss roll every day, 12,500,000 pieces of chocolate and sugar confectionery every week, 10,000,000 cakes weekly and 30,000,000 portions of ice cream in a peak summer week.

BANQUET

Greatest *World Outdoors* The greatest banquet ever staged was that by President Loubet, President of France, in the gardens of the Tuileries, Paris, on 22 Sept. 1900. He invited every one of the 22,000 mayors in France and their deputies. With the Gallic *penchant* for round numbers, the event has always been referred to as "le banquet des 100,000 maires".

Indoors The largest banquet ever held has been one for 10,158 at a $15 a plate dinner in support of Mayor Richard J. Daley of Chicago at McCormick Place Convention Hall on the Lake on 3 March 1971.

Great Britain Britain's largest banquet was one catered for by J. Lyons & Co. Ltd., at Olympia, London, on 8 Aug. 1925. A total of 8,000 guests were seated at 5 miles of tables, served by 1,360 waitresses, supported by 700 cooks and porters. The occasion was a War Memorial fund-raising effort by Freemasons. Of the 86,000 glasses and plates used, 3,500 were broken. The world's largest tea party was one for 25,000 on the Gaslight Coke Company's annual sports day at East Ham, Greater London, in 1939, with Lyons again catering.

Shipbuilding In 1970 there were 21,689,513 gross tons of ships, excluding sailing ships, barges and vessels of less than 100 tons, launched throughout the world, excluding the U.S.S.R. and China (mainland). Japan launched 10,475,804 gross tons (48·3 per cent. of the world total), the greatest tonnage launched in peacetime by any single country. The United Kingdom ranked fourth, behind also Sweden and West Germany, with 1,237,134 gross tons.

The world's leading shipbuilding firm in 1970 was the Ishikawajima-Harima Co. of Japan, which launched 50 merchant ships of 2,035,313 gross tons from five shipyards.

Physically the largest shipyard in the United Kingdom is Harland and Wolff Ltd. of Queen's Island, Belfast, which covers some 250 acres. The largest shipyard in tonnage building is the Swan Hunter Group with 19 ships launched in 1970 of 495,000 gross tons.

Shipping line The largest shipping group in the world is that owned by the Peninsular and Oriental Steam Navigation Company, London. The company had total net assets of £301,600,000 at 30 Sept. 1969. The company was founded in 1837 by Willcox and Anderson, and among the principal members of the group are 23 shipping and shipowning companies, 20 transport and forwarding companies and two marine engineering companies. The group's fleet comprises 241 ships, including 185 cargo ships, 22 passenger ships and 6 ferries of 1,740,000 gross tons, 19 tankers and 9 bulk carriers of 1,950,000 deadweight tons. British Petroleum, by 1970, had increased its fleet of tankers to 4,278,000 d.w.t.

The world's largest shoe shop in Oxford Street, London, England

Shoe shop The largest shoe shop in the world is that of Lilley & Skinner, Ltd. at 356/360 Oxford Street, London, W.1. The shop has a floor area of 76,000 square feet, spread over four floors. With a total staff of more than 350 people it offers, in ten departments, a choice of 250,000 pairs of shoes. Every week, on average, over 45,000 people visit this store.

LARGEST SHOPPING CENTRE

The world's largest shopping centre is the Yorkdale Shopping Centre, six miles from the centre of Toronto, Canada. It was built on a 72-acre site with an additional 50 acres for a 6,750 car parking lot. A total of 125 stores and services provide 1,340,000 square feet (30·7 acres) of selling space for 25,000,000 customers per year. It was opened in February 1964 and the enclosed 1,000-foot-long mall is maintained at a temperature of 72° F.

Largest store The world's largest store is R. H. Macy & Co. Inc. at Broadway and 34th Street, New York City, N.Y., U.S.A. It has a floor space of 46·2 acres, and 11,000 employees who handle 400,000 items. Macy's have an average of 150,000 customers a day who make 4,500,000 transactions a year. The sales of the company and its subsidiaries reached a record $907,029,000 (£378 million) in 1969/70. Mr. Rowland Hussey Macy's sales on his first day at his fancy goods store on 6th Avenue, on 27 Oct. 1858, were recorded as $11·06 (now £4·61).

Largest supermarket *U.K.* The largest supermarket building in the United Kingdom is the Woolco One-Stop Shopping Centre opened in Bournemouth, Hampshire on 29 Oct. 1968. Currently it has an area of 114,000 square feet and parking space for 1,250 cars.

Soft drinks The world's top-selling soft drink is "Coca-Cola" with over 100,000,000 bottles per day in mid-1971 in 135 countries. "Coke" was invented by Dr. John S. Pemberton of Atlanta, Georgia in 1886 and the Coca-Cola company was formed in 1892. The fastest bottling line is the plant at Inagi, Tōkyō, Japan, which can fill, crown and pack bottles of Coca-Cola at the rate of 72,000 per hour.

STEEL COMPANY

The world's largest steel company is the United States Steel Company, with sales of $4,825,137,559 (£2,010 million) in 1969. The company had an average of 204,723 employees in 1969, and net assets valued at $5,228,639,713 (£2,179 million) at 31 Dec. 1969.

Largest steelworks *World* The largest steelworks in the world is the Bethlehem Steel Corporation's plant at Sparrow's Point, Maryland, U.S.A. with an annual ingot steel capacity of more than 9,000,000 short tons or 8,030,000 long tons.

United Kingdom The largest single British plant is the Port Talbot works of the British Steel Corporation, Glamorganshire, which stretch over a distance of 4½ miles, with an area of 2,600 acres. The total number employed at this plant is 13,500 and its capacity is 3,250,000 tons.

Tobacco company The world's largest tobacco company is the British-American Tobacco Company Ltd. (founded 1902), of London. The group's net assets were £790,200,000 at 30 Sept. 1970. The 1969/70 sales were £1,556,030,000. The group has more than 140 factories and 120,000 employees.

Toy manufacturer The world's largest toy manufacturer is Mattel Inc. of Hawthorne, Los Angeles, U.S.A. founded in 1945. Its total sales in 1970 were $358,000,000 (£149·1 million).

Toy shop *World* The world's biggest toy store is F.A.O. Schwarz, 745 Fifth Avenue at 58th Street, New York City, N.Y., U.S.A. with 50,000 square feet on three floors. Schwarz have 10 branch stores with a further 100,000 square feet.

United Kingdom Britain's biggest toy shop is that of Hamley Brothers, Ltd., founded in 1760 in Holborn and removed to Regent Street, London, W.1, in 1901. It has selling space of 20,000 square feet on 8 floors and up to 250 employees during the Christmas season.

Fisheries The highest recorded catch of fish was 59,540,000 tons in 1967. The highest proportion of the world catch was that of Peru, with 16·69 per cent. (9,940,000 tons, mostly anchoveta). The United Kingdom's highest figure was 1,187,000 tons in 1948. The world's largest fishmongers are MacFisheries, a subsidiary of Unilever Ltd., with 360 retail outlets as at April 1970.

Landowners The world's largest landowner is the United States Government, with a holding of 765,291,000 acres (1,185,787 square miles), including 529,000 acres outside the U.S. at 30 June 1966. The total value was $69,357,000,000 (£28,856 million). The United Kingdom's greatest ever private landowner was the 3rd

Duke of Sutherland, George Granville Sutherland-Leveson-Gower, K.G. (1828–92), who owned 1,358,000 acres in 1883. Currently the largest landowner in Great Britain is the Forestry Commission (instituted 1919) with more than 2,890,000 acres. The longest tenure is that by St. Paul's Cathedral of land at Tillingham, Essex, given by King Ethelbert before A.D. 616. Currently the landowner with the largest acreage is the 8th Duke of Buccleuch (b. 1894) with 336,000 acres.

LAND VALUES

Highest Currently the most expensive land in the world is that in the City of London. Prime freehold attained £300 per square foot in mid-1969. The 600-foot National Westminster Bank on a 2¼-acre site off Bishopsgate will become the world's highest valued building. At rents of £10 per square foot on 500,000 net square feet and on 18 years purchase, it will, by 1972, be worth £90 million. The value of the whole site of 6½ acres will be £225,000,000. On 1 Feb. 1926 a parcel of land of 1,275 square feet was bought by the One Wall Street Realty Corporation for $1,000 (then £206) per square foot. In February 1964 a woman paid $510 (£212·50) for a triangular piece of land measuring 3 inches by 6½ inches by 5¾ inches at a tax lien auction in North Hollywood, California, U.S.A.—equivalent to $365,182,470 (£152·1 million) per acre. The real estate value per square metre of the four topmost French vineyards has not been recently estimated.

Lowest The historic example of low land values is the Alaska Purchase of 30 March 1867, when William Henry Seward (1801–72), the United States Secretary of State, agreed that the U.S. should buy the whole territory from the Russian Government of Czar Alexander II for $7,200,000 (now £3,000,000), equivalent to 1·9 cents per acre. When Willem Verhulst bought Manhattan Island, New York, *ante* June in 1626, by paying the Brooklyn Indians (Canarsees) with trinkets and cloth valued at 60 guilders (equivalent to $39 or £16·25), he was buying land now worth up to $425 (£177) per square foot for 0·2 of a cent per acre—a capital appreciation of 9,000 million-fold.

Greatest auction The greatest ever auction was that at Anchorage, Alaska on 11 Sept. 1969 for 179 tracts totalling 450,858 acres of the oil-bearing North Slope, Alaska. An all-time record bid of $72,277,133 for a 2,560 acre lease was made by the Amerada Hess Corporation–Getty Oil consortium. This £30,115,472 bid indicated a price of $28,233 (£11,763) per acre.

Highest rent The highest recorded rental is one of £10 per square foot for office accommodation near the Guildhall, City of London, in 1970.

Companies The number of companies on the register in Great Britain at 1 Jan. 1969 was 553,282 of which 16,657 were public and the balance private companies.

Most directorships The world record for directorships was set in September 1959 by Harry O. Jasper, a London real estate financier, with 451. If he had attended all their Annual General Meetings this would have involved him, in normal office hours, in an A.G.M. every 4 hours 33 minutes.

STOCK EXCHANGES

The oldest Stock Exchange in the world is that at Amsterdam, in the Netherlands, founded in 1602. There were 121 throughout the world as of 1 May 1969.

Most markings The highest number of markings received in one day on the London Stock Exchange is 32,655 after the 1959 General Election on 14 Oct. 1959. The record for a year is 4,396,175 "marks" in the year ending 31 March 1960. There were 9,356 securities (gilt-edged 1,228, company 8,128) quoted on 31 March 1969. Their total nominal value was £46,528 million (gilt-edged £25,805 million, company £20,723 million) and their market value was £131,679 million (gilt-edged £18,459 million, company £113,220 million).

The greatest overall daily movement occurred on 24 Feb. 1955, when the market value of United Kingdom Ordinary shares fell by about £200,000,000 or 3·8 per cent.

The highest figure of *The Financial Times* Industrial Ordinary share index (1 July 1935=100) was 521·9 on 19 Sept. 1968. The lowest figure was 49·4 in 1940. The greatest rise in a day has been 20·5 points to 352·2 on Budget Day on 30 March 1971.

Highest and lowest par values The highest denomination of any share quoted on the London Stock Exchange is £100 for preference shares in Baring Brothers & Co. Ltd., the bankers. The lowest unit of quotation is one penny, in the case of the stock of City of San Paulo Improvements and Freehold Land Co. Ltd. and the capital shares in the Acorn Securities Co., Ltd.

U.S. records The highest index figure on the Dow Jones average (instituted 8 Oct. 1896) of selected industrial stocks at the close of a day's trading was 995·15 on 9 Feb. 1966, when the average of the daily "highs" of the 30 component stocks was 1,001·11. The old record trading volume in a day on the New York Stock Exchange of 16,410,030 shares on 29 Oct. 1929, the "Black Tuesday" of the famous "crash" was unsurpassed until April 1968. The Dow Jones industrial average, which had reached 381·17 on 3 Sept. 1929, plunged 48·31 points in the day, on its way to the Depression's lowest point of 41·22 on 8 July 1932. The total lost in security values was $125,000 million (now £52,083 million). World trade slumped 57 per cent. from 1929 to 1936. The greatest paper loss in a year was $55,925 million (£23,302 million) in 1957. The record daily increase of 28·40 points on 30 Oct. 1929 was beaten on 27 May 1970, when the index increased 32·04 points to 663·20. The day's trading record is now 28,250,000 shares on 9 Feb. 1971. The largest deal on record was for two 2,000,000 blocks of Greyhound shares at $20 each sold to Goldman Sachs and Saloman Brothers.

Largest issue The largest security offering in history was one of $1,200,000,000 (then £428·57 million) in American Telephone and Telegraph Company stock in 1964. The largest offering on the London Stock Exchange by a United Kingdom company was the £40 million of loan stock by I.C.I. in December 1970.

Greatest appreciation It is almost impossible to state categorically which shares have enjoyed the greatest appreciation in value. Spectacular "growth stocks" include the International Business Machines Corporation (IBM), in which 100 shares, costing $5,250 (now £2,187) in July 1932, grew to 13,472 shares with a market value of $4,230,000 (£1,762,500) on 28 March 1969. In addition $233,100 were paid in dividends. The greatest aggregate market value of any corporation is $35·5 billion, assuming a closing price of $314 multiplied by the 113,116,613 shares extant on 28 March 1969. In the United Kingdom an investment of £100 in Drage's Ltd. in 1951 would have been realizable at £108,000 in 1962. The same amount invested in 1947 in the late Mr. Jack Cotton's Mansion House Chambers Co. would have been worth £200,000 in City Centre Properties stock by 1964.

Largest investment house The largest investment company in the world, and also once the world's largest partnership (124 partners, but now 1,082 stockholders), is Merrill Lynch, Pierce, Fenner & Smith, Inc. (founded 6 Jan. 1914) of 70 Pine Street, New York City, N.Y., U.S.A. It has 16,000 employees, 176 offices and 1,090,000 separate accounts, for whom $18,000 million (£5,416 million) in securities have been held. The firm is referred to in United States stock exchange circles as "We" or "We, the people" or "The Thundering Herd". The company's assets totalled $1,856,557,035 at 30 Sept. 1970.

Largest bank The International Bank for Reconstruction and Development (founded 27 Dec. 1945), the United Nations

"World Bank" at 1818 H Street N.W., Washington, D.C., U.S.A., has an authorized share capital of $27,000 million (£11,250 million). There were 115 members with a subscribed capital of $23,457,600,000 (£9,774 million) at 1 Jan. 1971. The International Monetary Fund in Washington, D.C., U.S.A. has 117 members with total quotas of $28,433,000,000 (£11,847 million) at 30 April 1971. The private bank with the greatest deposits is the Bank of America National Trust and Savings Association, of San Francisco, California, U.S.A., with $22,171,463,000 at 31 Dec. 1969. Its total resources as at 31 Dec. 1970 were $29,739 million. Barclays Bank (with Barclays D.C.O. and other subsidiary companies) had more than 5,000 branches in 40 countries (over 3,200 in the United Kingdom) in December 1970. Deposits totalled £6,040,457,000 and assets £7,150,117,000 as at 31 Dec. 1970. The largest bank in the United Kingdom is the National Westminster with total assets of £5,392,261,000 and 3,600 branches as at 1 Jan. 1971.

Largest bank building The largest bank building in the world is the 813-foot-tall Chase Manhattan Building, completed in May 1961 in New York City, N.Y., U.S.A. It has 64 storeys and contains the largest bank vault in the world, measuring 350 feet × 100 feet × 8 feet and weighing 879 tons. Its six doors weigh up to 40 tons apiece but each can be closed by the pressure of a forefinger. The 60-storey First National Bank of Chicago, completed in 1969, is 850 feet tall.

2. MANUFACTURED ARTICLES

Guinness Superlatives Ltd. publishes fine art books in colour on English and Irish Glass; Pottery and Porcelain; English Furniture; Antique Firearms; Edged Weapons, Uniforms and British Gallantry Decorations, obtainable on order from the publishers or from any good bookshop.

Antique *Largest* The largest antique ever sold has been London Bridge in March 1968. The sale was made by Mr. Ivan F. Luckin of the Court of Common Council of the Corporation of London to the McCulloch Corporation of Los Angeles, California, U.S.A. for $2,460,000 (£1,029,000). The 10,000 tons of elevational stonework is being re-assembled at Lake Havasu City, Arizona for opening in 1971.

Armour The highest price paid for a suit of armour is £25,000, paid in 1924 for the Pembroke suit of armour, made at Greenwich in the 16th century, of the Earl of Pembroke.

BEDS

Largest In Bruges, Belgium, Philip, Duke of Burgundy had a bed 12½ feet wide and 19 feet long erected for the perfunctory *coucher officiel* ceremony with Princess Isabella of Portugal in 1430. The largest bed in Great Britain is the Great Bed of Ware, dating from *c.* 1580, from the Crown Inn, Ware, Hertfordshire, now preserved in the Victoria and Albert Museum, London. It is 10 feet 8½ inches wide, 11 feet 1 inch long and 8 feet 9 inches tall. The largest standard bed currently marketed in the United Kingdom is the London Bedding Centre's "King Size" bed, 7 feet wide by 7 feet long, with 1,600 springs, sold for £170.

Heaviest The world's most massive beds are waterbeds which first became a vogue in California, U.S.A. in 1970 when merchandised by Michael V. Zamoro, 53. When filled, king-sized versions measuring 8 feet square will weigh more than 14 cwt. (1,568 lb.) and are more advisably used on the ground floor.

Largest candle The largest candle made in Britain was one made at St. Michael's College, Tenbury Wells, Shropshire on 24 Jan. 1971. It stood 15 feet 8 inches tall and weighed 3 cwt. (336 lb.) when it was lit on Candlemas Day (2 Feb. 1971) to burn until Candlemas 1972.

The 15-foot 8-inch-tall candle built in Shropshire, England

CARPETS AND RUGS

Earliest The earliest carpet known is a white bordered black hair pelt from Pazyryk, U.S.S.R. dated to the 5th century B.C. now preserved in Leningrad. The earliest known in Britain were some depicted at the court of Edward IV *c.* 1480.

Largest Of ancient carpets the largest on record was the gold-enriched silk carpet of Hashim (dated A.D. 743) of the Abbasid caliphate in Baghdad, Iraq. It is reputed to have measured 180 feet by 300 feet.

The world's largest carpet now consists of 88,000 square feet (over two acres) of maroon carpeting in the Coliseum exhibition hall, Columbus Circle, New York City, N.Y., U.S.A. This was first used for the International Automobile Show on 28 April 1956.

Most expensive The most magnificent carpet ever made was the Spring carpet of Khusraw made for the audience hall of the Sassanian palace at Ctesiphon, Iraq. It was about 7,000 square feet of silk, gold thread and encrusted with emeralds. It was cut up as booty by a Persian army in A.D. 635 and from the known realization value of the pieces must have had an original value of some £80,000,000.

It was reported in March 1968 that a 16th century Persian silk hunting carpet was sold "recently" to an undisclosed U.S. museum by a member of the Rothschild family for "about $600,000" (£205,000).

Most finely woven The most finely woven carpet known is one with more than 2,490 knots per square inch from a fragment of an Imperial Mughal prayer carpet of the 17th century now in the Altman collections in the Metropolitan Museum of Art, New York City.

Christmas present *Most expensive* The most expensive Christmas present listed in any store's catalogue has been in the 1970 Nieman-Marcus, Dallas, Texas offering of a "Noah's Ark" for $588,247 (£245,102). This gift boat sleeps eight passengers and accommodates 92 mammals, 10 reptiles, 26 birds, 14 species of freshwater fish, 38 insects and a veterinarian, also a French chef and maid, an English valet and librarian, and a Park Avenue physician. The present is intended "for the pessimist".

CIGARS

Largest The largest cigar ever made is one 170 centimetres (5 feet 7 inches) long and 67 centimetres ($26\frac{3}{8}$ inches) in circumference, put into the Bünde Tobacco and Cigar Museum, Germany, in 1936. It would theoretically take an estimated 600 hours to smoke. The largest standard cigar in the world is the $9\frac{3}{4}$-inch-long "Partagas Visible Immensas". The Partagas factory in Havana, Cuba, manufactures special gift cigars 50 centimetres (19·7 inches) long, which retail in Europe for more than £5 each.

Most expensive The world's most expensive regular cigar has been the "Partagas Visible Immensas". This used to be retailed in the United States for $7·50 (£3·$12\frac{1}{2}$). The most expensive cigars imported into Britain, where the duty is £5·$48\frac{1}{2}$ per lb., are the Montecristo 'A', which normally retail for £1·$36\frac{1}{2}$ each.

The world's heaviest smoker in action

Most voracious cigar smoker The only man to master the esoteric art of smoking 12 full-sized cigars simultaneously is Mr. Simon Argevitch of Oakland, California, U.S.A.

CIGARETTES

Consumption The heaviest smokers in the world are the people of the United States, where about 542,000 million cigarettes (an average of nearly 4,000 per adult) were consumed at a cost of nearly $10,000 million (£4,166 million) in 1970. The peak consumption in the United Kingdom was 2,960 cigarettes per adult in 1969. The peak volume was 243,100,000 lb. in 1961, compared with about 216,000,000 lb. in 1969, when 125,000 million cigarettes were sold.

In the United Kingdom 68·6 per cent. of adult men and 43·2 per cent. of adult women smoke. Nicotine releases acetylcholine in the brain, so reducing tension and increasing resolve. It has thus been described as an anodyne to civilization.

Most expensive The most expensive cigarettes in the world are the gold-tipped "Royal Dragoons", made by Simon Arzt of Cairo, in the United Arab Republic (formerly Egypt). They have been retailed in the United Kingdom for more than 5p each.

Most popular The world's most popular cigarette is "Winston", a filter cigarette made by the R. J. Reynolds Tobacco Co., which sold 82,000 million of them in 1969. The largest selling British cigarette is W.D. & H.O. Wills' "Embassy Filter", which was introduced in the medium size class in August 1962, with coupons. They are estimated to have attained nearly 24 per cent. of the market in 1968.

Longest and shortest The longest cigarettes ever marketed were "Head Plays", each 11 inches long and sold in packets of five in the United States in about 1930, to save tax. The shortest were "Lilliput" cigarettes, each $1\frac{1}{4}$ inches long, made in Great Britain in 1956.

Earliest abstention The earliest recorded case of a man giving up smoking was on 5 April 1679 when Johan Kastu, Sheriff of Turku, Finland wrote in his diary "I quit smoking tobacco". He died one month later.

Largest collection The world's largest collection of cigarettes is that of Robert E. Kaufman, M.D., of 950 Park Avenue, New York City 28, N.Y., U.S.A. In May 1970 he had 6,300 different kinds of cigarettes from 158 countries. The oldest brand represented is "Lone Jack", made in the U.S.A. in *c.* 1885. Both the longest and shortest (see above) are represented.

Cigarette packets The world's largest collection of cigarette packets is that of Niels Ventegodt of Copenhagen, Denmark. He had 42,590 different packets from 194 countries by April 1970. The countries supplying the largest numbers were the United Kingdom (5,692) and the United States (3,592). The earliest is the Finnish "Petit Canon" packet for 25, made by Tollander & Klärich in 1860. The rarest is the Latvian 700-year-anniversary (1201–1901) Riga packet, believed to be unique.

Cigarette cards The earliest known and most valuable cigarette card is that bearing the portrait of the Marquess of Lorne published in the United States *c.* 1879. The only known specimen is in the Metropolitan Museum of Art, New York City. The earliest British example appeared in 1883 in the form of a calendar issued by Allen & Ginter, of Richmond, Virginia, trading from Holborn Viaduct, London. The largest known collection is that of Mr. Edward Wharton-Tigar (b. 1913) of London with a collection of more than 500,000 cigarette and trade cards in about 25,000 sets.

Largest curtain The world's largest curtain is that covering Jan Styka's painting *The Crucifixion* at Forest Lawn Memorial Park, Glendale, California, U.S.A. It is made of velvet, measures 195 feet wide and 45 feet long and weighs 3,500 lb. (1·56 tons).

Dinner service The highest price ever paid for a silver dinner service is £207,000 for the Berkeley Louis XV Service of 168 pieces, made by Jacques Roettiers between 1736 and 1738, sold at the salerooms of Sotheby & Co., London, in June 1960.

FABRICS

Most expensive The most expensive fabric obtainable is an evening wear fabric sequinned with a peacock feather, designed by Mr. Alan Hershman of London costing £105 per yard (36 inches in width) with 194,400 sequins per yard. Re-embroidered multi-coloured guipure lace in widths of only 15 inches retail for £40 per yard.

Finest cloth The finest of all cloths is Shahtoosh (or Shatusa), a brown-grey wool from the throats of Indian goats. It is sold by Neiman-Marcus of Dallas, Texas, U.S.A., at $18·50 (£7·71) per square foot and is both more expensive and finer than Vicuña. A simple hostess gown in Shahtoosh costs up to $5,000 (£2,083).

LARGEST FIREWORK

The most powerful firework obtainable is the Bouquet of Chrysanthemums *hanabi*, marketed by the Marutamaya Ogatsu Fireworks Co. Ltd., of Tōkyō, Japan.

It is fired to a height of over 3,000 feet from a 36-inch calibre mortar. Their chrysanthemum and peony flower shells produce a spherical flower with "twice-thrice changing colours", 2,000 feet in diameter. The largest firework produced in Britain is one fired from Brock's 25-inch, 22 cwt. mortar. The shell weighs 200 lb. and is 6½ feet in circumference and was first used in Lisbon in 1886. The last firing was in London on 8 June 1946 for the World War II Victory Celebration which was the most elaborate show of aerial pyrotechny ever fired. Brock's Fireworks Ltd. of Hemel Hempstead, Hertfordshire was established before 1720.

FLAGS

Oldest The oldest national flag in the world is that of Denmark (a large white cross on a red field), known as the Dannebrog ("Danish Cloth"), dating from 1219, adopted after the Battle of Lindanissa in Estonia, now part of the U.S.S.R. The crest in the centre of the Austrian flag has its origins in the 11th century. The origins of the Iranian flag, with its sword-carrying lion and sun, are obscure but "go beyond the 12th century".

Largest The largest flag in the world is the "Stars and Stripes" displayed annually on the Woodward Avenue side of J. L. Hudson Company's store in Detroit, Michigan, U.S.A. The flag, 104 feet by 235 feet and weighing 1,500 lb., was unfurled on 14 June 1949. The 50 stars are each 5½ feet high and each stripe is 8 feet deep. The largest Union Flag (or Union Jack) was one of 11,720 square feet (144 by 80 feet) used at a military tattoo in the Olympic Stadium, West Berlin in September 1967. The largest flag *flown* from a public building in Britain is a Union Flag measuring 36 feet by 18 feet, flown on occasions from the Victoria Tower of the Palace of Westminster, London.

Largest float The largest float used in any street carnival is the 200-foot-long dragon *Sun Loon* used in Bendigo, Victoria, Australia. It has 65,000 mirror scales. Six men are needed to carry its head alone.

FURNITURE

Most expensive The highest price ever paid for a single piece of furniture is £63,000 for a Louis XVI marquetry commode by David Röntgen (1743–1807) of Germany, owned by the 6th Earl of Rosebery and sold to Linsky of New York City, N.Y., U.S.A., at the salerooms of Sotheby & Co., London, on 17 April 1964.

Oldest British The oldest surviving piece of British furniture is a three-footed tub with metal bands found at Glastonbury, Somerset, and dating from between 300 and 150 B.C.

Gold plate The world's highest auction price for a single piece of gold plate is £40,000 for a 20 oz. 4 dwt. George II teapot made by James Ker for the King's Plate horserace for 100 guineas at Leith, Scotland in 1736. The sale was by Christie's of London on 13 Dec. 1967 to a dealer from Boston, Massachusetts, U.S.A.

Hat *Most expensive* The highest price ever paid for a hat is 165,570 francs (inc. tax) (£14,032) by Moët et Chandon at an auction by Maîtres Liery, Rheims et Laurin on 23 April 1970 for one last worn by Emperor Napoleon I (1769–1821) on 1 Jan. 1815.

Jade The highest price paid for jade has been £42,000 for a Chinese spinach green screen emblematic of the Four Seasons sold by auction at Christie's, London on 16 July 1963.

Largest jig-saw The largest jig-saw ever made is believed to be one of 10,400 pieces, measuring 15 feet by 10 feet, made in 1954, at the special request of a man in Texas, U.S.A., by Ponda Puzzle Products, Ltd., of St. Leonard's-on-Sea, Sussex.

Matchbox labels The oldest match label is that of John Walker, Stockton-on-Tees, County Durham, England in 1827. Collectors of labels are phillumenists, of bookmatch covers philliberumenists and of matchboxes cumyxaphists. The world's longest and perhaps dullest set is one in the U.S.S.R. comprising 600 variations on interior views of the Moscow Metro.

Sheerest nylon The lowest denier nylon yarn ever produced is the 6-denier used for stockings exhibited at the Nylon Fair in London in February 1956. The sheerest stockings normally available are 9 denier. An indication of the thinness is that a hair from the average human head is about 50 denier.

Paperweight The highest price ever paid for a paperweight is £8,500 at Sotheby & Co., London on 16 March 1970 for a Clichy lily-of-the-valley weight.

The penknife with most blades

Penknife *Most blades* The penknife with the greatest number of blades is the Year Knife made by the world's oldest firm of cutlers, Joseph Rodgers & Sons Ltd., of Sheffield, England, whose trade mark was granted in 1682. The knife was built in 1822 with 1,822 blades but now has 1,971 to match the year of the Christian era until A.D. 2000 beyond which there will be no further space. It was acquired by Britain's largest hand tool manufacturers, Stanley Works (Great Britain) Ltd. of Sheffield, in 1970.

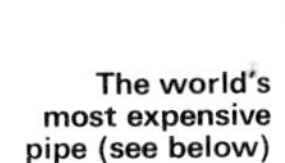

The world's most expensive pipe (see below)

Pipe *Most expensive* The most expensive smoker's pipe is the "H" standard, top quality straight grained briar pipe retailed by Alfred Dunhill Ltd. of Duke Street, London, S.W.1 at £250.

Longest In the Braunschweig Museum, Germany, there is exhibited an outsize late 19th century pipe, 15 feet in length, the bowl of which can accommodate 3 lb. of tobacco.

The world champion pieces of porcelain (left) and pottery (right) (see below)

Porcelain and pottery The highest price ever paid for a single piece of porcelain is £44,000 at auction at the salerooms of Sotheby & Co., London on 2 March 1971 for an early 15th century blue and white stem cup $8\frac{3}{8}$ inches high bearing the four-character mark of Emperor Hsüan Tê. It is the only undamaged example known. The highest price paid for any ceramic object is £94,500 for a 13th century Sung Dynasty Chinese octagonal flower vase, $8\frac{1}{4}$ inches high, sold at auction in the salerooms of Christie's on 12 Oct. 1970. This vase was previously sold in 1953 for only £2,400, thus exhibiting a *daily* rate of appreciation of £14·60.

Pistols *Most expensive* The highest price ever paid for antique firearms is £43,050 by Frank Partridge & Sons, Bond Street, London for a garniture of a flintlock rifle and a pair of pistols, inlaid with gold and silver, and accessories made between 1798 and 1809 by Nicolas Boutet of Versailles, gunsmith to Emperor Napoleon I. The sale was at Christie, Manson and Woods Ltd. of London on 8 July 1970.

Largest rope The largest rope ever made was a coir fibre launching rope with a circumference of 47 inches, made in 1858 for the British liner *Great Eastern* by John and Edwin Wright of Birmingham. It consisted of four strands, each of 3,780 yarns.

Ship in bottle The smallest ship in a bottle built is a sailing ship model $\frac{1}{16}$th of an inch long placed inside a minute computer bulb by Mr. Albert Stannard of Leyton, London E.17.

The smallest "ship in a bottle" (see above)

SHOES

Most expensive The most expensive standard shoes obtainable are the alligator shawl-tongued custom golf shoe, Style 5591, made by Brockton Footwear Inc. of Massachusetts, U.S.A., which retail for $195 (£81·25) per pair.

Largest Excluding cases of elephantiasis, the largest shoes ever sold are a pair size 42 built for the giant Harley Davidson of Avon Park, Florida, U.S.A.

Silverplate The highest price ever paid at auction for a single piece of silver is £78,000 at Christies of London on 1 July 1970 for a unique Charles I silver inkstand, hallmarked for 1639, weighing 172 oz. It had been sold also at Christies on 5 June 1893 for £446.

The highest price for English Silver is £56,000 paid by the London dealer Wartski for the Brownlow James II Tankards at Christie's, London, on 20 Nov. 1968. This pair made in 1686 was in mint condition and weighed nearly $7\frac{1}{2}$ lb. It has been calculated that they appreciated at the rate of 75p per hour since they were sold by Lord Astor for £17,000 in 1963.

Apostle spoons The highest price ever paid for a set of 13 apostle spoons is $30,000 (£10,700), paid by the Clark Institute of Williamstown, Massachusetts, U.S.A. There are only six other complete sets known.

Stuffed bird The highest price ever paid for a stuffed bird is £9,000. This was given in the salerooms of Messrs. Sotheby & Co., London by the Iceland Natural History Museum for a specimen of the Great Auk (*Alca impennis*) in summer plumage, which was taken in Iceland *c.* 1821; this particular specimen stood $22\frac{1}{2}$ inches high. The Great Auk was a flightless North Atlantic seabird, which was finally exterminated on Eldey, Iceland in 1844, becoming extinct through hunting. The last British sightings were at Co. Waterford in 1834 and St. Kilda *c.* 1840.

Sword The highest price recorded for a sword is £21,000 paid at Sotheby's on 23 March 1970 for a swept hilt rapier $48\frac{1}{2}$ inches long made by Israel Schuech in 1606 probably for Elector Christian II or Duke Johann Georg of Saxony. The hilt is inset with pearls and semi-precious stones. It should be noted that prices as high as £60,000 have been rumoured in Japan for important swords by master Japanese swordsmiths.

Most expensive snuff The most expensive snuff obtainable in Britain is "Café Royale" sold by G. Smith and Sons (inst. 1869) of Charing Cross Road, London. It sells at 92p per oz.

Snuff box The record price for a snuff box is £23,000 for a Louis Quinze box made by Daniel Govaers in 1726 containing miniatures of the king and his queen, realized at Sotheby's, London on 25 Nov. 1968.

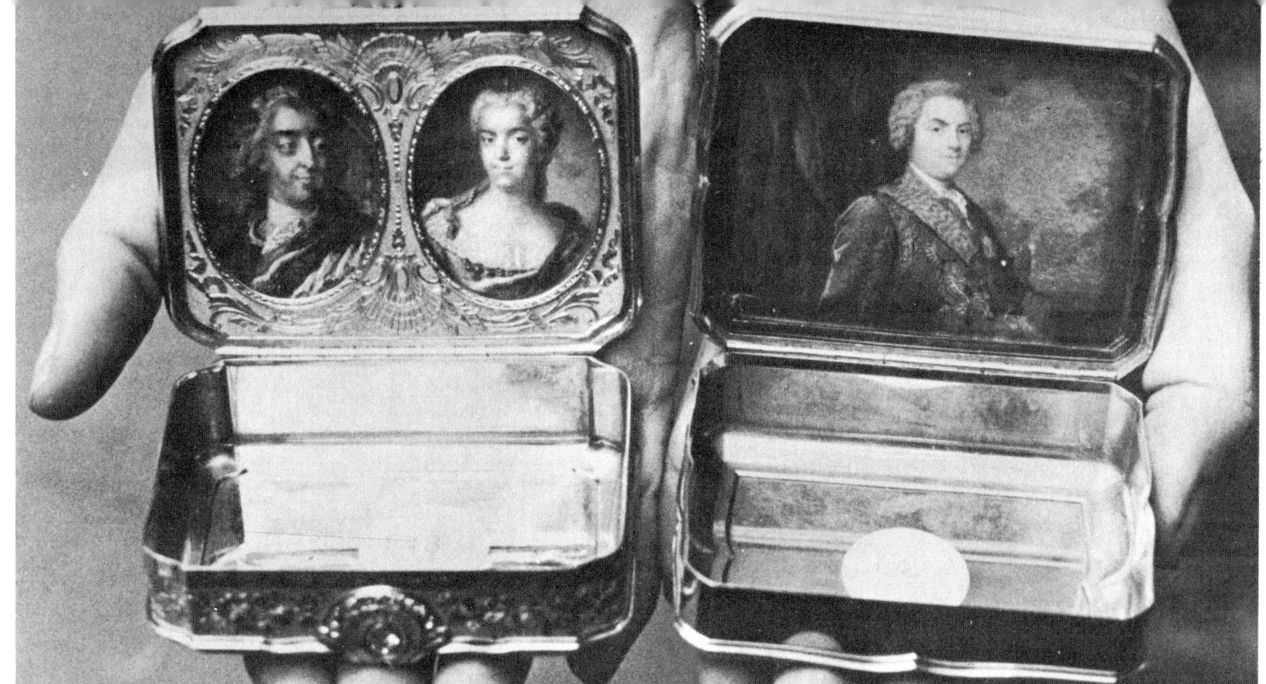

The snuff box which brought the all-time record auction price of £23,000 is shown on the left (see page 156)

TAPESTRY

Earliest The earliest known examples of tapestry weaved linen are three pieces from the tomb of Thutmose IV, the Egyptian pharaoh and dated to 1483 to 1411 B.C.

Largest The largest single piece of tapestry ever woven is "Christ in Glory", measuring 74 feet 8 inches by 38 feet, designed by Graham Vivian Sutherland, O.M. (b. 24 Aug. 1903) for an altar hanging in Coventry Cathedral, Warwickshire. It cost £10,500 and was delivered from Pinton Frères of Felletin, France, on 1 March 1962.

Longest The longest of all ancient tapestries is Queen Matilda of England's famous Bayeux tapestry of embroidery, a hanging 19½ inches wide by 231 feet in length. It depicts events of the period 1064–66 in 72 scenes and was probably worked in Canterbury, Kent, in *c.* 1086. It was "lost" from 1476 until 1724.

Most expensive The highest price paid for a set of tapestries is £200,000 for four Louis XV pieces at Sotheby & Co., London on 8 Dec. 1967.

Earliest tartan The earliest evidence of tartan is the so-called Falkirk tartan, found stuffed in a jar of coins in Bells Meadow, north of Callendar Park, Scotland. It is of a dark and light brown pattern and dates from *c.* A.D. 245. The earliest reference to a specific named tartan has been to a Murray tartan in 1618.

Vase *Most expensive* The highest price ever paid for a vase is 23,000,000 yen (£27,380), obtained by Messrs. Sotheby & Co., at a sale held at the department store of Mitsukoshi in Tōkyō, Japan on 2 Oct. 1969. This was for a 16th century Chinese Kinrade double-gourd green and orange vase 39·4 cms. (15½ inches) tall.

Largest wig The largest wig yet made is that made by Jean Leonard, owner of a salon in Copenhagen, Denmark. It is intended for bridal occasions, made from 24 tresses, measures nearly 8 feet in length and costs £416.

Writing paper The most expensive writing paper in the world is that sold by Cartier Inc. on Fifth Avenue, New York City at $1,904 (£793) per 100 sheets with envelopes. It is of hand made paper from Finland with deckle edges and a "personalized" portrait watermark.

3. AGRICULTURE

ORIGINS

It has been estimated that only 21 per cent. of the world's land surface is cultivable and that of this only two-fifths of this is cultivated. The earliest attested evidence of cultivated grain is that from Jarmo, Iraq, dated *c.* 6750 B.C. The earliest evidence of animal husbandry comes from sheep at Zawi Chemi Shanidar, Iraq, dating from *c.* 8800 B.C. The order in which animals have been domesticated is: dogs and reindeer (mesolithic period, possibly as early as 18000 B.C.); sheep (*c.* 9000 B.C.); goats (at Jarmo and Jericho, *c.* 6500 B.C.); pigs (at Jarmo, *c.* 6500 B.C.) and cattle (at Banahilk, northern Iraq, before 5000 B.C.).

FARMS

Earliest The earliest British farming site yet discovered is one at Staines, Greater London, dating from *c.* 2500 B.C., found in 1961.

Largest *World* The largest farms in the world are collective farms in the U.S.S.R. These have been reduced in number from 235,500 in 1940 to only 36,000 in 1969 and have been increased in size so that units of over 60,000 acres are not uncommon.

Britain The largest farms in the British Isles are Scottish hill farms in the Grampians. The largest arable farm is that of Elveden, Suffolk, farmed by the Earl of Iveagh. Here 11,356 acres are farmed on an estate of 23,000 acres, the greater part of which was formerly derelict land. The 1970 production included 833,602 gallons of milk, 2,190 tons of grain and 7,790 tons of sugar beet. The livestock includes 3,344 cattle, 948 ewes and 3,537 pigs.

Largest wheat field The world's largest single wheat field was probably one of more than 35,000 acres, sown in 1951 near Lethbridge, Alberta, Canada.

Largest hop field The largest hop field in the world is one of 710 acres at Toppenish, Washington State, U.S.A. It is owned by John I. Haas, Inc., the world's largest hop growers, with hop farms in British Columbia (Canada), California, Idaho, Oregon and Washington, with a total net area of 3,065 acres.

Cattle station The world's largest cattle station was Alexandria Station, Northern Territory, Australia, selected in 1873 by Robert Collins, who rode 1,600 miles to reach it. It has 66 wells, a staff of 90 and originally extended over 7,207,608 acres—more than the area of the English counties of Yorkshire, Devon, Norfolk and Cambridgeshire put together. The present area is 6,500 square miles which is stocked with 58,000 shorthorn cattle. Until 1915 the Victoria River Downs Station, Northern Territory, was over three times larger, with an area of 22,400,000 acres (35,000 square miles).

Sheep station The largest sheep station in the world is Commonwealth Hill, in the north-west of South Australia. It grazes between 70,000 and 90,000 sheep in an area of 3,640 square miles (2,329,006 acres) *i.e.* larger than the combined area of Norfolk and Suffolk.

The largest sheep move on record occurred when 27 horsemen moved a mob of 43,000 sheep 40 miles from Barealdine to Beaconsfield Station, Queensland, Australia, in 1886.

Mushroom farm The largest mushroom farm in the world is the Butler County Mushroom Farm, Inc., founded in 1937 in a disused limestone mine near West Winfield, Pennsylvania, U.S.A. It now has 875 employees working underground, in a maze of galleries 110 miles long, producing about 25,000,000 lb. (11,160 tons) of mushrooms per year.

Turkey farm Europe's largest turkey farm is that of Bernard Matthews, Ltd., at Weston Longville, Norfolk, with up to 300 workers tending 160,000 turkeys.

CROP YIELDS

Wheat Crop yields for highly tended small areas are of little significance. The greatest recorded wheat yield is 169·9 bushels (91 cwt.) per acre from 27·7 acres in 1964 by Yoshino Brothers Farms at Quincy, Washington State, U.S.A. The British record is 71·4 cwt. per acre (variety Viking) on a field of 9·453 acres by J. F. Oliver, near Doncaster, Yorkshire in 1962.

Barley A yield of 64¾ cwt. per acre of variety Pallas was reported in 1962 from a field of 20 acres by Colonel K. C. Lee of Blaco Hill Farm, Mattersey, near Doncaster, Yorkshire.

DIMENSIONS AND PROLIFICACY

Cattle Of heavyweight cattle the heaviest on record was a Hereford-Shorthorn named "Old Ben", owned by Mike and John Murphy of Miami, Indiana, U.S.A. When he died at the age of 8, in February 1910, he had attained a length of 16 feet 2 inches from nose to tail, a girth of 13 feet 8 inches, a height of 6 feet 4 inches at the forequarters and a weight of 4,720 lb. (42·1 cwt.). The stuffed and mounted steer is displayed in Highland Park, Kokomo, Indiana, as proof to all who would otherwise have said "there ain't no such animal". The British record is the 4,480 lb. (40 cwt.) of "The Bradwell Ox" owned by William Spurgin of Bradwell, Essex. He was 15 feet from nose to tail and had a girth of 11 feet.

The highest recorded birthweight for a calf is 225 lb. (16 stone 1 lb.) from a British Friesian cow at Rockhouse Farm, Bishopston, Swansea, Glamorganshire, in 1961.

On 25 April 1964 it was reported that a cow named "Lyubik" had given birth to seven calves at Mogilev, U.S.S.R. A case of five live calves at one birth was reported in 1928 by T. G. Yarwood of Manchester, Lancashire. The life-time prolificacy record is 30 in the case of a cross-bred cow owned by G. Page of Warren Farm, Wilmington, Sussex, which died in November 1957, aged 32. A cross-Hereford calved in 1916 and owned by A. J. Thomas of West Hook Farm, Marloes, Pembrokeshire, Wales, produced her 30th calf in May 1955 and died in May 1956, aged 40.

Pigs The heaviest pig ever recorded in Britain was one of 12 cwt. 66 lb. (1,410 lb.), bred by Joseph Lawton of Astbury, Cheshire. In 1774 it stood 4 feet 8½ inches in height and was 9 feet 8 inches long. The highest recorded weight for a piglet at weaning (8 weeks) is 81 lb. for a boar, one of nine piglets farrowed on 6 July 1962 by the Landrace gilt "Manorport Ballerina 53rd", *alias* "Mary", and sired by a Large White named "Johnny" at Kettle Lane Farm, West Ashton, Trowbridge, Wiltshire.

The highest recorded number of piglets in one litter is 34, thrown on 25–26 June 1961 by a sow owned by Aksel Egedee of Denmark. In February 1955 a Wessex sow owned by Mrs. E. C. Goodwin of Paul's Farm, Leigh, near Tonbridge, Kent, had a litter of 34, of which 30 were born dead. A litter of 32 piglets (26 live born) was thrown in February 1971 by a British saddleback owned by Mr. R. Spencer of Toddington, Gloucestershire. In September 1934 a Large White sow, owned by Mr. H. S. Pedlingham, died after having farrowed 385 piglets in 22 litters in 10 years 10 months.

Sheep The highest recorded birthweight for a lamb in Britain is 26 lb., in the case of a lamb delivered on 9 Feb. 1967 by Alan F. Baldry from a ewe belonging to J. L. H. Arkwright of Winkleigh, Devonshire. A case of eight lambs at a birth was reported by D. T. Jones of Priory Farm, Monmouthshire, in June 1956, but none lived.

Egg-laying The highest authenticated rate of egg-laying by a hen is 361 eggs in 364 days by a Black Orpington in an official test at Taranki, New Zealand, in 1930. The U.K. record is 353 eggs in 365 days in a National Laying Test at Milford, Surrey in 1957 by a Rhode Island Red owned by W. Lawson of Welham Grange, Retford, Nottinghamshire. In January 1957 a battery pullet owned by Mr. Thomas Whitwell of Goodies Farm, Firbank, Westmorland, laid 16 eggs in six days.

The largest egg reported is one of 16 ounces, with double yolk and double shell, laid by a white Leghorn at Vineland, New Jersey, U.S.A., on 25 Feb. 1956. The largest in the United Kingdom was one of 8¼ ounces, laid by "Daisy", owned by Peter Quarton, aged 8, at Lodge Farm, Kexby Bridge, near York, in March 1964.

MILK YIELDS

Cows The world lifetime record yield of milk is 334,292 lb. (149·2 tons) at 3·4 per cent. butter fat by the U.S. Holstein cow "College Ormsby Burke" which died at Fort Collins, Colorado in August 1966. The greatest yield of any British cow was that given by the British Friesian "Manningford Faith Jan Graceful", owned by R. and H. Jenkinson of Oxfordshire. This cow yielded 326,451 lb. (145·7 tons) before she died in November 1955, aged 17½ years. The greatest recorded yield for one lactation (365 days) is 45,081 lb (20·13 tons) by R. A. Pierson's British Friesian "Bridge Birch" in England in 1947–48. The British record for milk yield in a day is 198¼ lb. by R. A. Pierson's British Friesian "Garsdon Minnie" in 1948.

Milking The hand milking record for cows is 17 lb. 11 oz. in two minutes from two cows by Manuel Dutra of Stockton, California at the Cow Palace, San Francisco, California, U.S.A., on 27 Oct. 1970. Dutra, known as a fierce competitor, proclaimed "I credit my cows with the victory".

Goats The highest recorded milk yield for any goat is 6,661 pints in 365 days by "Malpas Melba", owned by Mr. J. R. Egerton of Bramford, East Anglia, in 1931.

SHEEP SHEARING

The highest recorded speed for lamb shearing in a working day was that of John Ferguson who machine-sheared 567 lambs (average 63 per hour) in 9 hours at Taupo, North Island, New Zealand, in 1969. Godfrey Bowen (New Zealand) sheared a Cheviot ewe in 46 seconds at the Royal Highland Show in Scotland in June 1957. The blade (*i.e.* hand-shearing) record in a 9-hour working day is 350, set in 1899. The female record is held by Mrs. Pamela Warren, aged 21, who machine-sheared 337 Romney Marsh ewes and lambs at Puketutu, near Piopio, North Island, New Zealand on 25 Nov. 1964.

LIVESTOCK PRICES

The highest nominal value ever placed on a bull is $1,050,000 (then £375,000), implicit in the $350,000 (£125,000) paid on 22 Jan. 1967 for a one-third share in the Aberdeen-Angus bull "Newhouse Jewror Eric", aged 7, by the Embassy Angus Farm of Mississippi, U.S.A.

The highest price ever paid for a bull in Britain is

dertis Evulse, the holder of the British uction record (see below)

60,000 guineas (£63,000), paid on 5 Feb. 1963 at Perth, Scotland, by Jock Dick, co-manager of Black Watch Farms, for "Lindertis Evulse", an Aberdeen-Angus owned by Sir Torquil and Lady Munro of Lindertis, Kirriemuir, Angus, Scotland. This bull failed a fertility test in August 1963 when 20 months old thus becoming the world's most expensive piece of beef.

Cow The highest price ever paid for a cow is Can. $62,000 (£23,890) for the Holstein-Friesian "Oak Ridges Royal Linda" by Mr. E. L. Vesley of Lapeer, Michigan, U.S.A. at the Oak Ridges, Canada dispersal sale on 12 Nov. 1968.

Sheep The highest price ever paid for a sheep is $A27,000 (£12,900) for a two-year-old Collinsville ram by the East Bungaree Pty. Ltd. of Mount Bryan, South Australia at the Perth Ram Sales in September 1969.

The British auction record is £5,000, paid by J. and A. Stoddart for a Scottish Blackface ram lamb owned by Ben Wilson, at Lanark in October 1963.

The highest price ever paid for wool is 1,800 Australian pence ($A15 or £6·98) per lb. for a bale from 120 selected sheep of the Hillcrest Merino stud, bought for Illingworth, Morris & Co. of Shipley, Yorkshire, at an auction at Goulbourn, New South Wales, Australia, on 3 Dec. 1964.

Pig The highest price ever paid for a pig is $10,200 (now £4,250), paid in 1953 for a Hampshire boar "Great Western" by a farm at Byron, Illinois, U.S.A. The U.K. record is 3,300 guineas (£3,465), paid by Malvern Farms for the Swedish Landrace gilt "Bluegate Ally 33rd" owned by Davidson Trust in a draft sale at Reading on 2 March 1955.

Horse The highest price ever given for a farm horse is £9,500, paid for the Clydesdale stallion "Baron of Buchlyvie" by William Dunlop at Ayr, Scotland, in December 1911.

Donkey Perhaps the lowest ever price for livestock was at a sale at Kuruman, Cape Province, South Africa in 1934 where donkeys were sold for less than 2p each.

Turkey The highest price ever paid for a turkey is $990 (then £353) for a 33 lb. stag bird bought at the Arkansas State Turkey Show at Springdale, Arkansas, U.S.A. on 3 Dec. 1955.

BUTTER FAT

The world record lifetime yield is 12,211 lb. by the U.S. Holstein cow "Minnow Creek Eden Delight" at Orange, Virginia, U.S.A. The British record butter fat yield in a lifetime is 12,144 lb. by the Friesian "Lavenham Wallen 87th" (b. 30 Nov. 1946, d. 17 Oct. 1967), owned by Mr. John Lindley of Nowers Farm, Wellington, Somerset. The world's lactation (365 days) record is 1,866 lb. by the U.S. Holstein-Friesian "Princess Breezewood R.A. Patsy" while the British record is 1,799 lb. (33,184 lb. milk at 5·42 per cent.) by A. Drexler's British Friesian "Zenda Bountiful" at Manor Farm, Kidlington, Oxfordshire, in the year ending 3 March 1953. This is sufficient to produce 2,116 lb. of butter. The United Kingdom record for butter fat in one day is 9·12 lb. (97 lb. milk at 9·40 per cent.) by Mr. and Mrs. K. McDonald's Jersey cow "Barings Flower".

CHEESE

The most active cheese-eaters are the people of France, with an annual average in 1969 of 29·98 lb. per person. The world's biggest producer is the United States with a factory production of 998,800 tons in 1970. The U.K. cheese consumption in 1970 was 11·4 lb. per head.

Oldest The oldest and most primitive cheeses are the Arabian *kishk*, made of the dried curd of goat's milk. There are today 450 named cheeses of 18 major varieties, but many are merely named after different towns and differ only in shape or the method of packing. France has 240 varieties.

Most expensive The most expensive of all cheeses is the small goat cheese Crottin de Chavignol, from the Berri area of France, which is marketed in Paris, at times, for 30 francs per kilogramme (£1·12½ per lb.). Britain's most costly cheeses are Blue Cheshire and Windsor Red both at 45p per lb.

Largest The largest cheese ever made was a cheddar of 34,591 lb. (15·44 tons), made in 43 hours on 20–22 Jan. 1964 by the Wisconsin Cheese Foundation for exhibition at the New York World's Fair, U.S.A. It was transported in a specially designed refrigerated tractor trailer "Cheese Mobile" 45 feet long.

Longest sausage The longest sausage ever recorded was one 3,124 feet long, made on 29 June 1966 by 30 butchers in Scunthorpe, Lincolnshire. It was made from 6½ cwt. of pork and 1½ cwt. of cereal and seasoning.

Piggery The world's largest piggery is the Sljeme pig unit in Yugoslavia which is able to process 300,000 pigs in a year. Even larger units may exist in Romania but details are at present lacking.

Cow shed The longest cow shed in Britain is that of the Yorkshire Agricultural Society at Harrogate. It is 456 feet in length with a capacity of 686 cows. The National Agricultural Centre, Kenilworth, Warwickshire, completed in 1967, has, however, capacity for 782 animals.

Foot-and-mouth disease The worst outbreak of foot-and-mouth disease in Great Britain was that from Shropshire on 25 Oct. 1967 to 25 June 1968 in which there were 2,364 outbreaks and 429,632 animals slaughtered at a direct and consequential loss of £150,000,000. The outbreak of 1871, when farms were much smaller, affected 42,531 farms. The disease first appeared in Great Britain at Stratford near London in August 1839.

Ploughing The world championship (instituted 1953) has been staged in 15 countries and won by ploughmen of eight nationalities of which the United Kingdom has been most successful with 6 champions. The only man to take the title three times has been Hugh Barr of Northern Ireland in 1954–55–56.

The fastest recorded time for ploughing an acre (minimum 32 right-hand turns and depth 9 inches) is 17 minutes 52·5 seconds by Mervyn Ford using a six-furrow 14-inch Ransomes plough towed by a Roadless 114 four-wheel drive tractor at Bowhay Farm, Ide, Exeter, Devon on 25 Sept. 1970.

The greatest recorded acreage ploughed in 24 hours is 84·1 acres by five farmers of the Exeter and District Young Farmers' Club near Ide, Exeter, Devon on 00–00 Sept. 1970.

1. ENDURANCE AND ENDEAVOUR

LUNAR CONQUEST

Neil Alden Armstrong (b. Wapakoneta, Ohio, U.S.A. of Scoto-Irish and German ancestry, on 5 Aug. 1930), command pilot of the Apollo XI mission, became the first man to set foot on the Moon on the Sea of Tranquillity at 02.56 and 20 seconds G.M.T. on 21 July 1969. He was followed out of the Lunar Module *Eagle* by Col. Edwin Eugene Aldrin, Jr. (b. Montclair, New Jersey, U.S.A. of Swedish, Dutch and British ancestry, on 20 Jan. 1930), while the Command Module *Columbia* piloted by Lt.-Col. Michael Collins (b. Rome, Italy, of Irish and pre-Revolutionary American ancestry, on 31 Oct. 1930) orbited above.

Eagle landed at 20.17 hrs. 42 secs. G.M.T. on 20 July and lifted off at 17.54 G.M.T. on 21 July, after a stay of 21 hours 36 minutes. The Apollo XI had blasted off from Cape Kennedy, Florida at 13.32 G.M.T. on 16 July and was a culmination of the U.S. space programme, which, at its peak, employed 376,600 people and attained in the year 1966–67 a peak budget of $5,900,000,000 (£2,460 million).

ALTITUDE

Man The greatest altitude attained by man was when the crew of the ill-fated Apollo XIII were at apocynthion (*i.e.* their furthest point behind the Moon) 158 miles above its surface and 248,655 miles above the Earth's surface at 1.21 a.m. B.S.T. on 15 April 1970. The crew were Capt. James Arthur Lovell, U.S.N., Frederick W. Haise and John L. Swigert.

Woman The greatest altitude attained by a woman is 231 kilometres (143·5 miles) by Jnr. Lt. (now Flt. Major) Valentina Vladimirovna Tereshkova (b. 6 March 1937) of the U.S.S.R., during her 48-orbit flight in *Vostok VI* on 16 June 1963. (See also Chapter 4.) The record for an aircraft is 24,336 metres (79,842 feet) by N. Prokhanova (U.S.S.R.) in an E-33 jet, on 22 May 1965.

SPEED

Man The fastest speed at which any human has travelled is 24,791 m.p.h. when the Command Module of Apollo X carrying Lt.-Col. Thomas P. Stafford and Cdrs. Eugene Andrew Cernan and John Watts Young, U.S.N., reached this maximum value at the 400,000-foot ($75\frac{3}{4}$-mile) altitude interface on its trans-Earth return flight on 26 May 1969. It was widely but incorrectly reported that the stricken Apollo XIII attained the highest recorded speed on its return on 17 April 1970. Its maximum value was in fact 24,689·2 m.p.h.

Woman The highest speed ever attained by a woman is 17,470 m.p.h. by Jnr. Lt. (now Flt. Major) Valentina Vladimirovna Tereshkova (b. 6 March 1937) of the U.S.S.R. in *Vostok VI* on 16 June 1963. The highest speed ever achieved in an aeroplane is 1,429·2 m.p.h. by Jacqueline Cochran (U.S.A.), in an F-104G1 "Starfighter" jet over Edwards Air Force Base, California, U.S.A., on 11 May 1964. The first woman in Britain to fly at over 1,000 m.p.h. was Flt. Off. Jean Oakes, who flew at 1,125 m.p.h. in an R.A.F. Lightning Mark 4 on 6 Sept. 1962.

LAND SPEED

The highest speed ever achieved on land is 650 m.p.h. momentarily during the 627·027 m.p.h. run of *Blue Flame* driven by Gary Gabelich (b. San Pedro, California, 29 Aug. 1940) on Bonneville Salt Flats, Utah, U.S.A., on 23 Oct. 1970 (see Mechanical World, page 129). The car built by Reaction Dynamics Inc. of Milwaukee, Wisconsin, is designed to withstand stresses up to 1,000 m.p.h. while the tyres have been tested to speeds of 850 m.p.h.

Man The highest speed ever achieved in a railed vehicle is 632 m.p.h. by Lt.-Col. John Paul Stapp (b. 1912) on a Northrop experimental rocket sled at the Holloman Air Force Base Development Center, Alamogordo, New Mexico, U.S.A., on 10 Dec. 1954. Running on rails and impelled by nine rockets with a total thrust of 40,000 lb., the top speed was reached within five seconds. In the deceleration, which lasted only $1\frac{1}{2}$ seconds, Stapp survived a force of 40g for 0·2 of a second but his haemorrhaged retinas left him partially blinded for 12 weeks. The normal experimental limit is 12g.

Woman The highest land speed recorded by a woman is 335·070 m.p.h. by Mrs. Lee Ann Breedlove (*née* Roberts) (born 1937) of Los Angeles, California, U.S.A., driving her husband's *Spirit of America—Sonic I* (see page 129) over the timing kilometre on the Bonneville Salt Flats, Utah, U.S.A., on 4 Nov. 1965.

Ray Munro (Canada), holder of 28 world hot air ballooning records. On Feb. 1970 he flew 158·34 miles across e Irish Sea in ours 52 mins.

WATER SPEED

Unofficial The highest speed ever achieved on water is 328 m.p.h. by Donald Malcolm Campbell, C.B.E. (1921–67) of the U.K., on his last and fatal run in the turbo-jet engined 2¼ ton *Bluebird* K7, on Coniston Water, Lancashire, England, on 4 Jan. 1967.

Official The official record is 285·213 m.p.h. (average of two 1 mile runs) by Lee Taylor, Jr. (b. 1934) of Downey, California, U.S.A., in the hydroplane *Hustler* on Lake Guntersville, Alabama, U.S.A., on 30 June 1967.

Propeller driven The world record for propeller-driven craft is 200·42 m.p.h. by Roy Duby (U.S.A.) in a Rolls-Royce-engined hydroplane on Lake Guntersville, Alabama, U.S.A., on 17 April 1962.

PROGRESSIVE HUMAN ALTITUDE RECORDS

Metres	Feet	Pilot	Vehicle	Place	Date
25	84	Jean François Pilâtre de Rozier (France)	Hot Air Balloon (tethered)	Fauxbourg, Paris	15 & 17 Oct. 1783
64	210	J. F. Pilâtre de Rozier (France)	Hot Air Balloon (tethered)	Fauxbourg, Paris	19 Oct. 1783
80	262	J. F. Pilâtre de Rozier (France)	Hot Air Balloon (tethered)	Fauxbourg, Paris	19 Oct. 1783
99	325	de Rozier and Girand de Villette (France)	Hot Air Balloon (tethered)	Fauxbourg, Paris	19 Oct. 1783
c. 100	*c.* 330	de Rozier and the Marquis François-Laurent d'Arlandes (1742–1809) (France)	Hot Air Balloon (free flight)	La Muette, Paris	21 Nov. 1783
c. 600	*c.* 2,000	Dr. Jâcques-Alexandre-César Charles (1746–1823) and Ainé Robert (France)	Charlière Hydrogen Balloon	Tuileries, Paris	1 Dec. 1783
c. 2 750	*c.* 9,000	J.-A.-C. Charles (France)	Hydrogen Balloon	Nesles, France	1 Dec. 1783
c. 4 000	*c.* 13,000	James Sadler (G.B.)	Hydrogen Balloon	Manchester	May 1785
c. 6 100	*c.* 20,000	E. G. R. Robertson (U.K.) and Loest (Germany)	Hydrogen Balloon	Hamburg, Germany	18 July 1803
7 000	22,965	Joseph Louis Gay-Lussac (France)	Hydrogen Balloon	Paris	15 Sept. 1804
c. 7 620	*c.* 25,000	Charles Green, Edward Spencer (G.B.)	Coal Gas Balloon *Nassau*	Vauxhall, London	24 July 1837
7 740	25,400[1]	James Glaisher (U.K.)	Hydrogen Balloon	Wolverhampton	17 July 1862
8 520	27,950	H. T. Sivel, J. E. Crocé-Spinelli, Gaston Tissandier (only survivor)	Coal Gas Balloon *Zénith*	La Villette, Paris	15 April 1875
9 615	31,500	Prof. A. Berson (Germany)	Hydrogen Balloon *Phoenix*	Strasbourg, France	4 Dec. 1894
10 800	35,433	Prof. Berson and Dr. R. J. Süring (Germany)	Hydrogen Balloon *Preussen*	Berlin, Germany	30 June 1901
11 145	36,565	Sadi Lecointe (France)	Nieuport Aircraft	Issy-les-Moulineaux, France	30 Oct. 1923
12 945	42,470[2]	Capt. Hawthorne C. Gray (U.S.A.)	Hydrogen Balloon	Scott Field, Illinois	4 May 1927
12 945	42,470	Capt. Hawthorne C. Gray (U.S.A.)	Hydrogen Balloon	Scott Field, Illinois	4 Nov. 1927
13 157	43,166	Lt. Apollo Soucek (U.S.A.)	U.S. Navy Wright *Apache*	Washington, D.C.	4 June 1930
15 837	51,961	Prof. Auguste Piccard and Paul Kipfer (Switzerland)	*F.N.R.S. I* Balloon	Augsburg	27 May 1931
16 196	53,139	Piccard & Dr. Max Cosyns (Belgium)	*F.N.R.S. I* Balloon	Dübendorf, nr. Zürich	18 Aug. 1932
18 500	60,695[3]	G. Profkoviev, F. N. Birnbaum and K. D. Godunov (U.S.S.R.)	Army Balloon *U.S.S.R.*	Moscow, U.S.S.R.	30 Sept. 1933
18 665	61,237	Lt.-Col. T. G. W. Settle, U.S.N. and Major Chester L. Fordney, U.S.M.C.	Hydrogen Balloon *Century of Progress*	Akron, Ohio	20 & 21 Nov. 1933
22 000	72,178[4]	Raul F. Fedoseyenko, A. B. Vasienko and E. D. Ususkin (U.S.S.R.)	*Osaviakhim* Balloon	Moscow, U.S.S.R.	30 Jan. 1934
22 060	72,377	Capts. Orvill A. Anderson and Albert W. Stevens (U.S. Army)	U.S. *Explorer II* Helium Balloon	Rapid City, South Dakota, U.S.A.	11 Nov. 1935
24 230	79,494	William Barton Bridgeman (U.S.A.)	U.S. Douglas D558-II *Skyrocket*	California, U.S.A.	15 Aug. 1951
25 370	83,235	Lt.-Col. Marion E. Carl, U.S.M.C.	U.S. Douglas D558-II *Skyrocket*	California, U.S.A.	21 Aug. 1953
c. 28 350	*c.* 93,000	Major Arthur Murray (U.S.A.F.)	U.S. *Bell X-1A* Rocket 'plane	California, U.S.A.	4 June 1954
38 465	126,200	Capt. Iven C. Kincheloe, Jnr. (U.S.A.F.)	U.S. *Bell X-2* Rocket 'plane	California, U.S.A.	7 Sept. 1956
41 605	136,500	Major Robert M. White (U.S.A.F.)	U.S. *X-15* Rocket 'plane	California, U.S.A.	12 Aug. 1960
51 694	169,600	Joseph A. Walker (U.S.A.)	U.S. *X-15* Rocket 'plane	California, U.S.A.	30 Mar. 1961

Kilometres	Statute Miles	Pilot	Vehicle	Place	Date
327	203·2	Flt.-Major Yuriy A. Gagarin (U.S.S.R.)	U.S.S.R. *Vostok I* Capsule	Orbital flight	12 April 1961
408	253·5	Col. Vladimir M. Komarov, Lt. Boris B. Yegorov and Konstantin P. Feoktistov	U.S.S.R. *Voskhod I* Capsule	Orbital flight	12 Oct. 1964
497·6	309·2	Col. Pavel I. Belyayev and Lt.-Col. Alexsey A. Leonov (U.S.S.R.)	U.S.S.R. *Voskhod II* Capsule	Orbital flight	18 Mar. 1965
763·4	474·4	Cdr. John Watts Young, U.S.N. and Major Michael Collins, U.S.A.F.	U.S. *Gemini X* Capsule	Orbital flight	19 July 1966
1 369·0	850·7	Cdr. Charles Conrad, Jr. and Lt.-Cdr. Richard F. Gordon, Jr., U.S.N.-	U.S. *Gemini XI* Capsule	Orbital flight	14 Sept. 1966
377 347	234,473	Col. Frank Borman, U.S.A.F., Capt. James A. Lovell, U.S.N. and Major William A. Anders, U.S.A.F.	U.S. *Apollo VIII* Command Module	Circum-lunar flight	25 Dec. 1968
399 814	248,433	Cdr. Eugene A. Cernan and Col. Thomas P. Stafford	U.S. *Apollo X* Lunar Module	Circum-lunar flight	22 May 1969
389 920	242,285[5]	Neil Alden Armstrong, Col. Edwin Eugene Aldrin, Jr. and Lt.-Col. Michael Collins	U.S. *Apollo XI* Lunar Module	Circum-lunar flight and first Moon landing	21–22 July 1969
400 187	248,655	Capt. James Arthur Lovell, U.S.N., Frederick W. Haise and John L. Swigert	U.S. *Apollo XIII*	Abortive lunar landing mission	15 April 1970

[1] *Glaisher, with Henry Coxwell, claimed 37,000 feet (11 275 metres) from Wolverhampton on 5 Sept. 1862. Some writers accept 30,000 feet (9 145 metres).*

[2] *Neither of Gray's altitudes were official records because he had to parachute on his first descent and he landed dead from his second ascent to an identical height.*

[3] *None survived the ascent.*

[4] *All died on descent.*

[5] *Note: This historic space flight* did not *establish an altitude record but has been included for reference only.*

PROGRESSIVE ABSOLUTE HUMAN SPEED RECORDS

The progression of the voluntary human speed record is listed below. It is perhaps noteworthy that the petrol-engined car at no time featured in this compilation.

Speed Km./h.	m.p.h.	Person and Vehicle	Place	Date
<40	<25	Running	—	*ante* 6500 B.C.
>40	>25	Sledging	Southern Finland	*c.* 6500 B.C.
>55	>35	Ski-ing	Fenno-Scandia	*c.* 3000 B.C.
>55	>35	Horse-riding	Anatolia, Turkey	*c.* 1400 B.C.
<80	<50	Ice Yachts (earliest patent)	Netherlands	A.D. 1600
95	59	Grand Junction Railway 2-2-2 *Lucifer*	Madeley Bank, Staffordshire, England	13 Nov. 1839
114	71[1]	Great Western Railway 2-2-2 *Ixion*	Twyford-Maidenhead, Berkshire, England	16 Dec. 1845
119·8	74·5	Great Western Railway 4-2-2 8 ft. single *Great Western*	Wootton Bassett, Wiltshire, England	1 June 1846
125·5	78	Great Western Railway 4-2-2 8 ft. single *Great Britain*	Wootton Bassett, Wiltshire, England	11 May 1848
131·6	81·8	Bristol & Exeter Railway 4-2-4 tank 9 ft. single No. 41	Wellington Bank, Somerset, England	June 1854
141·3	87·8	Tommy Todd, downhill skier	La Porte, California, U.S.A.	Mar. 1873
144	89·48	Crompton No. 604 engine	Champigny-Pont sur Yonne, France	20 June 1890
144·8	90·0	Midland Railway 4-2-2 7 ft. 9 in. single	Ampthill, Bedford, England	Mar. 1897
162·5	101·0	Siemens und Halske electric engine	near Berlin, Germany	1901
201	124·89	Siemens und Halske electric engine	Marienfeld-Zossen, near Berlin	6 Oct. 1903
206·7	128·43	Siemens und Halske electric engine	Marienfeld-Zossen, near Berlin	23 Oct. 1903
210·2	130·61	Siemens und Halske electric engine	Marienfeld-Zossen, near Berlin	27 Oct. 1903
>257·5	>150	Frank H. Marriott, Stanley Steamer *Rocket*	Ormond Beach, Florida, U.S.A.	26 Jan. 1907
>338	>210	World War I fighters in dives including Martinsyde F.4's and Nieuport *Nighthawks*	over England and Flanders	1918–19
339	210·64	Sadi Lecointe (France) Nieuport-Delage 29	Villesauvage, France	25 Sept. 1921
341	211·91	Sadi Lecointe (France) Nieuport-Delage 29	Villesauvage, France	21 Sept. 1922
392·64	243·94	Brig.-Gen. William A. Mitchell (U.S.A.) Curtiss H.S. D-12	Detroit, Michigan	18 Oct. 1922
435·3	270·5	Lt. Alford J. Williams (U.S.N.), Curtiss R.2 C-1	Mitchell Field, Long Is., N.Y.	4 Nov. 1923
441·3	274·2	Lt. A. Brown (U.S.N.), Curtiss H.S. D-12	Mitchell Field, Long Is., N.Y.	4 Nov. 1923
448·15	278·47[2]	Adj. Chef A. Bonnet (France) Ferbois V-2	Istres, France	11 Dec. 1924
457·39	284·21[3]	Fg. Off. Sidney Norman Webster, A.F.C., Supermarine S.5	Venice, Italy	26 Sept. 1927
504·67	313·59[4]	Major Mario de Bernardi (Italy) Macchi M-32	Venice, Italy	6 Nov. 1927
519·1	322·6[5]	Lt. Alford J. Williams (U.S.N.)	Mitchell Field, Long Is., N.Y.	7 Nov. 1927
561	348·6	Major Mario de Bernardi (Italy) Macchi M-52 *bis*	Venice, Italy	30 Mar. 1928
>595·4	>370	Fg. Off. Richard D. Waghorn, A.F.C. and Fg. Off. Richard L. R. Atcherley (1903–70) Supermarine S.6.'s	Solent, Hampshire, England	7 Sept. 1929
c. 611·5	*c.* 380	Flt. Lt. J. N. Boothman (b. 1901) Supermarine S.6B	Solent, Hampshire, England	13 Sept. 1931
624	388	Flt. Lt. George Hedley Stainforth, A.F.C. (1899–1942) Supermarine S.6B	Ryde, Isle of Wight, England	13 Sept. 1931
668·2	415·2	Flt. Lt. George Hedley Stainforth, A.F.C. Supermarine S.6B	Ryde, Isle of Wight, England	29 Sept. 1931
692·529	430·32[6]	W.O. Francesco Agello (Italy) Macchi-Castoldi 72	Lago di Garda, Italy	10 April 1934
>700	>434·96[7]	Col. Bernasconi (Italy) Macchi-Castoldi 72	Desenzano, Italy	18 April 1934
710·07	441·22	Sec. Lt. Francesco Agello (Italy) Macchi-Castoldi 72	Lago di Garda, Italy	23 Oct. 1934
746·64	463·94[2]	Hans Dieterle (Germany) Heinkel He.100V-8	Oranienburg, E. Germany	30 Mar. 1939
782	486	Fritz Wendel (Germany) Messerschmitt 209 V-1	Augsburg, E. Germany	26 April 1939
c. 845	*c.* 525	Heinkel 176 test flight	Peenemünde, Germany	3 July 1939
920·2	571·78	Flugkapitan Heinz Dittmar Me.163V-1	Peenemünde, Germany	July–August 1941
1,005	624·62	Flugkapitan Heinz Dittmar Me.163V-1	Peenemünde, Germany	2 Oct. 1941
1,005	624·62	Unnamed test pilot—possibly Gerd Linter Me.262V-12	Insterburg, Germany	July 1944
c. 1,050	*c.* 652	Franz Rösle Me.163B	Brandis, Germany	March–April 1945
c. 1,030–1,060	*c.* 640–660	Geoffrey Raoul de Havilland, O.B.E., D.H. 108 *Swallow*	Egypt Bay, Kent, England	27 Sept. 1946
1,050·3	652·6	Cdr. Turner F. Caldwell, U.S.N., Douglas *Skystreak* D-558-I	Muroc Dry Lake, California	20 Aug. 1947
1,051·5	653·4	Major Marion E. Carl, U.S.M.C., Douglas *Skystreak* D-558-I	Muroc Dry Lake, California	14 Oct. 1947
1,078	670	Capt. Charles E. Yeager, U.S.A.F., *Bell XS-1 Glamerous Glennis* (Mach 1·015)	Muroc Dry Lake, California	14 Oct. 1947
1,556	967	Capt. Charles E. Yeager, U.S.A.F., *Bell XS-1*	Muroc Dry Lake, California	1948
1,826·6	1,135	William Bridgeman, Douglas *Skyrocket* D-558-II	Muroc Dry Lake, California	June 1951
1,900·6	1,181	William Bridgeman, Douglas *Skyrocket* D-558-II	Muroc Dry Lake, California	11 June 1951
1,965·0	1,221	William Bridgeman, Douglas *Skyrocket* D-558-II	Muroc Dry Lake, California	June 1951
1,992·3	1,238	William Bridgeman, Douglas *Skyrocket* D-558-II	Muroc Dry Lake, California	7 Aug. 1951
2,013·2	1,241	William Bridgeman, Douglas *Skyrocket* D-558-II	Muroc Dry Lake, California	Dec. 1951
2,047·0	1,272	Albert Scott Crossfield, Douglas *Skyrocket* D-558-II	Muroc Dry Lake, California	14 Oct. 1953
2,137·2	1,328	Albert Scott Crossfield, Douglas *Skyrocket* D-558-II	Muroc Dry Lake, California	14 Oct. 1953
2,594·2	1,612	Major Charles E. Yeager, *Bell X-1A*	Muroc Dry Lake, California	12 Dec. 1953
3,112·4	1,934	Lt.-Col. Frank Everest, *Bell X-2*	Muroc Dry Lake, California	23 July 1956
3,369·9	2,094	Capt. Milburn G. Apt, *Bell X-2*	Muroc Dry Lake, California	27 Sept. 1956
3,397·3	2,111	Joseph A. Walker, North America *X-15*	Muroc Dry Lake, California	12 May 1960
3,534·1	2,196	Joseph A. Walker, North America *X-15*	Muroc Dry Lake, California	4 Aug. 1960
3,661·1	2,275	Major Robert M. White, North America *X-15*	Muroc Dry Lake, California	7 Feb. 1961
4,675·1	2,905	Major Robert M. White, North America *X-15*	Muroc Dry Lake, California	7 Mar. 1961
c. 28,260	*c.* 17,560	Flt. Maj. Yuriy Alekseyevich Gagarin, *Vostok I*	Earth orbit	12 April 1961
28,257	17,558	Cdr. Walter Marty Schirra, U.S.N., *Sigma 7*	Earth orbit	3 Oct. 1962
c. 28,325	*c.* 17,600	Air Eng. Col. Vladimir Mikhaylovich Komarov, Lt. Boris Borisovich Yegorov and Konstantin Petrovich Feoktistov, *Voskhod I*	Earth orbit	12 Oct. 1964
c. 28,565	*c.* 17,750	Col. Pavel Ivanovitch Belyayev and Lt. Col. Aleksey Arkhipovich Leonov, *Voskhod II*	Earth orbit	18 Mar. 1965

PROGRESSIVE ABSOLUTE HUMAN SPEED RECORDS—Continued

Speed Km./h.	m.p.h.	Person and Vehicle	Place	Date
28,876	17,943	Cdr. Charles Conrad, Jr., Lt.-Cdr. Richard F. Gordon, Jr., *Gemini XI*	Earth orbit	14 Sept. 1966
38,988	24,226	Col. Frank Borman, Capt. James Arthur Lovell, Major William A. Anders, *Apollo VIII*	Trans lunar flight	21 Dec. 1968
39,834	24,752	Col. Frank Borman, Capt. James Arthur Lovell, Major William A. Anders, *Apollo VIII*	Re-entry from lunar orbit	27 Dec. 1968
39,897	24,791	Cdrs. Eugene Andrew Cernan and John Watts Young and Col. Thomas P. Stafford, *Apollo X*	Re-entry from lunar orbit	26 May 1969

[1] *A speed of 85 m.p.h. (137 Km./h.) was claimed by Frank Elrington in a run-away compressed air railway from Kingstown (now Dún Laoghaire) to Dalkey, County Dublin on 19 Aug. 1843. It was, however, self-timed.*
[2] *Average of 4 runs, individual runs not officially published.*
[3] *Earlier runs 280·61 m.p.h., 451·59 Km./h. and 281·09 m.p.h., 452·37 Km./h.*
[4] *Earlier run 290·34 m.p.h., 467·25 Km./h.*
[5] *Self-timed unofficial run.*
[6] *Earlier runs at 421·58 m.p.h., 678·477 Km./h. and 424·17 m.p.h., 682·637 Km./h.*
[7] *Unofficial single run.*

The only car er to hold an solute human speed record, he 150 m.p.h. nley Steamer *Rocket* built in 1906

TRAVELLING

Most velled man *Most countries* The man who has visited more countries than anyone is J. Hart Rosdail (b. 1915) of Elmhurst, Illinois, U.S.A. Since 1934 he has visited 140 of the 146 sovereign countries and 69 of the 80 non-sovereign territories of the world making a total of 209. He estimates his mileage surpassed one million miles during 1970.

Flying The greatest number of flying hours claimed is more than 40,000 by the light aircraft pilot Max. A. Conrad (b. 1903) of the U.S.A., who began his flying career on 13 March 1928. Capt. Charles Blair (Pan American World Airways) logged 35,000 flying hours and more than 10,000,000 miles including 1,450 Atlantic crossings up to July 1969. Capt. Gordon R. Buxton surpassed 8,000,000 miles in 22,750 flying hours in 38 years to 22 May 1966. He retired as Senior B.O.A.C. captain, aged 60, having passed all medicals.

Space The most travelled man in space is Capt. James Arthur Lovell, U.S.N. with 717 hours 4 mins. 16 secs. and an estimated mileage of 7,270,000.

ss-Channel record The record for travelling the 214 miles between Paris (Arc de Triomphe) and London (Marble Arch) is 40 minutes 44 seconds by Sqn. Ldr. Charles G. Maughan, R.A.F. (b. 1924), by motorcycle, helicopter and Hunter jet aircraft on 22 July 1959, so winning the *Daily Mail* award.

Most lefatigable cruise passenger Mrs. Clara Macbeth, the 98-year-old Manhattan millionairess, having lived on the cruise liner *Caronia* for 17 years with a companion at £165 a day, booked four round trips on the *Queen Elizabeth 2* in July 1969.

CIRCUMNAVIGATION

Earliest A true circumnavigation of the world must pass through two points antipodean to each other. Man's earliest circumnavigation of the world was achieved by Juan Sebastián de Elcano (died August 1526) and 17 others in the Spanish ship *Vittoria* on 6 Sept. 1522. De Elcano was a navigator to the Portuguese-born explorer Fernão de Magalhães (Ferdinand Magellan) (*c.* 1480–1521), who, having sailed westward from the estuary of the Guadalquivir, Spain, on 20 Sept. 1519, with five ships and about 270 men, was killed on Mactan Island, in the Philippines, on 27 April 1521. The distance sailed was 30,700 miles. Among the crew was one Englishman, Andrews of Bristol. No woman completed the circle until 243 years later in 1764 when it was discovered that the valet of M. de Commerson aboard the Frenchman *La Boudeuse* was a female.

First solo The first man to complete a solo circumnavigation was Capt. Joshua Slocum, aged 51, who sailed from Newport, Rhode Island, U.S.A., in his 36-foot oyster boat *Spray* and returned after his 46,000-mile voyage 3 years 2 months and 2 days later at 1 a.m. on 27 June 1898. He was a non-swimmer.

First solo with a single stop-over The first ever solo circumnavigation with a single port of call was the 274-day voyage from Plymouth *via* Sydney and Cape Horn by Sir Francis C. Chichester, K.B.E. (born Shirwell, Devon 17 Sept. 1901) in his 53-foot 18 ton ketch *Gipsy Moth IV*, ending at 7.56 p.m. G.M.T. on 28 May 1967. The first leg of 14,109 miles from Plymouth to Sydney lasted 107 days, from 27 Aug. to 12 Dec. 1966. He left Sydney on 29 Jan. 1967 arriving home 15,517 miles distant 119 days later.

First non-stop solo The first ever technically non-stop circumnavigation was achieved in 312 days by Robin Knox-Johnston, C.B.E., aged 30, from 14 June 1968 to 22 April 1969 in his 32-foot ketch *Suhaili* from Falmouth, England. He made some unaided repairs at Otago, New Zealand on 21 Nov. 1968. He covered 28,800 miles.

Fastest solo Lt.-Cdr. Nigel C. W. Tetley, R.N., in his 40-foot trimaran *Victress* "tied the knot" before sinking off the Azores on 21 May 1969. By 10 May he had sailed 26,000 miles (a multi-hull record, solo or with crew) in 236 days at an average of 110·1 miles per day.

Longest voyage The longest voyage on record is one of about 38,000 miles by Bernard Moitessier (France) (b. Saigon, Viet-Nam, 1926) in his 39-foot $13\frac{1}{4}$-ton steel sailing boat *Joshua*. He left Plymouth, England on 21 Aug. 1968, reached the Cape via Cape Horn but then redoubled to Tahiti, arriving on 22 June 1969.

Submarine The first submarine circumnavigation was achieved between 24 Feb. and 25 April 1960, during an 84-day 10-hour 41,519-mile voyage ("Operation Magellan") by the U.S. nuclear submarine *Triton* (Capt. Edward Latimer Beach), beginning at New London, Connecticut, U.S.A., on 16 Feb. 1960 and ending on 10 May 1960. The circumnavigation from St. Paul's Rock, South Atlantic, required 30,708 statute miles at an average of 18 knots. There was one brief surfacing off Montevideo, Uruguay, to transfer a sick member of the 183-man crew. On 3 April 1966 it was announced that a flotilla of U.S.S.R. nuclear submarines, under the command of Vice-Admiral A. I. Sorokin, had completed a submerged circumnavigation covering 40,000 kilometres (24,800 miles).

ATLANTIC CROSSINGS

Smallest boat *Westwards* The smallest boat ever to cross the Atlantic was the *April Fool*, a 6-foot boat sailed by Hugo Vihlen (U.S.) (born 1932) in 84 days from 29 March 1968 out of Casablanca 4,100 miles to Miami Beach, Florida, U.S.A. Because of the off-setting current the craft had to be brought in the last 23 miles by a U.S. Coastguard cutter.

Eastwards The smallest boat to sail non-stop across the Atlantic eastwards was the 13-foot 6-inch long sloop *Tinkerbelle*, sailed by Robert Manry, aged 48, of Cleveland, Ohio, U.S.A. from Falmouth, Massachusetts, to Falmouth, Cornwall, in 78 days from 31 May to 17 Aug. 1965.

Rowing *Earliest World* The first two men to have rowed the Atlantic were the Norwegians George Harbo (1865–1945) and Frank Samuelsen (1869–1946) who left the Battery, Manhattan Island, New York, U.S.A., on 6 June 1896, and covered 3,075 miles in 56 days, landing at St. Mary's, Isles of Scilly, on 1 Aug. 1896. Their boat, the *Richard K. Fox*, was an 18-foot-long clinker built double ender with a 5-foot beam, and had no mast or sails in its equipment. They stowed five pairs of oars. On 15 July they were picked up, given a meal and new provisions, and climbed back into their boat to complete their journey.

British The first Britons to complete a row across the Atlantic were Capt. John Ridgway, M.B.E., aged 27 and Sergeant Charles "Chay" Blyth, B.E.M., aged 26, in the 22-foot dory *English Rose III*. They left Orleans, Cape Cod, Massachusetts on 4 June and arrived at Inishmore, Aran Isles, Ireland after 91 days on 3 Sept. 1966.

Earliest solo The first west-east solo row across the Atlantic was achieved by the paratrooper Tom McClean (b. Dublin 1943), from St. John's, Newfoundland 2,058 miles to Blacksod Bay, County Mayo, Ireland in 70 days 17 hours from 17 May to 27 July 1969 in his 20-foot dory *Super Silver*.

The first east-west crossing was achieved by John Fairfax (U.K.) (born 21 May 1937) in his 22-foot-long rowing boat *Britannia*. He left Las Palmas on 20 Jan. 1969 and arrived at Fort Lauderdale, Florida, U.S.A. on 20 July 1969 after a record 182 days in an open boat.

The record for a solo Britain–U.S.A. crossing is 26 days 20 hours 32 minutes by Geoffrey Williams, aged 25, of Redruth, Cornwall in the 57-foot ketch *Sir Thomas Lipton* (waterline length 42 feet). He sailed 3,700 nautical miles from Plymouth, Devon on 1 June reaching Brenton Reef light tower, near Newport, Rhode Island, U.S.A., 2,860 miles distant on a Great Circle course on 27 June 1968.

Fastest The fastest solo crossing of the Atlantic is 20 days achieved by Bernard Rhodes, 24 of Newby Bridge, Lancashire, England in his 22-foot trimaran *Klis* from Las Palmas to Bridgetown, Barbados, landing on 11 Feb. 1967.

Rounding the Horn The earliest rounding of Cape Horn (Cabo de Hornos), Chile by a yacht was by the 36-foot *Pandora* (G. D. Blythe [G.B.] and Peter Arapakis [Greece], crew) on 16 Jan. 1911.

Robert E. Peary and his Eskimos at their most northerly camp, Camp Jessup, in 1909

POLAR CONQUESTS

North Pole The claims of neither of the two U.S. Arctic explorers, Dr. Frederick Albert Cook (1865–1940) nor Civil Engineer Robert Edwin Peary, U.S.N. (1856–1920) in reaching the North Pole is subject to positive proof. Cook, accompanied by the Eskimos, Ah-pellah and Etukishook, two sledges and 26 dogs, struck north from a point 60 miles north of Svartevoeg, on Axel Heiberg Is., Canada, 460 miles from the Pole on 21 March 1908, allegedly reaching Lat. 89° 31′ N. on 19 April and the Pole on 21 April. Peary, accompanied by his negro assistant, Matthew Alexander Henson (1866–1955) and the four Eskimos, Ooqueah, Egingwah, Seegloo, and Ootah (1875–1955), struck north from his Camp Bartlett (Lat. 87° 44′ N.) at 5 a.m. on 2 April 1909. After travelling another 134 miles, he allegedly established his final camp, Camp Jessup, in the proximity of the Pole at 10 a.m. on 6 April and marched a further 42 miles quartering the sea-ice before turning south at 4 p.m. on 7 April. Peary's longest claimed 3-day march for a record 163 geographical miles must be regarded as highly improbable. Cook's comparative maximum claim was for 68 geographical miles in 3 days.

The earliest indisputable attainment of the North Pole over the sea-ice was at 3 p.m. (Central Standard Time) on 19 April 1968 by Ralph Plaisted (U.S.) and three companions after a 42-day trek in four Skidoos (snow-mobiles). Their arrival was independently verified 18 hours later by a U.S. Air Force weather aircraft.

Arctic crossing The first crossing of the Arctic sea-ice was achieved by the British Trans-Arctic Expedition which left Point Barrow, Alaska on 21 Feb. 1968 and arrived at the Seven Island Archipelago north-east of Spitzbergen 464 days later on 29 May 1969 after a haul of 3,620 statute miles. The team was Wally Herbert (leader), 34, Major Ken Hedges, 34, R.A.M.C., Allan Gill, 38, and Dr. Roy Koerner (glaciologist), and 40 huskies. This was the longest sustained journey ever made on polar pack ice.

South Pole The first ship to cross the Antarctic circle (Lat. 66° 30′ S.) was the *Resolution* (462 tons), under Capt. James

The British Trans-Arctic Expedition 1968–69, which made the longest sledge journey in history

Cook (1728–79), on 17 Jan. 1773. The first person definitely to sight the Antarctic continent was Edward Bransfield (*c.* 1795–1852), Master of the R.N. ship *Williams* who, on 30 Jan. 1820, discovered "Trinity Land", believed to be the island now called Trinity Island, off the coast of Graham Land (Palmer Peninsula). The crew of the U.S. vessel *Cecilia* (Capt. John Davis) were the first men to land on the continent when they went ashore at Hughes Bay, on the Danco Coast of Graham Land (Palmer Peninsula), at 10 a.m. on 7 Feb. 1821. On 15 June 1960 it was claimed in Moscow, U.S.S.R., that Lt. Mikhail P. Lazarev sighted the Princess Marthaland coast of the mainland two days *before* Bransfield from the masthead of the sloop *Mirny* in Lat. 69° 23′ S., Long. 2° 35′ W. Capt. Fabian Gottlieb von Bellingshausen (1779–1852), it was claimed, also sighted the mainland on the same day from his *Vostok*. Photostats of correspondence were produced to support these claims.

The South Pole was first reached on 14 Dec. 1911 by a Norwegian party, led by Roald Amundsen (1872–1928), after a 53-day march with dog sledges from the Bay of Whales, to which he had penetrated in the *Fram*. Olav Bjaaland, the first to arrive, was the last survivor, dying in June 1961, aged 88. The others were the late Helmer Hanssen, Sverre Hassel and Oskar Wisting.

ld Amundsen orway) at the South Pole in 1911

Antarctic crossing The first crossing of the Antarctic continent was completed at 1.47 p.m. on 2 March 1958, after a 2,158-mile trek lasting 99 days from 24 Nov. 1957, from Shackleton Base to Scott Base *via* the Pole. The crossing party of twelve was led by Dr. (now Sir) Vivian Ernest Fuchs (born 11 Feb. 1908).

Longest sledge journey The longest polar sledge journey was one of 3,720 statute route miles in 476 days by the British Trans-Arctic Expedition from 21 Feb. 1968 to 10 June 1969 (see page 164).

MOUNTAINEERING

Highest by man The conquest of the highest point on Earth, Mount Everest (29,028 feet) was first achieved at 11.30 a.m. on 29 May 1953, by Edmund Percival Hillary (New Zealand) and the Sherpa Tenzing Norkhay (see Mountaineering, Chapter 12).

Highest by women The greatest altitude attained by a woman mountaineer is 26,208 feet by Miss Setsuko Watanabe, 31, on Everest in May 1970. The highest mountain summit reached by women is Qungur I (Kongur Tiube Tagh) (*c.* 25,146 feet), climbed in 1961 by Shierab and another (unnamed) Tibetan woman.

GREATEST OCEAN DESCENT

The record ocean descent was achieved in the Challenger Deep of the Marianas Trench, 250 miles south-west of Guam, in the Pacific Ocean, when the Swiss-built U.S. Navy bathyscaphe *Trieste*, manned by Dr. Jacques Piccard (Switzerland), and Lt. Donald Walsh, U.S.N., reached the ocean bed 35,802 feet (6·78 miles) down, at 1.10 p.m. on 23 Jan. 1960 (but see also Chapter 3). The pressure of the water was 16,883 lb. per square inch (1,085·3 tons per square foot), and the temperature 37·4° F. The descent required 4 hours 48 minutes and the ascent 3 hours 17 minutes.

Deep sea diving The world's record depth for a salvage observation chamber is that established by the Admiralty salvage ship *Reclaim* on 28 June 1956. In an observation chamber measuring 7 feet long and 3 feet internal diameter, Senior Com. Boatswain (now Lt.-Cdr.) G. A. M. Wookey, M.B.E., R.N., descended to a depth of 1,060 feet in Oslo Fjord, Norway.

SALVAGING

Deepest The deepest salvaging operation ever carried out was on the wreck of the S.S. *Niagara*, sunk by a mine in 1940, 438 feet down off Bream Head, Whangarei, North Island, New Zealand. All but 6 per cent. of the

£2,250,000 of gold in her holds was recovered in 7 weeks. The record recovery was that from the White Star Liner *Laurentic*, which was torpedoed in 114 feet of water off Malin Head, Donegal, Ireland, in 1917, with £5,000,000 of gold ingots in her Second Class baggage room. By 1924, 3,186 of the 3,211 gold bricks had been recovered with immense difficulty.

Largest vessel The largest vessel ever salvaged was the U.S.S. *Lafayette*, formerly the French liner *Normandie* (83,423 tons), which keeled over during fire-fighting operations at the West 49th Street Pier, New York Harbour, U.S.A., on 9 Feb. 1942. She was righted in October 1943, at a cost of $4,500,000 (then £1,250,000), and was broken up at Newark, New Jersey, beginning September 1946.

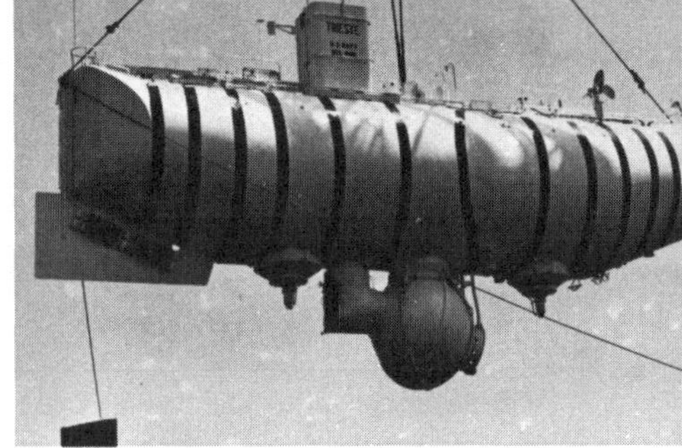

The bathyscaphe *Trieste*, which in 1960 carried two men 6·8 miles down into the Pacific Ocean

OCEAN DESCENTS—PROGRESSIVE RECORDS

Feet	Vehicle	Divers	Location	Date
c. 245	Steel Sphere	Ernest Bazin (France)	Belle Île	1865
c. 830	Diving Bell	Balsamello Bella Nautica (Italy)		1889
c. 1,650	Hydrostat	Hartman		1911
1,426	Bathysphere	Dr. C. William Beebe and Dr. Otis Barton (U.S.A.)	S.E. Bermuda	11 June 1930
2,200	Bathysphere	Dr. C. W. Beebe and Dr. O. Barton (U.S.A.)	S.E. Bermuda	22 Sept. 1932
2,510	Bathysphere	Dr. C. W. Beebe and Dr. O. Barton (U.S.A.)	S.E. Bermuda	11 Aug. 1934
3,028	Bathysphere	Dr. C. W. Beebe and Dr. O. Barton (U.S.A.)	S.E. Bermuda	15 Aug. 1934
7,850	*Converted U-boat*	*Heinz Sellner (Germany) (unwitnessed)*	*Murmansk*	*Aug. 1947*
4,500	Benthoscope	Dr. Otis Barton (U.S.A.)	off Santa Cruz, California	16 Aug. 1949
5,085	Bathyscaphe *F.N.R.S. 3*	Lt.-Cdr. Georges S. Houet and Lt. Pierre-Henri Willm (France)	off Toulon	12 Aug. 1953
6,890	Bathyscaphe *F.N.R.S. 3*	Lt.-Cdr. G. S. Houet and Lt. P.-H. Willm (France)	off Cap Ferrat	14 Aug. 1953
10,335	Bathyscaphe *Trieste*	Prof. Auguste and Dr. Jacques Piccard (Switzerland)	Ponza Is.	30 Sept. 1953
13,287	Bathyscaphe *F.N.R.S. 3*	Lt.-Cdr. G. S. Houet and Eng. Off. P.-H. Willm (France)	off Dakar, Senegal	15 Feb. 1954
18,600	Bathyscaphe *Trieste*	Dr. J. Piccard (Swiss) and Andreas B. Rechnitzer (U.S.A.)	Marianas Trench	14 Nov. 1959
24,000	Bathyscaphe *Trieste*	Dr. J. Piccard (Swiss) and Lt. D. Walsh, U.S.N.	Marianas Trench	7 Jan. 1960
35,802	Bathyscaphe *Trieste*	Dr. J. Piccard (Swiss) and Lt. D. Walsh, U.S.N.	Marianas Trench	23 Jan. 1960

DEEP DIVING—PROGRESSIVE RECORDS

BREATH-HOLDING

Feet	Divers	Location	Date
c. 50	Mother-of-pearl divers	Mediterranean	*c.* 3,300 B.C.
c. 120	Sponge and oyster divers (limit)	various	—
c. 200	Stotti Georghios (Greece)	Adriatic	1913
198	Jacques Mayol (France)	off Freeport, Grand Bahama	July 1966
212½	P.O. Robert Croft, U.S.N.	Floridian coast, U.S.A.	8 Feb. 1967
#125	Evelyn Patterson (Zambia)	off Freeport, Grand Bahama	1967
217½	P.O. Robert Croft, U.S.N.	off Ft. Lauderdale, U.S.A.	19 Dec. 1967
231	Jacques Mayol (France)	Mediterranean	14 Jan. 1968
240	P.O. Robert Croft, U.S.N.	Floridian coast, U.S.A.	12 Aug. 1968

BREATHING AIR

Feet	Divers	Location	Date
162[1]	A. Lambert (U.K.)	Grand Canary Is.	1885
190[1]	Greek and Swedish divers	off Patras, Greece	1904
210[1]	Lt. G. C. C. Damant, R.N.	Loch Striven, Scotland	1906
274[2]	Chief Gunner S. J. Drellifsak, U.S.N.	from U.S.S. *Walke*	9 Oct. 1914
304[2]	F. Crilley, W. F. Loughman, F. C. L. Nielson, U.S.N.	off Hawaii	1915
344[2]	Diver Hilton, R.N.	British waters	1932
307[3]	Frederick Dumas (France)	Mediterranean	1947
†396[3]	Lt. Maurice Farques (France)	Mediterranean	1947
††400[3]	Hope Root (U.S.A.)	U.S. waters	1953
350[3]	Jean Clarke-Samazen	off Santa Catalina, U.S.A.	Aug. 1954
#320[3]	Katherine Troutt (Australia)	Sydney Heads, Australia	7 Sept. 1964
355[3]	Hal D. Watts and Herb Johnson (U.S.A.)	off Loo Key, Fla., U.S.A.	4 Sept. 1966
380[3]	Hal D. Watts and Arthur J. Muns (U.S.A.)	off Miami Beach, U.S.A.	3 Sept. 1967
#325[3]	Kitty Giesler	off Freeport, Grand Bahama	31 Oct. 1967
437[3]	John J. Gruener and R. Neal Watson (U.S.A.)	off Freeport, Grand Bahama	14 Oct. 1968

BREATHING GAS MIXTURES

Feet	Divers	Location	Date
420[4]	M. G. Nohl (U.S.A.)	Lake Michigan, U.S.A.	1 Dec. 1937
440[5]	R. M. Metzger and Claude Conger, U.S.N.	Portsmouth, N.H., U.S.A.	22 June 1941
†528[5]	A. Zetterström (Sweden)	Baltic	7 Aug. 1945
450[4]	P.O.'s Wilfred H. Bollard and W. Soper, R.N.	Loch Fyne, Scotland	26 Aug. 1948
540[4]	P.O. W. H. Bollard, R.N.	Loch Fyne, Scotland	28 Aug. 1948
550	Diver J. E. Johnson	Hauriki Gulf, N.Z.	1949
600[4]	Lt.-Cdr. George A. M. Wookey, M.B.E., R.N.	Oslo Fjord, Norway	13 Oct. 1956
728[6]	Hannes Keller (Switzerland) and Kenneth MacLeish (U.S.A.)	Lake Maggiore, Italy	30 June 1961
*1,000[6]	H. Keller (Switzerland) and Peter Small †(U.K.)	off Santa Catalina, U.S.A.	3 Dec. 1962
**1,025[4]	U.S. Navy Aquanauts		Feb. 1968
**1,100[4]	Carl Deckman (Int. Underwater Contractors, Inc.)	Murray Hill, N.J., U.S.A.	12 Mar. 1968
**1,197[4]	Ralph W. Brauer (U.S.A.) and Réné Veyrunes (France)	Comex Chamber, France	27 June 1968
**1,500[4]	John Bevan and Peter Sharphouse (U.K.)	Alverstoke, Hampshire	11 Mar. 1970

 # Female record.
† Died on the ascent.
†† Died on the descent.
** Emerged from a diving bell.*
*** Simulated chamber dive.*
1 Surface supplied, helmet.
2 Surface supplied, flexible dress.
3 Scuba (self-contained underwater breathing apparatus).
4 Oxygen-helium.
5 Oxygen-hydrogen.
6 Oxygen-helium plus an additive.

Most expensive The most expensive salvage operation ever conducted was that by the U.S. Navy off Palomares, southern Spain, for the recovery of a 2,800 lb. 20 megaton H-bomb, between 17 Jan. and 7 April 1966, at a cost of $30,000,000 (£12·5 million). A fleet of 18 ships and 2,200 men took part. A CURV (Cable-controlled Underwater Research Vehicle) was flown from California and retrieved the bomb, dropped from a crashing B-52 bomber, from a depth of 2,850 feet.

ghest award The highest salvage award ever paid out was £575,000 to the salvors of the S.S. *Toledo* (4,581 gross tons), stranded off Karachi, West Pakistan, in July 1952.

MINING DEPTHS

Greatest penetration Man's deepest penetration made into the ground is in the East Rand Proprietary Mine in Boksburg, Transvaal. In November 1959 a level of 11,246 feet or 2·13 miles below ground level was attained in a pilot winze in the Hercules section. The rock temperature at this depth was 126° F. Incline shafts to a planned depth of 12,000 feet are being worked at Western Deep Levels mine, Klerksdorp, South Africa.

haft sinking record The one month (31 days) world record is 1,251 feet for a standard shaft 26 feet in diameter at Buffelsfontein Mine, Transvaal, South Africa, in March 1962. The British record is 336 feet in 31 days in January 1961 at the No. 2 shaft of Kellingley Colliery, Knottingley, Yorkshire.

RUNNING

Mensen Ehrnst (1799–1846) of Norway is reputed to have run from Istanbul, Turkey, to Calcutta, in West Bengal, India, and back in 59 days in 1836, so averaging an improbable 94·2 miles per day. The greatest non-stop run recorded is 121 miles 440 yards in 22 hours 27 minutes by Jared R. Beads, 41, of Westport, Maryland in October 1969. The greatest distance covered in 24 hours is the 162 miles 704 yards of George Littlewood (England) on 25 Nov. 1884. The distance comprised 5 miles 154 yards more than six marathons and would entail more than 649 laps of a quarter-mile track.

x-day races The greatest distance covered by a man in six days (*i.e.* the 144 permissible hours between Sundays in Victorian times) was 623¾ miles by George Littlewood (England), who required only 139 hours 1 min. for this feat in December 1888 at the old Madison Square Gardens, New York City, U.S.A.

ongest race The longest race ever staged was the 1929 Trans-continental Race (3,665 miles) from New York City, N.Y., to Los Angeles, California, U.S.A. The Finnish-born Johnny Salo (killed 6 Oct. 1931) was the winner in 79 days, from 31 March to 17 June. His elapsed time of 525 hours 57 minutes 20 seconds gave a running average of 6·97 m.p.h.

th America ast to coast Bruce Tulloh (Great Britain), aged 33, the 1962 European 5,000 metre champion, lowered the North-American trans-continental record from Los Angeles to New York (2,876 miles) to 64 days 21 hours 50 minutes (average 44·3 miles per day) from 10 a.m. on 21 April to 11.50 a.m. on 25 June 1969. His weight dropped from 8 st. 4 lb. to 7 st. 12 lb.

Hottest run The traverse of the 120-mile-long Death Valley, California in both directions was uniquely accomplished by Paul Pfau with ground temperatures reaching 140° F. on 22–24 Jan. (30½ elapsed hours) for the southbound and on 3–5 March 1971 (26 hours 10 minutes) for the northbound traverse.

WALKING

The greatest distance ever walked non-stop is 215 miles 1,670 yards by John Sinclair, 51, of Great Britain, in 47 hours 42 minutes round the perimeter of the Wingfield Aerodrome, Cape Town, South Africa on 21–23 April 1969. The greatest distance achieved in a non-stop walking endurance test held under continuous surveillance in Great Britain is 201 miles 722 yards by Bob Thirtle, 49, of King's Lynn, Norfolk around the perimeter of the R.A.F. station Marham, Norfolk (4 miles 627 yards per lap) in 55 hours 40 minutes on 4–6 April 1969. A claim for 211 miles non-stop by Edward Frederick Westcott from Land's End to Bristol in 54 hours 5 minutes on 21–23 Aug. 1967 is not subject to proof.

The longest officially controlled walking race was that of 3,415 miles from New York to San Francisco, U.S.A., from 3 May to 24 July 1926, won by A. L. Monteverde aged 60, occupying 79 days 10 hours 10 minutes. In 1909 Edward Payson Weston walked 7,495 miles on a Trans-continental and return walk in 181 days.

Duration The longest *duration* recorded non-stop walk is one of 66½ hours by Michael Potter, 27, at Sittingbourne, Kent in July 1970. He covered 185 miles.

SWIMMING

The greatest recorded distance ever swum is 1,826 miles down the Mississippi, U.S.A. by Fred P. Newton, 27, from 6 July to 29 Dec. 1933. He was 742 hours in the water between Ford Dam near Minneapolis and Carrollte Ave., New Orleans, Louisiana. The water temperature fell to 47° F. and Newton used olive oil and axle grease.

The longest duration swim ever achieved was one of 168 continuous hours, ending on 24 Feb. 1941, by the legless Charles Zibbelman, *alias* Zimmy (born 1894) of the U.S.A., in a pool in Honolulu, Hawaii, U.S.A.

The longest duration swim by a woman was 87 hours 27 minutes in a pool by Mrs. Myrtle Huddleston of New York City, N.Y., U.S.A., in 1931.

Longest on a raft The longest recorded survival alone on a raft is 133 days (4½ months) by Second Steward Poon Lim (born Hong Kong) of the U.K. Merchant Navy, whose ship, the S.S. *Ben Lomond*, was torpedoed in the Atlantic 750 miles off the Azores at 11.45 a.m. on 23 Nov. 1942. He was picked up by a Brazilian fishing boat off Salinas, Brazil, on 5 April 1943 and was able to walk ashore. In July 1943, he was awarded the B.E.M.

Poon Lim, B.E.M., who survived 4½ months alone on a raft in the Atlantic

Dr. Alain Bombard (France) drifted from Casablanca, Morocco to Barbados on his 15-foot inflatable dinghy *Hérétique* in 64 days in 1952. The seals on his food and water rations were unbroken.

The longest intentional single-handed voyage on a raft was one of 7,450 miles by William Willis (born in Germany, 1893) of the U.S.A., who arrived at Upolu, Western Samoa, on 12 Nov. 1963, accompanied by two cats, on his steel-hulled trimaran raft *Age Unlimited* (32 by 20 feet), after a 130-day voyage across the Pacific Ocean. He had been cast off 50 miles off Callao, Peru, on 5 July 1963.

CYCLING

The duration record for cycling on a track is 168 hours (7 days) by Syed Muhammed Nawab, aged 22, of Lucknow, India, in Addis Ababa, Ethiopia, in 1964. The monocycle duration record is 11 hours 21 minutes (83·4 miles) by Raymond Le Grand at Maubeuge, France, on 12 Sept. 1955. The longest cycle tour on record is one of 135,000 miles by Mishreelal Jaiswal (born 1924) of India, through 107 countries from 1950 to 5 April 1964, ending in San Francisco, California, U.S.A. He wore out five machines.

MARRIAGE AND DIVORCE

Most Mrs. Beverly Nina Avery, then aged 48, a barmaid from Los Angeles, California, U.S.A., set a monogamous world record in October 1957 by obtaining her sixteenth divorce from her fourteenth husband, Gabriel Avery. She alleged outside the court that five of the 14 had broken her nose. In Malaya, Abdul Rahman, aged 55, of Kuala Lumpur, married his 23rd wife aged 16 in October 1967 but voluntarily never had more than one wife at a time.

Beverly Nina O'Malley with one of her 14 husbands

The greatest number of marriages accumulated in the monogamous world is 19 by Glynn de Moss Wolfe (U.S.) (b. 1908) who married for the 19th time since 1930 his 17th wife Gloria, aged 23, on 22 Feb. 1969. His total number of children is, he says, 31. In 1955 he was reputedly worth $500,000 but recently testified to be living on welfare. The most often marrying millionaire was Thomas F. Manville (1894–1967) who contracted his 13th marriage to his 11th wife Christine Erdlen, aged 20, in New York City, U.S.A., on 11 Jan. 1960 when aged 65. His shortest marriage (to his seventh wife) effectively lasted only 34 minutes. His fortune came from asbestos, none of which he could take with him.

Reports in April 1959 that Francis Van Wie, a conductor on the street-cars of the San Francisco Municipal Railway, California, U.S.A., had married his 18th wife, one Minnie Reardon, were later revised when it was discovered that some of his earlier marriages were undissolved. The widely publicized story of Bora Mičić, 44, of Milesevo, Boznia who reputedly married 79 times and divorced 78 times between 1944 and 1970, is not regarded as authentic by Yugoslav diplomatic sources.

Longest engagement The longest engagement on record is one of 67 years between Octavio Guillen, 82 and Adriana Martinez, 82. They finally took the plunge in June 1969 in Mexico City, Mexico.

Longest marriage The longest recorded marriage is one of 86 years between Sir Temulji Bhicaji Nariman and Lady Nariman from 1853 to 1940 resulting from a cousin marriage when both were five. Sir Temulji (born 3 Sept. 1848) died, aged 91 years 11 months, in August 1940 at Bombay.

Probably the longest marriage now existing is that between Ward McDaniel (b. 19 June 1868) and his wife Annie *née* Hays (b. 8 May 1869) who celebrated their 81st anniversary on 21 Jan 1971. They were married at Winterset, Iowa on 21 Jan. 1890 when Benjamin Harrison was President.

James Frederick Burgess (born 3 March 1861, died 27 Nov. 1966) and his wife Sarah Ann, *née* Gregory (born 11 July 1865, died 22 June 1965) were married on 21 June 1883 at St. James's, Bermondsey, London, and celebrated their 82nd anniversary in 1965.

Most married James and Mary Grady of Illinois, U.S.A. have married each other 27 times as a protest against the existence of divorce in the period 1964–69. They have married in 25 different States, 3 times in a day (16 Dec. 1968), twice in an hour and twice on television.

Mass ceremony The largest mass wedding ceremony was one of 791 couples officiated over by Sun Myung Moon of the Holy Spirit Association for the Unification of World Christianity in Seoul, South Korea in October 1970. The response to the question "Will you swear to love your spouse for ever?" is "Ye".

Eating out The world champion for eating out is Fred E. Magel of Chicago, Illinois, U.S.A. who since 1928 has dined in more than 32,300 restaurants in 60 nations as a restaurant grader. He asserts the most expensive is Voisins, Park Avenue, New York City, U.S.A. where a solo lunch cost him $26.50 (more than £11) and the one serving the largest helpings is Zehnder's Hotel, Frankenmuth, Michigan, U.S.A. Mr. Magel's favourite dishes are South African rock lobster and mousse of fresh English strawberries.

Party giving The most expensive private party ever thrown was that of Mr. and Mrs. Bradley Martin of Troy, N.Y., U.S.A. staged at the Waldorf Hotel, Manhattan in February 1897. The cost to the host and hostess was estimated to be $369,200 in the days when dollars were made of gold.

Toastmasters The Guild of Professional Toastmasters (founded 1962) has only 12 members. Its founder, Ivor Spencer, has listened to 21,670 speeches to 7 May 1969, including one in excess of 2 hours by the maudlin victim of a retirement luncheon. Winners of the After Dinner Speaker of the Year Trophy (inst. 1967) have been Lord Redcliffe-Maud, G.C.B., C.B.E. in 1967 and the Rt. Hon. J. H. Wilson, O.B.E., M.P. in 1968. The Guild also elects the most boring speaker of the year, but for professional reasons, does not publicize the winner's name. Red coats were introduced by the earliest professional William Knight-Smith (d. 1932) *c.* 1900.

Working week The longest working week (maximum possible 168 hours) is up to 136 hours at times by some housemen and registrars in some of the teaching hospitals in London. This figure has been given in evidence by the Action Group of Junior Hospital Medical Staff.

Working career The longest working career in one job in Britain is believed to belong to Mr. Mark Hicks of Crookham,

Hampshire (d. July 1966 aged 92). He started work for the Basingstoke Canal Co., aged 10, and was still working as bailiff of the canal four days before his death after 82 years.

Longest pension Miss Millicent Barclay, daughter of Col. William Barclay was born posthumously on 10 July 1872 and became eligible for a Madras Military Fund pension to continue until her marriage. She died unmarried on 26 Oct. 1969 having drawn the pension for every day of her life of 97 years 3 months.

MISCELLANEOUS ENDEAVOURS

pple peeling The longest single unbroken apple peel on record is one of 912 inches (76 feet) peeled by Fritz Wafler of Wolcott, New York, U.S.A., in November 1970.

pple picking The greatest recorded performance is 151 U.S. bushels (146·3 Imperial bushels) picked in 8 hours by Ray Craig at Ben Nardie's Fruit Farm, Parke County, Indiana, U.S.A. in October 1967.

Autographs The largest collection of autographed photographs signed by celebrities is one of 1,460 amassed by Peter Clark of London, England to mid-May 1970.

Peter Clark, the most successful collector of signed photographs

ag carrying The record time for the annual "World Coal Carrying Championship" over the uphill 1,080 yards course at Ossett cum Gawthorpe, Yorkshire, England with a 112 lb. sack is 4 minutes 42 seconds by Ruben L. Parsons, 26, of Kendal, Westmorland on 30 March 1970. The non-stop distance record carrying 1 cwt. is $12\frac{1}{4}$ miles in 3 hours 40 minutes from Perranporth to Cambourne, Cornwall by E. John Rapson on 4 April 1953.

Bag-pipes The longest duration pipe has been one of 50 hours by William Donaldson, Donald Grant, John Lovie and William Wotherspoon of Aberdeen University on 21–23 April 1969. The comment of some local inhabitants after the "lang blaw" was "Thank God there's nae smell".

Balloon racing The largest release of balloons was 20,000 at the Great Beefeater Gin Balloon Race from Harleyford Manor, Marlow, Buckinghamshire, England on 21 April 1971. The winner of the 1970 Alcan Race was Mrs. Jean Bridgens whose balloon, released from Webbs Garden Centre, Wordsley on 26 Sept. 1970, landed 665 miles away near Starnberg-am-See, West Germany. The only authenticated case of a balloon landing 1,000 miles away was one released by J. Kingdom at Trowbridge, Wiltshire on 5 Sept. 1970 and recovered at Marmentini, Italy.

The mass release of 20,000 balloons in the Beefeater Gin Race

Ball punching Ron Renaulf (Australia) equalled his own world duration ball punching record of 125 hours 20 minutes at 10.20 p.m. on 31 Dec. 1955, at the Esplanade, Southport, Queensland, Australia.

Barrel jumping The greatest number of barrels jumped by a skater is 17 (total length 28 feet 8 inches) by Kenneth LeBel at the Grossinger Country Club, New York State, U.S.A., on 9 Jan. 1965.

Bed carrying The longest solo bed carrying walk on record with a bed weighing more than 50 kg. (114 lb.) is one of 9·6 miles by Peter Amstutz, between Lucerne and Hoch-Ybrig, Switzerland on 4 Nov. 1970.

Bed of nails The duration record for lying on a bed of nails (needle-sharp 6-inch nails 2 inches apart) is 25 hours 9 minutes by Zjane Azzar at Walton Store, Park and George Street, Sydney, Australia on 20–21 Nov. 1969. Much longer durations are claimed by uninvigilated *fakirs*—the most extreme case being *Silki* who claimed 111 days in Sao Paulo, Brazil ending on 24 Aug. 1969.

Bed-pushing The longest recorded push of a normally sessile object is of 411 miles in the case of a wheeled hospital bed by a team of ten from the Aldbourne Methodist Youth Club, Marlborough, Wiltshire on 1–6 Aug. 1970. A push of 408 miles in extreme weather conditions down to 17° F. below zero was achieved by 12 students from Dalhousie University, Nova Scotia, Canada on 15–21 Dec. 1970.

Best man The world's champion "best man" is Mr. Wally Gant, a bachelor fishmonger from Wakefield, Yorkshire, who officiated for the 50th time since 1931 in December 1964.

Big wheel riding The endurance record for riding a Big Wheel is 14 days 21 hours by David Trumayne, 22, at Ramsgate, Kent ending on 8 June 1969. He completed 62,207 revolutions. Richard Ford, 30, sat for 20 days $16\frac{1}{2}$ hours in a 40-foot Ferris Wheel in San Francisco, California in January 1971. It did not, however, revolve at night.

Blanket making On 11 June 1969 fifty blankets were made from fleece to the finished dyed article in 14 hours 4 minutes by 150 members of Charles Early & Marriott (Witney) Ltd. at Witney, Oxfordshire, England. The first blanket was completed in 8 hours 11 minutes.

Body jump The greatest number of "bodies" cleared in a motorcycle ramp jump is 41 by Sgt.-Maj. Gledhill, B.E.M., 41, on a B.S.A. 441 c.c. Victor Grand Prix of the Royal Artillery Motorcycle Team at Woolwich, Greater London on 4 June 1970. The 41st man was Capt. Tony Scarisbrick.

The build-up to the ultimate in car-cramming—103 in and on a Volkswagen in the *Blue Peter* studio

Bomb defusing The highest reported number of unexploded bombs defused by any individual is 8,000 by Werner Stephan in West Berlin, Germany, in the 12 years from 1945 to 1957. He was killed by a small grenade on the Grunewald blasting site on 17 Aug. 1957.

Bond signing The greatest feat of bond signing was that performed by L. E. Chittenden (d. 1902), the Registrar of the United States Treasury. In 48 hours (20–22 March 1863) he signed 12,500 bonds worth $10,000,000 (now £4,166,666), which had to catch a steam packet to England. He suffered years of pain and the bonds were never used.

Boomerang throwing Two types of boomerang are used by the natives of Australia: the return type, aimed against birds and used as a plaything, and the war boomerang. The longest measured throws for a return type are ones of 90 yards with an orbital perimeter of 250 yards with a 6 oz. vulcanized fibre boomerang by Bob and Jack Burwell of Slack's Creek, Queensland. These have been kept airborne for 18·4 seconds.

Brick carrying The record for the annual Narrogin Brick Carrying contest in Western Australia (instituted in 1960) is 40·0 miles by Ronald D. Hamilton on 10 Oct. 1970. The 8 lb. 12 oz. wire-cut semi-pressed brick has to be carried in a downward position with a nominated ungloved hand. The feminine record for a 7¾ lb. brick is 1·6 miles by Pat McDougall, aged 16, but Jeanette Bartlett of Swindon, Wiltshire carried an 8 lb. 13¾ oz. brick more than 1·49 miles on 4 July 1969.

Bricklaying The world record for bricklaying was established in 1937 by Joseph Raglon of East St. Louis, Illinois, U.S.A., who, supported by assistants, placed 3,472 bricks in 60 minutes of foundation-work—at a rate of nearly 58 a minute.

The record for constructional bricklaying was set when J. E. Bloxham, of Stratford-upon-Avon, England laid a 13½-foot wall of 5,188 bricks in 7 hours 35 minutes with two assistants on 28th May 1960. It was also reported that Mr. C. Hull of Sheffield, Yorkshire laid 860 bricks in 60 minutes on 24 Nov. 1924.

Brick throwing The greatest reported distance for throwing a standard 5 lb. building brick is 135 feet 8 inches by Robert Gardner at Stroud, Gloucestershire, England, in the annual contest on 18 July 1970.

Burial alive The longest recorded burial alive is one of 100 days ending on 17 Sept. 1968 in Skegness by Mrs. Emma Smith of Ravenshead, Nottinghamshire, England. The male record is 78 days by Bill Kearns, 36, of South Hiendley, Yorkshire, from 21 June to 7 Sept. 1969.

The record in a "regulation" size coffin is 240 hours 18 minutes 50 seconds by Tim Hayes of Cóbh, Ireland ending on 2 Sept. 1970. His coffin was 6 feet 3 inches long, 14 inches deep and 21 inches wide at the shoulder tapering to 12 inches at the ankle.

Car cramming Car cramming is potentially a most dangerous and inadvisable exercise since the weight of 100 bodies is about 6 tons. The highest total of "bodies" crammed into and on a small car is 103 students from Bournemouth College on the *Blue Peter* T.V. programme at the B.B.C. Centre, Wood Lane, London on 12 Nov. 1970. The loaded Volkswagen 1300 was driven 5 metres.

Circuit training The most protracted test was one of 100 hours by Jim Hyde and John Pike of King Alfred Boy's Club, Winchester, England on 9–13 Sept. 1969. The work was a mixture of punch bag, weight lifting, medicine ball, chest expanders, trampoline, floor exercises, skipping and merely running.

Clapping The duration record for continuous clapping is 14 hours 6 minutes by Nicholas Willey, 18 and Christopher Floyd, 17 of Canford School, Dorset, England on 13–14 Dec. 1968. They sustained an average of 140 claps per minute and an audibility range of at least 100 yards.

Club swinging Bill Franks set a world record of 17,280 revolutions (4·8 per second) in 60 minutes at Webb's Gymnasium, Newcastle, N.S.W., Australia on 2 Aug. 1934. M. Dobrilla swung continuously for 144 hours at Cobar, N.S.W. finishing on 15 Sept. 1913.

Coal shovelling The record for filling a half-ton hopper with coal is 56·6 seconds by D. Coghlan of Reefton, New Zealand on 3 Jan. 1969.

Commuter Most durable Bruno Leuthardt commuted 370 miles each day for the 11 years 1957–67 from Hamburg to teach in the Bodelschwingh School, Dortmund, West Germany. He was late only once due to the 1962 Hamburg floods.

Competition winnings The champion winner of consumer and newspaper reader competitions in the United Kingdom over the 8-year period June 1962 to June 1970 has been Mrs. S. G. Bray of Huddersfield, Yorkshire, with 507 prizes valued in cash and kind at £15,267.

The largest single competition prize awarded in Britain has been £10,000 for the first prize in the 1965 Stork Margarine Family Album Competition. The winner was Mrs. V. Laurie of Brentford, Middlesex.

DANCING

The largest dance ever staged was that put on by the Houston Livestock Show at the Astro Hall, Houston, Texas, U.S.A. on 8 Feb. 1969. The attendance was more than 16,500 with 4,000 turned away.

Marathon dancing must be distinguished from dancing mania, which is a pathological condition. The worst outbreak of dancing mania was at Aachen, Germany, in July 1374, when hordes of men and women broke into a frenzied dance in the streets which lasted for hours till injury or complete exhaustion ensued.

The most severe marathon dance staged as a public spectacle in the U.S.A. was one lasting 3,780 hours (22 weeks 3½ days) completed by Callum L. deVillier, 24 and Vonny Kuchinski, 20 at Sommerville, Massachusetts, U.S.A. from 28 Dec. 1932 to 3 June 1933. In the last two weeks the rest allowance was cut from 15 minutes per hour to only 3 minutes while the last 52½ hours were continuous. The prize of $1,000 was equivalent to less than 26½ cents per hour.

Ballet Among the world's greatest ballet dancers, Vatslav Fomich Nijinsky (1890–1950), a Russian-born Pole, was alone in being credited with being able to achieve the *entrechat dix*—crossing and uncrossing the feet 10 times in a single elevation. This is not believed by physical education experts since no high jumper can stay off the ground for more than 1 second and no analysable film exists.

Most turns The greatest number of spins called for in classical ballet choreography is the 32 *fouettés en tournant* in "Swan Lake" by Pyotr Ilyich Chaykovskiy (Tschaikovsky) (1840–1893). Miss Rowena Jackson, of New Zealand, achieved 121 such turns at her class in Melbourne, Victoria, Australia, in 1940.

Most curtain calls The greatest recorded number of curtain calls ever received by ballet dancers is 89 by Dame Peggy Arias, D.B.E. *née* Hookham (born Reigate, Surrey, 18 May 1919), *alias* Margot Fonteyn, and Rudolf Nureyev (born in a train near Ufa, U.S.S.R., 1938) after a performance of "Swan Lake" at the Vienna Staatsoper, Austria, in October 1964.

Ballroom *Marathon* The individual continuous world record for ballroom dancing is 106 hours 5 minutes 10 seconds by Carlos Sandrini in Buenos Aires, Argentina, in September 1955. Three girls worked shifts as his partner.

Champions The world's most successful professional ballroom dancing champions have been Bill Irvine, M.B.E. and Bobby Irvine, M.B.E., who have been undefeated as World Professional Champions since 1960.

Charleston The Charleston duration record is 22½ hours by John Giola, aged 23, at the Roseland Ballroom, Broadway, New York City, N.Y., U.S.A., in 1926.

Flamenco The fastest flamenco dancer ever measured is Solero de Jerez aged 17 who in Brisbane, Australia in Sept. 1967 in an electrifying routine attained 16 heel taps per second or a rate of 1,000 a minute.

Go-go The duration record for go-go dancing (Boogoloo or Reggae) is 108 hours (with 5 minute breaks each hour) by Jane Berins, 16, of Glinton, Peterborough on 24-28 March 1970.

Jiving The duration record for non-stop jiving is 40 hours by Gordon Lightfoot and Kathleen Fowler at Penrith, on 22–24 April 1960. Breaks of 3½ minutes per hour were permitted for massage. This time was equalled by Terry Ratcliffe, aged 16, and Christina Woodcroft, aged 17, at Traralgon, Victoria, Australia, from 10.15 p.m. on 28 May to 2.13 p.m. on 30 May 1965.

Limbo The lowest height for a bar under which a clothed limbo dancer has passed is 6½ inches by Teresa Marquis of St. Lucia, West Indies, at the Guinness Distribution Depot, Grosvenor Road, Belfast, Northern Ireland on 15 April 1970. Her vital statistics are 34–24–36.

Twist The duration record for the twist is 102 hours by Mrs. Cathie Harvey (then Mrs. Cathy Connelly) at the Theatre Royal, Tyldesley, Lancashire ending on 29 Nov. 1964. She had 5 minutes time out per hour and 20 minutes every 4 hours.

Most expensive course The world's most expensive dance course has been the "Lifetime Executive Course" of Arthur Murray (b. Murray Teichmann, 4 April 1895) in the United States. It came after the Lifetime Course ($7,300) and the $9,000 "Gold Medal Course" and cost $12,000, making a total of $28,300 or now equivalent to £11,791.

Modern The longest recorded dancing marathon (50 minutes per hour) in popular style is one of 54 hours by Miss Gillian Smith at Wigan Technical College, Wigan, Lancashire on March 3–5 1970.

Dance band The most protracted session for a dance band is one of 321 hours (13 days 9 hours) by the Black Brothers of West Germany at Bonn ending on 2 Feb. 1968. Never less than a quartet were in action during the marathon.

Disc-jockey The longest continuous period of acting as a disc-jockey is 360 hours (15 days) by Pete Grooves, 19, of Basingstoke, Hampshire on 15–30 Nov. 1970. Melvyn Pace worked 400 hours, sleeping during some L.P.s at Granny's Club, Leicester ending at noon on 19 Oct. 1970. Four R.A.F. men from the Avon Club, Upavon, Wiltshire played singles in shifts for 334 hours on 8–22 April 1970.

Drumming The world's duration drumming record is 150 hours by Robert Sturgill of Aberdeen, Washington, U.S.A., in October 1970.

Egg and spoon racing David Smith and Peter Dilley of Chigwell, Essex completed a local 20-mile fresh egg and dessert spoon marathon in 5 hours 25 minutes on 27 July 1969.

Egg throwing The longest recorded distance for throwing a fresh hen's egg without breaking is 268 feet 7 inches by James Shepherd Anthony, 22 and John Wilson (catcher) at Old Lyonian sports ground, Harrow, Middlesex, England on 25 May 1971.

Escapology The most renowned of all escape artists has been Ehrich Weiss *alias* Harry Houdini (1874–1926), who pioneered underwater escapes from locked, roped and weighted containers while handcuffed and shackled with irons.

Face-slapping The face-slapping contest duration record was set in Kiev, U.S.S.R., in 1931, when a draw was declared between Vasiliy Bezbordny and Goniusch after 30 hours.

Fruit machines Using 6d. discs a team of four from the Vale of Pewsey Young Conservatives succeeded in feeding in £1,512·60 worth of discs (*viz* 60,504) in 48 hours, a lever pulling rate of better than once every 3 seconds.

Grave digging It is recorded that Johann Heinrich Karl Thieme, sexton of Aldenburg, Germany, dug 23,311 graves during a 50-year career. In 1826 his understudy dug *his* grave.

Guitar playing The longest recorded solo guitar playing marathon is one of 93 hours by Peter Baco, 21, in Winnipeg, Canada in July 1970.

Gun running The record for the Royal Tournament naval gun run competition (instituted 1900, with present rules since 1919) is 2 minutes 50·5 seconds by the Fleet Air Arm Gun Crew at Earl's Court, London in 1969. The barrel alone weighs 8 cwt. The wall is 5 feet high and the chasm

28 feet across. The same team in 1968 achieved an unofficial 2 minutes 47·6 seconds in a practice run at Lee-on-the-Solent, Hampshire.

Hairdressing The world record for non-stop barbering is 80 hours (610 heads) by Rolf Elfso at Engelen, Stockholm, Sweden on 27–30 Nov. 1970. During the same marathon Gabino Padron dried and blow-waved 442 customers in 51 hours. The world's most expensive men's hairdresser is Tristan of Hollywood, California, U.S.A. who charges any "client" $100 (£41·66) on their first visit. This consists of a "consultation" followed by "remedial grooming". Miss Iris M. Rennell of St. Helier, Jersey dressed women's hair non-stop for 77 hours at her Aphrodite Salon in March 1970.

Handbell ringing The longest recorded handbell ringing recital was one of 7 hours 1 minute by 12 ringers of the Silverdale Handbell Ringers, Lancashire playing in unison with 1 minute breaks between pieces and 5 minute breaks each hour.

Handshaking The world record for handshaking was set up by Theodore Roosevelt (1858–1919), President of the U.S.A., who shook hands with 8,513 people at a New Year's Day, White House Presentation in Washington, D.C., U.S.A. on 1 Jan. 1907. Outside public life the record has become meaningless because aspirants merely arrange circular queues and shake the same hands repetitively.

HIGH DIVING

The highest regularly performed dive is that of professional divers from La Quebrada ("the break in the rocks") at Acapulco, Mexico, a height of 118 feet. The leader of the 25 divers in the exclusive Club de Clavadistas is Raúl Garcia (b. 1928). The base rocks, 21 feet out from the take-off, necessitate a leap of 27 feet out. The water is 12 feet deep.

On 18 May 1885, Sarah Ann Henley, aged 24, jumped from the Clifton Suspension Bridge, which crosses the Avon, England. Her 250-foot fall was slighty cushioned by her voluminous dress and petticoat acting as a parachute. She landed, bruised and bedraggled, in the mud on the Gloucestershire bank and was carried to hospital by four policemen. On 11 Feb. 1968 Jeffrey Kramer, 24, leapt off the George Washington Bridge 250 feet above the Hudson River, New York City, N.Y. and survived. Of the 367 people who have made suicide dives from the Golden Gate Bridge, San Francisco, California, U.S.A. since 1937, the third to have survived was Claud Layton on 17 July 1969. On 10 July 1921 a stuntman named Terry leapt from a seaplane into the Ohio River at Louisville, Kentucky. The alleged altitude was 310 feet.

Samuel Scott (U.S.A.) is reputed to have made a dive of 497 feet at Pattison Fall (now Manitou Falls) in Wisconsin, U.S.A., in 1840, but this would have entailed an entry speed of 86 m.p.h. The actual height was probably 165 feet.

Hitch-hiking The hitch-hiking record for the 873 miles from Land's End, Cornwall, to John o' Groats, Caithness, Scotland, is 29½ hours by Ian Crawford of Edinburgh on 4–5 April 1965. The time before the first "hitch" on the first day is excluded. This time was equalled in the reverse direction by Bernard Atkins, aged 18, of Donington, Lincolnshire in 11 lifts on 28 July 1966. The fastest time recorded for the round trip is 77 hours 20 minutes by Christine Elvery, 20 and Gwendolen Sherwin, 20, of which 61 hours 20 minutes was travelling on 24–27 March 1969.

The longest recorded hike is one of 18,500 miles through 14 countries from Singapore to London by David Kwan, aged 22, which occupied 81 weeks from 4 May 1957, or an average of 32 miles a day.

Hoop rolling In 1968 it was reported that Zolilio Diaz (Spain) had rolled a hoop 600 miles from Mieres to Madrid and back in 18 days.

Hopscotch The most protracted game of hopscotch on record is 125 hours by 10 students from Flint Central High School, Michigan, U.S.A. on 12–17 April 1971 and by 10 from Dundee University, Scotland on 23 April 1971.

House of cards The greatest number of storeys (8 cards per storey) achieved in building houses of cards is 14 by B. Ameringen in Enfield, Middlesex on 9 Jan. 1971. Malcolm Rossiter, 17, of Salisbury, Rhodesia built a card tower of 22 storeys on 5 Dec. 1963.

The world's longest range human cannon-ball—the 145 m.p.h. Florinda Zacchini

Human cannon-ball The record distance for firing a human from a cannon is 175 feet in the case of Emanuel Zacchini in the Ringling Bros. and Barnum & Bailey Circus, Madison Square Garden, New York City, U.S.A., in 1940. His muzzle velocity was 145 m.p.h. On his retirement the management were fortunate in finding that his daughter Florinda was of the same calibre.

Juggling The only juggler in history able to juggle—as opposed to "shower"—10 balls or eight plates was the Italian Enrico Rastelli, who was born in Samara, Russia, on 19 Dec. 1896 and died in Bergamo, Italy, on 13 Dec. 1931.

Kissing The most prolonged osculatory marathon on record is one of 30 hours 27 minutes from 8 a.m. 9 Jan. to 2.27 p.m. 10 Jan. 1971 at U.C.L.A., California, U.S.A. by Gregory Wike, 19 and Miss Pat Lacy, 18.

Kite-flying The greatest reported height attained by kites is 35,530 feet by a train of 19 flown near Portage by 10 Gary, Indiana high school boys in 1969. The flight took 7 hours and was assessed by telescopic triangulation.

Knitting The longest recorded knitting marathon is one of 55 hours 6 minutes by Mrs. Rita Campbell at Adair Brothers Store, Gisborne, New Zealand (with 5-minute time out allowances per hour) on 1–3 Sept. 1970. The world's most prolific hand-knitter of all time has been Mrs. Gwen Matthewman (b. 1927) of Featherstone, Yorkshire, who retired on 31 Dec. 1970. In her last year she knitted 615 garments involving 438 lb. 14 oz. (7,022 oz.) of wool (equivalent to the fleece of 57 sheep). She had been timed to average 108 stitches per minute in a 30-minute test. Her technique has been filmed by the world's only Professor of Knitting—a Japanese.

The longest scarf knitted was one 438 feet long (minimum width 10 inches) by a team from Castle Vale Comprehensive School, Birmingham reported on 7 Feb. 1970. The longest non-stop figure on record is one of 60 hours by 6 students of West London College, London W.14 on 13–16 March 1970. The finest recorded knitting is a piece of 2,464 stitches per square inch by Douglas Milne of Mount Florida, Glasgow, Scotland in May 1969.

Knot-tying The non-stop knot-tying marathon record is 76,504 links of a drummer's chain knot in $\frac{3}{4}$ inch tarred sisal rope in $50\frac{1}{2}$ hours by four members of the 9th Beds. (Biggleswade) Scout Troop on 29–31 May 1969.

Lion-taming The greatest number of lions mastered and fed in a cage by an unaided lion-tamer was 40, by "Captain" Alfred Schneider in 1925. Clyde Raymond Beatty (1903–65) handled more than 40 "cats" (mixed lions and tigers) simultaneously. Twenty-one lion-tamers have died of injuries since 1900.

Log rolling The most protracted log rolling contest on record was one in Chequamegon Bay, Ashland, Wisconsin, U.S.A., in 1900, when Allan Stewart dislodged Joe Oliver from a 24-inch diameter log after 3 hours 15 minutes birling.

Message in a bottle The longest voyage recorded for a message in a bottle was one of 25,000 miles, from the Pacific to the shore of the island of Sylt in the North Sea on 3 Dec. 1968. The bottle had been dropped on 27 May 1947.

Morse The highest recorded speed at which anyone has received morse code is 75·2 words per minute—over 17 symbols per second. This was achieved by Ted R. McElroy of the United States in a tournament at Asheville, North Carolina, U.S.A. on 2 July 1939.

Needle threading The record number of strands of cotton threaded through a number 13 needle (eye $\frac{1}{2}$ an inch by $\frac{1}{16}$ of an inch) in 2 hours is 3,795 by Miss Brenda Robinson of the College of Further Education, Chippenham, Wiltshire on 20 March 1971.

Omelette making The greatest number of two-egg omelettes made in 30 minutes is 77 by Leonard C. Andrew at West Jesmond School Hall, Newcastle upon Tyne, England on 29 Nov. 1969.

The world's champion omelette maker Leonard Andrew

Quiz league The largest and oldest (established 1959) Quiz league in the world is the Merseyside Quiz League, England with 82 teams and five major trophies.

Quoit throwing The world's record for rope quoit throwing is an unbroken sequence of 4,002 pegs by Bill Irby, Snr. of Australia in 1968.

PARACHUTING

Earliest descent The earliest demonstration of a quasi-parachute was by Sebastien Lenormand of Lyons, France, with a conical canopy from an observation tower in Montpellier, France, in 1783. The first successful parachute jump from a balloon was by André-Jacques Garnerin (1769–1823) from 2,230 feet over Monceau Park, Paris, on 22 Oct. 1797. The earliest descent from an aeroplane was that of Captain Albert Berry, U.S. Army, over St. Louis, Missouri, on 1 March 1912. The first free fall from an aircraft was by Leslie Lehoy Irvin (1895–1966) at McCook Field near Dayton, Ohio, U.S.A. on 19 April 1919.

Longest delayed drop *Male* The longest delayed drop and the greatest altitude for any parachute descent was achieved by U.S.A.F. doctor Captain Joseph W. Kittinger, D.F.C., aged 32, over Tularosa, New Mexico, U.S.A. on 16 Aug. 1960. He stepped out of a balloon at 102,200 feet for a free fall of 84,700 feet (16·04 miles) lasting 4 minutes 38 seconds, during which he reached a speed of 614 m.p.h., despite a stabilizing drogue. He experienced a temperature of −94° F. His 28-foot parachute opened at 17,500 feet and he landed after a total time of 13 minutes 45 seconds. The step by the gondola door was inscribed "This is the highest step in the world".

The British record for a group delayed drop is 39,183 feet (7·43 miles) (from 41,383 feet) by 5 R.A.F. Parachute Jumping Instructors over Boscombe Down, Wiltshire on 16 June 1967. They were Sq.-Ldr. J. Thirtle; Flt.-Sgt. A. K. Kidd and Sgts. L. Hicks, P. P. Keane and K. J. Teesdale.

Female The women's delayed drop record is 46,250 feet (8·76 miles) by O. Komissarova (U.S.S.R.) on 21 Sept. 1965.

Highest escape The greatest altitude from which a successful parachute *escape* has been made from an aircraft is from a *Canberra* jet bomber by Flt.-Lt. John de Salis, aged 29, of Southampton, and Fg. Off. Patrick Lowe, aged 23, of Potters Bar, Hertfordshire, over Monyash, Derbyshire, on 9 April 1958. Their plane exploded at 56,000 feet (10·60 miles) and they fell free in a temperature of −70° F. to a height of 10,000 feet at which altitude their parachutes were automatically opened. The longest descent recorded was one by Lt.-Col. William H. Rankin, U.S.M.C., from a Chance Vought F8U *Crusader* jet fighter at 47,000 feet on 26 July 1959. His "descent" through a thunderstorm over North Carolina took 40 minutes instead of the expected 11 minutes because of violent upward air currents.

Heaviest load The greatest single load ever dropped by parachute is 50,450 lb. (22·52 tons) of steel plates from a U.S. Air Force C-130 *Hercules* with 6 'chutes near El Centro, California on 28 Jan. 1970. The largest parachute made is a U.S. Air Force cargo parachute with a 100-foot diameter, reported in September 1964.

Most descents The greatest number of parachute jumps is over 5,000 by Lt.-Col. Ivan Savkin (U.S.S.R.) (b. 1913), who reached 5,000 on 12 Aug. 1967. Since 1935 he has spent 27 hours in free fall, 587 hours floating and has dropped 7,800 miles. The British record was set by Sq.-Ldr. Charles Agate, A.F.C. (b. March 1905) of the R.A.F., who totalled 1,601 descents with packed parachutes between 1939 and 1946. The speed record is 81 jumps in 8 hours 22 minutes by Michael Davis, 24, and Richard Bingham, 25, at Columbus, Ohio, U.S.A., on 26 June 1966.

Longest fall without a parachute The greatest altitude from which anyone has bailed out without a parachute and survived is 22,000 feet. This occurred in January 1942, when Lt. (now Lt.-Col.) I. M. Chisov (U.S.S.R.) fell from an Ilyushin 4 which had been severely damaged. He struck the ground a glancing blow on the edge of a snow-covered ravine and slid to the bottom. He suffered a fractured pelvis and severe spinal damage. It is estimated that the human body reaches 99 per cent. of its low level terminal velocity after falling 1,880 feet. This is 117–125 m.p.h. at normal atmospheric pressure in a random posture, but up to 185 m.p.h. in a head down position.

The British record is 18,000 feet by Flt.-Sgt. Nicholas Stephen Alkemade, aged 21, who jumped from a blazing R.A.F. *Lancaster* bomber over Germany on 23 March 1944. His headlong fall was broken by a fir tree and he landed without a broken bone in an 18-inch snow bank.

Highest landing The record landing height for parachute jumps is 23,405 feet by 10 U.S.S.R. parachutists onto the summit of Lenina Peak reported in May 1969. Four of the ten were killed.

Highest tower jump The highest jump ever achieved from a building is from the top of the 1,984-foot-tall KTUL-TV tower at Tulsa, Oklahoma, U.S.A. by Herb. Schmidt on 4 Oct. 1970.

Most northerly The most northerly parachute jump was made in 87° 30′ N. on the polar ice cap on 31 March 1969 by Ray Munro, 47, of Lancaster, Ontario, Canada. His eyes were frozen shut instantly in the temperature of −39° F.

Piano-playing The longest piano-playing marathon has been one of 1,088 hours (45 days 8 hours) playing 22 hours every day from 11 Oct. to 24 Nov. 1970 by James Crowley, Jr., 30 at Scranton, Pennsylvania, U.S.A. The British record is 195 hours 17 minutes (with 5 minute breaks each hour) set in Manchester by Michael George, 24, of Heaton Norris, Cheshire, ending on 24 July 1969.

The women's world record is 133 hours (5 days 13 hours) by Mrs. Marie Ashton, aged 40, in a theatre in Blyth, Northumberland, on 18–23 Aug. 1958.

Piano smashing The record time for demolishing an upright piano and passing the entire wreckage through a circle 9 inches in diameter is 2 minutes 26 seconds by six men representing Ireland led by Johnny Leydon of Sligo, at Merton, Surrey, England on 7 Sept. 1968. The fastest time in which an upright piano has been sawn in half is 125 minutes 5 seconds by a team of four from the Earl's Court pm Club on the steps of St. Martin's in the Field, Trafalgar Square, London on 26 Oct. 1970 using an Eclipse all-purpose saw.

Pillar box standing The record number of people to pile on top of a pillar box (6 square foot oval top) is 26, all students of the City of London College, Moorgate, in Finsbury Circus, London, E.C.2 on London Weekend T.V. on 21 Sept. 1968.

Pilot *Youngest* The youngest age at which anyone has ever qualified as a military pilot is 15 years 5 months in the case of Sgt. Thomas Dobney (b. 6 May 1926) of the R.A.F. He had understated his age (14 years) on entry.

Pipe smoking The duration record for keeping a pipe (3·3 grammes of tobacco) continuously alight with only an initial match is 253 minutes 28 seconds by Yrjö Pentikäinen of Kuopio, Finland on 15–16 March 1968.

Plate spinning The greatest number of plates spun simultaneously is 44 by Holley Gray, on the *Blue Peter* T.V. show at the B.B.C. T.V. Centre, Wood Lane, London W.12 on 18 May 1970.

Pole-squatting There being no international rules, the "standards of living" atop poles vary widely. The record squat is 211 days 9 hours by Miss Maurie Rose Kirby, aged 17, ending on 4 March 1959, on a 71-foot-tall pole at Indianapolis, Indiana, U.S.A. She staged the test as a protest against being called a juvenile delinquent.

The British record is 32 days 14 hours by John Stokes, aged 32, of Moseley, in a barrel on a 45-foot pole in Birmingham, ending on 27 June 1966. This is claimed as a world record for a barrel.

Modern records do not, however, compare with that of St. Daniel (A.D. 409–493), called Stylites (Greek, *stylos*=pillar), a monk who spent 33 years 3 months on a stone pillar in Syria. This is probably the oldest of all human records.

Pop group The duration record for a 6-man pop-playing group is 104 hours 50 minutes by one in King's Lynn, Norfolk on 3–7 Sept. 1970.

Pram pushing The greatest distance covered in pushing a pram in 24 hours is 261 miles by the 45 strong Cholsey Scout and Guide Association, Berkshire on 16–17 Oct. 1970. A team of 10 from Skelmersdale, Lancashire set a distance of 190¼ miles with a "baby" (a sizeable teenage girl) aboard on 23–24 April 1971.

Fastest "psychiatrist" The world's fastest "psychiatrist" was the osteopath Dr. Albert L. Weiner of Erlton, New Jersey, U.S.A., who dealt with up to 50 patients a day in four treatment rooms. He relied heavily on narcoanalysis, muscle relaxants and electro-shock treatments. In December 1961 he was found guilty on 12 counts of manslaughter from using unsterilized needles.

Pub-crawling The world's champion pub-crawler is the abstemious Mr. Barry Cameron-Lunn of New Zealand. In Britain alone he has visited 11,700 pubs up to October 1969. His ration is half a pint per pub and his record in one night is 24. The only known example of a blanket coverage of every pub in a city with a 7 figure population is the visitation of all Birmingham's 742 licensed premises by Roger Walker and Ronald Smith from January 1968 to 17 Oct. 1970.

Riding in armour The longest recorded ride in full armour is one of 145 miles from Wednesfield to London *via* Birmingham and Oxford in six days by Kenneth Quicke in August 1956.

Riveting The world's record for riveting is 11,209 in 9 hours by J. Moir at the Workman Clark Ltd. shipyard, Belfast, Northern Ireland, in June 1918. His peak hour was his seventh with 1,409, an average of nearly 23½ per minute.

Rocking-chair The longest recorded duration of a "Rockathon" is 125 hours 3 minutes by Bret Edmonds in Bath Abbey Churchyard, Somerset, England from 10.27 a.m. 6 Nov. to 3.30 p.m. 11 Nov. 1970.

Rolling pin The record distance for a woman to throw a 2 lb. rolling pin is 140 feet 4 inches by Sheri Salyer at Stroud, Oklahoma on 18 July 1970. The British record is 134 feet 2 inches by Ann Cook at Stroud, Gloucestershire on 20 July 1968.

Rope tricks Will Rogers (1879–1935) of the United States demonstrated an ability to rope three separate objects with 3 lariats at a single throw.

Longest safari The world's longest safari was one mounted in Africa by Peter Parnwell of Johannesburg, South Africa. It lasted 365 days, embraced 37 African countries and territories and extended over 30,000 miles.

Scooter riding The greatest distance covered by a team (18 boys, 7 girls) in 24 hours is 276·5 miles by the Wagga Wagga Methodist Youth Fellowship, N.S.W., Australia on 2–3 April 1971.

See-saw The duration record for see-sawing is 270 hours by Dave Bennett, 34, and Don Cox, 24, on Cannery Row, Monterey, California ending on 8 Nov. 1970. The longest see-saw marathon in which the participants did not leave the see-saw is one of 80 hours by David Turner and David Such of the Twyford & Rushcombe Youth Club on 27–30 Dec. 1969.

Sermon The longest sermon on record was delivered by Clinton Locy of West Richland, Washington, U.S.A., in February 1955. It lasted 48 hours 18 minutes and ranged through texts from every book in the Bible. A congregation of eight was on hand at the close. From 31 May to 10 June 1969 the Dalai Lama, the exiled ruler of Tibet, completed a sermon on Tantric Buddhism for five to seven hours per day to total 60 hours in India.

Sewing machines The fastest time recorded for sewing down a piece of tape 9 yards long with a treadle machine is 4 minutes 41·4 seconds by Harry Walgate at the Joint Reading

Clinton Locy, the most prolix preacher in the world, being shaved while in full spate

Round Table competition, Reading, Berkshire on 19 Nov. 1969.

Shaving The fastest barber on record is Gerry Harley, who shaved 130 men in 60 minutes at The Plough, Gillingham, Kent on 1 April 1971.

Sheaf tossing The world's best performance for tossing an 8-lb. sheaf is 56 feet by C. R. Wiltshire of Geelong, Victoria, Australia in 1956. Contests date from 1914.

Fastest shorthand The highest recorded speeds ever attained under championship conditions are: 300 words per minute (99·64 per cent. accuracy) for five minutes and 350 w.p.m. (99·72 per cent. accuracy, that is, two insignificant errors) for two minutes by Nathan Behrin (U.S.A.), in New York in December 1922. Behrin (b. 1887) used the Pitman system invented in 1837. Morris I. Kligman of New York currently claims to be the world's fastest shorthand writer at 300 w.p.m. He has taken 50,000 words in five hours and transcribed them in under five hours.

Mr. G. W. Bunbury of Dublin, Ireland, holds the unique distinction of writing at 250 w.p.m. for 10 minutes on 23 Jan. 1894.

Currently the fastest shorthand writer in Britain is Jane Swan (Mrs. Kenneth Meader) of North Finchley with a Pitman's Certificate for 230 w.p.m.

In the British Isles only five shorthand writers have passed the official Pitman tests at 250 w.p.m. for five minutes:

Miss Edith Ulrica Pearson of London, on 30 June 1927.
Miss Emily Doris Smith of London, on 22 March 1934.
Miss Beatrice W. Solomon of London, in March 1942.
Mrs. Audrey Boyes (*née* Bell) of Finchley, London, in 1956.

Shouting The greatest number of wins in the national town criers' contest is eight by Herbert T. Waldron of Great Torrington, Devon. He won every year from 1957 to 1965, except for 1959. (See also Longest-ranged voice, Chapter I.) In a test in November 1970 Richard Smith (b. 1947), the 1969 and 1970 champion, registered 97 decibels.

Showering The most prolonged continuous shower bath on record is one of 168 hours by Peter Schell, aged 36, of Munich, West Germany ending on 19 Jan. 1968. The feminine record is 97 hours 1 minute by an anonymous co-ed from Holmes Hall, East Lansing, Michigan, U.S.A. ending on 28 Jan. 1969. She is believed to be the world's only anonymous record-holder.

Singing The longest recorded singing marathon is one of 26 hours 15 minutes by Tony Coleno at the *Jenny Wren* public house, Cambridge, England on 26–27 Sept. 1970. The longest recorded group marathon was performed by five students (at least four singing at any one time) from Brighton Polytechnic, Sussex who sang the two line refrain "Lloyd George knew my Father—Father knew Lloyd George" to the tune of Onward Christian Soldiers for 34 hours from 1.30 p.m. Monday to 11.30 p.m. Tuesday 8–9 March 1971.

Skipping The greatest number of turns ever performed without a break is variously reported as 32,089 and 32,809 by J. P. Hughes of Melbourne, Victoria, Australia, in 3 hours 10 minutes on 26 Oct. 1953.

Other records made without a break:

Most turns in one jump	5 by Katsumi Suzuki, Tōkyō, early 1968.
Most turns in 1 minute	286 by J. Rogers, Melbourne, 10 Nov. 1937. and T. Lewis, Melbourne, 16 Sept. 1938.
Most turns in 2 hours	22,806 by Tom Morris, Sydney, 21 Nov. 1937.
Double turns	2,001 by K. Brooks, Brisbane, January 1955.
Treble turns	70 by J. Rogers, Melbourne, 17 Sept. 1951.
Duration	1,264 miles by Tom Morris, Brisbane–Cairns, Queensland, 1967

Slinging The greatest distance recorded for a sling-shot is 1,147 feet 4 inches using a 34-inch-long sling and a $7\frac{1}{2}$ ounce stone by Melvin Gaylor on Newport Golf Course, Shide, Isle of Wight on 25 Sept. 1970.

Smoke ring blowing The highest recorded number of smoke rings formed from a single pull of a cigarette is 53 by Wilf Kristian Whitaker in the University Union, Leeds, Yorkshire in October 1970. An uncorroborated claim for 74 rings is outstanding.

Snakes and Ladders The longest recorded game of Snakes and Ladders has been one of 45 hours by a team of 10 scouts and guides of Water Orton, Birmingham, England on 26–27 Feb. 1971.

Spinning The duration record for spinning a clock balance wheel by hand is 5 minutes 26·8 seconds by Philip Ashley, aged 16, of Leigh, Lancashire, on 20 May 1968.

Spitting The greatest distance achieved in a national spitting title contest is 27 feet 8 inches (with following wind) by William Koster at St. Louis, Missouri, U.S.A., on 8 May 1971. The record at the annual classic at Raleigh, Mississippi is 25 feet 10 inches by Don Snyder, 22, set in August 1970. A distance of 26 feet $10\frac{1}{2}$ inches was attained in a spit-off by D. McIntosh at the Annual Gordon Highlanders Band contest at Minden, West Germany on 23 May 1970. Distance is dependent on the quality of salivation, absence of cross wind and the co-ordination of the quick hip and neck snap. The record for projecting a melon seed is 33 feet $3\frac{1}{2}$ inches by Craig Jones at the "world" championship at Pardeeville, Wisconsin, U.S.A., on 16 Sept. 1969. Serious spitters wear 12-inch boots so practice spits can be measured without a tape.

Stilt-walking The highest stilts ever successfully mastered were 22 feet from the ankle to the ground by Harry Yelding ("Harry Sloan") of Great Yarmouth, Norfolk. Hop stringers use stilts up to 15 feet. In 1892 M. Garisoain of Bayonne stilt-walked the last 8 kilometres into Biarritz in 42 minutes to average 7·1 m.p.h. In 1891 Sylvain Dornon stilt-walked from Paris to Moscow *via* Vilno in 50 stages for the 1,830 miles. Another source gives his time as 58 days.

Stretcher bearing The longest recorded carry of a stretcher case is one of 21·22 miles by eight Venture Scouts from Ewell Spring Mixed Unit, Epsom, Surrey on 9 April 1971.

Submergence The longest submergence in a frogman's suit is 100 hours 3 minutes by Mrs. Jane Lisle Baldasare, aged 24, at Pensacola, Florida, U.S.A., ending on 24 Jan. 1960. Mrs. Baldasare also holds the feminine underwater distance record at 14 miles. Her ex-husband, Fred Baldasare, aged 38, set the underwater distance record of nearly 50 miles in his France-England Channel crossing of 18 hours 1 minute ending on 11 July 1962.

Suggestion boxes The most prolific example on record of the use of any suggestion box scheme is that of Mr. John Drayton of Pontypool, Monmouthshire, who plied British Rail with a total of 25,000 suggestions.

Switchback riding The world endurance record for rides on a roller coaster is 465 circuits of the John Collins Pleasure Park switchback at Barry Island, Glamorgan by a group of four men and two girls. The test lasted 31 hours, with two brief breaks, on 15–16 Aug. 1968.

Tailoring The highest speed at which a three-piece man's suit has been made is 84 minutes including measuring and pressing by Wallis and Linnell Ltd. of Kettering, Northamptonshire on 18 Dec. 1969 on the occasion of a retirement presentation to Mr. Ernie Earl after 50 years service.

Talking The world record for non-stop talking is 138 hours (5 days 18 hours) by Victor Villimas of Cleveland, Ohio, U.S.A. in Leeds, Yorkshire, England, from 25–31 Oct. 1967. The longest continuous political speech on record was one of 29 hours 5 minutes by Gerard O'Donnell in Kingston-upon-Hull, Yorkshire, on 23–24 June 1959. The longest recorded lecture was one of 45 hours on "The Christian Faith and its Response" by the Rev. Roger North, 26, at Hartley Victoria Methodist College, Manchester on 15–17 May 1971.

A feminine non-stop talking record was set by Mrs. Alton Clapp of Greenville, North Carolina, U.S.A., in August 1958, with 96 hours 45 minutes 11 seconds. In the U.S.A. such contests have been referred to as "gab fests".

T-bone dive The greatest T-bone dive performed was by Evel Knievel (U.S.) who crashed after clearing 17 cars on his 750 c.c. Laverda motorcycle at Pocono, Pennsylvania, U.S.A. in September 1970.

Teeth-pulling The man with the "strongest teeth in the world" is John Massis of Belgium, who in 1969 demonstrated the ability to pull a 36-ton train along rails with a bit in his teeth.

TIGHTROPE WALKING

The greatest 19th century tightrope walker was Jean François Gravelet, *alias* Charles Blondin (1824–1897), of France, who made the earliest crossing of the Niagara Falls on a 3-inch rope, 1,100 feet long, 160 feet above the Falls on 30 July 1855. He also made a crossing with Harry Colcord, pick-a-back on 15 Sept. 1860. Though this is difficult to believe, Colcord was his agent.

Endurance The world tightrope endurance record is 214 hours by Henri Rochetain (born 1926) of France on a wire 4,950 feet long, 550 feet above La Seuge river at Le Puy, France, on 13–21 Aug. 1966. The feminine record is 34 hours 15 minutes by Francine Pary, aged 17, on a wire 50 feet high at Toulouse, France, in February 1957.

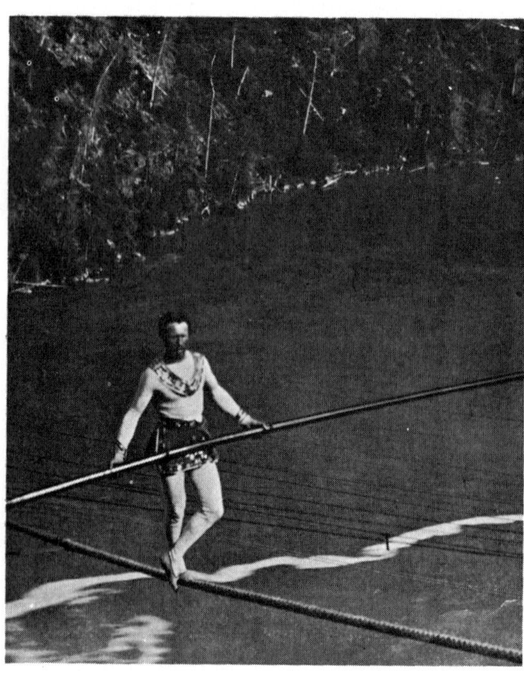

The great Blondin crossing above the Niagara Falls

Longest The longest walk by any funambulist was achieved by Henri Rochetain (b. 1926) of France on a wire 3,790 yards long slung across a gorge at Clermont Ferrand, France on 13 July 1969. He required 3 hours 20 minutes to negotiate the crossing.

High-wire act *Highest* The greatest drop beneath any high wire act was over the 750-foot-deep Tallulah Gorge, Georgia, U.S.A. where, on 18 July 1970, Karl Wallenda, 66, walked 821 feet in 616 steps with a 35 lb. pole in 20 minutes including pauses for two headstands. The highest altitude high-wire act was that of the Germans Alfred and Henry Traber on a 520-foot rope stretched from the Zugspitze (9,738 feet) to the Western Peak, Bavaria, Germany, during July and August 1953.

Tree-climbing The fastest tree-climbing record is one of 36 seconds for a 90-foot pine by Kelly Stanley (Canada) at the Toowoomba Show, Queensland, Australia in 1968.

Tree-sitting The duration record for sitting in a tree is 55 days from 10 a.m. 22 July to 10 a.m. 15 Sept. 1930 by David William Haskell (born 1920) on a 4-foot by 6-foot platform up a backyard walnut tree in Wilmar (now Rosemund), California, U.S.A.

Tunnel of fire The longest tunnel of fire (petrol-soaked hoops of straw) negotiated by a trick motorcyclist is one of 51 feet 5 inches by Wayne Harris of the "Destruction Squad" of Leicester at the Oxford Stadium, Cowley, England on 7 Nov. 1970.

TYPEWRITING

Fastest The highest recorded speeds attained with a ten-word penalty per error on a manual machine are:

One Minute: 170 words, Margaret Owen (U.S.A.) (Underwood Standard), New York, 21 Oct. 1918.
One Hour: 147 words (net rate per minute), Albert Tangora (U.S.A.) (Underwood Standard), 22 Oct. 1923.

The official hour record on an electric machine is 9,316 words (40 errors) on an I.B.M. machine, giving a net rate of 149 words per minute, by Margaret Hamma, now Mrs. Dilmore (U.S.A.), in Brooklyn, New York City, N.Y., U.S.A. on 20 June 1941.

In an official test in 1946 Stella Pajunas, now Mrs. Garnand, attained a speed of 216 words per minute on an I.B.M. machine.

Slowest Chinese typewriters are so complex that even the most skilled operator cannot select characters from the 1,500 offered at a rate of more than 11 words a minute. The Hoang typewriter produced in 1962 has 5,700 Chinese characters. The keyboard is 2 feet wide and 17 inches high.

Longest The world duration record for typewriting on an electric machine is 150 hours by David J. Carnochan, 22 of the University College London Union from noon on 24 Feb. to 6 p.m. 2 March 1970. His breaks were 70 minutes less than the permitted 5 minutes per hour.

The longest duration typing marathon on a manual machine is 120 hours 15 minutes by Mike Howell, a 23-year-old blind office worker from Greenfield, Oldham, Lancashire on 25–30 Nov. 1969 on an Olympia manual typewriter in Liverpool. In aggregating 561,006 strokes he performed a weight movement of 2,482 tons plus a further 155 tons on moving the carriage for line spacing. On an electric machine the total figure would have been 565 tons.

Most travelled typewriter The world's most travelled typewriter is the Underwood Noiseless portable (rebuilt 1938) of Britain's most

CIRCUS RECORDS

The following circus acrobatic feats represent the greatest performed, either for the first time or, if marked with an asterisk, uniquely. A "mechanic" is a safety harness.

Flying Trapeze	Earliest Act	Jules Leotard (France)	Circus Napoleon, Paris	12 Nov. 1859
	Double back somersault	Eddie Silbon	Paris Hippodrome	1879
	Triple back somersault (female)	Lena Jordan (Latvia) to Lew Jordan (U.S.A.)	Sydney, Australia	April 1897
	Triple back somersault (male)	Ernest Clarke to Charles Clarke	Publiones Circus, Cuba	1909
	Triple and a half back somersault	Tony Steele to Lee Strath Marilees	Durango, Mexico	30 Sept. 1962
	Quadruple back somersault (in practice)	*Ernest Clarke to Charles Clarke	Orrin Bros. Circus, Mexico City, Mexico	1915
	Triple back somersault (bar to bar, practice)	Edmund Ramat and Raoul Monbar	Various	1905–10
	Head to head stand on swinging bar (no holding)	*Ed. and Ira Millette (*née* Wolf)	Various	1910–20
Horse back	Running leaps on and off	*26 by "Poodles" Hanneford	New York	1915
	Three-high column without "mechanic"	*Willy, Baby and Rene Fredianis	Nouveau Cirque, Paris	1908
	Double back somersault mounted	(John or Charles) Frederic Clarke	Various	*c.* 1905
	Double back somersault from a 2-high to a trailing horse with "mechanic"	Aleksandr Sergey	Moscow Circus	1956
Fixed Bars	Pass from 1st to 3rd bar with a double back somersault	Phil Shevette, Andres Atayde	Woods Gymnasium, New York, European tours	1925–27
	Triple fly-away to ground (male)	Phil Shevette	Folies Bergère, Paris	May 1896
	Triple fly-away to ground (female)	Loretto Twins, Ora and Pauline	Los Angeles	1914
Giant Spring Board	Running forward triple back somersault	John Cornish Worland, (1855–1933) of the U.S.A.	St. Louis, Missouri	1874
Risley (Human Juggling)	Back somersault feet to feet	Richard Risley Carlisle (1814–74) and son (U.S.A.)	Theatre Royal, Edinburgh	Feb. 1844
Acrobatics	Quadruple back somersault to a chair	Sylvester Mezzetti (voltiger) to Butch Mezzetti (catcher)	New York Hippodrome	1915–17
Aerialist	One arm swings 125 (no net) 32 feet up	Vicky Unus (La Toria) (U.S.A.)	Ringling Bros., Barnum & Bailey circuit	Nov. 1962
Teeter Board	Seat to seat triple back somersault	The 5 Draytons		1896
Wire-Juggling	16 hoops (hands and feet)	Ala Naito (Japan) (female)	Madison Square Garden, N.Y.	1937
Low Wire (7 feet)	Feet to feet forward somersault	Con Colleano	Empire Theatre, Johannesburg	1923
		Ala Naito (Japan) (female)	Madison Square Garden, N.Y.	1937
High Wire (30–40 feet)	Four high column (with mechanic)	*The Solokhin Brothers (U.S.S.R.)	Moscow Circus	1962
	Three layer, 7 man pyramid	Great Wallendas (Germany)	U.S.A.	1961
Ground Acrobatics	Stationary double back somersault	François Gouleau (France)		1905
	Four high column	The Picchianis (Italy)		1905
	Five high pyramids	The Yacopis (Argentina) with 3 understanders, 3 second layer understanders, 1 middleman, 1 upper middleman and a top mounter	Ringling Bros., Barnum & Bailey circuit	1941

famous sportswriter, Peter Wilson of the *Daily Mirror*. It has accompanied him in covering 45 sports in 51 countries and 60 trans-Atlantic flights for 36 years (1935–1971).

Walking on hands The duration record for walking on hands is 871 miles by Johann Hurlinger, of Austria, who in 55 daily 10-hour stints, averaged 1·58 m.p.h. from Vienna to Paris in 1900.

Wall of death The greatest endurance feat on a wall of death was 3 hours 4 minutes by the motorcyclist Louis W. "Speedy" Babbs on a 32-foot diameter silo at the Venice Amusement Pier, California on 11 Oct. 1929. In 1934 Babbs performed 1,003 consecutive loop the loops in an 18-foot diameter silo at Ocean Park Pier, California, U.S.A.

Whip cracking The longest stock whip ever "cracked" (*i.e.* the end made to travel above the speed of sound—760 m.p.h.) is one of 55 feet by "Saltbush" Bill Mills of Australia.

Wood-cutting The world record for cutting six "shoes" to ascend and sever the top of a 16-foot high 15-inch diameter log is the 1 minute 31 seconds set by the Tasmanian axeman, Doug Youd (born 1938). His brother Roy felled a tree 12 inches in diameter in 1961 in 1 minute 52·3 seconds.

The world record for sawing (hand-bucking) through a 32-inch log is 1 minute 26·4 seconds by Paul M. Searls, aged 46, in Seattle, Washington State, U.S.A.on 5 Nov. 1953. The world record for double-handed sawing through an 18-inch white pine log is 10·2 seconds by Bill Donnelly and Ernie Hogg at Southland, South Island, New Zealand, on 4 Dec. 1955, equalled by N. J. Thorburn and M. Reed at Whangarei, New Zealand, on 3 March 1956. Donnelly and Hogg sawed through a 20-inch white pine log in 12·9 seconds at Invercargill, New Zealand, on 11 Feb. 1956. The 24-inch white pine record is 18·8 seconds by Denis Organ and Graham Sanson at Stratford, North Island, New Zealand on 27 Nov. 1965.

Yo-yo The yo-yo originates from a Filipino jungle fighting weapon recorded in the 16th century weighing 4 lb. with a 20-foot cord. The word means "come-come". The craze was started by Louis Marx (U.S.A.) in 1929. The most difficult modern yo-yo trick is the double-handed cross-over loop the loop. Art Pickles of East Sheen, London, the 1933–53 world champion once achieved 1,269 consecutive loop the loops. The individual endurance record is 8 hours 7 minutes 13 seconds by David Rose, 14, at Chadds Department Store, Hereford on 23 May 1970. The group marathon record is 76 hours set by six students with 3 yo-yos at Brierley's Store, Leicester, England on 1–8 March 1969.

Largest circus The world's largest permanent circus is Circus Circus Las Vegas, Nevada, U.S.A. opened on 18 Oct. 1968 at a cost of $15,000,000 (£6,250,000). It covers an area of 129,000 square feet capped by a 90-foot-high tent-shaped flexiglass roof. The new Moscow Circus, completed in 1968, has a seating capacity of 3,200.

WEALTH AND POVERTY

Richest rulers The Kingdom of Saudi Arabia derived an income of about $560,000,000 (then £200 million) from oil royalties in 1964, but the Royal Family's share was understood to be not more than £25,000,000. The Shaikh of Abu Dhabi, Zaid ibn Sultan Zaid al Nahayyan (b. 1917), has become extremely wealthy since the Murban oilfield began yielding in 1963, and by 1966 Abu Dhabi was estimated to have an income of $67,000,000 (then £23·9 million) which if divided equally would result in an income of $3,350 per head. Before World War II the income of Maj.-Gen. H. H. Maharajadhiraj Raj Rajeshwar Sawai Shree Yeshwant Rao Holkar Bahadur, G.C.I.E. (1908–61), the Maharaja of Indore, was estimated to be as high as £25,000,000 per annum. The state incomes of the 279 surviving rulers of India's 554 Princely States granted in 1947 were cut off in September 1970. It had been estimated that the Nizam of Hyderabad was worth nearly £900 million at the time of his death.

The man with once the highest income in the world was H.H. Shaikh Sir Abdullah as-Salim as-Sabah, G.C.M.G., C.I.E. (1895–1965), the 11th Amir of Kuwait, with an estimated £2,600,000 per week or £135 million a year.

Private citizen According to a survey researched by *Fortune* magazine published in May 1968 the world's two richest private citizens were Jean Paul Getty (b. Minneapolis, Minnesota, 15 Dec. 1892), and Howard Robard Hughes (b. Houston, Texas, 24 Dec. 1905) with evaluations of $1,338,000,000 (£557·5 million) and $1,373,000,000 (£572 million) respectively. Getty, now resident in Surrey, England, made his first million dollars, "the hardest", in his first 19 months in the oil business in Tulsa, Oklahoma, in June 1916, when aged 22. Getty maintains that "if you can count your millions, you are not a billionaire". More recent estimates suggest that the assets owned and controlled by Mr. Hughes, a recluse since 1954, exceed $2 billion (£833 million). The United States' only other possible living dollar billionaire (a "billion" in the U.S.A. is 1,000 million) is Haroldson Lafayette Hunt (b. 1889) of Dallas, Texas, owner of the Hunt Oil Company, with an annual income of reputedly $60 million (£25 million), of which 27½ per cent. is tax free under the Federal oil depletion allowance. One estimate puts his fortune at $2,000 million.

Billionaires Probably the only other dollar "billionaires" in the United States have been John Davison Rockefeller, the first (1839–1937), Henry Ford, the first (1863–1947) and Andrew William Mellon (1855–1937). A "billion" dollars is now equivalent to £416,666,666. Rockefeller kept account of his personal expenditure in Ledger No. 1 all his life. He referred to competitors, all of whom he regarded as redundant, as "the dear people".

Centi-millionaires and millionaires *World* *Fortune* Magazine in May 1968 estimated that there were 153 U.S. Centimillionaires (*i.e.* those with disposable assets of more than $100 million). The fastest centimillionaire has been Henry Ross Perot (b. Texarkana, Texas 1930), founder and President of Electronic Data Systems Corporation of Dallas, Texas in 1962. By 1968 his personal fortune was estimated at $320 million (£133,000,000). By December 1969 it was estimated that the value of his stock holdings might have reached $1,500 million, but he later said he could raise $100 million from his own resources to buy the release of 1,361 U.S. P.o.W.'s in North Vietnam. It was estimated in 1961 that there were 50,000 millionaires in the United States of whom 13,500 came from the State of California. The 1967 total probably surpassed 100,000 of whom 21 succeeded in paying no taxation.

United Kingdom The wealthiest United Kingdom citizen is believed to be Sir John Reeves Ellerman, 2nd baronet (born 21 Dec. 1909), a director of Ellerman Lines Ltd., whose father, Sir John Reeves Ellerman, Bt., C.H. (1862–1933), left £36,684,994, the largest will ever proved in the United Kingdom. His fortune is estimated to be worth about £500 million. The highest death duties ever paid have been £18,000,000 on the estate of Hugh Richard Arthur Grosvenor, G.C.V.O., D.S.O., the 2nd Duke of Westminster (1879–1953), paid between July 1953 and August 1964.

The greatest will proved in Ireland was that of the 1st Earl of Iveagh (1847–1927), who left £13,486,146.

Millionairesses The world's wealthiest woman was probably Princess Wilhelmina Helena Pauline Maria of Orange-Nassau (1880–1962), formerly Queen of the Netherlands (from 1890 to her abdication, 4 Sept. 1948), with a fortune which was estimated at over £200 million.

The largest amount proved in the will of a woman in the United Kingdom has been the £4,075,550 (duty paid £3,233,454) of Miss Gladys Meryl Yule, daughter of Sir David Yule, Bt. (1858–1928), in August 1957. Mrs. Anna Dodge (later Mrs. Hugh Dillman) who was born in Dundee, Scotland, died on 3 June 1970 in the United States, aged 103, and left an estate of £40,000,000.

Youngest The youngest person ever to accumulate a millionaire estate was the child film actress Shirley Temple (b. Santa Monica, California 23 April 1928), formerly Mrs. John Agar, Jr., now Mrs. Charles Black, of the U.S.A. Her accumulated wealth exceeded $1,000,000 (then £209,000) before she was 10 years old.

Earliest The earliest recorded self-made millionairess was Mrs. Annie M. Pope-Turnbo Malone (d. 1957), a laundress from St. Louis, Missouri, U.S.A., who in 1905 perfected the permanent straight treatment for those with crinkly hair.

Richest families In May 1968 it was estimated that three members of the Irish-American Mellon family of the U.S.A., from Omagh, County Tyrone: Mrs. Alisa Mellon Bruce (1902–1969), Paul Mellon (b. 1907) and Richard King Mellon (b. 1900), were each worth between $500 million and $1,000 million (£416·6 million). Another 1968 estimate put the family fortune at more than $3,000 million (about £1,255 million). It has also been tentatively estimated that the combined wealth of the much larger du Pont family of some 2,100 members may be in excess of this figure.

The largest number of millionaires estates in one family in the British Isles is that of the Wills family of the Imperial Tobacco Company, of whom 14 members have left estates in excess of £1,000,000 since 1910. These totalled £55 million, of which death duties (introduced in 1894) have taken over £27,000,000.

Largest dowry The largest recorded dowry was that of Elena Patiño, daughter of Don Simon Iturbi Patiño (1861–1947), the Bolivian tin millionaire, who in 1929 bestowed £8,000,000 from a fortune at one time estimated to be worth £125,000,000.

Greatest miser Henrietta (Hetty) Howland Green (*née* Robinson) (1835–1916) who kept a balance of over $31,400,000 (then £6·2 million) in one bank alone was so mean that her son had to have his leg amputated because of the delays in finding a *free* medical clinic. She herself lived off cold porridge because she was too mean to heat it and died of apoplexy in an argument over the virtues of skimmed milk. Her estate proved to be of $95 million (then £19 million).

SALARIES

Highest *World* The world's highest salary in 1968 was earned by Mr. Konosuke Matsushita the business executive of Tōkyō, Japan. His total income (including dividends) was £851,991 of which only 80 per cent. was removed in tax. The highest salary in the United States is that of the Chairman of the Board and Chief Executive Officer of the General Motors Corporation, of Detroit, Michigan, U.S.A. James Roche (b. 1905) succeeded to this appointment on 30 Oct. 1967. His 1969–70 salary with bonuses was $765,858 (£319,107). In June 1969 he won a Cadillac in a local draw but returned it on the grounds that he was already provided. The record gain from stock options was that of Ralph Cordiner, Chairman of the General Electric Co., who made a paper profit of $1,262,260 (now £525,941) on options exercised in 1957.

United Kingdom Britain's highest paid business executive was reputed to be Sir William Lyons (b. Blackpool 4 Sept. 1901), Chairman and Managing Director of Jaguar Cars Ltd. of Coventry, Warwickshire, who, prior to Jaguar's incorporation in British Motor Holdings in July 1966, is said to have received about £120,000. The highest salary initially disclosed under the 1967 Companies Act was that of Mr. Owen Aisher with £91,722 as Chairman of Marley Tiles Ltd. In 1968 he drew only £77,400 of the £108,600 to which he was entitled. In July 1965 it was reported that Mr. Wilfred Harvey, then Chairman of the British Printing Corporation, was eligible under his commission agreement to have drawn £270,000 in 1964–65. The highest amount paid in a straight salary in 1970 was that of Sir David Barran (b. 23 May 1912), Chairman of Shell Transport and Trading Co. Ltd. at £76,574. His net take home pay from this would be about £13,000.

Highest wage The highest recorded wage in Britain is £290 in a week paid to Jimmy Houston, 43, a stovepipe welder for a 6-day week including two all-night stints on the Isle of Grain, Kent, in 1970.

Highest income The highest gross income ever achieved in a single year by a private citizen is an estimated $105,000,000 (now £43¾ million) in 1927 by the Sicilian born Chicago gangster Alphonse ("Scarface Al") Capone (1899–1947). This was derived from illegal liquor trading and alky-cookers (illicit stills), gambling establishments, dog tracks, dance halls, "protection" rackets and vice. On his business card Capone described himself as a "Second Hand Furniture Dealer". Henry Ford, the first (1863–1947) earned about £25 million per annum at his peak.

Lowest incomes The poorest people in the world are the surviving Pintibu (or Bindibu) of whom 42 were found in the Northern Territory of Australia in July 1957. They subsist with water from soak holes and by eating rats. In September 1957 Chinese Government sources admitted that in some areas of the mainland the average annual income of peasants was 42 yuans (£6·90) per head. In 1964 China's average income per head was estimated at £25 per annum and the daily calorie intake at 2,200 (see calorific comparative data, Chapter 11).

"Golden handshake" record The most golden "golden handshake" was the £83,575 tax-free compensation for loss of office received in 1954 by Sir Charles Blampied Colston, C.B.E., M.C., D.C.M. (1891–1969), Chairman and Managing Director of Hoover Ltd. Since the Finance Act of 1960, which made such payments taxable after the first £5,000, the greatest amount ever paid out is believed to be £124,000, which was announced on 29 June 1964 to have been paid to Philip Gordon Walker (b. 9 June 1912), the Managing Director of Albert E. Reed & Co. Ltd. (since renamed Reed International Ltd.) from 1951 until his resignation on 9 July 1963, shortly after the company had been merged with the International Publishing Corporation. After tax he received an estimated £35,000. The largest leaving present recorded in trade union history was one aggregating a reported £25,000 from branches of the Transport and General Workers' Union to its secretary the Rt. Hon. Frank Cousins (b. 1904) in September 1969.

Return of cash The largest amount of cash ever found and returned to its owners was $240,000 (£85,714) in unmarked $10 (£3·56½) and $20 (£7·13) bills found in a street in Los Angeles, California, U.S.A., by Douglas William Johnston, an unemployed negro, in March 1961. He received many letters, of which 25 per cent. suggested that he was insane.

Greatest bequests The greatest bequests in a life-time of a millionaire were those of the late John Davison Rockefeller (1839–1937), who gave away sums totalling $750,000,000 (now £312·5 million). The greatest benefactions of a British millionaire were those of William Richard Morris, later the Viscount Nuffield, G.B.E., C.H. (1877–1963), which totalled more than £30,000,000 between 1926 and his death on 22 Aug. 1963. The Scottish-born U.S. citizen Andrew Carnegie (1835–1919) is estimated to have made benefactions totalling £70 million during the last 18 years of his life. These included 7,689 church organs and 2,811 libraries. He had started life in a bobbin factory at $1·20 per week.

The largest bequest made in the history of philanthropy was the $500,000,000 (£178,570,000) gift, announced on 12 Dec. 1955, to 4,157 educational and other institutions by the Ford Foundation (established 1936) of New York City, N.Y., U.S.A. The assets of the Foundation had a book value of $2,477,984,000 (now £1,032 million) in 1967.

Best dressed women The longest reign as the "Best Dressed Woman" was 15 years from 1938 to 1953 by the Duchess of Windsor (b. Bessie Wallis Warfield at Blue Ridge Summit, Pennsylvania, 19 June 1896, formerly Mrs. Spencer, formerly Mrs. Simpson). In January 1959 the New York Dress Institute put the Duchess and Mrs. William S. "Babe" Paley beyond annual comparison by elevating them to an ageless "Hall of Fame". Also later elevated was Mrs. Jacqueline Lee Kennedy-Onassis *née* Bouvier (born at Southampton, Long Island, New York, 28 July 1929). Including furs and jewellery, some perennials, such as Mrs. Winston F. C. "Ceezee" Guest, Mrs. Paley and Mrs. Gloria Guinness, known as "The Ultimate", are reputed to spend up to $100,000 (£41,666) a year on their wardrobes. Mrs. Henry M. Flagler, the chatelaine of Whitehall, her husband's $300,000 establishment in Palm Beach, Florida, U.S.A. in the era 1902–1914, never wore any dress a second time. Her closets were nonetheless moth proof.

In January 1960 the Institute decided it was politic to list a Top Twelve, not in order of merit, but alphabetically. The youngest winner was Mrs. Amanda Carter Burden, aged 22, a step-daughter of the twice blessed Mr. William Paley (see above), on 13 Jan. 1966. After 1966 rankings were re-established.

GASTRONOMIC RECORDS

Records for eating and drinking by trenchermen do not match those suffering from the rare disease of bulimia (morbid desire to eat) and polydipsia (pathological thirst). Some bulimia patients have to spend 15 hours a day eating, with an extreme consumption of 384 lb. 2 oz. of food in six days by Matthew Daking, aged 12, in 1743 (known as Mortimer's case). Some polydipsomaniacs have been said to be unsatisfied by less than 96 pints of liquid a day. Miss Helge Andersson (b. 1908) of Lindesberg, Sweden was reported in January 1971 to have been drinking 40 pints of water a day since 1922—a total of 87,600 gallons.

The world's greatest trencherman is Edward Abraham ("Bozo") Miller (b. 1909) of Oakland, California, U.S.A. He consumes up to 25,000 calories per day or more than 11 times that recommended. He stands 5 feet 7½ inches tall but weighs from 20 to 21½ stone, with a 57-inch waist. He has been undefeated in eating contests since 1931 (see below). The bargees on the Rhine are reputed to be the world's heaviest eaters with 5,200 calories a day.

While no healthy person has been reported to have succumbed in any eating or drinking contest, from a medical point of view, record attempts must be regarded as *extremely* inadvisable, particularly among young people.

Specific records have been claimed as follows:

Baked Beans 40 lb. in 30 minutes by 8 boys from the Coseley Youth Centre, Staffordshire, on 1 Feb. 1970.

Bananas 50½ in 10 minutes by Steyen Nel in Port Elizabeth, S. Africa, on 12 July 1970.

Beer Lawrence Hill (b. 1942) of Bolton, Lancashire, drained a 2½-pint Yard of Ale in 6½ seconds on 17 Dec. 1964. A 3-pint yard was downed in 10·15 seconds by Jack Boyle, 52, at The Bay Horse, Ormsgill, Barrow-in-Furness, Lancashire on 14 May 1971. Lionel Tutt (b. 1931) of Toddington, Bedfordshire, the 1968 and 1969 winner of the "World Beer Drinking Championship", downed 1 gallon in 7 minutes 33 seconds at the Royal Lancaster Hotel, London on 17 Dec. 1968.

The Oxford University "sconce" record is 12·0 seconds for 2 pints of beer set by the Australian, R. Hawke (University College) in 1955 and Clive Anderson (Magdalen) on 26 Feb. 1967. The record for a single pint (1/100th second watch) is 2·20 seconds by Jack Boyle (see above) also on 14 May 1971. The record for 2 litres (3·52 Imperial pints) is 11 seconds by J. H. Cochran (Class of 1925, Princeton University, New Jersey, U.S.A.) in Harry's New York Bar, Paris, on 26 June 1932.

The most extreme recorded drinking feat was one recorded in 1810 at Wroxham, Norfolk, England where a man was witnessed to have lowered 54½ pints of porter in 55 minutes. This must be regarded as an exaggerated report and the true record is closer to 31 pints in 56 minutes (32 pints in 58 minutes) by Fleet Air Arm Radio Mechanic Philip Davies, 29, at The Woodpecker, Todmorton, Lancashire in April 1971.

Beer Upsidedown 3¾ pints by Ernie Driver at Welland Valley, Yorkshire (in 3 minutes 58 seconds) on 1 Nov. 1970. 2 pints in 45 seconds by Mr. Southcombe at Victoria Hotel, Newcastle under Lyme on 25 Feb. 1971.

Boiled Eggs 44 in 30 minutes by Georges Grogniet of Belgium on 31 May 1956.

Cheese 16 oz. of Cheddar in 4 minutes 55 seconds by George Inchmore at Arnside, Westmorland on 25 May 1970.

Chicken 27 (2 lb. pullets) by "Bozo" Miller (see above) at Trader Vic's, San Francisco, California, U.S.A., in 1963.

Clams 437 in 10 minutes by Joe Gagnon (U.S.) at Everett, Washington, U.S.A. in January 1971.

Gherkins 1 lb. in 4 minutes 27 seconds by Robert Harari, 21, at Palmer's Green, London N.13, 6 Nov. 1968.

Goldfish (live) 225 by Roger Martinez at St. Mary's University, San Antonio, Texas, U.S.A. on 6 Feb. 1970.

Grapes 1 lb. (unpipped) in 86 seconds by Malcolm Heygate-Browne at High Wycombe, Buckinghamshire on 23 April 1971.

Haggis 19 oz. haggis in 65 seconds at Waterloo Station, London on 1 Jan. 1967.

Hamburgers 77 at a 2½-hour sitting by Philip Yazdizk (U.S.A.), Chicago, Illinois, U.S.A., on 25 April 1955.

Ice Cream 7 lb. 3 oz. (46 2½-oz. scoops) in 30 minutes by Peter Morrow, Brisbane, Queensland, Australia on 27 April 1970.

Lemons 12 quarters (3 lemons) whole (including skin and pips) in 162 seconds by John Wood at Wakefield Youth Hostel, Yorkshire on 16 April 1971.

Meat One whole roast ox in 42 days by Johann Ketzler of Munich, Germany in 1880.

Meat Pies 10 8-oz. pies (Steak & Kidney), by John Taylor, 25, at Rugby, Warwickshire in January 1969.

Milk 1 U.S. quart (0·83 of an Imperial quart) by L.M.E.M. Frank Fowler in 6·0 seconds in H.M.S. *Puma* at Monterey, California, U.S.A. on 1 April 1971.

Oysters 480 in 60 minutes by Joe Garcia (Australia), in Melbourne, on 5 Feb. 1955. The official record for opening oysters is 100 in 3 minutes 37 seconds in Paris in 1954 by le Champion du Monde des Ecaillers M. Williams Bley.

Pickled Onions 60 in 15 minutes 12 seconds by Paul Besley, 20, outside Trinity College, Cambridge on 20 March 1971.

Potato Crisps 30 2-oz. bags in 24 minutes 3·6 seconds, without a drink, by Paul G. Tully of Brisbane University in May 1969. The largest single crisp on record is one measured to be 5 inches × 3 inches found at Reeds School, Cobham, Surrey by John Nichol, 16, on 2 Feb. 1971.

Prunes 130 in 116 seconds (stoned and soaked), Edward Baxter at St. Edward's Hall, Leek, Staffordshire, 12 Oct. 1968. 200 in 90 minutes by Robert Muery, West Senior High School, Michigan, U.S.A., on 23 Feb. 1971.

Ravioli 324 (first 250 in 70 minutes) by "Bozo" Miller (see above) at Rendezvous Room, Oakland, California, U.S.A., in 1963.

Raw Eggs 26 in 9·0 seconds by Leslie Jones on Harlech T.V., Cardiff on 10 Nov. 1970. David Taylor at St. Leonards-on-Sea, Sussex ate 16 raw eggs with their shells in 3 minutes 20 seconds on 8 Jan. 1970.

Sandwiches 17 (jam "butties" $5 \times 3 \times \frac{1}{2}$ inch) in 10 minutes by Leslie Biddlestone at South Hylton Secondary Modern School, Sunderland on 21 July 1970.

Sausages 25 2-oz. sausages in 4 minutes 37 seconds by Rodney Harrison, 22, at Much Wenlock, Shropshire on 26 May 1969. 30 2-oz. sausages in 10 minutes 11·8 seconds by Walter Cornelius, 43, at Peterborough on 8 May 1969.

Spaghetti 100 yards in 1 minute 34 seconds (by 4 people in a 3 ft. diameter circle) at St. Mary's Youth Club, Balham, London in October 1967.

Tea Drinking 78 cups (⅓ pint) by Mrs. Marion Tindall of Barton-on-Sea, Hampshire, England, in September 1970.

Whelks 81 (unshelled) in 15 minutes by William Corfield at the Helyar Arms, East Coker, Somerset on 6 Sept. 1969.

2. HONOURS, DECORATIONS AND AWARDS

Eponymous record The largest object to which a human name is attached is the super cluster of galaxies known as Abell 7, after the astronomer Dr. George O. Abell of the University of California, U.S.A. The group of clusters has an estimated linear dimension of 300,000,000 light years and was announced in 1961.

ORDERS AND DECORATIONS

Oldest The earliest of the orders of chivalry is the Venetian order of St. Marc, reputedly founded in A.D. 831. The Castilian order of Calatrava has an established date of foundation in 1158. The prototype of the princely Orders of Chivalry is the Most Noble Order of the Garter founded by King Edward III in *c.* 1348.

Most titles The most titled person in the world is the 18th Duchess of Alba (Albade Tormes), Doña Maria del Rosario Cayetana Fitz-James Stuart y Silva. She is 8 times a duchess, 15 times a marchioness, 21 times a countess and is 19 times a Spanish grandee.

British *Rarest* The rarest British medal is the Union of South Africa King's Medal for Bravery in Gold. The unique recipient was Francis C. Drake, aged 14, who rescued a child from a deep well at Parys, in the Orange Free State, on 6 Jan. 1943. However, the Queen's Fire Services Medal for Gallantry (instituted in 1954), which can only be won posthumously, has yet to be awarded.

Of War Medals, only two Naval General Service Medals (1793–1840) were issued with seven bars (the one legged Admiral of the Fleet Sir James Alexander Gordon, G.C.B. [1782–1869] and the one-eyed Rear Admiral Sir John Hindmarsh, K.H. [d. 1860]) and only two Military General Service Medals (1793–1814) with 15 bars (James Talbot of the 45th Foot and Daniel Loochstadt of the 60th Foot).

ommonest Of gallantry decorations, the most unsparingly given was the Military Medal, which was awarded to 115,589 recipients between 1916 and 1919. The most frequently awarded decoration in the 1939–45 war was the Distinguished Flying Cross, which was awarded (including bars) 21,281 times.

Most expensive The highest price paid for any United Kingdom decoration is £3,500 for the Victoria Cross won by Able Seaman Edward Robinson at the Relief of Lucknow during the Indian Mutiny of 1858. The purchaser at the auction at Glendining's, London W.1 on 22 Oct. 1970 was Mr. John E. G. Bartholomew, 46, of Windlesham, Surrey.

VICTORIA CROSS

Most bars The only three men ever to have been awarded a bar to the Victoria Cross (instituted 1856) are:—

Surg.-Capt. (later Lt.-Col.) Arthur Martin-Leake, V.C.*, V.D., R.A.M.C. (1874–1953) (1902 and bar 1915).
Capt. Noel Godfrey Chavasse, V.C.*, M.C., R.A.M.C. (1884–1917) (1916 and bar posthumously 14 Sept. 1917).
Second Lieut. (later Capt.) Charles Hazlett Upham, V.C.*, N.Z.M.F. (born 1911) (1941 and bar 1942).

v Zealand's es Upham, only living ouble V.C.

Oldest The greatest reported age at which a man has won the V.C. is 69 in the case of Lieut. (later Capt.) William Raynor of the Bengal Veteran Establishment, in defence of the magazine at Delhi, India, on 11 May 1857. Recent evidence indicates that he was not older than 66.

Youngest The lowest established age for a V.C. is 15 years 100 days for Hospital Apprentice Arthur Fitzgibbon (born at Peteragurh, northern India, 13 May 1845) of the 67th (The Hampshire) Regt. for bravery at the Taku Forts in northern China on 21 Aug. 1860. Later, as an assistant surgeon, he was dismissed for insubordination. The youngest living V.C. is Lance-Corporal Rambahadur Limbu (b. Nepal, 1939) of the 10th Princess Mary's Own Gurkha Rifles. The award, announced on 22 April 1966, was for his courage while fighting in the Bau district of Sarawak, East Malaysia, on 21 Nov. 1965.

Longest lived The longest lived of all the 1,349 winners of the Victoria Cross was Captain (later General Sir) Lewis Stratford Tollemache Halliday, V.C., K.C.B., of the Royal Marine Light Infantry. He was born on 14 May 1870, won his V.C. in China in 1900, and died on 9 March 1966, aged 95 years 299 days. The oldest living V.C. is Maj. Gen. Dudley Graham Johnson, V.C., C.B., D.S.O. and bar, M.C. (b. 13 Feb. 1884), who won his decoration as an Acting Lt.-Col. attached to the 2nd Batt. Royal Sussex Regt. at the Sumbre Canal, France on 4 Nov. 1918. He also received the Queen's South Africa Medal in 1900 aged 16.

Most awards The two organizations which have won most V.C.s are Eton College (23 this century) and The Church Lads' Brigade with 22.

RECORD NUMBER OF BARS (repeat awards) EVER GAZETTED TO BRITISH GALLANTRY DECORATIONS

* = a bar

V.C.*	A first bar has been three times awarded to the Victoria Cross (see above).
D.S.O.***	A third bar has been 16 times awarded to the Distinguished Service Order.
D.S.C.***	A third bar has been uniquely awarded to the Distinguished Service Cross won by Cdr. Norman Eyre Morley, R.N.V.R.
M.C.***	A third bar has been four times awarded to the Military Cross.
D.F.C.**	A second bar has been 54 times awarded to the Distinguished Flying Cross.
A.F.C.**	A second bar has been 12 times awarded to the Air Force Cross.
D.C.M.**	A second bar has been 11 times awarded to the Distinguished Conduct Medal.
C.G.M.*	A first bar has been uniquely awarded to the Conspicuous Gallantry Medal won by C.P.O. A. R. Blore and a second medal to Able Seaman D. Barry.
G.M.*	A first bar has been 25 times awarded to the George Medal.
K.P.M.**	A second bar has been uniquely awarded to the King's/Queen's Police Medal for Gallantry won by Supt. F. W. O'Gormon.
E.M.*	A first bar has twice been awarded to the Edward Medal (1st Class).
D.S.M.***	A third bar has been uniquely awarded to the Distinguished Service Medal won by Petty Officer William Henry Kelly.
M.M.***	A third bar has been uniquely awarded to the Military Medal won by Cpl. Ernest A. Correy.
D.F.M.**	A second bar has been uniquely awarded to the Distinguished Flying Medal won by Flt.-Sgt. (now Group Capt.) Donald Ernest Kingaby, D.S.O., A.F.C.
A.F.M.*	A first bar has been 7 times awarded to the Air Force Medal.
S.G.M.*	A first bar has been uniquely awarded to the Sea Gallantry Medal won by Chief Officer James Whiteley.
B.E.M.*	A first bar has been 4 times awarded to the British Empire Medal for Gallantry (as instituted in 1957).

No bars have yet been awarded to the George Cross (G.C.), the Conspicuous Gallantry Medal (Flying) (C.G.M.). No bars were ever awarded to the Albert Medal in Gold (A.M.), the Albert Medal (A.M.), the Edward Medal (E.M.) or the Empire Gallantry Medal (E.G.M.).

Most mentions in despatches The record number of "mentions" is 24 by Field Marshal the Rt. Hon. the Earl Roberts, V.C., K.G., K.P., G.C.B., O.M., G.C.S.I., G.C.I.E., V.D. (1832–1914). He was also the only subject with 8 sets of official post-nominal letters.

U.S.S.R. The U.S.S.R.'s highest award for valour is the Gold Star of a Hero of the Soviet Union. Over 10,000 were awarded in World War II. Among the 109 awards of a second star were those to Marshal Iosif Vissarionovich Dzhugashvili, *alias* Stalin (1879–1953) and Lt.-General Nikita Sergeyevich Khrushchyov (born 17 April 1894). The only war-time triple awards were to Marshal Georgiy Konstantinovich Zhukov, Hon. G.C.B. (born 1896) (subsequently awarded a fourth Gold Star, unique until Mr. Khrushchyov's fourth award) and the leading air aces Guards' Colonel (now Aviation Maj.-Gen.) Aleksandr Ivanovich Polkyrshkin and Aviation Maj.-Gen. Ivan Nikitaevich Kozhedub.

U.S.A. The highest U.S. decoration is the Congressional Medal of Honor. Five marines received both the Army and Navy Medals of Honor for the same acts in 1918 and 14 officers and men from 1863 to 1915 have received the medal on two occasions.

Most bemedalled The most bemedalled chest is that of H.I.M. Field-Marshal Hailé Selassié, K.G., G.C.B. (Hon.), G.C.M.G. (Hon.) (born, as Ras Tafari Makonnen, on 23 July 1892), Emperor of Ethiopia, who has over 50 medal ribbons worn in up to 14 rows.

TOP SCORING AIR ACES

World 80 Rittmeister Manfred, Freiherr (Baron) von Richthofen (Germany).
352[2] Major Erich Hartman (Germany).

United Kingdom 73[1] Capt. (acting Major) Edward Mannock, V.C., D.S.O.**, M.C.*.
38[3] Wg.-Cdr. (now Air Vice Marshal) James Edgar Johnson, C.B., C.B.E., D.S.O.**, D.F.C.*.

A compilation of the top air aces of 13 combatant nations in World War I and of 22 nations in World War II was included in the 13th edition of *The Guinness Book of Records.*

1 *Recent research suggests that Mannock's total may have been lower than that of Major James Thomas Byford McCudden, V.C. D.S.O.*, M.C.*, M.M.* (57 victories).

2 *All except one of the aircraft in this unrivalled total were Soviet combat aircraft on the Eastern Front in 1942–45. The German air ace with most victories against the R.A.F. was Oberleutnant Hans-Joachim Marseille (killed 30 Sept. 1942), who, in 388 actions, shot down 158 Allied aircraft, 151 of them over North Africa.*

3 *The greatest number of successes against flying bombs (V.1's) was by Sqn. Ldr. Joseph Berry, D.F.C.** (b. Nottingham, 1920, killed 2 Oct. 1944), who brought down 60. The most successful R.A.F. fighter pilot was Sqn. Ldr. Marmaduke Thomas St. John Pattle, D.F.C.*, of South Africa, with a known total of at least 40.*

Top jet ace The greatest number of kills in jet to jet battles is 16 by Capt. Joseph Christopher McConnell, Jr., U.S.A.F. (b. Dover, New Hampshire, 30 Jan. 1922) in the Korean war (1950–53). He was killed on 25 Aug. 1954. It is possible that an Israeli ace may have surpassed this total in the period 1967–70 but the identity of pilots is subject to strict security.

Top woman ace The record score for any woman fighter pilot is 13 by Jnr. Lt. Lila Litvak (U.S.S.R.) in the Eastern Front campaign of 1941–45.

Anti-submarine successes The highest number of U-boat kills attributed to one ship in the 1939–45 war was 13 to H.M.S. *Starling* (Capt. Frederick J. Walker, C.B., D.S.O.***, R.N.). Captain Walker was in overall command at the sinking of a total of 25 U-boats between 1941 and the time of his death on 9 July 1944. The U.S. Destroyer Escort *England* sank six Japanese submarines in the Pacific between 18 and 30 May 1944.

Most successful U-boat captain The most successful of all World War II submarine commanders was Korvetten-Kapitän (now Kapitän zur See) Otto Kretschmer (b. 1911), captain of the U.23 and later the U.99. He sank one allied destroyer and 43 merchantmen totalling 263,682 gross registered tons in 16 patrols before his capture on 17 March 1941. He is a Knight's Cross of the Iron Cross with Oakleaves and Swords. In World War I Kapitän-Leutnant Lothar von Arnauld de la Periere, in the U.35 and U.139, sank 194 allied ships totalling 453,716 gross tons. The most successful boats were U.48, which in World War I sank 54 ships of 90,350 g.r.t. in a single voyage and 535,900 g.r.t. all told, and U.53 which sank 53 ships of 318,111 g.r.t. in World War II.

NOBEL PRIZES

The Nobel Foundation of £3,200,000 was set up under the will of Alfred Bernhard Nobel (1833–96), the unmarried Swedish chemist and chemical engineer, who invented dynamite in 1866. The Nobel Prizes are presented annually on 10 Dec., the anniversary of Nobel's death and the festival day of the Foundation. Since the first Prizes were awarded in 1901, the highest cash value of the award, in each of the six fields of Physics, Chemistry, Medicine and Physiology, Literature, Peace and Economics was £32,000 in 1970.

MOST AWARDS

By countries The United States has shared in the greatest number of awards (including those made in 1970) with a total of 77, made up of 20 for Physics, 13 for Chemistry, 23 for Medicine-Physiology, 6 for Literature, 14 for Peace and 1 for Economics.

The United Kingdom has shared in 54 awards, comprising 14 for Physics, 15 for Chemistry, 11 for Medicine-Physiology, 6 for Literature and 8 for Peace.

By classes, the United States holds the records for Medicine-Physiology with 23, for Physics with 20 and for Peace with 14; Germany for Chemistry with 20; and France for Literature with 12.

Greatest reception The greatest ticker-tape reception ever given on Broadway, New York City, N.Y., U.S.A., was that for Lt.-Col. (now Col.) John Herschel Glenn, Jr. (born 18 July 1921) on 1 March 1962, after his return from his tri-orbital flight. The New York Street Cleaning Department estimated that 3,474 tons of paper descended. This total compared with 3,249 tons for General of the Army Douglas MacArthur (1880–1964) in 1951 and 1,800 tons for Col. Charles Augustus Lindbergh (born 4 Feb. 1902) in June 1927.

Most statues The world record for raising statues to oneself was set by Generalissimo Dr. Rafael Leónidas Trujillo y Molina (1891–1961), former President of the Dominican Republic. In March 1960 a count showed that there were "over 2,000". The country's highest mountain was named Pico Trujillo (now Pico Duarte). One Province was called Trujillo and another Trujillo Valdez. The capital was named Ciudad Trujillo (Trujillo City) in 1936, but reverted to its old name of Santo Domingo de Guzmán on 23 Nov. 1961. Trujillo was assassinated in a car ambush on 30 May 1961, and 30 May is now celebrated annually as a public holiday. The man to whom most statues have been raised is undoubtedly Vladimir Ilyich Ulyanov, *alias* Lenin (1877–1924), busts of whom have been mass-produced as also in the case of Mao Tse-tung.

Individuals Individually the only person to have won two Prizes outright is Dr. Linus Carl Pauling (born 28 Feb. 1901), the Professor of Chemistry since 1931 at the California Institute of Technology, Pasadena, California, U.S.A. He was awarded the Chemistry Prize for 1954 and the Peace Prize for 1962. The only other person to have won two prizes was Madame Marie Curie (1867–1934), who was born in Poland as Marja Sklodowska. She shared the 1903 Physics Prize with her husband Pierre Curie (1859–1906) and Antoine Henri Becquerel (1852–1908), and won the 1911 Chemistry Prize outright. The Peace Prize has been awarded three times to the International Committee of the Red Cross (founded 29 Oct. 1863), of Geneva, Switzerland, namely in 1917, 1944 and in 1963, when it was shared with the International League of Red Cross Societies.

Oldest The oldest prizeman has been Professor Francis Peyton Rous (1879–1970) of the United States. He shared the Medicine Prize in 1966, at the age of 87.

Youngest The youngest laureate has been Professor Sir William Lawrence Bragg, C.H., O.B.E., M.C. (born in Adelaide, South Australia, 31 March 1890), of the U.K., who, at the age of 25, shared the 1915 Physics Prize with his father, Sir William Henry Bragg, O.M., K.B.E. (1862–1942), for work on X-rays and crystal structures. Bragg and also Theodore William Richards (1868–1928) of the U.S.A., who won the 1914 Chemistry prize, carried out their prize work when aged 23. The youngest Literature prizeman has been Joseph Rudyard Kipling (1865–1936) at the age of 41 in 1907. The youngest Peace prize-winner has been the Rev. Dr. Martin Luther King, Jr. (1929–68) of the U.S.A., in 1964.

PEERAGE

Most ancient creation The year 1223 has been ascribed to the premier Irish barony of Kingsale (formerly de Courcy), though on the Order of Precedence the date is listed as 1397. The premier English barony, de Ros, was held until her death on 8 Oct. 1956, by a Baroness in her own right and 26th in her line, dating from 1264. It was called out of abeyance on 29 Aug. 1958 in favour of a granddaughter, Mrs. Georgiana Angela Maxwell (born 1933). The earldom of Arundel, a subsidiary title of the Duke of Norfolk, dates from 1139.

Oldest creation The oldest age at which any person has been raised to the peerage is 94 in the case of Sir William Francis Kyffin Taylor, G.B.E., K.C. (born 9 July 1854), who was created Baron Maenan of Ellesmere, County Salop (Shropshire), in 1948, and died, aged 97, on 22 Sept. 1951, when the title became extinct.

ldest peer The oldest peer ever recorded was the Rt. Hon. Frank Douglas-Pennant, the 5th Baron Penrhyn (born 21 Nov. 1865), who died on 3 Feb. 1967, aged 101 years 74 days. Currently the oldest peer is the Rt. Hon. Sir John Frederick Whitworth Aylmer, Bt., the 9th Baron Aylmer (b. 23 April 1880). His family motto is "Steady". He lives in Canada. The oldest peeress recorded was the Countess Desmond, who was alleged to be 140 when she died in 1604. This claim is patently exaggerated but it is accepted that she may have been 104. Currently the oldest peeress of parliament is the Countess of Kintore, Ethel Sydney Keith-Falconer, Dowager Viscountess Stonehaven, born on 20 Sept. 1874.

ongest and shortest peerages The peer who has sat longest in the House of Lords was Lt.-Col. Charles Henry FitzRoy, O.B.E., the 4th Baron Southampton (b. 11 May 1867), who succeeded to his father's title on 6 July 1872, took his seat on 23 Jan. 1891, 18 months before Mr. W. E. Gladstone's fourth administration began, and died, aged 91, on 7 Dec. 1958, having held the title for more than 86 years.

The shortest enjoyment of a peerage was the "split second" by which the law assumes that the Hon. Wilfrid Carlyle Stamp (born 28 Oct. 1904), the 2nd Baron Stamp, survived his father, Sir Josiah Charles Stamp, G.C.B., G.B.E., the 1st Baron Stamp, when both were killed as a result of German bombing of London on 16 April 1941. Apart from this legal fiction, the shortest recorded peerage was one of 30 minutes in the case of Sir Charles Brandon, K.B., the 3rd Duke of Suffolk, who died, aged 13 or 14, just after succeeding his brother, the 2nd Duke, when both were suffering a fatal illness, at Buckden, Huntingdonshire, on 14 July 1551.

Highest numbering The highest succession number borne by any peer is that of the present 35th Baron Kingsale (John de Courcy, b. 1941), who succeeded to the 746-year-old Barony on 7 Nov. 1969.

Most creations The largest number of new hereditary peerages created in any year was the 54 in 1296. The record for all peerages (including life peerages) is 55 in 1964. The greatest number of extinctions in a year was 16 in 1923 and the greatest number of deaths was 44 in 1935.

Longest abeyance The longest abeyance of any peerage was that of the baronies of Burgh and Strabolgi, which were called out on 9 May 1916, after 547 years in abeyance since 6 April 1369.

ost prolific The most prolific peer of all time is believed to be Sir Robert Shirley, the 1st Earl Ferrers (1650–1717). By his first wife, Elizabeth (*née* Washington) (died 1693), he had 17 children (10 sons and 7 daughters), and by his second wife Selina (*née* Finch) (died 1762) 10 children (5 sons and 5 daughters), making a total of 27 legitimate children (15 boys and 12 girls). In addition, he fathered 30 illegitimate children. Currently the peer with the largest family is the Rt. Hon. Bryan Walter Guinness, 2nd Baron Moyne, with 6 sons and 5 daughters.

The most prolific peeress is believed to be Elizabeth (*née* Barnard), who bore 22 children to her husband Lord Chandos of Sudeley (1642–1714).

BARONETS

Oldest The greatest age to which a baronet has lived is 101 years 6 months, in the case of Sir Fitzroy Maclean, 10th Bt., K.C.B., who was born on 18 May 1835 and died on 22 Nov. 1936. He was the last survivor of the Charge of the Light Brigade at Balaclava in the Crimea, Russia, on 25 Oct. 1854.

Most and least creations The largest number of creations this century was 51 in 1919. There were none in 1940 or since 1965.

KNIGHTS

Youngest The youngest age at which a knighthood has been conferred is 2 years 9 months in the case of Richard, Duke of York, who was born at Shrewsbury on 17 Aug. 1472 and invested a K.G. on 15 May 1475. He is believed to have been murdered in the Tower of London with his elder brother, ex-King Edward V, probably between July and September 1483.

ORDER OF MERIT

The Order of Merit (instituted on 23 June 1902) is limited to 24 members. Up to 1971 there were 127 awards including only 3 women, plus 9 honorary awards to non-British citizens. The longest lived holder has been the Rt. Hon. Bertrand Arthur William Russell, 3rd Earl Russell, who died on 2 Feb. 1970 aged 97 years 260 days. The oldest recipient was Admiral of the Fleet the Hon. Sir Henry Keppel, G.C.B., O.M. (1809–1904), who received the Order aged 93 years 56 days on 9 Aug. 1902. The youngest recipient has been H.R.H. the Duke of Edinburgh, K.G., K.T., O.M., G.B.E. who was appointed on his 47th birthday on 10 June 1968.

Most freedoms Probably the greatest number of freedoms ever conferred on any man was 54 in the case of Andrew Carnegie (1835–1919), who was born in Dunfermline, Fife but emigrated to the United States in 1848. The most freedoms conferred upon any citizen of the United Kingdom is 42, in the case of the Rt. Hon. Sir Winston Leonard Spencer Churchill, K.G., O.M., C.H., T.D. (1874–1965).

Most honorary degrees The greatest number of honorary degrees awarded to any individual is 89, given to Herbert Clark Hoover (1874–1964), former President of the United States (1929–33).

Greatest vote The largest monetary vote made by Parliament to a subject was the £400,000 given to the 1st Duke of Wellington (1769–1852) on 12 April 1814. He received in all £864,000. The total received by the 1st, 2nd and 3rd Dukes to January 1900 was £1,052,000.

Who's Who The longest entry in *Who's Who* (founded 1849) was that of the Rt. Hon. Sir Winston Leonard Spencer Churchill, K.G., O.M., C.H., T.D. (1874–1965), who had 211 lines in the 1965 edition. Apart from those who qualify for inclusion by hereditary title, the youngest entry has been Yehudi Menuhin, Hon. K.B.E. (b. New York City, U.S.A. 22 April 1916), the concert violinist, who first appeared in the 1932 edition. The longest entry of the 66,000 entries in *Who's Who in America* is that of Richard Buckminster Fuller whose all-time record of 139 lines compares with the 23 line sketch on President Nixon.

"Time" magazine cover The most frequent subject has been President Johnson with 41 treatments to the end of 1967. The youngest subject for a *Time* (first issued 3 March 1923) cover was Charles Augustus Lindbergh, Jr. (born in June 1930), during the kidnapping case of 1932. The oldest subject was the veteran sports coach Amos Alonzo Stagg (1862–1965) in the issue of 20 Oct. 1958. Summing up his life's work he agreed with the dictum of the Brooklyn baseball manager of 1948 "Lippy" Leo Durocher that "Nice guys come last".

Longest obituary The obituary of Thomas Alva Edison (U.S.) (11 Feb. 1847–18 Nov. 1931) occupied 4½ pages in the *New York Times* of the next day.

ACCIDENTS AND DISASTERS

WORST IN THE WORLD

Category	Number	Details	Date
Pandemic	75,000,000	The Black Death (bubonic, pneumonic and septicaemic plague)	1337–1351
	21,640,000	Influenza	April–Nov. 1918
Famine	9,500,000[1]	Northern China	Feb. 1877–Sept. 1878
Flood	3,700,000	Hwang-ho River, China	Aug. 1931
Earthquake	830,000	Shensi Province, China	23 Jan. 1556
Circular Storm[2]	300,000	Haiphong, North Viet-Nam	8 Oct. 1881
Landslide	200,000	Kansu Province, China	16 Dec. 1920
Conventional Bombing[3]	c. 168,000	Tōkyō, Japan	9–10 Mar. 1945
Atomic Bomb	91,223[4]	Hiroshima, Japan	6 Aug. 1945
Snow Avalanche	c. 5,000[5]	Huarás, Peru	13 Dec. 1941
Marine (single ship)	4,120	*Wilhelm Gustloff* (25,484 tons) torpedoed off Danzig by U.S.S.R. submarine S-13	30 Jan. 1945
Panic	c. 4,000	Chungking (Zhong qing) China air raid shelter	c. 8 June 1941
Dam Burst	2,209	South Fork Dam, Johnstown, Pennsylvania	31 May 1889
Explosion	1,963[6]	Halifax, Nova Scotia, Canada	6 Dec. 1917
Fire[7] (single building)	1,670	The Theatre, Canton, China	May 1845
Mining[8]	1,572	Honkeiko Colliery, China (coal dust explosion)	26 April 1942
Riot	c. 1,200	New York City anti-conscription riots	13-16 July 1863
Crocodiles	c. 900	Japanese soldiers, Ramree Is., Burma	19–20 Feb. 1945
Tornado	689	South Central States, U.S.A.	18 Mar. 1925
Railway	543	Modane, France	12 Dec. 1917
Man-eating Tigress[9]	436	Champawat district, India, shot by Col. Jim Corbett	pre-1945
Hail	246	Moradabad, Uttar Pradesh, India	30 April 1888
Aircraft (Civil)	155[10]	Maracaibo, Venezuela, Douglas DC-9-30 jet airliner	16 Mar. 1969
Submarine	129	U.S.S. *Thresher* off Cape Cod, Massachusetts, U.S.A.	10 April 1963
Road[11]	>125	Two trucks crashed into a crowd of dancers, Sotouboua, Togo	6 Dec. 1965
Mountaineering	40[12]	U.S.S.R. Expedition on Mount Everest	Dec. 1952
Fireworks	18	Hearst election celebration, Madison Square, New York City, N.Y., U.S.A.	1902
Space Exploration	3	Apollo oxygen fire, Cape Kennedy, Fla., U.S.A.	27 Jan. 1967

WORST IN THE UNITED KINGDOM

Number	Details	Date
800,000	The Black Death (bubonic, pneumonic and septicaemic plague)	1347–1350
225,000	Influenza	Sept.–Nov. 1918
1,500,000[13]	Ireland (famine and typhus)	1846–1851
c. 2,000[14]	Severn Estuary	20 Jan. 1606
1	City of London	6 April 1580
1	Rowhedge, Essex	22 April 1884
c. 8,000	"The Channel Storm"	26 Nov. 1703
144	Pantglas coal tip No. 7, Aberfan, Glamorganshire	21 Oct. 1966
1,436	London	10–11 May 1941
8	Lewes, Sussex (snowdrifts)	27 Dec. 1836
c. 4,000	H.M. Troopship *Lancastria* (16,243 tons) off St. Nazaire	17 June 1940
173	Bethnal Green Tube Station (air raid siren)	3 Mar. 1943
270	Bradfield Dam, Dale Dyke, near Sheffield (burst)	11 Mar. 1864
134	Chilwell, Notts. (explosives factory)	1 July 1918
86[15]	New Royal Theatre, Exeter	5 Sept. 1887
439	Universal Colliery, Senghenydd, Caerphilly, Glamorganshire, Wales	14 Oct. 1913
565 (min.)	London anti-Catholic Gordon riots	2–13 June 1780
60[16]	Widecombe, Devon	21 Oct. 1638
227[17]	Triple collision at Quintins Hill, Dumfries-shire, Scotland	22 May 1915
81[18]	Avro Tudor V at Sigginston, near Llandow, Glamorgan	12 Mar. 1950
99	H.M.S. *Thetis*, during trials, Liverpool Bay	1 June 1939
24	R.M. Cadets, run down by bus, Gillingham, Kent	4 Dec. 1951
5	On Ben Nevis, Scotland	19 Dec. 1954

1 *In 1770 the great Indian famine carried away a proportion of the population estimated as high as one third, hence a figure of tens of millions. The figure for Bengal alone was also probably about 10 million. It has been estimated that more than 5,000,000 died in the post-World War I famine in the U.S.S.R. The U.S.S.R. government in July 1923 informed Mr. (later President) Herbert Hoover that the A.R.A. (American Relief Administration) had since August 1921 saved 20,000,000 lives from famine and famine diseases.*

2 *The total death roll on the 12–13 Nov. 1970 East Pakistan cyclone though officially "more than 200,000" remains unofficially up to 500,000. One report asserted that less than half of the population of the 4 islands of Bhola, Charjabbar, Hatia and Ramagati (1961 Census 1·4 million) survived. The most damaging hurricane recorded was the billion dollar Betsy (name now retired) in 1965 with an estimated insurance pay-out of $750 million.*

3 *The number of civilians killed by the bombing of Germany has been put variously as 593,000 and "over 635,000". The death roll in Dresden, Germany on 13–15 Feb. 1945 is believed to have been 135,000.*

4 *United States Casualty Commission figure in 1960 was 79,400, while the Hiroshima Peace Memorial Museum gives a figure of 240,000.*

5 *A total of 10,000 Austrian and Italian troops is reputed to have been lost in the Dolomite valley of Northern Italy on 13 Dec. 1916 in more than 100 avalanches. The total is probably exaggerated though bodies were still being found in 1952.*

6 *Some sources maintain that the final death roll was over 3,000.*

7 *84,000 were killed in the U.S. fire raid on Tokyo, Japan, on 9–10 March 1945.*

8 *The worst gold mining disaster in South Africa was 152 killed due to flooding in the Witwatersrand Gold Mining Co. Gold Mine in 1909.*

9 *In the period 1941–42* c. *1,500 Kenyans were killed by a pride of 22 man-eating lions. Eighteen of these were shot by a hunter named Rushby.*

10 *Viasa (Venezuelan Air Lines): 84 on board and a toll last reported at 71 on the ground. The highest toll in the air was when a Boeing 727 of All-Nippon Airways, Japan, crashed into Tōkyō Bay on 4 Feb. 1966, killing all 133 aboard (126 passengers and 7 crew).*

11 *The worst ever years for road deaths in the U.S.A. and the U.K. have been, respectively, 1970 (55,500) and 1941 (9,169). In the U.S.A. in 1968 4,400,000 were injured. The world's highest death rate is said to be in Queensland, Australia but global statistics are not available. The greatest pile-up on British roads was on the M6 near Wigan, Lancashire on 8 Dec. 1969 when 3 were killed and 120 injured in more than 100 vehicles.*

12 *According to Polish sources, not confirmed by the U.S.S.R.*

13 *Based on the net rate of natural increase between 1841 and 1851, a supportable case for a loss of population of 3 million can be made out if rates of under-enumeration of 25 per cent. (1841) and 10 per cent. (1851) are accepted. Potato rot* (Phytophthora infestans) *was first reported on 13 Sept. 1845.*

14 *Death rolls of 100,000 were reputed in England and Holland in the floods of 1099, 1421 and 1446.*

15 *In July 1212, 3,000 were killed in the crush, burned or drowned when London Bridge caught fire at both ends. The death roll in the Great Fire of London of 1666 was only 8. History's first "fire storm" occurred in the Quebec Yard, Surrey Docks, London during the 300-pump fire in the Blitz on 7–8 Sept. 1940. Dockland casualties were 306 killed.*

16 *Killed and injured.*

17 *The 213-yard-long troop train was telescoped to 67 yards. Signalmen Meakin and Tinsley were sentenced for manslaughter.*

18 *The worst crash by a U.K. operated aircraft was that of the B.O.A.C. Boeing 707 which broke up in mid-air near Mount Fuji, Japan, on 5 March 1966. The crew of 11 and all 113 passengers (total 124) were killed. The cause was violent CAT (Clear Air Turbulence).*

The rat flea, which was the carrying agent of man's greatest killing pandemic—the Black Death

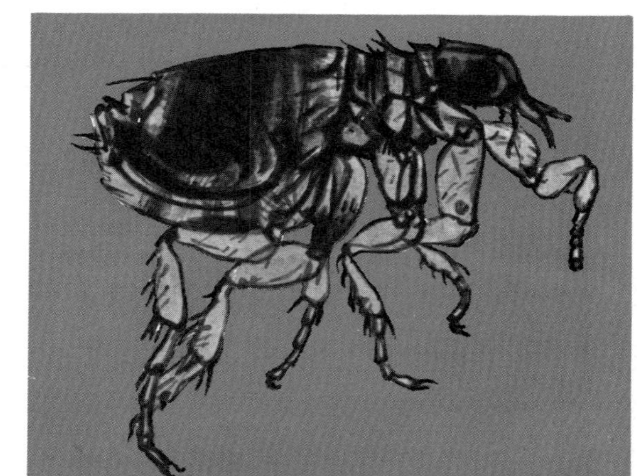

11 THE HUMAN WORLD

1. POLITICAL AND SOCIAL

The land area of the Earth is estimated at 57,700,000 square miles (including inland waters), or 29·3 per cent. of the world's surface area. The permanently inhabited continents (*i.e.* excluding Antarctica) and island groups have an estimated area of 52,430,000 square miles, including inland waters.

Largest political division The British Commonwealth of Nations, a free association of 31 independent sovereign states together with their dependencies, covers an area of about 13,700,000 square miles and had an estimated population of 970,000,000 at mid-1971.

COUNTRIES

Total The total number of separately administered territories in the world is 226, of which 146 are independent countries. Of these 24 sovereign and 65 non-sovereign are insular countries. Only 29 sovereign and 3 non-sovereign countries are entirely without a seaboard. Territorial waters vary between extremes of 3 miles (*e.g.* United Kingdom, Australia, France, Ireland and the U.S.A.) up to 200 miles (*e.g.* Argentina, Ecuador, El Salvador and Panama).

Largest The country with the greatest area is the Union of Soviet Socialist Republics (the Soviet Union), comprising 15 Union (constituent) Republics with a total area of 8,649,550 square miles, or 15·0 per cent. of the world's total land area, and a total coastline (including islands) of 66,090 miles. The country measures 5,580 miles from east to west and 2,790 miles from north to south.

The United Kingdom covers 94,221 square miles (including 1,197 square miles of inland water), or 0·16 per cent. of the total land area of the world. Great Britain is the world's eighth largest island, with an area of 84,186 square miles and a coastline 5,126 miles long, of which Scotland accounts for 2,573 miles, Wales 601 miles and England 1,952 miles.

Smallest The smallest independent country in the world is the State of the Vatican City (Stato della Città del Vaticano), which was made an enclave within the city of Rome, Italy on 11 Feb. 1929. It has an area of 44 hectares (108·7 acres).

The world's smallest republic is Nauru, less than 1 degree south of the equator in the Western Pacific, which became independent on 31 Jan. 1968, has an area of 5,263 acres (8·2 square miles) and a population of 7,000 (estimate mid-1969).

The smallest colony in the world is Pitcairn Island with an area of 960 acres (1·5 square miles) and a population of 74 (1 Jan. 1970).

The official residence, since 1834, of the Grand Master of the Order of the Knights of Malta totalling 3 acres and comprising the Villa del Priorato di Malta on the lowest of Rome's seven hills, the 151-foot Aventine, retains certain diplomatic privileges and has accredited representatives to foreign governments and is hence sometimes cited as the smallest state in the world.

FRONTIERS

Most The country with the most frontiers is the U.S.S.R., with 13—Norway, Finland, Poland, Czechoslovakia, Hungary, Romania, Turkey, Iran (Persia), Afghanistan, Mongolia, China (mainland), North Korea and Japan (territorial waters).

Longest The longest continuous frontier in the world is that between Canada and the United States, which (including the Great Lakes boundaries) extends for 3,987 miles (excluding 1,538 miles with Alaska). The frontier which is crossed most frequently is that between the United States and Mexico. It extends for 1,933 miles and there are more than 120,000,000 crossings every year. The Sino-Soviet frontier extends for 4,500 miles with virtually nil crossings.

Most impenetrable boundary The 858-mile-long Iron Curtain, dividing the Federal Republican (West) and the Democratic Republican (East) parts of Germany, utilises 2,230,000 land mines and 50,000 miles of barbed wire, much of it of British manufacture, in addition to many watch-towers containing detection devices. The whole 270-yard-wide strip occupies 133 square miles of East German territory.

POPULATIONS

World Estimates of the human population of the world depend largely on the component figure for the population of mainland China (see Most populous, p. 186). Including the higher assumed figure, the world total at mid-1971 can be estimated to be 3,670 million, giving an average density of 69·7 people per square mile of land (including inland waters). This excludes Antarctica and uninhabited island groups. The daily increase in the world's population was probably running at 190,000 in 1969. It is estimated that about 14,500 were born and about 6,600 died every hour in 1970. The world's population has doubled in the last 63 years and is expected to double again in the next 40 years. It is now estimated that the world's population in the year 2000 will be more than 6,000 million, and possibly closer to 7,000 million. The present population "explosion" is of such a magnitude that it has been fancifully calculated that, if it were to continue unabated, there would be one person to each square yard by A.D. 2600, and humanity would weigh more than the Earth itself by A.D. 3700. It is estimated that 74,000,000,000 humans have been born and have died in the last 600,000 years.

WORLD POPULATION—
Progressive mid-year estimates

Date	Millions	Date	Millions
4000 B.C.	85		
A.D. 1	c. 200–300	1967	3,420
1650	c. 500–550	1968	3,483
1750	750	1969	3,552
1800	960	1970	3,610
1850	1,240	1971	3,670
1900	1,650	1975	3,944*
1920	1,862	1980	4,330*
1930	2,070	1985	4,746*
1940	2,295	1990	5,188*
1950	2,517	1995	5,648*
1960	3,005	2000	6,130*
1965	3,297	2050	16,700*
1966	3,353	2070	25,000*

** Assessed in 1964, based on an underestimate of 2,998 million for mid-1960, rising to 3,592 million by mid-1970. These estimates will be raised if the higher estimate for China (732 against 722 million) for 31 Dec. 1967 is corroborated.*

Most populous country The country with the largest population in the world is China (mainland only). Owing to the scarcity of available data, estimates vary considerably, but officials of the United Nations have assumed that the total was about 650,000,000 at mid-1960, increasing to 695,000,000 by mid-1965, and rose to 740,000,000 by mid-1969. According to the Japanese newspaper *Mainichi*, estimates made from Chinese Revolutionary Committee announcements indicate that the Chinese population as of 31 Dec. 1967 was 732 million and hence should have reached over 750,000,000 by mid-1969. Some estimates run considerably higher including the passing of the 800 million mark in late 1968. Only 12 per cent. of China is under cultivation.

Colonial The most populous colony in the world is Mozambique, South East Africa with an estimated mid-1969 figure of 7,376,000. The capital city is Lorenzo Marques.

Least populous The independent state with the smallest population is the Vatican City or the Holy See (see Smallest country, page 185), with 880 inhabitants at 1 Jan. 1966.

Most densely populated The most densely populated territory in the world is the Portuguese province of Macau (or Macao), on the southern coast of China. It has an estimated population

The world's most densely populated country—Monaco (see below)

of 260,000 (30 June 1969) in an area of 6·2 square miles, giving a density of 41,935 per square mile. At the census of 31 Aug. 1940, Macau had a population of 374,737, giving a density of 60,660 per square mile. The population has, since 1960, increased from 170,000 largely as a result of the influx of refugees from China (mainland).

The Principality of Monaco, on the south coast of France, has a population of 24,000 (estimated 1 Jan. 1970) in an area of 369·9 acres, giving a density of 41,500 per square mile. Singapore has 2,085,000 (mid-1971 estimate) people in an inhabited area of 73 square miles.

Of territories with an area of more than 200 square miles, Hong Kong (398¼ square miles) contains 4,089,000 people (estimate 1 July 1970), giving the territory a density of 10,267 per square mile. The name Hong Kong is the transcription of the local pronunciation of the Peking dialect version of Xiang gang (a port for incense). About 80 per cent. of the population lives in the urban areas of Hong Kong island and Kowloon, on the mainland, and the density there is greater than 200,000 per square mile. At North Point there are 12,400 people living in 6½ acres, giving an unsurpassed spot density of more than 1,200,000 per square mile. In 1959 it was reported that in one house designed for 12 people the number of occupants was 459, including 104 in one room and 4 living on the roof.

Of countries over 1,000 square miles, the most densely populated is the Netherlands, with a population of 13,033,000 (estimate 1 July 1970) on 12,978 square miles of land, giving a density of 1,004 people per square mile. The Indonesian islands of Java and Madura (combined area 51,033 square miles) have a population of 73,400,000 (estimate for mid-1969), giving a density of 1,438 per square mile. The United Kingdom (94,221 square miles) had an estimated home population of 55,711,000 at 30 June 1970, giving a density of 591·3 people per square mile. The projected population figures for 1980 and 2000 are 59,548,000 and 66,100,000. The population density for England alone (50,869 square miles) is 959·8 per square mile, while that of south-eastern England is more than 1,640 per square mile.

BRITISH ISLES—LARGEST AND SMALLEST COUNTIES

	By Area (in acres)				By Home Population (estimate, 30 June 1969)*			
	Largest		Smallest		Largest			
England	Yorkshire	3,923,359	Rutland	97,273	London	7,703,410	Rutland	29,680
Wales	Carmarthen	588,472	Flint	163,707	Glamorgan	1,258,320	Radnorshire	18,210
Scotland	Inverness-shire	2,695,094	Clackmannan	34,937	Lanarkshire	1,551,900	Kinross	6,300
Northern Ireland	Tyrone	806,918	Armagh	327,907	Antrim	717,100	Fermanagh	50,100
Republic of Ireland	Cork	1,843,408	Louth	202,806	Dublin	794,047	Longford	28,989

** Figures for the Republic of Ireland refer to the mid-1966 inter-censal estimate.*
NOTE: *Lanarkshire includes the City of Glasgow (945,000); Antrim includes Belfast County Borough (390,700) and Dublin includes Dublin County Borough (650,153). The largest Welsh town is the City of Cardiff (population 287,460 at 30 June 1968).*

The English county with the longest coastline is Cornwall (320 miles) and that with the longest in Wales is Pembrokeshire with 183 miles. Westmorland has the shortest coastline with 5¼ miles. Of the 91 counties of the United Kingdom all but 28 have a coastline. Fermanagh in Northern Ireland comprises 9·04 per cent. inland water.

Most sparsely populated Antarctica became permanently occupied by relays of scientists from October 1956. The population varies seasonally and reaches 1,500 at times.

The least populated territory, apart from Antarctica, is Greenland, with a population of 47,000 (estimate 1 July 1969) in an area of 840,000 square miles, giving a density of about 0·055 of a person per square mile, or one person to every 17·8 square miles. The ice-free area of the island (now believed to be several islands) is only 132,000 square miles.

CITIES

Most populous *World* The most populous city in the world is Tōkyō, the capital of Japan since 1868. The 23 wards (*ku*) of the old City contained 9,037,215 people at July 1969, while Tōkyō-to (Tōkyō Prefecture) had 11,462,230 in its 823·6 square miles at 31 July 1969. The population of this area had surpassed that of Greater London and New York in early 1957 and in January 1962 it became the first urban area in history whose recorded population exceeded 10,000,000. At the census of 1 Oct. 1965, the "Keihin Metropolitan Area" (Tōkyō-Yokohama Metropolitan Area) of 1,081 square miles contained 14,770,727 people. The density in the 23 wards is 39,655 people per square mile.

In December 1964 the population of Shanghai, in China, was unofficially reported to be 10,700,000. The city proper population figure in the 1957 census was 6,900,000.

United Kingdom The largest conurbation in Europe is Greater London (established on 1 April 1965), with an estimated home population of 7,703,410 (30 June 1969) in an area of 396,516 acres (619·5 square miles). The residential population of the City of London (677 acres) is 4,210 compared with 128,000 in 1801.

Largest The largest metropolitan census area in the world is that of New York and north-eastern New Jersey, which includes the cities of New York, Jersey City and Newark, N.J., U.S.A. It has a population of 16,131,300 (estimate 1 July 1968) and an area of 4,409·4 square miles, giving a density of 3,624 per square mile. The area extends to an extreme of 136 miles from Columbus Circle (New York City centre) to Pine Hill in Ulster county. The population for the Standard Metropolitan Statistical Area for New York City was estimated at 11,550,600 in mid-1968.

The world's largest city not built by the sea or on a river is Mexico City (Ciudad de México), the capital of Mexico, with an estimated population of 3,483,649 at 30 June 1969. Greater Mexico City's population was 7,123,000 (mid-1968 estimate).

Largest in area The world's largest town, in area, is Kiruna, in Sweden. Its boundaries have, for fiscal avoidance purposes, been extended to embrace an area of 5,458 square miles. The largest city in the United Kingdom is Greater London with an area of 619·5 square miles.

Smallest hamlet The only hamlet in Great Britain with an official population of one is Gallowhill in the parish of Inveravon, Banffshire, Scotland.

Highest *World* The highest capital city in the world, before the domination of Tibet by China, was Lhasa, at an elevation of 12,087 feet above sea-level. La Paz, the administrative and *de facto* capital of Bolivia, stands at an altitude of 11,916 feet above sea-level. The city was founded in 1548 by Capt. Alonso de Mendoza on the site of an Indian village named Chuquiapu. It was originally called Ciudad de Nuestra Señora de La Paz (City of Our Lady of Peace), but in 1825 was renamed La Paz de Ayacucho, its present official name. Sucre, the legal capital of Bolivia, stands at 9,301 feet above sea-level. The new town of Wenchuan, founded in 1955 on the Chinghai-Tibet road, north of the Tangla range, is the highest in the world at 5,100 metres (16,732 feet) above sea-level. The highest village in the world is the Andean mining village of Aucanquilca, in Chile, at 17,500 feet above sea-level.

Great Britain The highest village in England is Flash, in northern Staffordshire, at 1,518 feet above sea-level. The term "flash" money probably relates to the former winter-time counterfeiting activities of the villagers. The highest in Scotland is Wanlockhead, in Dumfries-shire at 1,380 feet above sea-level.

Oldest *World* The oldest known walled town in the world is Arīhā (Jericho), in Jordan. Radio-carbon dating on specimens from the lowest levels reached by archaeologists indicate habitation there by perhaps 3,000 people as early as 7800 B.C. The village of Zawi Chemi Shanidar, discovered in 1957 in northern Iraq, has been dated to 8910 B.C. The oldest capital city in the world is Dimashq (Damascus), the capital of Syria. It has been continuously inhabited since *c.* 2500 B.C.

Great Britain The oldest town in Great Britain is often cited as Colchester, the old British Camulodunon, headquarters of Belgic chiefs in the 1st century B.C. However, the place called Ictis, referred to by Pytheas in *c.* 308 B.C., has been identified with Marazion, close to St. Michael's Mount, Cornwall.

Northernmost The world's northernmost town with a population of more than 10,000 is the Arctic port of Dikson, U.S.S.R. in 73° 32′ N. The northernmost village is Ny Ålesund (78° 55′ N.), a coalmining settlement on King's Bay, Vest Spitsbergen, in the Norwegian territory of Svalbard, inhabited only during the winter season. The northernmost capital is Reykjavík, the capital of Iceland, in 64° 06′ N. Its population was estimated to be 81,026 at 1 Dec. 1969. The northernmost permanent human occupation is the base at Alert (82° 31′ N.), on Dumb Bell Bay, on the north-east coast of Ellesmere Island, northern Canada.

The world's most southerly "capital"—Port Stanley, Falkland Islands

Southernmost The world's southernmost village is Puerto Williams (population about 350), on the north coast of Isla Navarino, in Tierra del Fuego, Chile, about 680 miles north of Antarctica. Wellington, North Island, New Zealand is the southernmost capital city on 41° 17′ S. The world's southernmost administrative centre is Port Stanley (51° 43′ S.), in the Falkland Islands, off South America.

Most remote from sea The large town most remote from the sea is Wulumuchi (Urumchi) formerly Tihwa, Sinkiang, capital of the Uighur Autonomous Region of China, at a distance of about 1,400 miles from the nearest coastline. Its population was estimated to be 275,000 at 31 Dec. 1957.

EMIGRATION

More people emigrate from the United Kingdom than from any other country. A total of 299,600 emigrated from the U.K. from mid-1969 to mid-1970 (latest available data). The largest number of emigrants in any one year was 360,000 in 1852, mainly from Ireland in the post-famine period.

IMMIGRATION

The country which regularly receives the most immigrants is the United States, with 358,579 in 1969. It has been estimated that, in the period 1820–1969, the U.S.A. has received 44,789,312 immigrants. The peak year for immigration into the United Kingdom was the 12 months from 1 July 1961 to 30 June 1962, when about 430,000 Commonwealth citizens arrived. The number of immigrants from mid-1969 to mid-1970 was 208,400.

MOST TOURISTS

In 1969 Italy received 31,201,699 foreign visitors—more than any other country except Canada, which in 1967 received 40,514,602, of whom more than 61 per cent. entered and left the same day. In 1970 the United Kingdom received 6,750,000 visitors who spent an estimated £433,000,000.

BIRTH RATE

Highest and lowest Based on latest data available, the highest recorded crude live birth rate is 62 live births per each 1,000 of the population in Guinea (Africans only, based on births reported for the 12-month period preceding the sample survey of 15 Jan. to 31 May 1955). The highest up-to-date figure is 61·2 for Kuwait in 1968. The rate for the whole world was 33 per 1,000 in 1963–69.

The lowest of the latest available recorded rates is 12·0 per 1,000 in the Panama Canal Zone; 13·4 in Luxembourg (1969) and 13·5 in Sweden (1969).

The 1969 rate in the United Kingdom was 16·6 per 1,000 (16·3 in England and Wales, 17·4 in Scotland and 21·5 in Northern Ireland), while the 1967 rate for the Republic of Ireland was 21·1 registered births per 1,000.

DEATH RATE

Highest and lowest The highest of the latest available recorded death rates is 40 deaths per each 1,000 of the population in Guinea (Africans only, 12 months preceding 1955 sample survey). The next highest figure is 35 per 1,000 in Burma in 1955 (still latest available). The rate for the whole world was 14 per 1,000 in 1963–69.

The lowest of the latest available recorded rates is 1·3 deaths per 1,000 in Mozambique in 1968. The lowest rate in an independent country in 1967 was 4·1 per 1,000 registered in Iraq and 4·4 in Syria in 1968.

The 1969 rate in the United Kingdom was 11·9 per 1,000 (11·8 in England and Wales, 12·3 in Scotland and 10·8 in Northern Ireland), while the 1968 rate for the Republic of Ireland was 11·3 registered deaths per 1,000. The highest S.M.I. (Standardized Mortality Index where the national average is 100) is in Salford, Lancashire with a figure of 133.

NATURAL INCREASE

The highest of the latest available recorded rates of natural increase is 55·0 per 1,000 in Kuwait (births 61·2, deaths 6·2) in 1968. The rate for the whole world was 33−14=19 per 1,000 in 1963–1969.

The 1969 rate for the United Kingdom was 4·7 per 1,000 (4·5 in England and Wales, 5·1 in Scotland and 10·7 in Northern Ireland). The figure for the Republic of Ireland was 10·3 per 1,000 in 1967.

There are three territories in which the death rate exceeds the birth rate, and which thus have a rate of natural decrease: West Berlin, Germany, 8·5 per 1,000 (birth rate 10·9, death rate 19·4) in 1968; East Berlin 1·0 per 1,000 and the Isle of Man 3·6 per 1,000 (registered births 13·7, registed deaths 17·3) in 1968. The lowest rate of natural increase in an independent country in 1968 was 0·0 per 1,000 in East Germany (birth rate 14·3, death rate 14·3).

Marriage ages The country with the lowest average ages for marriage is India, with 20·0 years for males and 14·5 years for females. At the other extreme is Ireland, with 31·4 for males and 26·5 years for females. In the People's Republic of China marriage for men is reportedly not approved before the age of 28.

SEX RATIO

The country with the largest recorded shortage of males is the U.S.S.R., with 1,171·6 females to every 1,000 males at 15 Jan. 1970. The country with the largest recorded woman shortage is Pakistan, with 900·7 to every 1,000 males at 1 Feb. 1961. The ratio in the United Kingdom was 1,052·1 females to every 1,000 males at 30 June 1966, and is expected to be 1,014·2 per 1,000 by A.D. 2000.

INFANT MORTALITY

Based on deaths before one year of age, the lowest of the latest available recorded rates is 9·2 deaths per 1,000 live births in Gibraltar in 1968, compared with 12·9 per 1,000 in Sweden in 1967.

The highest recorded infant mortality rate recently reported has been 259 per 1,000 live births among the indigenous African population of Zambia (then Northern Rhodesia) in the 12 months preceding the sample survey of 30 June 1950. Among most recent estimates the highest is an annual average of 64·2 per 1,000 for Mexico in 1968. Many countries with rates more than twice as high have apparently ceased to make returns. Among these is Ethiopia, where the infant mortality rate was unofficially estimated to be nearly 550 per 1,000 live births in 1969.

The United Kingdom figure for 1969 was 18·4 per 1,000 live births (England and Wales 17·9, Scotland 21·1 Northern Ireland 24·3).

LIFE EXPECTATION

There is evidence that life expectation in Britain in the 5th century A.D. was 33 years for males and 27 years for females. In the decade 1890–1900 the expectation of life among the population of India was 23·7 years. The British figure for 1901–1910 was 48·53 years for males and 52·83 years for females.

Based on the latest available data, the highest recorded expectation of life for males at birth is 71·85 years and the highest for females is 76·54 years, both in Sweden in 1969.

The lowest recorded expectation of life at birth is 27 years for both sexes in the Vallée du Niger area of Mali in 1957 (sample survey, 1957–58). The figure for males in Gabon was 25 years in 1960–61.

The latest available figures for England and Wales (1966–68) are 68·7 years for males and 74·9 years for females; for Scotland (1968) 66·92 years for males and 73·05 years for females; for Northern Ireland (1966–68) 68·19 years for males and 73·45 years for females; and for the Republic of Ireland (1960–62) 68·13 years for males and 71·86 years for females.

At the age of 60, the highest recorded expectation of life for males is in Bolivia, with 20·39 years (1949–51). More reliable figures include 18·64 years in Puerto Rico (1959–61), 18·6 years in Iceland (1961–65). The highest recorded figure for females is 21·66 years in Ryukyu Islands (1960), 20·99 years in Puerto Rico (1959–61) and 20·9 years in Iceland (1961–65).

The figures for England and Wales (1965–67) are 15·[illegible] years for men and 19·8 years for women; for Scotland (1968) 14·52 years for men and 18·50 years for women for Northern Ireland (1966–68) 15·38 years for men and

18·86 years for women; and for the Republic of Ireland (1960–62) 15·83 years for men and 18·10 years for women.

STANDARDS OF LIVING

National incomes The country with the highest income per person in 1969 was Nauru, with nearly $4,000 (£1,666) per head, followed by Kuwait and the U.S.A. The U.S.A. in 1967 leads on the basis of major industrial countries measured by real product per head at 190 (U.K. = 100).

COST OF LIVING

The greatest increase since 1963 (= 100) has been in Djakarta, the capital of Indonesia, where the index figure reached 57,712 (food 62,876) by 1968.

In the United Kingdom the official index of retail prices (16 Jan. 1962 = 100) was 149·0 on 16 March 1971—a rise of 12·0 points or 8·76 per cent. in 12 months.

:apital city *t and least expensive* According to data published by the U.N. Statistical Office in June 1970, the world's most expensive capital city is Saigon, South Viet-Nam (122) and the world's cheapest is Damascus, Syria (69). These indices compare with the cost of living in New York of 100 in 1968. The figure for London is 80.

HOUSING

For comparison, dwelling units are defined as a structurally separated room or rooms occupied by private households of one or more people and having separate access or a common passageway to the street.

The country with the greatest recorded number of private housing units is India, with 79,193,602 occupied in 1960. These contain 83,523,895 private households.

Great Britain comes fourth among reporting countries, with 18,488,000 dwellings (England 15,773,000, Wales 943,000, Scotland 1,772,000) at December 1969. The 1968 figure for Northern Ireland was 435,000. The Republic of Ireland had 687,304 private households in 1966.

'iped water Austria reported that 100 per cent. of its dwellings had piped water inside or outside (63·6 per cent. inside) in 1961. This is matched by the urban areas of the Panama Canal Zone, which have 100 per cent. with piped water inside. In England and Wales 98·3 per cent. of dwellings (where an occupier was present) had piped water inside in 1961. In Scotland 98·6 per cent. of dwellings had piped water inside or outside in 1961, while in Northern Ireland 80·7 per cent. of private households had piped water inside in 1961. In the Republic of Ireland 57·2 per cent. of dwellings had piped water inside or outside (51·0 per cent. inside) in 1961.

Baths The country with the highest recorded proportion of dwellings with a bath is New Zealand, with 97·1 per cent. (1961), compared with 100 per cent. in the urban areas of the Panama Canal Zone (1958).

Subject to the qualifications given above (under "Piped water"), and excluding dwellings with only shower installations, the 1968 United Kingdom figure was 84 per cent.

Electricity Luxembourg had 99·9 per cent. of its dwellings equipped with electricity in 1960, compared with 100 per cent. in the Cocos (Keeling) Islands in 1960, and 100 per cent. in the urban areas of Hong Kong (1960), the Panama Canal Zone (1958) and Switzerland where in October 1968 Furna, Graubünden, ceased to be the last village without electricity.

PHYSICIANS

The country with the most physicians is the U.S.S.R., with 550,389 in 1967, or one to every 427 persons. In England and Wales there were 24,131 doctors employed by the National Health Service on 30 Sept. 1969.

The country with the highest proportion of physicians is Israel, where there were 6,312 (one for every 420 inhabitants) in 1967. The country with the lowest recorded proportion is Upper Volta, with 68 physicians (one for every 74,320 people) in 1967.

Dentists The country with the most dentists is the United States, where 112,000 were registered members of the American Dental Association in 1970.

Psychiatrists The country with the most psychiatrists is the United States. The registered membership of the American Psychiatric Association was 17,050 in 1970. The membership of the American Psychological Association was 30,635 in 1970.

HOSPITALS

Largest *World* The largest medical centre in the world is the District Medical Center in Chicago, Illinois, U.S.A. It covers 478 acres and includes five hospitals, with a total of 5,600 beds, and eight professional schools with more than 3,000 students.

The largest hospital in the world is Danderyd Hospital in northern Stockholm, Sweden. In 1969 it had 12,000 beds.

The largest mental hospital in the world is the Pilgrim State Hospital, on Long Island, New York State, U.S.A., with 12,800 beds. It formerly contained 14,200 beds.

The largest maternity hospital in the world is the Kandang Kerbau Government Maternity Hospital in Singapore. It has 239 midwives, 151 beds for gynaecological cases, 388 maternity beds and an output of 31,255 babies in 1969 compared with the record "birthquake" of 39,856 babies (more than 109 per day) in 1966.

United Kingdom The largest hospitals of any kind in the United Kingdom are the Rainhill Hospital near Liverpool, and St. Bernard's Hospital, Southall, Middlesex, which each have 2,267 staffed beds for mental patients.

The largest general hospital in the United Kingdom is the St. James Hospital, Leeds, Yorkshire, with 1,350 available staffed beds.

The largest maternity hospital in the United Kingdom is the Mill Road Maternity Hospital, Liverpool, with 214 staffed beds.

The largest children's hospital in the United Kingdom is Queen Mary's Hospital for Children, at Carshalton, Surrey, with 736 staffed beds.

Largest baby-sitting service The world's largest baby-sitting organization is the Carol Agency (est. 1950), Washington Blvd., Los Angeles, California, U.S.A., with 800 registered "sitters" serving 25,000 families.

2. ROYALTY

Oldest ruling house The Emperor of Japan, Hirohito (born 29 April 1901), is the 124th in line from the first Emperor, Jimmu Tenno or Zinmu, whose reign was traditionally from 660 to 581 B.C., but probably from *c.* 40 to *c.* 10 B.C. His Imperial Majesty Muhammad Rizā Shāh Pahlavi of Iran (b. 26 Oct. 1919) claims descent from Cyrus the Great (reigned *c.* 559–529 B.C.).

Her Majesty Queen Elizabeth II (b. 21 April 1926) represents a dynasty which has ruled since about A.D. 500—that of Eirc of Dalriada (now Lorne, Argyllshire, Scotland), who is believed to be her 48-greats grandfather.

REIGNS

Longest The longest recorded reign of any monarch is that of

Pepi II, a Sixth Dynasty Pharaoh of ancient Egypt. His reign began in *c.* 2272 B.C., when he was aged 6, and lasted 91 years. Musoma Kanijo, chief of the Nzega district of western Tanganyika (now part of Tanzania), reputedly reigned for more than 98 years from 1864, when aged 8, until his death on 2 Feb. 1963. The 6th Japanese Emperor Koo-an traditionally reigned for 102 years (from 392 to 290 B.C.), but probably his actual reign was from about A.D. 110 to about A.D. 140. The reign of the 11th Emperor Suinin was traditionally from 29 B.C. to A.D. 71 (99 years), but probably from A.D. 259 to 291. The longest reign in European history was that of King Louis XIV of France, who ascended the throne on 14 May 1643, aged 4 years 8 months, and reigned for 72 years 110 days until his death on 1 Sept. 1715, four days before his 77th birthday.

Currently the longest reigning monarch in the world is King Sobhuza II, K.B.E. (b. July 1899), the *Ngwenyama* (Paramount Chief) of Swaziland, under United Kingdom protection, since December 1899, and independent since 6 Sept. 1968. Hirohito (see page 189) has been Emperor of Japan since 25 Dec. 1926.

Shortest The shortest recorded reign was that of the Dauphin Louis Antoine, who was technically King Louis XIX of France for the fifteen minutes between the signature of Charles X (1757–1836) and his own signature to the act of abdication, in favour of Henri V, which was executed at the Château de Rambouillet on 2 Aug. 1830.

BRITISH MONARCHS

Reign *Longest* The longest reign of any King of Great Britain was that of George III, from 25 Oct. 1760 to 29 Jan. 1820 (59 years 96 days) and the longest of a Queen was that of Victoria, from 20 June 1837 to 22 Jan. 1901 (63 years 216 days). James Francis Edward (born 10 June 1688), the Old Pretender, known to his supporters as James III, styled his reign from 16 Sept. 1701 until his death on 1 Jan. 1766, thus lasting over 64 years.

Shortest The shortest reign of any post-Conquest King of England was that of Edward V, from 9 April until he was deposed on 25 June 1483 (seventy-seven days). He died probably between July and September 1483. If Sweyn "Forkbeard", the Danish King of England, reigned from "Christmas to Candlemas" in 1013–14, it was for a period of perhaps 40 days but there is, however, doubt as to when, in the autumn of 1013, he in fact acceded. The shortest reign of a Queen was that of Jane, who acceded on 6 July 1553, was proclaimed Queen on 10 July and was deposed on 19 July 1553, after a reign of only 13 days (or nine days from proclamation).

Longest lived Excluding the 8 who suffered violent death, English monarchs have had an average life span of 57 years. The longest lived British monarchs were King George III, who died on 29 Jan. 1820 aged 81 years 239 days, and Queen Victoria, who, at the time of her death on 22 Jan. 1901, had surpassed his age by four days. The oldest monarch at the time of succession was William IV, who became King on 26 June 1830, aged 64 years 10 months.

The oldest member of the Royal Family was H.R.H. Princess Augusta Caroline Charlotte Elizabeth Mary Sophia Louise of Cambridge, C.I., the Grand Duchess of Mecklenburg-Strelitz, the elder daughter of H.R.H. Prince Adolphus Frederick, the 1st Duke of Cambridge, seventh son of King George III. She was born on 18 July 1822 and died, aged 94 years 139 days, on 4 Dec. 1916. The oldest male member of the Royal Family was H.R.H. Prince Arthur William Patrick Albert, the 1st Duke of Connaught and Strathearn, K.G., K.T., K.P., G.M.B., G.C.S.I., G.C.M.G., G.C.I.E., G.C.V.O., G.B.E., V.D., T.D., the third son of Queen Victoria. He was born on 1 May 1850 and died, aged 91 years 260 days, on 16 Jan. 1942.

The longest lived male member of any English Royal House—Queen Victoria's third son, the 91-year-old H.R.H. the Duke of Connaught

Youngest The youngest English monarch to accede was Henry VI who was born on 6 Dec. 1421 and came to the throne on 1 Sept. 1422, aged less than 9 months. Scotland's youngest was Queen Mary, born on 7 or 8 Dec. 1542. She succeeded to the Scottish throne on 14 Dec. 1542 aged 6 or 7 days.

Britain's youngest monarch, Mary, Queen of Scots" from the age of 6 or 7 days

England's youngest Queen was Isabella, daughter of King Charles VI of France. She was born on 9 Nov 1389 and became the second wife of Richard II at Calais, probably on 4 Nov. 1396, when a few days short of her seventh birthday.

Most children The King with the most legitimate children was Edward I (1239–1307), who had 16 by his two queens, Eleanor of Castille (d. 1290) and Margaret of France (1282–1317).

The monarch with the greatest number of illegitimate children was Henry I (1068–1135), who had at least 20 (9 sons, 11 daughters) and possibly 22, by six mistresses in addition to one (possibly two) sons and a daughter born legitimately.

The largest number of children born to a Queen regnant was nine to Queen Victoria (1819–1901) and the largest number to a Queen consort was 15 to Queen Charlotte Sophia (1744–1818), the wife of George III (1738–1820). Before coming to the throne in 1702, Queen Anne (1665–1714) conceived 18 children, of whom only five were live-born and all of these died in infancy. Prince William, K.G. (1689–1700), the Duke of Gloucester, survived to the age of 11 years 6 days.

Iost often married The most often married English King was Henry VIII whose sixth and last wife, Catherine Parr (*c.* 1512–1548), was England's most married Queen. She was first married to the Hon. Sir Edward Burgh (died 1529 or earlier), secondly to John Neville, the 3rd Lord Latimer (died 1542 or 1543), thirdly on 12 July 1543 to Henry VIII, and fourthly and finally on 3 March 1547, five weeks after Henry's death, to Thomas, Lord Seymour of Sudeley, K.G. She died on 7 Sept. 1548, eight days after giving birth to a daughter.

land's most ried Queen, 4 times wed herine Parr, sixth wife of Henry VIII

Royal absences The longest absence of a British monarch from his realm was that of James I, King of Scots, who was a prisoner of the English from before the time of his accession aged 11 on 4 April 1406 for nearly 18 years until late March 1424. The longest absence of an English monarch from his country was that of Richard I from his accession on 12 Dec. 1189 until 13 March 1194 (4 years 91 days). George III never once left the country in his reign of 59 years 96 days (1760–1820).

allest and shortest England's tallest monarch was Edward IV (reigned 1461–1483), who was between 6 feet 3 inches and 6 feet 4 inches and was regarded as a giant in his time. Charles I (reigned 1625–1649) was, on the evidence of his armour, barely over 5 feet tall. This compares with the 4 feet 9½ inches of the 12-year-old Edward V. Queen Matilda, wife of William I, who died in 1083, was 4 feet 2 inches.

3. LEGISLATURES

PARLIAMENTS

Oldest The oldest legislative body is the *Alpingi* (Althing) of Iceland, founded in A.D. 930. This body, which originally comprised 39 local chieftains, was abolished in 1800, but restored by Denmark to a consultative status in 1843 and a legislative status in 1874. The legislative assembly with the oldest continuous history is the Tynwald Court in the Isle of Man, which is believed to have originated more than 1,000 years ago.

Largest The largest legislative assembly in the world is the National People's Congress of China (mainland). The fourth Congress, which met in March 1969, had 3,500 members.

Smallest quorum The House of Lords has the smallest quorum, expressed as a percentage of eligible voters, of any legislative body in the world, namely one-third of one per cent. To transact business there must be three peers present, including the Lord Chancellor or his deputy. The House of Commons quorum of 40 M.P.'s, including the Speaker or his deputy, is nearly 20 times as exacting.

Highest paid legislators The most highly paid of all the world's legislators are Senators of the United States, who receive a basic annual salary of $42,500 (£17,708). Of this, up to $3,000 (£1,250) is exempt from taxation. In addition, up to $130,000 (£54,166) per annum is allowed for office help, with a salary limit of $13,345 (£5,560) per assistant per year. Senators also enjoy free travel, telephones, postage, medical care, telegrams (to a limit of $2,000 (£833) per session), flowers and haircuts. They also command very low rates for stationery, filming, speech and radio transcriptions and, in the case of women senators, beauty treatment. When abroad they have access to "counterpart funds".

Longest membership The longest span as a legislator was 83 years by József Madarász (1814–1915). He first attended the Hungarian Parliament in 1832–36 as *ablegatus absentium* (*i.e.* on behalf of an absent deputy). He was a full member in 1848–50 and from 1861 until his death on 31 Jan. 1915.

Filibusters The longest continuous speech in the history of the United States Senate was that of Senator Wayne Morse of Oregon on 24–25 April 1953, when he spoke on the Tidelands Oil Bill for 22 hours 26 minutes without resuming his seat. Interrupted only briefly by the swearing-in of a new senator, Senator Strom Thurmond (South Carolina, Democrat) spoke against the Civil Rights Bill for 24 hours 19 minutes on 28–29 Aug. 1957. The United States national record duration for a filibuster is 28 hours 15 minutes by Texas State Senator Kilmer Corbin of Lubbock at Austin, Texas, on 17–18 May 1955. He was speaking against the financing of water projects by taxation.

ELECTIONS

Largest The largest election ever held was that for the Indian *Lok Sabha* (House of the People) on 15–21 Feb. 1967 (except in certain snow-bound areas of Himachal Pradesh where the election was held in June 1967). About 165,000,000 of the electorate of 250,681,530 chose from 1,979 candidates for 520 seats.

Closest The ultimate in close general elections occurred in Zanzibar (now part of Tanzania) on 18 Jan. 1961, when the Afro-Shirazi Party won by a single seat, after the seat of Chake-Chake on Pemba Island had been gained by a single vote.

Most one-sided North Korea recorded a 100 per cent. turn-out of electors and a 100 per cent. vote for the Workers' Party of Korea in the general election of 8 Oct. 1962. The previous record had been set in the Albanian election of 4 June 1962, when all but seven of the electorate of 889,875 went to the polls—a 99·9992 per cent. turn-out. Of the 889,868 voters, 889,828 voted for the candidates of the Albanian Party of Labour, *i.e.* 99·9955 per cent. of the total poll.

Highest personal majority The highest personal majority was 157,692 from 192,909 votes cast, by H.H. Maharani of Jaipur (born 23 May 1919) in the Indian general election of Feb. 1962.

Communist parties The largest national Communist party outside the Soviet Union (about 12,400,000 members in 1966) and Communist states has been the Partito Communista Italiano (Italian Communist Party), with a membership of 2,300,000 in 1946. The total fell to 1,350,000 by 1965, but rose to 1,575,000 in 1966. The now illegal Partai Komunis Indonesia had about 2,000,000 members in 1964. The membership in mainland China was estimated to be 21,000,000 in 1966. The Communist Party of Great Britain, formed on 31 July 1920 in Cannon Street Station Hotel, London, attained its peak membership of 56,000 in December 1942, compared with 30,607 in June 1969 (latest available figure).

Most parties The country with the greatest number of political parties is Italy with 73 registered for the elections of 19 May 1968. These included "Friends of the Moon" with one candidate.

PRIME MINISTERS

Oldest The longest lived Prime Minister of any country is believed to have been Christopher Hornsrud, Prime Minister of Norway from 28 Jan. to 15 Feb. 1928. He was born on 15 Nov. 1859 and died on 13 Dec. 1960, aged 101 years 28 days.

El Hadji Muhammad el Mokri, Grand Vizier of Morocco, died on 16 Sept. 1957, at a reputed age of 116 Muslim (*Hijri*) years, equivalent to 112·5 Gregorian years.

Longest term of office Prof. Dr. António de Oliveira Salazar, G.C.M.G. (Hon.) (1889–1969) was the President of the Council of Ministers (*i.e.* Prime Minister) of Portugal from 5 July 1932 until 27 Sept. 1968—36 years 84 days. He was superseded 11 days after going into a coma.

UNITED KINGDOM

Parliament *Earliest* The earliest known use of the term "parliament" in an official English royal document, in the meaning of a summons to the King's council, dates from 19 Dec. 1241.

The Houses of Parliament of the United Kingdom, in the Palace of Westminster, London, had 1,698 members (House of Lords 1,068, House of Commons 630) in 1971.

Longest The longest English Parliament was the "Pensioners" Parliament of Charles II, which lasted from 8 May 1661 to 24 Jan. 1679, a period of 17 years 8 months and 16 days. The longest United Kingdom Parliament was that of George V, Edward VIII and George VI, lasting from 26 Nov. 1935 to 15 June 1945, a span of 9 years 6 months and 20 days.

Shortest The parliament of Edward I, summoned to Westminster for 30 May 1306, lasted only one day. The parliament of Charles I from 13 April to 5 May 1640 lasted only 22 days. The shortest United Kingdom Parliament was that of George III, lasting from 15 Dec. 1806 to 29 April 1807, a period of only 4 months and 14 days.

Longest sittings The longest sitting in the House of Commons was one of 41½ hours from 4 p.m. on 31 Jan. 1881 to 9.30 a.m. on 2 Feb. 1881, on the question of better Protection of Person and Property in Ireland. The longest sitting of the Lords has been 13 hours 32 minutes, from 2.30 p.m. on 2 July 1963 to 4.02 a.m. on 3 July 1963, on the fourth day of the report stage of the London Government Bill.

Most divisions The record number of divisions in the House of Commons is 43 in the single session of 20–21 March 1907.

ELECTORATES

Largest and smallest The largest electorate of all time was the estimated 217,900 for Hendon, Middlesex, now part of Greater London, prior to redistribution in 1941. The largest electorate for any seat in Great Britain on the register in force until February 1971 was 123,297 in Billericay, Essex. In Antrim South, Northern Ireland the figure was 143,544. The smallest electorate of all time was in Old Sarum (number of houses nil, population nil since *c.* 1540) in Wiltshire, with eight electors who returned two members in 1821, thus being 54,475 times as well represented as the Hendon electorate of 120 years later. There were no contested elections in Old Sarum for the 536 years from 1295 to 1831. The smallest electorate for any seat on the register prior to redistribution was Ladywood, Birmingham with 18,734 electors.

MAJORITIES

Party The largest party majorities were those of the Liberals, with 307 seats in 1832 and 356 seats in 1906. In 1931 the Coalition of Conservatives, Liberals and National Labour candidates had a majority of 425. The narrowest party majority was that of the Whigs in 1847, with a single seat.

The largest majority on a division was one of 463 (464 votes to 1), on a motion of "no confidence" in the conduct of World War II, on 29 Jan. 1942. Since the war the largest majority has been one of 461 (487 votes to 26) on 10 May 1967, during the debate on the government's application for Britain to join the European Economic Community (the "Common Market").

Largest personal *All-time* The largest individual majority of any Member of Parliament was the 62,253 of Sir A. Cooper Rawson, M.P. (Conservative) at Brighton in 1931. He polled 75,205 votes against 12,952 votes for his closer opponent, the Labour Candidate Lewis Coleman Cohen, later Lord Cohen of Brighton (1897–1966), from an electorate of 128,779. The largest majority of any woman M.P. was 38,823 in the same General Election by the Countess of Iveagh (*née* Lady Gwendolen Florence Mary Onslow), C.B.E. (1881–1966), the Conservative member for Southend-on-Sea, Essex, from November 1927 to October 1935.

Current The largest majority in the 1970 Parliament is 41,433 held by James Kilfedder (Ulster Unionist) in Down North where he received 55,679 votes.

Narrowest personal *All-time* The closest result occurred in the General Election of 1886 at Ashton-under-Lyne, Lancashire when the Conservative and Liberal candidates both received 3,049 votes. The Returning Officer, Mr. James Walker, gave his casting vote for John E. W. Addison (Con.), who was duly returned while Alexander B. Rowley (Gladstone-Liberal) was declared unelected. On 13 Oct. 1892 there was a by-election at Cirencester, Gloucestershire, which resulted in an election petition after which the number of votes cast for the Conservative and Liberal were found to have been equal. A new election was ordered.

Two examples of majorities of one have occurred. At Durham in the 1895 General Election, Matthew Fowler (Lib.) with 1,111 votes defeated the Hon. Arthur R. D. Elliott (Liberal-Unionist) (1,110 votes) after a recount.

At Exeter in the General Election of December 1910 a Liberal victory over the Conservatives by 4 votes was reversed on an election petition to a Conservative win by H. E. Duke, K.C. (later the 1st Lord Merrivale) (Unionist) with 4,777 votes to R. H. St. Maur's (Lib.) 4,776 votes.

The smallest majority since "universal" franchise was one of two votes by Abraham John Flint (b. 1903), the National Labour candidate at Ilkeston, Derbyshire, on 27 Oct. 1931. He received 17,587 votes, compared with 17,585 for G. H. Oliver, D.C.M. (Labour).

Current The finest economy of effort in getting elected by any member of the 1970 Parliament was a majority of 13 votes by Ernle Money (Conservative) in Ipswich, Suffolk with 27,704 votes over Sir Dingle Foot, Q.C. (Labour) with 27,691.

Most recounts The greatest recorded number of recounts has been 7 in the case of Brighton, Kemptown on 16 Oct. 1964 when Dennis H. Hobden (Labour) won by 7 votes and at Northampton on 31 March–1 April 1966 when Sir Harmer Nicholls (Conservative) won by 3 votes. The later counts from the point of view of the loser M. J. Ward (Labour) went +163, +163, +2, −2, −6, +1, −2, −3.

Fewest votes The smallest number of votes received by any candidate in a parliamentary election since "universal" franchise is 23 in the case of Richard Wort (Independent Conservative) in the Kinross and West Perthshire by-election of 7 Nov. 1963.

Most rapid change of fortune In 1874 Hardinge Stanley Giffard (Con.), later the 1st Earl of Halsbury (1823–1921), received one vote at Launceston, Cornwall. On 3 July 1877 he was returned unopposed for the same seat.

Greatest swing The greatest swing, at least since 1832, was that at Dartford, Kent when on 27 March 1920 Labour turned a Coalition majority of 9,370 to a win of 9,048. This represented a swing of 38·7 per cent. compared with the swing of 26·8 per cent. at Orpington, Kent on 14 March 1962 to the Liberals. In the 1970 General Election an Ulster Unionist majority of 22,986 was turned into a Protestant Unionist majority of 2,679 over the sitting Member by Ian Richard Kyle Paisley. Since there was no Protestant Unionist candidate in 1966 no swing figure is calculable.

Highest poll The highest poll in any constituency since "universal" franchise was 93·42 per cent. in Fermanagh and South Tyrone, Northern Ireland, at the General Election of 25 Oct. 1951, when there were 62,799 voters from an electorate of 67,219. The Anti-Partition candidate, Mr. Cahir Healy (b. 1877), was elected with a majority of 2,635 votes. The highest poll in any constituency in the 1970 General Election was 92·18 per cent. in Fermanagh and South Tyrone. The highest figure in Great Britain was, as in 1966, North Cornwall with 85·11 per cent.

M.P.s

Youngest Edmund Waller (1606–1687) was the Member of Parliament for Amersham, Buckinghamshire, in the Parliament of 1621, in which year he was 15. The official returns, however, do not show him as actually having taken his seat until two years later when, in the Parliament of 1623–24, he sat as Member for Ilchester. In 1435 Henry Long (1420–1490) was returned for an Old Sarum seat also at the age of 15. His precise date of birth is unknown. Minors were debarred in law in 1695 and in fact in 1832. Since that time the youngest Member of Parliament has been the Hon. Esmond Cecil Harmsworth (now the 2nd Viscount Rothermere), who was elected for the Isle of Thanet, Kent, on 28 Nov. 1919, when one day short of being 21 years 6 months. The youngest M.P. in 1970 was Miss Bernadette Devlin (b. 23 April 1947) who was elected for Mid Ulster on 17 April 1969 and who made her maiden speech the day before her twenty-second birthday.

nuel Young, M.P., who represented ast Cavan in is 97th year

Oldest The oldest of all members was Samuel Young (b. 14 Feb. 1822), Nationalist M.P. for East Cavan (1892–1918), who died on 18 April 1918, aged 96 years 63 days. The oldest "Father of the House" in Parliamentary history was the Rt. Hon. Charles Pelham Villiers (b. 3 Jan. 1802), who was the Member for Wolverhampton when he died on 16 Jan. 1898, aged 96. He was a Member of Parliament for 63 years 6 days, having been returned at 16 elections. The oldest member sitting in the present Parliament is Stephen Owen Davis (Ind. Labour), M.P. for Merthyr Tydfil who was born in November 1886.

Longest span The longest span of service of any M.P. is 63 years 10 months (October 1900 to September 1964) by the Rt. Hon. Sir Winston Leonard Spencer Churchill, K.G., O.M., C.H., T.D. (1874–1965), with a break only from November 1922 to October 1924. The longest unbroken span was that of C. P. Villiers (see below). The longest span in the Palace of Westminster (both Houses of Parliament) has been 73 years by the 10th Earl of Wemyss, G.C.V.O., who, as Sir Francis Wemyss-Charteris-Douglas, served as M.P. for East Gloucestershire (1841–46) and Haddingtonshire (1847–83) and then took his seat in the House of Lords, dying on 30 June 1914, aged 95 years 330 days.

Viscountess Astor, the first woman to take her seat in the House of Commons

Earliest women M.P.s The first woman to be elected to the House of Commons was Mme. Constance Georgine Markievicz (*née* Gore Booth). She was elected as member (Sinn Fein) for St. Patrick's, Dublin, in December 1918. The first woman to take her seat was the Viscountess Astor, C.H. (1879–1964) (b. Nancy Witcher Langhorne at Danville, Virginia, U.S.A.; formerly Mrs. Robert Gould Shaw), who was elected Unionist member for the Sutton Division of Plymouth, Devonshire, on 28 Nov. 1919, and took her seat three days later.

HOUSE OF LORDS

Oldest Member The oldest member ever was the Rt. Hon. the 5th Baron Penrhyn, who was born on 21 Nov. 1865 and died on 3 Feb. 1967, aged 101 years 74 days. The oldest now is the Rt. Hon. Lord Aylmer (b. 23 March 1880).

Youngest Member The youngest member of the House of Lords is H.R.H. the Prince Charles Philip Arthur George, K.G., the Prince of Wales (b. 14 Nov. 1948). All Dukes of Cornwall, of whom Prince Charles is the 24th, are technically eligible to sit, regardless of age—in his case from his succession on 6 Feb. 1952, aged 3. The 20th and 21st holders, later King George IV (b. 1762) and King Edward VII (b. 1841), were technically entitled to sit from birth.

Longest speech The longest recorded continuous speech in the House of Commons was that of Henry Peter Brougham (1778–1868) on 7 Feb. 1828, when he spoke for 6 hours on Law Reform. He ended at 10.40 p.m. and the report of this speech occupied 12 columns of the next day's edition of *The Times*. Brougham, created the 1st Lord Brougham and Vaux on 22 Nov. 1830, also holds the

House of Lords record, also with six hours, on 7 Oct. 1831, speaking on the second reading of the Reform Bill.

The longest post-war speech has been one of 2 hours 37 minutes by Malcolm K. Macmillan (b. 1913), the Labour member for the Western Isles, on 15–16 March 1961.

Greatest parliamentary petition The greatest petition was supposed to be the Great Chartist Petition of 1848 but of the 5,706,000 "signatures" only 1,975,496 were valid. The all time largest was for the abolition of Entertainment Duty with 3,107,080 signatures presented on 5 June 1951.

PREMIERSHIP

Longest term No United Kingdom Prime Minister has yet matched in duration the continuous term of office of Great Britain's first Prime Minister, the Rt. Hon. Sir Robert Walpole, K.G., later the 1st Earl of Orford (1676–1745), First Lord of the Treasury and Chancellor of the Exchequer from 3 April 1721 to 12 Feb. 1742. The office was not, however, officially recognised until 1905, since when the longest tenure has been that of Herbert Henry Asquith, later the 1st Earl of Oxford and Asquith (1852–1928), with 8 years 243 days from 8 April 1908 to 7 Dec. 1916. This was 7 days longer than the three terms of Sir Winston Churchill, between 1940 and 1955. The Hon. Sir Thomas Playford, G.C.M.G. (b. 5 July 1896) was State Premier of South Australia from 5 Nov. 1938 to 10 March 1965.

Shortest term The Rt. Hon. Sir James Waldegrave, K.G., 2nd Earl of Waldegrave (1715–63) held office for 5 days from 8–12 June 1757 but was unable to form a ministry. The shortest term of any ministry was that of the 1st Duke of Wellington, K.G., G.C.B., G.C.H. (1769–1852), whose third ministry survived only 22 days from 17 Nov. to 9 Dec. 1834.

Most times The only Prime Minister to have accepted office five times was the Rt. Hon. Stanley Baldwin, later the 1st Earl Baldwin of Bewdley (1867–1947). His ministries were those of 22 May 1923 to 22 Jan. 1924, 4 Nov. 1924 to 5 June 1929, 7 June 1935 to 21 Jan. 1936, from then until 12 Dec. 1936 and from then until 28 May 1937.

Great Britain's most durable Prime Minister and most durable Speaker, Walpole and Onslow (centre), conferring

Longest lived The oldest Prime Minister of the United Kingdom has been the Rt. Hon. Sir Winston Leonard Spencer Churchill, K.G., O.M., C.H., T.D. (b. 30 Nov. 1874), who surpassed the age of the Rt. Hon. William Ewart Gladstone (1809–98) on 21 April 1963 and died on 24 Jan. 1965, aged 90 years 55 days.

Youngest The youngest of Great Britain's 47 prime ministers has been the Rt. Hon. the Hon. William Pitt (b. 28 May 1759), who accepted the King's invitation to be First Lord of the Treasury on 19 Dec. 1783, aged 24 years 205 days. He had previously declined on 27 Feb. 1783, when aged 23 years 275 days.

CHANCELLORSHIP

Longest and shortest tenures The Rt. Hon. Sir Robert Walpole, K.G., later the 1st Earl of Orford (1676–1745), served 22 years 5 months as Chancellor of the Exchequer, holding office continuously from 12 Oct. 1715 to 12 Feb. 1742, except for the period from 16 April 1717 to 2 April 1721. The briefest tenure of this office was 26 days in the case of the Baron (later the 1st Earl of) Mansfield (1705–93), from 11 Sept. to 6 Oct. 1767.

Most appointments The only man with four terms in this office was the Rt. Hon. William Ewart Gladstone (1809–98) in 1852–55, 1859–66, 1873–74 and 1880–82.

SPEAKERSHIP

Longest Arthur Onslow (1691–1768) was elected Mr. Speaker on 23 Jan. 1728, at the age of 36. He held the position for 33 years 54 days, until 18 March 1761.

4. MILITARY AND DEFENCE

WAR

Longest The longest of history's countless wars was the "Hundred Years War" between England and France, which lasted from 1338 to 1453 (115 years), although it may be said that the Holy War, comprising the nine Crusades from the First (1096–1104) to the Ninth (1270–91), extended over 195 years. It has been calculated that in the 3,467 years since 1496 B.C. there have been only 230 years of peace throughout the civilized world.

Last battle on British soil The last pitched land battle in Britain was at Culloden Field, Drummossie Moor, Inverness-shire, on 16 April 1746. The last Clan battle in Scotland was between Clan Mackintosh and Clan MacDonald at Mulroy, Inverness-shire, in 1689. The last battle on English soil was the Battle of Sedgemoor, Somerset, on 6 July 1685, when the forces of James II defeated the supporters of Charles II's illegitimate son, James Scott (formerly called Fitzroy or Crofts), the Duke of Monmouth (1649–85). During the Jacobite rising of 1745–46, there was a skirmish at Clifton Moor, Westmorland, on 18 Dec. 1745, when the British forces under Prince William, the Duke of Cumberland (1721–65), brushed with the rebels of Prince Charles Edward Stuart (1720–88) with about 12 killed on each side. This was a tactical victory for the Scots under Lord George Murray.

Shortest war The shortest war on record was that between the United Kingdom and Zanzibar (now part of Tanzania) from 9.02 to 9.40 a.m. on 27 Aug. 1896. The U.K. battle fleet under Rear-Admiral (later Admiral Sir) Harry Holdsworth Rawson (1843–1910) delivered an ultimatum to the self-appointed Sultan Sa'īd Khalid to evacuate his palace and surrender. This was not forthcoming until after 38 minutes of bombardment. Admiral Rawson received the Brilliant Star of Zanzibar (first class) from the new Sultan Hamud ibn Muhammad. It was proposed at one time that elements of the local populace should be compelled to defray the cost of the ammunition used.

Bloodiest war By far the most costly war in terms of human life was World War II (1939–45), in which the total number of fatalities, including battle deaths and civilians of all countries, is estimated to have been 54,800,000 assuming 25 million U.S.S.R. fatalities and 7,800,000 Chinese civilians killed. The country which suffered most was Poland with 6,028,000 or 22·2 per cent. of her population of 27,007,000 killed.

In the case of the United Kingdom, however, the heaviest casualties occurred in World War I (1914–18), with 765,399 killed out of 5,500,000 engaged (13·9 per cent.), compared with 265,000 out of 5,896,000 engaged (4·49 per cent.) in World War II. The heaviest total for one day was 21,392 fatalities and 35,493 wounded in the First Battle of the Somme on 1 July 1916. The total casualties in the Third Battle of Ypres (Passchendaele), from 31 July to 6 Nov. 1917, were about 575,000 (238,313 British and 337,000 German). The total death roll from World War I was only 17·7 per cent. of that of World War II, *viz*. 9,700,000.

Most costly Although no satisfactory computation has been published, it is certain that the material cost of World War II far transcended that of the rest of history's wars put together. In the case of the United Kingdom the cost of £34,423 million was over five times as great as that of World War I (£6,700 million) and 158·6 times that of the Boer War of 1899–1902 (£217 million). The total cost of World War II to the Soviet Union was estimated semi-officially in May 1959 at 2,500,000,000,000 roubles (£100,000 million).

Bloodiest civil war The bloodiest civil war in history was the T'ai-p'ing ("Peace") rebellion, in which peasant sympathizers of the Southern Ming dynasty fought the Manchu Government troops in China from 1853 to 1864. The rebellion was led by the deranged Hung Hsiu-ch'üan (poisoned himself in June 1864), who imagined himself to be a younger brother of Jesus Christ. His force was named *T'ai-p'ing Tien Kuo* (Heavenly Kingdom of Great Peace). According to the best estimates, the loss of life was between 20,000,000 and 30,000,000, including more than 100,000 killed by Government forces in the sack of Nanking on 19–21 July 1864.

Bloodiest battle *Modern* The battle with the greatest recorded number of fatalities was the First Battle of the Somme from 1 July to 19 Nov. 1916, with more than 1,030,000—614,105 British and French and *c.* 420,000 (*not* 650,000) German. The gunfire was heard on Hampstead Heath, London. The greatest battle of World War II and the greatest ever conflict of armour was the Battle of Kursk of 5–22 July 1943 on the Eastern front, which involved 1,300,000 Red Army troops with 3,600 tanks, 20,000 guns and 3,130 aircraft in repelling a German Army Group which had 2,500 tanks. The final investment of Berlin by the Red Army in 1945 is, however, said to have involved 3,500,000 men; 52,000 guns and mortars; 7,750 tanks and 11,000 aircraft on both sides.

Ancient Modern historians give no credence to the casualty figures attached to ancient battles, such as the 250,000 reputedly killed at Plataea (Greeks *v.* Persians) in 479 B.C. or the 200,000 allegedly killed in a single day at Châlons-sur-Marne, France, in A.D. 451. This view is on the grounds that it must have been logistically quite impossible to maintain forces of such a size in the field at that time.

British soil The bloodiest battle fought on British soil was the Battle of Towton, in Yorkshire, on 29 March 1461, when 36,000 Yorkists defeated 40,000 Lancastrians. The total loss has been estimated at between 28,000 and 38,000 killed. A figure of 80,000 British dead was attributed by Tacitus to the battle of A.D. 61 between Queen Boudicca (Boadicea) of the Iceni and the Roman Governor of Britain Suetonius Paulinus, for the loss of 400 Romans in an Army of 10,000. The site of the battle is unknown but may have been near Borough Hill, Daventry, Northamptonshire, or more probably near Hampstead Heath, London. It is improbable that, for such a small loss, the Romans could have killed more than 20,000 Britons.

GREATEST INVASION

Seaborne The greatest invasion in military history was the Allied land, air and sea operation against the Normandy coasts of France on D-day, 6 June 1944. Thirty-eight convoys of 745 ships moved in on the first three days, supported by 4,066 landing craft, carrying 185,000 men and 20,000 vehicles, and 347 minesweepers. The air assault comprised 18,000 paratroopers from 1,087 aircraft. The 42 available divisions possessed an air support from 13,175 aircraft. Within a month 1,100,000 troops, 200,000 vehicles and 750,000 tons of stores were landed.

The greatest invasion in military history—when a million men were landed in Normandy in 28 days in 1944

Airborne The largest airborne invasion was the Anglo-American assault of three divisions (34,000 men), with 2,800 aircraft and 1,600 gliders, near Arnhem, in the Netherlands, on 17 Sept. 1944.

Last on British soil The last invasion of Great Britain occurred on 12 Feb. 1797, when the Irish-American adventurer General Tate landed at Carreg Gwastad with 1,400 French troops. They surrendered near Fishguard, Pembrokeshire, to Lord Cawdor's force of the Castlemartin Yeomanry and some local inhabitants armed with pitchforks.

Worst sieges The worst siege in history was the 880-day siege of Leningrad, U.S.S.R. by the German Army from 30 Aug. 1941 until 27 Jan. 1944. The best estimate is that between 1·3 and 1·5 million defenders and citizens died. The longest siege in military history was that of Centa which was besieged by the Moors under Mulai Ismail for the 26 years 1674 to 1700.

LARGEST ARMED FORCES

Numerically, the country with the largest regular armed force is the U.S.S.R., with 3,305,000 at mid-1970, compared with the U.S.A.'s 3,161,000 at the same date. The Chinese People's Liberation Army, which includes naval and air services, has nearly 2,800,000 regulars, but there is also a civilian home guard militia claimed to be 200 million strong but regarded by the Institute for Strategic Studies to have an effective element of not more than 7,000,000.

DEFENCE

The estimated level of spending on armaments throughout the world in 1970 was $167,000 million (£69,800 million). This represents £19 per person per annum, or close to 10 per cent. of the world's total production of goods and services. It was estimated in 1970 that there were 15,400,000 full-time military and naval personnel and 30,000,000 armament workers.

The expenditure on "defence" by the government of the United States in the year ending 30 June 1970 was $81,240 million (£33,850 million), or about 9·2 per cent. of the country's gross national product. The budget for 1970–71 was $79,432 million (£33,097 million).

The U.S.S.R.'s official "defence" budget for 1968–69 was 17,700 million roubles (£8,200 million at the official exchange rate). Almost certainly, this does not include space research costs or the research and development budget for advanced weapons systems. If considered in terms of purchasing power equivalent to U.S. dollars, total military expenditure by the U.S.S.R., including elements not in the official budget, is probably nearer $53,000 million (£22,080 million) per year, or 11·7 per cent. of the country's G.N.P.

At the other extreme is Andorra, whose defence budget, voted in 1970, amounted to £4·08.

NAVIES

Largest The largest navy in the world is the United States Navy, with a manpower of 694,000 and 294,000 Marines at 30 June 1970. The active strength in 1970 included 16 attack and 4 anti-submarine carriers, 41 *Polaris-* or *Poseidon*-armed and 103 other submarines, 73 guided missile ships including 8 cruisers, 29 destroyers and 30 frigates, and 139 amphibious assault ships. The total number of ships in commission was 780.

The strength of the Royal Navy in mid-1971 was 2 aircraft carriers, 2 commando ships, 2 assault ships, 15 destroyers (6 guided missiles), 66 frigates, 8 nuclear and 27 other submarines and 54 minesweepers. The uniformed strength was run down to 79,900 by 1 April 1971 though there are more than 100,000 Navy Department civilians. In 1914 the Royal Navy had 542 warships including 31 battleships with 5 building.

Greatest naval battle The greatest number of ships and aircraft ever involved in a sea-air action was 231 ships and 1,996 aircraft in the Battle of Leyte Gulf, in the Philippines. It raged from 22 to 27 Oct. 1944, with 166 United States and 65 Japanese warships engaged, of which 26 Japanese and 6 U.S. ships were sunk. In addition 1,280 U.S. and 716 Japanese aircraft were engaged. The greatest naval battle of modern times was the Battle of Jutland on 31 May 1916, in which 151 Royal Navy warships were involved against 101 German warships. The Royal Navy lost 14 ships and 6,097 men and the German fleet 11 ships and 2,545 men. The greatest of ancient naval battles was the Battle of Lepanto on 7 Oct. 1571, when an estimated 25,000 Turks were lost in 250 galleys, sunk by the Spanish, Venetian and Papal forces of more than 300 ships in the Gulf of Lepanto, now called Korinthiakós Kólpos, or the Gulf of Kórinthos (Corinth), Greece.

Greatest evacuation The greatest evacuation in military history was that carried out by 1,200 Allied naval and civil craft from the beachhead at Dunkerque (Dunkirk), France, between 27 May and 4 June 1940. A total of 338,226 British and French troops were taken off.

ARMIES

Largest Numerically, the world's largest army is that of China (mainland), with a total strength of about 2,400,000 in mid-1970. The total size of the U.S.S.R.'s army (including the ground elements of the Air Defence Command) in mid-1970 was estimated at 2,000,000 men, believed to be organized into about 157 divisions. The strength of the British Army was 165,900 on 1 April 1971.

Smallest The smallest army in the world is that of San Marino, with a strength of 11, while Costa Rica (since 1948), Iceland, Liechtenstein, Monaco and Nauru have no army at all.

Oldest The oldest army in the world is the 83-strong Swiss Guard in the Vatican City, with a regular foundation dating back to 21 Jan. 1506. Its origins, however, extend back before 1400.

John B. Salling, who faded away in 1959

Oldest old soldiers The oldest old soldier of all time was probably John B. Salling of the army of the Confederate States of America and the last accepted survivor of the U.S. Civil War (1861–65). He died in Kingsport, Tennessee, U.S.A., on 16 March 1959, aged 112 years 305 days. The oldest Chelsea pensioner, based only on the evidence of his tombstone, was the 111-year-old William Hiseland (b. 6 Aug. 1620, d. 7 Feb. 1732). The last survivor of the Afghan war of 1878–79 was Alfred Hawker, who died on 10 Dec. 1962, aged 104 years 41 days.

Tallest soldiers The tallest soldier of all time was Väinö Myllyrinne (1909–63) who was inducted into the Finnish Army when he was 7 feet 3 inches and later grew to 8 feet $1\frac{1}{4}$ inches. The British Army's tallest soldier was Benjamin Crow who was signed on at Litchfield in November 1947 when he was 7 feet 1 inch tall. Edward Evans (1924–58), who later grew to 7 feet $8\frac{1}{2}$ inches, was in the Army when he was 6 feet 10 inches.

Oldest British Army regiment The oldest regular regiment in the British Army is the Royal Scots, raised in French service in 1633, though the Buffs (Royal East Kent Regiment) can trace back their origin to independent companies in Dutch pay as early as 1572. The Coldstream Guards, raised in 1650, were, however, placed on the establishment of the British Army before the Royal Scots and the Buffs. The oldest armed body in the United Kingdom is the Honourable Artillery Company. Formed from the Finsbury Archers, it received its charter from Henry VIII in 1537, and is now the senior regiment of the Territorial and Army Volunteer Reserve.

TANKS

Earliest The prototype of all tanks was the "Little Willie", built by William Foster & Co. Ltd. of Lincoln, and first tested in September 1915. Tanks were first taken into action by the Machine Gun Corps (Heavy Section), which later became the Royal Tank Corps, at the battle

The most heavily gunned British tank—a Chieftain with her 120 mm. armament

of Flers, in France, on 15 Sept. 1916. The Mark I was armed with a pair of 6-lb. guns and four machine-guns. The Mark I Male weighed 28 tons and was driven by a motor developing 105 horse-power which gave it a maximum road speed of 4 to 5 m.p.h.

Heaviest The heaviest tank ever constructed was the German Panzer Kampfwagen Maus II, which weighed 189 tons. By 1945 it had reached only the experimental stage and was not proceeded with.

The heaviest operational tank used by any army was the 81·5-ton 13-man French Char di Rupture 3C of 1923. It carried a 155 mm. howitzer and had two 250 h.p. engines giving a maximum speed of 8 m.p.h. On 7 Nov. 1957, in the annual military parade in Moscow, U.S.S.R., a Soviet tank possibly heavier than the German Jagd Tiger II (71·7 tons), built by Henschel, and certainly heavier than the Stalin III, was displayed.

The heaviest British tank ever built is the 76-ton prototype "Tortoise". With a crew of seven and a designed speed of 12 m.p.h., this tank has a width two inches less than that of the operational 65-ton "Conqueror". The most heavily armed is the 52-ton "Chieftain", put into service in November 1966, with a 120 mm. gun.

GUNS

Earliest Although it cannot be accepted as proved, the best opinion is that the earliest guns were constructed in North Africa, possibly by Arabs, in *c*. 1250. The earliest representation of an English gun is contained in an illustrated manuscript dated 1326 at Oxford. The earliest anti-aircraft gun was an artillery piece on a high angle mounting used in the Franco-Prussian War of 1870 by the Prussians against French balloons.

Largest The remains of the most massive guns ever constructed were found near Frankfurt am Main, Germany, in 1945. They were "Schwerer Gustav" and "Dora", each of which had a barrel 94 feet 9 inches long, with a calibre of 800 millimetres (31·5 inches), and a breech weighing 108 tons. The maximum charge was 2,000 kilogrammes (4,409 lb.) of cordite to fire a shell weighing 4,800 kilogrammes (4·7 tons) a distance of 55 kilometres (34 miles). The maximum projectile was one of 7 tons with a range of 22 miles. Each gun with its carriage weighed 1,323 tons and required a crew of 1,500 men.

During the 1914–18 war the British Army used a gun of 18 inches calibre. The barrel alone weighed 125 tons. In World War II the "Bochebuster", a train-mounted howitzer with a calibre of 18 inches, firing a 2,500 lb. shell to a maximum range of 22,800 yards, was used from 1940 onwards as part of the Kent coast defences.

Greatest range The greatest range ever attained by a gun is by the H.A.R.P. (High Altitude Research Project) gun consisting of two 16-inch calibre barrels in tandem in Barbados. In 1968 a 200 lb. projectile had been fired to a height of 400,000 feet (75¾ miles).

The famous "Big Bertha" guns, which shelled Paris in World War I, were the "Lange Berta" of which seven were built with a calibre of 21 cm. (8·26 inches), a designed range of 79·5 miles and an achieved range of more than 75 miles.

Mortars The largest mortars ever constructed were Mallets mortar (Woolwich Arsenal, London, 1857), and the "Little David" of World War II, made in the U.S.A. Each had a calibre of 36¼ inches (920 mm.), but neither was ever used in action.

Largest cannon The highest calibre cannon ever constructed is the *Tsar Puchka* (King of Cannons), now housed in the Kremlin, Moscow, U.S.S.R. It was built in the 16th century with a bore of 36 inches (915 mm.) and a barrel 17 feet long. It was designed to fire cannon balls weighing 2 tons but was never used. The Turks fired up to seven shots per day from a bombard 26 feet long, with an internal calibre of 42 inches, against the walls of Constantinople (now Istanbul) from 12 April to 29 May 1453. It was dragged by 60 oxen and 200 men and fired a stone cannon ball weighing 1,200 lb.

Military engines The largest military catapults, or onagers, were capable of throwing a missile weighing 60 lb. a distance of 500 yards.

Longest march The longest march in military history was the famous Long March by the Chinese Communists in 1934–35. In 368 days, of which 268 days were of movement, from October to October, their force of 90,000 covered 6,000 miles northward from Kiangsi to Yünnan. They crossed 18 mountain ranges and six major rivers and lost all but 22,000 of their force in continual rear-guard actions against Nationalist Kuo-min-tang (K.M.T.) forces.

Most rapid march The most rapid recorded march by foot-soldiers was one of 62 miles in 26 hours on 28–29 July 1809, by the Light Brigade under Brigadier- (later Major-) General Robert Craufurd (1764–1812), coming to the relief of Lieut.-Gen. Sir Arthur Wellesley, later Field Marshal the 1st Duke of Wellington (1769–1852), after the Battle of Talavera (Talavera de la Reina, Toledo, Spain) in the Peninsular War.

The longest recorded march by a body of 60 without any fall-outs was one of 14 hours 23 minutes by the London Rifle Brigade on 18–19 April 1914. On 8 April 1922, two officers and 27 other ranks of the London Scottish Regiment covered the 53 miles from London to Brighton in 13 hours 59 minutes, each carrying 46 lb. of equipment, but two men failed to finish.

AIR FORCES

The earliest autonomous air force is the Royal Air Force whose origins began with the Royal Flying Corps (created 13 May 1912); the Air Battalion of the Royal Engineers (1 April 1911) and the Corps of Royal Engineers Balloon Section (1878) which was first operational in Bechuanaland (now Botswana) in 1884.

Largest The greatest Air Force of all time was the United States Army Air Force (now called the U.S. Air Force), which had 79,908 aircraft in July 1944 and 2,411,294 personnel in March 1944. The U.S. Air Force had 810,000 personnel and 6,500 first-line combat aircraft in mid-1970. The U.S.S.R. Air Force, with about 480,000 men in mid-1970, had 4,000 tactical aircraft. In addition, the U.S.S.R.'s Strategic Rocket Forces had about 350,000 operational personnel in mid-1970. The strength of the

of the Royal Air Force was 105,100 on 1 April 1971.

BOMBS

The heaviest conventional bomb ever used operationally was the Royal Air Force's "Grand Slam", weighing 22,000 lb. and measuring 25 feet 5 inches long, dropped on Bielefeld railway viaduct, Germany, on 14 March 1945. In 1949 the United States Air Force tested a bomb weighing 42,000 lb. at Muroc Dry Lake, California, U.S.A.

Atomic The two atom bombs dropped on Japan by the United States in 1945 each had an explosive power equivalent to that of 20,000 tons (20 kilotons) of trinitrotoluene ($C_7H_5O_6N_3$), called T.N.T. The one dropped on Hiroshima, known as "Little Boy", was 10 feet long and weighed 9,000 lb. The most powerful thermo-nuclear device so far tested is one with a power equivalent to 57,000,000 tons of T.N.T., or 57 megatons, detonated by the U.S.S.R. in the Novaya Zemlya area at 8.33 a.m. G.M.T. on 30 Oct. 1961. The shock wave was detected to have circled the world three times, taking 36 hours 27 minutes for the first circuit. Some estimates put the power of this device at between 62 and 90 megatons. On 9 Aug. 1961, Nikita Khrushchyov, then the Chairman of the Council of Ministers of the U.S.S.R., declared that the Soviet Union was capable of constructing a 100-megaton bomb, and announced the possession of one in East Berlin, Germany, on 16 Jan. 1963. It has been estimated that such a bomb would make a crater 19 miles in diameter and would cause serious fires at a range of from 36 to 40 miles. Work started in the U.S.S.R. on atomic bombs in June 1942 although their first chain reaction was not achieved until December 1945 by Dr. Igor Kurchatov. The patent for the fusion or H bomb was filed in the United States on 26 May 1946 by Dr. Janos (John) von Neumann (1903–57), a Hungarian-born mathematician, and Dr. Klaus Emil Julius Fuchs (born in Germany, 1911), the defected physicist.

Largest atomic arsenal It was estimated early in 1970 that the United States possessed 4,250 deliverable thermo-nuclear warheads including 1,054 land-based I.C.B.M.s. The U.S.S.R.'s arsenal was estimated at 2,300 including 1,300 I.C.B.M.s (Inter-Continental Ballistic Missiles).

No official estimate has been published of the potential power of the device known as Doomsday, but this far surpasses any tested weapon. A 50,000 megaton cobalt-salted device has been mooted which could kill the entire human race except those who were deep underground and who stayed there for more than five years.

Largest "conventional" explosion The largest military use of conventional explosive was in tunnels under the German positions on the Messines Ridge, Belgium. These were mined from January 1916 to June 1917, and packed 416·6 tons of ammonal, blastine, guncotton and dynamite. The bombardment which accompanied the detonation at 3.10 a.m. on 7 June 1917 was reportedly heard or felt in London. A missing 30,000-lb. charge of ammonal near Floegsteert Wood blew up on 17 July 1955—possibly set off by an electrical storm.

5. JUDICIAL

LEGISLATION AND LITIGATION

STATUTES

Oldest The earliest known judicial code was that of King Urnammu during the third dynasty of Ur, Iraq, in *c.* 2145 B.C. The oldest English statute is a section of the Statute of Marlborough of 1267, retitled in 1948 "The Distress Act, 1267". Some statutes enacted by Henry II (d. 1189) and earlier kings are even more durable as they have been assimilated into the Common Law. An extreme example is Alfred, Dooms, c43 of *c.* A.D. 890 which contains the passage "judge thou not one doom to the rich, another to the poor".

Longest in the United Kingdom Measured in bulk the longest statute of the United Kingdom is the Income Tax and Corporation Tax Act, 1970, which runs to 540 sections, 15 schedules and 670 pages. It is 1½ inches thick and costs £2·80. However, its 540 sections are surpassed in number by the 748 of the Merchant Shipping Act, 1894.

Of old statutes, 31 George III XIV, the Land Tax Act of 1791, written on parchment, consists of 780 skins forming a roll 1,170 feet long.

Shortest The shortest statute is the Parliament (Qualification of Women) Act, 1918, which runs to 27 operative words—"A woman shall not be disqualified by sex or marriage from being elected to or sitting or voting as a Member of the Common House of Parliament". Section 2 contains a further 14 words giving the short title.

Most It was computed in March 1959 that the total number of laws on Federal and State statute books in the United States was 1,156,644. The Illinois State Legislature only discovered in April 1967 that it had made the sale of cigarettes illegal and punishable by a $100 fine for a second offence in 1907.

Earliest English patent The earliest of all known English patents was that granted by Henry VI in 1449 to Flemish-born John of Utynam for making the coloured glass required for the windows of Eton College. The peak number of applications for patents filed in the United Kingdom in any one year was 63,614 in 1969.

Most protracted litigation The longest contested law suit ever recorded ended in Poona, India, on 28 April 1966, when Balasaheb Patloji Thorat received a favourable judgment on a suit filed by his ancestor Maloji Thorat 761 years earlier in 1205. The points at issue were rights of presiding over public functions and precedences at religious festivals.

The dispute over the claim of the Prior and Convent of Durham Cathedral to administer the spiritualities of the diocese during a vacancy in the See grew fierce in 1283. It smouldered until 1939, having flared up in 1672, 1890 and 1920. In 1939 the Archbishop of Canterbury exercised his metropolitan rights and appointed the Dean as guardian of spiritualities of Durham "without prejudice to the general issue", then 656 years old.

A Messines Ridge crater—the ultimate in trench warfare from 1917

Longest British trial The longest trial in the annals of British justice was the Tichborne personation case. The civil trial began on 11 May 1871, lasted 103 days and collapsed on 6 March 1872. The criminal trial went on for 188 days, resulting in a sentence on 28 Feb. 1874 for two counts of perjury (14 years imprisonment and hard labour) on the London-born Arthur Orton, *alias* Thomas Castro (1834–98), who claimed to be Roger Charles Tichborne (1829–54), the elder brother of Sir Alfred Joseph Doughty-Tichborne, 11th Bt. (1839–66). The whole case, during which, miraculously, no juryman fell ill, thus spanned 827 days and cost £55,315. The jury were out for only 30 minutes.

The impeachment of Warren Hastings (1732–1818), which began in 1788, dragged on for seven years until 23 April 1795, but the trial lasted only 149 days. He was appointed a member of the Privy Council in 1814.

Murder The longest murder trial in Britain was that in which Ronald and Reginald Kray (twins), 35, were found guilty of the murder by shooting of George Cornell, 38, at the Blind Beggar public house on 9 June 1966, and by stabbing of Jack "The Hat" McVitie, 38, in Evering Road, Stoke Newington in October 1967. They were sentenced by Mr. Justice Melford Stevenson to imprisonment for not less than 30 years on 5 March 1969 after a 39-day trial at the Old Bailey, London. The costs of the trial were estimated at more than £200,000.

The shortest recorded British murder hearings were *R. v. Murray* on 28 Feb. 1957 and *R. v. Cawley* at Winchester Assizes on 14 Dec. 1959. The proceedings occupied only 30 seconds on each occasion.

Divorce The longest trial of a divorce case in Britain was *Gibbons v. Gibbons and Roman and Halperin*. On 19 March 1962, after 28 days, Mr. Alfred George Boyd Gibbons was granted a decree *nisi* against his wife Dorothy for adultery with Mr. John Halperin of New York City, N.Y., U.S.A.

Longest address The longest address in a British court was in *Globe and Phoenix Gold Mining Co. Ltd. v. Amalgamated Properties of Rhodesia*. Mr. William Henry Upjohn, K.C. (1853–1941) concluded his speech on 22 Sept. 1916, having addressed the court for 45 days.

st attended trial The greatest attendance at any trial was at that of Major Jesús Sosa Blanco, aged 51, for an alleged 108 murders. At one point in the 12½-hour trial (5.30 p.m. to 6 a.m., 22–23 Jan. 1959), 17,000 people were present in the Havana Sports Palace, Cuba.

ighest bail The highest amount ever demanded as bail was $46,500,000 (then £16,608,333) against Antonio De Angelis in a civil damages suit by the Harbor Tank Storage Co. filed in the Superior Court, Jersey City, New Jersey, U.S.A. on 16 Jan. 1964. (See also Greatest swindle, page 205.)

The highest bail figure in a British court is £140,000, granted to Manick Banthia at Uxbridge Court, Middlesex on 14 Oct. 1966. The amount involved £30,000 on his own recognizances, a surety of £50,000 and three of £20,000 each. He was charged with an attempt illegally to export £30,000 from London Airport in 60 Bank envelopes. Two other men, Joe Cohen and Amarendra Goswami also charged, had a combined bail of £170,000.

On 2 June 1959 the original bail fixed at Dublin, Ireland, for Dr. Paul Singer, aged 48, managing director of Shanahan's Stamp Auctions Ltd., was £100,000. This was later reduced to £15,000.

Greatest pensation The greatest Crown compensation for wrongful imprisonment was £10,000, paid on 23 Sept. 1931 to T. Boevey Barrett, who had been wrongfully convicted of alleged frauds in 1921. After serving three years' imprisonment in Accra, Ghana, he was granted a free pardon in 1930.

The greatest compensation paid for wrongful imprisonment in the United Kingdom was £6,000, paid in 1929 to Oscar Slater (*né* Leschziner), who had been arraigned for the murder of Miss Marion Gilchrist, aged 83, in Glasgow on 6 May 1909.

GREATEST DAMAGES

Loss of life The greatest damages awarded as compensation for loss of life were $2,000,000 (£714,285), awarded in 1965 to Mrs. Trese Hollerich, whose husband died when a Boeing 720-B airliner owned by Northwest Airlines crashed on 12 Feb. 1963 near Miami, Florida, U.S.A. In July 1965 the Boeing Company and Northwest Airlines settled the case out of court for $1,225,000 (£437,500).

Breach of contract The greatest damages ever awarded for a breach of contract were £610,392, awarded on 16 July 1930 to the Bank of Portugal against the printers Waterlow & Sons Ltd., of London, arising from their unauthorized printing of 580,000 five-hundred escudo notes in 1925. This award was upheld in the House of Lords on 28 April 1932. One of the perpetrators, Arthur Virgilio Alves Reis, served 16 years (1930–46) in gaol.

Personal injury The greatest damages ever awarded for personal injury are $3,600,000 (£1,500,000) on 18 Oct. 1970 to Keith Bush, 30, of Ely, Nevada, U.S.A., at Reno, Nevada against General Electric and Westinghouse Air Brake Co. in connection with an industrial accident which left him blind, speechless and paralyzed.

The greatest damages ever awarded for personal injury in a British court were £78,398, awarded to Christopher Povey, 19, of Hale, Cheshire for injuries sustained in a gymnasium accident at Rydal School, Colwyn Bay, by Mr. Justice Crichton at Manchester Assizes on 12 Mar. 1969. This figure was later reduced to £62,500 on appeal on 8 Dec. 1969. On 22 April 1969 £74,500 was awarded for road accident damage to Mr. John Rodney de Winton Kitcat of Buntingford, Hertfordshire in 1966 by Mr. Justice Paull with a stay granted in respect of £24,500.

An award of £66,447, subsequently reduced on appeal by £15,000 to £51,447, was made by Mr. Justice Cantley to Mr. William Henry Fletcher (b. 1908) of Walton, Liverpool on 15 June 1967 for severe brain damage (and serious physical injuries) sustained in a road accident (in July 1964).

On 5 Feb. 1960, the Dublin High Court awarded £87,402 damages for motor injuries to Mr. Kevin P. McMorrow, aged 38, of County Leitrim, against his driver Mr. Edward Knott. It is understood that, after an appeal, a settlement was made out of court for £50,000.

Breach of promise The largest sum involved in a breach of promise suit in the United Kingdom was £50,000, accepted in 1913 by Miss Daisy Markham, *alias* Mrs. Annie Moss (d. 20 Aug. 1962, aged 76), in settlement against the 6th Marquess of Northampton (b. 6 Aug. 1885).

Defamation The greatest damages for defamation ever awarded in the United Kingdom were £117,000, awarded on 21 July 1961 in *The Rubber Improvement Co. Ltd. v. Associated Newspapers Ltd.* for 51 words which appeared in the *Daily Mail* of 23 Dec. 1958. The company was represented by Colin Duncan, M.C. (now a Q.C.) and Mr. (now Sir) Helenus Patrick Joseph Milmo, Q.C. (b. 24 Aug. 1908), who has since become a judge. After appeal proceedings by both sides this action was settled out of court for a substantially smaller amount.

Divorce The highest award made to the dispossessed party in a divorce suit was $70,000 (£25,000), awarded to Mr. Demetrus Sophocles Constandinidi against Dr. Henry William Lance for bigamous adultery with his wife Mrs. Julia Constandinidi. She married Dr. Lance after going through a form of divorce in Sioux Falls, South Dakota, U.S.A., on 27 Feb. 1902.

ALIMONY

World The greatest alimony ever paid was $11,550,000 (£4,125,000), paid by Reuben Hollis Fleet, the United States millionaire aircraft manufacturer, to his second wife Dorothy (*née* Mitchell) in 1945, after their separation, following "verbal abuse".

Britain The highest alimony awarded in a British court is £5,000 per annum, but in 1919 the 2nd Duke of Westminster, G.C.V.O., D.S.O. (1879–1953) settled £13,000 per annum upon his first wife, Constance Edwina (*née* Cornwallis-West), C.B.E., later Mrs. Lewis.

HIGHEST SETTLEMENT

Divorce The greatest amount ever paid in a divorce settlement is $9,500,000 (£3,393,000), paid by Edward J. Hudson to Mrs. Cecil Amelia Blaffer Hudson, aged 43. This award was made on 28 Feb. 1963 at the Domestic Relations Court, Houston, Texas, U.S.A. Mrs. Hudson was, reputedly, already worth $14,000,000 (£5,000,000).

Patent case The greatest settlement ever made in a patent infringement suit is $9,250,000 (£3,303,000), paid in April 1952 by the Ford Motor Company to the Ferguson Tractor Co. for a claim filed in January 1948.

HIGHEST COSTS

The highest costs in English legal history arose from the case of the *Société Rateau v. Rolls-Royce,* an action concerning the alleged infringement of a French patent of 4 Dec. 1939 for an axial flow jet engine. Mr. Justice Lloyd-Jacob held in April 1967 that the patent had not been infringed. Costs were estimated at £325,000.

Income tax *Highest reward* The greatest amount paid for information concerning a case of income tax delinquency was $79,999·93 (£28,571), paid by the United States Internal Revenue Service to a group of informers. Payments are limited to 10 per cent. of the amount recovered as a direct result of information laid. Informants are often low-income accountants or women scorned. The total of payments in 1965 was $597,731 (then £213,475).

Greatest lien The greatest lien ever imposed by the U.S. Internal Revenue Service was one of $21,261,818 (£7,593,500), filed against the California property of John A. T. Galvin in March 1963, in respect of alleged tax arrears for 1954–57.

WILLS

Shortest The shortest valid will in the world is "Vše zene", the Czech for "All to wife", written and dated 19 Jan. 1967 by Herr Karl Tausch of Langen, Hesse, Germany. The shortest will contested but subsequently admitted to probate in English law was the case of *Thorn v. Dickens* in 1906. It consisted of the three words "All for Mother".

Longest The longest will on record was that of Mrs. Frederica Cook (U.S.A.), in the early part of the century. It consisted of four bound volumes containing 95,940 words.

JUDGE

Oldest *World* The oldest recorded active judge was Judge Albert R. Alexander (1859–1966) of Plattsburg, Missouri, U.S.A. He was the magistrate and probate judge of Clinton County until his retirement aged 105 years 8 months on 9 July 1965.

Britain The greatest recorded age at which any British judge has sat on a bench was 93 years 9 months in the case of Sir William Francis Kyffin Taylor, G.B.E., K.C. (later Lord Maenan), who was born on 9 July 1854 and retired as presiding judge of the Liverpool Court of Passage in April 1948, having held that position since 1903. The greatest age at which a House of Lords judgment has been given is 92 in the case of the 1st Earl of Halsbury (b. 3 Sept. 1823) in 1916.

Youngest The youngest certain age at which any English judge has been appointed is 31, in the case of Sir Francis Buller (b. 17 March 1746), who was appointed Second Judge of the County Palatine of Chester on 27 Nov. 1777, and Puisne Judge of the King's Bench on 6 May 1778, aged 32 years 1 month. The Hon. Daines Barrington (*c.* 1727–1800) was appointed Justice of the Counties of Merioneth and Anglesey sometime in 1757 and may have been even younger.

Youngest Q.C. The earliest age at which a barrister has taken silk since 1900 is 33 years 8 months in the case of Mr. (later the Rt. Hon. Sir) Francis Raymond Evershed (1899–1966) in April 1933. He was later Lord Evershed, a Lord of Appeal in Ordinary.

Highest paid lawyer It was estimated that Jerry Giesler (1886–1962), an attorney in Los Angeles, California, U.S.A., averaged $50,000 (£17,850) in fees for each case which he handled during the latter part of his career. Currently, the most highly paid lawyer is generally believed to be Louis Nizer of New York City, N.Y., U.S.A.

CRIME AND PUNISHMENT

GREATEST MASS KILLINGS

China The greatest massacre in human history ever imputed is that of 26,300,000 Chinese during the régime of Mao tse Tung between 1949 and May 1965. This accusation was made by an agency of the U.S.S.R. Government in a radio broadcast on 7 April 1969. The broadcast broke down the total into four periods:—2·8 million (1949–52); 3·5 million (1953–57); 6·7 million (1958–60); and 13·3 million (1961–May 1965). The highest reported death figures in single monthly announcements on Peking radio were 1,176,000 in the provinces of Anhwei, Chekiang, Kiangsu, and Shantung, and 1,150,000 in the Central South Provinces. Po-ipo, Minister of Finance, is alleged to have stated in the organ *For a lasting peace, for a people's democracy* "in the past three years (1950–1952) we have liquidated more than 2 million bandits". General Jacques Guillermaz, a French diplomat estimated the total executions between February 1951 and May 1952 at between 1 million and 3 million. In April 1971 the Executive *Yuan* or cabinet of the implacably hostile government of The Republic of China in Taipai, Taiwan announced its official estimate of the mainland death roll in the period 1949–69 as "at least 39,940,000". This figure, however, excluded "tens of thousands" killed in the Great Proletarian Cultural Revolution, which began in late 1966.

U.S.S.R. The total death roll in the Great Purge, or *Yezhovshchina*, in the U.S.S.R., in 1936–38 has never been published, though evidence of its magnitude may be found in population statistics which show a deficiency of males from before the outbreak of the 1941–45 war. The reign of terror was administered by the *Narodny Kommissariat Vnutrennykh Del* (N.K.V.D.), or People's Commissariat of Internal Affairs, the Soviet security service headed by Nikolay Ivanovich Yezhov (1895–?1939), described by Nikita Khrushchyov in 1956 as "a degenerate". S. V. Utechin, an expert on Soviet affairs, regards estimates of 8,000,000 or 10,000,000 victims as "probably not exaggerations".

Nazi Germany At the S.S. (*Schutzstaffel*) extermination camp (*Vernichtungslager*) called Auschwitz-Birkenau (Oswiecim-Brzezinka), near Oswiecim (Auschwitz), in southern Poland, where a minimum of 900,000 people (Soviet estimate is 4,000,000) were exterminated from 14 June 1940 to 29 Jan. 1945, the greatest number killed in a day was 6,000. The man who operated the release of the "Zyklon B" cyanide pellets into the gas chambers there during this time was Sergeant Mold. The Nazi (*Nationalsozialistiche Deutsche Arbeiter Partei*) Commandant during the period 1940–43 was Rudolf Franz Ferdinand Höss, who was tried in Warsaw from 11 March to 2 April 1947 and hanged, aged 47, at Oswiecim on 15 April 1947. Erich Koch, the war-time *Gauleiter* of East Prussia and *Reichskommissar* for German-occupied Ukraine, was arrested near Hamburg on 24 May 1949, tried in Warsaw from 20 Oct. 1958 to 9 March 1959 and sentenced to death for his responsibility for, or complicity in, the deaths of 4,232,000 people. The death sentence was later commuted to imprisonment.

Obersturmbannführer (Lt.-Col.) Karl Adolf Eichmann (b. Solingen, West Germany 19 March 1906) of the S.S. was hanged in a small room inside Ramleh Prison, near Tel Aviv, Israel, at just before midnight (local time) on 31 May 1962, for his complicity in the deaths of 5,700,000 Jews during World War II, under the instruction given in April 1941 by Adolf Hitler (1889–1945) for the "Final Solution" (*Endlösung*), *i.e.* the extermination of European Jewry.

ced labour No official figures have been published of the death roll in Corrective Labour Camps in the U.S.S.R., first established in 1918. The total number of such camps was known to be more than 200 in 1946 but in 1956 many were converted to less severe Corrective Labour Colonies. An estimate published in the Netherlands puts the death roll between 1921 and 1960 at 19,000,000. The camps were administered by the *Cheka* until 1922, the O.G.P.U. (1922–34), the N.K.V.D. (1934–1946), the M.V.D. (1946–1953) and the K.G.B. since 1953. Daily intake has been limited to only 2,400 calories since 1961.

Largest criminal ganization The largest syndicate of organized crime is the Mafia or La Cosa Nostra, which has infiltrated the executive, judiciary and legislature of the United States. It consists of some 3,000 to 5,000 individuals in 24 "families" federated under "The Commission", which has a Sicilian-Jewish axis and an estimated annual turnover in vice, gambling, protection rackets and rigged trading of $30,000 million per annum of which some 25 per cent. is profit. The biggest Mafia (means *swank* from a Sicilian word for beauty or pride) killing was on 10 Sept. 1931 when the topmost man Salvatore Maranzano, *Il Capo di Tutti Capi*, and 40 allies were liquidated.

rder rate *Highest* The country with the highest recorded murder rate is Nicaragua, with 29·3 registered homicides per each 100,000 of the population in 1965. It has been estimated that the total number of murders in Colombia during *La Violencia* (1945–62) was about 300,000, giving a rate over a 17-year period of more than 48 a day. A total of 592 deaths was attributed to one bandit leader, Teófilo ("Sparks") Rojas, aged 27, between 1948 and his death in an ambush near Armenia on 22 Jan. 1963. Some sources attribute 3,500 slayings to him.

Britain In Great Britain the highest annual total of murders since 1900 has been 242 in 1945, and the lowest 124 in 1937 and 125 in 1958.

Lowest The country with the lowest officially recorded rate in the world is Spain, with 42 murders (a rate of 1·35 per each million of the population) in 1963, or one murder every 9 days. In the Indian protectorate of Sikkim, in the Himalayas, murder is, however, practically unknown, while in the Hunza area of Kashmir, in the Karakoram, only one definite case has been recorded since 1900.

MOST PROLIFIC MURDERER

World The greatest number of victims ascribed to anyone has been 610 in the case of Countess Erszebet Báthory (1560–1614) of Hungary. At her trial which began on 2 Jan. 1611 a witness testified to seeing a list of her victims in her own handwriting totalling this number. All were alleged to be young girls from the neighbourhood of her castle at Csejthe where she died on 21 Aug. 1614. She had been walled up in her room for the 3½ years, after being found guilty.

Gille de Rays (Raies or Retz) (1404–40) was reputed to have murdered ritually between 140 and 200 kidnapped children. The best estimates put the total of his victims at about 60. He was hanged and burnt at Nantes, France, on 25 Oct. 1440.

The most prolific murderer known in recent criminal history was Herman Webster Mudgett (b. 16 May 1860), better known as H. H. Holmes. It has been estimated that he disposed of some 150 young women "paying guests" in his "Castle" on 63rd Street, Chicago, Illinois, U.S.A. After a suspicious fire on 22 Nov. 1893, the "Castle" was investigated and found to contain secret passages, stairways and a maze of odd rooms, some windowless or padded, containing hidden gas inlets and electric indicators. There was also a hoist, two chutes, a furnace, an acid bath, a dissecting table, a selection of surgical instruments and fragmentary human remains. Holmes was hanged on 7 May 1896, on a charge of murdering his associate, Benjamin F. Pitezel.

Murderess The greatest total of victims ascribed to a recent murderess is 16, together with a further 12 possible victims, making a total of 28. This was in the case of Bella Poulsdatter Sorensen Gunness *née* Grunt (1859–1908) of La Porte, Indiana, U.S.A. Evidence came to light when her farm was set on fire on 28 April 1908, when she herself was found by a jury to have committed suicide by strychnine poisoning. Her victims, remains of many of whom were dug from her hog-lot, are believed to comprise two husbands, at least eight and possibly 20 would-be suitors lured by "Lonely Hearts" advertisements, three women and three children. A claim that Vera Renczi murdered 35 persons in Romania this century lacks authority.

Britain The only man to be arraigned on a charge of nine murders was Peter Thomas Anthony Manuel, aged 32, a New York born Lanarkshire woodworker. He was found guilty, on 29 May 1958, after a 16-day trial at Glasgow High Court, of the capital murders of five females and two males. Two other charges were not proceeded with and three other murders were later admitted by him, making a total of twelve. He was hanged at Barlinnie Prison, near Glasgow, at 8 a.m. on 11 July 1958. The total number of murders committed by "Doctor" William Palmer (b. 1824) of Rugeley, Staffordshire, is not definitely known but was at least 13 and most probably 16, the victims having been poisoned by strychnine or antimony. He was hanged at Stafford on 14 June 1856. Scotland's most prolific known murderer was the Irish-born William Burke (1792–1829), who, in partnership with William Hare, murdered at least 13 derelicts in Edinburgh within 12 months, to sell their corpses. Hare turned King's evidence and Burke was hanged on 28 Jan. 1829.

Gang murders During the period of open gang warfare in Chicago, Illinois, U.S.A., the peak year was 1926, when there were 76 unsolved killings. The 1,000th gang murder in Chicago since 1919 occurred on 1 Feb. 1967. Only 13 cases have ended in convictions.

Thuggee It has been estimated that at least 2,000,000 Indians were strangled by Thugs (*burtotes*) during the period of the Thuggee cult, from 1550 until finally suppressed in 1852. It was established at the trial of Buhram that he had strangled at least 931 victims with his yellow and white cloth strip or *ruhmal* in the Oudh district between 1790 and 1830.

The bomb outrage at Clerkenwell, London in 1868 resulting in the last public execution

"Smelling out" The greatest "smelling out" recorded in African history occurred before Shaka (1787–1828) and 30,000 Nguni subjects near the River Umhlatuzana, Zululand (now Natal, South Africa) in March 1824. After 9 hours, over 300 were "smelt out" as guilty of smearing the Royal *Kraal* with blood, by 150 witch-finders led by the hideous female *isangoma* Nobela. The victims were declared innocent when Shaka admitted to having done the smearing himself to expose the falsity of the power of his diviners. Nobela poisoned herself with atropine ($C_{17}H_{23}NO_3$), but the other 149 witch-finders were thereupon skewered or clubbed to death.

Suicide The estimated daily total of suicides throughout the world surpassed 1,000 in 1965. The country with the highest recorded suicide rate is Hungary, with 33·9 per each 100,000 of the population in 1965, or an average of 9·3 suicides each day. The latest available figure for West Berlin, Germany, is 55 per 100,000 in 1966. The country with the lowest recorded rate is the United Arab Republic (formerly called Egypt), with 16 suicides (0·1 per 100,000) registered in Health Bureau localities (about 48 per cent. of the population) in 1963.

In England and Wales there were 4,226 suicides in 1969, or an average of 11 per day. In the northern hemisphere April and May tend to be peak months.

CAPITAL PUNISHMENT

Capital punishment was first abolished *de facto* in Liechtenstein in 1798. Capital punishment in the British Isles dates from A.D. 450, but fell into disuse in the 11th century, only to be revived in the Middle Ages, reaching a peak in the reign of Edward VI (1547–1553), when an average of 560 persons were executed annually at Tyburn alone. The most people executed at one hanging was 24 at Tyburn (Marble Arch, London) in 1571. Even into the 19th century, there were 223 capital crimes, though people were, in practice, hanged for only 25 of these.

Between 1830 and 1955 the largest number hanged in a year was 27 (24 men, 3 women) in 1903. The least was 5 in 1854, 1921 and 1930.

In 1956 there were no hangings in England, Wales or Scotland, since when the highest number in any year has been 5. The last hangings were those of Peter Anthony Allen (b. 4 April 1943) at Walton Prison, Liverpool, and John Robson Walby (b. 1 April 1940), *alias* Gwynne Owen Evans, at Strangeways Gaol, Manchester, both on 13 Aug. 1964. They had been found guilty of the capital murder of John Alan West, aged 53, a laundry van driver, who was stabbed and battered to death at his home in Workington, Cumberland, on 7 April 1964.

The death penalty for murder was abolished on a free vote in the House of Commons by a majority of 158 (343–185) on 16 Dec. and a majority of 46 in the House of Lords on 18 Dec. 1969.

Last public hanging The last public execution in England took place outside Newgate Prison, London, at 8 a.m. on 26 May 1868, when Michael Barrett was hanged for his part in the Fenian bomb outrage on 13 Dec. 1867, when 12 were killed outside the Clerkenwell House of Detention, London. The earliest non-public execution was of the murderer Thomas Wells on 13 Aug. 1868. The last public hanging in Scotland was that of the murderer Joe Bell in Perth in 1866. The last in the United States occurred at Owensboro, Kentucky in 1936.

Last from yard-arm The last naval execution at the yard-arm was the hanging of Marine John Dalliger aboard H.M.S. *Leven* in the River Yangtze, China, on 13 July 1860. Dalliger had been found guilty of two attempted murders.

Youngest Although the hanging of persons under 18 was expressly excluded only in the Children's and Young Persons Act, 1933 (Sec. 33), no person under that age had, in fact, been executed since 1887. Though it has been published widely that a girl of seven was hanged in 1808 and a boy of nine in 1831, the name of neither can be produced. In 1801 Andrew Benning, aged 13, was executed for housebreaking. The youngest persons hanged since 1900 have been 18 years old:— J. H Clarkson at Leeds on 29 March 1904; Henry Jacoby on 7 Jan. 1922; Bishop in 1925; another case in 1932 James Farrell on 29 March 1949; and Francis Robert George ("Flossie") Forsyth on 10 Nov. 1960.

Oldest The oldest person hanged in the United Kingdom since 1900 was a man of 71 named Charles Frembd (*sic*) at Chelmsford Gaol on 4 Nov. 1914, for the murder of his wife at Leytonstone, Essex. In 1822 John Smith said to be 80, of Greenwich, London, was hanged for the murder of a woman.

Last public guillotining The last person to be publicly guillotined in France was the murderer Eugen Weidmann before a large crowd at Versailles, near Paris, at 4.50 a.m. on 17 June 1939. Dr. Joseph Ignace Guillotin (1738–1812) died a natural death. He had advocated the use of the machine designed by Dr. Antoine Louis in 1789 in the French constituent assembly.

Most attempts The only man in Britain to survive three attempts to hang him was John Lee at Exeter Gaol, Devonshire, on 23 Feb. 1885. Lee had been found guilty of murdering, on 15 Nov. 1884, Emma Ann Whitehead Keyse of Babbacombe, who had employed him as a footman. The attempts, in which the executioner, James Berry, failed three times to get the trap open, occupied about seven minutes. Sir William Harcourt, the Home Secretary, commuted the sentence to life imprisonment. After release, Lee emigrated to the United States in 1917, was married and lived until 1933. The rope is now owned by Mr. D. A. Dale of Histon, Cambridge. In 1803 it was reported that Joseph Samuels was reprieved in Sydney, Australia after three unsuccessful attempts to hang him in which the rope twice broke.

Slowest The longest delay in carrying out a death sentence in recent history is in the case of Sadamichi Hirasawa (b. 1906) of Tōkyō, Japan, who was sentenced to death in January 1950, after a trial lasting 16 months, on charges of poisoning twelve people with potassium cyanide in a Tōkyō bank. In November 1962 he was transferred to a prison at Sendai, in northern Honshū, where he was still awaiting execution in May 1970. The longest stay on "death row" in the United States has been one of more than 14 years by Edgar Labat, aged 44, and Clifton A. Paret, aged 38, in Angola Penitentiary, Louisiana, U.S.A. In March 1953 they were sentenced to death, after being found guilty of rape in 1950. They were released on 5 May 1967, only to be immediately re-arrested on a local jury indictment arising from the original charge.

Caryl Chessman, aged 39 and convicted of 17 felonies, was executed on 2 May 1960 in the gas chamber at the California State Prison, San Quentin, California, U.S.A. In 11 years 10 months and one week on "death row", Chessman had won eight stays.

EXECUTIONER

The longest period of office of a Public Executioner was that of William Calcraft (1800–1879), who was in office from 1828 to 1871 and officiated at nearly every hanging outside and later inside Newgate Prison, London. The most "suitably qualified" executioner on the Home Office list for the last remaining gallows at Wandsworth Prison, London against possible use for traitors, violent pirates and Royal dockyard arsonists is believed to be Mr. Harry Allen (b. 1918).

BLOODIEST ASSIZES

In the West Country Assizes of 1685 (Winchester to Wells), George Jeffreys, the 1st Baron Jeffreys of Wem (1645–1689), sentenced 330 persons to be hanged, 841 to be transported for periods of ten or more years and larger numbers to be imprisoned and flogged. These sentences followed the Duke of Monmouth's insurrections.

LONGEST SENTENCES

World The longest recorded prison sentence is one of 7,109 years awarded to a pair of confidence tricksters by an Iranian court on 15 June 1969. The duration of sentences are proportional to the amount of the defalcations involved.

Richard Honeck was sentenced to life imprisonment in the United States in 1899, after having murdered his former schoolteacher. It was reported in November 1963 that Honeck, then aged 84, who was in Menard Penitentiary, Chester, Illinois, was due to be paroled after 64 years in prison, during which time he had received one letter (a four-line note from his brother in 1904) and two visitors, a friend in 1904 and a newspaper reporter in 1963. He was released on 20 Dec. 1963.

United Kingdom On 17 May 1939, William Burkitt, three times acquitted of murder by a jury (1915, 1925 and 1939), was sentenced by Mr. Justice Cassells "to be kept in prison for the rest of your natural life". Burkitt, whose appeal against the sentence failed in 1948, had served 34 years for manslaughter up to 1954, when he was released. He died on 24 Dec. 1956. The longest single period served by a reprieved murderer in Great Britain this century was 40 years 11 months by John Watson Laurie, the Goat Fell or Arran murderer, who was reprieved on the grounds of insanity in November 1889 and who died in Perth Penitentiary on 4 Oct. 1930.

The longest prison sentence ever passed under United Kingdom law was one of three consecutive and two concurrent terms of 14 years, thus totalling 42 years, imposed on 3 May 1961 on George Blake (b. Rotterdam, 11 Nov. 1922 of an Egyptian-born Jewish-British father and a Dutch mother as George Behar), for treachery. Blake, formerly U.K. vice-consul in Seoul, South Korea, has been converted to Communism during 34 months' internment there from 2 July 1950 to April 1953. It has been alleged that his betrayals may have cost the lives of up to 42 United Kingdom agents. He was "sprung" from Wormwood Scrubs Prison, London, W.12, on 22 Oct. 1966.

The longest fixed prison sentence imposed on a woman in the United Kingdom was 20 years for Mrs. Lona Teresa Cohen (*née* Petra, 1913), *alias* Helen Joyce Kroger, for conspiring to commit a breach of Section 1 of the Official Secrets Act, 1911. The sentence was passed at the Old Bailey, London, on 22 March 1961. She had conspired with her husband to transmit to Moscow United Kingdom defence data collected by Col. Konon Trofimovich Molody, *alias* Gordon Arnold Lonsdale (1924–70), of the U.S.S.R. Committee of State Security (*Komitet Gosudarstvennoi Besopasnosty* or K.G.B.). A remission of sentence was announced by the Foreign Secretary on 24 July 1969.

Mrs. Carol Hanson (*née* King) (b. Ramsgate, Kent, 1946) was sentenced at Hertfordshire Assizes on 10 July 1970 to life imprisonment with a recommendation she should serve at least 20 years for her part in the murder by stabbing of 10-year-old Christine Beck on 16 March 1970.

Recipient of the longest prison sentence for a woman—Mrs. Carol Ann Hanson

Broadmoor The longest period for which any person has been detained in the Broadmoor hospital for the criminally insane, near Crowthorne, Berkshire, is 76 years in the case of William Giles. He was admitted as an insane arsonist at the age of 11 and died there on 10 March 1962, at the age of 87.

Oldest prisoner The oldest known prisoner in the United States is John Weber, 95, at the Chillicothe Correctional Institute, Ohio who began his 44th year in prison on 29 Oct. 1970.

Greatest mass arrest The greatest mass arrest in the United Kingdom occurred on 17 Sept. 1961, when 1,314 demonstrators supporting the unilateral nuclear disarmament of the United Kingdom were arrested for wilfully disregarding the directions of the police and thereby obstructing highways leading to Parliament Square, London, by sitting down.

Lynching The worst year in the 20th century for lynchings in the United States has been 1901, with 130 lynchings (105 Negroes, 25 Whites), while the first year with no reported cases was 1952.

The last lynching recorded in Britain was that of Panglam Godolan, a Pakistani and a suspected murderer, in London on 27 Oct. 1958. The last case previous to this was of a kidnapping suspect in Glasgow in 1922.

LONGEST PRISON ESCAPES

The longest recorded escape from prison was that of Leonard T. Fristoe, 77, who escaped from Nevada State Prison, U.S.A., on 15 Dec. 1923 and was turned in by his son on 15 Nov. 1969 at Compton, California. He had had 46 years of freedom under the name Claude R. Willis. He had killed two sheriff's deputies in 1920.

The longest period of freedom achieved by a British gaol breaker is more than 15½ years by Irish-born John Patrick Hannan, who escaped from Verne Open Prison at Portland, Dorset, on 22 Dec. 1955 and was still at large in May 1971. He had served only 1 month of a 21-month term for car-stealing and assaulting two policemen.

Broadmoor The longest escape from Broadmoor was one of 39 years by the Liverpool wife murderer James Kelly, who got away on 28 Jan. 1888, using a pass key made from a corset spring. After an adventurous life in Paris, in New York and at sea he returned in April 1927, to ask for re-admission. After some difficulties this was arranged. He died in 1930.

Greatest gaol break The greatest gaol break in Britain was that from Wandsworth, South London, on 24 June 1961. Eleven men got away, of whom one was immediately recaptured with a broken leg. The other ten were all rounded up within a few days.

ROBBERY

Greatest The greatest robbery on record was that of the Reichbank's reserves by a combine of U.S. military personnel and Germans. Gold bars, 728 in number, valued at £3,518,334 were removed from a caché on Klausenkopf mountainside, near Einsiedel, Bavaria on 7 June 1945 together with six sacks of bank notes of 404,840 U.S. dollars and £405 (possibly forged) from a garden in Oberaer. The book *Gold Is Where You Hide It* by W. Stanley Moss (Andre Deutsch, 1956) named the Town Major of Garmisch-Partenkirkan Capt. Robert Mackenzie, *alias* Ben F. Harpman of the Third U.S. Army and the local military governor Captain (later Major) Martin Borg as the instigators. Mackenzie was reputedly sentenced to 10 years after an F.B.I. investigation but Borg vanished from Vitznau, Switzerland on 30 March 1946. In the same area, in which 6 apparently associated murders occurred, 630 cubes of uranium and six boxes of platinum bars and precious stones and 34 forging plates also disappeared. (See, however, Industrial Espionage, page 205.)

Embezzlement In 1959 the Venezuelan Government asked the United States Government for the extradition of Col. Marcos Pérez Jiménez to face charges of embezzling more than $13,000,000 (about £4,600,000) in Government funds during his Presidency. He had been President of Venezuela from 3 Dec. 1952 until being deposed on 23 Jan. 1958, after which he fled the country and went to live in Miami, Florida, where he was finally turned over to the Venezuelan authorities on 16 Aug. 1963 and flown to Venezuela. His fortune has been estimated at $700,000,000 (£250 million).

Bank On 23 March 1962, 150 *plastiqueurs* of the *Organisation de l'Armée Secrète* (O.A.S.) removed by force 23,500,000 francs (£1,703,000) from the Banque d'Algérie in Oran, Algeria, after the collapse of civil order.

The biggest "inside job" was that at the National City Bank of New York, from which the Assistant Manager, Richard Crowe, removed $883,660 (£315,593). He was arrested on 11 April 1949. On 23 Oct. 1969 it was disclosed that $13,193,000 (£5,497,000) of U.S. Treasury bills were inexplicably missing from the Morgan Trust, Wall Street, New York City, U.S.A.

Train The greatest recorded train robbery occurred between about 3.10 a.m. and 3.45 a.m. on 8 Aug. 1963, when a General Post Office mail train from Glasgow, Scotland, was ambushed between Sears Crossing and Bridego Bridge at Mentmore, near Cheddington, Buckinghamshire. The gang escaped with about 120 mailbags containing £2,595,998 worth of bank notes being taken to London for pulping. Only £343,448 had been recovered by 9 Dec. 1966.

The only uncaptured member of the Great Train Robbers gang —Ronald Biggs

Art The greatest recorded art robbery was the theft of eight paintings, valued at £1,500,000, taken during the night of 30–31 Dec. 1966 from the Dulwich College Picture Gallery in London. The haul included three paintings by Peter Paul Rubens (1577–1640), one by Adam Ehlsheimer (1578–1610), three by Rembrandt van Rijn (1606–69) and one by Gerard Dou (1613–75). Three of the paintings were recovered on 2 Jan. 1967 and the remaining five on 4 Jan. 1967.

Jewels The greatest recorded theft of gem stones occurred on 13 Nov. 1969 in Freetown, Sierra Leone, when an armed gang stole diamonds belonging to the Sierra Leone Selection Trust worth £1,500,000. The haul from Carrington & Co. Ltd. of Regent Street, London, on 21 Nov. 1965 was estimated to be £500,000.

Coins The largest numismatic robbery ever made was in the home of Willis H. Du Pont at Coconut Grove, Miami, Florida on 5 Oct. 1967 when $1,500,000's (£625,000) worth of Russian and United States material were removed by five men.

Industrial espionage It has been alleged that about 1966 a division of the American Cyanamid Company lost some papers and vials of micro-organisms through industrial espionage, allegedly organized from Italy, which data had cost them $24,000,000 (then £8·57 million) in research and development. It is arguable that this represents the greatest robbery of all-time.

Greatest kidnapping ransom The greatest ransom ever extracted in a kidnapping case was $600,000 (£214,285), obtained by Carl Austin Hall and Mrs. Bonny Brown Heady for the release of Robert C. Greenlease, Jr., aged 6, who was kidnapped on 28 Sept. 1953 and found dead nine days later. Both kidnappers were executed on 18 Dec. 1953 at Missouri State Prison, Jefferson City, Missouri, U.S.A. Of the ransom money, $301,690 (£107,746) is still missing.

The greatest amount paid for the return of a live child is $250,000 (£89,285) by Herbert King, President of the Gibraltar Finance Corporation of Beverly Hills, California, for the return of his son Kenneth, aged 11, in April 1967. On 13 Oct. 1968 it was reported that a ransom equivalent to £1,250,000 was being demanded by some Sardinian bandits for the return of Giuseppe (Peppino) Ticca, aged 69.

Largest narcotics haul The largest recorded haul of narcotics was made by police in Hong Kong on 7 Feb. 1965, when they seized almost 4,000 lb. of opium and morphine which had been smuggled into Hong Kong aboard a British ship from Bangkok, Thailand. Such an amount would produce about 830 lb. of pure heroin, now marketable at $75,000,000 (£31,250,000). On 5 June 1971 the Spanish police seized £17 million worth of heroin, which was believed to be part of a half-ton consignment worth £40,000,000 dispersed by smugglers in Western Europe.

Greatest bigamists It has been recorded that Mrs. Theresa Vaughan (or Vaughn), aged 24, while on trial in Sheffield, Yorkshire, on 19 Dec. 1922, confessed to 61 bigamous marriages within five years. No confirmation of this case is obtainable from local police records. A male record of 72 has been claimed.

Largest court The largest judicial building in the world is the Johannesburg Central Magistrates' Court, opened in 1941 at the junction of Fox and West Streets, Johannesburg, South Africa. There are 42 court-rooms (8 civil and 34 criminal), with a further seven criminal court-rooms under construction. The court has a panel of 70 magistrates and deals with an average of 2,500 criminal cases every week, excluding petty cases in which guilt has been admitted in writing.

Penal camps The largest penal camp systems in the world were those near Karaganda and Kolyma, in the U.S.S.R., each with a population estimated in 1958 at between 1,200,000 and 1,500,000. The official N.A.T.O. estimate for all Soviet camps was "more than one million" in March 1960. It was estimated in 1966 that the total population of penal camps in China was about 10,000,000.

Devil's Island The largest French penal settlement was that of St. Laurent du Maroni, which comprised the notorious Îles du Diable, Royale and St. Joseph (for incorrigibles) off the coast of French Guiana, in South America. It remained in operation for 99 years from 1854 until the last group of repatriated prisoners, including Théodore Rouselle, who had served 50 years, was returned to Bordeaux on 22 Aug. 1953. It has been estimated that barely 2,000 *bagnard* (ex-convicts) of the 70,000 deportees ever returned. These, however, include the executioner Ladurelle (imprisoned 1921–37), who was murdered in Paris in 1938.

PRISONS

Largest *World* The largest prison in the world is Kharkov Prison, in the U.S.S.R., which has at times accommodated 40,000 prisoners.

British Isles The largest prison in the United Kingdom is Wormwood Scrubs, West London, with 1,240 cells. The highest prison walls in Great Britain are those of Leicester Prison, measuring 30 feet high.

The largest prison in Scotland is Barlinnie, near Glasgow, with 962 single cells. Ireland's largest prison is Mountjoy Prison, Dublin, with 808 cells.

Smallest The smallest prison in the world is usually cited as that on the island of Sark, in the Channel Islands, which has a capacity of two. In fact the prison on Herm, a neighbouring island, is smaller, with a diameter of 13 feet 6 inches, and must rank with the single person lock-ups such as that at Shenley, Hertfordshire. The smallest prison in England is Oxford Prison (also the oldest, built in *c.* 1640), with 120 cells. The smallest in Scotland is Penninghame Open Prison, Wigtownshire with accommodation for 63. Ireland's smallest prison is that at Sligo, with 100 cells.

Highest population The highest prison population, including Borstals and detention centres, for England and Wales was the figure for 30 April 1971 of 40,352. In Scotland the average prison population was 4,834 and in Northern Ireland 721 in 1969.

Most secure prison After it became a maximum security Federal prison in 1934, no convict was known to have lived to tell of a successful escape from the prison on Alcatraz ("Pelican") Island in San Francisco Bay, California, U.S.A. A total of 23 men attempted it but 12 were recaptured, 5 shot dead, one drowned and 5 presumed drowned. On 16 Dec. 1962, three months before the prison was closed, one man reached the mainland alive, only to be recaptured on the spot.

Largest bribe An alleged bribe of £30,000,000 offered to Shaikh Zaid ibn Sultan of Abu Dhabi, Trucial Oman, by a Saudi Arabian official in August 1955, is the highest on record. The affair concerned oil concessions in the disputed territory of Buraimi on the Persian Gulf.

Greatest forgery The greatest recorded forgery was the German Third Reich government's forging operation, code name "Bernhard", engineered by Herr Naujocks in 1940–41. It involved £150,000,000's worth of £5 notes.

Greatest swindle The greatest swindle ever perpetrated in commercial history was that of Antonio (Tino) De Angelis (born 1915), a 5 ft. 5 in. 290 lb. ex-hog-cutter from New York City, U.S.A. His Allied Crude Vegetable Oil Refining Corporation (formed 19 Nov. 1955) operated from an uncarpeted office adjoining a converted tank farm in Bayonne, New Jersey. The tanks were rigged with false dipping compartments and were interconnected such that sea water could be pumped to substitute for phantom salad oil which served as collateral for warehouse receipts. A deficiency of 927,000 short tons of oil valued at $175,000,000 (then £62·5 million) was discovered.

Passing bad cheques The record for passing bad cheques was set by Frederick Emerson Peters (1886–1959), who, by dint of some 200 impersonations, netted $250,000 (£89,300) with 28,000 bad cheques. Among his many philanthropies was a silver chalice presented to a cathedral in Washington, D.C., U.S.A., also paid for with a bad cheque.

FINES

A fine equivalent to £9·83 million was imposed on Juan Vila Reyes, president of the Barcelona textile machinery manufacturer Matesa, by the Currency Crime Court, Madrid, Spain on 19 May 1970 for converting export development funds to his own use.

Heaviest The heaviest fine ever imposed in the United Kingdom was one of £277,500, plus £3,717 costs, on I. Hennig & Co. Ltd., the London diamond merchants, at Clerkenwell Magistrates' Court, London, on 14 Dec. 1949. The amount was later reduced on appeal.

Smallest The smallest recorded fine in Britain was one penny, imposed on Philip Cathie of Hove, Sussex, at Marlborough Street, London, on 19 April 1960, for reversing in a Soho one-way street to allow a taxi to pass. On 23 Feb. 1962, the same stipendiary fined George Shrimpton and Hamish Smith one penny for moving a locked car owned by a woman.

Rarest prosecution There are a number of crimes in English law for which there have never been prosecutions. Among unique prosecutions are *Rex v. Crook* in 1662 for praemunire and *Rex v. Gregory* for selling honours under the Honours (Prevention of Abuses) Act, 1924, in 1933. Maundy Gregory (d. 1941) was the honours broker of Lloyd George's 1919–20 Coalition Government.

Maundy Gregory, the defendant in the rarest of prosecutions in 1933

It is a specific offence on Pitcairn Island in the Pacific to shout "Sail Ho!" when no vessel is in sight. The fine is 25p, which can be commuted to one day's labour on the public roads (there are no cars) or making an oar for the public boat.

6. ECONOMIC

MONETARY AND FINANCE

Largest budget *World* The greatest annual expenditure budgeted by any country has been $229,200 million (£95,500 million) by the United States government for the fiscal year ending 30 June 1972.

The highest budgeted revenue in the United States has been $217,600 million (£90,666 million) in 1971–72. The estimated revenue receipts of the U.S.S.R. Government in 1969 were 139,000 million roubles (*officially* equivalent to $148,800 million or £62,000 million).

In the United States, the greatest surplus was $8,419,469,844 (then £2,104 million) in 1947–48, and the greatest deficit was $57,420,430,365 (then £1,935 million) in 1942–43.

United Kingdom The greatest annual budgeted expenditure of the United Kingdom was £18,833 million for the fiscal year 1971–72. The highest budgeted current revenue has been £23,401 million in 1971–72.

The greatest annual surplus achieved was £4,610,000,000 in 1970–71 and the greatest deficit was £2,825 million in 1944–45.

Foreign aid The total net foreign aid given by the United States government between 1 July 1945 and 31 Dec. 1969 was $121,181 million (£50,492 million), of which $4,117 million has gone into Vietnam, Cambodia and Laos. The country which received most U.S. aid in 1969 was India, with $458, 000,000 (£190·8 million). U.S. foreign aid began with $50,000 to Venezuela for earthquake relief in 1812.

TAXATION

Most taxed The major national economy with the highest rate of taxation (central and local taxes, plus social security contribution) is that of Sweden, with 46·6 per cent. of her Gross National Product in 1967. The lowest proportion for any advanced national economy in 1967 was 20·3 per cent. in Japan, which also enjoys the highest economic growth rate. The comparable figure for the United Kingdom in 1967 was 37·7 per cent. but more than 41·0 per cent. in 1969.

Least taxed There is no income tax paid by residents on Lundy Island off North Devon, England.

Highest surtax The country with the most confiscatory marginal rate of income tax is Burma, where the rate is 99 per cent. for annual incomes exceeding 300,000 kyats (pronounced chuts) (£22,540). In November 1969 Premier Ne Win proclaimed "the way of true Socialism—the Burmese way". The second highest marginal rate was in the United Kingdom, where the topmost surtax level was 97·5 per cent. in 1950–51 and 96·25 per cent. in 1965–66. In 1967–68 a "special charge" of up to 9s. (45p) in the £ additional to surtax brought the top rate to 27s. 3d. (136p) in the £. In 1971 the top rate was reduced to 75·4 per cent. A married man with two children earning £5,000 per year in 1938 would, in March 1970, have to have earned nearly £75,000 to have enjoyed the same standard of living.

In volume, as opposed to *per caput*, the most taxed country is the United States, where the total of individual income taxes collected in the year ended 30 June 1969 was $97,440,405,000 (£40,600 million), compared with total personal income of $748,874 million (£312,030 million) in the year to mid-1969.

Highest and lowest rates in United Kingdom

Income tax was introduced in Great Britain in 1799 at the standard rate of 2s. (10p) in the £. It was discontinued in 1815, only to be re-introduced in 1842 at the rate of 7d. (3p) in the £. It was at its lowest at 2d. (0·83p) in the £ in 1875, gradually climbing to 1s. 3d. (6p) by 1913. From April 1941 until 1946 the record peak of 10s. (50p) in the £ was maintained to assist in the financing of World War II. Death Duties (introduced in 1894) on millionaire estates began at 8 per cent. (1894–1907) and were raised to a peak of 80 per cent. by 1949.

NATIONAL DEBT

The largest national debt of any country in the world is that of the United States, where the gross federal public debt of the Federal Government will reach its peak figure of $429,400,000,000 (£178,916 million), equivalent to $1,834 (£764) per person, in the fiscal year 1971–72. This amount in dollar bills would make a pile 25,421 miles high, weighing 356,150 tons.

The United Kingdom National Debt, which became a permanent feature of Britain's economy as early as 1692, was £33,079 million, or £592 per person, at 31 March 1971. This amount placed in a pile of brand new £1 notes would be 2,032·5 miles in height.

Gross National Product

The estimated world aggregate of Gross National Products in 1968 exceeded £800,000 million. The country with the largest Gross National Product is the United States, with $976,500 million (£406,875 million) for 1970. The long awaited "Trillion Dollars" should be attained in 1971. The estimated G.N.P. of the United Kingdom was £42,667 million in 1970.

National wealth

The richest large nation, measured by real Gross National Product per head, has been the U.S.A. since about 1910. The average share G.N.P. in the U.S.A. was $4,700 (£1,958) in 1970. It has been estimated that the value of all physical assets in the U.S.A. in 1966 was $2,460,000,000,000 or $12,443 (£5,184) per head. The comparative figure for the United Kingdom was £85,423 million at 31 Dec. 1961 (latest available data).

National Savings

The highest total of National Savings recorded in a year was £573,549,000 (net receipts) in 1945–46. The highest net receipts in a week were £42,423,000 for the week ending 11 May 1946. The total amount invested was £8,750,300,000 as at 31 March 1971. The greatest withdrawals in a week were £21,208,000 (including interest) in the week ending 23 Dec. 1967. Mr. Arthur Ellis of Saltergate, Chesterfield between 1958 and 1970 has won one £250, two £100 and 39 £25 premium bond draw prizes. All his winnings are donated to the local parish church.

GOLD RESERVES

The country with the greatest monetary gold reserve is the United States, whose Treasury had $11,039 million (£4,599 million) on hand on 1 March 1971. The United States Bullion Depository at Fort Knox, 30 miles south-west of Louisville, Kentucky, U.S.A. is the principal depository. Gold is stored in standard mint bars of 400 troy ounces (439 oz. avoirdupois), measuring 7 inches by $3\frac{5}{8}$ inches by $1\frac{5}{8}$ inches, and each worth $14,000 (£5,833).

The greatest accumulation of gold in the world is now in the Federal Reserve Bank at 33 Liberty Street, New York City, N.Y., U.S.A. The bank has admitted to having had gold valued at $13,000 million (£5,416 million) owned by foreign central banks and stored 85 feet below street level, in a vault 50 feet by 100 feet behind a steel door weighing 89 tons.

United Kingdom

The highest published figure for the sterling area's gold and convertible currency reserves was $4,190 million (then £860 million) on 31 Aug. 1938, and the lowest of recent times $298,000,000 (then £74 million) on 31 Dec. 1940. The figure was £1,425 million ($3,420 million) at 1 May 1970.

BANK RATE

In 1971 the highest bank rate in the world was that of South Korea at 26 per cent. and the lowest that of Portugal at $2\frac{3}{4}$ per cent. The lowest that the Bank of England bank rate has ever been is 2 per cent., first from 22 April 1852 to 6 Jan. 1853. The highest ever figure was 10 per cent., first on 9 Nov. 1857, and most recently on 6 Aug. 1914. The highest yearly average was 7·35 per cent. in 1864 (6 per cent. to 9 per cent.). The longest period without a change was the 12 years 13 days from 26 Oct. 1939 to 7 Nov. 1951, during which time the rate stayed at 2 per cent.

PAPER MONEY

Paper money is an invention of the Chinese and, although the date of 119 B.C. has been suggested, the innovation is believed to date from the T'ang dynasty of the 7th century A.D. The world's earliest bank notes were issued by the Stockholms Banco, Sweden, in July 1661. The oldest surviving note is one for 5 dalers dated 6 Dec. 1662. The oldest surviving printed Bank of England note is one for £555 to bearer, dated 19 Dec. 1699 ($4\frac{1}{2} \times 7\frac{3}{4}$ inches).

Largest and smallest notes

The largest paper money ever issued was the one kwan note of the Chinese Ming dynasty issue of 1368–99, which measured 9 inches by 13 inches. The smallest bank note ever issued was the 5 cent. note of the Chekiang Provincial Bank (established 1908) in China. It measured 55 millimetres (2·16 inches) by 30 millimetres (1·18 inches).

Highest denominations *World*

The highest denomination of paper currency ever authorized in the world are United States gold certificates for $100,000 (£41,666), bearing the head of former President Thomas Woodrow Wilson (1856–1924), issued by the U.S. Treasury in 1934. There also exists in the U.S. Bureau of Engraving and Printing an example of a U.S. Treasury note for $500,000,000 bearing interest coupons for $15,625 each 6 months for 14 years at $6\frac{1}{4}$ per cent.

The world's highest denomination note in circulation—the U.S. $10,000 bill

The highest denomination notes in circulation are U.S. Federal Reserve Bank notes for $10,000 (£4,166). They bear the head of Salmon Portland Chase (1808–73). None has been printed since July 1944 and their circulation fell from 4,600 at 31 Dec. 1941 to only 394 at 30 June 1967 but rose to 1,900 by March 1969. On 15 July 1969 the U.S. Treasury announced that no further notes higher than $100 would be issued. By June 1971 only 400 were in circulation.

United Kingdom

Two Bank of England notes for £1,000,000 still exist, dated before 1812, but these were used only for internal accounting. Facsimile million pound notes were reproduced by J. Arthur Rank Productions Ltd. to publicize their film *The Million Pound Note* made in 1954. These were dated 20 June 1903. The highest issued denominations were £1,000 notes, first printed in 1725, discontinued in 1943 and withdrawn on 30 April 1945. A total of 63 of these notes were still unaccounted for up to

Britain's highest denomination note—a Scottish £100 note

July 1968 after which no data has been issued by the Bank.

The highest denomination notes currently issued by the Bank of England are those for £20 (reintroduced 8 July 1970), but Scottish banks issue notes up to £100 denomination. The rarest Bank of England notes of low denomination are the 10 shilling notes signed by Cyril Patrick Mahon, who was in office for only 4 months from their issue on 22 Nov. 1928 to 26 March 1929.

The lowest ever denomination Bank of England note was for a penny, dated 10 Jan. 1828, which was adapted from a £5 note and doubtless used to adjust an overnight difference. In 1868 it was purchased by the Bank for £1 from the landlord of the "Blue Last", Bell Alley, in the City of London.

Most expensive The highest price paid for a note no longer valid currency is believed to be $3,600 (£1,500), paid in 1900 for the first Ming note (see page 207) ever found. About £2,500 was paid for a £1,000 note of 1933 in London in 1970.

Highest circulation The highest ever Bank of England note circulation in the United Kingdom was £3,695,000,000 on 14 April 1971—equivalent to a pile of £1 notes 220·7 miles high.

DEVALUATION

Devaluation was practised by Emperor Nero of Rome (A.D. 54–68), who debased his coinage. Since 1945, 112 of the world's 120 currencies have devalued including the pound twice, the rouble 3 times and the Chilean currency 46 times (since 1 Jan. 1949). The U.S. dollar has only once been devalued vis-à-vis gold (in 1934).

WORST INFLATION

The world's worst inflation occurred in Hungary in June 1946, when the 1931 gold pengö was valued at 130 trillion ($1·3 \times 10^{20}$) paper pengös. Notes were issued for szazmillio billion (100 trillion or 10^{20}) pengös. Currently the worst inflation is in Brazil, where the cruzeiro depreciated 42 times, in terms of the United States dollar, between 1 Feb. 1957 (64·80 per $) and March 1967 (2,720 per $). A new cruzeiro, equivalent to 1,000 old cruzeiros, was introduced on 8 Feb. 1967. In 1966–67 there was a further 21·2 per cent. inflation.

CHEQUES

Largest *World* The greatest amount paid by a single cheque in the history of banking was $960,242,000·00 (£342,943,571), paid on 31 Jan. 1961 by the Continental Illinois National Bank and Trust Company of Chicago, Illinois, U.S.A. This bank headed a group which bought the accounts receivable of Sears, Roebuck & Co., to whom the cheque was paid.

United Kingdom The largest cheque drawn in Britain was one for £119,595,645, drawn on 24 Jan. 1961 by Lazard Brothers & Co. Ltd. and payable to the National Provincial Bank, in connection with the takeover of the British Ford Motor Company. The rate of cheque clearing was, by May 1971, 1,100,000,000 per annum.

Oldest The oldest surviving English cheque is one drawn on 14 March 1664.

COINS

Oldest *World* The earliest certainly dated coins are the electrum (alloy of gold and silver) staters of Lydia, in Asia Minor (now Turkey), which were coined in the reign of King Gyges (*c.* 685–652 B.C.). Primitive uninscribed "spade" money of the Chou dynasty of China is now *believed* to date from *c.* 770 B.C. Countries without any coins are Paraguay, Laos and Indonesia.

British The earliest coins to circulate in Britain were Gallo-Belgic gold imitations of the Macedonian staters of Philip II (359–336 B.C.). The Bellovaci type has been tentatively dated *c.* 130 B.C. The earliest date attributed to coins minted in Britain is *c.* 95 B.C. for the Westerham type gold stater.

Heaviest The Swedish copper 10 daler coins of 1659 attained a weight of up to 43½ lb. Of primitive exchange tokens, the most massive are the holed stone discs, or *Fé*, from the Yap Islands, in the western Pacific Ocean, with diameters of up to 12 feet. A medium-sized one was worth one Yapese wife or an 18-foot canoe.

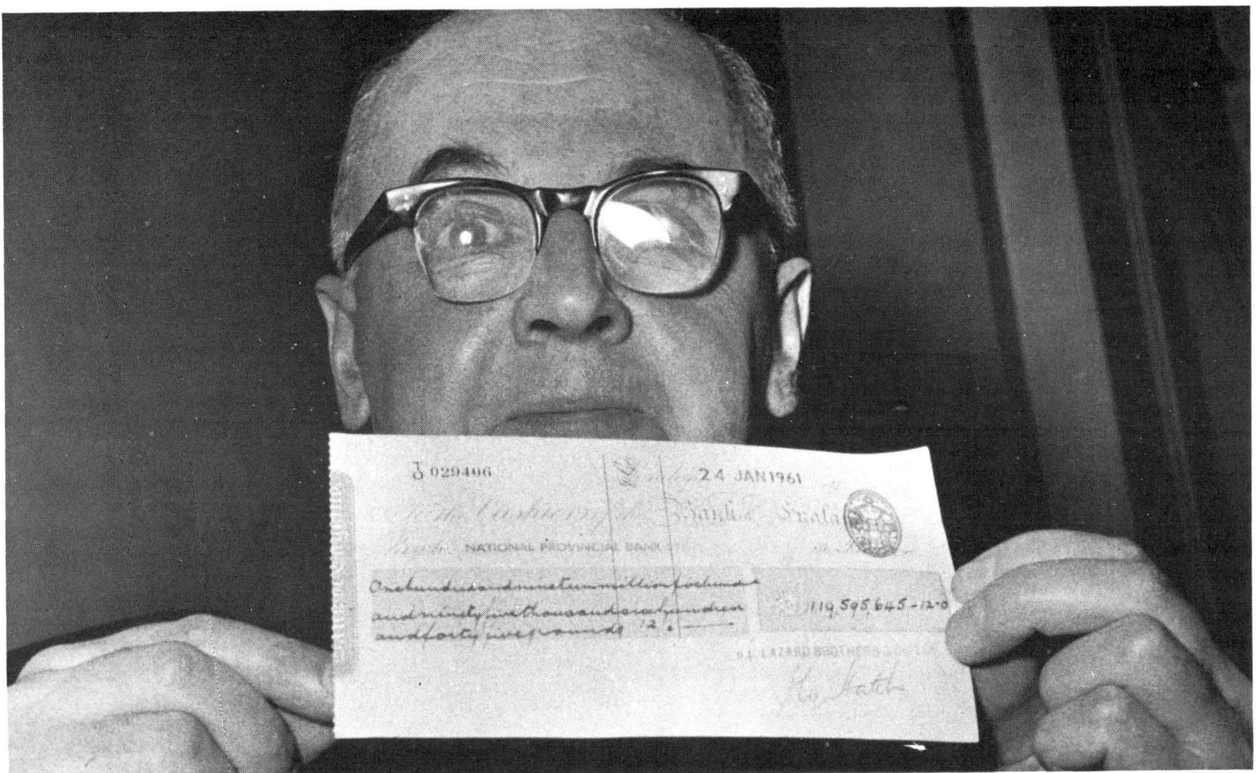

A cheque 250 times bigger than that ever received by a pools winner —one for £119,595,645

Smallest The smallest coins in the world were the gold "pin-head" coins used in Colpata, southern India, in *c.* 1800, which weighed as little as one grain, or 480 to the troy ounce.

Highest enomination *World* The 1654 Indian gold 200 mohur (£500) coin of the Mughal Emperor Khurram Shihāb-ud-dīn Muhammad, Shāh Jahān (reigned 1628–57), is both the highest denomination coin and that of the greatest intrinsic worth ever struck. It weighed 33,600 grains (70 troy oz.) and hence has an intrinsic worth of £875. It had a diameter of $5\frac{3}{8}$ inches. The only known example disappeared in Patna, Bihar, India, in *c.* 1820, but a plaster-cast of this coin exists in the British Museum, London.

British Gold five-guinea pieces were minted from the reign of Charles II (1660–1685) until 1753 in the reign of George II. A pattern 5 guinea piece of George III dated 1777 also exists.

Lowest enomination *World* The 1 aurar piece of Iceland, had a face value of 0·0114 of a penny in 1971. Quarter farthings (sixteen to the penny) were struck in copper at the Royal Mint, London, in the Imperial coinage for use in Ceylon, in 1839 and 1851–53. The lowest denomination gold coins ever struck are the Kruger gold 3d. pieces struck in South Africa at the behest of Mr. Solly Marks. One is dated 1894 and 215 are dated 1898. They are now worth £250 each.

Rarest *British* During the period 1526–44 several new coins were introduced, among them the George noble (third of a £) and its half. Only a single specimen of the half George noble is known to exist. A unique half sovereign of Edward VI was sold for £620 in October 1956.

Bronze coinage was introduced in Queen Victoria's reign in 1860. There are known to be single examples extant of an Edward VIII 1937 penny, halfpenny and farthing. There is only a single specimen of a penny dated 1954 in private hands. Its insurance value was put at £15,000 by its owners. It was reported on 12 July 1967 that a unique half-crown dated 1952, bearing the head of George VI, had been found by Mr. Horace Burrows of London. It was sold for £1,700 on 7 Sept. 1967 but a second specimen was reported in January 1968. Only two specimens are also known of the English shilling dated 1952.

Most expensive *World* The highest price paid in auction for a single coin is $77,500 (£32,292) for a U.S. 1804 silver dollar, struck in 1834 (*sic*) of which only seven exist, at Stack's of New York City on 23 Oct. 1970. It was sold by the Massachusetts Historical Society and bought by an anonymous collector. This specimen was spotted by Henry C. Young, a teller, in the ordinary course of his work in the Bank of Pennsylvania in 1850. The two U.S. gold $50 pieces of 1877 in the Smithsonian Institution, Washington, D.C., have been valued at $100,000 (£41,666) each as have the seven surviving examples of the U.S. Brasher Doubloon of 1787. Among the many unique coins that which would attract logically the greatest price on the market would be the unique 1873 dime (U.S. 10 cent piece) with the CC mint mark, since dimes are the most avidly collected series of any coins in the world.

One of the U.S. $50 gold pieces held in Washington, D.C.

H.M. The Queen distributing the lowest denomination coin at the annual Maundy ceremony

British The highest auction price paid for an English coin is £10,500 paid by the London dealer Spink at the salerooms of Messrs. Glendining and Co. on 17 Oct. 1968 for a gold Edward IV London Noble of the Heavy Coinage period (1461–1464). This coin, together with 85 others, was part of the Fishpool Hoard discovered on 22 March 1966. The coins were sold by Mr. Bernard Beeton, a retired lorry driver, one of the 6 people accredited with the discovery, and one of only two who wisely complied with the law in relation to Treasure Trove. The coins fetched a total of £85,000, about one-sixth of the value of the entire hoard (see Treasure Trove).

Legal tender coins *Oldest* The oldest legal tender Imperial coins in circulation are the now rare silver shillings and sixpences of the reign of George III, dated 1816. All gold coinage of or above the least current weight dated onward from 1838 is still legal tender.

Heaviest and highest denomination The gold five-pound (£5) piece or quintuple sovereign is both the highest current denomination coin in the United Kingdom and also, at 616·37 grains (1·4066 oz.), the heaviest. The most recent specimens available to the public are dated 1937, of which only 5,501 were minted. The rarest are the six surviving pattern pieces of William IV, dated 1831, of which an example was sold by private treaty for £4,250 in July 1966.

Lightest and smallest The silver Maundy (new) penny piece is the smallest of the British legal tender coins and, at 7·27 grains (just under 1/60th of an ounce), the lightest. These coins exist for every date since 1822 and are 0·453 of an inch in diameter.

Greatest collection It was estimated in November 1967 that the Lilly coin collection of 1,227 U.S. gold pieces now at the Smithsonian Institution, Washington, D.C., U.S.A., had a market value of $5½ million (£2,290,000). The greatest single coin collection ever amassed in Britain was that of Richard Cyril Lockett (1873–1950) of Liverpool, Lancashire. The collection realized a record of £387,457.

The greatest hoard of gold of unknown ownership ever recovered is one valued at about $3,000,000 (£1,070,000), from the lost $8,000,000 (£2,860,000) carried in 10 ships of a Spanish bullion fleet which was sunk by a hurricane off Florida, U.S.A., on 31 July 1715. The biggest single haul was by the diver Kip Wagner on 30 May 1965.

Largest Treasure Trove The largest hoard of coins ever found in the United Kingdom was the Tutbury hoard, discovered on the bed of the River Dove in Staffordshire in June 1831. It consisted of about 20,000 silver coins of Edward I and Edward II and some of Henry III. The chest is believed to have been deposited in *c.* 1324–25. The most valuable hoard ever found was one of more than 1,200 gold coins from the reigns of King Richard II to Edward IV, worth more than £500,000, found on 22 March 1966 by John Craughwell, aged 47, at Fishpool, near Mansfield, Nottinghamshire.

Largest mint The largest mint in the world is the U.S. Treasury's mint built in 1965–69 on Independence Mall, Philadelphia, covering 500,000 square feet with an annual capacity on a 3 shift seven day a week production of 8,000 million coins. A single stamping machine can produce coins at a rate of 10,000 per minute.

Greatest hoarders It was estimated in November 1968 that about $22,500 million (£9,375 million) worth of gold is being retained in personal possession throughout the world and that $4,800 million (£2,000 million) of this total is held by the population of France.

Largest pile The tallest column of pennies on record was one 11 feet 10 inches tall containing some 99,600 coins (worth £415)

collected for Muscular Dystrophy at the A.B.C. Bowl, North Harrow, London. The pile was pulled over on 27 Feb. 1970. Lower pyramids but of 145,080 pennies (£604 10s.), collected by the licensee Mr. Frank Steele, were "knocked down" in the Coffee House Hotel, Wavertree, Liverpool, for the Royal Wavertree School for Blind Children in January 1969.

Mile of pennies A mile of old pennies (52,800 or 436 more than mathematically necessary) were laid in Victoria Park by boys and girls of Clark's College, Finchley, North London on 16 July 1970.

TRADE UNIONS

Largest *World* The world's largest union is the Industrie-Gewerkschaft Metall (Metal Workers' Union) of West Germany, with a membership of 2,070,000 at 1 Jan. 1970. The union with the longest name is probably the F.N.O.M. M.C.F.E.T.M.F., the National Federation of Officers, Machinists, Motormen, Drivers, Firemen and Electricians in Sea and River Transportation of Brazil.

Britain The largest trade union in the United Kingdom is the Transport and General Workers' Union, with 1,638,686 members at 1 Jan. 1971.

Oldest The oldest of the 150 trade unions affiliated to the Trade Union Congress (founded 1868) is the National Society of Brushmakers (current membership 2,700) founded in 1747.

Smallest The smallest union is the Sheffield Wool Shear Workers' Trade Union with a membership of 25.

LABOUR DISPUTES

Largest The highest total of stoppages due to industrial disputes occurring in any year was 3,888 (plus 37 from 1969) in 1970. The disputes involved about 1,784,000 people and a total of 10,970,000 working days were lost. The total of working days lost in 1920 was 26,500,000. The British average of 294 days lost per 1,000 persons employed in the 5 years 1965–69 compares with extremes of 1,574 in Italy, 1,556 in Canada and 4 in Sweden.

The most serious single labour dispute in the United Kingdom was the General Strike of 4–12 May 1926, called by the Trades Union Congress in support of the Miners' Federation. During the nine days of the strike 1,580,000 people were involved and 14,500,000 working days were lost.

During the year 1926 a total of 2,750,000 people were involved in 323 different labour disputes and the working days lost during the year amounted to 162,300,000, the highest figure ever recorded.

Longest The world's longest recorded strike ended on 4 Jan. 1961, after 33 years. It concerned the employment of barbers' assistants in Copenhagen, Denmark. The longest recorded major strike was that at the plumbing fixtures factory of the Kohler Co. in Sheboygan, Wisconsin, U.S.A., between April 1954 and October 1962. The strike is alleged to have cost the United Automobile Workers' Union about $12,000,000 (£4·3 million) to sustain.

UNEMPLOYMENT

Highest The highest recorded unemployment in Great Britain was on 23 Jan. 1933, when the total of unemployed persons on the Employment Exchange registers was 2,903,065, representing 22·8 per cent. of the insured working population. The highest figure for Wales was 244,579 (39·1 per cent.) on 22 Aug. 1932.

Lowest The lowest recorded peace-time level of unemployment was 0·9 per cent. on 11 July 1955, when 184,929 persons were registered. The peak figure for the total working population in the United Kingdom has been 26,290,000 in September 1966. The figure for June 1970 was 25,637,000.

Largest association The largest single association in the world is the Blue Cross, the U.S.-based medical insurance organization with a membership at 1 Jan. 1970 of 76,177,236. Benefits paid out exceeded $4·39 billion (£1,829 million). The largest association in the United Kingdom is the Automobile Association, with a membership of 4,233,718 on 1 Jan. 1971.

FOOD CONSUMPTION

Calories Of all countries in the world, based on the latest available data, Ireland has the largest available total of calories per person. The net supply averaged 3,460 per day in 1967. The United Kingdom average was 3,160 per day in 1967–68. The highest calorific value of any foodstuff is that of pure animal fat, with 930 calories per 100 grammes (3·5 oz.). Pure alcohol provides 710 calories per 100 grammes.

Protein New Zealand has the highest recorded consumption of protein per person, an average of 107 grammes (3·76 oz.) per day in 1967. The United Kingdom average was 88 grammes (3·10 oz.) per day in 1967–68.

The lowest *reported* figures are 1,780 calories per day in Somalia in 1961–63 and 37 grammes (1·30 oz.) of protein per day in Gabon in 1963–65.

Cereals The greatest consumers of cereal products—flour, milled rice, etc.—are the people of Turkey, with an average of 492 lb. per person in 1960–61. The United Kingdom average was 160·9 lb. in 1967–68 and the figure for the Republic of Ireland was 210 lb. in 1967.

Potatoes The greatest eaters of potatoes and root flour are the people of Ghana, who consumed 2·52 lb. per head per day in 1961–63. The United Kingdom average was 9·77 oz. per day in 1970. The average for Ireland was 12·48 oz. in 1967.

Sugar The greatest consumers of refined sugar are the people of Dominican Republic, with an average of 6·17 oz. per person per day in 1966. The United Kingdom average was 5·08 oz. in 1970 and the average in Ireland was 4·90 oz. in 1967.

Meat The greatest meat eaters in the world—figures include offal and poultry—are the people of Uruguay, with an average consumption of 10·93 oz. per person per day in 1966. The United Kingdom average was 5·74 oz. in 1970 and the Irish average was 7·34 oz. in 1967.

BEER

Of reporting countries, the nation with the highest beer consumption per person is West Germany, with 29·9 gallons per person in 1969. In the Northern Territory of Australia, however, the annual intake has been estimated to be as high as 52 gallons per person. A society for the prevention of alcoholism in Darwin had to disband in June 1966 for lack of support. The United Kingdom average was 21·6 gallons, or 172·8 pints, per person in 1969. The January 1970 edition of the U.S.S.R. periodical *Sotsialisticheskaya Industria* claimed that the Russians invented beer.

SPIRITS

The freest spirit drinkers are the white population of South Africa, with 1·71 gallons of proof spirit per person per year, and the most abstemious are the people of Belgium, with 2 pints per person. It was estimated in 1969 that 13 per cent. of all males between 20 and 55 years in France were suffering from alcoholism.

Largest dish The largest single dish in the world is roasted camel, prepared occasionally for Bedouin wedding feasts. Cooked eggs are stuffed in fish, the fish stuffed in cooked chickens, the chickens stuffed into a roasted sheep carcass and the sheep stuffed into a whole camel.

Most expensive food The most expensive food is white truffle of Alba which in 1969 fetched £35 per lb. in the market.

Largest cake The largest cake ever baked was a six-sided "birthday" cake weighing 25,000 lb., made in August 1962 by Van de Kemp's Holland Dutch Bakers of Seattle, Washington State, U.S.A., for the Seattle World's Fair (the "Century 21 Exposition"). The cake was 23 feet high, with a circumference of 60 feet. The ingredients included 18,000 eggs, 10,500 lb. of flour, 4,000 lb. of cane sugar, 7,000 lb. of raisins, 2,200 lb. of pecans and 100 lb. of salt.

Largest Easter egg The largest Easter egg ever made was one of 550 lb. and £120 worth of chocolate made at the Liverpool College of Crafts and Catering in March 1971.

Largest pizza pie The largest pizza ever baked was one measuring 11 feet 8 inches by 3 feet 7 inches at Cambridge, New York, U.S.A. on 9 Jan. 1971.

SPICES

Most expensive The most expensive of all spices is Mediterranean saffron (*Crocus sativus*). It takes 96,000 stigmas and therefore 32,000 flowers to make a pound, which retails for £33·60 in the United Kingdom.

"Hottest" The hottest of all spices is the capsicum hot pepper known as Tabasco, first reported in 1888 by Mr. Edmund McIlhenny on Avery Island, Louisiana, U.S.A.

Rarest condiment The world's most prized condiment is Cà Cuong, a secretion recovered in minute amounts from beetles in North Vietnam. Owing to war conditions, the price rose to $100 (now £41·60) per ounce before supplies virtually ceased.

Sweets The biggest sweet eaters in the world are the people of Britain, with 7·6 oz. of confectionery per person per week in early 1970. The figure for Scotland was more than 9 oz. in 1968.

Tea The most expensive tea marketed in the United Kingdom is "Oolong", specially imported for Fortnum and Mason of Piccadilly, London, W.1, where, in 1971, it retailed for £4·40 per lb. It is blended from very young Formosan leaves. In Britain the *per caput* consumption of tea in 1970 was 139·2 oz. followed by Ireland and Libya.

The world's largest tea company is Brooke Bond Liebig Limited (a merger of Brooke Bond Tea Ltd. of London founded 1869 and Liebig's Extract of Meat Co. Ltd. made in May 1968), with a turnover of £229,800,000 in the year ended 30 June 1970. The company has 36,799 acres of mature plantations in India, Ceylon and East Africa, and ranches in Argentina, Paraguay and Rhodesia extending over 2,686,180 acres and employs over 50,000 people.

Coffee The world's greatest coffee drinkers are the people of Sweden, who consumed 13·43 kg. (29·61 lb.) of coffee per person in 1968. This compares with 1·59 kg. (3·5 lb.) for the United Kingdom in 1969.

Oldest tinned food The oldest tinned food known was roast beef canned by Donkin, Hall and Gamble in 1823 and salvaged from H.M.S. *Fury* in the Northwest Passage, Canada. It was opened on 11 Dec. 1958.

Recipe The oldest known surviving recipe is one dated 1657 handed down from Bernice Bardolf of the Black Horse Tavern, Barnsley, Yorkshire found buried in September 1969 in the yard of the Alhambra Hotel, Barnsley. Barnsley Bardolf, a variant, is now on the menu.

Fresh water The world's greatest consumers of fresh water are the people of the United States, whose average daily consumption reached 411,200 million gallons in 1970. By 31 Dec. 1967, 40·6 per cent. was fluoridized.

ENERGY

To express the various forms of available energy (coal, liquid fuels and water power, etc., but omitting vegetable fuels and peat), it is the practice to convert them all into terms of coal. On this basis the world average consumption was the equivalent of 1,733 kg. (32·4 cwt.) of coal, or its energy equivalents, per person in 1968.

The highest consumption in the world is in the United States, with an average of 203·3 cwt. per person in 1968. The United Kingdom average was 98·5 cwt. per person. The lowest recorded average for 1968 was 15·4 lb. per person in Burundi.

MASS COMMUNICATIONS

AIRLINES

The country with the busiest airlines system is the United States, where 125,414 million revenue passenger miles were flown on scheduled domestic and regional services in 1969. This was equivalent to an annual trip of 618 miles for every one of the inhabitants of the U.S.A. The United Kingdom airlines flew 182,208,000 miles and carried 13,870,800 passengers in 1970. This is equivalent to an annual flight of 194 miles for every person in the United Kingdom.

MERCHANT SHIPPING

The world total of merchant shipping excluding vessels of less than 100 tons gross, sailing vessels and barges was 52,444 vessels of 227,489,864 tons gross on 1 July 1970. The largest merchant fleet in the world as at mid-1970 was that under the flag of Liberia with 33,296,644 tons gross. Liberian registration overtook the United Kingdom Merchant fleet of 21,716,148 tons gross in 1967. The U.K. figure for mid-1970 was 25,824,820 tons gross but the British Commonwealth was 7,369 ships of 36,276,511 tons gross.

Largest and busiest ports Physically, the largest port in the world is New York Harbor, N.Y., U.S.A. The port has a navigable waterfront of 755 miles (460 miles in New York State and 295 miles in New Jersey) stretching over 92 square miles. A total of 261 general cargo berths and 130 other piers give a total berthing capacity of 391 ships at one time. The total warehousing floor space is 18,400,000 square feet (422·4 acres). The world's busiest port and largest artificial harbour is the Rotterdam-Europoort in the Netherlands which covers 38·88 square miles. It handled 32,023 sea-going vessels and about 250,000 barges in 1970. It is able to handle 310 sea-going vessels simultaneously up to 225,000 tons and 65 feet draught. In 1970 225,000,000 tons of seaborne cargo was handled.

RAILWAYS

The country with the greatest length of railway is the United States, with 208,111 miles of track at 31 Dec. 1968.

The farthest anyone can get from a railway on the mainland island of Great Britain is 54 miles in the case of Cape Wrath, Sutherland, Scotland.

The number of journeys made on British Rail in 1970 was 823,867,000, with an average journey of 22·85 miles, compared with the peak year of 1957, when 1,101 million journeys (average 20·51 miles) were made.

ROADS

The country with the greatest length of road is the United States (50 States), with 3,704,914 miles of graded roads at 1 Jan. 1968. The average speed of cars at off-peak times has risen from 45·0 m.p.h. in 1945 to 58·8 m.p.h. by 1966. There is no speed limit in Nevada.

The country with the greatest number of motor vehicles per mile of road is the United Kingdom, with 220,184 miles of road including 655 miles of Motorway at 31 March 1969 and 15,120,303 vehicles in September 1969. A total of 36,000,000 vehicles by 2010 has been forecast.

Busiest The highest traffic volume of any point in the world is at the Harbor and Santa Monica Freeways interchange in Los Angeles, California, U.S.A. with a 24-hour average on Fridays of 420,000 vehicles in 1970.

The territory with the highest traffic density in the world is Hong Kong. On 31 May 1970 there were 122,274 motor vehicles on 600 miles of serviceable roads giving a density of 8·64 yards per vehicle. The comparative figure for the United Kingdom is 25 yards.

The greatest traffic density at any one point in the United Kingdom is at Hyde Park Corner, London. The average daytime 8 a.m.–8 p.m. flow in 1970 was 164,338 vehicles every 12 hours. The busiest Thames bridge in 1968 was Putney Bridge, with a 12-hour average of 36,249 vehicles. The greatest reported aggregation of London buses was 38, bumper to bumper, along the Vauxhall Bridge Road on 18 Nov. 1965. Censuses are biennial.

Widest

The widest street in the world is the Monumental Axis, running for 1½ miles from the Municipal Plaza to the Plaza of the Three Powers in Brasília, the capital of Brazil. The six-lane boulevard was opened in April 1960 and is 250 metres (273·4 yards) wide. The Bay Bridge Toll Plaza has 34 lanes (17 in each direction) serving the Bay Bridge, San Francisco, California.

Narrowest

The world's narrowest street is St. John's Lane in Rome, with a width of 19 inches. The narrowest street in the United Kingdom is Parliament Street, Exeter, Devon, which at one point measures 26 inches across.

Longest straight road

The longest straight road in the United Kingdom was a stretch of 22¾ miles between Bailgate in the City of Lincoln and Broughton village, Lincolnshire. Part of the Roman road Ermine Street, it now comprises sections of Class I (A.15), Class III and unclassified road, with only two slight deviations of less than 50 feet from the true straight line. Part of the road was closed for an airfield, reducing the straight section to 16½ miles.

Longest
World

The longest motorable road in the world is the Pan-American Highway, which will stretch 13,859 miles from Anchorage, Alaska, to southern Chile. There remains a gap of 450 miles, known as the Darien gap, in Panama and Colombia.

Most complex interchange

The most complex interchange on the British road system is that at Gravelly Hill, north of Birmingham on the Midland Link road joining the M1 with the M5 and M6. There are 18 routes on 6 levels together with a diverted canal and river, which consumed 26,000 tons of steel, 250,000 tons of concrete and 300,000 tons of earth.

Longest street

This title has been accorded to Figueroa Street which stretches 30 miles from Pasadena at Colorado Blvd. to the Pacific Coast Highway, Los Angeles, U.S.A.

Britain

The longest designated road in Great Britain is the 404-mile-long A1 from London to Edinburgh. The longest Roman roads were Watling Street, from Dubrae (Dover) 215 miles through Londinium (London) to Viroconium (Wroxeter), and Fosse Way, which ran 218 miles from Lindum (Lincoln) through Aquae Sulis (Bath) to Isca Dumnoniorum (Exeter). However, a 10-mile section of Fosse Way between Ilchester and Seaton remains indistinct. The oldest roads in Britain are trackways dating from pre-Celtic times (*i.e.* before 550 B.C.). An example is the Ridgeway running across the Berkshire Downs. The commonest street name in Greater London is Park Road, of which there are 43.

Longest hill

The longest steep hill on any road in the United Kingdom is on the road westwards from Lochcarron toward Applecross in Ross and Cromarty, Scotland. In 6 miles this road rises from sea-level to 2,054 feet, with an average gradient of 1 in 15·4, the steepest part being 1 in 4.

Highest
World

The highest pass ever used by traffic is the Bódpo La (19,412 feet above sea-level), in western Tibet. It was used in 1929 by a caravan from the Shipki Pass on the trade route to Rudok. The highest carriageable road in the world is one 1,180 kilometres (733·2 miles) long between Tibet and south-western Sinkiang, completed in October 1957, which takes in passes of an altitude up to 18,480 feet above sea-level. Europe's highest pass (excluding the Caucasian passes) is the Col de Restefond (9,193 feet) between Jausiers and Saint-Etienne-de-Tinée, France. It is usually closed between early October and early June. The highest motor road in Europe is the Pico de Veleta in the Sierra Nevada, southern Spain. The shadeless climb of 22·4 miles brings the motorist to 11,384 feet above sea-level.

United Kingdom

The highest road in the United Kingdom is the A6293 tarmac extension at Great Dun Fell, Westmorland (2,780 feet) leading to a Ministry of Defence radar installation. A permit is required to use it. The highest classified road in England is the B6293 at Killhope Cross (2,056 feet) on the Cumberland-Durham border near Nenthead. The highest classified road in Scotland is the A93 road over the Grampians through Cairnwell, a pass between Blairgowrie, Perthshire, and Braemar, Aberdeenshire, which reaches a height of 2,199 feet. The highest classified road in Wales is the Rhondda-Afan Inter-Valley road (A4107), which reaches 1,750 feet 2½ miles east of Abergwynfi, Glamorganshire.

Lowest

The lowest road in the world is that along the Israeli shores of the Dead Sea, 1,290 feet below sea-level. The lowest in Great Britain are just below sea-level in the Holme Fen area of Huntingdon and Peterborough.

Highest motorway

The highest motorway in Great Britain is the trans-Pennine M62, which, at the Windy Hill interchange, reaches an altitude of 1,220 feet. Its 183-foot-deep Dean Head cutting is the deepest roadway cutting in Europe.

Longest viaduct

The longest elevated road viaduct in Europe is the 9,680-foot-long Chiswick-Langley section of the M4 motorway in West London. It was completed at a cost of £19,000,000 on 24 March 1965.

Traffic jams

The worst traffic jams in the world are in Tōkyō, Japan. Only 9 per cent. of the city area is roadway, compared with London (23 per cent.), Paris (25 per cent.), New York (35 per cent.) and Washington, D.C. (43 per cent.). The longest traffic jam reported in Britain was one of 35 miles in length between Torquay and Yarcombe, Devonshire, on 25 July 1964 and 35 miles on the A30 between Egham, Surrey and Micheldever, Hampshire on 23 May 1970.

Traffic lights

Automatic electric traffic lights were introduced into New York City in 1918 and into Great Britain with a one day trial in Wolverhampton on 11 Feb. 1928. They were first permanently operated in Leeds, Yorkshire on 16 March and in Edinburgh, Scotland on 19 March 1928. Semaphore-type traffic signals were set up in Westminster Square, London in 1868. It was not an offence to disobey traffic signals until assent was given to the 1930 Road Traffic bill.

Parking meters

The earliest parking meters ever installed were those put in the business district of Oklahoma City, Oklahoma, U.S.A., on 19 July 1935. They were the invention of Carl C. Magee (U.S.A.) and reached London in 1958.

Briefest offence

On 7 March 1963 Mr. Charles William Rossiter of Willesden, London, N.W.10, was fined £1 in the West London Court for exceeding a parking limit in Gloucester Road, London, from 3.20 to 3.21 p.m. on 10 Dec. 1962. In May 1970 Mr. Arthur Randall unwittingly parked on a clearway to visit a baker's shop. On emerging after 60 seconds his car was gone. At the pound the ticket showed this offence to have been between 9.03 and 9.04 a.m. The cost of recovery of £6·50 worked out at 11p per second.

The 1,800-year-old Roman milestone at Chesterholm, Northumberland

Worst driver It was reported that a 75-year-old *male* driver received 10 traffic tickets, drove on the wrong side of the road four times, committed four hit-and-run offences and caused six accidents, all within 20 minutes, in McKinney, Texas, U.S.A., on 15 Oct. 1966.

Milestone Britain's oldest milestone *in situ* is a Roman stone dating from about A.D. 150 on the Stanegate, at Chesterholm, near Badron Mill, Northumberland.

TELEPHONES

There were an estimated 255,200,000 telephones in the world at 1 Jan. 1970. The country with the greatest number was the United States, with 115,222,000 instruments, equivalent to 563·8 for every 1,000 people, compared with the United Kingdom figure of 13,748,000 (third largest in the world to the U.S.A. and Japan), or 249·6 per 1,000 people, at 31 March 1969.

The only one of the world's 146 sovereign countries without telephones is Bhutān. The territory with fewest telephones is Pitcairn Island with 15.

The country with the most telephones per head of population is Monaco, with 643·8 per 1,000 of the population at 1 Jan. 1970. The country with the least is Upper Volta with 0·3 of a telephone per 1,000 people at 1 Jan. 1970.

The greatest total of calls made in any country is in the United States, with 151,504 million (745·0 calls per person) in 1969.

The lowest recorded figure was Pakistan with 0·3 of a call per person in 1969.

The United Kingdom telephone service connected 9,686,000,000 calls in the year 1969, an average of 174·2 per person.

The city with most telephones is New York City, N.Y., U.S.A., with 5,904,933 (739 per 1,000 people) at 1 Jan. 1970. In 1969 Washington, D.C. surpassed the level of one for one with 1,002 telephones per 1,000 people though in some small areas there are still higher densities such as in Beverly Hills, north of Los Angeles with a return of about 1,600 per 1,000.

Longest call The longest telephone connection on record was one of 550 hours from 28 Nov. to 21 Dec. 1966 between co-eds of Ford Hall (7th floor) and the 7th floor of Moore Hall at Kansas State University.

Longest cable The world's longest submarine telephone cable is the Commonwealth Pacific Cable (COMPAC), which runs for more than 9,000 miles from Australia, *via* Auckland, New Zealand and the Hawaiian Islands to Port Alberni, Canada. It cost about £35,000,000 and was inaugurated on 2 Dec. 1963.

POSTAL SERVICES

The country with the largest mail in the world is the United States, whose population posted 95,000 million letters and packages in 1970 when the U.S. Postal Service employed 715,970 people. The United Kingdom total was 11,300 million letters in the year ending 31 March 1969.

The United States also takes first place in the average number of letters which each person posts during one year. The figure was 460 in 1970. The United Kingdom figure was 203·6 per head in 1968–69. Of all countries the greatest discrepancy between incoming and outgoing mail is for the U.S.A. whence in 1967 only 627 million items were mailed in response to 1,198 million items received from foreign sources.

POSTAGE STAMPS

Earliest The earliest adhesive postage stamps in the world were the "Penny Blacks" of the United Kingdom, bearing the head of Queen Victoria, placed on sale on 1 May for use on 6 May 1840. A total of 64,000,000 were printed. The National Postal Museum possesses a unique full proof sheet of 240 stamps, printed in April 1840, before the corner letters, plate numbers or marginal inscriptions were added.

Largest The largest postage stamps ever issued were the 1913 Express Delivery stamps of China, which measured 9¾ inches by 2¾ inches. The largest standard postage stamps ever issued were the 10 RLS (ten riyal) airmail stamps issued by the Trucial State of Fujeira (Fujairah) measuring 3¼ by 5¾ inches (18·68 square inches).

Smallest The smallest stamps ever issued were the 10 cents and 1 peso of the Colombian State of Bolívar in 1863–66. They measured 8 millimetres (0·31 of an inch) by 9·5 millimetres (0·37 of an inch).

Highest and lowest denomination The highest denomination stamp ever issued was a red and black stamp for £100, issued in Kenya in 1925–27. The highest denomination stamp ever issued in the United Kingdom was the £5 orange Victoria stamp issued on 21 March 1882. Owing to inflations it is difficult to determine the lowest denomination stamp but it was probably the 1946 3,000 pengö Hungarian stamp, worth at one time only $1{\cdot}6 \times 10^{-14}$d.

Highest price *World* The highest price ever paid for a single philatelic item is the $380,000 (£158,333) for two 1d. orange "Post Office" Mauritius stamps of 1847 on a cover bought at H. R. Harmer's Inc., New York City, U.S.A. by Raymond H. Weill Co. of New Orleans, Louisiana for their own account from the Liechtenstein-Dale collection on 21 Oct. 1968. The item was discovered in 1897 in an Indian bazaar by a Mr. Charles Williams who paid less than £1 for it.

Most valuable *World* There are a number of stamps of which but a single specimen is known. Of these the most celebrated is the one cent black on magenta issued in British Guiana (now Guyana) in February 1856. It was originally bought for six shillings from L. Vernon Vaughan, a schoolboy, in 1873. This is the world's most renowned stamp, for which £A16,000 (£12,774 sterling) was paid in 1940, when it was sold by Mrs. Arthur Hind. It was insured for £200,000, when it was displayed in 1965 at the Royal Festival Hall, London. It was sold on 24 March 1970 by Frederick T. Small by auction at the Siegel Galleries, New York City, U.S.A. for $280,000 (£116,666) by Irwin Weinberg. It was alleged in October 1938 that Hind had, in 1928, purchased and burned his stamp's twin.

Great Britain The highest price paid for stamps in Britain is £28,000, paid on 1 Oct. 1963 for a 1d. orange-red and a 2d. deep blue of Mauritius on an 1847 envelope. The most valuable philatelic piece of Great Britain is the Buccleuch block of 48 (4×12) unused Plate 2 imperforate 2d. Blues printed on 21 July 1840. These were found in 1945 by Mr. A. Martin at Dalkeith House, Scotland, and were auctioned, along with some minor pieces, by H. R. Harmer Ltd. for £6,300 in June 1946.

There are three unique British stamps. They are an unissued 1860, 1½d. rosy-mauve error, corner-lettered with an O for a C and an Edward VII 1d. War Office error overprinted "Official", which are both in the Royal Collection; and an unused 9d. straw of 1862 on azure paper, discovered in 1938. The rarest British stamp which is not an error is the King Edward VII 6d. dull purple Inland Revenue Official stamp issued and withdrawn on 14 May 1904. Only 11 or 12 are known and one was sold for £3,500 unused in Feb. 1967.

Commonest British stamp The most frequently reproduced United Kingdom stamp has been the definitive Elizabeth II 3d. violet, issued from 1 Oct. 1953 to 17 May 1965, of which 19,920 million were issued.

Largest collection The greatest private stamp collection ever auctioned has been that of Maurice Burrus (d. 1959) of Alsace, France, which realised an estimated £1,500,000.

The largest national collection in the world is that at the British Museum, London, which has had the General Post Office collection on permanent loan since March 1963. The British Royal collection, housed in 400 volumes, is also believed to be worth more than £1,000,000. The collection of the Universal Postal Union (founded 9 Oct. 1874) in Geneva, Switzerland receives 400 copies of each new issue of each member nation but the largest international collections are those of the Swiss, Swedish, German, Dutch and U.S.A. (Smithsonian Institution) authorities.

A pioneer pillar-box dating from 1853 at Barnes Cross, Dorset

POSTAL ADDRESSES

Highest numbering The practice of numbering houses began in 1463 on the Pont Notre Dame, Paris, France. The highest numbered house in Britain is No. 2,679 Stratford Road, Solihull, Warwickshire, occupied since 1966 by Mr. & Mrs. H. Hughes. The highest numbered house in Scotland is No. 2,629 London Road, Mount Vernon, Glasgow, which is part of the local police station.

Pillar-boxes Pillar-boxes were introduced into Great Britain at the suggestion of the novelist Anthony Trollope (1815–82). The oldest site on which one is still in service is one dating from 8 Feb. 1853 in Union Street, St. Peter Port, Guernsey though the present box is not the original. The oldest original box in Great Britain is another Victorian example at Barnes Cross, Holwell, near Bishop's Caundle, Dorset, also dating from probably later in 1853.

Post Offices The Post Office's northernmost post office is at Haroldswick, Unst, Shetland Islands. The most southerly in the British Isles is at Samarès, Jersey.

The British Isles' most southerly post office at Samarès, Jersey

TELEGRAMS
The country where most telegrams are sent is the U.S.S.R., whose population sent 322,800,000 telegrams in 1967. The United Kingdom total was 18,177,000, including 7,561,000 sent overseas, in the year ending 31 March 1970.

The world's largest telegraph company is the Western Union Telegraph Company of New York City, N.Y., U.S.A. It had 26,269 employees on 1 Jan. 1969, a total of 11,000 telegraphic offices and agencies and 5,734,792 miles of telegraph channels.

The largest British telegraphic undertaking is Cable and Wireless Ltd., which operates 58,000 nautical miles of ocean cables (including 20,000 miles of telephone cable) and about 300,000 miles of radio circuits. It has a fleet of seven cable ships, more than 80 overseas stations and 10,392 employees.

INLAND WATERWAYS
The country with the greatest length of inland waterways is Finland. The total length of navigable lakes and rivers is about 50,000 kilometres (31,000 miles). In the United Kingdom the total length of navigable rivers and canals is 3,940 miles.

Longest navigable river The longest navigable natural waterway in the world is the River Amazon, which sea-going vessels can ascend as far as Iquitos, in Peru, 2,236 miles from the Atlantic seaboard. On a National Geographic Society expedition ending on 10 March 1969, Helen and Frank Schreider navigated downstream from San Francisco, Peru, 3,845 miles up the Amazon, by a balsa raft named *Mamuri* 249 miles to Atalaya, thence 356 miles to Pucallpa by outboard motor dug-out canoe and thence the last 3,240 miles towards Belem in the 30-foot petrol-engined cabin cruiser *Amazon Queen*.

The oldest college at Cambridge University—the 687-year-old Peterhouse

7. EDUCATION

ILLITERACY
Literacy is variously defined as "ability to read simple subjects" and "ability to read and write a simple letter". The looseness of definition and the scarcity of data for some countries preclude anything more than approximations, but the extent of illiteracy among adults (15 years old and over) is estimated to have been 39·3 per cent. throughout the world at the opening of the last decade in 1961. In 1969 a United Nations' estimate put the level at 810 million out of 2,335 million adults or 34·7 per cent. The continent with the greatest proportion of illiterates is Africa, where 81·5 per cent. of adults are illiterate. The latest figure available for the Niger Republic is 99·1 per cent. A U.S.S.R. report published in June 1968, affirms that more than 300 million people in China are still "completely illiterate".

UNIVERSITIES
World Probably the oldest educational institution in the world is the University of Karueein, founded in A.D. 859 in Fez, Morocco. The European university with the earliest date of foundation is that of Naples, Italy, founded in 1224 by charter of Frederick II (1194–1250), Holy Roman Emperor.

United Kingdom The oldest university in the United Kingdom is the University of Oxford, which came into being in *c.* 1167. The oldest college is quoted as University College (1249), though its foundation is less well documented than that of Merton College in 1264. The earliest college at Cambridge University is Peterhouse, founded in 1284. The largest college at either university is Trinity College, Cambridge. It was founded in 1546. The oldest university in Scotland is the University of St. Andrews, Fife. It was established in 1411.

Greatest enrolment The university with the greatest enrolment in the world is the University of Calcutta (founded 1857) in India, with more than 196,257 students (internal and external) and 31 professors in 1969. Owing to the inadequacy of the buildings and number of lecturers, the students are handled in three shifts per day. The enrolment at all branches of the State University of New York, U.S.A., was 149,211 in January 1970 and is expected to reach 290,400 by 1974. The University of London had 38,551 internal students in 1970.

Part of the world's most heavily endowed university—the Harvard Business School

Largest building The largest university building in the world is the M. V. Lomonosov State University on the Lenin Hills, south of Moscow, U.S.S.R. It stands 240 metres (787·4 feet) tall, has 32 storeys and contains 40,000 rooms. It was constructed in 1949–53.

Richest The richest university in the world is Harvard University in Cambridge, Massachusetts, U.S.A. Its endowments had a book value of $621,795,041 (£259 million) in 1968.

PROFESSORS

Youngest The youngest at which anybody has been elected to a chair in a major university is 21 years 10 months, in the case of William Rowan Hamilton (b. 4 Aug. 1805), Andrews Professor of Astronomy at the University of Dublin, Trinity College, Dublin, Ireland, on 16 June 1827. He died of alcoholism at the age of 60 on 2 Sept. 1865. In July 1967 Dr. Harvey Friedman, Ph.D., was appointed Assistant Professor of Mathematics at Stanford University, California, U.S.A. aged just 19 years.

Most durable The longest period for which any professorship has been held is 63 years in the case of Thomäs Martyn (1735–1825), Professor of Botany at Cambridge University from 1762 until his death. His father, John Martyn (1699–1768), had occupied the chair from 1733 to 1762.

Senior Wranglers Since 1910 the Wranglers (first class honours students in the Cambridge University mathematical Tripos, part 2) have been placed in alphabetical order only. In 1890 Miss P. G. Fawcett of Newnham was placed "above the Senior Wrangler".

Youngest undergraduate The most extreme recorded cases of undergraduate juvenility were those of John Donne (1573–1631), who entered Hart Hall, Oxford, aged 11, and William Thomson (1824–1907), later Lord Kelvin, O.M., G.C.V.O., who entered Glasgow University also aged 11.

Longest studentship No central records are kept but the closest approach in Britain to an eternal student appears to be that of George A. Goulty of Guildford, Surrey who entered the Southern College of Art, Winchester in 1942 and who, in 1971, after 15 years further education, is at Reading University reading for his seventh qualification, a Ph.D.

Oldest student The oldest student enrolled by the Open University is Miss Mary Carr of Gosforth, Northumberland, aged 79.

SCHOOLS

Largest *World* The largest school in the world was the De Witt Clinton High School in the Bronx, New York City, N.Y., U.S.A., where the enrolment attained a peak of 12,000 in 1934. It was founded in 1897 and now has an enrolment of 6,000.

United Kingdom The school with the most pupils in the United Kingdom in May 1971 was the Portobello Senior Secondary School, Edinburgh with 2,250. England's largest is Thomas Bennett School, Crawley, Sussex with 2,144 in January 1970.

Oldest in Britain The title of the oldest school in Britain is contested. It is claimed that King's School in Canterbury, Kent, was a foundation of Saint Augustine, some time between his arrival in Kent in A.D. 597 and his death in *c.* 604.

Oldest old school tie The practice of wearing distinctive neckties bearing the colours or registered designs of schools, universities, sports clubs, regiments, etc., appears to date from *c.* 1880. The practice originated in Oxford University, where boater bands were converted into use as "ribbon ties". The earliest definitive evidence stems from an order from Exeter College for college ties, dated 25 June, 1880.

Most expensive *World* The most expensive school in the world is the Oxford Academy (established 1906) in Pleasantville, New Jersey, U.S.A. It is a private college-preparatory boarding school for boys with "academic deficiencies". The school has 15 masters and each of the 47 boys is taught individually in each course. The tuition fee for the school year is $8,400 (£3,500).

United Kingdom The most expensive school in the United Kingdom is Millfield at Street, Somerset, founded by R. J. O. Meyer in 1937. The termly fees for late entrant pupils may amount to £1,300 per annum. The most expensive girls' school in 1970–71 was Benenden, Kent (founded 1924) with annual fees of £750.

Greatest disenrolment Between June 1966 and March 1967 about 110,000,000 Chinese schoolchildren over 9 years were excused attendance to aid the 22,000,000 Red Guards (*Hung*

H. M. Butler— Headmaster of Harrow

Wei Pings) in prosecuting the "Great Cultural Revolution".

Most 'O' and 'A' levels Ruth Felicity Chadwick (b. Birmingham 16 Oct. 1951) now of Lichfield, Staffordshire between summer 1966 and summer 1969 passed 23 G.C.E. examinations (17 'O' and 6 'A' levels). In August 1970 she awaited the results of one further 'O' and one further 'A' level. F. L. Thomason of Cleobury Mortimer, Worcestershire had by June 1971 accumulated 18 'O', 4 'A' and 1 'S' levels and was sitting 3 further 'O' and 3 further 'A' levels.

Youngest headmaster The youngest headmaster of a major public school was Henry Montagh Butler (b. 2 July 1835), appointed Headmaster of Harrow School on 16 Nov. 1859, when aged 24 years 137 days. His first term in office began in January 1860.

8. RELIGIONS

LARGEST

Religious statistics are necessarily highly approximations. The test of adherence to a religion varies widely in rigour, while many individuals, particularly in the East, belong to two or more religions.

Christianity is the world's prevailing religion, with over 945,000,000 adherents in 1971 and probably an additional 150,000,000 Protestants who are not in membership with the Church of their baptism. The total of 175,000,000 practising and 150,000,000 non-practising Protestants is easily outnumbered by the 590,000,000 who have received baptism into the Roman Catholic Church. The largest non-Christian religion is Islām, with about 500,000,000 adherents in 1970.

In the United Kingdom the Anglicans comprise members of the Established Church of England, the Dis-established Church in Wales, the Episcopal Church in Scotland and the Church of Ireland. In 1968 there were 27,756,000 living persons who had been baptized in Anglican churches in the provinces of Canterbury and York. In the same area it is estimated that there were 9,691,000 persons confirmed, of whom nearly 2,000,000 were Easter communicants in 1968. In Scotland the most numerous group is the Church of Scotland (the Presbyterians), which had 1,201,933 members, apart from adherents, at 1 Jan. 1969.

SMALLEST

In New Zealand the 1966 Census revealed 94 religious sects with a single follower each. These included a Millenarian Heretic and an Aesthetic Hedonist. Such followers might alternatively be described as leaders.

Largest clergy The world's largest religious organization is the Roman Catholic Church, with over 500,000,000 members, 418,000 priests and 946,000 nuns in 1964. The total number of cardinals, patriarchs, metropolitans, archbishops, bishops, abbots and superiors is 2,800. There are about 416,000 churches.

Jews The total of world Jewry was estimated to be 14,351,000 in 1970. The highest concentration was in the United States, with 5,870,000, of whom 2,381,000 were in Greater New York. The total in Israel was 2,530,000. The total of British Jewry is 450,000, of whom 280,000 are in Greater London, 31,500 in Manchester and Salford, and 13,500 in Glasgow. The total in Tōkyō, Japan, is only 250.

Largest Temple The largest religious structure ever built is Angkor Wat (City Temple), covering 402 acres, in Cambodia, south-east Asia. It was built to the God Vishnu by the Khmer King Suryavarman II in the period 1113–50. Its curtain wall measures 1,400 yards by 1,400 yards and its population, before it was abandoned in 1432, was 80,000.

Part of Angkor Wat—the world's largest temple

CATHEDRALS

Largest *World* The world's largest cathedral is the cathedral church of the Diocese of New York, St. John the Divine, with a floor area of 121,000 square feet and a volume of 16,822,000 cubic feet. The corner stone was laid on 27 Dec. 1892, and the Gothic building was still uncompleted in 1967. In New York it is referred to as "Saint John the Unfinished". The nave is the longest in the world, 601 feet in length, with a vaulting 124 feet in height.

The cathedral covering the largest area is that of Santa María de la Sede in Sevilla (Seville), Spain. It was built in Spanish Gothic style between 1402 and 1519 and is 414 feet long, 271 feet wide and 100 feet high to the vault of the nave.

United Kingdom The largest cathedral in the British Isles is the Anglican Cathedral of Liverpool. Built in modernized Gothic style, work was begun on 19 July 1904, and when completed will have cost over £3,000,000. The building encloses 100,000 square feet and has an overall length of 671 feet. The Vestey Tower is 331 feet high.

Smallest *United Kingdom* The smallest cathedral in use in the United Kingdom (excluding converted parish churches) is St. Asaph in Flintshire, Wales. It is 182 feet long, 68 feet wide and has a tower 100 feet high. Oxford Cathedral in Christ Church (College) is 155 feet long. The nave of the Cathedral of the Isles on the Isle of Cumbrae, Buteshire measures only 40 × 20 feet. The total floor area is 2,124 square feet.

Longest The longest Gothic church in the United Kingdom is Winchester Cathedral, Hampshire, which is 560 feet long (internal length 526 feet).

Longest nave The longest nave in the United Kingdom is that of St. Albans Cathedral, Hertfordshire, which is 285 feet long.

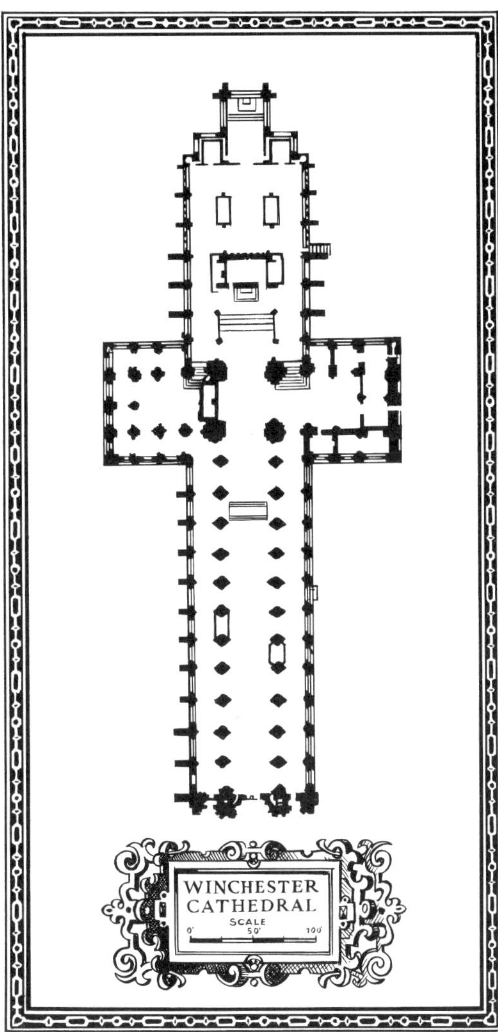

CHURCHES

Largest *World* The largest church in the world is the basilica of St. Peter, built between 1492 and 1612 in the Vatican City, Rome. The length of the church, measured from the apse, is 611 feet 4 inches. The area is 18,110 square yards. The inner diameter of the famous dome is 137 feet 9 inches and its centre is 119 metres (390 feet 5 inches) high. The external height is 457 feet 9 inches.

The elliptical Basilique of St. Pie X at Lourdes, France, completed in 1957 at a cost of £2,000,000 has a capacity of 20,000 under its giant span arches and a length of 659 feet.

The crypt of the underground Civil War Memorial Church in the Guadarrama Mountains, 28 miles from Madrid, Spain, is 853 feet in length. It took 21 years (1937–58) to build, at a reported cost of £140,000,000 and is surmounted by a cross 492 feet tall.

United Kingdom The largest parish church in the United Kingdom is Holy Trinity Parish Church, Kingston-upon-Hull, Yorkshire. The church exterior is 295 feet long and 104 feet wide, and parts of the transept date from 1285. The internal area is 26,384 square feet. The parish church of St. Nicholas at Great Yarmouth, Norfolk, formerly the largest in England, was destroyed by bombing in 1942 but was rededicated in May 1961. Its side aisles are 40 feet wide.

Smallest *World* The world's smallest church is the Union Church at Wiscasset, Maine, U.S.A., with a floor area of 31½ square feet (7 feet by 4½ feet). Les Vaubelets Church in Guernsey has an area of 16 feet by 12 feet, room for one priest and a congregation of two.

Britain The smallest church in use in England is Bremitham Church, Cowage Farm, Foxley near Malmesbury, Wiltshire which measures 12 feet by 12 feet and is used for service twice a year. The smallest completed English church in regular use is that at Culbone, Somerset, which measures 35 feet by 12 feet. The smallest Welsh chapel is St. Trillo's Chapel, Rhôs-on-Sea (Llandrillo-yn-Rhos), Denbighshire, measuring only 12 feet by 6 feet. The smallest chapel in Scotland is St. Margaret's, Edinburgh, measuring 16½ feet by 10½ feet, giving an area of 173¼ square feet.

OLDEST

World The earliest known shrine dates from the proto-neolithic Natufian culture in Jericho, where a site on virgin soil has been dated to the ninth millennium B.C. A simple rectilinear red-plastered room with a niche housing a stone pillar believed to be the shrine of a Pre-Pottery fertility cult dating from *c.* 6500 B.C. was also uncovered in Jericho (now Arīhā) in Jordan. The oldest surviving Christian church in the world is Qal'at es Salihige in eastern Syria, dating from A.D. 232. A list of the oldest religious buildings in 43 countries was included in the 11th edition of *The Guinness Book of Records*, at page 117. The oldest wooden church in Great Britain and probably in the world is St. Andrew's, Greensted, near Ongar, Essex dating to A.D. 835 though some of the timbers date to the original building of *c.* A.D. 650.

United Kingdom The oldest church in the United Kingdom is St. Martin's Church in Canterbury, Kent. It was built in A.D. 560 on the foundations of a 1st century Roman church. The oldest church in Ireland is the Gallerus Oratory, built in *c.* 750 at Ballyferriter, near Kilmalkedar, County Kerry. Britain's oldest nunnery is St. Peter and Paul Minster, on the Isle of Thanet, Kent. It was founded in *c.* 748 by the Abbess Eadburga of Bugga.

England's tallest spire for 410 years—the 404-foot spire of Salisbury Cathedral

TALLEST SPIRES

World The tallest cathedral spire in the world is that of the Protestant Cathedral of Ulm in Germany. The building is early Gothic and was begun in 1377. The tower, in the centre of the west façade, was not finally completed until 1890 and is 528 feet high. The world's tallest church spire is that of the Chicago Temple of the First Methodist Church on Clark Street, Chicago, Illinois, U.S.A. The building consists of a 22-storey skyscraper (erected in 1924) surmounted by a parsonage at 330 feet, a "Sky Chapel" at 400 feet and a steeple cross at 568 feet above street level.

United Kingdom The highest spire in the United Kingdom is that of the church of St. Mary, called Salisbury Cathedral, Wiltshire. The Lady Chapel was built in the years 1220–25 and the main fabric of the cathedral was finished and consecrated in 1258. The spire was added later, 1334–65, and reaches a height of 404 feet. St. Paul's Cathedral, London, possessed a 489-foot spire, built in 1315, but this was struck by lightning in June 1561. The height of the present cross above the dome is 365 feet.

LARGEST SYNAGOGUES

World The largest synagogue in the world is the Temple Emanu-El on Fifth Avenue at 65th Street, New York City, N.Y., U.S.A. The temple, completed in September 1929, has a frontage of 150 feet on Fifth Avenue and 253 feet on 65th Street. The Sanctuary proper can accommodate 2,500 people, and the adjoining Beth-El Chapel seats 350. When all the facilities are in use, more than 6,000 people can be accommodated.

Great Britain The largest synagogue in Great Britain is the Edgware Synagogue, Greater London, completed in 1959, with a capacity of 1,630 seats.

Largest mosque The largest mosque ever built was the now ruinous al-Malawiya mosque of al-Mutawakil in Samarra, Iraq built in A.D. 842–852 and measuring 401,408 square feet (9·21 acres) with dimensions of 784 feet by 512 feet. The world's largest mosque in use is the Jama Masjid (1644–58) in Delhi, India, with an area of more than 10,000 square feet and two 108-foot-tall minarets. The largest mosque will be the Merdeka Mosque in Djakarta, Indonesia, which was begun in 1962. The cupola will be 45 metres (147·6 feet) in diameter and the capacity in excess of 50,000 people.

Tallest minaret The world's tallest minaret is the Qutb Minar, south of New Delhi, India, built in 1194 to a height of 238 feet.

Tallest pagoda The world's tallest pagoda is the 288-foot-tall Shwemawdaw in Pegu, Burma. It was restored by April 1954 having been damaged by an earthquake in 1930. The tallest Chinese temple is the 13-storey Pagoda of the Six Harmonies (*Liu he ta*) outside Hang zhou (Hangchow). It is "nearly 200 feet high".

The world's tallest pagoda at Pegu, Burma

SAINTS

Most and least rapidly Canonized The shortest interval that has elapsed between the death of a Saint and his canonization was in the case of St. Anthony of Padua, Italy, who died on 13 June 1251 and was canonized 352 days later on 30 May 1252. This was one day faster than St. Peter of Verona (1206–52) canonized on 6 April 1253.

The other extreme is represented by St. Bernard of Thiron, for 20 years Prior of St. Sabinus, who died in 1117 and was made a Saint in 1861—744 years later. The Italian monk and painter, Fra Giovanni da Fiesole (*né* Guido di Pietro), called *Il Beato* ("The Blessed") Fra Angelico (*c.* 1400–1455), is still in the first stage of canonization.

POPES

Reign *Longest* The longest reign of any of the 262 Popes has been that of Pius IX (Giovanni Maria Mastai-Ferretti), who reigned for 31 years 236 days from 16 June 1846 until his death aged 85, on 7 Feb. 1878.

Shortest Pope Stephen II was elected on 24 March 752 and died two days later, but he is not included in the *Liber pontificalis* or the Catalogue of the Popes. The shortest reign of any genuine Pope is that of Giambattista Castagna (1521–90), who was elected Pope Urban VII on 15 Sept. 1590 and died twelve days later on 27 Sept. 1590.

Oldest It is recorded that Pope St. Agatho (reigned 678–681) was elected at the age of 103 and lived to 106, but recent scholars have expressed doubts. The oldest of recent

Pope Pius XII, who in 1939 reputedly came within a vote of unanimous election

Pontiffs has been Pope Leo XIII (Vincenzo Gioacchino Pecci), who was born on 2 March 1810, elected Pope at the third ballot on 20 Feb. 1878 and died on 20 July 1903, aged 93 years 140 days.

Youngest The youngest of all Popes was Pope Benedict IX (Theophylact), who had three terms as Pope: in 1032–44; April to May 1045; and 8 Nov. 1047 to 17 July 1048. It would appear that he was aged only 11 or 12 in 1032, though the Catalogue of the Popes admits only to his "extreme youth"

Last non-Italian Cardinalate and English Popes The last non-Italian Pope was the Utrecht-born Cardinal Priest Adrian Dedel (1459–1523) of the Netherlands. He was elected on 9 Jan. 1522, crowned Pope Adrian VI on 31 Aug. 1522 and died on 14 Sept. 1523. The last Pope elected from outside the College of Cardinals was Bartolomeo Prignano (1318–89), Archbishop of Bari, who was elected Pope Urban VI on 8 April 1378. The only Englishman to be elected Pope was Nicholas Breakspear (born at Abbots Langley, near Watford, Hertfordshire, in *c.* 1100), who, as Cardinal Bishop of Albano, was elected Pope Adrian IV on 4 Dec. 1154, and died on 1 Sept. 1159.

Last married The first 37 Popes had no specific obligation to celibacy. The last married Pope was Adrian II (867–872). Rodrigo Borgia was the father of at least four children before being elected Pope Alexander VI in 1492.

Slowest election After 31 months without declaring *Habemus Papam* ("We have a Pope"), the cardinals were subjected to a bread and water diet and the removal of the roof of their conclave by the Mayor before electing Teobaldo Visconti (*c.* 1210–76), the Archbishop of Liège, as Pope Gregory X at Viterbo on 1 Sept. 1271. Cardinal Eugenio Maria Guiseppe Giovanni Pacelli (1876–1958), who took the title of Pius XII, was reputedly elected by 61 votes out of 62 at only the third ballot on 2 March 1939, his 63rd birthday.

CARDINALS

Oldest By May 1971 the Sacred College of Cardinals contained 125 declared members compared with 136 a year earlier. The oldest is Cardinal Bishop Paolo Giobbe of Italy (b. 10 Jan. 1880).

Youngest The youngest Cardinal of all time was Giovanni de' Medici (b. 11 Dec. 1475), later Pope Leo X, who was made a Cardinal Deacon in March 1489, when aged 13 years 3 months. The youngest in 1971 is Cardinal Bishop Stephan Sou Hwan Kim of South Korea (b. 6 May 1922). He was named as a Cardinal in April 1969 when aged 46.

Giovanni de' Medici—see Youngest Cardinal above

The Church of England's youngest Bishop—the Rt. Rev. Stuart Blanch

BISHOPS

Oldest The oldest serving Bishop (excluding Suffragans and Assistants) in the Church of England at 1 Jan. 1971 was the Rt. Rev. Cyril Easthaugh, M.C. (b. 22 Dec. 1897), the 34th Bishop of Peterborough.

The oldest Roman Catholic bishop in recent years was Mgr. Alfonso Carinci (b. 9 Nov. 1862), who was titular Archbishop of Seleucia, in Isauria, from 1945 until his death on 6 Dec. 1963, at the age of 101 years 27 days. He had celebrated Mass about 24,800 times. He was the oldest bishop at the first session of the Second Vatican Council (the 21st Oecumenical Council), held in Rome from 11 Oct. to 8 Dec. 1962.

Youngest The youngest bishop of all time was Hugnes, whose father, the Comte de Vermandois, successfully demanded for him the archbishopric of Reims from the feeble Pope John X (reigned 914–928), when he was only five years old.

The youngest serving Bishop (excluding Suffragans and Assistants) in the Church of England at 1 Jan 1971 was the Rt. Rev. Stuart Yarworth Blanch (b. 2 Feb. 1918), the 5th Bishop of Liverpool.

BISHOPRIC

Longest tenure The longest tenure of any Church of England bishopric is 57 years in the case of the Rt. Rev. Thomas Wilson, who was consecrated Bishop of Sodor and Man on 16 Jan. 1698 and died in office on 7 March 1755. Of English bishoprics the longest tenure, if one excludes the unsubstantiated case of Aethelwulf, reputedly bishop of Hereford from 937 to 1012, are those of 47 years by Jocelin de Bohun (Salisbury) 1142–1189 and Nathaniel Crew or Crewe (Durham) 1674–1721.

STAINED GLASS

Oldest The oldest stained glass in the world represents the Prophets in a window of the cathedral of Augsburg, Bavaria, Germany, dating from *c.* 1050. The oldest stained glass in the United Kingdom is represented by 12th century fragments in the Tree of Jesse in the north aisle of the nave of York Minster, dated *c.* 1150. An earlier date (*c.* 1080) has been attributed to glass in a window of the church at Compton, Surrey. The oldest complete window in Britain is the Norman window in St. Mary the Virgin, Brabourne, Kent dating from *c.* 1090.

York Minster lit by the oldest and largest area of stained glass in Britain

A scene from history's most thronged funeral procession

Largest The largest stained glass window is one measuring 300 feet long by 23 feet high at the John F. Kennedy International Airport (formerly Idlewild), Long Island, New York State, U.S.A. The largest single stained glass window in Great Britain is the East window in Gloucester Cathedral measuring 72 feet by 38 feet, set up to commemorate the Battle of Crécy (1346), while the largest area of stained glass is 125 windows, totalling 25,000 square feet in York Minster.

BRASSES

The world's oldest monumental brass is that commemorating Bishop Ysowilpe in St. Andrew's Church, Verden, near Hanover, West Germany, dating from 1231. The oldest in Great Britain is of Sir John D'Abernon at Stoke D'Abernon, near Leatherhead, Surrey, dating from 1277.

PARISHES

Largest and smallest The latest population figures for parishes in the United Kingdom are from the census of 23 April 1961. The most populous parish was the Parish of Kirkby St. Chad, Liverpool, with 52,177 parishioners. Of the nine parishes uninhabited in 1961, Iham Parish, in the diocese of Chichester, Sussex, has had a nil population since 1931.

Longest incumbency The longest incumbency on record is one of 76 years by the Rev. Bartholomew Edwards, Rector of St. Nicholas, Ashill, Norfolk from 1813 to 1889. There appears to be some doubt as to whether the Rev. Richard Sherinton was installed at Folkestone from 1524 or 1529 to 1601. If the former is correct it would surpass the Norfolk record. The parish of Iden, East Sussex had only two incumbents in the 117-year period from 1807 to 1924.

Oldest parish register The oldest parish registers in England are those of St. James Garlickhythe and St. Mary Bothaw, two old City of London parishes, dating from 1536. Scotland's oldest surviving register is that for Anstruther-Wester, Fife, with burial entries from 1549.

Largest crowd The greatest recorded number of human beings assembled with a common purpose was more than 5,000,000 at the 21-day Hindu festival of Kumbh-Mela, which is held every 12 years at the confluence of the Yamuna (formerly called the Jumna), the Ganges and the invisible "Sarasviti" at Allahabad, Uttar Pradesh, India, on 21 Jan. 1966. According to the Jacob Formula for estimating the size of crowds, the allowance of area per person varies from 4 square feet (tight) to 9½ square feet (loose). Thus such a crowd must have occupied an area of more than 700 acres.

Largest funeral The greatest attendance at any funeral is the estimated 5 million who thronged Cairo, United Arab Republic, for the funeral of President Gamal Abdel Nasser (b. 15 Jan. 1918) on 1 Oct. 1970.

Biggest demonstrations A figure of 2·7 million was published from China for the demonstration against the U.S.S.R. in Shanghai on 3–4 April 1969 following the border clashes, and one of 10 million for the May Day celebrations of 1963 in Peking.

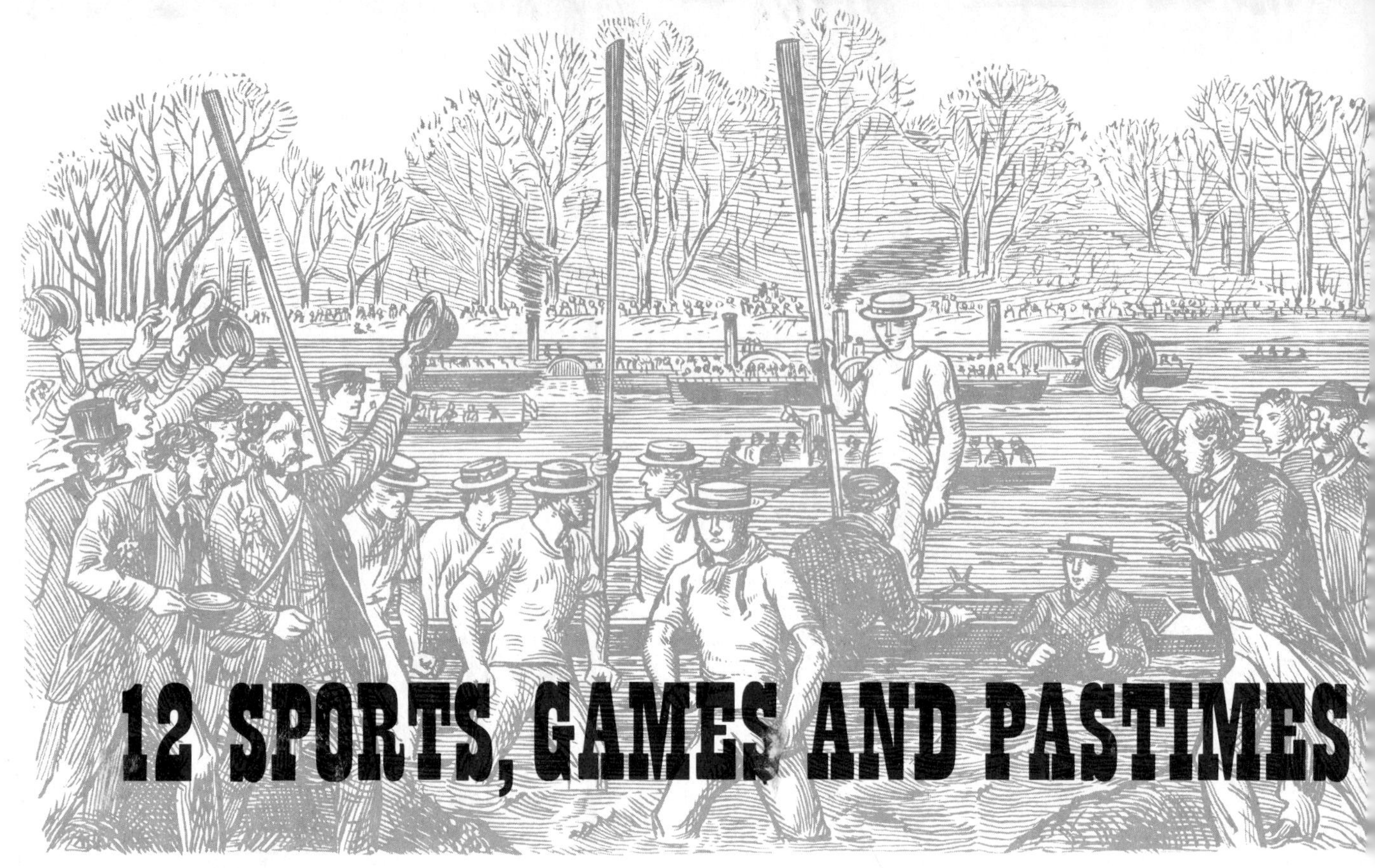

Earliest The origins of sport stem from the time when self-preservation ceased to be the all-consuming human preoccupation. Archery was a hunting skill in mesolithic times (before 20,000 B.C.), but did not become an organized sport until *c.* A.D. 300, among the Genoese. The earliest dated origin for any sport is *c.* 3000 B.C. for wrestling, depicted on pre-dynastic murals at Ben Hasan, Egypt (now the United Arab Republic), and also from early Sumerian sources at Kyafefe, Iraq.

Fastest The governing body for aviation, *La Fédération Aéronautique Internationale,* records maximum speeds in lunar flight of up to 24,791 m.p.h. However, these achievements, like all air speed records since 1923, have been para-military rather than sporting. In shooting, muzzle velocities of up to 7,100 feet per second (4,840 m.p.h.) are reached in the case of a U.S. Army Ordnance Department standard 0·30 calibre M1903 rifle. The highest speed reached in a non-mechanical sport is in sky-diving, in which a speed of 185 m.p.h. is attained in a head-down free falling position, even in the lower atmosphere. In delayed drops a speed of 614 m.p.h. has been recorded at high rarefied altitudes. The highest projectile speed in any moving ball game is *c.* 160 m.p.h. in pelota. This compares with 170 m.p.h. (electronically-timed) for a golf ball driven off a tee.

Slowest In wrestling, before the rules were modified towards "brighter wrestling", contestants could be locked in holds for so long that single bouts could last for up to 11 hours. In the extreme case of the 2 hours 41 minutes pull in the regimental tug o' war in Jubbulpore, India, on 12 Aug. 1889, the winning team moved a net distance of 12 feet at an average speed of 0·00084 m.p.h.

Longest The most protracted sporting test was an automobile duration test of 222,618 miles by Appaurchaux and others in a Ford Taunus. This was contested over 142 days in 1963. The distance was equivalent to 8·93 times around the equator.

The most protracted non-mechanical sporting event is the *Tour de France* cycling race. In 1926 this was over 3,569 miles, lasting 29 days. The total damage to the French national economy of this annual event, now reduced to 23 days, is immense. If it is assumed that one-third of the total working population works for only two-thirds of the time during the currency of *Le Tour* this would account for a loss of more than three-quarters of one per cent. of the nation's annual Gross National Product. In 1970 this was more than £40,000 million, so the loss would have been about £300,000,000.

Shortest Of sports with timed events the briefest recognized for official record purposes is the quick draw in shooting in which electronic times down to 0·06 of a second have been returned.

Most expensive The most expensive of all sports is the racing of large yachts—"J" type boats, last built in 1937, and International 12-metre boats. The owning and racing of these is beyond the means of individual millionaires and is confined to multi-millionaires or syndicates.

Largest crowd The greatest number of live spectators for any sporting spectacle is the estimated 1,000,000 (more than 20 per cent. of the population) who line the route of the annual San Sylvestre road race of 8,600 metres (5 miles 605 yards) through the streets of São Paulo, Brazil, on New Year's night. However, spread over 23 days, it is estimated that more than 10,000,000 see the annual *Tour de France* along the route (see also above).

The largest crowd travelling to any sporting venue is "more than 400,000" for the annual *Grand Prix d'Endurance* motor race on the Sarthe circuit near Le Mans, France. The record stadium crowd was one of 199,854 for the Brazil *v.* Uruguay match in the Maracaña Municipal Stadium, Rio de Janeiro, Brazil, on 16 July 1950.

Largest field The largest pitch of any ball game is that of polo, with 12·4 acres, or a maximum length of 300 yards and a width, without side boards, of 200 yards.

Most participants The annual Nijmegen Vierdaagse march in the Netherlands over distances up to 50 kilometres (31 miles 120 yards) attracted 16,667 participants in 1968.

Heaviest sportsmen The heaviest sportsman of all-time was the wrestler William J. Cobb of Macon, Georgia, U.S.A., who in 1962 was billed as the 802 lb. (57 st. 4 lb.) "Happy

ti-millionaire Commodore Vanderbilt (U.S.A.), actitioner of the most ensive sport

Humphrey". The heaviest player of a ball-game was Bob Pointer, aged 18, the 447 lb. (31 st. 13 lb.) tackle on the 1967 Santa Barbara High School team, California, U.S.A.

Worst disasters The worst sports disaster in recent history was when an estimated 604 were killed after some stands at the Hong Kong Jockey Club racecourse collapsed and caught fire on 26 Feb. 1918. During the reign of Antoninus Pius (A.D. 138–161) the upper wooden tiers in the Circus Maximus, Rome collapsed during a gladiatorial combat killing some 1,112 spectators. Britain's worst sports disaster was when 66 were killed and 145 injured at the Rangers *v.* Celtic football match at Exit 13 of Ibrox Park stadium, Glasgow on 2 Jan. 1971. The casualties occurred on the terraces when an exiting crowd stampeded back to see a last minute equalizing goal by Rangers so colliding with those leaving behind them. At the same ground on 5 April 1902 there were 325 casualties with 25 killed due to the collapse of part of the wooden terracing.

Youngest world record breaker The youngest age at which any person has broken a world record is 12 years 328 days in the case of Karen Yvette Muir (born 16 Sept. 1952) of Kimberley, South Africa, who broke the women's 110 yards backstroke world record with 1 minute 08·7 seconds at Blackpool on 10 Aug. 1965.

Youngest and oldest internationals The youngest age at which any person has won international honours is 8 years in the case of Miss Joy Foster, the Jamaican singles and mixed doubles table tennis champion in 1958. It would appear that the greatest age at which anyone has actively competed for his country is 73 years in the case of Oscar G. Swahn (Sweden), who won a silver medal for shooting in the Olympic Games at Antwerp in 1920.

Youngest and oldest champions The youngest age at which anyone has successfully participated in a world title event is 12 years in the case of Bernard Malvoire (France), cox of the winning coxed fours in the Olympic regatta at Helsinki in 1952. The youngest individual Olympic winner was Miss Marjorie Gestring (U.S.A.), who took the springboard diving title at the age of 13 years 9 months at the Olympic Games in Berlin in 1936. The greatest age at which anyone has held a world title is 60 years in the case of Pierre Etchbaster, who retired in 1955, after 27 years as undefeated world tennis champion from May 1928.

Longest reign The longest reign as a world champion is 27 years by Pierre Etchbaster (France) (see above).

The longest reign as a British champion is 41 years by the archer Miss Legh who first won the Championship in 1881 and for the 23rd and final time in 1922.

Greatest earnings The greatest fortune amassed by an individual in sport is an estimated £17,000,000 by the late Sonja Henie of Norway (1912–1969), the triple Olympic figure skating champion (1928–32–36), when later (1936–56) a professional ice skating promoter starring in her own ice shows and 11 films. The most earned for a single event is the reported $2,500,000 (£1,041,666) each by the boxers Bob Frazier and Mohammed Ali (*né* Cassius Clay) in their heavyweight world title fight over 15 rounds in Madison Square Gardens, New York City on 8 March 1971. This works out at £23,148·14 per minute of actual fighting.

The world's fastest earners in action at £385 per second

Largest trophy The world's largest sporting trophy is the Helms World Trophy for the sportsman of the year which stands 6 feet 2 inches in height on a marble base, which is 21 inches in height, making an overall height of 7 feet 11 inches. It is housed at the Helms Hall, 8760 Venice Boulevard, Los Angeles, California, U.S.A.

Largest following The sport with most participants in Britain is swimming with $6\frac{3}{4}$ million. The highest number of paid admissions is $7\frac{3}{4}$ million for Association Football, which also attracts more than 21 million T.V. viewers.

Most sportsmen According to a report issued in April 1971, 28,400,000 men and 15,200,000 women are actively involved in 209,000 physical culture and sports groups in the U.S.S.R. where there are 6·1 million track athletes, 5·6 million volleyball players, 3·9 million footballers and 891,000 weightlifters. The report lists 2,918 stadiums, 430 indoor and 475 outdoor swimming pools for 791,000 swimmers.

ANGLING

LARGEST CATCH

The largest fish ever caught on a rod is an officially ratified man-eating great white shark (*Carcharodon carcharias*) weighing 2,664 lb., and measuring 16 feet 10 inches long, caught on a 130 lb. test line by Alf Dean at Denial Bay, near Ceduna, South Australia, on 21 April 1959. Capt. Frank Mundus (U.S.A.) harpooned a 17-foot-long 4,500 lb. white shark, after a 5-hour battle, off Montauk Point, New York, U.S.A., in 1964.

The largest marine animal ever killed by hand harpoon was a blue whale 97 feet in length, killed by Archer Davidson in Twofold Bay, New South Wales, Australia, in 1910. Its tail flukes measured 20 feet across and its jaw bone 23 feet 4 inches. To date this has provided the ultimate in "fishing stories".

SMALLEST CATCH

The smallest full-grown fish ever caught is the *Schindleria praematurus*, weighing 1/14,000 of an ounce (see page 39) found in Samoa, in the Pacific. The smallest mature shark is the rare *Squalidus laticaudus*, found off the Philippines, which measures only 6 inches in length.

Spear fishing The largest fish ever taken underwater was an 804 lb. Giant Black Grouper or Jewfish by Don Pinder of the Miami Triton Club, Florida, U.S.A., in 1955. The British spearfishing record is 89 lb. 0 oz. for an angler fish by J. Brown (Weymouth Association Divers) in 1969.

Casting record The longest surf casting distance ever reported is one of 1,000 feet achieved on a beach in South Africa. The official world record under I.C.F. (International Casting Federation) rules is 161 metres (528 feet 2½ inches) by Walter Kummerow (West Germany).

Longest fight The longest recorded fight with a fish is 32 hours 5 minutes by Donal Heatley (b. 1938) (New Zealand) with a black marlin (estimated length 20 feet and weight 1,500 lb.) off Mayor Island off Tauranga, North Island on 21–22 Jan. 1968. It towed the 12-ton launch 50 miles before breaking the line.

Rarest fish The burbot, the rarest British fish, is "almost extinct", so it has been agreed that no record for this species should be published, at least until 1974, in the interests of conservation.

The heaviest British rod-caught fish is the tunny

WORLD RECORDS (All tackle)

(Sea fish as ratified by the International Game Fish Association to 1 Jan. 1971. Freshwater fish, ratified by *"Field & Stream"*, are marked *)

Species	Weight lb.	oz.	Name of Angler	Location	Date
Amberjack	149	0	Peter Simons	Bermuda	21 June 1964
Barracuda	103	4	C. E. Benet	West End, Bahamas	11 Aug. 1932
Bass (Californian Black Sea)	563	8	James D. McAdam	Anacapa Island, California, U.S.A.	20 Aug. 1968
Bass (Giant Sea)	680	0	Lynn Joyner	Fernandina Beach, Florida, U.S.A.	20 May 1961
*Carp†	55	5	Frank J. Ledwein	Clearwater Lake, Minnesota, U.S.A.	10 July 1952
Cod	98	12	Alphonse J. Bielevich	Isle of Shoals, Massachusetts, U.S.A.	8 June 1969
Marlin (Black)	1,560	0	Alfred C. Glassell, Jr.	Cabo Blanco, Peru	4 Aug. 1953
Marlin (Blue)	845	0	Elliot J. Fishman	St. Thomas, Virgin Is.	4 July 1968
Marlin (Pacific Blue)	1,153	0	Greg. D. Perez	Ritidian Point, Guam	21 Aug. 1969
Marlin (Striped)	465	0	James Black	Mayor Island, New Zealand	27 Feb. 1948
Marlin (White)	161	0	L. F. Hooper	Miami Beach, Florida, U.S.A.	20 Mar. 1938
*Pike (Northern)	46	2	Peter Dubuc	Sacandaga Reservoir, New York State, U.S.A.	15 Sept. 1940
Sailfish (Atlantic)	141	1	Tony Burnand	Ivory Coast, Africa	26 Jan. 1961
Sailfish (Pacific)	221	0	C. W. Stewart	Santa Cruz I., Galapagos Is.	12 Feb. 1947
*Salmon (Chinook)††	92	0	H. Wichmann	Skeena River, British Columbia, Canada	19 July 1959
Sawfish	890	8	Jack Wagner	Fort Amador, Canal Zone	26 May 1960
Shark (Blue)	410	0	Richard C. Webster	Rockport, Massachusetts, U.S.A.	1 Sept. 1960
	410	0	Martha C. Webster	Rockport, Massachusetts, U.S.A.	17 Aug. 1967
**Shark (Mako)	1,061	0	J. B. Penwarden	Mayor Island, New Zealand	17 Feb. 1970
Shark (White or Man-eating)	2,664	0	Alfred Dean	Denial Bay, Ceduna, South Australia	21 April 1959
Shark (Porbeagle)	430	0	Desmond Bougourd	South of Jersey, C.I.	29 June 1969
Shark (Thresher)	922	0	W. W. Dowding	Bay of Islands, New Zealand	21 Mar. 1937
Shark (Tiger)	1,780	0	Walter Maxwell	Cherry Grove, South Carolina, U.S.A.	14 June 1964
*Sturgeon (White)	360	0	Willard Cravens	Snake River, Idaho, U.S.A.	24 April 1956
Swordfish	1,182	0	L. E. Marron	Iquique, Chile	7 May 1953
Tarpon	283	0	M. Salazar	Lago de Maracaibo, Venezuela	19 Mar. 1956
*Trout (Lake)#	63	2	Hubert Hammers	Lake Superior	25 May 1952
Tuna (Allison or Yellowfin)	269	8	Henry Nishikawa	Hanalei, Hawaii, U.S.A.	30 May 1962
Tuna (Atlantic Big-eyed)	295	0	Dr. Arsenio Cordeiro	San Miguel, Azores	8 July 1960
Tuna (Pacific Big-eyed)	435	0	Dr. Russel V. A. Lee	Cabo Blanco, Peru	17 April 1957
Tuna (Bluefin)	1,040	0	M. M. Immergut	Prince Edward Island, Canada	23 Sept. 1970
Wahoo	149	0	John Pirovano	Cat Cay, Bahamas	15 June 1962

† *A carp weighing 83 lb. 8 oz. was taken (not by rod) near Pretoria, South Africa.*

†† *A salmon weighing 126 lb. 8 oz. was taken (not by rod) near Petersburg, Alaska, U.S.A.*

** *A 1,295 lb. specimen was taken by two anglers off Natal, South Africa on 17 March 1939 and a 1,500 lb. specimen harpooned inside Durban Harbour, South Africa in 1933.*

A 102 lb. trout was taken from Lake Athabasca, northern Saskatchewan, Canada, on 8 Aug. 1961.

BRITISH ROD-CAUGHT RECORDS (as ratified by the British Record [rod-caught] Fish Committee of the National Anglers' Council)
(Selected from the complete list of about 100 species)

SEA FISH

Species	Weight		Name of Angler	Location	Year
	lb.	oz.			
Angler Fish	68	2	H. G. T. Legerton	Canvey Island, Essex	1967
Bass	18	2	F. C. Borley	Felixstowe Beach, Suffolk	1943
Black Bream	6	1	F. W. Richards	The Skerries, Dartmouth	1969
Red Bream	7	8	A. F. Bell	Fowey, Cornwall	1925
Brill	16	0	A. H. Fisher	Derby Haven, Isle of Man	1950
Bull Huss (Greater Spotted Dogfish)	21	3	J. Holmes	Hat Rock, Cornwall	1955
Coalfish	23	8	H. Millais	Land's End, Cornwall	1921
Cod	46	0½	R. Baird	Firth of Clyde	1970
Conger	92	13	P. H. Ascott	Torquay, Devon	1970
Dab	2	10¾	A. B. Hare	The Skerries, Dartmouth	1968
Dogfish (Lesser Spotted)	4	8	J. Beattie	off Ayr Pier, Ayrshire	1969
Dogfish (Spur)	16	12½	W. R. Legg	Abbotsbury, Chesil Beach, Dorset	1964
Flounder	5	11½	A. G. L. Cobbledick	Fowey, Cornwall	1956
Garfish	2	9⅛	A. W. Bodfield	Dartmouth, Devonshire	1963
Grey Mullet	10	1	P/O. P. C. Libby	Portland, Dorset	1952
Gurnard	11	7¼	C. W. King	Wallasey, Cheshire	1952
Gurnard (Red)	3	2	W. S. Blunn	Stoke, nr. Plymouth, Devon	1970
Haddock	9	4½	Mrs. L. Morley	Mevagissey, Cornwall	1969
Hake	25	5½	Herbert W. Steele	Belfast Lough	1962
Halibut	161	12	W. E. Knight	Orkney	1968
John Dory	10	12	B. Perry	Porthallow, Cornwall	1963
Ling	45	0	H. C. Nicholl	Penzance, Cornwall	1912
Lumpsucker	6	3¼	F. Harrison	Redcar, Yorkshire	1968
Mackerel	5	6½	S. Beasley	N. of Eddystone Lighthouse	1969
Megrim	3	10	D. DiCicco	Ullapool, Ross-shire	1966
Monkfish	66	0	G. C. Chalk	Shoreham, Sussex	1965
Mullet (Red)	3	10	John E. Martel	St. Martin's, Guernsey	1967
Plaice	7	15	Ian B. Brodie	Salcombe, Devon	1964
Pollack	23	8	G. Bartholomew	Newquay, Cornwall	1957
Pouting	5	8	R. S. Armstrong	off Berry Head, Devon	1969
Ray (Spotted)	16	3	E. Lockwood	Lerwick Harbour, Shetland	1970
Ray (Thornback)	38	0	J. Patterson	Rustington, Sussex	1935
Scad	3	3	J. B. Thornton	Deal, Kent	1934
Allis Shad	3	4½	Bernard H. Sloane	Torquay, Devon	1964
Twaite Shad	3	2	S. Jenkins	Tor Bay, Devon	1954
	3	2	T. Hayward	Deal, Kent	1949
Shark (Blue)	218	0	N. Sutcliffe	Looe, Cornwall	1959
Shark (Mako)	498	8	Ken C. Burgess	Looe, Cornwall	1966
Shark (Porbeagle)	430	0	see world record left		
Shark (Thresher)	280	0	H. A. Kelly	Dungeness, Kent	1933
Skate (Common)	226	8	R. S. Macpherson	Dury Voe, Shetland	1970
Sole	4	1⅞	R. A. Austin	Bordeaux Vale, Guernsey	1967
Sting Ray	59	0	J. M. Buckley	Clacton-on-Sea, Essex	1952
Three-bearded Rockling	2	13⅛	K. Westaway	Portland Harbour, Dorset	1966
Tope	74	11	A. B. Harries	Caldy Island, Pembrokeshire	1964
Tunny	851	0	L. Mitchell-Henry	Whitby, Yorkshire	1933
Turbot	29	0	G. M. W. Garnsey	The Manacles, Cornwall	1964
Greater Weever	2	4	P. Ainslie	Brighton, Sussex	1927
Whiting	6	3	Mrs. R. Barrett	Rame Head, Cornwall	1971
Wrasse (Ballan)	7	10	B. K. Lawrence	Trevose Head, Cornwall	1970

FRESHWATER FISH

It will be noted that seven former "records" achieved between 1923 and 1955 have been discarded because they cannot be substantiated under the existing rules. These are noted as being "open to claim" if a specimen comes up to or over the "minimum qualifying standard".

Species	Weight		Name of Angler	Location	Year
	lb.	oz.			
Barbel[1]	13	2	J. H. Harrigan	Royalty Fishery, Christchurch, Hampshire	1965
	13	2	E. Upton	Royalty Fishery, Christchurch, Hampshire	1970
Bleak	0	3½	N. D. Sizmur	Walton-on-Thames, Surrey	1963
Bream (Common)	11	12	W. Gollins	nr. Ellesmere, Shropshire	1970
Bream (Silver)	record open to claim				
Carp	44	0	Richard Walker	Redmire Pool, Herefordshire	1952
Chub	record open to claim				
Crucian Carp	4	6¼	P. H. Oliver	Private lake, Surrey	1970
Dace	record open to claim				
Eel	8	10	A. Dart	Hunstrete Lake	1969
Grayling	record open to claim				
Gudgeon	record open to claim				
Gwyniad (Whitefish)	1	4	J. R. Williams	Llyn Tegid, Merionethshire	1965
Loch Lomond Powan	1	5¾	D. J. Warren	Loch Lomond	1970
Perch	4	12	S. F. Baker	Oulton Broad, Norfolk	1962
Pike[3]	record open to claim				
Roach	3	14	W. Penney	Lambeth Reservoir, Molesey, Surrey	1938
	3	14	A. Brown	Pit, near Stamford, Lincolnshire	1964
Rudd	4	8	Rev. E. C. Alston	Mere, near Thetford, Norfolk	1933
"Ruffe"		4	B. B. Poyner	River Stour, Warwickshire	1969
Salmon[3]	64	0	Miss G. W. Ballantyne	River Tay	1922
Tench	9	1	John Salisbury	Hemingford Grey, Huntingdonshire	1963
Trout (Brown)[4]	18	2	K. J. Grant	Loch Garry, Inverness-shire	1965
Trout (Rainbow)*	10	0¼	M. Parker	From a private lake	1970
Trout (Sea)	record open to claim				

* *This fish was cultivated.*

1 *A 16 lb. 4 oz. Barbel was caught in the close season by R. Beddington in the R. Avon at Christchurch, Hants. in April 1934.*

2 *A Pike of allegedly 52 lb. was recovered when Whittlesea Mere, Cambridgeshire and Isle of Ely, was drained in 1851.*

3 *The 8th Earl of Home is recorded as having caught a 69¾ lb. specimen in the R. Tweed in 1730. J. Wallace claimed a 67-pounder at Barjarg, Dumfries-shire in 1812.*

4 *In 1866 W. C. Muir is reputed to have caught a 39½ lb. specimen in Loch Awe, and in 1816 a 36 lb. specimen was reported from the R. Colne, near Watford, Hertfordshire.*

IRISH ANGLING RECORDS (as ratified by the Irish Specimen Fish Committee)

Species	Weight lb. oz.	Name of Angler	Location	Date
SEA FISH				
Angler Fish	71 8	M. Fitzgerald	Cork (Cóbh) Harbour	5 July 1964
Bass	16 0	Major Ashe Windham	Waterville, Kerry	Aug. 1909
Sea Bream (Red)	9 6	P. Maguire	Valentia, Kerry	24 Aug. 1963
Coalfish	24 7	J. E. Hornibrook	Kinsale, Cork	26 Aug. 1967
Cod	42 0	I. L. Stewart	Ballycotton, Cork	1921
Conger	72 0	J. Greene	Valentia, Kerry	June 1914
Dab	1 12½	Ian V. Kerr	Kinsale, Cork	10 Sept. 1963
Dogfish (Greater Spotted)	19 12	Michael Courage	Bray, Co. Wicklow	6 July 1969
Dogfish (Spur)	16 4	C. McIvor	Strangford Lough, Co. Down	20 June 1969
Flounder	4 3	J. L. McMonagle	Killala Bay, Co. Mayo	5 Aug. 1963
Garfish	3 10¼	Evan G. Bazzard	Kinsale, Cork	16 Sept. 1967
Gurnard (Grey)	3 1	Brendan Walsh	Rosslare Bay	21 Sept. 1967
Gurnard (Red)	3 9½	James Prescott	Broadhaven Bay, Co. Mayo	17 July 1968
Gurnard (Tub)	10 8	Clive Gammon	Belmullet, Co. Mayo	18 June 1970
Haddock	10 13½	F. A. E. Bull	Kinsale, Cork	15 July 1964
Hake	25 5½	Herbert W. Steele	Belfast Lough	28 April 1962
Halibut	152 12	E. C. Henning	Valentia, Kerry	1926
John Dory	7 1	Stanley Morrow	Tory Island, Co. Donegal	6 Sept. 1970
Ling	46 8	Andrew J. C. Bull	Kinsale, Cork	26 July 1965
Mackerel	3 6	J. O'Connell	Valentia, Kerry	24 Sept. 1969
Monkfish	69 0	Mons. Michael Fuchs	Westport, Co. Mayo	1 July 1958
Mullet (Grey)	6 0	N. Fitchett	Ballycotton, Cork	8 Sept. 1965
Plaice	7 0	Ernest Yemen	Portrush, Antrim	28 Sept. 1964
Pollack	19 3	J. N. Hearne	Ballycotton, Cork	1904
Pouting	4 10	W. G. Pales	Ballycotton, Cork	1937
Ray (Blonde)	36 8	D. Minchin	Cork (Cóbh) Harbour	9 Sept. 1964
Ray (Thornback)	37 0	M. J. Fitzgerald	Kinsale, Cork	28 May 1961
Shark (Blue)	206 0	J. L. McMonagle	Achill, Co. Mayo	7 Oct. 1959
Shark (Porbeagle)	365 0	Dr. M. O'Donel Browne	Keem Bay, Achill, Co. Mayo	28 Sept. 1932
Skate (Common)	221 0	T. Tucker	Ballycotton, Cork	1913
Skate (White)	165 0	Jack Stack	Clew Bay, Westport, Co. Mayo	7 Aug. 1966
Sting Ray	51 0	John K. White	Kilfenora Strand, Fenet	8 Aug. 1970
Tope	60 12	Crawford McIvor	Strangford Lough, Co. Down	12 Sept. 1968
Turbot	26 8	J. F. Eldridge	Valentia, Kerry	1915
Whiting	4 8½	Eddie Boyle	Kinsale, Cork	4 Aug. 1969
Wrasse (Ballan)	7 6	Anthony J. King	Killybegs, Donegal	26 July 1964
FRESHWATER				
Bream	11 12	A. Pike	River Blackwater, Co. Monaghan	July 1882
Carp	18 12	John Roberts	Abbey Lake	6 June 1958
Dace	1 2	John T. Henry	River Blackwater, Cappoquin	8 Aug. 1966
Eel (River)	5 15	Edmund Hawksworth	River Shannon, Clondra	25 Sept. 1968
Perch	5 8	S. Drum	Lough Erne	1946
Pike	42 0*	M. Watkins	River Barrow	22 Mar. 1964
Roach	2 13½	Lawrie Robinson	River Blackwater, Cappoquin	11 Aug. 1970
Rudd	3 1	A. E. Biddlecombe	Kilglass Lake	27 June 1959
Rudd-Bream hybrid	5 5	W. Walker	Coosan Lough, Garnafailagh, Athlone	5 June 1963
Salmon	57 0†	M. Maher	River Suir	1874
Tench	7 12	Edmund Hawksworth	River Shannon, Clondra	4 June 1966
Brown Trout (Lake)	26 2††	William Meares	Lough Ennell	15 July 1894
Brown Trout (River)	20 0	Major H. H. Place	River Shannon, Corbally	22 Feb. 1957
Rainbow Trout	8 7	Dr. J. P. C. Purdon	Lough Eyes, Co. Fermanagh	11 Mar. 1968
Sea Trout	12 0	T. Regan	River Dargle, Co. Wicklow	3 Oct. 1958

* *A Pike in excess of 92 lb. is reputed to have been landed from the Shannon at Portumna, County Galway, in c. 1796.*

† *A 58 lb. Salmon was reported from the River Shannon in 1872 while one of 62 lb. was taken in a net on the lower Shannon on 27 March 1925.*

†† *A 35½ lb. Brown Trout is reputed to have been caught at Turlaghvan, near Tuam, in August 1738. "Pepper's Ghost", the 30 lb. 8 oz. fish caught by J. W. Pepper in Lough Derg in 1860, has now been shown to have been a salmon.*

ARCHERY

Earliest references Palaeolithic drawings of archers indicate that bows and arrows are an invention of at least 20,000 years ago. Archery developed as an organized sport at least as early as the 4th century A.D. The oldest archery body in the British Isles is the Royal Company of Archers, the Sovereign's bodyguard for Scotland, dating from 1676, though the Ancient Scorton Arrow meeting in Yorkshire was first staged in 1673. The world governing body is the *Fédération Internationale de Tir à l'Arc* (FITA), founded in 1931.

Flight shooting The longest recorded distance ever shot is 1 mile 101 yards 1 foot 9 inches in the unlimited footbow class by the professional Harry Drake of Lakeside, California, U.S.A. at Ivanpah Dry Lake, California on 3 Oct. 1970. Drake also holds the flight records for the handbow at 856 yards 1 foot 8 inches and the crossbow at 1,359 yards 2 feet 5 inches both at Ivanpah Dry Lake on 14–15 Oct. 1967.

The British record is 647 yards 1 foot 11 inches by Alan Webster at York on 20 April 1969.

HIGHEST SCORES

World The world records for FITA Rounds (see below) are: men 1,250 points by Jorma Sandelen (Finland) at Varkaus, Finland on 2–3 Sept. 1969, and women 1,208 points by Mrs. Nancy E. Myrick (U.S.A.) at the World Championships at Amersfoort, Netherlands, 23–28 July 1967.

The record for a FITA Double Round is 2,467 points by Jorma Sandelen (Finland) at Varkaus, Finland on 2–3 Sept. 1969. The feminine record is 2,361 points by Mrs. Dorothy Lidstone (Canada) at Valley Forge, Pennsylvania, U.S.A. on 17–18 Aug. 1969.

British York Round (6 dozen at 100 yards, 4 dozen at 80 yards and 2 dozen at 60 yards).

The only archer to have shot an arrow over a mile—
Harry Drake (U.S.A.) in action

Single Round, 1,097 J. Ian Dixon at Oxford, on 4 July 1968.
Double Round, 2,138 Roy D. Matthews at Oxford, on 3–4 July 1968.
Hereford (Women) (6 dozen at 80 yards, 4 dozen at 60 yards and 2 dozen at 50 yards).
Single Round, 1,090 Mrs. Sandra Simester at Slough, Buckinghamshire, 6 Sept. 1970.
Double Round, 2,122 Miss Lynne A. Thomas at Leeds, on 4–5 Sept. 1969.
FITA Round (Men) (3 dozen each at 90, 70, 50 and 30 metres).
Single Round, 1,216 Roy D. Matthews at Warsaw, Poland, on 18–19 Sept. 1970.
Double Round, 2,305 J. Ian Dixon at Valley Forge, Pennsylvania, U.S.A., on 17–18 Aug. 1969.
FITA Round (Women's) (3 dozen each at 70, 60, 50 and 30 metres).
Single Round, 1,211 Miss Lynne A. Thomas at Warsaw, Poland, on 18–19 Sept. 1970.
Double Round, 2,274 Miss Pauline Edwards at Valley Forge, Pennsylvania, U.S.A., on 17–18 Aug. 1969.

Most titles The greatest number of world titles (instituted 1931) ever won by a man is four by H. Deutgen (Sweden) in 1947–48–49–50. The greatest number won by a woman is seven by Mrs. Janina Spychajowa-Kurkowska (Poland) in 1931–32–33–34, 1936, 1939 and 1947.

The greatest number of British Championships is 12 by Horace A. Ford between 1849 and 1867, and 23 by Miss B. M. Legh in 1881, 1886–87–88–89–90–91–92, 1895, 1898–99–1900, 1902–03–04–05–06–07–08–09, 1913 and 1921–22.

Marathon The highest recorded score over 24 hours by a pair of archers is 21,700 out of a possible 24,000 during 20 Portsmouth Rounds (60 arrows at 20 yards) shot by Paul Templar and David Dakers of the Heugh Bowmen at Peterlee Community Centre, Peterlee, Co. Durham from 10.30 a.m. to 10.30 a.m. on 7–8 April 1971.

ATHLETICS

Earliest references Track and field athletics date from the ancient Olympic Games. The earliest accurately known Olympiad dates from 21 or 22 July 776 B.C., at which celebration Coroebus won the foot race. The oldest surviving measurements are a long jump of 23 feet $1\frac{1}{2}$ inches (7·05 metres) by Chionis of Sparta in *c.* 656 B.C. and a discus throw of 100 cubits by Protesilaus.

Fastest runner Robert Lee Hayes (b. 20 Dec. 1942) of Jacksonville, Florida, U.S.A., was timed at 26·9 m.p.h. at the 75-yard mark of a 100-yard race in May 1964. Wyomia Tyus (b. Griffin, Georgia, U.S.A., 29 Aug. 1945) was timed at 23·78 m.p.h. in Kiev, U.S.S.R. on 31 July 1965.

Highest jumper There are several reported instances of high jumpers exceeding the official world record height of 7 feet $5\frac{3}{4}$ inches. The earliest of these came from unsubstantiated reports of Tutsi tribesmen in Central Africa (see page 15) clearing up to 8 feet $2\frac{1}{2}$ inches, definitely however, from inclined take-offs. The greatest height cleared above an athlete's own head is $17\frac{5}{8}$ inches, achieved by Ni Chih-chin of China (Mainland) when clearing 2·29 metres (7 feet $6\frac{1}{8}$ inches) in an exhibition at Changsha, Hunan on 8 Nov. 1970. He stands 6 feet $0\frac{1}{2}$ inch tall and was born on 14 April 1942. The greatest height cleared by a woman above her own head is 6 inches by Miroslava Rezkova (Czechoslovakia), standing 5 feet $6\frac{1}{2}$ inches when she jumped 6 feet $0\frac{1}{2}$ inch at Povazka Bystrica, Czechoslovakia on 20 July 1969.

Most Olympic gold medals Ray C. Ewry (U.S.A.) won eight individual Olympic gold medals, three in 1900, three in 1904 and two in 1908. Paavo Johannes Nurmi (Finland) won six individual and three team race gold medals between 1920 and 1928. The greatest number of gold medals won in a single celebration is five by Paavo Nurmi (Finland) in 1924 (1,500 metres, 3,000 metres team, 5,000 metres, cross-country team and individual). The most individual wins is four by Alvin C. Kraenzlein (U.S.A.) in 1900 (60 metres, 110 metres and 200 metres hurdles and long jump). The most wins by a woman is four by Francina E. Blankers-Koen (b. 26 April 1918) of the Netherlands in 1948 (100 and 200 metres, 80 metres hurdles, and the last stage in the 4 × 100 metres relay), and four by Betty Cuthbert (b. 20 April 1938) of Australia in 1956 (100 metres, 200 metres and the last stage in the 4 × 100 metres relay) and 1964 (400 metres).

Fanny Blankers-Koen—the Flying Dutchwoman who won 4 Olympic gold medals in 1948

Most medals The most Olympic medals (of any metal) won by a man is 12 (nine gold and three silver) by Nurmi. The most won by a woman is seven by Shirley de la Hunty (*née* Strickland) of Australia between 1948 and 1956. The United Kingdom record is four by Guy M. Butler in 1920 and 1924 and for women three by Dorothy Hyman, M.B.E., in 1960 and 1964, and Mrs. Mary Denise Rand, M.B.E. (now Toomey, *née* Bignal), (b. Wells, Somerset 10 Feb. 1940) in 1964.

Emmanuel McDonald Bailey, winner of 14 A.A.A. sprint titles

Most national titles The greatest number of national A.A.A. titles won by one athlete is fourteen individual and two relay titles by Emmanuel McDonald Bailey (b. Williamsville, Trinidad 8 Dec. 1920), between 1946 and 1953.

The greatest number of consecutive title wins is seven by Denis Horgan (Ireland) in the shot putt (1893–99), Albert A. Cooper (2 miles walk, 1932–38), Donald Osborne Finlay, D.F.C., A.F.C. (1909–70) (120 yards hurdles, 1932–38), Harry Whittle (440 yards hurdles, 1947–1953) and Maurice Herriott (3,000 metres steeplechase, 1961–67). The record for consecutive W.A.A.A titles is eight by Mrs. Judy U. Farr (Trowbridge & District A.C.) (b. 24 Jan. 1942), who won the $1\frac{1}{2}$ mile/2,500 metre walk from 1962–69.

James Ray Hines (U.S.A.)—first man to break 10·0 secs. for 100 metres

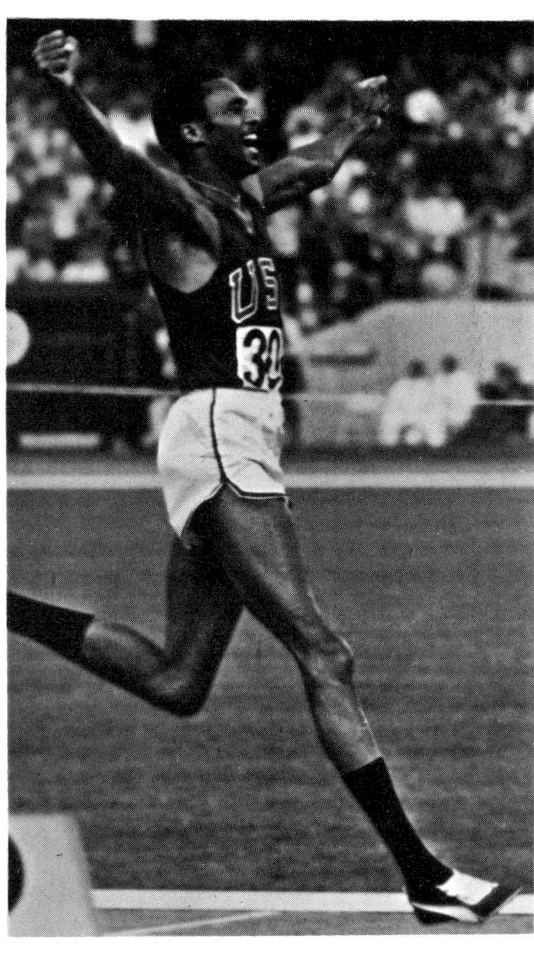

rld 200-metre and 220 yards record holder ommie Smith (U.S.A.)

Co-holder of the world's 800-metre record, Ralph Doubell

WORLD RECORDS—MEN

The complete list of World Records for the 54 scheduled men's events (excluding the 6 walking records, see under WALKING) passed by the International Amateur Athletic Federation as at 30 June 1971.

RUNNING

Event	Mins. secs.	Name and Nationality	Place	Date
100 yards	9·1	Robert Lee Hayes (U.S.A.)	St. Louis, Missouri, U.S.A.	21 June 1963
	9·1	Harry Winston Jerome (Canada)	Edmonton, Alberta, Canada	15 July 1966
	9·1	James Ray Hines (U.S.A.)	Houston, Texas, U.S.A.	13 May 1967
	9·1	Charles Edward Greene (U.S.A.)	Provo, Utah, U.S.A.	15 June 1967
	9·1	John W. Carlos (U.S.A.)	Fresno, California, U.S.A.	10 May 1969
220 yards (straight)	19·5	Tommie C. Smith (U.S.A.)	San Jose, California, U.S.A.	7 May 1966
220 yards (turn)	20·0	Tommie C. Smith (U.S.A.)	Sacramento, California, U.S.A.	11 June 1966
440 yards	44·5	John Smith (U.S.A.)	Eugene, Oregon, U.S.A.	26 June 1971
880 yards	1:44·9	James Ronald Ryun (U.S.A.)	Terre Haute, Indiana, U.S.A.	10 June 1966
1 mile	3:51·1	James Ronald Ryun (U.S.A.)	Bakersfield, California, U.S.A.	23 June 1967
2 miles	8:19·6	Ronald William Clarke, M.B.E. (Australia)	London, England	24 Aug. 1968
3 miles	12:50·4	Ronald William Clarke, M.B.E. (Australia)	Stockholm, Sweden	5 July 1966
6 miles	26:47·0	Ronald William Clarke, M.B.E. (Australia)	Oslo, Norway	14 July 1965
10 miles	46:37·8	Jerome Drayton	Toronto, Ontario, Canada	6 Sept. 1970
15 miles	1H 12:48·2	Ronald Hill (United Kingdom)	Bolton, Lancashire, England	21 July 1965
100 metres	9·9	James Ray Hines (U.S.A.)	Sacramento, California, U.S.A.	20 June 1968
	9·9	Ronald Ray Smith (U.S.A.)	Sacramento, California, U.S.A.	20 June 1968
	9·9	Charles Edward Greene (U.S.A.)	Sacramento, California, U.S.A.	20 June 1968
	9·9	James Ray Hines (U.S.A.)	Mexico City, Mexico	14 Oct. 1968
200 metres (straight)	19·5	Tommie C. Smith (U.S.A.)	San Jose, California, U.S.A.	7 May 1966
200 metres (turn)	19·8	Tommie C. Smith (U.S.A.)	Mexico City, Mexico	16 Oct. 1968
400 metres	43·8	Lee Edward Evans (U.S.A.)	Mexico City, Mexico	18 Oct. 1968
800 metres	1:44·3	Peter George Snell (New Zealand)	Christchurch, New Zealand	3 Feb. 1962
	1:44·3	Ralph D. Doubell (Australia)	Mexico City, Mexico	15 Oct. 1968
1,000 metres	2:16·2	Jürgen May (East Germany)	Erfurt, East Germany	20 July 1965
	2:16·2	Franz-Josef Kemper (West Germany)	Hanover, West Germany	21 Sept. 1966
1,500 metres	3:33·1	James Ronald Ryun (U.S.A.)	Los Angeles, California, U.S.A.	8 July 1967
2,000 metres	4:56·2	Michel Jazy (France)	St. Maur des Fosses, France	12 Oct. 1966
3,000 metres	7:39·6	Kipchoge Keino (Kenya)	Hälsingborg, Sweden	27 Aug. 1965
5,000 metres	13:16·6	Ronald William Clarke, M.B.E. (Australia)	Stockholm, Sweden	5 July 1966
10,000 metres	27:39·4	Ronald William Clarke, M.B.E. (Australia)	Oslo, Norway	14 July 1965
20,000 metres	58:06·2	Gaston Roelants (Belgium)	Louvain, Belgium	28 Oct. 1966
25,000 metres	1H 15:22·6	Ronald Hill (United Kingdom)	Bolton, Lancashire, England	21 July 1965
30,000 metres	1H 31:30·4	James Noel Carroll Alder (U.K.)	London (Crystal Palace)	5 Sept. 1970
1 hour	12 miles 1,478 yards (20,664 metres)	Gaston Roelants (Belgium)	Louvain, Belgium	28 Oct. 1966

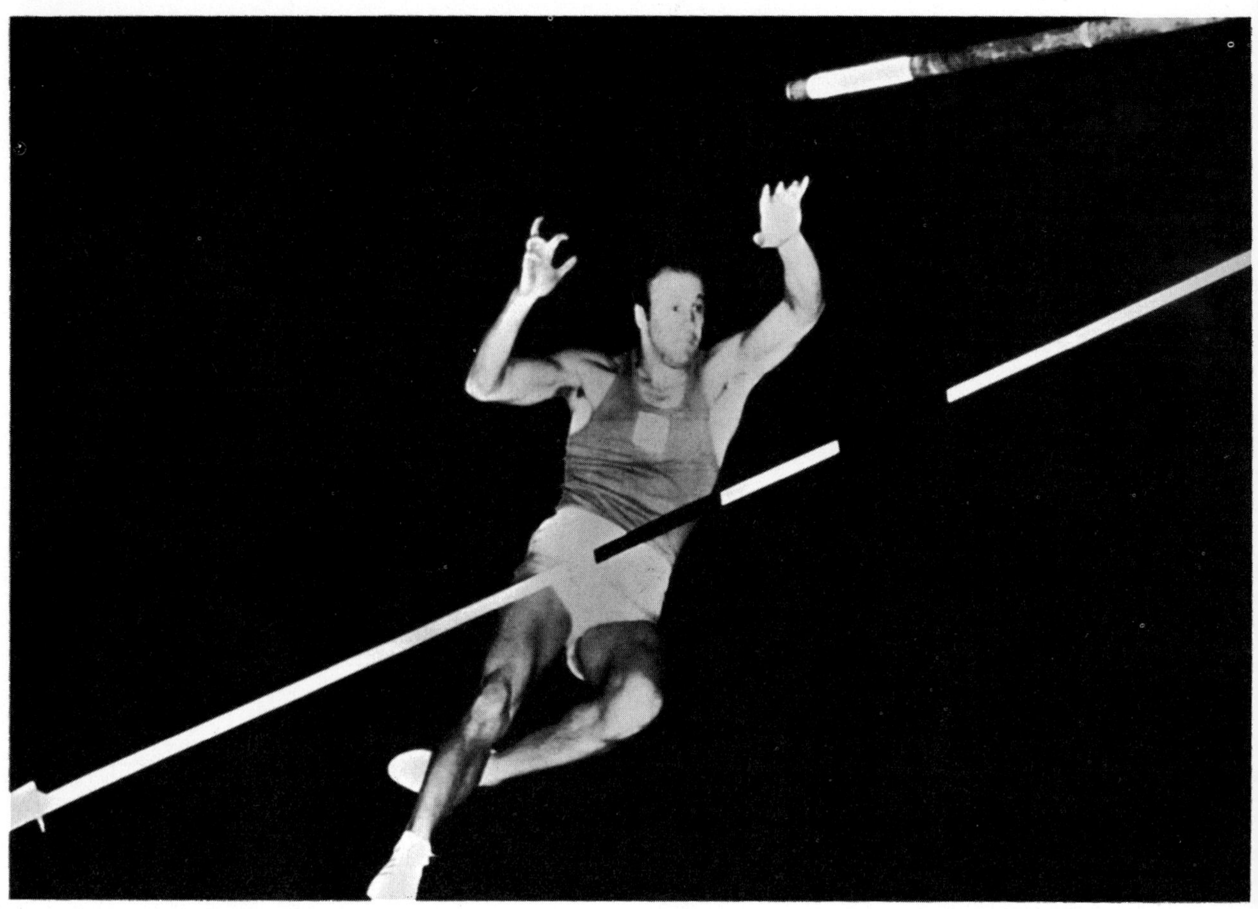

Christos Papanikolaou (Greece) at the high point of history's first 18-foot vault

HURDLING

120 yards (3′ 6″ hurdles)	13·2	Karl Martin Lauer (West Germany)	Zürich, Switzerland	7 July 1959
	13·2	Lee Quency Calhoun (U.S.A.)	Bern, Switzerland	21 Aug. 1960
	13·2	Earl Ray McCullouch (U.S.A.)	Minneapolis, Minnesota, U.S.A.	16 July 1967
	13·2	Erv. Hall (U.S.A.)	Knoxville, Tennessee, U.S.A.	19 June 1969
220 yards (2′ 6″) (straight)	21·9	Donald Augustus Styron (U.S.A.)	Baton Rouge, Louisiana, U.S.A.	2 April 1960
440 yards (3′ 0″)	48·8	Ralph Mann (U.S.A.)	Des Moines, Iowa, U.S.A.	20 June 1970
110 metres (3′ 6″)	13·2	Karl Martin Lauer (West Germany)	Zürich, Switzerland	7 July 1959
	13·2	Lee Quency Calhoun (U.S.A.)	Bern, Switzerland	21 Aug. 1960
	13·2	Earl Ray McCullouch (U.S.A.)	Minneapolis, Minnesota, U.S.A.	16 July 1967
200 metres (2′ 6″) (straight)	21·9	Donald Augustus Styron (U.S.A.)	Baton Rouge, Louisiana, U.S.A.	2 April 1960
200 metres (2′ 6″) (turn)	22·5	Karl Martin Lauer (West Germany)	Zürich, Switzerland	7 July 1959
	22·5	Glenn Ashby Davis (U.S.A.)	Bern, Switzerland	20 Aug. 1960
400 metres (3′ 0″)	48·1	David Peter Hemery (United Kingdom)	Mexico City, Mexico	15 Oct. 1968
3,000 metres Steeplechase	8:22·0	Kerry O'Brien (Australia)	Berlin (West), West Germany	4 July 1970

FIELD EVENTS

Event	ft.	ins.	Metres	Name and Nationality	Place	Date
High Jump	7	6¼	2·29†	Patrick Matzdorf (U.S.A.)	Berkeley, California, U.S.A.	3 July 1971
Pole Vault	18	0	5·49	Christos Papanikolaou (Greece)	Athens, Greece	24 Oct. 1970
Long Jump	29	2½	8·90	Robert Beamon (U.S.A.)	Mexico City, Mexico	18 Oct. 1968
Triple Jump	57	0¾	17·39	Viktor Sanyeyev (U.S.S.R.)	Mexico City, Mexico	17 Oct. 1968
Shot Putt	71	5½	21·78	James Randel Matson (U.S.A.)	College Station, Texas, U.S.A.	22 April 1967
Discus Throw	224	5	68·40	L Jay Silvester (U.S.A.)	Reno, Nevada, U.S.A.	18 Sept. 1968
Hammer Throw	245	0	74·68	Anatoliy Bondarchuk (U.S.S.R.)	Athens, Greece	20 Sept. 1969
Javelin Throw	304	1	92·70	Jorma V. P. Kinnunen (Finland)	Tampere, Finland	18 June 1969

† *Ni Chih-chin (China, Mainland) cleared a non-ratifiable 2·29 (7 feet 6⅛ inches) in an exhibition jump at Changsha, Hunan, China (Mainland), on 8 Nov. 1970.*

DECATHLON

8,417 points	William Toomey (U.S.A.) (1st day: 100m. 10·3s., Long Jump 25′ 5½″, Shot Putt 47′ 2¼″, High Jump 6′ 4″, 400m. 47·1s.)	Los Angeles, California, U.S.A. (2nd day: 110m. Hurdles 14·8s., Discus 152′ 6″, Pole Vault 14′ 0¼″, Javelin 215′ 8″, 1,500m. 4:39·4s.)	10–11 Dec. 1969

THE MARATHON

There is no official marathon record because of the varying severity of courses. The best time over 26 miles 385 yards (standardized in 1924) is 2 hours 08 minutes 33·6 seconds (av. 12·24 m.p.h.) by Derek Clayton (b. 1942, at Barrow-in-Furness, England) of Australia, at Antwerp, Belgium, on 30 May 1969.

The best time by a British international is 2 hours 9 minutes 28·0 seconds by Ronald Hill of Bolton United Harriers, at Edinburgh, Scotland on 22 July 1970.

The best time by a female is 3 hours 02 minutes 53 seconds (av. 8·60 m.p.h.) by Caroline Walker (U.S.A.), aged 16, at Seaside, Oregon, U.S.A. on 28 Feb. 1970. She finished 42nd of 149 starters in a mixed race contrary to I.A.A.F. rules.

RELAYS

Event	Mins. secs.	Team	Place	Date
4 × 110 yards (two turns)	38·6	University of Southern California, U.S.A. (Earl Ray McCullouch, Fred Kuller, Orenthal James Simpson, Lennox Miller [Jamaica])	Provo, Utah, U.S.A.	17 June 1967
4 × 220 yards and 4 × 200 metres	1:21·7	Texas Agricultural & Mechanical College (Donald Rogers, Rocklie Woods, Marvin Mills, Curtis Mills)	Des Moines, Iowa, U.S.A.	24 April 1970
4 × 440 yards	3:02·8	Trinidad and Tobago (Lennox Yearwood, Kent Bernard, Edwin Roberts, Wendell A. Mottley)	Kingston, Jamaica	13 Aug. 1966
4 × 880 yards	7:11·6	Kenyan National Team (Naftali Bon, Hezekiah Nyamau, Thomas Saisi, Robert Ouko)	London (Crystal Palace)	5 Sept. 1970
4 × 1 mile	16:05·0	Oregon Track Club (U.S.A.) (Roscoe Divine, C. Wade Bell, Arne Kvalheim [Norway], David Wilborn)	Eugene, Oregon, U.S.A.	30 May 1968
4 × 100 metres (two turns)	38·2	United States National Team (Charles Edward Greene, Melvin Pender, Ronald Ray Smith, James Ray Hines)	Mexico City, Mexico	20 Oct. 1968
4 × 400 metres	2:56·1	United States National Team (Vincent Matthews, Ronald Freeman, G. Lawrence James, Lee Edward Evans)	Mexico City, Mexico	20 Oct. 1968
4 × 800 metres	7:08·6	West Germany "A" Team (Manfred Kinder, Walter Adams, Dieter Bogatzki, Franz-Josef Kemper)	Wiesbaden, West Germany	13 Aug. 1966
4 × 1,500 metres	14:49·0	France "A" Team (Gérard Vervoort, Claude Nicolas, Michel Jazy, Jean Wadoux)	St. Maur des Fosses, France	25 June 1965

Earliest landmarks The first time 10 seconds ("even time") was bettered for 100 yards under championship conditions was when John Owen recorded $9\frac{4}{5}$ seconds in the United States A.A.U. Championships at Analostan Island, Washington, D.C., U.S.A., on 11 Oct. 1890. The first recorded instance of 6 feet being cleared in the high jump was when Marshall Jones Brooks jumped 6 feet $0\frac{1}{8}$ inch at Marston, near Oxford, England, on 17 March 1876. The breaking of the "4-minute barrier" in the one mile was first achieved by Dr. Roger Gilbert Bannister, C.B.E. (b. Harrow, England 23 March 1929), when he recorded 3 minutes 59·4 seconds on the Iffley Road track, Oxford, at 6.10 p.m. on 6 May 1954.

World record breakers *Oldest* The greatest age at which anyone has broken a world athletics record in a standard Olympic event is 35 years 255 days in the case of Dana Zátopkova, *née* Ingrova (b. 19 Sept. 1922) of Czechoslovakia, who broke the women's javelin record with 182 feet 10 inches (55·73 metres) at Prague, Czechoslovakia, on 1 June 1958. On 20 June 1948 Mikko Hietanen (Finland) (b. 22 Sept. 1911) bettered his own world 30,000 metres record with 1 hour 40 minutes 46·4 seconds at Jyväskylä, Finland, when aged 36 years 272 days.

Youngest Doreen Lumley (b. September 1921) of New Zealand equalled the world record for the women's 100 yards of 11·0 seconds at Auckland, New Zealand on 11 March 1939, when aged 17 years 6 months.

Professional records Professional records include: 100 yards, 9·3 seconds by Ken Irvine (Australia) at Dubbo, New South Wales, Australia, on 9 March 1963; Mile, 3 minutes 59·7 seconds from scratch by Harold Downes (Australia) in a handicap race at Bendigo, Victoria, Australia, on 9 March 1963; Shot Putt, 64 feet (19·507 metres) by Arthur Rowe (b. 17 Aug. 1936) of Barnsley, Yorkshire, at Keswick, Cumberland, on 6 Aug. 1962.

History's fastest 400-metre runner—Lee Edward Evans (U.S.A.)

Shot putt both hands The greatest combined distance for putting the shot is 106 feet $10\frac{1}{4}$ inches (61 feet $0\frac{3}{4}$ inch with the right hand and 45 feet $9\frac{1}{2}$ inches left hand) by William Parry O'Brien (b. 28 Jan. 1932) of the U.S.A., at Culver City, California, U.S.A., on 17 Aug. 1962.

Longest tug o' war The longest recorded pull is one of 2 hours 41 minutes between "H" Company and "E" Company of the 2nd Battalion of the Sherwood Foresters (Derbyshire Regiment) at Jubbulpore, India, on 12 Aug. 1889. "E" Company won.

The longest recorded pull under A.A.A. Rules (in which lying on the ground or entrenching the feet is not permitted) is one of 8 minutes 18·2 seconds for the first pull between the R.A.S.C. (Feltham) and the Royal Marines (Portsmouth Division) at the Royal Tournament of June 1938.

Three-legged race The fastest recorded time for a 100 yards three-legged race is 11·0 seconds by Harry L. Hillman and Lawson Robertson at Brooklyn, New York City, N.Y., U.S.A., on 24 April 1909.

WORLD RECORDS—WOMEN

The complete list of World Records for the 27 scheduled women's events passed by the International Amateur Athletic Federation as at 30 June 1971. Those marked with an asterisk are awaiting ratification.

RUNNING

Event	Mins. secs.	Name and Nationality	Place	Date
100 yards	10·0	Chi Cheng (Taiwan, China)	Portland, Oregon, U.S.A.	13 June 1970
220 yards (turn)	22·6	Chi Cheng (Taiwan, China)	Los Angeles, U.S.A.	3 July 1970
440 yards	52·4	Judith Florence Pollock (*née* Amoore) (Australia)	Perth, Western Australia	27 Feb. 1965
880 yards	2:02·0	Dixie Isobel Willis (Australia)	Perth, Western Australia	3 Mar. 1962
	2:02·0	Judith Florence Pollock (*née* Amoore) (Australia)	Stockholm, Sweden	5 July 1967
1 mile	4:36·8	Maria Francesca Gommers (Netherlands)	Leicester, England	14 June 1969
60 metres	7·2	Betty Cuthbert (Australia)	Sydney, N.S.W., Australia	21 Feb. 1960
	7·2	Irina Robertovna Bochkaryova (*née* Turova) (U.S.S.R.)	Moscow, U.S.S.R.	28 Aug. 1961
100 metres	11·0	Wyomia Tyus (U.S.A.)	Mexico City, Mexico	15 Oct. 1968
	11·0	Renate Stecher (*née* Meissner) (East Germany)	Berlin (East), East Germany	2 Aug. 1970
	11·0	Chi Cheng (Taiwan, China)	Vienna, Austria	18 July 1970
200 metres (turn)	22·4	Chi Cheng (Taiwan, China)	Munich, West Germany	12 July 1970
400 metres	51·0	Marilyn Fay Neufville (Jamaica)	Edinburgh, Scotland	23 July 1970
800 metres†	1:58·3*	Hildegard Falck (West Germany)	Stuttgart, West Germany	11 July 1971
1,500 metres	4:10·7	Jaroslava Jehličková (Czechoslovakia)	Athens, Greece	20 Sept. 1969

† *Shin Geum Dan (North Korea) has achieved 1:59·1 at Djakarta, Indonesia, on 12 Nov. 1963, and 1:58·0 at P'yongyang, North Korea, on 5 Sept. 1964; but the meeting in Indonesia, the Games of the New Emerging Forces (GANEFO), was not recognized by the I.A.A.F., and she was under suspension by the I.A.A.F. at the time of the other performance.*

HURDLING

Event	Secs.	Name and Nationality	Place	Date
100 metres (2′ 9″)	12·7	Karen Balzer (East Germany)	Berlin (East), East Germany	26 July 1970
	12·7	Teresa Sukniewicz (Poland)	Warsaw, Poland	20 Sept. 1970
200 metres (2′ 6″)	25·8	Pamela Kilborn (Australia)	Melbourne, Australia	17 Dec. 1969
	25·8	Annelie Jahns (East Germany)	Erfurt, East Germany	5 July 1970
	25·8	Teresa Sukniewicz (Poland)	Warsaw, Poland	9 Aug. 1970

FIELD EVENTS

Event	ft.	ins.	Metres	Name and Nationality	Place	Date
High Jump	6	3¼	1·91	Iolanda Söter (*née* Balas) (Romania)	Sofia, Bulgaria	16 July 1961
Long Jump	22	5¼	6·84	Heide Rosendahl (West Germany)	Turin, Italy	3 Sept. 1970
Shot Putt	67	0½	20·43	Nadyezhda Chizhova (U.S.S.R.)	Athens, Greece	16 Sept. 1969
Discus Throw	209	10	63·96	Liesel Westermann (West Germany)	Hamburg, West Germany	27 Sept. 1969
Javelin Throw	204	8½	62·40	Yelena Yegorovna Gorchakova (U.S.S.R.)	Tōkyō, Japan	16 Oct. 1964

PENTATHLON (1969 Scoring Tables)

	Name and Nationality	Place	Date
5,406 points	Burglinde Pollak (East Germany) (100m. hurdles 13·3s.; Shot Putt 15·57m. (51′ 1″); High Jump 1·75m. (5′ 8¾″); Long Jump 6·20m. (20′ 4″); 200m. 23·8s.)	Erfurt, East Germany	5–6 Sept. 1970

RELAYS

Event	Mins. Secs.	Team	Place	Date
4 × 110 yards	45·0	United Kingdom National Team (Anita D. Neil, Maureen Dorothy Tranter, Janet Mary Simpson, Lillian Barbara Board)	Portsmouth, England	14 Sept. 1968
4 × 220 yards	1:35·8*	Australia (Marian Hoffman, Jennifer Lamy, Raelene Boyle, Pamela Kilborn)	Brisbane, Australia	9 Nov. 1969
4 × 100 metres	42·8	United States National Team (Barbara Ferrell, Margaret Bailes [*née* Johnson], Mildrette Netter, Wyomia Tyus)	Mexico City, Mexico	20 Oct. 1968
4 × 200 metres	1:33·8	United Kingdom National Team (Maureen Dorothy Tranter, Della P. James, Janet Mary Simpson, Valerie Peat [*née* Wild])	London (Crystal Palace)	24 Aug. 1968
4 × 400 metres	3:30·8	United Kingdom National Team (Rosemary Olivia Stirling, Patricia Barbara Lowe, Janet Mary Simpson, Lillian Barbara Board)	Athens, Greece	16 Sept. 1969
	3:30·8	French Team (Bernadette Martin, Nicole Duclos, Eliane Jacq, Colette Besson)	Athens, Greece	16 Sept. 1969
4 × 800 metres	8:25·0	United Kingdom National Team (Rosemary Olivia Stirling, Georgena Craig, Patricia Barbara Lowe, Sheila Carey [*née* Taylor])	London (Crystal Palace)	5 Sept. 1970

UNITED KINGDOM (NATIONAL) RECORDS—MEN

Event	Mins. secs.	Name	Place	Date
100 yards	9·4	Peter Frank Radford	Wolverhampton	28 May 1960
220 yards (turn)	20·5	Peter Frank Radford	Wolverhampton	28 May 1960
440 yards	45·9	Robbie Ian Brightwell, M.B.E.	London (White City)	14 July 1962
880 yards	1:47·2	Christopher Sydney Carter	London (White City)	3 June 1968
1 mile	3:55·7	Alan Simpson	London (White City)	30 Aug. 1965
2 miles	8:26·8	Peter John Stewart	London (Crystal Palace)	5 Sept. 1970
3 miles	13:04·6	Richard George Taylor	London (White City)	13 Aug. 1969
6 miles	26:51·6	David Colin Bedford	Portsmouth, Hampshire	10 July 1971
10 miles	46:44·0	Ronald Hill	Leicester	9 Nov. 1968
15 miles	1H 12:48·2	Ronald Hill	Bolton, Lancashire	21 July 1965
100 metres	10·2	Emmanuel McDonald Bailey	Belgrade, Yugoslavia	25 Aug. 1951
	10·2	Walter Menzies Campbell	San Jose, California, U.S.A.	20 May 1967
	10·2	Walter Menzies Campbell	Modesto, California, U.S.A.	27 May 1967
200 metres (turn)	20·5	Peter Frank Radford	Wolverhampton	28 May 1960
400 metres	45·7	Adrian Peter Metcalfe	Dortmund, West Germany	2 Sept. 1961
	45·7	Robbie Ian Brightwell, M.B.E.	Tōkyō, Japan	18 Oct. 1964
	45·7	Robbie Ian Brightwell, M.B.E.	Tōkyō, Japan	19 Oct. 1964
800 metres	1:46·3	Christopher Sydney Carter	Budapest, Hungary	4 Sept. 1966
1,000 metres	2:18·2	John Peter Boulter	London (Crystal Palace)	6 Sept. 1969
1,500 metres	3:39·0	Peter John Stewart	Warsaw, Poland	12 Sept. 1970
2,000 metres	5:08·2	Colin Robinson	Stretford, Lancashire	7 Sept. 1968
3,000 metres	7:47·6	Richard George Taylor	London (Crystal Palace)	6 Sept. 1969
5,000 metres	13:22·2	David Colin Bedford	Edinburgh, Scotland	12 June 1971
10,000 metres	27:47·0	David Colin Bedford	Portsmouth, Hampshire	10 July 1971
20,000 metres	58:39·0	Ronald Hill	Leicester	9 Nov. 1968
25,000 metres	1H 15:22·6	Ronald Hill	Bolton, Lancashire	21 July 1965
30,000 metres	1H 31:30·4	James Noel Carroll Alder	London (Crystal Palace)	5 Sept. 1970
1 hour	12 miles 1,268 yards	Ronald Hill	Leicester	9 Nov. 1968

HURDLING

Event	Secs.	Name	Place	Date
120 yards/110 metres	13·6	David Peter Hemery	Brno, Czechoslovakia	5 July 1969
	13·6	David Peter Hemery	Warsaw, Poland	13 Sept. 1970
200 metres (turn)	23·0	Alan Peter Pascoe	Loughborough, Leicestershire	5 June 1969
200 metres/220 yards (straight)	23·3	Peter Burke Hildreth	Imber Court, Surrey	27 Aug. 1955
200 metres/220 yards (turn)	23·7	Paul Ashley Laurence Vine	London (White City)	15 July 1955
	23·7	John Michael Walter Hogan	London (White City)	9 May 1964
400 metres	48·1	David Peter Hemery	Mexico City, Mexico	15 Oct. 1968
440 yards	50·2	David Peter Hemery	London (White City)	13 July 1968
3,000 metres Steeplechase	8:30·8	Gerald Stevens	London (White City)	1 Sept. 1969

FIELD EVENTS

Event	ft. ins.	Metres	Name	Place	Date
High Jump	6 10	2·08	Gordon Albert Miller	London (White City)	18 May 1964
Pole Vault	16 8¾	5·10	Michael Anthony Bull	Edinburgh, Scotland	23 July 1970
Long Jump	27 0	8·23	Lynn Davies, M.B.E.	Bern, Switzerland	30 June 1968
Triple Jump	54 0	16·46	Frederick John Alsop	Tōkyō, Japan	16 Oct. 1964
Shot Putt	64 2	19·56	Arthur Rowe	Mansfield, Nottinghamshire	7 Aug. 1961
Discus Throw	190 3	58·00	William Tancred	Shotley, Suffolk	1 May 1971
Hammer Throw	227 2	69·24	Andrew Howard Payne	Solihull, Warwickshire	26 Sept. 1970
Javelin Throw	273 9	83·44	David Howard Travis	Zürich, Switzerland	2 Aug. 1970

DECATHLON (1962 Scoring Tables)

Points	Name	Place	Date
7,903 points	Peter Gabbett (1st day: 100m. 10·5s., Long Jump 24′ 7¾″ (7·51m.), Shot Putt 43′ 8″ (13·31m.), High Jump 6′ 1¼″ (1·85m.), 400m. 47·4s.)	Kassel, West Germany (2nd day: 110m. Hurdles 15·2s., Discus 151′ 0″ (46·02m.), Pole Vault 13′ 9½″ (4·20m.), Javelin 181′ 10″ (55·42m.), 1500m. 4:39·8s.)	5–6 June 1971

RELAYS

Event	Time	Team	Place	Date
4 × 110 yards	40·0	United Kingdom National Team (Peter Frank Radford, Ronald Jones, David Henry Jones, Thomas Berwyn Jones)	London (White City)	3 Aug. 1963
4 × 200 metres and 4 × 220 yards	1:26·0	London Team (David Henry Jones, Brian Andrew Smouha, Peter Frank Radford, David Hugh Segal)	London (White City)	30 Sept. 1959
4 × 440 yards	3:06·5	England Team (Martin John Winbolt-Lewis, John Austin Adey, Peter Warden, Timothy Joseph Michael Graham)	Kingston, Jamaica	13 Aug. 1966
4 × 800 metres and 4 × 880 yards†	7:17·4	United Kingdom National Team Martin Bilham, David Cropper, Michael John Maclean, Peter Miles Browne	London (Crystal Palace)	7 Sept. 1970
4 × 1 mile	16:24·8	Northern Counties Team (Stanley George Taylor, John Paul Anderson, Alan Simpson, Brian Hall)	Dublin, Ireland	17 July 1961
4 × 100 metres	39·3	United Kingdom National Team (Joseph William Speake, Ronald Jones, Ralph Banthorpe, Barrie Harrison Kelly)	Mexico City, Mexico	19 Oct. 1968
4 × 400 metres	3:01·2	United Kingdom National Team (Martin John Winbolt-Lewis, Colin William Ashburner Campbell, David Peter Hemery, John Sherwood)	Mexico City, Mexico	20 Oct. 1968
4 × 1,500 metres	15:27·2	United Kingdom National Team (Ralph Henry Dunkley, David Charles Law, Douglas Alastair Gordon Pirie, George William Nankeville)	London (White City)	23 Sept. 1953

† *A U.K. National Team recorded 7:14·6 for 4 × 880 yards at the Crystal Palace, London, on 22 June 1966, but lap times were illegally communicated to the runners.*

UNITED KINGDOM (NATIONAL) RECORDS—WOMEN

Event	Mins. secs.	Name	Place	Date
100 yards	10·6	Heather Joy Young (*née* Armitage)	Cardiff	22 July 1958
	10·6	Dorothy Hyman, M.B.E.	London (White City)	7 July 1962
	10·6	Dorothy Hyman, M.B.E.	London (White City)	4 July 1964
	10·6	Mary Denise Toomey (formerly Rand *née* Bignal), M.B.E.	London (White City)	4 July 1964
	10·6	Daphne Arden (now Slater)	London (White City)	4 July 1964
220 yards (turn)	23·6	Daphne Arden (now Slater)	London (White City)	4 July 1964
440 yards	54·1	Deirdre Ann Watkinson	Kingston, Jamaica	8 Aug. 1966
880 yards	2:04·2	Anne Rosemary Smith	London (White City)	2 July 1966
1 mile	4:37·0	Anne Rosemary Smith	Chiswick, Greater London	3 June 1967
100 metres	11·3	Dorothy Hyman, M.B.E.	Budapest, Hungary	2 Oct. 1963
	11·3	Dorothy Hyman, M.B.E.	Budapest, Hungary	3 Oct. 1963
	11·3	Valerie Peat (*née* Wild)	Mexico City, Mexico	14 Oct. 1968
200 metres	23·2	Dorothy Hyman, M.B.E.	Budapest, Hungary	3 Oct. 1963
400 metres	52·1	Lillian Barbara Board, M.B.E.	Mexico City, Mexico	16 Oct. 1968
800 metres	2:01·1	Ann Elizabeth Packer (now Brightwell), M.B.E.	Tōkyō, Japan	20 Oct. 1964
1,500 metres	4:15·4	Rita Ridley (*née* Lincoln)	London (Crystal Palace)	20 June 1970

HURDLING

Event	Secs.	Name	Place	Date
100 metres	13·4	Christine Bell (*née* Perera)	Berlin (East), East Germany	2 Aug. 1970
200 metres	27·3	Patricia Ann Jones	Stretford, Lancashire	22 July 1967
	27·3	Sheila Garnett	Watford, Hertfordshire	5 June 1971

FIELD EVENTS

Event	ft. ins.	Metres	Name	Place	Date
High Jump	5 10½	1·79	Linda Hedmark (*née* Knowles)	Skellefteå, Sweden	17 June 1969
	5 10½	1·79	Barbara Jean Inkpen	London (White City)	11 July 1970
Long Jump	22 2¼	6·76	Mary Denise Toomey (formerly Rand *née* Bignal), M.B.E.	Tōkyō, Japan	14 Oct. 1964
Shot Putt	53 6¼	16·31	Mary Elizabeth Peters	Belfast, Northern Ireland	1 June 1966
Discus Throw	180 7	55·04	Christine Rosemary Payne (*née* Charters)	The Hague, Netherlands	17 May 1970
Javelin Throw	182 5	55·60	Susan Mary Platt	London (Chiswick)	15 June 1968

PENTATHLON

Event	Name	Place	Date
5,148 points	Mary Elizabeth Peters (100m. Hurdles 13·6s., Shot Putt 52′ 11″ (16·13m.), High Jump 5′ 5¼″ (1·66m.), Long Jump 18′ 9½″ (5·73m.), 200m. 24·3s.)	Edinburgh, Scotland	21–22 July 1970

RELAYS

Event	Mins. secs.	Name	Place	Date
4 × 110 yards	45·0	United Kingdom National Team (Anita Doris Neil, Maureen Dorothy Tranter, Janet Mary Simpson, Lillian Barbara Board)	Portsmouth, Hampshire	14 Sept. 1968
4 × 220 yards	1:37·6	London Olympiades A.C. (Della Patricia James, Barbara M. Jones, Lillian Barbara Board, Janet Mary Simpson)	Solihull, Warwickshire	10 June 1967
4 × 100 metres	43·7	United Kingdom National Team (Anita Doris Neil, Maureen Dorothy Tranter, Janet Mary Simpson, Lillian Barbara Board)	Mexico City, Mexico	19 Oct. 1968
4 × 200 metres	1:33·8	(for details see World record)		
4 × 400 metres	3:30·8	(for details see World record)		
4 × 800 metres	8:25·0	(for details see World record)	London (Crystal Palace)	5 Sept. 1970

Greatest caber toss The 230 lb. Braemar Caber, originally 21 feet in length, defied all comers until it was successfully tossed by George Clark at the Braemar Gathering, Aberdeenshire, Scotland, in September 1951.

INTERNATIONALS

Most The greatest number of full Great Britain internationals won by a British male athlete is 51 by Crawford William Fairbrother (b. 1 Dec. 1936), the high jumper, from 1957 to mid-1970. The feminine record is 34 full internationals by Suzanne Allday (*née* Farmer) from 1951 to 1964.

Oldest and youngest Of full Great Britain (outdoor) internationals the oldest have been Harold Whitlock (b. 16 Dec. 1903) at the 1952 Olympic Games, aged 48 years 218 days, and Mrs. Dorothy Tyler (*née* Odam) (b. 19 March 1920) at the 1956 Olympic Games, aged 36 years 269 days. The youngest have been William Land (b. 29 Nov. 1914) *versus* Italy in 1931, aged 16 years 271 days, and Miss Sylvia Needham (b. 28 March 1935) *versus* France in 1950, aged 15 years 166 days. Sonia Lannaman (b. King's Heath, Birmingham of Jamaican parentage, 1946) represented Great Britain *versus* East Germany indoors in East Berlin on 4 Dec. 1970 before she was 15.

Blind 100 yards The fastest time recorded for a 100 yards by a blind man is 11·0 seconds by George Bull, aged 19, of Chippenham, Wiltshire, in a race at the Worcester College for the Blind, on 26 Oct. 1954.

Pancake race record The annual Housewives Pancake Race at Olney, Buckinghamshire, was first mentioned in 1445. The record for the winding 415-yard course is 63·0 seconds, set by Miss Janet Bunker, aged 17, on 7 Feb. 1967. The record for the counterpart race at Liberal, Kansas, U.S.A. is 59·1 seconds by Kathleen West, 19, on 10 Feb. 1970.

Standing high jump The best standing high jump is 5 feet 9¼ inches by Johan Christian Evandt (Norway) at Oslo on 4 March 1962.

BADMINTON

Origins The game was devised *c.* 1863 at Badminton Hall in Gloucestershire, the seat of the Dukes of Beaufort.

International Championships The International Championship or Thomas Cup (instituted 1948) has been won 4 times by Malaya (now part of Malaysia) in 1948–49, 1951–52 and 1954–55, and as Malaysia, by the default of Indonesia in the final in 1966–67 and by Indonesia in 1957–58, 1960–61, 1963–64 and 1970–71.

The inaugural Ladies International Championship or Uber Cup (instituted 1956) was won by the United States, who successfully defended in 1960 and 1963, since when Japan have won and retained the Cup (1966 and 1969).

Longest hit Frank Rugani drove a shuttlecock 79 feet $8\frac{1}{2}$ inches in tests at San Jose, California, U.S.A., on 29 Feb. 1964.

Longest games The longest recorded game has been one of 267 hours by 5 players from the Anglia T.V. Badminton Club on 8–19 April, who maintained continuous singles. The longest doubles marathon has been one of 144 hours maintained by 9 players from St. John's Youth Hall, Lurgan, Armagh, Northern Ireland on 11–17 April 1971.

Most titles Most wins in the All-England Championships (instituted 1899):—

Event	Times	Holder	Dates
Men's Singles	7	Erland Kops (Denmark)	1958, 1960–63, 1965, 1967
Women's Singles	10	Mrs. G. C. K. Hashman (*née* Judy Devlin) (U.S.A.)	1954, 1957–58, 1960–64, 1966–67
Most titles (*i.e.* including doubles):—			
Men	21	G. A. Thomas (later Sir George Thomas, Bt.)	from 1903 to 1928
Women	17	Miss M. Lucas (U.K.)	from 1899 to 1910
	17	Mrs. G. C. K. Hashman (*née* Judy Devlin) (U.S.A.)	from 1954 to 1967

Most Internationals Most international appearances:—

	Times	Men	Times	Women
England	100	A. D. Jordan, 1951 to 1970	52	Mrs. W. C. E. Rogers (*née* Cooley), 1955 to 1969
Ireland	45	K. Carlisle, 1954 to 1970	43	Miss Y. Kelly, 1955 to 1970
Scotland	37	R. S. McCoig, 1956 to 1970	28	Miss C. E. Dunglison, 1956 to 1967
Wales	20	D. Colmer, 1964 to 1970	22	Mrs. L. W. Myers, 1928 to 1939

BASEBALL

Earliest game "Baste-Ball" was a pursuit banned at Princeton, New Jersey, U.S.A., as early as 1786. On 4 Feb. 1962, it was claimed in *Nedelya*, the weekly supplement to the Soviet newspaper *Izvestiya*, that "Beizbol" was an old Russian game. The earliest baseball game under the Cartwright rules was at Hoboken, New Jersey, U.S.A., on 19 June 1846, with the New York Nine beating the Knickerbockers 23–1 in 4 innings.

Highest batting average The highest average in a career is 0·367 by Tyrus Raymond Cobb (1886–1961), the "Georgia Peach" of Augusta, Anniston, Detroit (1905–26) and Philadelphia (1927–28). During his career Ty Cobb made a record 2,244 runs from a record 4,191 hits made during a record 11,429 times at bat in a record 3,033 major league games.

HOME RUNS

Most The highest number of home runs hit in a career is the 714 by George Herman ("Babe") Ruth (1895–1948) of Baltimore-Providence, Boston Red Sox (American League), New York Yankees and Boston (National League), between 1914 and 1935. His major league record for home runs in one year is 60 in 154 games between 15 April and 30 Sept. 1927. Roger Maris (b. 1935) (New York Yankees) hit 61 homers in a 162-game schedule in 1961. Left-hander Joe Baumann of Roswell, New Mexico, hit 72 homers in the minor league in 1954.

Longest The longest home run ever measured was one of 618 feet by Roy Edward Carlyle in a minor league game at Emeryville Ball Park, California, U.S.A., on 4 July 1929. In 1919 "Babe" Ruth hit a 587-foot homer in a Boston Red Sox *v.* New York Giants match at Tampa, Florida, U.S.A. The longest throw (ball weighs between 5 and $5\frac{1}{4}$ oz.) is 445 feet 10 inches by Glen Gorbaus on 1 Aug. 1957. The longest throw by a woman is 296 feet by Miss Mildred "Babe" Didrikson (later Mrs. George Zaharis) (U.S.) (1914–56) at Jersey City, New Jersey, U.S.A. on 25 July 1931. The fastest time for circling bases is 13·3 seconds by Evar Swanson at Columbus, Ohio, in 1932.

Pitching The first "perfect game" (no hits, no runs) pitched in a World Series was by Don Larsen (New York Yankees) with 97 pitches (71 in the strike zone) against Brooklyn Dodgers on 8 Oct. 1956.

Highest earnings The greatest earnings of a baseball player is $1,091,477 (now £454,782) amassed by "Babe" Ruth between 1914 and 1938.

Record attendances and receipts The World Series record attendance is 420,784 (6 games with total receipts of $2,626,973·44, then £938,205), when the Los Angeles (ex-Brooklyn) Dodgers beat the Chicago White Sox 4–2 on 1–8 Oct. 1959. The single game record is 92,706 for the fifth game (receipts $552,774·77, then £197,420) at the Memorial Coliseum, Los Angeles, California, on 6 Oct. 1959. The record net receipts for a series has been $3,018,113 (then £1,257,547) from a paid attendance of 379,670, who saw the Detroit Tigers beat the St. Louis Cardinals 4–3 on 2–10 Oct. 1968. The highest seating capacity in a baseball stadium is 74,056 in the Cleveland Municipal Stadium, Ohio, U.S.A.

Highest catch Joe Sprinx (Cleveland Indians) caught a baseball dropped from an airship at 800 feet in July 1931. The force of the ball broke his jaw.

BASKETBALL

Origins *Ollamalitzli* was a 16th century Aztec precursor of basketball played in Mexico. If the solid rubber ball was put through a fixed stone ring the player was entitled to the clothing of all the spectators. Modern basketball was devised by the Canadian-born Dr. James A. Naismith (1861–1939) at the Training School of the International Y.M.C.A. College at Springfield, Massachusetts, U.S.A., in December 1891 and first played on 20 Jan. 1892. The first public contest was on 11 March 1892. The game is now a global activity. The Amateur Basketball Association of England and Wales was founded in 1936.

World Olympic champions The U.S.A. have won the Olympic title since its inception at Berlin in 1936 (7 times with 54 successive victories) and also the 1954 world title (instituted 1950). Brazil won in 1959 and 1963.

Largest ever gate The Harlem Globetrotters (U.S.A.) played an exhibition to 75,000 in the Olympic Stadium, West Berlin, Germany, in 1951. The largest indoor basketball stadium is the Astrodome, Houston, Texas, U.S.A., where 52,693 watched a match on 20 Jan. 1968.

Greatest playing record The Harlem Globetrotters set unapproached attendance and scoring records in their silver jubilee season of 1951–52. They won 333 games and lost 8 before over 3,000,000 spectators.

The team was founded by the London-born Abraham M. Saperstein (1903–66) of Chicago, Illinois, U.S.A., and the first game was played at Hinckley, Illinois, on 7 Jan. 1927. In the 39 seasons to 1965 they won 8,434 games and lost 322. They have travelled almost 5,000,000 miles, visited 87 countries on six continents, and have been seen by an estimated 53,000,000 people.

U.S.A. professional records The greatest number of points scored in a career is 30,000 by Wilton ("Wilt the Stilt") Norman Chamberlain (b. 21 Aug. 1936) in the 11 seasons 1959–1970. He stands 7 feet $1\frac{1}{10}$ inches tall and weighs 20 st. (280 lb.).

Most points scored in a season: Chamberlain, now with the Philadelphia 76ers, scored 4,029 points for the Philadelphia Warriors in the 1961–62 season. Most points scored in a single game: Chamberlain scored 100 points against the New York Knickerbockers at Hershey, Pennsylvania, on 2 March 1962. Most points scored by a team: 173, by Boston Celtics, against Minnesota Lakers (139 points) at Boston, Massachusetts, on 28 Feb. 1959. Most points in a match: 316, between the Philadelphia Warriors (169 points) and the New York Knickerbockers (147 points), as above. The longest field goal on record is 84 feet 11 inches by George Linn, aged 20, of Alabama against North Carolina at Tuscaloosa, Alabama, in January 1955.

Non-A.B.A. scoring record Clarence (Bevo) Francis of Rio Grande College, Rio Grande, Ohio, U.S.A., scored 3,964 points (an average of 101 points per game) in the 1953–54 season. This total includes 150 points scored in one game.

Tallest players The tallest player of all time was Vasiliy Akhtayev (b. 1935) of the U.S.S.R., who played for Kazakhastan in 1956, when measuring 232 centimetres (7 feet 7·3 inches). The tallest woman player is Ulyana Semyonova (b. 1950), who plays for T.T.T. Riga, Latvia and stands 6 feet $9\frac{1}{2}$ inches. The tallest international player in the world is the 7-foot $4\frac{3}{4}$-inch tall Christopher Greener (see Chapter 1) of L.L.S.K., London whose debut for England was *v.* France on 17 Dec. 1969.

Most expensive In 1969 Ferdinand Lewis Alcindor (b. 16 April 1947) signed a five year contract for $1,400,000 (£583,333) with Milwaukee Bucks. Alcindor stands 7 feet $1\frac{3}{8}$ inches tall.

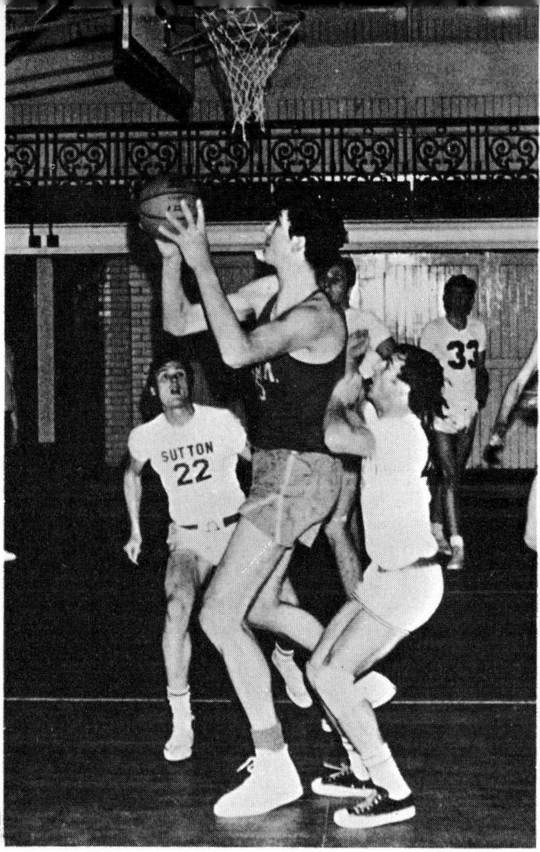

Christopher Greener (England), the world's tallest international player

Most accurate The greatest goal shooting demonstration has been by the professional trick specialist Wilfred Hetzel (b. 1912) who once achieved a run of 144 straight baskets from the foul line off one foot.

Longest games marathon record The longest recorded basketball marathon was of 86 hours by 18 players from Sir Frederic Osborn School, Welwyn Garden City, Hertfordshire on 19–22 Feb. 1971. The longest recorded match between two teams of five without substitutes is 32 hours by 10 students of Dundee University on 18–19 April 1971.

Britain The most A.B.B.A. titles (initiated 1936) have been won by the London Central Y.M.C.A. with eight wins in 1957–58, 1960 and 1962–63–64–67–69. The highest score in a final was 98 points by London Polytechnic *v.* Nottingham Y.M.C.A. in 1954. Four women's titles (instituted 1965) have been won by Malory.

The record score by an England international team is 101–33, when beating Wales at Belfast in 1962.

The highest tournament score in Britain has been 132 points by Aldershot Warriors *v.* Highbury Hawks (52) on 3 Oct. 1970.

BILLIARDS

Earliest mention The earliest recorded mention of billiards was in a poem by Clément Marot (1496–1544) of France, and it was mentioned in England in 1591 by Edmund Spenser (*c.* 1552–99). The first recorded public billiards room in England was the Piazza, Covent Garden, London, in the early part of the 19th century. Rubber cushions were introduced in 1835 and slate beds in 1836.

Highest breaks Tom Reece (1873–1953) made an unfinished break of 499,135, including 249,152 cradle cannons (2 points each), in 85 hours 49 minutes against Joe Chapman at Burroughes' Hall, Soho Square, London, between 3 June and 6 July 1907. This was not recognized because press and public were not continuously present. The highest certified break made by the anchor cannon is 42,746 by W. Cook (England) from 29 May to 7 June 1907. The official world record under the then baulk-line rule is 1,784 by Joe Davis, O.B.E. (b. 15 April 1901) in the United Kingdom Championship on 29 May 1936. Walter Lindrum (Australia) made an official break of

4,137 in 2 hours 55 minutes against Joe Davis at Thurston's on 19–20 Jan. 1932, before the baulk-line rule was in force. The amateur record is 702 by Robert Marshall *v.* Tom Cleary, both of Australia, in the Australian Amateur Championship at Brisbane on 17 Sept. 1953. Davis has an unofficial personal best of 2,502 (mostly pendulum cannons) in a match against Tom Newman (1894–1943) (England) in Manchester in 1930.

Fastest century Walter Lindrum, M.B.E. (1898–1960) of Australia made an unofficial 100 break in 27·5 seconds in Australia on 10 Oct. 1952. His official record is 100 in 46·0 seconds, set in Sydney in 1941.

Most world titles The greatest number of world championship titles (instituted 1870) won by one player is eight by John Roberts, Jnr. (England) in 1870 (twice), 1871, 1875 (twice), 1877 and 1885 (twice). The greatest number of United Kingdom titles (instituted 1934) won by any player is seven (1934–39 and 1947) by Joe Davis (England), who also won four world titles (1928–30 and 1932) before the series was discontinued in 1934. Willie Hoppe (U.S.A.) won 51 "world" titles in the United States variants of the game between 1906 and 1952.

Most amateur titles The record for world amateur titles is four by Robert Marshall (Australia) in 1936–38–51–62. The greatest number of British Amateur Championships (instituted 1888) ever won is eight by Sidney H. Fry (1893 to 1925) and A. Leslie Driffield (1952–54, 1957–59, 1962 and 1967).

Bar billiards marathon The duration record for bar billiards is 72 hours by 5 players from Harrow County Grammar School who scored a total of 772,550 points on 6–9 April 1970.

The highest recorded pin fall in 72 hours is 904,670 by 5 players at the Albion Hotel, Eastbourne, Sussex on 6–9 Dec. 1970.

BOBSLEIGH

Origins The oldest known sledge is dated *c.* 6500 B.C. and came from Heinola, southern Finland. The word toboggan comes from the Micmac American Indian word *tobaakan*. The oldest bobsleigh club in the world is St. Moritz Tobogganing Club, home of the Cresta Run, founded in 1887. Modern world championships were inaugurated in 1924. Four-man bobs were included in the first Winter Olympic Games at Chamonix in 1924 and two-man boblets from the third Games at Lake Placid, U.S.A., in 1932.

Cresta Run The skeleton one-man toboggan dates, in its present form, from 1892. On the 1,325-yard-long Cresta Run at St. Moritz, Switzerland, dating from 1884 speeds of up to 83·8 m.p.h. were reached by Flt.-Lt. (now Sqn. Ldr.) Colin Mitchell (Great Britain) in February 1959. The record from the Junction (2,868 feet) is 43·59 seconds by Nino Bibbia (b. 9 Sept. 1924) of Italy on 16 Jan. 1965. The record from Top (3,981 feet) is 54·67 seconds by Bibbia on 13 Feb. 1965.

The greatest number of wins in the Cresta Run Grand National (inst. 1885) is seven by the 1948 Olympic champion Nino Bibbia (Italy) in 1960–61–62–63–64–66–68. The greatest number of wins in the Cresta Run Curzon Cup (inst. in 1910) is eight by Bibbia in 1950–57–58–60–62–63–64–69 who hence won the Double in 1960–62–63–64.

Olympic and world titles The Olympic four-man bob title has been won three times each by the U.S.A. (1928–32–48) and Switzerland (1924–36–56). Only the U.S.A. (1932, 1936) and Italy (1956, 1968) have won the Olympic boblet event twice.

The world four-man bob title has been won nine times by Switzerland (1924–36–39–47–54–55–56–57–71). Italy won the two-man title 13 times (1954–56–57–58–59–60–61–62–63–66–68–69–71). Eugenio Monti (Italy) (b. 1927) has been a member of eleven world championship crews.

LUGEING

In lugeing the rider adopts a sitting, as opposed to a prone position. It was largely developed by British tourists at Klosters, Switzerland, from 1883. The first European championships were at Reichenberg, East Germany, in 1914 and the first world championships at Oslo, Norway, in 1953. The International Luge Federation was formed in 1957. Lugeing attracts more than 20,000 competitors in Austria.

Most world titles The most successful rider in the world championships is Thomas Köhler (East Germany), who won the single-seater title in 1962, 1966 and 1967 and shared in the two-seater title in 1967 and 1968 (Olympic). Otrun Enderlein (East Germany) has won thrice (1965, 1966 and 1967).

Highest speed The fastest luge run is at Krynica, Poland, where speeds of more than 80 m.p.h. have been recorded.

BOWLING (TEN PIN)

Origins The ancient German game of nine-pins was exported to the United States in the early 17th century. In about 1845 the Connecticut and New Haven State Legislatures prohibited the game so a tenth pin was added to evade the ban; but there is some evidence of 10 pins being used in Suffolk about 300 years ago.

In the United States there were 9,140 bowling establishments with 141,492 bowling lanes and 29,000,000 bowlers in 1969–70. The world's largest bowling centre is a bowling centre in Japan with 250 lanes which is almost complete. The largest in Europe is the Excel Bowl at Nottingham, England, where the game was introduced in 1960, with 48 lanes on two floors (24 on each floor).

Highest scores The highest individual score for three sanctioned games (possible 900) is 886 by Albert (Allie) Brandt of Lockport, New York State, U.S.A., on 25 Oct. 1939. The record for consecutive strikes in sanctioned match play is 29 by Frank Caruana at Buffalo, New York, on 5 March 1924, and 29 by Max Stein at Los Angeles, California, on 8 Oct. 1939. The highest number of sanctioned 300 games is 23 (till 1970) by Elvin Mesger of Sullivan, Missouri, U.S.A. The maximum 900 for a three-game series has been recorded three times in unsanctioned games—by Leo Bentley at Lorain, Ohio, U.S.A., on 26 March 1931; by Joe Sargent at Rochester, New York State, U.S.A., in 1934; and by Jim Margie in Philadelphia, Pennsylvania, U.S.A., on 4 Feb. 1937. Such series must have consisted of 36 consecutive strikes (*i.e.* all pins down with one ball).

The United Kingdom record for a three-game series is 772 by Brian Wilkins at Dagenham, Greater London on 27 Feb. 1971. The record score for a single game is 300 by Albert Kirkham, aged 34, of Burslem, Staffordshire, on 5 Dec. 1965, which was equalled by Terence Saunders (now of Dagenham) at Stamford Hill, Greater London in 1969.

World championships The world championships were instituted in 1954. The highest pinfall in the individual men's event is 5,708 by David Pond (G.B.) of Harlow, Essex, at Malmö, Sweden, in 1967.

Marathon Bill Halstead (U.S.A.) bowled 1,201 games (knocked down 165,959 pins) scoring 1,948 strikes, lifted 130·3 tons and walked 127·2 miles in 151 hours 25 minutes at Tampa, Florida, U.S.A., on 27 Nov. to 3 Dec. 1966.

SKITTLES

The duration record for knocking down skittles (9-pins) is 53 hours (56,191 pins down) by 9 men at the Plymouth Inn alley, Totnes, Devon on 30 June–2 July 1969.

The highest score in 24 hours is 55,143 pins by 12 members of The Cinderford Band in the Swan Hotel alley, Cinderford, Gloucestershire, on 22–23 Aug. 1970. The duration record is 48 hours by 8 players (68,744 pin falls) at Yeovil, Somerset, on 19–21 Feb. 1971.

BOWLS

LAWN

Origins Bowls can be traced back to at least the 13th century in England. The Southampton Town Bowling was formed in 1299. After falling into disrepute, the game was rescued by the bowlers of Scotland who, headed by W. W. Mitchell, framed the modern rules in 1848–49.

World title In the inaugural World Championship held in Sydney, Australia in October 1966 the Singles Title was won by David John Bryant (b. 1931) (England) and the team title (Leonard Cup) by Australia.

Most title wins In the annual International Championships (instituted 1903) Scotland have won 23 times to England's 19. The most consecutive wins is five by England from 1958 to 1962 and five by Scotland from 1965 to 1969.

English titles The only man to have won four Singles Titles (instituted 1905) is E. Percy C. Baker (Poole Park, Dorset) in 1932, 1946, 1952 and 1955. He has also shared two pairs wins (1950 and 1962) and a triples win in 1960. The most Pairs Titles (instituted 1912) is four by Worthing, in 1937–38, 1955 and 1957. The Triples Title (instituted 1945) has never been won twice. The Rinks (instituted 1905) have been won three times by Belgrave (Leicester) in 1919, 1922 and 1954 and by Clevedon (Somerset) in 1957, 1968, 1969. David Bryant, M.B.E., skipped Clevedon to the E.B.A. Triple Title in 1966 and so became the only man ever to have won all four titles. In 1969 he participated in his 8th E.B.A. title win.

Most internationals The greatest number of international seasons by an English bowler is 21 by R. Kivell (Exonia, Devon) between 1947 and 1969.

CROWN GREEN BOWLS

The British Crown Green Amateur Bowling Association was founded in 1907. The game is played in 8 English Midland and Northern counties and in North Wales.

R. G. Meyrick (Shropshire) has won the British Amateur title four times (1948, 61, 62 and 66).

BOXING

Earliest references The origins of fist-fighting belong to Greek mythology. The earliest prize-ring code of rules was formulated in England on 16 Aug. 1743 by the champion pugilist Jack Broughton (1704–89), who reigned from 1729 to 1750. Boxing, which had, in 1867, come under the Queensberry Rules formulated for John Sholto Douglas, 8th Marquess of Queensberry, was not established as a legal sport in Britain until after the ruling of Mr. Justice Grantham on 24 April 1901, following the death of Billy Smith.

Longest fight The longest recorded fight with gloves was between Andy Bowen of New Orleans (k. 1894) and Jack Burke in New Orleans, Louisiana, U.S.A., on 6–7 April 1893. The fight lasted 110 rounds and 7 hours 19 minutes from 9.15 p.m. to 4.34 a.m., but was declared a no contest when both men were unable to continue. The longest recorded bare knuckle fight was one of 6 hours 15 minutes between James Kelly and Jack Smith at Melbourne, Australia, on 19 Oct. 1856. The greatest recorded number of rounds is 278 in 4 hours 30 minutes, when Jack Jones beat Patsy Tunney in Cheshire in 1825.

Shortest fight There is a distinction between the quickest knock-out and the shortest fight. A knock-out in 10½ seconds (including a 10-second count) occurred on 26 Sept. 1946, when Al Couture struck Ralph Walton while the latter was adjusting a gum shield in his corner at Lewiston, Maine, U.S.A. If the time was accurately taken it is clear that Couture must have been more than half-way across the ring from his own corner at the opening bell. The shortest fight on record appears to be one at Palmerston, New Zealand on 8 July 1952 when Ross Cleverley (R.N.Z.A.F.) floored D. Emerson (Pahiatua) with the first punch and the referee stopped the contest without a count 7 seconds from the bell. Teddie Barker (Swindon) scored a technical knock-out over Bob Roberts (Nigeria) at the first blow in a welter-weight fight at Maesteg, Glamorganshire, Wales, on 2 Sept. 1957. The referee, Joe Brimell, stopped the fight without a count 10 seconds from the bell.

The shortest world heavyweight title fight occurred when Tommy Burns (1881–1955) (*né* Noah Brusso) of Canada knocked out Jem Roche in 1 minute 28 seconds in Dublin, Ireland, on 17 March 1908. The duration of the Clay *v.* Liston fight at Lewiston, Maine, U.S.A. on 25 May 1965 was 1 minute 52 seconds (including the count) as timed from the video tape recordings, despite a ringside announcement giving a time of 1 minute. Charles "Sonny" Liston (b. 1932) died in 1970. The shortest world title fight was when Al McCoy knocked out George Chip in 45 seconds for the middleweight crown in New York on 7 April 1914. The shortest ever British title fight was one of 40 seconds (including the count), when Dave Charnley knocked out David "Darkie" Hughes in a lightweight championship defence in Nottingham on 20 Nov. 1961.

Tallest The tallest boxer to fight professionally was Gogea Mitu (b. 1914) of Romania in 1935. He was 7 feet 4 inches and weighed 23 stone 5 lb. (327 lb.). John Rankin, who won a fight in New Orleans, Louisiana, U.S.A., in November 1967, was reputedly also 7 feet 4 inches.

WORLD HEAVYWEIGHT CHAMPIONS

Longest and shortest reigns The longest reign of any world heavyweight champion is 11 years 8 months and 9 days by Joe Louis (born Joseph Louis Barrow, Lafayette, Alabama, 13 May 1914), from 22 June 1937, when he knocked out James J. Braddock in the eighth round at Chicago, Illinois, U.S.A., until announcing his retirement on 1 March 1949. During his reign Louis made a record 25 defences of his title. The shortest reign was by Primo Carnera (Italy) for 350 days from 29 June 1933 to 14 June 1934. However, if the disputed title claim of Marvin Hart is allowed, his reign from 3 July 1905 to 23 Feb. 1906 was only 235 days.

Heaviest and lightest The heaviest world champion was Primo Carnera (1906–67) of Italy, the "Ambling Alp", who won the title from Jack Sharkey in 6 rounds in New York City, N.Y., U.S.A., on 29 June 1933. He scaled 270 lb. (19 stone 4 lb.), had a chest measurement of 53 inches, the longest reach at 85½ inches (finger tip to finger tip) and also the largest fists with a 14¾-inch circumference. The lightest champion was Robert Prometheus Fitz-simmons (1862–1917), who was born at Helston, Cornwall, and, at a weight of 167 lb. (11 stone 13 lb.), won the title by knocking out James J. Corbett in 14 rounds at Carson City, Nevada, U.S.A., on 17 March 1897.

Jersey Joe alcott (U.S.A.), world heavyweight champion at 38

The greatest differential in a world title fight was 86 lb. between Carnera (270 lb. or 19 stone 4 lb.) and Tommy Loughran (184 lb. or 13 stone 2 lb.) of the U.S.A., when the former won on points at Miami, Florida, U.S.A., on 1 March 1934.

Tallest and shortest The tallest world champion was the 6-foot $6\frac{1}{4}$-inch tall Jess Willard (1881–1968) (U.S.A.), who won the title at 17 stone 12 lb. by knocking out Jack Johnson (U.S.A.) in the 26th round at Havana, Cuba, on 5 April 1915. Carnera was 6 feet $5\frac{3}{4}$ inches. The shortest was Tommy Burns (1881–1955) of Canada, world champion from 23 Feb. 1906 to 26 Dec. 1908, who stood 5 feet 7 inches and weighed 12 stone 11 lb.

Oldest and youngest The oldest man to win the heavyweight crown was Jersey Joe Walcott (b. Arnold Raymond Cream, 31 Jan. 1914 at Merchantville, New Jersey, U.S.A.) who knocked out Ezzard Charles on 18 July 1951 in Pittsburgh, Pennsylvania, when aged 37 years 168 days. Walcott was the oldest holder at 38 years 7 months 23 days losing his title on 23 Sept. 1952 and in 1953 the oldest challenger. The youngest age at which the world title has been won is 21 years 331 days by Floyd Patterson (b. Waco, North Carolina, 4 Jan. 1935) of the U.S.A. After the retirement of Rocky Marciano, Patterson won the vacant title by beating Archie Moore in 5 rounds in Chicago, Illinois, U.S.A., on 30 Nov. 1956. He is also the only man ever to regain the heavyweight championship. He lost to Ingemar Johansson (Sweden) on 26 June 1959 but defeated him on 20 June 1960 at the New York Polo Grounds Stadium.

Longest lived The longest lived of any heavyweight champion of the world has been Jess Willard (U.S.A.), who was born 29 Dec. 1881 at St. Clere, Kansas, and died 15 Dec. 1968 at Pacoima, California aged 86 years 351 days.

Earliest title fight The first world heavyweight title fight, with gloves and 3-minute rounds, was that between John Lawrence Sullivan (1858–1918) and "Gentleman" James J. Corbett (1866–1933) in New Orleans, Louisiana, U.S.A., on 7 Sept. 1892. Corbett won in 21 rounds.

Undefeated Only James Joseph (Gene) Tunney (b. Greenwich Village, New York City, 25 May 1898) (1926–1928) and Rocky Marciano (1952–56) *finally* retired as undefeated champions.

WORLD CHAMPIONS (any weight)

Longest and shortest reign Joe Louis's heavyweight duration record of 11 years 252 days stands for all divisions. The shortest reign has been 54 days by the French featherweight Eugène Criqui from 2 June to 26 July 1923. The disputed flyweight champion Emile Pladner (France) reigned only 47 days from 2 March to 18 April 1929, and the disputed featherweight champion Dave Sullivan, from 26 Sept. to 11 Nov. 1898, reigned 46 days.

Youngest and oldest The youngest age at which any world championship has been claimed is 19 years 6 days by Pedlar Palmer (b. 19 Nov. 1876), who won the disputed bantamweight title in London on 25 Nov. 1895. Willie Pep (b. William Papaleo, 20 Nov. 1922), of the U.S.A., won the featherweight crown in New York on his 20th birthday, 22 Nov. 1942. After Young Corbett III knocked out Terry McGovern (1880–1918) in two rounds at Hartford, Connecticut, U.S.A., on 28 Nov. 1901, neither was able to get his weight down to nine stone, and the featherweight title was claimed by Abe Attell, when aged only 17 years 251 days. The oldest world champion was Archie Moore (b. Archibald Lee Wright, Collinsville, Illinois on either 13 Dec. 1913 or 1916) (U.S.A.) who was recognized as a light-heavyweight champion up to early 1962 when his title was removed. He was then believed to be between 44 and 47. Bob Fitzsimmons (1862–1917) had the longest career of any official world title-holder with over 32 years from 1882 to 1914. He won his last world title aged 41 years 174 days in San Francisco, California on 25 Nov. 1903. He was an amateur from 1880 to 1882.

Longest fight The longest world title fight (under Queensberry Rules) was that between the lightweights Joe Gans (1874–1910), of the U.S.A., and Oscar Matthew "Battling" Nelson (1882–1954), the "Durable Dane", at Goldfield, Nevada, U.S.A., on 3 Sept. 1906. It was terminated in the 42nd round when Gans was declared the winner on a foul.

Most recaptures The only boxer to win a world title five times at one weight is "Sugar" Ray Robinson (b. Walker Smith, Jr., in Detroit, 3 May 1920) of the U.S.A., who beat Carmen Basilio (U.S.A.) in the Chicago Stadium on 25 March 1958, to regain the world middleweight title for the fourth time. The other title wins were over Jake LaMotta (U.S.A.) in Chicago on 14 Feb. 1951, Randolph Turpin (United Kingdom) in New York on 12 Sept. 1951, Carl "Bobo" Olson (U.S.A.) in Chicago on 9 Dec. 1955, and Gene Fullmer (U.S.A.) in Chicago on 1 May 1957. The record number of title bouts in a career is 33 or 34 (at bantam and featherweight) by George Dixon (1870–1909), *alias* Little Chocolate, of the U.S.A., between 1890 and 1901.

Greatest weight span The only man to hold world titles at three weights *simultaneously* was Henry ("Homicide Hank") Armstrong (b. 22 Dec. 1912), now the Rev. Harry Jackson, of the U.S.A., at featherweight, lightweight and welterweight from August to December 1938.

Greatest "tonnage" The greatest "tonnage" recorded in any fight is 601 lb. when Ewart Potgieter (South Africa) at 335 lb. (23 stone 13 lb.), the heaviest ever fighter, knocked out Bruce Olson (U.S.A.) at 266 lb. (19 stone) at Portland, Oregon, on 2 March 1957. The greatest "tonnage" in a world title fight was $488\frac{3}{4}$ lb. (34 stone $12\frac{3}{4}$ lb.) when Carnera (then $259\frac{1}{4}$ lb.) fought Paolino Uzcuden ($229\frac{1}{2}$ lb.) of Spain in Rome on 22 Oct. 1933.

Most knock-downs in title fights Vic Toweel (South Africa) knocked down Danny O'Sullivan of London 14 times in 10 rounds in their world bantamweight fight at Johannesburg on 2 Dec. 1950, before the latter retired.

ALL FIGHTS

Largest purse The greatest purse has been \$2,500,000 (£1,041,667) guaranteed to Joe Frazier (b. South Carolina, U.S.A., February 1944) and Cassius Marcellus Clay 7th (later Muhammad Ali Haj) (b. Louisville, Kentucky, U.S.A., 17 Jan. 1942) for their 15-round fight at Madison Square Gardens, New York City, on 8 March 1971.

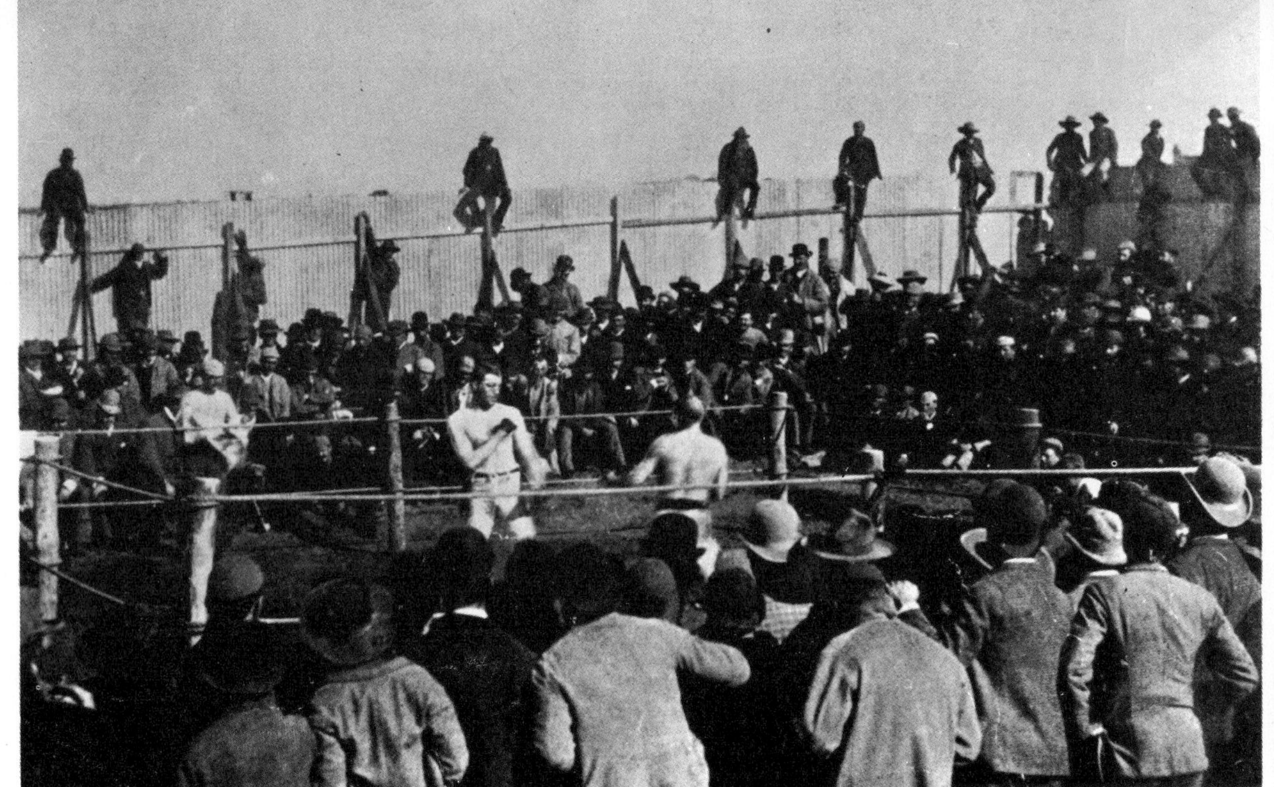

The top purse fight of the bare-knuckle era in 1889 (see below)

Bare knuckle stake The largest stake ever fought for in the bare-knuckle era was $22,500 (then £4,633) in the 27-round fight between Jack Cooper and Wolf Bendoff at Port Elizabeth, South Africa on 29 July 1889.

Attendances *Highest* The greatest paid attendance at any boxing fight has been 120,757 (with a ringside price of $27.50) for the Tunney *v.* Dempsey world heavyweight title fight at the Sesqui-centennial Stadium, Philadelphia, Pennsylvania, U.S.A., on 23 Sept. 1926. The indoor record is 37,321 at the Clay *v.* Ernie Terrell fight in the Astrodome, Houston, Texas, on 6 Feb. 1967.

The highest non-paying attendance is 135,132 at the Tony Zale *v.* Billy Prior fight at Juneau Park, Milwaukee, Wisconsin, U.S.A., on 18 Aug. 1941.

Lowest The smallest attendance at a world heavyweight title fight was 2,434 at the Clay *v.* Liston fight at Lewiston, Maine, U.S.A. on 25 May 1965.

Highest earnings in career The largest known fortune ever made in a fighting career was $4,760,338 (now £1,983,474), amassed by Rocky Marciano (b. Rocco Francis Marchegiano) of the U.S.A. (1923–1969) from 39 of his 49 professional bouts (43 knock-outs and 6 on points) between 21 Feb. 1947 and 21 Sept. 1955. He retired, undefeated, on 27 April 1956 and was killed in an air crash in central Iowa, U.S.A. on 31 Aug. 1969. Including earnings for refereeing and promoting, Jack Dempsey has grossed over $10,000,000 (now £4,166,666) to 1967. Floyd Patterson (U.S.A.) received $2,384,737 (then £851,692) for his three fights against Ingemar Johansson (Sweden) on 26 June 1959, 20 June 1960, and 13 March 1961 and possibly grossed $7,500,000 (£3,125,000) since 1952. The total known earnings from title fights by Clay (Muhammad Ali Haj) to March 1967 were $3,135,302 (then £1,119,750). His career gross has been estimated at $5½ million (£2,290,000).

Most knock-outs The greatest number of finishes classed by the rules prevailing as "knock-outs" in a career is 136 by Archie Moore of the U.S.A. The record for consecutive K.O.s is 44, set by Lamar Clark of Utah at Las Vegas, Nevada, U.S.A., on 11 Jan. 1960. He knocked out 6 in one night (5 in the first round) at Bingham, Utah, on 1 Dec. 1958.

Most fights The greatest recorded number of fights in a career is 1,309 by Abraham Hollandersky, *alias* Abe the Newsboy (U.S.A.), in the fourteen years from 1905 to 1918. He filled in the time with 387 wrestling bouts (1905–1916).

Most fights without loss Hal Bagwell of Gloucester, England, was undefeated in 183 consecutive fights, of which only 5 were draws, between 10 Aug. 1938 and 29 Nov. 1948.

Greatest weight difference The greatest weight difference recorded in a major bout is 10 stone (140 lb.) between Bob Fitzsimmons (12 stone 4 lb.) and Ed Dunkhorst (22 stone 4 lb.) at Brooklyn, New York City, N.Y., U.S.A., on 30 April 1900. Fitzsimmons won in two rounds.

Longest career The heavyweight Jem Mace, known as "the gypsy" (b. Beeston, Norwich, 8 April 1831), had a career lasting 35 years from 1855 to 1890, but there were several years in which he had only one fight. He died, aged 78, in Liverpool on 3 March 1910. Walter Edgerton, the "Kentucky Rosebud", knocked out John Henry Johnson, aged 45, in 4 rounds at the Broadway A.C., New York City, N.Y., U.S.A., on 4 Feb. 1916, when aged 63.

British titles The most defences of a British heavyweight title is 13 by "Bombardier" Billy Wells (1887–1967) from 1911 to 1919. The only British boxer to win three Lonsdale Belts outright has been Henry William Cooper, O.B.E. (b. Camberwell, London, 3 May 1934), heavyweight champion (1959–1969, 1970–71).

Father and son British titles won by father and son were at featherweight by "Spider" Jim Kelly (23 Nov. 1938 to 28 June 1939) and "Spider" Billy Kelly (22 Jan. 1955 to 4 Feb. 1956) and at heavyweight by Jack London (1913–63) from 15 Sept. 1944 to 17 July 1945 and Brian London (b. Brian Sydney Harper at West Hartlepool June 1934) from 3 June 1958 to 12 Jan. 1959.

Most Olympic gold medals The only amateur boxer ever to win three Olympic gold medals is the southpaw László Papp (b. 1926) (Hungary), who took the middleweight (1948) and the light-middleweight titles (1952 and 1956). The only man to win two titles in one celebration was O. L. Kirk (U.S.A.), who took both the bantam and featherweight titles at St. Louis, Missouri, U.S.A., in 1904, when the U.S. won all the titles. In 1908 Great Britain won all the titles.

A.B.A. TITLES

Most The greatest number of A.B.A. titles won by any boxer is 6 by Joseph Steers at middleweight and heavyweight between 1890 and 1893.

Longest span The greatest span of A.B.A. title-winning performances is that of the heavyweight H. Pat Floyd, who won in 1929 and gained his fourth title 17 years later in 1946.

Class	Instituted	Wins	Name	Years
Flyweight (8 stone or under)	1920	5	T. Pardoe	1929–33
Bantamweight (8 stone 7lb. or under)	1884	4	W. W. Allen	1911–12, 1914, 1919
Featherweight (9 stone or under)	1888	5	G. R. Baker	1912–14, 1919, 1921
Lightweight (9 stone 7 lb. or under)	1881	4	M. Wells	1904–07
		4	F. Grace	1909, 1913, 1919–20
Light-Welterweight (10 stone or under)	1951	2	D. Stone	1956–57
		2	R. Kane	1958–59
		2	L./Cpl. B. Brazier	1961–62
		2	R. McTaggart	1963, 1965
Welterweight (10 stone 8 lb. or under)	1920	3	N. Gargano	1954–55–56
Light-Middleweight (11 stone 2 lb. or under)	1951	2	B. Wells	1953–54
		2	B. Foster	1952, 1955
		2	S. Pearson	1958–59
		2	T. Imrie	1966, 1969
Middleweight (11 stone 11 lb. or under)	1881	5	R. C. Warnes	1899, 1901, 1903, 1907, 1910
		5	H. W. Mallin	1919–23
		5	F. Mallin	1928–32
Light-Heavyweight (12 stone 10 lb. or under)	1920	4	H. J. Mitchell	1922–25
Heavyweight (any weight)	1881	5	F. Parks	1899, 1901–02, 1905–06

El Cordobés in an ncharacteristic pose

BULLFIGHTING

The first renowned professional bullfighter was Francisco Romero of Ronda, in Andalusia, Spain, who fought in about 1700. The earliest treatise was *Tauromaquia o Arte torear* by José Delgado y Galvez. Spain now has some 190 active matadors. Since 1700, 42 major matadors have died in the ring.

Largest stadiums The world's largest bullfighting ring is the Plaza, Mexico City, with a capacity of 48,000. The largest of Spain's 312 bullrings is the Plaza Monumental, Madrid with a capacity of 23,663. The record gate has been $75,000 (now £31,250), taken at the Tijuana Plaza Monumental, Mexico, on 13 May 1962.

Most successful matadors The most successful matador measured by bulls killed was Lagartijo (1841–1900), born Rafael Molina, whose lifetime total was 4,867. The longest career of any 20th century *espada* was that of Juan Belmonte (1892–1962) of Spain who survived 29 seasons from 1909–1937, killing 3,000 bulls and being gored 50 times. In 1919 he killed 200 bulls in 109 *corridas*. In 1884 Romano set a record by killing 18 bulls in a day in Seville and in 1949 El Litri (Miguel Báes) set a Spanish record with 114 *novilladas* in a season.

Highest paid The highest paid bullfighter in history is El Cordobés (b. Manuel Benítez Pérez, probably on 4 May 1936, Palma del Rio, Spain), who became a sterling millionaire in 1966, when he fought 111 *corridas* up to 4 October of that year, latterly receiving a minimum fee of 1 million pesetas (then £6,945) for each half-hour in the ring. On 19 May 1968 he received £9,000 for a *corrida* in Madrid. In 1970 he received an estimated £750,000 for 121 fights.

CANOEING

Origins The acknowledged pioneer of canoeing as a sport was John Macgregor, a British barrister, in 1865. The Canoe Club was formed on 26 July 1866.

Most Olympic gold medals Gert Fredriksson of Sweden won the 1,000 metres Kayak singles in 1948, 1952 and 1956, the 10,000 metres Kayak singles in 1948 and 1956 and the 1,000 metres Kayak doubles in 1960. With 6 Olympic titles and 3 others (1,000 metres K.1 in 1950 and 1954 and 500 metres K.1 in 1954) his total individual world titles is 9. The Olympic 1,000 metre record of 3 minutes 14·38 seconds represents an average speed of 11·51 m.p.h. and a striking rate of 125 strokes per minute.

Most British titles The most British Open titles (instituted 1936) ever won is 23, of which 11 were individual, by Alistair Wilson (Ayrshire Kayak Club) with K.1 500 metres 1962–64–65–66; 1,000 metres 1962–64–65–66; 10,000 metres 1963–66–67; K.2 500 metres 1963–68; 1,000 metres 1965; 10,000 metres 1963–66; K.4 1,000 metres

1964–65–66 and K.1 4×500 metres Relay 1963–64–65–66. David Mitchell (Chester S. & C.C.) won his sixth consecutive British slalom title in 1968.

The only United Kingdom canoeists to win world titles have been Paul Farrant (died 18 April 1960) of Chalfont Park Canoe Club, who won the canoe slalom at Geneva, Switzerland, in August 1959, and Alan Emus, who won the canoe sailing at Hayling Island, Hampshire, in August 1961 and on the Boden See (Lake of Constance) in August 1965. Emus also won this event in the European Championship at Stockholm, Sweden, in August 1963.

Trans-Atlantic In 1928 E. Romer (Germany) crossed the North Atlantic from Lisbon to the West Indies in a 19½-foot Klepper folding canvas kayak named *Deutsches Sport* canoeing and sailing for 58 days.

Circum-navigation The first man to circumnavigate Great Britain by canoe is Geoffrey Hunter, 26, who started from and returned to Maidstone Bridge, Kent in 188 days (3 May–7 Nov. 1970). He lost one canoe and had to cling to a buoy for 14 hours in the Solway Firth.

Cross-Channel The singles record for canoeing across the English Channel is 3 hours 36 minutes by David Shankland, aged 29, of Cardiff, in a home-made N.C.K.I. named "Jelly Roll", from Shakespeare Bay, Dover, to Cap Gris-Nez, France, on 21 June 1965. The doubles record is 3 hours 20 minutes 30 seconds by Capt. William Stanley Crook and the late Ronald Ernest Rhodes in their glass-fibre K.2 "Accord", from St. Margaret's Bay, Dover, to Cap Blanc Nez, France, on 20 Sept. 1961.

The greatest mass start was on 24 Aug. 1970 by 34 C.2s or K.2s. Only two were successful one of which was crewed by the only girl—Gillian Tarrant, 19.

Devizes-Westminster The Senior Class record for the annual Devizes-Westminster Challenge Cup race (instituted 1948) over 125 miles with 77 locks is 19 hours 14 minutes 20 seconds by R. Evans and P. Pagnanelli (16 Parachute Brigade C.C.) in a K.2 Glider on 27–28 March 1970 on their third consecutive win. The record for the Junior Class event (held over 4 days) is 18 hours 51 seconds by A. Hunter and J. West (Leander Sea Scouts) on 27–30 March 1970. There are 77 portages and 21 miles of tidal water.

Eskimo rolls The record for Eskimo rolls is 325 in 22 minutes 44 seconds by Robert A. Hignell in a Merano kayak in the Denstone College, Staffordshire swimming pool on 2 March 1971.

DOWN STREAM CANOEING

River	Miles			Date	
Rhine	820	Sgt. Charles Kavanagh	Chur, Switzerland to Willemstad, Neths.	13 Feb. 1961	17½ days
Murray	1,300	Phillip Davis, 16, and Robert S. Lodge (15½-foot canoe)	Albury, N.S.W. to Murray Bridge	27 Dec. 1970–1 Feb. 1971	36 days
Nile	4,000	John Goddard (U.S.), Jean Laporte and André Davy (France)	Kagera to the Delta	Nov. 1953–July 1954	9 months

CAVING

Duration (trogging) The endurance record for staying in a cave is 463 days by Milutin Veljković (b. 1935) (Yugoslavia) in the Samar Cavern, Svrljig Mountains, northern Yugoslavia from 24 June 1969 to 30 Sept. 1970. The British record is 130 days by David Lafferty, aged 27, of Hampstead, who stayed in Boulder Chamber, Gough's Cave, Cheddar Gorge, Somerset, from 27 March to 4 Aug. 1966. He was alone until 1 Aug. when he thought it was 7 July.

PROGRESSIVE WORLD DEPTH RECORDS

Feet	Cave	Cavers	Date
210	Lamb Lair, near West Harptree, Somerset	John Beaumont (explored)	*c.* 1676
454	Macocha, Moravia	Joseph Nagel	May 1748
742	Grotta di Padriciano, Trieste	Antonio Lindner, Svetina	1839
1,079	Grotta di Trebiciano, Trieste	Antonio Lindner	6 April 1841
1,293	Nidlenloch, Switzerland	—	1909
1,433	Geldloch, Austria	—	1923
1,476	Abisso Bertarelli, Yugoslavia	R. Battelini, G. Cesca	24 Aug. 1925
1,491	Spluga della Preta, Venezia, Italy	*L. de Battisti	18 Sept. 1927
1,775	Antro di Corchia, Tuscany, Italy	E. Fiorentino Club	1934
1,980	Trou de Glaz, Isère, France	F. Petzl, C. Petit-Didier	4 May 1947
2,389	Gouffre de la Pierre Saint Martin, Basses-Pyrénées, France	*Georges Lépineux	15 Aug. 1953
2,428	Gouffre Berger, Sornin Plateau, Vercors, France	J. Cadoux, G. Garby	11 Sept. 1954
2,963	Gouffre Berger, Sornin Plateau, Vercors, France	*F. Petzl and 6 men	25 Sept. 1954
3,230	Gouffre Berger, Sornin Plateau, Vercors, France	L. Potié, G. Garby *et al.*	29 July 1955
⟩3,600	Gouffre Berger, Sornin Plateau, Vercors, France	Jean Cadoux and 2 others	11 Aug. 1956
⟩3,600	Gouffre Berger, Sornin Plateau, Vercors, France	*Frank Salt and 7 others	23 Aug. 1962
⟩3,700	Gouffre Berger, Sornin Plateau, Vercors, France	Kenneth Pearce	4 Aug. 1963
3,799	Gouffre de la Pierre Saint Martin, Basses-Pyrénées, France	C. Queffélec and 3 others	Aug. 1966
3,872	Gouffre de la Pierre Saint Martin, Basses-Pyrénées, France	C. Queffélec and 10 others	Aug. 1968
4,300	Gouffre de la Pierre Saint Martin, Basses-Pyrénées, France	Ass. de Rech. Spéléo Internat.	8–11 Nov. 1969

* *Leader*

WORLD'S DEEPEST CAVES

According to the latest available revised measurements, the deepest caves in the world are:—

Feet	Cave	Location
4,300	Gouffre de la Pierre Saint Martin	Basses-Pyrénées, France/Spain
3,750	Gouffre Berger	Sornin Plateau, Vercors, France
3,051	Réseau Trombe	Pyrénées, Haute-Garonne, France
2,872	Spluga della Preta	Lessinische Alps, Italy
2,641	Antro di Corchia	Apuanian Alps, Italy
2,573	Grotta del Monte Cucco	Perugia, Italy

NOTE: *The Provetina Cave, Greece has the world's longest vertical pitch of 1,298 feet. The highest known cave entrance in the world is that of the Rakhiot Cave, Nanga Parbat, Kashmir at 21,860 feet.*

CHESS

Origins The name chess is derived from the Persian word *shah* (a king or ruler). It is a descendant of the game *Chaturanga*. The earliest reference is from the Middle Persian Karnamak (*c.* A.D. 590–628), though there are grounds for believing its origins are from the 4th century in north west India. It reached Britain in *c.* 1255. The *Fédération Internationale des Éschecs* was established in 1924. There were an estimated 5,000,000 competitive players in the U.S.S.R. in 1967.

World champions François André Danican, *alias* Philidor (1726–95), of France claimed the title of "world champion" from 1747 until his death. World champions have been generally recognized since 1843. The longest tenures were 28 years by Wilhelm Steinitz (1836–1900) of Austria, from 1866 to 1894, and 27 years by Dr. Emanuel Lasker (1868–1941) of Germany, from 1894 to 1921. The youngest was Paul Charles Morphy (1837–84) of New Orleans, Louisiana, U.S.A., who won the title in 1858, when aged 21, and held it until 1862. The women's world championship was won three times by Yelizaveta Bykova (U.S.S.R.) in 1953, 1958 and 1960. The biennial world team championship (instituted 1927) has been won most often by the U.S.S.R.—11 times consecutively starting in 1952.

British titles Most British titles have been won by Dr. Jonathan Penrose, O.B.E. (b. 1934) of East Finchley, London with 10 titles in 1958–63, 1966–69. Mrs. Rowena M. Bruce (b. 1919) of Plymouth won 8 titles in 1950–51–54–55 (shared)–59–60–63–66.

Longest games The most protracted chess match on record was one drawn on the 191st move between H. Pilnik (Argentina) and Moshe Czerniak (Israel) at Mar del Plata, Argentina, in April 1950. The total playing time was 20 hours. A game of 21½ hours, but drawn on the 171st move (average over 7½ minutes per move), was played between Makagonov and Chekover at Baku, U.S.S.R., in 1945. A game of 221 moves between Arthur Williams (G.B.) and Kenneth Pogoff (U.S.A.) occurred at Stockholm, Sweden in August 1969 but required only 4 hours 25 minutes.

Marathon The longest recorded session is one of 101 hours between John P. Cameron and Jon Stevens at Ipswich Civic College, Suffolk, England, on 21–25 March 1970. The longest game at "lightning chess" (*i.e.* all moves completed by a player in five minutes) is 50 hours 2 minutes by Michael Dales, 15 and Martin Clarke, 14, of Cordeaux High School, Lincolnshire on 21–23 July 1970. At Otago University, New Zealand, Grant Kerr, 20 and Aldis Skuja, 21, played for 73 hours 6 minutes (520 games) against a succession of opponents on 1–4 Aug. 1969.

Slowest Lawrence Grant and Dr. J. Munro MacLennan, the latter now in Sydney, New South Wales, Australia, are still playing a match begun at Aberdeen University on 24 Nov. 1926. They make one move each time they correspond which is most often by an annual Christmas card.

Shortest game The shortest recorded game between masters was one of four moves when Lazard (Black) beat Gibaud in a Paris chess café in 1924. The moves were: 1. P–Q4, Kt–KB3; 2. Kt–Q2, P–K4; 3. PxP, Kt–Kt5; 4. P–KR3, Kt–K6. White then resigned because if he played 5. PxKt there would have followed Q–KR5 check and the loss of his Queen for a Knight by any other move.

Most opponents Records by chess masters for numbers of opponents tackled simultaneously depend very much on whether or not the opponents are replaced as defeated, are in relays, or whether they are taken on in a simultaneous start. The greatest number tackled on a replacement basis is 400 (379 defeated) by the Swedish master Gideon Ståhlberg (died 26 May 1967) in 36 hours of play in Buenos Aires, Argentina, in 1940. Georges Koltanowski (Belgium, now of U.S.A.) tackled 56 opponents "blindfold" and won 50, drew 6, lost 0 in 9¾ hours at Fairmont Hotel, San Francisco, California, U.S.A., on 13 Dec. 1960.

CONTRACT BRIDGE

Earliest references Bridge (a corruption of Biritch) is of Levantine origin, having been played in Greece in the early 1880s. The game was known in London in 1886 under the title of "Biritch" or Russian Whist.

Auction Bridge (highest bidder names trump) was introduced in 1904 but was swamped by the Contract game, which was devised by Harold S. Vanderbilt (U.S.A.) on a Caribbean voyage in November 1925. The new version became a world-wide craze after the U.S.A. *v.* Great Britain challenge match between Ely Culbertson (b. Romania, 1891) and Lt.-Col. Walter Buller at Almack's Club, London, on 15 Sept. 1930. The U.S.A. won the 54-hand match by 4,845 points.

World titles The World Championship (Bermuda Bowl) has been won most often by Italy (1957–58–59, 1961–62–63, 1965–66–67, 1969), whose team also won the Olympiad in 1964 and 1968. Three of the Italian players, Massimo D'Alelio, Giorgio Belladonna and Pietro Forquet, were in 11 of these winning teams.

Perfect deals The mathematical odds against dealing 13 cards of one suit are 158,753,389,899 to 1, while the odds against receiving a "perfect hand" consisting of all 13 spades are 635,013,559,596 to 1. The odds against each of the 4 players receiving a complete suit (a "perfect deal") are 2,235,197,406,895,366,368,301,559,999 to 1. Instances of this are reported frequently but the chances of it happening genuinely are extraordinarily remote—in fact if all the people in the world were grouped in bridge fours, and each four were dealt 120 hands a day, it would require 62×10^{12} years before one "perfect deal" should recur.

A "perfect" perfect deal with the dealer (South) with 13 clubs, round to East with 13 spades was the subject of affidavits by Mrs. E. F. Gyde (dealer), Mrs. Hennion, David Rex-Taylor and Mrs. P. Dawson at Richmond Community Centre, Surrey, on 25 Aug. 1964. This deal, 24 times more remote than a "perfect deal", the second of the rubber, was with a pack *not* used for the first deal. In view of the fact that there should be 31,201,794 deals with two perfect hands for each deal with four perfect hands and that reports of the latter far outnumber the former, it can be safely assumed that reported occurrences of perfect deals are almost without exception bogus.

Longest session The longest recorded session is one of 176¾ hours by David Shapira, Michael Robertson, Richard Melville and Brian Moffett in Belmont Hall, Dundee University, Scotland on 18–24 April 1971.

Most master points The player with the highest-lifetime total of master points is Barry Crane, a Hollywood television producer, with 11,357 points by May 1970. The most points scored in tournaments in one year is 1,434 by Paul Soloway of Los Angeles, California, U.S.A., in 1969.

At June 1970 the leading scorers of master points in the United Kingdom were the twin brothers Robert Sharples (2,025 points) and James (2,016).

HIGHEST POSSIBLE SCORES (excluding penalties)

Opponents bid 7 of any suit or No Trumps doubled and redoubled and vulnerable

	Opponents make no trick	
Above Line	1st undertrick	400
	12 subsequent undertricks at 600 each	7,200
	All Honours	150
		7,750

Bid 1 No Trump, double and redouble, vulnerable

Below Line	1st trick (40 × 4)	160
Above Line	6 over tricks (400 × 6)	2,400
	2nd game of 2-Game Rubber	*350
	All Honours	150
	Bonus for making redoubled contract	50
	(Highest Possible Positive Score)	3,110

* *In practice, the full bonus of 700 points is awarded after the completion of the second winning game rather than 350 after each game.*

COURSING

Origins The sport of dogs chasing hares was probably of Egyptian origin in *c.* 3000 B.C. and brought to England by the Normans in 1067. The classic event is the annual Waterloo Cup, instituted at Altcar, near Liverpool, in 1836. A government bill to declare the sport illegal was "lost" owing to the dissolution of Parliament on 29 May 1970.

Most successful dog The most successful Waterloo Cup dog recorded was Colonel North's *Fullerton,* sired by *Greentich,* who tied for first in 1889 and then won outright in 1890–91–92.

The only dogs to win the Victorian Waterloo Cup (instituted 1873) three times have been *Bulwark* in 1906–07–09, at which time it was known as the Australian Waterloo Cup, and *Byamee* in 1953–54–55.

Longest course The longest authenticated course is one of 4 minutes 10 seconds, when Major C. Blundell's *Blackmore* beat *Boldon* in a Barbican Cup decider on 2 March 1934.

CRICKET

Earliest match The earliest evidence of the game of cricket is from a drawing depicting two men playing with a bat and ball dated *c.* 1250. The game was played in Guildford, Surrey, at least as early as 1550. The earliest major match of which the score survives was one in which a team representing England (40 and 70) was beaten by Kent (53 and 58 for 9) by one wicket at the Artillery Ground in Finsbury, London, on 18 June 1744. Cricket was played in Australia as early as 1803.

BATTING

Highest innings The highest recorded innings by any team was one of 1,107 runs by Victoria against New South Wales in an Australian inter-State match at Melbourne, Victoria, on 27–28 Dec. 1926.

England The highest innings made in England is 903 runs for 7 wickets declared, by England in the 5th Test against Australia at the Oval, London, on 20, 22 and 23 Aug. 1938. The highest innings in a county championship match is 887 by Yorkshire *v.* Warwickshire at Edgbaston on 7–8 May 1896.

Lowest The lowest recorded innings is 12 made by Oxford University *v.* the Marylebone Cricket Club (M.C.C.) at Oxford on 24 May 1877, and 12 by Northamptonshire *v.* Gloucestershire at Gloucester on 11 June 1907. On the occasion of the Oxford match, however, the University batted a man short. The lowest score in a Test match is 26 by New Zealand *v.* England in the 2nd Test at Auckland on 28 March 1955.

The lowest aggregate for two innings is 34 (16 in first and 18 in second) by Border *v.* Natal in the South African Currie Cup at East London on 19 and 21 Dec. 1959.

Greatest victory The greatest recorded margin of victory is an innings and 851 runs, when Pakistan Railways (910 for 6 wickets declared) beat Dera Ismail Khan (32 and 27) at Lahore on 2–4 Dec. 1964. The largest margin in England is one of an innings and 579 runs by England over Australia in the 5th Test at the Oval on 20–24 Aug. 1938 when Australia scored 201 and 123 with two men short in both innings. The most one-sided county match was when Surrey (698) defeated Sussex (114 and 99) by an innings and 485 runs at the Oval on 9–11 Aug. 1888.

FASTEST SCORING

The greatest number of runs scored in a day is 721 runs all out (10 wickets) in 6 hours by the Australians *v.* Essex at Southchurch Park, Southend-on-Sea on the first day on 15 May 1948.

The Test record for runs in a day is 588 at Old Trafford on 27 July 1936 when England put on 398 and India were 190 for 0 in their second innings by the close.

Innings of 200 or more The fastest recorded exhibition of hitting occurred in a Kent *v.* Gloucestershire match at Dover on 20 Aug. 1937, when Kent scored 219 runs for 2 wickets in 71 minutes, at the rate of 156 runs for each 100 balls bowled.

Fastest 50 The fastest 50 ever hit was completed in 8 minutes (1.22 to 1.30 p.m.) and in 11 scoring strokes by Clive C. Inman (b. Colombo, Ceylon, 29 Jan. 1936) in an innings of 57 not out for Leicestershire *v.* Nottinghamshire at Trent Bridge, Nottingham on 20 Aug. 1965.

Century The fastest century ever hit was completed in 35 minutes by Percy George Herbert Fender (b. 22 Aug. 1892), when scoring 113 not out for Surrey *v.* Northamptonshire at Northampton on 26 Aug. 1920. The most prolific scorer of centuries in an hour or less was Gilbert Laird Jessop (1874–1955), with 11 between 1897 and 1913. The fastest Test century was one of 70 minutes by Jack Morrison Gregory (b. 14 Aug. 1895) of New South Wales, for Australia *v.* South Africa in the 2nd Test at Johannesburg on 12 Nov. 1921. Edwin Boaler Alletson (1884–1963) scored 189 runs in 90 minutes for Nottinghamshire *v.* Sussex at Hove on 20 May 1911.

Double century The fastest double century was completed in 120 minutes by Gilbert Jessop (1874–1955) (286) for Gloucestershire *v.* Sussex at Hove on 1 June 1903.

Treble century The fastest treble century was completed in 181 minutes by Denis Charles Scott Compton, C.B.E. (b. Hendon, 23 May 1918) of Middlesex, who scored 300 for the M.C.C. *v.* North-Eastern Transvaal at Benoni on 3–4 Dec. 1948.

1,000 in May The most recent example of scoring 1,000 runs *in May* was by Charles Hallows (Lancashire) (b. 4 April 1895), who made precisely 1,000 between 5–31 May 1928. Dr. W. G. Grace (9–30 May 1895) and W. R. Hammond (7–31 May 1927) surpassed this feat with 1,016 and 1,042 runs. The greatest number of runs made *before*

Denis Compton, scorer of most runs and most centuries in a season

the end of May was by T. W. Hayward with 1,074 from 16 April to 31 May in 1900.

Slowest scoring The longest time a batsman has ever taken to open his scoring is 1 hour 37 minutes by Thomas Godfrey Evans (b. Finchley, 18 Aug. 1920) of Kent, who scored 10 not out for England *v.* Australia in the 4th Test at Adelaide on 5–6 Feb. 1947. Richard Gorton Barlow (1850–1919) utilized 2½ hours to score 5 not out for Lancashire *v.* Nottinghamshire at Nottingham on 8 July 1882. During his innings his score remained unchanged for 80 minutes.

The slowest century on record was by Derrick John (Jackie) McGlew (b. 11 March 1929) of South Africa in the Third Test *v.* Australia at Durban on 25 and 27 Jan. 1958. He required 9 hours 35 minutes for 105, reaching the 100 in 9 hours 5 minutes. The slowest double century recorded is one of 10 hours 8 minutes by Robert Baddeley Simpson (b. 3 Feb. 1936) of New South Wales, during an innings of 311, lasting 12 hours 42 minutes, for Australia *v.* England in the Fourth Test at Old Trafford on 23, 24 and 25 July 1964.

Highest individual innings The highest individual innings recorded is 499 in 10 hours 40 minutes by Hanif Muhammad (b. Junagadh, Pakistan, 21 Dec. 1934) for Karachi *v.* Bahawalpur at Karachi, Pakistan, on 8, 9 and 11 Jan. 1959. The record for a Test match is 365 not out in 10 hours 8 minutes by Garfield St. Aubrun Sobers (b. Barbados, 28 July 1936) playing for the West Indies in the Third Test against Pakistan at Sabina Park, Kingston, Jamaica, on 27 Feb.–1 March 1958. The England Test record is 364 by Sir Leonard Hutton (b. Fulneck, Pudsey, Yorkshire, 23 June 1916) *v.* Australia in the 5th Test at the Oval on 20, 22 and 23 Aug. 1938. The highest score in England is 424 in 7 hours 50 minutes by Archibald Campbell MacLaren (1871–1944) for Lancashire *v.* Somerset at Taunton on 15–16 July 1895.

Longest innings The longest innings on record is one of 16 hours 39 minutes for 337 runs by Hanif Muhammad (Pakistan) *v.* the West Indies in the 1st Test at Bridgetown, Barbados, on 20–23 Jan. 1958. The English record is 13 hours 17 minutes by Hutton (see above).

Least runs in a career S. Clarke, the Somerset wicket-keeper, played five matches for his county in 1930, scoring no runs in each of his nine innings of which 7 were ducks.

Most runs off an over The first batsman to score the possible of 36 runs off a six-ball over was Garfield Sobers (Nottingham) off Malcolm Andrew Nash (Glamorgan) at Swansea on 31 Aug. 1968. The ball (recovered from the last hit from the road by a small boy) resides in Nottingham's Museum.

BIGGEST SCORERS

Season The greatest number of runs ever scored in a season is 3,816 in 50 innings (8 not out) by Denis Compton (Middlesex) in 1947. His batting average was 90·85.

Most runs in a career The greatest aggregate of runs in a career is 61,237 in 1,315 innings (106 not out) between 1905 and 1934 by Sir John (Jack) Berry Hobbs (1882–1963) of Surrey and England. His career average was 50·65.

Test matches The greatest number of runs scored in Test matches is 7,459 in 179 innings (15 not out) by Michael Colin Cowdrey (b. Bangalore, India, 24 Dec. 1932) of Kent, playing for England between 1954–55 and 1971. His average is 45·48.

CENTURIES

Season The record for the greatest number of centuries in a season is also held by Compton with eighteen in 1947. With their restricted fixture list the Australian record is eight by Sir Donald George Bradman (b. 27 Aug. 1908) in only 12 innings in the 1947–48 season.

Career The most centuries in a career is 197 by Sir John Hobbs between 1905 and 1934. The Australian record is Sir Donald Bradman's 117 centuries between 1927 and 1949.

Test matches The greatest number of centuries scored in Test matches is 29 by Sir Donald Bradman (Australia) between 1928 and 1948. The English record is 22 by Walter Hammond (1903–65) of Gloucestershire, between 1927 and 1947, and 22 by Colin Cowdrey (Kent) between 1954–55 and 1971.

Highest averages The highest recorded seasonal batting average in England is 115·66 for 26 innings (2,429 runs) by Don Bradman (Australia) in England in 1938. The English record is 96·96 by Herbert Sutcliffe (b. 24 Nov. 1894) of Yorkshire, for 42 innings (3,006 runs) in 1931. The world record for a complete career is 95·14 for 338 innings (28,067 runs) by Bradman between 1927 and 1949. The record for Test matches is 99·94 in 80 innings (6,996 runs) by Bradman in 1928–48. The English career record is 56·37 for 500 innings (62 not out) by Kumar Shri Ranjitsinhji (1872–1933), later H.H. the Jam Saheb of Nawanagar, with 24,692 runs between 1893 and 1920.

Double centuries The only batsman to score double centuries in both innings is Arthur Edward Fagg (b. 18 June 1915), who made 244 and 202 not out for Kent *v.* Essex at Colchester on 13–15 July 1938.

Wally Hammond (1903–65), who held 78 catches in a season (see page 249)

Longest hit The longest measured drive is one of 175 yards by Walter (later the Rev.) Fellows (1834–1901) of Christ Church, Oxford University, in a practice on their ground, off Charles Rogers in 1856. J. E. C. Moore made a measured hit of 170 yards 1 foot 5 inches at Griffith, New South Wales, Australia, in February 1930. Peter Samuel Heine (b. 28 June 1929) of the Orange Free State is said to have driven a ball bowled by Hugh Joseph Tayfield (b. 30 Jan. 1929) of Natal for approximately 180 yards at Bloemfontein on 3 Jan. 1955.

Most sixes in an innings The highest number of sixes hit in an innings is 15 by John Richard Reid, O.B.E. (b. 3 June 1928), in an innings of 296, lasting 3 hours 47 minutes, for Wellington *v.* Northern Districts in the Plunket Shield Tournament at Wellington, New Zealand, on 14–15 Jan. 1963. The Test record is 10 by Walter Hammond in an innings of 336 not out for England *v.* New Zealand at Auckland on 31 March and 1 April 1933.

Most sixes in a match The highest number of sixes in a match is 17 (10 in the first and 7 in the second innings) by William James Stewart (b. 31 Aug. 1934) for Warwickshire *v.* Lancashire at Blackpool on 29–31 July 1959. His two innings were of 155 and 125.

Most boundaries in an innings The highest number of boundaries in an innings was 68 (all in fours) by Percival Albert Perrin (1876–1945) in an innings of 343 not out for Essex *v.* Derbyshire at Chesterfield on 18–19 July 1904.

Most runs off a ball The most runs scored off a single hit is 10 by Samuel Hill Hill-Wood (1872–1949) off Cuthbert James Burnup (1875–1960) in the Derbyshire *v.* M.C.C. match at Lord's, London, on 26 May 1900.

GREATEST PARTNERSHIP

World The record stand for any partnership is the fourth wicket stand of 577 by Gul Muhammad (b. 15 Oct. 1921), who scored 319, and Vijay Samuel Hazare (b. 11 March 1915) (288) in the Baroda *v.* Holkar match at Baroda, India, on 8–10 March 1947.

England The highest stand in English cricket, and the world record for a first wicket partnership, is 555 by Percy Holmes (b. 25 Nov. 1886) (224 not out) and Herbert Sutcliffe (313) for Yorkshire *v.* Essex at Leyton on 15–16 June 1932.

Highest score by a No. 11 The highest score by a No. 11 batsman is 163 by Thomas Peter Bromly Smith (1908–67) for Essex *v.* Derbyshire at Chesterfield in August 1947.

BOWLING

Most wickets The largest number of wickets ever taken in a season is 304 by Alfred Percy ("Tich") Freeman (1888–1965) of Kent, in 1928. Freeman bowled 1,976·1 overs, of which 423 were maidens, with an average of 18·05 runs per wicket. The greatest wicket-taker in history is Wilfred Rhodes (b. Kirkheaton, Yorkshire, 29 Oct. 1877), who took 4,187 wickets for 69,993 runs (average 16·71 runs per wicket) between 1898 and 1930.

Tests The greatest number of wickets taken in Test matches is 307 for 6,625 runs (average 21·57) by Frederick Sewards Trueman (b. Scotch Springs, Yorkshire, 6 Feb. 1931), in 67 Tests between June 1952 and June 1965. The lowest bowling average in a Test career (minimum 15 wickets) is 61 wickets for 775 runs (12·70 runs per wicket) by John James Ferris (1867–1900) in 9 Tests (8 for Australia and 1 for England) between 1886 and 1892.

Fastest The highest measured speed for a ball bowled by any bowler is 93 m.p.h. by Harold Larwood (b. Nuncargate, Notts., 14 Nov. 1904) in 1933. The fastest bowler of all time is regarded by many as Charles Jesse Kortright (1871–1952), who played for Essex from 1889 to 1907. Albert Cotter (1883–1917) of New South Wales, Australia, is reputed to have broken a stump more than 20 times. Wesley Winfield Hall (b. 12 Sept. 1937) of Barbados was timed to bowl at 91 m.p.h. in practice in 1962–63, when playing for Queensland, Australia.

Freddie Trueman (Yorkshire and England), who took 307 Test wickets

Most consecutive wickets No bowler in first class cricket has yet achieved five wickets with five consecutive balls. The nearest approach was that of Charles Warrington Leonard Parker (1884–1959) (Gloucestershire) in his own benefit match against Yorkshire at Bristol on 10 Aug. 1922, when he struck the stumps with five successive balls but the second was called as a no-ball. The only man to have taken 4 wickets with consecutive balls more than once is Robert James Crisp (b. 28 May 1911) for Western Province *v.* Griqualand West at Johannesburg on 23–24 Dec. 1931 and against Natal at Durban on 3 March 1934.

Most "hat tricks" The greatest number of "hat tricks" is seven by Douglas Vivian Parson Wright (b. 21 Sept. 1914) on 3 and 29 July, 1937, 18 May 1938, 13 Jan. and 1 July 1939, 11 Aug. 1947 and 1 Aug. 1949. In his own benefit match at Lord's on 22 May 1907, Albert Edwin Trott (Middlesex) took four Somerset wickets with four consecutive balls and then later in the same innings achieved a "hat trick".

Most wickets in an innings The taking of all ten wickets by a single bowler has been recorded many times but only one bowler has achieved this feat on three occasions—Alfred Percy Freeman of Kent, against Lancashire at Maidstone on 24 July 1929, against Essex at Southend on 13–14 Aug. 1930 and against Lancashire at Old Trafford on 27 May 1931. The fewest runs scored off a bowler taking all 10 wickets is 10, when Hedley Verity (1905–43) of Yorkshire dismissed (8 caught, 1 l.b.w., 1 stumped) every Nottinghamshire batsman in 118 balls at Leeds on 12 July 1932. The only bowler to have "cleaned bowled" a whole side out was John Wisden (1826–84) of Sussex, playing for the North *v.* the South at Lord's in 1850.

Most wickets in a match James Charles Laker (b. Bradford, Yorkshire, 9 Feb. 1922) of Surrey took 19 wickets for 90 runs (9–37 and 10–53) for England *v.* Australia in the 4th Test at Old Trafford on 26–31 July 1956. No other bowler has taken more than 17 wickets in a first class match. Henry Arkwright (1837–66) took 18 wickets for 96 runs in a 12-a-side match, M.C.C. *v.* Gentlemen of Kent, at Canterbury on 14–17 Aug. 1861. Alfred Percy Freeman (Kent) took ten or more wickets in a match on 140 occasions between 1914 and 1936.

Most wickets in a day The greatest number of wickets taken in a day's play is 17 by Colin Blythe (1879–1917) for 48 runs, for Kent against Northamptonshire at Northampton on 1 June 1907; by Hedley Verity for 91 runs, for Yorkshire *v.*

Essex at Leyton on 14 July 1933; and by Thomas William John Goddard (1900–66) for 106 runs, for Gloucestershire *v.* Kent at Bristol on 3 July 1939.

Most expensive bowling The greatest number of runs hit off one bowler in one innings is 362, scored off Arthur Alfred Mailey (b. 3 Jan. 1888) in the New South Wales *v.* Victoria inter-State match at Melbourne on 24–28 Dec. 1926. The greatest number of runs ever conceded by a bowler in one match is 428 by C. S. Nayudu in the Holkar *v.* Bombay match at Bombay on 4–9 March 1945, when he also made the record number of 917 deliveries.

Most maidens Hugh Joseph Tayfield bowled 16 consecutive 8-ball maiden overs (137 balls without conceding a run) for South Africa *v.* England at Durban on 25–27 Jan. 1957. The greatest number of consecutive 6-ball maiden overs bowled is 21 (130 balls) by Ragunath G. ("Bapu") Nadkarni (b. 4 April 1932) for India *v.* England at Madras on 12 Jan. 1964. The English record is 17 overs (105 balls) by Horace L. Hazell (born 30 Sept. 1909) for Somerset *v.* Gloucestershire at Taunton on 4 June 1949, and 17 (104 balls) by Graham Anthony (Tony) Richard Lock (b. 5 July 1929) of Surrey, playing for the M.C.C. *v.* the Governor-General's XI at Karachi, Pakistan, on 31 Dec. 1955. Alfred Shaw (1842–1907) of Nottinghamshire bowled 23 consecutive 4-ball maiden overs (92 balls) for North *v.* the South at Nottingham in 1876.

Most balls The greatest number of balls sent down by any bowler in one season is 12,234 (651 maidens: 298 wickets) by Alfred Percy Freeman (Kent) in 1933. The most balls bowled in an innings is 588 (98 overs) by Sonny Ramadhin (b. 1 May 1930) of Trinidad, playing for the West Indies in the First Test *v.* England at Birmingham on 30 May and 1, 3 and 4 June 1957. He took 2 for 179.

Best average The lowest recorded bowling average for a season is one of 8·61 runs per wicket (177 wickets for 1,525 runs) by Alfred Shaw of Nottinghamshire in 1880.

FIELDING

Most catches in an innings The greatest number of catches in an innings is seven, by Michael James Stewart (b. 16 Sept. 1932) for Surrey *v.* Northamptonshire at Northampton on 7 June 1957, and by Anthony Stephen Brown (b. 24 June 1936) for Gloucestershire *v.* Nottinghamshire at Trent Bridge on 26 July 1966.

In a match Walter Reginald Hammond (1903–65) held a record total of 10 catches (4 in the first innings, 6 in the second) for Gloucestershire *v.* Surrey at Cheltenham on 16–17 Aug. 1928. The record for a wicket-keeper is 11 (see right).

In a season and in a career The greatest number of catches in a season is 78 by Walter Hammond (Gloucestershire) in 1928, and 77 by Michael James Stewart (Surrey) in 1957. The most catches in a career is 1,011 by Frank Edward Woolley (b. 27 May 1887) of Kent in 1906–1938. The Test record is 117 by Michael Colin Cowdrey between 1954–55 and 1971.

Longest throw The longest recorded throw of a cricket ball ($5\frac{1}{2}$ oz.) is 140 yards 2 feet (422 feet) by R. Percival on Durham Sands Racecourse on Easter Monday, 14 April 1884.

WICKET-KEEPING

In an innings The most dismissals by a wicket-keeper in an innings is eight (all caught) by Arthur Theodore Wallace Grout (1927–68) for Queensland against Western Australia at Brisbane on 15 Feb. 1960. The Test record is six (all caught) by A. T. W. Grout (see above) for the First Australia *v.* South Africa Test at Johannesburg on 27–28 Dec. 1957; six (all caught) by Denis Lindsay (b. 4 Sept. 1939) of North-Eastern Transvaal, for South Africa *v.* Australia in the First Test at Johannesburg on 24 Dec. 1966; six (all caught) by John Thomas Murray (b. 1 April 1935) of Middlesex, for England *v.* India in the Second Test at Lord's, London on 22 June 1967.

In a match The greatest number of dismissals by a wicket-keeper in a match is 12 by Edward Pooley (1838–1907) (eight caught, four stumped) for Surrey *v.* Sussex at the Oval on 6–7 July 1868; nine caught, three stumped by Don Tallon (b. 17 Feb. 1916) of Australia for Queensland *v.* New South Wales at Sydney on 2–4 Jan. 1939; and also nine caught, three stumped by Hedley Brian Taber (b. 29 April 1940) of New South Wales against South Australia at Adelaide 17–19 Dec. 1968. The record for catches is 11 (seven in the first innings and four in the second) by Arnold Long (b. 18 Dec. 1940), for Surrey *v.* Sussex at Hove on 18 and 21 July 1964. The Test record for dismissals is 9 (eight caught, one stumped) by Gilbert Roche Andrews Langley of South Australia, playing for Australia *v.* England in the 2nd Test at Lords, London, on 22–26 June 1956.

In a season The record number of dismissals for any wicket-keeper in a season is 127 (79 caught, 48 stumped) by Leslie Ethelbert George Ames (b. 3 Dec. 1905) of Kent in 1929. The record for the number stumped is 64 by Ames in 1932. The record for catches is 96 by James Graham Binks (b. 5 Oct. 1935) of Yorkshire in 1960.

In a career The highest total of dismissals in a wicket-keeping career is 1,468 (a record 1,215 catches, plus 253 stumpings) by Herbert Strudwick (1880–1970) of Surrey between 1902 and 1927. The most stumpings in a career is 415 by Ames (1926–1951). The Test record is 219 in 91 innings by Godfrey Evans.

Least byes The best wicket-keeping record for preventing byes is that of Archdale Palmer Wickham (1855–1935) when, keeping for Somerset *v.* Hampshire at Taunton on 20–22 July 1899, he did not concede a single bye in a total of 672 runs. The record for Test matches is no byes in 659 runs by Godfrey Evans for England in the 2nd Test *v.* Australia at Sydney, New South Wales, on 14, 16, 17 and 18 Dec. 1946.

Most byes The records at the other extreme are those of Philip Harman Stewart-Brown (born 30 April 1904) of Harlequins, who let through 46 byes in an Oxford University innings of only 188 on 21–23 May 1927 and 58 byes let through by Anthony William Catt of Kent in a Northamptonshire total of 374 at Northampton on 20–22 Aug. 1955.

ENGLISH COUNTY CHAMPIONSHIP

The greatest number of victories has been secured by Yorkshire, with 29 outright wins up to 1968, and one shared with Middlesex in 1949. They have never been lower than twelfth (in 1953) on the table. The most "wooden spoons" have been won by Northamptonshire, with ten since 1923. They did not win a single match between May 1935 and May 1939. The record number of consecutive title wins is 7 by Surrey from 1952 to 1958. The greatest number of consecutive appearances for one county is 421 by Joe Vine (1875–1946) of Sussex.

Oldest and youngest county cricketers The youngest player to represent his county was William Wade Fitzherbert Pullen (1866–1937), for Gloucestershire against Middlesex at Lord's on 5 June 1882, when aged 15 years 346 days. The oldest regular County players have been William George Quaife (1872–1951) of Sussex and Warwickshire, who played his last match for Warwickshire against Hampshire at Portsmouth on 27–30 Aug. 1927, when aged 55, and John Herbert King (1871–1946) of Leicestershire, who played his last match for his county against Yorkshire at Leicester on 5–7 Aug. 1925, when aged 54.

Largest crowds The greatest recorded attendance at a cricket match is 350,534 (receipts £30,124) for the Third Test between Australia and England at Melbourne on 1–7 Jan. 1937. For the whole series the figure was a record 933,513 (receipts £87,963). The greatest recorded attendance at a cricket match on one day was 90,800 on the second day of the Fifth Test between Australia and the West Indies at Melbourne on 11 Feb. 1961, when the receipts were £A13,132 (£10,484 sterling). The English record is 159,000 for the Fourth Test between England and Australia at Headingley, Leeds, on 22–27 July 1948, and the record for one day probably a capacity of 46,000 for a match between Lancashire and Yorkshire at Old Trafford on 2 Aug. 1926. The English record for a Test series is 549,650 (receipts £200,428) for the series against Australia in 1953.

Greatest receipts The world record for receipts from a match is £72,882, from the attendance paid by 91,149 at the Second Test between England and Australia at Lord's, London, on 20–25 June 1968. The Test series record is £245,286 paid by 298,631 for the five England *v.* Australia Tests of June–August 1968.

Highest benefit The highest "benefit" ever accorded a player is £14,000 for Cyril Washbrook (b. 6 Dec. 1914) in the Lancashire *v.* Australians match at Old Trafford on 7–10 Aug. 1948.

Most Test appearances The record number of Test appearances is 109 by Michael Colin Cowdrey (England) between 1954–55 and 1971. The highest number of Test captaincies is 41, including 35 consecutive games, by Peter Barker Howard May (b. 31 Dec. 1929) of Cambridge University and Surrey, who captained England from 1955 to 1961 and played in a total of 66 Tests. The most innings batted in Test matches is 179 in 109 Tests by Cowdrey of Kent, playing for England between 1954–55 and 1971. Garfield Sobers (West Indies) holds the record for consecutive Tests, with 80 from April 1955 to April 1971.

Longest match The lengthiest recorded cricket match was the "timeless" Test between England and South Africa at Durban on 3–14 March 1939. It was abandoned after 10 days (8th day rained off) because the boat taking the England team home was due to leave. The lengthiest in England was the 6-day 5th England *v.* Australia Test on 6–12 Aug. 1930, when rain prevented play on the fifth day.

MINOR CRICKET RECORDS
(where excelling those in First Class Cricket)

Bowling Stephen Fleming bowling for Marlborough College "A" XI, New Zealand *v.* Bohally Intermediate at Blenheim, New Zealand in Dec. 1967 took 9 wickets in 9 consecutive balls. In February 1931 in a schools match in South Africa Paul Hugo also took 9 wickets with 9 consecutive balls for Smithfield School *v.* Aliwal North.

Highest individual innings In a Junior House match between Clarke's House and North Town, at Clifton College, Bristol, in June 1899, A. E. J. Collins, aged 13, scored an unprecedented 628 not out in 6 hours 50 minutes, over five afternoons' batting, carrying his bat through the innings of 836. The scorer, E. W. Pegler, gave the score as "628—plus or minus 20, shall we say".

Fastest individual scoring S. K. Coen (South Africa) scored 50 runs (11 fours and 1 six) in 7 minutes for Gezira *v.* the R.A.F. in 1942, compared with the First Class record of 8 minutes. Cecil George Pepper hit a century in 24 minutes in a Services match in Palestine in 1943. Cedric Ivan James Smith hit 9 successive sixes for a Middlesex XI *v.* Harrow and District at Rayners' Lane, Harrow, in 1935. This feat was repeated by Arthur Dudley Nourse, Jr. in a South African XI *v.* Military Police match at Cairo in 1942–43. Nourse's feat included six sixes in one over.

Highest scoring rate In the match Royal Naval College, Dartmouth *v.* Seale Hayne Agricultural College in 1923, K. A. Sellar (now Cdr. "Monkey" Sellar, D.S.O., D.S.C., R.N.) and L. K. A. Block (now Judge Block, D.S.C.) were set to score 174 runs in 105 minutes but achieved this total in 33 minutes, so averaging 5·27 runs per minute.

Lowest score There are at least 60 recorded instances of sides being dismissed for 0. A recent instance was in July 1970 when, in a 2nd XI House match at Brentwood School, West dismissed North for 0 with 13 balls.

Greatest stand T. Patten and N. Rippon made a third wicket stand of 641 for Buffalo *v.* Whorouly at Gapsted, Victoria, Australia, on 19 March 1914.

Wicket-keeping In a Repton School match for Priory *v.* Mitre, H. W. P. Middleton caught one and stumped eight batsmen in one innings on 10 July 1930.

John Solomon (left), winner of most Open Croquet championships with Prof. Bernard Neal

CROQUET

Earliest references Croquet, in its present-day form, originated as a country-house lawn game in Ireland in 1852.

Most championships The greatest number of victories in the Open Croquet Championships (instituted at Evesham, Worcestershire, 1867) is ten by John William Solomon (b. 1932) (1953, 1956, 1959, 1961, 1963 to 68). He has also won the Men's Championship on 9 occasions (1951, 1953, 1958 to 60, 1962, 1964–65 and 1971), the Open Doubles (with E. Patrick C. Cotter) on 10 occasions (1954–55, 1958–59, 1961 to 65 and 1969) and the Mixed Doubles once (with Mrs. N. Oddie) in 1954, making a total of 30 titles. Solomon has also won the President's Cup on 8 occasions (1955, 1957 to 59, 1962 to 64 and 1968). He has also been Champion of Champions on all four occasions since this competition was instituted in 1967.

Miss Dorothy D. Steel, fifteen times winner of the Women's Championship (1919 to 39), won the Open Croquet Championship four times (1925, 1933, 1935–36). She had also five Doubles and seven Mixed Doubles titles making a total of 31 titles.

Lowest handicap The lowest playing handicap has been that of Humphrey O. Hicks (Devon) with minus $5\frac{1}{2}$. In 1964 the limit was fixed at minus 5, which handicap is held by J. W. Solomon, E. Patrick C. Cotter, H. O. Hicks, G. N. Aspinall, K. F. Wylie and Dr. W. P. Ormerod.

Largest club The largest number of courts at any one club is eleven, at the Sussex County (Brighton) Croquet and Lawn Tennis Club.

CROSS-COUNTRY RUNNING

International Championships The earliest recorded international cross-country race took place over 9 miles 20 yards from Ville d'Avray, outside Paris, on 20 March 1898, between England and France (England won by 21 points to 69). The inaugural International Cross-Country Championships took place at the Hamilton Park Racecourse, Glasgow, on 28 March 1903. The greatest margin of victory is 56 seconds or 390 yards by Jack T. Holden (England) at Ayr Racecourse, Scotland, on 24 March 1934. The narrowest win was that of Jean-Claude Fayolle (France) at Ostend, Belgium, on 20 March 1965, when the timekeepers were unable to separate his time from that of Melvyn Richard Batty (England), who was placed second.

The greatest team wins have been those of England, with a minimum of 21 points (the first six runners to finish) on two occasions, at Gosforth Park, Newcastle upon Tyne, Northumberland, on 22 March 1924, and at the Hippodrome de Stockel, Brussels, Belgium, on 20 March 1932.

Most wins The greatest number of victories in the International Cross-Country Race is four by Jack Holden (England) in 1933–34–35 and 1939, and four by Alain Mimoun-o-Kacha (France) in 1949, 1952, 1954 and 1956. England have won 41 times to 1971.

Most appearances The runners of participating countries with the largest number of international championship appearances are:—

Belgium	20	M. Van de Wattyne, 1946–65
Wales	14	D. Phillips, 1922, 1924, 1926–37
England	12	J. T. Holden, 1929–39, 1946
Spain	12	A. L. Amoros, 1951–62
Scotland	11	D. McL. Wright, 1920–30
	11	J. C. Flockhart, 1933–39, 1946–49
France	11	A. Mimoun-o-Kacha, 1949–50, 1952, 1954, 1956, 1958–62, 1964

English Championship The English Cross-Country Championship was inaugurated at Roehampton, South London, in 1877. The greatest number of individual titles achieved is four by P. H. Stenning (Thames Hare and Hounds) in 1877–80 and Alfred E. Shrubb (1878–1964) (South London Harriers) in 1901–04. The most successful club in the team race has been Birchfield Harriers from Birmingham with 27 wins and one tie between 1880 and 1953.

Largest field The largest recorded field was one of 1,815 starters (1,020 completed the course) at Gosforth Park, Newcastle upon Tyne in the summer of 1916. It was staged by the Northern Command of the Army and was won by Sapper G. Barber in 35 minutes 7·2 seconds, by a margin of over 40 yards.

CURLING

Origins An early form of the sport is believed to have originated in the Netherlands about 450 years ago. The first club was formed at Kilsyth, near Glasgow, in 1510. Organized administration began in 1838 with the formation of the Royal Caledonian Curling Club, the international legislative body based in Edinburgh. The first indoor ice rink to introduce curling was at Southport in 1879.

The U.S.A. won the first Gordon International Medal series of matches, between Canada and the U.S.A., at Montreal in 1884. The first Strathcona Cup match between Canada and Scotland was won by Canada in 1903. Although demonstrated at the Winter Olympics of 1924, 1932 and 1964, curling is not yet included in the official Olympic programme.

Most titles The most Strathcona Cup wins is seven by Canada (1903–09–12–23–38–57–65) against Scotland. The record for international team matches for the Scotch Cup and Silver Broom (instituted 1959) is ten wins by Canada, in 1959–60–61–62–63–64–66–68–69–70.

Marathon The longest recorded curling match is one of 32 hours and 151 ends by two Rinks from the Glasgow Young Curlers Club skipped by D. Horton and B. Methuen on 7–8 March 1970.

Largest rink The world's largest curling rink is the Big Four Curling Rink, Calgary, Alberta, Canada opened in 1959 at a cost of $Can2,250,000 (£867,050). Each of the two floors has 24 sheets of ice, accommodating 48 teams of 192 players.

Mrs. Beryl Burton, O.B.E., holder of every women's British Road record from 10 to 100 miles

CYCLING

Earliest race The earliest recorded bicycle race was a velocipede race over two kilometres (1·24 miles) at the Parc de St. Cloud, Paris, on 31 May 1868, won by James Moore (G.B.).

Slow cycling Slow bicycling records came to a virtual end in 1965 when Tsugunobu Mitsuishi, aged 39, of Tōkyō, Japan stayed stationary for 5 hours 25 minutes.

Highest speed The highest speed ever achieved on a bicycle is 127·243 m.p.h. by Jose Meiffret (b. April 1913) of France, using a 275-inch gear behind a windshield on a racing car at Freiburg, West Germany, on 19 July 1962. Antonio Maspes (Italy) recorded an unofficial unpaced 10·8 secs. for 200 metres (42·21 m.p.h.) at Milan on 28 Aug. 1962.

The greatest distance ever covered in one hour is 76 miles 604 yards by Leon Vanderstuyft (Belgium) on the Montlhéry Motor Circuit, France, on 30 Sept. 1928. This was achieved from a standing start paced by a motorcycle. The 24-hour record behind pace is 860 miles 367 yards by Hubert Opperman in Australia in 1932.

Most world titles The greatest number of world titles for a particular event won since the institution of the amateur championships in 1893 and the professional championships in 1895 are:—

Amateur Sprint	4	William J. Bailey (U.K.)	1909–10–11, 1913
	4	Daniel Morelon (France)	1966–67, 1969–70
Amateur 100 kms. Paced	7	Leon Meredith (U.K.)	1904–05, 1907–09, 1911, 1913
Amateur Road Race	2	Giuseppe Martano (Italy)	1930, 1932
	2	Gustave Schur (East Germany)	1958–59
Professional Sprint	7	Jeff Scherens (Belgium)	1932–37, 1947
	7	Antonio Maspes (Italy)	1955–56, 1959–62, 1964
Professional 100 kms. Paced	6	Guillermo Timoner (Spain)	1955, 1959–60, 1962, 1964–65
Professional Road Race	3	Alfredo Binda (Italy)	1927, 1930, 1932
	3	Henri (Rik) Van Steenbergen (Belgium)	1949, 1956–57

Tour de France The greatest number of wins in the Tour de France (inaugurated 1903) is five by Jacques Anquetil (b. 8 Jan. 1934) of France, who won in 1957, 1961, 1962, 1963 and 1964. The closest race ever was that of 1968 when after 2,898·7 miles over the 25 days (27 June–21 July) Jan Janssen (Netherlands) (b. 1940) beat Herman van Springel (Belgium) in Paris by 38 seconds. The longest course was 3,569 miles on 20 June–18 July 1926.

Most Olympic titles Cycling has been on the Olympic programme since the revival of the Games in 1896. The greatest number of gold medals ever won is four by Marcus Hurley (U.S.A.) over the ¼, ⅓, ½ and 1 mile in 1904.

The Land's End to John o' Groats (879 miles) feminine record is 2 days 11 hours 7 minutes (average speed 14·75 m.p.h.) by Mrs. Eileen Sheridan on 9–11 June 1954. She continued to complete 1,000 miles in 3 days 1 hour.

Roller cycling The greatest recorded distance registered in a 12-hour roller team cycling test is 508 miles 330 yards by Adrian Perkin, John Pugh, Bernard Trudgill and Lindsay Wigby of the Godric C.C. at Bungay, Suffolk on 23 March 1968.

The eight-man 24-hour record is 1,008 miles 1,320 yards by the Barnwell C.R.S. at Cambridge on 9–10 Jan. 1970. The team was Jim Bowyer, Ian Cannell, Colin Chapman, John Day, Bob Sampson, Peter Scarth, Chris Stevens and Richard Voss.

WORLD RECORDS — OPEN AIR TRACKS

MEN

Professional unpaced standing start:

Distance	*hrs. mins. secs.*	*Name and nationality*	*Place*	*Date*
1 km.	1 08·6	Reginald Hargreaves Harris (U.K.)	Milan	20 Oct. 1952
5 kms.	5 51·6	Ole Ritter (Denmark)	Mexico City	4 Oct. 1968
10 kms.	11 58·4	Ole Ritter (Denmark)	Mexico City	4 Oct. 1968
20 kms.	24 17·4	Ole Ritter (Denmark)	Mexico City	4 Oct. 1968
1 hour	30 miles 214 yards	Ole Ritter (Denmark)	Mexico City	10 Oct. 1968
Professional unpaced flying start:				
200 metres	10·8	Antonio Maspes (Italy)	Rome	21 July 1960
500 metres	28·8	Marino Morettini (Italy)	Milan	29 Aug. 1955
1,000 metres	1 02·6	Marino Morettini (Italy)	Milan	26 July 1961
Professional motor-paced:				
100 kms.	1 03 40·0	Walter Lohmann (W. Germany)	Wuppertal	24 Oct. 1955
1 hour	58 miles 737 yards	Walter Lohmann (W. Germany)	Wuppertal	24 Oct. 1955
Amateur unpaced standing start:				
1 km.	1 02·44	Pierre Trentin (France)	Zürich	15 Nov. 1970
4 kms.	4 37·54	Mogens Frey (Denmark)	Mexico City	17 Oct. 1968
5 kms.	6 01·6	Mogens Frey (Denmark)	Mexico City	5 Oct. 1969
10 kms.	12 23·8	Mogens Frey (Denmark)	Mexico City	5 Oct. 1969
20 kms.	25 00·5	Mogens Frey (Denmark)	Mexico City	5 Oct. 1969
100 kms.	2 19 01·6	Ole Ritter (Denmark)	Rome	19 Sept. 1965
1 hour	29 miles 921 yards	Mogens Frey (Denmark)	Mexico City	5 Oct. 1969
Amateur unpaced flying start:				
200 metres	10·61	Omari Phakadze (U.S.S.R.)	Mexico City	22 Oct. 1967
500 metres	27·85	Pierre Trentin (France)	Mexico City	21 Oct. 1967
1,000 metres	1	Luigi Borghetti (Italy)	Mexico City	21 Oct. 1967

WOMEN

Amateur unpaced standing start:

Distance	*hrs. mins. secs.*	*Name and nationality*	*Place*	*Date*
1 km.	1 15·1	Irena Kirichenko (U.S.S.R.)	Yerevan	8 Oct. 1966
3 kms.	4 01·7	Raisa Obdovskaya (U.S.S.R.)	Brno	20 Aug. 1969
5 kms.	7 03·3	Nina Sadovaya (U.S.S.R.)	Irkutsk	2 July 1955
10 kms.	14 27·0	Elsy Jacobs (Luxembourg)	Milan	9 Nov. 1958
20 kms.	28 58·4	Mrs. Beryl Burton, O.B.E. (U.K.)	Milan	11 Oct. 1960
100 kms.	2 44 57·0	Leena Turunen (Finland)	Helsinki	8 Sept. 1967
1 hour	25 miles 1,207 yards	Elsy Jacobs (Luxembourg)	Milan	9 Nov. 1958
Amateur unpaced flying start:				
200 metres	12·3	Lyubov Razuvayeva (U.S.S.R.)	Irkutsk	17 July 1955
500 metres	32·5	Irena Kirichenko (U.S.S.R.)	Irkutsk	1967
1,000 metres	1 10·6	Irena Kirichenko (U.S.S.R.)	Irkutsk	1967

COVERED TRACKS

MEN

Professional unpaced standing start:

1 km.	1 08·0	Reginald Hargreaves Harris (U.K.)	Zürich	19 July 1957
5 kms.	6 05·6	Ferdinand Bracke (Belgium)	Brussels	5 Dec. 1964
10 kms.	12 26·8	Roger Rivière (France)	Paris	19 Oct. 1958
20 kms.	25 18·0	Siegfried Adler (W. Germany)	Zürich	2 Aug. 1968
1 hour	29 miles 162 yards	Siegfried Adler (W. Germany)	Zürich	2 Aug. 1968

Professional unpaced flying start:

200 metres	10·99	Oscar Plattner (Switzerland)	Zürich	1 Dec. 1961
500 metres	28·6	Oscar Plattner (Switzerland)	Zürich	17 Aug. 1956
1,000 metres	1 01·23	Patrick Sercu (Belgium)	Antwerp	3 Feb. 1967

Professional motor-paced:

100 kms.	1 23 59·8	Guillermo Timoner (Spain)	San Sebastian	12 Sept. 1965
1 hour	46 miles 669 yards	Guy Solente (France)	Paris	13 Feb. 1955

Amateur unpaced standing start:

1 km.	1 06·76	Patrick Sercu (Belgium)	Brussels	12 Dec. 1964
5 kms.	6 06·0	Xavier Kurmann (Switzerland)	Zürich	28 Nov. 1968
10 kms.	12 26·2	Xavier Kurmann (Switzerland)	Zürich	1 Dec. 1968
20 kms.	25 14·6	Ole Ritter (Denmark)	Zürich	30 Oct. 1966
1 hour	28 miles 575 yards	Alfred Ruegg (Switzerland)	Zürich	16 Nov. 1958

Amateur unpaced flying start:

200 metres	10·72	Daniel Morelon (France)	Zürich	4 Nov. 1967
500 metres	28·89	Pierre Trentin (France)	Zürich	4 Nov. 1967
1,000 metres	1 02·44	Pierre Trentin (France)	Zürich	15 Nov. 1970

WOMEN

Amateur unpaced standing start:

1,000 metres	1 15·5	Elizabeth Eichholz (Germany)	Berlin	4 Mar. 1964

Amateur unpaced flying start:

200 metres	13·2	Karla Günther (Germany)	Berlin	7 Mar. 1964
500 metres	35·0	Karla Günther (Germany)	Berlin	7 Mar. 1964

Most British titles The greatest number of National individual track cycling championships secured by any one rider is 12 by Albert White (1920–25), ranging from the quarter mile to 25 miles. White also shared in three one-mile tandem championships.

ROAD CYCLING RECORDS

(British) as recognized by the Road Time Trials Council (out-and-home records).

MEN

Distance	*hrs.*	*mins.*	*secs.*	*Name*	*Course area*	*Date*
25 miles		51	0	Alf Engers	Catterick	30 Aug. 1969
30 miles	1	04	56	Dave Dungworth	Derby	10 June 1967
50 miles	1	43	46	John Watson	Boroughbridge	23 Aug. 1970
100 miles	3	46	37	Anthony Taylor	Boroughbridge	31 Aug. 1969
12 hours	281·87 miles			John Watson	Blyth, Nottinghamshire	7 Sept. 1969
24 hours	507·00 miles			Roy Cromack	Cheshire	26–27 July 1969

WOMEN

Distance	*hrs.*	*mins.*	*secs.*	*Name*	*Course area*	*Date*
10 miles		22	43	Beryl Burton, O.B.E.	Worcester	30 June 1967
25 miles		54	55	Beryl Burton, O.B.E.	Catterick	2 Aug. 1970
30 miles	1	12	20	Beryl Burton, O.B.E.	St. Neots	3 May 1969
50 miles	1	55	4	Beryl Burton, O.B.E.	Catterick	21 Sept. 1969
100 miles	3	55	5	Beryl Burton, O.B.E.	Essex	4 Aug. 1968
12 hours	277·25 miles			Beryl Burton, O.B.E.	Wetherby	17 Sept. 1967
24 hours	427·86 miles			Christine Moody	Cheshire	26–27 July 1969

ROAD RECORDS ASSOCIATION'S STRAIGHT-OUT DISTANCE RECORDS

Distance	*days*	*hrs.*	*mins.*	*secs.*	*Name*	*Date*
25 miles			47	55	Derek Cottington	2 May 1970
50 miles		1	39	23	Derek Cottington	2 May 1970
100 miles		3	28	40	Ray Booty	28 Sept. 1956
1,000 miles	2	10	40	0	Reg Randall	19–21 Aug. 1960
12 hours			276½ miles		Harry Earnshaw	4 July 1939
24 hours			475¾ miles		Ken Joy	26–27 July 1954

PLACE TO PLACE RECORDS

(British) as recognized by the Road Records Association.

	days	*hrs.*	*mins.*	*secs.*	*Name*	*Date*
London to Edinburgh (380 miles)		18	49	42	Cliff Smith	2 Nov. 1965
London to Bath and back (210 miles)		9	36	23	Ken Joy	14 June 1953
London to York (197 miles)		8	23	0	Harry Earnshaw	4 July 1939
London to Brighton and back (107 miles)		4	18	18	Les West	3 Oct. 1970
Land's End to London (287 miles)		12	34	0	Robert Maitland	17 Sept. 1954
Land's End to John o' Groats (879 miles)	1	23	46	35	Richard W. E. Poole	18 June 1965

The setting of the 1,000,001 up record by a Royal Hussars military operation

DARTS

Origins The origins of darts date from the use by archers of heavily weighted ten-inch throwing arrows for self-defence in close quarters fighting. The "dartes" were used in Ireland in the 16th century and darts was played on the *Mayflower* by the Plymouth pilgrims in 1620. Today there are an estimated 6,000,000 dart players in the British Isles—a higher participation than in any other sporting pastime. No national or international controlling organization for the game has existed which has collated records and conditions of play. The throwing distances and boards vary considerably from one locality to another.

Lowest possible scores The lowest number of darts to achieve standard scores are: 201 four darts, 301 six darts, 501 nine darts, 1,001 seventeen darts. The four and six darts "possibles" have been many times achieved, the nine darts 501 occasionally but never the seventeen darts 1,001 which would require 15 treble 20's, a treble 17 and a 50. The lowest even number which cannot be scored with three darts (ending on a double) is 162. The lowest odd number which cannot be scored with three darts (ending on a double) is 159.

Fastest match The fastest time taken for a match of three games of 301 is $2\frac{1}{2}$ minutes by Jim Pike (1903–1960) at Broadcasting House, Broad Street, Birmingham, in 1952.

Fastest "round the board" The record time for going round the board in "doubles" at arm's length is 14·5 seconds by Jim Pike at the Craven Club, Newmarket, in March 1944. His match record for this feat at the nine-feet throwing distance, retrieving his own darts, is 3 minutes 30 seconds at King John's Head, Blackfriars, London, in 1937.

Million and one up The shortest recorded time to score 1,000,001 up *on one board*, under the rules of darts, is 9 hours 48 minutes 31 seconds (scoring rate of 28·32 per second) by eight players from the Sergeant's Mess of the 13th/18th Royal Hussars (Q.M.O.) at Munster, West Germany on 15 March 1969.

Most doubles The recorded number of doubles scored in 10 hours is 1,948 (in 8,393 darts) by John Latham, 33, at the Queen's Arms Hotel, Acomb, Northumberland on 17 Oct. 1970 at the throwing distance of $7\frac{1}{2}$ feet.

Marathon record The most protracted recorded darts marathon was one of 112 hours 15 minutes at The Plough, White Notley, Essex by Peter Tilbrook, Arthur Clarke, Robert Reeve and Malcolm Bright.

Greatest crowd The largest attendance at any darts match was the 17,000 at the Agricultural Hall, Islington, London, at the finals of the 1939 *News of the World* contest.

Most titles Re-instituted in 1947, the annual *News of the World* England and Wales individual Championships consist of the best of 3 legs 501 up, "straight" start and finish on a double with an 8-feet throwing distance. The only men to win twice are Tommy Gibbons (Ivanhoe Working Men's Club) of Conisbrough, Yorkshire, in 1952 and 1958; Tom Reddington (Derbyshire) in 1955 and 1960; and Tom M. Barrett (Odco Sports Club, London) in 1964 and 1965.

EQUESTRIAN SPORTS
SHOW JUMPING

Origins Evidence of horse-riding dates from an Anatolian statuette dated *c.* 1400 B.C. Pignatelli's academy of horsemanship at Naples dates from the 16th century. The earliest show jumping was in Paris in 1886. Equestrian events have been included in the Olympic Games since 1912.

Most Olympic medals The greatest number of Olympic gold medals is four by three horsemen:— Lt. C. Ferdinand Pahud de Mortanges (Netherlands), who won the individual three-day event in 1928 and 1932 and was in the winning team in 1924 and 1928; by Major (later Col.) Henri St. Cyr (Sweden), who won the individual Grand Prix de dressage event in 1952 and 1956 and who was also in the winning teams; and by Hans Winkler (Germany), who won the Grand Prix jumping in 1956 and was in the winning team of 1956, 1960 and 1964. The most team wins in the Prix des Nations is four by Germany in 1936, 1956, 1960 and 1964. The lowest score obtained by a winner was no faults, by F. Ventura (Czechoslovakia) in 1928 and by Pierre Jonqueres d'Oriola (France), the only two-time winner (1952 and 1964), in 1952.

Jumping records The official *Fédération Equestre Internationale* high jump record is 8 feet $1\frac{1}{4}$ inches by *Huasó*, ridden by Capt. Alberto Larraguibel Morales (Chile) at Vina del Mar, Santiago, Chile, on 5 Feb. 1949, and 27 feet $2\frac{3}{4}$ inches for long jump over water by *Amado Mio* ridden by Lt.-Col. Lopez del Hierro (Spain), at Barcelona, Spain on 12 Nov. 1951. *Heatherbloom*, ridden by Dick Donnelly was reputed to have covered 37 feet in clearing an 8-foot 3-inch *puissance* jump at Richmond, Virginia, U.S.A. in 1903. *Solid Gold* cleared 36 feet 3 inches over water at the Wagga Show, New South Wales, Australia in August 1936 for an Australian record. *Jerry M.*

Two B.S.J.A. record holders—Alan Oliver and *Red Admiral*

allegedly cleared 40 feet over the water at Aintree in 1912.

At Cairns, Queensland, *Golden Meade* ridden by Jack Martin cleared an unofficially measured 8 feet 6 inches on 25 July 1946. *Ben Bolt* was credited with clearing 9 feet 6 inches at the 1938 Royal Horse Show, Sydney, Australia. The Australian record is 8 feet 4 inches by *Flyaway* (C. Russell) in 1939 and *Golden Meade* (A. L. Payne) in 1946. The world's unofficial best for a woman is 7 feet 5½ inches by Miss B. Perry (Australia) on *Plain Bill* at Cairns, Queensland, Australia in 1940. The greatest recorded height reached bareback is 6 feet 7 inches by *Silver Wood* at Heidelberg, Victoria, Australia, on 10 Dec. 1938.

The highest British performance is 7 feet 6¼ inches by the 16·2 hands bay gelding *Swank*, ridden by Donald Beard, at Olympia, London, on 25 June 1937. On the same day, the Lady Wright (*née* Margery Avis Bullows) set the best recorded height for a British equestrienne on her liver chestnut *Jimmy Brown* at 7 feet 4 inches. These records were over the now unused sloping poles. Harvey Smith on *O'Malley* cleared 7 feet 3 inches in Toronto, Canada in 1967.

Most titles The most B.S.J.A. championships won is four by Alan Oliver (1951–54–59–69). The only horses to have won twice are *Maguire* (Lt.-Col. Nathaniel Kindersley) in 1945 and 1947, *Sheila* (Hayes) in 1949–50 and *Red Admiral* (Oliver) in 1951 and 1954. The record for the Ladies' Championship is 8 by Miss Patricia Smythe (born 22 Nov. 1928), now Mrs. Samuel Koechlin, O.B.E. (1952–53–55–57–58–59–61–62). She was on Robert Hanson's *Flanagan* in 1955, 1958 and 1962—the only three time winner.

Marathon The longest continuous period spent in the saddle is 38 hours by Joseph Roberts of the Leicester School of Equitation in the Wimbledon Common-Putney Heath area, Greater London on 15–17 May 1968.

FENCING

Origins Fencing was practised as a sport in Egypt as early as the 12th century B.C. The first governing body for fencing in Britain was the Corporation of Masters of Defence founded by Henry VIII before 1540 and fencing was practised as sport, notably in prize fights, since that time. The foil was the practice weapon for the short court sword from the 17th century. The épée was established in the mid-19th century and the light sabre was introduced by the Italians in the late 19th century.

Most Olympic titles The greatest number of individual Olympic gold medals won is three by Nedo Nadi (Italy) in 1912 and 1920 (2) and Ramon Fonst (Cuba) in 1900 and 1904 (2). Nadi also won three team gold medals in 1920 making an unprecedented total of five gold medals at one celebration. Italy has won the épée team title six times. France has won the foil team title five times. Hungary has won nine sabre team titles. Aladàr Gerevich (Hungary) was in the winning sabre team in 1932–36 1948–52–56–60. Allan Jay, M.B.E. (G.B.) competed in 5 Olympics (1952–68).

Most world titles The greatest number of individual world titles won is four by Christian d'Oriola (France) with the foil in 1947–49–53–54. He also won the Olympic titles in 1952 and 1956. Ellen Müller-Priess (Austria) won the women's foil in 1947 and 1949 and shared it in 1950. She also won the Olympic title in 1932. Italy won the men's foil teams thirteen times; Hungary the ladies' foil teams eleven times; Italy the épée teams ten times and Hungary the sabre teams thirteen times.

Most A.F.A. titles The greatest number of Amateur Fencing Association titles have been won as follows:—

Foil	(Instituted 1898)	7	J. Emrys Lloyd	1928, 1930–33, 1937–38
Épée	(Instituted 1904)	5	R. Montgomerie	1905, 1907, 1909, 1912, 1914
Sabre	(Instituted 1898)	6	Dr. R. F. Tredgold	1937, 1939, 1947–49, 1955
Foil (Ladies)	(Instituted 1907)	10	Miss Gillian M. Sheen (now Mrs. R. G. Donaldson)	1949, 1951–58, 1960

FIVES

ETON FIVES

A handball game against the buttress of Eton College Chapel was recorded in 1825, but a court existed at Lord Weymouth's School, Warminster, as early as 1773 and a handball game against the church wall at Babcary, Somerset, was recorded in June 1765. New courts were built at Eton in 1840, the rules were codified in 1877, rewritten laws were introduced in 1931 and the laws were last drawn up in 1950.

Most titles Only one pair have won the Amateur Championship (Kinnaird Cup) six times—Anthony Hughes and Arthur James Gordon Campbell (1958, 1965–68 and 1971). Hughes also was in the winning pair in 1963 making seven titles in all.

RUGBY FIVES

As now known, this game dates from *c.* 1850 with the first inter-public school matches recorded in the early 1870s. The Oxford *v.* Cambridge contest was inaugurated in 1925 and the Rugby Fives Association was founded in the home of Dr. Cyriax, in Welbeck Street, London, on 29 Oct. 1927. The dimensions of the Standard Rugby Fives court were approved by the Association in 1931.

Most titles The greatest number of Amateur Singles Championships (instituted 1932) ever won is four by John Frederick Pretlove in 1953, 1955–56 and 1958, and by Eric Marsh in 1960–61–62–63. Pretlove also holds the record for the Amateur Doubles Championship (instituted 1925), being co-champion in 1952, 1954, 1956–57–58–59 and 1961. The first person to have held all ten National and Provincial titles during his playing career is David E. Gardner. To 1971 he had won 11 Scottish titles (5 singles and 6 doubles), 13 North of England titles (4 singles and 9 doubles), 7 West of England titles (2 singles and 5 doubles), Lancashire Open (1 singles, 1 doubles), the Amateur Singles in 1964 and the Amateur Doubles in 1960, 1965, 1966, 1970 and 1971.

FOOTBALL (Soccer)

Origins A game with some similarities termed *Tsu-chin* was played in China in the 3rd and 4th centuries B.C. The earliest clear representation of the game is an Edinburgh print dated 1672–73. It became standardized with the formation of the Football Association in England on 26 Oct. 1863. A 26-a-side game, however, existed in Florence, Italy, as early as 1530, for which rules were codified in *Discorsa Calcio* in 1580. The oldest club is Sheffield F.C., formed on 24 Oct. 1857. Eleven per side was standardized in 1870.

HIGHEST SCORES

Teams The highest score recorded in a British first-class match is 36. This occurred in the Scottish Cup match between Arbroath and Bon Accord on 5 Sept. 1885, when Arbroath won 36–0 on their home ground. The goals were not fitted with nets.

The highest margin recorded in an international match is 17. This occurred in the England *v.* Australia match at Sydney on 30 June 1951, when England won 17–0. The highest in the British Isles was when England beat Ireland 13–0 at Belfast on 18 Feb. 1882. The highest score in an F.A. Cup match is 26, when Preston North End beat Hyde 26–0 at Deepdale, Preston on 15 Oct. 1887. This is also the highest score between English clubs. The biggest victory in a final tie is 6 when Bury beat Derby County 6–0 at Crystal Palace on 18 April 1903, in which year Bury did not concede a single goal in the five Cup matches.

The highest score by one side in a Football League (Division I) match is 12 goals when West Bromwich Albion beat Darwen 12–0 at West Bromwich on 4 March 1892; when Nottingham Forest beat Leicester Fosse by the same score at Nottingham on 21 April 1909; and when Aston Villa beat Accrington 12–2 at Villa Park on 12 March 1892.

The highest aggregate in League Football was 17 goals when Tranmere Rovers beat Oldham Athletic 13–4 in a 3rd Division (North) match at Prenton Park, Birkenhead, on Boxing Day, 1935. The record margin in a League match has been 13 in the Newcastle United 13, Newport County 0 Division II match in 1946 and in the Stockport County 13, Halifax 0 Division III (North) match in 1934.

Individuals The most scored by one player in a first-class match is 16 by Stains for Racing Club de Lens *v.* Aubry-Asturies, in Lens, France, on 13 Dec. 1942. The record for any British first-class match is 13 by John Petrie in the Arbroath *v.* Bon Accord Scottish Cup match in 1885 (see above). The record in League Football is 10 by Joe Payne (b. Bolsover, Derbyshire) for Luton Town *v.* Bristol Rovers in a 3rd Division (South) match at Luton on 13 April 1936. The English 1st Division record is 7 goals by Ted Drake (b. Southampton, Hampshire) for Arsenal *v.* Aston Villa at Birmingham on 14 Dec. 1935, and James Ross for Preston North End *v.* Stoke at Preston on 6 Oct. 1888. The Scottish 1st Division record is 8 goals by James McGrory for Celtic *v.* Dunfermline Athletic at Celtic Park, Glasgow, on 14 Jan. 1928.

The record for individual goal-scoring in a British home international is 6 by Joe Bambrick for Ireland *v.* Wales at Belfast on 1 Feb. 1930.

Career The greatest total of goals scored in a career is 1,026 by Edson Arantes do Nascimento (b. Baurú, Brazil, 28 June 1940), known as Pelé, the Brazilian inside left from 1957 to the World Cup final on 21 June 1970. His best year was 1958 with 139 and the *milesimo* (1,000th) came in a penalty for his club Santos in the Maracanã Stadium, Rio de Janeiro on 19 Nov. 1969 when playing in his 909th first-class match.

The best season League records are 60 goals in 39 League games by William Ralph ("Dixie") Dean (b. Birkenhead, Cheshire, 1906) for Everton (Division I) in 1927–28 and 66 goals in 38 games by Jim Smith for Ayr United (Scottish Division II) in the same season. With 3 more in Cup ties and 19 in representative matches Dean's total was 82.

The greatest number of goals scored in British first-class football is 550 (410 in League matches) by James McGrory of Glasgow Celtic (1922–38). The most scored in League matches is 434, for West Bromwich Albion, Fulham, Leicester City and Shrewsbury Town, by George Arthur Rowley (b. 1926) between 1946 and April 1965. Rowley also scored 32 goals in the F.A. Cup and 1 for England "B".

Fastest goals The fastest goal on record was one variously claimed to be from 4 to 13 seconds after the kick-off by Jim Fryatt of Bradford in a Fourth Division match against Tranmere Rovers at Park Avenue, Bradford on 25 April 1964. John Scarth (Gillingham) scored 3 goals in 2 minutes against Leyton Orient at Priestfield Stadium, Gillingham on 1 Nov. 1952. John McIntyre (Blackburn Rovers) scored 4 goals in 5 minutes *v.* Everton at Ewood Park, Blackburn, on 16 Sept. 1922. W. G. ("Billy") Richardson (West Bromwich Albion) scored 4 goals in 5 minutes against West Ham United at Upton Park on 7 Nov. 1931.

The international record is 3 goals in $3\frac{1}{2}$ minutes by Willie Hall (Tottenham Hotspur) for England against Ireland on 16 Nov. 1938 at Old Trafford, Manchester.

Pelé (Brazil), who retired in July 1971 after playing for Brazil 110 times (and scoring 95 international goals)

MOST APPEARANCES

The greatest total of full international appearances by a British footballer is 106 by Bobby Charlton, O.B.E. (b. Ashington, Northumberland, 11 Oct. 1937) of Manchester United. His first was *v.* Scotland on 19 April 1958 and his 106th in the World Cup in Mexico City on 14 June 1970. Pelé retired from international play on 18 July 1971 having played for Brazil in 110 matches (95 goals).

England The greatest number of appearances for England secured in the International Championship is 38 by William (Billy) Ambrose Wright, C.B.E. (b. Ironbridge, Shropshire, 6 Feb. 1924) in 1946–1959.

Wales The record number of appearances for Wales in the International Championship is 48 by William (Billy) Meredith (Manchester City and United) in the longest international span of 26 years (1895–1920). This is a record for any of the four home countries. Ivor Allchurch, M.B.E. (born 29 Dec. 1929) of Swansea, Newcastle, Cardiff City and Worcester City played 67 times for Wales, including 37 times against the home countries, between 15 Nov. 1950 and Feb. 1968.

Scotland The Scottish record for International Championship matches is 30 by Alan Morton (Queen's Park and Glasgow Rangers) from 1920 to 1932. Morton also had a single foreign international making a total of 31 caps. George Young (Glasgow Rangers) has a record total of 53 appearances for Scotland, of which 29 were for International Championship matches, between 1946 and 1957.

Ireland The greatest number of appearances for Ireland is 56 by Billy Bingham (b. Belfast) (Sunderland, Luton, Everton and Port Vale) (1951 to 1963) and by Danny Blanchflower (Barnsley, Aston Villa and Tottenham Hotspur) (1949 to 1963).

Oldest cap The oldest cap has been William Henry (Billy) Meredith (1874–1958), who played outside right for Wales *v.* England at Highbury, London, on 15 March 1920 when aged 45 years 229 days.

Youngest caps *World* The world's youngest international footballer has been G. Dorval who played for Brazil *v.* Argentina in 1957 while still 15.

British Isles The youngest cap in the British Isles has been Norman Kernaghan (Belfast Celtic) who played for Ireland *v.* Wales in 1936 aged 17 years 80 days. It is possible, however, that W. K. Gibson (Cliftonville) who played for Ireland *v.* Wales in 1894 at 17 was slightly younger. England's youngest international was Duncan Edwards (b. Dudley, Staffordshire, 1 Oct. 1936, d. 21 Feb. 1958, 15 days after the Munich air crash) the Manchester United left half, against Scotland at Wembley on 2 April 1955, aged 18 years 6 months. The youngest Welsh cap was John Charles (b. Swansea, 19 Jan. 1932) the Leeds United centre half, against Ireland at Wrexham on 8 March 1950, aged 18 years 1 month. Scotland's youngest international has been Denis Law (b. Aberdeen, 24 Feb. 1940) of Huddersfield Town, who played against Wales on 18 Oct. 1958, aged 18 years 236 days. Research remains to be completed on the date of birth of David Black of Hurlford, Ayrshire, who may have been 17 when he played for Scotland *v.* Ireland in 1889.

Longest match The world duration record was set in the Western Hemisphere club championship in Santos, Brazil, on 2–3 Aug. 1962, when Santos drew 3–3 with Penarol F.C. of Montevideo, Uruguay. The game lasted $3\frac{1}{2}$ hours, from 9.30 p.m. to 1.00 a.m.

The longest British match on record was one of 3 hours 23 minutes between Stockport County and Doncaster Rovers in the second leg of the 3rd Division (North) Cup at Edgeley Park, Stockport, on 30 March 1946.

Billy Bingham, who shares with Danny Blanchflower the Irish record of 56 caps

The world's heftiest goalkeeper: Willie Foulke, who weighed 26 stone (364 lb.)

Heaviest goalkeeper The biggest goalkeeper in representative football was the England international Willie J. Foulke (1874–1916), who stood 6 feet 3 inches and weighed 22 stone 3 lb. His last games were for Bradford, by which time he was 26 stone.

TRANSFER FEES

The world's highest reported transfer fee is more than £400,000 for the Varese centre forward Pietro Anastasi signed by Juventus, of Turin, Italy on 18 May 1968. The British cash record is *c.* £190,000 for the Burnley forward Ralph Coates (b. Helton-le-Hole, Co. Durham, 1945) paid by Tottenham Hotspur on 5 May 1971. The overall British record is £200,000 for the West Ham United player Martin Peters (b. 1944) of which £125,000 was in cash and £75,000 for the reverse transfer of Jimmy Greaves from the buying club, Tottenham Hotspur on 16 March 1970.

The British aggregate record is held by the centre forward Tony Hateley (b. Derby, 1942) who in six moves from July 1963 to 28 Oct. 1970 was reportedly valued at £393,500.

Signing fee On 26 May 1961, Luis Suarez, the Barcelona inside forward, was transferred to Internazionale (Milan) for £144,000, of which Suarez himself received a record £59,000. The British record is £10,000 for John Charles (Leeds United to Juventus, Turin on 19 April 1957), for Denis Law (Manchester City to Torino, Italy on 13 June 1961) and Martin Peters (see above).

CROWD AND GATES

The greatest recorded crowd at any football match was 205,000 (199,854 paid) for the Brazil *v.* Uruguay World Cup final in the Maracanã Municipal Stadium, Rio de Janeiro, Brazil, on 16 July 1950.

The British record paid attendance is 149,547 at the Scotland *v.* England international at Hampden Park, Glasgow, on 17 April 1937. It is, however, probable that this total was exceeded (estimated 160,000) on the occasion of the F.A. Cup Final between Bolton Wanderers and West Ham United at Wembley Stadium on 28 April 1923, when the crowd broke in on the pitch and the start was delayed 40 minutes until the pitch was cleared. The counted admissions were 126,047. The record gross F.A. Cup receipts at Wembley, Greater London, are a reported £185,000 (excluding radio and television fees) for the final between Arsenal and Liverpool on 8 May 1971.

The Scottish Cup record attendance is an estimated 170,000 when Celtic played Aberdeen at Hampden Park on 24 April 1937. The record for a League match between British club teams is 143,570 at the Rangers *v.* Hibernian match at Hampden Park, Glasgow, on 27 March 1948. The highest attendance at a friendly match has been when Glasgow Rangers played Eintracht, Frankfurt at Hampden Park in 1961.

Smallest The smallest crowd at a full home international was 7,483 for the Scotland *v.* Northern Ireland match of 6 May 1969 at Hampden Park. The smallest crowd at a Football League fixture was for the Stockport County *v.* Leicester City Match at Old Trafford, Manchester, on 7 May 1921. Stockport's own ground was under suspension and the "crowd" numbered 13.

RECEIPTS

The greatest receipts at any match were £204,805, from an attendance of 96,924 at the World Cup final between England and West Germany at the Empire Stadium, Wembley, on 30 July 1966.

The record for a British international match is £105,000 for the England *v.* Scotland match at Wembley on 10 May 1969 (attendance 100,000). The receipts for the Manchester United *v.* Benfica match at Wembley on 29 May 1968 were £118,000 (attendance 100,000).

F.A. CHALLENGE CUP

Wins The greatest number of F.A. Cup wins is 7 by Aston Villa in 1887, 1895, 1897, 1905, 1913, 1920 and 1957 (nine final appearances). Of the 6-time winners Newcastle United have been in the final 10 times, as have 5-time winners West Bromwich Albion. The highest scores have been 6–1 in 1890, 6–0 in 1903 and 4–3 in 1953.

The greatest number of Scottish F.A. Cup wins is 21 by Celtic in 1892, 1899, 1900, 1904, 1907–8, 1911–12, 1914, 1923, 1925, 1927, 1931, 1933, 1937, 1951, 1954, 1965, 1967, 1969 and 1971.

Youngest player The youngest player in a Cup Final was Howard Kendall (b. 22 May 1946) of Preston North End, who played against West Ham United on 2 May 1964, 20 days before his 18th birthday.

Longest tie The most protracted F.A. Cup tie in the competition proper was that between Stoke City and Bury in the 3rd round with Stoke winning 3–2 in the fifth meeting after

9 hours 22 minutes of play in January 1955. The matches were at Bury (1–1) on 8 January; Stoke on 12 January (abandoned after 22 minutes of extra time with Stoke leading 1–0); Goodison Park (3–3) on 17 January; Anfield (2–2) on 19 January; and finally at Old Trafford on 24 January.

MOST LEAGUE CHAMPIONSHIPS
The greatest number of League Championships (Division I) is 8 by Arsenal in 1931, 1933, 1934, 1935, 1938, 1948, 1953 and 1971. The record number of points is 67 by Leeds United in 1969 while the lowest has been 8 by Doncaster Rovers (Division II) in 1904–5.

The only F.A. Cup and League Championship "doubles" are those of Preston North End in 1889, Aston Villa in 1897, Tottenham Hotspur in 1961 and Arsenal in 1971. Preston won the League without losing a match and the Cup without having a goal scored against them throughout the whole competition. Glasgow Rangers have won the Scottish League Championship 33 times between 1899 and 1964 and were joint champions on another occasion. Their 76 points in the Scottish 1st Division in 1921 represents a record in any division.

Closest win In 1923–24 Huddersfield won the Division I championship over Cardiff by 0·02 of a goal with a goal average of 1·81.

WORLD CUP
The *Fédération Internationale de Football* (F.I.F.A.) was founded in Paris on 21 May 1904 and instituted the World Cup Competition in 1930, two years after the four British Isles' associations had resigned.

The only country to win three times has been Brazil in 1958, 1962 and 1970. Brazil was also third in 1938 and second in 1950. Antonion Carbajal (b. 1923) played for Mexico in goal in the competitions of 1950–54–58–62 and 1966. The record goal scorer has been Just Fontaine (France) with 13 goals in 6 games in the 1958 competition in Sweden. The most goals scored in a final is 3 by Geoffrey Hurst (b. Ashton-under-Lyne, 1941) (West Ham United) for England *v.* West Germany on 30 July 1966.

EUROPEAN NATIONS CUP
The European F.A. started in 1958 a tournament to be staged every 4 years. Each tournament takes 2 years to run with the semi-finals and final on the same territory. The U.S.S.R. won the first when they beat Yugoslavia 2–1 in Paris on 10 July 1960 followed by Spain (1964) and Italy (1968).

EUROPEAN CHAMPIONS CUP
The European Cup for the League champions of the respective nations was approved by F.I.F.A. on 8 May 1955 and was run by the European F.A. which came into being in the previous year. Real Madrid defeated Rheims 4–3 in the first final in 1956 and went on to win the Cup in the next 4 seasons and in 1966. They took part in all competitions, either as holders or Spanish champions up to and including 1969–70.

Glasgow Celtic became the first British club to win the Cup when they beat Inter Milan 2–1 in the National Stadium, Lisbon, Portugal, on 25 May 1967. At the same time they established the record of being the only club to win the European Cup and the two senior domestic tournaments (League and Cup) in the same season.

EUROPEAN CUP WINNERS CUP
A tournament for the national Cup winners started in 1960–1 with 10 entries. Fiorentina beat Glasgow Rangers on 4–1 aggregate in a two-leg final in May 1961. Tottenham Hotspur were the first British club to win the trophy, beating Atletico Madrid 5–1 in Rotterdam on 15 May 1963 and were followed by West Ham United in 1965, Manchester City on 29 April 1970 and Chelsea in 1971.

FOOTBALL (Amateur)

Most Olympic wins The only countries to have won the Olympic football title twice are the United Kingdom (1908 and 1912); Uruguay (1924 and 1928) and Hungary (1952 and 1964). The United Kingdom also won the unofficial tournament in 1900. The highest Olympic score is Denmark 17 *v.* France "A" 1 in 1908.

Highest scores The highest score in a home Amateur International is 11 goals in the England *v.* Scotland match (8–3) at Dulwich on 11 March 1939. The foreign record was when England beat France 15–0 in Paris on 1 Nov. 1906.

The highest score in an F.A. Amateur Cup Final is 8, when Northern Nomads beat Stockton 7–1 at Sunderland in 1926, and when Dulwich Hamlet beat Marine (Liverpool) by the same score at Upton Park in 1932.

Individual The highest individual scores in amateur internationals are 6 by W. O. Jordan for England *v.* France (12–0) at Park Royal, London, on 23 March 1908; 6 by Vivian J. Woodward for England *v.* Holland (9–1) at Stamford Bridge, London, on 11 Dec. 1909; and 6 also by Harold A. Walden for Great Britain *v.* Hungary in Stockholm, Sweden, on 1 July 1912.

Most caps The record number of England amateur caps is 51 by Mike Pinner of Hendon, the former Pegasus goalkeeper who played for England between 1955 and 1963, when he became a professional with Leyton Orient.

F.A. Amateur Cup wins The greatest number of F.A. Amateur Cup (instituted 1893) wins is 10 by Bishop Auckland who won in 1896, 1900, 1914, 1921–22, 1935, 1939, 1955, 1956 and 1957.

Largest crowd The highest attendance at an amateur match is 100,000 at the Cup Final between Pegasus and Bishop Auckland at Wembley on 21 April 1951. The amateur gate record is £29,305 at the final between Bishop Auckland and Hendon on 16 April 1955.

Heading The highest recorded number of repetitions for heading a ball is 3,412 in 34 minutes 8 seconds by Colin Jones, aged 15, at Queensferry, near Chester, on 8 March 1961.

Least successful goalkeeper The goalkeeper of the Victoria Boys' and Girls' Club Intermediate "B" team in the 1967–68 season in the Association for the Jewish Youth League Under 16 Division 2 in London, England, let through 252 goals in the 12 league matches, an average of better (or worse) than 21 per match.

Longest ties The aggregate duration of ties in amateur soccer have not been collated but it is recorded that in the London F.A. Intermediate Cup first qualifying round Highfield F.C. Reserves had to meet Mansfield House F.C. on 19 and 26 Sept. and 3, 10 and 14 Oct. 1970 to get a decision after 9 hours 50 minutes play with scores of 0–0, 1–1, 1–1, 3–3 and 0–2.

Highest score In the match between Eastbourne United *v.* St. Mary's Youth Club in Sussex, England on 18 Jan. 1970, Eastbourne won 49–3 with one of their players scoring 10 goals and their goalkeeper contributing seven.

Most indisciplined In the local Cup match between Tongham Youth Club, Surrey and Hawley, Hampshire, England on 3 Nov. 1969 the referee booked all 22 players including one who went to hospital, and one of the linesmen. The match, won by Tongham 2–0, was described by a player as "A good, hard game".

Longest marathon The longest recorded 11-a-side football match played under F.A. rules without substitutes has been one of 18 hours by two teams from Edge Hill College of Education, Ormskirk, Lancashire on 27 June 1971. A record equalling this claim by two teams at Wadhurst,

Sussex on 3 July 1971 has yet to be authenticated.

The longest recorded authenticated 5-a-side games have been:- outdoors: 38 hours 5 minutes by two teams (no substitutes) from Portishead Youth Centre, Bristol ending at 10.15 a.m. on 15 Nov. 1970, and indoors: 51 hours by two teams (no substitutes) from the Beaconsfield Youth Club, Buckinghamshire ending at 11.20 p.m. on 27 June 1971.

Table football The most protracted game of 2-a-side table football on record was one of 170 hours maintained by 8 students from Hatfield Polytechnic, Hertfordshire on 19–26 Feb. 1971.

FOOTBALL (AUSTRALIAN RULES)

Origins The game evolved among the Irish diggers in the Ballarat goldfields in the 1840s and the rules were first formulated on 7 Aug. 1858 after a schools match in Melbourne umpired by Thomas W. Wills.

Most league premierships Since the Victorian Football League's inception in 1897 the greatest number of these league premierships has been won by Collingwood with 13 (1902–03–10–17–19–27–28–29–30–35–36–53 and 1958). Essendon won in 1897, 1901–11–12–23–24–42–46–49–50–62–65 and Melbourne in 1900–26–39–40–41–48–55–56–57–59–60–64. The record for successive league premierships is 10 by Fremantle in the West Australian League from 1887 to 1896.

Most Carnival wins Of the 16 triennial Carnival Matches played (instituted 1908) Victoria has won all but those in 1911, 1921 and 1961.

Highest team scores The highest recorded score occurred when Port Melbourne beat Sandringham 287 to 51, scoring 43 goals and 29 behinds against 7 goals and 9 behinds, in an Association match on 30 Aug. 1941.

Lowest The lowest score in senior competition occurred in August 1962, when Liverpool failed to score against St. George (122 points) at Rosedale Oval in the Sydney competition.

Highest individual score The most goals scored in a match is 28 by Bill Wood of South Sydney against Sydney on 21 Aug. 1943. The record for a season is 188 goals by Ron Todd of Williamstown in 1945. W. Pearson of the Melbourne Amateur F.A. kicked 220 goals in 1934. Ken Farmer kicked 1,419 goals between 1929 and 1941 for a career record. In junior competition Kim Albiston, aged 15, kicked 40 goals and 8 behinds for Doncaster Youth Club against Vermont Under-15's in Melbourne on 13 May 1967. The score was 473 to nil.

Highest attendance The attendance record is 118,828 for the Grand Final between Carlton and Essendon at Melbourne Cricket Ground in 1968.

Brownlow Medal The Victorian League's Brownlow Medal (instituted 1924) has been won three times by three players—Haydn Bunton of Fitzroy (1931–32–35), R. "Dick" Reynolds (1934–37–38), who played a League record of 320 games for Essendon and Bob Skilton (1959–63–68).

Herald Trophy The Herald Trophy (instituted 1944) has been won three times by Bill Hutchinson (Essendon), in 1948 (shared), 1952 and 1953, and by R. Skilton (South Melbourne) in 1959, 1962 and 1963.

Kicking records

Place	107 yds. 2 ft. (practice)	A. Thurgood (Essendon) at East Melbourne, June 1899
	93 yds. (with wind)	D. McNamara at Melbourne, 19 May 1923
	91 yds. 1 ft.	F. Cooper at Fremantle, June 1895
Punt	91 yds. (with wind)	R. Kercheval (U.S.A.) at Chicago, Illinois, 1935
	87 yds.	S. Francis (U.S.A.) at Stanford, California, 30 Dec. 1936
Drop	84 yds.	P. Vinar (Geelong), 1965

FOOTBALL (GAELIC)

Earliest references The game developed from inter-parish "free for all" with no time-limit, no defined playing area nor specific rules. The formation of the Gaelic Athletic Association was in Thurles, Ireland, on 1 Nov. 1884.

Most titles The greatest number of All-Ireland Championships ever won by one team is 22 by Ciarraidhe (Kerry) between 1903 and 1970. The greatest number of successive wins is four by Wexford (1915–18) and four by Kerry (1929–32).

Highest scores The highest score in an All-Ireland final was when Cork (6 goals, 6 points) beat Antrim (1 goal, 2 points) in 1911. The highest combined score was when Kerry (2 goals, 19 points) beat Meath (no goals, 18 points) in 1970. A goal equals 3 points.

Lowest scores In four All-Ireland finals the combined totals have been 7 points: 1893 Wexford (1 goal [till 1894 worth 5 points], 1 point) *v.* Cork (1 point); 1895 Tipperary (4 points) *v.* Meath (3 points); 1904 Kerry (5 points) *v.* Dublin (2 points); 1924 Kerry (4 points) *v.* Dublin (3 points).

Most appearances The most appearances in All-Ireland finals is ten by Dan O'Keeffe (Kerry) of which seven (a record) were on the winning side.

Individual score The highest recorded individual score in an All-Ireland final has been 2 goals, 5 points by Frank Stockwell (Galway) in the match against Cork in 1956.

Largest crowd The record crowd is 90,556 for the Down *v.* Offaly final at Croke Park, Dublin, in 1961.

Inter-provincials The province of Leinster has won most championships (Railway Cup) with 17 between 1928 and 1962. Sean O'Neill (Down) holds the record of 8 medals with Ulster (1960–71).

FOOTBALL (RUGBY LEAGUE)

Origins The Rugby League was formed originally in 1895 as "The Northern Rugby Football Union" by the secession of 22 clubs in Lancashire and Yorkshire from the parent Rugby Union. Though payment for loss of working time was a major cause of the breakaway the "Northern Union" did not itself embrace full professionalism until 1898. A reduction in the number of players per team from 15 to 13 took place in 1906 and the present title of "Rugby League" was adopted in 1922.

Most wins Under the one-league Championship system (1907–1962 and 1965–71) the club with the most wins was Wigan with nine (1909, 1922, 1926, 1934, 1946, 1947, 1950, 1952 and 1960).

In the Rugby League Challenge Cup (inaugurated

1896–97) the club with the most wins is Leeds with 8 in 1910–23–32–36, 1941–42 (wartime), 1957 and 1968. Oldham is the only club to appear in four consecutive Cup Finals (1924–27) and Bradford Northern is the only football club (Rugby League or Association) to have appeared at Wembley in three consecutive years (1947–48–49).

Only three clubs have won all four major Rugby League trophies (Challenge Cup, League Championship, County Cup and County League) in one season: Hunslet in 1907–08, Huddersfield in 1914–15 and Swinton in 1927–28.

In addition to the three "All Four Cup clubs", on only five other occasions has a club taken the Cup and League honours in one season: Broughton Rangers (1902); Halifax (1903); Huddersfield (1913); Warrington (1954); and St. Helens (1966).

World Cup The record aggregate score in a World Cup match is 60 points, when Great Britain beat The Rest by 33 points to 27 at Bradford on 10 Oct. 1960.

There have been five World Cup Competitions. Australia were winners in 1957, 1968 and 1970. Great Britain won in 1954 and 1960.

Senior match The highest aggregate score in Cup or League football, in a game where a senior club has been concerned, was 121 points, when Huddersfield beat Swinton Park Rangers by 119 points (19 goals, 27 tries) to 2 points (one goal) in the first round of the Northern Union Cup on 28 Feb. 1914.

Cup Final The record aggregate in a Cup Final is 43 points, when Wigan beat Hull 30–13 at Wembley on 9 May 1959, and when Wakefield Trinity beat Hull 38–5 at Wembley on 14 May 1960.

The greatest winning margin was 34 points when Huddersfield beat St. Helens 37–3 at Oldham on 1 May 1915.

Touring teams The record score for a British team touring the Commonwealth is 101 points by England *v.* South Australia (nil) at Adelaide in May 1914.

The record for a Commonwealth touring team in Britain is 92 points (10 goals, 24 tries) by Australia against Bramley's 7 points (2 goals, one try) at the Barley Mow Ground, Bramley, near Leeds, on 9 Nov. 1921.

Record crowds and receipts The greatest attendance at any Rugby League match is 102,569 for the Warrington *v.* Halifax Cup Final replay at Odsal Stadium, Bradford, on 5 May 1954.

The highest receipts for a match in the United Kingdom have been £90,000 for the Castleford *v.* Wigan R.L. Cup Final at Wembley Stadium, Greater London on 9 May 1970.

Most international caps Test Matches between Great Britain (formerly England) and Australia are regarded as the highest distinction for a R.L. player in either hemisphere and Jim Sullivan, the Wigan full-back and captain, holds a Test record for a British player with 15 appearances in these games between 1924 and 1933, though Mick Sullivan (no kin) of Huddersfield, Wigan, St. Helens and York, played in 16 G.B. *v.* Australia games in 1954–1964, of which 13 were Tests and 3 World Cup matches.

In all Tests, including those against New Zealand and France, Mick Sullivan made the record number of 47 appearances and scored 43 tries.

Most Cup Finals Two players have appeared in seven Cup Finals: Alan Edwards (Salford, Dewsbury and Bradford Northern) between 1938 and 1949, and Eric Batten (Leeds, Bradford Northern and Featherstone Rovers) between 1941 and 1952.

Eric Ashton, M.B.E., Wigan and Great Britain centre has the distinction of captaining Wigan at Wembley in six R.L. Cup Finals in nine years 1958–1966, taking the trophy three times (1958, 1959 and 1965).

The youngest player in a Cup Final was Reg Lloyd (Keighley) who was 17 years 8 months when he played at Wembley on 8 May 1937.

Most goals The record number of goals in a season is 224 by Bernard Ganley (Oldham) in the 1957–58 season. His total was made up of 219 in League, Cup and representative games and five in a "friendly" fixture.

MOST TRIES

Season Albert Aaron Rosenfeld (Huddersfield), an Australian-born wing-threequarter, scored 80 tries in the 1913–14 season.

Career Brian Bevan, an Australian-born wing-threequarter, scored 834 tries in League, Cup, representative or charity games in the 18 seasons (16 with Warrington, 2 with Blackpool Borough) from 1946 to 1964.

MOST POINTS

Cup C. H. ("Tich") West of Hull Kingston Rovers scored 53 points (10 goals and 11 tries) in a 1st Round Challenge Cup-tie *v.* Brookland Rovers on 4 March 1905.

League Lionel Cooper of Huddersfield scored 10 tries and kicked two goals against Keighley on 17 Nov. 1951.

Season B. Lewis Jones (Leeds) is the only player to have scored over 500 points in a season, with 505 (197 goals and 37 tries) in 1956–57. The record number of points in a single season by a team is 1,269 by Huddersfield (1914–15) and Wigan (1949–50).

Career Jim Sullivan (Wigan) scored 6,192 points (2,955 goals and 94 tries) in a senior Rugby League career extending from 1921 to 1946.

HIGHEST SCORES

The highest aggregate scores in international Rugby League football are:

Match	Points	Score
Great Britain *v.* Australia (*Test Matches*)	62	Australia won 50–12 (Swinton, 9 Nov. 1963)
Great Britain *v.* New Zealand (*Test Matches*)	72	Great Britain won 52–20 (Wellington, 30 July 1910)
Great Britain *v.* France (*Test Matches*)	65	Great Britain won 50–15 (Leeds, 14 March 1959)
England *v.* Wales	63	England won 40–23 (Leeds, 18 Oct. 1969)
England *v.* France	55	France won 42–13 (Marseille, 25 Nov. 1951)
England *v.* Other Nationalities	61	England won 34–27 (Workington, 30 March 1933)
Wales *v.* France	50	France won 29–21 (Bordeaux, 23 Nov. 1947)
Wales *v.* Other Nationalities	48	Other Nationalities won 27–21 (Swansea, 31 March 1951)
Australia *v.* Great Britain	76	Australia won 63–13 (Paris, 31 Dec. 1933)
Australia *v.* Wales	70	Australia won 51–19 (Wembley, 30 Dec. 1933)
Australia *v.* France (*Test Matches*)	62	Australia won 56–6 (Brisbane, 2 July 1960)
Australia *v.* New Zealand (*Test Matches*)	74	New Zealand won 49–25 (Brisbane, 28 June 1952)
New Zealand *v.* France (*Test Matches*)	53	France won 31–22 (Lyon, 15 Jan. 1956)

Record transfer fees The highest R.L. transfer fee is the reputed £15,000 deal which took Colin Dixon, the Halifax forward, to Salford on 19 Dec. 1968. Halifax were stated to have received £12,000 in cash and the winger M. Kelly, who was valued at £3,000.

Longest kick The longest claimed place kick was one of 80 yards by H. H. (Dally) Messenger for Australia *v.* Hull in Hull, Yorkshire in 1908 but this was apparently only estimated. In April 1940 Martin Hodgson (Swinton) kicked a goal on the Rochdale ground later measured to be 77¾ yards.

Australian Premiership The St. George (Sydney) R.L. club won the Sydney Premiership (club championship) in September 1966 for the eleventh successive season.

FOOTBALL (RUGBY UNION)

Origins The game is traditionally said to have originated from a breach of the rules of the football played in November 1823 at Rugby School by William Webb Ellis (later the Rev.) (*c.* 1807–72). This handling code of football evolved gradually and was known to have been played at Cambridge University by 1839. The Rugby Football Union was not founded until 1871.

MOST CAPPED PLAYERS

The totals below are limited to matches between the seven member countries of the "International Rugby Football Board" and France. Michel Crauste (b. 7 July 1934) of France has appeared in 62 internationals of all kinds since 1958.

New Zealand	53	Colin E. Meads	1957–71
Ireland	48	Thomas J. Kiernan	1960–70
Wales	44	Kenneth J. Jones, M.B.E.	1947–57
France	43	Michel Crauste, L.d'H.	1958–66
Scotland	40	Hugh F. McLeod, O.B.E.	1954–62
	40	David M. D. Rollo	1959–68
Australia	37	John E. Thornett, M.B.E.	1955–67
England	34	Derek Prior Rogers, O.B.E.	1961–69
South Africa	33	J. P. Engelbrecht	1960–69
	33	Frik C. H. Du Preez	1960–70

John Thornett, Australia's most capped player: 37 times in 13 years

HIGHEST SCORES

Internationals The highest aggregate for any match played under the auspices of the International Board since 1905, when modern scoring values came in, is 55 points when Wales beat England by 34 points to 21 at Cardiff in 1967. It has to be noted, however, that in 1881 England beat Wales by 7 goals, 1 drop goal and 6 tries to nil, which would amount in modern terms to a score of 56 points.

The highest score by any Overseas side in an international in the British Isles was when South Africa beat Scotland by 44 points to 0 at Murrayfield on 24 Nov. 1951.

The highest score in any full international was when France beat Romania by 59 points (7 goals, 6 tries and 2 penalty goals) to 3 in the Olympic Games at Colombes, Paris, on 24 May 1924. Fiji scored 113 points to 3 versus British Solomon Islands and 113 points to 13 versus New Caledonia at the 1969 South Pacific Games at Port Moresby.

The highest score in the "International Championship" in which France (which is not a member of the International Board) takes part, was when Wales beat France by 49 points to 14 at Swansea in 1910. The greatest winning margin in the "International Championship" was 42 points when Wales beat France by 47 points to 5 in Paris in 1909.

Ian S. Smith (Scotland) has scored most consecutive tries in international matches with 6; 3 in the second half of Scotland *v.* France in 1925 and 3 in the first half against Wales two weeks later.

Tour match The record score for any international tour match is 103–0 (17 goals, 5 tries and 1 penalty goal) when New Zealand beat Northern New South Wales at Quirindi, Australia, on 30 May 1962. Rod Heeps scored 8 tries (24 points) and Don B. Clarke kicked 10 conversions and the penalty goal (23 points).

George Nepia, the Maori full back, played in all 30 of New Zealand's (All Blacks) tour matches of 1924–25 in the British Isles.

Schools Scores of over 100 points have been recorded in club matches, for example Radford School beat Hills Court by 31 goals and 7 tries (in modern values 176 points) to nil on 20 Nov. 1886.

Individual The highest individual points score in any match between members of the International Board is 24 by W. Fergie McCormick—1 drop goal, 3 conversions and 5 penalty goals for New Zealand against Wales at Auckland on 14 June 1969.

In a match between Stucley's and Darracott's in a junior house match at Bideford G.S., Devon the scrum-half, Alan McKenzie, 14, contributed 73 points (13 tries and 17 conversions) to Stucley's 113 to nil win in November 1963.

Longest kicks The longest recorded successful drop-goal is 90 yards by G. Brand for South Africa *v.* England at Twickenham, London, in 1932. This was taken 7 yards inside

The world's highest Rugby Union posts at Barberton, Transvaal, South Africa

the England "half" 55 yards from the posts and dropped over the dead ball line.

The place kick record is reputed to be 100 yards at Richmond Athletic Ground, Surrey, by D. F. T. Morkell in an unsuccessful penalty for South Africa *v.* Surrey on 19 Dec. 1906. This was not measured until 1932.

Greatest crowd A crowd of 95,000 has twice been reported: when the British Lions beat South Africa 23–22 at Ellis Park, Johannesburg, on 6 Aug. 1955, and when France met Romania at Bucharest on 19 May 1957, as a curtain raiser for an Association match. The British record is over 76,000 for the Calcutta Cup match (England *v.* Scotland) at Murrayfield, Edinburgh, on 17 March 1962.

Middlesex Seven-a-Sides The Middlesex Seven-a-Sides were inaugurated in 1926. The most successful side has been Harlequins with 7 wins (1926–27–28–29–33–35–67).

The only players to be in five winning "sevens" have been N. M. Hall (St. Mary's Hospital 1944–1946 and Richmond 1951–53–55), and J. A. P. Shackleton and I. H. P. Laughland both of London Scottish (1960–61–62–63–65).

Highest posts The world's highest Rugby Union goal posts measure 93 feet $10\frac{1}{2}$ inches and are made of metal. They are at the Municipal Grounds, Barberton, Transvaal, South Africa.

SCORING RECORDS—AGGREGATE and MARGIN of VICTORY in the ten annual internationals in the "International Championship" (since modern scoring values came in in 1905).

Match	*Pts.*	*Record aggregate*	*Pts.*	*Record margin*
1. England *v.* Scotland	47	Scotland won 28–19 in 1931	19	England won by 19–0 in 1924 and 24–5 in 1947
2. England *v.* Wales	55	Wales won 34–21 in 1967	22	Wales won by 22–0 in 1907 and by 28–6 in 1922
3. England *v.* Ireland	50	England won 36–14 in 1938	22	England won by 36–14 in 1938 and Ireland by 22–0 in 1947
4. England *v.* France	54	England won 41–13 in 1907	37	England won by 37–0 in 1911
5. Scotland *v.* Wales	45	Scotland won 35–10 in 1924	25	Scotland won by 35–10 in 1924
6. Scotland *v.* Ireland	46	Scotland won 29–17 in 1913	21	Ireland won by 21–0 in 1950
7. Scotland *v.* France	34	Scotland won 31–3 in 1912	28	Scotland won by 31–3 in 1912
8. Wales *v.* Ireland	32	Wales won 28–4 in 1920	29	Wales won by 29–0 in 1907
9. Wales *v.* France	63	Wales won 49–14 in 1910	42	Wales won by 47–5 in 1909
10. Ireland *v.* France	33	France won 27–6 in 1964	24	Ireland won by 24–0 in 1913

FOX HUNTING

EARLIEST REFERENCES

Hunting the fox in Britain dates only from the middle of the 17th century. Prior to that time hunting was confined principally to the deer or the hare with the fox being hunted only by mistake. It is now estimated that huntsmen account for 10,000 of the 50,000 foxes killed each year.

PACK

Oldest The oldest pack of foxhounds in existence in England is the Sinnington (1680), but the old Charlton Hunt in Sussex, now extinct, the Mid-Devon and the Duke of Buckingham in the Bilsdale country, Yorkshire, hunted foxes prior to that time.

Largest The pack with the greatest number of hounds has been the Duke of Beaufort's hounds maintained at Badminton, Gloucestershire, since *c.* 1780. At times hunting eight times a week, this pack had 120 couples.

HUNT

Longest The longest recorded hunt was one led by Squire Sandys which ran from Holmbank, northern Lancashire, to Ulpha, Cumberland, a total of nearly 80 miles in reputedly only six hours, in January or February 1743. The longest hunt in Ireland is probably a run of 24 miles made by the Scarteen Hunt, County Limerick, from Pallas, to Knockoura in 1914. The longest duration hunt was one of 10 hours 5 minutes by the Charlton Hunt of Sussex, which ran from East Dean Wood at 7.45 a.m. to kill over $24\frac{1}{2}$ miles away at 5.50 p.m. on 26 Jan. 1736.

Largest fox The largest fox ever killed by a hunt in England was a $23\frac{3}{4}$ lb. dog on Cross Fell, Cumberland, by an Ullswater Hunt in 1936. A fox weighing 28 lb. 2 oz. measuring 54 inches from nose to tail was shot on the Staffordshire-Worcestershire border on 11 March 1956.

BEAGLING

The oldest beagle hunt is the Royal Rock Beagle Hunt, Wirral, Cheshire, whose first outing was on 28 March 1845. The Newcastle and District Beagles claim their origin from the municipally-supported Newcastle Harriers existing in 1787. The Royal Agricultural College beagle pack killed $75\frac{1}{2}$ brace of hares in the 1966–67 season.

GAMBLING

World's biggest lottery prize The world's biggest lottery is Spain's *Lotería de Navidad* (Christmas Lottery) drawn annually on 22 December. Ticket sales reach more than £60 million and the distribution of 85,000 prizes, worth more than £25 million, includes *El Gordo* (the fat one) worth about £410,000 for a full £66 ticket.

BINGO

Origins Bingo is a lottery game which, as keno, was developed in the 1880s from lotto, whose origin is thought to be the 17th century Italian game *tumbule*. It has long been known in the British Army (called Housey-Housey) and the Royal Navy (called Tombola). The winner was the first to complete a random selection of numbers from 1–90. The U.S.A. version called Bingo differs in that the selection is from 1–75. With the introduction of the Betting and Gaming Act on 1 Jan. 1961, large scale Bingo sessions were introduced in Britain by Mecca Ltd., which played to more than 250,000 entrants in an average week during the summer of 1962.

Largest house The largest "house" in Bingo sessions was staged at the Empire Pool, Wembley, Greater London, on 25 April 1965 when 10,000 attended.

Largest prize Prizes have been controlled since 1 July 1970 by the Betting and Gaming Act 1968. Prior to limitation, prizes in linked games between more than 50 clubs reached £16,000. The largest in a single game was £5,000 won in the Mecca National Rally at the Empire Pool, Wembley on 29 March 1970.

Longest session A session of 60 hours (two callers) was held at St. Mark's Church Hall, London W.1 on 1–3 April 1970 and at the Royal Bingo, Haverfordwest, Pembrokeshire by Ron Taylor and Ron McKenzie (1,255 games and 72,790 calls) later in April 1970.

FOOTBALL POOLS

The winning dividend paid out by Littlewoods Pools Ltd. in their first week in February 1923 was £2 12s. 0d. In April 1937 a record £30,780 was paid to R. Levy of London on 4 away wins, and in April 1947 a record £64,450 for a 1d. points pool.

Progressive list of individual record winnings

Amount	Recipient	Date
£75,000	P. C. Frank H. Chivers, 54, Aldershot, Hampshire	6 April 1948
£91,832	George A. Borrett, Huyton, Lancashire	26 Sept. 1950
£94,335	Thomas A. Wood, 42, Carlisle	10 Oct. 1950
£104,990	Mrs. Evelyn Knowlson, 43, Manchester	7 Nov. 1950
£75,000 (limit)	(45 limit winners)	from 20 Nov. 1951 to 10 Sept. 1957
£205,235	Mrs. Nellie McGrail (now Mrs. Albert Cooper), 37, of Reddish, Cheshire	5 Nov. 1957
£206,028	W. John Brockwell, 29, Epsom, Surrey	18 Feb. 1958
£209,079	Tom Riley, 58, of Horden, Co. Durham	1 April 1958
£209,837	Ronald Smith of Liverpool	23 Dec. 1958
£260,104	John Dunn, 45, of Chelsea, London	27 Oct. 1959
£265,352	Arther Webb, 70, of Scarborough, Yorkshire	24 Nov. 1959
£301,739·45	Lawrence Freedman, 54, of Willesden, London	8 Dec. 1964
£316,000	Geoffrey Liddiard	Mar. 1965
£338,356·80	Percy Harrison, 52, of East Stockwith, Lincolnshire	30 Aug. 1966
£401,792	Albert Crocker, 54, of Dobwalls, Cornwall	17 April 1971

The odds for selecting 8 draws (if there are 8 draws) from 54 matches for an all-correct line are 1,040,465,789 to 1 against.

Shared winnings The largest first dividend ever paid was one of £458,270, paid by Littlewoods and shared between 4,722 people on 1 March 1966. The most paid on one coupon for a first dividend is £331,196 received by Percy Harrison.

Summer record The greatest amount won in out of season summer pools is £286,962 by Tom Woods, 44, of Blackburn, Lancashire on Littlewoods Treble Chance on 19 May 1971.

Tom Woods, the record holder for a win on the summer pools, receives his cheque from the singer Anita Harris

HORSE RACING

Highest ever odds The highest recorded odds ever secured by a backer were 560,000 to 1 by A. Stone in the Penny Jackpot Accumulator run by A. Williams Ltd. betting shop branch at Kingston, Surrey, England on 18 April 1970. On the Newbury card he won 6 races and was paid out £2,337·30 for 1 (old) penny. The world record odds on a "double" are 24,741 to 1 secured by Mr. Montague Harry Parker of Windsor, England, for a £1 each-way "double" on *Ivernia* and *Golden Sparkle* with William Hill.

Biggest tote win The best recorded tote win was one of £341 2s. 6d. to 2s. (£341·12½ to 10p) by Mrs. Catharine Unsworth of Blundellsands, Liverpool at Haydock Park on a race won by *Coole* on 30 Nov. 1929. The highest odds in Irish tote history were £184 7s. 6d. on a 2s. 6d. (£184·37½ on a 12½p) stake, *viz.* 1,475 to 1 on *Hillhead VI* at Baldoyle on 31 Jan. 1970.

Most complicated bet The most complicated bet is the Harlequin, a compounc wager on 4 horses with 2,028 possible ways of winning It was invented by Monty H. Preston of London wh is reputed to be the fastest settler of bets in the world He once completed 3,000 bets in a 4½-hour test.

Largest bookmaker The world's largest bookmaker is William Hill with a estimated annual turnover reaching £65,000,000. Th largest chain of Betting Shops is Ladbroke's with 48 shops in the United Kingdom.

Topmost tipster The only recorded instance of a racing corresponden forecasting 8 out of 8 winners on a race card was a Taunton, Somerset, on 15 April 1969 by Tom Cosgrov of the London *Evening News*.

ROULETTE

The longest run on an ungaffed (*i.e.* true) whee recorded is 28 coups at Monte Carlo, Monaco fo which the probability is 1 in 268,435,456. A run of 3 might be expected every 50 years from 1,000 true whee spun 250 times a day.

Greatest pay out The greatest published pay out on a single bet is £62,50 by William Hill to the Hon. Raymond Guest, U.S Ambassador to Ireland, on 29 May 1968 for a £50 each-way bet at 100–1 placed on his *Sir Ivor* in Septemb 1967 for the 1968 Derby. In 1944 it was said that backer won £200,000 in an ante post bet on *Garden Pat* which won the 2,000 Guineas.

GLIDING

Emanuel Swedenborg (1688–1772) made sketches of gliders in the 18th century.

The earliest man-carrying glider was designed by Sir George Cayley (1773–1857) and carried his coachman (possibly John Appleby) about 500 yards across a valley near Brompton Hall, Yorkshire, in the summer of 1853. Gliders now attain speeds of 145 m.p.h. and the Jastrzab aerobatic sailplane is designed to withstand vertical dives at up to 280 m.p.h.

Highest standard A Gold C with three diamonds (for goal flight, distance and height) is the highest standard in gliding. This has been gained by eighteen British pilots up to July 1971.

Most titles The British national championship (instituted 1939) has been won most often by Philip A. Wills (b. 26 May 1907), in 1948–49–50 and 1955. The first woman to win this title was Mrs. Anne Burns of Farnham, Surrey on 30 May 1966.

SELECTED WORLD RECORDS

Distance	716·94 miles	Walter A. Scott (U.S.A.) in an ASW-12, on 26 July 1970 Ben W. Greene (U.S.A.) in an ASW-12, on 26 July 1970
Declared Goal Flight	641·3 miles	Hans-Werner Grosse (Germany) in an ASW-12, on 4 June 1970
Absolute Altitude	46,266 feet	Paul F. Bikle, Jr. (U.S.A.) in a Schweizer SGS-123E, over Mojave, California (released at 3,963 feet) on 25 Feb. 1961 (also record altitude gain—42,303 feet)
Goal and Return	534 miles	Walter A. Scott (U.S.A.) in an ASW-12, on 3 Aug. 1970
Speed over Triangular Course		
100 km.	96·34 m.p.h.	Walter Neubert (Germany) in a Kestrel 22m over the U.S.A. on 5 July 1970
300 km.	74·48 m.p.h.	A. Roehm (Germany) in a BS-1 on 4 June 1967
500 km.	85·25 m.p.h.	M. Jackson (South Africa) in a BJ-3 in South Africa on 28 Dec. 1967

BRITISH NATIONAL RECORDS[1]

	Single-seater
460·5 miles	P. D. Lane, in a Skylark 3F, Geilenkirchen to Hiersac, Germany on 1 June 1962
360 miles	Rear-Ad. H. C. N. Goodhart, R.N., in a Skylark 3, Lasham, Hants to Portmoak, Scotland on 10 May 1959
37,050 feet	Rear-Ad. H. C. N. Goodhart, R.N., in a Schweizer 1-23, at Bishop, California, U.S.A. on 12 May 1955
374 miles[2]	Alfred H. Warminger, in a Standard Austria, South Africa on 13 Jan. 1966
78·5 m.p.h.	Edward P. Hodge in a Diamant 16·5 over Rhodesia on 1 Nov. 1970
69·1 m.p.h.	John Delafield in a Phoebus 17 over South Africa on 22 Dec. 1969
64·20 m.p.h.[3]	Anne Burns, in a Standard Austria, at Kimberley, South Africa on 25 Dec. 1963

[1] *British National records may be set up by British pilots in any part of the world.*
[2] *Edward Pearson's 392 miles (approx.) over South Africa in a Cirrus on 4 Jan. 1971 awaits ratification.*
[3] *Also women's world record. Mrs. Burns with Janie Oesch set a multi-seat altitude record of 31,600 feet from Colorado Springs, U.S.A. in a Schweizer 2-32 on 5 Jan. 1967.*

GOLF

Origins The earliest mention of golf occurs in a prohibiting law passed by the Scottish Parliament in March 1457 under which "golfe be utterly cryed downe". The Romans had a cognate game called *paganica*, which may have been carried to Britain before A.D. 400. In February 1962 the Soviet newspaper *Izvestiya* claimed that the game was of 15th-century Danish origin. Gutta percha balls succeeded feather balls in 1848 and were in turn succeeded in 1902 by rubber-cored balls, invented in 1899 by Haskell (U.S.A.). Steel shafts were authorized in 1929.

CLUBS

The oldest club of which there is written evidence is the Gentlemen Golfers (now the Honourable Company of Edinburgh Golfers) formed in March 1744—10 years prior to the institution of the Royal and Ancient Club at St. Andrews, Fife. The oldest existing club in North America is the Royal Montreal Club (1873) and the oldest in the U.S.A. is St. Andrew's, New York (1888).

Largest The only club in the world with 15 courses is the Eldorado Golf Club, California, U.S.A. The club with the highest membership in the world is the Wanderer's Club, Johannesburg, South Africa, with 9,120 members, of whom 850 are golfers. The club with the highest membership in the British Isles is the Royal and Ancient Golf Club at St. Andrews, Fife (1,750). The largest in England is Wentworth Club, Virginia Water, Surrey, with 1,702 members, and the largest in Ireland is Royal Portrush with 594 full gentlemen members.

COURSES

Highest The highest golf course in the world is the Tuctu Golf Club in Morococha, Peru, which is 14,335 feet above sea-level at its lowest point. Golf has, however, been played in Tibet at an altitude of over 16,000 feet.

The highest golf course in Great Britain is one of 9 holes at Leadhills, Lanarkshire, 1,500 feet above sea-level.

Lowest The lowest golf course in the world was that of the Sodom and Gomorrah Golfing Society at Kallia, on the north-eastern shores of the Dead Sea, 1,250 feet below sea-level. The clubhouse was burnt down in 1948 and it is now no longer in use.

Longest hole The longest hole in the world is the 17th hole (par 6) of 745 yards at the Black Mountain Golf Club, North Carolina, U.S.A. It was opened in 1964. In August 1927 the 6th hole at Prescott Country Club in Arkansas, U.S.A., measured 838 yards. The longest hole on a championship course in Great Britain is the sixth at Troon, Ayrshire, which stretches 580 yards. The 9th at Hillsborough Golf Course, Wadsley, Sheffield, Yorkshire is 654 yards.

Largest green Probably the largest green in the world is the 5th green at Runaway Brook G.C., Bolton, Massachusetts, U.S.A. with an area greater than 28,000 square feet.

Biggest bunker The world's biggest bunker (called a trap in the U.S.A.) is Hell's Half Acre on the seventh hole of the Pine

Valley course, New Jersey, U.S.A., built in 1912 and generally regarded as the world's most trying course.

LOWEST SCORES

9 holes and 18 holes *Men* The lowest recorded score on any 18-hole course with a par score of 70 or more is 55 (15 under bogey) by A. E. Smith, the Woolacombe professional, on his home course on 1 Jan. 1936. The course measured 4,248 yards. The detail was 4, 2, 3, 4, 2, 4, 3, 4, 3 = 29 out, and 2, 3, 3, 3, 3, 2, 5, 4, 1 = 26 in. Nine holes in 25 (4, 3, 3, 2, 3, 3, 1, 4, 2) was recorded by A. J. "Bill" Burke in a round in 57 (32 + 25) on the 6,389-yard par 71 Normandie course, St. Louis, Missouri, U.S.A. on 20 May 1970. Homero Blancas (b. 1938, of Houston, Texas) also scored 55 (27 + 28) on a course of 5,002 yards (par 70) in a tournament at the Premier Golf Course, Longview, Texas, U.S.A., on 19 Aug. 1962. The lowest recorded score on a long course (over 6,000 yards) in Britain is 58 by Harry Weetman (b. 25 Oct. 1920), the British Ryder Cup golfer, for the 6,171-yard Croham Hurst Course, Croydon, on 30 Jan. 1956.

The United States P.G.A. tournament record for 18 holes is 60 by Al Brosch (30 + 30) in the Texas Open on 10 Feb. 1951; William Nary in the El Paso Open, Texas on 9 Feb. 1952; Ted Kroll (b. August 1919) in the Texas Open on Feb. 20 1954; Wally Ulrich in the Virginia Beach Open on 11 June 1954; Tommy Bolt (b. March 1918) in the Insurance City Open on 25 June 1954; Mike Souchak (b. May 1927) in the Texas Open on 17 Feb. 1955 and Samuel Jackson Snead (b. 27 May 1912) in the Dallas Open, Texas on 14 Sept. 1957. Snead went round in 59 in the 3rd round of the Sam Snead Festival, a non-P.G.A. tournament, at White Sulphur Springs, West Virginia, U.S.A., on 16 May 1959.

Women The lowest recorded score on an 18-hole course for a woman is 62 (30 + 32) by Mary (Mickey) Kathryn Wright (b. May 1935) of Dallas, Texas, on the Hogan Park Course (6,286 yards) at Midland, Texas, U.S.A., in November 1964.

United Kingdom The British Tournament 9-hole record is 28 by John Panton (b. 1917, Scotland) in the Swallow-Penfold Tournament at Harrogate, Yorkshire, in 1952; by Bernard John Hunt (b. 2 Feb. 1930) of Hartsbourne in the Spalding Tournament at Worthing, Sussex, in August 1953; and by Lionel Platts (b. 10 Oct. 1934, Yorkshire), of Wanstead in the Ulster Open at Shandon Park, Belfast, on 11 Sept. 1965. The lowest score recorded in a first class professional tournament on a course of more than 6,000 yards in Great Britain was set at 61 (29 + 32), by Thomas Bruce Haliburton (b. Scotland, on 5 June 1915) of Wentworth G.C. in the Spalding Tournament at Worthing, Sussex, in June 1952. Peter Butler equalled the 18-hole record with 61 (32 + 29) in the Bowmaker Tournament on the Old Course at Sunningdale, Berkshire, on 4 July 1967.

36 holes The record for 36 holes is 122 (59+63) by Snead in the 1959 Sam Snead Festival on 16–17 May 1959. On a short course Horton Smith (see below) scored 121. The lowest score by a British golfer has been 61+65=126 by Tom Haliburton (see below left).

72 holes The lowest recorded score on a first-class course is 257 (27 under par) by Mike Souchak (born May 1927) in the Texas Open at San Antonio in February 1955, made up of 60 (33 + 27), 68, 64, 65 (average 64·25 per round).

The late Horton Smith (born 1908), a U.S. Masters Champion, scored 245 (63, 58, 61 and 63) for 72 holes on the 4,700-yard course (par 64) at Catalina Country Club, California, U.S.A., to win the Catalina Open on 21–23 Dec. 1928.

The lowest 72 holes in a national championship is 262 by Percy Alliss (G.B.) in the 1932 Italian Open at San Remo, and by Liang Huan Lu (Formosa) in the 1971 French Open at Biarritz. The lowest for four rounds in a British first-class tournament is 262 (66, 63, 66 and 67) by Bernard Hunt in the Piccadilly Stroke Play tournament on Wentworth East Course, Virginia Water, Surrey, on 4–5 Oct. 1966. Kel Nagle of Australia shot 260 (64, 65, 66, and 65) in the Irish Hospitals Golf Tournament at Woodbrook Golf Club, near Bray, Ireland, on 21–23 July 1961.

Eclectic record The lowest recorded eclectic (from the Greek *eklektikos* = choosing) score, *i.e.* the sum of a player's all-time personal low scores for each hole, for a course of more than 6,000 yards is 33 by the club professional Jack McKinnon on the 6,538-yard Capilano Golf and Country Club course, Vancouver, British Columbia, Canada. This was compiled over the period 1937–1964 and reads 2–2–2–1–2–2–2–2–1 (=16 out) and 2–1–2–2–1–2–2–2–3 (=17 in) =33. The British record is 39 by John W. Ellmore at Elsham Golf Club, Lincolnshire (6,070 yards). This is made up of 2, 3, 2, 2, 2, 2, 2, 3, 2 = 20 (out) and 3, 1, 2, 1, 2, 2, 3, 3, 2 = 19 (in).

Highest scores The highest score for a single hole in the British Open is 21 by a player in the inaugural meeting at Prestwick in 1860. Double figures have been recorded on the card of the winner only once, when Willie Fernie (1851–1924) scored a 10 at Musselburgh, Midlothian, in 1883. Ray Ainsley of Ojai, California, took 19 strokes for the par-4 16th hole during the second round of the U.S. Open at Cherry Hills Country Club, Denver, Colorado, on 10 June 1938. Most of the strokes were used in trying to extricate the ball from a brook. Hans Merrell of Mogadore, Ohio, took 19 strokes on the par-3 16th (222 yards) during the third round of the Bing Crosby National Tournament at Cypress Point Club, Del Monte, California, U.S.A., on 17 Jan. 1959. It is recorded that Chevalier von Cittern went round 18 holes in 316 at Biarritz, France, in 1888.

Name JOCK McKINNON Attested Date

HOLES	1	2	3	4	5	6	7	8	9	OUT	10	11	12	13	14	15	16	17	18	IN	TOTAL	HDCP	NET
MEN'S YARDAGE	453	403	451	168	504	401	436	369	183	3368	445	155	368	402	136	420	254	415	575	3170	6538		
MEN'S PAR	5	4	5	3	5	4	4	4	3	37	5	3	4	4	3	4	3	4	5	35	72		
HANDICAP STROKES	15	5	9	17	3	13	1	7	11		10	16	8	4	18	2	14	12	6				
Eclectic 1937 – 1964	2	2	2	1	2	2	2	2	1	16	2	1	2	2	1	2	2	2	3	17	33		
WOMEN'S YARDAGE	453	403	451	126	447	401	405	316	169	3171	425	127	328	402	136	420	254	396	460	2948	6119		
WOMEN'S PAR	5	4	5	3	5	4	4	4	3	37	5	3	4	4	3	5	4	4	5	37	74		

NATIONAL RATING: MEN'S BLUE TEES - 71 MEN'S WHITE TEES - 70 WOMEN'S TEES - 74 DISTANCE IS MEASURED HORIZONTALLY FROM FIXED YARDAGE MARKERS TO CENTRE OF GREEN

Jock McKinnon's eclectic record score card

A ball being propelled round 18 holes at Dungannon, Co. Tyrone in record time

Most shots for one hole A woman player in the qualifying round of the Shawnee Invitational for Ladies at Shawnee-on-Delaware, Pennsylvania, U.S.A. in *c.* 1912, took 166 strokes for the short 130-yard 16th hole. Her tee shot went into the Binniekill River and the ball floated. She put out in a boat with her exemplary, but statistically minded husband at the oars. She eventually beached the ball $1\frac{1}{2}$ miles downstream but was not yet out of the wood. She had to play through one on the home run.

Fastest and slowest rounds With such variations in the lengths of courses, speed records, even for rounds under par, are of little comparative value.

On 18 Sept. 1970 a golf ball was propelled from the first tee to the eighteenth green (and 18 times holed out) by 45 members of the Mickleover Golf Club (5,253 yards), Derbyshire, England in 14 minutes 17 seconds

The slowest stroke play tournament round was one of 5 hours 15 minutes by Sam Snead and Ben W. Hogan (b. 13 Aug. 1912) of the U.S.A. *v.* Stan Leonard and Al Balding (b. April 1924) of Canada in the Canada Cup contest on the West Course, at Wentworth, Surrey, in 1956. This was a 4-ball medal round, everything holed out.

Most rounds in a day Col. Bill Farnham played 376 holes (20 rounds plus 16 holes) at his home course at Guilford Lakes, Connecticut, U.S.A., in 24 hours 10 minutes, from 2.40 p.m. on 11 Aug. to 2.50 p.m. on 12 Aug. 1934. Edward A. Ferguson of Detroit, Michigan, U.S.A., played 828 holes (46 rounds) in 158 hours from 6.00 p.m. 25 Aug. to 8.00 a.m. 1 Sept. 1930. He walked $327\frac{1}{2}$ miles.

Peter Chambers, 23, played 257 holes (14 rounds plus 5 holes) in under 24 hours on the 5,827-yard South Cliff G.C. course, Scarborough, Yorkshire on 19–20 June 1970. No cart was used. The best rounds were 76 and the worst 90. On 28 May 1970 Capt. Roland (Roger) Halford Ayers played 6 rounds on the par-70, 6,271-yard Chigwell G.C. course, Essex in 9 hours 45 minutes (last round in 79 [net 69] in 81 minutes) as a sexagenarian's protest against slow players and the International rule that an airline Captain may not fly "in command" of an aircraft over 45,000 lb. all-up weight when over 60.

Youngest and oldest champions The youngest winner of the British Open was Tom Morris, Jr. (born 1850, died 25 Dec. 1875) at Prestwick, Ayrshire, in 1868. The youngest winner of the British Amateur title was John Charles Beharrel (born 2 May 1938) at Troon, Ayrshire, on 2 June 1956, aged 18 years 1 month. The oldest winner of the British Amateur was the Hon. Michael Scott at Hoylake, Cheshire, in 1933, when 54. The oldest British Open Champion was "Old Tom" Morris (b. 1821), who was aged 46 in 1867. In recent times the 1967 champion, Roberto de Vicenzo (Argentina) was aged 44 years 93 days. The oldest United States Amateur Champion was Jack Westland (b. 1905) at Seattle, Washington, in 1952.

Longest drives In long-driving contests 325 yards is rarely surpassed at sea level. The United States P.G.A. record is 341 yards by Jack William Nicklaus (born Columbus, Ohio, 21 Jan. 1940), weighing $14\frac{3}{4}$ stone, in July 1963. The Irish Professional Golfers Association record is however 392 yards by their amateur member William Thomas (Tommie) Campbell (Foxrock Golf Club) made at Dun Laoghaire, Co. Dublin, in July 1964. Under freak conditions of wind, slope, parched or frozen surfaces, or ricochet from a stone or flint, even greater distances are achieved. The greatest recorded drive is one of 445 yards by Edward C. Bliss (1863–1917), a 12 handicap player, at the 9th hole of the Old Course, Herne Bay, Kent, in August 1913. Bliss, 6 feet tall and over 13 stone, drove to the back of the green on the left-handed dog-leg. The drive was measured by a government surveyor, Capt. L. H. Lloyd, who also measured the drop from the tee to resting place as 57 feet.

Other freak drives include the driving of the 483-yard 13th at Westward Ho! by F. Lemarchand, backed by a gale; and to the edge of the 465-yard downhill 9th on the East Devon Course, Budleigh Salterton, by T. H. V. Haydon in September 1934. Neither drive was accurately measured.

Perhaps the longest recorded drive on level ground was one of an estimated 430 yards by Craig Ralph Wood (born 18 Nov. 1901) of the U.S.A. on the 530-yard fifth hole at the Old Course, St. Andrews, Fife, in the Open Championship in June 1933. The ground was parched and there was a strong following wind.

Tony Jacklin drove a ball from the roof of the Savoy Hotel (125 feet above the pavement) 353 yards to splash into the River Thames on 26 Nov. 1969. A drive of 2,640 yards ($1\frac{1}{2}$ miles) across ice was achieved by an Australian meteorologist named Nils Lied at Mawson

"Old Tom" Morris, the oldest ever winner of The Open, at 46

Base, Antarctica, in 1962. On the Moon the energy expended on a mundane 300-yard drive would achieve, craters permitting, a distance of a mile.

Longest hitter The golfer regarded as the longest consistent hitter the game has ever known is the 6 feet 5 inches tall, 17 st. 2 lb. George Bayer (U.S.A.), the 1957 Canadian Open Champion. His longest measured drive was one of 420 yards at the fourth in the Las Vegas Invitational, Nevada, in 1953. It was measured as a precaution against litigation since the ball struck a spectator. Bayer also drove a ball pin high on a 426-yard hole in Tucson, Arizona, U.S.A. Radar measurements show that an 87 m.p.h. impact velocity for a golf ball falls to 46 m.p.h. in 3·0 seconds.

The Open The Open Championship was inaugurated in 1860 at Prestwick, Ayrshire, Scotland. The lowest score for 9 holes is 29 by Tom Haliburton (Wentworth) and Peter W. Thomson, M.B.E. (Australia) in the first round of the Open on the Royal Lytham and St. Anne's course at Lytham St. Anne's, Lancashire, on 10 July 1963.

The lowest scoring round is 63 (all in qualifying rounds) by Frank Jowle (b. 14 May 1912) at the New Course, St. Andrews (6,526 yards), on 4 July 1955; by Peter William Thomson, M.B.E. (b. 23 Aug. 1929) of Melbourne, Australia at Royal Lytham and St. Anne's (6,635 yards) on 30 June 1958; and Maurice Bembridge (Little Aston) at Delamere Forest, Cheshire, on 7 July 1967. The best by an amateur is 65 by Ronnie David Bell Mitchell Shade, M.B.E. (b. 15 Oct. 1938) in a qualifying round on the Eden Course (6,250 yards), St. Andrews, on 4 July 1964. The lowest rounds in The Open itself have been 65 by (Thomas) Henry Cotton, M.B.E. (b. Holmes Chapel, Cheshire, 26 Jan. 1907) at Royal St. George's, Sandwich, Kent in the 2nd round on 27 June 1934 to complete a 36-hole record of 132 (67+65); by Christy O'Connor (b. County Donegal, Ireland, 1925) (Royal Dublin) at Royal Lytham and St. Anne's, Lancashire in the 2nd round on 10 July 1969; and by Neil C. Coles (b. 26 Sept. 1934) (Coombe Hill) on the Old Course, St. Andrews in the 1st round on 8 July 1970. The lowest 72-hole aggregate is 276 (71, 69, 67, 69) by Arnold Daniel Palmer (b. 10 Sept. 1929) of Latrobe, Pennsylvania, U.S.A., at Troon, Ayrshire, ending on 13 July 1962.

British Amateur The lowest score for nine holes in the British Amateur Championship (inaugurated in 1885) is 29 by Richard Davol Chapman (born 23 March 1911) of the U.S.A. at Sandwich in 1948.

Michael Francis Bonallack, O.B.E. (b. 1935) shot a 61 (32+29) on the par-71 6,905-yard course at Ganton, Yorkshire, on 27 July 1968 in the 1st round of the English Amateur championship.

U.S. Open The United States Open Championship was inaugurated in 1894. The lowest 72-hole aggregate is 275 (71, 67, 72 and 65) by Jack Nicklaus on the Lower Course (7,015 yards) at Baltusrol Country Club, Springfield, New Jersey, on 15–18 June 1967 and 275 (69, 68, 69 and 69) by Lee Trevino (born near Horizon City, Texas 1940) at Oak Hill Country Club, Rochester, N.Y., on 13–16 June 1968. The lowest score for 18 holes is 64, achieved three times: by Lee Mackey, Jr., at Merion Country Club in Ardmore, Pennsylvania, on 8 June 1950; by Tommy Jacobs on the 7,053-yard course at the Congressional Country Club, Washington, D.C., on 19 June 1964; and by Rives McBee at the Olympic Country Club in San Francisco, California, on 17 June 1966.

U.S. Masters The lowest score in the U.S. Masters (instituted on the par-72 6,980-yard Augusta National Golf Course, Georgia, in 1934) has been 271 by Jack Nicklaus in 1965. The lowest rounds have been 64 by Lloyd Mangrum (1st round, 1940) and Jack Nicklaus (3rd round, 1965).

Bobby Jones (U.S.A.), winner of 13 major titles (1923–30)

Most internationals The greatest number of amateur international appearances to the end of 1970 is:

England	Michael Francis Bonallack, O.B.E. (Thorpe Hall)	65 times	1957–1970
Ireland	Joseph Boyton Carr (Sutton)	82 times	1947–1969
Scotland	Ronnie David Bell Mitchell Shade, M.B.E. (Duddingston)	46 times	1957–1968
Wales	W. I. Tucker (Monmouth)	57 times	1949–1970

Richest prizes The greatest first place prize money was $60,000 (total purse $300,000 [£125,000]) in the Dow Jones Open Invitational played at Upper Montclair Country Club,

MOST TITLES

The most titles won in the world's major championships are as follows:

The Open	Harry Vardon (1870–1937)	6	1896–98–99, 1903–11–14
British Amateur	John Ball (1861–1940)	8	1888–90–92–94–99, 1907–10–12
U.S. Open	W. Anderson	4	1901–03–04–05
	Robert Tyre Jones, Jr. (b. 17 Mar. 1902)	4	1923–26–29–30
	Ben William Hogan (b. 13 Aug. 1912)	4	1948–50–51–53
U.S. Amateur	R. T. Jones, Jr.	5	1924–25–27–28–30
P.G.A. Championship (U.S.A.)	Walter Charles Hagen	5	1921–24–25–26–27
Masters Championship (U.S.A.)	Arnold D. Palmer	4	1958–60–62–64
U.S. Women's Open	Miss Elizabeth (Betsy) Earle-Rawls	4	1951–53–57–60
	Miss "Mickey" Wright	4	1958–59–61–64
U.S. Women's Amateur	Mrs. Glenna C. Vare (*née* Collett)	6	1922–25–28–29–30–35
British Women's	Miss Charlotte Cecilia Pitcairn Leitch	4	1914–20–21–26
	Miss Joyce Wethered (born 1901) (now Lady Heathcoat-Amory)	4	1922–24–25–29

NOTE: *Jones won 13 major titles in 1923–30 while Nicklaus is the only golfer to have won 5 different such titles.*

Harry Vardon, 6 times winner of The Open

Clifton, New Jersey on 27–30 Aug. 1970 and £25,000 ($60,000) in the John Player Golf Classic at Hollinwell, Nottinghamshire, England on 3–6 Sept. 1970.

Highest earnings The greatest amount ever won in official golf prizes is $1,249,000 (£520,416), by Arnold Palmer from 1954 to 1 Jan 1971. During this period Palmer won 53 tournaments. The highest earnings in a season (all tournaments) are $267,000 by Jack Nicklaus in 1968, who reached the $1 million mark on 26 Jan. 1970.

Most tournament wins The record for winning tournaments in a single season is 19 (out of 31) by Byron Nelson (b. 4 Feb. 1912) of Fort Worth, Texas, in 1945. Of these 11 were consecutive, including the P.G.A., Canadian P.G.A. and Canadian Open, from 16 March to 15 August. He was a money prize winner in 113 consecutive tournaments.

Steadiest player William Earl Casper (b. 24 June 1931, San Diego, California) in the 11 years 1958–68 was only once (1963) outside the top 4 money winners on the U.S. professional circuit surpassing the $1 million mark on 12 Jan. 1970. He has won the Vardon Trophy in 1960, 1963, 1965, 1966 and 1968.

Most club championships The British record for club championships is 20 consecutive wins (1937–39 and 1946–62) by R. W. H. Taylor at the Dyke Golf Club, Brighton, Sussex. He retired unbeaten in July 1963.

HOLES IN ONE

Longest The longest hole ever holed in one shot is the 10th hole (444 yards) at Miracle Hills Golf Club, Omaha, Nebraska, U.S.A. Robert Mitera achieved a hole-in-one there on 7 Oct. 1965. Mitera, aged 21, stands 5 feet 6 inches tall and weighs 165 lb. (11 st. 11 lb.). He is a two handicap player who can normally drive 245 yards. A 50 m.p.h. gust carried his shot over a 290-yard drop-off. The group in front testified to the remaining 154 yards. The feminine record is 393 yards by Marie Robie of Wollaston, Massachusetts, U.S.A., on the first hole at the Furnace Brook Golf Club, western Massachusetts, on 4 Sept. 1949.

Billy Casper, generally considered the steadiest golfer of all time

The longest hole in one performed in the British Isles is the 5th (380 yards) on Tankersley Park course, near Sheffield, Yorkshire, by David Hulley in 1961.

Most The record total number of "aces" recorded in the United States in a year has been 18,319 (indicating more than 100 on some days) in 1969. The greatest number of holes-in-one in a career is 35 by Art Wall, Jr. (b. November 1923) between 1936 and 1966. The British record is 30 by Charles T. Chevalier (b. 22 July 1902) of Heaton Moor Golf Club, Stockport, Lancashire between 20 June 1918 and 17 July 1965. Dr. Joseph O. Boydstone scored holes-in-one at the 3rd, 4th and 9th holes on the Bakersfield Public Golf Course, California, U.S.A., on 10 Oct. 1961. The holes measured 210, 132 and 135 yards.

Double albatross There is no recorded instance of a golfer performing three consecutive holes-in-one but there are at least 13 cases of "aces" being achieved in two consecutive holes of which the greatest was Norman L. Manley's unique "double albatross" on the par-4 330-yard 7th and par-4 290-yard 8th holes on the Del Valle Country Club course, Saugus, California, on 2 Sept. 1964. Three examples by Britons have been by Roger Game at Walmer and Kingsdown, Kent in 1964; Charles Fairlie at Gourock in June 1968 and by the professional John Hudson, 25, of Hendon at Royal Norwich (11th eagle and 12th albatross) in the Martini International on 11 June 1971.

Youngest and oldest The youngest golfer recorded to have shot a hole-in-one was Tommy Moore (6 years 36 days) of Hagerstown, Maryland on the 145-yard 4th at the Woodbrier Golf Course, Martinsville, West Virginia, on 8 March 1968. The oldest golfer to have performed the feat is Walter Fast, aged 91 years 339 days, at Madison G.C., Peoria, Illinois on the 140-yard 13th hole on 12 Nov. 1970.

Shooting your age The record for scoring one's age in years over an 18-hole round is held by William Edmonds (b. 7 March 1888) of Maritzburg Golf Club, Natal, South Africa, who has won the Senior Golfers' Championship of South Africa and Rhodesia five times. On his 70th birthday, on 7 March 1958, he scored a 69. On 7 March 1964, aged 76, he went round a course of 6,565 yards at his club in 74. He had scored his age, or under his age, 228 times gross by 10 July 1970.

The oldest player to score under his age is C. Arthur Thompson (b. 1869) of Victoria, British Columbia, Canada, who scored 96 on the Uplands course of 6,215 yards on 3 Oct. 1966. He was reported to be still in action aged 101 in April 1971.

World Cup (formerly Canada Cup) The World Cup (instituted as the Canada Cup in 1953) has been won most often by the U.S.A., with ten victories in 1955–56–60–61–62–63–64–66–67–69. The only man to have been on six winning teams has been Arnold Palmer (1960, 62–64, 66–67). The lowest aggregate score for 144 holes is 545 by Australia (Bruce Devlin and David Graham) at San Isidro, Buenos Aires, Argentina on 12–15 Nov. 1970. The lowest individual score has been 269 by Roberto de Vicenzo (Argentina) also in 1970.

Throwing the golf ball The lowest recorded score for throwing a golf ball round 18 holes is 113 by David Hawkins at Sheerness Golf Club, Kent (5,895 yards) on 13 Sept. 1968.

GREYHOUND RACING

Earliest meeting Modern greyhound racing originated with the perfecting of the mechanical hare by Oliver P. Smith at Emeryville, California, U.S.A., in 1919. The earliest greyhound track race in the British Isles was at Belle Vue, Manchester, opened on 24 July 1926.

Derby The only dog to have twice won the English Greyhound Derby (held since 1945 over 525 yards at the White City Stadium, London) was *Mick the Miller* (whelped in Ireland, June 1926 and died 1939) on 25 July 1929, when owned by Albert H. Williams, and on 28 June 1930 (owned by Mrs. Arundel H. Kempton). This dog won a record sequence of 19 consecutive races from 19 March to 20 Aug. 1930. The highest prize was £7,728 for *Faithful Hope* in 1966. The only dogs to win the English, Scottish and Welsh Derby "triple" are *Trev's Perfection*, owned by Fred Trevillion, in 1947, and *Mile Bush Pride*, owned by Noel W. Purvis, in 1959.

Grand National The only dogs to have twice won the Greyhound Grand National (instituted 1927) over 525 yards and 4 flights are *Juvenile Classic* in 1938 and 1940 at the White City Stadium, London, and *Blossom of Annagura* on 21 May 1949 and 20 May 1950 (in the then record time of 29·38 secs.). The latter also won the 1951 Irish Grand National.

The fastest *photo*-timing is 29·43 seconds by *Barrowside* in May 1955. *Barrowside* failed to secure the "double" by placing second in the Derby—27 inches behind the winner, but displaced the previous record of *Dangerous Prince*, who was second in both races in 1949.

Fastest dog The highest speed at which any greyhound has been timed is 41·26 m.p.h. (345 yards in 17·1 secs.) by *Highland Dew* for a track record at Dapto, New South Wales, Australia. The highest speed recorded for a greyhound in Great Britain is 39·13 m.p.h. by *Beef Cutlet*, when covering a straight course of 500 yards in 26·13 seconds at Blackpool, Lancashire, on 13 May 1933. The highest speed on an oval course is 37·94 m.p.h. by *Yellow Printer*, the Derby record-holder at 28·44 secs., at White City, London on 3 June 1968 when he recorded 28·30 secs. for 525 yards.

GYMNASTICS

Earliest references Gymnastics were widely practised in Greece during the period of the ancient Olympic Games (776 B.C. to A.D. 393), but they were not revived until *c*. 1780.

World Championships The greatest number of individual titles won by a man in the World Championships is 10 by Boris Shakhlin (U.S.S.R.) between 1954 and 1964. He also won 3 team titles. The female record is 10 individual wins and 5 team titles by Larissa Semyonovna Latynina (born 1935, retired 1966) of the U.S.S.R., between 1956 and 1964.

Olympic Games Italy has won most Olympic team titles with four victories in 1912, 1920, 1924 and 1932.

The only man to win six individual gold medals is Boris Shakhlin (U.S.S.R.), with one in 1956, four (two shared) in 1960 and one in 1964. He also was a member of the winning Combined Exercises team in 1956.

The most successful woman has been Vera Caslavska-Odlozil (Czechoslovakia), with 7 individual Gold Medals, three in 1964 and four (one shared) in 1968. She also won a team Silver Medal in 1960, 1964 and 1968 and an individual Silver Medal in 1968. Latynina won six individual Gold Medals and first places in three team events in 1956–64.

Arthur Whitford, holder of a record number of 10 British gymnastic championships

British Championship The most times that the British Gymnastic Championship has been won is 10 by Arthur Whitford in 1928–36 and 39. He was also in four winning Championship teams. The women's record is 5 wins by Miss Margaret Bell, 1965–69.

Rope climbing The United States Amateur Athletic Union records are tantamount to world records: 20 feet (hands alone) 2·8 seconds, Don Perry (U.S.A.) at Champaign, Illinois, U.S.A., on 3 April 1954; 25 feet (hands alone), 4·7 seconds, Garvin S. Smith at Los Angeles, California, U.S.A., on 19 April 1947.

Chinning the bar The greatest number of chin-ups (from a dead hang position) recorded is 106 by William D. Reed at the Weightman Hall, University of Pennsylvania, U.S.A. on 23 June 1969. The feminine record for one-handed chin-ups is 27 in Hermann's Gym, Philadelphia, Pennsylvania, U.S.A. in 1918 by Lillian Leitzel (Mrs. Alfredo Codona) (U.S.A.), who was killed in Copenhagen, Denmark, on 12 Feb. 1931. Her total would be unmatched by any male but it is doubtful if they were achieved from a "dead hang" position. It is believed that only one person in 100,000 can chin a bar one-handed. Francis Lewis (b. 1896) of Beatrice, Nebraska, U.S.A. in May 1914 achieved 7 consecutive chins using only the middle finger of his left hand. His bodyweight was 158 lb.

Press-ups The greatest recorded number of consecutive press-ups is 6,006 in 3 hours 54 minutes by Chick Linster, aged 16, of Wilmette, Illinois, U.S.A., on 5 Oct. 1965. Masura Noma of Mihara, Japan did 1,227 press-ups in 37 minutes in January 1968. Jim Slegh of Long Beach, California did 72 one-arm press-ups on 9 Oct. 1939.

Sit-ups The greatest recorded number of consecutive sit-ups on a hard surface is 15,011 in less than six hours by Special Agent John R. Greenshields of the F.B.I. on 6 June 1966.

Greatest tumbler The greatest tumbler of all time is Dick Browning (U.S.A.) who made a backward somersault over a 7-foot 3-inch bar at Santa Barbara, California, in April 1954. In his unique repertoire was a "round-off", backward handspring, backward somersault with half-twist, walk-out, tinsica tigna round-off, backward handspring, double backward somersault.

Hand-to-hand balancing The longest horizontal dive achieved in any hand-to-hand balancing act is 22 feet by Harry Berry (top mounter) and the late Nelson Soule (understander) of the Bell-Thazer Brothers from Kentucky, U.S.A., who played at State fairs and vaudevilles from 1912 to 1918. Berry used a 10-foot tower and trampoline for impetus.

Largest gymnasium The world's largest gymnasium is Yale University's Payne Whitney Gymnasium at New Haven, Connecticut, U.S.A., completed in 1932 and valued at $18,000,000 (£7,500,000). The building, known as the "Cathedral of Muscle", has nine storeys with wings of five storeys each. It is equipped with four basketball courts, three rowing tanks, 28 squash courts, 12 handball courts, a roof jogging track and a 25-yard by 42-foot swimming pool on the first floor and a 55-yard long pool on the third floor.

HANDBALL (COURT)

Handball played against walls or in a court is a game of ancient Celtic origin. In the early 19th century only a front wall was used but gradually side and back walls were added. The earliest international contest was in New York City, U.S.A. in 1887 between the champion of the U.S.A. and Ireland. The court is now a standardized 60 feet by 30 feet in Ireland, Ghana and Australia, and 40 feet by 20 feet in Canada, Mexico and the U.S.A. The game is played with both a hard and a soft ball.

Championship World championships were inaugurated in New York in October 1964 with competitors from Australia, Canada, Ireland, Mexico and the U.S.A. U.S.A. won in 1964; Canada and U.S.A. shared the title in 1967 and Ireland won in 1970.

Most titles In Ireland the most titles (instituted 1925) have been won as follows:

Hardball
Singles John J. Gilmartin (Kilkerry)
10 1936–42, 1945–47
Doubles John Ryan and John Doyle (Wexford)
6 1952, 1954–58
Softball
Singles Paddy Perry (Roscommon)
8 1930–37
Doubles James O'Brien and Patrick Downey (Kerry)
7 1955–56, 1960–64

HANDBALL (FIELD)

Handball, similar to association football with a substitution of the hands for the feet, was first played *c.* 1895. It was introduced into the Olympic Games at Berlin in 1936 as an 11-a-side outdoor game with Germany winning, but in 1972 it will be an indoor game with 7-a-side, which has been the standard size of team since 1952.

By 1971 there were 41 countries affiliated to the International Handball Federation, a World Cup competition and an estimated 5 million participants. The earliest international match was when Sweden beat Denmark on 8 March 1935.

HOCKEY

Origins A representation of two hockey players apparently in an orthodox "bully" position was found in Tomb No. 16 at Beni Hasan, United Arab Republic (formerly Egypt) and has been dated to *c.* 2000 B.C. There is a British reference to the game in Lincolnshire in 1277. The oldest club is Blackheath, founded in 1861. The first country to form a national association was England (The Hockey Association) in 1886.

MEN

Earliest international The first international match was the Wales *v.* Ireland match at Rhyl on 26 Jan. 1895. Ireland won 3–0.

Highest international score The highest score in international hockey was when India defeated the United States 24–1 at Los Angeles, California, U.S.A., in the 1932 Olympic Games. The Indians were Olympic Champions from the re-inception of Olympic hockey in 1928 until 1960, when Pakistan beat them 1–0 at Rome. They had their seventh win in 1964. Three Indians have won 3 Olympic gold medals—Dhyan Chand and R. J. Allen (1928, 1932, 1936), Randhir Gentle (1948, 1952, 1956). The greatest number of goals in a home international match was when England defeated France 16–0 at Beckenham on 25 March 1922.

Longest game The longest international game on record was one of 145 minutes (into the sixth period of extra time), when Netherlands beat Spain 1–0 in the Olympic tournament at Mexico City on 25 Oct. 1968. After Moss Sports had played Symington's in the County mixed senior competition at Leicester on 22 March 1969 for 170 minutes without decision, a coin was tossed and Symington's won.

Most appearances The most by a Briton is 89 by John W. Neill with 56 for Great Britain and 33 for England won from 1959 until the 1968 Olympic Games.

England 46, Michael W. Corby (Middlesex) (1961–71)
Wales 61, David J. Prosser (1961–71)
Scotland 63, F. H. Scott (Hounslow) (up to 1971)
Ireland 60, Harold Cahill (1947–71)
Great Britain 56, John W. Neill (England) (1959–68)

Greatest scoring feat M. C. Marckx (Bowdon 2nd XI) scored 19 goals against Brooklands 2nd XI (score 23–0) on 31 Dec. 1910. He was selected for England in March 1912 but declined due to business priorities.

WOMEN

Origins The earliest women's club was East Molesey in Surrey, England formed in *c.* 1887. The first national association was the Irish Ladies' Hockey Union founded in 1894. The All England Women's Hockey Association held its first formal meeting in Westminster Town Hall, London, on 23 Nov. 1895. The first international match was an England *v.* Ireland game in Dublin in 1896. Ireland won 2–0.

Highest international score The highest score in a women's international match occurred when England defeated France 23–0 at Merton, Surrey, on 3 Feb. 1923.

Most appearances The England records are 53 caps by Miss Mildred Mary Knott (1923–39) and 17 seasons by Miss Mabel Bryant (1907–1929), who won 39 caps. The Irish record is 58 (46 full caps and 12 touring) by Mrs. Sean Kyle (born Maeve Esther Enid Shankey, 6 Oct. 1928) between November 1947 and 1966.

Highest attendance The highest attendance at a women's hockey match was 65,000 for the match between England and Wales at the Empire Stadium, Wembley, Greater London, on 8 March 1969.

HORSE RACING

Origins Stone and bone carvings prove that horse racing is a sport at least thirty centuries old. The 23rd ancient Olympic Games of 624 B.C. in Greece featured horse racing. The earliest horse race recorded in England was one held in about A.D. 210 at Netherby, Yorkshire, among Arabians brought to Britain by Lucius Septimius Severus (A.D. 146–211), Emperor of Rome. The oldest race still being run annually is the Lanark Silver Bell, instituted in Scotland by William Lion (1165–1214).

The Jockey Club was formed in 1750–51 and the General Stud Book started in 1791. Racing colours (silks) became compulsory in 1889.

RACECOURSES

Largest The world's largest racecourse is the Newmarket course

The world's smallest racecourse at Lebong, Darjeeling, India

(founded 1636), on which the Beacon Course, the longest of the 19 courses, is 4 miles 397 yards long and the Rowley Mile is 167 feet wide. The border between Suffolk and Cambridgeshire runs through the Newmarket course. The world's largest grandstand is that opened in 1968 at Belmont Park, Nassau County, Long Island, N.Y., U.S.A. at a cost of $30,700,000 (£12·8 million). It is 110 feet tall, 440 yards long and contains 908 mutule windows. The highest seating capacity at any racetrack is 40,000 at Atlantic City Audit, New Jersey, U.S.A.

Smallest The world's smallest racecourse is the Lebong racecourse, Darjeeling, West Bengal, India (altitude 7,000 feet), where the complete lap is 481 yards. It was laid out *c.* 1885 and used as a parade ground.

HORSES

Greatest record The horse with the best recorded win-loss record and the only one on which it was safe to bet was *Kincsem*, a Hungarian mare foaled in 1874, who was unbeaten in 54 races (1877–1880), including the Goodwood Cup of 1878. It is reported from Puerto Rico that the horse *Camarero* won 56 races in succession.

Tallest The tallest horse ever to race is *Fort d'Or*, owned by Lady Elizabeth (Eliza) Nugent (*née* Guinness), which stands 18 hands 2 inches.

Highest price The highest price ever paid for a stallion is $5,440,000 (£2,666,666) paid after the 1970 season by a 32-share syndicate for the Canadian-bred *Nijinsky* owned by Charles Engelhard of Far Hills, New Jersey, U.S.A.

Greatest winnings The greatest amount ever won by a horse is $1,977,896 (then £706,391) by *Kelso* (foaled in 1957) in the U.S.A., between 1959 and his retirement on 10 March 1966. He is now the supreme status symbol of the hunt under Mrs. Richard C. du Pont. In 63 races he won 39, came second in 12 and third in 2. The most successful horse of all time has been *Buckpasser*, whose career winnings were $1,462,014 (£609,172) in 1965–66–67. He won 25 races out of 31. The most won by a mare is $783,674 (£279,883) by *Cicada*. In 42 races she won 23, came second in 8 and third in 6. The most won in a year is $817,941 (£340,808) by *Damascus* in 1967. His total reached $1,176,781.

Largest prizes The richest race ever held is the All-American Futurity, a race for quarter-horses over 400 yards at Ruidoso Downs, New Mexico, U.S.A. The prizes in 1970 totalled $670,000 (£279,150). *Laico Bird*, the winner in 1967 in 20·11 seconds, received $228,300 (£81,535). The largest single prize ever paid was 1,094,126 francs, plus 78 per cent. of the entry fees, making 1,480,000 francs (then £107,000) to the owner of *Prince Royal II*, winner of the 43rd Prix de l'Arc de Triomphe at Longchamp, Paris, on 4 Oct. 1964.

JOCKEYS

The most successful jockey of all time has been Willie Shoemaker (b. weighing 2½ lb. on 19 Aug. 1931) now weighing 98 lb. after 22 years in the saddle, beating Johnny Longden's life-time record of 6,032 winners at Del Mar, California, U.S.A. on 7 Sept. 1970. Shoemaker, known as The Ice Man, stands 4 feet 11½ inches. His mounts won more than $43 million (£17,916,666) from 19 March 1949 to this time. Herve Filion surpassed Shoemaker's record of 485 winners in a year.

The greatest amount ever won by any jockey in a year is $3,088,888 by Braulio Baeza (b. Panama) in the U.S.A. in 1967. The oldest jockey was Levi Barlingame (U.S.A.), who rode his last race at Stafford, Kansas, U.S.A., in 1932 aged 80. The youngest jockey was

Fort d'Or, the tallest race horse of all time at 18 hands 2 inches

SPEED RECORDS

Distance	Time	m.p.h.	Name	Course	Date
¼ mile	20·8s.	43·26	*Big Racket* (U.S.A.)	Lomas de Sotelo, Mexico	5 Feb. 1945
½ mile (straight)	45·0s.	40·00	*Gloaming* (N.Z.)	Wellington, New Zealand	12 Jan. 1921
½ mile	45·0s.	40·00	*Beau Madison* (U.S.A.)	Phoenix, Arizona, U.S.A.	30 Mar. 1957
	45·0s.	40·00	*Another Nell* (U.S.A.)	Cicero, Ill., U.S.A.	8 May 1967
⅝ mile	53·6s.	41·98	*Indigenous* (G.B.)	Epsom, Surrey	2 June 1960
¾ mile	1m. 07·4s.	40·06	*Zip Pocket* (U.S.A.)	Phoenix, Arizona, U.S.A.	6 Dec. 1966
	1m. 07·4s.	40·06	*Vale of Tears* (U.S.A.)	Ab Sar Ben, Omaha, Neb., U.S.A.	7 June 1969
	1m. 06·2s.	40·78	*Broken Tindril* (G.B.)	*Brighton, Sussex	6 Aug. 1929
Mile	1m. 31·8s.	39·21	*Soueida* (G.B.)	*Brighton, Sussex	19 Sept. 1963
	1m. 31·8s.	39·21	*Loose Cover* (G.B.)	*Brighton, Sussex	9 June 1966
	1m. 32·2s.	39·04	*Dr. Fager* (U.S.A.)	Arlington, Ill., U.S.A.	24 Aug. 1968
1½ miles	2m. 26·0s.	36·98	*Meneleck* (G.B.)	Haydock Park, Lancashire	1 July 1961
2 miles	3m. 15·0s.	36·93	*Polazel* (G.B.)	Salisbury, Wiltshire	8 July 1924
3 miles	5m. 15·0s.	34·29	*Farragut* (Mexico)	Agua Caliente	9 Mar. 1941

** Course downhill for two-thirds of a mile.*

Frank Wootton (English Champion jockey 1909–12), who rode his first winner in South Africa aged 9 years 10 months. The lightest recorded jockey was Kitchener (died 1872), who won the Chester Cup on *Red Deer* in 1844 at 3 stone 7 lb. He was said to have weighed only 2 stone 12 lb. in 1840.

Trainers The greatest amount ever won by a trainer in one year is $2,456,250 (then £881,519) by Eddie A. Neloy (U.S.A.) in 1966 when his horses won 93 races.

Dead heats There is no recorded case in turf history of a quintuple dead heat. The nearest approach was in the Astley Stakes, at Lewes, England, in August 1880 when *Mazurka, Wandering Nun* and *Scobell* triple dead-heated for first place, just ahead of *Cumberland* and *Thora,* who dead-heated for fourth place. Each of the five jockeys thought he had won. The only two known examples of a quadruple dead heat were between *The Defaulter, Squire of Malton, Reindeer* and *Pulcherrima* in the Omnibus Stakes at The Hoo, England, on 26 April 1851, and between *Overreach, Lady Go-Lightly, Gamester* and *The Unexpected* at the Houghton Meeting at Newmarket on 22 Oct. 1855. The earliest recorded photo-finish dead heat in Britain was between *Phantom Bridge* and *Resistance* in the 5-furlong Beechfield Handicap at Doncaster on 22 Oct. 1947.

Longest race The longest recorded horse race was one of 1,200 miles in Portugal, won by a horse *Emir* bred from Egyptian-bred Blunt Arab stock. The holder of the world's record for long distance racing and speed is *Champion Crabbet,* who covered 300 miles in 52 hours 33 minutes, carrying 17½ stone, in 1920. In 1831 Squire George Osbaldeston (1787–1866), M.P. of East Retford, covered 200 miles in 8 hours 42 minutes at Newmarket, using 50 mounts, so averaging 22·99 m.p.h. In 1967 G. Steecher covered 100 miles on a single horse in 11 hours 4 minutes in Victoria, Australia.

Shortest price The shortest odds ever quoted for any racehorse are 10,000 to 1 on for *Dragon Blood,* ridden by Lester Piggott (G.B.) in the Premio Naviglio in Milan, Italy on 1 June 1967. Odds of 100 to 1 on were quoted for the United States horse *Man o' War* (foaled 29 March 1917, died 1 Nov. 1947) on three separate occasions in 1920, and for the two British horses, *Ormonde* in the Champion Stakes on 14 Oct. 1886 (three runners), and *Sceptre* in the Limekiln Stakes on 27 Oct. 1903 (two runners).

BRITISH TURF RECORDS

Most expensive horses The highest price ever paid for a horse in the British Isles is £250,000, paid in February 1953 for *Tulyar* by the Irish National Stud to the Rt. Hon. Aga Sultan Sir Mohammed Shah, H.H. Aga Khan III, G.C.S.I., G.C.M.G., G.C.I.E., G.C.V.O. (1877–1957) of Iran (Persia). *Sir Ivor* commands a covering fee of £8,000. A sum of £250,000 was also paid for *Ballymoss* by a syndicate in September 1958. The French horse *Charlottesville* was bought by a syndicate for £336,000 from H.H. Shah Karim, Aga Khan IV (b. 13 Dec. 1936), in November 1960. The record payment for a horse in training is 136,000 guineas (£142,800) for *Vaguely Noble* at Park Paddocks, Newmarket auction sale by Dr. Robert A. Franklyn (U.S.) on 7 Dec. 1967.

Most successful horses No horse has yet won all five classics. The nearest approach was in 1902, when *Sceptre* won the 1,000 Guineas, 2,000 Guineas, Oaks and St. Leger. In 1868 *Formosa* won the same four but dead-heated in the 2,000 Guineas. The most races won in a season is 23 by *Fisherman* in 1856. *Catherina* won 79 out of 174 races between 1833 and 1841. The only horse to win the same race in seven successive years was *Dr. Syntax*, who won the Preston Gold Cup from 1815 to 1821. The most successful sire was *Stockwell,* whose progeny won 1,153 races (1858–76) and in 1866 set a record of 132 races won. The greatest amount of prize money ever won by an English horse on English racecourses is £163,949·75 by *Royal Palace* in 1966–67–68.

Most successful owners The greatest amount of stake money won is £1,025,592 from 784 races by H.H. Aga Khan III (1877–1957) from 1922 until his death. These included 35 classics, of which 17 were English classics. The record for a season was set by Mr. H. J. Joel, who surpassed the previous record of £100,668 by winning £120,924 in 1967. The most wins in a season is 106 by Mr. David Robinson. The most English classics won is 20 by the 4th Duke of Grafton, K.G. (1760–1844), from 1813 to 1831.

Most successful trainers Captain Sir Cecil Charles Boyd-Rochfort, K.C.V.O. (b. 16 April 1887) has earned more than £1,500,000 for his patrons. The record for a season is £256,899 by Charles Francis Noel Murless (born 1910) in 1967. The most classics won by a trainer is 40 or 41 by John Scott, including 16 St. Leger winners between 1827 and 1862.

Most successful jockeys Sir Gordon Richards (b. 5 March 1904) retired in 1954, having won 4,870 races from 21,834 mounts since his first win at Leicester on 21 March 1921. In 1953, after 27 attempts, he won the Derby, six days after being knighted. He set a record of 12 consecutive wins by winning the last race in which he rode at Nottingham on 3 Oct. 1933, all six at Chepstow on the 4th and the first five on the 5th. In 1947 he won a record 269 races. The most classic races won by a jockey is 27 by Frank Buckle (1766–1832), between 1792 and 1827.

Most runners The most horses in a race is 66 (a world record) in the Grand National of 22 March 1929. The record for the flat is 58 in the Lincolnshire Handicap on 13 March 1948. The most runners at a meeting were 214 (flat) in seven races at Newmarket on 15 June 1915 and 229 (National Hunt) in eight races at Worcester on 13 Jan. 1965.

THE DERBY

The greatest of England's five classic races, the Epsom Derby, was inaugurated on 4 May 1780 by the 12th Earl of Derby (1752–1834). It has been run over 1 mile 885 yards since 1784 (1½ miles since World War I) on Epsom Downs, Surrey, except for the two war periods, when it was run at Newmarket. Since 1884 the race has been for three-year-old colts carrying 9 stone and fillies carrying 8 stone 9 lb.

Highest prize The highest prize for winning any English race was £74,489·50 for *Charlottown* in the Derby on 25 May 1966.

Most winning owners The only owner with five outright winners was the 3rd Earl of Egremont (1751–1837) with *Assassin* (1782), *Hannibal* (1804), *Cardinal Beaufort* (1805), *Election* (1807), and *Lapdog* (1826). H.H. Aga Khan III (1877–1957) had four winners in *Blenheim* (1930), *Bahram* (1935), *Mahmoud* (1936) and *Tulyar* (1952) and a half-share in *My Love* (1948).

Trainer The only two trainers with seven winners were John Porter with *Blue Gown* (1868), *Shotover* (1882), *St. Blaise* (1883), *Ormonde* (1886), *Sainfoin* (1890), *Common* (1891) and *Flying Fox* (1899), and Robert Robson with *Waxy* (1793), *Tyrant* (1802), *Pope* (1809), *Whalebone* (1810), *Whisker* (1815), *Azor* (1817), and *Emilius* (1823). Fred Darling had seven winners, including two in the war-time meetings at Newmarket (1940–41).

Jockey The most successful jockey was Jem Robinson, who won six times in 1817, 1824–25, 1827–28 and 1836. Steve Donoghue (1884–1945) rode six winners in 1915, 1917, 1921–23 and 1925, but the first two were war-time races not on the Epsom Course.

Record time The record time for the Derby is 2 minutes 33·8 seconds (average speed 35·06 m.p.h.) by *Mahmoud,* ridden by Charlie Smirke, owned by H.H. Aga Khan III, trained by Frank Butters (1878–1957), winning at 100 to 8 by three lengths from a field of 22 in 1936. The fastest time recorded over the Derby course is, however, 2 minutes

33·0 seconds by the four-year-old *Apelle* in winning the 1928 Coronation Cup.

Dead heats The two instances of dead heats were in 1828, when *Cadland* beat *The Colonel* in the run off, and in 1884 between *Harvester* and *St. Gatien* (stakes divided).

Disqualifications The two disqualifications were of *Running Rein* (race awarded to *Orlando*) in 1844 and of *Craganour* (race awarded to *Aboyeur*) in the "Suffragette Derby" on 4 June 1913, when Miss Emily Davison killed herself by impeding King George V's horse *Anmer*.

Other records The only greys to have won were *Gustavus* (1821), *Tagalie* (1912), *Mahmoud* (1936) and *Airborne* (1946). Only two black horses have ever won—*Smolensko* (1813) and *Grand Parade* (1919). The longest odds quoted on a placed Derby horse were 200–1 against for *Black Tommy*, second to *Blink Bonny* in 1857. The shortest priced winner was *Ladas* (1894) at 9–2 on and the highest priced winners were *Jeddah* (1898), *Signorinetta* (1908) and *Aboyeur* (1913), all at 100 to 1 against. The smallest field was four in 1794 and the largest 34 in 1862. The smallest winner was *Little Wonder* (14 hands 3½ inches) in 1840.

GRAND NATIONAL

Most wins *Horse* The first official Grand National Steeplechase may be regarded as the Grand Liverpool Steeplechase of 26 Feb. 1839 though the race was not so named until some years later. The first winner of the Grand Liverpool Steeplechase was Mr. Pott's *The Duke* in 1837. The race is for six-year-olds and over (since 1930) and is run over a course of 4 miles 856 yards, with 30 jumps, at Aintree, near Liverpool. No horse has won three times but six share the record of two wins:

Peter Simple	1849 and 1853	*The Colonel*	1869 and 1870
Abd-el-Kader	1850 and 1851	*Manifesto*	1897 and 1899
The Lamb	1868 and 1871	*Reynoldstown*	1935 and 1936

Manifesto was entered eight times (1895–1904) and won twice, came third three times and fourth once. *Poethlyn* won in 1919 having won the war-time Gatwick race in 1918.

Jockey The only jockey to ride five winners was G. Stevens on *Free Trader* (1856), *Emblem* (1863), *Emblematic* (1864) and *The Colonel* (1869–70).

Owner The only owners with three winners, since the race became a handicap in 1843, are Captain Machell with *Disturbance* (1873), *Reughy* (1874) and *Regal* (1876); and Sir Charles Assheton-Smith with *Cloister* (1893), *Jerry M* (1912) and *Covertcoat* (1913).

Trainer The only trainer with four winners was the Hon. Aubrey Hastings with *Ascetic's Silver* (1906), *Ally Sloper* (1915), *Ballymacad* (1917, Gatwick) and *Master Robert* (1924).

Highest prize The highest prize was £22,334·25 won by *Anglo* on 26 March 1966.

Fastest time Times before the 1939–45 War were not officially returned. In 1935 the eight-year-old *Reynoldstown* ridden by Mr. F. Furlong won by 3 lengths from a field of 27 in times variously reported as 9 minutes 21·0 seconds or 9 minutes 20·2 seconds. *Golden Miller*, a seven-year-old ridden by G. Wilson, carrying 12 stone 2 lb., and owned by the Hon. Miss Dorothy Paget, won by 5 lengths from a field of 30 in 9 minutes 20·4 seconds (28·82 m.p.h.) in 1934.

Highest jump The 15th jump, known as the "Open Ditch", is 5 feet 2 inches high and 3 feet 9 inches thick. The ditch on the take-off side is 6 feet wide, and the guard rail in front of the ditch is 1 foot 6 inches in height.

STEEPLECHASING

Golden Miller won the Cheltenham Gold Cup on 14 March 1935 in very heavy conditions carrying 12 stone over 3 miles 3 furlongs in 6 minutes 30 seconds, so averaging an unsurpassed 31·15 m.p.h.

HURLING

Earliest reference A game of very ancient origin, hurling only became standardized with the formation of the Gaelic Athletic Association in Thurles, Ireland, on 1 Nov. 1884.

Most titles The greatest number of All-Ireland Championships won by one team is 21 shared by Tipperary in 1887, 1895–96, 1898–99–1900, 1906, 1908, 1916, 1925, 1930, 1937, 1945, 1949–50–51, 1958, 1961–62 and 1964–65 and by Cork in 1890, 1892–93–94, 1902–03, 1919, 1926, 1928–29, 1931, 1941–42–43–44, 1946, 1952–53–54, 1966 and 1970. The greatest number of successive wins is the four by Cork (1941–44).

Highest score The highest score in an All-Ireland final was in 1896 when Tipperary (8 goals, 14 points) beat Dublin (no goals, 4 points). The record aggregate score was when Cork (6 goals, 21 points) defeated Wexford (5 goals, 10 points) in 1970. A goal equals 3 points.

Lowest score The lowest score in an All-Ireland final was when Tipperary (1 goal, 1 point) beat Galway (nil) in the first championship at Birr in 1887.

Most The most appearances in All-Ireland finals is ten shared by Christy Ring (Cork) and John Doyle (Tipperary). They also share the record of All-Ireland medals won with 8 each. Ring's appearances on the winning side were in 1941–42–43–44, 1946 and 1952–53–54, while Doyle's were in 1949–50–51, 1958, 1961–62 and 1964–65.

Individual score The highest recorded individual score was by Nick Rackard (Wexford), who scored 7 goals and 7 points against Antrim in the 1954 All-Ireland semi-final.

Largest crowd The largest crowd was 84,856 for the final between Cork and Wexford at Croke Park, Dublin, in 1954.

Inter-provincials Munster holds the greatest number of inter-provincial (Railway Cup) championships with 32 (1928–1970). Christy Ring (Cork and Munster) played in a record 22 finals (1942–1963) and was on the winning side 18 times.

Longest stroke The greatest distance for a "lift and stroke" is one of 129 yards credited to Tom Murphy of Three Castles, Kilkenny, in a "long puck" contest in 1906. The record for the annual *An Poc Fada* (Long Puck) contest (instituted 1961) in the ravines of the Cooley Hills, north of Dundalk, County Louth, is 65 pucks (drives) plus 87 yards over the course of 3 miles 320 yards by Fionnbar O'Neill (Cork) in 1966. This represents an average of 84·8 yards per drive.

ICE HOCKEY

Origins There is pictorial evidence that hockey was played on ice in the 17th century in The Netherlands. The game was probably first played in North America in 1860 at Kingston, Ontario, Canada, but Montreal and Halifax also lay claim to priority.

Olympic Games Canada has won the Olympic title six times (1920–24–28–32–48–52) and the world title 19 times, the last being at Geneva in 1961. The longest Olympic career is that of Richard Torriani (Switzerland) from 1928 to 1948. The most gold medals won by any player is two, this was achieved by nine U.S.S.R. players in the 1968 Games, who had been in the 1964 gold medal team.

Stanley Cup The Stanley Cup, presented by the Governor-General Lord Stanley (original cost $48·67), became emblematic of world professional team supremacy several years after the first contest at Montreal in 1893. It has been won most often by the Montreal Canadiens [*sic*], with 17 wins in 1916, 1924, 1930, 1931, 1944, 1946, 1953, 1956 (winning a record 45 games), 1957, 1958, 1959, 1960, 1965, 1966, 1968, 1969 and 1971. Henri Richard and Jean Beliveau played in their tenth finals in 1971.

Longest match The longest match was 2 hours 56 minutes 30 seconds when Detroit Red Wings eventually beat Montreal Maroons 1–0 in the sixth period of overtime at the Forum, Montreal, at 2.25 a.m. on 25 March 1936.

Most goals Ottawa defeated Dawson City 23–2 at Ottawa on 16 Jan. 1905.

Most cup goals in a season: 76 goals by Phil Esposito of the Boston Bruins in 1970–71. The most points in a season is 152 (76 goals and 76 assists) by Phil Esposito (Boston Bruins) also in 1970–71. The North American career record for goals is 786 by Gordie Howe (b. 1928) (Detroit Red Wings) in 25 seasons ending in 1970–71. He has also collected 500 stitches in his face. Two players have scored 1,000 goals in Great Britain—Chick Zamick (Nottingham Panthers and Wembley Lions) and George Beach (Wembley Monarchs and later Wembley Lions).

Fastest scoring Toronto scored 8 goals against the New York Americans in 4 minutes 52 seconds on 19 March 1938. Bill Mosienko (Chicago) scored three goals in 21 seconds against New York Rangers on 23 March 1952.

Fastest player The highest speed measured for any player is 29·7 m.p.h. for Bobby Hull (Chicago Black Hawks). The highest puck speed is also attributed to Hull, whose left-handed slap shot has been measured at 118·3 m.p.h.

BRITISH LEAGUE

The highest score on record was when Streatham beat Racing Club de Paris 23–3 in 1949–50. Bud McEachern shot seven goals for Streatham.

Most wins The British League championship (instituted 1934 but ended in 1960) has been won most often by the Wembley Lions with four victories in 1936–37, 1952 and 1957.

ICE SKATING

Origins The earliest reference to ice skating is that of a Danish writer dated 1134. The earliest English account of 1180 refers to skates made of bone. Metal blades date from probably *c.* 1600. The earliest skating club was the Edinburgh Skating Club formed in 1742. The earliest artificial ice rink in the world was the "Glaciarium" in Chelsea, London, in 1876.

Longest race The longest race regularly held is the "Elfstedentocht" ("Tour of the Eleven Towns") in the Netherlands. It covers 200 kilometres (124 miles 483 yards) and the fastest time is 7 hours 35 minutes by Jeen van den Berg (b. 8 Jan. 1928) on 3 Feb. 1954.

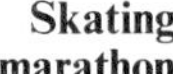

Skating marathon The longest recorded skating marathon is one of 279·46 miles (35 hours) by Colin Thomson at the Silver

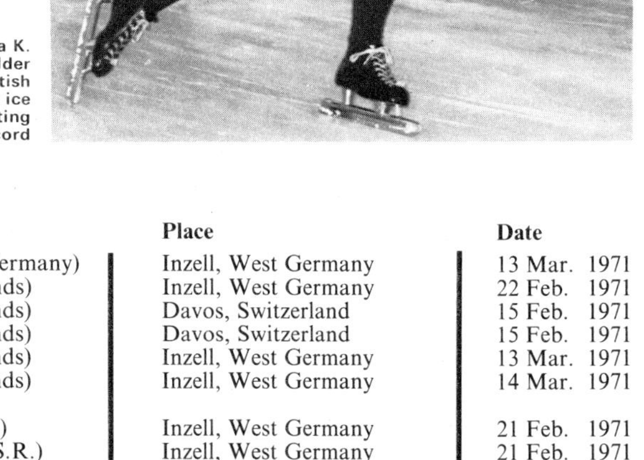

Patricia K. Tipper, holder of every British women's ice speed skating record

WORLD SPEED SKATING RECORDS

	Distance	mins. secs.	Name and Nationality	Place	Date
MEN	500 metres	38·42*	Erhard Keller (West Germany)	Inzell, West Germany	13 Mar. 1971
	1,000 metres	1:18·80	Ard Schenk (Netherlands)	Inzell, West Germany	22 Feb. 1971
	1,500 metres	1:58·70	Ard Schenk (Netherlands)	Davos, Switzerland	15 Feb. 1971
	3,000 metres	4:12·00	Ard Schenk (Netherlands)	Davos, Switzerland	15 Feb. 1971
	5,000 metres	7:12·00	Ard Schenk (Netherlands)	Inzell, West Germany	13 Mar. 1971
	10,000 metres	14:55·96	Ard Schenk (Netherlands)	Inzell, West Germany	14 Mar. 1971
WOMEN	500 metres	42·75	Anne Henning (U.S.A.)	Inzell, West Germany	21 Feb. 1971
	1,000 metres	1:27·70	Ludmilla Titova (U.S.S.R.)	Inzell, West Germany	21 Feb. 1971
	1,500 metres	2:17·82	Nina Statkevich (U.S.S.R.)	Medeo, U.S.S.R.	17 Jan. 1970
	3,000 metres	4:50·30	Ans Schut (Netherlands)	Inzell, West Germany	23 Feb. 1969
	5,000 metres	9:01·60	Rimma Zhukova (U.S.S.R.)	Medeo, U.S.S.R.	24 Jan. 1953

BRITISH OUTDOOR RECORDS

	Distance	mins. secs.	Name	Place	Date
MEN	500 metres	40·90	A. John Tipper	Cortina d'Ampezzo, Italy	28 Jan. 1970
	1,000 metres	1:24·00	A. John Tipper	Cortina d'Ampezzo, Italy	27 Jan. 1970
	1,500 metres	2:08·40	A. John Tipper	Cortina d'Ampezzo, Italy	28 Jan. 1970
	3,000 metres	4:34·70	John B. Blewitt	Cortina d'Ampezzo, Italy	16 Jan. 1968
	5,000 metres	7:57·10	Terence A. Malkin	Oslo, Norway	12 Feb. 1964
	10,000 metres	16:30·10	Terence A. Malkin	Oslo, Norway	19 Jan. 1964
WOMEN	500 metres	51·90	Patricia K. Tipper	Cortina d'Ampezzo, Italy	16 Jan. 1968
	1,000 metres	1:44·20	Patricia K. Tipper	Inzell, West Germany	7 Jan. 1968
	1,500 metres	2:42·80	Patricia K. Tipper	Cortina d'Ampezzo, Italy	17 Dec. 1967
	3,000 metres	5:39·40	Patricia K. Tipper	Cortina d'Ampezzo, Italy	16 Dec. 1967

* *This represents a speed of 29·11 m.p.h.*

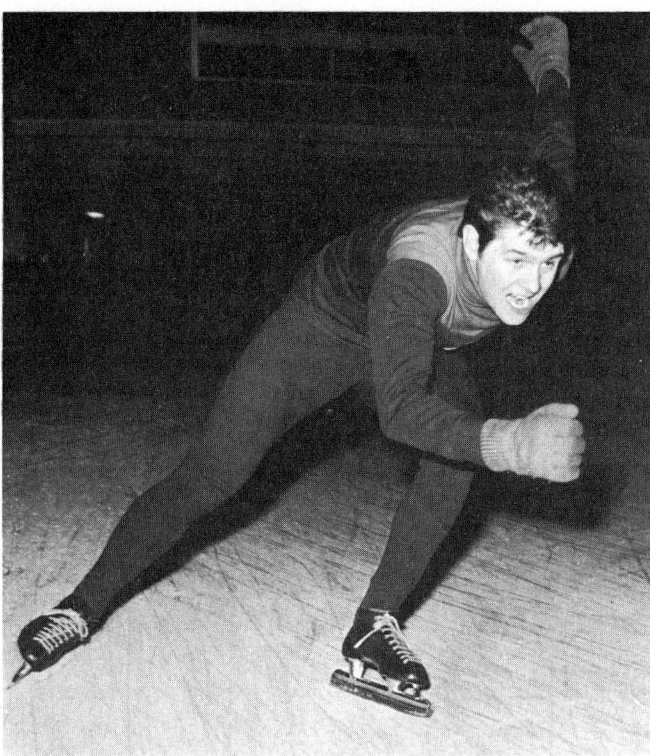

A. John Tipper, Britain's fastest ever sprint speed skater

Blades Ice Rink, Streatham, London on 14–15 June 1971. He was accompanied by Teny Yeo and Peter Bruce through the first 100 miles in 9 hours 7 minutes.

Largest rink The world's largest indoor ice rink is the Tōkyō Ice Rink, completed in 1960, which has an ice area of 43,000 sq. ft. (or 0·99 of an acre). The largest artificial outdoor rink is the Fujikyu Highland Promenade Rink, Japan opened at a cost of £335,000 in 1967 and with an area of 165,750 square feet (3·8 acres). The largest in the U.K. is the Crossmyloof Ice Rink, Glasgow, with an ice area of 225 feet by 97 feet.

SPEED SKATING

Most titles World The greatest number of world speed skating titles (instituted 1893) won by any skater is five by Oscar Mathisen (Norway) in 1908–09 and 1912–14, and Clas Thunberg (b. 5 April 1893) of Finland, in 1923, 1925, 1928–29 and 1931. The most titles won by a woman is four by Mrs. Inga Voronina, *née* Artomonova (1936–66) of Moscow, U.S.S.R., in 1957, 1958, 1962 and 1965.

Olympic The most Olympic gold medals won in speed skating is six by Lidia Skoblikova (b. 8 March 1939) of Chelyaminsk, U.S.S.R., in 1960 (2) and 1964 (4).

FIGURE SKATING

World The greatest number of world men's figure skating titles (instituted 1896) is ten by Ulrich Salchow (b. 7 Aug. 1877) of Sweden, in 1901–05 and 1907–11. The women's record (instituted 1906) is ten titles by Frk. Sonja Henie (b. 8 April 1912) of Norway, between 1927 and 1936.

Olympic The most Olympic gold medals won by a figure skater is three by Gillis Graftström (b. 7 June 1893) of Sweden in 1920, 1924 and 1928 (also silver medal in 1932); and by Sonja Henie (see above) in 1928, 1932 and 1936.

British The record number of British titles is 11 by Jack Page (Manchester S.C.) in 1922–31 and 1933, and six by Miss Cecilia Colledge (Park Lane F.S.C., London) in 1935–36–37(2)–38 and 1946.

ICE YACHTING

Origin The sport originated in The Netherlands from the year 1600 (earliest patent granted) and along the Baltic coast. The earliest authentic record is Dutch, dating from 1768. The largest known ice yacht was *Icicle*, built for Commodore John E. Roosevelt for racing on the Hudson River, New York, in *c.* 1870. It was 68 feet 11 inches long and carried 1,070 square feet of canvas. The highest speed officially recorded is 143 m.p.h. by John D. Buckstaff in a Class A stern-steerer on Lake Winnebago, Wisconsin, U.S.A., in 1938. Such a speed is possible in a wind of 72 m.p.h.

JUDO (JIU-JITSU)

Origins Judo is a modern combat sport which developed out of an amalgam of several old Japanese fighting arts, the most popular of which was ju-jitsu (jiu-jitsu), which is thought to be of pre-Christian Chinese origin. Judo has been greatly developed by the Japanese since 1882, when it was first devised by *Shihan* Dr. Jigoro Kano. World championships were inaugurated in 1956. Great Britain has won most consecutive European championships (instituted in 1951) with 3 victories (1957–58–59). France won in 1951–52, 1954–55 and 1962.

Highest grade The efficiency grades in Judo are divided into pupil (*kyu*) and master (*dan*) grades. The highest awarded is the extremely rare red belt *Judan* (*10th dan*), given only to seven men. The Judo protocol provides for an *11th dan* (*Juichidan*) who also would wear a red belt and even a *12th dan* who would wear a white belt twice as wide as an ordinary belt, but these have never been bestowed. The highest British native honorary grade is *7th dan* by Trevor P. Leggett.

Heaviest champion The heaviest world champion was Antonius (Anton) J. Geesink (b. 6 April 1934) of The Netherlands, who won the 1964 Olympic open title in Tōkyō at a weight of 17 stone. He was 19 stone in 1965 and stands 6 feet 6 inches tall.

KARATE

Origins Originally *karate* (empty hand) is known to have been developed by the unarmed populace as a method of attack on, and defence against, armed oppressors in Okinawa, in the Ryukyu Islands, in the 17th century. It is accepted that it may have been of Chinese origin. It was introduced into Japan in 1916. The four major schools of *Karate* in Japan are *Shotokan*, *Wado-ryu*, *Goju-ryu* and *Shito-ryu*. Military *Karate* for killing, as used by Korean troops, is *tae kwan do*.

Top exponents The only winner of two All-Japanese titles was Hirokazu Kanazawa (*6th dan*) in 1957 and 1958. He won his first title with a broken arm. The highest *dan* among *karatekas* is Yamaguchi Gogen (b. 1907) a *10th dan* of the Goju-ryu Karate Do.

The leading exponents in the United Kingdom are Tatsuo Suzuki (*7th dan*, *Wado-ryu*), chief instructor to the All-Britain Karate-Do Association; Hirokazu Kanazawa (*5th dan*, *Shotokan*), resident instructor to the K.U.G.B. (Karate Union of Great Britain); and Steve Arneil (b. in South Africa), who is a *5th dan*.

Greatest force The force needed to break a brick with the abductor digiti quinti muscle of the hand is normally 130–140 lb. The highest measured impact is 196 lb.

LACROSSE

Origin The game is of American Indian origin, derived from the inter-tribal game *baggataway*, and was played before 1492 by Iroquois Indians in lower Ontario, Canada and upper New York State, U.S.A. It was introduced into Great Britain in 1867. The English Lacrosse Union was formed in 1892. The Oxford *v.* Cambridge match was instituted in 1903 and the game was included in the Olympic Games of 1908 and featured as an exhibition sport in the 1928 and 1948 Games.

World championship The first World Tournament was held at Toronto, Canada in 1967 and the U.S.A. won.

Longest throw The longest recorded throw is 162·86 yards by Barney Quinn of Ottawa on 10 Sept. 1892.

Most titles The English Club Championship (Iroquois Cup), instituted in 1890, has been won most often by Stockport with 15 wins between 1897 and 1934.

Highest score The highest score in any international match was England's 18–2 win over Wales at Cardiff in 1907.

The record number of international representations for England is 13 by G. A. MacDonald of Mellor, Cheshire to 1967. (No internationals were played in 1968.)

Mrs. Margaret Court, winner of the record number of major championships

LAWN TENNIS

Origins The modern game is generally agreed to have evolved as an outdoor form of Tennis (see separate entry) and to have first become organized with the court and equipment devised, and patented in February 1874, by Major Walter Clopton Wingfield, M.V.O. (1833–1912). This was introduced as "sphairistike" but the game soon became known as lawn tennis. Open lawn tennis was introduced in 1968.

ALL TIME RECORDS

GREATEST DOMINATION

The earliest occasion upon which any player secured all four of the world's major titles was in 1935 when Frederick John Perry (U.K.) won the French title having won Wimbledon (1934), the United States title (1933–34) and the Australian title (1934).

The earliest example of a man holding all four titles at the same time was J. Donald Budge (U.S.A.) who won the championships of Wimbledon (1937), the U.S.A. (1937), Australia (1938), France (1938). He subsequently retained Wimbledon (1938) and the U.S.A. (1938). Rodney George Laver (Australia) repeated the grand slam of the four major championships in 1962 and again, when the events were open, in 1969.

The first example of a woman player holding all four titles at the same time was Miss Maureen Catherine Connolly (1935–1969) (U.S.A.). She won the United States title in 1951, Wimbledon in 1952, retained the U.S. title in 1952, won the Australian in 1953, the French in 1953 and Wimbledon again in 1953. She won her third U.S. title in 1953, her second French title in 1954, and her third Wimbledon title in 1954. Miss Connolly (later Mrs. Norman Brinker) was seriously injured in a riding accident shortly before the 1954 U.S. championships and died in June 1969 aged only 34.

In the course of her playing career (from 1960) Miss Margaret Jean Smith (later Mrs. Barry M. Court, M.B.E.) (Australia) won the singles, the women's doubles and the mixed doubles titles in all four of the leading championships, those of Australia, France, Wimbledon and the U.S. She won a total of 53 titles in all at these meetings, including all four singles in 1970.

MOST GAMES

Singles match The greatest number of games ever played in a singles match is 126. Roger Taylor (U.K.) beat Wieslaw Gasiorek (Poland) 27–29, 31–29, 6–4 on an indoor court in Warsaw, Poland, on 5 Nov, 1966, in a King's Cup tie. The match lasted 4 hours 35 minutes.

Doubles match The greatest number of games ever played in a doubles match is 147. Dick Leach and Dick Dell of Michigan University beat Tommy Mozur and Lenny Schloss 3–6, 49–47, 22–20 at Newport, Rhode Island, U.S.A. on 18–19 Aug. 1967.

Longest match Mark Cox and Robert K. Wilson (G.B.) beat Charles M. Pasarell and Ron E. Holmberg (U.S.A.) 26–24, 17–19, 30–28 in a match lasting 6 hours 23 minutes at the U.S. Indoor Championships at Salisbury, Maryland on 16 Feb. 1968.

Fastest service The fastest service ever *measured* was one of 154 m.p.h. by Michael J. Sangster (U.K.) in June 1963. Crossing the net the ball was travelling at 108 m.p.h. Some players consider the service of Robert Falkenberg (U.S.A.) the 1948 Wimbledon Champion as the fastest ever used.

Greatest crowd The greatest crowd at a tennis match was 25,578 at the first day of the Davis Cup Challenge Round between Australia and the United States at the White City, Sydney, New South Wales, Australia, on 27 Dec. 1954.

WIMBLEDON RECORDS

(The first Championship was in June 1877. Professionals first played in 1968.) *Note:* From 1971 the likelihood of long matches and sets were deliberately diminished by the introduction of a tie-break system, which prevents most sets from proceeding beyond a 17th game (*i.e.* 9–8).

MOST GAMES

Singles The most games in a singles match at Wimbledon was 112 when Ricardo Alonzo Gonzalez (United States)

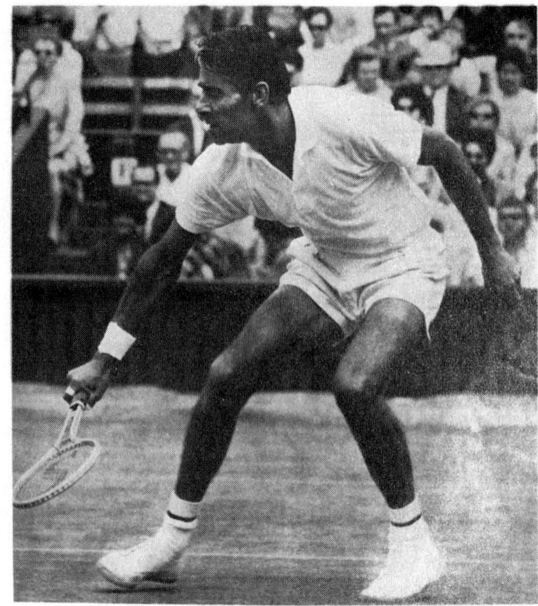

Pancho Gonzalez, winner of Wimbledon's longest ever match

beat Charles M. Pasarell (United States) 22–24, 1–6, 16–14, 6–3, 11–9 in the first round on 24–25 June 1969. The match, which was interrupted by nightfall, lasted a Wimbledon record total of 5 hours and 12 minutes.

Doubles The most games in a doubles match at Wimbledon was 98 when Eugene L. Scott (U.S.A.) and Nicola Pilic (Yugoslavia) beat G. Cliff Richey (U.S.A.) and Torben Ulrich (Denmark) by 19–21, 12–10, 6–4, 4–6, 9–7 in the first round of the men's doubles on 22 June 1966.

Set The most games in a set at Wimbledon was 62 when Pancho Segura (Ecuador) and Alex Olmedo (Peru) beat Abe A. Segal and Gordon L. Forbes (South Africa) 32–30 in a second round match in 1968.

MOST GAMES IN FINALS

The most games in a Wimbledon men's singles final was 58 when Jaroslav Drobny (then Egypt) beat Kenneth R. Rosewall (Australia) 13–11, 4–6, 6–2, 9–7 in 1954.

The most games in a Wimbledon ladies' singles final was 46 when Mrs. Barry M. Court, M.B.E., 27, beat Mrs. L. W. King (U.S.A.) by 14–12, 11–9 on 3 July 1970 in a match lasting 2 hours 25 minutes.

The most games in a Wimbledon men's doubles final was 70 when John D. Newcombe and Anthony D. Roche (Australia) beat Kenneth R. Rosewall and Frederick S. Stolle (Australia) 3–6, 8–6, 5–7, 14–12, 6–3 in 1968.

The most games in a Wimbledon ladies' doubles final was 38, on two occasions. Mme. Simone Mathieu (France) and Miss Elizabeth ("Bunny") Ryan (U.S.A.) beat Miss Freda James (now Mrs. S. H. Hammersley) and Miss Adeline Maud Yorke (now Mrs. D. E. C. Eyres) (both U.K.) by 6–2, 9–11, 6–4 in 1933, and Miss Rosemary Casals and Mrs. Billie Jean King (U.S.A.) beat Miss Maria Bueno (Brazil) and Miss Nancy Richey (U.S.A.) 9–11, 6–4, 6–2 in 1967.

The most games in a Wimbledon mixed doubles final was 48 when Eric W. Sturgess and Mrs. Sheila Summers (South Africa) beat John E. Bromwich (Australia) and Miss A. Louise Brough (U.S.A.) 9–7, 9–11, 7–5 in 1949.

Longest match The longest Wimbledon match was the 5 hours 12 minutes required by the Gonzalez *v.* Pasarell match (*see* Most games, singles).

Youngest champions The youngest ever champion at Wimbledon was Miss Charlotte Dod (1871–1960), who was 15 years 8 months when she won in 1887.

The youngest male singles champion was Wilfred Baddeley (b. 11 Jan. 1872) who won the Wimbledon title in 1891 at the age of 19.

Richard Dennis Ralston (b. 27 July 1942) of Bakersfield, California, U.S.A. was 25 days short of his 18th birthday when he won the men's doubles with Rafael H. Osuna (1938–1969) of Mexico in 1960.

Most appearances Arthur W. Gore (1868–1928) of the U.K. made 36 appearances between 1888 and 1927, and was in 1909 at 41 years the oldest ever singles winner. In 1964, Jean Borotra (b. 13 Aug. 1898) of France made his 35th appearance since 1922.

Most wins Miss Elizabeth Ryan (U.S.A.) won her first title in 1914 and her nineteenth in 1934 (12 women's doubles with 5 different partners and 7 mixed doubles with 5 different partners).

The greatest number of wins by a man at Wimbledon has been 14 by William Charles Renshaw (b. 1861) (G.B.) who won 7 singles titles (1881–2–3–4–5–6–9) and 7 doubles (1880–1–4–5–6–8–9), partnered by his twin brother (James) Ernest. Hugh Lawrence Doherty (1875–1919) won 5 singles (1902–3–4–5–6), 8 men's doubles (1897–8–9–1900–01 and 1903–4–5), partnered by his brother Reginald Frank Doherty (1872–1910), and two mixed doubles (then unofficial) in 1901–02, partnered by Mrs. A. Sterry.

J. Ernest Renshaw, who contributed as doubles partner to his twin brother's Wimbledon record of 14 titles

The greatest number of singles wins was eight by Mrs. F. S. Moody (*née* Helen N. Wills), now Mrs. Aiden Roark, of the U.S.A., who won in 1927, 1928, 1929, 1930, 1932, 1933, 1935 and 1938.

The greatest number of singles wins by a man was seven by William C. Renshaw (G.B.), as quoted above.

The greatest number of doubles wins by men was 8 by the brothers R. F. and H. L. Doherty (G.B.). They won each year from 1897 to 1905 except for 1902.

The most wins in women's doubles were 12 by Miss Elizabeth Ryan (U.S.A.) between 1914 and 1934 (see above).

The most wins in mixed doubles was 7 by Miss Elizabeth Ryan (U.S.A.) between 1919 and 1932. The male record is four wins shared by Elias Victor Seixas

(U.S.A.) in 1953–54–55–56 and Kenneth N. Fletcher (Australia) in 1963–65–66–68.

Professional tennis The professional game became established in 1934 with William Tatem Tilden II (1893–1953) and H. Ellsworth Vines (both U.S.A.). The longest domination was achieved by Ricardo Alonzo ("Pancho") Gonzalez (b. 9 May 1928) of the U.S.A., who was ranked No. 1 for 8 years, from 1954 to 1961.

Lawn tennis marathons The longest recorded non-stop lawn tennis doubles game is one of 28 hours by Ian Fetters, 18; Norman Pillans, 18; Iain Beattie, 16 and Douglas Wilson, 23, of Raith L.T.C., Kirkcaldy on 26–27 June 1971. The duration record for the maintenance of continuous singles by 4 players is 50 hours 1 minute by Chris Dalleson, Chris Goodes, Ray Turner and Stuart Richards of Conway L.T.C., Southgate, Greater London, ending at 8.01 p.m. on 15 July 1971.

DAVIS CUP

Most victories The greatest number of wins in the Davis Cup (instituted 1900) has been (inclusive of 1970) Australia and Australasia 22 times and U.S.A. 22 times. The British Isles/Great Britain have won 9 times, in 1903–04–05–06, 1912, 1933–34–35–36.

Individual performance Nicola Pietrangeli (Italy) played 161 rubbers, 1954 to 1971, winning 117. He played 110 singles (winning 77) and 51 doubles (winning 40). He took part in 63 ties.

Greatest number of games In a tie the greatest number of games played was 281 in Perth in 1960 when in the Inter-Zone final Italy beat the U.S.A. 3–2.

In a match the greatest number of games played was 95 when at Edgbaston, Birmingham in 1969 in the quarter-final of the European Zone Wilhelm Bungert and Christian Kuhnke (Germany) beat Mark Cox and Peter Curtis (Great Britain) 10–8, 17–19, 13–11, 3–6, 6–2.

In a singles match the greatest number of games played was 86 when at Cleveland, Ohio, in the 1970 Challenge Round, Arthur Ashe (U.S.A.) beat Christian Kuhnke (Germany) 6–8, 10–12, 9–7, 13–11, 6–4.

MODERN PENTATHLON

Points scores in riding, fencing, cross country and hence overall scores have no comparative value between one competition and another. In shooting and swimming (300 metres) the scores are of record significance.

The Modern Pentathlon (Riding, Fencing, Shooting, Swimming and Running) was inaugurated into the Olympic Games at Stockholm in 1912. The Modern Pentathlon Association of Great Britain was formed in 1922.

MOST TITLES

World The record number of world titles won is 5 by András Balczo (Hungary) in 1963, 1965, 1966, 1967 and 1969.

British The pentathlete with most British titles is Sgt. Jeremy Robert Fox, R.E.M.E. (b. 1941) with 6 (1963, 1965, 1966, 1967, 1968 and 1970).

	World			British		
Shooting	1,066	P. Macken (Australia) and R. Phelps (U.K.), Leipzig	21 Sept. 1965	1,066	R. Phelps, Leipzig	21 Sept. 1965
	1,066	I. Mona (Hungary), Jönköping	11 Sept. 1967			
Swimming	1,240	C. Richards (U.S.A.), Warendorf, West Germany	4 Aug. 1970	1,042	L/Cpl. B. Lillywhite, Melbourne	Oct. 1966

MOTORCYCLING

Earliest races The first motorcycle race was one from Paris to Dieppe, France, in 1897. The oldest motorcycle races in the world are the Auto-Cycle Union Tourist Trophy (T.T.) series, first held on the 15¾-mile "Peel" ("St. John's") course in the Isle of Man in 1907, and still run in the island, on the "Mountain" circuit (37·73 miles) and, until 1959, on the Clypse circuit of 10·79 miles.

FASTEST CIRCUITS

World The highest average lap speed attained on any closed circuit is 157·343 m.p.h. by Eugene R. "Burrito" Romero (b. Martinez, California, U.S.A., 22 May 1947) when he lapped the 2·50-mile Daytona International Speedway, Daytona Beach, Florida, U.S.A., which is banked at 31 degrees, in 57·20 seconds on a 741 c.c. three-cylinder Triumph Trident, in practice, on 12 March 1970.

The fastest road circuit is the Francorchamps circuit near Spa, Belgium. It is 14·10 kilometres (8 miles 1,340 yards) in length and was lapped in 4 minutes 1·4 seconds (average speed of 130·658 m.p.h.) by Giacomo Agostini (b. Lovere, Italy, 16 June 1942) on a 500 c.c. three-cylinder M.V.-Agusta on lap 7 of the 500 c.c. Belgian Grand Prix on 6 July 1969.

United Kingdom The fastest circuit in the United Kingdom is the 10·637-mile Portstewart-Coleraine-Portrush circuit in Londonderry, Northern Ireland. The race lap record is 5 minutes 50·6 seconds (average speed 109·222 m.p.h.) by Ralph Bryans (b. Belfast, Northern Ireland, 7 March 1942) on a 250 c.c. six-cylinder Honda, during the North-West 200, on 18 May 1968. Rodney Alfred Gould (b. Banbury, Oxfordshire, 10 March 1943) lapped in 5 minutes 47·6 seconds (110·165 m.p.h.) on a 350 c.c. parallel twin TR2 Yamaha, in practice, on 22 May 1969.

The record for the outer circuit lap (2·767 miles) at the Brooklands Motor Course near Weybridge, Surrey (open between 1907 and 1939) was 80·0 seconds (average speed 124·51 m.p.h.) by Noel Baddow "Bill" Pope (later Major) (1909–1971) of the United Kingdom on a Brough Superior powered by a supercharged 996 c.c. V-twin "8–80" J.A.P. engine developing 110 b.h.p., on 4 July 1939. The race lap record for the outer circuit at Brooklands was 80·6 seconds (average speed 123·588 m.p.h.) by Eric Crudgington Fernihough (1905–1938) of the United Kingdom on a Brough Superior powered by an unsupercharged 996 c.c. V-twin J.A.P. engine, on 28 July 1935.

FASTEST RACES

World The fastest race in the world was held over 10 laps of the A.V.U.S. track, Berlin, East Germany (5 miles 273 yards lap). It was won by H. Reginald Armstrong of Dublin in 24 minutes 23·3 seconds (average speed 126·882 m.p.h.) on a 493 c.c. four-cylinder Gilera, on 16 September 1956.

The fastest road race is the 500 c.c. Belgian Grand Prix held on the Francorchamps circuit (8 miles 1,340 yards) near Spa, Belgium. The record for this 13-lap (113·898 miles) race is 54 minutes 18·1 seconds (average speed 125·850 m.p.h.) by Giacomo Agostini, on a 500 c.c. three-cylinder M.V.-Agusta, on 6 July 1969.

United Kingdom The fastest race in the United Kingdom is the 350 c.c. event of the North-West 200 held on the Londonderry circuit (see above). The record for this 7-lap (74·459 miles) race is 41 minutes 25·0 seconds (average speed 107·868 m.p.h.) by Rodney Gould on a 350 c.c. parallel twin TR2 Yamaha on 24 May 1969.

Longest race The longest race is the 24 heures Bol d'Or at Montlhéry, Paris, France (3 miles 1,610 yards lap). The greatest distance ever covered is 1,835·95 miles (average speed 76·498 m.p.h.) by Thomas Dickie and Paul Anthony Smart on a 741 c.c. three-cylinder Triumph Trident on 12–13 Sept. 1970.

Longest circuit The 37·73-mile "Mountain" circuit, over which the two main T.T. races have been run since 1911, has 264 curves and corners and is the longest used for any motorcycle race.

MOST SUCCESSFUL RIDERS

The record number of victories in the Isle of Man T.T. races is 12 by Stanley Michael Bailey Hailwood, M.B.E. (b. Oxford, 2 April 1940), now of Durban, South Africa, between 1961 and 1967. The first man to win three consecutive T.T. titles in two events was James A. Redman (Rhodesia) (b. Hampstead, London, 8 Nov. 1931). He won the 250 c.c. and 350 c.c. events in 1963–64–65. Mike Hailwood is the only man to win three events in one year, in 1961 and 1967.

World championships Most world championship titles (instituted by the *Fédération Internationale Motorcycliste* in 1949) won are:

10 Giacomo Agostini (Italy)
350 c.c. 1968, 69, 70, 71
500 c.c. 1966, 67, 68, 69, 70, 71.

Giacomo Agostini is the only man to win two world championships in four consecutive years (350 and 500 c.c. titles in 1968–69–70–71).

Giacomo Agostini won 77 races in the world championship series between 1965 and 26 June 1971, including a record 19 in 1970, also achieved by Mike Hailwood in 1966.

Trials Sammy Hamilton Miller (b. Belfast, Northern Ireland, 11 Nov. 1935), won eleven A.-C.U. Solo Trials Drivers' Stars in 1959–60–61–62–63–64–65–66–67–68–69.

Scrambles Jeffrey Vincent Smith, M.B.E. (b. Colne, Lancashire, 14 Oct. 1934) won nine A.-C.U. 500 c.c. Scrambles Stars in 1955–56, 1960–61–62–63–64–65 and 1967.

Torsten Hallman (b. Uppsala, Sweden, 1939) and Joel Robert (b. Belgium, 1943) have each won four 250 c.c. moto-cross world championships, 1962–63, 1966–67 and 1964, 1968–69–70 respectively. Joel Robert won a record 38th 250 c.c. Grand Prix on 23 May 1971.

Most successful machines Italian M.V.-Agusta machines won 32 world championships between 1952 and 1970 and 222 world championship races between 1952 and 1970. Japanese Honda machines won 29 world championship races and five world championships in 1966.

SPEED RECORDS

The official world speed record (average speed for two runs over a 1 kilometre course) is 224·569 m.p.h. (average time 9·961 seconds) by Bill A. Johnson, aged 38, of Garden Grove, Los Angeles, California, U.S.A., riding a Triumph Bonneville T120 streamliner, with a 667·25 c.c. parallel twin-cylinder engine running on methanol and nitro-methane and developing 75 to 80 b.h.p., at Bonneville Salt Flats, Tooele County, Utah, U.S.A., on 5 Sept. 1962. His machine was 17 feet long and weighed 400 lb. His first run was made in 9·847 seconds (227·169 m.p.h.).

Calvin G. Rayborn (b. San Diego, California, U.S.A., 20 Feb. 1940) recorded higher speeds over the measured mile, without F.I.M. observers, at Bonneville on 16 Oct. 1970 riding his 10-foot 3-inch long, 1,480 c.c. V-twin Harley-Davidson streamliner running on methanol and nitro-methane. On the first run he covered the mile in 13·494 seconds (266·785 m.p.h.). On the second run his time was 13·626 seconds (264·201 m.p.h.). The average time for the two runs was 13·560 seconds (average speed 265·487 m.p.h.).

Robert Leppan, 32, of Detroit, achieved a speed of 268 m.p.h. over a measured mile one-way at Bonneville on 20 Oct. 1970 riding his 17-foot 9-inch long *Gyronaut X-1* streamliner powered by two 741 c.c. in-line three-cylinder Triumph Trident engines.

The world record for two runs over 1 kilometre (1,093·6 yards) from a standing start is 116·903 m.p.h. (19·135 seconds) by Alfred Joseph Hagon (b. Ilford, Essex, 3 Oct. 1931) on his supercharged 1,260 c.c. Hagon-J.A.P. V-twin developing 140 b.h.p., at Elvington Airfield, Yorkshire on 16 Oct. 1966. The faster run was made in 18·964 seconds.

On 27 Sept. 1970 at Elvington Dave Lecoq riding Drag-Waye averaged 19·02 seconds (117·610 m.p.h.), but failed to better the previous record by the necessary one per cent. margin.

The world record for two runs over 440 yards from a standing start is 92·879 m.p.h. (9·69 seconds) by Dave Lecoq on the supercharged 1,287 c.c. Drag-Waye powered by a flat-four Volkswagen engine developing 150 b.h.p., at Elvington Airfield, Yorkshire on 27 Sept. 1970. The faster run was made in 9·60 seconds.

The fastest time for a single run over 440 yards from a standing start is 8·68 seconds by E. J. Potter of Ithaca, Michigan, U.S.A., on his 5,359 c.c. Chevrolet Corvette V8 Special at Castlereagh Airstrip near Sydney, Australia on 26 Jan. 1970.

MOTOR RACING

Earliest races The first automobile trial was one of 20 miles from Paris to Versailles and back on 20 April 1887, won by Georges Bouton's steam quadricycle in 74 minutes, at an average of 16·22 m.p.h. The first "real" race was from Paris to Rouen on 23 July 1894. The winner was Count de Dion (France), driving a de Dion Bouton steam car at an average of 11·6 m.p.h.

The oldest motor race in the world, still being regularly run, is the R.A.C. Tourist Trophy (36th race held in 1971), first staged on 14 Sept. 1905 in the Isle of Man. The oldest continental races are the Targa Florio (55th in 1971), in Sicily, first held on 9 May 1906, and the French Grand Prix (49th in 1971), first held on 26–27 June 1906.

ackie Stewart, holder of the ace lap record on Britain's fastest circuit

FASTEST CIRCUITS

World The highest average lap speed attained on any closed circuit is 201·105 m.p.h. (47·617 seconds) by Bobby Isaac (U.S.A.) driving a 1969 Dodge Charger, powered by a 600 b.h.p., 426 cubic inch V8 engine, at the Alabama International Motor Speedway, Talladega, Alabama, U.S.A., in November 1970. The race lap average for this 2·66-mile, 33-degree banked tri-oval is also a record. On 14 Sept. 1969 it was lapped at over 195 m.p.h. during a 500-mile race by Richard Brickhouse (U.S.A.) driving a 1969 Dodge Daytona.

The fastest road circuit is the Francorchamps circuit near Spa, Belgium. It is 14·10 kilometres (8 miles 1,340 yards) in length and was lapped in 3 minutes 14·6 seconds (average speed 162·080 m.p.h.) during the Francorchamps 1,000 kilometre sports car race on 9 May 1971, by Joseph Siffert (b. Fribourg, Switzerland, 7 July 1936) driving a 4,990 c.c. flat-12 Porsche 917 Group 5 sports car.

United Kingdom The fastest circuit in the United Kingdom is the ex-aerodrome course of 2·927 miles at Silverstone, Northamptonshire (opened 1948). The race lap record is 1 minute 19·9 seconds (131·880 m.p.h.) by John Young "Jackie" Stewart (b. Milton, Dunbartonshire, 11 June 1939) driving a 2,993 c.c. Tyrrell-Cosworth V8 on lap 45 of the 24th British Grand Prix, on 17 June 1971. The practice lap record is 1 minute 17·0 seconds (136·847 m.p.h.) by Frank Gardner (b. Australia, 1927) driving a 7·9 litre Lola T260-Chevrolet Group 7 sports car early in June 1971.

The record for the outer circuit lap (2·767 miles) at the Brooklands Motor Course near Weybridge, Surrey (open between 1907 and 1939) was 1 minute 9·44 seconds (average speed 143·44 m.p.h.) by John Rhodes Cobb (1899–1952) in his 3-ton 23,856 c.c. Napier-Railton, with a Napier *Lion* 12-cylinder aero-engine developing 450 b.h.p., on 7 Oct. 1935. His average speed over a kilometre was 151·97 m.p.h. (14·72 seconds). The race lap record at Brooklands was 1 minute 9·6 seconds (average speed 143·11 m.p.h.) by Oliver Henry Julius Bertram (b. Kensington, London, 26 Feb. 1910), driving a 7,963 c.c. Barnato-Hassan Special (Bentley engine), during the 7-lap "Dunlop Jubilee Cup" handicap race on 24 Sept. 1938.

The Motor Industry Research Association (MIRA) High Speed Circuit (2·82-mile lap with 33-degree banking on the bends) at Lindley, Warwickshire, was lapped in 1 minute 2·8 seconds (average speed 161·655 m.p.h.) by Norman Dewis (b. 20 Aug. 1920) driving a Jaguar development car on an officially undisclosed date prior to 1967.

FASTEST RACES

World The fastest race in the world was the 50-mile event at the NASCAR Grand National meeting at the 2·50-mile, 31-degree banked Daytona International Speedway, Daytona Beach, Florida, U.S.A. on 8 Feb. 1964. It was won by Richard Petty (b. 2 July 1937) of Randleman, North Carolina in 17 minutes 27 seconds (average speed 171·920 m.p.h.), driving a 405 b.h.p. 1964 Plymouth V8.

The fastest road race is the Francorchamps 1,000 kilometre sports car race held on the Francorchamps circuit (8 miles 1,340 yards) near Spa, Belgium. The record time for this 71-lap (622·055 miles) race is 4 hours 1 minute 9·7 seconds (average speed 154·765 m.p.h.) by the Mexican, Pedro Rodriguez (1940–1971) and (Keith) Jack "Jackie" Oliver (b. Chadwell Heath, Essex, 14 Aug. 1942), driving a 4,990 c.c. flat-12 Porsche 917K Group 5 sports car, on 9 May 1971.

United Kingdom The fastest currently held race in the United Kingdom is the British Grand Prix. The record for this 68-lap (199·036-mile) race is 1 hour 31 minutes 31·5 seconds (average speed 130·480 m.p.h.) by Jackie Stewart, driving a 2,993 c.c. Tyrrell-Cosworth V8, at Silverstone (see left), in the 24th race, on 17 July 1971.

The fastest race ever held in the United Kingdom was the Broadcast Trophy Handicap held on the Brooklands outer circuit on 29 March 1937. The 29-mile race was won by John Cobb driving his 23,970 c.c. 12-cylinder Napier-Railton at an average speed of 136·03 m.p.h.

John R. Cobb, setting the Brooklands track record at 143·44 m.p.h.

TOUGHEST CIRCUITS

The Targa Florio (first run 1906) is widely acknowledged to be the most arduous race. Held on the Piccolo Madonie Circuit in Sicily, it now covers eleven laps (492·126 miles) and involves the negotiation of 9,350 corners, over severe mountain gradients, and narrow rough roads. The record time is 6 hours 35 minutes 30·0 seconds (average speed 74·659 m.p.h.) by Joseph Siffert and Brian Herman Thomas Redman (b. Burnley, Lancashire, 9 March 1937) driving a 2,997 c.c. flat-8 Porsche 908/3 Spyder Group 6 prototype sports car in the 54th race on 3 May 1970. The lap record is 33 minutes 36·0 seconds (average speed 79·890 m.p.h.) by Leo Juhani Kinnunen (b. Tampere, Finland, 5 Aug. 1943) on lap 11 of this race in a similar Porsche.

The most difficult Grand Prix circuit is generally regarded to be that for the Monaco Grand Prix (first run 1929), run round the streets and the harbour of Monte Carlo. It is 3,145 metres (1 mile 1,679 yards) in length and has ten pronounced corners and several

A British Bentley wins the Le Mans for the fifth time in 1930

sharp changes of gradient. The race is run over 80 laps (156·337 miles) and involves on average more than 2,000 gear changes. The record for the race is 1 hour 52 minutes 21·3 seconds (average speed 83·487 m.p.h.) by Jackie Stewart driving a 2,993 c.c. Tyrrell-Cosworth V8, on 23 May 1971. The lap record is 1 minute 22·2 seconds (average speed 85·586 m.p.h.) by Stewart on lap 57 of the above race.

LE MANS

The world's most important race for sports cars is the 24-hour *Grand Prix d'Endurance* (first held 1923) on the Sarthe circuit at Le Mans, France. The greatest distance ever covered is 3,315·210 miles (average speed 138·134 m.p.h.) by Dr. Helmut Marko (b. Austria, April 1943) and Gijs van Lennep (Netherlands) driving a 4,907 c.c. flat-12 Porsche 917K Group 5 sports car, on 12–13 June 1971. The race lap record (8 miles 650 yards lap) is 3 minutes 18·7 seconds (average speed 151·632 m.p.h.) by Pedro Rodriguez (1940–1971) driving a Porsche 917L on 12 June 1971. The record practice lap is 3 minutes 13·6 seconds (average speed 155·627 m.p.h.) by Jackie Oliver driving a similar car on 18 April 1971. The pre-war record average speed was 86·85 m.p.h. by a 3·3 litre Bugatti in 1939.

Most wins The race has been won by Ferrari cars nine times, in 1949, 1954, 1958 and 1960–61–62–63–64–65. The most wins by one man is four by Olivier Gendebien (b. 1924) (Belgium), who won in 1958 and 1960–61–62.

British wins The race has been won 12 times by British cars, thus: Bentley in 1924 and 1927–28–29–30, once by Lagonda in 1935, five times by Jaguar in 1951, 1953 and 1955–56–57 and once by Aston Martin in 1959.

INDIANAPOLIS 500

The Indianapolis 500-mile race (200 laps) was inaugurated in the U.S.A. in 1911. The most successful drivers have been Warren Wilbur Shaw (1902–1954), who won in 1937, 1939 and 1940, Louis Meyer, who won in 1928, 1933 and 1936, and Anthony Joseph Foyt, Jr. (b. Houston, Texas, U.S.A., 1935), who won in 1961, 1964 and 1967. Mauri Rose won in 1947 and 1948 and was the co-driver of Floyd Davis in 1941. The record time is 3 hours 10 minutes 11·56 seconds (average speed 157·735 m.p.h.) by Al Unser (b. Albuquerque, New Mexico, U.S.A., 30 May 1939) driving a 2·65 litre 700 b.h.p. turbocharged Johnny Lightning-P. J. Colt-Ford Special on 29 May 1971. He received $238,454·31 from a record prize fund of $1,001,604·22 for winning this, the 55th, race. The race lap record is 51·44 seconds (average speed 174·961 m.p.h.) by Mark Donohue of Media, Pennsylvania, U.S.A., driving a 2·6 litre 700 b.h.p. turbocharged McLaren M16-Offenhauser, on lap 66, on 29 May 1971. The practice lap record is 49·73 seconds (average speed 180·977 m.p.h.) by Donohue on 13 May 1971.

Fastest pit stop A. J. Foyt, Jr.'s first fuel stop on lap 14 during the Indianapolis 500 on 29 May 1971 took only 9 seconds.

Duration record The greatest distance ever covered in one year is 400,000 kilometres (248,548·5 miles) by François Lecot (1879–1949), an innkeeper from Rochetaillée, near Lyon, France, in an 11 c.v. Citroën (1,900 c.c., 66 b.h.p.), mainly between Paris and Monte Carlo, from 22 July 1935 to 26 July 1936. He drove on 363 of the 370 days.

The world's duration record is 185,353 miles 1,741 yards in 133 days 17 hours 37 minutes 38·64 seconds (average speed 58·07 m.p.h.) by Marchand, Presalé and six others in a Citroën on the Montlhéry track near Paris, France, during March–July 1933.

MOST SUCCESSFUL DRIVERS

Based on the World Drivers' Championships, inaugurated in 1950, the most successful driver is Juan-Manuel Fangio y Cia (b. Balcarce, Argentina, 24 June 1911) who won five times in 1951–54–55–56–57. He retired in 1958, after having won 24 Grand Prix races (2 shared). The most successful driver in terms of race wins is Stirling Craufurd Moss, O.B.E. (b. Paddington, London, 17 Sept. 1929), with 167 (11 shared) races won, including 16 Grand Prix victories (1 shared), from 18 Sept. 1948 to 11 Feb. 1962. Moss was awarded the annual Gold Star of the British Racing Drivers' Club in 1950–51–52, 1954–55–56–57–58–59 and 1961, a record total of ten awards.

Juan-Manuel Fangio (Argentina), 5 times winner of the World Drivers' Championships

The most Grand Prix victories is 25 by Jim Clark, O.B.E. (1936–1968) of Scotland between 17 June 1962 and 1 January 1968. Clark also holds the record for Grand Prix victories in one year with 7 in 1963. He won a record 61 Formula One and Formula Libre races between 1959 and 1968.

Oldest and youngest G.P. winners The youngest Grand Prix winner was Bruce Leslie McLaren (1937–1970) of New Zealand, who won the United States Grand Prix at Sebring, Florida, U.S.A. on 12 December 1959 aged 22 years 104 days. The oldest Grand Prix winner was Tazio Giorgio Nuvolari (1892–1953) of Italy, who won the Albi Grand Prix at Albi, France on 14 July 1946 aged 53 years 240 days. The oldest Grand Prix driver was Louis Alexandre Chiron, O. St.-C., L.d'H., C.d'I. (b. Monaco, 3 Aug. 1899), who finished 6th in the Monaco Grand Prix on 22 May 1955 aged 55 years 292 days.

The world's first long distance rally—Peking to Paris in 1907

Pike's Peak race The Pike's Peak Auto Hill Climb, Colorado, U.S.A. (instituted 1916) has been won by Bobby Unser (b. Colorado Springs, Colorado, U.S.A., 1934) 11 times between 1956 and 1969 (9 championship, 1 stock and 1 sports car title). On 30 June 1968 in the 46th race, he set a record of 11 minutes 54·9 seconds in his 336 cubic inch Chevrolet championship car for the 12·42-mile course rising from 9,402 feet to 14,110 feet through 157 curves.

Hill climbing The British National Hill Climb Championship inaugurated in 1947 has been won six times by Anthony Ernest Marsh (b. Stourbridge, Worcestershire, 20 July 1913), 1955–56–57, 1965–66–67. Raymond Mays (b. Bourne, Lincolnshire, 1 Aug. 1899) won the Shelsley Walsh hill climb, near Worcester, 19 times between 1923 and 1950.

RALLIES

Earliest The earliest long rally was promoted by the Parisian daily *Le Matin* in 1907 from Peking, China, to Paris over a route of about 7,500 miles. Five cars left Peking on 10 June. The winner, Prince Scipione Borghesi, arrived in Paris on 10 Aug. 1907 in his 40 h.p. Itala.

Longest The world's longest ever rally was the £10,000 *Daily Mirror* World Cup Rally run over 16,243 miles starting from Wembley, London on 19 April 1970 to Mexico City *via* Sofia, Bulgaria and Buenos Aires, Argentina passing through 25 countries. It was won on 27 May 1970 by Hannu Mikkola (b. Joensuu, Finland, 24 May 1942) and Gunnar Palm (b. Kristinehamn, Sweden, 25 Feb. 1937) in a 1,834 c.c. Ford Escort. The longest held annually is the East African Safari (first run 1953), run through Kenya, Tanzania and Uganda, which is up to 3,874 miles long, as in the 17th Safari held between 8–12 April 1971. The smallest car to win the Monte Carlo Rally (founded 1911) was an 841 c.c. Saab driven by Erik Carlsson (b. Sweden, 1929) and Gunnar Haggbom of Sweden on 25 Jan. 1962, and by Carlsson and Gunnar Palm (Sweden) on 24 Jan. 1963.

DRAGGING

Piston engined The highest terminal velocity recorded by a piston-engined dragster is 240·00 m.p.h. by Donald Glenn "Big Daddy" Garlits (b. 1932) of Tampa, Florida driving his 426 cubic inch supercharged V8 Dodge *Swamp Rat* in the United States on 13 July 1968. The lowest elapsed time is 6·3 seconds (terminal velocity 228·42 m.p.h.) by Sarge Arcieró of Broomal, Pennsylvania, U.S.A., driving a 392 cubic inch Chrysler AA/F during the National Hot Rod Association's 2nd Annual Galornationals at Gainesville Dragway, Florida, U.S.A., in April 1971.

Rocket or jet-engined The highest terminal velocity recorded by any dragster is 273·555 m.p.h. (elapsed time 6·14 seconds) by Arthur Eugene Arfons (b. Akron, Ohio, 3 Feb. 1926) driving *Cyclops*, powered by a General Electric J79 GE-2 jet engine developing 17,500 lb. s.t., at Rockingham, North Carolina, U.S.A. on 25 Sept. 1969. The lowest elapsed time by any dragster is 5·41 seconds (terminal velocity 229 m.p.h.) by the Reaction Dynamics X-1 *Rislone Rocket* powered by a hydrogen peroxide rocket motor developing 2,500 lb. static thrust, driven by Chuck Suba (U.S.A.) in the U.S.A. early in 1968.

Terminal velocity is the speed attained at the end of a 440-yard run made from a standing start and elapsed time is the time taken for the run.

LAND SPEED RECORDS

The highest speed ever recorded by a wheeled vehicle was achieved by Gary Gabelich (b. San Pedro, California, U.S.A., 1940), at Bonneville Salt Flats, Utah, U.S.A., on 23 Oct. 1970. He drove the Reaction Dynamics *The Blue Flame,* weighing 4,950 lb. and measuring 37 feet long, powered by a liquid natural gas—hydrogen peroxide rocket engine developing a maximum static thrust of 22,000 lb. On his first run he covered the measured mile in 5·829 seconds (average speed 617·602 m.p.h.). On the second run his time was 5·739 seconds (average speed 627·287 m.p.h.) giving an average for the two runs of 5·784 seconds (622·407 m.p.h.). During the attempt only 13,000 lb. s.t. was used and a peak speed of 650 m.p.h. was momentarily attained.

The most successful land speed record breaker was Major Sir Malcolm Campbell (1885–1948) of the United Kingdom. He broke the official record nine times between 25 Sept. 1924, with 146·157 m.p.h. in a Sunbeam, and 3 Sept. 1935, when he achieved 301·129 m.p.h. in the Rolls-Royce engined *Bluebird.*

The first of the three Bluebirds in which Sir Malcolm Campbell raised the land speed record from 246·63 m.p.h. to 304·31 m.p.h.

The world speed record for compression ignition engined cars is 169·3 m.p.h. (average for 2 runs over 1 kilometre) by Dana Fuller, Jr., in the 6,974 c.c. Fuller Diesel 6/71 at Bonneville Salt Flats, Utah, U.S.A., on 11 Sept. 1953.

Go-kart circumnavigation The only recorded instance of a go-kart being driven round the world was a circumnavigation by Stan Mott, of New York, U.S.A., who drove a Lambretta engined 175 c.c. "Italkart" with a ground clearance of two inches, 23,300 land miles through 28 countries from 15 Feb. 1961 to 5 June 1964, starting and finishing in New York, U.S.A.

MOUNTAINEERING

Origins Although bronze-age artifacts have been found on the summit of the Riffelhorn, mountaineering, as a sport, has a continuous history dating back only to 1854. Isolated instances of climbing for its own sake exist back to the 14th century. The Atacamenans built sacrificial platforms near the summit of Llullaillaco (22,058 feet) in late pre-Columbian times *c.* 1490. The earliest recorded rock climb in the British Isles was of Stacna Biorrach, St. Kilda by Sir Robert Moray in 1698.

Mount Everest Mount Everest (29,028 feet) was first climbed at 11.30 a.m. on 29 May 1953, when the summit was reached by Edmund Percival Hillary (born 20 July 1919), created K.B.E., of New Zealand, and the Sherpa, Tenzing Norkhay (born, as Namgyal Wangdi, in Nepal in 1914, formerly called Tenzing Khumjung Bhutia), who was awarded the G.M. The successful expedition was led by Col. (later Hon. Brigadier) Henry Cecil John Hunt, C.B.E., D.S.O. (born 22 June 1910), who was created a Knight Bachelor in 1953 and a life peer on 11 June 1966.

Greatest wall The greatest wall in the world is the 14,500-foot-high south face of Annapurna I (26,504 feet), which starts at 12,000 feet. It was climbed by the British expedition led by Christian Bonnington when on 27 May 1970 Donald Whillans, 36 and Dougal Haston, 27 scaled to the summit.

Europe's greatest wall is the Eiger-wand (North face) which was first climbed by Heckmair, Vörg, Harrer and Kasparek of the 1938 Austro-German group.

Rock climbing The world's most demanding XS (extremely severe) rock climb is regarded as the sheer almost totally holdless Muir wall of the 3,000-foot El Capitan, Yosemite, California, U.S.A. first climbed in November 1958. In 1968 Royal Robbins (U.S.A.) climbed this solo with pitons.

MOUNTAIN RACING

The record time for the race from Fort William to the summit of Ben Nevis and return is 1 hour 38 minutes 50 seconds by Peter Hall (Barrow A.C.) on 5 Sept. 1964. The feminine record is 1 hour 51 minutes for the ascent only, by Elizabeth Wilson-Smith on 14 Sept. 1909, and 3 hours 2 minutes for the ascent and return by Kathleen Connachie, aged 16, on 3 Sept. 1965. The full course by the bridle path is about 14 miles but distance can be saved by crossing the open hillside. The mountain was first climbed in about 1720 and the earliest race was in 1895.

The Lakeland 24-hour record is 60 peaks achieved by Alan Heaton in the summer of 1965. The Yorkshire three peak record is 2 hours 40 minutes 34 seconds by Michael P. Davies (Reading A.C.) in 1968.

The "Three Thousander" record over the 14 Welsh peaks of over 3,000 feet is 5 hours 13 minutes by the late Eric Beard (Leeds A.C.) on 17 June 1965.

Three peaks record The Three Peaks record from sea level at Fort William, Inverness-shire, to sea level at Caernarvon, *via* the summits of Ben Nevis, Scafell Pike and Snowdon, is 11 hours 54 minutes by Josh Naylor of Wasdale (running) with Frank Davies as driver for the 480 miles on the road, on 8–9 July 1971. From summit to summit the time was 10 hours 9 minutes. This course was achieved on foot by the late Eric Beard, 37, of Leeds Athletic Club, in 10 days in June 1969.

Greatest fall The greatest recorded fall survived by a mountaineer was when Christopher Timms (Christchurch University) slid 7,500 feet down an ice face into a crevasse on Mt. Elie de Beaumont (10,200 feet), New Zealand on 7 Dec. 1966. His companion was killed but he survived with concussion, bruises and a hand injury.

Fell running Bill Teasdale won the Guides' Race at the Grasmere Sports, Westmorland, for the eleventh time in 1966. It involves running to a turning point on Butter Crag (966 feet above sea level) and back, a distance of about $1\frac{1}{2}$ miles.

SUBSEQUENT ASCENTS OF MOUNT EVEREST

Climbers	Date	
Ernst Schmidt, Jürg Marmet	23 May	1956
Hans Rudolf von Gunten, Adolf Reist	24 May	1956
*Wang Fu-chou, Chu Yin-hua, Konbu	25 May	1960
James Warren Whittaker, Sherpa Nawang Gombu	1 May	1963
Barry C. Bishop, Luther G. Jerstad	22 May	1963
Dr. William F. Unsoeld, Dr. Thomas F. Hornbein	22 May	1963
Capt. A. S. Cheema, Sherpa Nawang Gombu	20 May	1965
Sonam Gyaltso, Sonam Wangyal	22 May	1965
C. P. Vohra, Sherpa Ang Kami	24 May	1965
Capt. H. P. S. Ahluwalia, H. C. S. Rawat, Phu Dorji	29 May	1965
Nomi Uemura, Tero Matsuura (Japan)	11 May	1970
Katsutoshi Hirabayoshi (Japan), Sherpa Chotari	12 May	1970

* *Not internationally accepted as authentic.*

NETBALL

Origins The game was invented in the U.S.A. in 1891 and introduced into England in 1895 by Dr. Toles. The All England Women's Netball Association was formed in 1926.

World title World championships were inaugurated in August 1963 at Eastbourne, Sussex and were won by Australia. The 1971 world championships at Kingston, Jamaica were also won by Australia. The record number of goals in the World Tournament is 402 by Mrs. Judith Heath in 1971.

Highest scores England has never been beaten in a home international. England's record score is 94 goals to 12 *v.* Wales in 1970 and 94 goals *v.* Northern Ireland in Jamaica in January 1971. The highest international score recorded was when New Zealand beat Northern Ireland 112–4 at Eastbourne, Sussex on 2 Aug. 1963.

Most internationals The record number of internationals is 36 by Annette Cairncross in 1954–63. Miss Anne Miles, as England's captain, is expected to overtake this record on 16 Oct. 1971 *v.* Wales with a 37th international.

Marathon A longest netball marathon match lasting 44 hours by 6 teams of 7 girls was played by Street Youth Club, Somerset on 6–8 Nov. 1970.

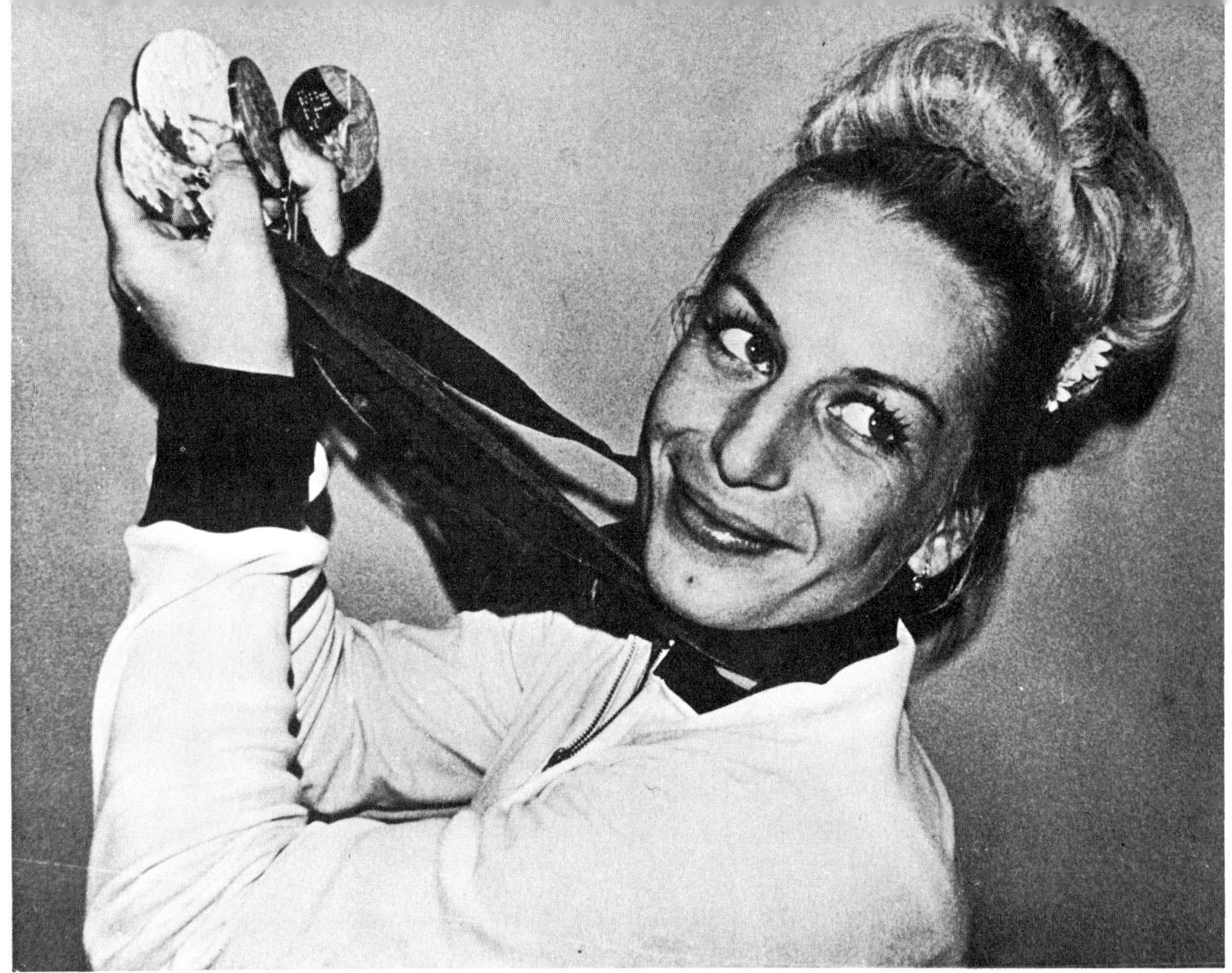

Vera Caslavska-Odlozil, the Czech gymnast, who has won the Olympic female record of 7 gold medals

OLYMPIC GAMES

Note: *The Guinness Book of Olympic Records* (3rd Edition, 1971) contains a complete roll of all the medal winners in currently contested events and their performances from 1896 to 1968 and the schedule for the 1972 Games at Sapporo and Munich.

Origins The earliest celebration of the ancient Olympic Games of which there is a certain record is that of July 776 B.C., when Koroibos, a cook from Elis, won a foot race, though their origin probably dates from *c.* 1370 B.C. The ancient Games were terminated by an order issued in Milan in A.D. 393 by Theodosius I, "the Great" (*c.* 346–395), Emperor of Rome. At the instigation of Pierre de Fredi, Baron de Coubertin (1863–1937), the Olympic Games of the modern era were inaugurated in Athens on 6 April 1896.

Largest crowd The largest crowd at any Olympic site was 150,000 at the 1952 ski-jumping at the Holmenkollen, outside Oslo, Norway. Estimates of the number of spectators of the marathon race through Tōkyō, Japan on 21 Oct. 1964 have ranged from 500,000 to 1,500,000.

MOST GOLD MEDALS

Individual In the ancient Olympic Games victors were given a chaplet of olive leaves. Milo (Milon of Krotōn) won 6 titles at *palaisma* (wrestling) 540–516 B.C. The most individual gold medals won by a male competitor in the modern Games is eight by Ray C. Ewry (U.S.A.) (see Athletics). The female record is seven by Vera Caslavska-Odlozil (see Gymnastics). The most won by a British competitor is four by Paul Radmilovic (1886–1968) in Water Polo in 1908, 1912 and 1920 and in the 800 metres team swimming event in 1908. The sculler and oarsman Jack Beresford won three gold and two silver medals in the five Olympics from 1920 to 1936.

National The United States has won most medals in all Olympic events (summer and winter) with (gold, silver, bronze) 574–415–363 = 1,352, with U.S.S.R. (formerly Russia) (did not compete 1920 to 1948 inclusive) second with 191–176–172 = 539, and the United Kingdom third with 143–193–158 = 494.

Oldest and youngest competitors The oldest recorded competitor was Oscar G. Swahn (Sweden), who won a silver medal for shooting running deer in 1920, when aged 73. The youngest-ever female gold medal winner is Miss Marjorie Gestring (U.S.A.) (b. 18 Nov. 1922, now Mrs. Bowman), aged 13 years 9 months, in the 1936 women's springboard event. Bernard Malivoire, aged 12, coxed the winning French pairs in 1952.

Longest span The longest competitive span of any Olympic competitor is 40 years by Dr. Ivan Osiier (Denmark), who competed as a fencer in 1908, 1912 (silver medal), 1920, 1924, 1928, 1932 and 1948, totalling seven celebrations. He refused to compete in the 1936 Games on the grounds that they were Nazi-dominated. The longest feminine span is 24 years (1932–1956) by the Austrian fencer Ellen Müller-Preiss. The longest span of any British competitor is 20 years by George Mackenzie who wrestled in the Games of 1908, 1912, 1920, 1924 and 1928, and by Mrs. Dorothy J. B. Tyler (*née* Odam), who high-jumped in 1936–48–52 and 56. The only Olympian to win 4 consecutive titles in athletics has been Alfred A. Oerter (b. 19 Sept. 1936, Astoria, N.Y.) of the U.S.A. who won the discus title in 1956–60–64–68.

Celebrations have been allocated as follows:—

I	Athens	6–15 April 1896
II	Paris	2–22 July 1900
III	St. Louis	29 Aug.–7 Sept. 1904
†	Athens	22 April–2 May 1906
IV	London	13–25 July 1908
V	Stockholm	6–15 July 1912
VI	*Berlin	1916
VII	Antwerp	14–29 Aug. 1920
VIII	Paris	5–27 July 1924
IX	Amsterdam	28 July–12 Aug. 1928
X	Los Angeles	30 July–14 Aug. 1932
XI	Berlin	1–16 Aug. 1936
XII	*Tōkyō, then Helsinki	1940
XIII	*London	1944
XIV	London	29 July–14 Aug. 1948
XV	Helsinki	19 July–3 Aug. 1952
XVI	Melbourne	22 Nov.–8 Dec. 1956
XVII	Rome	25 Aug.–11 Sept. 1960
XVIII	Tōkyō	10–24 Oct. 1964
XIX	Mexico City	12–27 Oct. 1968
XX	Munich	26 Aug.–10 Sept. 1972
XXI	Montreal	18 July–1 Aug. 1976

** Cancelled due to World Wars.*
† Intercalated Celebration.

The Winter Olympics were inaugurated in 1924 and have been allocated as follows:—

I	Chamonix, France	25 Jan.–4 Feb. 1924
II	St. Moritz, Switzerland	11–19 Feb. 1928
III	Lake Placid, U.S.A.	4–13 Feb. 1932
IV	Garmisch-Partenkirchen, Germany	6–16 Feb. 1936
V	St. Moritz, Switzerland	30 Jan.–8 Feb. 1948
VI	Oslo, Norway	14–25 Feb. 1952
VII	Cortina d'Ampezzo, Italy	26 Jan.–5 Feb. 1956
VIII	Squaw Valley, California	18–28 Feb. 1960
IX	Innsbruck, Austria	29 Jan.–9 Feb. 1964
X	Grenoble, France	6–18 Feb. 1968
XI	Sapporo, Japan	3–13 Feb. 1972
XII	Denver, Colorado, U.S.A.	20–29 Feb. 1976

ORIENTEERING

Origins Orienteering was invented by Major Ernst Killander in Sweden in 1918. World championships were inaugurated in 1966 and are held biennially. Annual British championships were instituted in 1967.

Most titles *World* Sweden won the world men's relay titles in 1966 and 1968 and the women's relay in 1966 with Ulla Lindkvist (Sweden) winning the individual titles in both 1966 and 1968.

Britain The most successful British team has been Southern Navigators, who won both the men's and women's titles in 1967 and retained the latter in 1968. Gordon Pirie won the men's individual title in 1967 and 1968 and Carol McNeill won the women's title in 1967 and 1969.

PELOTA VASCA (JAI ALAI)

Origins The game, which originated in Italy as *longue paume* and was introduced into France in the 13th century, is said to be the fastest of all ball games with speeds of up to 160 m.p.h. Gloves were introduced *c.* 1840 and the *chisterak* was invented *c.* 1860 by Gantchiki Dithurbide of Sainte Pée. The long *chistera* was

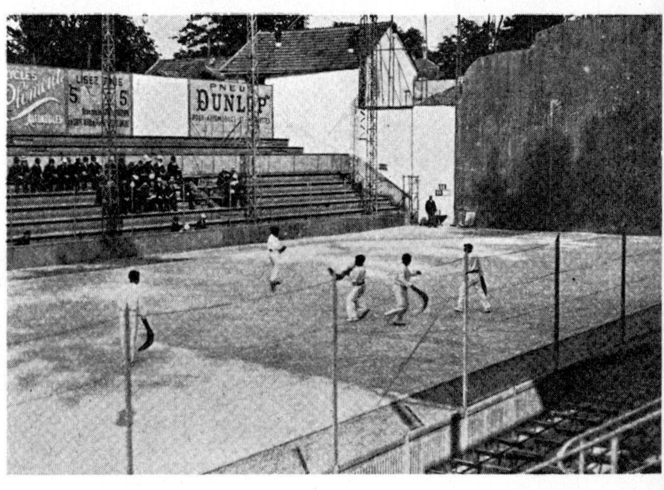

The fastest of ball games, Pelota Vasca, being played in Spain

invented by Melchior Curuchage of Buenos Aires, Argentina in 1888. The world's largest *fronton* (the playing court) is that built for $4,500,000 (now £1,875,000) at Miami, Florida, U.S.A.

Games played in a *fronton* are *Frontenis, pelote* and *paleta* with both leather and rubber balls. The sport is governed by the International Federation of Basque Pelote.

PIGEON RACING

Earliest references Pigeon Racing was the natural development of the use of homing pigeons for the carrying of messages—a quality utilized in the ancient Olympic Games (776 B.C.–A.D. 393). The sport originated in Belgium and came to Britain *c.* 1820. The earliest major long-distance race was from Crystal Palace, South London, in 1871. The earliest recorded occasion on which 500 miles was flown in a day was by "Motor" (owned by G. P. Pointer of Alexander Park Racing Club) which was released from Thurso, Scotland, on 30 June 1896 and covered 501 miles at an average speed of 1,454 yards per minute (49½ m.p.h.).

Longest flights The greatest recorded homing flight by a pigeon was made by one owned by the 1st Duke of Wellington (1769–1852). Released from a sailing ship off the Ichabo Islands, West Africa, on 8 April, it dropped dead a mile from its loft at Nine Elms, London, on 1 June 1845, 55 days later, having flown an airline route of 5,400 miles, but an actual distance of possibly 7,000 miles to avoid the Sahara Desert. The official British duration record (into Great Britain) is 1,141 miles by A. Bruce's bird in the 1960 Barcelona Race which was liberated on 9 July and homed at Fraserburgh, Aberdeenshire, Scotland on 5 August.

Highest speeds In level flight in windless condition it is very doubtful if any pigeon can exceed 60 m.p.h.

The 500 miles record is 2,095 yards per minute (71·42 m.p.h.) by W. Reed's winner of the Thurso Race in 1948. The world's longest reputed distance in 24 hours is 803 miles (velocity 1,525 yards per minute) by E. S. Peterson's winner of the 1941 San Antonio R.C. event, Texas, U.S.A.

The best 24-hour performance into the United Kingdom is 686 miles by A. R. Hill's winner of the 1952 race from Hanover, Germany to St. Just, Cornwall—average speed 1,300 yards per minute (44·31 m.p.h.).

POLO

Earliest games The earliest polo club was the Kachar Club (founded in 1859) in Assam, India. The game was introduced into England from India in 1869 by the 10th Hussars at Aldershot, Hampshire and the earliest match was one between the 9th Lancers and the 10th Hussars on Hounslow Heath, west of London, in July 1871. The first All-Ireland Cup match was at Phoenix Park, Dublin, in 1878. The earliest international match between England and the U.S.A. was in 1886.

The game is played on the largest pitch of any ball game in the world. A ground measures 300 yards long by 160 yards wide with side boards or, as in India, 200 yards wide without boards.

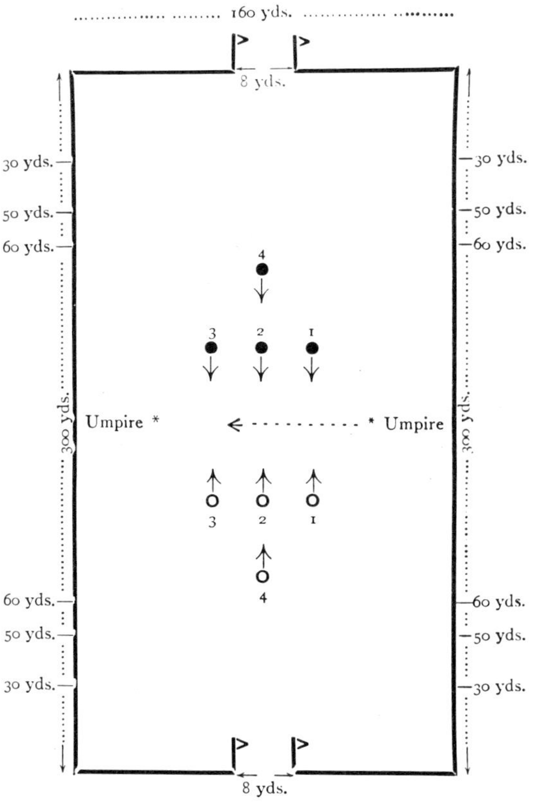

PLAN OF POLO GROUND.

lan of a Polo Field, which requires the est standard pitch of any ball game

Highest handicap The highest handicap based on eight $7\frac{1}{2}$-minute "chukkas" is 10 goals introduced in the U.S.A. in 1891 and in the United Kingdom and in Argentina in 1910. The most recent additions to the select ranks of the 32 players ever to receive 10-goal handicaps are H. Heguy, F. Dorignal and G. Dorignal all of Argentina. The last (of six) 10-goal handicap players from Great Britain was G. Balding in 1939.

The highest handicap of any of the United Kingdom's 300 players is 7, achieved in the Argentine in October 1966 by Paul Withers and John Lucas. H.R.H. the Prince Philip, the Duke of Edinburgh (b. 10 June 1921) has a handicap of 5 at back and thus ranks among the highest handicapped players in the United Kingdom.

Highest score The highest aggregate number of goals scored in an international match is 30, when Argentina beat the U.S.A. 21–9 at Meadow Brook, Long Island, New York, U.S.A., in September 1936.

Most internationals The greatest number of times any player has represented England is four in the case of Frederick M. Freake in 1900, 1902, 1909 and 1913. Thomas Hitchcock, Jr. (1900–44) played five times for the U.S.A. *v.* England (1921–24–27–30–39) and twice *v.* Argentina (1928–36).

Most expensive pony The highest price ever paid for a polo pony was $22,000 (now £7,857), paid by Stephen Sanford for Lewis Lacey's *Jupiter* after the U.S.A. *v.* Argentina international in 1928.

Largest trophy The world's largest trophy for a particular sport is the Bangalore Limited Handicap Polo Tournament Trophy. This massive cup standing on its plinth is 6 feet tall and was presented in 1936 by the Raja of Kolanke.

POWER BOAT RACING

Origins The earliest application of the petrol engine to a boat was Gottlieb Daimler's experimental power boat on the River Seine, Paris, France, in 1887. The sport was given impetus by the presentation of an international championship cup by Sir Alfred Harmsworth in 1903, which was also the year of the first off-shore race from Calais to Dover.

Harmsworth Cup Of the 25 contests from 1903 to 1961, the United States has won 16, the United Kingdom 5, Canada 3 and France 1.

The greatest number of wins has been achieved by Garfield A. Wood with 8 (1920–21, 1926, 1928–29–30, 1932–33). The only boat to win three times is *Miss Supertest III*, owned by James G. Thompson (Canada), in 1959–60–61. This boat also achieved the record speed of 115·972 m.p.h. at Picton, Ontario, Canada in 1960.

Gold Cup The Gold Cup (instituted 1903) has been won four times by Garfield A. Wood (1917, 1919–20–21) and by Bill Muncey (1956–57, 1961–62). The record speed is 120·356 m.p.h. for a 3-mile lap by Rolls-Royce-engined *Miss Exide*, owned by Milo Stoen, driven by Bill Brow at Seattle, Washington, U.S.A. on 4 Aug. 1965.

Highest off-shore speeds The highest race speed attained is 73·1 m.p.h. by Don Aronow (U.S.A.) in his 32-foot *The Cigarette*, powered by two 475 h.p. Mercruiser engines over 214 miles at Viarreggio, Italy on 20 July 1969. The highest average race speed off British shores has been 69·5 m.p.h. by Vincenzo Balastrieri (Italy) and D. Pruett in *Red Tornado* over 184 miles from Southsea Pier, Hampshire to Weymouth, Dorset to Hillhead Buoy, south of the Isle of Wight in the Wills International Race on 14 June 1969.

Longest race The longest race is the *Daily Telegraph and B.P.* Round Britain event inaugurated on 26 July 1969 at Portsmouth with 1,403 miles in 10 stages west-about England, Wales and across Northern Scotland *via* the Caledonian Canal. The 1969 race (26 July to 7 August) was won by *Avenger Too* (Timo Makinen and Pascoe Watson) in 39 hours 9 minutes 37·7 seconds. Of the 42 starters 24 finished.

Cowes-Torquay race The record average for the *Daily Express* International Off-Shore Race (instituted 1961) is 66·47 m.p.h. by *The Cigarette* (Don Aronow) (see above) over the 236-mile course from Cowes, Isle of Wight to Torquay, Devon and back in 3 hours 33 minutes.

RACKETS

Earliest world champion The first world rackets champion was Robert Mackay, who claimed the title in London in 1820. The first closed court champion was Francis Erwood at Woolwich in 1860. The first new court built in Great Britain since 1914 was the Second Court opened at Harrow School in 1965.

Longest reign Of the 18 world champions since 1820 the longest reign is held by British-born U.S. resident Geoffrey W. T. Atkins, who has held the title since beating the professional James Dear in 1954 and completed a fourth successful defence of it in April 1970.

Most amateur titles Since the Amateur singles championship was instituted in 1888 the most titles won by an individual is nine by Edgar M. Baerlein between 1903 and 1923. Since the institution of the Amateur doubles championship in 1890 the most shares in titles has been eleven by David Sumner Milford, between 1938 and 1959. He also has seven Amateur singles titles (1930–52), an open title (1936) and held the world title from 1937 to 1947.

RODEO

Origins Rodeo came into being with the early days of the North American cattle industry. The earliest references to the sport are from Sante Fe, New Mexico, U.S.A., in 1847. Steer wrestling came in with Bill Pickett (Oklahoma) in 1903. The other events are calf roping, bull riding, saddle and bare-back bronc riding.

The largest rodeo in the world is the Calgary Exhibition and Stampede at Calgary, Alberta, Canada. The record attendance has been 853,620 on 9–18 July 1969. The record for one day is 127,043 on 15 July 1967.

Most world titles The record number of all-round titles is five by Jim Shoulders (U.S.A.), in 1949 and 1956–57–58–59 and by Larry Mahan (U.S.A.) in 1966–67–68–69–70. The record figure for prize money in a single season is $57,726 (£24,052) in the three riding events by Larry Mahan, aged 25, of Brooks, Oregon, U.S.A. in 1969.

Time records Records for timed events, such as calf-roping and steer-wrestling, are meaningless, because of the widely varying conditions due to the size of arenas and amount of start given the stock. The fastest time recorded for roping a calf is 7·5 seconds by Junior Garrison of Marlow, Oklahoma, at Evergreen, Colorado, U.S.A. in 1967, and the fastest time for overcoming a steer was 2·4 seconds by James Bynum of Waxahachie, Texas, at Marietta, Oklahoma, in 1955.

The standard required time to stay on in bareback events is 8 seconds and in saddle bronc riding 10 seconds. In the now obsolete ride-to-a-finish events, rodeo riders have been recorded to have survived 90+ minutes, until the horse had not a buck left in it.

Champion bull The top bucking bull is *V-61*, a 1,800-lb. Brahma owned by the Henry Knight Rodeo Company of Fowler, Colorado, U.S.A. He was never ridden in 9 years until John Quintana, 23, of Milwaukee, Oregon, succeeded in June 1971, so scoring 94 points—an absolute Rodeo record.

Champion bronc The greatest bucking bronco of all time was *Midnight*, owned by Verne Elliott of Platteville, Colorado. In seven years (1923–1930) he was ridden by only four riders once each, and of these only Frank Studnick (at Pendleton, Oregon, in 1929) was not subsequently thrown because he did not mount him again.

ROLLER SKATING

Origins The first roller skate was devised by Joseph Merlin of Huy, Belgium, in 1760. Several "improved" versions appeared during the next century, but a really satisfactory roller skate did not materialize before 1866, when James L. Plimpton of New York produced the present four-wheeled type, patented it, and opened the first public rink in the world at Newport, Rhode Island, that year. The great boom periods were 1870–75, 1908–12 and 1948–54, each originating in the United States.

Largest rink The largest indoor rink ever to operate was located in the Grand Hall, Olympia, London. It had an actual skating area of 68,000 square feet. It first opened in 1890, for one season, then again from 1909 to 1912.

Roller hockey Roller hockey (previously known as Rink Hockey in Europe) was first introduced in this country as Rink Polo, at the old Lava rink, Denmark Hill, London, in the late 1870s. The Amateur Rink Hockey Association was formed in 1905, and in 1913 became the National Rink Hockey (now Roller Hockey) Association. Britain won the inaugural World Championship in 1936 since when Portugal has won most titles with 10 between 1947 and 1970.

Most titles Leslie E. Woodley of Birmingham won 12 British national individual titles over the three regulation distances (880 yards, one mile and five miles) between 1957 and 1964. Mrs. Chloe Ronaldson of London won 17 ladies' titles over 440 yards, 800 metres and 880 yards in 1958–71.

Records The fastest speed put up in an official world record is 25·78 m.p.h. when Giuseppe Cantarello (Italy) recorded 34·9 seconds for 440 yards on a road at Catania, Sicily on 28 Sept. 1963. The world mile record on a rink is 2 minutes 25·1 seconds by Johnny Ferriti (Italy). The greatest distance skated in one hour on a rink by a woman is 20 miles 1,355 yards by C. Patricia Barnett (G.B.) at Brixton, London on 24 June 1962. The men's record on a closed road circuit is 22 miles 465·9 yards (35 km. 831 m.) by Alberto Civolani (Italy) at Bologna, Italy on 15 Oct. 1967.

Marathon record The longest recorded continuous roller skating marathon was performed by Professor Eckard with 108 hours at Rockhampton, Queensland, Australia in 1913. The longest reported skate was by Clinton Shaw from Victoria, British Columbia to St. John's, Newfoundland (4,900 miles) on the Trans-Canadian Highway *via* Montreal from 1 April to 11 Nov. 1967.

ROWING

Oldest race The earliest established sculling race is the Doggett's Coat and Badge, which was rowed on 1 Aug. 1716 over 5 miles from London Bridge to Chelsea and is still being rowed every year over the same course, under the administration of the Fishmongers' Company. The first English regatta probably took place on the Thames by the Ranelagh Gardens, near Putney in 1775. Boating began at Eton in 1793, 72 years before the "song". The Leander Club was formed *c.* 1818.

BOAT RACE

The earliest University Boat Race, which Oxford won, was from Hambleden Lock to Henley Bridge on

S.H. Princess Grace of Monaco's father—John Kelly one of only three rsmen to win 3 Olympic gold medals

10 June 1829. In the 117 races to 1971, Cambridge won 65 times, Oxford 51 times and there was a dead heat on 24 March 1877.

Record time The race record time for the course of 4 miles 374 yards (Putney to Mortlake) is 17 minutes 50 seconds by Cambridge in 1948. Oxford returned 17 minutes 37 seconds in practice on 19 March 1965. The smallest winning margin was Oxford's win by a canvas in 1952. The greatest margin (apart from sinking) was Cambridge's win by 20 lengths in 1900. The record for the distance (rowed on the ebb from Mortlake to Putney) is 17 minutes 24 seconds by the Tideway Scullers School in the Head of the River Race on 21 March 1964.

termediate times The record to the Mile Post is 3 minutes 47 seconds (Oxford 1960 and 25 March 1967); Hammersmith Bridge 6 minutes 42 seconds (Oxford 25 March 1967); Chiswick Steps 10 minutes 45 seconds (Oxford 1965, in practice) and Barnes Bridge 14 minutes 39 seconds (Oxford 19 March 1965, in practice).

Oarsman *Heaviest* The heaviest man ever to row in a University boat has been David L. Cruttenden (b. Hartlepool, 1947) the No. 6 in the 1970 Cambridge boat at 16 st. 0 lb. The 1969 Cambridge crew averaged a record 13 st. 9⅜ lb.

Lightest The lightest oarsman was the 1882 Oxford Stroke, A. H. Higgins, at 9 stone 6½ lb. The lightest cox was F. H. Archer (Oxford) in 1862 at 5 stone 2 lb.

OLYMPIC GAMES

Since 1900 there have been 93 Olympic finals, of which the U.S.A. have won 27, Germany 16 and the United Kingdom 14. Four oarsmen have won 3 gold medals: John B. Kelly (U.S.A.), father of Princess Grace of Monaco, in the sculls (1920) and double sculls (1920 and 1924); Paul V. Costello (U.S.A.) in the double sculls (1920, 1924 and 1928); Jack Beresford, Jr. (G.B.) in the sculls (1924), coxless fours (1932) and double sculls (1936) and Vyacheslav Ivanov (U.S.S.R.) in the sculls (1956, 1960 and 1964).

HENLEY ROYAL REGATTA

The annual regatta at Henley-on-Thames, Oxfordshire, was inaugurated on 26 March 1839.

Since 1839 the course, except in 1923, has been about 1 mile 550 yards, varying slightly according to the length of boat. In 1967 the shorter craft were "drawn up" so all bows start level. Prior to 1922 there were two slight angles. Classic Records (year in brackets indicates the date instituted):

HENLEY ROYAL REGATTA—Classic Records

			mins. secs.	
Grand Challenge Cup (1839)	8 oars	Ratzeburger Ruderclub (West Germany)	6:16	3 July 1965
Ladies' Challenge Plate (1845)	8 oars	G.S.R., Aegir (Netherlands)	6:42	3 July 1970
Thames Challenge Cup (1868)	8 oars	Isis	6:35	3 July 1965
Princess Elizabeth Challenge Cup (1946)	8 oars	Emmanuel School	6:44	1 July 1965
		Tabor Academy, U.S.A. (twice)	6:44	3 July 1965
Stewards' Challenge Cup (1841)	4 oars	Quintin	6:55	3 July 1965
Visitors' Challenge Cup (1847)	4 oars	St. Edmund Hall, Oxford	7:13	3 July 1965
Wyfold Challenge Cup (1855)	4 oars	Derby R.C.	7:06	3 July 1965
Prince Philip Cup (1963)	4 oars	Leander	7:03	3 July 1965
Britannia Challenge Cup	4 oars	Thame R.C. (coxed)	7:26	6 July 1968
Silver Goblets and Nickalls' Cup (1895)	Pair oar	Peter Gorny and Gunther Bergau (ASK Vorwaerts Rostock, East Germany)	7:35	1 July 1965
Double Sculls Challenge Cup (1939)	Sculls	Melch Buergin and Martin Studach (Grasshoppers Club, Zürich)	7:01	3 July 1965
Diamond Challenge Sculls (1844)	Sculls	Donald M. Spero (New York A.C., U.S.A.)	7:42	3 July 1965

Sculling The record number of wins in the Wingfield Sculls (instituted on the Thames 1830) is seven by Jack Beresford, Jr. (see Olympics), from 1920 to 1926. The fastest time (Putney to Mortlake) has been 21 minutes 11 seconds by L. F. Southworth in 1933. The record number of world professional sculling titles (instituted 1831) won is seven by W. Beach (Australia) between 1884 and 1887. Stuart A. Mackenzie (Great Britain and Australia) performed the unique feat of winning the Diamond Sculls at Henley for the sixth consecutive occasion on 7 July 1962. In 1960 and 1962 he was in Leander colours.

Highest speed Speeds in tidal or flowing water are of no comparative value. The highest recorded speed for 2,000 metres by an eight in the World Championships is 5 minutes 43·61 seconds by Norway at St. Catherine's, Ontario, Canada, on 4 Sept. 1970 and in the Olympic Games 5 minutes 54·02 seconds (12·64 m.p.h.) by Germany at Toda, Japan on 12 Oct. 1964.

Loch Ness Loch Ness, the longest stretch of inland water in Great Britain (22·7 miles), was rowed by a coxed four jolly-boat from Eastern Amatern Rowing Club of Portobello on 11 Oct. 1969 in 4 hours 11 minutes.

Oxford–London The fastest time registered between Folly Bridge, Oxford through 33 locks and 112 miles to Westminster Bridge, London is 15 hours 16 minutes by an eight (no substitutes) from the Wallingford R.C. on 18 Oct. 1970 so beating a military record set in 1824.

SHOOTING

Olympic Games The record number of gold medals won is five by Morris Fisher (U.S.A.) with three in 1920 and two in 1924.

Record heads The world's finest head is the 23-pointer stag head in the Maritzburg collection, Germany. The outside span is $75\frac{1}{2}$ inches, the length $47\frac{1}{2}$ inches and the weight $41\frac{1}{2}$ lb. The greatest number of points is probably 33 (plus 29) on the stag shot in 1696 by Frederick III (1657–1713), the Elector of Brandenburg, later King Frederick I of Prussia.

The record head for a British Red Deer is a 47-pointer (length $33\frac{1}{2}$ inches) from the Great Warnham Deer Park, Sussex, in 1892. The record for a semi-feral stag is a 20-pointer with an antler length of $45\frac{3}{8}$ inches from Endsleigh Wood, Devon, found in December 1950 and owned by G. Kenneth Whitehead.

Largest shoulder guns The largest bore shoulder guns made were 2 bores. Less than a dozen of these were made by two English wild-fowl gunmakers *c.* 1885. Normally the largest guns made are double-barrelled 4-bore weighing up to 26 lb., which can be handled only by men of exceptional physique. Larger smooth-bore guns have been made, but these are for use as punt-guns.

Highest muzzle velocity The highest muzzle velocity of any rifle bullet is 7,100 feet per second (4,840 m.p.h.) by a 1937 0·30 calibre, M 1903 Standard U.S. Army Ordnance Department rifle.

Clay pigeon The record number of clay birds shot in an hour is 1,308 by Joseph Nother (formerly Wheater) (born 1918) of Kingston-upon-Hull, Yorkshire, at Bedford on 21 Sept. 1957. Using 5 guns and 7 loaders he shot 1,000 in 42 minutes 22·5 seconds.

BISLEY
The National Rifle Association was instituted in 1859. The Queen's (King's) Prize has been shot since 1860 and has only once been won by a woman—Miss Marjorie Elaine Foster, M.B.E. (score 280) in 1930. Only Arthur G. Fulton, M.B.E. has won 3 times (1912, 1926, 1931).

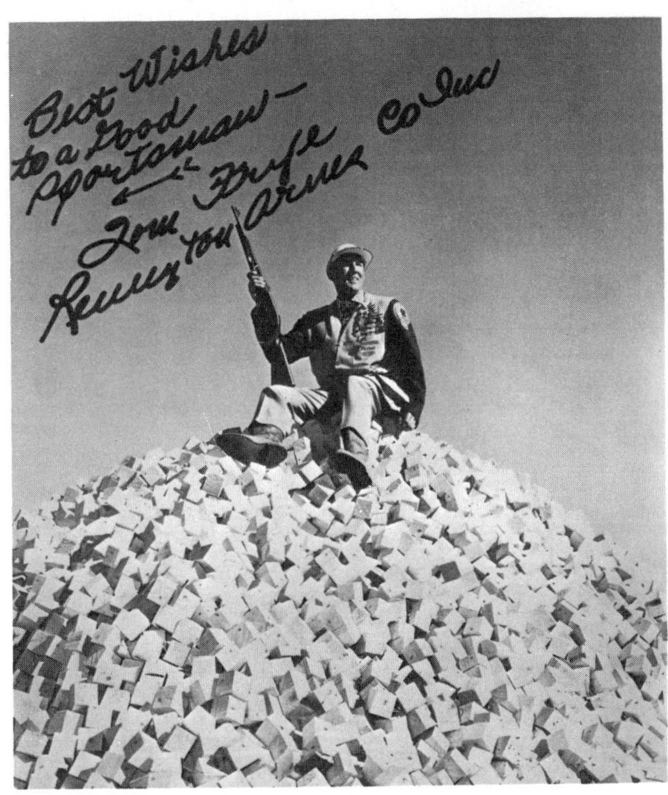

Tom Frye the American marksman who missed only 6 pine blocks in 100,010 attempts with a pair of ·22 Remingtons

The highest score (possible 300) is 292 by Capt. C. H. Vernon, with 146 in both the 2nd and 3rd stages, on 15–16 July 1927. The record for the Silver Medal, shot at 300, 500 and 600 yards, is 148 (possible 150) by four marksmen in 1927, C. A. Sutherland on 19 July 1935, Warrant Officer Norman L. Beckett (Canada) on 21 July 1961 and Keith M. Pilcher on 19 July 1963.

Block tossing Using a pair of auto-loading Remington Nylon 66 ·22 calibre guns, Tom Frye (U.S.A.) tossed 100,010 blocks ($2\frac{1}{2}$-inch pine cubes) and hit 100,004—his longest run was 32,860—on 5–17 Oct. 1959.

Biggest bag The largest animal ever shot by any big game hunter was a bull African elephant (*Loxodonta africana*) shot by J. J. Fénykövi (Hungary), 48 miles north-northwest of Macusso, Angola, on 13 Nov. 1955. It required 16 heavy calibre bullets from an 0·416 Rigby and weighed an estimated 24,000 lb. (10·7 tons), standing 13 feet 2 inches at the shoulders. In November 1965 Simon Fletcher, 28, a Kenyan farmer, claimed to have killed two elephants with one 0·458 bullet.

The greatest recorded lifetime bag is 556,000 birds, including 241,000 pheasants, by the 2nd Marquess of Ripon (1867–1923). He himself dropped dead on a grouse moor after shooting his 52nd bird on the morning of 22 Sept. 1923.

Revolver shooting The greatest rapid fire feat was that of Ed. McGivern (U.S.A.), who twice fired from 15 feet 5 shots which could be covered by a silver half-dollar piece (diameter 1·1875 inches) in 0·45 seconds at the Lead Club Range, South Dakota, U.S.A., on 20 Aug. 1932.

Quickest draw The super-star of fast drawing and winner of the annual "World's Fastest Gun" award from 1960–1971 is Bob Munden (b. Kansas City, Missouri, 8 Feb. 1942). His records include Walk and Draw Level Blanks in 21/100ths sec. and Standing Reaction Blanks (4-inch balloons at 8 feet) in 20/100ths sec. both at Las Vegas, Nevada on 9 Aug. 1966 and Self Start Blanks in 2/100ths sec. at Baldwin Park, California on 17 Aug. 1968.

WORLD RECORDS

		Possible—Score			
Free Pistol	50m. 6 × 10 shot series	600—570	A. Yegrishchin (U.S.S.R.)	Lahti	1968
Free Rifle	300 m. 3 × 40 shot series	1,200—1,157	G. L. Anderson (U.S.A.)	Mexico City	23 Oct. 1968
Small Bore Rifle	50 m. 3 × 40 shot series	1,200—1,164	L. W. Wigger, Jr. (U.S.A.)	Tōkyō	20 Oct. 1964
		1,200—1,164	G. L. Anderson (U.S.A.)	Johannesburg	1969
Small Bore Rifle	50 m. 60 shots prone	600—598	D. Boyd (U.S.A.)	Wiesbaden	1966
		598	A. Mayer (Canada)	Winnipeg	1967
		598	J. Kurka (Czechoslovakia)	Mexico City	19 Oct. 1968
		598	L. Hammerl (Hungary)	Mexico City	19 Oct. 1968
Centre-Fire Pistol	25 m. 60 shots	600—597	T. D. Smith (U.S.A.)	São Paulo	1963
Rapid Fire Pistol	25 m. silhouettes 60 shots	600—598	G. Liverzani (Italy)	Phoenix, Arizona	1970
Running Target	50 m. 40 shots	200—171	M. Nordfors (Sweden)	Pistoia, Italy	1967
Trap	300 birds	300—297	K. Jones (U.S.A.)	Wiesbaden	1966
Skeet	200 birds	200—200	N. Durnev (U.S.S.R.)	Cairo	1962
		200—200	E. Petrov (U.S.S.R.)	Phoenix, Arizona	1970

Bench Rest Open Rifle: five shots put through a hole 0·0630 of an inch in diameter at 100 yards by Zeiser (U.S.A.) on 30 Aug. 1958.

LARGEST BRITISH BAGS

Woodpigeon	550	1 gun	Major A. J. Coates, near Winchester	10 Jan. 1962
Snipe	1,108	2 guns	Tiree, Inner Hebrides	25 Oct.–3 Nov. 1906
Hares	1,215	11 guns	Holkham, Norfolk	19 Dec. 1877
Woodcock	228	6 guns	Ashford, County Galway	28 Jan. 1910
Grouse	2,929	8 guns	Littledale and Abbeystead, Lancashire	12 Aug. 1915
Grouse	1,070	1 gun	Lord Walsingham in Yorkshire	30 Aug. 1888
Geese (Brent)	704*	32 punt-guns	Colonel Russell i/c, River Blackwater, Essex	*c.* 1860
Rabbits	6,943	5 guns	Blenheim, Oxfordshire	17 Oct. 1898
Partridges	2,015†	6 guns	Rothwell, Lincolnshire	12 Oct. 1952
Pheasants	3,937	7 guns	Hall Barn, Beaconsfield, Buckinghamshire	18 Dec. 1913
Pigeons	561	1 gun	K. Ransford, Shropshire-Montgomery	22 July 1970

**Plus about 250 later picked up.* *†Plus 104 later picked up.*

SKI-ING

Origins The earliest dated skis found in Fenno-Scandian bogs have been dated to *c.* 2500 B.C. A rock carving of a skier at Rødøy, Tjøtta, North Norway, dates from 2000 B.C. The earliest recorded military competition was an isolated one in Oslo, Norway, in 1767. Ski-ing did not develop into a sport until 1843 at Tromsø. Ski-ing was known in California by 1856, having been introduced by "Snowshoe" Thompson from Norway. The Kiandra Snow Shoe Club (founded 1878), Australia, claims it is the world's oldest. Ski-ing was not introduced into the Alps until 1883, though there is some evidence of earlier use in the Carniola district. The first Slalom event was run at Mürren, Switzerland, on 21 Jan. 1922. The Winter Olympics were inaugurated in 1924. The Ski Club of Great Britain was founded on 6 May 1903. The National Ski Federation of Great Britain was formed in 1964.

Most Olympic wins The most Olympic gold medals won by an individual for ski-ing is four (including one for a relay) by Sixten Jernberg (b. 6 Feb. 1929) of Sweden, in 1956–60–64. In addition, Jernberg has won three silver and two bronze medals. The only woman to win three gold medals is Klavdiya Boyarskikh (U.S.S.R.), who won the 5 kilometres and 10 kilometres, and was a member of the winning 3 × 5 kilometres Nordic relay team, at Innsbruck, Austria, in 1964.

Most world titles The world alpine championships were inaugurated at Mürren, Switzerland, in 1931. The greatest number of titles won is 12 by Christel Cranz (b. 1 July 1914) of Germany, with four Slalom (1934–37–38–39), three Downhill (1935–37–39) and five Combined (1934–35–37–38–39). She also won the gold medal for the Combined in the 1936 Olympics. The most titles won by a man is seven by Anton ("Toni") Sailer (b. 17 Nov. 1935) of Austria, who won all four in 1956 (Giant Slalom, Slalom, Downhill and the non-Olympic Alpine Combination) and the Downhill, Giant Slalom and Combined in 1958.

Pioneer skier "Snowshoe" Thompson who introduced the sport to California in 1856—104 years before the Winter Olympics were held in that State

In the Nordic events Johan Gröttumsbraaten (b. 24 Feb. 1899) of Norway won six titles (two at 18 kilometres and four Combined) in 1931–32. The record for a jumper is five by Birger Ruud (b. 23 Aug. 1911) of Norway, in 1931–32 and 1935–36–37.

The World Cup, instituted in 1967, has been twice won by Jean-Claude Killy (France) (b. 30 Aug. 1943) in 1967 and 1968 and by Karl Schranz (Austria) in 1969

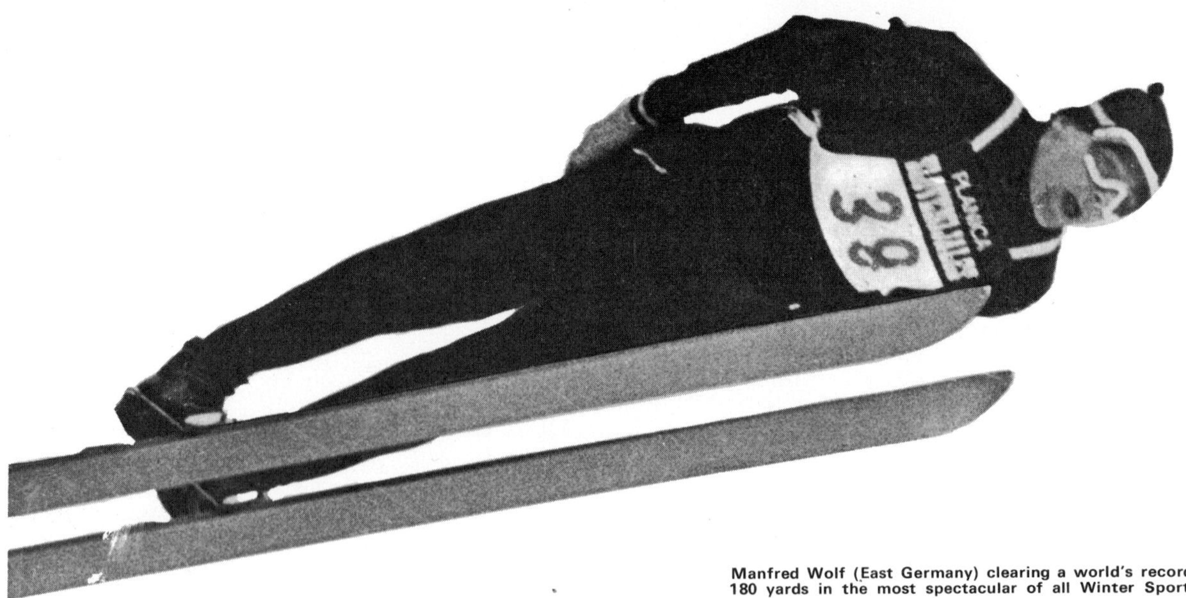

Manfred Wolf (East Germany) clearing a world's record of over 180 yards in the most spectacular of all Winter Sports events

and 1970. The women's cup has been twice won by Miss Nancy Greene (Canada) in 1967 and 1968.

Most British titles The greatest number of British Ski-running titles won is three by Leonard Dobbs (1921, 1923–24), William R. Bracken (1929–31) and Jeremy Palmer-Tomkinson (1965–66–68). The most Ladies Titles is four by Miss Isobel M. Roe (1938–39, 1948–49) and Miss Gina Hathorn (1966–68–69–70). The most wins in the British Ski-jumping Championship (discontinued 1936) is three, by Colin Wyatt (1931, 1934, 1936).

Highest speed The highest speed claimed for any skier is 109·14 m.p.h. by Ralph Miller (U.S.A.) on the 62 degree slopes of the Garganta *Schuss* at Portillo, Chile, on 25 Aug. 1955. Since the timing was only manual by two time-keepers standing half a kilometre back from a marked 50-metre section of *piste*, this claim cannot be regarded as reliable. Some error is further indicated by the fact that to achieve such a speed 50 metres would have to be covered in 1·0248 seconds—an accuracy quite impossible on a stopwatch. The highest speed recorded in Europe is 108·589 m.p.h. over a flying 100 metres by Luigi de Marco (Italy) on a 62·8 degree gradient on the Rosa plateau above Cervinia, Italy, on 18 July 1964. The average race speeds by the 1968 Olympic downhill champion on the Chamrousse course, Grenoble, France were Jean-Claude Killy (France) (53·93 m.p.h.) and Olga Pall (Austria) (47·90 m.p.h.).

Duration The longest non-stop ski-ing marathon was one lasting 48 hours by Onni Savi, aged 35, of Padasjoki, Finland, who covered 305·9 kilometres (190·1 miles) between noon on 19 April and noon on 21 April 1966.

Largest entry The world's greatest Nordic ski race is the "Vasa Lopp", which commemorates an event of 1521 when Gustav Vasa (1496–1560), later King Gustavus Eriksson, skied 85 kilometres (52·8) miles from Mora to Sälen, Sweden. The re-enactment of this journey in reverse direction is now an annual event, with 9,397 starters on 4 March 1970. The record time is 4 hours 39 minutes 49 seconds by Janne Stefansson on 3 March 1968.

Longest jump *World* The longest ski-jump ever recorded is one of 165 metres (541·3 feet) by Manfred Wolf (East Germany) at Planica, Jugoslavia on 23 March 1969.

British The British record is 61 metres (200·1 feet) by Guy John Nixon (b. 9 Jan. 1909) at Davos on 24 Feb. 1931. The record at Hampstead, London, on artificial snow is 28 metres (90·8 feet) by Reidar Andersen (b. 20 April 1911) of Norway on 24 March 1950.

Longest run The longest all-downhill ski run in the world is the Weissfluhjoch-Küblis Parsenn course (9 miles long), near Davos, Switzerland. The run from the Aiguille du Midi top of the Chamonix lift (vertical lift 8,176 feet) across the Vallée Blanche is 13 miles.

Longest lift The longest chair lift in the world is the Alpine Way to Kosciusko Châlet lift above Thredbo, near the Snowy Mountains, New South Wales, Australia. It takes from 45 to 75 minutes to ascend the 3·5 miles, according to the weather. The highest is at Chactaltaya, Bolivia, rising to 16,500 feet.

SKIJORING

The record speed reached in aircraft skijoring (being towed by an aircraft) is 109·23 m.p.h. by Reto Pitsch on the Silsersee, St. Moritz, Switzerland, in 1956.

SKI-BOB

The ski-bob was invented by Mr. Stevens of Hartford, Connecticut, U.S.A., and patented (No. 47334) on 19 April 1892 as a "bicycle with ski-runners". The Fédération Internationale de Skibob was founded on 14 Jan. 1961 in Innsbruck, Austria. The Ski-Bob Association of Great Britain was registered on 23 Aug. 1967. The highest speed attained is 103·4 m.p.h. by Erich Brenter (Austria) at Cervinia, N. Italy, in 1964.

Highest altitude Yuichiro Miura (Japan) skied 1·6 miles down Mt. Everest starting from 26,200 feet. In a run from a height of 24,418 feet he reached speeds of 93·6 m.p.h. on 6 May 1970.

SNOWMOBILE

Ky Michaelson, in the 3,000 h.p. snowmobile *Sonic Challenger*, was timed at 114·5 m.p.h. over 440 yards on Lake Champlain, Vermont, U.S.A., on 15 Feb. 1970.

SNOOKER

Earliest mention Research shows that snooker was originated by Lt.-Gen. Sir Neville Chamberlain (1820–1902) as a variation of "black pool", in the Ootacamund Club, Nilgiris, South India in 1875. It did not reach England until 1885.

Highest breaks It is possible if an opponent commits a foul with 15 reds on the table that his opponent can exercise an option of nominating a colour as a red and then pots this free ball and then goes on to pot the black with 15 reds still on the table, he can score 155. The official world record break is the maximum possible (excluding handicaps or penalties) of 147 by Joe Davis, O.B.E. (b. 15 April 1901) against Willie Smith at Leicester Square Hall, London, on 22 Jan. 1955 and by Rex Williams (G.B.) against Manuel Francisco at Cape Town, South Africa, on 22 Dec. 1965. Horace Lindrum "cleared the table" with an unofficial 147 in Sydney in 1941. The highest officially recognized break by an amateur is one of 122 by Ratan Badar (India) in 1964. On 11 Jan. 1970 Eric Baxter, 45, scored 136 at Wombwell Reform Club, Yorkshire which score is being submitted for ratification.

Three Bristolian snooker players after setting a 202 frame marathon record

Most centuries Joe Davis secured his 500th century on 18 Feb. 1953, at which time the game's next most prolific scorer was his brother, Fred, with 144 centuries. His record of centuries made in public exhibitions reached 687 before he retired in 1965. The highest total of centuries logged in public and private is over 2,000 by Norman Squire (Australia). Rex Williams recorded 682 centuries to March 1967.

Marathon The official snooker endurance record is 104 hours by Tim Wallis, Tony Porter and Mark Crowley of Harvey Sports & Social Club, Bristol, England on 13–17 May 1971. They played 202 frames—17,332 points.

SPEEDWAY

Origins The first organized races were at the Maitland (New South Wales, Australia) Agricultural Show of 1925. The sport was introduced to Great Britain at High Beech, Essex, on 19 Feb. 1928. After three seasons of competition in southern and northern leagues, the National League was instituted in 1932. The best record is that of the Wembley Lions who won in 1932, 1946–47, 1949–53, making a record total of eight victories. Since the National Trophy knock-out competition was instituted in 1931, Belle Vue (Manchester) have been most successful with nine victories in 1933–34–35–36–37, 1946–47, 1949 and 1958. In 1965 the League was replaced by the British League.

Most world titles The world speedway championship was inaugurated in 1936. The only five-time winner has been Ove Fundin (b. Tranås, 1933) (Sweden), who won in 1956, 1960, 1961, 1963 and 1967. In addition he was second in 1957–58–59 and third in 1962, 1964 and 1965.

Lap speed The fastest recorded speed on a British speedway track is 54·62 m.p.h. on the 470-yard 2nd Division track at Crewe by Barry Meeks.

SQUASH RACKETS

(Note: "1970", for example, refers to the 1970–71 season.)

Earliest champion Although rackets (U.S. spelling, racquets) with a soft ball was evolved *c.* 1850 at Harrow School (England), there was no recognized champion of any country until J. A. Miskey of Philadelphia won the American Amateur Singles Championship in 1906.

World title The inaugural international (world) championships were staged in Australia in August 1967 when Australia won the team title in Sydney and Geoffrey B. Hunt (Victoria) took the individual title, both titles being retained at the second championships played in London (individual) and Birmingham (team), England in February 1969.

MOST WINS

Open Championship The most wins in the Open Championship (amateur or professional), held annually in Britain, is seven by Hashim Khan (Pakistan) in 1950–51–52–53–54–55 and 1957.

Amateur Championship The most wins in the Amateur Championship is six by Abdel Fattah Amr Bey (Egypt, now the United Arab Republic), later appointed Ambassador in London, who won in 1931–32–33 and 1935–36–37. Norman F. Borrett of England won in 1946–47–48–49–50.

Professional Championship The most wins in the Professional Championship is five by J. P. Dear (Great Britain) in 1935–36–37–38 and 1949, and Hashim Khan (Pakistan) in 1950–51–52–53–54.

Most international selections The record for international selections is held by O. L. Balfour (Scotland) with 45 between 1954 and 1968. The record for England is 43 by G. J. A. Lyon from 1956 to 1968; for Ireland 39 by D. M. Pratt from 1956 to 1970 and for Wales 44 by L. J. Verney between 1949 and 1965.

Longest span of internationals P. Harding-Edgar first played for Scotland in 1938 and last played 21 years later in 1959.

Longest championship match The longest recorded championship match was one of 2 hours 13 minutes in the final of the Open Championship of the British Isles at the Edgbaston-Priory Club, Birmingham in December 1969 when Jonah P. Barrington (Ireland) beat Geoffrey B. Hunt (Australia) 9–7, 3–9, 3–9, 9–4, 9–4 with the last game lasting 37 minutes.

Most wins in the women's championship The most wins in the Women's Squash Rackets Championship is ten by Miss Janet R. M. Morgan (now Mrs. Shardlow) of England in 1949–50–51–52–53–54–55–56–57–58 and by Mrs. Heather McKay, M.B.E. (*née* Blundell) of Australia, 1961 to 1970.

Marathon record The longest recorded squash singles marathon (under competition conditions) has been one of 43 hours at Devonport, Tasmania on 10 Jan. 1971 by Guy Grant, aged 30, and Ray Schulz, aged 37.

SURFING

Origins The traditional Polynesian sport of surfing in a canoe (*ehorooe*) was first recorded by Captain James Cook, R.N., F.R.S. (1728–79) on his third voyage at Tahiti in December 1771. Surfing on a board (*Amo Amo iluna ka lau oka nalu*) was first described ("most perilous and extraordinary . . . altogether astonishing, and is scarcely to be credited") by Lt. (later Capt.) James King, R.N., F.R.S. in March 1779 at Kealakekua Bay, Hawaii Island. A surfer was first depicted by this voyage's official artist John Webber.

The sport was revived at Waikiki by 1900. Australia's first club, the Bondi Surf Bathers Lifesaving Club, was formed in February 1906. Australia's most successful champion has been Bob Newbiggin, who won the senior title in 1939–40–45–46–47 and the senior Belt Race in 1940. Hollow boards came in in 1929.

Highest waves ridden Makaha Beach, Hawaii provides the reputedly highest consistently high waves often reaching the rideable limit of 30–35 feet. The highest wave ever ridden was the *tsunami* of "perhaps 50 feet", which struck Minole,

Hawaii on 3 April 1868, and was ridden to save his life by a Hawaiian named Holua.

Longest ride *Sea wave* About 4 to 6 times each year rideable surfing waves break in Matanchen Bay near San Blas, Nayarit, Mexico which make rides of *c.* 5,700 feet possible.

River bore The longest recorded rides on a river bore have been set on the Severn bore, England. On 18 Sept. 1970 Colin Prior and Charles Williams (G.B.) and Neil Reading and John Ryland (Australia) rode 2 miles in an expedition organized by *Drive* magazine. In 1968 local residents reported a ride of 4 to 6 miles by Rodney Sumpter of Sussex.

SWIMMING

Earliest references It is recorded that inter-school swimming contests in Japan were ordered by Imperial edict of Emperor Go-Yoozei as early as 1603. In Great Britain competitive swimming originated in London *c.* 1837, at which time there were five or more pools, the earliest of which had been opened at St. George's Pier, Liverpool in 1828.

Largest pools The largest swimming pool in the world is the sea-water Orthlieb Pool in Casablanca, Morocco. It is 480 metres (1,547 feet) long and 75 metres (246 feet) wide, and has an area of 3·6 hectares (8·9 acres). The largest land-locked swimming pool with heated water is the Fleishhacker Pool on Sloat Boulevard, near Great Highway, San Francisco, California, U.S.A. It measures 1,000 feet by 150 feet (3·44 acres) and up to 14 feet deep, and contains 7,500,000 gallons of heated water. The world's largest competition pool is that at Osaka, Japan, which accommodates 25,000 spectators. The largest in the United Kingdom is the Empire Pool, Cardiff, completed in 1958.

Mark Spitz (U.S.A.), the fastest free style swimmer of all-time

WORLD RECORDS—MEN (at distances recognized by the *Fédération Internationale de Natation Amateur*)

Those marked with an asterisk are awaiting ratification. †=salt water ††=fresh and salt water mixed.
Only performances set up in 50 metres or 55 yards baths are recognized as World Records.
F.I.N.A. no longer recognize any records made for distances over non-metric distances.

Distance	Time mins. secs.	Name and Nationality	Place	Date
FREE STYLE				
100 metres	51·9	Mark Spitz (U.S.A.)	Los Angeles, California, U.S.A.	23 Aug. 197
200 metres	1:54·3	Donald Arthur Schollander (U.S.A.)	Long Beach, California, U.S.A.	30 Aug. 196
	1:54·3	Mark Spitz (U.S.A.)	Santa Clara, California, U.S.A.	12 July 196
400 metres	4:02·6	Gunnar Larsson (Sweden)	Barcelona, Spain	7 Sept. 197
800 metres	8:28·8	Michael J. Burton (U.S.A.)	Louisville, Kentucky, U.S.A.	17 Aug. 196
	8:28·6*	Graham Windeatt (Australia)	Sydney, Australia	4 April 197
1,500 metres	15:57·1	John Kinsella (U.S.A.)	Los Angeles, California, U.S.A.	23 Aug. 197
BREASTSTROKE				
100 metres	1:05·8	Nikolai Pankin (U.S.S.R.)	Magdeburg, East Germany	20 April 196
200 metres	2:23·5	Brian Job (U.S.A.)	Los Angeles, California, U.S.A.	22 Aug. 197
BUTTERFLY STROKE				
100 metres	55·6	Mark Spitz (U.S.A.)	Long Beach, California, U.S.A.	30 Aug. 196
200 metres	2:05·0	Gary Hall (U.S.A.)	Los Angeles, California, U.S.A.	22 Aug. 197
BACKSTROKE				
100 metres	56·9	Roland Matthes (East Germany)	Barcelona, Spain	8 Sept. 197
200 metres	2:06·1	Roland Matthes (East Germany)	Barcelona, Spain	11 Sept. 197
INDIVIDUAL MEDLEY				
200 metres	2:09·3	Gunnar Larsson (Sweden)	Barcelona, Spain	12 Sept. 197
400 metres	4:31·0	Gary Hall (U.S.A.)	Los Angeles, California, U.S.A.	21 Aug. 197
FREE STYLE RELAYS				
4 × 100 metres	3:28·8	Los Angeles S.C., U.S.A. (Don Havens, Mike Weston, Bill Frawley, Frank Heckl)	Los Angeles, California, U.S.A.	23 Aug. 197
4 × 200 metres	7:48·0	United States National Team (John Kinsella, Tim McBreen, Gary Hall, Mark Lambert)	Tōkyō, Japan	28 Aug. 197
MEDLEY RELAY				
4 × 100 metres	3:54·4	East Germany (Roland Matthes, Klaus Katzur, Udo Poser, Lutz Unger)	Barcelona, Spain	8 Sept. 197

WORLD RECORDS—WOMEN

Distance	Time mins. secs.	Name and Nationality	Place	Date
FREE STYLE				
100 metres	58·9	Dawn Fraser (now Ware), M.B.E. (Australia)	North Sydney††	29 Feb. 1964
200 metres	2:06·7	Deborah Meyer (U.S.A.)	Los Angeles, California, U.S.A.	24 Aug. 1968
	2:06·5*	Shane Gould (Australia)	London, England	1 May 1971
400 metres	4:24·3	Deborah Meyer (U.S.A.)	Los Angeles, California, U.S.A.	20 Aug. 1970
	4:22·6*	Karen Moras (Australia)	London, England	30 April 1971
800 metres	9:02·4	Karen Moras (Australia)	Edinburgh, Scotland	18 July 1970
1,500 metres	17:19·9	Deborah Meyer (U.S.A.)	Louisville, Kentucky, U.S.A.	17 Aug. 1969
BREASTSTROKE				
100 metres	1:14·2	Catharine Ball (U.S.A.)	Los Angeles, California, U.S.A.	25 Aug. 1968
200 metres	2:38·5	Catharine Ball (U.S.A.)	Los Angeles, California, U.S.A.	26 Aug. 1968
BUTTERFLY STROKE				
100 metres	1:04·1	Alice Jones (U.S.A.)	Los Angeles, California, U.S.A.	20 Aug. 1970
200 metres	2:19·3	Alice Jones (U.S.A.)	Los Angeles, California, U.S.A.	22 Aug. 1970
BACKSTROKE				
100 metres	1:05·6	Karen Yvette Muir (South Africa)	Utrecht, Netherlands	6 July 1969
200 metres	2:21·5	Susan Atwood (U.S.A.)	Louisville, Kentucky, U.S.A.	14 Aug. 1969
INDIVIDUAL MEDLEY				
200 metres	2:23·5	Claudia Anne Kolb (U.S.A.)	Los Angeles, California, U.S.A.	25 Aug. 1968
400 metres	5:04·7	Claudia Anne Kolb (U.S.A.)	Los Angeles, California, U.S.A.	24 Aug. 1968
FREE STYLE RELAY				
4 × 100 metres	4:00·8	East Germany (Gabriele Wetzko, Iris Komor, Elke Schmisch, Carola Schulze)	Barcelona, Spain	11 Sept. 1970
MEDLEY RELAY				
4 × 100 metres	4:27·4	United States (Susan Atwood, Kim Brecht, Alice Jones, Cindy Schilling)	Tōkyō, Japan	1 Sept. 1970

Fastest swimmer Excluding relay stages with their anticipatory starts, the highest speed reached by a swimmer is 4·89 m.p.h. by Stephen Edward Clark (U.S.A.), who recorded 20·9 seconds for a heat of 50 yards in a 25-yard pool at Yale University, New Haven, Connecticut, U.S.A., on 26 March 1964. Spitz's 100 metre record of 51·9 seconds required an average of 4·363 m.p.h.

ost world records Men, 32, Arne Borg (Sweden) (b. 1901), 1921–1929. Women, 42, Ragnhild Hveger (Denmark) (b. 10 Dec. 1920), 1936–1942.

Most Olympic titles The greatest number of individual Olympic gold medals ever won is five by John Weissmuller (U.S.A.), who won 3 individual and 2 relay medals in 1924 and 1928. The most gold medals won at one Games is four by Donald Arthur Schollander (U.S.A.), who won the individual 100 metres and 400 metres free style races, and swam on the last stage in the 4 × 100 metres and 4 × 200 metres free style relays, in Tōkyō, Japan, in 1964, Dawn Fraser, M.B.E. (b. Sydney, Australia, 1937), now Mrs. Gary Ware, won the 100 metres free style in 1956, 1960 and 1964 and a fourth gold medal in the 4 × 100 metres free style relay in 1956. Mrs. Patricia McCormick (U.S.A.) won four gold medals in the highboard and springboard diving contests in 1952 and 1956. The greatest number by a British swimmer is three by John A. Jarvis (1872–1933), who won the 100 metres, 1,000 and 4,000 metres in Paris in 1900.

Most difficult dives Those with the highest tariff (degree of difficulty 2·9) are the "1½ forward somersaults with triple twist"; the "2½ forward somersaults with double twist" and the "1½ reverse with 2½ twists". Joaquin Capilla of Mexico has performed a 4½ somersaults dive from a 10-metre board, but this is not on the international tariff.

The only diver to win an Olympic double twice—Mrs Pat McCormick (U.S.A.)

LONG DISTANCE SWIMMING

A unique achievement in long distance swimming was established in 1966 by the cross-Channel swimmer Mihir Sen of Calcutta, India. These were the Palk Strait from India to Ceylon (in 25 hours 36 minutes on 5–6 April); the Straits of Gibraltar (Europe to Africa in 8 hours 1 minute on 24 August); the Dardanelles (Gallipoli, Europe to Sedulbahir, Asia Minor in 13 hours 55 minutes on 12 September) and the entire length of the Panama Canal in 34 hours 15 minutes on 29–31 October. He had earlier swum the English Channel in 14 hours 45 minutes on 27 Sept. 1958.

CHANNEL SWIMMING

Earliest *Man* The first man to swim across the English Channel (without a life jacket) was the Merchant Navy captain Matthew Webb, A.M. (1848–83), who swam breaststroke from Dover, England, to Cap Gris-Nez, France, in 21 hours 45 minutes from 12.56 p.m. to 10.41 a.m., 24–25 Aug. 1875. He swam an estimated 38 miles to make the 21-mile crossing. Paul Boyton (U.S.A.) had swum from Cap Gris-Nez to the South Foreland in his patent life-saving suit in 23 hours 30 minutes on 28–29 May 1875. There is good evidence that Jean-Marie Saletti, a French soldier, escaped from a British prison hulk off Dover by swimming to Boulogne in July or August 1815. The first crossing from France to England was made by Enrique Tiraboschi, a wealthy Italian living in Argentina, who crossed in 16 hours 33 minutes on 11 Aug. 1923, to win the *Daily Sketch* prize of £1,000.

Woman The first woman to succeed was Gertrude Ederle (U.S.A.) who swam from Cap Gris-Nez, France to Dover, England on 6 Aug. 1926, in the then record time of 14 hours 39 minutes. The first woman to swim from England to France was Florence Chadwick of California, U.S.A., in 16 hours 19 minutes on 11 Sept. 1951. She repeated this on 4 Sept. 1953 and 12 Oct. 1955.

Fastest The fastest swim is one of 9 hours 35 minutes by Barry Watson, aged 25, of Bingley, Yorkshire, who left Cap Gris-Nez, France, at 2 a.m. and arrived at St. Margaret's Bay, near Dover, at 11.35 a.m. on 16 Aug. 1964. The record for an England-France crossing (recognized by the *Channel Swimming Association*, founded in 1927) is 10 hours 23 minutes by Helge Jensen (Canada) on 31 Aug. 1960. The feminine record is 9 hours 59 minutes 57 seconds by Linda McGill, M.B.E., 21, of Sydney, Australia who left Cap Gris-Nez at 4 a.m. on 29 Sept. 1967 and landed at St. Margaret's Bay. The feminine record for an England to France crossing is 13 hours 40 minutes by Greta Andersen (b. Denmark, now of Los Alamitos, California, U.S.A.) from Dover to Cap Gris-Nez on 29–30 Sept. 1964. The fastest crossing by a relay team is one of 9 hours 29 minutes by Radcliffe Swimming Club of Lancashire, from Cap Gris-Nez to Walmer on 13 June 1966.

Slowest The slowest crossing was the third ever made, when Henry Sullivan (U.S.A.) swam from England to France in 26 hours 50 minutes on 5–6 Aug. 1923. The slowest from France to England and the slowest ever by a Briton was one of 23 hours 48 minutes by Philip Mickman (born Ossett, Yorkshire, 1931) on 23–24 Aug. 1949.

Earliest and latest The earliest time in the year on which the Channel has been swum is 6 June by Dorothy Perkins (England), aged 19, in 1961, and the latest is 14 October by Ivy Gill (England) in 1927. Both swims were from France to England.

Youngest The youngest conqueror is Leonore Modell of Sacramento, California, U.S.A., who swam from Cap Gris-Nez to near Dover in 15 hours 33 minutes on 3 Sept. 1964, when aged 14 years 5 months. The youngest relay team to cross are from the Royal Tunbridge Wells Monson S.C. from England to France on 4 Sept. 1968. The team, coached by John Wrapson, had an average age of 12 years 4 months and were David Young, Richard Field, Kim Taylor, Peter Chapman, Stephen Underdown and Peter Burns.

The youngest English Channel relay team—Royal Tunbridge Wells Monson S.C. Average age 12 years 4 months

Oldest The oldest swimmer to swim the Channel has been William E. (Ned) Barnie, aged 55, when he swam from France to England in 15 hours 1 minute on 16 Aug. 1951.

Double crossing *First* Antonio Abertondo (b. Buenos Aires, Argentina), aged 42, swam from England to France in 18 hours 50 minutes (8.35 a.m. on 20 Sept. to 3.25 a.m. on 21 Sept 1961) and after about 4 minutes rest returned to England in 24 hours 16 minutes, landing at St. Margaret's Bay at 3.45 a.m. on 22 Sept. 1961, to complete the first "double crossing" in 43 hours 10 minutes. Kevin Murphy, 21, completed the first double crossing by a Briton in 35 hours 10 minutes on 6 Aug. 1970. The first swimmer to achieve a crossing both ways was Edward H Temme (b. 1904) on 5 Aug. 1927 and 19 Aug. 1934.

Fastest The fastest double crossing, and the second to be achieved, was one of 30 hours 3 minutes by Edward (Ted) Erikson, aged 37, a physiochemist from Chicago, Illinois, U.S.A. He left St. Margaret's Bay, near Dover at 8.20 p.m. on 19 Sept. 1965 and landed at a beach about a mile west of Calais, after a swim of 14 hours 15 minutes. After a rest of about 10 minutes he returned and landed at South Foreland Point, east of Dover, at 2.23 a.m. on 21 Sept. 1965.

Most conquests Brojan Das (Pakistan) attempted a Channel crossing six times in 1958–61, succeeding on each occasion. Greta Andersen (U.S.A.) has also swum the Channel six times (1957–65).

Underwater The first underwater cross-Channel swim was achieved by Fred Baldasare (U.S.A.), aged 38, a frogman, who completed the distance from France to England in 1[illegible] hours 1 minute on 11 July 1962. The fastest underwater swim was by Simon Paterson, aged 20, a frogman from Egham, Surrey, who swam from France to England in 14 hours 50 minutes on 28 July 1962.

Tom Blower, conqueror of the notoriously-cold Irish Channel swim in 1947

Irish Channel The swimming of the 22-mile wide Irish Channel from Donaghadee, Northern Ireland to Portpatrick, Scotland was accomplished by Tom Blower of Nottingham in 1947.

Bristol Channel The first person to achieve a double crossing of the Bristol Channel is Jenny James who swam from Sully, Glamorganshire to Weston-super-Mare, Somerset in 10 hours 2 minutes on 18 Sept. 1949 and the return course in 8 hours 21 minutes on 9 July 1950.

Loch Ness The first person to swim the length of Great Britain's longest lake, the 22¾-mile-long Loch Ness, was Brenda Sherratt of West Bollington, Cheshire, aged 18, in 31 hours 27 minutes on 26–27 July 1966.

Treading water The duration record for treading water (vertical posture without touching the lane markers) is 17½ hours by Peter Strawson of Lawford, Essex on 25–26 July 1967.

Ice swimming Wilhelm Simons (b. 1899) of Berlin, Germany, covered a frozen 100-metre course with two 15-metre swims in 2 minutes 29·6 seconds on the Schliersee, Bavaria on 21 Jan. 1971. The ice had to be broken and the water temperature was 2° C (35·6° F).

Relays The longest recorded mileage in a 24-hour swim relay (team of 5) is 63 miles 487 yards by a relay team from the Paarl Amateur Swimming Club, South Africa, on 5–6 Jan. 1970. The fastest time recorded for 100 miles by a team of 20 swimmers is 31 hours 35 minutes 21·3 seconds by Piedmont Swim Club, California, U.S.A., on 3–4 Sept. 1970.

Marathon relays In Buttermere, Westmorland, England on 18–28 July 1968 six boys, aged 13 to 15, covered 300 miles in 230 hours 39 minutes.

Underground swimming The longest recorded underground swim is one of 3,402 yards in 87 minutes by David Stanley Gale through the Dudley Old Canal Tunnel, Worcestershire, in August 1967.

Sponsored swimming The greatest amount of money raised in a sponsored swim is £2,466 by Grimsby Round Table, Lincolnshire with 576 swimmers covering 355·8 miles at the Scartho Road pool on 4 April 1970.

Underwater swimming Vitalyi Bardashevich covered 100 metres underwater with an aqualung in 42·6 seconds in Moscow, U.S.S.R. in April 1971. Nadezhda Turukalo swam 100 metres (with scuba) in 49·4 seconds in Minsk, U.S.S.R. on 2 Aug. 1970.

TABLE TENNIS

Earliest reference The earliest evidence relating to a game resembling table tennis has been found in the catalogues of London sports goods manufacturers in the 1880s. The old Ping Pong Association was formed in 1902 but the game proved only a temporary craze until resuscitated in 1921. The English Table Tennis Association was formed on 24 April 1927.

The highest total of English men's titles is 20 by G. Viktor Barna. The women's record is 18 by Diane Rowe (b. 14 April 1933), now Mrs. Eberhard Scholer. Her twin Rosalind (now Mrs. Cornett) has won 9 (two in singles).

Youngest international The youngest ever international (probably in any sport) was Joy Foster, aged 8, the 1958 Jamaican singles and mixed doubles champion.

Marathon records In the Swaythling Cup final match between Austria and Romania in Prague, Czechoslovakia, in 1936, the play lasted for 25 or 26 hours, spread over three nights.

The longest recorded time for a marathon singles match by two players is 59 hours 30 minutes by Graham Shires and Peter Shaw of the Leigh Park Community Centre Youth Club, Havant, Hampshire on 29–31 May 1971.

The longest recorded marathon by 4 players maintaining continuous singles is 500 hours (20 days 20 hours) by 8 players (all aged 16) (two sets of four players at separate tables) from the Maryborough Boys' High School Interact Club, Queensland, Australia on 30 Nov.–21 Dec. 1970.

Highest speed No conclusive measurements have been published, but Chuang Tse-tung (China) the world champion of 1961–63–65, has probably smashed at a speed of more than 60 m.p.h.

Fastest striker in table tennis, Chuang Tse-tung (China, mainland), who reputedly could smash at 60 m.p.h.

MOST WINS IN WORLD CHAMPIONSHIPS (Instituted 1926–27)

Event	Name and Nationality	Times	Years
Men's Singles (St. Bride's Vase)	G. Viktor Barna (Hungary)	5	1930, 1932–33–34–35
Women's Singles (G. Geist Prize)	Angelica Rozeanu (Romania)	6	1950–51–52–53–54–55
Men's Doubles	G. Viktor Barna (Hungary) with two different partners	8	1929–35, 1939
Women's Doubles	Maria Mednyanszky (Hungary) with three different partners	7	1928, 1930–31–32–33–34–35
Mixed Doubles (Men)	Ferenc Sido (Hungary) with two different partners	4	1949–50, 1952–53
(Women)	Maria Mednyanszky (Hungary) with three different partners	6	1927–28, 1930–31, 1933–34

G. Viktor Barna gained a personal total of 15 world titles, while 18 have been won by Miss Maria Mednyanszky.

MOST TEAM TITLES

Event	Team	Times	Years
Men's Team (Swaythling Cup)	Hungary	11	1927–31, 1933–35, 1938, 1949, 1952
Women's Team (Marcel Corbillon Cup)	Japan	7	1952, 1954, 1957, 1959, 1961, 1963, 1967

MOST WINS IN ENGLISH OPEN CHAMPIONSHIPS (Instituted 1921)

Event	Name and Nationality	Times	Years
Men's Singles	Richard Bergmann (Austria, then G.B.)	6	1939–40, 1948, 1950, 1952, 1954
Women's Singles	Miss K. M. Berry (G.B.)	3	1923–24–25
	Miss G. Farkas (Hungary)	3	1947–48, 1956
Men's Doubles	G. Viktor Barna (Hungary, then G.B.) with five different partners	7	1931, 1933–34–35, 1938–39, 1949
Women's Doubles	Miss Diane Rowe (G.B.) with four different partners	12	1950–56, 1960, 1962–65
Mixed Doubles (Men)	G. Viktor Barna (Hungary, then G.B.) with four different partners	8	1933–36, 1938, 1940, 1951, 1953
(Women)	Miss Diane Rowe (G.B.) (now Scholer) with three different partners	4	1952, 1954, 1956, 1960, 1969

TENNIS (REAL OR ROYAL)

Origins The game originated in French monasteries *c.* 1050.

Oldest court The oldest of the 18 surviving Tennis Courts in the British Isles is the Royal Tennis Court at Hampton Court Palace, which was built by order of King Henry VIII in 1529–30 and rebuilt by order of Charles II in 1660. The oldest court in the world is one built in Paris in 1496. There are estimated to be 3,000 players and 29 courts in the world.

World titles The first recorded World Tennis Champion was Clerge (France) *c.* 1740. Pierre Etchebaster won the title at Prince's, Paris, in May 1928, last defended it in New York (winning 7–1) in December 1949 and retired undefeated in 1955, after 27 years. Etchebaster, a Basque, also holds the record for the greatest number of successful defences of his title, with six.

British titles The Amateur Championship of the British Isles (instituted 1780) has been won 13 times by Edgar M. Baerlein (b. 1879) (1912 to 1930). The greatest number of international appearances has been 18 by Sir Clarance Napier Bruce, G.B.E., 3rd Baron Aberdare (1885–1957).

TIDDLYWINKS

Accuracy The lowest number of shots taken to pot 12 winks from 3 feet is 23, achieved by M. Brogden (Hull University) on 18 Oct. 1962. This record was equalled by A. Cooper (Altrincham Grammar School) in December 1963 and by J. King (Ealing Grammar School) on 2 May 1965.

Speed The record for potting 24 winks from 18 inches is 21·8 seconds by Stephen Williams (Altrincham Grammar School) in May 1966.

Marathon Allen R. Astles (University of Wales) potted 10,000 winks in 3 hours 51 minutes 46 seconds at Aberystwyth, Cardiganshire in February 1966. The most protracted game on record is one of 144 hours 2 minutes (with a team of six) by the 1st Helston Venture Scout Unit, Cornwall on 28 Dec. 1970 to 3 Jan. 1971.

TRAMPOLINING

Origins The sport of trampolining (from the Spanish word *trampolin*, a springboard) dates from 1936, when the prototype "T" model trampoline was developed by George Nissen (U.S.A.). Trampolines were used in show business at least as early as "The Walloons" of the period 1910–12.

Most difficult manoeuvres The three most difficult manoeuvres yet achieved are the triple twisting double back somersault, known as a Miller after the first trampolinist to achieve it—Wayne Miller (b. 1947) of the U.S.A.; four consecutive triple somersaults by Len Ranson (1970 Australian champion) and the women's Wills (5½ twisting back somersault), named after the five-time world champion Judy Wills (b. 1948) of the U.S.A.

Most titles The only man to retain a world title (instituted 1964) is Dave Jacobs (U.S.) the 1967–68 champion. Judy Wills has won every women's title (1964–65–66–67–68). Both European men's titles (1969 and 1971) were won by Paul Luxon (G.B.). Three United Kingdom titles have been won by David Curtis (1966–67–68) and Paul Luxon (1969–70–71), while Miss Jackie Allen (1960–61), Mary Hunkin (*née* Chamberlaine) (1963–64) and Lynda Ball (1965–66) have each won twice.

Marathon record The longest recorded trampoline bouncing marathon is one of 460 hours, set by a team of 15 members, aged 9 to 17, of the Police and Citizens Youth Club, Western Australia from 7–26 May 1971. The record for a 6-man team is 127 hours by Teddington Youth Centre, Middlesex, England on 13–18 April 1971. The solo record is 44 hours 25 minutes (with 5-minute breaks per hour permissible) by Gavin Jury of Richmond, New Zealand on 24–26 Oct. 1970.

TROTTING AND PACING

The trotting gait (the simultaneous use of the diagonally opposite legs) was first recorded in England in *c.* 1750. The sulky first appeared in harness-racing in 1829. Pacers thrust out their fore and hind legs simultaneously on one side.

Highest price The highest price paid for a trotter is $3,000,000 (£1,250,000) for *Nevele Pride* by the Stoner Creek Stud of Lexington, Kentucky from Louis Resnick and Nevele Acres in the autumn of 1969. The highest price ever paid for a pacer is $2,000,000 (now £833,333) for *Bret Hanover* in August 1966.

Greatest winnings The greatest amount won by a trotting horse is $956,161 (£398,400) by *Roquepine*, a French mare, from 1963 to 1969. The record for a pacing horse is $1,000,837 (£417,015) by the New Zealand-bred *Cardigan Bay* from 1959 to his retirement in September 1968. In 134 starts he had 66 wins and 24 seconds.

Records against time	Trotting			Pacing		
World (mile track)	1:54·8	Nevele Pride (U.S.A.), Indianapolis, Indiana	31 Aug. 1969	1:53·6	Bret Hanover (U.S.A.) Lexington, Kentucky	7 Oct. 1966
Australia	2:01·2	Gramel, Harold Park, Sydney	1964	1:57·3	Halwes, Harold Park, Sydney	1968
New Zealand	2:02·4	Control, Addington, Christchurch	1964	1:56·2	Cardigan Bay, Hutt Park, Wellington	1963

VOLLEYBALL

Origins The game was invented as *Minnonette* in 1895 by William G. Morgan at the Y.M.C.A. gymnasium at Springfield, Massachusetts, U.S.A. The International Volleyball Association was formed in Paris in April 1947. The Amateur Volleyball Association of Great Britain was formed in May 1955. The ball travels at a speed of up to 70 m.p.h. when smashed over the net, which measures 2·43 metres (7 feet 11·6 inches). In the women's game the net is 2·24 metres (7 feet 4·1 inches).

World titles World Championships were instituted in 1949. The U.S.S.R. has won six men's titles (1949, 1952, 1960, 1962, 1964 and 1968) in the eight meetings held. The U.S.S.R. won the women's championship in 1952, 1956, 1960, 1968 and 1970. The record crowd is 60,000 for the 1952 world title matches in Moscow, U.S.S.R.

Marathon The longest recorded volleyball marathon is one of 72 hours by four sets of 6-a-side teams (8 minutes playing time per game and no breaks) from the Cardinal Wiseman R.C. School, Coventry, England on 24–27 Oct. 1969.

WALKING

Walking on crutches David Ryder, 21, a polio victim from Chigwell, Essex, arrived at Land's End from John o' Groats on 18 Aug. 1969 having completed the entire course on crutches. From 30 March to 14 Aug. 1970 he succeeded in walking on crutches 2,960 miles across North America.

London to Brighton The record time for the London to Brighton walk is 7 hours 35 minutes 12 seconds by Donald James Thompson (b. 20 Jan. 1933) on 14 Sept. 1957. The record time for London to Brighton and back is 18 hours 5 minutes 51 seconds by William Frederick Baker (b. 5 April 1889) of Queen's Park Harriers, London, on 18–19 June 1926.

Trans-Continental The record for walking across the United States from San Francisco, California, to New York is 66 days by Flt. Sgt. P. Maloney and Staff Sgt. M. Evans, ending on 17 June 1960. The feminine record for the 3,207-mile route is 86 days by Dr. Barbara Moore (b. Varvara Belayeva, in Kalouga, Russia, 22 Dec. 1903), ending on 6 July 1960.

End to end The record for walking from John o' Groats to Land's End (route varies between 876 and 891 miles) is 11 days 23 hours 45 minutes achieved by Malcolm Taylor of Milnsbridge, Huddersfield, Yorkshire on 18–30 July 1969. The feminine record is 17 days 7 hours by Miss Wendy Lewis ending on 15 March 1960. End to end and back has twice been achieved. Frederick E. Westcott, aged 31, finished on 18 Dec. 1966 and David Tremayne (Australia), aged 27, finished on 28 May 1971.

OFFICIAL WORLD RECORDS (Track Walking)

(As recognized by the International Amateur Athletic Federation) (*Awaiting ratification)

Distance	Time Hrs.	mins.	secs.	Name and Nationality	Place	Date
20,000 metres	1	25	50·0	Peter Frenkel (East Germany)	Erfurt, East Germany	4 July 1970
30,000 metres	2	17	16·8	Anatoliy I. Yegorov (U.S.S.R.)	Leningrad, U.S.S.R.	15 July 1959
20 miles	2	31	33·0	Anatoliy S. Vedyakov (U.S.S.R.)	Moscow, U.S.S.R.	23 Aug. 1958
30 miles	4	00	06·4*	Christoph Höhne (East Germany)	Berlin, East Germany	18 Oct. 1969
50,000 metres	4	08	05·0*	Christoph Höhne (East Germany)	Berlin, East Germany	18 Oct. 1969
2 hours	26,657 metres (16 miles 992 yards)*			Boris Khrolovich (U.S.S.R.)	Minsk, U.S.S.R.	15 Sept. 1966

UNOFFICIAL WORLD BEST PERFORMANCES (Track Walking)

(Best valid performances over distances or times for which records are no longer recognized by the I.A.A.F.)

Distance	Hrs.	mins.	secs.	Name and Nationality	Place	Date
5 miles		34	21·2	Kenneth Joseph Matthews (U.K.)	White City, London	28 Sept. 1960
10 miles	1	09	40·6	Kenneth Joseph Matthews (U.K.)	Walton-on-Thames	6 June 1964
50,000 metres (road)	4	02	43·0	Christoph Höhne (East Germany)	Podebrady, Czechoslovakia	6 Aug. 1967
1 hour	8 miles 1,294 yards			Grigoriy Panichkin (U.S.S.R.)	Stalinabad, U.S.S.R.	1 Nov. 1959
24 hours	133 miles 21 yards			Huw D. M. N. Neilson (U.K.)	Walton-on-Thames	14–15 Oct. 1960

Gyorgy Karparti, Water Polo's most capped international, who played 151 times for Hungary

WATER POLO

Origins Water Polo was developed in England as "Water Soccer" in 1869 and was first included in the Olympic Games in Paris in 1900.

Olympic Games Hungary has won the Olympic tournament five times, in 1932, 1936, 1952, 1956 and 1964. Great Britain won in 1900, 1908, 1912 and 1920.

A.S.A. championships The club with the greatest number of Amateur Swimming Association titles is Plaistow United Swimming Club of Greater London, with eleven from 1928 to 1954.

Most goals The greatest number of goals scored by an individual in a home international is eleven by Terry C. Miller (Plaistow United), when England defeated Wales 13–3 at Newport, Monmouthshire, in 1951.

Most caps The greatest number of internationals is 151 by Gyorgy Karparti of Hungary to 1966.

WATER SKI-ING

Origins The origins of water ski-ing lie in plank gliding or aquaplaning. A photograph exists of a "plank-riding" contest in a regatta won by a Mr. S. Storry at Scarborough, Yorkshire on 15 July 1914. Competitors were towed on a *single* plank by a motor launch. The present day sport of water ski-ing was pioneered by Ralph W. Samuelson on Lake Pepin, Minnesota, U.S.A., on two curved pine boards in the summer of 1922, though claims have been made for the birth of the sport on Lake Annecy (Haute Savoie), France, in 1920. The British Water Ski Federation was founded in London in 1954.

Longest jumps The first recorded jump on water skis was by Dick Pope, Sr., at Miami Beach, Florida, U.S.A. in 1928. The longest jumps ever recorded are ones of 165 feet by Mike Suyderhoud (U.S.A.) at Fall River Mills, near Redding, California, U.S.A. on 9 Aug. 1970 and 165 feet 5¾ inches at Bedfont, near London also in August 1970. The official women's record is 106 feet by Elizabeth Allen (b. 1951) of Florida, U.S.A., at Callaway Gardens, Pine Mountain, Georgia, U.S.A., on 17 July 1966.

The British record is 156 feet 1½ inches by Ian Walker at Halstead, Essex on 18 July 1970. The Irish record is 128 feet by Alan Dagg (Golden Falls W.S.C.) at Dublin on 25 Aug. 1970. The women's record is 106 feet 3½ inches by Jeannette Stewart-Wood (b. 1946) at Ruislip, Greater London on 11 June 1967. This could not be ratified as a world record because a minimum improvement of 8 inches is required.

Buoys and tricks The world record for slalom is 38 buoys (6 passes through the course plus two buoys with the 75-foot rope shortened by 36 feet) by Mike Suyderhoud (U.S.) at Ruislip, Middlesex on 6 June 1970 and Roby Zucchi (Italy) at Canzo, Italy on 6 Sept. 1970. The record for tricks is 5,970 points by Ricky McCormick (U.S.) at Bedfont, near London, in August 1970. The British records are 33 buoys by Ian Walker (Ruislip) at Canzo, Italy in September 1970 (5 passes plus 3 buoys with the 75-foot rope shortened by 32 feet) and 3,765 points by Paul Adlington (Ruislip) at Princes in August 1969.

Mike Suyderhoud (U.S.A.), world record holder for water ski jumping

Longest run The greatest distance travelled non-stop is 818·2 miles by Marvin G. Shackleford round McKellar Lake, Memphis, Tennessee, U.S.A. in 35 hours 15 minutes in September 1960. The British record is 470·67 miles (in 15 hours 1 minute 53·2 seconds) by Charles Phipps, 30, on Lake Windermere from 4.4 a.m. to 7.5 p.m. on 4 Oct. 1959. The chief driver was George Price and the co-ordinator Charles Hulme.

Highest speed The water ski-ing speed record is 122·11 m.p.h. by Chuck Stearns of Bellflower, California, U.S.A., at the Marine Stadium, Long Beach, California, U.S.A., on 11 Jan. 1969 towed by the nitromethane alcohol burner *Panic Mouse*. He survived a fall at *c.* 125 m.p.h. Sally Younger (b. 1953), set a feminine record of 105·14 m.p.h. at Perris, California on 17 June 1970.

Water ski racing The record for the 50-mile Cross Channel race from Greatstone-on-Sea, near New Romney, England to Cap Gris-Nez, France and back is 1 hour 58 minutes 45 seconds by Tim Hardy of Hunstanton behind a Fletcher 170 (Mercury 135) on 13 June 1971.

Most titles World overall championships (instituted 1949) have been won twice by Alfredo Mendoza (U.S.A.) in 1953–55 and Mike Suyderhoud (U.S.A.) in 1967–69 and three times by Mrs. Willa McGuire (*née* Worthington) of the U.S.A., in 1949–50 and 1955. Mendoza won five championship events and McGuire and Elizabeth Allen (U.S.A.) seven each. The most British overall titles (instituted 1953) ever won by a man is four by Lance Callingham in 1959–60 and 1962–63, and the most by a woman is three by Maureen Lynn-Taylor in 1959–60–61 and by Jeanette Stewart-Wood in 1963–66–67.

Barefoot The barefoot duration record is 67 minutes over about 36 miles by Stephen Z. Northrup (U.S.A.) in 1969. The backwards barefoot record is 33 minutes 19 seconds by Paul McManus (Australia) in 1969. A barefoot jump of 43 feet was reported from Australia. The barefoot speed records are 75 m.p.h. by Wayne Jones (Australia) and 61 m.p.h. by Haidee Jones (Australia).

Water ski flying The altitude record is 2,890 feet by Bill Moyes of Sydney, Australia over Lake Ellesmere, New Zealand on 4 Feb. 1969. The endurance record surpassed 24 hours in 1969.

WEIGHTLIFTING

The greatest weightlifter yet seen—Vasili Alexeev (U.S.S.R.) holder of every Super-heavyweight record

Origins Amateur weightlifting is of comparatively modern origin, and the first world championship was staged at the Café Monico, Piccadilly, London, on 28 March 1891. Prior to that time, weightlifting consisted of professional exhibitions in which some of the advertised poundages were open to doubt. The first 400 lb. clean and jerk is, however, attributed to Charles Rigoulot (1903–62), a French professional, in Paris, with 402½ lb. on 1 Feb. 1929.

Greatest back lift The greatest weight ever raised by a human being is 6,270 lb. (2·80 tons) in a back lift (weight raised off trestles) by the 26-stone Paul Anderson (U.S.A.) (born 1933), the 1956 Olympic heavyweight champion, at Toccoa, Georgia, U.S.A., on 12 June 1957. The heaviest Rolls-Royce, the Phantom VI, weighs 5,600 lb. (2½ tons). The greatest lift by a woman is 3,564 lb. with a hip and harness lift by Mrs. Josephine Blatt *née* Schauer (1869–1923) at the Bijou Theatre, Hoboken, New Jersey, U.S.A., on 15 April 1895.

Greatest overhead lift The greatest overhead lifts made from the ground are the clean and jerks achieved by super-heavyweights which now exceed 4½ cwt. (504 lb.) (see table p. 302). The greatest overhead lift ever made by a woman is 286 lb. in a continental clean and jerk by Katie Sandwina, *née* Brummbach (Germany) (b. 21 Jan. 1884, d. as Mrs. Max Heymann in New York City, U.S.A., on 21 Jan. 1952) in *c.* 1911. This is equivalent to seven 40-pound office typewriters. She stood 6 feet 1 inch tall, weighed 220 lb. (15 stone 10 lb.) and is reputed to have unofficially lifted 312½ lb. and to have shouldered a cannon taken from the tailboard of a Barnum and Bailey circus wagon which allegedly weighed 1,200 lb.

Power lifts Paul Anderson, as a professional, has bench-pressed 627 lb. and has achieved 1,200 lb. in a squat so aggregating, with an 820 lb. dead lift, a career total of 2,647 lb. The A.A.U. of America record for a single contest is an aggregate of 2,040 lb. by Bob Weaver set in 1967.

The highest recorded two-handed dead lift is 820 lb. by Paul Anderson. Hermann Gorner (Germany) performed a one-handed dead lift of 734½ lb. in Dresden on 20 July 1920. Peter B. Cortese (U.S.A.) achieved a one-armed dead lift of 370 lb. *i.e.* 22 lb. over triple his bodyweight at York, Pennsylvania on 4 Sept. 1954.

Gorner (see above) raised 24 men weighing 4,123 lb. on a plank on the soles of his feet in London on 12 Oct. 1927 and also carried on his back a 1,444 lb. piano for a distance of 52½ feet on 3 June 1921.

The highest competitive two-handed dead lift by a woman is 392 lb. by Mlle. Jane de Vesley (France) in Paris on 14 Oct. 1926.

It was reported that an hysterical 8 stone 11 lb. woman, Mrs. Maxwell Rogers, lifted one end of a 3,600 lb. (1·60 ton) station wagon which, after the collapsing of a jack, had fallen on top of her son at Tampa, Florida, U.S.A., on 24 April 1960. She cracked some vertebrae.

Cue levering The only man ever to have levered six 16 oz. billiard cues simultaneously by their tips through 90 degrees to the horizontal, is W. J. (Bill) Hunt of Darwen, Lancashire at the Unity Club, Great Harwood, Lancashire on 25 June 1954.

Olympic Games The U.S.S.R. has won 18, the U.S.A. 14 and France 9 of the 68 titles at stake. Eight lifters have so far succeeded in winning Olympic titles in successive Games. Three lifters have won 2 gold and 1 silver medal:—

Louis Hostin (France) Light-heavy: Silver 1928; Gold 1932 and 1936.
Tommy Kono (Hawaii/U.S.A.) Lightweight: Gold 1952; Light-heavy: Gold 1956; Middleweight: Silver 1960.
Yoshinobu Miyake (Japan) Bantam: Silver 1960; Featherweight: Gold 1964 and 1968.

OFFICIAL WORLD WEIGHTLIFTING RECORDS

Bodyweight Class	Lift	Lifted lb.	kg.	Name and Nationality	Place	Date
Flyweight (114½ lb.–52 kg.)	Press	252¼	114·5	Adam Gnatov (U.S.S.R.)	Rostov-on-Don, U.S.S.R.	10 Mar. 1971
	Snatch	225¾	102·5	Takeshi Horikoshi (Japan)	Sapporo, Japan	30 May 1971
	Jerk	286½	130	Vladislav Krishchishin (U.S.S.R.)	Szombathely, Hungary	20 June 1970
	Total	749¼	340	Vladislav Krishchishin (U.S.S.R.)	Szombathely, Hungary	20 June 1970
Bantamweight (123¼ lb.–56 kg.)	Press	277¾	126	Sandor Holczreiter (Hungary)	Budapest, Hungary	14 May 1971
	Snatch	250	113·5	Koji Miki (Japan)	Osaka, Japan	15 Nov. 1968
	Jerk	330½	150	Mohamed Nassiri (Iran)	Mexico City, Mexico	13 Oct. 1968
	Total	820¾	372·5	Imre Földi (Hungary)	Szombathely, Hungary	21 June 1970
Featherweight (132¼ lb.–60 kg.)	Press	302	137	Imre Földi (Hungary)	Rostov-on-Don, U.S.S.R.	11 Mar. 1971
	Snatch	276½	125·5	Yoshinobu Miyake (Japan)	Matsuura, Japan	28 Oct. 1969
	Jerk	338¼	153·5	Dito Shanidze (U.S.S.R.)	Rostov-on-Don, U.S.S.R.	11 Mar. 1971
	Total	881½	400	Yoshinobu Miyake (Japan)	Matsuura, Japan	28 Oct. 1969
Lightweight (148¾ lb.–67·5 kg.)	Press	327¼	148·5	Vladimir Drexler (U.S.S.R.)	Balkhash, U.S.S.R.	31 May 1971
	Snatch	303	137·5	Waldemar Baszanowski (Poland)	Lublin, Poland	23 April 1971
	Jerk	382¼	173·5	Peter Korol (U.S.S.R.)	Sofia, Bulgaria	22 June 1971
	Total	991¾	450	Waldemar Baszanowski (Poland)	Sofia, Bulgaria	22 June 1971
Middleweight (165¼ lb.–75 kg.)	Press	359¼	163	Alexander Kolotkov (U.S.S.R.)	Balkhash, U.S.S.R.	31 May 1971
	Snatch	319½	145	Masashi Ohuchi (Japan)	Yufuin, Japan	18 June 1967
	Jerk	413¼	187·5	Viktor Kurentsov (U.S.S.R.)	Mexico City, Mexico	16 Oct. 1968
	Total	1,063¼	482·5	Viktor Kurentsov (U.S.S.R.)	Dubna, U.S.S.R.	31 Aug. 1968
Light-heavyweight (181¾ lb.–82·5 kg.)	Press	388	176	Hans Bettembourg (Sweden)	Falun, Sweden	21 Aug. 1970
	Snatch	357	162	David Rigert (U.S.S.R.)	Volgograd, U.S.S.R.	16 Nov. 1970
	Jerk	425¼	193	Boris Pavlov (U.S.S.R.)	Podolsk, U.S.S.R.	8 June 1971
	Total	1,118½	507·5	Boris Pavlov (U.S.S.R.)	Kharkov, U.S.S.R.	11 Oct. 1970
Middle-heavyweight (198¼ lb.–90 kg.)	Press	425¼	193	Hans Bettembourg (Sweden)	Falun, Sweden	18 April 1971
	Snatch	370¼	168	Pavel Pervushin (U.S.S.R.)	Odessa, U.S.S.R.	21 Feb. 1971
	Jerk	451¾	205	David Rigert (U.S.S.R.)	Sofia, Bulgaria	25 June 1971
	Total	1,201	545	David Rigert (U.S.S.R.)	Taganrog, U.S.S.R.	17 April 1971
Heavyweight (242½ lb.–110 kg.)	Press	448½	203·5	Valeri Yakubovsky (U.S.S.R.)	Moscow, U.S.S.R.	25 April 1971
	Snatch	371¼	168·5	Karl Utsar (U.S.S.R.)	Rostov-on-Don, U.S.S.R.	14 Mar. 1971
	Jerk	473¾	215	Yan Talts (U.S.S.R.)	Szombathely, Hungary	27 June 1970
	Total	1,250½	567·5	Valeri Yakubovsky (U.S.S.R.)	Moscow, U.S.S.R.	25 April 1971
Super-heavyweight (Above 242½ lb.–110 kg.)	Press	497	225·5	Vasili Alexeev	Moscow, U.S.S.R.	24 July 1971
	Snatch	396¾	180	Vasili Alexeev	Moscow, U.S.S.R.	24 July 1971
	Jerk	518	235	Vasili Alexeev	Moscow, U.S.S.R.	24 July 1971
	Total	1,410¾	640	Vasili Alexeev	Moscow, U.S.S.R.	24 July 1971

(As supplied by Mr. Oscar State, O.B.E., General Secretary of the *Fédération Haltérophile Internationale*)

WRESTLING

Earliest references Wrestling holds and falls, depicted on the walls of the Egyptian tombs of Beni Hasan, prove that wrestling dates from 3000 B.C. or earlier. It was introduced into the ancient Olympic Games in the 18th Olympiad in *c.* 704 B.C. The Graeco-Roman style is of French origin and arose about 1860. The International Amateur Wrestling Federation (F.I.L.A.) was founded in 1912.

Most Olympic titles Two wrestlers have won three Olympic titles. They are:

Carl Westergran (Sweden)

Graeco-Roman Middleweight A	1920
Graeco-Roman Middleweight B	1924
Graeco-Roman Heavyweight	1932

Ivar Johansson (Sweden)

Freestyle Middleweight	1932
Graeco-Roman Welterweight	1932
Graeco-Roman Middleweight	1936

Best record Osamu Watanabe (Japan) won the freestyle featherweight event in the 1964 Olympic Games. This was his 186th successive win and he had never been defeated. The flyweight Ali Aliyer (U.S.S.R.) won 3 world freestyle titles (1959, 1961, 1962).

Longest bout The longest recorded bout was one of nearly 11 hours between Max Klein (Russia) and Alfred Asikainen (Finland) in the Graeco-Roman middleweight "A" event in the 1912 Olympic Games in Stockholm, Sweden.

Great Britain *Most titles*

Heavyweight	10	Ken Richmond, 1949–60
Middleweight	7	Thomas Albert Baldwin (b. 27 Sept. 1905), 1942, 1944–46, 1948, 1951–52 (also Welterweight in 1941)
Welterweight	9	Joe Feeney, 1957–60, 1962, 1964–66, 1968
Lightweight	8	Arthur Thompson, 1933–40
Featherweight	8	H. Hall, 1952–57, 1961, 1963 and Lightweight 1958–59
Bantamweight	6	Joe Reid, 1930–35

Longest span The longest span for B.A.W.A. titles is 24 years by G. Mackenzie, who won his first title in 1909 and his last in 1933. Mackenzie also jointly holds (see Fencing) the record of having represented Great Britain in five successive Olympiads from 1908 to 1928.

Heaviest heavyweight The heaviest heavyweight champion in British wrestling history was A. Dudgeon (Scotland), who won the 1936 and 1937 B.A.W.A. heavyweight titles, scaling 22 stone.

Professional wrestling Professional wrestling dates from *c.* 1875 in the United States. Georges Karl Julius Hackenschmidt (1877–1968) made no submissions in the period 1898–1908. The highest paid professional wrestler ever is Antonio ("Tony") Rocca of Puerto Rico, with $180,000 (£75,000) in 1958. The heaviest ever wrestler has been William J. Cobb of Macon, Georgia, U.S.A. (b. 1926), who was billed in 1962 as the 802 lb. (57 st. 4 lb.) "Happy" Humphrey. What he lacked in mobility he possessed in suffocating powers. By July 1965 he had reduced to a more modest 232 lb. (16 st. 8 lb.).

Ranger, the U.S. yacht of 1937 that could crowd on over two-fifths of an acre of sail

Sumo wrestling The sport's legendary origins in Japan were 2,000 years ago. The heaviest ever performer was probably Dewagatake, a wrestler of the 1920s who was 6 feet 5 inches tall and weighed up to 30 stone. Weight is amassed by over alimentation with a high protein sea food stew called *chanko-rigori.* The tallest was probably Ozora, an early 19th century performer, who stood 7 feet 3 inches tall. The most successful wrestler has been Koki Naya (b. 1940), *alias* Taiho ("Great Bird"), who won his 26th Emperor's Cup on 10–24 Sept. 1967. He was first a *Yokozuna* (Grand Champion) in 1967. The highest *dan* is Makuuchi.

YACHTING

Origin Yachting in England dates from the £100 stake race between Charles II and his brother James, Duke of York, on the Thames on 1 Sept. 1661 over 23 miles, from Greenwich to Gravesend. The earliest club is the Royal Cork Yacht Club (formerly the Cork Harbour Water Club), established in Ireland in 1720.

Highest speed A speed of 30 knots was attained in September 1966 by *Lady Helmsman,* the 25-foot C class catamaran built by Reg. White (b. 1936) of Brightlingsea, Essex. The aerodynamic mast accounts for a third of the 300 square feet of sail area permitted. She won the Little America's Cup in 1966–67–68.

Most successful The most successful racing yacht in history was the Royal Yacht *Britannia* (1893–1935), owned by King George V, which won 231 races in 625 starts.

America's Cup The America's Cup races, open to challenge by any nation's yachts, began on 8 Aug. 1870 with the unsuccessful attempt by J. Ashbury's *Cambria* (G.B.) to capture the trophy from the *Magic,* owned by F. Osgood (U.S.A.). Since then the Cup has been challenged by Great Britain in 15 contests, by Canada in two contests, and by Australia thrice, but the United States holders have never been defeated. The closest race ever was the fourth race of the 1962 series, when the 12-metre sloop *Weatherly* beat her Australian challenger *Gretel* by about 3½ lengths (75 yards), a margin of only 26 seconds, on 22 Sept. 1962. The fastest time ever recorded by a 12-metre boat for the triangular course of 24 miles is 2 hours 46 minutes 58 seconds by *Gretel* in 1962.

Little America's Cup The catamaran counterpart to the America's Cup was instituted in 1961. The British club entry has won on each annual occasion to 1968 *v.* the U.S.A. (1961–66 and 1968) and *v.* Australia in 1967.

Largest yacht The largest private yacht ever built was Mrs. Emily Roebling Cadwalader's *Savarona* of 4,600 gross tons, completed in Hamburg, Germany, in Oct. 1931, at a cost of $4,000,000 (now £1·66 million). She (the yacht), with a 53-foot beam and measuring 407 feet 10 inches overall, was sold to the Turkish government in March 1938. Operating expenses for a full crew of 107 men approached $500,000 (now £208,000) per annum.

The largest private sailing yacht ever built was the full-rigged 350-foot auxiliary barque *Sea Cloud* (formerly *Hussar*), owned by the oft-married Mrs. Marjorie Merriweather Post-Close-Hutton-Davies-May (born 1888), one-time wife of the U.S. Ambassador in the U.S.S.R. Her four masts carried 30 sails with the total canvas area of 36,000 square feet.

Largest sail The largest sail ever made was a parachute spinnaker with an area of 18,000 square feet (more than two-fifths of an acre) for Vanderbilt's *Ranger* in 1937.

Olympic Games The first sportsman ever to win individual gold medals in four successive Olympic Games was Paul B. Elvstrom of Denmark in the Firefly class in 1948 and the Finn class in 1952, 1956 and 1960. He has also won 8 other world titles in a total of 6 classes. The lowest number of penalty points by the winner of any class in an Olympic regatta is 3 points (6 wins [1 disqualified] and 1 second in 7 starts) by *Super-docius* of the Flying Dutchman class (Lt. Rodney Pattisson, M.B.E., R.N. and Iain Macdonald-Smith, M.B.E.) at Acapulco, Mexico in October 1968.

CHAPTER 1—THE HUMAN BEING

Page 11

Tallest giantess The most recent research into the identity of the Northfield giantess indicates that she died in 1922.

Pages 15–16

Centenarians Miss Stevenson celebrated her 110th birthday on 9 July 1971.

Page 19

Multiple births It was announced by Dr. Gennaro Montanino of Rome that he had removed the foetuses of 10 girls and 5 boys from the womb of a 35-year-old housewife on 22 July 1971. A fertility drug was responsible for the unique and record instance of quindecaplets.

CHAPTER 2—THE ANIMAL AND PLANT KINGDOMS

Page 33

Oldest cat "Buncle" died on 13 Feb. 1971, aged 26 years and 2 months.

Largest litter "Tarawood Antigone", owned by Mrs. Valerie Gane of Stow-in-the-Wold, Gloucestershire, was reported to have given birth to 19 kittens in October 1970.

Page 34

Heaviest rabbit "Chewer", a 4-year-old Norfolk Star from Attleborough, Norfolk, is reported to have weighed 25 lb. in May 1971.

Page 36

Cagebirds Oldest A budgerigar, hatched in November 1948 and living in March 1971, aged 22 years 4 months was reportedly owned by Mrs. Dolan of Loughton, Essex.

Reptile Fastest A young ora (*Varanus komodoensis*) can outrun a dog over 300 yards and thus can probably touch 30 m.p.h.

Chelonian Largest The scientific name for the giant tortoise is now *Geochelone gigantea*.

Page 37

Snake Longest Recent research shows that the 37½-foot anaconda reported in 1944 was not fatally shot. Hence the measurement quoted becomes speculative. On 8 July 1971 a 38-inch adder (*Vipera berus*) was killed on Walberswick common, East Suffolk.

Oldest An Indian python (*Phyton moluras*) at Philadelphia Zoo, Pennsylvania, U.S.A. was living, aged 34 years 1 month, on 1 Jan. 1971.

Most poisonous The minimal lethal dose of the beaked sea-snake *Hydrophis fasciatus* is reported to be 1·5 mg.

Page 38

Toad Oldest The 54-year claim from Copenhagen is now reported as defective.

Page 39

Fish Shortest lived Killifish (spp *Cyprinodontidae*) have a normal life span of 8 months in their natural habitat.

Page 40

Lobster Largest A specimen weighing 14 lb. 12 oz. has been reported from Ringhaddy, Co. Down, N. Ireland.

Page 46

Earliest life The oldest known living life-form was announced in December 1970 by Drs. Sanford and Barbara Siegel of Harvard University, U.S.A., to be a microscopic organism, similar in form to an orange slice, first collected near Harlech, Merionethshire, Wales in 1964. It has been named *Kakabekia barghoorniana* and has existed from 2,000 million years ago.

Page 47

Britain's greatest oaks In April 1971 the girth of the Chirk oak (*q.v.*) was measured at 40 feet 2 inches.

Page 48

Longest daisy chain A team from Coronation Secondary School, Pembroke Dock, Wales completed a daisy chain 244 feet long on 12 May 1971.

Rarest British plant There were only 2 or 3 plants of the Lady's Slipper orchid (*Cyripedium calceolus*) in a single locality in 1971.

Page 49

Pineapple Dole Co. Plantation report a pineapple weighing 16 lb. 8 oz. gathered in Mindanao, Philippine Islands, in 1967.

Pumpkins In October 1970 George F. Ould picked five pumpkins off one plant at Feniton, Devon weighing 298 lb., the largest weighing 82 lb.

Commonest British plant The most widely distributed plant in Great Britain appears to be Ribwort plantain.

Page 51

Ten-leafed clover A certified ten-leafed clover (*Trifolium pratense*) found by Phillipa Smith in Woodborough, Nottinghamshire in 1966 was exhibited on the *Magpie* T.V. programme on 8 July 1971.

Largest zoo The San Diego Zoo, California, U.S.A., at its 31 Dec. 1970 census, had 287 mammalian, 1,010 avian and 275 reptilian and amphibian species and sub-species.

CHAPTER 3—THE NATURAL WORLD

Page 52

Earthquake Greatest Kamchatka—for Lat. 50° 45′ N. read Lat. 52° 45′ N.

Page 57

Highest points by counties Several highest points in counties have been reassessed in 1971 by a few feet. The following revisions are significant:- Shropshire—Brown Clee Hill now 1,772 feet; Roxburghshire —Spot Height, 2,433 feet.

Page 59

Largest lakes Wales The total surface area of Lake Vyrnwy is 1,120 acres.

Page 60

Deepest caves by countries 2,006 feet, Sotano del San Agustin, Mexico. 1,885 feet, Raggefavreraige, Norway.

Longest caves by countries Flint Ridge, Kentucky, U.S.A. now surveyed to 72·9 miles. Lancaster Hole, Westmorland now has 12·5 surveyed miles.

Page 62

eatest snowfall World At 5,400 feet in Mount Rainer Park, 1,014 inches of snow fell in the year ending 18 May 1971.

ongest drought Scotland This occurred on 3 April to 10 May 1938 (38 days) at Port William, Wigtownshire.

viest hailstone The Coffeyville stone is now accepted. Circumference 17·5 inches.

CHAPTER 4—THE UNIVERSE AND SPACE

Page 63

argest craters U.S.S.R. scientists reported in late 1970 an astrobleme with a 60-mile diameter in the River Popigai basin.

Page 66

Constellations A recently published measurement of Crux Australis indicates its size as 68 square degrees.

Page 67

Universe In April 1971 the heaviest galaxy was found to be 41C 31:04 (a "binary" system) with a mass 45 times that of the Milky Way, thus indicating a figure of 12,000 sextillion tons ($1{\cdot}2 \times 10^{40}$ tons).

Page 69

Duration on the Moon Capt. Shepard was promoted to Rear Admiral, U.S.N., on 28 April 1971. The crew of the Apollo XV lunar exploration module *Falcon,* manned by Col. David R. Scott and Lt.-Col. James B. Irwin, was on the lunar surface for 66 hours 55 minutes from 23.16 hours B.S.T. 30 July to 18.11 hours B.S.T. 2 Aug. 1971.

Longest lunar mission Apollo XV's command module *Endeavour* set a duration record for manned lunar orbit of 6 days 1 hour in the longest ever lunar mission of 12 days 8 hours from 26 July to 7 Aug. 1971.

CHAPTER 5—THE SCIENTIFIC WORLD

Page 73

Champagne cork flight Clement Freud, of the *Daily Telegraph* colour supplement, at the cellars of Grants of St. James's, Whitcombe Street, London S.W.1, fired a cork from a bottle of non-vintage Pommery and Greno champagne 54 feet $1\frac{3}{4}$ inches.

ost expensive wine A bottle (one of five left) of *Château Lafite* Rothschild 1846 was bought at the Hublein Inc. auction in New York City on 26 May 1971 by Laurence H. Bender, 25, for an undisclosed client, for $5,000 (£2,083·33) or £86·80 per fluid oz.

Page 76

dio telescope The Effelsberg 100-metre dish became operative in April 1971. Its total cost was £14·2 million.

Page 78

Lowest temperature It was reported in November 1970 that by adiabatic demagnetization of helium 3 a temperature of 1×10^{-8} K has been achieved.

Smallest microscope The smallest high power microscope in the world is the 2,000× 18 oz. McArthur microscope measuring $4 \times 2\frac{1}{2} \times 2$ inches. It provides immersion dark ground, phase contrast, polarising and incident illumination and is produced at Landbeach, Cambridge, England.

st inaccurate rsion of "pi" In 1897 the State legislature of Indiana came within a single vote of "simplifying" the numerical value of pi to 3·2.

HAPTER 6—THE ARTS AND ENTERTAINMENTS

Page 81

Painting Longest Sixty students of the St. Albans College of Art, Hertfordshire, painted non-stop for 60 hours to produce a painting on a 3-mile long roll of cartridge paper on 1–3 July 1971.

The world's most expensive piece of Sculpture—£158,333

Page 82

Art auction sale Highest total The highest total ever achieved for a single auction of works of art is £3,638,825 achieved by a sale of 27 paintings by old masters at the salerooms of Messrs. Christie, Manson and Wood, London on 25 June 1971. The highest price in the sale was paid for *The Death of Acteon* by Titian (£1,680,000).

Miniature portrait The highest price ever paid for a portrait miniature is the £65,100 given by an anonymous buyer at a sale held by Messrs. Christie, Manson and Wood, London on 8 June 1971 for a miniature of Frances Howard, Countess of Essex and Somerset by Isaac Oliver, painted *c.* 1605. This miniature, sent for sale by Lord Derby, measured $5\frac{1}{8}$ inches in diameter.

Woman artist Most expensive The highest price known to have been paid for the work of a woman artist is the $150,000 (£62,500) paid at the New York salerooms of Sotheby and Co., Parke-Bernet, on 10 March 1971 for the painting *Summertime*, measuring $29 \times 39\frac{1}{2}$ inches by the American-born Impressionist painter Mary Cassatt.

Page 83

Sculpture Most expensive The highest price ever paid for a piece of sculpture is the $380,000 (£158,333) given at Sotheby's New York salerooms, Parke-Bernet, on 5 May 1971 for Edgar Degas' bronze *Petite Danseuse de Quatorze Ans,* executed in an edition of about 12 casts in 1880. This bronze is $37\frac{1}{2}$ inches high and the figure of the young girl wears a real tutu, hair ribbon and ballet shoes. This particular cast was sold by one millionaire, Norton Simon of California, and purchased by Jack Linsky of New York.

Page 86

Longest sentence The President of Columbia University, New York, in his report for 1943 used a sentence of 4,284 words punctuated as a single sentence extending over 11 pages.

Page 87

Most Christian names The daughter of Arthur Pepper of West Derby, Lancashire, born on 19 Dec. 1882, was christened Ann Bertha Cecilia Diana Emily Fanny Gertrude Hypatia Inez Jane Kate Louisa Maud Nora Orphelia Quince Rebecca Starkey Teresa Ulysis Venus Winifred Xenophen Yetty Zeus Pepper.

Commonest forenames The four names most commonly given in 1969 changed in order to Paul, Andrew, Mark and David and to Sharon, Karen, Joanne and Julie.

Shortest names Other single letter place names are U in the Caroline Islands, Pacific Ocean; and the Japanese town of Sosei which is alternatively called Aioi or O-o or even O. Other U.S. two letter places are O.K., Kentucky; Ti, Oklahoma and T.B., Maryland. There was once a 6 in West Virginia and there are currently 17, Ohio; 30, Iowa; 56, Arkansas; 76, Kentucky; 84, Pennsylvania and Zero, Montana.

Page 88

Earliest encyclopaedias The earliest known encyclopaedia was compiled by Speusippas (*post* 408–*c.* 388 B.C.) a nephew of Plato, in Athens *c.* 370 B.C. The earliest encyclopaedia compiled by a Briton was *Liber excerptionum* by the Scottish monk Richard (d. 1173) at St. Victor's Abbey, Paris *c.* 1140.

STOP PRESS

Page 90

Oldest authoress The oldest authoress in the world is Mrs. Alice Pollock (*née* Wykeham-Martin) (b. 2 July 1868) of Haslemere, Surrey, whose book "Portrait of My Victorian Youth" (Johnson Publications) was published in March 1971 when she was aged 102 years 8 months.

Longest literary gestation Brig.-Gen. Sir Harold Hartley, G.C.V.O., C.H., C.B.E., M.C., F.R.S. (b. 3 Sept. 1878), made an agreement with Oxford University Press to publish "Studies in the History of Chemistry" on 22 Feb. 1901. The book appeared in April 1971—more than 70 years later.

Page 91

The Katzenjammer Kids were created by Rudolph Dirks.

Page 94

Largest organ The Auditorium organ in Atlantic City is now reported to be only partially functional. The Grand organ at Wanamaker's Store, Philadelphia, installed in 1911, was enlarged until by 1930 it had 6 manuals and 30,067 pipes including a 64-foot Gravissima.

Pages 94–95

Most expensive violin The Lady Anne Blunt Stradivarius, made in 1721, was bought at auction at Sothebys by W. E. Hill & Son, London on 3 June 1971 for £84,000. On this valuation the Messie 'Strad' is now worth some £200,000.

Page 96

Opera singer Youngest The youngest opera singer in the world has been Jeanette Gloria La Bianca, born in Buffalo, New York on 12 May 1934, who made her debut as Rosina in *The Barber of Seville* at the Teatro dell'Opera, Rome on 8 May 1950 aged 15 years 361 days. Ginetta La Bianca was taught by Lucia Carlino and managed by Angelo Carlino.

Page 99

Play reading The fastest time for reading the complete works of Shakespeare is 53 hours 17 minutes by a team of 11 from Leeds Polytechnic Union Drama Society, Yorkshire, England on 28–30 April 1971.

CHAPTER 7—THE WORLD'S STRUCTURES

Page 105

Earliest structures Ireland The carbon dating of the earliest known settlement in Ireland at Ballynagilly, Co. Tyrone was announced in June 1971 to be from 3675±50 B.C. This site is thus probably at least a century earlier than the earliest dated neolithic site in England at Sindon, Sussex.

Page 107

Largest underground garage The three-level Orly Airport underground car park near Paris, France, accommodates 2,000 vehicles and measures 590 feet × 282 feet.

Grain elevators The total capacity at Port Arthur, Ontario is reportedly 100 million short tons or 3,300 million bushels.

Page 110

Largest stadium United Kingdom Hampden Park was opened on 31 Oct. 1903. It was surveyed to accommodate 184,000 and is, in the interests of public safety, now limited to take 135,000 of which 15,000 can be seated.

Page 112

Tallest structures The Eiffel Tower is of iron construction. The 356th suicide was committed on 2 July 1971.

Page 113

Longest cable suspension bridges An Italian government report published on 21 April 1971 called for a 9,000-foot-long span across the Straits of Messina to Sicily.

Page 115

Panama Canal tolls The highest toll paid has been $30,466·10 (£12,694) by the U.S. tanker Orion Hunter (39,287 gross tons) on 4 Jan. 1963. The lowest was 45 cents (19p) charged to Albert H. Oshiver for swimming through.

Page 121

Largest mirror The world's largest mirrors are made by a covering of vacuum aluminium coated melinex. Pearson Mirrorlite Ltd. of Sheffield, England reported in 1970 a mirror 40 feet 6 inches by 4 feet 9 inches in a single piece.

The world's most expensive-ever car—the U.S.A.'s Moon buggy *Rover*, which cost £15,833,333

CHAPTER 8—THE MECHANICAL WORLD

Page 127

Largest cargo vessel The *Polysaga* is currently carrying oil but is capable of carrying dry cargo. Excluding all combined purpose vessels, the largest dry cargo ship is *Universe Kure* of 76,004 gross tons.

Most powerful tug M.T. *Oceania* was built *for* Bugsier und Bergungs A.G. by Rickmers Werft at Bremerhaven, West Germany.

Largest tankers The largest tankers ordered from a British yard are nine tankers from Harland & Wolff, Belfast, each with a deadweight tonnage of 264,000 tons. The deadweight tonnage of *Esso Northumbria* (q.v.) is 253,000 tons and its length is 1,141 feet.

Page 128

Largest propeller The diameter is 30 feet 5 inches and the weight 58 tons. The securing cap weighs 8 cwt.

Page 129

Registration plates New research by P. H. Robertson shows that the earliest legislation on registration plates is contained in the Paris Police Ordinance of 14 Aug. 1893 (Rule II, Para. 17).

Page 130

Most expensive cars An auction record was set at Parke-Bernet, New York City, on 12 June 1971, when Dr. Peter Williamson bought one of the two existing 1936 Bugatti type 57 SC "Atlantique" coupés for $59,000 (£24,583).

World's most expensive vehicle The total research, development and construction cost of the Apollo XV Lunar Rover has been estimated at "more than $38,000,000" or £15,833,333.

Page 131

Oldest drivers In June 1971 the magistrates at Petersfield, Hampshire, requested the Rev. Wilfred Lionel de Burckenhold Thorold, 98, to take a driving test. In 1968 a U.S. Social Security survey reported a centenarian named Mr. Dring, who drove to work every day in an aged car.

Page 132

Round Britain motoring The *Guinness Book of Records* does not publish place to place or rally records made on public roads due to public policy unless these are under the aegis of H.M. Armed Forces, the R.A.C. or the Police.

On 7–11 May 1971 an R.A.F. team of Corporals Peter Mitchell and Ken Jones, and Junior Technician John Housley from Leuchars, Fife, completed 3,542 miles in 97¾ hours in a rally round the coast of Great Britain in a 1961 Mark 2, 2·4 Jaguar.

Page 134

Fastest trains British Rail announced in June 1971 that the APT (Advanced Passenger Train) service prototype trains would be in operation in 1974, running at speeds of 125 m.p.h. raised eventually to 155 m.p.h. London would be reached in 4¼ hours from Glasgow and 1 hour 35 minutes from Cardiff.

Permanent way The Castleton–Dunkirk, New York State, track has been reduced to *two* lanes.

Page 136

Supersonic flight The present rank of Charles E. Yeager is not Lt. Gen. but Brig.-Gen.

Page 139

Busiest airport Bien Hoa, South Vietnam, handled 1,019,437 take-offs and landings in 1970. The world's largest heliport is the U.S. Army's Hanchey Heliport, Fort Rucker, Alabama, with an area of 111·9 acres.

Page 140

Blackpool Tower to Snaefell, Isle of Man record over 61 miles is 29 minutes 35 seconds set by Billy Gill (Kirkby Boys' Club) Liverpool, using a Bell Jet Ranger helicopter in the 1970 race.

Page 142

Largest generator A 690,000 kW generator in service at Longannet, Fife since January 1970 has delivered 700,000 kW for short periods.

Page 143

Shortest lift The travel is 29 (not 34) inches. It was installed in 1959 and requires 16 seconds to travel.

Page 145

Most expensive watch The Patek Philippe Type 3448 self-winding calendar watch is the most complete available since it automatically indicates leap days each fourth year. The U.K. retail price, with an 18-carat bracelet, is £1,900.

CHAPTER 9—THE BUSINESS WORLD

Page 148

Chemist shop chain Boots had 1,441 branches in the United Kingdom and 10 in New Zealand as at 1 April 1971.

Largest brewery The Bass-Charrington brewery at Runcorn will have a capacity of 2,500,000 barrels.

Page 151

Shipbuilding By June 1971 Swan Hunter had 61 ships of 1,363,000 grt. and 2,120,000 dwt. tons on order worth £241 million.

Page 152

Companies The number of companies at 1 Jan. 1971 was 559,497 of which 16,639 were public and the balance private companies.

Page 154

Largest curtain The largest curtain ever built has been the bright orange 4-ton 250,000-sq.-ft. curtain suspended across the Rifle Gap, Grand Hogback, Colorado, U.S.A. by the Bulgarian-born sculptor Christo, 36 (*né* Javacheff) in the summer of 1971.

Cigarette packets The Ventegodt collection had by 20 July 1971 grown to 44,918 for 197 countries with 6,006 from the U.K. and 3,692 from the U.S.A.

Biggest offer The American Telegraph & Telephone Co. offered $1,375 million's worth of shares in a rights offer on 27,500,000 shares of convertible preferred stock on the New York market on 2 June 1971.

Page 155

Furniture The highest price ever paid for a single piece of furniture is 165,000 guineas (£173,250) at auction at Christies, London on 24 June 1971, for a Louis XVI bureau plat by Martin Carlin in 1778 and once belonging to the Empress Marie-Feodorovna in 1784, sold by the estate of Mrs. Anna Thomson Dodge and bought by Mr. Henri Sabet of Tehran, Iran. It is 51½ inches wide, 30 inches deep and 30 inches high in veneered pale tulipwood with a tooled and guilded black leather top and 14 Sèvres porcelain plaques in ormolu frames.

Page 156

Silver plate This side-heading should read Silver.

Snuff box The highest price ever paid for a snuff box is the 825,570 francs (inc. tax £61,609) given in a sale held by Maitres Ader and Picard at the Palais Galliera in Paris for a gold and lapis lazuli example by J. A. Meissonnier (d. 1750), dated Paris 1728. This is the only signed example of a snuff box by Meissonnier to have survived although he is known to have been one of the most patronised of French 18th-century goldsmiths. It was made for Marie-Anne de Vaviere-Neubourg, wife of Charles II of Spain. It measures 84 × 29 millimetres. It was sent for sale by the executors of the estate of the late D. David-Weill, and was purchased by Messrs. Wartski of Regent Street, London.

Page 157

Most expensive wreath The most expensive wreath on record was that sent to the funeral of President Kennedy in Washington, D.C. on 25 Nov. 1963 by the civic authority of Paris. It was handled by Interflora Inc. and cost $1,200 (now £500). The only rival was a floral tribute sent to the Mayor of Moscow in 1970 by Umberto Farmichello, general manager of Interflora which is never slow to scent an opportunity.

Agriculture Origins The earliest certain date for the domestication of dogs is *c.* 7700 B.C., *e.g.* at Star Carr, Yorkshire.

Earliest British farm The earliest dated British farming site is a neolithic one, enclosed within the Iron Age hill-fort at Hembury, Devon, excavated during 1934–5 and now dated to *c.* 3140 B.C.

Page 158

Sheep shearing British records for 9 hours have been set at 555 by Roger Poyntz-Roberts (300) and John Savery (255) on 9 June 1971 (sheep caught *by* shearers), and 610 by the same pair (sheep caught *for* shearers) in July 1970. In a shearing marathon by the Kingsbridge Young Farmers' Club, four men machine-shore 776 sheep in 24 hours on 4–5 June 1971.

Page 159

Ploughing The dates in September 1970 were 25–26.

CHAPTER 10—HUMAN ACHIEVEMENTS

Page 163

Most travelled men Lester Nixon of Sarasota, Florida, U.S.A. has visited 112 countries in a wheel-chair—South Korea being his 112th in July 1971.

Page 164

Atlantic crossings The fastest east-west crossing by a rowing boat has been 73 days by Donald Allum, 33, and Geoffrey Allum, 23, in *Q.E.3*, a 20-foot Yorkshire dinghy, from Las Palmas to Barbados on 12 Jan.–26 March 1971.

The solo east-west record is 166 days by Sidney Genders, 51 (Great Britain), in *Khaggavisana* from Sennen Cove, Cornwall, England to Miami, Florida, U.S.A. *via* the Canary Islands and Antigua arriving on 27 June 1970.

Sailing Earliest feminine The first solo feminine crossing was achieved by Mrs. Ann Davison in the 23-foot 2½-ton Bermuda sloop *Felicity Ann* sailing from Plymouth on 18 May 1952. She arrived at Miami, Florida, U.S.A. on 13 Aug. 1954 having called at ports in France, The Azores, Barbados and The Bahamas. Miss Nicolette Milnes-Walker, 28, sailing in the 30-foot *Aziz*, achieved the first non-stop crossing by the northern route arriving off Newport, Rhode Island, U.S.A. on 26 July 1971 after 46 days.

Most crossings Between 1950 and 1971 Humphrey Barton (G.B.) has completed 16 Atlantic crossings in boats between 25¼ and 35¼ feet overall, including 12 in his *Rose Rambler*.

Page 167

Running Ken Baily, of Bournemouth, England total lifetime logged running mileage reached 150,255 miles by 8 June 1971. Baily surpassed 6 times the Earth's circumference.

The 24-hour running record is 159 miles 562 yards (6 marathons plus 3,532 yards) by Wally H. Hayward, 45 (South Africa) at Motspur Park, Surrey on 20–21 Nov. 1954. The best distance by a 19th century "wobbler" was 150 miles 395 yards by Charles Rowell in New York City in February 1882.

Endurance walking Tony Rafferty, 32, at the Olympic Park, Melbourne, Australia on 16 July 1971 completed a 71-hour non-stop walk of 218¾ miles. This superseded in duration a 70-hour walk (with 5 minute intervals per hour) by Terry Godden (b. 5 Dec. 1943) at Ashford, Kent on 18–21 June 1971. The times of Michael Potter's walk were from midnight on 24–25 to 6.30 p.m. on 27 July 1971.

Walkathon At the Polar Palace "Walkathon", Van Ness Ave., Hollywood, California, U.S.A. between 27 March and 26 May 1934, Noble "Kid" Chissell established an unbroken world solo record of 468 hours (19½ days).

Walking backwards The only man to walk across the United States backwards has been Plennie L. Wingo of Abilene, Texas who started on 15 April 1931. His longest non-stop stint was 45 miles in 12½ hours.

Page 168

Eating out Fred E. Magel's total of restaurants reached 34,000 by May 1971.

STOP PRESS

Page 168

Most jobs Norman Darwood (b. 1928) of Surrey, who left school aged 14, has had a total of 36 jobs in 28 years from tea-boy to mathematician and author of technical papers on computing.

Page 169

Bed-making Karen Brunner and Marge Bowyer claimed a world's record of 79·9 seconds for making up a King Size double bed with sheets and pillow slips at the Seattle Sea Fair, Washington, U.S.A., on 1 Aug. 1971.

Bed of nails Vernon E. Craig *alias* Komar of Wooster, Ohio, U.S.A., in Barberton, Ohio supported two men weighing 475 lb. (33 st. 13 lb.) and 350 lb. (25 st.) on his chest while lying on a bed of nails at an exhibition in May 1969.

Bed-pushing Nine students from Highbury Technical College, Portsmouth pushed a bed from John o' Groats to Ryhope, Co. Durham, an estimated distance of 500 miles, from 9–16 April 1971.

Bed race The record time for the annual Knaresborough bed race (established 1962) in Yorkshire is 15 minutes 54 seconds for the 2½-mile course across the River Nidd by the Leeds Regional Hospital Board team (from 34 teams) on 5 June 1971.

Body jump For 4 June 1970 record 4 June 197*1*.

Page 170

Burial alive Tim Hayes raised his record to 242 hours 58 minutes in a "regulation"-sized coffin 14-foot down in Naas, Co. Kildare, Ireland from 23 May to 2 June 1971.

Page 171

Limbo A record for a flaming bar was established by "Safari", at the Côte du Nord Hotel, Jersey on 5 June 1971, at 9 inches.

Modern dance marathon Vic Jones and Julia Reece danced 74¼ hours from 1.00 p.m. 9 July, to 3.15 p.m. 12 July 1970 (with 10-minute intervals for each hour), at the Starlight Ballroom, Crawley, Sussex.

Disc jockey marathon Robert Airbright, 20, completed 506 hours from noon on 4 June, to 2.00 p.m. on 25 June 1971 at the Sighthill Community Centre, Edinburgh, Scotland.

Egg throwing Edward Nunn threw an egg 270 feet 3 inches to the catcher Nicholas Brittain at Stourport-on-Severn in the Round Table contest on 24 April 1971.

Escapology Houdini's escapes from a strait jacket were usually protracted and "agonized" with the fastest being 138 seconds. On 26 July 1971 Jack Gently effected an escape from a standard jacket in 45 seconds at Neath, Glamorgan, Wales before 600 witnesses.

Page 172

Hitch hiking The fastest possible time to travel from John o' Groats to Land's End by public transport is 28 hours 46 minutes using two buses and 4 trains. This journey was covered in 28 hours 22 minutes (owing to a bus excelling itself) on 5–6 Aug. 1970 by A. I. Ferguson.

House of cards A tower of cards of 34 storeys using 7 packs was erected by R. F. Gompers of Darwin College, The University, Canterbury, Kent on 3 May 1971. David J. Wilson of the Applied Mathematics Dept. of the University of Adelaide, South Australia built a 7-card per storey "house" to 22 storeys.

Longest screen kiss The longest kiss in cinematic history was in the film *You're In The Army Now*, released in 1940, when Regis Toomey kissed Jane Wyman for a duration of 185 seconds.

Kite flying record The date in 1969 was 13 June. A duration record of 37 hours 17 minutes over Sarasota, Florida, U.S.A. was claimed by Will Yolen in January 1971.

Page 173

Leapfrogging The longest recorded leapfrog (gaps of not more than 10 yards between each leap) has been 14 miles 1,442 yards by Ian Craft, Rae Johnson and John Sparts, survivors from a 14-man team in 4 hours 50 minutes at Colchester, Essex on 27th May 1971.

Lion taming (animal training) The most accomplished of all animal training acts is believed to be the animal pyramid uniquely performed by Günther Gebel-Williams (Germany) (b. 1936), who sits astride a tiger on the back of its mortal enemy the African elephant. He also employs both his blonde wife and his blonde ex-wife simultaneously under the Big Top.

Omelette making Clement Freud made 105 two-egg omelettes at The Victoria, Nottingham, England on 15 July 1971, in 26 minutes 25 seconds.

Page 174

Piano sawing A team of four at the Highland Games, Dronfield Woodhouse, near Sheffield on 3 July 1971 returned a time of 28 minutes 29 seconds for sawing a piano in half with an Eclipse saw.

Rocking chair Rande Dahl, 18, achieved 150 hours 18 minutes at the Seattle Sea Fair, Washington, U.S.A., ending on 30 July 1971.

See-saw marathon Martin Ashton and Graham Stokes kept a see-saw in constant motion for 100 hours at Willenhall, Staffordshire from 1–5 June 1971.

Page 175

Singing Paddy Corbett, 20, is reported to have sung for 27 hours 30 minutes at the University College, Galway, Ireland's College Week in January 1971.

Spitting Snyder achieved 31½ feet at Mississippi State University, U.S.A. on 21 April 1971.

Submergence Malcolm Hatton, 21, remained under water at Marineland, Morecambe, Lancashire on 29–30 May 1971 for 31 hours 5 minutes in a wet suit.

Swinging Jim Anderson and Lyle Hendrickson completed a 100-hour marathon on a swing at the Seattle Sea Fair, Washington, U.S.A., on 1 Aug. 1971.

Page 176

Typewriting Using the Dvorak Simplified Keyboard, Lenore Fenton achieved 165 set words per minute in a test at Seattle, Washington, U.S.A. in 1942. The youngest person to reach 100 w.p.m. has been 12-year-old Kelley McCanley (U.S.A.) on 8 April 1971. She also used the D.S. Keyboard.

Page 180

Beer upside down Jimmy Aitken, 27, drank 3 pints in 21 seconds on 18 May 1971 at the Skinner's Arms, Oakwood, Leeds, Yorkshire.

Beer drinking 1 pint in 1·8 seconds by P. C. Thomas Boland on the A.T.V. programme *Today* on 3 Aug. 1971.

Cheese 16 oz. in 4 minutes 30 seconds by John Lombino of Alhambra High School, California, U.S.A. on 25 May 1971.

Gherkin eating Peter L. Citron ate 1 lb. of gherkins at Roffman's House of Delicacies, Omaha, Nebraska, U.S.A. on 20 May 1971.

Grapes 1 lb. (unpipped) in 82·5 seconds by Leslie Jones at the Boot and Ship Hotel, Bagillt, Flintshire in June 1971.

Prunes John Lombino ate 265 prunes in 45 minutes at Alhambra High School, California, U.S.A. on 21 May 1971.

Sandwiches 39 (jam "butties" $5 \times 4 \times \frac{1}{2}$ inch) in 60 minutes by Paul Hughes at Ruffwood School, Kirkby, Liverpool on 16 July 1971.

Page 181

Most decorated American Lt. Audie Murphy (b. 20 June 1924) of the U.S. Third Infantry Division had the Congressional Medal of Honor, D.S.C., Legion of Merit, Silver Star with cluster, Bronze Star and Purple Heart with two clusters. He was killed in June 1971 in an aircraft.

Page 183

Most freedoms Another estimate puts Mr. Carnegie's total of Freedoms at 57 in the years 1890–1919.

Page 184

Air disaster On 30 July 1971 a Sabre jet fighter (1 killed) crashed into an All Nippon Airways Boeing 727 over Morioka, Japan, in which all 161 passengers and crew were killed.

Road accident A death toll of 69 was caused by a single lorry ploughing into a street crowd in Palam village, Hyderabad, India on 25 May 1971.

Space disaster Lt.-Col. Georgiy Timofeyevich Dobrovolsky; Flt.-Eng. Vladislav Nikolayevitch Volkov and Test Eng. Viktor Ivanovich Patsayev were found dead when *Soyuz 11* landed in the U.S.S.R. on 30 June 1971.

Footnote 11: The 1969 total of U.S. road deaths was 56,400.

CHAPTER 11—THE HUMAN WORLD

Page 189

Baths The United Kingdom figure of 84 per cent. relates to 1966 (latest available data).

Physicians The total number of doctors in Great Britain "economically active" on 30 Sept. 1969 has been estimated as 67,000 of whom 22,131 were in the N.H.S. hospital service in England and Wales.

Largest hospitals Rainhill Hospital, Lancashire has 2,350 staffed beds; St. James's Hospital, Leeds 1,337 and Queen Mary's Hospital for Children, Carshalton, Surrey 716 beds.

The Danderyd Hospital, Stockholm is due to be completed in 1972–73 with a total of 1,300 to 1,400 (*sic*) beds.

Page 191

Filibuster Texas State Senator Don Kennard "discussed" his amendment to an educational measure in the Capitol Building, Austin, Texas, U.S.A. from 4.28 p.m. 29 May to 9.50 p.m. 30 May 1971—a total of 29 hours 22 minutes without a break.

Page 197

Greatest range gun The H.A.R.P. 16-inch barrels were bored out to 16·5 inches.

Page 198

Earliest treaty The earliest English treaty of which record exists is one between Henry I and Robert, Count of Flanders who agreed to send 500 soldiers to the service of the King in exchange for 400 Marks of silver. This was signed on 17 May 1101.

Page 206

Welfare swindle The greatest welfare swindle yet worked was that of the gypsy Anthony Moreno on the French Social Security in Marseilles. By forging birth certificates and school registration forms, he invented 197 fictitious families and 3,000 children on which he claimed benefits from 1960 to mid-1968. Moreno, nicknamed "El Chorro" (the fountain), was last reported free of extradition worries and living in luxury in his native Spain having absquatulated with an estimated £2,300,000.

Page 211

Largest pile A column of 189,372 old pennies (£789·05) was knocked down by Lord Vesty at the Boar's Head, Berkeley, Gloucestershire on 14 May 1971.

Mile of pennies On 20 Feb. 1971 the Wombwell and District Round Table, Yorkshire, completed a 1½-mile course of (old) pennies (6 lines round the 440-yard Dorothy Hyman Stadium) totalling some £330 in value.

Page 212

Longest loaf The longest loaf on record was one 72 feet 6 inches weighing 280 lb. made by the Gais Bakery which was escorted by police during the annual Seattle Sea Fair, Washington, U.S.A., on 1 Aug. 1971.

CHAPTER 12—SPORTS, GAMES AND PASTIMES

Page 226

Angling Surf casting A British record of 202 yards 1 foot 7 inches was set by Nigel Forrester at Kessingland, Suffolk on 18 July 1971 using a 6 oz. weight.

Pages 232–237

The following unratified world records have been set: 200 metres (turn) 19·8 secs. Donald Quarrie (Jamaica) Cali, Colombia 4 Aug. 1971; Hammer Throw 245 ft. 8¾ ins. (74·90 metres) Uwe Beyer (West Germany) Stuttgart, West Germany 17 July 1971; Women's 800 metres 1 min. 58·3 secs. Hildegard Falk (*née* Jonze) Stuttgart, West Germany 11 July 1971; Women's 4 × 110 yards relay 44·7 secs. Tennessee Tigerbelles (U.S.A.) (Diane Hughes, Debbie Wedgeworth, Mattline Render, Iris Davis) Bakersfield, California, U.S.A. 17 June 1971.

Page 233

Athletics Three-legged walk Dale Stenson and Gerry Muns walked 32·9 miles three-legged in 35 hours 39 minutes on 1 Aug. 1971 at the Seattle Sea Fair, Washington, U.S.A.

Page 238

Basketball Britain In a match between Wellington & District and The Light Infantry, Shrewsbury at Shrewsbury in March 1971 the score was 145–60. Colin Turner (Wellington) scored 105 points in two 20-minute periods of play.

Page 239

Bowling (Ten Pin) marathon Richard Dewey, 42, bowled 1,206 consecutive games in Kansas City, U.S.A. ending on 25 May 1971.

Page 245

Chess Longest games: for Pogoff read Rogoff.

Page 250

Croquet marathon The most protracted croquet game on record is one of 40 hours by Jan White, 24 (height 4 feet 9 inches) and Peter Ryland, 19 (height 6 feet 9 inches) of New College, University of London at Hampstead, Greater London against a relay of opponents ending at 00·30 on 17 May 1971.

Page 251

Curling marathon The longest curling match on record is one of 32 hours 6 minutes played at the Stranraer Ice Rink between two rinks (*i.e.* 4 players=1 rink) from Newton Stewart and District Round Table, Kirkcudbrightshire on 2–3 May 1971.

Page 258

Football (soccer) Most F.A. Cup Winner's medals. Three players have won five:— J. H. Forrest (Blackburn Rovers) in 1884–85–86–90–91; the Hon. A. F. Kinnaird (Wanderers) in 1873–77–78 and (Old Etonians) in 1879–82 and C. H. R. Wolleston (Wanderers) in 1872–73–76–77–78.

Page 264

Ice skating World records ratified in July 1971 were Men's Overall: 168·248 points, Ard Schenk (Netherlands), Inzell, 13–14 Nov. 1970; Women's Overall: 182·817 points, Stien Kaiser (Netherlands), Davos, Switzerland, 15–16 Jan. 1971; 1,500 metres: 2 minutes 15·8 seconds, Kaiser, 15 Jan. 1971 and 3,000 metres: 4 minutes 46·5 seconds, Kaiser, 16 Jan. 1971.

Page 279

Lawn Tennis Longest rally against a wall R. J. Simons achieved a rally of 6,470 strikes in a squash court at Stowe School, Buckinghamshire on 10 Oct. 1970.

Singles marathon Mel Baleson, 21 and Glen Grisillo, 24, both of South Africa played 1,224 games in 73 hours 25 minutes at the University of Nevada, Reno, Nevada, U.S.A., on 6–9 May 1971.

Page 280

Motorcycling Giacomo Agostini, 29 (Italy), won his 10th world title with the 1971 350 c.c. title at Imatra, Finland in July 1971 on an M.V. Agusta. He also won the 500 c.c. and the overall world championship titles.

Pages 280–283

Motor racing The mileage of the 1970 World Cup Rally was 16,208 miles and was conceived by Wylton Dickson Associates Ltd.

Page 291

Shooting Bench-rest 1,000-yard shooting Smallest group $7\frac{11}{16}$ths inches by Mary Louise DeVito on 11 Oct. 1970 (7 mm-300 Wetherby); 10-shot possibles (score 5 × 10) Clifford Hocker, 8 June 1969 (300 Winchester Magnum) and Frank Weber, 25 Oct. 1970 (6·5 × 300 Wetherby). All records at Pennsylvania 1,000-yard Benchrest Club Inc., U.S.A.

Page 297

Swimming marathon The longest sponsored swim was one of 403¼ miles in seven hours in the Quarry Pool, Shrewsbury, England on 26–27 June 1971 by 140 members of the Shrewsbury Amateur Swimming Club which raised more than £1,400 for the Shropshire Spastics Society.

Page 298

Trampoline marathon Six trampolinists in Townsville, Queensland, Australia bounced for 254 hours from 30 April to 11 May 1971.

Page 299

Trotting and pacing The career winnings of the French horse *Une de Mai* were $1,116,000 (£465,000) by July 1971.

Volleyball The governing body is now described as the English Volleyball Association. Four Grace Baptist Church Youth teams of 6 in Seattle, Washington, U.S.A. completed a 125-hour marathon on 31 July 1971.

Walking The fastest end to end walk of Ireland (the world's 20th largest island) is 13 days 5 hours for the 370-mile route from Malin Head, County Donegal to Mizen Head, County Cork by Feardorcha Mac Aogáin on 20 Dec. 1970 to 2 Jan. 1971.

Page 303

Yachting Robert Johnson's 73-foot ketch *Windward Passage* set the Trans-Pacific record (2,225 miles from Los Angeles to Honolulu) in 9 days 9 hours 6 minutes in July 1971.

INDEX

PHOTOGRAPHIC CREDITS

Allied Breweries, 111
American Museum of Natural History, 39 (top right)
Associated Press, 168, 289, 303

Barberton Iron & Steel Ltd., 263
Barratts, 281 (bottom)
B.I.P.S., 14 (bottoms)
John Bland, 215
Boots Pure Drug Co., 148 (top right)
Boston Deep Sea Fishers Ltd., 128 (middle left)
British Aircraft Corporation, 137
B.O.A.C. British TransArctic Expedition, 165 (top)
British Travel Association, 108
Brown & Root Inc., 145
Bugatti Owners' Club Ltd., 130 (bottom)

California State Library, 291
Camera Press Ltd., 79, 221, 222 (bottom), 257 (top), 297 (bottom)
J. Campbell Harper, Edinburgh, 208
Central Press Photos, 301
T. Chettleburgh, 214
Compagnie Generale Transatlantique, 125
Conway Studios Corporation, 90 (top left)
George Craig, 267 (top)
Christie, Manson & Wood, 82, 156 (top left)
Crown Copyright, 55, 76, 119, 126 (bottom left, top right and middle left), 190 (top right), 197
Croydon Advertiser Ltd., 16
Cryer & Marchant Ltd., 130 (middle left)

Daily Express, 209 (top)
Daily Mirror, 18
Decca Records, 100 (top left)
Dell Publishing Co. Inc., 121
Alfred Dunhill Ltd., 155 (bottom right)
A. Dupont, 100 (bottom right)

Eljay Photo Service Inc., 74 (bottom left)
Essex County Standard, 203
Evening News, 14 (top), 29, 193 (right), 262, 264, 269 (bottom), 278 (top)

H. B. Fisher, 297 (top)
Foto Engler, Bremerhaven, W. Germany, 127
Fox Photos, 210
Marvin Frost, 50 (bottom left)

Gannon, Kingston-upon-Thames, 139
General Electric Research Laboratory, 73
Gloucester Newspapers Ltd., 58
Goodyear Aerospace Corporation, 107
Goodyear Tyre & Rubber Co. (G.B.) Ltd., 129
Arthur Guinness Son & Co. Ltd., 147, 163

Handford Photography, Croydon, 148 (middle right)
Herts Pictorial, Hitchin, 133 (top left)
Himalayan High Altitude Expedition, 106
Ron Howard, 169 (middle left)
Hungarian News Agency, 300 (top)

Illustrated London News, 187, 202
Imperial War Museum, 195, 198
Isle of Man Tourist Board, 120 (top right)
International News Photos, 13 (top)

Japanese T.V. Channel Eight, 24

Kent and Sussex Courier, 296
Keystone Press Agency Ltd., 169 (top)
Kingsport News, 196

E. D. Lacy, 281 (top), 294
R. G. Le Tourneau Inc. 131 (middle right)
Lilley & Skinner Ltd., 151
Loganair, 138 (top left)
London Brick Co., 148 (top left)

Massachusetts Institute of Technology, 80
C. E. May & Son, Reading, 49
the late Donald McGill, 91
Metropolitan Life Insurance Co., 149 (bottom right)
"The Motor", 282

N.A.S.A., 68, 306
National Coal Board, 123
National Galleries of Scotland, 190 (middle right)
National Geographic Society, School Services, 15 (top)
Normanns Kunstforlag A.S., 124
Northcliffe Newspapers Ltd., 257 (bottom)

Oberammergau Passionspiel, 99
Oxford University Press, 89

Parke-Bernet Galleries, 74 (top right), 83
Parker Bros. Inc., 149 (top left)
D. E. Pedgley, 62
Malcolm Pendrill Ltd., 90 (middle right)
Photo Detaille, 186
Photo-Reportage Ltd., 181
Picture Post, 146
Planet News, 167 (bottom right), 282 (bottom);
Elvis Presley Fan Club, 101
Press Association, 157, 277
Publicity Designs, 283 (bottom)

Radio Times Hilton Picture Library, 218 (top), 283 (top)
John Lawson Reay, Llandudno, 143
Remington Arms Co. Inc., 290
Reveille, 156 (bottom left)
Royal Danish Ministry for Foreign Affairs, 144

Shropshire Star & Journal, 153
Alan D. Smith, 170
Smithsonian Institution, 209 (bottom)
Sotheby & Co. Ltd., 44, 305
South West Picture Agency Ltd., 293
Sperryn's Ltd., 156 (top right)
Stanley Works (G.B.) Ltd., 155 (middle right)
The Studio, Royal Gardens, Kew, 50 (top left)
Milos Svobić, 292

The Times, 92
M. L. and H. V. Tipper, 275, 276

United Pictorial Press, 222 (top), 300 (bottom)
United Press International, 77, 94, 223, 285, 295
U.S. Forest Service, 47
U.S. Navy Photograph, 66, 166
U.S.S.R. Official Photograph, 33

Victoria Palace Theatre, 98
Fiona Vigers, 272 (bottom)
Volkswagen, 150

A. Waite, 215 (bottom)
Wide World Photos, 175
Peter Wilkes, 13 (bottom)
Wimpey News, 148 (bottom left)
G. L. Wood, 11, 38

Index by Myra Shaverin

AN EXPLANATORY NOTE

ENGLISH ROYAL PEDIGREE—FRONT AND BACK END-PAPERS

H.R.H. The Prince Charles, Prince of Wales, K.G. (b. 1948) shares the earliest historically provable English pedigree. This starts with Elesa the father of Cerdic, King of the West Saxons, a 12 greats grandfather of Alfred the Great. Cerdic flourished before the year A.D. 500 and died in 534. Elesa's pedigree is recited back for a further 23 generations (which includes the name of Woden) in the Anglo Saxon Chronicle of 855 but this rote, extending back well before the Christian era, lacks essential historicity.
The elapse of 1,414 years between the death of Cerdic in 534 and the birth of his 49 greats grandson, Prince Charles, in 1948 is occupied by 50 generations at an average of 28 years per generation.

Note: (a) Hyphened dates on the tables indicate the year of birth and death and *not* the duration of a reign.
(b) The number before a name indicates the number of "greats" in grandparentage; *e.g.* "3. H.M. Queen Victoria" means she is Prince Charles's great-great-great grandmother.

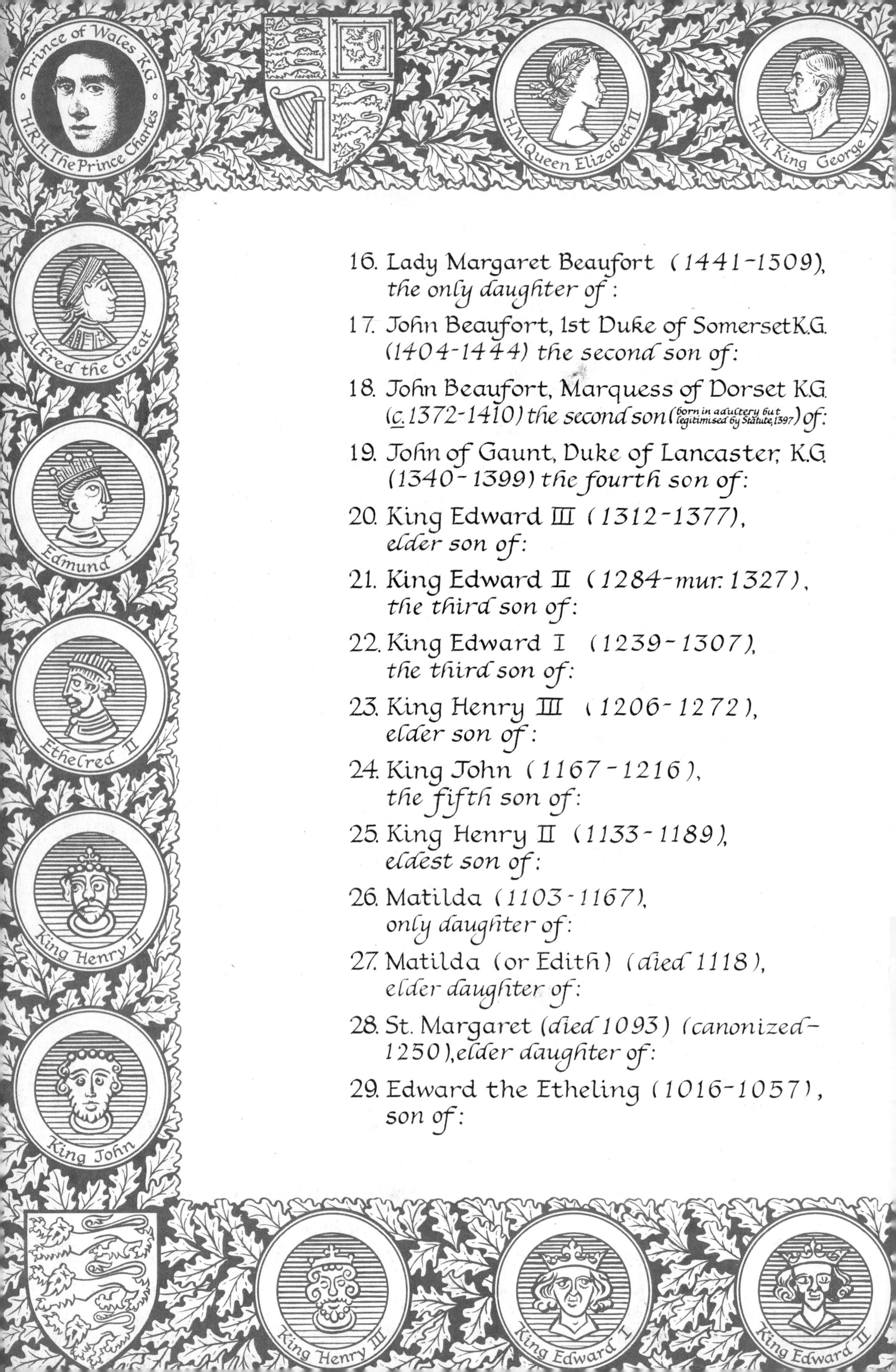

16. Lady Margaret Beaufort (1441-1509), *the only daughter of:*

17. John Beaufort, 1st Duke of Somerset K.G. (1404-1444) *the second son of:*

18. John Beaufort, Marquess of Dorset K.G. (c.1372-1410) *the second son (born in adultery but legitimised by Statute, 1397) of:*

19. John of Gaunt, Duke of Lancaster, K.G. (1340-1399) *the fourth son of:*

20. King Edward III (1312-1377), *elder son of:*

21. King Edward II (1284-mur. 1327), *the third son of:*

22. King Edward I (1239-1307), *the third son of:*

23. King Henry III (1206-1272), *elder son of:*

24. King John (1167-1216), *the fifth son of:*

25. King Henry II (1133-1189), *eldest son of:*

26. Matilda (1103-1167), *only daughter of:*

27. Matilda (or Edith) (died 1118), *elder daughter of:*

28. St. Margaret (died 1093) (canonized 1250), *elder daughter of:*

29. Edward the Etheling (1016-1057), *son of:*